A People & A Nation

A HISTORY OF THE UNITED STATES

Volume II: Since 1865

Eleventh Edition

Jane Kamensky
Harvard University

Carol Sheriff
College of William and Mary

David W. Blight
Yale University

Howard P. Chudacoff
Brown University

Fredrik Logevall
Harvard University

Beth Bailey
University of Kansas

Mary Beth Norton
Cornell University

Australia • Brazil • Mexico • Singapore • United Kingdom • United States

49°N

WASHINGTON
1889

Columbia R.

OREGON COUNTRY
(By Agreement
with Britain, 1846)

OREGON
1859

42°N

MONTANA
1889

Missouri R.

IDAHO
1890

WYOMING
1890

NORTH DAKOTA
1889

SOUTH DAKOTA
1889

NEVADA
1864

Great
Salt
Lake

UTAH
1896

MEXICAN CESSION
(1848)

NEBRASKA
1867

LOUISIANA
PURCHASE
(From France, 1803)

COLORADO
1876

Colorado R.

CALIFORNIA
1850

KANSAS
1861

ARIZONA
1912

NEW MEXICO
1912

OKLAHOMA
1907

PACIFIC

OCEAN

GADSDEN PURCHASE
(From Mexico, 1853)

TEXAS
(Independent Republic,
Annexed 1845)

Rio Grande

TEXAS
1845

Nueces R.

PACIFIC OCEAN

HAWAI'I
1959

HAWAI'I
(Annexed 1898)

RUSSIA

ALASKA
1959

CANADA

0   50 100 Km.

0   50   100 Mi.

MEXICO

ALASKA PURCHASE
(From Russia, 1867)

0   200   400 Km.

0   250   400 Mi.

PACIFIC OCEAN

Territorial Growth of the United States

1820 Date of states admission to the Union

● Geographic center of population by decade

CANADA

Lake Superior

MINNESOTA 1858

WISCONSIN 1848

Lake Michigan

Lake Huron

MICHIGAN 1837

Lake Ontario

Lake Erie

St. Lawrence R.

MAINE 1820

VT. 1791

N.H.

MASS.

CONN.

R.I.

NEW YORK

IOWA 1846

ILLINOIS 1818

INDIANA 1816

OHIO 1803

PENNSYLVANIA

NEW JERSEY 1790

DELAWARE

MARYLAND

MASON-DIXON LINE

THE THIRTEEN COLONIES

MISSOURI 1821

MISSOURI COMPROMISE LINE 36°30'N ● 2000

KENTUCKY 1792

WEST VIRGINIA 1863

VIRGINIA

THE ORIGINAL UNITED STATES (By Treaty with Britain, 1783)

THE ORIGINAL

NORTH CAROLINA

ARKANSAS 1836

TENNESSEE 1796

SOUTH CAROLINA

Mississippi R.

GEORGIA

ALABAMA 1819

MISSISSIPPI 1817

(Seized from Spain, 1810, 1813)

LOUISIANA 1812

FLORIDA (By Treaty with Spain, 1819)

FLORIDA 1845

Gulf of Mexico

ATLANTIC OCEAN

BAHAMAS

| 0 | 150 | 300 Km. |
| 0 | 150 | 300 Mi. |

PUERTO RICO (Acquired from Spain, 1898)

VIRGIN IS. (Acquired from Denmark, 1916–1917)

19°N

68°W

PUERTO RICO

VIRGIN ISLANDS

18°N

67°W

66°W

65°W

| 0 | 25 | 50 Km. |
| 0 | 25 | 50 Mi. |

CUBA

HAITI

DOMINICAN REPUBLIC

90°W   80°W   70°W   60°W

N

GREENLAND
(DENMARK)

ICELAND

ALASKA
(U.S.)

CANADA

60°N

80°N

UN
KING

IRELAND

UNITED STATES

40°N

PORTUGAL

S

Azores
(Port.)

ATLANTIC OCEAN

MOROC

Bermuda
(U.K.)

Midway Is.
(U.S.)

WESTERN
SAHARA
(MOROCCO)

Hawaiian Is.
(U.S.)

MEXICO

BAHAMAS

DOMINICAN REP.

CUBA

Virgin Is.
(U.S.)

20°N

MAURITANIA

JAMAICA

HAITI

ST. KITTS AND NEVIS
ANTIGUA AND BARBUDA

BELIZE

Puerto Rico
(U.S.)

DOMINICA

CAPE
VERDE

SENEGAL

HONDURAS

BARBADOS

GUATEMALA

ST. LUCIA

GAMBIA

EL SALVADOR

NICARAGUA

GRENADA

ST. VINCENT AND
THE GRENADINES

GUINEA-BISSAU

GUINEA

PACIFIC OCEAN

COSTA RICA

TRINIDAD AND TOBAGO

SIERRA
LEONE

IVOR
COAS

VENEZUELA

GUYANA

PANAMA

LIBERIA

GHA

COLOMBIA

FR. GUIANA
(FRANCE)

EQUAT

Equator

SURINAM

SÃO TOMÉ A

Galapagos Is.
(Ecuador)

ECUADOR

0°

PERU

BRAZIL

SAMOA

BOLIVIA

French Polynesia
(France)

TONGA

PARAGUAY

20°S

CHILE

Easter Is.
(Chile)

URUGUAY

ARGENTINA

40°S

| 0 | 1,000 | 2,000 Km. |
| 0 | 1,000 | 2,000 Mi. |

Falkland Is.
(U.K.)

60°S

160°W   140°W   120°W   100°W   80°W   60°W   40°W   20°W

80°S

TIC OCEAN

NORWAY FINLAND
SWEDEN ESTONIA
DEN.   LATVIA
              LITHUANIA
                BELARUS
GERMANY POLAND
CZ.   SLK.   UKRAINE
AUS. HUNG. MOLDOVA
SLN. CR. ROMANIA
ITALY B. H. SE.
ALBANIA MAC. BULGARIA
GREECE   GEORGIA
MALTA   CYPRUS ARMENIA
TUNISIA   SYRIA
          LEBANON
          ISRAEL
RIA   LIBYA   EGYPT   JORDAN KUWAIT
                        SAUDI
                        ARABIA
                              UNITED
                              ARAB EMIRATES OMAN

RUSSIA

KAZAKHSTAN

UZBEKISTAN

TURKMENISTAN

AZERBAIJAN

TURKEY

IRAQ

IRAN

AFGHANISTAN

KYRGYZSTAN

TAJIKISTAN

MONGOLIA

PEOPLE'S REPUBLIC OF CHINA

N. KOREA

S. KOREA   JAPAN

PACIFIC OCEAN

NIGER   CHAD
BENIN   SUDAN   ERITREA
NIGERIA   DJIBOUTI
CENTRAL   ETHIOPIA
AFRICAN REP.
CAMEROON
GO
NEA
PE GABON RWANDA
           DEM. REP.
           OF CONGO   UGANDA KENYA
OF CONGO   BURUNDI
                 TANZANIA

YEMEN

PAKISTAN

NEPAL

BHUTAN

BANGLADESH

INDIA

MYANMAR
(BURMA)

LAOS

THAILAND   VIETNAM

CAMBODIA
(KAMPUCHEA)

Taiwan

Mariana
Islands
(U.S.)

Guam
(U.S.)

Wake I.
(U.S.)

MARSHALL
ISLANDS

SRI LANKA

MALDIVES

PHILIPPINES

BRUNEI
DARUSSALAM

PALAU

FEDERATED STATES
OF MICRONESIA

KIRIBATI

MALAYSIA

SINGAPORE

NAURU

INDIAN OCEAN

SEYCHELLES

COMOROS

ANGOLA   ZAMBIA   MALAWI
NAMIBIA   ZIMBABWE
BOTSWANA   MADAGASCAR
                         MAURITIUS
      MOZAMBIQUE
      SWAZILAND
SOUTH   LESOTHO
AFRICA

INDONESIA

TIMOR LESTE

PAPUA
NEW
GUINEA

SOLOMON IS.

VANUATU

New Caledonia
(France)

TUVALU

FIJI

ABBREVIATIONS

AUS.	AUSTRIA
BEL.	BELGIUM
B. H.	BOSNIA AND HERZEGOVINA
CR.	CROATIA
CZ.	CZECH REPUBLIC
DEN.	DENMARK
HUNG.	HUNGARY
K.	KOSOVO
LUX.	LUXEMBOURG
MAC.	MACEDONIA
MO.	MONTENEGRO
NETH.	NETHERLANDS
SE.	SERBIA
SLK.	SLOVAKIA
SLN.	SLOVENIA
SWITZ.	SWITZERLAND

AUSTRALIA

NEW
ZEALAND

NTARCTICA

20°E   40°E   60°E   80°E   100°E   120°E   140°E   160°E

A People & A Nation, Eleventh Edition, Volume II: Since 1865
Jane Kamensky /Carol Sheriff/David W. Blight/ Howard P. Chudacoff/ Fredrik Logevall/ Beth Bailey /Mary Beth Norton

Product Manager: Joseph Potvin

Senior Content Developer: Kate MacLean

Associate Content Developer: Claire Branman

Product Assistant: Alexandra Shore

Senior Marketing Manager: Valerie Hartman

Senior Content Project Manager: Carol Newman

Manufacturing Planner: Julio Espera

IP Analyst: Alexandra Ricciardi

IP Project Manager: Betsy Hathaway

Production Service/Compositor: MPS Limited

Senior Art Director: Cate Rickard Barr

Text and Cover Designer: tani hasegawa, TT EYE.

Cover Image: *Santa Fe*, 1936-37 (oil on canvas)/ Nordfeldt, Bror Julius Olsson (1878-1955)/ Christies Images/Private Collection/Bridgeman Images.

For product information and technology assistance, contact us at
Cengage Customer & Sales Support, 1-800-354-9706

For permission to use material from this text or product, submit all requests online at **www.cengage.com/permissions**. Further permissions questions can be emailed to **permissionrequest@cengage.com.**

Library of Congress Control Number: 2017955520

Student Edition:
ISBN: 978-1-337-40273-6

Loose-leaf Edition:
ISBN: 978-1-337-40491-4

Cengage
20 Channel Center Street
Boston, MA 02210
USA

Cengage is a leading provider of customized learning solutions with employees residing in nearly 40 different countries and sales in more than 125 countries around the world. Find your local representative at **www.cengage.com.**

Cengage products are represented in Canada by Nelson Education, Ltd.

To learn more about Cengage platforms and services, visit **www.cengage.com.**

To register or access your online learning solution or purchase materials for your course, visit **www.cengagebrain.com.**

Printed in the United States of America
Print Number: 01   Print Year: 2017

BRIEF CONTENTS

CONTENTS

14 Reconstruction: An Unfinished Revolution, 1865–1877 410

15 The Ecology of the West and South, 1865–1900 440

16 Building Factories, Building Cities, 1877–1920   466

19   The Quest for Empire, 1865–1914   548

20   Americans in the Great War, 1914–1920   572

21   The New Era, 1920–1929   600

26 The Tumultuous Sixties, 1960–1968   754

29 Into the Global Millennium: America Since 1992   844

Appendix   A-1

Index   I-1

FEATURES

MAPS

FIGURES

TABLES

LINKS TO THE WORLD

LEGACY FOR A PEOPLE AND A NATION

VISUALIZING THE PAST

With this eleventh edition, *A People and A Nation* consolidates the last edition's broad structural changes, fine-tuning the streamlining and chapter combinations that made the text easier to assign over the course of an average academic semester. In this edition the authors introduced new interpretations, updated content to reflect recent research, and thought hard about what new features might engage our readers. This edition also more fully embraces the possibilities offered by digital platforms, as you will learn about in the MindTap description that follows later in this introduction.

A People and A Nation represents our continuing rediscovery of America's history—our evolving understandings of the people and the forces that have shaped the nation and our stories of the struggles, triumphs, and tragedies of America's past.

Key Themes in *A People and A Nation*

Published originally in 1982, *A People and A Nation* was the first U.S. history survey textbook to move beyond a political history to tell the story of the nation's people—the story of *all* its people—as well. That commitment remains. Our text encompasses the diversity of America's people and the changing texture of their everyday lives. The country's political narrative is here, too, as in previous editions. But as historical questions have evolved over the years and new authors have joined the textbook team, we have asked new questions about "a people" and "a nation." In our recent editions, we remind students that the "*A People*" and "*A Nation*" that appear in the book's title are neither timeless nor stable. European colonists and the land's indigenous inhabitants did not belong to this "nation" or work to create it, and Americans have struggled over the shape and meaning of their nation since its very beginning. The people about whom we write thought of themselves in various ways, and in ways that changed over time. Thus we emphasize not only the ongoing diversity of the nation's people, but their struggles, through time, over who belongs to that "people" and on what terms.

In *A People and A Nation*, the authors emphasize the changing global and transnational contexts within which the American colonies and the United States have acted. We pay attention to the economy, discussing the ways that an evolving market economy shaped the nation and the possibilities for its different peoples. We show how the meaning of identity—gender, race, class, sexuality, as well as region, religion, and family status—changes over time, and we find the nation's history in the mobility and contact and collision of its peoples. We discuss the role of the state and the expanding role and reach of the federal government; we pay attention to region and emphasize historical contests between federal power and local authority. We trace America's expansion and rise to unprecedented world power and examine its consequences. And we focus on the meaning of democracy and equality in American history, most particularly in tales of Americans' struggles for equal rights and social justice.

In *A People and A Nation*, we continue to challenge readers to think about the meaning of American history, not just to memorize facts. More than anything else, we want students to understand that the history of the American nation was not foreordained. Ours is a story of contingency. As, over time, people lived their day-to-day lives, made what choices they could, and fought for things they believed in, they helped to shape the future. What happened was not inevitable. Throughout the course of history, people faced difficult decisions, and those decisions mattered.

What's New in This Edition

Planning for the eleventh edition began at an authors' meeting near Cengage headquarters in Boston. Authors' meetings are always lively, and we discussed everything from recent scholarship and emerging trends in both U.S. and global history to the possibilities offered by digital platforms and the needs of the students who would be reading our work.

This edition continues to build on *A People and A Nation*'s hallmark themes, giving increased attention to the global perspective on American history that has characterized the book since its first edition. From the "Atlantic world" context of European colonies in North and South America to the discussion of international terrorism, the authors have incorporated the most recent globally oriented scholarship throughout the volume. We have stressed the incorporation of different peoples into the United States through territorial acquisition as well as through immigration. At the same time, we have integrated the discussion of such diversity into our narrative so as not to artificially isolate any group from the mainstream.

We have continued the practice of placing three probing questions at the end of each chapter's introduction to inspire and guide students' reading of the pages that follow. Additionally, focus questions and key terms have been added to this edition. The focus questions appear beneath each section title within every chapter to further support students in their reading and comprehension of the material. Key terms appear near the first mention of a term and are placed throughout each chapter.

Chapter-level Changes for the Eleventh Edition

For this edition, the authors reexamined every sentence, interpretation, map, chart, illustration, and caption, refined the narrative, presented new examples, updated bibliographies, and incorporated the best new scholarship. What follows here is a description of chapter-level changes for the eleventh edition:

11. **Chapter 14: Reconstruction: An Unfinished Revolution, 1865–1877**
    - Revised discussion of Radical Republican vision of Reconstruction
    - New scholarship on the military occupation of the South
    - New scholarship on the movement West
    - Revised discussion of railroad growth and expansion
    - Updated Legacy for a People and a Nation feature on the Lost Cause

12. **Chapter 21: The New Era, 1920–1929**
    - New Links to the World feature on Margaret Mead

13. **Chapter 22: The Great Depression and the New Deal, 1929–1939**
    - Added section on the voyage of the St. Louis and FDR responses to Nazi Germany

14. **Chapter 23: The Second World War at Home and Abroad, 1939–1945**
    - Revised discussion of U.S. path to war
    - Discussion of attack on Pearl Harbor has been recast to emphasize Japan's broader attack on U.S. and U.K. Pacific possessions
    - New scholarship on financing the war

15. **Chapter 25: America at Midcentury, 1945–1960**
    - Discussion of GI Bill updated to incorporate recent scholarship
    - Added material on relative income equality and tax rates
    - Updates made to recast Levvittown in the *Visualizing the Past* feature
    - New *Links to the World* feature: Sputnik

16. **Chapter 26: The Tumultuous Sixties, 1960–1968**
    - Added material on federal spending on social welfare programs
    - New section on Mexican American and Chicano activism
    - Updated and revised *Legacy for a People and a Nation* feature: "The Immigration Act of 1965"
    - Minor updates to the Vietnam section

17. **Chapter 27: A Pivotal Era, 1969–1980**
    - New chapter-opening vignette on the Iran hostage crisis
    - A section on Puerto Rican nationalism has been added
    - Updated *Legacy for A People and a Nation* feature: "The All-Volunteer Force"
    - Information on Pentagon Papers case has been added

18. **Chapter 28: Conservatism Revived, 1980–1992**
    - New chapter-opening vignette on 1980 "Washington for Jesus" rally
    - New scholarship on rise of conservatism
    - Revised discussion of economic policies and results
    - Additional material on computer technology

19. **Chapter 29: Into the Global Millennium: America Since 1992**
    - Added discussion of Obama's presidency and accomplishments
    - Fully recast and updated final section on Americans in the new millennium
    - Information added on the digital revolution
    - Significant changes to the section on Obama's foreign policy, including in the second term, including the rise of ISIS and the civil war in Syria

Format for Each Chapter

Opening Vignette

Each chapter opens with a brief story about a person, place, or event and includes an image related to the story. The stories highlight specific events with historical significance while bringing attention to the larger themes in U.S. History during that period.

Focus Questions

Each chapter section is accompanied by a set of focus questions that guide students in absorbing and interpreting the information in the section that follows. This is a new pedagogical feature added in this edition to help students retain the information they are learning as they move through the book.

Chapter Features: *Legacies, Links to the World,* and *Visualizing the Past*

The following three features— *Legacy for* A People and a Nation, *Links to the World*, and *Visualizing the Past*—are included in each chapter of *A People and A Nation*, eleventh edition:. These features all illustrate key themes of the text and give students alternative ways to experience historical content.

Legacy for A People and A Nation features appear toward the end of each chapter and offer compelling and timely answers to students who question the relevance of historical study by exploring the historical roots of contemporary topics. New *Legacies* in this edition include "Fictions of Salem: Witch-Hunting in the American Grain," "The Star-Spangled Banner," and "The Mexican-United States Border."

Links to the World features examine ties between America (and Americans) and the rest of the world. These brief essays detail the often little-known connections between developments here and abroad, vividly demonstrating that the geographical region that is now the United States has never been isolated from other peoples and countries. Essay topics range broadly over economic, political, social, technological, medical, and cultural history, and the feature appears near relevant discussions in each chapter. This edition includes new *Links* on anthropologist Margaret Mead and on Sputnik and American education. Each *Link* feature highlights global interconnections with unusual and lively examples that will both intrigue and inform students.

Visualizing the Past features offer striking images along with brief discussions intended to help students analyze the images as historical sources and to understand how visual materials can reveal aspects of America's story that otherwise might remain unknown. New to this edition is "A British View of the Colonial Army" in Chapter 6.

Summary

The core text of each chapter ends with a brief summary that helps students synthesize what they have just read and directs students to see long-term trends and recurring themes that appear across chapters.

Suggested Readings

A list of secondary sources appears at the end of each chapter for students and instructors who want to dig deeper into the content of the chapter.

Key Terms

Within each chapter, terms are boldfaced for students' attention with brief definitions appearing on the same page. Terms highlighted include concepts, laws, treaties, movements and organizations, legal cases, and battles.

MindTap for *A People and A Nation*

- MindTap 2-semester Instant Access Code: ISBN 9781337402750

- MindTap 2-semester Printed Access Card: ISBN - 9781337402767

- MindTap 1-semester Instant Access Code: ISBN 9781337404686

- MindTap 1-semester Printed Access Card: ISBN 9781337404693

MindTap for *A People and A Nation* is a flexible online learning platform that provides students with an immersive learning experience to build and foster critical thinking skills. Through a carefully designed chapter-based learning path, MindTap allows students to easily identify learning objectives; draw connections and improve writing skills by 1) completing unit-level essay assignments; 2) reading short, manageable sections from the ebook: 3) and testing their content knowledge with map-based critical thinking questions.

MindTap allows instructors to customize their content, providing tools that seamlessly integrate YouTube clips, outside websites, and personal content directly into the learning path. Instructors can assign additional primary source content through the Instructor Resource Center and Questia primary- and secondary-source databases that house thousands of peer-reviewed journals, newspapers, magazines, and full-length books.

The additional content available in MindTap mirrors and complements the authors' narrative, but also includes primary-source content and assessments not found in the printed text. To learn more, ask your Cengage sales representative to demo it for you—or go to www.Cengage.com/MindTap.

Supplements for *A People and A Nation*

- **Instructor's Companion Website.** The Instructor's Companion Website, accessed through the Instructor Resource Center (login.cengage.com), houses all of the supplemental materials you can use for your course. This includes a Test Bank, Instructor's Manual, and PowerPoint Lecture Presentations. The Test Bank, offered in Microsoft® Word® and Cognero® formats, contains multiple-choice, true-or-false, and essay questions for each chapter. Cognero® is a flexible, online system that allows you to author, edit, and manage test bank content for *A People and a Nation*, 11e. Create multiple test versions instantly and deliver through your LMS from your classroom, or wherever you may be, with no special installs or downloads required. The Instructor's Resource Manual includes chapter summaries, and outlines, learning objectives, suggested lecture topics, discussion questions class activities, and suggestions for additional films to watch. Finally, the PowerPoint Lectures are ADA-compliant slides collate the key takeaways from the chapter in concise visual formats perfect for in-class presentations or for student review.

- **Cengagebrain.com.** Save your students time and money. Direct them to www.cengagebrain.com for a choice in formats and savings and a better chance to succeed in your class. Cengagebrain.com, Cengage's online store, is a single destination for more than 10,000 new textbooks, eTextbooks, eChapters, study tools, and audio supplements. Students have the freedom to purchase à la carte exactly what they need when they need it. Students can save 50 percent on the electronic textbook and can purchase an individual eChapter for as little as $1.99.

- *Doing History: Research and Writing in the Digital Age,* 2e ISBN: 9781133587880 Prepared by Michael J. Galgano, J. Chris Arndt, and Raymond M. Hyser of James Madison University. Whether you're starting down the path as a history major or simply looking for a straightforward, systematic guide to writing a successful paper, this text's "soup to nuts" approach to researching and writing about history addresses every step of the process: locating your sources, gathering information, writing and citing according to various style guides, and avoiding plagiarism.

- *Writing for College History*, 1e ISBN: 9780618306039 Prepared by Robert M. Frakes of Clarion University. This brief handbook for survey courses in American, western, and world history guides students through the various types of writing assignments they may encounter in a history class. Providing examples of student writing and candid assessments of student work, this text focuses on the rules and conventions of writing for the college history course.

- *The Modern Researcher*, 6e ISBN: 9780495318705 Prepared by Jacques Barzun and Henry F. Graff of Columbia University. This classic introduction to the techniques of research and the art of expression thoroughly covers every aspect of research, from the selection of a topic through the gathering of materials, analysis, writing, revision, and publication of findings. They present the process not as a set of rules but through actual cases that put the subtleties of research in a useful context. Part One covers the principles and methods of research; Part Two covers writing, speaking, and getting one's work published.

- *Reader Program.* Cengage publishes a number of readers. Some contain exclusively primary sources, others are devoted to essays and secondary sources, and still others provide a combination of primary and secondary sources. All of these readers are designed to guide students through the process of historical inquiry. Visit www.cengage.com/history for a complete list of readers.

- *Custom Options.* Nobody knows your students like you, so why not give them a text that is tailor-fit to their needs? Cengage offers custom solutions for your course—whether it's making a small modification to *A People and a Nation*, 11e, to match your syllabus or combining multiple sources to create something truly unique. Contact your Cengage representative to explore custom solutions for your course.

Acknowledgments

The authors would like to thank Timothy Cole, David Farber, Mark Guerci, Anna Daileader Sheriff, and Benjamin Daileader Sheriff for their assistance with the preparation of this edition.

We also want to thank the many instructors who have adopted *APAN* over the years. We have been very grateful for the comments from the historian reviewers who read drafts of our chapters. Their suggestions, corrections, and pleas helped guide us through this revision. We could not include all of their recommendations, but the book is better for our having heeded most of their advice. We heartily thank:

Dawn Cioffoletti, *Florida Gulf Coast University*

Charles Cox, *Bridgewater State College*

Mary Daggett, *San Jacinto College - Central*

Jesse Esparza, *Texas Southern University*

Miriam Forman-Brunell, *University of Missouri, Kansas City*

Amy Forss, *Metropolitan Community College – South*

Devethia Guillory, *Lonestar College - North Harris*

Gordon Harvey, *Jacksonville State University*

Kathleen Gorman, *Minnesota State University, Mankato*

Jennifer Gross, *Jacksonville State University*

Donna Hoffa, *Wayne County Community College*

Richard Hughes, *Illinois State University*

Lesley Kauffman, *San Jacinto College – Central*

Karen Kossie-Chernyshev, *Texas Southern University*

Mary Hovanec, *Cuyahoga Community College*

Yu Shen, *Indiana University - Southeast*

Michael Swope, *Wayne County Community College*

Nancy Young, *University of Houston*

The authors thank the helpful Cengage people who designed, edited, produced, and nourished this book. Many thanks to Joseph Potvin, product manager; Kate MacLean, senior content developer; Claire Branman, associate content developer; Pembroke Herbert, photo researcher; Charlotte Miller, art editor; and Carol Newman, senior content project manager.

J. K.
C. S.
D. B.
H. C.
F. L.
B. B.
M. B. N.

Jane Kamensky

Born in New York City, Jane Kamensky earned her BA (1985) and PhD (1993) from Yale University. She is now Professor of History at Harvard University and the Pforzheimer Foundation Director of the Schlesinger Library on the History of Women in America. She is the author of *A Revolution in Color: The World of John Singleton Copley* (2016), winner of the New York Historical Society's Barbara and David Zalaznick Book Prize in American History and the Annibel Jenkins Biography Prize of the American Society for Eighteenth-Century Studies; *The Exchange Artist: A Tale of High-Flying Speculation and America's First Banking Collapse* (2008), a finalist for the 2009 George Washington Book Prize; *Governing the Tongue: The Politics of Speech in Early New England* (1997); and *The Colonial Mosaic: American Women, 1600–1760* (1995); and the coeditor of *The Oxford Handbook of the American Revolution* (2012). With Jill Lepore, she is the coauthor of the historical novel *Blindspot* (2008), a *New York Times* editor's choice and *Boston Globe* bestseller. In 1999, she and Lepore also cofounded *Common-place* (www.common-place.org), which remains a leading online journal of early American history and life. Jane has also served on the editorial boards of the *American Historical Review*, the *Journal of American History*, and the *Journal of the Early Republic*; as well as on the Council of the American Antiquarian Society, the Executive Board of the Organization of American Historians, and as a Commissioner of the Smithsonian's National Portrait Gallery. Called on frequently as an advisor to public history projects, she has appeared on PBS, C-SPAN, the History Channel, and NPR, among other media outlets. Jane, who was awarded two university-wide teaching prizes in her previous position at Brandeis, has won numerous major grants and fellowships to support her scholarship.

Carol Sheriff

Born in Washington, D.C., and raised in Bethesda, Maryland, Carol Sheriff received her BA from Wesleyan University (1985) and her PhD from Yale University (1993). Since 1993, she has taught history at the College of William and Mary, where she has won the Thomas Jefferson Teaching Award; the Alumni Teaching Fellowship Award; the University Professorship for Teaching Excellence; The Class of 2013 Distinguished Professorship for Excellence in Scholarship, Teaching, and Service; and the Arts and Sciences Award for Teaching Excellence. Her publications include *The Artificial River: The Erie Canal and the Paradox of Progress* (1996), which won the Dixon Ryan Fox Award from the New York State Historical Association and the Award for Excellence in Research from the New York State Archives, and *A People at War: Civilians and Soldiers in America's Civil War, 1854–1877* (with Scott Reynolds Nelson, 2007). In 2012, she won the John T. Hubbell Prize from *Civil War History* for her article on the state-commissioned Virginia history textbooks of the 1950s, and the controversies their portrayals of the Civil War era provoked in ensuing decades. Carol has written sections of a teaching manual for the New York State history curriculum, given presentations at Teaching American History grant projects, consulted on an exhibit for the Rochester Museum and Science Center, and appeared in The History Channel's Modern Marvels show on the Erie Canal. She worked on several public-history projects marking the sesquicentennial of the Civil War, and is involved in public and scholarly projects to commemorate the Erie Canal's bicentennial. At William and Mary, she teaches the U.S. history survey as well as upper-level classes on the Early Republic, the Civil War Era, and the American West.

David W. Blight

Born in Flint, Michigan, David W. Blight received his BA from Michigan State University (1971) and his PhD from the University of Wisconsin (1985). He is now professor of history and director of the Gilder Lehrman Center for the Study of Slavery, Resistance, and Abolition at Yale University. For the first seven years of his career, David was a public high school teacher in Flint. He has written *Frederick Douglass's Civil War* (1989) and *Race and Reunion: The Civil War in American Memory, 1863–1915* (2000), which received eight awards, including the Bancroft Prize, the Frederick Douglass Prize, the Abraham Lincoln Prize, and four prizes awarded by the Organization of American Historians. His most recent books are a biography of Frederick Douglass (forthcoming in 2018); *American Oracle: The Civil War in the Civil Rights Era* (2011) and *A Slave No More: The Emancipation of John Washington and Wallace Turnage* (2007), which won three book prizes. His edited works include *When This Cruel War Is Over: The Civil War Letters of Charles Harvey Brewster* (1992), *Narrative of the Life of Frederick Douglass* (1993), W. E. B. Du Bois, *The Souls of Black Folk* (with Robert Gooding Williams, 1997), *Union and Emancipation* (with Brooks Simpson, 1997), and *Caleb Bingham, The Columbian Orator* (1997). David's essays have appeared in the *Journal of American History* and *Civil War History*, among others. A consultant to several documentary films, David appeared in the 1998 PBS series, *Africans in America*. David also teaches summer seminars for secondary school teachers, as well as for park rangers and historians of the National Park Service. He has served on the Executive Board of the Organization of American Historians, and in 2012, he was elected to the American Academy of Arts and Sciences. In 2013–2014 David was Pitt Professor of American History and Institutions at the University of Cambridge in the United Kingdom.

Howard P. Chudacoff

Howard P. Chudacoff, the George L. Littlefield Professor of American History and Professor of Urban Studies at Brown University, was born in Omaha, Nebraska. He earned his AB (1965) and PhD (1969) from the University of Chicago. He has written *Mobile Americans* (1972), *How Old Are You?* (1989), *The Age of the Bachelor* (1999), *The Evolution of American Urban Society* (with Judith Smith, 2004), and *Children at Play: An American History* (2007) and *Changing the Playbook: How Power, Profit, and Politics Transformed College Sports* (2015). He has also coedited (with Peter Baldwin) *Major Problems in American Urban History* (2004). His articles have appeared in such journals as the *Journal of Family History, Reviews in American History*, and *Journal of American History*. At Brown University, Howard has cochaired the American Civilization Program and chaired the Department of History, and served as Brown's faculty representative to the NCAA. He has also served on the board of directors of the Urban History Association and the editorial board of *The National Journal of Play*. The National Endowment for the Humanities, Ford Foundation, and Rockefeller Foundation have given him awards to advance his scholarship.

Fredrik Logevall

A native of Stockholm, Sweden, Fredrik Logevall is Laurence D. Belfer Professor of International Affairs at Harvard University, where he holds appointments in the Department of History and the Kennedy School of Government. He received his BA from Simon Fraser University (1986) and his PhD from Yale University (1993). His most recent book is *Embers of War: The Fall of an Empire and the Making of America's Vietnam* (2012), which won the Pulitzer Prize in History and the Francis Parkman Prize, and which was named a best book of the year by the *Washington Post* and the *Christian Science Monitor*. His other publications include *Choosing War* (1999), which won three prizes, including the Warren F. Kuehl Book Prize from the Society for Historians of American Foreign Relations (SHAFR); *America's Cold War: The Politics of Insecurity* (with Campbell Craig; 2009); *The Origins of the Vietnam War* (2001); *Terrorism and 9/11: A Reader* (2002); and, as coeditor, *The First Vietnam War: Colonial Conflict and Cold War Crisis* (2007); and *Nixon and the World: American Foreign Relations, 1969–1977* (2008). Fred is a past recipient of the Stuart L. Bernath article, book, and lecture prizes from SHAFR, and a past member of the Cornell University Press faculty board. He serves on numerous editorial advisory boards. A past president of SHAFR, Fred is a member of the Society of American Historians and the Council of Foreign Relations.

Beth Bailey

Born in Atlanta, Georgia, Beth Bailey received her BA from Northwestern University (1979) and her PhD from the University of Chicago (1986). She is now Foundation Distinguished Professor of History and director of the Center for Military, War, and Society Studies at the University of Kansas. Beth served as the coordinating author for the tenth and eleventh editions of *A People and A Nation*. She is the author of *America's Army: Making the All-Volunteer Force* (2009), which won the Army Historical Foundation's Distinguished Writing Award; *The Columbia Companion to America in the 1960s* (with David Farber, 2001); *Sex in the Heartland* (1999); *The First Strange Place: The Alchemy of Race and Sex in WWII Hawaii* (with David Farber, 1992); and *From Front Porch to Back Seat: Courtship in 20th Century America* (1988). She also co-edited *Understanding the U.S. Wars in Iraq and Afghanistan* (2015); *America in the Seventies* (2004); and the reader *A History of Our Time* (multiple editions). Beth has lectured in Australia, Indonesia, France, Germany, the Netherlands, Great Britain, Japan, Saudi Arabia, Lebanon, and China. She is a trustee for the Society of Military History and was appointed by the Secretary of the Army to the Department of the Army Historical Advisory Committee. Beth has received several major grants or fellowships in support of her research. She teaches courses on the history of gender and sexuality and on U.S. Military, War, and Society.

Mary Beth Norton

Born in Ann Arbor, Michigan, Mary Beth Norton received her BA from the University of Michigan (1964) and her PhD from Harvard University (1969). She is the Mary Donlon Alger Professor of American History at Cornell University. Her dissertation won the Allan Nevins Prize. She has written *The British-Americans* (1972); *Liberty's Daughters* (1980, 1996); *Founding Mothers & Fathers* (1996), which was one of three finalists for the 1997 Pulitzer Prize in History; and *In the Devil's Snare* (2002), one of five finalists for the 2003 *L.A. Times* Book Prize in History and won the English-Speaking Union's Ambassador Book Award in American Studies for 2003. Her most recent book is *Separated by Their Sex* (2011). She has coedited three volumes on American women's history. She was also general editor of the *American Historical Association's Guide to Historical Literature* (1995). Her articles have appeared in such journals as the *American Historical Review, William and Mary Quarterly*, and *Journal of Women's History*. Mary Beth has served as president of the American Historical Association and the Berkshire Conference of Women Historians, as vice president for research of the American Historical Association, and as a presidential appointee to the National Council on the Humanities. She has appeared on Book TV, the History and Discovery Channels, PBS, and NBC as a commentator on Early American history, and she has lectured frequently to high school teachers. She has received four honorary degrees and is an elected member of both the American Academy of Arts and Sciences and the American Philosophical Society. She has held fellowships from the National Endowment for the Humanities; the Guggenheim, Rockefeller, and Starr Foundations; and the Henry E. Huntington Library. In 2005–2006, she was the Pitt Professor of American History and Institutions at the University of Cambridge and Newnham College.

A People & A Nation

14

Reconstruction: An Unfinished Revolution, 1865–1877

T he lower half of the city of Charleston, South Carolina, the seedbed of seces- sion, lay in ruin when most of the white population evacuated on February 18, 1865. A bombardment by Union batteries and gunboats around Charleston harbor had already destroyed many of the lovely, neoclassical townhomes of the low-country planters. Then, as the city was abandoned, fires broke out everywhere, ignited in bales of cotton left in huge stockpiles in public squares. To many observers, the flames were the funeral pyres of a dying civilization.

Among the first Union troops to enter Charleston was the Twenty-first U.S. Colored Regiment, which received the surrender of the city from its mayor. For black Charlestonians, most of whom were former slaves, this was a time of celebration. In symbolic ceremonies, they pro- claimed their freedom and announced their rebirth. Whatever the postwar order would bring, the freedpeople of Charleston converted Confederate ruin into a vision of Reconstruction based on Union victory and black liberation.

Still, in Charleston as elsewhere, death demanded attention. During the final year of the war, the Confederates had converted the planters' Race Course, a horse-racing track, and its famed Washington Jockey Club, into a prison. Union soldiers were kept in terrible conditions in the interior of the track, without shelter. The 257 who died there of exposure and disease were buried in a mass grave behind the grandstand. After the fall of the city, Charleston's black people organized to create a proper burial ground for the Union dead. During April,

◀ Photograph of the grandstand and clubhouse of the Washington Jockey Club and Race Course, Charleston, SC, site of Confederate prison and burial ground of more than 260 Union soldiers, as well as the first commemo- ration of Decoration Day, May 1, 1865. Library of Congress, Prints & Photographs Division [LC-DIG-stereo-1s02451]

Chronology

1865	■ Johnson begins rapid and lenient Reconstruction
	■ White southern governments pass restrictive black codes
	■ Congress refuses to seat southern representatives
	■ Thirteenth Amendment ratified, abolishing slavery
1866	■ Congress passes Civil Rights Act and renewal of Freedmen's Bureau over Johnson's veto
	■ Congress approves Fourteenth Amendment
	■ In *Ex parte Milligan*, the Supreme Court reasserts its influence
1867	■ Congress passes First Reconstruction Act and Tenure of Office Act
	■ Constitutional conventions called in southern states
1868	■ House impeaches and Senate acquits Johnson
	■ Most southern states readmitted to Union under Radical plan
	■ Fourteenth Amendment ratified
	■ Grant elected president
1869	■ Congress approves Fifteenth Amendment (ratified in 1870)
	■ Sharecropping takes hold across a cash-poor southern economy
1871	■ Congress passes second Enforcement Act and Ku Klux Klan Act
	■ Treaty with England settles *Alabama* claims
1872	■ Amnesty Act frees almost all remaining Confederates from restrictions on holding office
	■ Grant reelected
1873	■ Slaughter-House cases limit power of Fourteenth Amendment
	■ Panic of 1873 leads to widespread unemployment and labor strife
1874	■ Democrats win majority in House of Representatives
1875	■ Several Grant appointees indicted for corruption
	■ Congress passes weak Civil Rights Act
	■ Democratic Party increases control of southern states with white supremacy campaigns
1876	■ *U.S. v. Cruikshank* further weakens Fourteenth Amendment
	■ Presidential election disputed
1877	■ Congress elects Hayes president

more than twenty black workmen reinterred the dead in marked graves and built a high fence around the cemetery. On the archway over the cemetery's entrance they painted the inscription "Martyrs of the Race Course."

And then they planned an extraordinary ceremony. On the morning of May 1, 1865, a procession of ten thousand people marched around the planters' Race Course, led by three thousand children carrying armloads of roses and singing "John Brown's Body." The children were followed by black women with baskets of flowers and wreaths, and then by black men. The parade concluded with members of black and white Union regiments, along with white missionaries and teachers led by James Redpath, the supervisor of freedmen's schools in the region. All who could fit assembled at the gravesite; five black ministers read from scripture, and a black children's choir sang "America," "We'll Rally 'Round the Flag," "The Star-Spangled Banner," and Negro spirituals. When the ceremony ended, the huge crowd retired to the Race Course for speeches, picnics, and military festivities.

Experience an interactive version of this story in MindTap®.

The war was over in Charleston, and "Decoration Day"—now Memorial Day, the day to remember the war dead and decorate their graves with flowers—had been founded by African Americans and their allies. Black people—by their labor, their words, their songs, and their marching feet on the old planters' Race Course—had created an American tradition. In their vision, they were creating the Independence Day of a Second American Revolution.

Reconstruction would bring revolutionary circumstances, but revolutions can also go backward. The Civil War and its aftermath wrought unprecedented changes in American society, law, and politics, but the underlying realities of economic power, racism, and judicial conservatism limited Reconstruction's revolutionary potential. As never before, the nation had to determine the nature of federal-state relations, whether confiscated land could be redistributed, and how to bring justice to both freedpeople and aggrieved white southerners whose property and lives had been devastated. Americans were about to try to redefine citizenship, fundamental civil and political rights, and equality before law against unrelenting opposition. A disunited country faced the harrowing challenge of psychological healing from a bloody and fratricidal war. How they would negotiate the tangled relationship between healing and justice would determine the fate of Reconstruction.

Nowhere was the turmoil of Reconstruction more evident than in national politics. Lincoln's successor, Andrew Johnson, fought bitterly with Congress over the shaping of Reconstruction policies. Although a southerner, Johnson had always been a foe of the South's wealthy planters, and his first acts as president suggested that he would be tough on "traitors." Before the end of 1865, however, Johnson's policies changed direction, and he became the protector of white southern interests.

Johnson imagined a lenient and rapid "restoration" of the South to the Union rather than the fundamental "reconstruction" that Republican congressmen favored. Between 1866 and 1868, the president and the Republican leadership in Congress engaged in a bitter power struggle over how to put the United States back together again. Before the struggle ceased, Congress had impeached the president, enfranchised freedmen, and given them a role in reconstructing the South. The nation also adopted the Fourteenth and Fifteenth Amendments, ushering in equal protection of the law, a definition of birthright citizenship, and universal manhood suffrage into the Constitution.

By 1868–1869, the Ku Klux Klan employed extensive violence and terror to thwart Reconstruction and undermine black freedom. As white Democrats in the South took control of state governments in the 1870s, they encountered little opposition from the North. Moreover, the wartime industrial boom had created new opportunities and priorities. The West, with its seemingly limitless potential and its wars against Native peoples, drew American resources and consciousness like never before. Americans moved in huge numbers and sought new "homes" in the trans-Mississippi West and the homes of Native Americans were displaced or destroyed. Political corruption became a nationwide scandal, and bribery a way of doing business.

Thus, Reconstruction became a revolution eclipsed. The white South's desire to reclaim control of its states and of race relations overwhelmed the national interest in stopping it. But Reconstruction left enduring legacies from which the nation has benefited and with which it has struggled ever since. In every succeeding racial or constitutional reckoning, we often return to Reconstruction as a means of understanding ourselves anew.

- *Should the Reconstruction era be considered the Second American Revolution? By what criteria should we make such a judgment?*

- *What were the origins and meanings of the Fourteenth Amendment in the 1860s? What is its significance today?*

- *Reconstruction is judged to have "ended" in 1877. Over the course of the 1870s, what caused its end?*

14-1 Wartime Reconstruction

▶ **What were the features of Abraham Lincoln's vision for Reconstruction?**

▶ **Why did Abraham Lincoln and Congress differ over Reconstruction policy?**

▶ **How did the creation and operation of the Freedman's Bureau signify a new expansive role for the federal government in society?**

Civil wars leave immense challenges of healing, justice, and physical rebuilding. Anticipating that process, reconstruction of the Union was an issue as early as 1863, well before the war ended. Many key questions loomed on the horizon when and if the North succeeded on the battlefield: How would the nation be restored? How would southern states and leaders be treated—as errant brothers or as traitors? How would a devastated southern economy be revived? What was the constitutional basis for readmission of states to the Union, and where, if anywhere, could American statesmen look for precedence or guidance? As winners of the war, could radical Republicans take their emancipation and human equality agenda abroad and spread it to foreign lands? More specifically, four vexing problems compelled early thinking and would haunt the Reconstruction era throughout. One, who would rule in the South once it was defeated? Two, who would rule in the federal government—Congress or the president? Three, what were the dimensions of black freedom, and what rights under law would the freedmen enjoy? And four, would Reconstruction be a preservation of the old republic or a second Revolution, a reinvention of a new republic?

14-1a Lincoln's 10 Percent Plan

Abraham Lincoln had never been antisouthern, though he had become the leader of an antislavery war. He lost three brothers-in-law, killed in the war on the Confederate side. His worst fear was that the war would collapse at the end into guerrilla warfare across the South, with surviving bands of Confederates carrying on resistance. Lincoln insisted that his generals give lenient terms to southern soldiers once they surrendered. In his Second Inaugural Address, delivered only a month before his assassination, Lincoln promised "malice toward none; with charity for all," as Americans strove to "bind up the nation's wounds."

Lincoln planned early for a swift and moderate Reconstruction process. In his "Proclamation of Amnesty and Reconstruction," issued in December 1863, he proposed to replace majority rule with "loyal rule" as a means of reconstructing southern state governments. He proposed pardons to all ex-Confederates except the highest-ranking military and civilian officers. Then, as soon as 10 percent of the voting population in the 1860 general election in a given state had taken an oath to the United States and established a government, the new state would be recognized. Lincoln did not consult Congress in these plans, and "loyal" assemblies (known as "Lincoln governments") were created in Louisiana, Tennessee, and Arkansas in 1864, states largely occupied by Union troops. These governments were weak and dependent on northern armies for survival.

14-1b Congress and the Wade-Davis Bill

Congress responded with great hostility to Lincoln's moves to readmit southern states in what seemed such a premature manner. Many Radical Republicans, strong proponents of emancipation and of aggressive prosecution of the war against the South, considered the 10 percent plan a "mere mockery" of democracy. Led by Thaddeus Stevens of Pennsylvania in the House and Charles Sumner of Massachusetts

Thirteenth Amendment The constitutional amendment that abolished slavery; passed by Congress in 1865.

in the Senate, congressional Republicans locked horns with Lincoln and proposed a longer and harsher approach to Reconstruction. Stevens advocated a "conquered provinces" theory, arguing that southerners had organized as a foreign nation to make war on the United States and, by secession, had destroyed their status as states. They therefore must be treated as "conquered foreign lands" and returned to the status of "unorganized territories" before any process of readmission could be entertained by Congress.

In July 1864, the Wade-Davis bill, named for its sponsors, Senator Benjamin Wade of Ohio and Congressman Henry W. Davis of Maryland, emerged from Congress with three specific conditions for southern readmission.

1. It demanded a "majority" of white male citizens participate in the creation of a new government.
2. To vote or be a delegate to constitutional conventions, men had to take an "iron-clad" oath (declaring that they had never aided the Confederate war effort).
3. All officers above the rank of lieutenant and all civil officials in the Confederacy would be disfranchised and deemed "not a citizen of the United States."

The Confederate states were to be defined as "conquered enemies," said Davis, and the process of readmission was to be harsh and slow. Lincoln, ever the adroit politician, pocket-vetoed the bill and issued a conciliatory proclamation of his own, announcing that he would not be inflexibly committed to any "one plan" of Reconstruction.

This exchange came during Grant's bloody campaign against Lee in Virginia, when the outcome of the war and Lincoln's reelection were still in doubt. On August 5, Radical Republicans issued the "Wade-Davis Manifesto" to newspapers. An unprecedented attack on a sitting president by members of his own party, it accused Lincoln of usurpation of presidential powers and disgraceful leniency toward an eventually conquered South. What emerged in 1864–1865 was a clear debate and a potential constitutional crisis. Lincoln saw Reconstruction as a means of weakening the Confederacy and winning the war; the Radicals saw it as a longer-term transformation of the political and racial order of the country.

14-1c Thirteenth Amendment

In early 1865, Congress and Lincoln joined in two important measures that recognized slavery's centrality to the war. On January 31, with strong administration backing, Congress passed the **Thirteenth Amendment**, which had two provisions: first, it abolished involuntary servitude everywhere in the United States; second, it declared that Congress shall have the power to enforce this outcome by "appropriate legislation." When the measure passed by 119 to 56, a mere two votes more than the necessary two-thirds, rejoicing broke out in Congress. A Republican recorded in his diary, "Members joined in the shouting and kept it up for some minutes. Some embraced one another, others wept like children. I have felt ever since the vote, as if I were in a new country."

But the Thirteenth Amendment had emerged from a long congressional debate and considerable petitioning and public advocacy. One of the first and most remarkable petitions for a constitutional amendment abolishing slavery was submitted early in 1864 by Elizabeth Cady Stanton, Susan B. Anthony, and the Women's Loyal National League. Women throughout the Union accumulated thousands of signatures, even venturing into staunchly pro-Confederate regions of Kentucky and Missouri to secure supporters. It was a long road from the Emancipation Proclamation to the Thirteenth Amendment—through treacherous constitutional theory about individual "property rights," a bedrock of belief that the sacred document ought never to be altered, and partisan politics. There had not been a Constitutional amendment since 1789, when the Twelfth Amendment established what we today call the Electoral College. But the logic of winning the war by crushing slavery, and of securing a new beginning under law for the nation that so many had died to save, won the day.

14-1d Freedmen's Bureau

Potentially as significant, on March 3, 1865, Congress created the Bureau of Refugees, Freedmen, and Abandoned Lands—the Freedmen's Bureau, an unprecedented agency of social uplift necessitated by the ravages of the war. Americans had never engaged in federal aid to citizens on such a scale. With thousands of refugees, white and black, displaced in the South, the government continued what private freedmen's aid societies had started as early as 1862. In the mere four years of its existence, the Freedmen's Bureau supplied food and medical services, built several thousand schools and some colleges, negotiated several hundred thousand employment contracts between freedpeople and their former masters, and tried to manage confiscated land.

Throughout its existence—it lasted until 1872, when Congress refused to approve renewal legislation—the Bureau remained controversial within the South, where whites generally hated it, and within the federal government, where politicians divided over its constitutionality. Some bureau agents were devoted to freedmen's rights, whereas others were opportunists who exploited the chaos of the postwar South. The war had forced into the open an eternal question of republics: what are the social welfare obligations of the state toward its people, and what do people owe their governments in return? Apart from their conquest and displacement of eastern Native peoples, Americans were relatively inexperienced at the Freedmen's Bureau's task—social reform through military occupation. They were also unaccustomed to the sheer reality that *government* possessed the only resources and institutions capable of confronting the social and economic chaos wrought by the war. Military occupation of significant parts of the South lasted into the late 1860s, but Americans had little experience with this kind of federal power.

14-1e Ruins and Enmity

In 1865, due to the devastation of the war, America was now a land with ruins. Like the countries of Europe, it now seemed an older, more historic landscape. Physically, politically, and spiritually, it had torn itself asunder. Some of its cities lay in rubble, large stretches of the southern countryside were depopulated and defoliated, and thousands of people, white and black, were refugees. Some of this would in time seem romantic to northern travelers in the postwar South.

Thousands of yeoman farmer-soldiers, some paroled by surrenders, walked home too late in the season to plant a crop in a collapsed economy. Many white refugees faced genuine starvation. Of the approximately 18,300,000 rations distributed across the South in the first three years of the Freedmen's Bureau, 5,230,000 went to whites. In early 1866, in a proud agricultural society, the legislature of South Carolina issued $300,000 in state bonds to purchase corn for the destitute.

In October 1865, just after a five-month imprisonment in Boston, former Confederate vice president Alexander H. Stephens rode a slow train southward. In Virginia, he found "the desolation of the country . . . was horrible to behold." When Stephens reached northern Georgia, his native state, his shock ran over: "War has left a terrible impression. . . . Fences gone, fields all a-waste, houses burnt." A northern journalist visiting Richmond that same fall observed a city "mourning for her sins . . . in dust and ashes." The "burnt district" was a "bed of cinders . . . broken and blackened walls, impassable streets deluged with debris." Above all, every northern traveler encountered a wall of hatred among white southerners for their conquerors. An innkeeper in North Carolina told a journalist that Yankees had killed his sons in the war, burned his house, and stolen his slaves. "They left me one inestimable privilege," he said, "to hate 'em. I git up at half-past four in the morning, and sit up 'til twelve at night, to hate 'em."

14-2 The Meanings of Freedom

▶ How did African Americans respond to and explore their new freedom after the war?

▶ What challenges did freedpeople face in obtaining land?

▶ How did education for freedpeople develop after the war?

▶ How did sharecropping affect freedpeople's desire to be economically independent?

Black southerners entered into life after slavery with hope and circumspection. A Texas man recalled his father telling him, even before the war was over, "Our forever was going to be spent living among the Southerners, after they got licked." Freed men and women tried to gain as much as they could from their new circumstances. Often the changes they valued the most were personal—alterations in location, employer, or living arrangements.

14-2a The Feel of Freedom

For America's former slaves, Reconstruction had one paramount meaning: a chance to explore freedom. A southern white woman admitted in her diary that the black people "showed a natural and exultant joy at being free." Former slaves remembered singing far into the night after federal troops, who confirmed rumors of their emancipation, reached their plantations. The slaves on a Texas plantation shouted for joy, their leader proclaiming, "We is free—no more whippings and beatings." A few people gave in to the natural desire to do what had been impossible before. One angry grandmother dropped her hoe and ran to confront her mistress. "I'm free!" she yelled. "Yes, I'm free! Ain't got to work for you no more! You can't put me in your pocket now!" Another man recalled that he and others "started on the move," either to search for family members or just to exercise the human right of mobility.

Many freed men and women reacted more cautiously and shrewdly, taking care to test the boundaries of their new condition. "After the war was over," explained one man, "we was afraid to move. Just like terrapins or turtles after emancipation. Just stick our heads out to see how the land lay." As slaves, they had learned to expect hostility from white people, and they did not presume it would instantly disappear. Life in freedom might still be a matter of what was possible, not what was right. Many freedpeople evaluated potential employers with shrewd caution. "Most all the Negroes that had good owners stayed with 'em, but the others left. Some of 'em come back and some didn't," explained one man. After considerable wandering in search of better circumstances, a majority of blacks eventually settled as agricultural workers back on their former farms or plantations. They often relocated their houses and did their utmost to control the conditions of their labor.

14-2b Reunion of African American Families

Throughout the South, former slaves devoted themselves to reuniting their families, separated during slavery by sale or hardship, and during the war by dislocation and the emancipation process. With only shreds of information to guide them, thousands of freedpeople embarked on odysseys in search of a husband, wife, child, or parent. By relying on the black community for help and information, and by placing ads that continued to appear in black newspapers such as the *Christian Recorder*, a national journal published by the African Methodist Episcopal Church, well into the 1880s, some succeeded in their quest, while others searched in vain.

Husbands and wives who had belonged to different masters established homes together for the first time, and, as they had tried under slavery, parents asserted the right to raise their own children. A mother bristled when her old master claimed a right to whip her children. She informed him that "he warn't goin' to brush none of her chilluns no more." The

freed men and women were too much at risk to act recklessly, but, as one man put it, they were tired of punishment and "sure didn't take no more foolishness off of white folks."

14-2c African Americans' Search for Independence

Many black people wanted to minimize contact with whites because, as Reverend Garrison Frazier told General Sherman in January 1865, "There is a prejudice against us . . . that will take years to get over." To avoid contact with overbearing whites who were used to supervising them, blacks abandoned the slave quarters and fanned out to distant corners of the land they worked. "After the war my stepfather come," recalled Annie Young, "and got my mother and we moved out in the piney woods." Others described moving "across the creek" or building a "saplin house . . . back in the woods." Some rural dwellers established small, all-black settlements that still exist along the back roads of the South.

Even once-privileged slaves desired such independence and social separation. One man turned down his master's offer of the overseer's house and moved instead to a shack in "Freetown." He also declined to let the former owner grind his grain for free because it "make him feel like a free man to pay for things just like anyone else."

14-2d Freedpeople's Desire for Land

In addition to a fair employer, what freed men and women most wanted was the ownership of land. Land represented self-sufficiency and a chance to gain compensation for generations of bondage. General Sherman's special Field Order Number 15, issued in February 1865, set aside 400,000 acres of land in the Sea Islands region for the exclusive settlement of freedpeople. Hope swelled among ex-slaves as forty-acre plots, mules, and "possessary titles" were promised to them. But President Johnson ordered them removed in October and the land returned to its original owners under army enforcement. A northern observer noted that slaves freed in the Sea Islands of South Carolina and Georgia made "plain, straight-forward" inquiries as they settled on new land. They wanted to be sure the land "would be theirs after they had improved it." Everywhere, black people young and old thirsted for homes of their own.

But most members of both political parties opposed genuine land redistribution to the freedmen. Even northern reformers who had administered the Sea Islands during the war showed little sympathy for black aspirations. The former Sea Island slaves wanted to establish small, self-sufficient farms. Northern soldiers, officials, and missionaries of both races brought education and aid to the freedmen but also insisted that they grow cotton for the competitive market.

"The Yankees preach nothing but cotton, cotton!" complained one Sea Island black. "We wants land," wrote another, but tax officials "make the lots too big, and cut we out." Indeed, the U.S. government eventually sold thousands of acres in the Sea Islands, 90 percent of which went to wealthy investors from the North. At a protest against evictions from a contraband camp in Virginia in 1866, freedman Bayley Wyatt made black desires and claims clear: "We has a right to the land where we are located. For why? I tell you. Our wives, our children, our husbands, has been sold over and over again to purchase the lands we now locates upon; for that reason we have a divine right to the land."

14-2e Freed Men and Women Embrace Education

Ex-slaves everywhere reached out for education. Black people of all ages hungered for the knowledge in books that had been permitted only to white people. With freedom, they started schools and filled classrooms both day and night. On log seats and dirt floors, freed men and women studied their letters in old almanacs and in discarded dictionaries. Young children brought infants to school with them, and adults attended at night or after "the crops were laid by." Many a teacher had "to make herself heard over three other classes reciting in concert" in a small room. The desire to escape slavery's ignorance was so great that, despite their poverty, many blacks paid tuition, typically $1 or $1.50 a month. These small amounts constituted major portions of a person's agricultural wages and added up to more than $1 million by 1870.

The federal government and northern reformers of both races assisted this pursuit of education. In its brief life, the Freedmen's Bureau founded over four thousand schools, and idealistic men and women from the North established others funded by private philanthropy. The Yankee schoolmarm—dedicated, selfless, and religious—became an agent of progress in many southern communities. Thus did African Americans seek a break from their past through learning. More than 600,000 were enrolled in elementary school by 1877. In a rural agricultural society recovering from wartime devastation, this was a stunning achievement.

Black people and their white allies also saw the need for colleges and universities. The American Missionary Association founded seven colleges, including Fisk University and Atlanta University, between 1866 and 1869. The Freedmen's Bureau helped to establish Howard University in Washington, D.C., and northern religious groups, such as the Methodists, Baptists, and Congregationalists, supported dozens of seminaries and teachers' colleges.

During Reconstruction, African American leaders often were highly educated individuals; many were from the prewar elite of free people of color. Francis Cardozo, who held various offices in South Carolina, had attended universities in Scotland and England. P. B. S. Pinchback, who became lieutenant governor of Louisiana, was the son of a planter who had sent him to school in Cincinnati. Both of the two black senators from Mississippi, Blanche K. Bruce and Hiram Revels, possessed privileged educations. Bruce was the son of a planter who had provided tutoring at home; Revels was the son of free black North Carolinians who had sent him to Knox College in Illinois.

14-2f Growth of Black Churches

Freed from the restrictions and regulations of slavery, African Americans could build their own institutions as they saw fit. The secret churches of slavery came into the open; in countless communities throughout the South, ex-slaves "started a brush arbor." A brush arbor was merely "a sort of . . . shelter with leaves for a roof," but the freed men and women worshipped in it enthusiastically. "Preachin' and shouting sometimes lasted all day," they recalled, for the opportunity to worship together freely meant "glorious times."

Within a few years, independent branches of the Methodist and Baptist denominations had attracted the great majority of black Christians in the South. By 1877, in South Carolina alone, the African Methodist Episcopal (AME) Church had a thousand ministers, 44,000 members, and its own school of theology, while the AME Zion Church had 45,000 members. In the rapid growth of churches, some of which became the wealthiest and most autonomous institutions in black life, the freedpeople demonstrated their most secure claim on freedom.

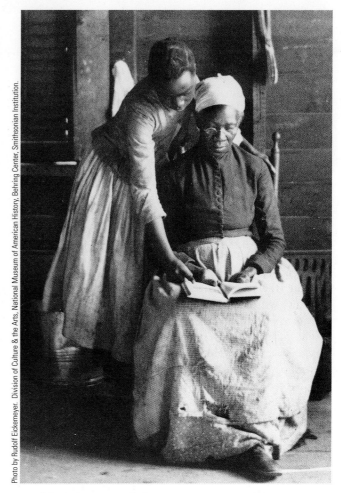

Photo by Rudolf Eickemeyer. Division of Culture & the Arts, National Museum of American History, Behring Center, Smithsonian Institution.

▲ African Americans of all ages eagerly pursued the opportunity to gain an education in freedom. This young woman in Mt. Meigs, Alabama, is helping her mother learn to read.

Library of Congress, Prints & Photographs Division, Reproduction number LC-USZ62-114267 (b&w film copy neg.)

◀ Churches became a center of African American life, both social and political, during and after Reconstruction. Churches large and small, like this one in Georgia became the first black-owned institutions for the postfreedom generation.

14-2g Rise of the Sharecropping System

The desire to gain as much independence as possible also shaped the former slaves' economic arrangements. Since most of them lacked money to buy land, they preferred the next best thing: renting the land they worked. But the South had a cash-poor economy with few sources of credit, and few whites would consider renting land to blacks. Most blacks had no means to get cash before the harvest, so other alternatives had to be tried.

Black farmers and white landowners therefore turned to **sharecropping**, a system in which farmers kept part of their crop and gave the rest to the landowner while living on his property. The landlord or a merchant "furnished" food and supplies, such as draft animals and seed, and he received payment from the crop. White landowners and black farmers bargained with one another; sharecroppers would hold out, or move and try to switch employers from one year to another. As the system matured during the 1870s and 1880s, most sharecroppers worked "on halves"—half for the owner and half for themselves.

The sharecropping system, which materialized as early as 1868 in parts of the South, originated as a desirable compromise between former slaves and landowners. It eased landowners' problems with cash and credit, and provided them a permanent, dependent labor force; blacks accepted it because it gave them freedom from daily supervision. In some districts women could leave field work, or even bargain for themselves to do less physical labor. Instead of working in the hated gangs under a white overseer, as in slavery, they farmed their own plots of land in family groups. But sharecropping later proved to be a disaster. Owners and merchants developed a monopoly of control over the agricultural economy, as sharecroppers found themselves mired in ever-increasing debt.

The fundamental problem, however, was that southern farmers as a whole still concentrated on cotton. In freedom, black women often chose to stay away from the fields and cotton picking to concentrate on domestic chores. Given the diminishing incentives of the system, they placed greater value on independent choices about gender roles and family organization than on reaching higher levels of production. The South did recover its prewar share of British cotton purchases, but cotton prices began a long decline, as world demand fell off.

Thus, southern agriculture slipped deeper and deeper into depression. Black sharecroppers struggled under a growing burden of debt that bound them to landowners and to "furnishing" merchants almost as oppressively as slavery had bound them to their masters. Many white farmers became debtors, too, gradually lost their land, and joined the ranks of sharecroppers. By the end of Reconstruction, over one-third of all southern farms were worked by sharecropping tenants, white and black.

sharecropping The system of tenant farming that replaced slavery; freedpeople "worked on halves," giving half of their crop to the landowner and taking half to market. The system left most freedpeople mired in debt with no social or geographic mobility.

Sharecropping: Enslaved to Debt

Sharecropping became an oppressive system in the postwar South. A new labor structure that began as a compromise between freedpeople who wanted independence and landowners who wanted a stable workforce evolved into a method of working on "halves," where tenants owed endless debts to the furnishing merchants, who owned plantation stores like this one, photographed in Mississippi in 1868. Merchants recorded in ledger books the debts that few sharecroppers were able to repay.

CRITICAL THINKING

- Why did both former slaves and former slave owners initially find sharecropping an agreeable, if difficult, new labor arrangement?
- What were the short- and long-term consequences of the sharecropping system for the freedpeople and for the southern economy?

◀ This Mississippi plantation store, shown in 1868, is a typical example of the new institution of the furnishing merchant and its power over postslavery agriculture in the South.

The Amistad Center of Art & Culture

◀ African Americans stand beside a log cabin home in Savannah, GA, c. 1867–1890.

Library of Congress, Prints & Photographs Division [LC-DIG-ppmsca-39591]

14-3 Johnson's Reconstruction Plan

▶ How did Andrew Johnson's political beliefs and personal background shape his views of former Confederates and freedpeople?

▶ What Reconstruction policies did Johnson enact?

▶ How did Johnson's Reconstruction policies affect freedpeople?

When Reconstruction began under President Andrew Johnson, many expected his policies to be harsh. Throughout his career in Tennessee, he had criticized the wealthy planters and championed the small farmers. When an assassin's bullet thrust Johnson into the presidency, many former slave owners shared the dismay of a North Carolina woman who wrote, "Think of Andy Johnson [as] the president! What will become of us—'the aristocrats of the South' as we are termed?" Northern Radicals also had reason to believe that Johnson would deal sternly with the South. When one of them suggested the exile or execution of ten or twelve leading rebels to set an example, Johnson replied, "How are you going to pick out so small a number? . . . Treason is a crime; and crime must be punished."

14-3a Andrew Johnson of Tennessee

Like his martyred predecessor, Johnson followed a path in antebellum politics from obscurity to power. With no formal education, he became a tailor's apprentice. But from 1829, while in his early twenties, he held nearly every office in Tennessee politics: alderman, state representative, congressman, two terms as governor, and U.S. senator by 1857. Although elected as a southern Democrat, Johnson was the only senator from a seceded state who refused to follow his state out of the Union. Lincoln appointed him war governor of Tennessee in 1862; hence his symbolic place on the ticket in the president's bid for reelection in 1864.

Although a Unionist, Johnson's political beliefs made him an old Jacksonian Democrat. And as they said in the mountainous region of east Tennessee, where Johnson established a reputation as a stump speaker, "Old Andy never went back on his raisin'." Johnson was also an ardent states' rightist. Before the war, he had supported tax-funded public schools and homestead legislation, fashioning himself as a champion of the common man. Although he vehemently opposed secession, Johnson advocated limited government. He shared none of the Radicals' expansive conception of federal power. His philosophy toward Reconstruction may be summed up in the slogan he adopted: "The Constitution as it is, and the Union as it was."

Through most of 1865, Johnson alone controlled Reconstruction policy, for Congress recessed shortly before he became president and did not reconvene until December. In the following eight months, Johnson formed new state governments in the South by using his power to grant pardons. He advanced Lincoln's leniency by extending even easier terms to former Confederates.

14-3b Johnson's Racial Views

Johnson had owned house slaves, although he had never been a planter. He accepted emancipation as a result of the war, but he did not favor black civil and political rights. Johnson believed that black suffrage could never be imposed on a southern state by the federal government, and that set him on a collision course with the Radicals. When it came to race, Johnson was a thoroughgoing white supremacist. He held what one politician called "unconquerable prejudices against the African race." In perhaps the most blatantly racist official statement ever delivered by an American president, Johnson declared in his annual message of 1867 that blacks possessed "less capacity for government than any other race of people. No independent government of any form has ever been successful in their hands; . . . wherever they have been left to their own devices they have shown a constant tendency to relapse into barbarism."

Such racial views had an enduring effect on Johnson's policies. Where whites were concerned, however, Johnson seemed to be pursuing changes in class relations. He proposed rules that would keep the wealthy planter class at least temporarily out of power.

Library of Congress Prints & Photographs Division (LC-B8184-10690)

▲ Combative and inflexible, President Andrew Johnson contributed greatly to the failure of his own Reconstruction program.

14-3c Johnson's Pardon Policy

White southerners were required to swear an oath of loyalty as a condition of gaining amnesty or pardon, but Johnson barred several categories of people from taking the oath: former federal officials, high-ranking Confederate officers, and political leaders or graduates of West Point or Annapolis who joined the Confederacy. To this list, Johnson added another important group: all ex-Confederates whose taxable property was worth more than $20,000. These individuals had to apply personally to the president for pardon and restoration of their political rights. The president, it seemed, meant to take revenge on the old planter elite.

Johnson appointed provisional governors, who began the Reconstruction process by calling state constitutional conventions. The delegates chosen for these conventions had to draft new constitutions that eliminated slavery and invalidated secession. After ratification of these constitutions, new governments could be elected, and the states would be restored to the Union with full congressional representation. But only those southerners who had taken the oath of amnesty and had been eligible to vote on the day the state seceded could participate in this process. Thus unpardoned whites and former slaves were not eligible.

14-3d Presidential Reconstruction

If Johnson intended to strip former aristocrats of their power, he did not hold to his plan. The old white leadership proved resilient and influential; prominent Confederates won elections and turned up in various appointive offices. Then Johnson started pardoning planters and leading rebels. He hired additional clerks to prepare the necessary documents and then began to issue pardons to large categories of people. By September 1865, hundreds were issued in a single day. These pardons, plus the rapid return of planters' abandoned lands, restored the old elite to power and quickly gave Johnson an image as the South's champion.

Why did Johnson allow the planters to regain power? He was determined to achieve a rapid Reconstruction in order to deny the Radicals any opportunity for the more thorough racial and political changes they desired in the South. And Johnson needed southern support in the 1866 elections; hence, he declared Reconstruction complete only eight months after Appomattox. Thus, in December 1865, many Confederate congressmen traveled to Washington to claim seats in the U.S. Congress. Even Alexander Stephens, vice president of the Confederacy, returned to Capitol Hill as a senator-elect from Georgia.

The election of such prominent rebels troubled many northerners. Some of the state conventions were slow to repudiate secession; others admitted only grudgingly that slavery was dead and wrote new laws to show it.

14-3e Black Codes

To define the status of freed men and women and control their labor, some legislatures merely revised large sections of the slave codes by substituting the word *freedmen* for *slaves.*

The new black codes compelled former slaves to carry passes, observe a curfew, live in housing provided by a landowner, and give up hope of entering many desirable occupations. Stiff vagrancy laws and restrictive labor contracts bound freedpeople to plantations, and "anti-enticement" laws punished anyone who tried to lure these workers to other employment. State-supported schools and orphanages excluded blacks entirely.

It seemed to some northerners that the South was intent on returning African Americans to servility and that Johnson's Reconstruction policy held no one responsible for the terrible war. But memories of the war—not yet even a year over—were still raw and would dominate political behavior for several elections to come. Thus, the Republican majority in Congress decided to call a halt to the results of Johnson's plan. On reconvening, the House and Senate considered the credentials of the newly elected southern representatives and decided not to admit them. Instead, they bluntly challenged the president's authority and established a joint committee to study and investigate a new direction for Reconstruction.

14-4 The Congressional Reconstruction Plan

▶ What political divisions existed in Congress?
▶ How did the relationship between the president and Congress evolve in the postwar period?
▶ What was the significance of the Fourteenth and Fifteenth Amendments?
▶ How did Congress re-incorporate former Confederate states into the Union?

Northern congressmen were hardly unified, but they did not doubt their right to shape Reconstruction policy. The Constitution mentioned neither secession nor reunion, but it gave Congress the primary role in the admission of states. Moreover, the Constitution declared that the United States shall guarantee to each state a "republican form of government." This provision, legislators believed, gave them the authority to devise policies for Reconstruction.

They soon faced other grave constitutional questions. What, for example, had rebellion done to the relationship between southern states and the Union? Lincoln had always believed secession impossible—the Confederate states had engaged in an "insurrection" within the Union in his view. Congressmen who favored vigorous Reconstruction measures argued that the war had broken the Union and that the South was subject to the victor's will. Moderate congressmen held that the states had forfeited their rights through rebellion and thus had come under congressional supervision.

14-4a The Radicals

These theories mirrored the diversity of Congress itself. Northern Democrats, weakened by their opposition to the war in its final year, denounced any idea of racial equality and supported Johnson's policies. Conservative Republicans, despite their party loyalty, favored a limited federal role in Reconstruction. The Radical Republicans, led by Thaddeus Stevens, Charles Sumner, and George Julian, wanted to transform the South. Although a minority in their party, they had the advantage of clearly defined goals. They believed it was essential to democratize the South, establish public education, and ensure the rights of the freedpeople. They favored black suffrage, supported some land confiscation and redistribution, and were willing to exclude the South from the Union for several years if necessary to achieve their goals.

Born of the war and its outcome, the Radicals brought a new civic vision to American life; they wanted to create an activist federal government and the beginnings of racial equality. A large group of moderate Republicans, led by Lyman Trumbull, opposed Johnson's leniency but wanted to restrain the Radicals. Trumbull and the moderates were, however, committed to federalizing the enforcement of civil, if not political, rights for the freedmen.

One overwhelming political reality faced all four groups: the 1866 elections. Ironically, Johnson and the Democrats sabotaged the possibility of a conservative coalition. They refused to cooperate with moderate Republicans and insisted that Reconstruction was over, that the new state governments were legitimate, and that southern representatives should be admitted to Congress. Among the Republicans, the Radicals' influence grew in proportion to Johnson's intransigence and outright provocation. It is an old story in American politics: when compromise or coalition fails, more radical visions will fill the void. Sometimes this leads to great social change, but other times to crisis and disaster.

14-4b Congress Versus Johnson

Trying to work with Johnson, Republicans believed a compromise had been reached in the spring of 1866. Under its terms, Johnson would agree to two modifications of his program: extension of the Freedmen's Bureau for another year and passage of a civil rights bill to counteract the black codes. This bill would force southern courts to practice equality under the ultimate scrutiny of the federal judiciary. Its provisions applied to public, not private, acts of discrimination. The Civil Rights Bill of 1866 was the first statutory definition of the rights of American citizens and is still on the books today.

Johnson destroyed the compromise, however, by vetoing both bills (they later became law when Congress overrode the president's veto). Denouncing any change in his program, the president condemned Congress's action and revealed his own racism. Because the Civil Rights Bill defined U.S. citizens as native-born persons who were taxed, Johnson claimed it discriminated against "large numbers of intelligent, worthy, and patriotic

Library of Congress Prints and Photographs Division [LC-US262-63460]

▲ Photograph of Thaddeus Stevens, Republican Congressman and staunch abolitionist from Pennsylvania, and leader of the "radicals" during the creation of Reconstruction policies, 1866–68.

foreigners . . . in favor of the negro." Anticipating arguments used by modern conservatives, the bill, he said, operated "in favor of the colored and against the white race."

All hope of presidential-congressional cooperation was now dead. In 1866, newspapers reported daily violations of black peoples' rights in the South and carried alarming accounts of anti-black violence—notably in Memphis and New Orleans, where police aided brutal mobs in their attacks. In Memphis, forty blacks were killed and twelve schools burned by white mobs, and in New Orleans, the toll was thirty-four African Americans dead and two hundred wounded. Such violence convinced Republicans, and the northern public, that more needed to be done. A new Republican plan took the form of the **Fourteenth Amendment** to the Constitution.

14-4c Fourteenth Amendment

Of the five sections of the Fourteenth Amendment, the first would have the greatest legal significance in later years. Written by John Bingham of Ohio, it conferred citizenship on "all persons born or naturalized in the United States" and prohibited states from abridging their constitutional "privileges and immunities" (see the Appendix for the Constitution and all amendments). It also barred any state from taking a person's life, liberty, or property "without due process of law" and from denying "equal protection of the laws." These resounding phrases have become powerful guarantees of African

Fourteenth Amendment
Defined U.S. citizens as anyone born or naturalized in the United States, barred states from interfering with citizens' constitutional rights, and stated for the first time that voters must be male.

Americans' civil rights—indeed, of the rights of all citizens, except for Native Americans, who were not granted citizenship rights until 1924.

Nearly universal agreement emerged among Republicans on the amendment's second and third sections. The fourth declared the Confederate debt null and void, and guaranteed the war debt of the United States. Northerners rejected the notion of paying taxes to reimburse those who had financed a rebellion, and business groups agreed on the necessity of upholding the credit of the U.S. government, an element of the Fourteenth Amendment that was invoked in bitter debates between congressional Republicans and the Obama administration over raising the federal "debt ceiling" in 2011 and again in 2013. The second and third sections barred Confederate leaders from holding state and federal office. Only Congress, by a two-thirds vote of each house, could remove the penalty. The amendment thus guaranteed a degree of punishment for the leaders of the Confederacy.

The second section of the amendment also dealt with representation and embodied the compromises that produced the document. Northerners disagreed about whether black people should have the right to vote. As a citizen of Indiana wrote to a southern relative, "[a]lthough there is a great deal [of] profession among us for the relief of the darkey yet I think much of it is far from being sincere. I guess we want to compel you to do right by them while we are not willing ourselves to do so." Those arched words are indicative not only of how revolutionary Reconstruction had become, but also of how far the public will, North and South, lagged behind the enactments that became new constitutional cornerstones. Many northern states still maintained black disfranchisement laws during Reconstruction.

Emancipation finally ended the three-fifths clause for the purpose of counting blacks, which would increase southern representation. Thus, the postwar South stood to gain power in Congress, and if white southerners did not allow black southerners to vote, former secessionists would derive the political benefit from emancipation. That was more irony than most northerners could bear. So Republicans determined that, if a southern state did not grant black men the vote, their representation would be reduced proportionally. If they did enfranchise black men, their representation would be increased proportionally. This compromise avoided a direct enactment of black suffrage but would deliver future black southern voters to the Republican Party.

The Fourteenth Amendment specified for the first time that voters were "male" and ignored female citizens, black and white. For this reason, it provoked a strong reaction from the women's rights movement. Advocates of women's equality had worked with abolitionists for decades, often subordinating their cause to that of the slaves. During the drafting of the Fourteenth Amendment, however, female activists demanded to be heard. Prominent leaders, such as Elizabeth Cady Stanton and Susan B. Anthony, ended their alliance with abolitionists and fought for women, while others remained committed to the idea that it was "the Negro's hour." Thus, the amendment infused new life into the women's rights movement and caused considerable strife among old allies.

14-4d The South's and Johnson's Defiance

In 1866, however, the major question in Reconstruction politics was how the public would respond to the congressional initiative. Johnson did his best to block the Fourteenth Amendment in both North and South. Condemning Congress for its refusal to seat southern representatives, the president urged state legislatures in the South to vote against ratification. Every southern legislature, except Tennessee's, rejected the amendment by a wide margin.

To present his case to northerners, Johnson organized a National Union Convention and took to the stump himself. In an age when active personal campaigning was rare for a president, Johnson boarded a special train for a "swing around the circle" that carried his message into the Northeast, the Midwest, and then back to Washington. In city after city, he criticized the Republicans in a ranting, undignified style. Increasingly, audiences rejected his views, hooting and jeering at him. In this whistle-stop tour, Johnson began to hand out American flags with thirty-six rather than twenty-five stars, declaring the Union already restored. At many towns, he likened himself to a "persecuted" Jesus who might now be martyred "upon the cross" for his magnanimity toward the South. And, repeatedly, he labeled the Radicals "traitors" for their efforts to take over Reconstruction.

The elections of 1866 were a resounding victory, though, for Republicans in Congress. Radicals and moderates whom Johnson had denounced won reelection by large margins, and the Republican majority grew to two-thirds of both houses of Congress. The North had spoken clearly: Johnson's official policies of states' rights and white supremacy were prematurely giving the advantage to former rebels and traitors. Thus, Republican congressional leaders won a mandate to pursue their Reconstruction plan.

But Johnson and southern intransigence had brought the plan to an impasse. Nothing could be accomplished as long as the "Johnson governments" existed and the southern electorate remained exclusively white. Republicans resolved to form new state governments in the South and enfranchise the freedmen.

14-4e Reconstruction Acts of 1867–1868

After some embittered debate in which Republicans and the remaining Democrats in Congress argued over the meaning and memory of the Civil War itself, the First Reconstruction Act passed in March 1867. This plan, under which the southern states were actually readmitted to the Union, incorporated only a part of the Radical program. Union generals, commanding small garrisons of troops and charged with supervising elections, assumed control in five military districts in the South (see Map 14.1). Confederate leaders designated in the Fourteenth Amendment were barred from voting until

Map 14.1 The Reconstruction Act of 1867

This map shows the five military districts established when Congress passed the Reconstruction Act of 1867. As the dates within each state indicate, conservative Democratic forces quickly regained control of government in four southern states. So-called Radical Reconstruction was curtailed in most of the others as factions within the weakened Republican Party began to cooperate with conservative Democrats.

new state constitutions were ratified. The act guaranteed freedmen the right to vote in elections as well as serve in state constitutional conventions and in subsequent elections. In addition, each southern state was required to ratify the Fourteenth Amendment, to approve its new constitution by majority vote, and to submit it to Congress for acceptance (see Table 14.1).

Thus, African Americans gained an opportunity to fight for a better life through the political process, and ex-Confederates were given what they interpreted as a bitter pill to swallow in order to return to the Union. The Second, Third, and Fourth Reconstruction Acts, passed between March 1867 and March 1868, provided the details of operation for voter registration boards, the adoption of constitutions, and the administration of "good faith" oaths on the part of white southerners.

14-4f Failure of Land Redistribution

In the words of one historian, the Radicals succeeded in "clipping Johnson's wings." But they had hoped Congress could do much more. Thaddeus Stevens, for example, argued that economic opportunity was essential to the freedmen. "If we do not furnish them with homesteads from forfeited and rebel property," Stevens declared, "and hedge them around with protective laws . . . we had better left them in bondage." Stevens therefore drew up a plan for extensive confiscation and redistribution of land, but it was never realized. Some historians see this as the great lost opportunity of Reconstruction.

Racial fears among whites and an American obsession with the sanctity of private property made land redistribution unpopular. Northerners were accustomed to a limited role for government, and the business community staunchly opposed any interference with private-property rights, even for former Confederates. Thus, black farmers were forced to seek work in a hostile environment in which landowners opposed their acquisition of land.

14-4g Constitutional Crisis

Congress's quarrels with Andrew Johnson grew still worse. To restrict Johnson's influence and safeguard its plan, Congress passed a number of controversial laws. First, it limited Johnson's power over the army by requiring the president to issue military orders through the General of the Army, Ulysses S. Grant, who could not be dismissed without the Senate's consent. Then Congress passed the Tenure of Office Act, which gave the Senate power to approve changes in the president's cabinet. Designed to protect Secretary of War Stanton, who sympathized with the Radicals, this law violated the tradition that a president controlled appointments to his own cabinet.

All of these measures, as well as each of the Reconstruction Acts, were passed by a two-thirds override of presidential vetoes. The situation led some to believe that the federal government had reached a stage of "congressional tyranny" and others to conclude that Johnson had become an obstacle to the legitimate will of the people in reconstructing the nation on a just and permanent basis.

Table 14.1 **Plans for Reconstruction Compared**

	Johnson's Plan	Radicals' Plan	Fourteenth Amendment	Reconstruction Act of 1867
Voting	Whites only; high-ranking Confederate leaders must seek pardons	Give vote to black males	Southern whites may decide but can lose representation if they deny black suffrage	Black men gain vote; whites barred from office by Fourteenth Amendment cannot vote while new state governments are being formed
Office holding	Many prominent Confederates regain power	Only loyal white and black males eligible	Confederate leaders barred until Congress votes amnesty	Fourteenth Amendment in effect
Time out of Union	Brief	Several years; until South is thoroughly democratized	Brief	3–5 years after war
Other change in southern society	Little; gain of power by yeomen not realized; emancipation grudgingly accepted, but no black civil or political rights	Expand education; confiscate land and provide farms for freedmen; expansion of activist federal government	Probably slight, depending on enforcement	Considerable, depending on action of new state governments

Johnson took several belligerent steps of his own. He issued orders to military commanders in the South, limiting their powers and increasing the powers of the civil governments he had created in 1865. Then he removed military officers who were conscientiously enforcing Congress's new law, preferring commanders who allowed disqualified Confederates to vote. Finally, he tried to remove Secretary of War Stanton. With that attempt, the confrontation reached its climax.

14-4h Impeachment of President Johnson

Impeachment is a political procedure provided for in the Constitution as a remedy for crimes or serious abuses of power by presidents, federal judges, and other high government officials. Those impeached (politically indicted) in the House are then tried in the Senate. Historically, this power has generally not been used as a means to investigate and judge the private lives of presidents, although in recent times it was used in this manner in the case of President Bill Clinton.

Twice in 1867, the House Judiciary Committee had considered impeachment of Johnson, rejecting the idea once and then recommending it by only a 5-to-4 vote. That recommendation was decisively defeated by the House. After Johnson tried to remove Stanton, however, a third attempt to impeach the president carried easily in early 1868. The indictment concentrated on his violation of the Tenure of Office Act, though many modern scholars regard his efforts to obstruct enforcement of the Reconstruction Act of 1867 as a far more serious offense.

Johnson's trial in the Senate lasted more than three months. The prosecution, led by Radicals, attempted to prove that Johnson was guilty of "high crimes and misdemeanors."

But they also argued that the trial was a means to judge Johnson's performance, not a judicial determination of guilt or innocence. The Senate ultimately rejected such reasoning, which could have made removal from office a political weapon against any chief executive who disagreed with Congress. Although a majority of senators voted to convict Johnson, the prosecution fell one vote short of the necessary two-thirds majority. Johnson remained in office, politically weakened and with less than a year left in his term. Some Republicans backed away from impeachment because they had their eyes on the 1868 election and did not want to hurt their prospects of regaining the White House.

14-4i Election of 1868

In the 1868 presidential election, Ulysses S. Grant, running as a Republican, defeated Horatio Seymour, a New York Democrat. Grant was not a Radical, but his platform supported **Congressional Reconstruction** and endorsed black suffrage in the South. (Significantly, Republicans stopped short of endorsing black suffrage in the North.) The Democrats, meanwhile, vigorously denounced Reconstruction and preached white supremacy. Indeed, in the 1868 election, the Democrats conducted the most openly racist campaign to that point in American history. Both sides waved the "bloody shirt," accusing each other as the villains of the war's sacrifices. By associating themselves

Impeachment Process to remove a president from office; attempted but failed in the case of Andrew Johnson.

Congressional Reconstruction The process by which the Republican-controlled Congress sought to make the Reconstruction of the ex-Confederate states longer, harsher, and under greater congressional control.

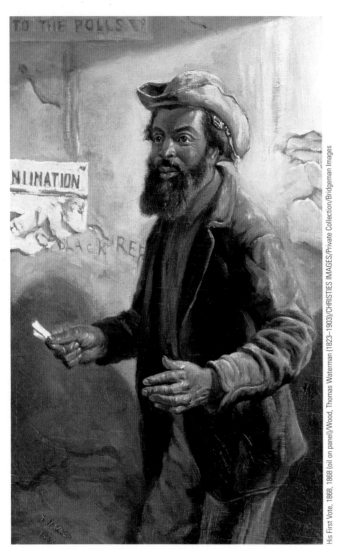

His First Vote, 1868, 1868 (oil on panel)/Wood, Thomas Waterman (1823–1903)/CHRISTIE'S IMAGES/Private Collection/Bridgeman Images

▲ *His First Vote*, 1868, by Thomas Waterman Wood, oil on canvas, invoking the power and significance of black male suffrage during Reconstruction.

with rebellion and with Johnson's repudiated program, the Democrats went down to defeat in all but eight states, though the popular vote was fairly close. Participating in their first presidential election ever on a wide scale, African Americans decisively voted en masse for General Grant.

In office, Grant acted as an administrator of Reconstruction but not as its enthusiastic advocate. He vacillated in his dealings with the southern states, sometimes defending Republican regimes and sometimes currying favor with Democrats. On occasion, Grant called out federal troops to stop violence or enforce acts of Congress. But he never imposed a true military occupation on the South. Rapid demobilization had reduced a federal army of more than 1 million to 57,000 within a year of the surrender at Appomattox. Thereafter, the number of troops in the South continued to fall,

Fifteenth Amendment
Prohibited states from denying the vote to any citizen on account of "race, color, or previous condition of servitude."

until in 1874 there were only 4,000 in the southern states outside Texas. The later legend of "military rule," so important to southern claims of victimization during Reconstruction, was steeped in myth.

14-4j Fifteenth Amendment

In 1869, the Radicals pushed through the **Fifteenth Amendment**, the final major measure in the constitutional revolution of Reconstruction. This measure forbade states to deny the right to vote "on account of race, color, or previous condition of servitude." Such wording did not guarantee the right to vote. It deliberately left states free to restrict suffrage on other grounds so that northern states could continue to deny suffrage to women and certain groups of men—Chinese immigrants, illiterate men, and those too poor to pay poll taxes.

Although several states outside the South refused to ratify, three-fourths of the states approved the measure, and the Fifteenth Amendment became law in 1870. It, too, had been a political compromise, and though African Americans rejoiced all across the land at its enactment, it left open the possibility for states to create countless qualification tests to obstruct voting in the future.

With passage of the Fifteenth Amendment, many Americans, especially supportive northerners, considered Reconstruction essentially completed. "Let us have done with Reconstruction," pleaded the *New York Tribune* in April 1870. "The country is tired and sick of it . . . . Let us have Peace!" But some northerners, like abolitionist Wendell Phillips, worried. "Our day," he warned, "is fast slipping away. Once let public thought float off from the great issue of the war, and it will take . . . more than a generation to bring it back again."

14-5 Politics and Reconstruction in the South

▶ **How did white Southerners resist the end of slavery and Reconstruction?**

▶ **How did Republican governments rule in the South?**

▶ **What was the relationship between African Americans and whites inside and outside of the Republican Party?**

▶ **How did white Southern conservatives seek to discredit Republican governments in the South?**

From the start, Reconstruction encountered the resistance of white southerners. In the black codes and in private attitudes, many whites stubbornly opposed emancipation, and the former planter class proved especially unbending because of its tremendous financial loss in slaves. In 1866, a Georgia newspaper frankly observed that "most of the white citizens believe that the institution of slavery was right, and . . . they will believe that the condition, which comes nearest to slavery, that can now be established will be the best." And for many poor whites who had never owned slaves and yet had sacrificed enormously in the war, destitution, plummeting agricultural prices, disease, and the uncertainties of a growing urban industrialization drove them off land, toward cities, and into hatred of the very idea of black equality.

14-5a White Resistance

Fearing loss of control over their slaves, some planters attempted to postpone freedom by denying or misrepresenting events. Former slaves reported that their owners "didn't tell them it was freedom" or "wouldn't let [them] go." Agents of the Freedmen's Bureau reported that "the old system of slavery [is] working with even more rigor than formerly at a few miles distant from any point where U.S. troops are stationed." To hold onto their workers, some landowners claimed control over black children and used guardianship and apprentice laws to bind black families to the plantation.

Whites also blocked blacks from acquiring land. A few planters divided up plots among their slaves, but most condemned the idea of making blacks landowners. A Georgia woman whose family was known for its support of religious education for slaves was outraged that two property owners planned to "rent their lands to the Negroes!" Such action was, she declared, "injurious to the best interest of the community."

Adamant resistance by whites soon manifested itself in other ways, including violence. In one North Carolina town, a local magistrate clubbed a black man on a public street, and in several states bands of "Regulators" terrorized blacks who displayed any independence. Amid their defeat, many planters believed, as a South Carolinian put it, that blacks "can't be governed except with the whip." And after President Johnson encouraged the South to resist congressional Reconstruction, many white conservatives worked hard to capture the new state governments.

14-5b Black Voters and the Southern Republican Party

Enthusiastically, black men voted Republican. Most agreed with one man who felt he should "stick to the end with the party that freed me." Illiteracy did not prohibit blacks (or uneducated whites) from making intelligent choices. Although Mississippi's William Henry could read only "a little," he testified that he and his friends had no difficulty selecting the Republican ballot. "We stood around and watched," he explained. "We saw D. Sledge vote; he owned half the county. We knowed he voted Democratic so we voted the other ticket so it would be Republican." Women, who could not vote, encouraged their husbands and sons, and preachers exhorted their congregations to use the franchise. Zeal for voting spread through entire black communities.

Thanks to a large black turnout and the restrictions on prominent Confederates, a new southern Republican Party came to power in the constitutional conventions of 1868–1870. Republican delegates consisted of a sizable contingent of blacks (265 out of the total of just over 1,000 delegates throughout the South), some northerners who had moved to the South, and native southern whites who favored change. The new constitutions drafted by this Republican coalition were more democratic than anything previously adopted in the history of the South. They eliminated property qualifications for voting and holding office, and they turned many appointed offices into elective posts. They provided for public schools and institutions to care for the mentally ill, the blind, the deaf, the destitute, and the orphaned.

The conventions broadened women's rights in property holding and divorce. Usually, the goal was not to make women equal with men but to provide relief to thousands of suffering debtors. In white families left poverty-stricken by the war and weighed down by debt, it was usually the husband who had contracted the debts. Thus, giving women legal control over their own property provided some protection to their families.

14-5c Triumph of Republican Governments

Under these new constitutions, the southern states elected Republican-controlled governments. For the first time, the ranks of state legislators in 1868 included black southerners. Contrary to what white southerners would later claim, the Republican state governments did not disfranchise ex-Confederates as a group. James Lynch, a leading black politician from Mississippi, explained why African Americans shunned the "folly" of disfranchising whites. Unlike northerners who "can leave when it becomes too uncomfortable," landless former slaves "must be in friendly relations with the great body of the whites in the state. Otherwise . . . peace can be maintained only by a standing army." Despised and

▲ Black Southerners attempting to vote are halted by White Leaguers in this engraving by J. H. Wares. The black man doffing his cap holds a "Republican ticket" but it will not get him to the ballot box, guarded by the election judge with a loaded pistol.

The Granger Collection, NYC.

lacking material or social power, southern Republicans strove for acceptance, legitimacy, and safe ways to gain a foothold in a depressed economy.

Far from being vindictive toward the race that had enslaved them, most black southerners treated leading rebels with generosity and appealed to white southerners to adopt a spirit of fairness. In this way, the South's Republican Party condemned itself to defeat if white voters would not cooperate. Within a few years, most of the fledgling Republican parties in the southern states would be struggling for survival against violent white hostility. Utter obstruction, the politics of fear, and violence has sometimes worked as a means to power in America. But for a time, some propertied whites accepted congressional Reconstruction as a reality.

14-5d Industrialization and Mill Towns

Reflecting northern ideals and southern necessity, the Reconstruction governments enthusiastically promoted industry. Accordingly, Reconstruction legislatures encouraged investment with loans, subsidies, and short-term exemptions from taxation. The southern railroad system was rebuilt and expanded, and coal and iron mining made possible Birmingham's steel plants. Between 1860 and 1880, the number of manufacturing establishments in the South nearly doubled.

This emphasis on business enterprise, however, produced higher state debts and taxes, drew money away from schools and other programs, and multiplied possibilities for corruption in state legislatures. The alliance between business and government took firm hold, often at the expense of the needs of common farmers and laborers. It also locked Republicans into a conservative strategy and doomed their chances with poorer whites.

Poverty remained the lot of vast numbers of southern whites. On a daily basis during the Reconstruction years, they had to subordinate politics to the struggle for livelihood. The war had caused a massive onetime loss of income-producing wealth, such as livestock, and a steep decline in land values. In many regions, the old planter class still ruled the best land and access to credit or markets.

As many poor whites and blacks found farming less tenable, they moved to cities and new mill towns. Industrialization did not sweep the South as it did the North, but it certainly laid deep roots. Attracting textile mills to southern towns became a competitive crusade. "Next to God," shouted a North Carolina evangelist, "what this town needs is a cotton mill!" In 1860, the South counted some 10,000 mill workers; by 1880, the number grew to 16,741 and, by the end of the century, to 97,559. Thus, poor southerners began the multi-generational journey from farmer to urban wage earner.

14-5e Republicans and Racial Equality

Policies appealing to African American voters rarely went beyond equality before the law. In fact, the whites who controlled the southern Republican Party were reluctant to allow blacks a share of offices proportionate to their electoral strength. Aware of their weakness, black leaders did not push very far for revolutionary economic or social change. In every

The Granger Collection

▲ *The Queen of Industry, or the New South*, cartoon by Thomas Nast, 1882, contrasting the pre-Civil War plantation economy with the more industrialized economy of the 1880s.

southern state, they led efforts to establish public schools, although they did not press for integrated facilities. In 1870, South Carolina passed the first comprehensive school law in the South. By 1875, in a major achievement for a Reconstruction government, 50 percent of black school-age children in that state were enrolled in school, and approximately one-third of the three thousand teachers were black.

Some African American politicians did fight for civil rights and integration. Many were from cities such as New Orleans or Mobile, where large populations of light-skinned free black people had existed before the war. Their experience in such communities had made them sensitive to issues of status, and they spoke out for open and equal public accommodations. Laws requiring equal accommodations won passage, but they often went unenforced.

The vexing questions of land reform and enforcement of racial equality, however, all but overwhelmed the Republican governments. Land reform largely failed because in most states whites were in the majority, and former slave owners controlled the best land and other sources of economic power. Economic progress was uppermost in the minds of most freedpeople. Black southerners needed land, and much land did fall into state hands for nonpayment of taxes. Such land was offered for sale in small lots. But most freedmen had too little cash to bid against investors or speculators. South Carolina established a land commission, but it could help only those with money to buy. Widespread redistribution of land had to arise from Congress, which never supported such action.

14-5f Myth of "Negro Rule"

Within a few years, white hostility to congressional Reconstruction began to dominate. Some conservatives had always wanted to fight Reconstruction through pressure and racist propaganda. They put economic and social pressure on black people: one black Republican reported that "my neighbors will not employ me, nor sell me a farthing's worth of anything." Charging that the South had been turned over to ignorant blacks, conservatives deplored "black domination," which became a rallying cry for a return to white supremacy.

Such attacks were inflammatory propaganda and part of the growing myth of "Negro rule," which would serve as a central theme in battles over the memory of Reconstruction. African Americans participated in politics but hardly dominated or controlled events. They were a majority in only two out of ten state constitutional writing conventions (transplanted northerners were a majority in one). In the state legislatures, only in the lower house in South Carolina did black legislators ever constitute a majority. Sixteen black men won seats in Congress before Reconstruction was over, but none was ever elected governor. Only eighteen served in a high state office, such as lieutenant governor, treasurer, superintendent of education, or secretary of state.

In all, some four hundred black men served in political office during the Reconstruction era, a signal achievement by any standard. Although they never dominated the process, they established a rich tradition of government service and civic activism. Elected officials, such as Robert Smalls in South Carolina, labored tirelessly for cheaper land prices, better health care, access to schools, and the enforcement of civil rights for black people. For too long, the black politicians of Reconstruction were the forgotten heroes of this seedtime of America's long civil rights movement.

14-5g Carpetbaggers and Scalawags

Conservatives also assailed the allies of black Republicans. Their propaganda denounced whites from the North as **"carpetbaggers,"** greedy crooks planning to pour stolen tax revenues into their sturdy luggage made of carpet material. Immigrants from the North, who held the largest share of Republican offices, were all tarred with this rhetorical brush.

In fact, most northerners who settled in the South had come seeking business opportunities, as schoolteachers, or to find a warmer climate; most never entered politics. Those who did enter politics generally wanted to democratize the South and to introduce northern ways, such as industry and public education. Carpetbaggers' ideals were tested by hard times and ostracism by white southerners.

Carpetbaggers' real actions never matched the sensational stereotypes, although by the mid-1870s even some

The Granger Collection, NYC

▲ *The Carpetbagger*, American lithograph song sheet music cover, ca. 1869. Emanating from the heyday of anti-carpetbagger propaganda, the figure seems to be part Uncle Sam and part scheming scoundrel with his bagful of Yankee notions, both religious and secular.

northerners who soured on Reconstruction or despaired over southern violence endorsed the images. Thomas Wentworth Higginson, a Union officer and commander of an African American regiment during the Civil War, suggested that any Yankee politician who remained in the South by 1874 was, more likely than not, a "mean man," a "scoundrel," and "like Shakespeare's Shylock." And that same year, the African American editors of the *Christian Recorder* distanced themselves from carpetbaggers. The "corrupt political vampires who rob and cheat and prey upon the prejudices of our people" and "feed upon the political carcass of a prostrate state," the paper insisted, were not black folks' allies. The white southern counterrevolutionaries seemed to be winning the propaganda war.

Conservatives also invented the term **scalawag** to discredit any native white southerner who cooperated with the Republicans.

"carpetbaggers" Derogatory nickname southerners gave to northerners who moved south after the Civil War, perceiving them as greedy opportunists who hoped to cash in on the South's plight.

scalawag Term used by conservative southerners to describe other white southerners who were perceived as aiding or benefiting from Reconstruction.

A substantial number of southerners did so, including some wealthy and prominent men. Most scalawags, however, were yeoman farmers, men from mountain areas and nonslaveholding districts who had been Unionists under the Confederacy. They saw that they could benefit from the education and opportunities promoted by Republicans. Sometimes banding together with freedmen, they pursued common class interests and hoped to make headway against the power of long-dominant planters. In the long run, however, the hope of such black-white coalitions floundered in the quicksand of racism.

14-5h Tax Policy and Corruption as Political Wedges

Taxation was a major problem for the Reconstruction governments. Republicans wanted to repair the war's destruction, stimulate industry, and support such new ventures as public schools. But the Civil War had destroyed much of the South's tax base. One category of valuable property—slaves—had disappeared entirely. And hundreds of thousands of citizens had lost much of the rest of their property—money, livestock, fences, and buildings—to the war. Thus, an increase in taxes (sales, excise, and property) was necessary even to maintain traditional services. Inevitably, Republican tax policies aroused strong opposition.

Corruption was another serious charge leveled against the Republicans. Unfortunately, it was often true. Many carpetbaggers and black politicians engaged in fraudulent schemes, sold their votes, or padded expenses, taking part in what scholars recognize was a nationwide surge of corruption in an age ruled by "spoilsmen." Corruption carried no

▲ Ku Klux Klan "Worse Than Slavery," an 1874 cartoon by Thomas Nast showing "White Leaguers" and the Klan combining in violence against blacks. The Granger Collection New York

party label, but the Democrats successfully pinned the blame on unqualified blacks and greedy carpetbaggers among southern Republicans.

14-5i Ku Klux Klan

All these problems hurt the Republicans, whose leaders also allowed factionalism along racial and class lines to undermine party unity. But in many southern states, the deathblow came through violence. The Ku Klux Klan (its members altered the Greek word for "circle," *kuklos*), a secret veterans' club that began in Tennessee in 1866, spread through the South, and rapidly evolved into a terrorist organization. Violence against African Americans occurred from the first days of Reconstruction but became far more organized and purposeful after 1867. Klansmen sought to frustrate Reconstruction and keep the freedmen in subjection. Nighttime harassment, whippings, beatings, rapes, and murders became common, as terrorism dominated some counties and regions.

Although the Klan tormented black people who stood up for their rights as laborers or individuals, its main purpose was political. Lawless night riders made active Republicans the target of their attacks. Leading white and black Republicans were killed in several states. After freedmen who worked for a South Carolina scalawag started voting, terrorists visited the plantation and, in the words of one victim, "whipped every . . . [black] man they could lay their hands on." Klansmen also attacked Union League clubs—Republican organizations that mobilized the black vote—and schoolteachers who were aiding the freedmen.

Klan violence was not a spontaneous outburst of racism; very specific social forces shaped and directed it. In North Carolina, for example, Alamance and Caswell counties were the sites of the worst Klan violence. Slim Republican majorities there rested on cooperation between black voters and white yeomen, particularly those whose Unionism or discontent with the Confederacy had turned them against local Democratic officials. Together, these black and white Republicans had ousted officials long entrenched in power. The wealthy and powerful men in Alamance and Caswell who had lost their accustomed political control were the Klan's county officers and local chieftains. They organized a deliberate campaign of terror, recruiting members and planning atrocities.

Klan violence injured and ultimately destroyed Republicans across the South. One of every ten black leaders who had been delegates to the 1867–1868 state constitutional conventions was attacked, seven fatally. In one judicial district of North Carolina, the Ku Klux Klan was responsible for twelve murders, over seven hundred beatings, and other acts of violence, including rape and arson. A single attack on Alabama Republicans in the town of Eutaw left four blacks dead and fifty-four wounded. In South Carolina, five hundred masked Klansmen lynched eight black prisoners at the Union County jail, and in nearby York County, the Klan committed at least eleven murders and hundreds of whippings. According to historian Eric Foner, the Klan "made it virtually impossible for Republicans to campaign or vote in large parts of Georgia."

Thus, a combination of difficult fiscal problems, Republican mistakes, racial hostility, and terror brought down the Republican regimes. In most southern states, Radical Reconstruction lasted only a few years (see Map 14.1). The most enduring failure of Reconstruction, however, was not political; it was social and economic.

14-6 Retreat from Reconstruction

▶ How did the federal government respond to white conservative resistance to Reconstruction?

▶ What developments inside and outside of the South contributed to declining support for federal Reconstruction policies?

▶ How did relations between various ethnic and racial groups in the West contribute to additional conflict over race in the post-war period?

▶ What was the impact of the Supreme Court's rulings, particularly related to the Fourteenth Amendment?

▶ How was the disputed election of 1876 resolved?

During the 1870s, northerners increasingly lost the political will to sustain Reconstruction in the South as a vast economic and social transformation occurred in their own region as well as in the West. Radical Republicans like Albion Tourgée, a former Union soldier who moved to North Carolina and was elected a judge, condemned Congress's timidity. Turning the freedman out on his own without protection, said Tourgée, constituted "cheap philanthropy." Indeed, many African Americans believed that, during Reconstruction, the North "threw all the Negroes on the world without any way of getting along." As the North underwent its own transformations and lost interest in the South's dilemmas, Reconstruction collapsed.

14-6a Political Implications of Klan Terrorism

In one southern state after another, Democrats regained control, and they threatened to defeat Republicans in the North as well. Whites in the old Confederacy referred to this decline of Reconstruction as "southern redemption," and during the 1870s, "redeemer" Democrats claimed to be the saviors of the South from alleged "black domination" and "carpetbag rule." And for one of only a few times in American history, violence and terror emerged as tactics in normal politics.

In 1870 and 1871, the violent campaigns of the Ku Klux Klan forced Congress to pass two **Enforcement Acts** and an anti-Klan law. These laws

Enforcement Acts Laws that sought to protect black voters, made violations of civil and political rights a federal offense, and sought to end Ku Klux Klan violence.

made actions by individuals against the civil and political rights of others a federal criminal offense for the first time. They also provided for election supervisors and permitted martial law and suspension of the writ of habeas corpus to combat murders, beatings, and threats by the Klan. Federal prosecutors used the laws rather selectively. In 1872 and 1873, Mississippi and the Carolinas saw many prosecutions; but in other states where violence flourished, the laws were virtually ignored. Southern juries sometimes refused to convict Klansmen; out of a total of 3,310 cases, only 1,143 ended in convictions. Although many Klansmen (roughly 2,000 in South Carolina alone) fled their state to avoid prosecution, and the Klan officially disbanded, the threat of violence did not end. Paramilitary organizations known as Rifle Clubs and Red Shirts often took the Klan's place.

Klan terrorism openly defied Congress, yet even on this issue there were ominous signs that the North's commitment to racial justice was fading. Some conservative but influential Republicans opposed the anti-Klan laws. Rejecting other Republicans' arguments that the Thirteenth, Fourteenth, and Fifteenth Amendments had made the federal government the protector of the rights of citizens, these dissenters echoed an old Democratic charge that Congress was infringing on states' rights. Senator Lyman Trumbull of Illinois, who had been a key author of the Thirteenth Amendment, declared that the states remained "the depositories of the rights of the individual." If Congress could punish crimes like assault or murder, he asked, "what is the need of the State governments?" For years, Democrats had complained of "centralization and consolidation"; now some Republicans seemed to agree with them. This opposition foreshadowed a more general revolt within Republican ranks in 1872.

14-6b Industrial Expansion and Reconstruction in the North

Both immigration and industrialization surged in the North. Between 1865 and 1873, 3 million immigrants entered the country, most settling in the industrial cities of the North and West. Within only eight years, postwar industrial production increased by 75 percent. For the first time, nonagricultural workers outnumbered farmers, and wage earners outnumbered independent craftsmen. And by 1873, only Britain's industrial output was greater than that of the United States. Government financial policies did much to bring about this rapid growth. Low taxes on investment and high tariffs on manufactured goods aided the growth of a new class of powerful industrialists, especially railroad entrepreneurs.

Railroads became the symbol of and the stimulus for the American age of capital. From 1865 to 1873, 35,000 miles of new track were laid, a total exceeding the entire national rail network of 1860. Railroad building fueled the banking industry and made Wall Street the center of American capitalism. Eastern railroad magnates, such as Thomas Scott of the Pennsylvania Railroad, the largest corporation

of its time, created economic empires with the assistance of huge government subsidies of cash and land. Railroad corporations also bought up mining operations, granaries, and lumber companies. In Congress and in every state legislature, big business now employed lobbyists to curry favor with government. Corruption ran rampant; some congressmen and legislators were paid annual retainers by major companies. Indeed, the transcontinental railroads helped Americans imagine how to conquer vast spaces, as well as conceive of time in new ways. The railroads brought modernity to the United States like almost nothing else; but they also taught the nation sordid lessons about the perils of monopoly and corruption, and by the late nineteenth century railroad entrepreneurs were the most hated men in the West. Moreover, in this laissez-faire world without rules, many railroads were overbuilt and thereby endangered the economy.

This soaring capitalist–politician alliance led as well to an intensified struggle between labor and capital. As captains of industry amassed unprecedented fortunes in an age with no income tax, gross economic inequality polarized American society. The workforce, worried a prominent Massachusetts business leader, was in a "transition state . . . living in boarding houses" and becoming a "permanent factory population." In Cincinnati, three large factories employed as many workers as the city's thousands of small shops. In New York or Philadelphia, workers increasingly lived in dark, unhealthy tenement housing. Thousands would list themselves on the census as "common laborer" or "general jobber." Many of the free-labor maxims of the Republican Party were now under great duress. Did the individual work ethic guarantee social mobility in America or erode, under the pressure of profit making, into a world of unsafe factories, child labor, and declining wages? In 1868, the Republicans managed to pass an eight-hour workday bill in Congress that applied to federal workers. The "labor question" now preoccupied northerners far more than the "southern" or the "freedmen" question (see Chapter 16).

Then, the Panic of 1873 ushered in more than five years of economic contraction. Three million people lost their jobs as class attitudes diverged, especially in large cities. Debtors and the unemployed sought easy-money policies to spur economic expansion (workers and farmers desperately needed cash). Businessmen, disturbed by the widespread strikes and industrial violence that accompanied the panic, fiercely defended property rights and demanded "sound money" policies as they sought to crush labor unions. The chasm between farmers and workers on the one hand, and wealthy industrialists on the other, grew ever wider.

14-6c Liberal Republican Revolt

Disenchanted with Reconstruction, a largely northern group calling itself the Liberal Republicans bolted the party in 1872 and nominated Horace Greeley, the famous editor of the

New York Tribune, for president. The Liberal Republicans were a varied group, including foes of corruption and advocates of a lower tariff. Normally such disparate elements would not cooperate with one another, but two popular and widespread attitudes united them: distaste for federal intervention in the South and an elitist desire to let market forces and the "best men" determine policy.

The Democrats also gave their nomination to Greeley in 1872. The combination was not enough to defeat Grant, who won reelection, but it reinforced Grant's desire to avoid confrontation with white southerners. Greeley's campaign for North-South reunion, for "clasping hands across the bloody chasm," was a bit premature to win at the polls but was a harbinger of the future in American politics. Organized Blue-Gray fraternalism (gatherings of Union and Confederate veterans) began as early as 1874. Grant continued to use military force sparingly and in 1875 refused a desperate request from the governor of Mississippi for troops to quell racial and political terrorism in that state.

Dissatisfaction with Grant's administration grew during his second term. Strong-willed but politically naive, Grant made a series of poor appointments. His secretary of war, his private secretary, and officials in the treasury department and navy were involved in bribery or tax-cheating scandals. Instead of exposing the corruption, Grant defended the culprits. In 1874, as Grant's popularity and his party's prestige declined, the Democrats recaptured the House of Representatives, signaling the end of the Radical Republican vision of Reconstruction. "Republican Party Struck by Lightning," read a Buffalo newspaper headline. And "Busted! The Republican Machine Gone to Smash!" said the *Louisville Courier-Journal* gleefully. Of thirty-five states holding legislative elections, twenty-three were won by Democrats.

14-6d General Amnesty

Such a political turnaround in Congress weakened legislative resolve on southern issues. Congress had already lifted the political disabilities of the Fourteenth Amendment from many former Confederates. In 1872, it had adopted a sweeping Amnesty Act, which pardoned most of the remaining rebels and left only five hundred barred from political office holding. In 1875, Congress passed a **Civil Rights Act**, partly as a tribute to the recently deceased Charles Sumner, purporting to guarantee black people equal accommodations in public places, such as inns and theaters, but the bill was watered down and contained no effective provisions for enforcement. (The Supreme Court later struck down this law.)

Democrats regained control of four state governments before 1872 and a total of eight by the end of January 1876 (see Map 14.1). In the North, Democrats successfully stressed the failure and scandals of Reconstruction governments. As opinion shifted, many Republicans sensed that their constituents were tiring of southern issues and the racial legacies of the war. Sectional reconciliation now seemed crucial for commerce. The nation was expanding westward rapidly, and the South was a new frontier for investment.

14-6e The West, Race, and Reconstruction

Nowhere did the new complexity and violence of American race relations play out so vividly as in the West. As the Fourteenth Amendment and other enactments granted to blacks the beginnings of citizenship, other nonwhite peoples faced continued persecution. Across the West, the federal government pursued a policy of containment against Native Americans. In California, where white farmers and ranchers often forced Native peoples into captive labor, some civilians practiced a more violent form of "Indian hunting." By 1880, thirty years of such violence left an estimated 4,500 Californian Native people dead at the hands of white settlers. Some historians have considered this policy a regional genocide.

In Texas and the Southwest, the rhetoric of national expansion still deemed Mexicans and other mixed-race Hispanics to be debased, "lazy," and incapable of self-government. And in California and other states of the Far West, thousands of Chinese immigrants became the victims of brutal violence. Few whites had objected to the Chinese who did the dangerous work of building railroads through the Rocky Mountains. But when the Chinese began to compete for urban, industrial jobs, great conflict emerged. Anti-coolie clubs appeared in California in the 1870s, seeking laws against Chinese labor, fanning the flames of racism, and organizing vigilante attacks on Chinese workers and the factories that employed them. Western politicians sought white votes by pandering to prejudice, and in 1879 the new California constitution denied the vote to Chinese immigrants.

If we view America from coast to coast, and not merely on the North–South axis, the Civil War and Reconstruction years both dismantled racial slavery and fostered a volatile new racial complexity, especially in the West. During the same age when early anthropologists employed elaborate theories of "scientific" racism to determine a hierarchy of racial types, the West was a vast region of racial mixing and conflict. Some African Americans, despite generations of mixture with Native Americans, asserted that they were more like whites than the nomadic, "uncivilized" Native Americans, while others, like the Creek freedmen of Indian Territory, sought Native identities. In Texas, whites, Native peoples, blacks, and Hispanics had mixed for decades, and by the 1870s forced reconsideration in law and custom of who was white and who was not.

During Reconstruction, America was undergoing what one historian has called a reconstruction of the very idea of *race* itself. As it did so, tumbling into some of the darkest years of American race relations, the turbulence of the expanding

Civil Rights Act An act that was designed to desegregate public places, but that lacked enforcement provisions.

◄ Anti-Chinese cartoon, "Every Dog (No Distinction of Color) Has His Day." The imagery here links Native Americans, African Americans, and Chinese immigrants in the same racist and xenophobic fear.

The Granger Collection, NYC

West reinforced the new nationalism and the reconciliation of North and South based on a resurgent white supremacy.

14-6f Foreign Expansion

Following the Civil War, pressure for expansion reemerged, and in 1867 Secretary of State William H. Seward arranged a vast addition of territory to the national domain through the purchase of Alaska from Russia (see Chapter 19). Opponents ridiculed Seward's $7.2 million venture, calling Alaska "Frigidia," "the Polar Bear Garden," and "Walrussia." But Seward convinced important congressmen of Alaska's economic potential, and other lawmakers favored the dawning of friendship with Russia.

Also in 1867, the United States took control of the Midway Islands, a thousand miles northwest of Hawai'i. And in 1870, President Grant tried unsuccessfully to annex the Dominican Republic. Leaders of American foreign policy, including some former abolitionists, believed that the new United States, re-founded by the war and emancipation, should export its values of antislavery and equality to

the world, especially in the Caribbean. This brand of liberal imperialism mixed with the pursuit of commerce and naval coaling stations, animated American expansion for the rest of the century.

Seward and his successor, Hamilton Fish, also resolved troubling Civil War grievances against Great Britain. Through diplomacy they arranged a financial settlement of claims on Britain for damage done by the *Alabama* and other cruisers built in England and sold to the Confederacy. They recognized that sectional reconciliation in Reconstruction America would serve new foreign ambitions.

14-6g Judicial Retreat from Reconstruction

Meanwhile, the Supreme Court played a major part in the northern retreat from Reconstruction. During the Civil War, the Court had been cautious and inactive. Reaction to the *Dred Scott* decision (1857) had been so vehement, and the Union's wartime emergency so great, that the Court had avoided interference with government actions. The justices breathed a collective sigh of relief, for example, when legal

The "Back to Africa" Movement

In the wake of the Civil War, and especially after the despairing end of Reconstruction, some African Americans sought to leave the South for the American West or North, but also to relocate to Africa. Liberia had been founded in the 1820s by the white-led American Colonization Society (ACS), an organization dedicated to relocating blacks "back" in Africa. Some eleven thousand African Americans had emigrated voluntarily to Liberia by 1860, with largely disastrous results. Many died of disease, and others felt disoriented in the strange new land and ultimately returned to the United States.

Reconstruction reinvigorated the emigration impulse, especially in cotton-growing districts where blacks had achieved political power before 1870 but were crushed by violence and intimidation in the following decade. When blacks felt confident in their future, the idea of leaving America fell quiet; but when threatened or under assault, whole black communities dreamed of a place where they could become an independent "race," a "people," or a "nation" as their appeals often announced. Often that dream, more imagined than realized, lay in West Africa. Before the Civil War, most blacks had denounced the ACS for its racism and its hostility to their sense of American birthright. But letters of

inquiry flooded into the organization's headquarters after 1875. Wherever blacks felt the reversal of the promise of emancipation the keenest, they formed local groups such as the Liberia Exodus Association of Pinesville, Florida; or the Liberian Exodus Arkansas Colony; and many others.

At emigration conventions, and especially in churches, blacks penned letters to the ACS asking for maps or any information about a new African homeland. Some local organizers would announce eighty or a hundred recruits "widawake for Liberia," although such enthusiasm rarely converted into an Atlantic voyage. The impulse was genuine, however. "We wants to be a People,'" wrote the leader of a Mississippi emigration committee; "we can't be it heare and find that we ar compel to leve this Cuntry." Henry Adams, a former Louisiana slave, Union soldier, and itinerant emigration organizer, advocated Liberia, but also supported "Kansas fever" with both biblical and natural rights arguments. "God . . . has a place and a land for all his people," he wrote in 1879. "It is not that we think the soil climate or temperature" elsewhere is "more congenial to us— but it is the idea that pervades our breast 'that at last we will be free,' free from oppression, free from tyranny,

free from bulldozing, murderous southern whites."

By the 1890s, Henry McNeal Turner, a freeborn former Georgia Reconstruction politician, and now bishop of the African Methodist Episcopal Church, made three trips to Africa and vigorously campaigned through press and pulpit for blacks to "Christianize" and "civilize" Africa. Two shiploads of African Americans sailed to Liberia, although most returned disillusioned or ill. Turner's plan of "Africa for the Africans" was as much a religious vision as an emigration system, but like all such efforts then and since, it reflected the despair of racial conditions in America more than realities in Africa. The numbers do not tell the tale of the depth of the impulse in this link to the world: in 1879–1880, approximately 25,000 southern blacks moved to Kansas, whereas from 1865 to 1900, just under 4,000 emigrated to West Africa.

CRITICAL THINKING

■ While there were certainly practical reasons some African Americans did not want to emigrate to West Africa, what other reasons might compel an African American person to prefer to remain in the United States, and perhaps even in the South, despite the unfulfilled promises of freedom and equality?

◀ Departure of African American emigrants to Liberia aboard the *Laurada*, Savannah, Georgia, March 1896. The large crowd bidding farewell to the much smaller group aboard the ship may indicate both the fascination with and the ambivalence about this issue among blacks in the South.

Library of Congress/Getty Images

technicalities prevented them from reviewing the case of Clement Vallandigham, a Democratic opponent of Lincoln's war effort who had been convicted by a military tribunal of aiding the enemy. But in 1866, a similar case, *Ex parte Milligan*, reached the Court.

Lambdin P. Milligan of Indiana had plotted to free Confederate prisoners of war and overthrow state governments. For these acts, a military court sentenced Milligan, a civilian, to death. Milligan challenged the authority of the military tribunal, claiming he had a right to a civil trial. Reasserting its authority, the Supreme Court declared that military trials were illegal when civil courts were open and functioning.

In the 1870s, the Court successfully renewed its challenge to Congress's actions when it narrowed the meaning and effectiveness of the Fourteenth Amendment. The *Slaughter-House* cases (1873) began in 1869, when the Louisiana legislature granted one company a monopoly on the slaughtering of livestock in New Orleans. Rival butchers in the city promptly sued. Their attorney, former Supreme Court Justice John A. Campbell, argued that Louisiana had violated the rights of some of its citizens in favor of others. The Fourteenth Amendment, Campbell contended, had revolutionized the constitutional system by bringing individual rights under federal protection, safeguarding them from state interference.

But in the *Slaughter-House* decision, the Supreme Court dealt a stunning blow to the scope of the Fourteenth Amendment. The Court declared state citizenship and national citizenship separate. National citizenship involved only matters such as the right to travel freely from state to state, and only such narrow rights, held the Court, were protected by the Fourteenth Amendment.

The Supreme Court also concluded that the butchers who sued had not been deprived of their rights or property in violation of the due-process clause of the amendment. Shrinking from a role as "perpetual censor" for civil rights, the Court's majority declared that the framers of the recent amendments had not intended to "destroy" the federal system, in which the states exercised "powers for domestic and local government, including the regulation of civil rights." Thus, the justices severely limited the amendment's potential for securing and protecting the rights of black citizens—its original intent.

The next day, the Court decided *Bradwell v. Illinois*, a case in which Myra Bradwell, a female attorney, had been denied the right to practice law in Illinois because she was a married woman, and hence not considered a free agent. Pointing to the Fourteenth Amendment, Bradwell's attorneys contended the state had unconstitutionally abridged her "privileges and immunities" as a citizen. The Supreme Court rejected her claim, declaring a woman's "paramount destiny ... to fulfill the noble and benign offices of wife and mother."

In 1876, the Court weakened the Reconstruction-era amendments even further by emasculating the enforcement clause of the Fourteenth Amendment and revealing deficiencies inherent in the Fifteenth Amendment. In *U.S. v. Cruikshank,* the Court overruled the conviction under the 1870 Enforcement Act of Louisiana whites who had attacked a meeting of blacks and conspired to deprive them of their rights. The justices ruled that the Fourteenth Amendment did not give the federal government power to act against these whites, who had murdered possibly as many as one hundred blacks. The duty of protecting citizens' equal rights, the Court said, "rests alone with the States." Such judicial conservatism as well as states' rights doctrine, practiced by justices who had all been appointed by Republican presidents Lincoln and Grant, left a profound imprint down through the next century, blunting the revolutionary potential in the Civil War amendments.

14-6h Disputed Election of 1876 and Compromise of 1877

As the 1876 elections approached, Americans increasingly focused on economic issues. The North was no longer willing to pursue the goals of Reconstruction. The results of a disputed presidential election confirmed this fact. Samuel J. Tilden, the Democratic governor of New York, ran strongly in the South and needed only one more electoral vote to triumph over Rutherford B. Hayes, the Republican nominee. Nineteen electoral votes from Louisiana, South Carolina, and Florida (the only southern states not yet under Democratic rule) were disputed; both Democrats and Republicans claimed to have won in those states despite fraud committed by their opponents (see Map 14.2).

To resolve this unprecedented situation, Congress established a fifteen-member electoral commission. Membership on the commission was to be balanced between Democrats and Republicans. Because the Republicans held the majority in Congress, they prevailed, 8 to 7, on every attempt to count the returns, with commission members voting along strict party lines. Hayes would become president if Congress accepted the commission's findings.

Congressional acceptance was not certain. Democrats controlled the House and could filibuster to block action on the vote. Many citizens worried that the nation would slip once again into civil war, as some southerners vowed, "Tilden or Fight!" The crisis was resolved when Democrats acquiesced in the election of Hayes based on a "deal" cut in a Washington hotel between Hayes's supporters and southerners who wanted federal aid to railroads, internal improvements, federal patronage, and removal of troops from southern states. Northern and southern Democrats simply decided not to contest the election of a Republican who was not going to continue Reconstruction policies in the South. Thus, Hayes became president, inaugurated privately inside the White House to avoid any threat of violence. Southerners relished their promises of economic aid, and Reconstruction was unmistakably over. Tilden had won the popular vote, but

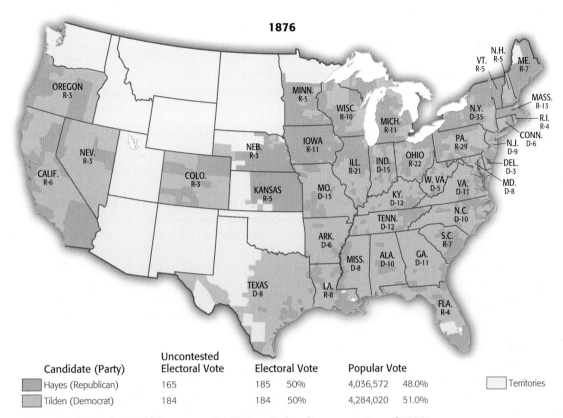

1876

Candidate (Party)	Uncontested Electoral Vote	Electoral Vote		Popular Vote	
Hayes (Republican)	165	185	50%	4,036,572	48.0%
Tilden (Democrat)	184	184	50%	4,284,020	51.0%

Territories

Map 14.2 Presidential Election of 1876 and the Compromise of 1877

In 1876, a combination of solid southern support and Democratic gains in the North gave Samuel Tilden the majority of popular votes, but Rutherford B. Hayes won the disputed election in the electoral college, after a deal satisfied Democratic wishes for an end to Reconstruction.

narrowly, not winning the Electoral College, the first of four such times in American history when the presidential winner did not win the most votes, a constitutional anomaly that still mystifies much of the world.

Southern Democrats rejoiced, but African Americans grieved over the betrayal of their hopes for equality. The Civil War had brought emancipation, and Reconstruction had guaranteed their rights under law. But events and attitudes in larger white America were foreboding. In a Fourth of July speech in Washington, D.C., in 1875, Frederick Douglass anticipated this predicament. He reflected anxiously on the American centennial to be celebrated the following year. The nation, Douglass feared, would "lift to the sky its million voices in one grand Centennial hosanna of peace and good will to all the white race . . . from gulf to lakes and from sea to sea." Douglass looked back on fifteen years of unparalleled change for his people and worried about the hold of white supremacy on America's historical memory: "If war among the whites brought peace and liberty to the blacks, what will peace among the whites bring?" Douglass's question would echo down through American political culture for decades.

Summary

Reconstruction left a contradictory record. It was an era of tragic aspirations and failures, but also of unprecedented legal, political, and social change. The Union victory brought about an increase in federal power, stronger nationalism, sweeping federal intervention in the southern states, and landmark amendments to the Constitution. It also sparked a revolution in how people would see the role of the state in their lives, often resulting in positive modes of dependence on government heretofore unimagined. But northern commitment to make these changes endure eroded, and the revolution remained unfinished. The mystic sense of promise for new lives and liberties among the freedpeople, demonstrated in that first Decoration Day in Charleston, was tarnished although not dead by 1877.

The North embraced emancipation, black suffrage, and constitutional alterations strengthening the central government. But it did so to defeat the rebellion and secure the peace. As the pressure of these crises declined, Americans, especially in the North, retreated from Reconstruction. The American people and the courts maintained a preference for

The Lost Cause

All major wars and their aftermath compel a struggle over their memory. Sometimes losers prevail over winners in contests to shape historical memory. After the Civil War, white southerners and their northern allies constructed a "Lost Cause" tradition, a potent and racially exclusive version of the war and Reconstruction that persists in American culture today.

The Lost Cause emerged among ex-Confederates as a mourning ritual and a psychological response to the trauma of defeat. But with time it also took root in selective reinterpretations of the war's causes; in southern resistance to Reconstruction; in doctrines of white supremacy; and in a nostalgic popular culture enjoyed and promoted by northerners and southerners alike. Lost Cause advocates—from high-ranking officers to common soldiers writing reminiscences to women leading memorial associations—argued that the war had never been about slavery, that the Confederates had only lost to Yankee numbers and resources, and that the nation should reconcile by equally honoring both southern and northern sacrifice. In the industrial, urban, multiethnic America of the emerging twentieth century, an Old South of benevolent masters and faithful slaves, of Robert E. Lee portrayed as America's truest Christian soldier, provided a sentimentalized road to reunion.

From 1865 to the 1880s, this Confederate legend had been forged by wartime participants determined to vindicate the Confederacy. By the 1890s, however, Lost Cause culture emerged especially with the United Daughters of the Confederacy. Elite southern white women built monuments, lobbied congressmen, delivered lectures, ran essay contests for schoolchildren, and strove to control the content of history textbooks, all in the service of an exalted South. Above all, Lost Causers advocated a story not at all about loss, but about what one historian has called a "victory narrative." This new victory was the nation's triumph over the racial revolution and constitutional transformations of Reconstruction. In his 1881 memoir, Jefferson Davis argued that slavery "was in no wise the cause of the conflict" and that slaves had been "contented with their lot." He also declared the Lost Cause not lost: "Well may we rejoice in the regained possession of self-government. . . . This is the great victory . . . a total noninterference by the Federal government in the domestic affairs of the States."

These stories and images reverberated in the very heartbeat of Jim Crow America, and they endure in modern tastes for Civil War memorabilia, such as the epic *Gone with the Wind,* the 2003 film *Gods and Generals*, and uses of the Confederate flag to oppose civil rights and represent southern identity. And the Confederate state rights tradition has been employed by some states and advocacy groups to suppress the voting rights of certain minority groups, to resist federal environmental policy, national health care reform, and the presidency of Barack Obama. Confederate mythology also inspired a horrendous mass murder by a young white supremacist in the Emanuel AME church in Charleston, South Carolina in June, 2015.

CRITICAL THINKING

- The Lost Cause mythology emerged originally as part of southern whites' mourning for those who died in the war and for the loss of the war. Over time, it transformed the nation's historical memory of the antebellum South, slavery, the war, and Reconstruction, quite literally whitewashing the past. Many modern proponents of the Lost Cause claim that their purpose is "heritage, not hate." Is it possible for the Lost Cause to be solely about heritage?

state authority and a distrust of federal power. The ideology of free labor dictated that property should be respected and that individuals should be self-reliant. Racism endured and transformed into the even more virulent forms of Klan terror and theories of black degeneration. Concern for the human rights of African Americans and other reforms frequently had less appeal than moneymaking in an individualistic, industrializing society.

New challenges began to overwhelm the aims of Reconstruction. How would the country develop its immense resources in an increasingly interconnected national economy? Could farmers, industrial workers, immigrants, and capitalists coexist? Industrialization not only promised prosperity but also wrought increased exploitation of labor. Moreover, industry increased the nation's power and laid the foundation for an enlarged American role in international affairs.

In the wake of the Civil War, Americans faced two profound tasks—the achievement of healing and the dispensing of justice. Both had to occur, but they never developed in historical balance. Making sectional reunion compatible with black freedom and equality overwhelmed the imagination in American political culture, and the nation still faced much of this dilemma more than a century later.

Suggestions for Further Reading

David W. Blight, *Race and Reunion: The Civil War in American Memory* (2001)

Gregory P. Downs, *Declarations of Dependence: The Long Reconstruction of Popular Politics in the South, 1861–1908* (2011)

W. E. B. Du Bois, *Black Reconstruction in America* (1935)

Eric Foner, *Reconstruction: America's Unfinished Revolution, 1863–1877* (1988)

William Gillette, *Retreat from Reconstruction, 1869–1879* (1980)

Gerald Jaynes, *Branches Without Roots: The Genesis of the Black Working Class in the American South, 1862–1882* (1986)

George Rable, *But There Was No Peace* (1984)

Heather Cox Richardson, *West from Appomattox: The Reconstruction of America after the Civil War* (2007)

Elliot West, "Reconstructing Race," *Western Historical Quarterly* (Spring 2003)

Richard White, *Railroaded: The Transcontinentals and the Making of Modern America* (2011)

Richard White, *The Republic for Which It Stands: The United States During Reconstruction and the Gilded Age* (2017)

MINDTAP
From Cengage

MindTap® is a fully online personalized learning experience built upon Cengage Learning content. MindTap® combines student learning tools—readings, multimedia, activities, and assessments—into a singular Learning Path that guides students through the course and helps students develop the critical thinking, analysis, and communication skills that are essential to academic and professional success.

The Ecology of the West and South, 1865–1900

Surrounded by eastern Arkansas lowlands that flooded every year, Nannie Stillwell Jackson kept a diary of her life as a farmwife in late-nineteenth-century America. Her everyday routine of tedious work and heartwarming generosity represented the human ecology—the interaction between people and their environment—that ordinary individuals experienced as they coped with challenges that they faced.

Nannie was headstrong and compassionate. She had to be. Her husband, ten years younger than herself—both she and he had been widowed and this was their second marriage—drank, stayed out late, and often disliked her independence. One Saturday in 1890, for example, Nannie went to town and bought a pair of stockings, then later wrote in her diary, ". . . Mr. Jackson got mad because I bought what I did today but I can't help it if he did." She also participated in a supporting network of neighboring farm women, who exchanged visits, food, clothing, meals, and aid almost daily. On August 6, 1890, for example, Nannie wrote, ". . . Aunt Mary Williams she brought me a nice mess of squash for dinner. Caroline Coalman is sick & sent Rosa to me to send her a piece of beef I sent her a bucket full of cold victuals . . ." Nature was both Nannie's ally and enemy. She often sent her teenage daughter to bring "water from the bayou to wash with," but she also complained "no rain yet & we do need rain so bad." And water-born typhoid fever killed several of her neighbors.

The humdrum events of Nannie's life occurred innumerable times in the American West and South as people worked hard with each other and with—sometimes against—the environment. Though much of this life was timeless, the human ecology of these regions was changing. In the part of the South where Nannie Jackson lived, the Missouri Pacific Railroad was nearby, and she had access to the outside world and its goods, such as the store-bought stockings she brought home, much to her husband's displeasure. During her lifetime, a "New South" emerged, built upon railroads, factories, and

◀ This Montana farm woman resembled Nannie Jackson in her hard work taking care of her farm. And like Nannie, she probably had gone to a nearby town to purchase the clothes she wore while milking her cows. Montana Historical Society

Chronology

1862	■ Homestead Act grants free land to citizens who live on and improve the land
	■ Morrill Land Grant Act gives states public land to sell in order to finance agricultural and industrial colleges
1864	■ Chivington's militia massacres Black Kettle's Cheyennes at Sand Creek
1869	■ First transcontinental railroad completed
1872	■ Yellowstone becomes first national park
1876	■ Custer's federal troops attack Lakotas and Cheyenne at Little Big Horn, Montana; suffer major defeat
1877	■ Nez Percé Indians under Young Joseph surrender to U.S. troops
1878	■ Timber and Stone Act allows citizens to buy timberland cheaply but also enables large companies to acquire huge tracts of forest land
1879	■ Carlisle School for Indians established in Pennsylvania
1880	■ Cigarette-making machine invented
1881–82	■ Chinese Exclusion Acts prohibit Chinese immigration to the United States
1883	■ National time zones established
1884	■ U.S. Supreme Court first denies Indians as wards under government protection
1887	■ Dawes Severalty Act ends communal ownership of Indian lands and grants land allotments to individual Native families; "California Plan" advances irrigation
1887–88	■ Devastating winter on Plains destroys countless livestock and forces farmers into economic hardship
1889	■ Asa Candler buys and develops Coca-Cola Company
1890	■ Final suppression of Plains Indians by U.S. Army at Wounded Knee
	■ Census Bureau announces closing of the frontier
	■ Yosemite National Park established
1892	■ John Muir helps found Sierra Club
1902	■ Newlands Reclamation Act passed

cities. Farther west, population grew at a furious pace as new migrants streamed in to develop the land and extract its wealth.

Experience an interactive version of this story in MindTap®.

Throughout the nation's history, the region known as the "South" had a relatively stable definition. It encompassed most of the states and territories beneath the 39th parallel westward to the Mississippi River and sometimes including Oklahoma and Texas. The meaning of the "West," however, changed. In the eighteenth century, the West encompassed the entire area beyond the Appalachian Mountains. As the result of settlement of the Midwest following the Civil War, the West came to be defined by the land between the Mississippi River and the Pacific Ocean, including the plains between the Mississippi and the Rocky Mountains, the Rockies themselves, and the mountains and valleys of the Far West.

Before migrants arrived, much of the West was not empty. It was occupied by long-time indigenous inhabitants, whose human ecology of communities working with natural resources operated in quite different ways from those that became common once others occupied the region. On the Plains, for example, the Pawnees planted crops in springtime, left their fields in summer to hunt buffalo, then returned for harvesting. They sometimes battled with nearby Cheyenne and Arapahoe peoples, who wanted hunting grounds and crops for their own purposes. In what now is the American Southwest, including Southern California, Native peoples shared the land and sometimes integrated with descendants of Spanish colonists. All these peoples survived by developing and using natural resources in limited ways, and they had at most only occasional access to outside markets. After the Civil War, however, white Americans flooded into the West, overwhelming Native and Hispanic communities. Between 1870 and 1890, the white population living in the region swelled from 7 million to nearly 17 million.

As newcomers built communities in the West and South in the late nineteenth century, however, they exploited the environment for profit far more extensively than did Native peoples. They excavated the earth to remove minerals, felled forests for timber to construct and heat homes, pierced the countryside with railroads to carry goods and link markets, and dammed rivers and plowed soil with machines to grow crops. Their goal was not mere survival; it included buying and selling in regional, national, and international markets. Nannie Jackson partook of only a tiny portion of this change when she went to town to buy stockings, but it surrounded her nonetheless. The abundance of exploitable land and raw materials of these regions filled Americans with faith that anyone eager and persistent enough could succeed and that faith fueled the new human ecology. But the confidence also rested on a belief that white people were somehow superior, and individual ambition often asserted itself at the expense of minority people and the environment. As new settlers transformed the landscape in both the West and South, the triumph of their market economies transformed the nation. Both optimism and discrimination, hope and hardship, were parts of the new human ecology.

- ▣ *How did the interaction between people and the environment shape the physical landscapes of the West and South?*

- ▣ *Describe the societal and technological changes the revolutionized lives of farmers in the West and South.*

- ▣ *How did the U.S. government's relations with Native Americans change over time throughout the late nineteenth century?*

15-1 The Transformation of Native Cultures

▶ **How did Native American peoples simultaneously depend upon and shape their surrounding environment?**

▶ **Why did Native American economic systems weaken in the late nineteenth century?**

▶ **What policies did the U.S. government pursue in relationship to Native American peoples?**

▶ **How did Native American peoples resist encroachment by settlers and the U.S. government?**

Indigenous peoples settled the West long before other Americans migrated there. Neither passive nor powerless in the face of nature, these Native peoples had been shaping their environment—for better and for worse—for centuries. Nevertheless, almost all Native peoples' economic systems weakened in the late nineteenth century. Several factors explain why and how these declines happened.

15-1a Subsistence Cultures

Among Native peoples, ecologies varied. Some Native peoples inhabited permanent settlements; others lived in a series of temporary camps. Seldom completely isolated, most were both participants and recipients in a flow of goods, culture, language, and disease carried by bands that migrated from one region to another. Regardless of their type of community, all Native peoples based their economies to differing degrees on four activities: 1) crop growing; 2) livestock raising; 3) hunting, fishing, and gathering; and 4) trading and raiding. Corn was the most common crop; sheep and horses, acquired from Spanish colonizers and from enemies, were the livestock; and buffalo (American bison) and salmon were the primary prey of hunting and fishing. Native peoples raided one another for food, tools, and horses, which in turn they used in trading with other Native groups and with whites. They also attacked to avenge wrongs and to oust competitors from hunting grounds. To achieve their standards of living, Native peoples tried to balance their economic systems. When a buffalo hunt failed, they subsisted on crops. When crops failed, they could still hunt buffalo and steal food and horses in a raid or trade livestock and furs for necessities.

For indigenous peoples on the Plains, whether nomads, such as the Lakotas ("Sioux"), or village dwellers, such as the Pawnees, everyday life focused on buffalo. They cooked and preserved buffalo meat; fashioned hides into clothing, moccasins, and blankets; used sinew for thread and bowstrings; and carved tools from bones and horns. Buffalo were so valuable that Pawnees and Lakotas often fought over access to herds. Plains communities also depended on horses, which they used for hunting, and as symbols of wealth. To provide food for their herds, **Plains Indians** altered the environment by periodically setting fire to tall-grass prairies. The fires burned away dead plants, facilitating growth of new grass in the spring so that horses could feed all summer.

In the Southwest, Native peoples led varying lifestyles, depending upon the environment. For example, among the O'odham of southeastern Arizona and northwest Mexico, whose name translates into "The People" to distinguish themselves from "others," some groups grew irrigated crops in the region's few river valleys while those who inhabited mountainous and desert territories followed more of a hunter-gatherer existence. Once foreigners arrived, The People traded for what was useful—tools, cloth, tobacco, livestock—and aided in raids against the Apache, who were enemies of O'odham. (Significantly, the Apache called themselves Nnee, which also means "The People.") The Navaho (or Dine', also meaning "The People") were herders, whose sheep, goats, and horses provided food, transportation, and status.

What buffalo were to Plains communities and sheep were to the ecology of southwestern natives, salmon were to Native peoples of the Northwest. Before the mid-nineteenth century, the Columbia River and its tributaries supported the densest population of Native peoples in North America, all of whom fished for salmon in the summer and stored dried fish for the winter. To harvest fish, the Clatsops, Klamath, and S'Klallams developed technologies of stream diversion, platform

Plains Indians Diverse Native American societies inhabiting the region from the Dakotas to Texas.

Library of Congress Prints and Photographs Division Washington, D.C. [LC-DIG-ppmsca-39873]

▲ Outfitted in elaborate attire, including a headdress with buffalo horns, metal armbands, and an animal hide shirt decorated with metal medallions, Cloud Man was a member of the Assisisboine people of the Northern Great Plains. His father was French and his mother Native American, but Cloud Man served as chief of his band and always identified himself as Native American.

construction over the water, and special baskets to catch fish from the platforms. Like native societies of other regions, many of these Indians traded for horses, buffalo robes, beads, cloth, and knives.

15-1b Slaughter of Buffalo

On the Plains and in parts of the Southwest, indigenous ecologies began to dissolve after 1850, when white migrants entered and competed with Native peoples for access to and control over natural resources. Perceiving buffalo and indigenous peoples as hindrances to their ambitions, whites endeavored to eliminate both. Huge herds of buffalo sometimes blocked trains from moving, so railroads made concerted efforts to remove them permanently. When the U.S. Army failed to enforce treaties that reserved hunting grounds for exclusive use by Native peoples, railroads sponsored buffalo hunts in which eastern sportsmen shot at the bulky targets from slow-moving trains, killing thousands. Some hunters collected from $1 to $3 each for hides that were sent east for use mainly as belts to drive industrial machinery; others did not even stop to pick up their kill.

Unbeknownst to both Native peoples and white migrants, however, a complex combination of circumstances had already doomed the buffalo before the slaughter of the late 1800s. Native peoples contributed to the depletion of the herds by increasing their kills, especially to trade hides with whites and other Native communities. Also, a period of dry years in the 1840s and 1850s had forced Native peoples such as the Lakota to set up camps in river basins, where they competed with buffalo for space and water. As a result, the buffalo were pushed out of nourishing grazing territory and faced threats of starvation. When whites arrived on the Plains, they, too, sought to settle in river basins, further depriving buffalo from nutritious grasslands. At the same time, lethal animal diseases, such as anthrax and brucellosis, brought in by white-owned livestock, decimated buffalo already weakened by malnutrition and drought. Increasing numbers of horses, oxen, and sheep, owned by white newcomers as well as by some Native peoples, also upset the buffalo's grazing patterns by devouring vital grass supplies. In sum, human and ecological shocks created vulnerability among the buffalo, to which mass killing only struck the final blow. By the 1880s only a few hundred of the 25 million buffalo estimated on the Plains in 1820 remained.

15-1c Decline of Salmon

In the Northwest, the basic wild source of Native peoples' food supply, salmon, suffered a fate similar to that of the buffalo, but for different reasons. White commercial fishermen and canneries moved into the Columbia and Willamette River valleys during the 1860s and 1870s. When commercial fishermen harvested increasing numbers of salmon running upriver to spawn before laying their eggs, the fish supply was not replenished. By the 1880s whites had greatly diminished salmon runs on the Columbia, and by the early 1900s, construction of dams on the river and its tributaries further impeded the salmon's ability to reproduce. The U.S. government protected Native peoples' fishing rights, but not the supply of fish on the river. Hatcheries helped restore some of this supply, but dams built to provide power, combined with overfishing and pollution, diminished salmon stocks.

15-1d Influence of Young White Men

Buffalo slaughter and salmon reduction undermined western native subsistence, but a unique mix of human demography contributed as well. For most of the nineteenth century, white populations that migrated into western lands inhabited by indigenous peoples were overwhelmingly young and male. In 1870 white men outnumbered white women by three to two in California, two to one in Colorado, and two to one in Dakota Territory. By 1900, preponderances of men remained throughout these places. Most of these males were unmarried and in their twenties and thirties, the stage of life when they were most prone to violent behavior. In other words, the whites with whom Native peoples were most likely to come into contact first were traders, trappers, soldiers, prospectors, and cowboys—almost all of whom owned guns and had few qualms about using them against animals and humans who got in their way.

Moreover, these men subscribed to prevailing attitudes that Native peoples were primitive, lazy, devious, and cruel. Such contempt made exploiting and killing Native peoples all the easier, and whites often justified violence against Native peoples by claiming preemptive defense against threats to life and property. When Native bands raided white settlements, they sometimes mutilated bodies, burned buildings, and kidnapped women, acts that were embellished in campfire stories, pamphlets, and popular fiction—all of which reinforced images of Native peoples as savages. Inside the bachelor society of saloons and cabins, white men boasted of exploits in Indian fighting and showed off trophies of scalps and other body parts taken from victims.

Native warriors, too, were young, armed, and prone to violence. Valuing bravery and vengeance, they boasted of fighting white interlopers. But indigenous communities contrasted with those of whites in that they contained excesses of women, the elderly, and children, making Native bands less mobile and therefore vulnerable to attack. They also were susceptible to bad habits of bachelor white society. Native men copied white males' behavior of bingeing on cheap whiskey and indulging in prostitution. The syphilis and gonorrhea that Native men contracted from Native women infected by white men killed many and reduced Native peoples' ability to reproduce, a consequence that their populations, already declining from smallpox and other diseases spread by whites, could not afford. Thus age and gender structures of the white frontier population, combined with attitudes of racial contempt, created a further threat to western Native peoples' existence.

15-1e Government Policy and Treaties

U.S. government policy reinforced efforts to remove Native peoples from the path of white ambitions, but the cultural organization of indigenous groups caused confusion. North American Native peoples were constituted not so much into tribes, as whites believed, as into countless bands and confederacies that shifted in composition. In the West, some two hundred languages and dialects separated these groups, making it difficult for indigenous groups to unite against white invaders. Although a language group could be defined as a tribe, separate bands and clans within each group had their own leaders, and seldom did a chief hold widespread power. Moreover, bands often spent more time battling among themselves than with white settlers.

Nevertheless, the government needed some way of categorizing Native peoples so as to fashion a policy toward them. It did so by imputing more meaning to tribal organization than was warranted. After 1795, American officials considered Indian tribes to be separate nations with which they could make treaties that ensured peace and defined boundaries between Native and white lands. This was a faulty assumption because chiefs who agreed to a treaty did not always speak for all members of a band and the group would not necessarily abide by an agreement. Moreover, white settlers seldom accepted treaties as guarantees of natives' land rights. On the Plains, whites assumed that they could settle wherever they wished, and they rarely hesitated to commandeer choice farmland along river valleys. In the Northwest, whites considered treaties protecting Native peoples' fishing rights on the Columbia River to be nuisances and ousted Native peoples from the best locations so that they could use mechanical devices to harvest fish. As white migrants pressed into indigenous territories, treaties made one week were violated the next.

15-1f Reservation Policy

Prior to the 1880s, the federal government tried to force western indigenous peoples onto reservations, where, it was thought, Native peoples could be "civilized." Reservations usually consisted of those areas of a group's previous territory that were least desirable to whites. When assigning Native groups to such parcels, the government promised protection from white encroachment and agreed to provide food, clothing, and other necessities.

Reservation policy helped make way for the market economy. In early years of contact in the West, trade had benefited both Native peoples and whites and had taken place on a nearly equal footing, much as it had between eastern Native peoples and whites in the preceding century. Native peoples acquired clothing, guns, and horses from whites in return for furs, hides, jewelry, and, sometimes, military assistance against enemy Native groups. In the West, however, whites' needs and economic power grew disproportionate to Native peoples' needs and power. Native peoples became more dependent, and whites increasingly dictated what was to be traded and on what terms. For example, white traders persuaded Navajo weavers in the Southwest to produce heavy rugs, which the Native groups rarely could use but appealed to eastern customers, and to adopt new designs and colors to boost sales. Meanwhile, by focusing on commercial production, Navajos raised fewer crops and were forced to buy food because the market economy undermined their subsistence agriculture. Soon they were selling land and labor to whites as well, and their dependency made it easier to force them onto reservations.

Reservation policy had degrading consequences. First, Native communities had no say over their own affairs on reservations. Supreme Court decisions in 1884 and 1886 defined them as wards (like helpless children under government protection) and denied them the right to become U.S. citizens. Thus they were unprotected by the Fourteenth and Fifteenth Amendments, which had extended the privileges and legal protections of citizenship to African Americans. Second, pressure from white farmers, miners, and herders who continually sought Native lands made it difficult for the government to preserve reservations intact. Third, the government ignored Native peoples' history, even combining on the same reservation Indian bands that habitually had warred against each other. Rather than serving as civilizing communities, reservations weakened every aspect of Native life, except the resolve to survive.

15-1g Native Resistance

Not all Native peoples succumbed to market forces and reservation restrictions. Apache bands long had raided white settlements in the Southwest and continued their insurgence even after most of their people had been forced onto reservations. Their raiding ended only after the last of their leaders, the Chiricahua chief Geronimo, was captured in 1886. Pawnees in the Midwest resisted disadvantageous deals that white traders tried to impose on them. In the Northwest, Nez Percé Indians defied being forced onto a reservation in Idaho by fleeing in 1877. They successfully eluded U.S. troops and the military's Crow and Cheyenne scouts over 1,800 miles of rugged terrain, but when they reached Montana, their leader, Young Joseph, decided that they could not escape, and he ended the flight. Sent to a reservation, Joseph repeatedly petitioned the government to return his peoples' ancestral lands, but his appeals went unheeded.

As they had done earlier in the East, whites responded to western Native peoples' defiance with military aggression. The attitude of many resembled that of an Arizona journalist who wrote, "Extermination is our only hope, and the sooner the better." In 1860, for example, Navajos, reacting to U.S. military pressure, carried out a destructive raid on Fort Defiance in Arizona Territory. In reprisal, the army eventually attacked and starved the Navajo into submission, destroying their fields, houses, and livestock, and in 1863–1864 forced them on a "Long Walk" from their homelands to a reservation at Bosque Redondo in New Mexico. Also in 1864, in order to eliminate Native peoples who blocked white ambitions in the Sand Creek region of Colorado, a militia commanded by Methodist minister John Chivington attacked a Cheyenne band led by Black Kettle, killing almost every warrior. In 1879, 4,000 U.S. soldiers forced surrender from Utes who already had given up most of their ancestral territory in western Colorado but were resisting further concessions.

The most publicized battle occurred in June 1876, when 2,500 Lakotas and Cheyennes led by Chiefs Rain-in-the-Face, Sitting Bull, and Crazy Horse surrounded and annihilated 256 government troops led by Colonel George A. Custer near Little Big Horn River in southern Montana. Although Native peoples consistently demonstrated military skill in such battles, shortages of supplies and relentless pursuit by U.S. soldiers, including African American units of Union Army veterans called Buffalo Soldiers (so named by the Cheyennes and Comanches they fought), eventually overwhelmed armed Native groups' resistance. Indigenous people were not so much conquered in battle as they were harassed and starved into submission.

15-1h Reform of Indian Policy

In the 1870s and 1880s, reformers and government officials sought more purposely than in the past to "civilize" and "uplift" Native peoples through landholding and education. This meant changing Native identities and outlawing customs deemed to be "savage and barbarous." In this regard, the United States copied imperialist policies of other nations, such as the French, who banned native religious ceremonies in their Pacific island colonies, and the British, who jailed Native African religious leaders. The American government determined to persuade indigenous peoples to abandon their

◀ The O'odham people kept track of historical events by carving scratches, dots, and notches year by year into wooden rods or cactus ribs. The "calendar sticks" were made by one man who functioned as a historian and who would retell the stories symbolized by his carvings. Markings of different colors served to remind the calendar stick recorder of details about an event.

traditional cultures and adopt American values of ambition, thrift, and materialism.

At the same time, other groups argued for sympathetic—and sometimes patronizing—treatment. Reform treatises, such as George Manypenny's *Our Indian Wards* (1880) and Helen Hunt Jackson's *A Century of Dishonor* (1881), plus unfavorable comparison with Canada's management of Indian affairs aroused American humanitarianism. Canada had granted Native peoples the rights of British subjects and proceeded more slowly than the United States in efforts to acculturate Native peoples. A high rate of intermarriage between Canadian Native peoples and Canadian whites also promoted smoother relations.

In the United States, the most active reform organizations were the Women's National Indian Association (WNIA) and the Indian Rights Association (IRA). The WNIA sought to use women's domestic qualities of nurture and compassion to help people in need and urged gradual assimilation. The IRA, which was more influential but numbered few Native Americans among its members, advocated citizenship and landholding by individual Native families. Most reformers believed Native Americans were culturally inferior to whites and assumed Native peoples could succeed economically only if they embraced middle-class values of diligence and education.

Reformers particularly deplored Native communities' sexual division of labor. Native women seemed to do all the work—tending crops, raising children, cooking, making tools and clothes—while being servile to men, who hunted but were otherwise idle. Ignoring the fact that white men sometimes mistreated white women, groups such as the WNIA and IRA wanted Native men to bear more responsibilities, treat women more respectfully, and resemble male heads of white middle-class households. But when Native men and women adopted this model of white society, in which women were supposed to be submissive and private, Native women lost much of the economic independence and power over daily life that they once had.

15-1i Zitkala-Sa

Some exceptional Native Americans managed to use white-controlled education to their advantage. Zitkala-Sa (Red Bird) was a Yankton Sioux born on Pine Ridge reservation in South Dakota in 1876. At age twelve, she was sent to a Quaker boarding school in Indiana and later attended Earlham College and the Boston Conservatory of Music. She became an accomplished orator and violinist, but her major contribution was her writing on behalf of her people's needs and the preservation of their cultures. In 1901 Zitkala-Sa published *Old Indian Legends,* in which she translated Sioux oral tradition into stories. She wrote other pieces for *Harper's* and *Atlantic Monthly,* and served in various capacities on the Standing Rock and Ute reservations. In 1902 Zitkala-Sa married a mixed-race army captain who had taken the name Ray Bonnin, and she became known as Gertrude Bonnin. Subsequently, she was elected the first full-blooded Native American secretary of the Society of American Indians and served as editor of *American Indian Magazine,* all the while advocating for Indian rights.

15-1j Dawes Severalty Act

In 1887 Congress reversed its reservation policy and passed the **Dawes Severalty Act.** The act, supported by reformers, authorized dissolution of community-owned Native American property and granted land allotments to individual native families. A family head received 160 acres; each child under eighteen received 40 acres. The government held that land in trust for twenty-five years, so families could not sell their allotments. The law also awarded citizenship to all who accepted allotments (an act of Congress in 1906 delayed citizenship for those who had not yet taken their allotment). It also entitled the government to sell unallocated land to whites.

Indian policy, as implemented by the Interior Department, now assumed two main features, both of which aimed at assimilating Native peoples into white American culture. First and foremost, as required by the Dawes Act, the government distributed reservation land to families in the belief that property ownership would create productive citizens and integrate indigenous peoples into the larger society. As one official stated, the goal was to "weaken and destroy tribal relations and individualize them by giving each a separate home and having them subsist by industry." Second, officials believed that Native peoples would abandon their "barbaric" habits more quickly if their children were educated in boarding schools away from the reservations.

The Dawes Act represented a Euro-American and Christian worldview, an earnest but narrow belief that a society of landholding families headed by men was the most desired model. Government agents and reformers were joined by educators who viewed schools as tools to create a patriotic, industrious citizenry. Using the model of Hampton Institute, founded in Virginia in 1869 to educate newly freed slaves, educators helped establish the Carlisle School in Pennsylvania in 1879, which served as the flagship of the government's school system for Native Americans. In keeping with Euro-American custom, the boarding schools imposed white-defined sex roles: boys were taught farming and carpentry, and girls learned sewing, cleaning, and cooking.

15-1k Ghost Dance

In 1890 the government made one final show of force. With active resistance having been suppressed, some Lakotas and other groups turned to **Ghost Dance** religious movement as a spiritual means of preserving native cultures. Inspired by a

Dawes Severalty Act U.S. Dawes Severalty Act law designed to "civilize" Indians by dividing up and distributing communal tribal lands to individuals.

Ghost Dance Ritual where Ghost Dance Sioux dancers moved in a circle, accelerating until they reached a trancelike state and experienced visions of the future where white society would vanish from Native American lands.

Attempts to Make Native Americans Look and Act Like "Americans"

Government officials believed that they could "civilize" indigenous children in boarding schools by not only educating them to act like white people but also by making them look like white people. Thus the boys in the photograph on the left were given baseball uniforms and the girl on the right was made to wear a dress and carry a purse and umbrella, all of which were foreign to Native peoples. These images convey information about how indigenous peoples were treated, but they also suggest attitudes of the photographer and the artist who made the images.

CRITICAL THINKING

■ What messages about "civilizing" Native peoples did the person who photographed the baseball team and the artist who drew the picture of the girl reuniting with her people want the viewer to receive?

University of Washington Libraries, Special Collections NA4117

▲ In an attempt to inculcate "American" customs into its Native students, the Fort Spokane Indian School in Spokane, Washington, created a baseball team for the young men who boarded there.

Library of Congress Prints and Photographs Division [LC-USZ62-100543]

▲ In an 1884 edition, *Frank Leslie's Weekly*, one of the most popular illustrated news and fiction publications of the late nineteenth and early twentieth centuries, depicted an "Americanized" Native girl dressed as a proper young lady returning from the Carlisle boarding school to visit her home at the Pine Ridge Agency in South Dakota.

Paiute prophet named Wovoka, the Ghost Dance consisted of movement in a circle until dancers reached a trancelike state and envisioned dead ancestors who, dancers believed, heralded a day when buffalo would return and all elements of white civilization, including guns and whiskey, would be buried. The ritual expressed this messianic vision in several days of dancing and meditation.

Ghost Dancers forswore violence but appeared threatening when they donned sacred shirts that they believed would repel the white man's bullets. As the religion spread, government agents became alarmed about the possibility of renewed native uprisings. Charging that the cult was anti-Christian, the army began arresting Ghost Dancers. Late in 1890, the government sent the Seventh Cavalry, Custer's old regiment, to detain Lakota moving toward Pine Ridge, South Dakota. Although the Lakotas were starving and seeking shelter, the army assumed they were armed for revolt. Overtaking the band at a creek called **Wounded Knee**, the troops massacred an estimated three hundred men, women, and children in the snow.

15-1l **The Losing of the West**

American Indian wars and the Dawes Act effectively accomplished what whites wanted and Native peoples feared: they reduced Native peoples' independence and dissolved their human ecology. Speculators induced indigenous peoples to sell newly acquired property, in spite of federal safeguards against such practices. Between 1887 and the 1930s, Native peoples' landholdings dwindled from 138 million acres to 52 million. Land-grabbing whites were particularly cruel to Ojibwas in the northern plains. In 1906 Minnesota Senator Moses E. Clapp attached to an Indian appropriations bill a rider declaring that mixed-blood adults on the White Earth reservation were "competent" (meaning educated in white ways) enough to sell their land without having to observe the twenty-five-year waiting period stipulated in the Dawes Act. When the bill became law, speculators duped many Ojibwas into signing away their property in return for counterfeit money and worthless merchandise. The Ojibwas lost more than half their original holdings, and economic ruin overtook them.

Government policy had other injurious effects on Native peoples' ways of life. The boarding-school program enrolled thousands of children and tried to teach them that their inherited customs were inferior, but most schoolchildren returned to reservations demoralized rather than ready to assimilate into white society. Polingaysi Qoyawayma, a Hopi woman forced to take the Christian name Elizabeth Q. White, recalled after four years spent at the Sherman Institute in Riverside, California, "As a Hopi, I was misunderstood by the white man; as a convert of the missionaries, I was looked upon with suspicion by the Hopi people."

Ultimately, political and ecological crises overwhelmed western indigenous groups. White violence and military superiority alone did not defeat them. Their economic systems had started to break down before military campaigns occurred. Buffalo extinction, enemy raids, and disease combined to hobble subsistence culture to the point where Native Americans had no alternative but to yield their lands to market-oriented whites. Believing their culture to be superior, whites determined to transform Native peoples into successful farmers by teaching them the value of private property, educating them in American ideals, and eradicating their "backward" languages, lifestyles, and religions. Although Native peoples tried to retain their culture and adapt to the demands they faced, by the end of the century they had lost control of the land and were under increasing pressure to shed their group identity. The West was won at their expense, and to this day they remain casualties of an aggressive age.

15-2 The Extraction of Natural Resources

▶ **What methods were used to extract natural resources in the West?**

▶ **What role did the Government play in the economic development of the West?**

▶ **What role did racial groups and race play in the development of the West?**

In contrast to indigenous peoples, who used natural resources to meet subsistence needs and small-scale trading, most whites who migrated to the West and Great Plains in the late nineteenth century were driven by the desire for material success. To their eyes, the vast stretches of territory promised untapped sources of wealth that could bring about a better life (see Map 15.1). Extraction of these resources advanced settlement and created new markets at home and abroad; it also fueled revolutions in transportation, agriculture, and industry that swept across the United States. This ecological relationship between nature and humans also gave rise to wasteful practices and fed habits of racial and sexual oppression.

15-2a **Mining**

In the mid-1800s, prospectors began to comb western terrain for gold, silver, copper, and other minerals. The mining frontier advanced rapidly, drawing thousands of people, mostly men, to Nevada, Idaho, Montana, Utah, and Colorado. California, where a gold rush helped populate a thriving state by 1850, furnished many of the miners, who traveled to nearby states in search of riches. Others seeking mineral riches followed traditional routes, moving from the East and Midwest to western mining regions.

Wounded Knee South Dakota site of a bloody clash between Sioux Indians and whites. Within minutes, white troops—mistakenly assuming the starving Sioux were armed for revolt—slaughtered three hundred people, including seven infants.

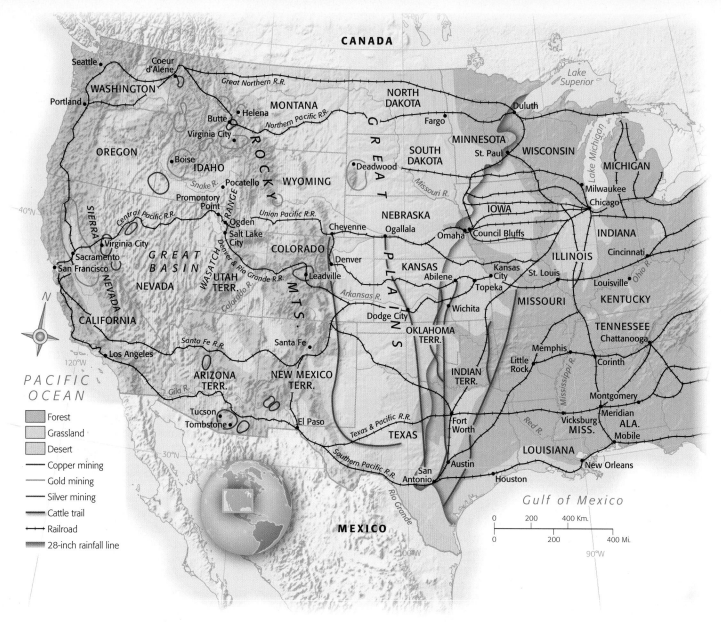

Map 15.1 The Development and Natural Resources of the West

By 1890, mining, lumbering, and cattle ranching had penetrated many areas west of the Mississippi River, and railroad construction had linked together the western economy. These activities, along with the spread of mechanized agriculture, altered both the economy and the people who were involved in them.

Prospectors tended to be restless optimists, willing to climb mountains and trek across deserts in search of a tell-tale glint of precious metal. They lived outdoors, shot animals for food, and financed their explorations by convincing merchants to advance credit for equipment in return for a share of the as-yet-undiscovered lode. Unlucky prospectors whose credit ran out took jobs and saved up for another search.

Digging up and transporting minerals was extremely expensive, so prospectors who did discover veins of metal seldom mined them. Instead, they sold their claims to large mining syndicates, such as the Anaconda Copper Company. Financed by eastern capital, these companies brought in engineers, heavy machinery, railroad lines, and work crews. Workers and businesses to serve the mining operations also settled cities and helped boost populations in places such as El Paso and Tucson. In doing so, they made western mining

corporate, just like eastern manufacturing. Though discoveries of gold and silver sparked national publicity, mining companies usually exploited less romantic but usually more-lucrative bonanzas of lead, zinc, tin, quartz, and copper.

15-2b Lumbering and Oil Drilling

Unlike mining, cutting trees to supply demands for construction and heating materials required vast tracts of forest land to be profitable. Because timber supplies in the upper Midwest and South had been depleted by earlier logging, lumber corporations moved into forests of the Northwest, where they felled trees, used horses and oxen to drag them to a nearby river, then floated the logs downstream to sawmills to be cut into boards. Large companies often grabbed millions of western acres under the Timber and Stone Act, passed by Congress in 1878 to stimulate settlement in California, Nevada,

The Australian Frontier

America's frontier West was not unique. Australia, founded like the United States as a European colony, had a frontier society that resembled the American West in several ways, especially in its mining development, its folk society, and its treatment of racial minorities. Australia experienced a gold rush in 1851, just two years after the United States did, and large-scale mining companies quickly moved into its western regions to extract mineral deposits. In 1897 future U.S. president Herbert Hoover, who at that time was a twenty-two-year-old geology graduate, went to work in Australia and began his successful career as a mining engineer.

Promise of mineral wealth lured thousands of immigrants to Australia in the late nineteenth century. Many of the newcomers arrived from China, and, as in the United States, these immigrants, most of them men, encountered abusive treatment. Anti-Chinese riots erupted in ports in New South Wales in 1861 and 1873, and beginning in 1854, the Australian government passed several laws restricting Chinese immigration. When the country became an independent British federation in 1901, one of its first acts applied a strict literacy test that virtually terminated Chinese immigration for over fifty years.

As in the American West, the Australian frontier bred folk heroes who came to symbolize white masculinity. In a society where men vastly outnumbered women, Australians glorified the tough, aggressive individual who displayed self-reliance and quick judgment that made the Australian backcountry man as idealized as the American cowboy. Similarly, Australian outlaws (called "bushrangers") such as Ned Kelly, an infamous bandit who was hanged in 1880, achieved the same notoriety as Americans Jesse James and Billy the Kid.

Although Australians celebrated white men who brought a spirit of personal liberty and opportunism to a new country, they also considered indigenous peoples, whom they called "Aborigines," as savages needing to be conquered and civilized. Christian missionaries viewed aborigines as lost in pagan darkness and tried to convert them. In 1869 the government of Victoria Province passed an Aborigine Protection Act that, like United States' policy toward Native Americans, encouraged removal of indigenous children from their families so they could learn European customs in schools run by whites. Australian natives adapted in their own ways. They formed cricket teams, and those with light skin sometimes hid their identity by telling census takers they were white. In the end, though, assimilation did not work, and Australians resorted to reservations as a means of "protecting" Native peoples, just as Americans isolated Native peoples on reserved land. Like the Americans, white Australians could not find a place for indigenous peoples in a land of opportunity.

▲ Much like the American counterpart, the Australian frontier involved mining operations and was populated by indigenous peoples. Here, the "Aborigines," as the natives were called, are using track to bring down ore extracted from a hill.

CRITICAL THINKING

- How can white attitudes toward natural resources in both the United States and Australia explain treatment of indigenous peoples in both places?
- Can attitudes toward Asian immigrants in both places also be explained in this manner? Why or why not?

◄ After gold was discovered along the Klondike River in northwest Canada in 1896, tens of thousands of eager Americans flocked to the area, leaving jobs and families in hopes of striking it rich. These jubilant miners found a gold nugget, but most were not so lucky. The gold rush subsided by the end of the century as the remoteness of the area, difficulties in prospecting without heavy machinery, and discoveries of gold elsewhere in Canada forced most prospectors to give up their quest.

Hulton Archive/Getty Images

Oregon, and Washington. The law allowed private citizens to buy, at a low price, 160-acre plots "unfit for cultivation" and "valuable chiefly for timber." Lumber companies hired seamen from waterfront boarding houses to register claims to timberland and then transfer those claims to the company owners. By 1900, private citizens had bought over 3.5 million acres, but most of that land belonged to corporations.

While mining corporations were excavating western mineral deposits and lumber corporations were cutting down Northwest timberlands, oil companies were beginning to drill wells in the Southwest. In 1900, most of the nation's petroleum still came from the Appalachians and Midwest, but rich oil reserves had been discovered in Southern California and eastern Texas, creating not only new wealth but also boosting boom cities, such as Los Angeles and Houston. Although oil and kerosene were still used mostly for lubrication and lighting, oil discovered in the Southwest soon became a vital source of fuel for autos and other machines.

15-2c Water and Irrigation

Glittering gold, tall trees, and gushing oil shaped popular images of the West, but water gave it life. If western lands promised wealth from mining, cutting, and drilling, their agricultural potential promised more—but only if settlers could find a way to bring water to the arid soil. Western economic development is the story of how public and private interests used technology and organization to utilize the region's sometimes scarce water resources to make the land agriculturally productive. Just as control of land was central to western ecology, so, too, was control of water.

For centuries, Native Americans irrigated southwestern fields to sustain their subsistence farming. When the

Spanish arrived, they began tapping the Rio Grande River to irrigate farms in southwest Texas and New Mexico. Later they channeled water to California mission communities of San Diego and Los Angeles. The first Americans of European ancestry to practice extensive irrigation were the Mormons. After arriving in Utah in 1847, they diverted streams and rivers into networks of canals, whose water enabled them to farm the hard-baked soil. By 1890 Utah boasted over 263,000 irrigated acres supporting more than 200,000 people.

15-2d Rights to Water

Efforts at land reclamation through irrigation in Colorado and California sparked conflict over rights to precious streams that flowed through the West. Americans inherited the English common-law principle of riparian rights, which held that only those who owned land along a river's banks could appropriate from the water's flow. The stream itself, according to riparianism, belonged to God; those who lived near it could take water for normal needs but were not to diminish the river. According to business owners, this principle, intended to protect nature, discouraged economic development because it prohibited property owners from damming or diverting water for large-scale economic development.

Americans who settled the West rejected riparianism in favor of prior appropriation, which awarded a river's water to the first person who claimed it. Westerners, taking cues in part from eastern Americans who had diverted waterways to power mills and factories, asserted that water, like timber, minerals, and other natural resources, existed to serve human needs and advance profits. They argued that anyone intending a "reasonable" or "beneficial" (economically productive) use of river water should have the right to appropriation, and the courts generally agreed.

15-2e Government Supervision of Water Rights

Under appropriation, someone who dammed and diverted water often reduced the flow of water downstream. People disadvantaged by such action could protect their interests either by suing those who deprived them of water or by establishing a public authority to regulate water usage. Thus in 1879 the state of Colorado created several regional water divisions throughout the state, each with a commissioner to regulate water rights. In 1890 Wyoming enlarged the concept of government control with a constitutional provision declaring that the state's rivers were public property subject to supervision.

Destined to become the most productive agricultural state, California devised a dramatic response to the problem of water rights, sometimes called the California Solution. In the 1860s, a few individuals controlled huge tracts of land in the fertile Sacramento and San Joaquin River valleys, which they used for speculating in real estate, raising cattle, and growing wheat. But around the edges of the wheat fields lay unoccupied lands that could profitably support vegetable and fruit farming if irrigated properly.

Unlike western states that had favored appropriation rights over riparian rights, California maintained a mixed legal system that upheld riparianism while allowing for some appropriation. This system disadvantaged irrigators and prompted them to seek to change state law. In 1887 the legislature passed a bill permitting farmers to organize into districts that would construct and operate irrigation projects. An irrigation district could use its authority to purchase water rights, seize private property to build irrigation canals, and finance projects through taxation or by issuing bonds. As a result of this legislation, California became the nation's leader in irrigated acreage, with more than 1 million irrigated acres by 1890, making the state's fruit and vegetable agriculture the most profitable in the country.

15-2f Newlands Reclamation Act

Although state-supervised irrigation stimulated farming, the federal government still owned most western land in the 1890s, ranging from 64 percent of California to 96 percent of Nevada. Prodded by land-hungry developers, state governments wanted the federal government to transfer to them at least part of public domain lands. States claimed that they could make these lands profitable through reclamation—providing them with irrigated water. Congress generally refused such transfers because of the controversies they raised. If one state sponsored irrigation to develop its own land, who would regulate waterways that flowed through more than one state? If, for example, California assumed control of the Truckee River, which flowed westward out of Lake Tahoe on the California-Nevada border, how would Nevadans be assured that California would allow

them sufficient water? Only the federal government, it seemed, had the power to regulate interstate water development.

In 1902, after years of debate, Congress passed the **Newlands Reclamation Act**. Named for the bill's sponsor, Nevada's Democratic congressman Francis Newlands, the law allowed the federal government to sell western public lands to individuals in parcels not to exceed 160 acres and to use proceeds from such sales to finance irrigation projects. The Newlands Act provided for control of water but did not address conservation, even though three-fourths of the water used in open-ditch irrigation, the most common form, was lost to evaporation. Thus the Newlands Reclamation Act fell squarely within the tradition of development of nature for human profit. It represented a decision by the federal government to aid the agricultural and general economic expansion of the West.

15-2g Complex Communities

As the West developed, it became a rich multiracial society, including not only Native Americans and white migrants but also Mexicans, African Americans, and Asians, all involved in community building. A crescent of territory, a borderland stretching from western Texas through New Mexico and Arizona to Northern California, but also including Mexico, supported ranchers and sheepherders, descendants of the Spanish who had originally claimed the land from the natives. In New Mexico, Spaniards intermarried with Native peoples to form a *mestizo* population of small farmers and ranchers. All along the Southwest frontier, Mexican immigrants moved into American territory to find work. Some returned to Mexico seasonally; others stayed. Although the Treaty of Guadalupe Hidalgo (1848) had guaranteed property rights to Hispanics, "Anglo" (the Mexican name for a white American) miners, speculators, and railroads used fraud and other means to obtain much of Hispanic landholdings. As a result, many Mexicanos moved to cities such as San Antonio and Tucson, and became wage laborers.

Before the Chinese Exclusion Act of 1882 prohibited the immigration of Chinese laborers, some 200,000 Chinese—mostly young, single males—entered the United States and built communities in California, Oregon, and Washington. Many came with five-year contracts to work on railroad construction, then return home, presumably with resources for a better life. They also labored in the fields. By the 1870s, Chinese people composed half of California's agricultural work force. The state's farms and citrus groves demanded a huge migrant work force to harvest the crops, and Chinese laborers moved from one ripening crop to another, working as pickers and packers. In cities such as San Francisco, they labored in textile and cigar factories and lived in large, densely-packed boarding houses. Few married because Chinese women were scarce.

Like Chinese and Mexicans, Japanese and European immigrants, especially Irish, moved from place to place as they worked on railroads and in mining

Newlands Reclamation Act Federal legislation that authorized the U.S. government to sell western public lands to finance dams and irrigation projects in the West.

and agricultural communities. The region consequently developed its own migrant economy, with workers traveling across a large geographical area as they took short-term jobs in mining, farming, and railroad construction.

African Americans tended to be more settled, many of them **"exodusters"** or former slaves who had fled the South and built all-black towns, mostly in Kansas. Nicodemus, Kansas, for example, was founded in 1877 by black migrants from Lexington, Kentucky, and grew to 600 residents within two years. Early experiences were challenging, but eventually the town boasted newspapers, shops, churches, a hotel, and a bank. When attempts to obtain railroad connections failed, however, the town declined, and many of its businesses moved across the Solomon River to the town of Bogue, where a Union Pacific Railroad camp was located. Other black migrants, encouraged by editors and land speculators, went to Oklahoma Territory. In the 1890s and early 1900s, African American settlers founded thirty-two all-black communities in Oklahoma, and the territory boasted several successful black farmers.

15-2h Western Women

Although unmarried men numerically dominated the western natural-resource frontier, many communities contained populations of white women who had come for the same reason as men: to make their fortune. But in the West as elsewhere, women's independence was limited; they usually accompanied a husband or father and seldom prospected themselves. Even so, many women used their labor as a resource and earned money by cooking and laundering, and in some cases providing sexual services for miners in houses of prostitution. In the Northwest, they worked in canneries, cleaning and salting the fish that their husbands caught. Mexicano women took jobs in cities as laundresses and seamstresses.

A number of white women helped to bolster family and community life as members of the home mission movement. Protestant missions had long sponsored benevolent activities abroad, such as in China, and had aided the settlement of Oregon in the 1830s and 1840s. But in the mid-nineteenth century, some women broke away from male-dominated missionary organizations. Using the slogan "Woman's work for women," they exerted moral authority in the West by establishing their own missionary societies and aiding women—unmarried mothers, Mormons, Native Americans, and Chinese—who they believed had fallen prey to men or who had not yet accepted principles of Christian virtue.

15-2i Significance of Race

To control labor and social relations within this human ecological complex, white settlers made race an important distinguishing characteristic within a hierarchy that included numerous categories. At the top were those descended from white Europeans, but this group had many sub-ranks, with Anglo-Saxons first, followed by less valued white groups, such as Celts, Turks, Slavs, Hebrews, and many more. Below whites were people considered (by whites) as nonwhite and inferior: Native Americans, Mexicans (both Mexican Americans, who had originally inhabited western lands, and Mexican immigrants), "Mongolians" (a term applied to Chinese), and "Negroes." In applying these categories, whites imposed racial distinctions on people who, with the possible exception of African Americans, had never before considered themselves to be a "race." Whites using these categories ascribed demeaning characteristics to all others, judging them to be permanently inferior. In 1878, for example, a federal judge in California ruled that Chinese could not become U.S. citizens because they were not "white persons."

Racial and ethnic minorities in western communities occupied the bottom segment of a two-tiered labor system. Whites dominated the top tier of managerial and skilled labor positions, while Irish, Chinese, Mexican, and African Americans generally held unskilled positions. All non-Anglo groups encountered prejudice, especially as dominant whites tried to reserve for themselves whatever riches the West might yield. Anti-Chinese violence erupted during hard times. For example, when the Union Pacific Railroad tried to replace white workers with lower-waged Chinese in Rock Springs, Wyoming, in 1885, unemployed whites invaded and burned down the Chinese part of town, killing twenty-eight. Mexicans, many of whom had been the original owners of the land in California and elsewhere, saw their property claims ignored or stolen by white miners and farmers.

The multiracial quality of western communities, however, also included a cross-racial dimension. Because so many white male migrants were single, intermarriages, or at least cohabitation, with Mexican and Native American women were common. Such unions were acceptable for white men, but not for white women, especially where Asian immigrants were involved. Most miscegenation laws passed by western legislatures were intended to prevent Chinese and Japanese men from marrying white women.

15-2j Conservation Movement

As whites were wresting ownership of the land from Native American and Mexican inhabitants, questions arose over who should control the nation's animal, mineral, and timber resources. Much of the undeveloped territory west of the Mississippi was in the public domain, and some people believed that the federal government, as its owner, should limit its exploitation. Others, however, believed that their own and the nation's prosperity depended on unlimited utilization of the land and its contents.

Questions about natural resources caught Americans between a desire for progress and a fear of spoiling nature. After the Civil War, people eager to protect the natural landscape began to organize a conservation movement. Sports hunters, concerned about depletion of wildlife, opposed mass commercial hunting and lobbied state legislatures to pass hunting regulations. Artists and tourists in 1864 persuaded

"exodusters" Freed people who migrated from the South to the North and Midwest for better opportunities.

Congress to preserve the beautiful Yosemite Valley by granting it to the state of California, which reserved it for public use. Then, in 1872, Congress designated the Yellowstone River region in Wyoming as the first national park. And in 1891 conservationists, led by naturalist John Muir, pressured Congress to authorize President Benjamin Harrison to create forest reserves—public lands protected from private timber cutters.

Such policies met with strong objections from lumber companies and railroads. Despite Muir's activism and efforts by the Sierra Club (which Muir helped found in 1892) and by such corporations as the Southern Pacific Railroad, which supported rational resource development, opposition was loudest in the West, where people remained eager to take advantage of nature's bounty. Ironically, however, by prohibiting trespass in areas such as Yosemite and Yellowstone, conservation policy deprived Native Americans and white settlers of the wildlife, water, and firewood that they had previously taken from federal lands.

15-2k Admission of New States

Development of mining and forest regions, as well as of farms and cities, brought western territories to the economic and population threshold of statehood (see Map 15.2). In 1889 Republicans seeking to solidify control of Congress passed an omnibus bill granting statehood to North Dakota, South Dakota, Washington, and Montana, where Republican politicians dominated. Wyoming and Idaho, both of which allowed

women to vote in state elections, were admitted the following year. Congress denied statehood to Utah until 1896, wanting assurances from the Mormons, who constituted a majority of the territory's population and controlled its government, that they would prohibit polygamy.

Western states' varied communities fostered a "go-getter" optimism that distinguished the American spirit. The lawlessness and hedonism of places such as Deadwood, in Dakota Territory, and Tombstone, in Arizona Territory, gave the region notoriety and romance. Legends, only partly true, arose about characters whose lives both typified and magnified western experience.

15-2l Western Folk Heroes

Arizona's mining towns, with their free-flowing cash and loose law enforcement, attracted gamblers, thieves, and opportunists whose names came to stand for the Wild West. Near Tombstone, the infamous Clanton family and their partner Johnny Ringo engaged in smuggling and cattle rustling. Inside the town, the Earp brothers—Wyatt, Jim, Morgan, Virgil, and Warren—and their friends William ("Bat") Masterson and John Henry ("Doc") Holliday operated on both sides of the law as gunmen, gamblers, and politicians. A feud between the Clantons and Earps climaxed on October 26, 1881, in a shootout at the O.K. Corral, where three members of the Clanton group were killed and Holliday and Morgan Earp were wounded. These characters and their exploits provided material for future novels, movies, and television programs.

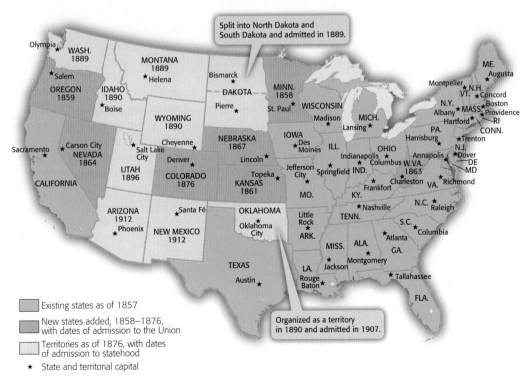

Map 15.2 The United States, 1876–1912

A wave of admissions between 1889 and 1912 brought remaining territories to statehood and marked the final creation of new states until Alaska and Hawai'i were admitted in the 1950s.

Writers Mark Twain, Bret Harte, and others captured the flavor of western life, and characters such as Buffalo Bill, Annie Oakley, and Wild Bill Hickok became western folk heroes. But violence and eccentricity were not widely common. Most miners and lumbermen worked long hours, often for corporations rather than as rugged individuals, and had little time, energy, or money for gambling, carousing, or gunfights. Women worked as long or longer as teachers, laundresses, storekeepers, and housewives. Only a few were sharpshooters or dance-hall queens. For most, western life was a matter of adapting and surviving.

15-3 The Age of Railroad Expansion

▶ How did railroad construction contribute to changes in social organization?

Between 1865 and 1890, railroad construction boomed, as total track grew from 35,000 to 200,000 miles, mostly from construction west of the Mississippi River (see Map 15.1). By 1900 the United States contained one-third of all railroad track in the world. A diverse mix of workers made up construction crews. The Central Pacific, built eastward from San Francisco, employed thousands of Chinese; the Union Pacific, extending westward from Omaha, Nebraska, used mainly Irish labor. Workers lived in shacks and tents that they dismantled, loaded on flatcars, and relocated each day.

Railroad expansion had powerful economic effects. After 1880, when steel rails replaced iron rails, railroads helped to boost the nation's steel industry to international leadership. Railroads also spawned related industries, including coal mining (for fuel), passenger- and freight-car manufacture, and depot construction. Influential and essential, railroads gave important impetus to western urbanization. With their ability to transport large loads of people and freight, lines such as the Union Pacific and the Southern Pacific accelerated the growth of western hubs, such as Chicago, Omaha, Kansas City, Cheyenne, Los Angeles, Portland, and Seattle.

15-3a Railroad Subsidies

Unlike European countries, where railroads were state-owned, American railroads were privately owned and managed. Yet, American railroads accomplished their massive construction feats with help from some of the largest government subsidies in American history. Promoters argued that because railroads were a public benefit, the government should grant them land from the public domain, which they could then sell to finance construction. During the Civil War, Congress, dominated by business-minded Republicans, was sympathetic, as it had been when it aided steamboat companies earlier in the century. As a result,

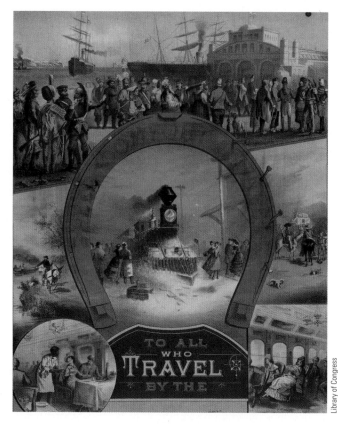

Library of Congress

▲ The rim of the horseshoe in this advertisement depicts reasons why railroad travel was better than other forms: one could avoid crowds of immigrants on steamships, move faster than a canal boat being towed by a mule, and be safe from bandits holding up a stagecoach. At the bottom of the poster are two depictions of luxurious dining and relaxed travel in a chair car that a railroad offered.

the federal government granted railroad corporations over 180 million acres, mostly for interstate routes. These grants usually consisted of a right-of-way, plus alternate sections of land in a strip 20 to 80 miles wide along the right-of-way. Railroads funded construction by using these lands as security for bonds—loans from investors—or by selling parcels for cash. States and localities heaped on further subsidies. State legislators, many of whom had financial interests in a railroad's success, granted some 50 million acres. Cities and towns also assisted, usually by offering loans or by purchasing railroad bonds or stocks.

Government subsidies had mixed effects. Although capitalists often opposed government involvement in the economic affairs of private businesses, railroads nevertheless readily accepted public aid and pressured governments into meeting their needs. The Southern Pacific, for example, threatened to bypass Los Angeles unless the city paid a bonus and built a depot. Without government help, few railroads could have prospered sufficiently to attract private investment, yet such aid was not always salutary. During the 1880s, the policy of generosity haunted communities whose zeal had prompted them to commit too much to railroads that were never built or that defaulted on loans. Some laborers and farmers fought subsidies, arguing that companies such as the Southern Pacific would become too powerful. Many communities boomed, however, because they had linked their fortunes to the iron horse. Moreover, railroads helped attract investment into the West and drew farmers into the market economy.

15-3b Standard Gauge, Standard Time

Railroad construction brought about important technological and organizational reforms. By the late 1880s, almost all lines had adopted standard-gauge rails so that tracks built by different companies could connect with one another. Air brakes, automatic car couplers, and other devices made rail transportation safer and more efficient. The need for gradings, tunnels, and bridges spurred the growth of the American engineering profession. Organizational advances included systems for coordinating passenger and freight schedules. Railroads also, however, reinforced racial segregation by separating black from white passengers on railroad cars and in stations.

Rail transportation altered conceptions of time and space. First, as they surmounted physical barriers by bridging rivers and tunneling through mountains, railroads transformed space into time. Instead of expressing distance between places in miles, people began to refer to the amount of time it took to travel from one place to another. Second, railroad scheduling required nationwide standardization of time so that shippers could be certain about when a train would depart or arrive. Before railroads, local clocks struck noon when the sun was directly overhead, and people set clocks and watches accordingly. But because the sun was not overhead at exactly the same moment everywhere, time varied from place to place. Boston's clocks, for instance, differed from those in New York by almost twelve minutes. To impose regularity, railroads created their own time zones. In 1883, without authority from Congress, the nation's railroads agreed to establish four standard time zones for the country. Most communities adjusted accordingly, and railroad time became national time.

15-4 Farming the Plains

▶ What environmental, social, and economic challenges did settlers face in the West?

▶ How did settlers adapt to life and farming in the West?

▶ How did ranching evolve over the course of the nineteenth century?

While California emerged as the nation's highest-yielding agricultural state, extraordinary ecological development occurred in the Great Plains. There, farming in the late 1800s exemplified two important achievements: the transformation by people of arid, windswept prairies into arable land that would feed the nation, and the transformation of agriculture into big business by means of mechanization, long-distance transportation, and scientific cultivation. These feats did not come easily. The region's climate and terrain presented formidable challenges, and overcoming them did not guarantee success. Irrigation and mechanized agriculture enabled farmers to feed the nation's burgeoning population and turned the United States into the world's breadbasket, but the experience also scarred the lives of countless people who made that accomplishment possible.

15-4a Settlement of the Plains

During the 1870s and 1880s, more acres were put under cultivation in states such as Kansas, Nebraska, and Texas than in the entire nation during the previous 250 years. The number of farms tripled between 1860 and 1910, as hundreds of thousands of hopeful migrants streamed into the Plains region. The Homestead Act of 1862 and other measures to encourage western settlement offered cheap or free plots to people who would reside on and improve their property. Railroads that had received land subsidies were especially active in recruiting settlers, advertising cheap land, arranging credit, offering reduced fares, and promising instant success. Railroad agents—often former immigrants—traveled to Denmark, Sweden, Germany, and other European nations to encourage immigration, and greeted newcomers at eastern ports.

Most families who occupied western farmlands migrated because opportunities there seemed to promise a second chance, a better existence than their previous one. Railroad expansion gave farmers in remote regions a way to ship crops to market, and construction of grain elevators eased problems of storage. As a result of worldwide as well as national population growth, demand for farm products burgeoned, and the prospects for commercial agriculture—growing crops for profit and shipment to distant, including international, markets—became more favorable than ever.

15-4b Hardship on the Plains

Farm life, however, was much harder than advertisements and railroad agents insinuated. Migrants often encountered scarcities of essentials that they had once taken for granted, and they had to adapt to the environment. Barren prairies contained insufficient lumber for housing and fuel, so pioneer families built houses of sod and burned buffalo dung for heat. Water for cooking and cleaning was sometimes scarce also. Machinery for drilling wells was expensive, as were windmills for drawing water to the surface.

Weather was even more forbidding than the terrain. The climate between the Missouri River and the Rocky Mountains divides along a line running from Minnesota southwest through Oklahoma, then south, bisecting Texas. West of this line, annual rainfall averages less than twenty-eight inches,

◀ Three adults and a child are posing alongside a road and in front of a sod house with their horse team in the background. Much of the farm frontier was virtually treeless, dry, and dusty. This family at least had enough resources to afford a relatively "high-toned" house and a windmill to bring up scarce water.

Library of Congress

not enough for most crops, and even scant life-giving rain was never certain (see Map 15.3). Heartened by adequate water one year, farmers gagged on dust and broke plows on hardened soil the next.

Weather seldom followed predictable cycles. Weeks of summer heat and parching winds suddenly gave way to violent storms that washed away crops and property. Frigid winter blizzards piled up mountainous snowdrifts that halted outdoor movement and froze livestock. During the winter of 1887–87, it snowed almost constantly on the Plains, prompting one farmer to observe that it "seemed as if all the world's ice from time's beginning had come on a wind that howled and screamed with the fury of demons." In springtime, melting snow swelled streams, and floods threatened millions of acres. In fall, a week without rain turned dry grasslands into tinder, and the slightest spark could ignite a raging prairie fire. Severe drought in Texas between 1884 and 1886 drove many farmers off the land, and a more widespread drought in 1886 struck areas as diverse as Dakota, Wyoming, and California.

Nature could be cruel even under good conditions. Weather that was favorable for crops also benefitted breeding insects. Worms and flying pests ravaged fields. In the 1870s and 1880s, grasshopper swarms ate up entire farms. Heralded only by the din of buzzing wings, a mile-long cloud of insects would smother the land and devour everything: plants, tree bark, and clothing. As one farmer lamented, the "hoppers left behind nothing but the mortgage."

15-4c Social Isolation

Settlers also had to cope with social isolation. In New England and Europe, farmers lived in villages and traveled daily to and from nearby fields. This pattern of community life was rare in the expanses of the Plains—and in the Far West and South as well—where peculiarities of land division compelled rural dwellers to live apart from each other. Because most farm plots

were rectangular—usually encompassing 160 acres—at most four families could live near one another, but only if they built homes around their shared four-corner intersection. In practice, households usually lived back from their boundary lines, and at least a half-mile separated farmhouses. Women were especially isolated, confined by domestic chores to the household. Like Nannie Jackson, they visited and exchanged food and services with neighbor women when they could and occasionally went to town, but, as one writer observed, a farm woman's life was "a weary, monotonous round of cooking and washing and mending."

Letters that Ed Donnell, a young Nebraska homesteader, wrote to his family in Missouri reveal how time and circumstances could dull optimism. In the fall of 1885, Donnell rejoiced to his mother, "I like Nebr first rate. . . . I have saw a pretty tuff time a part of the time since I have been out here, but I started out to get a home and I was determined to win or die in the attempt. . . . Have got a good crop of corn, a floor in my house and got it ceiled overhead." Already, though, Donnell was lonely. He went on, "There is lots of other bachelors here but I am the only one I know who doesn't have kinfolks living handy. . . . You wanted to know when I was going to get married. Just as quick as I can get money ahead to get a cow."

A year and a half later, Donnell's dreams were dissolving and, still a bachelor, he was beginning to look for a second chance elsewhere. He wrote to his brother, "The rats eat my sod stable down. . . . I may sell out this summer, ... If I sell I am going west and grow up with the country." By fall, conditions had worsened. Donnell lamented, "We have been having wet weather for 3 weeks. . . . My health has been so poor this summer and the wind and the sun hurts my head so. I think if I can sell I will . . . move to town for I can get $40 a month working in a grist mill and I would not be exposed to the weather." Donnell's doubts and hardships, shared by thousands of people, fed the cityward migration of farm folk that fueled late-nineteenth-century

Map 15.3 Agricultural Regions of the United States, 1890

In the Pacific Northwest and east of the twenty-eight-inch-rainfall line, farmers could grow a greater variety of crops. Territory west of the line was either too mountainous or too arid to support agriculture without irrigation. The grasslands that once fed buffalo herds could now feed beef cattle.

urban growth (see "Growth of the Modern American City," Section 16-4).

15-4d Mail-Order Companies and Rural Free Delivery

Farm families survived by sheer resolve and by organizing churches and clubs where they could socialize a few times a month. By 1900 two developments had brought rural settlers who lived east of the rainfall line into closer contact with modern consumer society. First, mail-order companies, such as Montgomery Ward (founded 1872) and Sears, Roebuck (founded 1893), made new products attainable through catalog sales. Emphasizing personal attention to customers, Ward and Sears received letters that often reported family news and sought advice on needs from gifts to childcare. A Washington man wrote to Mr. Ward, "As you advertise everything for sale that a

◀ Farm women sometimes relieved their isolation by getting together and creating a quilt. Note the different age groups represented in this activity and the animal trophy hanging conspicuously above them.

person wants, I thought I would write you, as I am in need of a wife, and see what you could do for me." Another reported, "I suppose you wonder why we haven't ordered anything from you since the fall. The cow kicked my arm and broke it and besides my wife was sick, and there was the doctor bill. But now, thank God, that is paid, and we are all well again, and we have a fine new baby boy, and please send plush bonnet number 29d8077."

Second, in 1896, after farmers petitioned Congress for extension of the postal service, the government made Rural Free Delivery (RFD) widely available. Farmers previously had to go to town to pick up mail. Now they could receive letters, newspapers, and catalogs in a roadside mailbox nearly every day. In 1913 the postal service inaugurated parcel post, which enabled people to receive packages, such as orders from Ward and Sears, more cheaply.

15-4e Mechanization of Agriculture

As with industrial production (see "Technology and the Triumph of Industrialism," Section 16-1), the late-nineteenth-century agricultural revolution was driven by expanded use of machinery. When the Civil War drew men away from farms in the upper Mississippi River Valley to fight in the army, women and older men who remained behind began using mechanical implements to grow crops to satisfy demand for food and take advantage of high grain prices. After the war, high demand encouraged farmers to continue utilizing machines, and inventors developed new implements to facilitate planting and harvesting. Seeders, combines, binders, reapers, and rotary plows, carried westward by railroads, facilitated grain-growing on the Plains and in California. Technology also aided dairy and poultry farming. The centrifugal cream separator, patented in 1879, sped the process of skimming cream from milk, and a mechanized incubator, invented in 1885, made chicken-raising more profitable.

For centuries, the acreage of grain a farmer planted was limited by the amount that could be harvested by hand. Machines significantly increased productivity. Before mechanization, a farmer working alone could harvest about 7.5 acres of wheat. Using an automatic binder that cut and bundled the grain, a farmer could harvest 135 acres. Machines dramatically reduced the time and cost of farming other crops as well.

15-4f Legislative and Scientific Aids

Meanwhile, Congress and scientists worked to improve existing crops and develop new ones. The 1862 Morrill Land Grant Act gave each state federal lands to sell in order to finance agricultural research at educational institutions. The act prompted establishment of public universities in Wisconsin, Illinois, Minnesota, California, and other states. A second Morrill Act in 1890 aided more schools, including several all-black colleges. The Hatch Act of 1887 provided for agricultural experiment stations in every state, further encouraging the advancement of agricultural science and technology.

Science also enabled farmers to use the soil more efficiently. Researchers developed dry farming, a technique of plowing and harrowing that minimized evaporation of precious moisture. Botanists perfected varieties of "hard" wheat whose seeds could withstand northern winters, and millers invented a process for grinding the tougher wheat kernels into flour. Agriculturists adapted new varieties of wheat from Russia and rice from Asia. Horticulturist Luther Burbank developed new food plants and flowers at a garden laboratory in Sebastopol, California. George Washington Carver, son of black slaves who became a chemist and taught at Alabama's Tuskegee Institute, created hundreds of products from peanuts, soybeans, and sweet potatoes. Other scientists devised means of combating plant and animal diseases. Just as in mining and manufacturing, science and technology provided American farming with means for expanding productivity in the market economy (see Table 15.1).

15-4g The Ranching Frontier

When commercial farming overspread the West, it ran headlong into one of the region's most romantic industries—ranching. Beginning in the sixteenth century, Spanish landholders raised cattle commercially in Mexico and what would become the American Southwest. They employed indigenous peoples and Mexicans as cowboys, known as *vaqueros*, who tended herds and rounded up cattle to be branded and slaughtered. Anglo ranchers moving into Texas and California in the early nineteenth century hired *vaqueros*, who in turn taught skills in roping, branding, and horse training to white and African American cowboys.

Table 15.1 Summary: Government Land Policy

Railroad land grants (1850–1871)	Granted 181 million acres to railroads to encourage construction and development
Homestead Act (1862)	Gave 80 million acres to settlers to encourage settlement
Morrill Act (1862)	Granted 11 million acres to states to sell to fund public agricultural colleges
Other grants	Granted 129 million acres to states to sell for other educational and related purposes
Dawes Act (1887)	Allotted some reservation lands to individual Native Americans to promote private property and weaken tribal values among Native groups and offered remaining reservation lands for sale to whites (by 1906, some 75 million acres had been acquired by whites)
Various laws	Permitted direct sales of 100 million acres by the Land Office

Source: Goldfield, David; Abbott, Carl; Anderson, Virginia Dejohn; Argersinger, Jo Ann; Argersinger, Peter H.; Barney, William L.; and Weir, Robert M., The American Journey, Volume II, 3rd ed., © 2004. Reproduced by permission of Pearson Education, Inc., Upper Saddle River, New Jersey.

▲ This lithograph, drawn from a photo in 1878, displays the transition from old means of farming, using horses and wagons, to new machines, such as the steam-powered wheat thresher depicted on this Dakota Territory farm.

By the 1860s, cattle ranching became increasingly profitable, as population growth boosted demand for beef and railroads simplified transportation of food. By 1870 drovers were herding thousands of Texas cattle on long drives northward to Kansas, Missouri, and Wyoming (see Map 15.1). At the northern terminus, the cattle were sold to northern feed lots or loaded onto trains bound for Chicago and St. Louis for slaughter and distribution to national and international markets.

The long drive gave rise to images of bellowing cattle, buckskin-clad cowboys, and smoky campfires under starry skies, but the process was not very efficient. Trekking 1,000 miles or more for two to three months made cattle sinewy and tough. Herds traveling through Native peoples' territories and farmers' fields were sometimes shot at and later prohibited from such trespass by state laws. Ranchers adjusted by raising herds nearer to railroad routes. When cattlemen discovered that crossing Texas longhorns with heavier Hereford and Angus breeds produced animals better able to survive harsh winters, cattle raising expanded northward, and proliferating herds in Kansas, Nebraska, Colorado, Wyoming, Montana, and Dakota crowded out already declining buffalo populations. Profits were considerable. A rancher could purchase a calf for $5, let it feed on grasslands for a few years, recapture it in a roundup, and sell it at a market price of $40 or $45.

15-4h The Open Range

Cattle raisers needed vast pastures to graze their herds while spending as little as possible on land acquisition. Thus they often bought a few acres bordering a stream and turned their herds loose on adjacent public domain that no one wanted because it lacked water access. By this method, called open-range ranching, a cattleman could utilize thousands of acres by owning only a hundred or so. Neighboring ranchers often formed associations

and allowed herds to graze together. Owners identified their cattle by burning a brand into each animal's hide. Each ranch had its own unique brand—a shorthand method for labeling movable property. But as more profit-seeking ranchers flowed into the Plains, cattle began to overrun the range, and other groups challenged ranchers over use of the land.

In California and New Mexico, sheepherders also grazed herds on public land, sparking territorial clashes. Ranchers complained that sheep ruined grassland by eating down to the roots and that cattle refused to graze where sheep had been. Occasionally ranchers and sheepherders resorted to armed conflict rather than settle disagreements in court, where a judge might discover that both were using public land illegally.

More importantly, however, the advancing farming frontier was generating new demands for acreage. Devising a way to mark property resulted in an unheralded but significant change in land management. The problem was fencing. Lacking sufficient timber and stone for fencing, western settlers could not easily define and protect their property. Tensions flared when farmers accused cattlemen of allowing their herds to trespass on cropland and when herders in turn charged that farmers should fence their property against grazing animals. Ranchers and farmers alike lacked an economical means of enclosing herds and fields.

15-4i Barbed Wire

The solution was barbed wire. Patented in 1873 by Joseph Glidden, a DeKalb, Illinois, farmer, this fencing consisted of twisted wire strands that held sharp wire barbs in place at regular intervals. Mass produced by the Washburn and Moen Manufacturing Company of Worcester, Massachusetts—80.5 million pounds in 1880 alone—barbed wire provided a cheap and durable means of enclosure. It benefited homesteaders by enabling them to protect their property from grazing cattle. It also ended open-range ranching and made roundups unnecessary, because it enabled ranchers to enclose their herds. In addition, the development of the round silo for storing hay without it spoiling enabled cattle raisers to feed their herds without grazing them on vast stretches of land.

15-4k Ranching as Big Business

By 1890 big businesses were taking over the cattle industry and applying scientific methods of breeding and feeding. Corporations also used technology to squeeze larger returns out of meatpacking. Like buffalo, all parts of a cow had uses. Only about half of it consisted of salable meat. Larger profits came from by-products: hides for leather, bones for fertilizer, hooves for glue, and fat for candles and soap. But cattle processing also had harmful environmental impact. What meatpackers could not sell they dumped into rivers and streams. By the late nineteenth century, the stench from the Chicago River, which flowed past the city's mammoth processing plants, made nearby residents sick.

Open-range ranching made beef a staple of the American diet and created a few fortunes, but it could not survive the rush of history. During the 1880s, overgrazing destroyed grass supplies on the Plains, and the brutal winter of 1886–1887 killed 90 percent of some herds and drove small ranchers out of business. By 1890, large-scale ranchers owned or leased the land they used, though some illegal fencing persisted. Cowboys formed labor organizations and participated in strikes for higher pay. The myth of the cowboy's freedom and individualism lived on, but ranching, like mining and farming, quickly became a corporate business.

15-5 The South After Reconstruction

▶ How did new forms of organizing agricultural labor and ranching practices impact white and black Southerners?

▶ How did the Southern industrial economy develop after Reconstruction?

▶ How was the South both "new" and "old" by 1890?

While the Great Plains and West were being transformed, the South developed its own human ecologies, involving resource exploitation, market economies, and land control. During and after Reconstruction, important shifts in the nature of agriculture swept the South. Between 1860 and 1880, the total number of farms in southern states more than doubled, from 450,000 to 1.1 million. The number of landowners, however, did not increase, because a growing proportion of southern farmers rented, rather than owned, their land. Meanwhile, average farm size actually decreased, from 347 to 156 acres. One-third of farmers counted in the 1880 federal census were sharecroppers and tenants; the proportion increased to two-thirds by 1920.

Ravaged by the Civil War, southern agriculture recovered slowly. Rather than diversify, farmers concentrated on growing cotton even more single-mindedly than before the war

in an attempt to recover a share of national and international markets. The effort did not work out well. High prices for seed and implements, declining prices for crops, taxes, and, most of all, debt trapped many white southerners in poverty. Conditions were even worse for African Americans, who endured brutal racism along with economic hardship.

15-5a Sharecropping and Tenant Farming in the South

Southern agriculture, unlike that of the Midwest, did not benefit much from mechanization. Tobacco and cotton, the principal southern crops, required constant hoeing and weeding by hand. Tobacco needed careful harvesting, because the leaves matured at different rates and the stems were too fragile for machines. Also, mechanical devices were not precise enough to pick cotton. Thus, southern agriculture remained labor-intensive, and laborlords who had once utilized slaves were replaced by landlords, who employed sharecroppers and tenant farmers.

Sharecropping and tenant farming—meaning that farmers rented their land rather than owned it—entangled millions of black and white southerners in webs of debt and humiliation, weighed down by the crop lien. Most farmers, too poor to have ready cash, borrowed in order to buy necessities such as seed, tools, and food. They could offer as collateral only what they could grow. A farmer helpless without supplies dealt with a "furnishing merchant," who would exchange provisions for a "lien," or legal claim, on the farmer's forthcoming crop. After the crop was harvested and brought to market, the merchant claimed the portion of the crop that would repay the loan. All too often, however, the debt exceeded the crop's value. The farmer could pay off only part of the loan but still needed supplies for the coming year. The only way to obtain these necessities was to sink deeper into debt by reborrowing and giving the merchant a lien on the next year's crop.

Merchants frequently exploited farmers' powerlessness by inflating prices and charging excessive interest on the advances farmers received. Suppose, for example, that a cash-poor farmer needed a 20-cent bag of seed or a 20-cent piece of cloth. The furnishing merchant would sell the item on credit but would boost the price to 28 cents. At year's end, that 28-cent loan would have accumulated interest of 50 percent, raising the farmer's debt to 42 cents—more than double the item's original cost. The farmer, having pledged more than his crop's worth against scores of such debts, fell behind in payments and never recovered. If he fell too far behind, he and his family could be evicted.

In the southern backcountry, which in antebellum times had been characterized by small, family-owned farms, few slaves, and diversified agriculture, economic changes compounded crop-lien problems. New spending habits illustrate these changes. In 1884 Jephta Dickson, who farmed land in the northern Georgia hills, bought $55.90 worth of flour, potatoes, peas, meat, and corn from merchants. Before the Civil War, farmers like Dickson grew almost all the food they needed and such expenditures would have been rare. But after the war, Dickson and others like him shifted to commercial farming; in the South that meant cotton rather than diversified agriculture. This specialization came about for two reasons: constant

▲ In the post-Reconstruction South, cotton remained central to the economy. Here, African American workers are sorting and baling the cotton for shipment, all under the watchful eye of a white supervisor.

debt forced farmers to grow crops that would bring in cash, and railroads enabled them to transport cotton to market more easily than before. As backcountry yeomen devoted more acres to cotton, they produced less of what they needed on a daily basis and found themselves at the mercy of merchants.

15-5b Closing the Southern Range

At the same time, many small black and white farmers who occupied settlements in the back-country suffered from laws that essentially closed the southern range—lands owned by the federal government but used freely by southern herders. This change resulted from the same commercialization of agriculture affecting farming in the West and Midwest. Before the 1870s, southern farmers, like western open-range ranchers, had let their livestock roam freely to search for food and water. By custom, farmers who wished to protect their crops would build fences to keep out foraging livestock. But as commercial agriculture reached the back-country, large landowners and merchants induced county and state governments to require the fencing-in of animals rather than crops. These laws hurt poor farmers who had little land, requiring them to use more of their acreage for pasture. Such laws undermined the cooperative customs that yeomen cherished and that people like Nannie Jackson practiced by forcing them to close themselves off from neighbors.

Poor whites in the rural South, facing economic hardship, also feared that newly enfranchised blacks would challenge whatever political and social superiority (real and imagined) they enjoyed. Wealthy white landowners and merchants fanned these fears, using racism to divide whites and blacks and to distract poor whites from protesting their economic subjugation.

15-5c Leading Industries

Southern agriculture had a close relationship with its two leading industries: cotton and tobacco. In the 1870s, textile mills began to appear in the old Cotton Belt. Powered by the region's abundant rivers, manned cheaply by whites eager to escape hardship on the land, and aided by low taxes and northern capital investment, such factories multiplied. By 1900, the South had four hundred mills with a total of 4 million spindles, and was on the verge of eclipsing New England in textile manufacturing supremacy. Proximity to raw materials and cheap labor also aided the tobacco industry, and the invention in 1880 of a cigarette-making machine enhanced the marketability of tobacco.

◄ Cigarette factories were among the few southern industries that employed African American workers. Here, a workforce of men are pressing and storing tobacco leaves in a Richmond, Virginia, tobacco company in 1899.

National Parks

The idea of embodying greatness in the natural splendor of national parks has been a uniquely American contribution to world culture. Initially, however, Congress did not recognize this possibility, even when in 1872 it created Yellowstone National Park to preserve its untouched beauty. No funds were appropriated for the park's protection and the government lacked sensitivity to the park's needs. For example, the area contained one of the country's few remaining buffalo herds, but poaching reduced the herd to just twenty-two animals. In 1886, however, the Secretary of the Interior requested and was granted cavalry soldiers to supervise the park; originally meant to be temporary, they stayed until 1922.

Slowly, Congress created other parks, including Yosemite and Sequoia in California in 1890 and sites in Oregon, Utah, Arizona, Montana, and Colorado between 1902 and 1915. From the beginning, conflicts arose between those who, like naturalist John Muir and the Sierra Club, wished to preserve parks in as pristine a quality as possible, and those, such as Senator William A. Clark of Montana, who wanted to lease the land to private businesses for logging, mining, railroads, and tourism. (Clark, who bribed and bullied his way

to power, was labeled by Mark Twain as "as rotten a human being as can be found under the flag.") To regularize park management, Congress in 1916 created the National Park Service (NPS) with the mission to conserve natural and historic territory while at the same time providing for their enjoyment by present and future generations. Stephen Mather, appointed head of the service, took his job of preservation seriously but also allowed hotel construction in parks for the comfort of visitors.

At first, all national parks were located in the West, but after 1920 the Park Service began establishing southern sites, beginning with the Great Smokies in Tennessee and North Carolina and Shenandoah in Virginia. A major turning point occurred in 1933 when President Franklin Roosevelt transferred supervision of all national monuments and historic sites to the NPS, giving the NPS jurisdiction over the Statue of Liberty and Civil War battlefields as well as Yosemite. A few years later, NPS began administering national seashores, and from the 1960s onward urban sites such as Golden Gate National Recreation Area near San Francisco and the Jean Lafitte area at New Orleans were included.

Success created problems for many sites because the American public was loving them to death. By 1950, 30 million people visited national parks annually. Roads fell into disrepair, campgrounds became dilapidated, and litter piled up. Moreover, those eager for the economic development of parklands continued to lobby for permission to expand roads, and build hotels, gas stations, and restaurants. In 1964, Congress passed a bill providing funds for future parkland acquisition, but achieving a balance between preserving natural beauty and allowing the public to enjoy it firsthand remains controversial. Today, there are almost 400 national park units, encompassing more than 84 million acres. They stand as a legacy from the past, and their status as national treasures poses challenges to the future.

CRITICAL THINKING

- With almost 400 national park units, encompassing more than 84 million acres, does the United States have enough such spaces?
- What should be the criteria for whether or not new areas should be designated as national parks?
- When should development and other economic interests take precedence?

Cigarette factories, located in cities, employed both black and white workers (though in segregated sections of the factories). Textile mills, concentrated in small towns, developed a separate labor system that employed women and children from poor white families and paid 50 cents a day for twelve or more hours of work. Such wages were barely half of those paid to northern workers. Many companies built villages around their mills, where they controlled housing, stores, schools, and churches. Inside these towns, companies banned criticism of the management and squelched attempts at union organization. Mill families soon found that factory jobs changed their status very little: the company store and the mill owner dominated their everyday lives.

Other industries utilizing nature were launched under the sponsorship of northern and European capital. Between 1890 and 1900, northern syndicates moved into pine forests of the Gulf States, boosting lumber production by 500 percent. During the 1880s, northern investors developed southern iron

deposits into steel manufacturing, much of it in the boom city of Birmingham, Alabama. What was to become the most famous southern product, Coca-Cola, was first formulated by Dr. John Pemberton, an Atlanta pharmacist, who in 1889 sold his recipe to another Atlantean, Asa Candler, who made a fortune marketing the drink nationally. Coal mining and railroad construction also expanded rapidly, though, as was the case with other southern industries, New York and London financiers dominated the boards of directors.

15-5d The New South

Regardless of outside influence, the new economy prompted local boosters to herald the emergence of a New South ready to compete with economies of the West and North by challenging the old economic order that had been dominated by the planter class. Believing that the South should put military defeat of the Civil War behind them—though never forgetting the heroism of Confederate soldiers—businessmen advocated emulating northern industrialism. Henry Grady, editor of the *Atlanta Constitution* and the voice of southern progress, proclaimed, "We have sowed towns and cities in the place of theories, and put business in place of politics. We have challenged your spinners in Massachusetts and your iron-makers in Pennsylvania. . . . We have fallen in love with work."

Yet in 1900 the South was as rural as it had been in 1860. Staple-crop agriculture remained central to its ecology, and white supremacy permeated its social and political relations. Furthermore, the South attracted few immigrants because of its low wages and except for only a few places, such as the city of New Orleans, did not benefit much from the energizing influence of foreign cultures. A New South would emerge, but not until after a world war and a massive African American exodus had shaken up old habits and attitudes.

Summary

The complex interactions between people and their environments transformed the West, the South, and the nation. In the West, indigenous people had used, and sometimes abused, the land to support subsistence cultures that included trade and war as well as hunting and farming. Living mostly in small groups, they depended on delicate resources, such as buffalo herds and salmon runs. When they came into contact with commerce-minded, migratory European Americans, their resistance to the market economy, diseases, and violence that whites brought into the West failed. The result was that the story of the American West became the story of the invaders, not that of the Native peoples.

Mexicans, Chinese, African Americans, and Anglos entered into a reciprocal relationship between human activities and the nonhuman world, with results that they had not always anticipated. Miners, timber cutters, farmers, and builders extracted raw minerals to supply eastern factories, used irrigation and machines to bring forth agricultural abundance from the land, filled pastures with cattle and sheep to expand food sources, and constructed railroads to tie the nation together. In doing so, they transformed half of the nation's territory within a few decades. But the environment also exerted its power over humans, through its climate, its insects and parasites, and its impenetrable hazards and barriers to human movement and agriculture.

The West's settlers, moreover, employed violence and greed that sustained discrimination within a multiracial society; left many farmers feeling cheated and betrayed; provoked contests over use of water and pastures; and sacrificed environmental

balance for market profits. The region's raw materials and agricultural products raised living standards and hastened industrial progress, but not without human and environmental costs.

Longer-settled, the South experienced its own set of changes. The end of slavery left African Americans still tied to the land as tenant farmers and sharecroppers and still subject to various forms of discrimination, while white farmers, landholders as well as tenants, found themselves at increasing disadvantage in expanding markets. To achieve sectional independence, some southerners tried to promote industrialization. Their efforts partially succeeded, but by 1900 many southern industries remained mere subsidiaries of northern firms. Moreover, southern planters, shippers, and manufacturers depended heavily on northern banks to finance their operations. Equally important, low wages and stunted opportunities discouraged potential migrants and immigrants who might have brought needed labor, skills, and capital. Thus although the South did grow economically in some ways, it remained a dependent region in the national economy. People of all sorts now belonged to one nation, indivisible, but sectional differences continued to make the nation increasingly diverse.

Suggestions for Further Reading

Edward Ayers, *The Promise of the New South: Life After Reconstruction* (1992)

William Cronon, *Nature's Metropolis: Chicago and the Great West* (1991)

Robert V. Hine and John Mack Faragher, *The American West: A New Interpretive History* (2000)

Andrew C. Isenberg, *The Destruction of the Bison: An Environmental History* (2000)

Karl Jacoby, *Shadows at Dawn: A Borderlands Massacre and the Violence of History* (2009)

Patricia Nelson Limerick, *Something in the Soil: Legacies and Reckoning in the New West* (2000)

Robert McMath, Jr., *The Populist Vanguard: A History of the Southern Farmers' Alliance* (1975)

Eugene P. Moehring, *Urbanism and Empire in the Far West, 1840–1890* (2004)

Robert M. Utley, *The Indian Frontier of the American West, 1846–1890* (1984)

Richard White, *"It's Your Misfortune and None of My Own": A New History of the American West* (1991)

Donald Worster, *A Passion for Nature: The Life of John Muir* (2008)

Building Factories, Building Cities, 1877–1920

As immigrants sailed into the New York harbor in the late nineteenth and early twentieth centuries, the first landmass they saw was Coney Island, a peninsula jutting out from Brooklyn. By this time, its easy access from New York City by carriage road and ferry lines, plus its beaches, parks, and other attractions had made Coney Island the largest entertainment resort in the world. A 300-foot tower, with an elevator to the top, was moved there after the 1876 World's Fair in Philadelphia. Electric arc lamps lighted the beaches for nighttime swimming. Racetracks and theaters attracted thousands of tourists. By 1904, the resort boasted three fantasy-filled amusement parks with the alluring names of Steeplechase, Luna, and Dreamland. Rides, such as the world's first roller coaster plus "A Trip to the Moon" (on a vehicle with flapping wings) and "Hell Gate" (a boat ride on swirling waters), dazzled visitors. Before it burned down in 1896, there was even a hotel shaped like an elephant that included guest rooms, a candy store, and a cigar shop. As one excited observer wrote of Coney Island, ". . . not to have seen it is not to have seen your own country."

Experience an interactive version of this story in MindTap®.

◀ Between 1884 and 1896, Coney Island featured an "Elephantine Colossus," at which visitors could stay overnight. According to an official description, each leg of the wooden behemoth was 60 feet high; its ears were 40 feet wide; and the trunk measured 72 feet. The forelegs housed a diorama and a cigar store, and the hind legs contained staircases leading to 31 hotel rooms, including "a main hall head room, 2 side body rooms, 2 thigh rooms, 2 shoulder rooms, 2 cheek rooms, 1 throat room, 1 stomach room, 4 hoof rooms, 6 leg rooms, 2 side rooms, and 2 hip rooms." Library of Congress Prints and Photographs Division Washington, D.C. [LC-USZ62-102887]

Chronology

1869	■ Knights of Labor founded
1873–78	■ Economy declines
1876	■ National League of Professional Baseball Clubs founded
1877	■ Widespread railroad strikes protest wage cuts
1878	■ Edison Electric Light Company founded
1880s	■ "New" immigrants from eastern and southern Europe begin to arrive in large numbers
1882	■ Standard Oil Trust founded
1883	■ Pulitzer buys *New York World*, creating major publication for yellow journalism
1886	■ Haymarket riot in Chicago protests police brutality against labor demonstrations
	■ American Federation of Labor (AFL) founded
1890	■ Sherman Anti-Trust Act outlaws "combinations in restraint of trade"
1892	■ Homestead (Pennsylvania) steelworkers strike against Carnegie Steel Company
1893–97	■ Economic depression causes high unemployment and business failures
1895	■ *U.S. v. E. C. Knight Co.* limits Congress's power to regulate manufacturing
1896	■ *Holden v. Harcy* upholds law regulating miners' working hours
1900–10	■ Immigration reaches peak
1905	■ *Lochner v. New York* overturns law limiting bakery workers' working hours and limits labor protection law
	■ Intercollegiate Athletic Association, forerunner of National Intercollegiate Athletic Association (NCAA), is formed, restructuring rules of football
1908	■ *Muller v. Oregon* upholds law limiting women to ten-hour workday
	■ First Ford Model T built
1911	■ Triangle Shirtwaist Company fire in New York City leaves 146 workers dead
1913	■ Ford begins moving assembly-line production
1920	■ Majority (51.4 percent) of Americans live in cities

Coney Island blended the ingredients of the modern American nation. Steel structures, inventions, electricity, consumer goods, and commercial amusement all combined to serve new needs and demands of a people ready to work but also eager to play in a burgeoning city. Everything at Coney Island was not permanent. A fire started by a carelessly thrown cigarette destroyed almost all of Steeplechase Park in 1907, and a combination of flammable materials and electric malfunction caused a huge fire that burned down Dreamland in 1911. But no one could deny that much about the way people lived was new and improved.

The industrialization that made Coney Island possible was a complex process whose chief feature was production of goods by new technology. In the mid-nineteenth century, an industrial revolution swept through parts of the United States, and the mechanization that characterized it powered a second round in the late 1800s. By that time, the United

States had become the world's most productive industrial nation, as well as the largest producer of raw materials and food (see Map 16.1). Four themes characterized American industrialization. First, inventors and manufacturers harnessed technology to serve production in ways never before imagined. Second, to increase production and maximize use of technology, factory owners divided work routines into repetitive tasks and organized them according to dictates of the clock, turning workers who once had thought of themselves as producers into employees. Third, a new consumer society took shape as goods such as canned foods and machine-made clothing became common. Fourth, in their quest for growth and profits, corporation owners amassed great power through new forms of corporate organization.

At the same time, technological advances and industrialization helped make cities a fact of national life. *Urbanization* is the process whereby cities and their areas expand

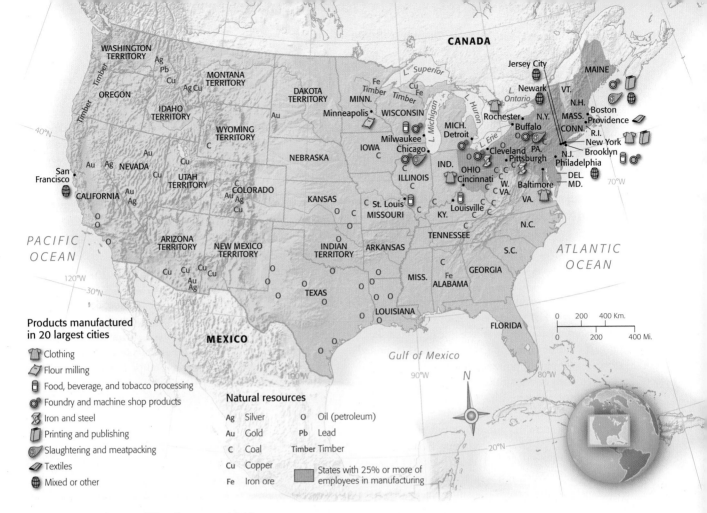

Map 16.1 Industrial Production, 1919

By the early twentieth century, each state could boast at least one kind of industrial production. Although the value of goods produced was still highest in the Northeast, states such as Minnesota and California had impressive dollar values of outputs. *Source: Data from the U.S. Bureau of the Census, Fourteenth Census of the United States, 1920, Vol. IX, Manufacturing (Washington, D.C.: US Government Printing Office, 1921).*

more rapidly than do their surrounding environments. This process accelerated after the Civil War and by 1920 a milestone of urbanization was passed: that year's census showed that, for the first time, a majority of Americans (51.4 percent) lived in cities. City dwellers both propelled industrialization by furnishing its workforces and benefited from it by consuming its goods and services, such as those offered at Coney Island. The many migrants and immigrants to cities utilized their economic and political opportunities to free themselves from uncertainties of the past. But poverty and discrimination also haunted many urban dwellers, combining the era's opportunities with the persistence of poverty and inequality. The ways that people built cities and adjusted to the industrial environment shaped modern American society.

◼ *How did mechanization affect the lives of average workers and the makeup of the labor force?*

◼ *What were the most important factors contributing to the urban growth of the period 1877–1920?*

◼ *How did immigrants adjust to and reshape their adopted homeland?*

16-1 Technology and the Triumph of Industrialism

▶ **How did technology contribute to the process of industrialization?**

▶ **How was electricity harnessed to produce goods?**

▶ **How did technology impact Americans in their day-to-day lives?**

While some people chased natural resource opportunities in the West and South, others employed a spirit of inventiveness to drive the new industrialization. Between 1860 and 1930, the U.S. Patent Office, created by the Constitution to "promote the Progress of science and the useful Arts," granted 1.5 million patents for new inventions; it granted only 36,000 between 1790 and 1860. Inventions often sprang from a marriage between technology and business organization. The harnessing of electricity, internal combustion, steelmaking, and chemistry illustrate how the marriage worked.

16-1a Birth of the Electrical Industry

Thomas Edison, America's most celebrated inventor, opened an "invention factory" in Menlo Park, New Jersey, in 1876. There, his application of electricity to light, sound, and images, plus his system for delivering electric power, brought new products to the nation and laid the foundation for how Americans live today. His most notable invention, created after tedious experimentation, was the incandescent light bulb. But also, his Edison Electric Light Company (founded in 1878) devised a system of power generation that provided electricity conveniently to manifold customers. Acting as his own publicist, Edison marketed his ideas by demonstrating how electric lighting could transform night into day. Such illumination not only lit homes and offices but enhanced the appeal of Coney Island parks and advertising signs.

Other entrepreneurs adapted electricity for countless purposes. George Westinghouse, for example, showed how alternating current could transmit electricity over long distances. Granville T. Woods, an African American engineer sometimes called "the black Edison," patented thirty-five devices vital to electronics and communications. Financiers Henry Villard and J. P. Morgan bought patents from inventors such as Woods, merged equipment manufacturing companies into the General Electric Company, and established research laboratories in which scientists created electrical products for practical use.

16-1b Henry Ford and the Automobile Industry

Meanwhile, the gas-powered internal combustion engine, developed in Germany, inspired one of America's most visionary manufacturers, **Henry Ford**. Originally an electrical engineer, Ford adapted the internal combustion engine to propel a vehicle. Though another inventor had already done the same thing, Ford applied organizational genius to the invention and spawned a massive industry, predicting in 1909, "I am going to democratize the automobile. When I'm through, everybody will be able to afford one, and about everyone will have one." Ford set about mass-producing identical cars on assembly lines that divided the manufacturing process into single tasks repeatedly performed by workers using the same specialized

Thomas Edison Inventor and founder of the first industrial research laboratory.

Henry Ford Founder of the Ford Motor Company and pioneer of modern assembly lines used in mass production.

Andrew Carnegie Scottish immigrant who built an enormous steel company and became a renowned philanthropist.

machines. By 1914, the Ford Motor Company outside of Detroit was producing 248,000 cars per year, and auto manufacturing spawned new industries in steel, oil, rubber, and glass, each of which utilized precision machines to standardize production and applied electricity to power assembly lines. A new Ford cost $490, still unaffordable to workers who earned at best $2 a day. To enable his employees to afford a car, as well as reduce labor turnover and head off unionization, Ford began a Five-Dollar-Day pay plan that combined wages and profit sharing.

In the 1850s, British engineer Henry Bessemer developed a process for producing steel, the strong, durable metal needed for many new products, from molten iron. In America, Scottish immigrant **Andrew Carnegie** recognized the benefits of the Bessemer process and in the 1870s built steelmaking plants near Pittsburgh that eventually furnished materials for rails and bridges, as well as barbed wire, tubing, and household appliances. In 1892, Carnegie combined his assets into the Carnegie Steel Company and by 1900 controlled 60 percent of the country's steel business. In 1901, he retired, selling his holdings to a group led by J. P. Morgan, who formed the huge U.S. Steel Corporation.

Industrial chemistry was pioneered by French immigrant E. I. du Pont, who manufactured gunpowder in Delaware in the early 1890s. In 1902, three du Pont cousins took over the company and expanded production into fertilizer, dyes, and other chemical products. In 1911, du Pont research labs adapted cellulose to the production of consumer goods such as photographic film, textile fibers, and plastics. The company also developed new methods of management and recordkeeping, all leading to higher profits.

16-1c Technology and Southern Industry

In the South, new industries developed around natural resources. The tobacco crop inspired North Carolinian James B. Duke to create a machine for making cigarettes. He began mass production in 1885. Like Edison and Ford, Duke used marketing and advertising to attract customers. By 1900, his American Tobacco Company was a global business with sales in England and Japan as well as the United States. Also, electric-powered cotton looms and a cheap labor force enabled the southern textile industry to surpass water-powered New England mills and attract investors. Many textile companies built villages around their mills and controlled housing, stores, schools, and churches. Northern capitalists also invested in southern iron and steel manufacturing, especially in the boom city of Birmingham, Alabama. And between 1890 and 1900, northern lumber syndicates moved into pine forests of the Gulf States, boosting wood production and prompting the relocation of furniture and paper production from North to South.

16-1d Technology and Everyday Life

In all regions, machines and technology altered everyday life. Telephones and typewriters made face-to-face communications less important and facilitated correspondence. Electric sewing machines made mass-produced clothing in standardized sizes available to almost everyone and gave homemakers more convenient ways of creating and mending clothing. Manufacturers

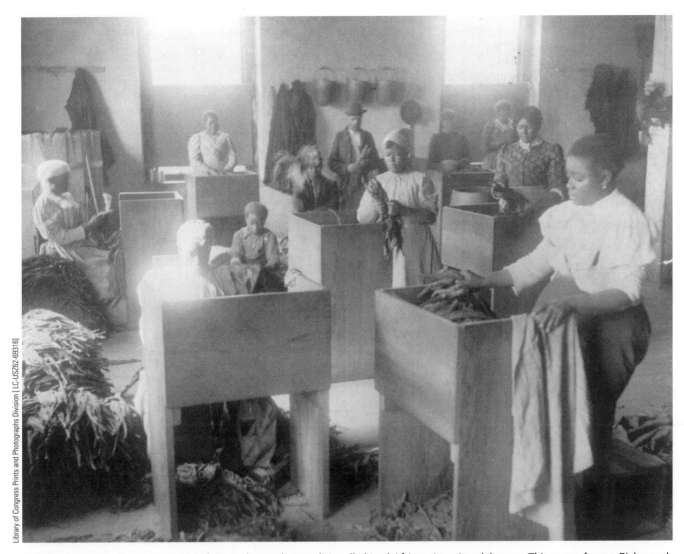

▲ Tobacco production was one southern industry that traditionally hired African American laborers. This scene from a Richmond tobacco factory around 1880 shows women and children preparing leaves for curing by tearing off the stems.

of "ready-to-wear" garments emphasized comfort, using less fabric for women's clothes and creating lighter-weight, yet durable suits for middle-class men and cheaper denim overalls for workingmen. Eating habits also changed. Refrigeration enabled preservation and shipment of fresh meat, produce, and dairy products; canning preserved foods such as tomatoes, fish, and milk that otherwise would have spoiled easily. Dietary reformers William K. Kellogg and Charles W. Post mass-produced new breakfast foods such as cornflakes and Grape-Nuts, and the discovery of vitamins heightened interest in food's health. Low-income families still consumed cheap dishes such as corn mush and hog fatback that were heavy in starches and carbohydrates, but increased availability and variety of processed foods meant that American workers never suffered the severe malnutrition that plagued other developing nations.

New technology even affected personal hygiene. Flush toilets, invented in England, reached American shores in the 1880s. More rapidly than Europeans, middle-class Americans combined a desire for cleanliness with an urge for convenience and began installing modern toilets in their urban houses,

making the bathroom a place of utmost privacy. At the same time, brothers Edward and Clarence Scott applied a new process for producing white tissue in rolls, providing Americans a form of toilet tissue more convenient than the rough paper they previously used. All these developments in communications, clothing, food, and plumbing contributed to a democratization of convenience that accompanied mass production and consumerism.

16-2 Big Business and Its Critics

▶ What structures of organization contributed to the expansion and consolidation of businesses in the late nineteenth and early twentieth century?

▶ What competing views of big business emerged in the late nineteenth and early twentieth century?

▶ How did state governments and the federal government seek to regulate big business?

You need only one soap

IVORY SOAP

Pure—First quality,
Not expensive
Will wash anything
No chapping

IT FLOATS

▲ As mass-produced brand-name products became more common, companies used visual images to advertise them. Artwork such as this ad for Ivory Soap captured attention more effectively than the written word.

All was not rosy for business, however. New technologies required large capital investments, and the more manufacturers produced, the more they needed to sell. To expand, businesses borrowed from banks and sought higher profits to repay loans and reward stockholders. This spiraling process strangled small firms that could not keep pace and caused uncertainty in transportation and banking. Optimism could vanish at the hint that a large debtor was about to fail. Economic downturns occurred with painful regularity—in 1871, 1884, and 1893—as overproduction, underconsumption, and unregulated banking strained the system, causing business owners to seek ways to create stability.

John D. Rockefeller Creator of Standard Oil and master of the use of pools and trusts to monopolize an industry.

horizontal integration Business strategy in which a holding company would seek to control all aspects of the industry in which it functioned, fusing related businesses together under one management.

Corporations proved to be the best instruments for industrial expansion. These were companies that raised capital by selling shares to stockholders who received a portion of company profits without personal risk because laws limited their liability for company debts to the amount of their own investments. Firms such as General Electric and the American Tobacco Corporation won judicial safeguards in 1886 when Chief Justice Morrison R. Waite of the Supreme Court accepted the contention by business interests that corporations, like ordinary individuals, are protected by laws preventing government from depriving them of property rights without due process of law, an opinion that has lasted to the present day. During the 1880s, a number of corporations in the same industry made agreements, called *pools*, to share markets and profits. But these arrangements often broke down because they lacked dependable enforcement.

16-2a Trusts and Holding Companies

Trusts soon came to dominate a few industries. These were large corporations formed to enable one company to control an industry by luring or forcing stockholders of smaller companies in that industry to yield control of their stock "in trust" to the larger company's board of trustees. This method enabled a company such as **John D. Rockefeller**'s Standard Oil to achieve domination by combining with, or *vertically integrating*, other oil refineries. In 1898, New Jersey adopted laws allowing companies chartered there to own stock in other states, facilitating creation of holding companies, which merged the buildings, equipment, inventory, and cash of several firms under single management. Using this **horizontal integration**, holding companies could dominate all aspects of an industry, including raw-material extraction, manufacture, and distribution. For example, Gustavus Swift's Chicago meat-processing operation controlled livestock, slaughterhouses, refrigerator cars, and marketing.

Trusts and holding companies provided solutions to big corporations' search for orderly profits. Between 1889 and 1903, some three hundred of these combinations formed, including American Sugar Refining Company and U.S. Rubber Company. A new species of businessman, the financier, aided the process by creating a holding company through stock sales and bank loans, then persuading firms to sell out to him. The practice often put small companies out of business and made huge fortunes for shrewd bankers such as J. P. Morgan and Jacob Schiff.

Growth of corporations turned stock and bond exchanges into hubs of activity. In 1869, only 145 industrial corporations traded on the New York Stock Exchange; by 1914, 511 did. Impressed by the safety and opportunity of the American economy, foreign investors poured huge sums into American companies. Banks and insurance companies also invested in railroads and industrial enterprises. As one journal proclaimed, "Nearly the whole country (including the typical widow and orphan) is interested in the stock market."

16-2b Social Darwinism

Business leaders involved in the formation of large corporations often justified their actions by invoking **Social Darwinism**, a theory developed by British philosopher Herbert Spencer. This philosophy loosely grafted Charles Darwin's theory of survival of the fittest onto laissez-faire, the doctrine that government should not interfere in private economic matters. Social Darwinists reasoned that in a free-market economy, wealth would naturally flow to those most capable of creating it. To them, acquisition of wealth thus was a sacred and deserved right. As one proponent argued, "If we do not have survival of the fittest, we have only one possible alternative, and that is survival of the unfittest."

Like western entrepreneurs who lauded individual effort while seeking government assistance for their railroads and timber companies, corporation heads praised private initiative while seeking public assistance. They denounced legislation that regulated work hours and factory conditions as interference with natural economic laws, but they lobbied forcefully for subsidies, tax relief, and tariffs that they said encouraged business growth.

16-2c Dissenting Voices

Critics charged that new forms of big business were unnatural because they stifled opportunity and fostered greed. Farmers, workers, and intellectuals feared that corporations were creating monopolies—domination of an economic activity by one powerful company—and that companies such as Standard Oil crushed small businesses, fixed prices, and corrupted politicians.

By the mid-1880s, a few intellectuals began to challenge Social Darwinism and laissez-faire. For example, sociologist Lester Ward, in his book *Dynamic Sociology* (1883), argued that human control of nature, not natural law, accounted for civilization's advance. A system that guaranteed survival only to the fittest, he wrote, was wasteful and brutal. Instead, cooperative activity fostered by government intervention was more just. Economists Richard Ely and Edward Bemis agreed that natural forces should be harnessed for the public good, and they denounced laissez-faire.

At the same time, visionaries such as Henry George and Edward Bellamy questioned why the United States had so many poor people while a few became fabulously wealthy. George, a printer alarmed by the poverty of working people like himself, came to believe that inequality stemmed from the ability of property owners to profit from rising land values and the rents they charged. To prevent profiteering, George proposed to replace all taxes with a "single tax" on the rise in property values caused by increased market demand. George's scheme, presented in *Progress and Poverty* (1879), had great popular appeal and influenced subsequent reformers.

Unlike George, who accepted private ownership, Edward Bellamy believed competitive capitalism promoted waste. Instead, he proposed a state in which government owned the means of production. Bellamy outlined his dream in *Looking Backward* (1888), a novel that depicted Boston in the year 2000

▲ A cartoon protesting John D. Rockefeller's power over the oil and railroad industries shows him wearing a golden crown and regal robe, and standing on an oil storage tank labeled "Standard Oil." The huge crown is topped with a dollar sign and made of oil tanks and railroad cars four railroad companies owned by Rockefeller: Lehigh Valley R.R., St. Paul R.R., Jersey Central R.R., and Reading Rail Road.

as a peaceful community where everyone had a job and a "principle of fraternal cooperation" replaced vicious competition and monopoly. Bellamy's vision, called "Nationalism," sparked formation of Nationalist clubs across the country and kindled efforts for political reform and government ownership of railroads and utilities.

16-2d Antitrust Legislation

Plans by George and Bellamy did not succeed, but several states took steps to prohibit monopolies and regulate business. By 1900, twenty-seven states had laws forbidding pools and

Social Darwinism Extended Charles Darwin's theory of "survival of the fittest" to the free-market system, arguing that competition would weed out weaker firms and allow stronger, fitter firms to thrive.

fifteen outlawed trusts. Most were agricultural states in the South and West whose politicians were responding to anti-monopolistic pressure from farmers (see "Agrarian Unrest and Populism," Section 17-5). But states lacked the staff and judicial support for effective attacks on big business, and corporations found ways to evade restrictions. Only national legislation, it seemed, could work.

Congress moved hesitantly but in 1890 passed the Sherman Anti-Trust Act that made illegal "every contract, combination in the form of trust or otherwise, or conspiracy in the restraint of trade." Those convicted of violating the law could receive fines and jail terms and victims could sue for triple damages. However, the law, under influence from pro-business eastern senators, was left purposefully vague. It did not clearly define "restraint of trade" and left interpretation of its provisions to the courts, which at the time were allies of business. When in 1895 the federal government prosecuted the Sugar Trust for owning 98 percent of the nation's sugar-refining capacity, eight of nine Supreme Court justices ruled in *U.S. v. E. C. Knight Co.* that control of sugar manufacturing did not necessarily mean control of trade. And because the Knight Company's manufacturing took place entirely within Pennsylvania, its business could not be considered as interstate commerce. Between 1890 and 1900, the federal government prosecuted only eighteen cases under the Sherman Anti-Trust Act, most of them against railroads. Ironically, the act equipped the government with a tool for breaking up labor unions, which, when they went on strike, were deemed in restraint of trade.

16-3 Mechanization and the Changing Status of Labor

▶ How did new means of organizing labor change the experience for workers in industry?

▶ How did laborers seek to advocate for their own interests in the workplace environment?

▶ How effective were unions in representing the interests of industrial workers?

Technology made possible higher profits for factory owners at lower costs. Workers faced less rewarding results. Skilled crafts such as cabinetmaking and metalworking survived, but as mechanized assembly lines made large-scale production more economical, owners invested in machines, hired fewer workers, and paid lower wages. Profitability relied as much on efficient methods of production as on the machines in use. Where previously workers controlled the methods and timing of production, by the 1890s, engineers and managers with expert knowledge were assuming this responsibility, using planning and standardization to reduce the need for human skills and judgment.

16-3a Frederick W. Taylor

The most influential advocate of efficiency was Frederick W. Taylor. As engineer for a Pennsylvania steel company in the 1880s, Taylor concluded that the best way a company could reduce costs and increase profits was to study "how quickly the various kinds of work . . . ought to be done." The "ought" in Taylor's scheme signified more output at lower costs, usually by eliminating workers. The "how quickly" meant that time and money were equivalent. He called his system "scientific management," which he later outlined in his book, *Principles of Scientific Management* (1911). In 1898, Taylor took a stopwatch to Bethlehem Steel Company to apply his principles. After observing workers shoveling iron ore, he designed fifteen kinds of shovels and prescribed proper motions for their use, enabling the plant to reduce a crew of 600 men to 140. Soon other companies began implementing Taylor's theories. Taylor had little respect for ordinary laborers, calling steelworkers "stupid" and "rarely able to comprehend the science of handling pig iron." Only managers, he argued, could understand and enforce his principles.

16-3b Workers Become Employees

Workers increasingly came to fear that they were becoming another kind of interchangeable part in an industrial machine. No longer able to consider themselves producers, who like farmers and craftsmen were paid according to the quality of what they produced, industrial workers instead were becoming employees, wage earners who worked not on their own but when someone hired them and paid them for time spent on the job. Mass production standardized manufacturing so that tasks were regulated by the clock, and carefully supervised. As a Massachusetts factory hand testified in 1879, "during working hours the men are not allowed to speak to each other, though working close together, on pain of discharge. Men are hired to watch and patrol the shop." Such work was dangerous as well as tedious. The slightest mistake on high-speed machinery could be serious, if not fatal, and accidents occurred often, killing hundreds of thousands each year. For those with mangled limbs, infections, and chronic illnesses, there was no insurance to replace lost income, and families stricken by such misfortune suffered acutely.

Workers attempted to retain autonomy and self-respect in the face of employers' ever-increasing power. Artisans such as glassworkers and printers fought to preserve traditional customs, such as appointing a fellow worker to read a newspaper aloud while they labored. Immigrants working in factories tried to persuade foremen to hire their relatives and friends. Off the job, workers gathered in saloons and parks for relaxation, drinking, and holiday celebrations, ignoring employers' attempts to control their social lives.

16-3c Women and Children in the Workforce

Employers cut labor costs another way by hiring women and children and paying them low wages. Between 1880 and 1900, numbers of employed women soared from 2.6 million to

8.6 million. As Figure 16.1 shows, the proportion of women working in domestic service (maids, cooks, laundresses), the most common and lowest paid form of female employment, dropped as clerical jobs (typists, filing clerks, and store clerks) expanded. Inventions such as the typewriter and cash register simplified clerical tasks, and employers replaced males with lower-paid females. By 1920, women filled nearly half of all clerical jobs; they held only 4 percent of them in 1880. Although poorly paid, women were attracted to sales and secretarial positions because of the respectability and pleasant surroundings compared with factory and domestic work. Nevertheless, for women lacking skills and education, jobs at low pay were the only choice. In manufacturing, women usually held menial positions in textile mills and food-processing plants that paid as little as $1.56 a week for seventy hours of work. (Unskilled men received $7 to $10 for a similar workweek.)

Although most children who worked toiled on their parents' farms, they too entered new occupations. In 1890, more than 18 percent of all children between ages ten and

fifteen held paying jobs. Mechanization in textile and shoe production created light tasks such as running errands and helping machine operators, which children could handle at a fraction of adult wages. In the South, textile mill owners induced sharecroppers, who desperately needed extra income, to bind their children over to factories at miserably low wages. Several states, especially in the Northeast, passed laws limiting ages and hours of child laborers. But large firms evaded regulations, which applied only to companies operating solely within a state's borders, exempting those involved in interstate commerce. Also, parents needing income from child labor lied about their children's ages, and employers seldom asked. Children also contributed to family needs by engaging in informal street trades, such as peddling newspapers, shining shoes, and scavenging for discarded wood, coal, and furniture.

16-3d Freedom of Contract

To justify their treatment of employees, employers said laborers had "freedom of contract," meaning that workers operated

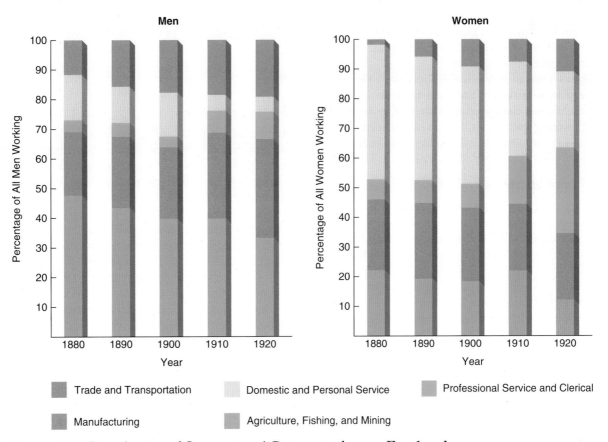

Figure 16.1 **Distribution of Occupational Categories Among Employed Men and Women, 1880–1920**

The changing lengths of the bar segments of each part of this graph represent trends in male and female employment. Over the forty years covered by this graph, the agriculture, fishing, and mining segment for men and the domestic service segment for women declined the most, whereas notable increases occurred in manufacturing for men and professional services (especially store clerks and teachers) for women. *Source: U.S. Bureau of the Census, Census of the United States, 1880, 1890, 1900, 1910, 1920 (Washington, D.C.: U.S. Government Printing Office).*

in a free market in which they sold their labor. By this principle, a worker who did not like the wages and hours being offered was free to decline a job and seek better conditions from another employer. In practice, however, employers used supply and demand to set wages as low as laborers would accept, forcing those needing work to take whatever they could get. When some states tried to improve working conditions through regulatory legislation, business interests enlisted courts, including the Supreme Court of the United States, to oppose such measures. Though the Court in *Holden v. Hardy* (1891) did uphold a law restricting miners' working hours because an overly long workday increased the threat of injury, it voided a law limiting bakery workers to a sixty-hour week and ten-hour day (*Lochner v. New York*, 1905), reasoning that baking was not dangerous enough to prevent workers from selling their labor freely.

In one case, *Muller v. Oregon* (1908), the Supreme Court made an exception for women. It concluded that a law regulating hours of female laundry workers was constitutional because a woman's well-being as bearer of children was "an object of public interest . . ." The case represented a victory for reform groups such as the Consumers' League, which wanted to safeguard women from exploitation. As a result of the *Muller* decision, however, labor laws effectively prevented women from being hired for physically demanding jobs such as printing and transportation, further confining women to low-paying, dead-end occupations.

Workers adjusted to mechanization as best they could. Some adapted to assembly lines and time clocks. Others resisted. Individuals challenged the system by ignoring management's rules or quitting. Still others, disgruntled over low wages and anxious to restore independence and better conditions, joined unions and went out on strikes (see Table 16.1).

16-3e Railroad Strikes of 1877

In 1877, a crisis in the railroad industry caused by four years of wage cuts, layoffs, and increased workloads climaxed with a series of violent strikes in which workers attacked railroad property from Pennsylvania and West Virginia to Texas and California. State militia, organized and commanded by employers, broke up picket lines and fired upon strikers, and railroads hired strikebreakers to replace union men. The worst violence occurred in Pittsburgh, where in July 1877, troopers attacked demonstrators, killing ten and wounding many more. After over a month of fighting in which more were killed and much property was destroyed, President Rutherford B. Hayes sent in federal soldiers—the first significant use of the army to quell labor unrest.

16-3f Knights of Labor

Railroadmen struck in their own interest, but about the same time an organization called the Knights of Labor tried to organize a broad base of laborers. Aided by Terrence Powderly, a machinist and mayor of Scranton, Pennsylvania, who was elected grand master in 1879, the Knights built a membership of 730,000 by 1886. In contrast to most craft unions, Knights welcomed unskilled and semiskilled workers, including women, African Americans, and immigrants (but not Chinese). The organization tried to bypass conflict between labor and management by establishing a cooperative society in which workers, not capitalists, owned factories, mines, and railroads. This ideal was difficult to achieve because employers held economic leverage and could outcompete laborers who might try to operate their own businesses. Powderly discouraged Knights members from going on strike, arguing that the goal of a cooperative society was more important than conflict and that workers too often lost strikes. Some Knights, however, chose militant action. In 1886, they struck against railroads in the Southwest. When owner **Jay Gould** refused to negotiate, the strike spread and violence increased. Powderly tried to negotiate, but Gould refused and the Knights gave in. Thereafter membership in the Knights dwindled, although its cooperative vision inspired the Populist movement of the 1890s (see "Agrarian Unrest and Populism," Section 17-5).

The same year that Knights struck against railroads, unionized and nonunionized workers staged strikes in favor of an eight-hour workday. On May 1, 1886, in Chicago, one hundred thousand workers massed for a huge demonstration. Two days later, fearing that anarchists in the crowd were fomenting antigovernment violence, Chicago police mobilized at the McCormick reaper plant and broke up a battle between unionists and strikebreakers, killing two

Jay Gould Captain of industry and owner of the Union Pacific Railroad.

Table 16.1 American Living Standards, 1890–1910

	1890	1910
Income and Earnings		
Annual income		
Clerical worker	$848	$1,156
Public schoolteacher	256	492
Industrial worker	486	630
Farm laborer	233	336
Hourly wage		
Soft-coal miner	0.18[a]	0.21
Ironworker	0.17[a]	0.23
Shoe worker	0.14[a]	0.19
Paper worker	0.12[a]	0.17
Labor Statistics		
Number of people in labor force	28.5 million	41.7 million[b]
Average workweek in manufacturing	60 hours	51 hours

[a]1892

[b]1920

Impact of the 1911 Triangle Shirtwaist Fire

On March 25, 1911, the worst factory fire in U.S. history occurred at the Triangle Shirtwaist Company, which occupied the top three floors of a building in New York City. Fed by piles of combustible fabric, the fire spread quickly, killing 146 of the 500 young women, mostly Jewish immigrants, employed in the factory. Many of the victims were burned to death because they were locked inside workrooms by their employer; others plunged from windows. These images show two ways the public received news of the tragedy: through friends and relatives who came to identify and claim the bodies of victims, and through a critical cartoon.

CRITICAL THINKING

- Which of these images seems more powerful and likely to inspire reform?
- How do mass tragedies get communicated to the public today?
- What limitations in communications existed in 1911?

▲ Many of the victims of the Triangle Shirtwaist fire of 1911 were lined up in coffins, and their bodies were identified by relatives arriving at a makeshift morgue.

Bettmann/Getty Images

The Granger Collection, NYC

▲ John French Sloan, an artist with radical leanings, drew this cartoon in the wake of the Triangle fire. Eager to assert that profit-minded capitalists were responsible for unnecessary deaths, Sloan used stark images to convey his message.

and wounding others. On May 4, demonstrators gathered at Haymarket Square near downtown Chicago to protest police brutality. As police approached, a bomb exploded, killing seven and injuring sixty-seven. In reaction, authorities arrested several anarchists, eight of whom were convicted of the bombing though evidence of their guilt was weak. Four were executed, one committed suicide in jail, and three received pardons from Governor John Altgeld in 1893. The presence of foreign-born anarchists and socialists at the Haymarket violence created fear among civic leaders that labor turmoil threatened social order. In response, governments strengthened police forces, and employer associations circulated blacklists of union activists whom they would not employ and began hiring private detectives to protect company property.

16-3g American Federation of Labor

The **American Federation of Labor (AFL)**, an alliance of craft unions, emerged from the 1886 upheavals as the major workers' organization. Led by English-born **Samuel Gompers**, former head of the Cigar Makers Union, the AFL avoided the Knights' idealistic goals in favor of concrete issues of higher wages, shorter hours, and the right to bargain collectively. A pragmatist rather than a radical, Gompers and the AFL accepted capitalism and worked to improve conditions within it.

The union avoided party politics, adhering instead to Gompers's policy of supporting labor's friends and opposing its enemies regardless of party. AFL membership grew from 140,000 in 1886 to 1 million in 1901 and 2.5 million in 1917, when it consisted of 111 national unions.

Organized by craft rather than by workplace, the AFL rebuffed unskilled laborers and excluded women. Male unionists insisted that women would depress wages and should stay at home because, as one put it, "Woman is not qualified for the conditions of wage labor. . . . The mental and physical makeup of woman is in revolt against wage service. She is competing with the man who is her father or husband or is to become her husband." Most unions also excluded immigrants and African Americans, fearing job competition from men who might work for less pay. Long-held prejudices

American Federation of Labor (AFL) Skilled craft unions united under leadership of Samuel Gompers.

Samuel Gompers AFL leader who focused on practical goals like improved wages, hours, and working conditions.

Homestead Strike Worker walkout after wage cuts at a Carnegie Steel plant in 1892; officials responded to the strike by shutting down the plant.

Eugene Debs Indiana labor leader who organized workers in the Pullman Strike of 1893; would be the Socialist Party of America's presidential candidate five times between 1900 and 1920.

Industrial Workers of the World (IWW) Radical labor organization that sought to unionize all workers; nicknamed Wobblies, the IWW embraced socialism and led mass strikes of mine workers in Nevada and Minnesota and timber workers in Louisiana, Texas, and the Northwest.

were reinforced when blacks and immigrants, eager for any work they could get, accepted jobs as strikebreakers to replace striking native whites.

16-3h Homestead and Pullman Strikes

The AFL and entire labor movement suffered setbacks in the early 1890s when once again violence stirred public fears. In July 1892, the AFL-affiliated Amalgamated Association of Iron and Steelworkers launched the **Homestead Strike** against Homestead Steel in Pennsylvania over pay cuts. Henry Frick, president of Carnegie Steel Company, Homestead's owner, hired three hundred guards from the Pinkerton Detective Agency to protect the factory, but angry strikers attacked the guards, sending them into retreat. State troopers intervened and, after five months, the strikers gave up.

In 1894, employees at the Pullman Palace Car Company, maker of railroad passenger cars, walked out over exploitive policies at the company town near Chicago. The owner, George Pullman, controlled nearly everything in the so-called model town of twelve thousand: land, buildings, school, bank, and rents. Pullman refused to negotiate with workers, and when he cut wages without reducing rents, the American Railway Union, led by charismatic **Eugene Debs**, went on strike. Pullman closed the factory and the union retaliated by refusing to handle all Pullman cars attached to any train. The railroad owners' association enlisted aid from the federal government and Debs was arrested for defying a court injunction against the strike. President Grover Cleveland ordered federal troops to Chicago, ostensibly to protect rail-carried mail, but in reality to crush the strike. The union ended the walkout and Debs received a six-month prison sentence.

16-3i Labor Violence in the West

In the West, unionized mine workers, led by the Western Federation of Miners (WFM), engaged in violent strikes during the 1890s. In 1894, fighting erupted in Cripple Creek, Colorado, when mine owners increased work hours without increasing pay. The governor called in state militia after two weeks of battles, and the owners agreed to restore the eight-hour workday. In Idaho, federal troops intervened three times in strikes by miners. In 1905, former Idaho governor Frank Steuenberg was assassinated and speculation arose that the WFM was exacting revenge for when Steuenberg imposed martial law during a strike in 1899. After the assassination, authorities arrested WFM activist William "Big Bill" Haywood, a brawny, one-eyed radical, and tried him for murder in 1907. He was acquitted after his famous defense attorney, Clarence Darrow, proved that a key witness was being paid by the mine owners.

In 1905, radical laborers formed the **Industrial Workers of the World (IWW)**. Unlike the AFL, but like the Knights of Labor, the IWW tried to unite unskilled workers under the motto, "An injury to one is an injury to all." Embracing violent tactics and the rhetoric of class conflict and socialism, the

"Wobblies," as IWW members were known, believed workers should seize and run the nation's industries. Their leaders, including Haywood, Mary "Mother" Jones, a coalfield organizer; Elizabeth Gurley Flynn, a fiery orator; Italian radical Carlo Tresca; and songwriter Joe Hill, headed strife-torn strikes in steel towns, textile communities, and lumber camps. The union attracted much publicity but collapsed during the First World War when federal prosecutors sent many of its leaders to prison and local police harassed IWW activities.

16-3j Women Unionists

Though generally excluded from unions, some female workers organized and battled employers as strenuously as men did. In 1909, male and female members of the International Ladies Garment Workers' Union, consisting mostly of Jewish immigrant shirtwaist workers, staged a strike known as "Uprising of the 20,000" in New York City. Women also were prominent in the 1912 "Bread and Roses" strike against textile owners in Lawrence, Massachusetts, and their Telephone Operators' Department of the International Brotherhood of Electrical Workers sponsored a strike over wage issues that paralyzed the New England Bell telephone system in 1919. Without aid from male electrical workers, the telephone operators nevertheless won concessions of higher wages and the right to bargain collectively.

The Women's Trade Union League (WTUL), founded in 1903, played a key role in representing laboring women. Patterned after a British women's league, WTUL sought legislation to establish shorter hours and better working conditions, supported strikes, sponsored educational activities, and campaigned for women's suffrage. At first, sympathetic middle-class women held most WTUL offices, but after 1910 control shifted to working-class leaders such as Agnes Nestor, a glove maker, and Rose Schneiderman, a capmaker. By inspiring working women to press for rights and by training leaders, WTUL provided a vital link between labor and the women's movement into the 1920s.

16-3k The Nonunionized Workforce

The high-profile activities of organized labor obscure the fact that the vast majority of American wage workers in these years did not belong to unions. In 1877, less than a million workers were unionized; by 1920, union membership had grown to 5 million but accounted for only 13 percent of the total labor force. For many, getting and keeping a job took priority over bargaining for higher pay and shorter hours. Few companies employed a full workforce year-round; they hired during peak seasons and laid off employees during slack times. Moreover, union organizers took no interest in unskilled laborers and intentionally excluded women, African Americans, and immigrants.

The men, women, and children who were not unionized coped with pressures of the industrial age as best they could. They joined societies such as the Polish Roman Catholic Union, African American Colored Brotherhood, and Jewish B'nai B'rith, which for small fees provided services such as life insurance, sickness benefits, and burial costs. For these Americans as well as for those in unions, the machine age had mixed results. Though wages generally rose between 1877 and 1914, boosting purchasing power and consumerism, hourly pay averaged around 20 cents for skilled work and 10 cents for unskilled. And even as wages rose, living costs rose faster. Those two dimensions of industrialism—work and lifestyle—displayed their most dramatic effects in cities.

◀ In 1919, telephone operators, mostly female, went on strike and shut down phone service throughout New England. The male-dominated leadership of the International Brotherhood of Electrical Workers, to which the operators belonged, opposed the strike, but the women refused to back down and eventually achieved several of their demands against the New England Telephone Company.

George Rinhart/Getty Images

16-4 Growth of the Modern American City

▶ How did transportation developments and population growth alter the urban landscape in the late nineteenth and early twentieth century?

▶ How did immigrants adapt to American society and retain features of their ethnic cultures?

▶ What systemic problems emerged in cities in the late nineteenth and early twentieth century?

▶ How did political machines and urban reformers seek to solve the systemic problems of city life?

Though their initial functions had been as centers for trade, cities became the arenas for industrial development in the late nineteenth century. As hubs for labor, transportation, communications, and consumption, cities supplied everything factories needed. Most cities housed a variety of manufacturing enterprises, but product specialization was common. Mass-produced clothing concentrated in New York City, the shoe industry in Philadelphia, food processing in Minneapolis, meat processing in Chicago, fish canning in Seattle, steelmaking in Pittsburgh and Birmingham, and oil refining in Houston and Los Angeles. Such activities increased cities' magnetic attraction for people and capital.

16-4a Mechanization of Mass Transportation

As cities grew, the compact landscape of earlier eras, where residences mingled among shops and factories, burst open as settlement sprawled beyond original boundaries. No longer did walking distance determine a city's size. Instead, cities separated into distinct districts: working- and middle-class neighborhoods, commercial strips, downtown, and suburbs. Two forces created this new arrangement: One, mass transportation, propelled people and enterprises outward; the other, economic change, drew human and material resources inward.

By the 1870s, horse-drawn vehicles began sharing city streets with motor-driven conveyances that moved riders faster and farther. Commuter railroads and cable cars came first, followed by electric-powered streetcars. In a few cities, such as New York and Chicago, companies raised track onto trestles, enabling "elevated" trains to move above jammed streets. In others, such as Boston and New York, underground subways avoided traffic congestion. Also, electric interurban railways, linking neighboring cities in the Midwest and West, furthered urban development.

These forms of mass transit launched urban dwellers into outlying neighborhoods and created a commuting public. The development mainly benefited the middle class. Working-class families, who needed every cent, found streetcar fares, usually five cents a ride, too high. But those with means could move to single-family bungalows in tree-lined, outlying neighborhoods and travel to the central city for work, shopping, and entertainment. Mass transit also altered commercial patterns. When consumers moved outward, shops, banks, and

restaurants followed, locating at trolley-line intersections and creating secondary business districts. Meanwhile, the urban core became a work zone, where tall buildings loomed over streets clogged with people, horses, and vehicles.

16-4b Population Growth

Between 1870 and 1920, the number of Americans living in cities increased from 10 million to 54 million, and the number of places with more than 100,000 people swelled from fifteen to sixty-four. Several cities grew big in a hurry. Chicago, with 109,000 people in 1860, swelled to 2.2 million by 1910. Pittsburgh had just 49,000 in 1860; by 1910, it housed 534,000. Cities in the South also grew, just not as explosively. Baltimore and New Orleans, the region's largest places in 1860 with 212,000 and 169,000, respectively, remained the largest in 1910, with 558,000 and 339,000.

Urban growth derived mainly from two sources. One was annexation of nearby territory, such as when Chicago tripled its area by adding three surrounding towns in 1889 and when New York City (Manhattan) merged with Brooklyn, Staten Island, and part of Queens in 1898, doubling from 1.5 million to 3 million people. Most communities agreed to be annexed

▲ Tall buildings, streetcars, offices, and shop characterized the new downtown of cities. The aptly-named Market Street of San Francisco resembled main streets in many other cities.

FIRST FLOOR PLAN   SECOND FLOOR PLAN

▲ Along with mass-produced consumer goods, such as clothing and household items, Sears, Roebuck and Company marketed architectural plans for middle-class housing. The "tiny house design," published in one of the company's catalogs, illustrates the layout and finished look of the kind of housing built on urban outskirts in the early twentieth century.

because they could take advantage of the schools, water, and fire protection that could be obtained from the nearby city.

More importantly, in-migration from the countryside and abroad contributed to urban population growth. As debt and crop prices worsened, many rural dwellers fled to big cities such as Chicago and San Francisco, and smaller places such as Indianapolis and Nashville. Both men and women, especially young adults, were attracted by the independence that city life offered. Rural African Americans felt the additional pressures of discrimination that drove them cityward. By 1900, thirty-two cities, mostly in the South but in the North also, had more than ten thousand black residents. Because few factories would employ African Americans, most found jobs in the service sector—cleaning, cooking, and driving—usually at very low wages. But such jobs were usually better than tenant farming.

16-4c New Foreign Immigrants

More newcomers were immigrants from a foreign country. They were part of a global movement resulting from population pressures, land redistribution, religious persecution, and industrialization that induced millions of families and individuals to leave Europe and Asia for Canada, Australia, Brazil, Argentina, and the United States. Migration has always characterized human history, but in the late nineteenth century advances in communications and transportation spread news of opportunities and made travel cheaper and safer. Before 1880, most immigrants had come from northern and western Europe—England, Ireland, and Germany. After 1880, a second wave from eastern and southern Europe, plus immigrants from Canada, Mexico, and Japan, joined the first groups (see Map 16.2).

Map 16.2 Sources of European-Born Population, 1900 and 1920

In just a few decades, the proportion of European immigrants to the United States who came from northern and western Europe decreased (Ireland and Germany) or remained relatively stable (England and Scandinavia), while the proportion from eastern and southern Europe increased dramatically. *Source: Data from U.S. Census Bureau, "Historical Census Statistics on the Foreign-Born Population of the United States: 1850–1990," February 1999, http://www.census.gov/population (accessed February 12, 2000).*

Between 1900 and 1910, two-thirds of immigrants came from Italy, Austria-Hungary, and Russia, and by 1910 arrivals from Mexico outnumbered those from Ireland. Some wanted only to make enough money to return home and live in greater security. Still, most of the 26 million arriving between 1870 and 1920 remained and settled in cities, where they helped to reshape American culture.

Many long-settled Americans feared those they called "new immigrants," whose customs, Catholic and Jewish faiths, unfamiliar languages, low-skill occupations, and poverty made them seem more alien than previous newcomers. Yet old and new immigrants resembled each other in their strategies for coping. The majority of both groups hailed from societies that made family the focus of life, and they sustained family bonds after reaching America. New arrivals often received aid from relatives who had already immigrated, and family members pooled resources to help them adapt.

16-4d Geographical and Social Mobility

Once they arrived in a city, newcomers seldom stayed put. Each year, millions of families packed up and moved, some to another neighborhood, others to a new town or the countryside. Migration was a means by which people tried to escape from poor housing and employment and move to a place where they hoped conditions and jobs would be better. Women migrated within and between cities, but they usually went with fathers and husbands whose economic standing defined their class. For African Americans, Native Americans, Mexican Americans, and Asian Americans, opportunities were scarcer. Assigned to low-paying occupations by prejudice, they made fewer gains.

Few individuals became rich from these moves, but many traveled the road from poverty to moderate success. Advances through work were available mostly to white males. Thousands of businesses were needed to serve burgeoning urban populations, and growing corporations were hiring new personnel. An aspiring merchant could open a saloon or shop for a few hundred dollars, and knowledge of accounting could qualify one for clerical jobs with higher income than manual labor. In fast-growing cities such as Atlanta and Los Angeles, approximately one in five white manual workers rose to white-collar or owner positions within ten years. In older cities, upward rates were slightly lower, perhaps one in six. Some men chose the security of a steady job over the risk of starting a business or the stigma of an unmanly clerical job. A Sicilian who lived in Bridgeport, Connecticut, observed, "The people that come here they afraid to get in business because they don't know how that business goes. In Italy these people don't know much about things because most of them work on farms or in a trade." Many, particularly unskilled workers, did not improve their status. They could not maintain Old World occupations and were forced to accept low-paying jobs and frustrated hopes. Still, the possibilities for upward mobility

seemed to temper people's dissatisfactions. Although gaps between rich and poor widened and discrimination dashed hopes, expanding urban economies created enough opportunities for those in between.

16-4e Cultural Retention

Despite the constant movement that made them turbulent places, cities contained collections of functioning subcommunities where people, most of whom had migrated from somewhere else, coped with daily challenges. Rather than yield completely to pressures to assimilate, migrants and immigrants interacted with their environment in a way that enabled them to retain their identity while also altering their outlook and the society in which they lived. Where the English language was a struggle, where clocks regulated their day, and where housing and employment were uncertain, immigrants first anchored their lives to

Photo by Lewis W. Hine/George Eastman House/Getty Images

▲ Male immigrants and an immigration official are looking through a wire fence at an Italian immigrant woman and her daughter who have recently arrived at the immigrant inspection station at Ellis Island, outside of New York City. The main port of entry for European immigrants after 1892, Ellis Island stands in the shadow of the Statue of Liberty.

what they knew best: their culture. Old World customs persisted in districts of Italians from the same province, Japanese from the same island, and Jews from the same Russian *shtetl*. Newcomers created aid organizations known in their homelands, such as Japanese *ken* societies that sponsored holiday celebrations and relief services and Chinese loan associations called *whey*, that helped members start businesses. Southern Italians transferred the *padrone* system, whereby for a payoff a boss found them jobs. Newcomers practiced religion as they always had, married within their group, and pursued long-standing feuds with people from rival villages.

16-4f Urban Borderlands

In large cities, such as Chicago and Philadelphia, immigrants initially clustered in inner-city neighborhoods where jobs and cheap housing were available. These districts often were multi-ethnic "urban borderlands," where diverse people and lifestyles coexisted. Even in districts identified with a specific group, such as "Little Italy" or "Greektown," rapid mobility constantly undermined stability as former inhabitants dispersed to other neighborhoods and new residents moved in. Often, an area's institutions such as bakeries, butcher shops, and churches, usually operated by and for one ethnic group and accessible by mass transportation, gave a neighborhood its identity more than the people who lived there.

For first- and second-generation immigrants, their neighborhoods acted as havens until they were ready to leave the borderlands for other districts where neighbors were of the same class but not necessarily the same nationality. Discrimination persisted as Jews were excluded from certain neighborhoods and Italians found it hard to break into political positions. But prejudice was rarely systematic for Europeans. For African Americans, Asians, and Mexicans, however, borderlands kept a more persistent and homogeneous character, largely due to discrimination.

16-4g Racial Segregation and Violence

By the late nineteenth century, racial bias forced African Americans into highly segregated ghettos. In cities such as Chicago, Cleveland, and Detroit, two-thirds or more of the black population was confined to only 10 percent of total residential area. Within their neighborhoods, blacks, like other urban dwellers, nurtured institutions such as churches, newspapers, and clubs that helped them cope with city life. Branches of Baptist and African Methodist Episcopal (AME) Protestantism were especially active in aiding members. In virtually all cities, religious associations dominated African American communities and fostered cooperation across class lines.

Often, the only way African Americans could relieve pressures of crowding in ghettos was to expand residential borders into surrounding, previously white neighborhoods, a process that resulted in harassment and attacks by white

residents whose intolerance intensified from fears that property values would decline if they had black neighbors. Competition between blacks and whites for housing, jobs, and political influence in the North and South sparked incidents of racial violence. In Atlanta in 1906, newspaper accounts alleging attacks by black men against white women provoked whites into an outburst of shooting that left twelve blacks dead and several injured. An influx of black strikebreakers into East St. Louis, Illinois, in 1917 heightened racial tensions. When some blacks fired back at a car from which they believed shots had been fired at their homes, they mistakenly killed two policemen. The next day, whites retaliated. The riot ended only after nine whites and thirty-nine blacks had been killed and three hundred buildings destroyed.

Though Chinese and Japanese immigrants usually preferred to live apart from Anglos and maintain their own business and social institutions in San Francisco, Seattle, Los Angeles, and New York, Anglos made every effort to keep them separate. In San Francisco, Denis Kearney, an Irish immigrant labor leader, blamed the Chinese for job competition and white unemployment in the 1870s. Promoting the slogan, "The Chinese must go," Kearney and his followers tried to prevent employers from hiring Chinese, often resorting to violence. In 1880, San Francisco banned Chinese laundries, which were social centers for immigrants, from locating in white neighborhoods, justifying the ban by saying they were fire hazards. In 1882, the U.S. Congress passed the Chinese Exclusion Act, suspending the immigration of Chinese laborers, and in 1892 the Geary Act extended previous restrictions and required Chinese Americans to carry certificates of residence. Japanese suffered similar restrictions, prevented by law from becoming citizens.

16-4h Mexican Barrios

In southwestern cities such as Los Angeles, Tucson, Albuquerque, and San Antonio, Mexicans had been the original inhabitants, Anglos the newcomers. But as Anglo arrivals increased, they pushed Mexicans into isolated residential and commercial districts called *barrios*. These areas tended to be located away from multi-ethnic borderlands housing European immigrants. To a considerable extent, then, racial and ethnic bias made urban experiences of African Americans, Asians, and Mexicans unique and hindered their opportunities to remake their lives.

Virtually everywhere newcomers lived, immigrant culture mingled with existing realities. Although many foreigners identified themselves by their village or regional birthplace, native-born Americans simplified by categorizing them by nationality. Thus people born in County Cork and County Limerick were all called Irish. Those from Calabria and Campobasso became Italians. At the same time, the diversity of American cities prompted foreigners to modify their attitudes and habits. They could not avoid contact with people different from themselves on the streets and in workplaces. They learned the English language, used locally grown foods for traditional meals, fashioned mass-produced clothing into Old World styles, and went to American doctors while still practicing folk medicine. Music especially revealed adaptation. Polish polka bands blended American and homeland folk music; Mexican ballads reflected new themes about hardship in the United States.

16-4i Religious Diversity

The influx of multiple immigrants transformed the United States into a religiously diverse nation. Newcomers from Italy, Polish lands, and Slovakia joined Irish and Germans to increase Catholic populations significantly in cities such as Buffalo, Cleveland, and Milwaukee. Catholic Mexicans constituted over half the population of El Paso, and New York City came to house one of the largest Jewish populations in the world. By 1920, Buddhism was well established among Japanese immigrants on the West Coast and in Hawai'i. As they coped with new conditions, Catholics and Jews tried to adjust their faiths to their environments by adopting English in services and altering traditional rituals. Changes were not complete, however. Catholic immigrant parishes pressured bishops into appointing priests of the same ethnicity as parishioners, and Orthodox Jews retained Old World customs such as separating men and women inside synagogues. An exchange of cultural patterns occurred when Catholics and Jews married co-religionists of different nationality groups—an Italian marrying a Pole, for example, kept religious identity strong while blending ethnic identities.

Each of the major migrant groups that peopled cities—native-born whites, foreigners, and native-born blacks—created the pluralism of modern American culture. The nation's broad diversity prevented domination by a single racial or ethnic majority and nurtured rich cultural variety: American folk literature, Italian and Mexican cuisine, Yiddish theater, African American music and dance, and much more. Newcomers changed their environment as much as it changed them.

Though rich in varied cultures, central sections of cities often were places challenged by crowding, poverty, crime, and disease. People coped as best they could, and technology, private enterprise, and government achieved some remarkable advances. But many problems evaded permanent solution.

16-4j Housing

Population growth created scarcity of adequate housing. Those with low incomes adapted to high rents and short supply by sharing space, resulting in homes and apartments intended for one family being occupied by two or three families plus boarders. The result was unprecedented crowding. In 1890, New York City's immigrant-packed Lower East Side averaged 702 people per acre, one of the highest population densities in the world. Inside tenements and row houses in New York, Philadelphia, and New Orleans spaces were cramped and interior rooms lacked light and fresh air. States such as New York passed regulations to establish ventilation and safety codes for new tenement buildings, but such measures could not remedy ills of existing buildings.

Eventually, technology and science brought about important changes in home life. Improved furnaces, electric lighting, and indoor plumbing created more comfort for middle-class households and, later, for most others. These advances occurred as a result of private enterprise; landlords and humanitarians alike opposed government financing of better housing, fearing that such a step would undermine profits. The major government-sponsored improvements occurred outside of buildings, where publicly financed street paving, modernized firefighting equipment, and electric street lighting made cities safer.

16-4k Poverty and Crime

Poverty, however, continued to burden many urbanites. Employment, especially for unskilled workers, fluctuated with business cycles, causing low-income families to live on the margins of survival. Since colonial days, an attitude that anyone could escape poverty through hard work and clean living had prevailed in American culture. According to this reasoning, poor people were morally weak and aiding them would encourage dependence on public support. Only those incapable of supporting themselves—orphans, people with disabilities, and widows—deserved relief. Close observance of the urban poor, however, prompted reformers such as Jacob Riis, a New York journalist, to conclude that people's environment contributed to hardship and that society ought to shoulder greater responsibility for improving conditions. Riis's series of articles, combined into a book, *How the Other Half Lives* (1890), alerted readers to the deplorable conditions of slum housing. Other reformers advocated public efforts to improve housing, education, and job opportunities to help the poor help themselves. Others, however, clung to the tenet that in a society of abundance, poverty relief could be tolerated but never encouraged. As one charity worker observed, relief "should be surrounded by circumstances that shall . . . repel everyone . . . from accepting it."

Crime and violence increased at an alarming rate in American cities in contrast to falling rates in other industrializing nations such as England and Germany. The American murder rate, for example, rose from 25 per million people in 1881 to 107 per million in 1898. Though police forces were becoming more professionalized, law enforcement was complicated because various urban groups differed in their views of how laws should be enforced. Ethnic and racial minorities were more likely to be arrested than those with economic or political influence. Also, while moralists clamored for crackdowns on drinking and gambling, those who enjoyed a drink or a card game favored personal freedom to indulge in these activities. Nativists were quick to blame immigrants for urban

▲ Inner-city dwellers used not only indoor space as efficiently as possible, but also what little outdoor space was available to them. Scores of families living in this cramped block of six-story tenements in New York strung clotheslines behind the buildings. Notice that there is virtually no space between buildings—only rooms at the front and back received daylight and fresh air.

crime, but urban lawlessness probably did not exceed that of mining camps and southern plantations, and the lawbreaking population included native-born offenders as well as foreigners.

16-4l Water Purity and Waste Disposal

Finding sources of pure water and a way to dispose of waste also challenged city dwellers. Old methods of sinking wells for water and dumping human and industrial waste into rivers and streams could no longer suffice. By the 1880s, doctors began to accept the theory that microorganisms caused disease, prompting new concerns over purity of water sources, where germs were believed to breed. Most cities replaced private water companies with more copious public supplies, but sewers, flush toilets, and factory waste created noxious pollution and sometimes disease. By 1900, for example, the Passaic River in New Jersey, once a popular recreation site, had been ruined by discharge from cities along its banks. Improvements came slowly as states passed laws prohibiting disposing of raw sewage into rivers, and a few cities began to filter their water and use chemicals to treat sewage. Though death rates from tuberculosis remained high, public regulation of water and food purity helped control diseases such as cholera, typhoid fever, and diphtheria.

Trash, however, was a growing problem. Experts in 1900 estimated that every New Yorker annually generated 160 pounds of garbage (food), 1,200 pounds of ashes (from stoves and furnaces), and 105 pounds of rubbish (other discarded items). Europeans of that era produced half as much trash. Factories created tons of solid waste (scrap metal, wood), and each of the 3.5 million horses in American cities daily dumped 20 pounds of manure and a gallon of urine on the streets. All this refuse created health and safety hazards. At the urging of women's groups, some cities hired engineers to address the dilemma. One such engineer, George Waring, Jr., designed efficient systems for sewage disposal and street cleaning in Memphis and New York. As a result of such efforts, cities became cleaner, but the trash problem continues to nag urban communities to the present.

16-4m Political Machines

The necessity for health and safety protection, schools, parks, and more strained the resources of growing cities. Most urban governments were complex entities, with power shared among a mayor, city council, and numerous boards and agencies. Philadelphia at one time had thirty different boards to administer health, poverty relief, public works, and more. Moreover, state laws usually limited a city's ability to levy taxes to fund its needs. Out of this complex system of urban

Photo courtesy of PhillyHistory.org, a project of the Philadelphia Department of Records.

▲ This scene, captured by a Philadelphia photographer in order to record the extent of trash that was littering city streets and sidewalks, illustrates the problems of disposal confronting inner-city, immigrant neighborhoods and the necessity for some form of public service to remove the refuse. Seemingly oblivious to the debris, the residents pose for the photographer.

management arose **political machines**, organizations whose goals were to obtain and retain power. Machine politicians used fraud and bribery to further their ends. But they also provided relief and service to those who voted for them. By meeting people's needs, machine politicians accomplished things that others had been unable or unwilling to attempt.

Most big cities were run by political machines at one time or another and for varying lengths of time. The most notable machines existed in New York, Philadelphia, and Chicago, but they also arose in places as varied as Cincinnati, Memphis, Kansas City, New Orleans, and San Francisco. These organizations bred leaders, called **bosses**, who built power bases among immigrant working classes. Bosses understood people's problems from firsthand experience and dealt with people on a personal basis. Martin Lomasney, a Boston boss, once remarked, "There's got to be in every ward somebody that any bloke can come to—no matter what he's done—and get help. Help, you understand, none of your law and justice, but help." To bosses, politics was a full-time profession. They attended weddings and wakes, sponsored picnics, and held open house in saloons where neighborhood folk could speak directly to them. In return for jobs, food, and intervention when someone got arrested, people gave machine politicians the votes that kept them in power.

To finance their activities, bosses used political influence to control the awarding of public contracts and streetcar and utility franchises. In return, recipients of city business and jobs were expected to repay the machine with a portion of their profits or salaries. Critics called this process graft; bosses called it gratitude. Though waste and corruption were often involved, bosses could boast major achievements. Aided by a new generation of professional engineers, machine-led governments constructed much of the new urban infrastructure—public buildings, sewer systems, schools, and streetcar lines—and expanded services such as firefighting, police, and public health.

Machines were rarely neutral or fair, however. Racial minorities and new immigrant groups such as Italians and Poles received only token favors and jobs, if any. Bribes and kickbacks made machine projects costly. Unable to raise enough revenue from taxes and fees, bosses financed

political machines Organizations that emerged in urban, often working-class and immigrant neighborhoods. They solicited votes for particular candidates and promised jobs and other services to supporters; putting their candidates in office gave them power over local government.

Bosses Headed political machines; often of similar background to constituents, these popular local figures exchanged votes for money, support, and other favors.

expansion with loans in the form of municipal bonds. As a result, public debts soared. Also, payoffs from gambling and illegal liquor traffic were important sources of machine revenues. But bosses likely were no guiltier of greed and discrimination than were those businessmen who exploited workers, spoiled the environment, and manipulated government in pursuit of profits. Sometimes humane, sometimes criminal, bosses acted as brokers between sectors of urban society and an uncertain world.

16-4n Civic and Social Reform

Reacting to ways bosses exercised power and disturbed by mounting costs and corruption in government, reformers tried to unseat machines. One group, mostly middle- and upper-class types called civic reformers, sought to replace machine politics with government run according to business principles of economy and efficiency. They advocated for structural changes such as tighter control of budgets, city manager and commission forms of government, and nonpartisan elections. In several places reform campaigns managed to oust machines, and a few reform mayors, such as Hazen Pingree of Detroit and Tom Johnson of Cleveland, worked not only for governmental change but to provide jobs and better housing for poor people. But most civic reformers only wanted to economize and root out dishonesty; they seldom held office for very long.

Beyond politics and government, another group, social reformers, undertook efforts to investigate and solve everyday problems. Mostly middle class, this group pressed government for building codes to ensure safer tenements, improved public and vocational schools to better prepare immigrants for citizenship, and medical care for those unable to afford it. Often led by women such as **Jane Addams** and **Florence Kelley**, social reformers also promoted safer food, public playgrounds, and school nurses. Environmental reformers, such as those in the City Beautiful movement, sought to improve cities' built environments. Inspired by the World's Columbian Exposition of 1893, a dazzling fair built on Chicago's South Side, architects and planners urged construction of civic centers, parks, and boulevards that would make cities economically efficient as well as more attractive. Many plans, however, were only dreams. Neither government nor private businesses could finance large-scale projects, and planners disagreed among themselves over whether beautification would really solve urban problems.

Regardless of their focus, urban reformers wanted to save cities, not abandon them. They believed they could improve urban society by fostering cooperation among all citizens. They often failed, however, to understand a city's diversity and that different people had conflicting goals. To civic reformers, appointing government workers on the basis of civil service exams rather than party loyalty meant progress, but to working-class men, jobs given for party loyalty were what counted. Moral reformers believed that restricting the sale of alcoholic beverages would prevent husbands from squandering wages and ruining their health, but immigrants saw such crusades as interference in their private lives. Planners envisioned boulevards and buildings as modern necessities, but such structures often displaced the poor. Well-meaning humanitarians tried to change the ways immigrant mothers shopped, cooked, and raised children without regard for mothers' inability to afford new products of the consumer economy. Thus urban reform merged idealism with insensitivity.

16-5 Family Life and Individual Life

▶ How did the makeup of a household and family alter in the late nineteenth and early twentieth century?

▶ What role did family play in the lives of the inhabitants of cities?

For the majority of urban dwellers, family, not government, was the most crucial institution. But increasingly, new institutions—schools, ethnic clubs, unions—competed with the family to provide education and security. Still, the family unit retained its fundamental role as a cushion in a harsh, uncertain world.

Throughout modern western history, most people have lived in two overlapping social units: household and family. A household is a grouping of related and/or unrelated people who share the same residence. A family is a group related by kinship, some of whom live together. Until recently, when the number of single people living alone has increased markedly, most American households (75 percent or more) have consisted of nuclear families—usually a married couple with or without children. About 15 to 20 percent of households have consisted of extended families—usually a nuclear family plus one or more adult relatives. This pattern held relatively consistent among various ethnic, racial, and socioeconomic groups.

Several factors explain this pattern. Because immigrants tended to be young, the population as a whole was young. In 1880, the median age of the American population was under twenty-one, and by 1920 it was still only twenty-five. (Median age at present is thirty-seven.) Moreover, death rates among people aged forty-five to sixty-four were double what they are today, and the proportion of the population aged sixty-five and older was just 4 percent in 1900; it is 14.5 percent today. Thus in the late nineteenth and early twentieth century, fewer children than today had living grandparents, and three-generation households of children, parents, and grandparents were rare.

Jane Addams Social worker, pioneer of the settlement house movement, and founder of Chicago's Hull House, which provided education, training, and social activities for immigrants and the poor.

Florence Kelley Settlement house worker who became the chief factory inspector for Illinois in 1893.

Falling birth rates reduced family sizes. In 1880, there were 40 live births per 1,000 people; by 1900 the rate had dropped to 32; and by 1920 it was 28. Several factors explain this pattern. First, the United States was becoming an urban nation, and birth rates are historically lower in cities than in rural areas. Second, as nutrition and medical care improved, infant mortality fell and families did not have to bear as many children to ensure that some would survive. Third, awareness that smaller families meant improved quality of life for each surviving child influenced parents' decisions to limit family size so that three or four children instead of five or six became the norm. Birth-control technology—diaphragms and condoms—had existed for centuries, but in this era new materials such as vulcanized rubber made devices more convenient and dependable.

16-5a Family as a Resource

Young adults who left home to work altered household composition, especially in cities, as many became boarders in homes and lodging houses. For people on the move, boarding was a transitional stage before setting up their own household. It also allowed families with spare space to obtain extra income by renting rooms to boarders. Families also took in widowed parents or unmarried adult siblings.

At a time when welfare agencies were rare, the family was the resource to which people turned in times of need. Relatives often resided near each other and aided one another with child care, meals, advice, and consolation. As one family member recalled, "After two days my brother took me to the shop he was working in and his boss saw me and he gave me the job." But obligations of kinship were not always welcome. Immigrant parents pressured daughters to stay at home to help with housework and child care, stifling opportunities for education and independence. Tensions also erupted when immigrant parents and their American-born children clashed over the abandonment of Old World ways or the amount of wages employed children should contribute to the household. Nevertheless, kinship helped people cope with the stresses of urban-industrial society.

16-5b The Unmarried

Although marriage rates were high, large numbers of city dwellers were unmarried, mainly because young people postponed marriage until their late twenties. In 1890 almost 42 percent of adult men and 37 percent of adult women were single, almost twice as high as in 1960 (though lower than today). About half lived with parents, but others inhabited rented rooms. Mostly young, they developed a subculture that patronized dance halls, saloons, cafes, and organizations such as the YMCA and YWCA.

Some unmarried people were part of homosexual populations that gathered in large cities such as New York, San Francisco, and Boston. Though numbers are difficult to estimate, gay men patronized their own clubs, restaurants, coffeehouses, and theaters. A number of same-sex couples, especially women, formed lasting relationships, sometimes called "Boston marriages." People in this subculture were categorized more by how they acted—men acting like women, women acting like men—than by who their sexual partners were. The term "homosexual" was not used. Men who dressed and acted like women were called "fairies." Gay women remained largely hidden, and a visible lesbian subculture was rare until the 1920s.

16-5c Stages of Life

Before the late nineteenth century, stages of life were less distinct than they are today. Childhood, for instance, had been regarded as a period during which youngsters prepared for adulthood by gradually assuming adult responsibilities. Subdivisions of youth—toddlers, schoolchildren, teenagers—were not recognized. Because married couples had more children over a longer time span, active parenthood occupied most of adult life. Children who cared for younger siblings might begin parenting responsibilities before reaching adulthood. Older people often did not retire; they worked until they were physically incapable.

In the late nineteenth century, demographic and social changes altered these patterns. Decreasing birth rates shortened the period of parenting, so more middle-aged couples experienced an "empty nest" once their children grew up and left home. Longer life expectancy and a tendency by employers to force aged workers to retire separated the old from the young. As states passed compulsory school attendance laws and established graded schools in the 1870s and 1880s, children spent more time with others of the same age than with older or younger people. Childhood and adolescence became distinct stages, and peers rather than family influenced youngsters' behavior more than previously. People's roles in school, in the family, on the job, and in the community came to be determined by age more than any other characteristic.

By 1900, new agencies were assuming tasks formerly performed by families. Schools made education a community responsibility. Employment agencies, political machines, and labor unions became responsible for getting people jobs and for job security. Age-based peer groups exerted influence over people's values and sociability. Yet kinship remained a dependable though not always appreciated institution. Family togetherness became especially visible at holiday celebrations. Thanksgiving, Christmas, and Easter were times for family reunions and child-centered activities. Birthdays, too, took on new festive qualities as milestones for measuring age-related norms and life stages. In 1914, President Woodrow Wilson proclaimed the second Sunday in May as Mother's Day, capping a six-year campaign by schoolteacher Anna Jarvis, who believed children were neglecting their mothers. Ethnic, religious, and racial groups adapted celebrations to their cultures, preparing special foods and engaging in special ceremonies. For many, holidays served as testimony to the vitality of family life.

16-6 New Leisure and Mass Culture

▶ What commercial activities emerged for amusement and leisure in the urban environments?

▶ How did sports and new forms of communication contribute to the creation of a mass culture?

▶ How did new forms of amusement and entertainment provide opportunities for minority groups in American society?

On December 2, 1889, as laborers paraded through Worcester, Massachusetts, seeking shorter working hours, a group of carpenters hoisted a banner proclaiming, "Eight Hours for Work, Eight Hours for Rest, Eight Hours for What We Will." That last phrase expressed claim to a new segment of daily life: leisure.

16-6a Increase in Leisure Time

By the late 1800s, technology had become truly time-saving. Machines and assembly lines cut average workweeks from sixty-six hours in 1860 to sixty in 1890 and forty-seven in 1920, giving workers shorter workdays and freer weekends. White-collar employees spent eight to ten hours a day on the job and often worked only half a day or not at all on weekends. Many Americans now had time for a variety of diversions, and entrepreneurs profited from their new leisure time.

Amusement became a new commercial activity. Production of games, toys, and musical instruments expanded. Improvements in cardboard production aided increased popularity of board games from manufacturers such as Milton Bradley and Parker Brothers. Significantly, the content of board games shifted from moral lessons to topics involving transportation, finance, and sports. Also, by the 1890s, middle-class families were buying mass-produced pianos and sheet music that made singing a popular home entertainment. The vanguard of new leisure pursuits, however, was sports. Formerly a fashionable indulgence of elites, organized sports became a favorite pastime of all classes.

16-6b Baseball

Baseball ruled as the most popular sport. Derived from older bat, ball, and base-circling games, baseball was formalized in 1845 by the Knickerbocker Club of New York City. By 1860 at least fifty baseball clubs existed, and youths played informal games on vacant city lots and rural fields across the nation. In 1866, the Cincinnati Red Stockings became the first fully professional baseball club, compiling a perfect 65–0 record playing local teams across the country. The founding of the National League of Professional Baseball Clubs in 1876 gave the sport a stable business structure, though as early as 1867, a "color line" excluded black players from major professional teams. In 1903 the National League and competing American League (formed in 1901) began a World Series between

their championship teams. The Boston Americans (later, Red Sox) defeated the Pittsburgh Pirates five games to three.

16-6c Croquet and Cycling

Croquet and cycling were popular pastimes attracting men and women alike. Played on lawns, sometimes with lighted wickets for nighttime competition, croquet encouraged socializing. Cycling was as popular as baseball, especially after 1885, when the cumbersome velocipede, with its huge front wheel and tall seat, gave way to safety bicycles with pneumatic tires and wheels of identical size. By 1900, Americans owned 10 million bicycles, and cycling clubs lobbied governments to build more paved roads. Cycle races brought international fame to professional riders such as Major Taylor, an African American. Also, bicycles helped free women from constraints of Victorian fashion. In order to ride safety bicycles, women had to wear divided skirts and simple undergarments. As the 1900 census proclaimed, "Few articles . . . have created so great a revolution in social conditions as the bicycle."

16-6d Football

American football, as an intercollegiate competition, attracted players and spectators wealthy enough to have access to higher education. By the late nineteenth century, however, the game was appealing to a wider audience. While the Princeton-Yale game drew fifty thousand spectators, informal games were played in yards and playgrounds throughout the country.

College football's violence and "tramp athletes"—nonstudents hired to help teams win—sparked a national scandal, climaxing in 1905 when 18 players died from game-related injuries and more than 150 were seriously injured. President Theodore Roosevelt, an advocate of athletics, convened a White House conference to discuss ways of eliminating brutality and foul play. The gathering founded the Intercollegiate Athletic Association (renamed the National Collegiate Athletic Association, or NCAA, in 1910) to police college sports. In 1906, the association altered football rules to make the game less violent by outlawing the "flying wedge," extending from five to ten yards the distance needed to make a first down, legalizing the forward pass, and tightening player eligibility.

As more women enrolled in college, they participated in sports such as rowing, track, swimming, archery, and baseball. Eventually, they made basketball their most popular intercollegiate sport. Basketball was invented in 1891 as a winter sport for men, but Senda Berenson of Smith College drafted special women's rules in 1899, limiting dribbling and running and encouraging passing.

16-6e Show Business

American show business matured in these years, becoming a mode of entertainment created by and for ordinary people. New theatrical performances offered audiences escape into

Japanese Baseball

Baseball, the "national pastime," was one new leisure-time pursuit that Americans took into different parts of the world. The Shanghai Base Ball Club was founded by Americans in China in 1863, but few Chinese paid much attention to the sport, largely because the Imperial Court denounced the game as spiritually corrupting. However, when Horace Wilson, an American teacher, taught baseball to his Japanese students in 1873, the game received an enthusiastic reception as a reinforcement of traditional virtues. In fact, baseball quickly became so much a part of Japanese culture that one Japanese writer commented, "Baseball is perfect for us. If the Americans hadn't invented it, we probably would have."

During the 1870s, scores of Japanese high schools and colleges sponsored organized baseball, and in 1883 Hiroshi Hiraoka, a railroad engineer who had studied in Boston, founded the first official local team, the Shimbashi Athletic Club Athletics. Fans displayed wild devotion to this and similar teams as they developed over the next several years.

Before Americans introduced baseball to Japan, the Japanese had no team sports and no predilection for recreational athletics. Once they learned about baseball, they found that the idea of a team sport fit their culture very well. But the Japanese had difficulty applying the American concept of leisure to the game. For them, baseball was serious business, involving hard and often brutal training. Practices at Ichiko, one of Japan's top high school baseball teams in the late nineteenth century, were dubbed "Bloody Urine" because many players passed blood after a day of drilling. There was a spiritual quality as well, linked to Buddhist values. According to one Japanese coach, "The purpose of [baseball] training is not health but the forging of the soul, and a strong soul is only born from strong practice. . . . Student baseball must be the baseball of self-discipline, or trying to attain the truth, just as in Zen Buddhism." This attitude prompted the Japanese to consider baseball a new method for pursuing the spirit of Bushido, the way of the samurai.

When Americans played baseball in Japan, the Japanese found them to be strong and talented but lacking in discipline and respect. Americans insulted the Japanese by refusing to remove their hats and bow when they stepped up to bat. An international dispute occurred in 1891 when William Imbrie, an American professor at Tokyo's Meijo University, arrived late for a game. Finding the gate locked, he climbed over the fence in order to enter the field. The fence, however, had sacred meaning, and Japanese fans attacked Imbrie for his sacrilege. Imbrie suffered facial injuries, prompting the American embassy to lodge a formal complaint. Americans assumed that their game would encourage Japanese to become like westerners, but the Japanese transformed the American pastime into an expression of team spirit, discipline, and nationalism that was uniquely Japanese.

CRITICAL THINKING

- The Japanese made baseball "their own" after Americans introduced it to their country. How are baseball and other professional sports today more like Japanese baseball than they are like their ancestral forms in the U.S.?
- How do we account for that change?

◀ Replete with bats, gloves, and uniforms, this Japanese baseball team of 1890 very much resembles its American counterpart of that era. The Japanese adopted baseball soon after Americans became involved in their country but also added their cultural qualities to the game.

Transcendental Graphics/Archive Photos/Getty Images

adventure, melodrama, and comedy. Plots were simple, heroes and villains recognizable. For urban people unfamiliar with other times and places, productions made the Wild West and Old South come alive through dramas of Buffalo Bill, Davy Crockett, and the Civil War. Musical comedies entertained with songs, humor, and dance. Folksy comedy and catchy tunes were performed by popular performers such as **George M. Cohan**. A singer and dancer born into an Irish family, Cohan drew on patriotism and traditional values in songs such as "The Yankee Doodle Boy" and "You're a Grand Old Flag."

By 1900, vaudeville was the most popular mass entertainment because it offered something for everyone. Shows, whose acts followed a fixed schedule just like trains and factory production, featured jugglers, magicians, acrobats, comedians, singers, dancers, and animal acts. Shrewd entrepreneurs made vaudeville a big business. The famous producer Florenz Ziegfeld packaged shows in a stylish format—the Ziegfeld Follies—and created a new form of femininity, the Ziegfeld Girl, whose graceful dancing and alluring costumes suggested a haunting sexuality.

16-6f Opportunities for Women and Minorities

Show business provided new opportunities for female, African American, and immigrant performers, but at the cost of stereotyping and exploitation. Comic opera diva Lillian Russell, vaudeville comedienne-singer Fanny Brice, and burlesque queen Eva Tanguay attracted loyal fans and handsome fees. In contrast to the demure Victorian female, they conveyed images of pluck and creativity. Tanguay exuded something both shocking and confident when she sang, "It's All Been Done Before But Not the Way I Do It." But lesser female performers were often exploited by male promoters and theater owners, who wanted to profit by titillating the public with scantily clad women onstage.

Before the 1890s, the chief form of commercial entertainment employing African Americans was the **minstrel show**. Vaudeville gave black artists new opportunities but reinforced demeaning social attitudes. Pandering to prejudices of white audiences, composers and white singers degraded blacks in songs such as "You May Be a Hawaiian on Old Broadway, But You're Just Another Nigger to Me." Black performers such as Bert Williams, a talented comedian and dancer who had graduated from high school at a time when most whites did not, achieved success by wearing blackface makeup and playing stereotypical roles of a smiling fool and dandy, living their lives tormented by the humiliation they had to suffer.

George M. Cohan Singer, dancer, and songwriter who drew on patriotic and traditional values in songs.

minstrel show Early stage show in which white men wore blackface makeup and played to the prejudices of white audiences by offering demeaning and caricatured portrayals of African Americans in songs, dances, and skits.

▲ Eva Tanguay was one of the most popular and highly-paid vaudeville entertainers of her era. She began performing in the 1890s, shown here, and her career lasted until the 1930s. An energetic singer who billed herself as "the girl who made vaudeville famous," Tanguay dressed in elaborate costumes and sang suggestive songs, many of which were written just for her and epitomized her carefree style.

Immigrants occupied the core of American popular entertainment. Vaudeville in particular used ethnic humor and exaggerated dialects in skits and songs. Performers reinforced ethnic stereotypes, but such distortions were more self-conscious and sympathetic than those involving blacks. Ethnic comedy often satirized everyday difficulties that immigrants faced. A typical scene featuring Italians, for example, highlighted a character's uncertain grasp of English, which caused him to confuse *diploma* with *the plumber* and *pallbearer* with *polar bear*. Such scenes allowed audiences to laugh with, rather than at, foibles of the human condition.

16-6g Movies

Shortly after 1900, live entertainment began to yield to motion pictures. Perfected by Thomas Edison in the 1880s, movies began as slot-machine peep shows in arcades and billiard parlors. Eventually, images were projected onto a screen so that large audiences could view them, and a new medium was born. Producers, many of them from Jewish immigrant backgrounds, discovered that a film could tell a dramatic story that catered to viewers' desires. Using themes of patriotism and working-class life, early filmmakers helped shift American culture away from straitlaced Victorian values to a more cosmopolitan outlook. And as new technology enabled movie lengths to expand from minutes to hours, producers presented social messages as well as intense drama. For example, *The Birth of a Nation* (1915), directed by D. W. Griffith, was a stunning epic about the Civil War and Reconstruction. But it also fanned racial prejudice by depicting African Americans as threats to white moral values. The National Association for the Advancement of Colored People (NAACP), formed in 1909, led organized protests against it. But the film's pioneering techniques—close-ups, fade-outs, and battle scenes—heightened its appeal.

By mass-producing sound and images, technology made entertainment an important consumer industry. The still camera, modernized by George Eastman, enabled ordinary people to record and preserve family memories. The phonograph, another Edison invention, brought musical performances into the home. News also became a consumer product. Using high-speed printing presses, cheap paper, and revenues from advertisements, shrewd publishers created a much-desired medium. Increased leisure time and high literacy rates nurtured a fascination with the sensational, and from the 1880s onward, popular urban newspapers increasingly whetted that appetite.

16-6h Yellow Journalism

Joseph Pulitzer, a Hungarian immigrant who bought the *New York World* in 1883, pioneered a new branch of journalism by filling *World* pages with stories of disasters, crimes, and scandals under screaming headlines set in large bold type. Pulitzer also popularized comics, and the yellow ink they were printed in brought about the term "yellow journalism" as a synonym for sensationalism. In one year, the *World*'s circulation rose from 20,000 to 100,000, and by the late 1890s it reached 1 million. Soon other publishers, such as William Randolph Hearst, who bought the *New York Journal* in 1895 and started a newspaper empire, adopted Pulitzer's techniques. Pulitzer, Hearst, and their rivals boosted circulations further by presenting sports and women's news in separate sections. Also, popular magazines, such as *Saturday Evening Post* and *Ladies Home Journal,* increased their circulation with human-interest stories, photographs, and eye-catching ads.

Other forms of communication also expanded, aided by technology. In 1891, there was less than one telephone for every hundred people in the United States; by 1901 the number had doubled, and by 1921 it had swelled to 12.6. In 1900, Americans used 4 billion postage stamps; in 1922, they bought 14.3 billion. The term *community*

took on new dimensions, as people used the media, mail, and telephone to extend their horizons far beyond their immediate locality. More than ever before, people in different parts of the country knew about and discussed the same news event, whether it was a sensational murder, sex scandal, or the fortunes of an entertainer or athlete. American was becoming a mass society where the same products, same technology, and same information dominated everyday life.

To some extent, the new amusements allowed ethnic and social groups to share common experiences. Amusement parks such as at Coney Island, ball fields, vaudeville shows, movies, and feature sections of newspapers and magazines were nonsectarian and apolitical. Yet different groups consumed them to suit their own needs. Immigrants, for example, used parks and amusement areas as sites for special ethnic gatherings. To the dismay of natives who hoped that public recreation and holidays would assimilate newcomers and teach them habits of restraint, immigrants converted picnics and Fourth of July celebrations into occasions for boisterous festivity. Young working-class men and women resisted parents' and moralizers' warnings and frequented dance halls, where they explored forms of courtship and sexual behavior free from adult oversight. And children often used streets, alleys, and rooftops to create their own recreation rather than participate in adult-supervised games in parks and playgrounds. Thus, as the American people learned to play, their leisure—like their work and politics—expressed, and was shaped by, the pluralistic forces that thrived in the new urban-industrial society.

Summary

Industrialization, propelled by machines and inventions, and urbanization, enriched by waves of newly arrived people and their diverse cultures, altered the United States and its human ecology in dramatic ways in the late nineteenth and early twentieth century. Industrial growth converted the country from a debtor, agricultural nation into a manufacturing, financial, and exporting power. Immigrants and their offspring outnumbered the native born in many cities, and the industrial economy depended on these new workers and consumers. And the era's new technologies, whether on assembly lines or in homes, also made cities safer and daily life more comfortable.

But in industry, massive size and aggressive consolidation of businesses engulfed the individual, changing the nature of work from a singular activity undertaken by skilled producers to mass production undertaken by wage earners. Laborers fought to retain control of their work and organized unions to advance their cause. Urban life, for its part, brought forward its own challenges, especially to newcomers, of finding adequate housing, a decent job, and a safe environment. In urban communities, politics and reform

Technology of Recorded Sound

Today's widespread markets for downloaded music come from a combination of technology, chemistry, and human resourcefulness that came together in the late nineteenth century. In 1877, even before he invented the light bulb, Thomas Edison devised a way to preserve and reproduce his own voice by storing it on indentations made in tinfoil. At first, Edison intended his "speaking machine" to help businesses store dictated messages and replace undependable secretaries. But in 1878 he was stirred by a rivalry with Alexander Graham Bell, inventor of the telephone, who also was working on a device that reproduced sounds, to invent a phonograph that played recorded music. By the 1890s, entrepreneurs were charging audiences admission to hear recorded sounds from these machines.

By 1901, companies such as the Columbia Phonograph Company and Victor Talking Machine Company began to produce machines that played music recorded on cylinders molded and hardened from a chemical wax compound more durable than the metal cylinders that Edison had used. Over the next ten years, various inventors improved the phonograph so that it played back sound from a stylus (needle) vibrating in grooves of a shellac disc. These developments increased the playing time of records from two minutes to four.

Phonograph records then replaced sheet music as the most popular medium of popular music, but soon another technological wonder—radio—rose to prominence and helped boost record sales. The popularity of the radio could not have been possible without another feat of electronic acoustic technology—the microphone. The microphone achieved better sound quality over previously used megaphones by picking up sound from a performance and turning it into electrical currents that were transmitted via wire from the microphone to a radio station, which then broadcast the sound. As phonograph prices declined and sound quality improved, more records became available.

The invention in 1938 of the idler wheel, which enabled a phonograph turntable to spin a disk at the speed necessary for the stylus to pick up the sound accurately, brought an important advance. Shortly thereafter, more significant inventions in sound recording, such as the magnetic tape recorder, allowed for more manipulation of sound in the recording studio than ever before. Tape and slower-speed turntables lengthened play time, and in 1963 Philips, a Dutch electronics firm, introduced the compact audiocassette. Two decades later, Philips joined with the Japanese corporation Sony to adapt digital laser discs, which an American had invented to store video images, to record music by transforming sound into sequences of numbers. The compact disc (CD) was born, and from there it was a short step for the Apple Computer Company to create the iPod, which housed CD-quality music on an internal hard drive. And more recently, online music sites have used compressed file sizes and marketed music for digital audio players, and downloaded music has replaced records, tapes, and discs, and has become a multi-billion-dollar industry.

CRITICAL THINKING

- As digital music downloads have begun to dominate all other forms of musical recording, the music industry has struggled to keep up in terms of artists' royalties and rights. This struggle is symptomatic of a larger problem regarding copyright and the dissemination of information digitally. What should the government's role be in regulating copyright and the web?

---

took on new meanings, and family life reflected both change and continuity.

An uneven distribution of power and wealth characterized the era. Corporations consolidated to control resources and make profits more certain. Workers and their allies had numbers and ideas but lacked influence, believing businesses were profiting at their expense. And the urban society that materialized when native inventiveness met the traditions of European, African, and Asian cultures seldom functioned smoothly, yet cities managed to thrive because of, rather than in spite of, their diverse fragments. When the desire to hold on to one's culture met with the need to fit in, often the results were compound identifications: Irish American, Italian American, Polish American, and the like.

By 1920, the foundation of the country's urban-industrial structure had been laid, climaxing an era of extraordinary dynamism.

Suggestions for Further Reading

John Bodnar, *The Transplanted: A History of Immigrants in Urban America* (1985)

Howard P. Chudacoff, *How Old Are You: Age Consciousness in American Culture* (1989)

Howard P. Chudacoff and Judith E. Smith, *The Evolution of American Urban Society*, 8th ed. (2014)

Steven J. Diner, *A Very Different Age: Americans of the Progressive Era* (1998)

Nancy Foner and George M. Frederickson, eds., *Not Just Black and White: Historical and Contemporary Perspectives on Immigration, Race, and Ethnicity in the United States* (2004)

Kenneth T. Jackson, *The Crabgrass Frontier: The Suburbanization of the United States* (1985)

Matthew Frye Jacobson, *Whiteness of a Different Color: European Immigrants and the Alchemy of Race* (1998)

John F. Kasson, *Amusing the Million: Coney Island at the Turn of the Century* (1978)

Alice Kessler-Harris, *Out to Work: A History of Wage-Earning Women in the United States* (2003)

T. J. Jackson Lears and Richard W. Fox, eds., *The Culture of Consumption: Critical Essays in American History, 1880–1980* (1983)

Robyn Muncy, *Creating a Female Dominion in American Reform, 1890–1935* (1991)

Kathy Peiss, *Cheap Amusements: Working Women and Leisure in Turn-of-the-Century New York* (1986)

Gilded Age Politics, 1877–1900

William Graham Sumner did not think much of people who were lazy, immoral, or criminal. He once observed, with regard to these people, "it would have been better for society and would have involved no pain to them, if they had never been born." Sumner, who distanced himself from those whom he considered objectional types, traveled several roads to success. Born in New Jersey, he was raised in Hartford, Connecticut, the son of a railroad employee and wife who both had immigrated from England. In spite of his family's modest means, Sumner was able to attend and graduate from Yale College (later Yale University) in 1863, after which he studied in Germany and England, then was ordained an Episcopal priest in 1869. But society and economics, rather than theology, were his real passions. So in 1872 he left his post at the Church of the Redeemer in Morristown, New Jersey, and accepted a professorship in political and social science at Yale, where he remained until retiring in 1909. Yale proved to be a good place for William's sister Alice as well as himself. In 1888, Alice fell in love with and married Yale's new football coach, Walter Camp, who shortly thereafter became one of the most influential powers in college sports.

Professor Sumner was a staunch believer in individual liberty and a champion of laissez-faire, the ideology that government involvement in private affairs should be kept to a minimum. He wrote numerous books and articles on these topics and has been credited among those who adapted Charles Darwin's theory of the survival of the fittest to social and economic relations. In an essay published in 1887, Sumner expressed his views on laissez-faire by asserting that the American people had "reached the point where individualism is possible" and that "legislative and administrative interference" should be resisted. Otherwise, he concluded, "whenever we try to get paternalized (meaning controlled by government) we only succeed in getting policed."

Experience an interactive version of this story in MindTap®.

◀ Politics in the late nineteenth century was an important community activity. In an age before movies, television, and shopping malls, forceful orators performed amidst lights, flags, streamers, and fireworks with speeches that sometimes lasted for hours.

Chronology

1873	▪ Congress ends coinage of silver dollars
1873–78	▪ Economic hard times hit
1877	▪ Georgia passes poll tax, disfranchising most African Americans
1878	▪ Bland-Allison Act requires U.S. Treasury to buy between $2 million and $4 million in silver each month
1881	▪ Garfield assassinated; Arthur assumes presidency
1883	▪ Pendleton Civil Service Act introduces merit system
	▪ Supreme Court strikes down 1883 Civil Rights Act
1886	▪ *Wabash* case declares that only Congress can limit interstate commerce rates
1887	▪ Farmers' Alliances form
	▪ Interstate Commerce Commission begins regulating rates and practices of interstate shipping
1890	▪ McKinley Tariff raises tariff rates
	▪ Sherman Silver Purchase Act commits the U.S. Treasury to buying 4.5 million ounces of silver each month
	▪ "Mississippi Plan" uses poll taxes and literacy tests to prevent African Americans from voting
	▪ National Woman Suffrage Association formed
1890s	▪ Jim Crow laws, discriminating against African Americans in legal treatment and public accommodations, passed by southern states
1892	▪ Populist convention in Omaha draws up reform platform
1893	▪ Sherman Silver Purchase Act repealed
1893–97	▪ Major economic depression hits United States
1894	▪ Wilson-Gorman Tariff passes
	▪ Coxey's Army marches on Washington, D.C.
1896	▪ *Plessy v. Ferguson* establishes separate but equal doctrine
1898	▪ Louisiana implements "grandfather clause" restricting voting by African Americans
1899	▪ *Cummings v. County Board of Education* applies separate but equal doctrine to schools

With his coarse opinions on individualism and people whom he deemed "unfit," Sumner can be seen as an icon of the age of the nation's rampant economic expansion. The traumatic Civil War and its aftermath plus the rise of large corporations between 1877 and 1900 influenced politics and government as much as they shaped everyday life. It was an era characterized by greed, special interest, and political exclusion. The obsession with corporation and individual profits prompted Mark Twain and his novelist friend Charles Dudley Warner to pen a novel titled *The Gilded Age 1874* that satirized America as a nation shiny and golden on the outside but in reality decadent and money-grubbing. Ever since, historians have used the expression "Gilded Age" to characterize the late nineteenth century.

At first glance, the Gilded Age may appear as the era in which laissez-faire, the doctrine that Sumner so passionately espoused, was triumphant. Corporations seemed to expand unfettered and government spending, especially on social programs, was kept to a minimum. The U.S. Congress was preoccupied with matters designed to aid business, and in a series of influential decisions, the Supreme Court limited the ability of government to control corporations.

Such a view, however, would miss some of the most vital developments of the era, developments that expanded government power at federal, state, and local levels far more than people at the time realized. Though certain groups resisted the imposition of government authority, others welcomed and actively sought it. Reformers could claim several accomplishments. In spite of partisan and regional rivalries, Congress achieved legislative landmarks in railroad regulation, tariff and currency reform, creation of the civil service, and other important issues. The presidency was occupied by honest, respectable men who, though not as exceptional as Washington, Jefferson, or Lincoln, asserted their authority and independence from Congress. And, state and local governments expanded their police power—the authority to protect the health, safety, and morals of their citizens. Nevertheless, past injustices continued, as exclusion prevented the majority of Americans—including women, African Americans, Native Americans, uneducated whites, and unnaturalized immigrants—from voting and from access to the tools of democracy.

From the 1870s to the 1890s, a stable party system and balance of power among geographic sections kept politics in a delicate equilibrium. Then, in the 1890s, rural discontent rumbled through the West and South, and a deep economic depression bared flaws in the industrial system. A presidential campaign in 1896 stirred the American people as they had not been stirred for a generation. Old parties split, a new party system arose, sectional unity dissolved, and fundamental disputes about the nation's future climaxed. The nation emerged from the turbulent 1890s with new economic configurations and new political alignments.

- ■ *What were the functions of government in the Gilded Age, and how did they change?*

- ■ *How did policies of exclusion and discrimination make their mark on the political culture of the age?*

- ■ *How did the economic climate give rise to the Populist movement?*

17-1 The Nature of Party Politics

▶ How did the public relate to party politics in the late nineteenth century?

▶ What was the relationship between and within the major political parties of the late nineteenth century?

At no other time in the nation's history was public interest in elections more avid than between 1870 and 1896. Consistently, around 80 percent of eligible voters (white and black males in the North and West, somewhat lower rates among mostly white males in the South) cast ballots in local, state, and national elections—a rate 20 to 30 percent higher than today's. Politics served as a form of recreation, more popular than baseball or circuses. Actual voting provided only the final step in a process that included parades, picnics, and speeches. As one observer remarked, "What the theatre is to the French, or the bull fight . . . to the Spanish . . . [election campaigns] are to our people."

17-1a Cultural–Political Alignments

In contrast to the present, when many voters consider themselves independents, in the Gilded Age party loyalty was vigorous and emotional. With some exceptions, people who opposed government interference in matters of personal liberty identified with the Democratic Party; those who believed government could be an agent of reform identified with the Republican Party. There was also a geographic dimension to these divisions. Northern Republicans tried to capitalize on bitter memories of the Civil War by "waving the bloody shirt" at northern and southern Democrats. As one Republican orator scolded in 1876, "Every man that tried to destroy this nation was a Democrat. . . . Soldiers, every scar you have on your heroic bodies was given you by a Democrat." Democrats

in the North tended to address urban and economic issues, but southern Democratic candidates waved a different bloody shirt, calling Republicans traitors to white supremacy and states' rights.

Issues of the era made politics a personal as well as a community activity. In an age before media celebrities occupied public attention, people formed emotional loyalties to individual politicians, loyalties that often overlooked crassness and corruption. James G. Blaine—Maine's flamboyant and powerful Republican congressman, senator, presidential aspirant, and two-time secretary of state—typified this appeal. Followers called him the "Plumed Knight," composed songs and organized parades in his honor, and sat mesmerized by his long speeches, while disregarding his corrupt alliances with businessmen and his animosities toward laborers and farmers.

Political allegiances were so evenly divided that no party gained dominance nationally for any sustained period of time. Between 1877 and 1897, Republicans held the presidency for three terms, Democrats for two. Rarely did the same party control both the presidency and Congress simultaneously. From 1876 through 1892, presidential elections were extremely close. The outcome often hinged on votes in a few populous northern states—Connecticut, New York, New Jersey, Ohio, Indiana, and Illinois. Both parties tried to gain advantages by nominating presidential and vice presidential candidates from these states (and by committing vote fraud on their candidates' behalf).

17-1b Party Factions

Internal quarrels split both the Republican and Democratic parties. Among Republicans, New York's Senator Roscoe Conkling led one faction, known as "Stalwarts." A physical fitness devotee labeled "the finest torso in public life," Conkling worked the spoils system to win government jobs for his supporters. Stalwarts' rivals were the "Half Breeds," led by James G. Blaine, who pursued influence as blatantly as Conkling did. On the sidelines stood more idealistic Republicans, or **"Mugwumps"** (supposedly an Algonquian term meaning "important person"). Mugwumps, such as Missouri Republican Senator Carl Schurz, scorned the political roguishness that tainted his party's leaders and believed that only righteous, educated men like themselves should govern. Republican allies of big business wanted gold to be the standard for currency, whereas those from western mining regions favored silver. Democrats also subdivided into interest groups: white supremacist southerners; working-class advocates; immigrant-stock supporters of urban political machines; business-oriented advocates of low tariffs and the gold standard; and debtor-oriented advocates of free silver. Like Republicans, Democrats avidly pursued the spoils of office.

In many states, one party usually dominated, and a few men typically held dictatorial sway. Often the state "boss" was a senator who doled out jobs and parlayed his clout into national influence.

"Mugwumps" Term used for idealistic Republican reformers.

(Until ratification of the Seventeenth Amendment to the Constitution in 1913, state legislatures elected U.S. senators.) Besides Conkling and Blaine, senatorial powers included Thomas C. Platt of New York, Nelson W. Aldrich of Rhode Island, Mark A. Hanna of Ohio, and Matthew S. Quay of Pennsylvania. These men exercised power brazenly. Quay once responded to an inquiry about using secret information from a Senate investigation to profit from an investment in the American Sugar Refining Company by pronouncing, "I do not feel that there is anything in my connection with the Senate to interfere with my buying or selling stock when I please, and I propose to do so in the future."

17-2 The Activism of Government

▶ How did government at all levels become more active in people's everyday lives?

▶ How did government seek to intervene in the operation of railroad businesses?

▶ What political divisions emerged over the development of economic policy in the late nineteenth century?

In spite of all the numerous divisions, government at every level came to play a much greater role in people's lives than ever before. Most of what governing bodies did for people was to pass laws and establish mechanisms intended to safeguard health and safety. These efforts evolved at state and local levels largely from the constitutional provision of "police power," meaning the authority, within certain limits, to regulate and enforce order to ensure the general welfare of the population.

17-2a Uses of Police Power

From the earliest days of the Republic, state and local governments intervened in people's lives to protect safety and morals. There were restrictions on where citizens could construct buildings (for fire protection), where they could dispose of waste, at what age they could marry, quarantines to prevent the spread of disease, and more. By the time of the Gilded Age, these laws and regulations extended into every corner of society. There were laws making it criminal to mistreat animals and children; laws providing for the purity of foods and medicines; laws establishing minimum requirements for professionals such as doctors, teachers, and ship captains; and laws to ensure the legitimacy of banks and insurance companies. Other laws required the licensing of, and sometimes prohibition of, liquor sales, prizefighting, and obscene literature; laws regulated rates and operations of streetcars and railroads; laws limited the working hours of women and

Interstate Commerce Act An 1887 law that established the Interstate Commerce Commission, the nation's first regulatory agency, to investigate railroad rate-making and discriminatory rate practices.

children; and laws mandated racial segregation. Though many of these measures met with some objection, representatives in state legislatures and city councils passed these laws with broad consent of the people they governed. Moreover, courts generally upheld them.

17-2b Due Process

When the exercise of police power was challenged, protestors asserted that governments were interfering with a person's or company's right to use of private property. This right was lodged in the clause of the Fifth Amendment to the Constitution that stated that no person could "be deprived of life, liberty, or property, without due process of law; nor shall private property be taken for public use without just compensation." The restriction originally applied to actions by the federal government, but Section 1 of the Fourteenth Amendment— in what is called the "due process clause"—extended the limitation to state governments as well.

The matter of railroad rates provides an example of how business interests tried to use due process as a protection against state and federal government regulation. As rail networks spread, so did competition. In their quest for customers, railroads reduced rates to outmaneuver rivals, but rate wars hurt profits, and inconsistent freight charges angered shippers and farmers. On noncompetitive routes, railroads often boosted charges as high as possible to compensate for unprofitably low rates on competitive routes, making pricing disproportionate to distance. Per mile charges for short-distance shipments served by only one line could exceed charges on long-distance shipments served by competing lines. Railroads also played favorites, reducing rates to large shippers and offering free passenger passes to preferred customers and politicians.

17-2c Railroad Regulation

Such favoritism stirred farmers, small merchants, and reform politicians to demand rate regulation to protect the welfare of all shippers. Their efforts succeeded first at the state level. By 1880, fourteen states had established commissions to limit freight and storage charges of state-chartered lines. Using lobbyists and pressure tactics, railroads fought these measures, arguing that the due process clause of the Fourteenth Amendment guaranteed them freedom to use their property without state government restraint. But in 1877, in *Munn v. Illinois*, the U.S. Supreme Court, using police power as a basis, upheld the principle of state regulation, declaring that grain warehouses owned by railroads acted in the public interest and therefore must submit to regulation for "the common good."

State legislatures, however, could not regulate commerce that crossed state lines, a limitation affirmed by the Supreme Court in the *Wabash* case of 1886, in which the Court declared that only Congress could limit rates involving interstate commerce. Reformers thereupon demanded action by the federal government. With support from businessmen who believed that they, like farmers, suffered from discriminatory rates, Congress passed the **Interstate Commerce Act** in 1887. The law prohibited rebates and rate discrimination and created the

▲ The patronage system—the practice of rewarding political supporters with jobs and favors—reached such an extent during the Gilded Age that critics likened it to the stock exchange, where traders clamored to be heard. President James A. Garfield is shown on a pedestal in the center of this cartoon surrounded by pleading job seekers while on the left, Senator Thomas C. Platt, Republican leader from New York State, is handcuffed to a man handing "orders from the boss" to Vice President Chester A. Arthur. The Pendleton Civil Service Act of 1883 was intended to replace patronage by making federal appointments based on merit rather than on political connections.

Interstate Commerce Commission (ICC), the nation's first regulatory agency, to investigate railroad rate-making, issue cease and desist orders against illegal practices, and seek court aid to enforce compliance. The legislation's weak provisions for enforcement, however, left railroads room for evasion, and federal judges reversed course and diminished both state and ICC powers. In the *Maximum Freight Rate* case (1897), for example, the Supreme Court evoked the due process provision, ruling that regulation interfered with a railroad's right to a "fair return" from its property. Even so, the principle of regulation, though weakened by a standoff between police power and due process, remained in force.

17-2d Veterans' Pensions

In addition to railroad regulation, issues of pensions, patronage abuses, tariffs, and currency provoked heated debates and partisan discord, but Congress nevertheless managed to pass significant legislation. From the end of the Civil War into the 1880s, Congress spent much time discussing soldiers' pensions. The **Grand Army of the Republic**, an organization of Union army veterans, allied with the Republican Party and cajoled the government into providing pensions for former northern soldiers and their widows. These grants were deserved but costly. Union troops had been poorly paid, and thousands of wives had been widowed. Although the North spent $2 billion to fight the Civil War, pensions to veterans ultimately cost

$8 billion, one of the largest welfare commitments the federal government has ever made. By 1900 soldiers' pensions accounted for roughly 40 percent of the federal budget. Soldiers who had fought for the Confederate cause, however, received none of this money, though some southern states funded small pensions and built old-age homes for ex-soldiers.

17-2e Civil Service Reform

Few politicians dared oppose pensions, but some attempted to dismantle the spoils system. During the Civil War, the federal government had expanded considerably, and the practice of awarding government jobs—spoils—to political supporters regardless of their qualifications flourished after the war. As the postal service, diplomatic corps, and other government agencies expanded, so did the public payroll. Between 1865 and 1891, the number of federal employees tripled, from 53,000 to 166,000. (There are about 2.1 million today.) Elected officials scrambled to control these jobs as a means to benefit themselves, their constituents, and their party. In return for comparatively short hours and high pay, appointees to federal positions pledged votes and a portion of their earnings to those who had caused them to be hired.

Grand Army of the Republic (GAR) A social and political lobbying organization of northern Civil War veterans that convinced Congress to provide $8 billion in pensions for former Union soldiers and widows.

A SENATE FOR REVENUE ONLY

The Granger Collection, NYC

◄ Federal economic policies such as tariffs sparked heated debates between businesses and their allies in Congress on one side and those who believed these policies benefited only special interests. This cartoon, clearly opposing the McKinley Tariff, depicts Uncle Sam, the symbol for America, bound up and held captive by the tariff and its raucous Senate supporters.

Shocked by such corruption, especially after revelations of scandals during the presidential administration of Ulysses S. Grant, some reformers began advocating appointments and promotions based on merit—civil service—rather than on political connections. Support for change accelerated in 1881 when a distraught job seeker assassinated President James Garfield. The **Pendleton Civil Service Act**, passed by Congress in 1882 and signed by President Chester Arthur in 1883, created the Civil Service Commission to oversee competitive examinations for government positions. The act gave the commission jurisdiction over only 10 percent of federal jobs, but the president could expand the list. Because the Constitution barred Congress from interfering in state affairs, civil service at state and local levels developed in a haphazard manner. Nevertheless, the Pendleton Act marked a beginning and provided a model for further reform.

17-2f Tariff Policy

Veterans' pensions and civil service reform were not the main issues of the Gilded Age, however. Rather, economic policy dominated congressional debates. The issue of tariffs carried strong political implications. From 1789 onward, Congress had created tariffs, which levied duties (taxes) on imported goods, to protect American manufactures and agricultural products from foreign competition. But tariffs quickly became a tool by which special interests could enhance their profits. By the 1880s these interests had succeeded in obtaining tariffs on more than four thousand items. A few economists and farmers argued for free trade (no tariffs), but most politicians insisted that tariffs were a necessary form of government assistance to support American industry and preserve jobs.

Pendleton Civil Service Act Attempt to end the spoils system; created the Civil Service Commission to oversee competitive exams for government jobs.

To support economic growth, the Republican Party put protective tariffs at the core of its political agenda. Democrats complained that tariffs made prices artificially high by discouraging importation of less-expensive goods, hurting farmers whose crops were not protected and consumers wanting to buy manufactured goods. For example, a yard of flannel produced in England might cost 10 cents, but an 8-cent-per-yard import duty raised the price to 18 cents. An American manufacturer of a similar yard of flannel, also costing 10 cents, could charge 17 cents, underselling foreign competition by 1 cent yet still pocketing a 7-cent profit.

During the Gilded Age, revenues from tariffs and other levies created a surplus in the federal treasury. Most Republicans liked the idea that the government was earning more than it spent and hoped to keep the surplus as a reserve or to spend it on projects such as harbor improvements, which would aid commerce. Democrats, however, asserted that the federal government should not be a profit-making operation. They acknowledged a need for protection of some manufactured goods and raw materials, but they favored lower tariff duties to encourage foreign trade and to reduce the treasury surplus.

Manufacturers and their congressional allies firmly controlled tariff policy. The Republican-sponsored McKinley Tariff of 1890 boosted already-high rates by 4 percent. When House Democrats, supported by President Grover Cleveland, passed a bill to trim tariffs in 1894, Senate Republicans, aided by southern Democrats eager to protect their region's infant textile and steel industries, added six hundred amendments restoring most cuts (the Wilson-Gorman Tariff). In 1897, the Dingley Tariff raised rates further. Attacks on duties, though unsuccessful, made tariffs a symbol of privileged business in the public mind and a continuing target for reformers.

17-2g Monetary Policy

Debates over monetary policy inflamed even stronger emotions than tariffs did because they represented conflict between haves and have-nots. When increased industrial and agricultural production caused prices to fall after the Civil War, debtors (have-nots) and creditors (haves) had opposing reactions. Farmers suffered because the prices they received for crops were dropping, but because high demand for a relatively limited supply of money in circulation raised interest rates on loans, it was costly for them to borrow funds to pay off mortgages and other debts. They favored the coinage of silver to increase the amount of currency in circulation, which in turn would reduce interest rates, making their debts less burdensome. Small businessmen, also in need of loans, agreed with farmers. Large merchants, manufacturers, and bankers favored a limited, more stable money supply backed only by gold. They feared the value of currency not backed by gold would fluctuate and that the resulting uncertainty would threaten investors' confidence in the U.S. economy. Arguments over the quantity and quality of money also reflected sectional cleavages: western silver-mining areas and agricultural regions of the South and West against the more conservative industrial Northeast.

Before the 1870s, the federal government had bought both gold and silver to back its paper money (dollars), setting a ratio that made a gold dollar worth sixteen times more than a silver dollar. In theory, a person holding a specific sum of dollar bills could exchange (redeem) them for one ounce of gold or sixteen ounces of silver. Discovery of gold in the West, however, increased the gold supply and lowered its market price relative to that of silver. Consequently, silver dollars disappeared from circulation—because of their inflated value relative to gold, owners hoarded them—and in 1873 a congressional act stopped the coinage of silver dollars. Through this action the United States unofficially adopted the gold standard, meaning that its currency was backed chiefly by gold.

But within a few years, new mines in the West began to flood the market with silver, and its price dropped. Because gold now became relatively less plentiful than silver and therefore worth *more* than sixteen times the value of silver, it became worthwhile for people to spend rather than hoard silver dollars. Silver producers wanted the government to resume buying silver at the old sixteen-to-one ratio, because they then could sell silver to the government above its market price. Debtors, hurt by the economic hard times of 1873–1878, saw silver as a means of expanding the currency supply, so they joined silver producers to press for resumption of silver coinage at the old sixteen-to-one ratio.

With both political parties split into silver and gold factions, Congress first tried to compromise. The Bland-Allison Act (1878) authorized the U.S. Treasury to buy between $2 million and $4 million worth of silver each month, and the **Sherman Silver Purchase Act** (1890) increased the government's monthly silver purchase by specifying weight (4.5 million ounces) rather than dollars. Neither measure satisfied the different interest groups. Creditors wanted the government to stop buying silver, whereas for debtors, the legislation failed to expand the money supply satisfactorily and still left the impression that the government favored creditors' interests. The issue would become even more emotional during the presidential election of 1896 (see "Silver Crusade and the Election of 1896," page 516).

17-2h Legislative Accomplishments

Members of Congress dealt with issues such as railroad regulation, civil service, and tariff policy under difficult conditions. Senators and representatives earned small salaries and usually had the financial burden of maintaining two residences: one in their home district and one in Washington. Most members of Congress had no private office space, only a desk. They worked long hours responding to constituents' requests, wrote their own speeches, and paid for staff out of their own pocket. Yet, though corruption and greed tainted several, most politicians were principled and dedicated. They managed to deal with important issues and pass significant legislation that increased the power of the federal government.

17-3 Presidential Initiative

▶ How did party politics between the Democrats and Republicans unfold in the Gilded Age?

▶ How did Gilded Age presidents use executive power to influence the development of legislation?

Operating under the cloud of Andrew Johnson's impeachment, Ulysses S. Grant's scandals, and doubts about the legitimacy of the 1876 election (see "Retreat from Reconstruction," Section 14-6), American presidents between 1877 and 1900 moved gingerly to restore authority to their office. Proper and honest, Presidents Rutherford Hayes (1877–1881), James Garfield (1881), Chester Arthur (1881–1885), Grover Cleveland (1885–1889 and 1893–1897), Benjamin Harrison (1889–1893), and William McKinley (1897–1901) tried to be legislative as well as administrative leaders. Like other politicians, they used symbols. Hayes served lemonade at the White House to emphasize that he, unlike his predecessor, Grant, was no hard drinker. McKinley set aside his cigar in public so photographers would not catch him setting a bad example for youth. More important, each president made cautious attempts to initiate legislation and use vetoes to guide national policy.

17-3a Hayes, Garfield, and Arthur

Rutherford B. Hayes had been a Union general and an Ohio congressman and governor before his disputed election to the presidency, an event that prompted opponents to label him "Rutherfraud." Although Republicans expected him to serve business interests, Hayes played a quiet role as conciliator. He emphasized national harmony over sectional rivalry and opposed

Sherman Silver Purchase Act Law that instructed the treasury to buy, at current market prices, 4.5 million ounces of silver monthly.

The Spectacle of Gilded Age Politics

During the Gilded Age, political events, especially presidential elections, provided opportunity for elaborate spectacle, and politicians occupied the limelight as major celebrities. A presidential campaign functioned as a public festival at a time when mass entertainments such as movies and sports did not exist to offer people outlets for their emotions. Campaigns often included parades, fireworks, and marching bands. This image, an artist's rendering, presents evidence of how people of the era might have expressed themselves politically.

CRITICAL THINKING

- How did Gilded Age presidents use executive power to influence the development of legislation?
- What similarities to modern-day campaign events and symbols does this image represent? In what ways is it different?
- Did politics and campaigning in the Gilded Age play a different role in the nation's culture than they do at present?

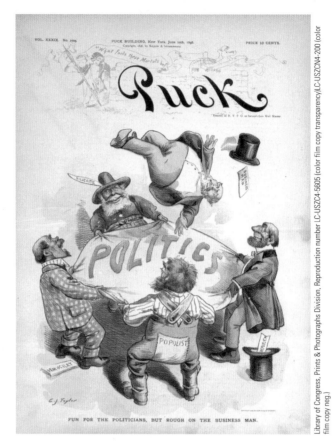

▲ Though business interests generally prevailed in the Gilded Age, various interest groups supported regulation. In this cartoon, a businessman is being tossed around by a "Silverite" (the man in the red shirt who is supporting free silver), a Republican (the bearded man in the frock coat), a Populist (the man in overalls), and a Democrat (the man in the checked suit).

racial violence. He tried to overhaul the spoils system by appointing civil service reformer Carl Schurz to his cabinet and by battling New York's patronage king, Senator Conkling. (He fired Conkling's protégé, Chester A. Arthur, from the post of New York customs house collector.) Though averse to using government power to aid the oppressed, Hayes believed society should not ignore the needs of the American Chinese and Native peoples, and after retiring from the presidency he worked to aid former slaves.

When Hayes declined to run for reelection in 1880, Republicans nominated another Ohio congressman and Civil War hero, James A. Garfield, who defeated Democrat Winfield Scott Hancock, also a Civil War hero, by only forty thousand votes out of 9 million cast. By winning the pivotal states of New York and Indiana, however, Garfield carried the electoral college by a comfortable margin, 214 to 155.

Solemn and cautious, Garfield tried to secure an independent position among party potentates. He hoped to reduce the tariff and develop economic relations with Latin America, and he pleased civil service reformers by rebuffing Conkling's patronage demands. But his chance to make lasting contributions ended in July 1881 when Charles Guiteau shot him in a Washington railroad station. Garfield lingered for seventy-nine days with a bullet in his spine that his inept doctor tried unsuccessfully to remove, but he succumbed to infection, heart ailments, and pneumonia and died September 19.

Garfield's successor was Vice President Chester A. Arthur, the New York Stalwart whom Hayes had fired. Republicans had nominated Arthur for vice president only to help Garfield win New York State's electoral votes. Although his elevation to the presidency made reformers shudder, Arthur became a dignified and temperate executive. He signed the Pendleton Civil Service Act, urged Congress to modify outdated tariff rates, and supported federal regulation of railroads. He wielded the veto aggressively, killing bills that excessively benefited railroads and corporations. Arthur wanted to run for president in 1884 but Republicans nominated James G. Blaine instead.

To oppose Blaine, Democrats picked New York's governor, Grover Cleveland, a bachelor who admitted during the campaign that he had fathered an out-of-wedlock son. The election reflected the nastiness of partisanship. Alluding to Cleveland's son, Republicans chided him with catcalls of "Ma! Ma! Where's my pa?" to which Democrats replied, "Gone to the White House, Ha! Ha! Ha!" Distaste for Blaine prompted some Mugwump Republicans to desert their party for Cleveland. On Election Day, Cleveland beat Blaine by only 29,000 popular votes; his tiny margin of 1,149 votes in New York gave him that state's 36 electoral votes, enough for a 219-to-182 victory in the electoral college. Cleveland may have won New York thanks to last-minute remarks of a Protestant minister, who equated Democrats with "rum, Romanism, and rebellion." Democrats eagerly publicized the slur among New York's large Irish Catholic population, urging voters to protest by supporting Cleveland.

17-3b Cleveland and Harrison

Cleveland, the first Democratic president since James Buchanan (1857–1861), tried to exert vigorous leadership. He expanded civil service, vetoed private pension bills, and urged Congress to cut tariff duties. When advisers warned that his actions might weaken his chances for reelection, the president retorted, "What is the use of being elected or reelected, unless you stand for something?" But Senate protectionists killed tariff reform passed by the House, and when Democrats renominated Cleveland for president in 1888, businessmen in the party convinced him to moderate his attacks on high tariffs.

Republicans in 1888 nominated Benjamin Harrison, former senator from Indiana and grandson of President William Henry Harrison (1841). During the campaign, some Republicans manipulated a British diplomat into stating that Cleveland's reelection would be good for England. Irish Democrats, who hated England's colonial rule over Ireland, took offense, as intended, and turned against Cleveland. Perhaps more beneficial to Harrison were the bribery and multiple voting that helped him win Indiana by 2,300 votes and New York by 14,000. (Democrats also indulged in fraud, but Republicans proved more successful at it.) Those states' electoral votes ensured Harrison's victory. Although Cleveland outpolled Harrison by 90,000 popular votes, Harrison carried the electoral college by 233 to 168.

The first president since 1875 whose party had majorities in both houses of Congress, Harrison used various methods, ranging from threats of vetoes to informal dinners and consultations with politicians, to influence the course of legislation. Partly in response, the Congress of 1889–1891 passed 517 bills, 200 more than the average passed by Congresses between 1875 and 1889. Harrison showed support for civil service by appointing reformer Theodore Roosevelt as civil service commissioner, but neither the president nor Congress could resist pressures from special interests, especially those waving the bloody shirt. Harrison signed the Dependents' Pension Act of 1890, which provided pensions for Union veterans who had suffered war-related disabilities and granted aid to their widows and children. The bill doubled the number of welfare recipients from 490,000 to 966,000.

The Pension Act and other appropriations pushed the 1890 federal budget past $1 billion for the first time in the nation's history. Democrats blamed the "Billion-Dollar Congress" on spendthrift Republicans. Voters reacted by unseating seventy-eight Republicans in the congressional elections of 1890. Seeking to capitalize on voter unrest, Democrats nominated Grover Cleveland to run against Harrison in 1892. This time Cleveland attracted large contributions from business and beat Harrison by 370,000 popular votes (3 percent of the total), easily winning the electoral vote.

In office again, Cleveland addressed problems of currency, tariffs, and labor unrest, but his actions reflected political weakness. During his campaign Cleveland had promised sweeping tariff reform, but he made little effort to line up support in the Senate, where protectionists undercut efforts to reduce rates. And he bowed to requests from railroad interests and sent federal troops to put down the Pullman strike of 1894. In spite of Cleveland's attempts to take initiative, major events—particularly economic downturn and agrarian ferment—pushed the nation in a different direction.

17-4 Discrimination and Disfranchisement

▶ **What forms of social and legal discrimination did African Americans face in the Gilded Age?**

▶ **How did African Americans respond to and challenge discrimination?**

▶ **How were women active in society and politics in the Gilded Age?**

Although speechmakers often spoke of freedom and opportunity during the Gilded Age, policies of discrimination and exclusion continued to haunt more than half of the nation's people. Just as during Reconstruction, issues of race shaped politics in the South, where white farmers and workers, facing economic insecurity, feared that newly enfranchised African American men would challenge whatever political and social superiority (real and imagined) they enjoyed. Wealthy landowners and merchants fanned these fears, using them to divide the races and to distract poor whites from protesting their own economic subjugation. Even some white feminists, such as Susan B. Anthony, opposed voting and other rights for African Americans on grounds that white women deserved such rights before black men did.

In the North, custom more than law limited opportunities of black people. Discrimination in housing, employment, and access to facilities such as parks, hotels, and department stores kept African Americans separate. Whites always were concerned that blacks should remain "in their place." Whether it was the wages they earned, the return they received for their crops, or the prices they paid for goods, African Americans felt the sting of their imposed inferiority.

17-4a Violence Against African Americans

The abolition of slavery altered the legal status of African Americans, but it did not markedly improve their economic opportunities. In 1880, the South was home to the vast majority of African Americans, and 90 percent of them depended for a living on farming or personal and domestic service—the same occupations they had held as slaves. Discrimination was rampant. Some communities considered themselves "sundown towns," where only whites were allowed on the streets at night. The New South, moreover, proved to be as violent as the Old South. Between 1889 and 1909, more than seventeen hundred African Americans were lynched in the South. About a quarter of **lynching** victims were accused of assault—rarely proved—on a white woman. Most of those lynched, however, had simply said something or acted in a way that made insecure whites feel disrespected, or they had succeeded in business or taken a job that made whites feel inferior.

African Americans did not suffer such violence silently. Their most notable activist at this time was **Ida B. Wells**, a Memphis, Tennessee, schoolteacher. In 1884 Wells was forcibly removed from a railroad car when she refused to surrender her seat to a white man. The incident sparked her career as a tireless spokesperson against white supremacy and violence. In 1889 Wells became partner of a Memphis newspaper, the *Free Speech and Headlight*, in which she published attacks against injustice. When three black Memphis grocers were lynched in 1892 after defending themselves against whites who had attacked them, Wells wrote an editorial urging local blacks to migrate to the West. She subsequently toured England and Europe, giving speeches and writing articles drumming up opposition to lynching and discrimination. Unable to return to hostile Memphis, she moved to Chicago, where she became a powerful advocate for racial justice.

lynching Vigilante hanging of those accused of crimes; used primarily against African Americans.

Ida B. Wells African American journalist and activist who mounted a national antilynching campaign.

17-4b Disfranchisement

In northern communities, whites sometimes made it uncomfortable for people of color to vote and hold office, but it was mainly in the South that white leaders instituted official measures of political discrimination. Despite threats and intimidation against them in the wake of Reconstruction's demise, blacks still formed the backbone of the southern Republican Party and won numerous elective positions. In North Carolina, for example, eleven African Americans served in the state senate and forty-three in the house between 1877 and 1890. Situations like these were unacceptable to many whites, and racist politicians reacted by depriving blacks of their right to vote. Beginning with Florida and Tennessee in 1889 and eventually in every southern state, governments levied taxes of $1 to $2 on all citizens wishing to vote. These poll taxes proved prohibitive to most blacks, who were so poor and deeply in debt that they rarely had cash for any purpose. Other schemes disfranchised African Americans who could not read.

Disfranchisement was also accomplished in other devious ways. The Supreme Court determined in *U.S. v. Reese* (1876) that Congress had no control over local and state elections other than the explicit provisions of the Fifteenth Amendment, which prohibits states from denying the vote "on account of race, color, or previous condition of servitude."

◀ Lynching could mean other than simple hanging. In 1893, a mob estimated at 10,000 gathered in Paris, Texas, to watch the torture and killing of an African American man believed to have assaulted and murdered a four-year-old white girl. This photo was taken just as Henry Smith, the alleged assailant, was tortured fifty times by red-hot iron brands, then doused with kerosene and set on fire. After the gruesome event, the vengeful crowd burned down the scaffold.

Library of Congress Prints and Photographs Division, LC-USZ62-68958

State legislators found ways to exclude black voters without mentioning race, color, or servitude. For instance, an 1890 state constitutional convention established the "Mississippi Plan," requiring prospective voters to pay a poll tax eight months before each election, present the tax receipt at election time, and prove that they could read and interpret the state constitution. South Carolina, Virginia, and Texas established similar provisions. Registration officials applied stiffer standards to blacks than to whites, even declaring black college graduates ineligible on grounds of illiteracy. In 1898 Louisiana enacted the first "grandfather clause," which established literacy and property qualifications for voting but exempted sons and grandsons of those eligible to vote before 1867—a year in which no blacks could vote in Louisiana. Other southern states initiated similar measures.

Such restrictions proved effective. In South Carolina, for example, 70 percent of eligible blacks voted in the 1880 election; by 1896, the rate dropped to 11 percent. By the 1900s, African Americans had effectively lost political rights in the South. More importantly, because voting is often considered a common right of citizenship, disfranchisement stripped African American men of their social standing as U.S. citizens. Disfranchisement also affected poor whites, few of whom could meet poll tax, property, and literacy requirements. Consequently, the total number of eligible voters in Mississippi shrank from 257,000 in 1876 to 77,000 in 1892.

17-4c Legal Segregation

Discrimination also stiffened in areas beyond voting, as existing customs of racial separation expanded. In all regions of the country, segregation by custom was common, as whites in power sought to keep racial minorities isolated by refusing them service and access. But in a series of cases during the 1870s, the Supreme Court opened the door to laws that strengthened racial discrimination by ruling that the Fourteenth Amendment protected citizens' rights only against infringement by state governments, not over what individuals, private businesses, or local governments might do. These rulings climaxed in 1883 when, in the *Civil Rights* cases, the Court struck down the 1875 Civil Rights Act, which prohibited segregation in facilities such as streetcars, theaters, and parks. Again, the Court declared that the federal government could not regulate private behavior in matters of race relations. Thus railroads, such as the Chesapeake & Ohio Railroad, which had forced Ida B. Wells out of her seat, could legally maintain discriminatory policies.

The Supreme Court also upheld legal segregation on a "separate but equal" basis in the case of **Plessy v. Ferguson** (1896). This case began in 1892 when a New Orleans organization of African Americans chose Homer Plessy, a fair-skinned, French-speaking Creole who was only one-eighth black (but still considered a "Negro" by Louisiana law), as a volunteer to violate a state law requiring "equal but separate accommodations" by sitting in a whites-only railroad car. As expected, Plessy was arrested. His lawyer appealed the conviction on grounds that the law violated Plessy's right to "life,

liberty," and property" under the Fourteenth Amendment, and the case reached the U.S. Supreme Court in 1896. The Court disappointed Plessy's supporters by affirming that a state law providing for separate facilities for the races was reasonable because it preserved "public peace and good order"—police power operating to the disadvantage of one group. Writing for the Court, Associate Justice Billings Brown asserted that legislation could not alter prejudice. "If the two races are to meet upon terms of social equality," he wrote, "it must be the result of . . . a voluntary consent of individuals." Thus, believed the Court, a law separating the races did not necessarily "destroy the legal equality of the races." Although the ruling did not specify the phrase "separate but equal," it legalized separate facilities for black and white people. In 1899 the Court applied the separate but equal doctrine to schools in *Cummins v. County Board of Education*, permitting school segregation until *Brown v. Board of Education* overturned the decision in 1954.

Segregation laws—known as Jim Crow laws—multiplied throughout the South, confronting African Americans with daily reminders of inferior status. State and local statutes, most of which were passed in the 1890s, restricted blacks to the rear of streetcars, to separate public drinking fountains and toilets, and to separate sections of hospitals and cemeteries. A Birmingham, Alabama, ordinance required that the races be "distinctly separated . . . by well defined physical barriers" in "any room, hall, theatre, picture house, auditorium, yard, court, ballpark, or other indoor or outdoor place." Mobile, Alabama, passed a curfew requiring blacks to be off the streets by 10 p.m., and Atlanta mandated separate Bibles for the swearing in of black witnesses in court. Jim Crow laws thus were products of active governments, but their goal was to restrict rather than expand liberty.

17-4d African American Activism

African American women and men challenged injustice in several ways. Some organized boycotts of segregated streetcars and discriminatory businesses; others promoted "Negro enterprise." In 1898, for example, Atlanta University professor John Hope called on blacks to become their own employers and supported formation of Negro Business Men's Leagues. A number of blacks used higher education as a means of elevating their status. In all-black teachers' colleges, young men and women sought to expand opportunities for themselves and all African Americans. Education could have presented a way to foster interracial cooperation. But the white supremacy that Jim Crow laws reflected taught southern blacks that they would have to negotiate in a biracial, rather than an interracial, society.

While disfranchisement diminished the public lives of African American men, who in contrast to women had previously been able to vote, African American women used traditional domestic roles as mothers, educators, and moral guardians to uplift the race and seek

Plessy v. Ferguson Supreme Court ruling validating legal segregation; legalized separate facilities for blacks and whites as long as they were equal.

Courtesy of Heritage Hall, Livingstone College, Salisbury, North Carolina

▲ Livingstone College in North Carolina was one of several institutions of higher learning established by and for African Americans in the late nineteenth century. With a curriculum that emphasized training for educational and religious work in the South and in Africa, these colleges were coeducational, operating on the belief that both men and women could have public roles.

better services for black communities. Their efforts signified political activity that was more subtle than voting—though they also did fight for the vote. They successfully lobbied southern governments for cleaner city streets, better public health, expanded charity services, and vocational education. In these efforts, black women found ways to join with white women in campaigns to negotiate with the white male power structure to achieve their goals. In many instances, however, white women sympathized with white men in support of racial exclusion.

17-4e Women's Suffrage

Though some women acquiesced to their inferior status, others challenged male power structures by seeking the right to vote. Some, such as Frances Willard, chose indirect tactics. Willard believed that religious faith would empower women, and she advocated what she called "home politics," a combination of women's traditional roles with an urge to improve society. From 1879 until her death in 1898, Willard served as president of the Woman's Christian Temperance Union (WCTU), the nation's largest female organization. She traveled the country making speeches and encouraged women who joined the WCTU to sign a pledge to abstain from alcohol as a first step toward protecting home and family from the evils of drink. But Willard also believed the WCTU could best do the Lord's work of improving society if women could vote. Thus, at its 1884 convention, the WCTU passed a resolution deploring the "disenfranchisement of 12 million people who are citizens." The 12 million, however, did not

include people of color. Willard confined black WCTU members to segregated branches and accused African Americans, who she said "multiply like the locusts of Egypt," of causing the defeat of temperance laws in the South. Ida Wells, for her part, criticized Willard for not speaking out against lynching and for making racial statements that led to white violence.

The direct crusade for suffrage was conducted by two organizations, the National Woman Suffrage Association (NWSA) and the American Woman Suffrage Association (AWSA). The NWSA, led by Elizabeth Cady Stanton and Susan B. Anthony, advocated women's rights in courts and workplaces as well as at the ballot box. The two women, both veterans of the women's rights movement of the 1840s, did not always agree. Anthony was less radical, believing that the NWSA should accommodate moderate suffragists. Stanton disdained religiosity and supported birth control, liberalized divorce laws, and property rights for women. She once wrote, "I would rather live under a government of man alone with religious liberty than under a mixed government without it." Nevertheless, Anthony and Stanton remained friends and worked tirelessly on behalf of their cause.

The AWSA, led by former abolitionist Lucy Stone, focused more narrowly on suffrage. Consisting of female and male moderate advocates of free suffrage, the AWSA worked especially at the state level. Personality conflicts, more than ideology, separated the NWSA and AWSA. But in the late 1880s, Stone proposed that the two groups overcome their differences, and they merged in 1890 to form the National American Woman Suffrage Association, with Stanton as its first president.

Congress failed to heed appeals for women's suffrage. Anthony's argument for a constitutional amendment giving women the vote received little support. On the few occasions when the Senate discussed a bill to create the amendment, senators voted it down, claiming that suffrage would interfere with women's family obligations. Moreover, the women's suffrage campaign was tainted by racial intolerance. Many movement leaders espoused the superiority of whites and accommodated racial prejudices of both the North and South in order to retain support from organization members. AWSA and NWSA membership was all white and mostly middle class. African Americans who joined the WCTU did

so within a separate Department of Colored Temperance. Also, leaders such as Anthony and Stanton resented that the Fifteenth Amendment enfranchised black men but not women. Such suffragists believed that "educated" white women should vote and that "illiterate" blacks, both men and women, should not have such a privilege.

Women did win partial victories. Between 1870 and 1910, eleven states, mostly in the West, gave women limited voting rights. By 1890 nineteen states allowed women to vote on school issues, and three granted suffrage on tax and bond issues. The right to vote in national elections awaited a later generation, but the efforts of leaders such as Wells, Anthony, and Stone proved that women did not have to vote to be politically active. And although their campaigns succeeded only slightly, they helped train a corps of female leaders in political organizing and public speaking.

▲ Frances Willard, shown here, became the second and best-known president of the national Woman's Christian Temperance Union (WCTU), founded in 1874. Beyond promoting abstinence from drinking alcohol, Willard and the WCTU were involved in other reforms, including women's suffrage. In 1893, Willard took her crusade worldwide and became the first president of the International Council of Women.

Library of Congress, Prints & Photographs Division, Reproduction number LC-USZ61-790 (b&w film copy neg.)

17-5 Agrarian Unrest and Populism

▶ How did farmers and rural populations respond to economic hardships and inequality?

▶ How did agrarian activism become politicized during the Gilded Age?

▶ How successful were farmers and rural populations in addressing economic hardships and inequality?

While ending voting exclusion and racial segregation had no major successes, economic inequality sparked a mass movement that would shake American society. Despite rapid industrialization and urbanization in the Gilded Age, the United States remained an agrarian nation. In 1890, 64 percent of the total population lived in rural areas, where they suffered economic hardship and were primed for protest. The expression of farmers' discontent—a mixture of strident rhetoric, nostalgic dreams, and hardheaded egalitarianism—began in Grange organizations in the early 1870s. It accelerated when Farmers' Alliances formed in the late 1870s and spread across the South and Great Plains in the 1880s. The Alliance movement flourished chiefly in areas where debt, weather, and insects demoralized struggling farmers. Once under way, the agrarian rebellion inspired visions of a cooperative, democratic society.

17-5a Hardship in the Midwest and West

In the Midwest, as growers cultivated more land, as mechanization boosted productivity, and as foreign competition increased, supplies of agricultural products exceeded national and worldwide demand. Consequently, prices for staple crops dropped steadily. A bushel of wheat selling for $1.45 in 1866 brought only 80 cents in the mid-1880s and 49 cents by the mid-1890s. Meanwhile, transportation and storage fees remained high. Expenses for seed, fertilizer, manufactured goods, taxes, and mortgage interest trapped many farm families in stressful and sometimes desperate

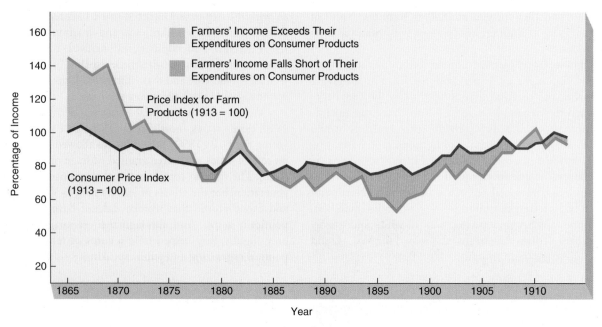

Figure 17.1 **Consumer Prices and Farm Product Prices, 1865–1913**

Until the late 1870s, in spite of falling farm prices, farmers were able to receive more income from their crops than they spent on consumer goods. But beginning in the mid-1880s, consumer prices leveled off and then rose, while prices for farm products continued to drop. As a result, farmers found it increasingly difficult to afford consumer goods, a problem that plagued them well into the twentieth century.

circumstances. In order to buy necessities and pay bills, farmers had to produce more. But the spiral wound ever more tightly: the more farmers produced, the lower crop prices dropped (see Figure 17.1).

The West suffered from special hardships. In Colorado, absentee capitalists seized control of access to transportation and water, and concentration of technology in the hands of large mining companies pushed out small firms. Charges of monopolistic behavior by railroads echoed among farmers, miners, and ranchers in Wyoming and Montana. In California, Washington, and Oregon, wheat and fruit growers found that railroads' control of transportation and storage rates blocked opportunities for higher incomes.

17-5b Grange Movement

Even before they felt the full impact of these developments, farmers began to organize. With aid from Oliver H. Kelley, a Bureau of Agriculture employee who wanted to elevate the status of farming, farmers in almost every state during the 1860s and 1870s founded chapters of the National Grange of the Patrons of Husbandry, or the Grange, dedicated to improving economic and social conditions. By 1875 the Grange had twenty thousand branches and a million members. Like voluntary organizations throughout the country, Granges wrote constitutions, elected officers, and required

Greenback Labor Party Advocated expanding the money supply through the government printing of money not backed by gold.

membership oaths. Strongest in the Midwest and South, Granges sponsored meetings and educational events to relieve the loneliness of rural life. Family oriented, Granges welcomed women's participation.

As membership flourished, Granges turned to economic and political action. Many members joined the **Greenback Labor Party**, formed in 1876 to advocate expanding the money supply by keeping "greenbacks"—paper money created by the government during the Civil War to help pay costs—in circulation. Grange branches formed cooperative associations to buy supplies and to market crops and livestock. In a few instances, Grangers ran farm implement factories and insurance companies. Most enterprises failed, however, because farmers lacked capital for large-scale buying and because competition from large manufacturers and dealers undercut them. For example, the mail-order firm Montgomery Ward could furnish rural customers with cheaper products more conveniently than could Granges.

Granges achieved some political successes in the late 1870s. They convinced states to establish agricultural colleges, elected sympathetic legislators, and pressed state legislatures for laws to regulate transportation and storage rates. But these ventures faltered when the U.S. Supreme Court denied states the power to regulate railroad rates (*Wabash* case, 1886). Granges disavowed party politics and thus would not challenge the power of business interests within the two major parties. Their attempts at economic and political influence declined, and today Granges exist mainly as social and service organizations.

▲ The Grange aimed not only to aid farmers but also to oppose oppressive policies against farmers by railroads. This cartoon, titled "Grange Awakening the Sleepers," depicts a farmer warning people complacently sleeping under railroad tracks that a train, with cars labeled "Consolidation Train, extortion, and bribery," is about to run them over.

17-5c The White Hats

In the Southwest, migration of English-speaking ranchers into pastureland used communally by Mexican farmers sparked resistance that sometimes turned violent. In the late 1880s, a group calling itself *Las Gorras Blancas*, or White Hats, struggled to control grazing areas that their ancestors had once held. In protest against Anglo intrusions, they burned buildings, destroyed fences, and threatened the town of Las Vegas in New Mexico territory. Sounding like the Grangers and Knights of Labor before them and the Populists after them, the White Hats proclaimed in 1889, "Our purpose is to protect the rights and interest of the people in general and especially those of the helpless classes." Their cause, however, could not halt Anglos from legally buying and using public land, and by 1900 many Mexicans had given up farm owning to work as agricultural laborers or migrate to cities.

17-5d Farmers' Alliances

By 1890, rural activism shifted to the Farmers' Alliances, two networks of organizations—one in the Great Plains, one in the South—that constituted a new mass movement. (The West had small Alliance groups, but they tended to be more closely linked to labor radicals and antimonopoly organizations.) The first Alliances arose in Texas, where hard-pressed farmers rallied against crop liens, merchants, and railroads in particular, and against money power in general. Using traveling

lecturers to recruit members, Alliance leaders expanded the movement into other southern states. By 1889 the southern Alliance boasted 2 million members, and a separate Colored Farmers' National Alliance claimed 1 million black members. A similar movement arose in the Plains, which in the late 1880s organized 2 million members in Kansas, Nebraska, and the Dakotas. Like Granges, Farmers' Alliances tried to foster community spirit. Women participated actively in Alliance activities, and members of the Knights of Labor were invited to join the "struggle against monopolistic oppression."

The Alliance remedy for economic woes combined a culture of generosity with government assistance. To bypass corporate power and control markets, Alliances, like the Grange, proposed that farmers form cooperatives, in which as a unified group they would sell crops and livestock, and buy supplies and manufactured goods. By pooling resources, Alliances reasoned, farmers could exert more economic pressure than they could individually, and they could share the benefits of their hard work rather than compete against each other.

To relieve the most serious rural problem, shortages of cash and credit, Alliances proposed a system of government aid called a *subtreasury*. The plan had two parts. One called for the federal government to construct warehouses where farmers could store nonperishable crops while awaiting higher market prices; during the wait, the government would loan farmers U.S. Treasury notes amounting to 80 percent of the market price that the stored crops would bring. Farmers could use these notes to pay debts and make purchases. Once the stored crops were sold, farmers would repay the loans plus small interest and storage fees. This provision would enable farmers to avoid the exploitative crop lien system.

Under the subtreasury plan's second part, the government would provide low-interest loans to farmers who wanted to buy land. These loans, along with the treasury notes loaned to farmers who temporarily stored crops in government warehouses, would inject cash into the economy and encourage the kind of inflation that advocates hoped would raise crop prices without raising other prices. If the government subsidized business through tariffs and land grants, reasoned Alliance members, it should help farmers earn a decent living, too.

17-5e Problems in Achieving Alliance Unity

If Farmers' Alliances had been able to unite politically, they could have wielded formidable power; but racial and sectional differences, plus personality clashes, thwarted early attempts at merging. Racial barriers weakened Alliance voter strength because southern white Democrats had succeeded in creating restrictions that prevented African Americans from voting. In addition, raw racism blocked acceptance of blacks by white Alliances. Some southern leaders, such as Georgia's Senator Tom Watson, tried to unite black and white farmers, realizing that both races suffered from similar burdens. But white farmers could not drop their prejudices. Many considered African Americans an inferior people and took comfort in the belief that there always would be people worse off than they were. At an 1889 meeting in St. Louis, white southerners rejected uniting with northern Alliances because such a merger would have ended their whites-only membership rules.

Differences on regional issues also prevented unity. Northern Alliances declined to unite with southerners, fearing domination by more politically experienced southern leaders. Northern farmers also favored protective tariffs to keep out foreign grain, whereas white southerners wanted low tariffs to curb costs of imported manufactured goods. Northern and southern Alliances agreed on some issues, however; both favored government regulation of railroads, equitable taxation, currency reform, ending election fraud that perpetuated special interests in office, and prohibition of landownership by foreign investors.

17-5f Rise of Populism

In spite of their divisions, growing membership and rising confidence drew Alliances into politics. By 1890, farmers had elected several officeholders sympathetic to their cause, especially in the South, where Alliance allies won four governorships, eight state legislatures, forty-four seats in the House of Representatives, and three in the Senate. In the Midwest, Alliance candidates running on third-party tickets, such as the Greenback Party, won victories in Kansas, Nebraska, and the Dakotas. During the summer of 1890, the Kansas Alliance held a "convention of the people" and nominated candidates who swept the state's fall elections. Formation of this People's, or Populist, Party gave a title to Alliance political activism. (Populism, derived from *populus*, the Latin word for "people," is the political doctrine that asserts the rights and powers of common people in their struggle against privileged elites.) Election successes in 1890 energized efforts to unite Alliance groups into a single **Populist Party**. By 1892, southern Alliance members decided to leave the Democratic Party and join northern counterparts in summoning a People's Party convention to draft a platform and nominate a presidential candidate. The gathering met in Omaha, Nebraska, on July 4.

The new party's platform was a sweeping reform document, reflecting goals of moral regeneration, political democracy, and antimonopolism. Its preamble charged that the nation had been "brought to the verge of moral, political, and material ruin. Corruption dominates the ballot box, the legislatures, the Congress, and . . . even the [courts]." Charging that inequality (between white classes) threatened to splinter society, the platform declared, "The fruits of the toil of millions are boldly stolen to build up colossal fortunes for a few," and that "wealth belongs to him that creates it." The document addressed three central sources of rural unrest: transportation, land, and money. Frustrated with weak state and federal regulation, Populists demanded government ownership of railroad and telegraph lines. They urged the federal government to reclaim all land owned for speculative purposes by railroads and foreigners. The monetary plank called on the government to expand the currency by making more money available for farm loans and by restoring unlimited coinage of silver. Other planks advocated a graduated income tax, direct election of U.S. senators, and a shorter workday. As its presidential candidate, the party nominated James B. Weaver of Iowa, a former Union general and supporter of an expanded money supply, who already had run for the presidency as the Greenback Party's candidate in 1880.

17-5g Populist Spokespeople

The Populist campaign featured dynamic personalities and rousing rhetoric. The Kansas plains rumbled with speeches by Mary Lease, who could allegedly "set a crowd hooting and harrahing at her will," and by "Sockless Jerry" Simpson, an unschooled but canny rural reformer who got his nickname after he ridiculed silk-stockinged wealthy people, causing a reporter to muse that Simpson probably never wore stockings. The South produced equally dynamic leaders, such as Georgia's Tom Watson and North Carolina's Leonidas Polk. Colorado's governor, Davis "Bloody Bridles" Waite, attacked mine owners, and Texas governor James Hogg battled railroads and other corporations. (Governor Hogg also saddled his daughter with the awkward name of Ima.) Minnesota's Ignatius Donnelly, pseudoscientist and writer of apocalyptic novels, became chief visionary of the northern plains and penned the Omaha platform's thunderous language. The campaign also attracted opportunists, such as the one-eyed, sharp-tongued South Carolina senator "Pitchfork Ben" Tillman, who exploited agrarian resentments for their own political ends.

In the 1892 presidential election, Populist candidate James Weaver garnered 8 percent of the popular vote, majorities in four states, and twenty-two electoral votes. Not since 1856 had a third party done so well in its first national effort. Nevertheless, the party had little national impact. The election had been successful for Populists only in the West. The vote-rich Northeast ignored Weaver, and Alabama was the only southern state that gave Populists as much as one-third of its votes.

Still, Populism gave rural dwellers faith in a future of cooperation and democracy. Although Populists were flawed egalitarians—they mistrusted blacks and foreigners—they sought change in order to fulfill their version of American ideals. Amid hardship and desperation, millions of people came to believe that a cooperative democracy in which government would ensure equal opportunity could overcome corporate power. A banner draped above the stage at the Omaha convention captured the movement's spirit: "We do not ask for sympathy or pity. We ask for justice." With this goal, Populists looked ahead to the presidential election of 1896 with hope.

Populist Party "People's Party" that raised an agrarian-based, third-party challenge to the Republicans and Democrats and advocated for the rights of the common man.

Russian Populism

Before American Populism arose late in the 1890s, a different form of populism took shape in another largely rural country: Russia. Whereas American Populism emerged from the Alliance organizations of farmers, Russian populism was the creation of intellectuals who wanted to educate peasants to agitate for social and economic freedom.

Propelled by reforms imposed by Czar Alexander II, Russian society had begun to modernize in the mid-nineteenth century. Government administration and the judiciary were reorganized, town governments were given control of taxation, and education became more widespread. Perhaps most importantly, in 1861 Alexander signed an Edict of Emancipation, freeing Russian serfs (slaves attached to specific lands) and granting them compensation to buy land from their landlords. The reforms were slow to take hold, however, prompting some young, educated Russians, called nihilists because they opposed the czar and feudalism, to press for more radical reforms, including socialism. The reformers became known as *narodniki*, or populists, from *narod*, the Russian term for "peasant."

Narodniki envisioned a society of self-governing village communes, somewhat like the cooperatives proposed by American Farmers' Alliances, and in the 1870s they visited Russian villages and attempted to educate peasants to their ideas. One of their leaders, Peter Lavrov, believed that intellectuals needed to bridge the gap between themselves and ordinary people, and help the masses improve their lives. This message, however, included a more radical tone than the American Populists' campaign for democracy, because Russian populists believed that only a revolutionary uprising against the czar could realize their goals. When Alexander instituted repressive policies against the narodniki in the late 1870s, many of them turned to terrorism, a move that resulted in the assassination of Alexander II in 1881.

Russian populism failed in different ways than American Populism. Russian peasants were not receptive to intervention from educated young people, and many peasants, still tied to tradition, could not abandon loyalty to the czar. Arrests and imprisonments after Alexander's assassination discouraged populists' efforts, and the movement declined. Nevertheless, just as many aims of American Populists were adopted by other reformers after the turn of the century, the ideas of Russian populism became the cornerstone of the Russian Revolution of 1917 and of Soviet social and political ideology that followed.

CRITICAL THINKING

- American populism did not turn toward socialism the way that Russian populism did. What factors explain this significant difference despite the many similarities between American and Russian populism?

◀ Russian peasants, like American tenant farmers and owners of small landholdings, suffered from poverty and pressures of the expanded market economy. The plight of struggling Russian farm families stirred up empathy from young populist intellectuals, who adopted radical solutions that did not capture as much political fervor among farmers as American Populism did.

Bettmann/Getty Images

Kean Collection/Getty Images

▲ The son of an Irish immigrant, Ignatius Donnelly was a Republican politician from Minnesota who wrote the rousing preamble to the Populist Party's platform presented at the party's historic convention in Omaha in 1892. Outside of politics, Donnelly published works asserting that there once was a continent named Atlantis that had been destroyed before the Great Flood of the Bible, and he argued that Shakespeare's plays had actually been written by Francis Bacon.

17-6 The Depression and Protests of the 1890s

▶ What were the characteristics of the economic depression of the 1890s?

▶ How did the federal government respond to the economic depression of the 1890s?

▶ How was the country's economic and industrial system challenged in the 1890s?

Before that election took place, economic crisis engulfed the nation. In 1893, shortly before Grover Cleveland's second presidency began, the Philadelphia & Reading Railroad, once a thriving and profitable line, went bankrupt. Like other railroads, it had borrowed heavily to lay track and build stations and bridges. But overexpansion cut into profits, and the company was unable to pay its debts. The same problem beset manufacturers. For example, output at McCormick farm machinery factories was nine times greater in 1893 than in 1879, but revenues only tripled. To compensate, the company bought more equipment and squeezed more work out of fewer laborers. This strategy, however, increased debt and unemployment. Jobless workers found themselves in the same plight as employers: they could not pay their bills. Banks

suffered, too, when their customers defaulted. The failure of the National Cordage Company in May 1893 sparked a chain reaction of business and bank closings. By year's end, five hundred banks and sixteen hundred businesses had failed. An adviser warned President Cleveland, "We are on the eve of a very dark night." He was right. Between 1893 and 1897, the nation suffered a staggering economic depression.

Personal hardship followed business collapse; nearly 20 percent of the labor force was jobless for a significant time during the depression. Falling demand caused prices to drop between 1892 and 1895, but layoffs and wage cuts more than offset declining living costs. Many people could not afford basic necessities. The New York police estimated that twenty thousand homeless and jobless people roamed the city's streets. Surveying the impact on Boston, Henry Adams wrote, "Men died like flies under the strain, and Boston grew suddenly old, haggard, and thin."

17-6a Continuing Currency Problems

As the depression deepened, so did the currency dilemma. The Sherman Silver Purchase Act of 1890 had committed the government to using treasury notes (silver certificates) to buy 4.5 million ounces of silver each month. Recipients could redeem these certificates for gold, at the ratio of one ounce of gold for every sixteen ounces of silver. But a western mining boom made silver more plentiful, causing its market value relative to gold to fall and prompting holders of silver certificates and greenback currency issued during the Civil War to cash in their notes in exchange for more valuable gold. As a result, the nation's gold reserves dwindled, falling below $100 million in early 1893.

The $100 million level had psychological importance. If investors believed that the country's gold reserves were disappearing, they would lose confidence in America's economic stability and refrain from investing. British capitalists, for example, owned $4 billion in American stocks and bonds. If dollars were to depreciate because there was too little gold to back them up, the British would stop investing in American economic growth. In fact, the lower the gold reserve dropped, the more people rushed to redeem their money—to get gold before it disappeared. Panic spread, causing more bankruptcies and unemployment.

Vowing to protect the gold reserves, President Cleveland called a special session of Congress to repeal the Sherman Silver Purchase Act. Repeal passed in late 1893, but the run on gold continued. In early 1895, reserves fell to $41 million. In desperation, Cleveland accepted an offer from a banking syndicate led by financier J. P. Morgan to sell the government 3.5 million ounces of gold in return for $65 million worth of federal bonds. When the bankers resold the bonds to the public, they made a $2 million profit. Cleveland claimed he had saved the reserves, but discontented farmers, workers, silver miners, and even some of Cleveland's Democratic allies saw only humiliation in the president's deal with big businessmen. "When Judas betrayed Christ," charged Senator Tillman, "his heart was not blacker than this scoundrel, Cleveland, in betraying the [Democratic Party]."

Few people knew what the president was privately enduring. At about the time Cleveland called Congress into special session, doctors discovered a tumor on his palate that required immediate removal. Fearful that publicity of his illness would hasten the run on gold, and intent on preventing Vice President Adlai E. Stevenson, a silver supporter, from gaining influence, Cleveland kept his condition a secret. He announced that he was going sailing, and doctors removed his cancer while the yacht floated outside New York City. Outfitted with a rubber jaw, Cleveland resumed a full schedule five days later, hiding terrible pain to dispel rumors that he was seriously ill. He eventually recovered, but those who knew of his surgery believed it had sapped his vitality.

The deal between Cleveland and Morgan did not end the depression. After improving slightly in 1895, the economy plunged again. Farm income, declining since 1887, slid further; factories closed; banks that remained open restricted withdrawals. The tight money supply depressed housing construction, drying up jobs and discouraging immigration. Cities encouraged citizens to cultivate "potato patches" on vacant land to help alleviate food shortages. Each night, urban police stations filled up with homeless persons with no place to stay.

17-6b Consequences of Depression

The depression ultimately ran its course. In the late 1890s, gold discoveries in Alaska, good harvests, and industrial revival brought relief. But the downturn hastened the crumbling of the old economic system and emergence of a new one. The American economy had expanded well beyond local and sectional bases; the fate of a large business in one part of the country now had repercussions elsewhere. When farmers fell into debt and lost purchasing power, their depressed condition in turn weakened railroads, farm implement manufacturers, and banks. Moreover, the trend toward corporate consolidation that characterized the new business system had tempted many companies to expand too rapidly. When the bubble burst in 1893, their reckless debts dragged them down, and they pulled other industries with them.

At the same time, a new global marketplace was emerging, forcing American farmers to contend not only with discriminatory transportation rates and falling crop prices at home, but also to compete with Canadian and Russian wheat growers, Argentine cattle ranchers, Indian and Egyptian cotton manufacturers, and Australian wool producers. More than ever before, the condition of one country's economy affected the economies of other countries. In addition, the glutted domestic market persuaded American businessmen to seek new markets abroad (see Chapter 19).

17-6c Depression-Era Protests

The depression exposed fundamental tensions in the industrial system. Technological and organizational changes had been widening the gap between employees and employers for half a century, prompting discord. An era of labor protest began with the railroad strikes of 1877. The vehemence of those strikes, and the support they drew from working-class people, raised fears that the United States would experience a popular uprising like the one in France in 1871, which had briefly overturned the government and introduced communist principles. The Haymarket riot of 1886, the prolonged strike at the Carnegie Homestead Steel plant in 1892, and the extensive labor violence among western miners heightened anxieties (see "Mechanization and the Changing Status of Labor," Section 16-3). To many middle- and upper-class people, it seemed as if worker protests portended an economic and political explosion. In 1894, the year the economy plunged into depression, there were more than thirteen hundred strikes and countless riots. Contrary to accusations of business leaders, few protesters were immigrant anarchists or communists come to sabotage American democracy. Rather, the disaffected included thousands of patriotic Americans who believed that in a democracy, their voices should be heard.

17-6d Socialists

Small numbers of socialists did participate in these confrontations. Some socialists believed that workers should control factories and businesses; others supported government ownership. All socialists, however, opposed capitalism. Their ideas derived from the writings of Karl Marx (1818–1883), the German philosopher and father of communism, who contended that whoever controls the means of production determines how well people live. Marx wrote that industrial capitalism generates profits by paying workers less than the value of their labor and that mechanization and mass production alienate workers from their labor. Thus, Marx contended, capitalists and laborers engage in an inescapable conflict over how much workers should benefit from their efforts. According to Marx, only by abolishing the return on capital—profits—could labor receive its true value, an outcome possible only if workers owned the means of production. Marx predicted that workers worldwide would become so discontented that they would revolt and seize factories, farms, banks, and transportation lines. This revolution would establish a socialist order of justice and equality. Marx's vision appealed to some workers, including many who did not consider themselves socialists, because it promised independence and security. It appealed to some intellectuals as well, because it promised to end class conflict and crass materialism.

In America, socialists disagreed over how to achieve Marx's vision. Much of the movement was influenced by immigrants, first from Germany but also by Russian Jews, Italians, Hungarians, and Poles. Although American socialism splintered into small groups, one of its main factions was the Socialist Labor Party, led by Daniel DeLeon, a fiery editor and lawyer born in Curaçao and educated in Germany, who criticized American labor organizations like the AFL as too conservative. Yet, as he and other socialists argued points of doctrine, they ignored everyday needs and thus failed to attract the mass of laborers. Nor could they rebut clergy and business leaders who celebrated opportunity, self-improvement, social mobility, and consumerism. Most workers hoped that they or their children would benefit through education and acquisition of property or by becoming their own boss; they thus sought individual advancement rather than the betterment of all.

17-6e Eugene V. Debs

As the nineteenth century closed, a new leader invigorated American socialism. Indiana-born Eugene V. Debs headed the American Railway Union, which had carried out the 1894 strike against the Pullman Company. Jailed for defying an injunction against striking rail workers, Debs read Marx's works in prison. Once released, he flirted briefly with Populism, then became leading spokesman for American socialism, combining visionary Marxism with Populist antimonopolism. Debs captivated audiences with passionate eloquence and indignant attacks on the free-enterprise system. "Many of you think you are competing," he would lecture. "Against whom? Against Rockefeller? About as I would if I had a wheelbarrow and competed with the Santa Fe [railroad] from here to Kansas City." By 1900 the group soon to be called the Socialist Party of America was uniting around Debs. It would make its presence felt more forcefully in the new century.

17-6f Coxey's Army

In 1894, not Debs but rather a quiet businessman named Jacob Coxey, a Civil War veteran and small business owner from Massillon, Ohio, captured public attention with his act of protest. Coxey had a vision. He was convinced that, to aid debtors, the federal government should issue $500 million of "legal tender" paper money and make low-interest loans to local governments, which would in turn use the funds to pay unemployed men to build roads and other public works. He planned to publicize his scheme by leading a march from Massillon to Washington, D.C., gathering a "petition in boots" of unemployed workers along the way. To emphasize his sincerity, Coxey named his newborn son Legal Tender and proposed that his teenage daughter lead the procession on a white horse.

Coxey's Army, about two hundred strong, left in March 1894. Hiking across Ohio into Pennsylvania, the marchers received food and housing in depressed industrial towns and rural villages and attracted additional recruits. Elsewhere, a dozen similar processions from places such as Seattle, San Francisco, and Los Angeles also began the trek eastward. Sore feet prompted some marchers to commandeer trains, but most marches were peaceful and law abiding.

Coxey's band, now of five hundred, including women and children, entered Washington, D.C., on April 30. The next day, the group, armed with "war clubs of peace," advanced to the Capitol. When Coxey and a few others vaulted a wall surrounding the grounds, mounted police moved in and routed the demonstrators. Coxey tried to speak from the Capitol steps, but police dragged him away. As arrests and clubbings continued, Coxey's dream of a demonstration of four hundred thousand jobless workers dissolved. Like the strikes, the first people's march on Washington yielded to police muscle.

Unlike socialists, who wished to replace the capitalist system, Coxey's troops merely wanted more jobs and better living standards. Today, in an age of union contracts, regulation of business, and government-sponsored unemployment relief, their goals do not appear radical. The brutal reactions of officials, however, reveal how threatening dissenters like Coxey and Debs seemed to defenders of the existing social order.

17-7 Silver Crusade and the Election of 1896

▸ What were the main issues during the election of 1896?

▸ What was the state of the political party system during the election of 1896?

▸ How did the election of 1896 impact the Populist Party?

Amid the tumult of social protest and economic depression, it appeared that the presidential election of 1896 would be pivotal. Debates over money and power were climaxing, Democrats and Republicans continued their battle over control of Congress and the presidency, and Populists stood at the center of a political whirlwind. The key question was whether voters would abandon old party loyalties for the Populist Party.

17-7a Free Silver

The Populist crusade against "money power" settled on the issue of silver, which many people saw as a simple solution to the nation's complex ills. To them, coinage of silver symbolized an end to special privileges for the rich and return of government to the people, because it would increase the amount of cash in circulation, reduce interest rates, and lift struggling families out of debt. Populists made free coinage of silver their political battle cry.

As the 1896 election approached, Populists had to decide how to translate their few previous electoral victories into broader success. Should they join with sympathetic factions of one of the major parties, risking a loss of identity? Or should they remain an independent third party and settle for minor wins at best? Except in mining areas of the Rocky Mountain states, where coinage of silver had strong support, Republicans were unlikely allies because their support for the gold standard and big business orientation represented what Populists opposed.

In the North and West, alliance with Democrats was more plausible. There, the Democratic Party retained vestiges of antimonopoly ideology and sympathy for a looser currency system, though "gold Democrats," such as President Cleveland and Senator David Hill of New York, held powerful

▲ Walking at the head of his informal "Commonweal Army" of protesters, Jacob Coxey marches toward Washington, D.C., in 1894. His troops, which included men on foot, on bicycles, and on horseback and his daughter riding a white horse, wanted the federal government to provide jobs to those made jobless by the depression of the 1890s.

Library of Congress Prints and Photographs Division Washington[LC-USZ62-96526]

influence. Populists assumed they shared common interests with Democratic urban workers, whom they believed suffered the same oppression that beset farmers. In the South, Alliances had supported a few Democratic candidates, but the failure of these candidates to carry out their promises once in office caused southern farmers to feel betrayed. Whichever option they chose, fusion (alliance with Democrats) or independence, Populists ensured that the election campaign of 1896 would be the most issue oriented since 1860.

17-7b Nomination of McKinley

As they prepared to nominate their presidential candidate, both major parties were divided. Republicans were guided by Ohio industrialist Marcus A. Hanna, who for a year had been maneuvering to win the nomination for Ohio's governor, William McKinley. By the time the party convened in St. Louis, Hanna had corralled enough delegates to succeed. "He had advertised McKinley," quipped Theodore Roosevelt, "as if he were a patent medicine." The Republicans' only distress occurred when they adopted a platform supporting the gold standard, rejecting a prosilver stance proposed by Colorado senator Henry M. Teller. Teller, who had been among the party's founders forty years earlier, walked out of the convention in tears, taking a small group of silver Republicans with him.

At the Democratic convention, prosilver delegates wearing silver badges and waving silver banners paraded through the Chicago Amphitheatre. Observing their tumultuous demonstrations, one delegate wrote, "For the first time I can understand the scenes of the French Revolution!" A *New York World* reporter remarked, "all the silverites need is a Moses." They found one in **William Jennings Bryan**.

17-7c William Jennings Bryan

Bryan arrived at the Democratic convention as a member of a contested Nebraska delegation. A former congressman whose support for coinage of silver had annoyed President Cleveland, Bryan found the depression's impact on midwestern farmers distressing. Shortly after the convention seated Bryan and his colleagues instead of a competing faction that supported the gold standard, Bryan joined the party's resolutions committee and helped write a platform calling for unlimited coinage of silver. When the committee presented the platform to the full convention, Bryan rose to speak on its behalf. His now-famous closing words ignited the delegates.

> Having behind us the producing masses of this nation and the world, supported by the commercial interests, the laboring interests, and the toilers everywhere, we will answer [the wealthy classes'] demand for a gold standard by saying to them: You shall not press down upon the brow of labor this crown of thorns, you shall not crucify mankind upon a cross of gold.

The speech could not have been better timed. Delegates who backed Bryan for president now began gathering support. It took five ballots to win the nomination, but the magnetic "Boy Orator" proved irresistible. In accepting the silverite goals of southerners and westerners and repudiating Cleveland's policies, the Democratic

William Jennings Bryan Orator, anti-imperialist, champion of farm interests, and three-time Democratic presidential candidate.

During the 1896 presidential campaign, Republicans depicted their candidate, William McKinley, as holding the key to prosperity for both the working man and the white-collar laborer, shown here raising their hats to the candidate. Republicans successfully made this economic theme—rather than the silver crusade of McKinley's unsuccessful opponent, William Jennings Bryan—the difference in the election's outcome.

William Jennings Bryan (1860–1925) posed for this photograph in 1896, when he first ran for president at the age of thirty-six. Bryan's emotional speeches turned agrarian unrest and the issue of free silver into a moral crusade.

Party became more attractive to discontented farmers. But, like the Republicans, it, too, alienated a minority wing. Some gold Democrats withdrew and nominated their own candidate.

Bryan's nomination presented the Populist Party meeting in St. Louis with a dilemma. Should Populists join Democrats in support of Bryan, or should they nominate their own candidate? Tom Watson, who opposed fusion with Democrats, warned, "the Democratic idea of fusion [is] that we play Jonah while they play whale." Others reasoned that supporting a separate candidate would split the anti-McKinley vote and guarantee a Republican victory. In the end, the convention compromised, first naming Watson as its vice-presidential nominee to preserve party identity (Democrats had nominated Maine shipping magnate Arthur Sewall for vice president) and then nominating Bryan for president.

The campaign, as Kansas journalist William Allen White observed, "took the form of religious frenzy . . . as the crusaders of the revolution rode home, praising the people's will as though it were God's will and cursing wealth for its iniquity." Bryan preached that "every great economic question is in reality a great moral question." Republicans countered Bryan's attacks on privilege by predicting chaos if he won. While Bryan raced around the country giving twenty speeches a day, Hanna invited thousands of people to McKinley's home in Canton, Ohio, where the candidate plied them with homilies on moderation and prosperity, promising something for everyone. In an appeal to working-class voters, Republicans stressed the new jobs that a protective tariff would create.

17-7d Election Results

The election results revealed that the political standoff had ended. McKinley, symbol of urban and corporate ascendancy, beat Bryan by 600,000 popular votes and won in the electoral college by 271 to 176 (see Map 17.1). It was the most lopsided presidential election since 1872.

Bryan had worked hard to rally the nation, but obsession with silver prevented Populists from building the urban-rural coalition that would have solidified their appeal. The silver issue diverted voters from focusing on broader reforms of cooperation and government aid that

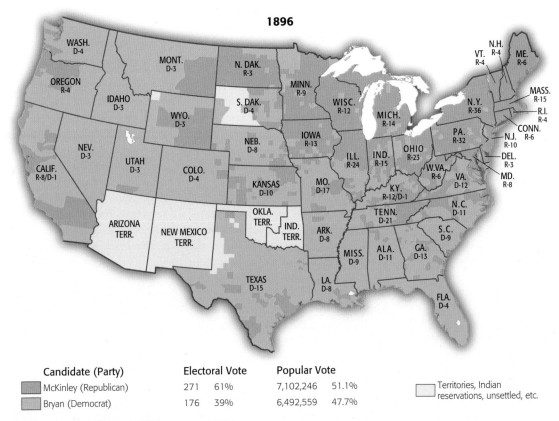

1896

Candidate (Party)	Electoral Vote		Popular Vote	
McKinley (Republican)	271	61%	7,102,246	51.1%
Bryan (Democrat)	176	39%	6,492,559	47.7%

Territories, Indian reservations, unsettled, etc.

Map 17.1 **Presidential Election, 1896**

William Jennings Bryan had strong voter support in the South and West, but the numerically superior industrial states, plus California, created majorities for William McKinley.

the Alliance movement and Omaha platform had proposed. Urban workers, who might have benefited from Populist goals, feared that silver coinage would shrink the value of their wages. Labor leaders, such as the AFL's Samuel Gompers, though partly sympathetic, would not commit themselves fully because they viewed farmers as businessmen, not workers. And socialists like Daniel DeLeon denounced Populists as "retrograde" because they, unlike socialists, believed in free enterprise. Thus the Populist crusade collapsed. Although Populists and fusion candidates won a few state and congressional elections, the Bryan-Watson ticket of the Populist Party polled only 222,600 votes nationwide.

17-7e The McKinley Presidency

As president, McKinley reinforced his support of business by signing the Gold Standard Act (1900), requiring that all paper money be backed by gold. A seasoned and personable politician, McKinley was best known for crafting protective tariffs; as a congressman, he had guided passage of record-high tariff rates in 1890. He accordingly supported the Dingley Tariff of 1897, which raised duties even higher. A believer in opening markets abroad to sustain profits

at home, McKinley encouraged imperialistic ventures in Latin America and the Pacific. Domestic tensions subsided as prosperity returned. Better times and victory in the Spanish-American War enabled him to beat Bryan again in 1900.

Summary

Though buffeted by special interests and lingering consequences of the Civil War, Gilded Age politicians succeeded in making many modest, and some major, accomplishments. Guided by well-meaning, generally competent people, much of what occurred in city halls, statehouses, the halls of Congress, and the White House prepared the nation for the twentieth century. Laws encouraging economic growth with some principles of regulation, measures expanding government agencies while reducing crass patronage, and federal intervention in trade and currency issues all evolved during the 1870s and 1880s, to the distress of Social Darwinists such as William Graham Sumner. Principles of police power clashed with those of due process, but many laws that were passed set the stage for the expanded government activism after the turn of the century.

Interpreting a Fairy Tale

The Wizard of Oz, released in 1939 and one of the most popular movies of all time, began as a work of juvenile literature penned by journalist L. Frank Baum in 1900. Originally titled *The Wonderful Wizard of Oz*, the story used memorable characters to create a fun-filled and adventurous quest.

Although children have viewed the tale and film as a fantasy, adults have been tempted to seek hidden meanings. In 1964 one scholar, Henry M. Littlefield, published an article in which he asserted that Baum really intended to write a Populist parable illustrating the conditions of overburdened farmers and laborers. The characters in *The Wonderful Wizard of Oz*, Littlefield opined, supported his theory. Dorothy symbolized the well-intentioned common person; the Scarecrow, the struggling farmer; the Tin Man, the industrial worker. Hoping for a better life, these friends, along with the Cowardly Lion (William Jennings Bryan with a loud roar but little power), followed a yellow brick road (the gold standard) that led nowhere. The Emerald City that they find is presided over by a wizard, who rules from behind a screen. A typical politician, the wizard tries to be all

things to all people, but Dorothy reveals him as a fraud. Dorothy is able to leave this muddled society and return to her simple Kansas farm family of Aunt Em and Uncle Henry by using her magical silver slippers (representing coinage of silver, though the movie made them red).

Subsequent theorists identified additional symbols, such as Oz being the abbreviation for ounces (oz.), the chief measurement of gold. The Wicked Witch of the East—who, Baum wrote, kept the little people (Munchkins) "in bondage, . . . making them slaves for her night and day"—could be seen as representing the force of industrial capitalism. Baum's story, viewed in film by most Americans, became a tool for explaining Populism to students, and by the 1970s its apparent message had strong appeal to critics of "the Establishment."

But then investigators began to take another look and offer different conclusions. In 1983 historian William R. Leach asserted that Baum's tale actually was a celebration of urban consumer culture. Its language exalted the opulence of Emerald City, which to Leach resembled the "White City" of the Chicago World's Fair of 1893, and

Dorothy's upbeat nature symbolized the optimism of the industrial era. Moreover, Baum's career supported this new interpretation. Before he was a writer, he had designed display windows and was involved in theater—activities that gave him an appreciation of modern urban life.

Rather than confusion, the real legacy of *The Wonderful Wizard of Oz* has been its ability to provoke differing interpretations. What matters is that Baum's turn-of-the-century fairy tale, the first truly American work of this sort, has bequeathed to the present so many fascinating images about the diversity and contradictions of American culture.

CRITICAL THINKING

- The legacy of *The Wonderful Wizard of Oz* lies in its ability to reveal the diversity and contradictions of American culture during the Populist era. Consider what message *The Wonderful Wizard of Oz* might have for Americans of today in light of the vast cultural and political divides within our nation revealed by the election of 2016. Based on your reading of this chapter, how do you interpret *The Wizard of Oz*?
- What are the merits and flaws in each of the interpretations presented here?

Nevertheless, the United States remained a nation of inconsistencies. Those who supported disfranchisement of African Americans and continued legal and social discrimination against women and racial minorities still dominated politics in the South, and extralegal inequities against these groups remained common in the North. People in power, often representing special-interest groups, could not tolerate radical views like those expressed by socialists, Coxey, or Populists, but many of the ideas raised by these groups continued to find supporters as the new century dawned.

The 1896 election realigned national politics. The Republican Party, founded in the 1850s amid a crusade against slavery and benefiting from northern victory in the Civil War, became the majority party by emphasizing government aid to business, expanding its social base among the urban middle class, and playing down its moralism. The Democratic Party miscalculated on the silver issue but held its support in the

South and inside urban political machines. At the national level, however, loyalties lacked the potency they once had. Suspicion of party politics increased, and voter participation rates declined. Populists tried to energize a third-party movement, but their success was fleeting. A new kind of politics was brewing, one in which technical experts and scientific organization would attempt to supplant the backroom deals and favoritism that had characterized the previous age.

Though the silver issue faded, many Populist goals eventually were incorporated by the major parties, including regulation of railroads, banks, and utilities; shorter workdays; a variant of the subtreasury plan; a graduated income tax; and direct election of senators. These reforms succeeded because a variety of groups united behind them. Immigration, urbanization, and industrialization had transformed the United States into a pluralistic nation in which compromise among interest groups had become a political fact of life. As the Gilded Age ended, business was still ascendant, and large segments of the population were still excluded from political and economic opportunity. But the winds of dissent and reform had begun to blow more strongly.

Suggestions for Further Reading

Edward L. Ayers, *The Promise of the New South: Life After Reconstruction* (1992)

Jean Baker, *Sisters: The Lives of America's Suffragists* (2005)

Ruth Bordin, *Frances Willard: A Biography (1986)*

Charles C. Calhoun, *Conceiving a New Republic* (2006)

Glenda Elizabeth Gilmore, *Gender and Jim Crow: Women and the Politics of White Supremacy in North Carolina, 1896–1920* (1996)

Steven Hahn, *A Nation Under Our Feet: Black Political Struggles in the Rural South, from Slavery to the Great Migration* (2003)

Michael Kazin, *A Godly Hero: The Life of William Jennings Bryan* (2006)

Jean V. Matthews, *The Rise of the New Woman: The Women's Movement in America, 1875–1930* (2003)

Robert C. McMath, *American Populism* (1993)

Nick Salvatore, *Eugene V. Debs: Citizen and Socialist* (1992)

MINDTAP
From Cengage

MindTap® is a fully online personalized learning experience built upon Cengage Learning content. MindTap® combines student learning tools—readings, multimedia, activities, and assessments—into a singular Learning Path that guides students through the course and helps students develop the critical thinking, analysis, and communication skills that are essential to academic and professional success.

18

The Progressive Era, 1895–1920

W hat Ben Lindsey saw made him furious. As a young Colorado lawyer in the 1890s, he was asked by a judge to defend two boys, about twelve years old, accused of burglary. The boys had already been imprisoned for sixty days without a trial and did not understand what the word *burglary* meant, let alone how the justice system worked. When Lindsey visited the youngsters in jail, he found them playing poker with two older cellmates, one a safecracker and the other a horse thief. Lindsey asked the warden how many other boys were in the jail. "Oh, quite a number" was the answer. Outraged that "good-natured" children were housed with hardened criminals, Lindsey later wrote, "Here were two boys, neither of them serious enemies of society, who were about to be convicted of burglary and have felony records for the rest of their lives. . . . I had made up my mind to smash the system that meant so much injustice to youth."

In 1901, Lindsey ran for county judge and began a long career "smashing the system" and advocating for the welfare of children. He spoke and wrote extensively about protecting juveniles from hard-hearted criminal prosecution, exploitive labor practices, and burdens of poverty. He and his wife, Henrietta, worked to promote a separate juvenile court system and aid to families whose children might be at risk of becoming lawbreakers. They wrote reform laws that were adopted by many states and foreign countries. The Lindseys' efforts to abolish injustice showed both genuine compassion and middle-class bias, and they occupied part of a broader movement aimed at finding solutions to the social and economic problems of modern American society.

◀ Judge Ben Lindsey (1869–1943) of Denver was a Progressive reformer who worked for children's legal protection. Like many reformers of his era, Lindsey had an earnest faith in the ability of humankind to build a better world. The Library of Congress

Chronology

1895
- Booker T. Washington gives Atlanta Compromise speech
- National Association of Colored Women founded

1898
- *Holden v. Hardy* upholds limits on miners' working hours

1901
- McKinley assassinated; T. Roosevelt assumes presidency

1904
- *Northern Securities* case dissolves railroad trust

1905
- *Lochner v. New York* removes limits on bakers' working hours

1906
- Hepburn Act tightens ICC control over railroads
- Meat Inspection Act passed
- Pure Food and Drug Act Passed

1908
- *Muller v. Oregon* upholds limits on women's working hours

1909
- NAACP founded

1910
- Mann-Elkins Act reinforces ICC powers
- White Slave Traffic Act (Mann Act) prohibits transportation of women for "immoral purposes"
- Taft fires Pinchot

1911
- Society of American Indians founded

1913
- Sixteenth Amendment ratified, legalizing income tax
- Seventeenth Amendment ratified, providing for direct election of senators
- Underwood Tariff institutes income tax
- Federal Reserve Act establishes central banking system

1914
- Federal Trade Commission created to investigate unfair trade practices
- Clayton Anti-Trust Act outlaws monopolistic business practices

1919
- Eighteenth Amendment ratified, establishing prohibition of alcoholic beverages

1920
- Nineteenth Amendment ratified, giving women the vote in federal elections

During the 1890s, economic depression, labor violence, political upheaval, and foreign entanglements shook the nation. Technology had fulfilled many promises, but numerous Americans continued to suffer from poverty and injustice. Some critics regarded industrialists as monsters who controlled markets and prices for the sole purpose of maximizing profits. Others believed government was corroded by bosses who enriched themselves through abuse of power. Still others felt that members of the new middle class overlooked the needs of the laboring classes. Tensions created by urbanization and industrialization seemed to be fragmenting society into conflicting interest groups.

Experience an interactive version of this story in MindTap®.

By 1900, the previous decade's political tumult had calmed, and economic depression subsided. The nation emerged victorious from a war against Spain (see Chapter 19), and an era of new political leaders, including a new brand of president, was dawning. A sense of renewal served both to intensify anxiety over continuing problems and to raise hopes that somehow those problems could be fixed so that democracy could be reconciled with capitalism.

From these circumstances emerged a complex and many-sided reform campaign. By the 1910s, reformers of various sorts were calling themselves Progressives; in 1912, they formed a political party by that name to embody their principles. Historians have uniformly used the term *Progressivism* to refer to the era's spirit, while disagreeing over its meaning and over who actually was a Progressive. Nonetheless, the era between 1895 and 1920 included a series of movements, each aiming in one way or another to renovate or restore American society, values, and institutions with hope that a better future lay ahead.

The reform impulse had many sources. Industrial capitalism had created awesome technology, unprecedented productivity, and a cornucopia of consumer goods. But it also brought harmful overproduction, domineering monopolies, labor strife, and destruction of natural resources. Burgeoning cities facilitated the amassing and distribution of goods, services, and cultural amenities; they also bred poverty, disease, and crime. The influx of immigrants and rise of a new class of managers and professionals reconfigured the social order. And the depression of the 1890s forced leading citizens to realize what working people already knew: the promise of American life was not being kept; equality of opportunity was elusive.

These problems galvanized members of both the middle and working classes to work toward change, though in differing ways. Middle-class reformers organized their ideas and actions around three goals. First, they sought to end abuses of power. Attacks on monopoly and corruption were not new; Jacksonian reformers of the 1830s and 1840s, as well as Populists of the 1890s, belonged to the same tradition. Progressives, however, broadened the offensive. Trust-busting, consumers' rights, and good government became compelling political issues. Second, Progressives such as Ben Lindsey wished to supplant corrupt power with humane institutions, such as schools, courts, and medical clinics. Though eager to protect individual rights, they asserted that society had the responsibility and power to improve individual lives, and they believed that government, acting for society at large, must intervene to protect the common good and elevate public interest above self-interest. Their revolt against fixed categories of thought challenged entrenched views on women's roles, race relations, education, legal and scientific thought, and morality. Third, Progressives wanted to enlist experts who would apply their special knowledge to end wasteful competition and promote social and economic order. Science and the scientific method—planning, control, predictability—were their central values. Just as corporations applied scientific management techniques to achieve economic efficiency, Progressives advocated expertise and planning to achieve social and political efficiency.

Another kind of reform arose from the everyday needs and problems of industrial working classes. Reformers representing this group sometimes allied with others interested in social welfare and sometimes worked on their own to promote greater public responsibility for the health, safety, and security of families and workers at risk in the new urban industrial world.

Befitting their name, Progressives had faith in the ability of humankind to create a better world. They voiced such phrases as "humanity's universal growth" and "the upward spiral of human development." Rising incomes, new educational opportunities, and increased availability of goods and services created an aura of confidence that social improvement would follow. Judge Lindsey expressed the Progressive creed when he wrote, "In the end the people

are bound to do the right thing, no matter how much they fail at times."

■ *What were the major characteristics of Progressivism?*

■ *In what ways did Progressive reform succeed, and in what ways did it fail?*

■ *How did women and racial minorities challenge previous ways of thinking about American society?*

18-1 The Varied Progressive Impulse

▶ How did politics become more oriented toward social issues in the Progressive Era?
▶ What role did the upper, middle, and working class play in the Progressive Era?
▶ How did religion influence the reformist impulse of the Progressive Era?
▶ How was Progressivism similar and different in the South and West from other regions?

Progressive reformers addressed vexing issues that had surfaced in the previous half-century, but they did so in a new political climate. After the heated election of 1896, party loyalties eroded and voter turnout declined. (As before, only adult males could vote, and some states still retained property qualifications for participation in some elections. Others used poll taxes and literacy tests to deny the voting privilege to nonwhite and poor white males.) In northern states, voter participation in presidential elections dropped from 80 percent of the eligible electorate in the 1880s to under 60 percent by 1912. In southern states, it fell below 30 percent. Parties, it seemed, were losing sway over the ways that the people viewed politics. At the same time, new interest groups—which championed their own special causes—gained influence, making Progressive reform issue-oriented rather than influenced by party ideologies.

18-1a National Associations and Foreign Influences

Many formerly local organizations that had formed around specific interests and issues became nationwide after 1890. These organizations included professional associations, such as the American Bar Association; women's organizations, such as the National American Woman Suffrage Association; problem-oriented groups, such as the National Consumers League; civic-minded clubs, such as the National Municipal

League; and minority group associations, such as the National Negro Business League and the Society of American Indians. Because they usually acted outside established parties, such groups made politics more fragmented and issue focused than in earlier eras.

American reformers also adopted foreign ideas. Some reform plans were introduced by Americans who had encountered them while studying in England, France, and Germany; others, by foreigners visiting the United States. (Europeans also learned from Americans, but the balance of the idea flow tilted toward the United States.) Americans copied from England such schemes as the settlement house, in which reformers went to live among and aid the urban poor, and workers' compensation for victims of industrial accidents. Ideas about city planning were imported from Germany. Other reforms, such as old-age insurance, subsidized workers' housing, and rural reconstruction, also originated abroad.

Issues and methods of implementation distinguished Progressive reform from the preceding Populist movement. Although goals of the rural-based Populists—moral regeneration, political democracy, and antimonopolism—continued after the movement faded, the Progressive quest for social justice, educational and legal reform, and government streamlining had a largely urban quality. Utilizing advances in mail, telephone, and telegraph communications, urban reformers could exchange information and coordinate efforts across the nation more easily than could rural reformers.

18-1b The New Middle Class and Muckrakers

Progressive goals—ending abuse of power, protecting the welfare of all people, reforming institutions, and promoting social efficiency—existed at all levels of society. But a new middle class of men and women in professions of law, medicine, engineering, social service, religion, teaching, and business formed an important reform vanguard. Offended by corruption and immorality in business, government, and human relations, these people were determined to apply the rational techniques that they had learned in their professions to problems of the larger society. They also believed they could create a unified nation by "Americanizing" immigrants and Native peoples—meaning educating them to conform to middle-class customs and ideals.

Indignation over abuses of power motivated many middle-class reformers. Their views were voiced by journalists whom Theodore Roosevelt dubbed "**muckrakers**" (after a character in the Puritan allegory *Pilgrim's Progress*, who, rather than looking heavenward at beauty, looked downward and raked the muck on the floor to expose evil). Muckrakers fed public tastes for scandal and sensation by exposing social, economic, and political wrongs. Their investigative articles in *McClure's, Cosmopolitan,* and other popular magazines attacked adulterated foods, fraudulent insurance, prostitution, and political corruption. Lincoln Steffens's articles in *McClure's,* later

muckrakers Journalists who wrote articles exposing urban political corruption and corporate wrongdoing.

published as *The Shame of the Cities* (1904), epitomized muckraking style. Steffens hoped his exposés of bosses' misrule in various cities would inspire outrage and, ultimately, reform. Other celebrated muckraking works included Upton Sinclair's *The Jungle* (1906), a novel that disclosed outrages of the meatpacking industry; Ida M. Tarbell's disparaging history of Standard Oil (first published in *McClure's,* 1902–1904); Burton J. Hendrick's *Story of Life Insurance* (1907); and David Graham Phillips's *Treason of the Senate* (1906).

To remedy corrupt politics, these Progressives advocated nonpartisan elections to prevent the fraud and bribery bred by party loyalties. To make officeholders more responsible, they urged adoption of the initiative, which permitted voters to propose new laws; the referendum, which enabled voters to accept or reject a law; and the recall, which allowed voters to remove offending officials and judges from office. The goal, like that of the business consolidation movement, was efficiency: middle-class Progressives would reclaim government by replacing the boss system with accountable managers chosen by a responsible electorate.

18-1c Upper-Class Reformers

The Progressive spirit also stirred some male business leaders and wealthy women. Executives like Alexander Cassatt of the Pennsylvania Railroad supported some—but not excessive—government regulation and political restructuring to protect their interests from more radical reformers. Others, like E. A. Filene, founder of a Boston department store, and Tom Johnson, a Cleveland streetcar magnate, were humanitarians who worked unselfishly for social justice. Business-dominated organizations like the Municipal Voters League and U.S. Chamber of Commerce thought that running schools, hospitals, and local government like efficient businesses would help stabilize society. Elite women led and gave financial support to organizations like the Young Women's Christian Association (YWCA), which aided unmarried workingwomen, and to settlement houses.

18-1d Settlement Houses

Young, educated middle-class women and men tried to bridge the gap between social classes that industrialism seemed to have opened by leaving their comfortable surroundings and living in inner-city outposts called settlement houses, an idea adopted from England. Residents envisioned the settlement house as a place where people could learn from each other and mutually mitigate modern problems through education, art, and reform. Between 1886 and 1910, over four hundred settlements were established, mostly in big cities, and they sponsored a variety of activities ranging from English language classes, kindergartens and nurseries, health clinics, vocational training, and playgrounds to art exhibits and amateur theater. As firsthand observers of urban poverty and poor housing, settlement house workers focused considerable energy on improving living conditions and marched at the vanguard of Progressivism. They backed housing and labor reform, offered meeting space to unions, and served as

Toynbee Hall, London

The settlement house movement, one of the Progressive Era's most idealized undertakings, owed most of its existence to Toynbee Hall in London, England. During the late nineteenth century, British middle-class university graduates began to feel uneasy about the failure of industrialization to provide adequate living conditions for the urban working class. Inspired by new curricula of social research, they sought to apply their knowledge to real situations. With this in mind, in 1884, Anglican clergyman Samuel Barnett and his wife Henrietta founded a residence in the London slums, where college students could live among working people and help them overcome their poverty. The Barnetts named the settlement Toynbee Hall after a friend, historian Arnold Toynbee (uncle of a famous historian of the same name), who had died the previous year. Their goal, as well as that of those who joined them, was to combine a religious mission to serve others with a scientific way of allaying class conflict by working with and learning from the masses through education and social welfare programs.

London and the nearby universities of Oxford and Cambridge at this time were destinations for young, idealistic Americans seeking to broaden their education and find a place for themselves in the modern world. The experiment at Toynbee Hall attracted them and several took up temporary residence there, then returned with motivation to establish similar reform centers in their own cities. Practically every founder of a settlement house established in American cities during the Progressive Era had been directly influenced by Toynbee Hall. Jane Addams, cofounder of Chicago's Hull House in 1889, visited Toynbee Hall in 1887 and called Hull House a "Toynbee Hall experiment." Vida Scudder, a Smith College graduate, undertook graduate studies at Oxford, and, influenced by Toynbee Hall, founded settlements in New York and Boston. Everett Wheeler visited Toynbee Hall in 1889 and established East Side House in New York in 1891. In 1893, George Hodges opened Kingsley House in Pittsburgh after spending a summer studying settlements in England. All these and more adopted the Toynbee philosophy "to bring men and women of education in to closer relations with the laboring classes for their mutual benefit."

American settlements diverged from their British model in a few respects. More women participated in American settlements than in British, mainly because many were graduates of new women's colleges established in the United States between the 1870s and 1890s. Also, because American settlement residents often were paid from funds raised from outside donors, they exhibited more of a sense of professionalism than their British counterparts, who normally were unpaid volunteers. And in the growing ethnic and racial diversity of the United States, which was less extensive in Great Britain, American settlements also adopted more explicit goals of assimilation.

CRITICAL THINKING

■ Despite many differences between them, American and English settlement houses both represent an attempt by well-meaning members of the upper and middle classes to impose reform on the working classes. What kinds of problems might these efforts have caused among the working classes even as they tried to resolve other problems?

Toynbee Hall, illustration from 'The Builder', February 14th, 1885 (litho)/ English School, (19th century)/Private Collection/Bridgeman Images

TOYNBEE·HALL·Commercial·Street·Whitechapel·London·E·   Mr E.Hoole·FRIBA·ARCHITECT·

◄ Founded in 1884 and located in a working-class district in East London, the settlement of Toynbee Hall attracted graduates from Oxford and Cambridge Universities who wished to live among impoverished industrial laborers, learn from them, and improve their conditions. The effort inspired young American social reformers to launch similar projects in American cities.

school nurses, juvenile probation officers, and teachers. They also worked in reform political campaigns.

Though several men helped initiate the settlement movement, the most influential participants were women. Jane Addams, Ellen Gates Starr, and Florence Kelley of Chicago's Hull House settlement, Lillian Wald of New York's Henry Street settlement, and Vida Scudder of Boston's Denison House were among many strong-minded leaders who not only broadened traditional roles of female service but also used settlement work as a springboard to larger roles in reform. Kelley's investigations into the exploitation of child labor prompted Illinois governor John Altgeld to appoint her state factory inspector; she later founded the National Consumers League. Wald helped make nursing a respected profession and cofounded the NAACP. And Addams had broad political influence, and her efforts on behalf of world peace garnered her the Nobel Peace Prize in 1931.

18-1e Working-Class Reformers

Vital elements of what became modern American liberalism derived from working-class urban experiences. By 1900, many urban workers were pressing for government intervention to ensure job safety and security. They advocated such bread-and-butter reforms as safe factories, shorter workdays, workers' compensation, protection of child and women laborers, better housing, and a more equitable tax structure. Politicians like Senator Robert F. Wagner of New York and Governor Edward F. Dunne of Illinois worked to alleviate hardships that resulted from urban-industrial growth. They trained in the trenches of machine politics, and their constituents were the same people who supported political bosses, supposedly the enemies of reform. Yet bossism was not necessarily incompatible with humanitarianism. When "Big Tim" Sullivan, an influential boss in New York's Tammany Hall machine, was asked why he supported shorter workdays for women, he explained, "I had seen me sister go out to work when she was only fourteen and I know we ought to help these gals by giving 'em a law which will prevent 'em from being broken down while they're still young." Those who represented working-class interests did not subscribe to all reforms. As protectors of individual liberty, they opposed schemes such as prohibition, Sunday closing laws, civil service, and nonpartisan elections, which conflicted with their constituents' interests. On the other hand, they joined with other reformers to pass laws aiding labor and promoting social welfare.

18-1f The Social Gospel

Much of Progressive reform rested on religious underpinnings from which arose new thoughts about how to fortify social relations with moral principles. In particular, a movement known as the **Social Gospel**, led by Protestant ministers Walter Rauschenbusch, Washington Gladden, and

Social Gospel Movement launched in the 1870s that stressed that true Christianity commits men and women to fight social injustice wherever it exists.

Charles Sheldon, would counter cutthroat capitalism by interjecting Christian churches into worldly matters, such as arbitrating industrial harmony and improving the conditions of the poor. Believing that service to fellow humans provided the way to securing individual salvation and creating God's kingdom on earth, Social Gospelers actively participated in social reform and governed their lives by asking, "What would Jesus do?"

Others took more secular pathways. Those who believed in service to all people tried to assimilate immigrants and Native peoples by expanding their educational, economic, and cultural opportunities. At times, well-intentioned humanitarians undermined their efforts by imposing their own values on people of different cultures. Working-class Catholic and Jewish immigrants, for example, sometimes rejected the Protestant creed and Americanization efforts of Social Gospelers and resented middle-class reformers' interference in their prerogative to raise children according to their own beliefs.

18-1g Socialists

Some people felt disillusioned and wanted to create a different society altogether. A blend of immigrant intellectuals, industrial workers, former Populists, and women's rights activists, they turned to socialism. Taking a cue from European counterparts—especially in Germany, England, and France, where the government sponsored such socialist goals as low-cost housing, workers' compensation, old-age pensions, public ownership of municipal services, and labor reform—they advocated that the United States adopt similar measures. By 1912, the Socialist Party of America, founded in 1901, claimed 150,000 members, and the socialist newspaper *Appeal to Reason* achieved the largest circulation—700,000 subscribers—of any weekly newspaper in the country.

In politics, socialists united behind Eugene V. Debs, the American Railway Union organizer who drew nearly 100,000 votes as Socialist Party candidate in the 1900 presidential election. A spellbinding orator who appealed to urban immigrants and western farmers alike, Debs won 400,000 votes in 1904 and polled 900,000 in 1912, at the pinnacle of his and his party's career. Although Debs and other Socialist Party leaders, such as Victor Berger of Wisconsin, the first socialist to be elected to the U.S. Congress, and New York labor lawyer Morris Hillquit, did not always agree on tactics, they made compelling overtures to reform-minded people.

Ultimately, American socialism had difficulty sustaining widespread acceptance. Some Progressives joined the Socialist Party, but most reformers favored capitalism too much to want it overthrown. Municipal ownership of public utilities represented their limit of drastic change. In Wisconsin, where Progressivism was most advanced, reformers refused to join forces with Berger's more radical group. In California, Progressives temporarily allied with conservatives to prevent socialists from gaining power in Los Angeles. Although some AFL unions supported socialist goals and candidates, many other unions opposed a reform like unemployment insurance

▲ Although their objectives sometimes differed from those of middle-class Progressive reformers, socialists also became a more active force in the early twentieth century. Socialist parades on May Day, like this one in 1910, were meant to express the solidarity of all working people.

because it would increase taxes. Moreover, private real estate interests opposed government intervention in housing, and manufacturers tried to suppress socialist activity by blacklisting militant laborers.

18-1h Southern and Western Progressivism

In some ways, Progressive reform in the South resembled that in other regions. Essentially urban and middle class in nature, it included the same goals of business regulation, factory safety, pure food and drug legislation, and moral reform as existed in the North. The South pioneered some political reforms; the direct primary originated in North Carolina; the city commission plan arose in Galveston, Texas; and the city manager plan began in Staunton, Virginia. Progressive governors, such as Braxton Bragg Comer of Alabama and Hoke Smith of Georgia, introduced business regulation, educational expansion, and other reforms that duplicated actions taken by their northern counterparts.

In the West, several politicians championed humanitarianism and regulation, putting the region at the forefront of campaigns to expand functions of federal and state governments. Nevada's Progressive Senator Francis Newlands advocated national planning and federal control of water resources. California governor Hiram Johnson fought for direct primaries, regulation of child and women's labor, workers' compensation, a pure food and drug act, and educational reform. Montana's Senator Thomas J. Walsh fought against corruption and for woman suffrage.

Southern and western women, white and black, made notable contributions to Progressive causes, just as they did in the North and East. In western states, women could vote on state and local matters and thus participated directly in political reform. But the more effective women's reform efforts in both regions took place outside politics, and their projects remained racially distinct. White women crusaded against child labor, founded social service organizations, and challenged unfair wage rates. African American women, using a nonpolitical guise as homemakers and religious leaders—roles that whites found more acceptable than political activism—served their communities by advocating for cleaner streets, better education, and health reforms.

18-1i Opponents of Progressivism

It would be a mistake to assume that a Progressive spirit captivated all of American society between 1895 and 1920. Large numbers of people, heavily represented in Congress, disliked government interference in economic affairs and found no fault with existing power structures. Defenders of free enterprise opposed regulatory measures out of fear that government programs undermined the initiative and competition that they believed were basic to a free-market system. "Old-guard" Republicans, such as Senator Nelson W. Aldrich of Rhode Island and House Speaker Joseph Cannon of Illinois, championed this ideology. Outside Washington, D.C., tycoons like J. P. Morgan and John D. Rockefeller insisted that progress would result only from maintaining the profit incentive and an unfettered economy.

Moreover, prominent Progressives were not "progressive" in every respect. Their attempts to Americanize immigrants reflected bigotry as well as naiveté. As governor,

Hiram Johnson promoted discrimination against Japanese Americans, and whether Progressive or not, most southern governors, such as Smith, Comer, Charles B. Aycock of North Carolina, and James K. Vardaman of Mississippi, rested their power on appeals to white supremacy. In the South, the disfranchisement of African Americans through poll taxes, literacy requirements, and other means meant that electoral reforms benefitted only whites—and then only white men with enough cash and schooling to satisfy voting prerequisites. Settlement houses in northern cities kept blacks and whites apart in separate programs and buildings.

Progressive reformers generally occupied the center of the ideological spectrum. Moderate, socially aware, sometimes contradictory, they believed on one hand that laissez-faire was obsolete and on the other that a radical departure from free enterprise was dangerous. Like Thomas Jefferson, they expressed faith in the conscience and will of the people; like Alexander Hamilton, they desired strong central government to act in the interest of conscience. Their goals were both idealistic and realistic. As minister-reformer Walter Rauschenbusch wrote, "We shall demand perfection and never expect to get it."

18-2 Government and Legislative Reform

▶ How did government become more active in society during the Progressive Era?

▶ What steps were taken by reformers to make government more efficient?

▶ How did reformers address concerns about matters of social and individual morality?

Mistrust of tyranny had traditionally prompted Americans to believe that democratic government should be small, interfere in private affairs only in unique circumstances, and withdraw when balance had been restored. But in the late 1800s, this laissez-faire viewpoint weakened when problems resulting from economic change seemed to overwhelm individual effort. Corporations pursued government aid and protection for their enterprises. Discontented farmers sought government regulation of railroads and other monopolistic businesses. And city dwellers, accustomed to favors performed by political machines, came to expect government to act on their behalf. Before 1900, state governments had been concerned largely with railroads and economic growth; the federal government had focused primarily on tariffs and the currency. But after 1900, issues of regulation, both economic and social, demanded attention. More than in the past, public opinion, roused by muckraking media, influenced change.

18-2a Restructuring Government

Middle-class Progressive reformers rejected the laissez-faire principle of government. Increasingly aware that a simple, inflexible government was inadequate in a complex industrial age, they reasoned that public authority needed to counteract inefficiency and exploitation. But before activists could effectively use such power, they would have to reclaim government from politicians—whose venality, they believed, had soiled the democratic system. Thus, eliminating corruption from government was one central thrust of Progressive activity.

Prior to the Progressive Era, reformers had attacked dishonesty in city governments through such reforms as civil service, nonpartisan elections, and close scrutiny of public expenditures. After 1900, campaigns to make cities run more efficiently resulted in city-manager and commission forms of government, in which urban officials were chosen for professional expertise rather than for political connections. But reforming city administration was not sufficient to realize the improvements reformers sought, and they turned to state and federal governments for help.

At the state level, faith in a reform-minded executive prompted Progressives to support a number of skillful and charismatic governors. Perhaps the most dynamic of these governors was Wisconsin's Robert M. La Follette. A small-town lawyer, La Follette rose through the state Republican Party to become governor in 1900. In office, he initiated a multipronged reform program, including direct primaries, more equitable taxes, and regulation of railroads. He also appointed commissions staffed by experts, who supplied him with data that he used in speeches to arouse support for his policies. After three terms as governor, La Follette became a U.S. senator and carried his ideals into national politics. "Fighting Bob" displayed a rare ability to approach reform scientifically while still exciting people with moving rhetoric. His goal, he proclaimed, was "not to 'smash' corporations, but to drive them out of politics, and then to treat them exactly the same as other people are treated."

Crusades against corrupt politics made the system more democratic. By 1916, all but three states had direct primaries, and many had adopted the initiative, referendum, and recall. Political reformers achieved a major goal in 1913 with adoption of the Seventeenth Amendment to the Constitution, which provided for direct election of U.S. senators, replacing election by state legislatures. Such measures, however, did not always achieve desired ends. Party bosses, better organized and more experienced than reformers, were still able to control elections, and special-interest groups spent large sums to influence voting. Moreover, courts usually aided entrenched power rather than reining it in.

18-2b Labor Reform

State laws resulting from Progressive efforts to improve labor conditions had more effect than did political reforms because middle-class and working-class reformers agreed on the need for them. Prodded by middle-class/working-class coalitions, many states enacted factory inspection laws, and by 1916 nearly two-thirds of states required compensation for victims of industrial accidents. The same

◀ Robert M. La Follette (1855–1925) was one of the most dynamic of Progressive politicians. As governor of Wisconsin, he sponsored a program of political reform and business regulation known as the Wisconsin Plan. In 1906, he entered the U.S. Senate and continued to champion Progressive reform. The National Progressive Republican League, which La Follette founded in 1911, became the core of the Progressive Party.

Library of Congress Prints and Photographs Division Washington, D.C[LC-US262-58275]

alliance induced some legislatures to grant aid to low-income mothers with dependent children. Under pressure from the National Child Labor Committee, nearly every state set a minimum age for employment (varying from twelve to sixteen) and limited hours that employers could make children work. Labor laws did not work perfectly, however. They seldom provided for the close inspection of factories that enforcement required. And families that needed extra income evaded child labor restrictions by falsifying their children's ages to employers.

Several middle- and working-class groups also united behind measures that restricted working hours for women and that aided retirees. After 1908, when the Supreme Court, in *Muller v. Oregon*, upheld Oregon's law prohibiting laundries from making female employees work more than ten hours a day, more states passed laws protecting female workers. Meanwhile, in 1914, efforts of the American Association for Old Age Security made progress when Arizona established old-age pensions. Judges struck down the law, but demand for pensions continued, and in the 1920s many states enacted laws to provide for needy elderly people.

18-2c Prohibition

Protecting women and children brought together reform coalitions. But when an issue involved regulating behavior such as drinking habits and sexual conduct, class differences emerged, especially when reformers used morality and social control as bases for their agenda. For example, the **Anti-Saloon League**, formed in 1893, intensified the long-standing campaign against drunkenness and its costs to society. This organization allied with the Woman's Christian Temperance Union (founded in 1874) to publicize alcoholism's role in causing health problems and family distress. The league was especially successful in shifting attention from the immorality of drunkenness to using law enforcement to break the alleged link between the drinking that saloons encouraged and the accidents, poverty, and poor productivity that resulted. Against the wishes of many working-class people who valued individual freedom to drink where and when they wanted, the war on saloons prompted many states and localities to restrict liquor consumption. By 1900, one-fourth of the nation's population lived in "dry" communities that prohibited the sale of liquor.

Nevertheless, consumption of alcohol increased as a result of the influx of immigrants whose cultures included social drinking, convincing prohibitionists that a nationwide ban was the best solution. They enlisted support from such notables as Supreme Court Justice Louis D. Brandeis and former president William Howard Taft, and in 1918 Congress passed the

Anti-Saloon League Advocacy group founded in 1893 that sought to ban alcohol by publicizing its harmful effects on families and individuals and its link to accidents and health problems.

Eighteenth Amendment (ratified in 1919 and implemented in 1920), outlawing the manufacture, sale, and transportation of intoxicating liquors. Not all prohibitionists were Progressive reformers, and not all Progressives were prohibitionists. Nevertheless, the Eighteenth Amendment represents an expression of the Progressive goal to protect family and workplace through reform legislation.

18-2d Controlling Prostitution

Moral outrage erupted when muckraking journalists charged that international gangs were kidnapping young white women and forcing them into prostitution, a practice called "white slavery." Accusations were exaggerated, but they alarmed some moralists who falsely perceived a link between immigration and prostitution, and who feared that prostitutes were producing genetically inferior children. (These moralists seldom expressed the same concern for African American women.) Although some women voluntarily entered "the profession" because it offered much higher income than other forms of work and other women occasionally performed sexual favors in return for gifts, those fearful about the social consequences of prostitution prodded governments to investigate and pass corrective legislation. The Chicago Vice Commission, for example, undertook a "scientific" survey of dance halls and illicit sex, and published its findings as *The Social Evil in Chicago* in 1911. The report concluded that poverty, gullibility, and desperation drove women into prostitution. Such investigations publicized rising numbers of prostitutes but failed to prove that criminal organizations deliberately lured women into "the trade."

Reformers nonetheless believed they could attack prostitution by punishing both those who promoted it and those who practiced it. In 1910, Congress passed the White Slave Traffic Act (Mann Act), prohibiting interstate and international transportation of a woman for immoral purposes. By 1915, nearly every state had outlawed brothels and solicitation of sex. Such laws ostensibly protected young women from exploitation, but in reality they failed to address the more serious problem of sexual violence that women suffered at the hands of family members, presumed friends, and employers.

Like prohibition, the Mann Act reflected sentiment that government could improve behavior by restricting it. Middle-class reformers believed that the source of evil was neither original sin nor human nature but the social environment. If evil was created by human will, it followed that sin could be eradicated by human effort. The new working classes, however, resented such meddling as unwarranted attempts to control them. Thus, when Chicagoans voted on a referendum to make their city dry shortly before the Eighteenth Amendment was passed, three-fourths of the city's immigrant voters opposed it, and the measure went down to defeat.

Eighteenth Amendment
Amendment to the Constitution that established national prohibition of alcohol.

18-3 New Ideas in Social Institutions

▶ What reforms were made in institutions of education in the Progressive Era?

▶ How did scientific principles impact the fields of the law and social sciences?

▶ How did Social Darwinism influence societal views of immigrants and persons of color?

In addition to legislative paths, Progressive reform opened new vistas in the ways social institutions were organized. Reformers' preoccupation with efficiency and scientific management infiltrated realms of education, law, religion, and social science. Darwin's theory of evolution had challenged traditional beliefs in a God-created world, immigration had created complex social diversity, and technology had made old habits of production obsolete. Thoughtful people in several professions grappled with how to respond to this new era yet preserve what was best from the past.

18-3a John Dewey and Progressive Education

Changing attitudes about childhood and increases in school attendance altered approaches to education. As late as 1870, when families needed children at home to do farmwork, Americans attended school for an average of only a few months a year for only four years. By 1900, however, the urban-industrial economy and its expanding middle class helped to create a more widespread appreciation of childhood as a special life stage requiring that youngsters be sheltered from society's dangers and promoting their physical and emotional growth. Those concerned about children's development believed that youngsters required forms of education and activity appropriate to a child's biological and cultural development.

Educators argued that expanded schooling, especially for swelling populations of immigrant and migrant children, produced responsible citizens and workers. Consequently, in the 1870s and 1880s, states passed laws that required children to attend school to age fourteen. Meanwhile, the number of public high schools grew from five hundred in 1870 to ten thousand in 1910. By 1900, educational reformers, such as psychologist G. Stanley Hall and philosopher John Dewey, asserted that to prepare children for a modern world, personal development should be the focus of the curriculum and that the school be the center of the community.

Progressive education, based on Dewey's *The School and Society* (1899) and *Democracy and Education* (1916), was a uniquely American phenomenon. Dewey believed that children should be taught to use intelligence and ingenuity as instruments for controlling their environments. From kindergarten through high school, Dewey argued, children needed to learn through direct experience, not by rote memorization. Dewey and his wife, Alice, put these ideas into practice in their own Laboratory School, located at the University of Chicago.

18-3b Growth of Colleges and Universities

A more practical curriculum also became the driving principle behind reform in higher education. Previously, the purpose of American colleges and universities had resembled that of their European counterparts: to train a select few for careers in law, medicine, and religion. But in the late 1800s, institutions of higher learning multiplied as states established public universities using federal funds from the Morrill Acts of 1862 and 1890. The number of private institutions also expanded. Between 1870 and 1910, the total number of BA degrees granted by American colleges and universities grew from 9,400 to 37,200. Curricula broadened as educators sought to keep pace with technological and social changes. Harvard University, under President Charles W. Eliot, pioneered in substituting electives for required courses and experimenting with new teaching methods. The University of Wisconsin and other state universities achieved distinction in new areas of study, such as political science, economics, and sociology. Many schools, private and public, considered athletics vital to a student's growth, and men's intercollegiate sports became a permanent feature of student life and source of school pride.

Southern states, in keeping with separate but equal policies, created segregated colleges for blacks in addition to institutions for whites. Aided by land grant funds, such schools as Alabama Agricultural and Mechanical University (A&M), South Carolina State University, and the A&M College for the Colored Race (North Carolina) opened their doors. "Separate" was a more accurate description of these institutions than "equal" as African Americans continued to suffer from inferior educational opportunities. Nevertheless, African American men and women found intellectual stimulation in all-black colleges and used education to promote the advancement of their race.

As higher education expanded, so did female enrollments. Between 1890 and 1910, the number of women attending colleges and universities swelled from 56,000 to 140,000. Of these, 106,000 attended coeducational institutions (mostly state universities); the rest enrolled in women's colleges, such as Wellesley and Barnard. By 1920, 283,000 women attended college, accounting for 47 percent of total enrollment. But discrimination lingered in admissions and curriculum policies. Women were encouraged (indeed, they usually sought) to take home economics and education courses rather than science and mathematics, and most medical schools refused to admit women or imposed stringent quotas. Separate women's medical schools, such as the Women's Medical College of Philadelphia and Women's Medical College of Chicago, trained female physicians, but most of these schools were absorbed or put out of business by larger institutions dominated by men.

American educators justifiably congratulated themselves for increasing enrollments and making instruction more meaningful. By 1920, 78 percent of children between ages five and seventeen were enrolled in public schools; another 8 percent attended private and parochial schools. These figures represented a huge increase over 1870 attendance rates. There were 600,000 college and graduate students in 1920, compared with only 52,000 in 1870. Yet few people

University of Michigan - Bentley Historical Library

▲ These members of the University of Michigan's Class of 1892 represent the student body of a publicly funded college in the late nineteenth century. With their varied curricula, inclusion of women, and increasing enrollments, such schools transformed American higher education in the Progressive Era.

looked beyond the numbers to assess how well schools were doing their job. Critical analysis seldom tested the faith that schools could promote equality as well as personal growth and responsible citizenship.

18-3c Progressive Legal Thought

The legal profession also embraced new emphases on experience and scientific principles. Harvard law professor Roscoe Pound and Oliver Wendell Holmes Jr., associate justice of the Supreme Court (1902–1932), led an attack on traditional views of law as universal and unchanging. "The life of the law," wrote Holmes, sounding like Dewey, "has not been logic; it has been experience." The opinion that law should reflect society's needs challenged the practice of invoking inflexible legal precedents that often obstructed social legislation. Louis D. Brandeis, a lawyer who later joined Holmes on the Supreme Court, insisted that judges' opinions be based on scientifically gathered information about social realities. Using this approach, Brandeis collected extensive data on harmful effects of long working hours to convince the Supreme Court, in *Muller v. Oregon*, to uphold Oregon's ten-hour limit on women's workday.

New legal thinking provoked some resistance. Judges loyal to laissez-faire economics and strict interpretation of the Constitution overturned laws that Progressives thought necessary for effective reform. Thus, despite Holmes's forceful dissent, in 1905 the Supreme Court, in *Lochner v. New York*, revoked a state law limiting bakers' working hours. In this and similar cases, the Court's majority argued that the Fourteenth Amendment protected an individual's right to make employment contracts without government interference. Judges also weakened federal regulations by invoking the Tenth Amendment, which prohibited the federal government from interfering in matters reserved to the states.

Courts did uphold some regulatory measures, particularly those intended to safeguard life and limb. A string of decisions, beginning with *Holden v. Hardy* (1898), in which the Supreme Court sustained a Utah law regulating working hours for miners, confirmed the use of state police power to protect health, safety, and morals. Judges also affirmed federal police power and Congress's authority over interstate commerce by upholding legislation, such as the Pure Food and Drug Act, the Meat Inspection Act, and the Mann Act. In these instances citizens' welfare took precedence over the Fourteenth and Tenth Amendments.

But the concept of general welfare often conflicted with the principle of equal rights when majorities imposed their will on minorities. Even if one agreed that laws should address society's needs, whose needs should prevail? The United States was (and remains) a mixed nation where interests of gender, race, religion, and ethnicity often conflict. Thus outcries resulted when a native-born Protestant majority imposed Bible reading in public schools (offending Catholics and Jews), required businesses to close on Sundays, limited women's rights, restricted religious practices of Mormons and other groups, prohibited interracial marriage, and enforced

racial segregation. Justice Holmes asserted that laws should be made for "people of fundamentally differing views," but fitting such laws to a nation of so many different interest groups sparked debates that continue to this day.

18-3d Social Science

Social science—the study of society and its institutions—experienced changes similar to those affecting education and law. In economics, scholars used statistics to argue that laws governing economic relationships were not timeless. Instead, they claimed, theory should reflect prevailing social conditions. Economist Richard T. Ely, for example, argued that poverty and impersonality resulting from industrialization required intervention by "the united efforts of Church, state, and science." A new breed of sociologists led by Lester Ward, Albion Small, and Edward A. Ross agreed, adding that citizens should work to cure social ills rather than passively wait for problems to solve themselves.

Meanwhile, historians Frederick Jackson Turner, Charles A. Beard, and Vernon L. Parrington examined the past to explain present American society. Beard, like other Progressives, believed that the Constitution was a flexible document amenable to growth and change, not a sacred code imposed by wise forefathers. His *Economic Interpretation of the Constitution* (1913) argued that a group of merchants and business-oriented lawyers created the Constitution to defend private property. If the Constitution had served special interests in one age, he argued, it could be changed to serve broader interests in another age.

Public health organizations such as the National Consumers League (NCL) joined physicians and social scientists to bring about some of the most far-reaching Progressive reforms. Founded by Florence Kelley in 1899, the NCL pursued protection of female and child laborers and elimination of health hazards in the marketplace. After aiding in the success of *Muller v. Oregon*, the organization supported reform lawyers Louis Brandeis and Felix Frankfurter in court cases to protect women workers. Local NCL branches united with women's clubs to advance consumer protection measures, such as the licensing of food vendors and inspection of dairies. They also urged city governments to fund neighborhood clinics that provided health education and medical care to the poor.

18-3e Eugenics

The Social Gospel served as a response to Social Darwinism, the application of natural selection and survival of the fittest to human interactions. But another movement that flourished during the Progressive Era, eugenics, sought to apply Darwinian principles to society in a more intrusive way. The brainchild of Francis Galton, an English statistician and cousin of Charles Darwin, eugenics rested on the belief that human character and habits could be inherited. If good traits could be inherited, so could unwanted traits, such as criminality and mental illness. Just as some Progressives believed that society had an obligation to intervene and erase poverty and injustice, eugenicists believed that society had an obligation to prevent the reproduction of those thought to be mentally defective and criminally inclined by preventing them from marrying and, in extreme cases, sterilizing them. Such ideas targeted immigrants and people of color. Though supported by such American notables as Alexander Graham Bell, Margaret Sanger, and **W. E. B. Du Bois**, eugenics was discredited, especially after it became a linchpin of Nazi racial policies, but modern genetic engineering has evolved from some of the eugenics legacy.

Some reformers saw immigration restriction as an acceptable way of controlling the composition of American society. A leading restrictionist was Madison Grant, whose *The Passing of the Great Race* (1916) strongly bolstered theories that immigrants from southern and eastern Europe threatened to weaken American society because they were inferior mentally and morally to earlier Nordic immigrants. Such ideas prompted many people, including some Progressives, to conclude that new laws should curtail the influx of Poles, Italians, Jews, and other eastern and southern Europeans, as well as Asians. Efforts to limit immigration reached fruition in the 1920s, when restrictive legislation drastically closed the door to "new" immigrants.

Thus, a new breed of men and women pressed for political reform and institutional change in the two decades before the First World War. Concerned middle-class professionals, confident that new ways of thinking and planning could bring about progress, and representatives of working classes, who experienced social problems firsthand, helped broaden government's role to meet the needs of a mature industrial society. But their questioning of prevailing assumptions also unsettled conventional attitudes toward race and gender.

18-4 Challenges to Racial and Sex Discrimination

▶ What were the competing views among African Americans regarding assimilation to new environments?

▶ How did Native Americans address questions of identity in the Progressive Era?

▶ How did the views and actions of the women's movement shift after 1910?

White male reformers of the Progressive Era dealt primarily with issues of politics and institutions, and in so doing often ignored issues directly affecting former slaves, nonwhite immigrants, American Indians, and women. Yet activists within these groups caught the Progressive spirit, challenged entrenched customs, and made strides toward their own advancement. Their efforts, however, posed a dilemma. Should women and nonwhites aim to imitate white men, with white men's values as well as their rights? Or was there something unique about racial and sexual cultures that they should preserve at the risk of sacrificing broader gains? Both

groups fluctuated between attraction to and rejection of the culture that excluded them.

18-4a Continued Discrimination for African Americans

In 1900, nine-tenths of African Americans lived in the South, where repressive Jim Crow laws had multiplied in the 1880s and 1890s (see "Discrimination and Disfranchisement," Section 17-4). Denied legal and voting rights, and officially segregated in almost all walks of life, southern blacks faced constant exclusion as well as relentless violence from lynching and countless acts of intimidation. In 1910, only 8,000 out of 970,000 high-school-age blacks were enrolled in southern high schools. In response, many African Americans moved northward in the 1880s, accelerating their migration after 1900. The conditions they found in places like Chicago, Cleveland, and Detroit represented relative improvement over rural sharecropping, but they still confronted job discrimination, inferior schools, and segregated housing.

African American leaders differed sharply over how—and whether—to pursue assimilation in their new environments. In the wake of emancipation, ex-slave Frederick Douglass urged "ultimate assimilation through self-assertion, and on no other terms." Others favored separation from white society and supported emigration to Africa or the establishment of all-black communities in Oklahoma Territory and Kansas. Others advocated militancy, believing, as Lewis H. Douglass, Frederick Douglass's son, wrote in the wake of a vicious attack on African Americans in Atlanta in 1906, "Our people must die to be saved and in dying must take as many along with them as it is possible to do with the aid of firearms and all other weapons."

18-4b Booker T. Washington and Self-Help

Most black people could neither escape nor conquer white society. They sought other routes to economic and social improvement. Self-help, a strategy articulated by educator **Booker T. Washington**, offered one popular alternative. Born into slavery in Virginia in 1856, Washington obtained an education and in 1881 founded Tuskegee Institute, an all-black vocational school, in Alabama. There he developed a philosophy that blacks' best hope for assimilation lay in at least temporarily accommodating to whites. Rather than fighting for political rights, Washington counseled African Americans to work hard, acquire property, and prove they were worthy of respect. Washington voiced his views in a speech at the Atlanta Exposition in 1895. "Dignify and glorify common labor," he

W. E. B. Du Bois African American educator and activist who demanded full racial equality, including the same educational opportunities open to whites, and called on black people to resist all forms of racism.

Booker T. Washington Leading African American activist of the late nineteenth century who advocated education and accommodation with white society as the best strategy for racial advancement.

urged, in what became known as the Atlanta Compromise. "Agitation of questions of racial equality is the extremest folly." Envisioning a society where blacks and whites would remain apart but share similar goals, Washington observed that "in all things that are purely social we can be as separate as the fingers, yet one as the hand in all matters essential to mutual progress."

Whites welcomed Washington's accommodation policy because it advised patience and reminded black people to stay in their place. Because he said what they wanted to hear, white businesspeople, reformers, and politicians chose to regard Washington as representing all African Americans. Although Washington endorsed a separate-but-equal policy, he projected a subtle racial pride that would find more direct expression in black nationalism in the twentieth century, when some African Americans would advocate control of their own businesses and schools. Washington never argued that blacks were inferior; rather, he asserted that they could enhance their dignity through self-improvement.

Some blacks, however, concluded that Washington endorsed second-class citizenship. His southern-based philosophy did not appeal to educated northern African Americans like newspaper editors William Monroe Trotter in Boston and T. Thomas Fortune in New York. In 1905, a group of "anti-Bookerites" convened near Niagara Falls and pledged militant pursuit of such rights as unrestricted voting, economic opportunity, integration, and equality before the law. Representing the Niagara movement was W. E. B. Du Bois, an outspoken critic of the Atlanta Compromise.

18-4c W. E. B. Du Bois and the "Talented Tenth"

A New Englander and the first African American to receive a PhD from Harvard, Du Bois was both a Progressive and a member of the black elite. He first studied at all-black Fisk University, then in Germany, where he learned about scientific investigation. While a faculty member at Atlanta University, Du Bois compiled fact-filled sociological studies of black urban life and wrote poetically in support of civil rights. He treated Washington politely but could not accept accommodation. "The way for a people to gain their reasonable rights," Du Bois asserted, "is not by voluntarily throwing them away." Instead, blacks must agitate for what was rightfully theirs. Du Bois believed that an intellectual vanguard of cultured, educated blacks, the "Talented Tenth," should lead in the pursuit of racial equality. In 1909, he joined white liberals who also were discontented with Washington's accommodationism to form the **National Association for the Advancement of Colored People (NAACP)**. The organization aimed to end racial discrimination, eradicate lynching, and obtain voting rights

National Association for the Advancement of Colored People (NAACP) Organization that called for sustained activism, including legal challenges, to achieve political equality for black people and full integration into American life.

through legal redress in the courts. By 1914, the NAACP had fifty branch offices and six thousand members.

Within the NAACP and in other ways, African Americans struggled with questions about their place in white society. Du Bois voiced this dilemma poignantly, admitting that "one ever feels his twoness—an American, a Negro, two souls, two thoughts, two unreconciled strivings, two warring ideals in one dark body." Somehow blacks had to reconcile that two-ness by combining racial pride with national identity. As Du Bois wrote in 1903, a black "would not Africanize America, for America has too much to teach the world and Africa. He would not bleach his Negro soul in a flood of white Americanism, for he knows that Negro blood has a message for the world. He simply wishes to make it possible for a man to be both a Negro and an American." That simple wish would haunt the nation for decades to come.

18-4d Society of American Indians

The dilemma of identity also vexed American Indians, but had an added tribal dimension. Since the 1880s, most Native American reformers had belonged to white-led organizations. In 1911, however, some middle-class Native Americans formed their own association, the Society of American Indians (SAI), to work for better education, civil rights, and health care. Under leadership of prominent professionals, who called themselves "Red Progressives," the SAI sought to promote unity among all Native peoples and, like white Progressives, invested faith in inevitable progress. To this end, the society advocated an annual "American Indian Days" to cultivate pride and offset images of savage peoples promulgated in Wild West shows.

The SAI's emphasis on racial pride, however, was squeezed between pressures for assimilation on one side and tribal allegiance on the other. Its small membership did not fully represent the diverse and unconnected Native American groups, and its attempt to establish a unifying governing body fizzled. Some tribal governments no longer existed to select representatives, and most SAI members simply promoted their self-interest. At the same time, the goal of achieving acceptance in white society proved elusive. Individual hard work was not enough to overcome prejudice and condescension, and attempts to redress grievances through legal action faltered for lack of funds. Ultimately, the SAI offered little to poverty-stricken Native Americans on reservations and elsewhere, who seldom knew that the organization even existed. Torn by internal disputes, the association folded in the early 1920s.

18-4e "The Woman Movement"

Challenges to established social assumptions also raised questions of identity among women. The ensuing quandaries resembled those faced by racial minorities: What tactics should women use to achieve rights? What should be women's role in society? Should they try to achieve equality within a male-dominated society? Or should they assert particular female virtues to create a new place for themselves within society?

Heavyweight Boxing Champion Jack Johnson as Race Hero

It is probable that more African Americans in the 1910s paid attention to Jack Johnson than they did to either Booker T. Washington or W. E. B. Du Bois. In 1908, Jackson became the first black heavyweight champion of the world by knocking out Tommy Burns. Immediately, white boxing fans began searching for a "Great White Hope" to recapture the title, and in 1910, former champion James J. Jeffries came out of retirement to fight Johnson, boasting that he would "demonstrate that a white man is king of them all." But after fifteen rounds of pummeling from Johnson, Jeffries gave up. African Americans around the nation celebrated their hero's victory, and in some places race riots erupted as angry whites attacked jubilant revelers. Racist reaction was particularly venomous because Johnson refused to accept white standards for the way a black man should behave. He courted and married white women, flaunted his taste for fast cars and fancy clothing, and dealt with opponents and reporters with a pompous attitude. In 1915, Johnson, then thirty-seven years old, lost his title to Jess Willard in Cuba. The fight took place outside the country because in 1913 Johnson had been convicted of violating the Mann Act for allegedly transporting Belle Schreiber, a white prostitute, across state lines for "immoral purposes." Sentenced to a year in jail, Johnson fled the country, but he returned in 1920 to serve his sentence.

CRITICAL THINKING

- How do these three images reveal racial attitudes, both black and white, toward Jack Johnson?
- What messages do they convey to the viewer?

▲ Jack Johnson successfully defends his championship against Jim Jeffries.

Bettmann/Getty Images

Library of Congress, Prints & Photographs Division, Reproduction number LC-DIG-ppmsca-31941 (digital file from original photo)LC-US262-28040 (b&w film copy neg.)

▲ Jack Johnson, posing with his white wife, Etta.

Library of Congress, Prints & Photographs Division, Reproduction number LC-US262-130087 (b&w film copy neg.)

▲ A crowd rushes to see their popular hero, Jack Johnson.

The answers that women found involved a subtle but important shift in their politics. Before 1910, crusaders for women's rights referred to themselves as "the woman movement." This label applied to middle-class women who strove to move beyond the household into higher education and paid professions. Like African American and Native American leaders, women argued that legal and voting rights were indispensable to such moves. They based their claims on the theory that women's special, even superior, traits as guardians of family and morality would humanize society. Settlement house founder Jane Addams, for example, endorsed woman suffrage by asking, "If women have in any sense been responsible for the gentler side of life which softens and blurs some of its harsher conditions, may not they have a duty to perform in our American cities?"

18-4f "Social Housekeeping"

Because female activists were generally barred from holding public office (except in a few western states), they asserted traditional female responsibilities for home and family as the rationale for reforming society through an enterprise that historians have called "social housekeeping." Rather than advocate reforms like trust-busting and direct primaries, female reformers formed organizations and worked collectively for factory inspection, regulation of children's and women's labor, improved housing, and consumer protection.

Such efforts were not confined to white women. Mostly excluded from white women's organizations, African American women had their own associations, including the Colored Women's Federation, which sought, among other goals, to establish a training school for "colored girls." Founded in 1895, the National Association of Colored Women was the nation's first African American social service organization; it concentrated on establishing nurseries, kindergartens, and retirement homes. Black women also developed reform organizations within Black Baptist and African Methodist Episcopal churches.

18-4g Feminism

Around 1910, some of those concerned with women's place in society began using the term *feminism* to represent their ideas. Whereas the woman movement spoke generally of duty and moral purity, feminists emphasized rights and self-development as key to economic and sexual independence. Charlotte Perkins Gilman, a major figure in the movement, denounced Victorian notions of womanhood and articulated feminist goals in her numerous writings. Her book *Women and Economics* (1898), for example, declared that domesticity and female innocence were obsolete, and attacked men's monopoly on economic opportunity. Arguing that paid employees should handle domestic chores, such as cooking, cleaning, and childcare, Gilman asserted that modern women must have access to jobs in industry and the professions.

18-4h Margaret Sanger's Crusade

Feminists also supported a single standard of behavior for men and women, and several feminists joined the birth control movement led by Margaret Sanger. A former visiting nurse who believed in a woman's right to sexual pleasure and to determine when to have a child, Sanger helped reverse state and federal laws that had banned publication and distribution of information about sex and contraception. Her speeches and actions aroused opposition from those who saw birth control as a threat to family and morality. Ironically, while she advocated greater reproductive freedom for women, her beliefs had a darker side; she also was a eugenicist who perceived birth control as a means of limiting the numbers of children born to "inferior" immigrant and nonwhite mothers. Regardless, Sanger persevered and in 1921 formed the American Birth Control League, enlisting physicians and social workers to convince judges to allow distribution of birth control information. Most states still prohibited the sale of contraceptives, but Sanger succeeded in introducing the issue into public debate.

18-4i Women's Suffrage

A new generation of Progressive feminists, represented by Harriot Stanton Blatch, daughter of nineteenth-century suffragist Elizabeth Cady Stanton, carried on women's battle for the vote. Blatch had broad experience in suffrage activities, having accompanied her mother on speaking tours, and participated in the British women's suffrage movement. In America, Blatch linked voting rights to the improvement of women's working conditions. She joined the Women's Trade Union League and founded the Equality League of Self Supporting Women in 1907. Declaring that every woman worked, whether she performed paid labor or unpaid housework, Blatch believed that all women's efforts contributed to society's betterment. In her view, achievement rather than wealth and refinement was the best criterion for public status. Thus, women should exercise the vote, not to enhance the power of elites, but to promote and protect women's economic roles.

Library of Congress Prints and Photographs Division Washington, D.C.[LC-DIG-nclc-04574]

▲ The rise of the settlement house movement provided young middle-class women with opportunities to aid inner-city working-class neighborhoods and formed the basis of the social work profession. In this photograph, a settlement worker is teaching neighborhood girls how to knit.

By the early twentieth century, suffragists had achieved some successes. Nine states, all in the West, allowed women to vote in state and local elections by 1912, and women continued to press for national suffrage (see Map 18.1). Their tactics ranged from letter writing and publications of the National American Woman Suffrage Association, led by **Carrie Chapman Catt**, to spirited meetings and militant marches of the National Woman's Party, led by Alice Paul and Harriot Stanton Blatch. All these activities heightened public awareness. More decisive, however, was women's service during the First World War as factory laborers, medical volunteers, and municipal workers. By convincing legislators that women could successfully shoulder public responsibilities, women's wartime contributions gave final impetus to passage of the national suffrage amendment (the Nineteenth Amendment) in 1920.

In spite of these accomplishments, the activities of women's organizations, feminists, and suffragists failed to create an interest group united or powerful enough to overcome men's political, economic, and social power. During the Progressive Era, the efforts of leaders like Blatch, Paul, and Catt helped clarify issues that concerned women and finally won women the right to vote, but that victory was only a step, not a conclusion. Discrimination in employment, education, and law continued to shadow women for decades to come. As feminist Crystal Eastman observed in the aftermath of the suffrage crusade: "Men are saying perhaps, 'Thank God, this everlasting women's fight is over!' But women, if I know them, are saying, 'Now at last we can begin.'... Now they can say what they are really after, in common with all the rest of the struggling world, is freedom."

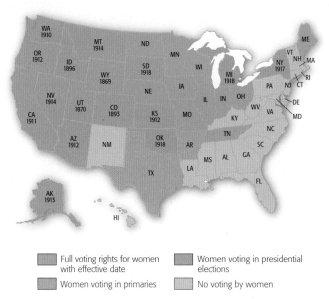

Map 18.1 **Woman Suffrage Before 1920**

Before Congress passed and the states ratified the Nineteenth Amendment, woman suffrage already existed, but mainly in the West. Several midwestern states allowed women to vote only in presidential elections, but legislatures in the South and the Northeast generally refused such rights until forced to do so by constitutional amendment.

18-5 Theodore Roosevelt and Revival of the Presidency

▶ How did Roosevelt employ the power of the federal government in the affairs of business and industry?

▶ What role did the federal government play in the use and regulation of the environment?

▶ What divisions emerged in the Republican Party after the election of William Howard Taft?

▶ How did New Nationalism differ from New Freedom?

The Progressive Era's theme of reform in politics, institutions, and social relations drew attention to government, especially the federal government, as the foremost agent of change. Although the federal government had notable accomplishments during the preceding Gilded Age, its role had been mainly to support rather than control economic expansion, as when it transferred western public lands and resources to private ownership. Then, in September 1901, the political climate suddenly shifted. The assassination of President William McKinley by anarchist Leon Czolgosz vaulted **Theodore Roosevelt**, the young vice president (he was forty-two), into the White House. As governor of New York, Roosevelt had angered state Republican bosses by showing sympathy for regulatory legislation, so they rid themselves of him by pushing him into national politics. Little did they anticipate that they provided the stepping-stone for the nation's most forceful president since Abraham Lincoln, one who imbued the office with much of its twentieth-century character.

18-5a **Theodore Roosevelt**

As a youth, Roosevelt suffered from asthma and nearsightedness. Driven throughout his life by an obsession to overcome his physical limitations, he exerted what he and his contemporaries called "manliness," meaning a zest for action and display of courage in a "strenuous life." In his teens, he became a marksman and horseman, and as a college student competed on Harvard's boxing and wrestling teams. In the 1880s, he went to live on a Dakota ranch, where he roped cattle and brawled with cowboys. Descended from a Dutch aristocratic family, Roosevelt had wealth to indulge in such pursuits. But he also inherited a sense of civic responsibility that guided him into a career in public service. He served three terms in the New York legislature, sat on the federal Civil Service Commission, served as New York City's police commissioner, was assistant secretary of the navy, and won election as governor of New York. In these offices Roosevelt earned a reputation as a combative, politically crafty leader. In 1898, he thrust himself into the

Carrie Chapman Catt President of the National American Woman Suffrage Association in the early twentieth century.

Theodore Roosevelt Youthful successor to slain president William McKinley in 1901; twenty-sixth president of the United States, 1901–1909; promoted an agenda of progressive reform.

▲ Looking eager for battle in his neatly-pressed new uniform from the elite haberdasher Brooks Brothers, Theodore Roosevelt served as a colonel in the U.S. Volunteers and joined the U.S. Army's campaign to oust Spain from Cuba in 1898. His bravado helped propel his political career into the governorship of New York and vice presidency of the United States.

Spanish-American War by organizing a volunteer cavalry brigade, called the Rough Riders, to fight in Cuba. Although his dramatic act had little impact on the war's outcome, it excited public imagination and made him a media hero.

Roosevelt carried his youthful exuberance into the White House. (A British diplomat once quipped, "You must always remember that the president is about six.") Considering himself a Progressive, he concurred with his allies that a small, uninvolved government would not suffice in the industrial era. Instead, economic progress necessitated a government powerful enough to guide national affairs. "A simple and poor society," he observed, "can exist as a democracy on the basis of sheer individualism. But a rich and complex society cannot so exist." Especially in economic matters, Roosevelt wanted government to act as an umpire, deciding when big business was good and when it was bad. But his brash patriotism and dislike of qualities that he considered effeminate also recalled earlier eras of unbridled expansion, when raw power prevailed in social and economic affairs.

Hepburn Act Legislation that strengthened regulatory powers of the Interstate Commerce Commission, particularly over railroads, and later other businesses and industries.

18-5b Regulation of Trusts

The federal regulation of business that has continued to the present began with Roosevelt's presidency. Roosevelt turned attention first to massive trusts created in previous decades by corporate consolidation. Although labeled a "trustbuster," Roosevelt actually considered business consolidation an efficient means to achieve material progress, but he distinguished between good and bad trusts; bad ones were those that unfairly manipulated markets. Thus, he instructed the Justice Department to use antitrust laws to prosecute railroad, meatpacking, and oil trusts, which he believed exploited the public. Roosevelt's policy triumphed in 1904 when the Supreme Court, convinced by the government's arguments, ordered the breakup of Northern Securities Company, the huge railroad combination created by J. P. Morgan. Roosevelt chose, however, not to attack other trusts, such as U.S. Steel, another of Morgan's creations.

When prosecution of Northern Securities began, Morgan reportedly collared Roosevelt and offered, "If we have done anything wrong, send your man to my man and they can fix it up." The president refused but was more sympathetic to cooperation between business and government than his rebuff might suggest. Rather than prosecute at every turn, he urged the Bureau of Corporations (part of the newly created Department of Labor and Commerce) to assist companies in merging and expanding. Through investigation and consultation, the administration cajoled businesses to regulate themselves; corporations often cooperated because government regulation helped them operate more efficiently and reduced overproduction.

Roosevelt also supported regulatory legislation, especially after his resounding victory in the presidential election of 1904, in which he won votes from Progressives and businesspeople alike. After a year of wrangling with railroads and their political allies, Roosevelt persuaded Congress to pass the **Hepburn Act** (1906), which strengthened the Interstate Commerce Commission (ICC) by giving it authority to inspect railroad financial records and set "just and reasonable" freight rates and extending that authority over ferries, express companies, storage facilities, and oil pipelines. The Hepburn Act still allowed courts to overturn ICC decisions, but in a break from previous laws, it required shippers to prove they were not in violation of regulations, rather than making the government demonstrate violations.

18-5c Pure Food and Drug Laws

Knowing that the political process made it difficult to achieve full business regulation, Roosevelt showed willingness to compromise on legislation to ensure the purity of food and drugs. For decades, reformers had been urging government regulation of processed meat and patent medicines. Public outrage at fraud and adulteration flared in 1906 when Upton Sinclair published *The Jungle*, a fictionalized exposé of Chicago meatpacking plants. Sinclair, a socialist whose objective was to improve working conditions, shocked public sensibilities with vivid descriptions. He wrote in one passage:

> There would be meat stored in great piles in rooms; and the water from the leaky roofs would drip over it, and thousands of rats would race about on it. It was too dark in these storage places to see well, but a man could run his hand over these piles of meat and sweep off handfuls of dried dung of rats. These rats were a nuisance, and the packers would put poisoned bread out for them; they would die, and then rats, bread, and meat would go into the hoppers together.

After reading the novel, Roosevelt ordered an investigation. Finding Sinclair's descriptions accurate, he supported the Meat Inspection Act, which, after considerable political maneuvering, passed Congress in 1906. Like the Hepburn Act, this law reinforced the principle of government regulation, requiring that government agents monitor the quality of processed meat. But as part of a compromise with meatpackers and their congressional allies, the bill provided that the government, rather than the meatpackers, had to finance inspections, and meatpackers could appeal adverse decisions in court. Nor were companies required to provide date-of-processing information on canned meats. Most large meatpackers welcomed the legislation anyway because it restored foreign confidence in American meat products.

The Pure Food and Drug Act (1906) not only prohibited dangerously adulterated foods but also addressed abuses in the patent medicine industry. Makers of tonics and pills had long been making undue claims about their products' effects and liberally using alcohol and narcotics as ingredients. Ads in popular publications, like one for a "Brain Stimulator and Nerve Tonic" in the Sears, Roebuck catalogue, made wildly exaggerated claims. Although the law did not ban such products, it required that labels list the ingredients—a goal consistent with Progressive confidence that if people knew the facts, they would make wiser purchases.

Roosevelt's approach to labor resembled his compromises with business over matters of regulation. When the United Mine Workers struck against Pennsylvania coal mine owners in 1902 over an eight-hour workday and higher pay, the president urged arbitration between the conflicting parties. Owners, however, refused to recognize the union or to discuss grievances. As winter approached and nationwide fuel shortages threatened, Roosevelt roused public opinion. He threatened to use federal troops to reopen the mines, thus forcing management to accept arbitration of the dispute by a special commission. The commission decided in favor of higher wages and reduced hours and required management to deal with grievance committees elected by the miners. But in a compromise with management, it did not mandate recognition of the union. The decision, according to Roosevelt, provided a "square deal" for all. The settlement also embodied Roosevelt's belief that the president or his representatives should determine which labor demands were legitimate and which were not. In Roosevelt's mind, there were good and

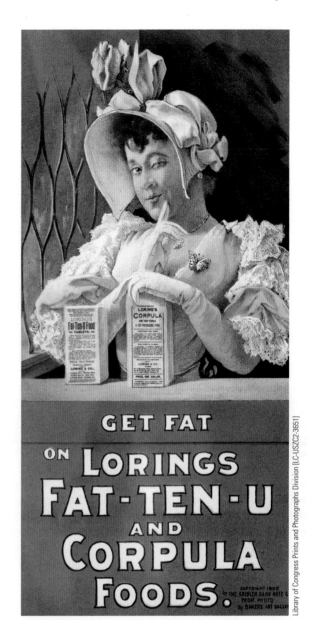

▲ Makers of unregulated patent medicines advertised their products' exorbitant abilities to cure almost any ailment and remedy any unwanted physical condition. Loring's Fat-Ten-U tablets and Loring's Corpula were two such products. The Pure Food and Drug Act of 1906 did not ban these items but tried to prevent manufacturers from making unsubstantiated claims.

bad labor organizations (socialists, for example, were bad), just as there were good and bad business combinations.

18-5d Race Relations

Although he angered southern congressmen by inviting Booker T. Washington to the White House to discuss racial matters, Roosevelt believed in white superiority and was neutral toward blacks only when it helped him politically. An incident in 1906 illustrates this belief. That year, the army transferred a battalion of African American soldiers from Nebraska to Brownsville, Texas. Anglo and Mexican residents resented their presence and banned them from parks and businesses. They also protested unsuccessfully to Washington. On August 14, a battle between blacks and whites broke out, and a white man was killed. Brownsville residents blamed the soldiers, but when army investigators asked the troops to identify who had participated in the riot, none of the soldiers cooperated. As a result, Roosevelt discharged 167 black soldiers without a hearing or trial, and prevented them from receiving their pay and pensions even though there was no evidence against them. Black leaders were outraged. Roosevelt, hoping that African Americans would support Republican candidates in the 1906 elections, had stalled before doing anything. But after the elections, he signed the discharge papers and offered no support when a bill was introduced in the Senate to allow the soldiers to reenlist.

18-5e Conservation

Roosevelt combined the Progressive impulse for efficiency with his love for the outdoors to make lasting contributions to resource conservation. Government involvement in this endeavor, especially the establishment of national parks, had begun in the late nineteenth century. Roosevelt advanced the movement by favoring *conservation* over *preservation*. He not only exercised presidential power to protect such natural wonders as the Olympic Peninsula in Washington and the Grand Canyon in Arizona, as well as such human marvels as the native cliff dwellings in Colorado and Arizona, by declaring them national monuments; he also backed a policy of "wise use" of forests, waterways, and other resources to conserve them for future generations. Previously, the government had transferred ownership and control of natural resources on federal land to the states and private interests. Roosevelt, however, believed the most efficient way to use and conserve resources would be for the federal government to retain management over lands that remained in the public domain.

Roosevelt used federal authority over resources in several ways. He created five national parks and fifty-one national bird reservations, and protected waterpower sites from sale to private interests. He also supported the Newlands Reclamation Act of 1902, which controlled sale of irrigated federal land in the West (see "Newlands Reclamation Act," Section 15-2f), and in 1908 brought the nation's governors to the White House to discuss the efficient use of resources. During his presidency, Roosevelt tripled the number and acreage of national forests and backed conservationist Gifford Pinchot in creating the U.S. Forest Service.

18-5f Gifford Pinchot

As chief forester of the United States and principal advocate of "wise use" policy, Pinchot promoted scientific management of the nation's woodlands. He obtained Roosevelt's support for transferring management of the national forests from the Interior Department to his bureau in the Agriculture Department, arguing that forests were crops grown on "tree farms." Under his guidance, the Forest Service charged fees for grazing livestock within national forests, supervised bidding for the cutting of timber, and hired university-trained foresters as federal employees.

Pinchot and Roosevelt did not seek to lock up—preserve—resources permanently; rather, they wanted to guarantee—conserve—their efficient use and make those who profited from using public lands pay the government for that privilege. Although antigovernment, pro-development attitudes still prevailed in the West, many of those involved in natural resource development welcomed such a policy because, like regulation of food and drugs, it enabled them to manage their operations more effectively, such as when Roosevelt and Pinchot encouraged lumber companies to engage in reforestation. As a result of new federal policies, the West and its resources fell under the Progressive spell of expert management.

18-5g Panic of 1907

In 1907, economic crisis forced Roosevelt to compromise his principles and work more closely with big business. That year, a financial panic caused by reckless speculation forced some New York banks to close in order to prevent frightened depositors from withdrawing money. J. P. Morgan helped stem the panic by persuading financiers to stop dumping stocks. In return for Morgan's aid, Roosevelt approved a deal allowing U.S. Steel to absorb the Tennessee Iron and Coal Company—a deal at odds with Roosevelt's trust-busting aims.

But during his last year in office, Roosevelt retreated from the Republican Party's traditional friendliness to big business. He lashed out at "malefactors of great wealth" and supported stronger business regulation and heavier taxation of the rich. Having promised that he would not seek reelection, Roosevelt backed his friend, Secretary of War **William Howard Taft**, for the Republican nomination in 1908, hoping that Taft would continue his initiatives. Democrats nominated William Jennings Bryan for the third time, but the "Great Commoner" lost again. Aided by Roosevelt, who still enjoyed great popularity, Taft won by 1.25 million popular votes and a 2-to-1 margin in the electoral college.

18-5h Taft Administration

Early in 1909, Roosevelt traveled to Africa to shoot game, leaving Taft to face political problems that Roosevelt had managed to postpone. Foremost was the tariff; rates had risen to excessive levels. Honoring Taft's pledge to cut tariffs, the House passed a bill sponsored by New York representative Sereno E. Payne that provided for numerous reductions. Protectionists in the Senate prepared, as in the past, to amend the bill and revise rates upward. But Senate Progressives, led by La Follette, attacked the tariff for benefiting special interests, trapping Taft between reformers who claimed to be preserving Roosevelt's antitrust campaign and protectionists who still dominated the Republican Party. In the end, Senator Aldrich restored most cuts the Payne bill had made, and Taft—who believed the bill had some positive provisions and understood that extreme cuts

William Howard Taft
Roosevelt's handpicked successor for president (1909–1913); later served as chief justice of the U.S. Supreme Court.

were not politically possible—signed what became known as the Payne-Aldrich Tariff (1909). In Progressives' eyes, Taft had failed the test of filling Roosevelt's shoes.

Progressive and conservative wings of the Republican Party openly split. Soon after the tariff controversy, a group of insurgents in the House, led by Nebraska's George Norris, challenged Speaker "Uncle Joe" Cannon of Illinois, whose power over committee assignments and the scheduling of debates could make or break a piece of legislation. Taft first supported, then abandoned, the insurgents, who nevertheless managed to liberalize procedures by enlarging the influential Rules Committee and removing selection of its members from Cannon's control. In 1910, Taft also angered conservationists by firing Gifford Pinchot, who had protested Secretary of the Interior Richard A. Ballinger's plans to aid private development by selling Alaskan coal lands and reducing federal supervision of western waterpower sites.

In reality, Taft was as sympathetic to reform as Roosevelt was. He prosecuted more trusts than Roosevelt; expanded national forest reserves; signed the Mann-Elkins Act (1910), which bolstered regulatory powers of the ICC; and supported such labor reforms as shorter work hours and mine safety legislation. The Sixteenth Amendment, which legalized the federal income tax as a permanent source of federal revenue, and the Seventeenth Amendment, which provided for direct election of U.S. senators, were initiated during Taft's presidency (and ratified in 1913). Like Roosevelt, Taft compromised with big business, but unlike Roosevelt, he lacked the ability to rouse the public with spirited rhetoric. Roosevelt had expanded presidential power and infused the presidency with vitality. "I believe in a strong executive," he once asserted. "I believe in power." Taft, by contrast, believed in the restraint of law. He had been a successful lawyer and judge, and returned to the bench as chief justice of the United States between 1921 and 1930. His caution and unwillingness to offend disappointed those accustomed to Roosevelt's magnetism.

18-5i Candidates in 1912

In 1910, when Roosevelt returned from Africa, he found his party torn and tormented. Reformers, angered by Taft's apparent insensitivity to their causes, formed the National Progressive Republican League and rallied behind Robert La Follette for president in 1912, though many hoped Roosevelt would run. Another wing of the party remained loyal to Taft. Disappointed by Taft's performance (particularly his firing of Pinchot), Roosevelt began to speak out. He filled speeches with references to "the welfare of the people" and stronger regulation of business. When La Follette became ill early in 1912, Roosevelt, proclaiming himself fit as a "bull moose," threw his hat into the ring for the Republican presidential nomination.

Taft's supporters controlled the Republican convention and nominated him for a second term. In protest, Roosevelt's supporters bolted the convention to form a third party—the Progressive, or Bull Moose, Party—and nominated the fifty-three-year-old former president. Meanwhile, Democrats took forty-six ballots to select their candidate, New Jersey's

Progressive governor **Woodrow Wilson**. Socialists, by now an organized and growing party, again nominated Eugene V. Debs. The ensuing campaign exposed voters to the most thorough debate on the nature of American democracy since 1896.

18-5j New Nationalism Versus New Freedom

Central to Theodore Roosevelt's campaign as Progressive Party nominee was a scheme called the "New Nationalism," a term coined by reform editor Herbert Croly. The New Nationalism envisioned an era of national unity in which government would coordinate and regulate economic activity. Echoing his statements made in the last years of his presidency, Roosevelt asserted that he would establish regulatory commissions of experts who would protect citizens' interests and ensure wise use of economic power. "The effort at prohibiting all combinations has substantially failed," he claimed. "The way out lies . . . in completely controlling them."

Wilson offered a more idealistic proposal, the "New Freedom," based on ideas of Progressive lawyer Louis Brandeis. Wilson argued that concentrated economic power threatened individual liberty and that monopolies should be broken up so that the marketplace could become genuinely open. But he would not restore laissez-faire. Like Roosevelt, Wilson would enhance government authority to protect and regulate. "Freedom today," he declared, "is something more than being let alone. Without the watchful . . . resolute interference of the government, there can be no fair play between individuals and such powerful institutions as the trust." Wilson stopped short, however, of advocating the cooperation between business and government inherent in Roosevelt's New Nationalism.

Roosevelt and Wilson stood closer together than their rhetoric implied. Despite his faith in experts as regulators, Roosevelt's belief in individual freedom was as strong as Wilson's. And Wilson was not completely hostile to concentrated economic power. Both men supported equality of opportunity (chiefly for white males), conservation of natural resources, fair wages, and social betterment. Neither would hesitate to expand government intervention through strong personal leadership and bureaucratic reform.

Amid passionate moral pronouncements from Roosevelt and Wilson, as well as a hard-hitting critique from Debs and a low-key defense of conservatism from Taft, the popular vote was inconclusive. The victorious Wilson won just 42 percent, though he did capture 435 out of 531 electoral votes (see Map 18.2). Roosevelt received 27 percent of the popular vote. Taft finished third, polling 23 percent and only 8 electoral votes. Debs won 6 percent but no electoral votes. One major outcome was evident, however; three-quarters of the electorate supported some alternative to the view of restrained government that Taft represented. Thus, Wilson could proclaim on Inauguration Day in 1913, "The Nation has been deeply stirred by a solemn passion. . . . The feelings with which we face this new age

Woodrow Wilson Democratic president whose election in 1912 ushered in a second wave of progressive reforms on the national level; served as president until 1921.

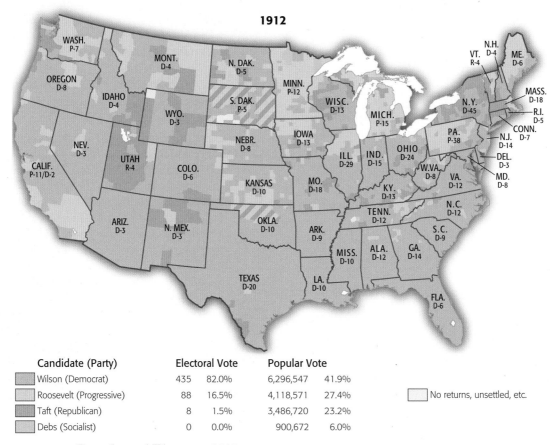

1912

Candidate (Party)	Electoral Vote		Popular Vote	
Wilson (Democrat)	435	82.0%	6,296,547	41.9%
Roosevelt (Progressive)	88	16.5%	4,118,571	27.4%
Taft (Republican)	8	1.5%	3,486,720	23.2%
Debs (Socialist)	0	0.0%	900,672	6.0%

No returns, unsettled, etc.

Map 18.2 Presidential Election, 1912

Although he had only a minority of the popular votes, Woodrow Wilson captured so many states that he achieved an easy victory in the electoral college.

of right and opportunity sweep across our heartstrings like some air out of God's own presence, where justice and mercy are reconciled and the judge and the brother are one."

18-6 Woodrow Wilson and Extension of Progressive Reform

▶ How did Woodrow Wilson's personality differ from that of Theodore Roosevelt?

▶ What economic regularity policies and reforms did Woodrow Wilson implement?

▶ What was Woodrow Wilson's position on race?

18-6a Woodrow Wilson

The public fondly called Roosevelt "Teddy" and "TR," but Thomas Woodrow Wilson was too aloof to be nicknamed "Woody" or "WW." Born in Virginia in 1856 and raised in the South, Wilson was the son of a Presbyterian minister. He earned a BA degree at Princeton, studied law at the University

of Virginia, received a PhD from Johns Hopkins University, and became a professor of history, jurisprudence, and political economy before returning to Princeton, where he served as the university's president from 1902 to 1910. Between 1885 and 1908, he published several respected books on American history and government.

Wilson's manner and attitudes reflected his background. On one hand, he was a superb orator who could inspire loyalty from white people with religious imagery and eloquent expressions of American ideals. But he harbored strong disdain for African Americans; he wrote that southern slaves had been treated "indulgently," belittled blacks who held office during Reconstruction, opposed admitting blacks to Princeton, and had no misgivings about Jim Crow laws. At Princeton, he upset tradition with curricular reforms and battles against the university's aristocratic elements, and he earned enough of a reputation as a reformer so that in 1910 New Jersey's Democrats, eager for respectability, nominated him for governor. After winning the election, Wilson repudiated the party bosses and promoted Progressive legislation. A poor administrator, he often lost his temper and stubbornly refused to compromise. His accomplishments nevertheless attracted national attention and won him the Democratic nomination for president in 1912.

18-6b Wilson's Policy on Business Regulation

As president, Wilson found it necessary to blend New Freedom competition with New Nationalism regulation; in so doing, he set the direction of future federal economic policy. Corporate consolidation had made restoration of open competition impossible. Wilson could only try to prevent abuses by expanding government's regulatory powers. He thus supported congressional passage in 1914 of the Clayton Anti-Trust Act and a bill creating the **Federal Trade Commission (FTC)**. The Clayton Act corrected deficiencies of the Sherman Anti-Trust Act of 1890 by outlawing such practices as price discrimination (lowering prices in some regions but not in others) and interlocking directorates (management of two or more competing companies by the same executives). The act also aided labor by exempting unions from its anti-combination provision, thereby making peaceful strikes, boycotts, and picketing less vulnerable to government interference. The FTC could investigate companies and issue cease and desist orders against unfair practices. Accused companies could appeal FTC orders in court; nevertheless, the FTC represented another step toward consumer protection.

Also under Wilson, the Federal Reserve Act (1913) established the nation's first central banking system since 1836. To break the power that syndicates like that of J. P. Morgan held over the money supply, the act created twelve district banks to hold reserves of member banks throughout the nation. The district banks, supervised by the Federal Reserve Board, would lend money to member banks at low interest, called the discount rate. By adjusting this rate (and thus the amount a member bank could afford to borrow), district banks could increase or decrease the supply of money in circulation. In other words, in response to the nation's economic needs, the Federal Reserve Board could loosen or tighten credit, making interest rates fairer, especially for small borrowers.

18-6c Tariff and Tax Reform

Wilson and Congress attempted to restore trade competition and aid consumers with the Underwood Tariff of 1913. By reducing or eliminating certain tariff rates, the Underwood Tariff encouraged importation of cheaper foreign materials and manufactured goods. To replace revenues lost because of tariff reductions, the act levied a graduated income tax on U.S. residents—an option made possible when the Sixteenth Amendment, which empowered Congress to create such a tax, was ratified earlier that year. The tax was tame by today's standards. Incomes under $4,000 ($98,000 in current dollars) were exempt; thus, almost all factory workers and most farmers escaped taxation. Individuals and corporations earning between $4,000 and $20,000 had to pay a 1 percent tax; thereafter rates rose to a maximum of 6 percent on earnings over $500,000.

The outbreak of the First World War (see Chapter 20) and approaching presidential election campaign prompted Wilson to support stronger reforms in 1916. To aid farmers, he backed the Federal Farm Loan Act. This measure created twelve federally supported banks (not to be confused with Federal Reserve banks), which could lend money at moderate interest

▲ Woodrow Wilson on the left, looking stiff and formal, stands with William Howard Taft, looking more at ease, outside the White House at Wilson's inauguration in March of 1917.

to farmers who belonged to credit institutions—a diluted version of the subtreasury plan that Populists had proposed a generation earlier (see "Farmers' Alliances," Section 17-5d). To forestall railroad strikes that might disrupt transportation at a time of national emergency, Wilson also pushed passage of the Adamson Act, which mandated eight-hour workdays and time-and-a-half overtime pay for railroad laborers. He pleased Progressives by appointing Brandeis, the "people's advocate," to the Supreme Court, though an anti-Semitic backlash almost blocked Senate approval of the Court's first Jewish justice. In addition, Wilson backed laws that regulated child labor and provided workers' compensation for federal employees who suffered work-related injuries or illness.

Amid his reforms, however, Wilson never overcame his racism. He fired several black federal officials, and his administration preserved racial separation in Washington, D.C. restrooms, restaurants, and government buildings. Wilson responded to protesting blacks that "segregation is not a humiliation but a benefit, and ought to be so regarded by you gentlemen." When the pathbreaking but inflammatory film about the Civil War and Reconstruction *The Birth of a Nation* was released in 1915, Wilson allowed a showing at the White House, though he subsequently prohibited it during the First World War.

Federal Trade Commission (FTC) Agency formed in 1914 to ensure fair trade practices.

Margaret Sanger, Planned Parenthood, and the Birth Control Controversy

Some reforms of the Progressive Era illustrate how earnest intentions to help can become tangled in divisive issues of morality. Such is the legacy of birth control advocate Margaret Sanger. In 1912, Sanger began writing a column on sex education in the *New York Call* entitled "What Every Girl Should Know." Almost immediately, moralists accused her of producing obscene literature because she publicly discussed venereal disease and contraception. The issue of limiting family size, however, became her passion, and she began counseling poor women on New York's Lower East Side about how to avoid the pain of frequent childbirth, miscarriage, and bungled abortion. In 1914, Sanger published the first issue of *The Woman Rebel*, a monthly newspaper that advocated a woman's right to practice birth control. Indicted for distributing obscenity through the mails, she fled to England. There she joined a set of radicals and gave speeches on behalf of family planning and a woman's need to enjoy sexual fulfillment without fear of pregnancy.

Returning to the United States, Sanger opened the country's first birth control clinic in Brooklyn in 1916. She was arrested, but when a court exempted physicians from a law prohibiting dissemination of contraceptive information, she set up a doctor-run clinic in 1923. Staffed by female doctors and social workers, the Birth Control Clinical Research Bureau acted as a model for other clinics. Sanger also organized the American Birth Control League (1921) and tried to win support from medical and social reformers, including some from the eugenics movement, for legalized

birth control. Eventually, her radical views caused her to fall out with some of her allies, and she resigned from the American Birth Control League in 1928.

The movement continued, however, and in 1938 the American Birth Control League and the Birth Control Clinical Research Bureau merged to form the Birth Control Federation of America, renamed the Planned Parenthood Federation of America (PPFA) in 1942. The organization's name defined its mission to strengthen the family and stabilize society with the help of governmental support, rather than to focus more directly on the feminist issue of whether or not a woman should have the right of voluntary motherhood. Throughout the 1940s, the PPFA emphasized family planning through making contraceptives more accessible. In 1970, it began receiving funds under a federal program to provide family-planning services.

In the 1960s, the emergence of new feminist agitation for women's rights and rising concerns about overpopulation moved issues of birth control and abortion into an arena of passionate controversy. Although the PPFA had initially dissociated itself from abortion as a means of family planning, the debate between a woman's "choice" and a fetus's "right to life" drew the organization into the fray, especially after 1973, when the Supreme Court validated women's right to an abortion in *Roe v. Wade*. The national PPFA and its local branches have fought legislative and court attempts to make abortions illegal ever since; most recently, in another landmark case in 2016, the Supreme Court overturned a Texas law that had restricted women's access to

clinics that provided abortions. In 1989, the PPFA helped organize a women's march on Washington for equality and abortion rights, but at the same time, some Latino and African American groups attacked the PPFA's stance, charging that legalized abortion was a kind of eugenics program meant to reduce births among nonwhite races.

Because of the PPFA's involvement in abortion politics, several of its clinics have been targets of picketing and even violence by those who believe abortion to be immoral. Also, debates have raged over whether government funding for Planned Parenthood clinics should be eliminated because the money might directly or indirectly be used to fund abortions. The PPFA now operates nearly nine hundred health centers providing medical services and education nationwide to more than 5 million women, most of whom are poor, and has fulfilled Margaret Sanger's dream of legalized contraception and family planning. But as with other reforms dealing with issues of morality and individual rights, birth control has left a legacy to a people and a nation of disagreement over whose rights and whose morality should prevail.

CRITICAL THINKING

- Should a person's health care decisions belong exclusively to that person or should the government play a role?
- If the government should play a role, how do we determine when the government should intervene in matters of a citizen's health?
- Consider this debate in terms of abortion rights; the use of alcohol, drugs, or tobacco; obesity; and medically-assisted suicide.

18-6d Election of 1916

In selecting a candidate to oppose Wilson in the presidential election of 1916, Republicans snubbed Theodore Roosevelt in favor of Charles Evans Hughes, Supreme Court justice and former reform governor of New York. Aware of public anxiety over the world war raging in Europe since 1914, Wilson ran on

a platform of neutrality, using the slogan "He Kept Us Out of War." Hughes advocated military preparedness, but Wilson's peace platform resonated with voters. The election was close. Wilson received 9.1 million votes to Hughes's 8.5 million and barely won in the electoral college, 277 to 254. The Socialist Party candidate, newspaperman Allan Benson, drew only

600,000 votes, down from 901,000 in 1912, largely because Wilson's reforms had won over some socialists and because the ailing Eugene Debs was no longer the party's standard-bearer.

During Wilson's second term, U.S. involvement in the First World War increased government regulation of the economy. Mobilization and war, he believed, required government-directed coordination of production and cooperation between the public and private sectors. The War Industries Board exemplified this cooperation: private businesses regulated by the board submitted to its control on condition that their profit motives would continue to be satisfied. After the war, Wilson's administration dropped most cooperative and regulatory measures, including farm price supports, guarantees of collective bargaining, and high taxes. This retreat from regulation, prompted in part by the election of a Republican Congress in 1918, stimulated a new era of business ascendancy in the 1920s.

Summary

By 1920, a quarter-century of reform had wrought momentous changes in the ways government, the economy, and society operated. In their efforts to end abuses of power, reform institutions, and apply scientific and efficient planning and management, Progressives established the principle of public intervention to ensure fairness, health, and safety. As well, concern over poverty and injustice reached new heights.

Multiple and sometimes contradictory goals characterized the era. By no means was there a single Progressive movement. Programs on the national level ranged from Roosevelt's faith in big government as a coordinator of big business to Wilson's promise to dissolve economic concentrations and legislate open competition. At state and local levels, reformers pursued causes as varied as neighborhood improvement, government reorganization, public ownership of utilities, and betterment of working conditions. National associations coordinated efforts on specific issues, but reformers with different goals often worked at cross-purposes, sometimes expanding rights but at other times restricting liberty. Women and African Americans developed a new consciousness about identity, and although women made some inroads into public life, both groups still found themselves in confined social positions and lacking white male support for their quest for dignity and recognition.

In spite of their successes, the failure of many Progressive initiatives indicates the strength of the opposition as well as weaknesses within reform movements themselves. As issues such as Americanization, eugenics, prohibition, education, and moral uplift illustrate, social reform often meant social control—attempting to impose one group's values on all of society and

to regulate behavior of immigrant and nonwhite racial groups. In political matters, courts asserted constitutional and liberty-of-contract doctrines in undercutting key Progressive legislation, notably the federal law prohibiting child labor. In states and cities, adoption of the initiative, referendum, and recall did not encourage greater participation in government as had been hoped; those mechanisms either were seldom used or became tools of special interests. Federal regulatory agencies lacked enough resources for thorough investigation and enforcement; they had to depend on information from the very companies they policed. Progressives thus failed in many respects to redistribute power. In 1920, as in 1900, government remained under the influence of business, a situation that many people in power considered quite satisfactory.

Yet the reform movements that characterized the Progressive Era reshaped the national outlook. Trust-busting, however faulty, made industrialists more sensitive to public opinion, and insurgents in Congress partially diluted the power of dictatorial politicians. Progressive legislation equipped government with tools to protect consumers against price fixing and dangerous products. Social reformers relieved some ills of urban and industrial life. And perhaps most important, Progressives challenged old ways of thinking. Although the questions they raised about the quality of American life remained unresolved, Progressives made the nation acutely aware of its principles and promises.

Suggestions for Further Reading

Nancy F. Cott, *The Grounding of Modern Feminism* (1987)

Steven J. Diner, *A Very Different Age: Americans of the Progressive Era* (1998)

Laurie Collier Hillstrom, *The Muckrakers and the Progressive Era* (2010)

Hugh D. Hindman, *Child Labor: An American History* (2002)

Alice Kessler-Harris, *Out to Work: A History of Wage-Earning Women in the United States*, 20th anniversary ed. (2003)

Michael McGerr, *A Fierce Discontent: The Rise and Fall of the Progressive Movement in America, 1870–1920* (2003)

Sidney Milkis and Jerome Mileur, eds., *Progressivism and the New Democracy* (1999)

Patricia A. Schecter, *Ida B. Wells and American Reform, 1880–1930* (2001)

David Tyack, *Seeking Common Ground: Public Schools in a Diverse Society* (2003)

Robert H. Wiebe, *The Search for Order, 1877–1920* (1967)

The Quest for Empire, 1865–1914

"Devil!" they shouted at Lottie Moon. "Foreign devil!" The Southern Baptist missionary, half a world away from home, braced herself against the cries of the Chinese "rabble" whom she had been determined to convert to Christianity. On that day in the 1880s, she walked "steadily and persistently" through the throng of hecklers, silently vowing to win their acceptance and then their souls.

Born in 1840 in Virginia and educated at what is now Hollins College, Charlotte Diggs Moon volunteered in 1873 for "woman's work" in northern China. There she taught and proselytized, largely among women and children, because women seldom preached to men and men were forbidden to preach to women. This compassionate, pious, and courageous single woman, "putting love into action," worked in China until her death in 1912.

In the 1870s and 1880s, Lottie Moon (Mu Ladi, or 幕拉第) made bold and sometimes dangerous evangelizing trips to isolated Chinese hamlets. "O! The torture of human eyes upon you; scanning every feature, every look, every gesture!" Curious peasant women pinched her, pulled on her skirts, and purred, "How white her hand is!" They peppered her with questions: "How old are you?" "Where do you get money to live on?" Speaking in Chinese, Lottie held high a picture book of Jesus Christ's birth and crucifixion, drawing the crowd's attention to the "foreign doctrine" that she hoped would displace Confucianism, Buddhism, and Taoism.

In the 1890s, a "storm of persecution" directed against foreigners swept China. Because missionaries were upending traditional ways and authority, they became hated targets. One missionary conceded that, in "believing Jesus," girls and women alarmed men who worried that "disobedient wives and daughters" would no longer "worship the idols when told." In the village of Shaling in early 1890, Lottie Moon's Christian converts were beaten and the "foreign devils" ordered to move out. Fearing for her life, she

◀ The missionary Lottie Moon (1840–1912) in 1901 with English-language students in Japan, during her refuge from the Boxer Rebellion in China. Virginia Baptist Historical Society

Chronology

1861–69	■ Seward sets expansionist course
1867	■ United States acquires Alaska and Midway
1876	■ Pro-U.S. Díaz begins thirty-four-year rule in Mexico
1878	■ United States gains naval rights in Samoa
1885	■ Strong's *Our Country* celebrates Anglo-Saxon destiny of dominance
1887	■ United States gains naval rights to Pearl Harbor, Hawai'i ■ McKinley Tariff hurts Hawaiian sugar exports
1893	■ Economic crisis leads to business failures and mass unemployment ■ Pro-U.S. interests stage successful coup against Queen Lili'uokalani of Hawai'i
1895	■ Cuban revolution against Spain begins ■ Japan defeats China in war, annexes Korea and Formosa (Taiwan)
1898	■ United States formally annexes Hawai'i ■ U.S. battleship *Maine* blows up in Havana harbor ■ United States defeats Spain in Spanish-American War
1899	■ Treaty of Paris enlarges U.S. empire ■ United Fruit Company forms and becomes influential in Central America ■ Philippine Insurrection breaks out, led by Emilio Aguinaldo
1901	■ McKinley assassinated; Theodore Roosevelt becomes president
1903	■ Panama grants canal rights to United States ■ Platt Amendment subjugates Cuba
1904	■ Roosevelt Corollary declares United States a hemispheric "police power"
1905	■ Portsmouth Conference ends Russo-Japanese War
1906	■ San Francisco School Board segregates Asian schoolchildren ■ United States invades Cuba to quell revolt
1907	■ "Great White Fleet" makes world tour
1910	■ Mexican revolution threatens U.S. interests
1914	■ U.S. troops invade Mexico ■ First World War begins ■ Panama Canal opens

had to flee. For several months in 1900, during the violent Boxer Rebellion, she had to leave China altogether, as a multinational force (including U.S. troops) intervened to save foreign missionaries, diplomats, and merchants.

Lottie Moon and thousands of other missionaries managed to convert to Christianity only a very small minority of the Chinese people. Although she, like other missionaries, probably never shed the Western view that she represented a superior religion and culture, she seldom wavered in her affection for the Chinese people and in her devotion to the foreign missionary project—in her "rejoicing to suffer." In frequent letters and articles directed to a U.S. audience, she lobbied to recruit "a band of ardent, enthusiastic, and experienced Christian women," to stir up "a mighty wave of enthusiasm for

Woman's Work for Woman." To this day, the Lottie Moon Christmas Offering in Southern Baptist churches raises millions of dollars for missions abroad.

Like so many other Americans who went overseas in the late nineteenth and early twentieth centuries, Lottie Moon helped spread American culture and influence abroad. In this complex process, other peoples sometimes adopted and sometimes rejected American ways. At the same time, American participants in this cultural expansion and the cultural collisions it generated became transformed. Lottie Moon, for example, strove to understand the Chinese people and to learn their language. She assumed their dress and abandoned such derogatory phrases as "heathen Chinese" and "great unwashed." She reminded other, less sensitive missionaries that the Chinese rightfully took pride in their own ancient history and thus had no reason to "gape in astonishment at Western civilization."

Lottie Moon also changed—again, in her own words—from "a timid self-distrustful girl into a brave self-reliant woman." As she questioned the Chinese confinement of women, most conspicuous in arranged marriages, foot binding, and sexual segregation, she advanced women's rights. She understood that she could not convert Chinese women unless they had the freedom to listen to her appeals. Bucking the gender ideology of the times, she also uneasily rose to challenge the male domination of America's religious missions. When the Southern Baptist Foreign Mission Board denied female missionaries the right to vote in meetings, she resigned in protest. The board soon reversed itself.

In later decades, critics labeled the activities of Lottie Moon and other missionaries "cultural imperialism," accusing them of seeking to subvert indigenous traditions and of sparking destructive cultural clashes. Defenders of missionary work, on the other hand, have celebrated their efforts to break down cultural barriers and to bring the world's peoples closer together. Either way, Lottie Moon's story illustrates how Americans in the late nineteenth century interacted with the world in diverse ways, how through their experiences the categories "domestic" and "foreign" came to intersect, and how they expanded abroad not only to seek land, trade, investments, and strategic bases, but also to promote American culture, including the Christian faith.

Experience an interactive version of this story in MindTap®.

Between the Civil War and the First World War, an expansionist United States joined the ranks of the great world powers. Before the Civil War, Americans had repeatedly extended the frontier: they bought Louisiana; annexed Florida, Oregon, and Texas; pushed Native Americans out of the path of white migration westward; seized California and other western areas from Mexico; and acquired southern parts of present-day Arizona and New Mexico from Mexico (the Gadsden Purchase). Americans had also developed a lucrative foreign trade with most of the world and promoted American culture wherever they traveled. They rekindled their expansionist course after the Civil War, building, managing, and protecting an overseas empire.

It was an age of empire. By the 1870s, most of Europe's powers were carving up Africa and large parts of Asia and Oceania for themselves. By 1900 the powers had conquered more than 10 million square miles (one-fifth of the earth's land) and 150 million people. As the century turned, France, Russia, and Germany were spending heavily on modern steel navies, challenging an overextended Great Britain. In Asia, meanwhile, a rapidly modernizing Japan expanded at the expense of both China and Russia.

Engineering advances altered the world's political geography through the Suez Canal (1869), the British Trans-Indian railroad (1870), and the Russian Trans-Siberian Railway (1904), while steamships, machine guns, telegraphs, and malaria drugs greatly facilitated the imperialists' task. Simultaneously, the optimistic spirit that had characterized

European political discourse in the 1850s and 1860s gave way to a brooding pessimism and a sense of impending warfare informed by notions of racial conflict and survival of the fittest.

This transformation of world politics did not escape notice by perceptive Americans. Some argued that the United States risked being "left behind" if it failed to join the scramble for territory and markets. Republican senator Henry Cabot Lodge of Massachusetts, claiming that the "great nations" were seizing "the waste areas of the world," advised that "the United States must not fall out of the line of march" because "civilization and the advancement of the [Anglo-Saxon] race" were at stake. Such thinking helped fuel Americans' desire in the years after the Civil War to exert their influence beyond the continental United States, to reach for more space, more land, more markets, more cultural penetration, and more power.

By 1900, the United States had emerged as a great power with particular clout in Latin America, especially as Spain declined and Britain disengaged from the Western Hemisphere. In the Pacific, the new U.S. empire included Hawai'i, American Samoa, and the Philippines. Theodore Roosevelt, who in the 1890s was a leading spokesman for the imperialist cause, would, as president in the decade that followed, seek to consolidate this newfound power.

Most Americans applauded expansionism—the outward movement of goods, ships, dollars, people, and ideas—as a traditional feature of their nation's history. But many became uneasy whenever expansionism gave way to imperialism—the imposition of control over other peoples, undermining their sovereignty and usurping their freedom to make their own decisions. Abroad, native nationalists, commercial competitors, and other imperial nations tried to block the spread of U.S. influence.

■ *What accounts for the increased importance of foreign policy concerns in American politics in the closing years of the nineteenth century?*

■ *What key arguments were made by American anti-imperialists?*

■ *How did late-nineteenth-century imperialism transform the United States?*

19-1 Imperial Dreams

▶ **Why did the United States take a more active role in international affairs and foreign policy in the late nineteenth century?**

▶ **What methods did expansionists seek to use to spread American influence abroad?**

▶ **What intellectual developments contributed to American activism abroad?**

Foreign policy assumed a new importance for Americans in the closing years of the nineteenth century. For much of the Gilded Age, they had been preoccupied by internal matters, such as industrialization, the construction of the railroads, and the settlement of the West. Over time, however, increasing numbers of political and business leaders began to look outward, and to advocate a more activist approach to world affairs. The motives of these expansionists were complex and varied, but all of them emphasized the supposed benefits of such an approach to the country's domestic health.

That proponents of overseas expansion stressed the benefits that would accrue at home should come as no surprise, for foreign policy has always sprung from the domestic setting of a nation—its needs and moods, its ideology and culture. The leaders who guided America's expansionist foreign relations were the same ones who guided the economic development of the machine age, forged the transcontinental railroad, built the nation's bustling cities and giant corporations, and shaped a mass culture. They unabashedly espoused the idea that the United States was an exceptional nation, so different from and superior to others because of its Anglo-Saxon heritage and its God-favored and prosperous history.

Exceptionalism was but one in an intertwined set of ideas that figured prominently in the American march toward empire. Nationalism, capitalism, Social Darwinism, and a paternalistic attitude toward foreigners influenced American

leaders as well. "They are children and we are men in these deep matters of government," future president Woodrow Wilson announced in 1898. The very words he chose reveal the gender and age bias of American attitudes. Where these attitudes intersected with foreign cultures, there came not only adoption but rejection, not only imitation but conflict, as Lottie Moon learned.

19-1a Foreign Policy Elite

It would take time for most Americans to grasp the changes under way. "The people" may influence domestic policy directly, but the making of foreign policy is usually dominated by what scholars have labeled the "foreign policy elite"—opinion leaders in politics, journalism, business, agriculture, religion, education, and the military. In the post–Civil War era, this small group, whom Secretary of State Walter Q. Gresham called "the thoughtful men of the country," expressed the opinions that counted. Better read and better traveled than most Americans, more cosmopolitan in outlook, and politically active, they believed that U.S. prosperity and security depended on the exertion of U.S. influence abroad. Increasingly in the late nineteenth century, and especially in the 1890s, the expansionist-minded elite urged both formal and informal imperialism. Ambitious and clannish, the imperialists often met in Washington, D.C., at the homes of historian Henry Adams and of writer and diplomat John Hay (who became secretary of state in 1898) or at the Metropolitan Club. They talked about building a bigger navy and digging a canal across Panama, Central America, or Mexico; establishing colonies; and selling surpluses abroad. Theodore Roosevelt, appointed assistant secretary of the navy in 1897, was among them; so were Senator Henry Cabot Lodge, who joined the Foreign Relations Committee in 1896, and corporate lawyer Elihu Root, who later would serve as both secretary of war and secretary of state. Such well-positioned luminaries kept up the drumbeat for empire.

These American leaders believed that selling, buying, and investing in foreign marketplaces were important to the United States. Why? One reason was profits from foreign sales. "It is my dream," declared the governor of Georgia in 1878, to see "in every valley . . . a cotton factory to convert the raw material of the neighborhood into fabrics which shall warm the limbs of Japanese and Chinese." Fear also helped make the case for foreign trade, as foreign commerce might serve as a safety valve to relieve overproduction, unemployment, economic depression, and the social tension that arose from them. The nation's farms and factories produced more than Americans could consume, all the more so during the 1890s depression. Surpluses had to be exported, the economist David A. Wells warned, or "we are certain to be smothered in our own grease." Economic ties also permitted political influence to be exerted abroad and helped spread the American way of life, especially capitalism, creating a world more hospitable to Americans. In an era when the most powerful nations in the world were also the greatest traders, vigorous foreign economic expansion symbolized national stature.

Figure 19.1 U.S. Trade Expansion, 1865–1914

This figure illustrates two key characteristics of U.S. foreign trade: first, that the United States began in the 1870s to enjoy a favorable balance of trade (exporting more than it imported), and second, that U.S. exports expanded tremendously, making the United States one of the world's economic giants. Adapted from Thomas G. Paterson, J. Garry Clifford, and Kenneth J. Hagan, *American Foreign Relations: A History*, 5th ed. Copyright 2000 by Houghton Mifflin Company.

19-1b Foreign Trade Expansion

Although most business leaders remained focused on the domestic marketplace, foreign trade figured prominently in the tremendous economic growth of the United States after the Civil War. Foreign commerce in turn stimulated the building of a larger protective navy, the professionalization of the foreign service, calls for more colonies,

and a more interventionist foreign policy. In 1865, U.S. exports totaled $234 million; by 1900, they had climbed to $1.5 billion (see Figure 19.1). By 1914, at the outbreak of the First World War, exports had reached $2.5 billion, prompting some Europeans to protest an American "invasion" of goods. In 1874, the United States reversed its historically unfavorable balance of trade (importing more than it exported) and began to enjoy a long-term favorable balance (exporting more than it imported)—though the balance of payments remained in the red. Most of America's products went to Britain, continental Europe, and Canada, but increasing amounts flowed to new markets in Latin America and Asia. Meanwhile, direct American investments abroad reached $3.5 billion by 1914, placing the United States among the top four investor countries.

Agricultural goods accounted for about three-fourths of total exports in 1870 and about two-thirds in 1900, with grain, cotton, meat, and dairy products topping the export list that year. More than half of the annual cotton crop was exported each year. Midwestern farmers transported their crops by railroad to seaboard cities and then on to foreign markets. Farmers' livelihoods thus became tied to world market conditions and the outcomes of foreign wars. Wisconsin cheesemakers shipped to Britain; the Swift and Armour meat companies exported refrigerated beef to Europe. To sell American grain abroad, James J. Hill of the Great Northern Railroad distributed wheat cookbooks translated into several Asian languages.

In 1913, when the United States outranked both Great Britain and Germany in manufacturing production, manufactured goods led U.S. exports for the first time. Substantial proportions of America's steel, copper, and petroleum were sold abroad, making many workers in those industries dependent on American exports. George Westinghouse marketed his air brakes in Europe; almost as many Singer sewing machines were exported as were sold at home; and Cyrus McCormick's "reaper kings" harvested the wheat of Russian fields (see Figure 19.2).

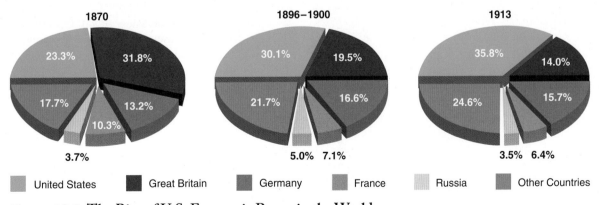

Figure 19.2 The Rise of U.S. Economic Power in the World

These pie charts showing percentage shares of world manufacturing production for the major nations of the world demonstrate that the United States came to surpass Great Britain in this significant economic measurement of power.
Adapted from Aaron L Friedberg, *The Weary Titan*, Princeton University Press, 1989 paperback edition. Reprinted by permission of Princeton University Press.

Messages in Advertising

The American march toward empire was also reflected in advertising. On the front and back covers of this 1901 promotional booklet, the Singer Sewing Machine Company is marketing not only its product but the idea that a sewing machine can unite nations.

The image that emerges of the United States is that of peacemaker and unifier.

CRITICAL THINKING

- In the 1892 Singer sewing machine advertisement card, the Zulu people are sewing American-style clothes. What message is being sent here, do you think?
- How does it compare to the recent advertising campaigns by firms such as Starbucks, Nike, and Subaru that push the product in question only indirectly and instead show people around the world connecting despite their differences?

▲ This Singer advertisement from 1892 shows people in national costumes using treadle machines.

▲ Singer sewing machine advertisement card, showing six people from Zululand (South Africa) with a Singer sewing machine.

19-1c Race Thinking and the Male Ethos

In promoting the expansion of U.S. influence overseas, many officials championed a nationalism based on notions of American supremacy. Some, echoing the articulations of European imperialists (who had their own conceptions of national supremacy), found justification for expansionism in racist theories then permeating Western thought and politics. For decades, the Western scientific establishment had classified humankind by race, and students of physical anthropology drew on phrenology and physiognomy—the analysis of skull size and shape, and the comparison of facial features—to produce a hierarchy of superior and inferior races. One well-known French researcher, for example, claimed that blacks represented a "female race" and "like the woman, the black is deprived of political and scientific intelligence; he has never created a great state . . . he has never accomplished anything in industrial mechanics. But on the other hand he has great virtues of sentiment. Like women he also likes jewelry, dancing, and singing."

The language of U.S. leaders was also weighted with words like *manliness* and *weakling*. Congressman Augustus P. Gardner, son-in-law of Senator Lodge and Spanish-American War veteran, extolled the "arena of lust and blood, where true men are to be found." The warrior and president Theodore Roosevelt viewed people of color (or "darkeys," as he called them) as effeminate weaklings who lacked the ability to govern themselves and could not cope with world politics. Americans regularly debased Latin Americans as half-breeds needing close supervision, distressed damsels begging for manly rescue, or children requiring tutelage. The gendered imagery prevalent in U.S. foreign relations joined race thinking to place women, people of color, and nations weaker than the United States in the low ranks of the hierarchy of power and, hence, in a necessarily dependent status justifying U.S. dominance.

Reverend Josiah Strong's popular and influential *Our Country* (1885) celebrated an Anglo-Saxon race destined to lead others. "As America goes, so goes the world," he declared. A few years later, he wrote that "to be a Christian and an Anglo-Saxon and an American . . . is to stand at the very mountaintop of privilege." Social Darwinists saw Americans as a superior people certain to overcome all competition. Secretary of State Thomas F. Bayard (1885–1889) applauded the "overflow of our population and capital" into Mexico to "saturate those regions with Americanism." But, he added, "we do not want them" until "they are fit."

Race thinking—popularized in magazine photos and cartoons, world's fairs, postcards, school textbooks, museums, and political orations—reinforced notions of American greatness, influenced the way U.S. leaders dealt with other peoples, and obviated the need to think about the subtle textures of other societies. The magazine *National Geographic*, which published its first issue in 1888, chronicled with photographs America's new overseas involvements in Asia and the Pacific. Even when smiling faces predominated in these shots, the image portrayed was that of strange, exotic, premodern peoples who had not become "Western." Fairs also put so-called uncivilized people of color on display in the "freak" or "midway" section. Dog-eating Filipinos aroused particular comment at the 1904 St. Louis World's Fair. Such racism downgraded diplomacy and justified domination and war because self-proclaimed superiors do not negotiate with people ranked as inferiors.

The same thinking permeated attitudes toward immigrants, whose entry into the United States was first restricted in these years. Although the Burlingame Treaty (1868) had provided for free immigration between the United States and China, riots against Chinese immigrants erupted again and again in the American West—in Los Angeles (1871), San Francisco (1877), Denver (1880), and Seattle (1886). A new treaty in 1880 permitted Congress to suspend Chinese immigration to the United States, and it did so two years later. A violent incident occurred in Rock Springs, Wyoming, in 1885, when white coal miners and railway workers rioted and massacred at least twenty-five Chinese.

In 1906, the San Francisco School Board, reflecting the anti-Asian bias of many West Coast Americans, ordered the segregation of all Chinese, Koreans, and Japanese in special schools. Tokyo protested the discrimination against its citizens. The following year, President Roosevelt quieted the crisis by striking a "gentleman's agreement" with Tokyo restricting the inflow of Japanese immigrants; San Francisco then rescinded its segregation order. Relations with Tokyo were jolted again in 1913 when the California legislature denied Japanese residents the right to own property in the state.

19-1d The "Civilizing" Impulse

With a mixture of self-interest and idealism typical of American thinking on foreign policy, expansionists believed that empire benefited both Americans and those who came under their control. When the United States intervened in other lands or lectured weaker states, Americans claimed that in remaking foreign societies they were extending liberty and prosperity to less-fortunate people. William Howard Taft, as civil governor of the Philippines (1901–1904), described the United States' mission in its new colony as lifting Filipinos up "to a point of civilization" that will make them "call the name of the United States blessed." Later, after becoming secretary of war (1904–1908), Taft said about the Chinese that "the more civilized they become . . . the wealthier they become, and the better market they become for us." "The world is to be Christianized and civilized," declared Reverend Josiah Strong. "And what is the process of civilizing but the creating of more and higher wants."

Missionaries dispatched to Africa and Asia, like Lottie Moon, helped spur the transfer of American culture and power abroad—"the peaceful conquest of the world," as Reverend Frederick Gates put it. One organization, the Student Volunteers for Foreign Missions, began in the 1880s on college campuses and by 1914 had placed some 6,000 missionaries abroad. In 1915 a total of 10,000 American

National Geographic

On a winter day in early 1888, thirty-three members of the elite Cosmos Club in Washington, D.C., convened around a mahogany table to consider "the advisability of organizing a society for the increase and diffusion of geographical knowledge." The result was the National Geographic Society, destined to become the largest nonprofit scientific and educational institution in the world.

At the heart of the enterprise would be a magazine designed to win broad support for the society. *National Geographic Magazine* (later simply *National Geographic*) appeared for the first time in October 1888. Early issues were brief, technical, and visually bland, and sales lagged. In 1898, however, Alexander Graham Bell became president of the society and made two key changes: he shifted emphasis from newsstand sales to society membership, reasoning correctly that armchair travelers would flock to join a distinguished fellowship, and he appointed a talented new editor, Gilbert H. Grosvenor, age twenty-three. Grosvenor commissioned articles of general interest and, in an unprecedented move, filled eleven pages of one issue with photographs.

These and other early photos showed people stiffly posed in their native costumes, displayed as anthropological specimens. But they caused a sensation. By 1908, pictures occupied 50 percent of the magazine's space. In 1910, the first color photographs appeared, in a twenty-four-page spread on Korea and China—at that time the largest collection of color photographs ever published in a single issue of any magazine. In later years, *National Geographic* would have several other photographic firsts, including the first natural-color photos of Arctic life and the undersea world.

The society also used membership dues to sponsor expeditions, such as the 1909 journey to the North Pole by Robert Peary and Matthew Henson and, later, Jacques Cousteau's many oceanic explorations and Jane Goodall's up-close observations of wild chimpanzees. The tales of these adventures then appeared in the magazine's pages, along with stunning photographs. By the end of Grosvenor's tenure as editor, in 1954, circulation had grown to more than 2 million.

Grosvenor's winning formula included less-admirable elements. His editors pressured photographers to provide "pictures of pretty girls" to the point at which, as one photographer recalled, "hundreds of bare-breasted women, all from poorer countries, were published at a time of booming subscription rates." Editors also developed a well-earned reputation for avoiding controversial issues and presenting a rosy view of the world. An article about Berlin published just before the start of World War II, for example, contained no criticism of the Nazi regime and no mention of its persecution of Jews. Recent years have seen the magazine take on more newsworthy items—AIDS, stem cell research, Hurricane Katrina, global warming—but in measured, generally nonpolitical tones.

Throughout, the society has continued to expand its reach, moving into the production of books, atlases, globes, and television documentaries. Targeting overseas readers, the society in 1995 launched a Japanese-language edition and subsequently added twenty-five other foreign editions. *National Geographic*, after a century of linking Americans to faraway places, now went in the other direction, connecting readers in many of those locales to the United States.

CRITICAL THINKING

- How was National Geographic a reflection of American imperialism?
- Does it continue to be so today?

◄ In 1916, as the National Geographic Society neared the end of its third decade, members gathered for this photo on the Society's front steps. On the front right is inventor Alexander Graham Bell. On the right two rows above, in the fur collar, is Gilbert H. Grosvenor.

PUCK.

ACCORDING TO THE IDEAS OF OUR MISSIONARY MANIACS,
THE CHINAMAN MUST BE CONVERTED, EVEN IF IT TAKES THE WHOLE MILITARY AND NAVAL FORCE OF THE TWO GREATEST NATIONS OF THE WORLD TO DO IT.

Library of Congress, Prints and Photographs Division[LC-DIG-ppmsca-28945]

▲ Cartoonists sometimes mocked the proselytizing efforts of U.S. and European missionaries. This illustration, from 1895, shows two missionaries, one British and one American, with bags of money and their respective militaries behind them, preaching to a Chinese man. The caption reads: "According to the ideas of our missionary maniacs, the Chinaman must be converted, even if it takes the whole military and naval forces of the two greatest nations of the world to do it." Note the labels on the guns.

missionaries worked overseas. In China by 1915, more than 2,500 American Protestant missionaries—most of them female—labored to preach the gospel, teach school, and administer medical care.

19-2 Ambitions and Strategies

▶ What early actions did the national government take to advance American interests abroad?

▶ What institutions and structures were established to help the United States expand its influence abroad?

The U.S. empire grew gradually, sometimes haltingly, as American leaders defined guiding principles and built institutions to support overseas ambitions. William H. Seward, one of its chief architects, argued relentlessly for extension of the American frontier as senator from New York (1849–1861) and secretary of state (1861–1869). "There is not in the history of the Roman Empire an ambition for aggrandizement so marked as that which characterizes the American people," he once said. Seward envisioned a large, coordinated U.S. empire encompassing Canada, the Caribbean, Cuba, Central America, Mexico, Hawai'i, Iceland, Greenland, and the Pacific islands. This empire would be built not by war but by a natural process of gravitation toward the United States. Commerce would hurry the process, as would a canal across Central America, a

transcontinental American railroad to link up with Asian markets, and a telegraph system to speed communications.

19-2a Seward's Quest for Empire

Most of Seward's grandiose plans did not reach fruition in his own day. In 1867, for example, he signed a treaty with Denmark to buy the Danish West Indies (Virgin Islands), but his domestic political foes in the Senate and a hurricane that wrecked St. Thomas scuttled his effort. The Virgin Islanders, who had voted for annexation, had to wait until 1917 for official U.S. status. Also doomed to failure was Seward's scheme with unscrupulous Dominican Republic leaders to gain a Caribbean naval base at Samana Bay. The stench of corruption rising over this unsavory dealmaking wafted into the Ulysses S. Grant administration and foiled Grant's initiative in 1870 to buy the entire island nation. The Senate rejected annexation.

Anti-imperialism, not just politics, blocked Seward. Opponents of the empire argued that the country already had enough unsettled land and that creating a showcase of democracy and prosperity at home would best persuade other peoples to adopt American institutions and principles. Some anti-imperialists, sharing the racism of the times, opposed the annexation of territory populated by dark-skinned people.

Seward did enjoy some successes. In 1866, citing the Monroe Doctrine (see "Monroe Doctrine," Section 8-6h), he sent troops to the border with Mexico and demanded

OUR NEW SENATORS.

SECRETARY SEWARD—"*My dear Mr. Kamskatca, you really must dine with me. I have some of the very finest tallow candles and the loveliest train oil you ever tasted, and my whale's blubber is exquisite—and pray bring your friend Mr. Seal along with you. The President will be one of the party.*"

▲ Humorists had a field day with the U.S. acquisition of Alaska. This cartoon, titled "Our New Senators," shows Secretary of State William H. Seward and President Andrew Johnson welcoming the representatives of the new territory to Washington.

that France abandon its puppet regime there. Also facing angry Mexican nationalists, Napoleon III abandoned the Maximilian monarchy that he had installed by force three years earlier. In 1867, Seward paid Russia $7.2 million for the 591,000 square miles of Alaska—land twice the size of Texas. Some critics lampooned "Seward's Icebox," but the secretary of state extolled the Russian territory's rich natural resources, and the Senate voted overwhelmingly for the treaty. That same year, Seward laid claim to the Midway Islands (two small islands and a coral atoll northwest of Hawai'i, so named because they are nearly halfway between North America and Asia) in the Pacific Ocean.

19-2b International Communications

Seward realized his dream of a world knit together by a giant communications system. In 1866, through the persevering efforts of financier Cyrus Field, an underwater transatlantic cable linked European and American telegraph networks. Backed by J. P. Morgan's capital, communications pioneer James A. Scrymser strung telegraph lines to Latin America, entering Chile in 1890. In 1903, a submarine cable reached across the Pacific to the Philippines; three years later, it extended to Japan and China. Information about markets, crises, and

Alfred Thayer Mahan U.S. Navy captain and author of *The Influence of Sea Power upon History* (1890) and an advocate of a stronger navy and imperialism.

war flowed steadily and quickly. Wire telegraphy—like radio (wireless telegraphy) later—shrank the globe. Drawn closer to one another through improved communications and transportation, nations found that faraway events had more and more impact on their prosperity and security.

More and more, American diplomats found that they could enter negotiations with their European counterparts on roughly equal terms—a sure sign that the United States had arrived on the international stage. Washington officials, for example, successfully confronted European powers in a contest over Samoa, a group of beautiful South Pacific islands located four thousand miles from San Francisco on the trade route to Australia. In 1878, the United States gained exclusive rights to a coaling station at Samoa's coveted port of Pago Pago (pronounced "Pango Pango"). Eyeing the same prize, Britain and Germany began to cultivate ties with Samoan leaders. Year by year, tensions grew as the powers dispatched warships to Samoa and aggravated factionalism among Samoa's chiefs. War seemed possible. At the eleventh hour, however, Britain, Germany, and the United States met in Berlin in 1889 and, without consulting the Samoans, devised a three-part protectorate that limited Samoa's independence. Ten years later, the three powers partitioned Samoa: the United States received Pago Pago through annexation of part of the islands (now called American Samoa and administered by the U.S. Department of the Interior); Germany took what is today independent Western Samoa; and Britain, for renouncing its claims to Samoa, obtained the Gilbert Islands and the Solomon Islands.

19-2c Alfred T. Mahan and Navalism

With eyes on all parts of the world, even on Africa, where U.S. interests were minimal, ardent expansionists embraced navalism—the campaign to build an imperial navy. Calling attention to the naval buildup by the European powers, notably Germany, they argued for a bigger, modernized navy, adding the "blue water" command of the seas to its traditional role of "brown water" coastline defense and riverine operations. Captain **Alfred Thayer Mahan** became a major popularizer for this "New Navy." Because foreign trade was vital to the United States, he argued, the nation required an efficient navy to protect its shipping; in turn, a navy required colonies for bases. "Whether they will or no," Mahan wrote, "Americans must now begin to look outward. The growing production of the country demands it." Mahan's lectures at the Naval War College in Newport, Rhode Island, where he served as president, were published as *The Influence of Sea Power upon History* (1890). This book sat on every serious expansionist's shelf, and foreign leaders read it too. Theodore Roosevelt and Henry Cabot Lodge eagerly consulted Mahan, sharing his belief in the links among trade, navy, and colonies, and his growing alarm over "the aggressive military spirit" of Germany.

Not to be outdone, Congress in 1883 moved toward naval authorization by authorizing construction of the first steel-hulled warships. American factories went to work to produce steam engines, high-velocity shells, powerful guns, and precision instruments. The navy shifted from sail power to steam and from wood construction to steel. Often named for states and cities to kindle patriotism and local support for naval expansion, New Navy ships, such as the *Maine, Oregon,* and *Boston,* thrust the United States into naval prominence, especially during crises in the 1890s.

19-3 Crises in the 1890s: Hawai'i, Venezuela, and Cuba

▶ How did American business and government actions serve to undermine the Native government in Hawai'i?

▶ How did Great Britain and the United States address a boundary dispute in Venezuela?

▶ How were the interests of Cubans and Americans intertwined with one another in the late nineteenth century?

▶ What developments drew the United States into war with Spain over Cuba?

In the depression-plagued 1890s, crises in Hawai'i and Cuba gave expansionist Americans opportunities to act on their zealous arguments for what Senator Lodge called a "large policy." Belief that the frontier at home had closed accentuated the expansionist case. In 1893, historian Frederick Jackson Turner postulated that an ever-expanding continental frontier had shaped the American character. That "frontier has gone," Turner pronounced, "and with its going has closed the first period of American history." He did not explicitly say that a new frontier had to be found overseas in order to sustain the U.S. way of life, but he did claim that "American energy will continually demand a wider field for its exercise."

19-3a Annexation of Hawai'i

Hawai'i, the Pacific Ocean archipelago of eight major islands located two thousand miles from the West Coast of the United States, emerged as a new frontier for Americans. The Hawaiian Islands had long commanded American attention—commercial, missionary religious, naval, and diplomatic. Wide-eyed U.S. expansionists envisioned ships sailing from the eastern seaboard through a Central American canal to Hawai'i and then on to the fabled China market. By 1881, Secretary of State James Blaine had already declared the Hawaiian Islands "essentially a part of the American system." By 1890, Americans owned about three-quarters of Hawai'i's wealth and subordinated its economy to that of the United States through sugar exports that entered the U.S. marketplace duty free.

In Hawai'i's multiracial society, Chinese and Japanese nationals far outnumbered Americans, who represented a mere 2.1 percent of the population. Prominent Americans on the islands—lawyers, businessmen, and sugar planters, many

of them the sons of missionaries—organized secret clubs and military units to contest the royal government. In 1887, they forced the king to accept a constitution that granted foreigners the right to vote and shifted decision-making authority from the monarchy to the legislature. The same year, Hawai'i granted the United States naval rights to Pearl Harbor. Many Native Hawai'ians (53 percent of the population in 1890) believed that the *haole* (foreigners)—especially Americans—were taking their country from them.

The McKinley Tariff of 1890 created an economic crisis for Hawai'i that further undermined the Native government. The tariff eliminated the duty-free status of Hawaiian sugar exports in the United States. Suffering declining sugar prices and profits, the American island elite pressed for annexation of the islands by the United States so that their sugar would be classified as domestic rather than foreign. When Princess Lili'uokalani assumed the throne in 1891, she sought to roll back the political power of the *haole*. The next year, the white oligarchy—questioning her moral rectitude, fearing Hawaiian nationalism, and reeling from the McKinley Tariff—formed the subversive Annexation Club.

The annexationists struck in January 1893 in collusion with John L. Stevens, the chief American diplomat in Hawai'i, who dispatched troops from the USS *Boston* to occupy Honolulu. The queen, arrested and confined, surrendered. However, rather than yield to the new provisional regime, headed by Sanford B. Dole, son of missionaries and a prominent attorney, she relinquished authority to the U.S. government. Up went the American flag. "The Hawaiian pear is now fully ripe and this is the golden hour to pluck it," a triumphant Stevens informed Washington. Against the queen's protests as well as those of Japan, President Benjamin Harrison hurriedly sent an annexation treaty to the Senate.

Sensing foul play, incoming president Grover Cleveland ordered an investigation, which confirmed a conspiracy by the economic elite in league with Stevens and noted that most Hawai'ians opposed annexation. Down came the American flag. But when Hawai'i gained renewed attention as a strategic and commercial way station to Asia and the Philippines during the Spanish-American War, President William McKinley maneuvered annexation through Congress on July 7, 1898, by means of a majority vote (the Newlands Resolution) rather than by a treaty, which would have required a two-thirds count. Under the Organic Act of June 1900, the people of Hawai'i became U.S. citizens with the right to vote in local elections and to send a nonvoting delegate to Congress. Statehood for Hawai'i came in 1959.

19-3b Venezuelan Boundary Dispute

The Venezuelan crisis of 1895 also saw the United States in an expansive mood. For decades Venezuela and Great Britain had quarreled over the border between Venezuela and British Guiana. The disputed territory contained rich gold deposits and the mouth of the Orinoco River, a commercial gateway to northern South America. Venezuela asked for U.S. help. President Cleveland decided that the "mean and hoggish" British had to be warned away. In July 1895, Secretary of State Richard Olney brashly lectured the British that the Monroe Doctrine prohibited European powers from denying self-government to nations in the Western Hemisphere. He aimed his spread-eagle words at an international audience, proclaiming the United States "a civilized state" whose "fiat is law" in the Americas. The United States, he declared, is "master of the situation and practically invulnerable as against any or all other powers." The British, seeking international friends to counter intensifying competition from Germany, quietly retreated from the crisis. In 1896, an Anglo-American arbitration board divided the disputed territory between Britain and Venezuela. The Venezuelans were barely consulted. Thus, the United States displayed a trait common to imperialists: disregard for the rights and sensibilities of small nations.

▲ Queen Lili'uokalani (1838–1917), ousted from her throne in 1893 by wealthy revolutionaries, vigorously protested the U.S. annexation of Hawai'i in 1898. In her autobiography and diary, as well as in interviews, she defended Hawaiian nationalism and emphasized that American officials in 1893 had conspired with Sanford B. Dole and others to overthrow the Native monarchy.

Bettmann/Getty Images

In 1895 came another crisis forced by U.S. policy, this one in Cuba. From 1868 to 1878, the Cubans had battled Spain for their independence. Slavery was abolished but independence denied. While the Cuban economy suffered depression, repressive Spanish rule continued. Insurgents committed to *Cuba libre* waited for another chance, and José Martí, one of the heroes of Cuban history, collected money, arms, and men in the United States.

19-3c Revolution in Cuba

American financial support of the Cuban cause was but one of the many ways the lives of Americans and Cubans intersected. Their cultures, for example, melded. Cubans of all classes had settled in Baltimore, New York, Boston, and Philadelphia. Prominent Cubans on the island had sent their children to schools in the United States. When Cuban expatriates returned home, many came in American clothes, spoke English, had American names, played baseball, and had jettisoned Catholicism for Protestant denominations. Struggling with competing identities, Cubans admired American culture but resented U.S. economic hegemony (predominance).

The Cuban and U.S. economies were also intertwined. American investments of $50 million, mostly in sugar plantations, dominated the Caribbean island. More than 90 percent of Cuba's sugar was exported to the United States, and most island imports came from the United States. Havana's famed cigar factories relocated to Key West and Tampa to evade protectionist U.S. tariff laws. Martí, however, feared that "economic union means political union," for "the nation that buys, commands" and "the nation that sells, serves." Watch out, he warned, for a U.S. "conquering policy" that reduced Latin American countries to "dependencies."

Martí's fears were prophetic. In 1894, the Wilson-Gorman Tariff imposed a duty on Cuban sugar, which had been entering the United States duty free under the McKinley Tariff. The Cuban economy, highly dependent on exports, plunged into deep crisis, hastening the island's revolution against Spain and its further incorporation into "the American system."

In 1895, from American soil, Martí launched a revolution against Spain that mounted in human and material costs. Rebels burned sugar cane fields and razed mills, conducting an economic war and using guerrilla tactics to avoid head-on clashes with Spanish soldiers. "It is necessary to burn the hive to disperse the swarm," explained insurgent leader Máximo Gómez. U.S. investments went up in smoke, and Cuban-American trade dwindled. To separate the insurgents from their supporters among the Cuban people, Spanish general Valeriano Weyler instituted a policy of "reconcentration." Some three hundred thousand Cubans were herded into fortified towns and camps, where hunger, starvation, and disease led to tens of thousands of deaths. As reports of atrocity and destruction became headline news in the American yellow press, Americans increasingly sympathized with the insurrectionists. In late 1897, a new government in Madrid modified reconcentration and promised some autonomy for Cuba, but the insurgents continued to gain ground.

19-3d Sinking of the *Maine*

President William McKinley had come to office as an imperialist who advocated foreign bases for the New Navy, the export of surplus production, and U.S. supremacy in the Western Hemisphere. Vexed by the turmoil in Cuba, he came to believe that Spain should give up its colony. At one point, he explored the purchase of Cuba by the United States for $300 million. Events in early 1898 caused McKinley to lose faith in Madrid's ability to bring peace to Cuba. In January, when antireform pro-Spanish loyalists and army personnel rioted in Havana, Washington ordered the battleship *Maine* to Havana harbor to demonstrate U.S. concern and to protect American citizens.

On February 15, an explosion ripped the *Maine*, killing 266 of 354 American officers and crew. Just a week earlier, William Randolph Hearst's inflammatory *New York Journal* had published a stolen private letter written by the Spanish minister in Washington, Enrique Dupuy de Lôme, who belittled McKinley as "weak and a bidder for the admiration of the crowd" and suggested that Spain would fight on. Congress soon complied unanimously with McKinley's request for $50 million in defense funds. The naval board investigating the *Maine* disaster then reported that a mine had caused the explosion. Vengeful Americans blamed Spain. (Later, official and unofficial studies attributed the sinking to an accidental internal explosion, most likely caused by spontaneous combustion of inadequately ventilated coal bunkers.)

19-3e McKinley's Ultimatum and War Decision

The impact of these events narrowed McKinley's diplomatic options. Though reluctant to go to war, he decided to send Spain an ultimatum. In late March, the United States insisted that Spain accept an armistice, end reconcentration altogether, and designate McKinley as arbiter. Madrid made concessions. It abolished reconcentration and rejected, then accepted, an armistice. The weary president hesitated, but he would no longer tolerate chronic disorder just ninety miles off the U.S. coast. On April 11, McKinley asked Congress for authorization to use force "to secure a full and final termination of hostilities between . . . Spain and . . . Cuba, and to secure in the island the establishment of a stable government, capable of maintaining order." American intervention, he said, meant "hostile constraint upon both the parties to the contest."

McKinley listed the reasons for war: the "cause of humanity"; the protection of American life and property; the "very serious injury to the commerce, trade, and business of our people"; and, referring to the destruction of the *Maine*, the "constant menace to our peace." At the end of his message, McKinley mentioned Spain's recent concessions but made little of them. He did not mention another possible motivation: de Lôme's depiction of him as "weak," a charge also leveled by Assistant Secretary of the Navy Theodore Roosevelt. On April 19, Congress declared Cuba free and independent and directed the president to use force to remove Spanish authority from the island. The legislators also passed the Teller Amendment, which disclaimed any U.S. intention to annex Cuba or control the island except to ensure its "pacification" (by which they meant the suppression of any actively hostile elements of the population). McKinley beat back a congressional amendment to recognize the rebel government.

THE DREAM OF THE ANTI-EXPANSIONIST.

◀ This 1899 print shows "the dream of the anti-expansionist," as Admiral George Dewey and General Elwell S. Otis, along with a sailor and a soldier, come ashore in the Philippines to offer their weapons and the U.S flag in surrender to Emilio Aguinaldo and a ragged but haughty group of Filipinos.

Believing that the Cubans were not ready for self-government, he argued that they needed a period of American tutoring.

19-4 The Spanish-American War and the Debate over Empire

▶ What motivated Americans to support and participate in war with Spain?

▶ What characteristics defined the debate over empire between anti-imperialists and imperialists?

Diplomacy had failed. By the time the Spanish concessions were on the table, events had already pushed the antagonists to the brink. Washington might have been more patient, and Madrid might have faced the fact that its once-grand empire had disintegrated. Still, prospects for compromise appeared dim because the advancing Cuban insurgents would settle for nothing less than full independence, and no Spanish government could have given up and remained in office. Nor did the United States welcome a truly independent Cuban government that might attempt to reduce U.S. interests. As historian Louis A. Perez Jr. has argued, McKinley's decision for war may have been "directed as much against Cuban independence as it was against Spanish sovereignty." Thus came a war some have titled (clumsily, but accurately) the "Spanish-American-Cuban-Filipino War" so as to represent all the major participants and identify where the war was fought and whose interests were most at stake.

19-4a Motives for War

The motives of Americans who favored war were mixed and complex. McKinley's April message expressed a humanitarian impulse to stop the bloodletting, a concern for commerce and property, and the psychological need to end the nightmarish anxiety once and for all. Republican politicians advised McKinley that their party would lose the upcoming congressional elections unless he solved the Cuba question. Many businesspeople, who had been hesitant before the crisis of early 1898, joined many farmers in the belief that ejecting Spain from Cuba would open new markets for surplus production.

Inveterate imperialists saw the war as an opportunity to fulfill expansionist dreams, while conservatives, alarmed by Populism and violent labor strikes, welcomed war as a national unifier. One senator commented that "internal discord" was disappearing in the "fervent heat of patriotism." Sensationalism also figured in the march to war, with the yellow press exaggerating stories of Spanish misdeeds. Theodore Roosevelt and others too young to remember the bloody Civil War looked on war as adventure and used masculine rhetoric to trumpet the call to arms.

More than 263,000 regulars and volunteers served in the army and another 25,000 in the navy during the war. Most of them never left the United States. The typical volunteer was young (early twenties), white, unmarried, native born, and working class. Many were southerners, a fact that helped the cause of reconciliation following the bitter divisions of the Civil War era. Deaths numbered 5,462—but only 379 in combat. The rest fell to yellow fever and typhoid, and most died in the United States, especially in camps in Tennessee, Virginia, and Florida, where in July and August a typhoid epidemic devastated the ranks. About 10,000 African American troops, assigned to segregated regiments, found no relief from racism and Jim Crow, even though black troops played a key role in the victorious battle for Santiago de Cuba. For all, food quality, sanitary conditions, and medical care were bad. Still, Roosevelt could hardly contain himself. Although his Rough Riders, a motley unit of Ivy Leaguers and cowboys, proved undisciplined and often ineffective, they nonetheless received good press largely because of Roosevelt's self-serving publicity efforts.

19-4b Dewey in the Philippines

To the surprise of most Americans, the first war news actually came from faraway Asia, from the Spanish colony of the Philippine Islands. Here, too, Madrid faced a rebellion from Filipinos seeking independence. On May 1, 1898, Commodore George Dewey's New Navy ship *Olympia* led an American squadron into Manila Bay and wrecked the outgunned Spanish fleet. Dewey and his sailors had been on alert in Hong Kong since February, when he received orders from imperial-minded Washington to attack the islands if war broke out. Manila ranked with Pearl Harbor and Pago Pago as a choice

▲ Like soldiers in all wars at all times, those in the Spanish-American War were keen to communicate with loved ones at home. Here two unidentified American soldiers write letters before taking part in the Siege of Santiago de Cuba.

The Granger Collection, NYC

▲ On July 1, 1898, U.S. troops stormed Spanish positions on San Juan Hill near Santiago, Cuba. Both sides suffered heavy casualties. A *Harper's* magazine correspondent reported a "ghastly" scene of hundreds killed and thousands wounded. The American painter William Glackens (1870–1938) put to canvas what he saw. Because Santiago surrendered on July 17, propelling the United States to victory in the war, and because Rough Rider Theodore Roosevelt fought at San Juan Hill and later gave a self-congratulatory account of the experience, the human toll has often gone unnoticed.

harbor, and the Philippines sat significantly on the way to China and its potentially huge market.

Facing Americans and rebels in both Cuba and the Philippines, Spanish resistance collapsed rapidly. U.S. ships blockaded Cuban ports to prevent Spain from resupplying its army, which suffered hunger and disease because Cuban insurgents had cut off supplies from the countryside. American troops saw their first ground-war action on June 22, the day several thousand of them landed near Santiago de Cuba and laid siege to the city. On July 3, U.S. warships sank the Spanish Caribbean squadron in Santiago harbor. American forces then assaulted the Spanish colony of Puerto Rico to obtain another Caribbean base for the navy and a strategic site to help protect a Central American canal. Losing on all fronts, Madrid sued for peace.

19-4c Treaty of Paris

On August 12, Spain and the United States signed an armistice to end the war. In Paris, in December 1898, American and Spanish negotiators agreed on the peace terms: independence for Cuba from Spain; cession of the Philippines, Puerto Rico, and the Pacific island of Guam to the United States; and American payment of $20 million to Spain for the territories. The U.S. empire now stretched deep into Asia, and the annexation of Wake Island (1898), Hawai'i (1898), and Samoa (1899) gave American traders, missionaries, and naval promoters other stepping-stones to China.

During the war with Spain, the *Washington Post* detected "a new appetite, a yearning to show our strength. . . . The taste of empire is in the mouth of the people." But as the nation debated the Treaty of Paris, anti-imperialists such as author Mark Twain, Nebraska politician William Jennings Bryan, intellectual William Graham Sumner, reformer Jane Addams, industrialist Andrew Carnegie, and Senator George Hoar of

◄ In this color illustration from 1899 we see the armored cruiser *USS Brooklyn*, under Commodore Winfield Scott Schley, which participated in the Battle of Santiago Bay on July 3, 1898. Later, in December 1899, the Brooklyn became the flagship of the Asiatic Squadron at Manila Bay, Philippines.

Library of Congress Prints and Photographs Division [LC-USZC4-3330]

Stock Montage/Archive Photos/Getty Images

Massachusetts argued vigorously against annexation of the Philippines. They were disturbed that a war to free Cuba had led to empire, and they stimulated a momentous debate over the fundamental course in American foreign policy.

19-4d Anti-Imperialist Arguments

Imperial control could be imposed either formally (by military occupation, annexation; or colonialism) or informally (by economic domination, political manipulation, or the threat of intervention). Anti-imperialist ire focused mostly on the formal kind of imperial control, involving an overseas territorial empire comprised of people of color living far from the mainland. Some critics appealed to principle, citing the Declaration of Independence and the Constitution: the conquest of people against their wills violated the right of self-determination. Philosopher William James charged that the United States was throwing away its special place among nations; it was, he warned, about to "puke up its heritage."

Other anti-imperialists feared that the American character was being corrupted by imperialist zeal. Jane Addams, seeing children play war games in the streets of Chicago, pointed out that they were not freeing Cubans but rather slaying Spaniards. Hoping to build a distinct foreign policy constituency out of networks of women's clubs and organizations, prominent women like Addams championed peace and an end to imperial conquest.

Some anti-imperialists protested that the United States was practicing a double standard—"offering liberty to the Cubans with one hand, cramming liberty down the throats of the Filipinos with the other, but with both feet planted upon the neck of the negro," as an African American politician from Massachusetts put it. Still other anti-imperialists warned that annexing people of color would undermine Anglo-Saxon purity and supremacy at home.

For Samuel Gompers and other anti-imperialist labor leaders, the issue was jobs: they worried that what Gompers called the "half-breeds and semi-barbaric people" of the new colonies would undercut American labor. Might not the new colonials be imported as cheap contract labor to drive down the wages of American workers? Would not exploitation of the weak abroad become contagious and lead to further exploitation of the weak at home? Would not an overseas empire drain interest and resources from pressing domestic problems, delaying reform?

The anti-imperialists entered the debate with many handicaps and never launched an effective campaign. Although they organized the Anti-Imperialist League in November 1898, they differed so profoundly on domestic issues that they found it difficult to speak with one voice on a foreign-policy question. They also appeared inconsistent: Gompers favored the war but not the postwar annexations; Carnegie would accept colonies if they were not acquired by force; Hoar voted for annexation of Hawai'i but not of the Philippines; Bryan backed the Treaty of Paris but only, he said, to hurry the process

Emilio Aguinaldo Nationalist leader of Filipino war against American occupation.

toward Philippine independence. Finally, possession of the Philippines was an established fact, very hard to undo.

19-4e Imperialist Arguments

The imperialists answered their critics with appeals to patriotism, destiny, and commerce. They sketched a scenario of American greatness: merchant ships plying the waters to boundless Asian markets; naval vessels cruising the Pacific to protect U.S. interests; missionaries uplifting inferior peoples. It was America's duty, they insisted, quoting a then-popular Rudyard Kipling poem, to "take up the white man's burden." Furthermore, Filipino insurgents were beginning to resist U.S. rule, and it seemed cowardly to pull out under fire. Germany and Japan, two powerful international competitors, were nosing around the Philippines, apparently ready to seize them if the United States' grip loosened. National honor dictated that Americans keep what they had shed blood to take. Republican Senator Albert Beveridge of Indiana asked, "Shall [history] say that, called by events to captain and command the proudest, ablest, purest race of history in history's noblest work, we declined that great commission?"

In February 1899, by a 57-to-27 vote (just one more than the necessary two-thirds majority), the Senate passed the Treaty of Paris, ending the war with Spain. Most Republicans voted yes and most Democrats no. An amendment promising independence as soon as the Filipinos formed a stable government lost by the slimmest margin possible: the tie-breaking ballot of the vice president. Democratic presidential candidate Bryan carried the anti-imperialist case into the election of 1900, warning that repudiation of self-government in the Philippines would weaken the principle at home. But the victorious McKinley refused to apologize for American imperialism, asserting that his policies had served the nation's interests.

19-5 Asian Encounters: War in the Philippines, Diplomacy in China

▶ What methods did Americans and Filipinos use against one another in the Philippine Insurrection?

▶ How did the United States seek to protect its commercial interests in China?

As McKinley knew, however, the Philippine crisis was far from over. He said he intended to "uplift and civilize" the Filipinos, but they denied that they needed U.S. help. **Emilio Aguinaldo**, the Philippine nationalist leader who had been battling the Spanish for years, believed that American officials had promised independence for his country. But after the victory over Spain, U.S. officers ordered Aguinaldo out of Manila and isolated him from decisions affecting his nation. In early 1899, feeling betrayed by the Treaty of Paris, he proclaimed an independent Philippine Republic and took up arms. U.S. officials responded with force.

19-5a Philippine Insurrection and Pacification

In a war fought viciously by both sides, American soldiers burned crops and villages and tortured captives, while Filipino forces staged hit-and-run ambushes that were often brutally effective. Like guerrillas in many later wars, they would strike suddenly and ferociously, and then melt into the jungle or friendly villages. Americans spoke of the "savage" Filipino; one soldier declared that the Philippines "won't be pacified until the niggers [Filipinos] are killed off like the Indians." U.S. troops introduced a variant of the Spanish reconcentration policy—in the province of Batangas, for instance, U.S. troops forced residents to live in designated zones in an effort to separate the insurgents from local supporters. Disaster followed. Poor sanitation, starvation, and malaria and cholera killed several thousand people. Outside the secure areas, Americans destroyed food supplies to starve out the rebels. At least one-quarter of the population of Batangas died or fled.

Before the Philippine Insurrection was suppressed in 1902, some 20,000 Filipinos had died in combat, and as many as 600,000 had succumbed to starvation and disease. More than 4,000 Americans lay dead. Resistance to U.S. rule, however, did not disappear. The fiercely independent, vehemently anti-Christian, and often violent Muslim Filipinos of Moro Province refused to knuckle under. The U.S. military ordered them to submit or be exterminated. In 1906, the Moros finally met defeat; 600 of them, including many women and children, were slaughtered at the Battle of Bud Dajo. As General Leonard Wood, the Moro provincial governor, wrote the president, "Work of this kind has its disagreeable side."

U.S. officials, with a stern military hand, soon tried to Americanize the Philippines. Architect Daniel Burnham, leader of the City Beautiful movement, planned modern Manila. U.S. authorities instituted a new educational system, with English as the main language of instruction. Thousands of young American educators, many of them motivated by idealism, were recruited to teach in the new schools. The Philippine economy grew while it was an American satellite, and a sedition act silenced critics of U.S. authority by sending them to prison. In 1916, the Jones Act vaguely promised independence once the Philippines established a "stable government." The United States finally ended its rule in 1946 during an intense period of decolonization after the Second World War.

19-5b China and the Open Door Policy

In China, McKinley opted for an approach that emphasized negotiations, with greater success. Outsiders had been pecking away at China since the 1840s, but the Japanese onslaught intensified the international scramble. Taking advantage of the Qing (Manchu) dynasty's weakness, the major imperial powers carved out spheres of influence (regions over which the outside powers claimed political control and exclusive commercial privileges): Germany in Shandong, Russia in Manchuria, France in Yunnan and Hainan, Britain in Kowloon and Hong Kong. Then, in 1895, the same year as the outbreak of the Cuban revolution, Japan claimed victory over China in a short war and assumed control of Formosa and Korea as well as parts of China proper (see Map 19.1). American religious and business leaders petitioned Washington to halt the dismemberment of China before they were closed out.

Secretary of State John Hay knew the United States could not force the imperial powers out of China, but he was determined to protect American commerce and missionaries like Lottie Moon. He knew that missionaries had become targets of Chinese nationalist anger and that American oil and textile companies had been disappointed in the results of their investments in the country. Thus, in September 1899, Hay sent the nations with spheres of influence in China a note asking them to respect the principle of equal trade opportunity—an **Open Door**. The recipients sent evasive replies, privately complaining that the United States was seeking, for free, the trade rights in China that they had gained at considerable military and administrative cost.

The next year, a Chinese secret society called the Boxers (so named in the Western press because some members were martial artists) incited riots that killed foreigners, including missionaries, and laid siege to the foreign legations in Beijing. The **Boxer Rebellion**, as it came to be known, sought ultimately to expel all foreigners from China. The United States, applauded by American merchants and missionaries alike, joined the other imperial powers in sending troops to lift the siege. Hay also sent a second Open Door note in July, which instructed other nations to preserve China's territorial integrity and to honor "equal and impartial trade." Hay's protests notwithstanding, China continued for years to be fertile soil for foreign exploitation, especially by the Japanese.

Although Hay's foray into Asian politics settled little, the Open Door policy became a cornerstone of U.S. diplomacy. The "open door" had actually been a long-standing American principle, for as a trading nation the United States opposed barriers to international commerce and demanded equal access to foreign markets. After 1900, however, when the United States began to emerge as the premier world trader, the Open Door policy became an instrument first to pry open markets and then to dominate them, not just in China but throughout the world. The Open Door also developed as an ideology with several tenets: first, that America's domestic well-being required exports; second, that foreign trade would suffer interruption unless the United States intervened abroad to implant American principles and keep markets open; and third, that the closing of any area to American products, citizens, or ideas threatened the survival of the United States itself.

Open Door Foreign policy proposed by U.S. Secretary of State John Hay, in which he asked the major European powers to ensure trading rights in China by opening the ports in their spheres of influence to all countries.

Boxer Rebellion Chinese insurgency against Christians and foreigners, defeated by an international force.

Map 19.1 Imperialism in Asia: Turn of the Century

China and the Pacific region had become imperialist hunting grounds by the turn of the century. The European powers and Japan controlled more areas than the United States, which nonetheless participated in the imperial race by annexing the Philippines, Wake, Guam, Hawai'i, and Samoa; announcing the Open Door policy; and expanding trade. As the spheres of influence in China demonstrate, that besieged nation succumbed to outsiders despite the Open Door policy.

19-6 TR's World

▶ What ideas guided Theodore Roosevelt in his views of U.S. foreign policy?

▶ How did Roosevelt use presidential power and authority on the international stage?

▶ How did Latin American countries respond to the expansion of American influence?

▶ What actions did the United States take to stem European threats to its hegemony?

Theodore Roosevelt played an important role in shaping U.S. foreign policy in the McKinley administration. As assistant secretary of the navy (1897–1898), as a Spanish-American War hero, and then as vice president in McKinley's second term, Roosevelt worked tirelessly to make the United States a key member of the great power club. He had long had a fascination with power and its uses. He also relished hunting and killing. After an argument with a girlfriend in his youth, he vented his anger by shooting

a neighbor's dog. When he killed his first buffalo in the West, he danced crazily around the carcass as his Indian guide watched in amazement. Roosevelt justified the slaughtering of American Indians, if necessary, and took his Rough Riders to Cuba, desperate to get in on the fighting. He was not disappointed. "Did I tell you," he wrote Henry Cabot Lodge afterward, "that I killed a Spaniard with my own hands?"

Like many other Americans of his day, Roosevelt took for granted the superiority of Protestant Anglo-American culture, and he believed in the importance of using American power to shape world affairs (a conviction he summarized by citing the West African proverb "Speak softly and carry a big stick, and you will go far"). In TR's world, there were "civilized" and "uncivilized" nations; the former, primarily white and Anglo-Saxon or Teutonic, had a right and a duty to intervene in the affairs of the latter (generally nonwhite, Latin, or Slavic, and therefore "backward") to preserve order and stability. If violent means had to be used to accomplish this task, so be it.

19-6a Presidential Authority

Roosevelt's love of the good fight caused many to rue his ascension to the presidency after McKinley's assassination in September 1901. But there was more to this "cowboy" than mere bluster; he was also an astute analyst of foreign policy and world affairs. TR understood that American power, though growing year by year, remained limited, and that in many parts of the world the United States would have to rely on diplomacy and nonmilitary means to achieve satisfactory outcomes. It would have to work in concert with other powers.

Roosevelt sought to centralize foreign policy in the White House. The president had to take charge of foreign relations, he believed, in the same way he took the lead in formulating domestic priorities of reorganization and reform. Congress was too large and unwieldy. As for public opinion, it was, Roosevelt said, "the voice of the devil, or what is still worse, the voice of the fool." This conviction that the executive branch should be supreme in foreign policy was to be shared by most presidents who followed TR in office, down to the present day.

With this bald assertion of presidential and national power, Roosevelt stepped onto the international stage. His first efforts were focused on Latin America, where U.S. economic and strategic interests and power towered (see Map 19.2), and on Europe, where repeated political and military disputes persuaded Americans to develop friendlier relations with Great Britain while avoiding entrapment in the continent's troubles, many of which Americans blamed on Germany.

As U.S. economic interests expanded in Latin America, so did U.S. political influence. Exports to Latin America, which exceeded $50 million in the 1870s, had risen to more than $120 million when Roosevelt became president in 1901, and then reached $300 million in 1914. Investments by U.S. citizens in Latin America climbed to a commanding $1.26 billion in 1914. In 1899, two large banana importers had merged to form the United Fruit Company. United Fruit owned much of the land in Central America (more than a million acres in 1913), as well as the railroad and steamship lines, and the firm became an influential economic and political force in the region. The company worked to eradicate yellow fever and malaria at the same time it manipulated Central American politics, partly by bankrolling favored officeholders.

Map 19.2 U.S. Hegemony in the Caribbean and Latin America

Through many interventions, territorial acquisitions, and robust economic expansion, the United States became the predominant power in Latin America in the early twentieth century. The United States often backed up the Roosevelt Corollary's declaration of a "police power" by dispatching troops to Caribbean nations, where they met nationalist opposition.

19-6b Cuba and the Platt Amendment

After the destructive war in Cuba, U.S. citizens and corporations continued to dominate the island's economy, controlling the sugar, mining, tobacco, and utilities industries, and most of the rural lands. Private U.S. investments in Cuba grew from $50 million before the revolution to $220 million by 1913, and U.S. exports to the island rose from $26 million in 1900 to $196 million in 1917. The Teller Amendment outlawed the annexation of Cuba, but officials in Washington soon used the document's call for "pacification" to justify U.S. control. American troops remained there until 1902.

Favoring the "better classes," U.S. authorities restricted voting rights largely to propertied Cuban males, excluding two-thirds of adult men and all women. American officials also forced the Cubans to append to their constitution a frank avowal of U.S. hegemony known as the **Platt Amendment**. This statement prohibited Cuba from making a treaty with another nation that might impair its independence; in practice, this meant that all treaties had to have U.S. approval. Most important, another Platt Amendment provision granted the United States "the right to intervene" to preserve the island's independence and to maintain domestic order. The amendment also required Cuba to lease a naval base to the United States (at Guantánamo Bay, still under U.S. jurisdiction today). Formalized in a 1903 treaty, the amendment governed Cuban-American relations until 1934. "There is, of course, little or no independence left Cuba under the Platt Amendment," General Wood, military governor of the island until 1902, told President Roosevelt.

The Cubans, like the Filipinos, chafed under U.S. mastery. Widespread demonstrations protested the Platt Amendment, and a rebellion against the Cuban government in 1906 prompted Roosevelt to order another invasion of Cuba. The marines stayed until 1909, returned briefly in 1912, and occupied the island again from 1917 to 1922. All the while, U.S. officials helped to develop a transportation system, expand the public school system, found a national army, and increase sugar production. When Dr. Walter Reed's experiments, based on the theory of the Cuban physician Carlos Juan Finlay, proved that mosquitoes transmitted yellow fever, sanitary engineers controlled the insect and eradicated the disease.

Puerto Rico, the Caribbean island taken as a spoil of war in the Treaty of Paris, also developed under U.S. tutelage. Although no Puerto Rican sat at the negotiating table for that treaty, the Puerto Rican elite at first welcomed the United States as an improvement over Spain. But disillusionment soon set in. The condescending U.S. military governor, General Guy V. Henry, regarded Puerto Ricans as naughty, ill-educated children who needed "kindergarten instruction in controlling themselves without allowing them too much liberty." Some residents warned against the "Yankee peril"; others applauded the "Yankee model" and futilely anticipated statehood.

19-6c Panama Canal

Panama, meanwhile, became the site of a bold U.S. expansionist venture. In 1869, the world had marveled at the completion of the Suez Canal, a waterway in northeast Africa that greatly facilitated travel between the Indian Ocean and Mediterranean Sea, and enhanced the power of the British empire. Surely that feat could be duplicated in the Western Hemisphere, possibly in Panama, a province of Colombia. One expansionist, U.S. Navy Captain Robert W. Shufeldt, predicted that a new canal would convert "the Gulf of Mexico into an American lake." Business interests joined politicians, diplomats, and navy officers in insisting that the United States control such an interoceanic canal.

To construct such a canal, however, the United States had to overcome daunting obstacles. The Clayton-Bulwer Treaty with Britain (1850) had provided for joint control of a canal. The British, recognizing their diminishing influence in the region and cultivating friendship with the United States as a counterweight to Germany, stepped aside in the Hay-Pauncefote Treaty (1901) to permit a solely U.S.-run canal. When Colombia hesitated to meet Washington's terms, Roosevelt encouraged Panamanian rebels to declare independence and ordered American warships to the isthmus to back them.

In 1903, the new Panama awarded the United States a canal zone and long-term rights to its control. The treaty also guaranteed Panama its independence. (In 1922, the United States paid Colombia $25 million in "conscience money" but did not apologize.) The completion of the **Panama Canal** in 1914 marked a major technological achievement. During the canal's first year of operation, more than one thousand merchant ships squeezed through its locks.

19-6d Roosevelt Corollary

As for the rest of the Caribbean, Theodore Roosevelt resisted challenges to U.S. hegemony. Worried that Latin American nations' defaults on debts owed to European banks were provoking European intervention (England, Germany, and Italy sent warships to Venezuela in 1902), the president in 1904 issued the Roosevelt Corollary to the Monroe Doctrine. He warned Latin Americans to stabilize their politics and finances. "Chronic wrongdoing," the corollary lectured, might require "intervention by some civilized nation," and "in flagrant cases of such wrongdoing or impotence," the United States would have to assume the role of "an international police power." Laced with presumptions of superiority, Roosevelt's declaration provided the rationale for frequent U.S. interventions in Latin America.

From 1900 to 1917, U.S. presidents ordered American troops to Cuba, Panama, Nicaragua, the Dominican Republic, Mexico, and Haiti to quell civil wars, thwart challenges to U.S. influence, gain ports and bases, and forestall European meddling (see Map 19.2). U.S. authorities

Platt Amendment Added to Cuba's constitution of 1903 under American pressure, it gave the United States the right to intervene if Cuban independence or internal order were threatened, and granted a naval base to the United States at Guantánamo Bay.

Panama Canal Major waterway that traverses the Isthmus of Panama in Central America, connecting the Atlantic and Pacific oceans. Built by the United States for $352 million; construction began in 1906 and was completed in 1914.

▲ In a suit and hat, President Theodore Roosevelt occupies the controls of a ninety-five-ton power shovel at a Panama Canal worksite. Roosevelt's November 1906 trip to inspect the massive project was the first time a sitting president left the United States.

ran elections, trained national guards that became politically powerful, and renegotiated foreign debts, shifting them to U.S. banks. They also took over customs houses to control tariff revenues and government budgets (as in the Dominican Republic, from 1905 to 1941).

19-6e U.S.-Mexican Relations

U.S. officials focused particular attention on Mexico, where longtime dictator Porfirio Díaz (1876–1910) aggressively recruited foreign investors through tax incentives and land grants. American capitalists came to own Mexico's railroads and mines and invested heavily in petroleum and banking. By the early 1890s, the United States dominated Mexico's foreign trade. By 1910, Americans controlled 43 percent of Mexican property and produced more than half of the country's oil; in the state of Sonora, 186 of 208 mining companies were American owned. The Mexican revolutionaries who ousted Díaz in 1910, like nationalists elsewhere in Latin America, set out to reclaim their nation's sovereignty by ending their economic dependency on the United States.

The revolution descended into a bloody civil war with strong anti-Yankee overtones, and the Mexican government intended to nationalize extensive American-owned properties. Washington leaders worked to thwart this aim, with President Woodrow Wilson twice ordering troops onto Mexican soil: once in 1914, at Veracruz, to avenge a slight to the U.S. uniform and flag and to overthrow the nationalistic government of President Victoriano Huerta; and again in 1916, in northern Mexico, where General John J. "Black Jack" Pershing spent months pursuing Pancho Villa after the Mexican rebel had

raided an American border town. Having failed to capture Villa and facing another nationalistic government led by Venustiano Carranza, U.S. forces departed in January 1917.

As the United States reaffirmed the Monroe Doctrine against European expansion in the hemisphere and demonstrated the power to enforce it, European nations reluctantly honored U.S. hegemony in Latin America. In turn, the United States held to its tradition of standing outside European embroilments. The balance of power in Europe was precarious, and seldom did an American president involve the United States directly. Theodore Roosevelt did help settle a Franco-German clash over Morocco by mediating a settlement at Algeciras, Spain (1906). But the president drew American criticism for entangling the United States in a European problem. Americans endorsed the ultimately futile Hague peace conferences (1899 and 1907) and negotiated various arbitration treaties, but on the whole stayed outside the European arena, except to profit from extensive trade with it.

19-6f Peacemaking in East Asia

In East Asia, though, both Roosevelt and his successor, William Howard Taft, took an activist approach. Both sought to preserve the Open Door and to contain Japan's

▲ Francisco "Pancho" Villa presented himself as a selfless Mexican patriot. Americans living along the border thought otherwise, particularly after Villa's forces murdered more than 30 U.S. civilians. American troops pursued Villa more than 300 miles into Mexico but never caught him.

Guantánamo Bay

Four hundred miles from Miami, near the southeastern corner of Cuba, sits U.S. Naval Base Guantánamo Bay. It is the oldest American base outside the United States, and the only one located in a country with which Washington does not have a fully open political and economic relationship. The United States has occupied the base for more than a century, since the aftermath of the Spanish-American War, leasing it from Cuba for $4,085 per year (originally, $2,000 in gold coins).

From an early point, Cuban leaders expressed dissatisfaction with the deal, and in the aftermath of Fidel Castro's communist takeover in 1959, Guantánamo was a source of constant tension between the two countries. Castro called the 45-square-mile base "a dagger pointed at Cuba's heart" and over the years he pointedly refused to cash the rent checks. He did cash the very first check, though, and Washington has used that fact to argue that his government accepts the terms of the lease.

Since late 2001, "Gitmo," as the base is known to U.S. service members, has contained a detainment camp for persons alleged to be militant combatants captured in Afghanistan and, later, Iraq and elsewhere. The first group of twenty detainees arrived in January 2002, after a twenty-hour flight from Afghanistan. By the end of 2005, the number exceeded five hundred, from more than forty countries. The George W. Bush administration called the detainees "unlawful enemy combatants" rather than "prisoners of war" but promised early on to abide by the Geneva accords governing prisoners of war. But soon there were allegations of abuse and complaints that holding detainees without trial, charges, or any prospect of release was cruel and unlawful. Some detainees committed suicide. For many critics, the camp became an international symbol of American heavy-handedness, and even some administration allies said that the controversy surrounding the camp was severely hurting America's image abroad.

In June 2006, the U.S. Supreme Court ruled that President Bush had overstepped his power in setting up the procedures for the Guantánamo detainees without specific authority from Congress. The Court further said that the procedures violated both the Uniform Code of Military Justice and the Geneva accords. In January 2009, President Barack Obama signed an executive order closing the detention center within one year, but strong opposition (even from some Democrats) as well as complications concerning detainee trials and resettlements ensured that the deadline would not be met. When Obama left office eight years later, the center remained in operation.

CRITICAL THINKING

- The question for a people and a nation thus remained: how would the United States balance its security needs with its commitment to due process and the rule of law?

---

rising power in the region. Many race-minded Japanese interpreted the U.S. advance into the Pacific as an attempt by whites to gain ascendancy over Asians. Japanese leaders nonetheless urged their citizens to go to America to study it as a model for industrializing and achieving world power. Although some Americans proudly proclaimed the Japanese the "Yankees of the East," the United States gradually had to make concessions to Japan to protect the vulnerable Philippines and to sustain the Open Door policy. Japan continued to plant interests in China and then smashed the Russians in the Russo-Japanese War (1904–1905). President Roosevelt mediated the negotiations at the Portsmouth Conference in New Hampshire and won the Nobel Peace Prize for this effort to preserve a balance of power in Asia and shrink Japan's "big head."

In 1905, in the Taft-Katsura Agreement, the United States conceded Japanese hegemony over Korea in return for Japan's pledge not to undermine the U.S. position in the Philippines. Three years later, in the Root-Takahira Agreement, Washington recognized Japan's interests in Manchuria, whereas Japan again pledged the security of the Pacific possessions held by the United States and endorsed the Open Door in China. Roosevelt also built up American

naval power to deter the Japanese; in late 1907, he sent on a world tour the navy's "Great White Fleet" (so named because the ships were painted white for the voyage). Duly impressed, the Japanese began to build a bigger navy of their own.

19-6g Dollar Diplomacy

President Taft, for his part, thought he might counter Japanese advances in Asia through dollar diplomacy—the use of private funds to serve American diplomatic goals and garner profits for American financiers—and at the same time bring reform to less-developed countries. In this case, Taft induced American bankers to join an international consortium to build a railway in China. Taft's venture, however, seemed only to embolden Japan to solidify and extend its holdings in China, where internal discord continued after the nationalist revolution of 1911 overthrew the Qing dynasty.

In 1914, when the First World War broke out in Europe, Japan seized Shandong and some Pacific islands from the Germans. In 1915, Japan issued its Twenty-One Demands, virtually insisting on hegemony over all of China. The Chinese door was being slammed shut, but the United States lacked adequate countervailing power in Asia to block Japan's imperial thrusts. A new president, Woodrow Wilson, worried about how the "white race" could blunt the rise of "the yellow race."

19-6h Anglo-American Rapprochement

British officials in London shared this concern, though their attention was focused primarily on rising tensions in Europe. A special feature of American-European relations in the TR-Taft years was the flowering of an Anglo-American cooperation that had been growing throughout the late nineteenth century. One outcome of the intense German-British rivalry and the rise of the United States to world power was London's quest for friendship with Washington. Already prepared by racial ideas of Anglo-Saxon kinship, a common language, and respect for representative government and private-property rights, Americans appreciated British support in the 1898 war and the Hay-Pauncefote Treaty, and London's virtual endorsement of the Roosevelt Corollary and withdrawal of British warships from the Caribbean. As Mark Twain said of the two imperialist powers, "We are kin in sin."

British-American trade and U.S. investment in Britain also secured ties. By 1914, more than 140 American companies operated in Britain, including H. J. Heinz's processed foods and F. W. Woolworth's "penny markets." Many Britons decried an Americanization of British culture. One journalist complained that a Briton "wakes in the morning at the sound of an American alarm clock; rises from his New England sheets, and shaves with . . . a Yankee safety razor. He . . . slips his Waterbury watch into his pocket [and] catches an electric train made in New York. . . . At his office . . . he sits on a Nebraskan swivel chair, before a Michigan roll-top desk." Such exaggerated fears and the always prickly character of the Anglo-American relationship, however, gave way to cooperation in world affairs, most evident in 1917 when the United States threw its weapons and soldiers into the First World War on the British side against Germany.

Summary

In the years from the Civil War to the First World War, expansionism and imperialism elevated the United States to world power status. By 1914, Americans held extensive economic, strategic, and political interests in a world made smaller by modern technology. The victory over Spain in 1898 was but the most dramatic moment in the long process. The outward reach of U.S. foreign policy from Seward to Wilson sparked opposition from domestic critics, other imperialist nations, and foreign nationalists, but expansionists prevailed, and the trend toward empire endured.

From Asia to Latin America, economic and strategic needs and ideology motivated and justified expansion and empire. The belief that the United States needed foreign markets to absorb surplus production in order to save the domestic economy joined missionary zeal in reforming other societies through the promotion of American products and culture. Notions of racial and male supremacy and appeals to national greatness also fed the appetite for foreign adventure and commitments. The greatly augmented navy became a primary means for satisfying American ideas and wants.

Revealing the great diversity of America's intersection with the world, missionaries like Moon in China, generals like Wood in Cuba, companies like Singer in Africa and Heinz in Britain, and politicians like Taft in the Philippines carried American ways, ideas, guns, and goods abroad to a mixed reception. The conspicuous declarations of Olney, Hay, Roosevelt, and other leaders became the guiding texts for U.S. principles and behavior in world affairs. A world power with far-flung interests to protect, the United States had to face a tough test of its self-proclaimed greatness and reconsider its political isolation from Europe when a world war broke out in August 1914.

Suggestions for Further Reading

Gail Bederman, *Manliness and Civilization: A Cultural History of Gender and Race in the United States, 1880–1917* (1995)

Julian Go, *American Empire and the Politics of Meaning: Elite Political Cultures in the Philippines and Puerto Rico* (2008)

Kristin L. Hoganson, *Fighting for American Manhood: How Gender Politics Provoked the Spanish-American and Philippine-American Wars* (1998)

Michael H. Hunt, *Ideology and U.S. Foreign Policy* (1987)

Paul A. Kramer, *The Blood of Government: Race, Empire, the United States, and the Philippines* (2006)

Walter LaFeber, *The American Search for Opportunity, 1865–1913* (2015)

Brian M. Linn, *The Philippine War, 1899–1902* (2000)

Eric T. Love, *Race over Empire: Racism and U.S. Imperialism, 1865–1900* (2004)

John Offner, *An Unwanted War: The Diplomacy of the United States and Spain over Cuba, 1895–1898* (1992)

Louis A. Perez Jr., *The War of 1898: The United States and Cuba in History and Historiography* (1998)

Americans in the Great War, 1914–1920

On May 7, 1915, Secretary of State William Jennings Bryan was having lunch with several cabinet members at the Shoreham Hotel in Washington when he received a bulletin: the luxurious British ocean liner *Lusitania* had been sunk, apparently by a German submarine. He rushed to his office, and at 3:06 pm came the confirmation from London: "THE LUSITANIA WAS TORPEDOED OFF THE IRISH COAST AND SANK IN HALF AN HOUR. NO NEWS YET OF PASSENGERS." In fact, 1,198 people had perished, including 128 Americans. The giant vessel had taken, not half an hour, but just eighteen minutes to go down. Bryan was deeply distraught but not altogether surprised. The European powers were at war, and he had feared precisely this kind of calamity. Britain had imposed a naval blockade on Germany, and the Germans had responded by launching submarine warfare against Allied shipping. Berlin authorities had proclaimed the North Atlantic a danger zone, and German submarines had already sunk numerous British and Allied ships. As a passenger liner, the *Lusitania* was supposed to be spared, but German officials had placed notices in U.S. newspapers warning that Americans who traveled on British or Allied ships did so at their own risk; passenger liners suspected of carrying munitions or other contraband were subject to attack. For weeks, Bryan had urged President Woodrow Wilson to stop Americans from booking passage on British ships; Wilson had refused.

That evening, Bryan mused to his wife, "I wonder if that ship carried munitions of war. . . . If she did carry them, it puts a different face on the whole matter! England has been using our citizens to protect her ammunition!" The *Lusitania*, it soon emerged, *was* carrying munitions, and Bryan set about urging a restrained U.S. response. Desperate to keep the United States

◀ This poster by Fred Spear, published in Boston not long after the *Lusitania* sinking, captured the anger Americans felt at the loss of 128 of their fellow citizens, among them women and children. Nearly two years before U.S. entry into the war, posters like this one urged Americans to enlist as preparation for the day when they must surely confront the German enemy. Library of Congress Prints and Photographs Division[LC-USZC4-1129]

Chronology

1914	■ First World War begins in Europe
1915	■ Germans sink RMS *Lusitania* off coast of Ireland
1916	■ After torpedoing the *Sussex*, Germany pledges not to attack merchant ships without warning
	■ National Defense Act expands military
1917	■ Germany declares unrestricted submarine warfare
	■ Russian Revolution ousts the czar; Bolsheviks later take power
	■ United States enters First World War
	■ Selective Service Act creates draft
	■ Espionage Act limits First Amendment rights
	■ Race riot breaks out in East St. Louis, Illinois
1918	■ Wilson announces Fourteen Points for new world order
	■ Sedition Act further limits free speech
	■ U.S. troops at Château-Thierry help blunt German offensive
	■ U.S. troops intervene in Russia against Bolsheviks
	■ Spanish flu pandemic kills 20 million worldwide
	■ Armistice ends First World War
1919	■ Paris Peace Conference punishes Germany and launches League of Nations
	■ May Day bombings help instigate Red Scare
	■ American Legion organizes for veterans' benefits and antiradicalism
	■ Wilson suffers stroke after speaking tour
	■ Senate rejects Treaty of Versailles and U.S. membership in League of Nations
	■ *Schenck v. U.S.* upholds Espionage Act
1920	■ Palmer Raids round up suspected radicals

Theodore Roosevelt, called the sinking "an act of piracy" and pressed for war. Wilson did not want war, but neither did he accept Bryan's argument that the British and German violations should be treated the same. He sent a strong protest note to Berlin, calling on the German government to end its submarine warfare.

For the next several weeks, as Bryan continued to press his case, he sensed his growing isolation within the administration. When in early June Wilson made it clear that he would not ban Americans from travel on belligerent ships and that he intended to send a second protest note to Germany, Bryan resigned. Privately, Wilson called Bryan a "strange man" who suffered from a "singular sort of moral blindness."

The division between the president and his secretary of state reflected divisions within the American populace over Europe's war. The split could be seen in the reaction to Bryan's resignation. Eastern newspapers charged him with "unspeakable treachery" and of stabbing the country in the back. But in the Midwest and South, Bryan was accorded respect, and he won praise from pacifists and German American groups for his "act of courage." A few weeks later, speaking to a capacity crowd of fifteen thousand at Madison Square Garden (another fifty thousand had been turned away), Bryan was loudly applauded when he warned against "war with any of the belligerent nations." Although many Americans felt, like President Wilson, that honor was more important than peace, others joined Bryan in thinking that some sacrifice of neutral rights was reasonable if the country could thereby stay out of the fighting. The debate would continue up until U.S. entry into the war in 1917, and the tensions would still ripple thereafter.

Experience an interactive version of this story in MindTap®.

out of the war, he urged Wilson to couple his condemnation of the German action with an equally tough note to Britain protesting its blockade and to ban Americans from traveling on belligerent ships. Wilson hesitated. Others, including former president

Like most Americans, Bryan had been stunned by the outbreak of the Great War (as it quickly became known) in 1914. For years, the United States had participated in the international competition for colonies, markets, and weapons supremacy. But full-scale war seemed unthinkable. The new machine guns, howitzers, submarines, and dreadnoughts were such awesome death engines that leaders surely would not use them. When they did, lamented one social reformer, "civilization is all gone, and barbarism comes."

For almost three years, President Wilson kept America out of the war. During this time, he sought to protect U.S. trade interests and improve the nation's military posture while also lecturing the belligerents to rediscover their humanity and to respect international law. But American property, lives, and neutrality fell victim to British and German naval warfare. When, two years after the *Lusitania* went down, the president finally asked Congress for a declaration of war, he did so with his characteristic crusading zeal. America entered the battle not just to win the war but to reform the postwar world: to "make the world safe for democracy."

A year and a half later, the Great War would be over. It exacted a terrible cost on Europe, for a whole generation of young men was cut down—some 10 million soldiers perished. Europeans looked at their gigantic cemeteries and could scarcely believe what had happened. They experienced an acute spiritual loss in the destruction of ideals, confidence, and goodwill. Economically, too, the damage was immense. Most portentous of all for the future of the twentieth century, the Great War toppled four empires of the Old World—the German, Austro-Hungarian, Russian, and Ottoman Turkish—and left two others, the British and French, drastically weakened.

For the United States, the human and material cost was comparatively small, yet Americans could rightly claim to have helped tip the scales in favor of the Allies with their infusion of war materiel and troops as well as their extension of loans and food supplies. The war years also witnessed a massive international transfer of wealth from Europe across the Atlantic, as the United States went from being the world's largest debtor nation to being its largest creditor nation. The conflict marked the United States' coming of age as a world power. In these and other respects, the Great War was a great triumph for Americans.

In other ways, though, World War I was a difficult, painful experience. It accentuated and intensified social divisions. Racial tensions accompanied the northward migration of southern blacks, and pacifists and German Americans were harassed. The federal government, eager to stimulate patriotism, trampled on civil liberties to silence critics. And following a communist revolution in Russia, a Red Scare in America repressed radicals and tarnished America's reputation as a democratic society. Although reformers continued after the armistice to devote themselves to issues like prohibition and woman suffrage, the war experience helped splinter the Progressive movement. Jane Addams sadly remarked that "the spirit of fighting burns away all those impulses . . . which foster the will to justice."

Abroad, Americans who had marched to battle as if on a crusade grew disillusioned with the peace process. They recoiled from the spectacle of the victors squabbling over the spoils, and they chided Wilson for failing to deliver the "peace without victory" that he had promised. As in the 1790s, the 1840s, and the 1890s, Americans once again engaged in a searching national debate about the fundamentals of their foreign policy. After negotiating the Treaty of Versailles at Paris following World War I, the president urged U.S. membership in the new League of Nations, which he promoted as a vehicle for reforming world politics. The Senate rejected his appeal (the League nonetheless organized without U.S. membership) because many Americans feared that the League might threaten U.S. interests and entangle Americans in Europe's problems.

- *Why did the United States try to remain neutral and then enter the European war in 1917?*
- *How was American society changed by the war?*
- *What were the main elements of Woodrow Wilson's postwar vision, and why did he fail to realize them?*

20-1 Precarious Neutrality

▶ Why was it difficult for Americans to remain neutral when war broke out in Europe in August 1914?
▶ What was "Wilsonianism"?
▶ How was American neutrality undermined by the actions of the Allies and Central Powers?

The war that erupted in August 1914 grew from years of European competition over trade, colonies, allies, and armaments. Two powerful alliance systems had formed: the Triple Alliance of Germany, Austria-Hungary, and Italy, and the Triple Entente of Britain, France, and Russia. All had imperial holdings and ambitions for more, but Germany seemed particularly bold, as it rivaled Great Britain for world leadership. Many Americans saw Germany as a threat to U.S. interests in the Western Hemisphere and viewed Germans as an excessively militaristic people who embraced autocracy and spurned democracy.

20-1a Outbreak of the First World War

Strategists said that Europe enjoyed a balance of power, but crises in the Balkan countries of southeastern Europe triggered a chain of events that shattered the "balance." Slavic nationalists sought to enlarge Serbia, an independent Slavic nation, by annexing regions such as Bosnia, then a province of the Austro-Hungarian Empire (see Map 20.1). On June 28, 1914, Archduke Franz Ferdinand, heir to the Austro-Hungarian throne, was assassinated by Gavrilo Princip, a Serbian nationalist, while on a state visit to Sarajevo, the capital of Bosnia. Alarmed by the prospect of an engorged Serbia on

its border, Austria-Hungary consulted its Triple Alliance partner Germany, which urged toughness. When Serbia called on its Slavic friend Russia for help, Russia in turn looked for backing from its ally France. In late July, Austria-Hungary declared war against Serbia. Russia then began to mobilize its armies.

Germany—having goaded Austria-Hungary toward war and believing war inevitable—struck first, declaring war against Russia on August 1 and against France two days later. Britain hesitated, but when German forces slashed into neutral Belgium to get at France, London declared war against Germany on August 4. Eventually, Turkey (the Ottoman Empire) joined Germany and Austria-Hungary as the Central Powers, and Italy (switching sides) and Japan teamed up with Britain, France, and Russia as the Allies. Japan took advantage of the European war to seize Shandong, Germany's area of influence in China.

Map 20.1 Europe Goes to War, Summer 1914

Bound by alliances and stirred by turmoil in the Balkans, where Serbs repeatedly upended peace, the nations of Europe descended into war in the summer of 1914. Step by step, a Balkan crisis escalated into the "Great War."

President Wilson at first sought to distance America from the conflagration by issuing a proclamation of neutrality—the traditional U.S. policy toward European wars. He also asked Americans to refrain from taking sides, to exhibit "the dignity of self-control." In private, the president said, "We definitely have to be neutral, since otherwise our mixed populations would wage war on each other." The United States, he fervently hoped, would stand apart as a sane, civilized nation in a deranged international system.

20-1b Taking Sides

Wilson's lofty appeal for American neutrality and unity at home collided with several realities. First, ethnic groups in the United States did take sides. Many German Americans and anti-British Irish Americans (Ireland was then trying to break free from British rule) cheered for the Central Powers. Americans of British and French ancestry, and others with roots in Allied nations, tended to champion the Allied cause. Germany's attack on Belgium confirmed in many people's minds that Germany had become the archetype of unbridled militarism.

The pro-Allied sympathies of Wilson's administration also weakened the U.S. neutrality proclamation. Honoring Anglo-American rapprochement, Wilson shared the conviction with British leaders that a German victory would destroy free enterprise and government by law. If Germany won the war, he prophesied, "it would change the course of our civilization and make the United States a military nation." Several of Wilson's chief advisers and diplomats—his assistant, Colonel Edward House; ambassador to London Walter Hines Page; and Robert Lansing, a counselor in the State Department who later became secretary of state—held similar anti-German views, which often translated into pro-Allied policies.

U.S. economic links with the Allies also rendered neutrality difficult, if not impossible. England had long been one of the nation's best customers. Now the British flooded America with new orders, especially for arms. Sales to the Allies helped pull the American economy out of its recession. Between 1914 and 1916, American exports to England and France grew 365 percent, from $753 million to $2.75 billion. In the same period, however, largely because of Britain's naval blockade, exports to Germany dropped by more than 90 percent, from $345 million to only $29 million. Loans to Britain and France from private American banks—totaling $2.3 billion during the neutrality period—financed much of U.S. trade with the Allies. Germany received only $27 million in the same period. The Wilson administration, which at first frowned on these transactions, came to see them as necessary to the economic health of the United States.

From Germany's perspective, the links between the American economy and the Allies meant that the United States had become the Allied arsenal and bank. Americans, however, faced a dilemma: cutting their economic ties with Britain would constitute a nonneutral act in favor of Germany. Under international law, Britain—which controlled the seas—could buy both contraband (war-related

goods) and noncontraband from neutrals. It was Germany's responsibility, not America's, to stop such trade in ways that international law prescribed—that is, by an effective blockade of the enemy's territory, by the seizure of contraband from neutral (American) ships, or by the confiscation of goods from belligerent (British) ships. Germans, of course, judged the huge U.S. trade with the Allies an act of nonneutrality that had to be stopped.

20-1c Wilsonianism

The president and his aides believed, finally, that Wilsonian principles stood a better chance of international acceptance if Britain, rather than the Central Powers, sat astride the postwar world. "Wilsonianism," the cluster of ideas that Wilson espoused, consisted of traditional American principles (such as democracy and the Open Door) and a conviction that the United States was a beacon of freedom to the world. Only the United States could lead the convulsed world into a new, peaceful era of unobstructed commerce, free-market capitalism, democratic politics, and open diplomacy. American Progressivism, it seemed, was to be projected onto the world.

"America had the infinite privilege of fulfilling her destiny and saving the world," Wilson claimed. Empires had to be dismantled to honor the principle of self-determination. Armaments had to be reduced. Critics charged that Wilson often violated his own credos in his eagerness to force them on others—as his military interventions in Mexico in 1914, Haiti in 1915, and the Dominican Republic in 1916 testified. All agreed, though, that such ideals served American commercial purposes; in this way idealism and self-interest were married.

To say that American neutrality was never a real possibility given ethnic loyalties, economic ties, and Wilsonian preferences is not to say that Wilson sought to enter the war. He emphatically wanted to keep the United States out. Time and again, he tried to mediate the crisis to prevent one power from crushing another. In early 1917, the president remarked that "we are the only one of the great white nations that is free from war today, and it would be a crime against civilization for us to go in." But go in the United States finally did. Why?

20-1d Violation of Neutral Rights

The short answer is that Americans got caught in the Allied–Central Power crossfire. British naval policy aimed to sever neutral trade with Germany in order to cripple the German economy. The British, "ruling the waves and waiving the rules," declared a blockade of water entrances to Germany and mined the North Sea. They also harassed neutral shipping by seizing cargoes and defining a broad list of contraband (including foodstuffs) that they prohibited neutrals from shipping to Germany. American commerce with Germany dwindled rapidly. Furthermore, to counter German submarines, the British flouted international law by arming their merchant ships and flying neutral (sometimes American) flags. Wilson frequently protested British violations of neutral rights, pointing out that neutrals had the right to sell and ship noncontraband goods to belligerents without interference. But London often deftly defused Washington's criticism by paying for confiscated cargoes, and German provocations made British behavior appear less offensive by comparison.

Unable to win the war on land and determined to lift the blockade and halt American-Allied commerce, Germany looked for victory at sea by using submarines. In February 1915, Berlin declared a war zone around the British Isles, warned neutral vessels to stay out so as not to be attacked by mistake, and advised passengers from neutral nations to stay off Allied ships. President Wilson informed Germany that the United States would hold it to "strict accountability" for any losses of American life and property.

Wilson was interpreting international law in the strictest possible sense. The law that an attacker had to warn a passenger or merchant ship before attacking, so that passengers and crew could disembark safely into lifeboats, predated the submarine. The Germans thought the slender, frail, and sluggish *Unterseebooten* (U-boats) should not be expected to surface to warn ships, for surfacing would cancel out the U-boats' advantage of surprise and leave them vulnerable to attack. Berlin protested that Wilson was denying it the one weapon that could break the British economic stranglehold, disrupt the Allies' substantial connection with U.S. producers and bankers, and win the war. To all concerned—British, Germans, and Americans—naval warfare became a matter of life and death.

20-2 The Decision for War

▶ Why did peace advocates oppose American involvement in World War I?

▶ What developments drew the United States into the war?

Ultimately, it was the war at sea that doomed the prospects for U.S. neutrality. In the early months of 1915, German U-boats sank ship after ship, most notably the British liner *Lusitania* on May 7. Of 159 Americans on board, 128 died. In mid-August, after a lull following Germany's promise to refrain from attacking passenger liners, another British vessel, the *Arabic*, was sunk off Ireland. Three Americans died. The Germans quickly pledged that an unarmed passenger ship would never again be attacked without warning. But the sinking of the *Arabic* fueled debate over American passengers on belligerent vessels. Echoing Bryan's plea from the previous spring (see the chapter-opening vignette), critics asked: why not require Americans to sail on American craft? From August 1914 to March 1917, after all, only 3 Americans died on an American ship (the tanker *Gulflight*, sunk by a German U-boat in May 1915), whereas about 190 were killed on belligerent ships.

20-2a Peace Advocates

In March 1916, a U-boat attack on the *Sussex*, a French vessel crossing the English Channel, took the United States a

Library of Congress

▲ Initially underestimated as a weapon, the German U-boat proved to be frighteningly effective against Allied ships. At the beginning of the war, Germany had about twenty operational submarines in its High Seas Fleet, but officials moved swiftly to speed up production. This 1914 German poster showing U-boats choking off supplies to Britain celebrates German submarine production.

step closer to war. Four Americans were injured on that ship, which the U-boat commander mistook for a minelayer. Stop the marauding submarines, Wilson lectured Berlin, or the United States would sever diplomatic relations. Again the Germans retreated, pledging not to attack merchant vessels without warning. At about the same time, U.S. relations with Britain soured. The British crushing of the Easter Rebellion in Ireland and further British restriction of U.S. trade with the Central Powers aroused American anger.

As the United States became more entangled in the Great War, many Americans urged Wilson to keep the nation out. In early 1915, Jane Addams, Carrie Chapman Catt, and other suffragists helped found the Woman's Peace Party, the U.S. section of the Women's International League for Peace and Freedom. "The mother half of humanity," claimed women peace advocates, had a special role as "the guardians of life." Later that same year, some pacifist Progressives—including

Oswald Garrison Villard, Paul Kellogg, and Lillian Wald—organized an antiwar coalition, the American Union Against Militarism. Businessman Andrew Carnegie, who in 1910 had established the Carnegie Endowment for International Peace, helped finance peace groups. So did Henry Ford, who in late 1915 traveled on a "peace ship" to Europe to propagandize for a negotiated settlement. Socialists like Eugene Debs added their voices to the peace movement.

Antiwar advocates emphasized several points: that war drained a nation of its youth, resources, and reform impulse; that it fostered repression at home; that it violated Christian morality; and that wartime business barons reaped huge profits at the expense of the people. Militarism and conscription, Addams pointed out, were what millions of immigrants had left behind in Europe. Were they now—in the United States—to be forced into the decadent system they had escaped? Although the peace movement was splintered—some wanted to keep the United States out of the conflict but did not endorse the pacifists' claim that intervention could never be justified—it carried political and intellectual weight that Wilson could not ignore, and it articulated several ideas that he shared. In fact, he campaigned on a peace platform in the 1916 presidential election. After his triumph, Wilson futilely labored once again to bring the belligerents to the conference table. In early 1917, he advised them to temper their acquisitive war aims, appealing for "peace without victory."

20-2b Unrestricted Submarine Warfare

In Germany, Wilson's overture went unheeded. Since August 1916, leaders in Berlin had debated whether to resume the unrestricted U-boat campaign. Opponents feared a break with the United States, but proponents claimed there was no choice. Only through an all-out attack on Britain's supply shipping, they argued, could Germany win the war before the British blockade and trench warfare in France had exhausted Germany's ability to keep fighting. If the U-boats could sink 600,000 tons of Allied shipping per month, the German admiralty estimated, Britain would be brought to the brink of starvation. True, the United States might enter the war, but that was a risk worth taking. Victory might be achieved before U.S. troops could be ferried across the Atlantic in sizable numbers. It proved a winning argument. In early February 1917, Germany launched unrestricted submarine warfare. All warships and merchant vessels—belligerent or neutral—would be attacked if sighted in the declared war zone. Wilson quickly broke diplomatic relations with Berlin.

This German challenge to American neutral rights and economic interests was soon followed by a German threat to U.S. security. In late February, British intelligence intercepted and passed to American officials a telegram addressed to the German minister in Mexico from German foreign secretary Arthur Zimmermann. Its message: if Mexico joined a military alliance against the United States, Germany would help Mexico recover the territories it had lost in 1848, including several western states. Zimmermann hoped to "set new

enemies on America's neck—enemies which give them plenty to take care of over there."

The Zimmermann telegram stiffened Wilson's resolve. Even though Mexico City rejected Germany's offer, the Wilson administration judged Zimmermann's telegram "a conspiracy against this country." Mexico still might let German agents use Mexican soil to propagandize against the United States, if not sabotage American properties. The prospect of a German-Mexican collaboration helped turn the tide of opinion in the American Southwest, where antiwar sentiment had been strong.

Soon afterward, Wilson asked Congress for "armed neutrality" to defend American lives and commerce. He requested authority to arm American merchant ships and to "employ any other instrumentalities or methods that may be necessary." In the midst of the debate, Wilson released Zimmermann's telegram to the press. Americans were outraged. Still, antiwar senators Robert M. La Follette and George Norris, among others, saw the armed-ship bill as a blank check for the president to move the country to war, and they filibustered it to death. Wilson proceeded to arm America's commercial vessels anyway. The action came too late to prevent the sinking of several American ships. War cries echoed across the nation. In late March, an agonized Wilson called Congress into special session.

20-2c War Message and War Declaration

On April 2, 1917, the president stepped before a hushed Congress. Solemnly, he accused the Germans of "warfare against mankind." Passionately and eloquently, Wilson enumerated U.S. grievances: Germany's violation of freedom of the seas, disruption of commerce, interference with Mexico, and breach of human rights by killing innocent Americans. The "Prussian autocracy" had to be punished by "the democracies." Russia was now among the latter, he was pleased to report, because the Russian Revolution had ousted the czar just weeks before. Congress declared war against Germany on April 6 by a vote of 373 to 50 in the House and 82 to 6 in the Senate. (This vote was for war against Germany only; a declaration of war against Austria-Hungary came several months later, on December 7.) Montana's Jeannette Rankin, the first woman ever to sit in Congress, cast a ringing no vote. "Peace is a woman's job," she declared, "because men have a natural fear of being classed as cowards if they oppose war" and because mothers should protect their children from death-dealing weapons.

For principle, for morality, for honor, for commerce, for security, for reform—for all of these reasons, Wilson took the United States into the Great War. The submarine was certainly the culprit that drew a reluctant president and nation into the maelstrom. Yet critics did not attribute the U.S. descent into war to the U-boat alone. They emphasized Wilson's rigid definition of international law, which did not accommodate the submarine's tactics. They faulted his contention that Americans should be entitled to travel anywhere, even on a belligerent ship loaded with

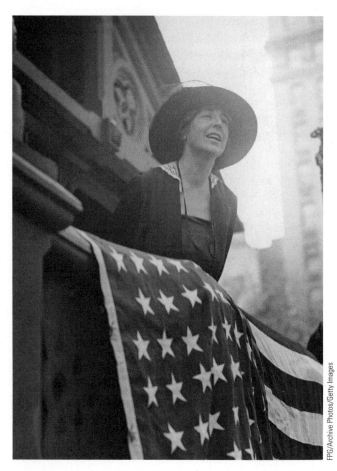

▲ Jeannette Rankin (1880–1973) of Montana was the first woman to sit in the House of Representatives (elected in 1916) and the only member of Congress to vote against U.S. entry into both world wars (in 1917 and 1941). A lifelong pacifist, she would later lead a march in Washington, D.C.—at age eighty-seven—against U.S. participation in the Vietnam War. Here she is addressing a rally in Union Square, New York City, September 1924.

contraband. They criticized his policies as nonneutral. But they lost the debate. Most Americans came to accept Wilson's view that the Germans had to be checked to ensure an open, orderly world in which U.S. principles and interests would be safe.

America went to war to reform world politics, not to destroy Germany. By early 1917, the president concluded that the United States would not be able to claim a seat at the postwar peace conference unless it became a combatant. At the peace conference, President Wilson intended to promote the principles he thought essential to a stable world order, to advance democracy and the Open Door, and to outlaw revolution and aggression. He tried to preserve part of his country's status as a neutral by designating the United States an "Associated" power rather than a full-fledged Allied nation, but this was akin to a hope of being only partly pregnant.

Selective Service Act Law that required all men between twenty-one and thirty (later expanded to eighteen through forty-five) to register with local draft boards.

20-3 Winning the War

▶ What actions did the federal government take to prepare for and prosecute the war?

▶ How did the nature of combat impact soldiers?

▶ How did Woodrow Wilson's vision for world affairs clash with that of Vladimir Lenin?

Even before the U.S. declaration of war, the Wilson administration—encouraged by such groups as the National Security League and the Navy League, and by mounting public outrage against Germany's submarine warfare—had been strengthening the military under the banner of "preparedness." When the pacifist song "I Didn't Raise My Boy to Be a Soldier" became popular, preparedness proponents retorted, "I Didn't Raise My Boy to Be a Coward." The National Defense Act of 1916 provided for increases in the army and National Guard and for summer training camps modeled on the one in Plattsburgh, New York, where a slice of America's social and economic elite had trained in 1915 as "citizen-soldiers." The Navy Act of 1916 started the largest naval expansion in American history.

20-3a The Draft and the Soldier

To raise an army after the declaration of war, Congress in May 1917 passed the **Selective Service Act**, requiring all males between the ages of twenty-one and thirty (later changed to eighteen and forty-five) to register. National service, proponents believed, would not only prepare the nation for battle but also instill patriotism and respect for order, democracy, and personal sacrifice. Critics feared it would lead to the militarization of American life.

On June 5, 1917, more than 9.5 million men signed up for the "great national lottery." By war's end, 24 million men had been registered by local draft boards. Of this number, 4.8 million had served in the armed forces, 2 million of that number in France. Among them were hundreds of thousands who had volunteered before December 1917, when the government prohibited enlistment because the military judged voluntarism too inefficient (many volunteers were more useful in civilian factories than in the army) and too competitive (enlistees got to choose the service they wanted, thus setting off recruiting wars). Millions of laborers received deferments from military duty because they worked in war industries or had dependents.

The typical soldier was a draftee in his early to mid-twenties, white, single, American born, and poorly educated (most had not attended high school, and perhaps 30 percent could not read or write). Tens of thousands of women enlisted in the army Nurse Corps, served as "hello girls" (volunteer bilingual telephone operators) in the army Signal Corps, and became clerks in the navy and Marine Corps. On college campuses, 150,000 students joined the Student Army Training Corps or similar navy and marine units. At officer training camps, the army turned out "ninety-day wonders."

FPG/Archive Photos/Getty Images

Some 400,000 African Americans also served in the military. Although many southern politicians feared arming blacks, the army drafted them into segregated units, where they were assigned to menial labor and endured crude abuse and miserable conditions. Ultimately, more than 40,000 African Americans would see combat in Europe, however, and several black units served with distinction in various divisions of the French army. The all-black 369th Infantry Regiment, for example, spent more time in the trenches—191 days—and received more medals than any other American outfit. The French government awarded the entire regiment the Croix de Guerre.

Although French officers had their share of racial prejudice and often treated the soldiers from their own African colonies poorly, black Americans serving with the French reported a degree of respect and cooperation generally lacking in the U.S. Army. They also spoke of getting a much warmer reception from French civilians than they were used to in the United States. The irony was not lost on African American leaders, such as W. E. B. Du Bois. Du Bois had endorsed the support of the National Association for the Advancement of Colored People (NAACP) for the war and echoed its call for blacks to volunteer for the fight so that they might help make the world safe for democracy and help blur the color lines at home.

But not everyone eligible for military service was eager to sign up. Approximately 3 million men evaded draft registration. Some were arrested, and others fled to Mexico or Canada, but most stayed at home and were never discovered. Another 338,000 men who had registered and been summoned by their draft boards failed to show up for induction. According to arrest records, most of these "deserters" and the more numerous "evaders" were lower-income agricultural and industrial laborers. Some simply felt overwhelmed by the government bureaucracy and stayed away; others were members of minority or ethnic groups who felt alienated. Although nearly 65,000 draftees initially applied for conscientious-objector status (refusing to bear arms for religious or pacifist reasons), some changed their minds or, like so many others, failed preinduction examinations. Quakers and Mennonites were numerous among the 4,000 inductees actually classified as conscientious objectors (COs). They did not have it easy. General Leonard Wood called COs "enemies of the Republic," and the military harassed them. COs who refused noncombat service, such as in the medical corps, faced imprisonment.

20-3b Trench Warfare

The U.S. troops who shipped out to France would do their fighting under American command. General **John J. Pershing**, head of the **American Expeditionary Forces (AEF)**, insisted that his "sturdy rookies" remain a separate, independent army. He was not about to turn over his "doughboys" (so termed, according to one theory, because the large buttons on American uniforms in the 1860s resembled a deep-fried bread of that name) to Allied commanders, who had become wedded to unimaginative and deadly trench warfare,

▲ Some fifteen thousand Native Americans served in the military in World War I. Most of them were enlistees who sought escape from restrictive Indian schools and lives of poverty, opportunities to develop new skills, and chances to prove their patriotism. This photo shows Fred Fast Horse, a Rosebud Sioux, as he recuperates in a New York hospital after suffering injury and paralysis during the Meuse-Argonne campaign of fall 1918. Unlike African Americans, Native Americans were not assigned to segregated units during the war. Native Americans participated in all major battles against German forces and suffered a high casualty rate in large part because they served as scouts, messengers, and snipers.

producing a military stalemate and ghastly casualties on the western front. Since the fall of 1914, zigzag trenches fronted by barbed wire and mines stretched across France. Between the muddy, stinking trenches lay "no man's land," denuded by artillery fire. When ordered out, soldiers would charge enemy trenches. If machine gun fire did not greet them, poison gas might.

First used by the Germans in April 1915, chlorine gas stimulated overproduction of fluid in the lungs, leading to death by drowning. One British officer tending to troops who had been gassed reported that "quite 200 men passed through my hands.... Some died with me, others on the way down ... I had to argue with many of them as to whether they were dead or not." Gas in a variety of forms (mustard and phosgene, in addition to chlorine) would continue in use throughout the war, sometimes blistering, sometimes incapacitating, often killing.

The extent of the dying in the trench warfare is hard to comprehend.

John J. Pershing Commander of American Expeditionary Forces that fought in Europe.

American Expeditionary Forces U.S. soldiers who fought in Europe during World War I.

At the Battle of the Somme in 1916, the British (who suffered nearly 60,000 casualties on the opening day) and French suffered 600,000 dead or wounded to earn only 125 square miles; the Germans lost 400,000 men. At Verdun that same year, 336,000 Germans perished, and at Passchendaele in 1917 more than 370,000 British men died to gain about 40 miles of mud and barbed wire. Ambassador Page grew sickened by what Europe had become—"a bankrupt slaughter-house inhabited by unmated women."

20-3c Shell Shock

The first American units landed in France on June 26, 1917, marched in a Fourth of July parade in Paris, and then moved by train toward the front. They soon learned about the horrors caused by advanced weaponry. Some suffered shell shock, a form of mental illness also known as war psychosis. Symptoms included a fixed, empty stare; violent tremors; paralyzed limbs; listlessness; jabbering and screaming; and haunting dreams. The illness could strike anyone; even those soldiers who appeared most manly and courageous cracked after days of incessant shelling and inescapable human carnage. "There was a limit to human endurance," one lieutenant explained. Providing some relief were Red Cross canteens, staffed by women volunteers, which gave soldiers way stations in a strange land and offered haircuts, food, and recreation. Some ten thousand Red Cross nurses also cared for the young warriors, while the American Library Association distributed 10 million books and magazines.

In Paris, where forty large houses of prostitution thrived, it became commonplace to hear that the British were drunkards, the French were whoremongers, and the Americans were both. Venereal disease became a serious problem. French Prime Minister Georges Clemenceau offered licensed, inspected prostitutes in "special houses" to the American army. When the generous Gallic offer reached Washington, Secretary of War Newton Baker gasped, "For God's sake . . . don't show this to the President or he'll stop the war." By war's end, about 15 percent of America's soldiers had contracted venereal disease, costing the army $50 million and 7 million days of active duty. Periodic inspections, chemical prophylactic treatments, and the threat of court-martial for infected soldiers kept the problem from being even greater.

20-3d American Units in France

The experience of being in Europe enlarged what for many American draftees had been a circumscribed world. Soldiers filled their diaries and letters with descriptions of the local customs and "ancient" architecture, and noted how the grimy and war-torn French countryside bore little resemblance to the groomed landscapes they had seen in paintings. Some felt both admiration for the spirit of endurance they saw in the populace and irritation that the locals were not more grateful for the Americans' arrival. "Life in France for the American soldier meant marching in the dirt and mud, living in cellars in filth, being wet and cold and fighting," the chief of staff of the Fourth Division remarked. "He had come to help France in the hour of distress and he was glad he came but these French people did not seem to appreciate him at all."

◀ A U.S. soldier of Company K, 110th Infantry Regiment, receives aid during fighting at Verennes, France.

National Archives

◀ During the First World War, the War Department promoted a film to combat sexually transmitted diseases. After the war, the New York State Board of Censors declared the film obscene.

The influx of American men and materiel—and the morale blow they delivered to the Central Powers—decided the outcome of the First World War. With both sides exhausted, the Americans tipped the balance toward the Allies. It took time, though, for the weight of the American military machine to make itself felt. From an early point, the U.S. Navy battled submarines and escorted troop carriers, and pilots in the U.S. Air Service, flying mostly British and French aircraft, saw limited action, mostly against German ground troops and transport. American "aces" like Eddie Rickenbacker took on their German counterparts in aerial "dogfights" and became heroes, as much in France as in their own country. But only ground troops could make a decisive difference, and American units actually did not engage in much combat until after the lull in the fighting during the harsh winter of 1917–1918.

20-3e The Bolshevik Revolution

By then, the military and diplomatic situation had changed dramatically because of an event that was arguably the most important political development of the twentieth century: the Bolshevik Revolution in Russia. In November 1917, the liberal-democratic government of Aleksander Kerensky, which had led the country since the czar's abdication early in the year, was overthrown by radical socialists led by Vladimir Ilyich Ulyanov, better known by the alias Lenin. Lenin seized power vowing to change world politics and end imperial rivalries on terms that challenged Woodrow Wilson's. Lenin saw the war as signaling the impending end of capitalism and looked for a global revolution, carried out by workers, that would sweep away the "imperialist order." For Western leaders, the prospect of Bolshevik-style revolutions spreading worldwide was too frightening to contemplate. The ascendancy of the world's laboring classes working in unity would destroy governments everywhere.

In the weeks following their takeover, the Bolsheviks attempted to embarrass the capitalist governments and incite world revolution by publishing several secret agreements among the Allies for dividing up the colonies and other territories of the Central Powers in the event of an Allied victory. Veteran watchers of world affairs found nothing particularly shocking in the documents, and Wilson had known of them, but the disclosures belied the noble rhetoric of Allied war aims. Wilson confided to Colonel House that he really wanted to tell the Bolsheviks to "go to hell," but he accepted the colonel's argument that he would have to address Lenin's claims that there was little to distinguish the two warring sides and that socialism represented the future.

20-3f Fourteen Points

The result was the **Fourteen Points**, unveiled in January 1918, in which Wilson reaffirmed America's commitment to an international system governed by laws and renounced territorial gains as a legitimate war aim. The first five points called for diplomacy "in the public view," freedom of the seas, lower tariffs, reductions in armaments, and the decolonization of empires. The next eight points

Fourteen Points President Wilson's program for world peace; presented to Congress in a 1918 speech, in the midst of World War I.

specified the evacuation of foreign troops from Russia, Belgium, and France, and appealed for self-determination for nationalities in Europe, such as the Poles. For Wilson, the fourteenth point was the most important—the mechanism for achieving all the others: "a general association of nations" or League of Nations.

Wilson's appeal did not impress Lenin, who called for an immediate end to the fighting, the eradication of colonialism, and self-determination for all peoples. Lenin also made a separate peace with Germany—the Treaty of Brest-Litovsk, signed on March 3, 1918. The deal erased centuries of Russian expansion, as Poland, Finland, and the Baltic states were taken from Russia and Ukraine was granted independence. One of Lenin's motives was to allow Russian troops loyal to the Bolsheviks to return home to fight anti-Bolshevik forces, who had launched a civil war to oust the new government.

The emerging feud between Lenin and Wilson contained the seeds of the superpower confrontation that would dominate the international system after 1945. Both men rejected the old diplomacy, which they claimed had created the conditions for the current war; both insisted on the need for a new world order. Although each professed adherence to democratic principles, they defined democracy differently. For Lenin, it meant workers everywhere seizing control from the owners of capital and establishing worker-led governments. For Wilson, it meant independent governments operating within capitalist systems and according to republican political practices.

20-3g Americans in Battle

In March 1918, with German troops released from the Russian front and transferred to France, the Germans launched a major offensive. By May, they had pushed to within fifty miles of Paris. Late that month, troops of the U.S. First Division helped blunt the German advance at Cantigny (see Map 20.2). In June, the Third Division and French forces held positions along the Marne River at Château-Thierry, and the Second Division soon attacked the Germans in the Belleau Wood. American soldiers won the battle after three weeks of fighting, but thousands died or were wounded after they made almost sacrificial frontal assaults against German machine guns.

Allied victory in the Second Battle of the Marne in July 1918 stemmed all German advances. In September, French and American forces took St. Mihiel in a ferocious battle in which American gunners fired 100,000 rounds of phosgene gas shells. Then the Allies began their massive Meuse-Argonne offensive. More than 1 million Americans joined British and French troops in weeks of fierce combat; some 26,000 Americans died before the Allies claimed the Argonne Forest on October 10. For Germany—its ground and submarine war stymied, its troops and cities mutinous, its allies Turkey and Austria dropping out, its kaiser

Map 20.2 **American Troops at the Western Front, 1918**

America's 2 million troops in France met German forces head-on, ensuring the defeat of the Central Powers in 1918.

The Influenza Pandemic of 1918

In the summer and fall of 1918, as World War I neared its end, a terrible plague swept the earth. It was a massive outbreak of influenza, and it would kill more than twice as many as the Great War itself—somewhere between 25 million and 40 million people. In the United States, 675,000 people died.

The first cases were identified in midwestern military camps in early March. Soldiers complained of flulike symptoms—headache, sore throat, fever—and many did not recover. At Fort Riley, Kansas, 48 men died. But with the war effort in full swing, few in government or the press took notice. Soldiers shipped out to Europe in large numbers (84,000 in March), some unknowingly carrying the virus in their lungs. The illness appeared on the western front in April. By the end of June, an estimated 8 million Spaniards were infected, thereby giving the disease its name, the Spanish flu.

In August, after a midsummer lull, a second, deadlier form of influenza began spreading. This time, the epidemic erupted simultaneously in three cities on three continents: Freetown, Sierra Leone, in Africa; Brest, France, the port of entry for many American soldiers; and Boston, Massachusetts. In September, the disease swept down the East Coast to New York, Philadelphia, and beyond. That month, 12,000 Americans died.

It was a flu like no other. People could be healthy at the start of the weekend and dead by the end of it. Some experienced a rapid accumulation of fluid in the lungs and would quite literally drown. Others died more slowly, of secondary infections with bacterial pneumonia. Mortality rates were highest for twenty- to twenty-nine-year-olds—the same group dying in huge numbers in the trenches.

In October, the epidemic hit full force. It spread to Japan, India, Africa, and Latin America. In the United States, 200,000 perished. There was a nationwide shortage of caskets and gravediggers, and funerals were limited to fifteen minutes. Bodies were left in gutters or on front porches, to be picked up by trucks that drove the streets. Stores were forbidden to hold sales; schools and cinemas closed. Army surgeon general Victor Vaughan made a frightening calculation: "If the epidemic continues its mathematical rate of acceleration, civilization could easily disappear from the face of the earth within a few weeks."

Then, suddenly, in November, for reasons still unclear, the epidemic eased, though the dying continued into 1919. In England and Wales, the final toll was 200,000. Samoa lost a quarter of its population, while in India the epidemic may have claimed a staggering 20 million. It was, in historian Roy Porter's words, "the greatest single demographic shock mankind has ever experienced."

World War I had helped spread the disease, but so had technological improvements that in previous decades facilitated global travel. The world was a smaller, more intimate place, often for good but sometimes for ill. Americans, accustomed to thinking that two great oceans could isolate them, were reminded that they were immutably linked to the rest of humankind.

CRITICAL THINKING

- World War I and the Spanish flu pandemic challenged many Americans' belief that the United States was protected by the vastness of the Atlantic and Pacific Oceans on either side of the continent. Even so, many Americans still assume a level of isolation. Does that assumption continue to color American foreign policy?

- What other events in the twentieth and twenty-first centuries have challenged the assumption of continental isolation?

PhotoQuest/Getty Images

◀ The rapid spread of the influenza pandemic required the construction of emergency hospitals in numerous locales, such as this one in Brookline, Massachusetts, pictured in October 1918.

abdicated, and facing the prospect of endless American troop reinforcements—peace became imperative. The Germans accepted a punishing armistice that took effect on the morning of November 11, 1918, at the eleventh hour of the eleventh day of the eleventh month.

20-3h Casualties

The cost of the war is impossible to compute, but the scale is clear enough: the belligerents counted 10 million soldiers and 6.6 million civilians dead and 21.3 million people wounded. Fifty-three thousand American soldiers died in battle, and another 62,000 died from disease. Many of the latter died from the virulent strain of influenza that ravaged the world in late 1918 and would ultimately claim more victims than the Great War itself. The economic damage was colossal as well, helping to account for the widespread starvation Europe experienced in the winter of 1918–1919. Economic output on the continent dwindled, and transport over any distance was in some countries virtually nonexistent. "We are at the dead season of our fortunes," wrote one British observer. "Never in the lifetime of men now living has the universal element in the soul of man burnt so dimly."

Casualties of the conflagration, the German, Austro-Hungarian, Ottoman, and Russian empires were no more. For a time, it appeared the Bolshevik Revolution might spread westward, as communist uprisings shook Germany and parts of central Europe. Even before the armistice, revolutionaries temporarily took power in the German cities of Bremen, Hamburg, and Lübeck. In Hungary, a revolutionary government actually held power for several months, while Austria was racked by left-wing demonstrations. In Moscow, meanwhile, the new Soviet state sought to consolidate its power. "We are sitting upon an open powder magazine," Colonel House worried, "and some day a spark may ignite it."

20-4 Mobilizing the Home Front

▶ What role did the federal government play in mobilizing the economy during World War I?

▶ What impact did wartime production needs have on workers?

▶ How did minority groups respond to wartime mobilization?

"It is not an army that we must shape and train for war," declared President Wilson, "it is a nation." The United States was a belligerent for only nineteen months, but the war had a tremendous impact at home. The federal government moved swiftly to expand its power over the economy to meet war needs and intervened in American life as never before. The vastly enlarged Washington bureaucracy managed the economy, labor force, military, public opinion, and more. Federal expenditures increased tremendously as the government spent more than $760 million a month from April 1917 to August 1919. As tax revenues lagged behind, the administration resorted to deficit spending (see Figure 20.1). The total cost of the war was difficult to calculate because future generations would have to pay veterans' benefits and interest on loans. To Progressives of the New Nationalist persuasion, the wartime expansion and centralization of government power were welcome. To others, these changes seemed excessive, leading to concentrated, hence dangerous, federal power.

20-4a Business-Government Cooperation

The federal government and private business became partners during the war. So-called dollar-a-year executives flocked to the nation's capital from major companies, retaining their corporate salaries while serving in official

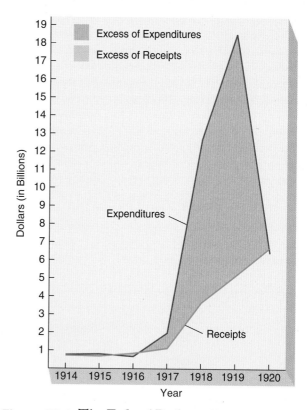

Figure 20.1 The Federal Budget, 1914–1920

During the First World War, the federal government spent more money than it received from increased taxes. It borrowed from banks or sold bonds through Liberty Loan drives. To meet the mounting costs of the war, in other words, the federal government had to resort to deficit spending. Expenditures topped receipts by more than $13 billion in 1919. Given this wartime fiscal pattern, moreover, the U.S. federal debt rose from $1 billion in 1914 to $25 billion in 1919. *Source: U.S. Department of Commerce, Historical Statistics of the United States: Colonial Times to 1957 (Washington, D.C.: Bureau of the Census, 1960), p. 711.*

administrative and consulting capacities. But evidence of self-interested businesspeople cashing in on the national interest aroused public protest. The head of the aluminum advisory committee, for example, was also president of the largest aluminum company. The assorted committees were disbanded in July 1917 in favor of a single manager, the **War Industries Board (WIB)**. But the federal government continued to work closely with business through trade associations, which grew significantly to two thousand by 1920. The government also suspended antitrust laws and signed cost-plus contracts, which guaranteed companies a healthy profit and a means to pay higher wages to head off labor strikes. Competitive bidding was virtually abandoned. Under such wartime practices, big business grew bigger.

Hundreds of new government agencies, staffed primarily by businesspeople, placed controls on the economy in order to shift the nation's resources to the Allies, the AEF, and war-related production. The Food Administration, led by engineer and investor Herbert Hoover, launched voluntary programs to increase production and conserve food—Americans were urged to grow "victory gardens" and to eat meatless and wheatless meals—but it also set prices and regulated distribution. The Railroad Administration took over the railway industry. The Fuel Administration controlled coal supplies and rationed gasoline. When strikes threatened the telephone and telegraph companies, the federal government seized and ran them.

The largest of the superagencies was the War Industries Board (WIB), headed by financier Bernard Baruch. At one point, this Wall Streeter told Henry Ford frankly that he would dispatch the military to seize his plants if the automaker did not accept WIB limits on car production. Ford relented. Although the WIB seemed all-powerful, in reality it had to conciliate competing interest groups and compromise with the business executives whose advice it so valued. Designed as a clearinghouse for coordinating the national economy, the WIB made purchases, allocated supplies, and fixed prices at levels that business requested. The WIB also ordered the standardization of goods to save materials and streamline production. The varieties of automobile tires, for example, were reduced from 287 to 3.

20-4b Economic Performance

The performance of the mobilized economy was mixed, but it delivered enough men and material to France to ensure the defeat of the Central Powers. About one-quarter of all American production was diverted to war needs. As farmers enjoyed boom years of higher prices, they put more acreage into production and mechanized as never before. From 1915 to 1920, the number of tractors in American fields jumped tenfold. Gross farm income for the period from 1914 to 1919 increased more than 230 percent. Although manufacturing output leveled off in 1918, some industries realized substantial growth because of wartime demand. Steel reached a peak production of 45 million tons in 1917, twice the prewar figure. As U.S. soldiers popularized American brands in Europe, tobacconists profited from a huge increase in cigarette sales: from 26 billion cigarettes in 1916 to 48 billion in 1918. Overall, the gross national product in 1920 stood 237 percent higher than in 1914.

The rush to complete massive assignments caused mistakes to be made. Weapons deliveries fell short of demand; the bloated bureaucracy of the War Shipping Board failed to build enough ships. In the severe winter of 1917–1918, millions of Americans could not get coal. Coal companies held back on production to raise prices; railroads did not have enough coal cars; and harbors froze, closing out coal barges. People died from pneumonia and freezing. A Brooklyn man went out in the morning to forage for coal and returned to find his two-month-old daughter frozen to death in her crib.

To help pay its wartime bills, the government dramatically increased taxes. The Revenue Act in 1916 started the process by raising the surtax on high incomes and corporate profits, imposing a federal tax on large estates, and significantly increasing the tax on munitions manufacturers. Still, the government financed only one-third of the war through taxes. The other two-thirds came from loans, including Liberty bonds sold to the American people through aggressive campaigns. The War Revenue Act of 1917 provided for a more steeply graduated personal income tax; a corporate income tax; an excess profits tax; and increased excise taxes on alcoholic beverages, tobacco, and luxury items.

Although these taxes did curb excessive corporate profiteering, there were loopholes. Sometimes companies inflated costs to conceal profits or paid high salaries and bonuses to their executives. Four officers of Bethlehem Steel, for example, divided bonuses of $2.3 million in 1917 and $2.1 million the next year. Corporate net earnings for 1913 totaled $4 billion; in 1917, they reached $7 billion; and in 1918, after the tax bite and the war's end, they still stood at $4.5 billion. Profits and patriotism went hand in hand in America's war experience.

20-4c Labor Shortage

For American workers, the full-employment wartime economy increased earnings and gave many of them time-and-a-half pay for overtime work. With the higher cost of living, however, workers saw minimal improvement in their economic standing. Turnover rates were high as workers switched jobs for higher pay and better conditions. Some employers sought to overcome labor shortages by expanding welfare and social programs, and by establishing personnel departments—"specialized human nature engineers to keep its human machinery frictionless," General Electric explained.

War Industries Board (WIB) Government agency established to coordinate military purchasing, ensure production efficiency, and provide weapons and supplies to the military.

Eating to Win

The war effort mobilized Americans as never before and also demanded that they make sacrifices. Herbert Hoover's Food Administration used colorful posters to persuade Americans to change their eating habits. The poster below uses bold type and a man standing over a fallen German soldier to send a patriotic message to eat less and save food for the troops. The poster at right has a 1940s Uncle Sam as teacher with a book promoting City and Farm Gardens and asking folks to learn more. The poster below and to the right uses religion (and guilt) to motivate the public.

CRITICAL THINKING

- Which poster do you find most effective, and why?
- How are Americans persuaded today to change their eating habits?

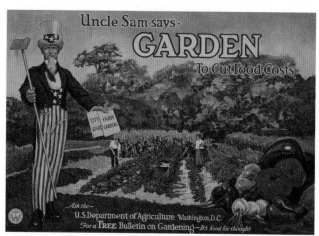

▲ In this colorful 1917 poster, Uncle Sam, posing as a teacher, says, "Garden to cut food costs." The poster offers a free Department of Agriculture "bulletin on gardening—it's food for thought."

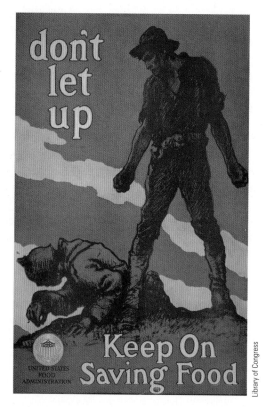

▲ Hispanic artist Francis Luis Mora used strong graphics for his 1918 poster showing a man standing over a fallen German soldier.

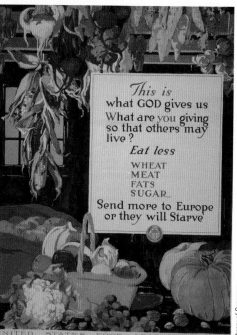

▲ This 1917 poster showing a bounty of fall harvest fruits and vegetables—"This is what God gives us"—uses richly detailed illustration and colorful red type to get attention and ask the question, "What are you giving so that others may live?"

To meet the labor crisis, the Department of Labor's U.S. Employment Service matched laborers with job vacancies, especially attracting workers from the South and Midwest to war industries in the East. The department also temporarily relaxed the literacy test and head tax provisions of immigration law to attract farm labor, miners, and railroad workers from Mexico. Because the labor crisis also generated a housing crisis as workers crammed into cities, the U.S. Housing Corporation and Emergency Fleet Corporation, following the British example, built row houses in Newport News, Virginia, and Eddystone, Pennsylvania.

The tight wartime labor market had another consequence: new work opportunities for women. In Connecticut, a special motion picture, *Mr. and Mrs. Hines of Stamford Do Their Bit*, appealed to housewives' patriotism, urging them to take factory jobs. Although the total number of women in the workforce increased slightly, the real story was that many changed jobs, sometimes moving into formerly male domains. Some white women left domestic service for factories, shifted from clerking in department stores to stenography and typing, or departed textile mills for employment in firearms plants. At least 20 percent of all workers in the wartime electrical machinery, airplane, and food industries were women. Some one hundred thousand women worked in the railroad industry. As white women took advantage of these new opportunities, black women took some of their places in domestic service and in textile factories. For the first time, department stores employed black women as elevator operators and cafeteria waitresses. Most working women were single and remained concentrated in sex-segregated occupations, serving as typists, nurses, teachers, and domestic servants.

Women also participated in the war effort in other ways. As volunteers, they made clothing for refugees and soldiers, served at Red Cross facilities, and taught French to nurses. Some drove ambulances in the war zone. Many worked for the Women's Committee of the Council of National Defense, whose leaders included Ida Tarbell and Carrie Chapman Catt. A vast network of state, county, and town volunteer organizations, the council publicized government mobilization programs, encouraged home gardens, sponsored drives to sell Liberty bonds, and continued the push for social welfare reforms. This patriotic work won praise from men and improved the prospects for passage of the Nineteenth Amendment granting woman suffrage. "We have made partners of women in this war," Wilson said as he endorsed woman suffrage in 1918. "Shall we admit them only to a partnership of suffering and sacrifice . . . and not to a partnership of privilege and right?"

Among African Americans, war mobilization wrought significant change as southern blacks undertook a great migration to northern cities to work in railroad yards, packinghouses, steel mills, shipyards, and coal mines. Between 1910 and 1920, Cleveland's black population swelled by more than 300 percent, Detroit's by more than 600 percent, and Chicago's by 150 percent. Much of the increase occurred between 1916 and 1919. All told, about a half-million African Americans

▲ Stella Young (1896–1989), a Canadian-born woman from Chelsea, Massachusetts, became widely known as the "Doughnut Girl" because of her service during the First World War with the American branch of the Salvation Army, an international organization devoted to social work. She arrived in France in March 1918 and worked in emergency canteens near the battlefront, providing U.S. troops with coffee, cocoa, sandwiches, doughnuts, pie, and fruit. Stella Young became famous when a picture of her wearing a khaki uniform and a "doughboy" steel helmet was widely circulated as a postcard. This piece of sheet music was even written about her, and her postcard image was used to create the cover. She served again in World War II. Chelsea named a city square in her honor in 1968.

uprooted themselves to move to the North. Families sometimes pooled savings to send one member; others sold their household goods to pay for the journey. Most of the migrants were males—young (in their early twenties), unmarried, and skilled or semiskilled. Wartime jobs in the North provided an escape from low wages, sharecropping, tenancy, crop liens, debt peonage, lynchings, and political disfranchisement. To a friend back in Mississippi, one African American wrote: "I just begin to feel like a man. . . . I don't have to humble to no one. I have registered. Will vote the next election."

20-4d National War Labor Board

To keep factories running smoothly, Wilson instituted the National War Labor Board (NWLB) in early 1918. The NWLB discouraged strikes and lockouts and urged management to negotiate with existing unions. In July, after the Western Union Company fired eight hundred union members for trying to organize the firm's workers and then defied an NWLB request to reinstate the employees, the president nationalized the telegraph lines and put the laborers back to work. That month, too, the NWLB directed General Electric to raise wages and stop discriminating against metal trades union members in Schenectady, New York. On the other hand, in September the NWLB ordered striking Bridgeport, Connecticut, machinists back to munitions factories, threatening to revoke their draft exemptions (granted earlier because they worked in an "essential" industry).

Many labor leaders hoped the war would offer opportunities for recognition and better pay through partnership with government. Samuel Gompers threw the AFL's loyalty to the Wilson administration, promising to deter strikes. He and other moderate labor leaders accepted appointments to federal agencies. The antiwar Socialist Party blasted the AFL for becoming a "fifth wheel on [the] capitalist war chariot," but union membership climbed from roughly 2.5 million in 1916 to more than 4 million in 1919.

The AFL, however, could not curb strikes by the radical Industrial Workers of the World (IWW, also known as "Wobblies") or rebellious AFL locals, especially those controlled by labor activists and socialists. In the nineteen war months, more than six thousand strikes expressed workers' demands for a "living wage" and improved working conditions (many called for an eight-hour workday). Exploiting Wilsonian wartime rhetoric, workers and their unions also sought to create "industrial democracy," a more representative workplace with a role for labor in determining job categories and content, and with workplace representation through shop committees. By 1920, in defiance of the national AFL, labor parties had sprung up in twenty-three states.

20-5 Civil Liberties Under Challenge

▶ How did the federal government seek to win and maintain public support for the war?

▶ What actions were taken by governmental and other actors to try to quash wartime dissent?

Gompers's backing of the call to arms meant a great deal to Wilson and his advisers, and they noted with satisfaction that most newspapers, religious leaders, and public officials were similarly supportive. They were less certain, however, about the attitudes of ordinary Americans. "Woe be to the man that seeks to stand in our way in this day of high resolution," the president

Committee on Public Information (CPI) Wartime propaganda agency, headed by journalist George Creel. While claiming merely to combat rumors with facts, the Creel committee in reality publicized the government's version of events and discredited all who questioned that version.

warned. An official and unofficial campaign soon began to silence dissenters who questioned Wilson's decision for war or who protested the draft. In the end, the Wilson administration compiled one of the worst civil liberties records in American history.

The targets of governmental and quasi-vigilante repression were the hundreds of thousands of Americans and aliens who refused to support the war: pacifists from all walks of life, conscientious objectors, socialists, radical labor groups, the debt-ridden tenant farmers of Oklahoma who staged the Green Corn Rebellion against the draft, the Non-Partisan League, reformers like Robert La Follette and Jane Addams, and countless others. In the wartime process of debating the question of the right to speak freely in a democracy, the concept of "civil liberties" emerged for the first time in American history as a major public policy issue (see "Legacy for a People and a Nation," at the end of this chapter).

20-5a The Committee on Public Information

The centerpiece of the administration's campaign to win support for the war was the **Committee on Public Information (CPI)**, formed in April 1917 and headed by Progressive journalist George Creel. Employing some of the nation's most talented writers and scholars, the CPI used propaganda to shape and mobilize public opinion. Pamphlets and films demonized the Germans, and CPI "Four-Minute Men" spoke at movie theaters, schools, and churches to pump up a patriotic mood. Encouraged by the CPI to promote American participation in the war, film companies and their trade association, the National Association of the Motion Picture Industry, produced documentaries, newsreels, and anti-German movies, such as *The Kaiser, the Beast of Berlin* (1918), and *To Hell with the Kaiser* (1918).

The committee also urged the press to practice "self-censorship" and encouraged people to spy on their neighbors. Ultrapatriotic groups, such as the Sedition Slammers and the American Defense Society, used vigilantism. A German-American miner in Illinois was wrapped in a flag and lynched. In Hilger, Montana, citizens burned history texts that mentioned Germany. By the end of the war, sixteen states had banned the teaching of the German language. To avoid trouble, the Kaiser-Kuhn grocery in St. Louis changed its name to Pioneer Grocery. Germantown, Nebraska, became Garland, and the townspeople in Berlin, Iowa, henceforth hailed from Lincoln. The German shepherd became the Alsatian shepherd.

Because towns had Liberty Loan quotas to fill, they sometimes bullied "slackers" into purchasing bonds. Nativist advocates of "100 percent Americanism" exploited the emotional atmosphere to exhort immigrants to throw off their Old World cultures. Companies offered English language and naturalization classes in their factories and refused jobs and promotions to those who did not make adequate strides toward learning English. Even labor's drive for compulsory health insurance, which before the

◀ A member of the Eighth Regiment of the Illinois National Guard with his family, circa 1918. Originally organized as a volunteer regiment during the Spanish-American War in 1898, the Eighth Regiment achieved its greatest fame during World War I. The only regiment to be entirely commanded by African Americans and headquartered at the only black armory in the United States, the "Fighting Eighth" served with distinction in France, with 143 of its members losing their lives.

Chicago History Museum/Getty Images

war had gained advocates in several states, including New York and California, became victimized by the poisoned war atmosphere. Many physicians and insurance companies had for years denounced health insurance as "socialistic"; after the United States entered the war, they discredited it as "Made in Germany."

Even institutions that had long prided themselves on tolerance became contaminated by the spirit of coercion. Wellesley College economics professor Emily Greene Balch was fired for her pacifist views (she won the Nobel Peace Prize in 1946). Three Columbia University students were apprehended in mid-1917 for circulating an antiwar petition. Columbia also fired Professor J. M. Cattell, a distinguished psychologist, for his antiwar stand. His colleague Charles Beard, a historian with a prowar perspective, resigned in protest, stating, "If we have to suppress everything we don't like to hear, this country is resting on a pretty wobbly basis." In a number of states, local school boards dismissed teachers who questioned the war.

20-5b Espionage and Sedition Acts

The Wilson administration also guided through an obliging Congress the **Espionage Act** (1917) and the Sedition Act (1918). The first statute forbade "false statements" designed to impede the draft or promote military insubordination, and it banned from the mails materials considered treasonous. The Sedition Act made it unlawful to obstruct the sale of war bonds and to use "disloyal, profane, scurrilous, or abusive" language to describe the government, the Constitution, the flag, or the military uniform. These loosely worded laws gave the government wide latitude to crack down on critics. More than two thousand people were prosecuted under the acts, and many others were intimidated into silence.

Progressives and conservatives alike used the war emergency to throttle the Industrial Workers of the World and the Socialist Party. Government agents raided IWW meetings, and the army marched into western mining and lumber regions to put down IWW strikes. By the end of the war, most of the union's leaders were in jail. In summer 1918, with a government stenographer present, Socialist Party leader Eugene V. Debs delivered a spirited oration extolling socialism and freedom of speech—including the freedom to criticize the Wilson administration for taking America into the war. Federal agents arrested him, and he was sentenced to ten years in prison. He remained incarcerated until late 1921, when he received a pardon.

The Supreme Court endorsed such convictions. In *Schenck v. U.S.* (1919), the Court unanimously upheld the conviction of a Socialist Party member who had mailed pamphlets urging resistance to the draft. In time of war, Justice Oliver Wendell Holmes wrote, the First Amendment could be restricted: "Free speech would not protect a man falsely shouting 'fire' in a theater and causing panic." If, according to Holmes, words "are of such a nature as to create a clear and present danger that they will bring about the substantial evils that Congress has a right to prevent," free speech could be limited.

Espionage Act Law that set fines and prison sentences for a variety of loosely defined antiwar activities.

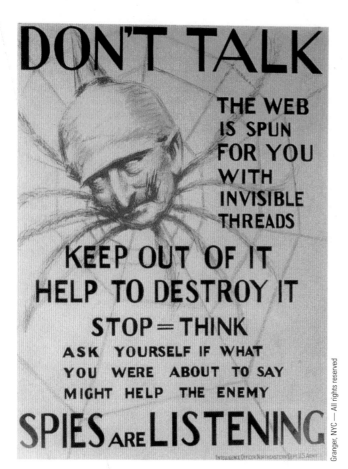

DON'T TALK

THE WEB
IS SPUN
FOR YOU
WITH
INVISIBLE
THREADS

KEEP OUT OF IT
HELP TO DESTROY IT
STOP = THINK
ASK YOURSELF IF WHAT
YOU WERE ABOUT TO SAY
MIGHT HELP THE ENEMY
SPIES ARE LISTENING

INTELLIGENCE OFFICER NORTHEASTERN DEPT. U.S. ARMY

▲ Through its concerted propaganda effort, the Committee on Public Information helped sell to the American people U.S. participation in the First World War. In this 1917 poster, the committee also warned against German spies, perhaps even German American spies, who might pick up secrets from unsuspecting citizens.

20-6 Red Scare, Red Summer

▶ What were the main characteristics of the Red Scare?

▶ Why did labor unions and immigrants stir up concern in postwar American society?

▶ Why did racial violence emerge in postwar American society?

The line between wartime suppression of dissent and the postwar Red Scare is not easily drawn. In the name of patriotism, both harassed suspected internal enemies and deprived them of their constitutional rights; both had government sanction. Together, they stabbed at the Bill of Rights and wounded radicalism in America. Yet in at least two respects, the phenomena were different. Whereas in wartime the main fear had been of subversion, after the armistice it was revolution; and whereas in 1917 the target had often been German Americans, in 1919 it was frequently organized labor. The Russian Revolution and the communist uprisings elsewhere in Europe alarmed many Americans, and the fears grew when in 1919 the Soviet

leadership announced the formation of the Communist International (or Comintern), whose purpose was to export revolution throughout the world. Terrified conservatives responded by looking for pro-Bolshevik sympathizers (or "Reds," from the red flag used by communists) in the United States, especially in immigrant groups and labor unions.

20-6a Labor Strikes

Labor union leaders emerged out of the war determined to secure higher wages for workers to meet rising prices and to retain wartime bargaining rights. Employers instead rescinded benefits they had been forced to grant to labor during the war, including recognition of unions. The result was a rash of labor strikes in 1919, which sparked the Red Scare. All told, more than 3,300 strikes involving 4 million laborers jolted the nation that year, including the Seattle general strike in January. On May 1, a day of celebration for workers around the world, bombs were sent through the mails to prominent Americans. Most of the devices were intercepted and dismantled, but police never captured the conspirators. Most people assumed, not unreasonably, that anarchists and others bent on the destruction of the American way of life were responsible.

Unrest in the steel industry in September stirred more ominous fears. Many steelworkers worked twelve hours a day, seven days a week, and lived in squalid housing. They looked to local steel unions, organized by the National Committee for Organizing Iron and Steel Workers, to help them improve their lives. When postwar unemployment in the industry climbed and the U.S. Steel Corporation refused to meet with committee representatives, some 350,000 workers walked off the job, demanding the right to collective bargaining, a shorter workday, and a living wage. The steel barons hired strikebreakers and sent agents to club strikers. Worried about both the 1919 strikes and Bolshevism, President Wilson warned against "the poison of disorder" and the "poison of revolt." But in the case of steel, the companies won; the strike collapsed in early 1920.

One of the leaders of the steel strike was William Z. Foster, a former IWW member and militant labor organizer who later joined the Communist Party. His presence in a labor movement seeking bread-and-butter goals permitted political and business leaders to dismiss the steel strike as a foreign threat orchestrated by American radicals. There was in fact no conspiracy, and the American left was badly splintered. Two defectors from the Socialist Party, John Reed and Benjamin Gitlow, founded the Communist Labor Party in 1919. The rival Communist Party of the United States of America, composed largely of immigrants, was launched the same year. Neither party commanded many followers—their combined membership probably did not exceed seventy thousand—and in 1919 the harassed Socialist Party could muster no more than thirty thousand members.

20-6b American Legion

Although divisiveness among radicals actually signified weakness, both Progressives and conservatives interpreted the advent of the new parties as strengthening the radical menace. That is certainly how the American Legion saw the question. Organized in May 1919 to lobby for veterans' benefits, the Legion soon preached an antiradicalism that fueled the Red Scare. By 1920, 843,000 Legion members, mostly middle and upper class, had become stalwarts of an impassioned Americanism that demanded conformity.

Wilson's attorney general, A. Mitchell Palmer, also insisted that Americans think alike. A Progressive reformer, Quaker, and ambitious politician, Palmer appointed J. Edgar Hoover to head the Radical Division of the Department of Justice. The zealous Hoover compiled index cards bearing the names of allegedly radical individuals and organizations. During 1919, agents jailed IWW members, and Palmer saw to it that 249 alien radicals, including the outspoken anarchist Emma Goldman, were deported to Russia.

Again, state and local governments took their cue from the Wilson administration. States passed peacetime sedition acts under which hundreds of people were arrested. Vigilante groups and mobs flourished once again, their numbers swelled by returning veterans. In November 1919, in Centralia, Washington, American Legionnaires broke from a parade to storm the IWW hall. Several were wounded. A number of Wobblies were soon arrested, and one of them, an ex-soldier, was taken from jail by a mob, then beaten, castrated, and shot. The New York State legislature expelled five duly elected Socialist Party members in early 1920.

20-6c Palmer Raids

The Red Scare reached a climax in January 1920 in the Palmer Raids. J. Edgar Hoover planned and directed the operation; government agents in thirty-three cities broke into meeting halls and homes without search warrants. More than four thousand people were jailed and denied counsel. In Boston, some four hundred people were kept in detainment on bitterly cold Deer Island; two died of pneumonia, one leaped to his death, and another went insane. Because of court rulings and the courageous efforts of Assistant Secretary of Labor Louis Post, who deliberately held up paperwork, most of the arrestees were released, although in 1920–1921 nearly six hundred aliens were deported.

Palmer's disregard for elementary civil liberties drew criticism, with many charging that his tactics violated the Constitution. Many of the arrested "communists" had committed no crimes. When Palmer called for a peacetime sedition act, he alarmed both liberal and conservative leaders. His dire prediction that pro-Soviet radicals would incite violence on May Day 1920 proved mistaken—not a single disturbance occurred anywhere in the country. Palmer, who had taken to calling himself the "Fighting Quaker," was jeered as the "Quaking Fighter."

20-6d Racial Unrest

Palmer also blamed communists for the racial violence that gripped the nation in these years. Here again, the charge was baseless. African Americans realized well before the end of the war that their participation did little to change discriminatory white attitudes. Segregation remained social custom. The Ku Klux Klan was reviving, and racist films like D.W. Griffith's *The Birth of a Nation* (1915) fed prejudice with its celebration of the Klan and its demeaning depiction of blacks. Lynching statistics exposed the wide gap between wartime declarations of humanity and the American practice of inhumanity at home: between 1914 and 1920, 382 blacks were lynched, some of them in military uniform.

Northern whites who resented "the Negro invasion" vented their anger in riots, as in East St. Louis, Illinois, in July 1917. The next month, in Houston, where African American soldiers faced white harassment and refused to obey segregation laws, whites and blacks exchanged gunfire. Seventeen whites and two African Americans died, and the army sentenced thirteen black soldiers to death and forty-one to life imprisonment for mutiny. During the bloody "Red Summer" of 1919 (so named by black author James Weldon Johnson for the blood that was spilled), race riots rocked two dozen cities and towns. The worst violence occurred in Chicago, a favorite destination for migrating blacks. In the very hot days of July 1919, a black youth swimming at a segregated white beach was hit by a thrown rock and drowned. Rumors spread, tempers flared, and soon blacks and whites were battling each other. Stabbings, burnings, and shootings went on for days until state police restored some calm. Thirty-eight people died, twenty-three African Americans and fifteen whites.

By the time of this tragedy, a disillusioned W. E. B. Du Bois had already concluded that black support for the war had not diminished whites' adherence to inequality and segregation. That spring he vowed a struggle: "We return. We return from fighting. We return fighting." Or as poet Claude McKay put it after the Chicago riot in a poem he titled "If We Must Die,"

Like men we'll face the murderous cowardly pack.
Pressed to the wall, dying, but fighting back.

20-6e Black Militancy

The exhortations of Du Bois and McKay reflected a newfound militancy among black veterans and in the growing black communities of the North. Editorials in African American newspapers subjected white politicians, including the president, to increasingly harsh criticism and at the same time implored readers to embrace their own prowess and beauty: "The black man is a power of great potentiality upon whom consciousness of his own strength is about to dawn." The NAACP stepped up its campaign for civil rights and equality, vowing in 1919 to publicize the terrors of the lynch law and to seek legislation to stop "Judge Lynch." Other blacks, doubting the potential for equality, turned instead to a charismatic Jamaican immigrant named Marcus Garvey (see "Marcus Garvey," Section 21-4a), who called on African Americans to abandon their hopes for integration and to seek a separate black nation.

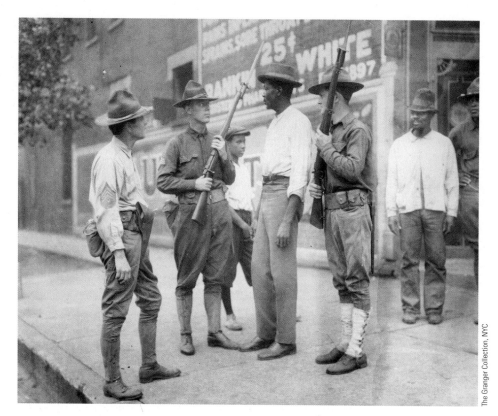

The Granger Collection, NYC

▲ An African American is confronted by state militia members during the race riots in Chicago in 1919. The troops were called in after Mayor Bill Thompson determined that the city police could not restore order.

The crackdown on laborers and radicals, and the resurgence of racism in 1919, dashed wartime hopes. Although the passage of the **Nineteenth Amendment** in 1920, guaranteeing women the right to vote, showed that reform could happen, it was the exception to the rule. Unemployment, inflation, racial conflict, labor upheaval, a campaign against free speech—all inspired disillusionment in the immediate postwar years.

20-7 The Defeat of Peace

▶ What actions did Woodrow Wilson seek to take to deter radicalism abroad?

▶ What provisions did Wilson seek to include in a peace treaty?

▶ Why did Wilson fail to achieve his main goals and objectives in the peace treaty?

President Wilson seemed more focused on confronting the threat of radicalism abroad than at home. Throughout the final months of the war, he fretted about the Soviet takeover in Russia, and he watched with apprehension the communist uprisings in various parts of central Europe. Months earlier, in mid-1918, Wilson had revealed his ardent anti-Bolshevism

Nineteenth Amendment Amendment to the Constitution that granted women the right to vote.

when he ordered five thousand American troops to northern Russia and ten thousand more to Siberia, where they joined other Allied contingents in fighting what was now a Russian civil war. They fought on the side of the "Whites" (various counterrevolutionary forces) against the "Reds" (the Bolsheviks). Wilson did not consult Congress. He said the military expeditions would guard Allied supplies and Russian railroads from German seizure and would also rescue a group of Czechs who wished to return home to fight the Germans.

Worried that the Japanese were building influence in Siberia and closing the Open Door, Wilson also hoped to deter Japan from further advances in Asia. Mostly, though, he wanted to smash the infant Bolshevik government, a challenge to his new world order. Thus, he backed an economic blockade of Russia, sent arms to anti-Bolshevik forces, and refused to recognize Lenin's government. The United States also secretly passed military information to anti-Bolshevik forces and used food relief to shore up opponents of the Soviets in the Baltic region. Later, at the Paris Peace Conference, representatives of the new Soviet government were denied a seat. U.S. troops did not leave Russia until spring 1920, after the Bolsheviks had demonstrated their staying power. The actions by Wilson and other Allied leaders in 1918–1920 generated powerful feelings of resentment and suspicion among many Russians.

Wilson faced a monumental task in securing a postwar settlement. When he departed for the Paris Peace Conference in December 1918, he faced obstacles erected by his political enemies, by the Allies, and by himself. Some observers suggested that a cocky Wilson underestimated his task. During the 1918 congressional elections, Wilson committed the blunder of suggesting that patriotism required the election of a Democratic Congress; Republicans had a field day blasting the president for questioning their love of country. The GOP gained control of both houses, and Wilson aggravated his political problems by not naming a senator to his advisory American Peace Commission. He also refused to take any prominent Republicans with him to Paris or to consult with the Senate Foreign Relations Committee before the conference. It did not help that the president denounced his critics as "blind and little provincial people."

Wilson was greeted with huge and adoring crowds in Paris, London, and Rome. Behind closed doors, however, the leaders of these countries—Georges Clemenceau of France, David Lloyd George of Britain, and Vittorio Orlando of Italy (with Wilson, the Big Four)—became formidable adversaries. Clemenceau mused, "God gave man the Ten Commandments, and he broke every one. Wilson has given us Fourteen Points. We shall see." After four years of horrible war, the Allies were not about to be cheated out of the fruits of victory. Wilson could wax lyrical about a "peace without victory," but the late-arriving Americans had not suffered the way the peoples of France and Great Britain had suffered. Germany would have to pay, and pay big, for the calamity it had caused.

20-7a Paris Peace Conference

At the conference, held at the ornate palace of Versailles, the Big Four tried to work out an agreement, mostly behind closed doors. Critics quickly pointed out that Wilson had immediately abandoned the first of his Fourteen Points: diplomacy "in the public view." The victors demanded that Germany (which had not been invited to the proceedings) pay a huge reparations bill. Wilson instead called for a small indemnity, fearing that a resentful and economically hobbled Germany might turn to Bolshevism or disrupt the postwar community in some other way. Unable to moderate the Allied position, the president reluctantly gave way, agreeing to a clause blaming the war on the Germans and to the creation of a commission to determine the amount of reparations (later set at $33 billion). Wilson acknowledged that the peace terms were "hard," but he also came to believe that "the German people must be made to hate war."

As for the breaking up of empires and the principle of self-determination, Wilson could deliver on only some of his goals. To the crushing disappointment of much of the world's nonwhite majority, the imperial system emerged largely unscathed, as the conferees created a League-administered "mandate" system that placed former German and Turkish colonies under the control of other imperial nations. Japan gained authority over Germany's colonies in the Pacific, while France and Britain obtained parts of the Middle East—the French obtained what became Lebanon and Syria, while the British received the three former Ottoman provinces that became Iraq. Britain also secured Palestine, on the condition that it uphold its wartime promise to promote "the establishment in Palestine of a national home for the Jewish people" without prejudice to "the civil and religious rights of existing non-Jewish communities"—the so-called Balfour Declaration of 1917.

In other arrangements, Japan replaced Germany as the imperial overlord of China's Shandong Peninsula, and France was permitted occupation rights in Germany's Rhineland. Elsewhere in Europe, Wilson's prescriptions fared better. Out of Austria-Hungary and Russia came the newly independent states of Austria, Hungary, Yugoslavia, Czechoslovakia, and Poland. Wilson and his colleagues also built a *cordon sanitaire* (buffer zone) of new westward-looking nations (Finland, Estonia, Latvia, and Lithuania) around Russia, to quarantine the Bolshevik contagion (see Map 20.3).

20-7b League of Nations and Article 10

Wilson worked hardest on the charter for the **League of Nations**, the centerpiece of his plans for the postwar world. He envisioned the League as having power over all disputes among states, including those that did not arise from the peace agreement; as such, it could transform international relations. Even so, the great powers would have a preponderant say: the organization would have an influential council of five permanent members and elected delegates from smaller states, an assembly of all members, and a World Court.

Wilson identified Article 10 as the "kingpin" of the League covenant: "The Members of the League undertake to respect and preserve as against external aggression the territorial integrity and existing political independence of all Members of the League. In case of any such aggression or in case of any threat or danger of such aggression the Council shall advise upon the means by which this obligation shall be fulfilled." This collective-security provision, along with the entire League charter, became part of the peace treaty because Wilson insisted there could be no future peace with Germany without a league to oversee it.

German representatives at first refused to sign the punitive treaty but submitted in June 1919. They gave up 13 percent of Germany's territory, 10 percent of its population, all of its colonies, and a huge portion of its national wealth. Many people wondered how the League could function in the poisoned postwar atmosphere of humiliation and revenge. But Wilson waxed euphoric: "The stage is set, the destiny disclosed. It has come about by no plan of our conceiving, but by the hand of God."

20-7c Critics of the Treaty

Critics in the United States were not so sure. In March 1919, thirty-nine senators (enough to deny the treaty the necessary two-thirds vote) had signed a petition stating that the League's structure did not adequately protect U.S. interests. Wilson denounced his critics as "pygmy" minds, but he persuaded the peace conference to exempt the Monroe Doctrine and domestic matters from League jurisdiction. Having made these concessions to senatorial advice, Wilson

League of Nations An international deliberative body, viewed as necessary to keep the peace; it was rejected by the U.S. Senate, and the United States never joined.

Map 20.3 Europe Transformed by War and Peace

After President Wilson and the other conferees at the Paris Peace Conference negotiated the Treaty of Versailles, empires were broken up. In eastern Europe in particular, new nations emerged.

would budge no more. Compromises with other nations had been necessary to keep the conference going, he insisted, and the League would rectify wrongs. Could his critics not see that membership in the League would give the United States "leadership in the world"?

By summer, criticism intensified: Wilson had bastardized his own principles. He had conceded Shandong to Japan. He had personally killed a provision affirming the racial equality of all peoples. The treaty did not mention freedom of the seas, and tariffs were not reduced. Reparations on Germany promised to be punishing. Senator La Follette and other critics on the left protested that the League would perpetuate empire. Conservative critics feared that the League would limit American freedom of action in world affairs, stymie U.S. expansion, and intrude on domestic questions. And Article 10 raised serious questions: Would the United States be *obligated*

to use armed force to ensure collective security? And what about colonial rebellions, such as in Ireland or India? Would the League feel compelled to crush them? "Were a League of Nations in existence in the days when George Washington fought and won," an Irish American editor wrote, "we would still be an English colony."

Henry Cabot Lodge of Massachusetts led the Senate opposition to the League. A Harvard-educated PhD and partisan Republican who also had an intense personal dislike of Wilson, Lodge packed the Foreign Relations Committee with critics and prolonged public hearings. He introduced several reservations to the treaty, the most important of which held that Congress had to approve any obligation under Article 10.

In September 1919, Wilson embarked on a speaking tour of the United States. Growing more exhausted every day, he dismissed his antagonists as "contemptible quitters." Provoked by Irish American and German American hecklers, he lashed out in Red Scare terms: "Any man who carries a hyphen about him carries a dagger which is ready to plunge into the vitals of the Republic." While doubts about Article 10 multiplied, Wilson tried to highlight neglected features of the League charter—such as the arbitration of disputes and an international conference to abolish child labor. In Colorado, a day after delivering another passionate speech, the president awoke to nausea and uncontrollable facial twitching. "I just feel as if I am going to pieces," he said. A few days later, he suffered a massive stroke that paralyzed his left side. He became peevish and even more stubborn, increasingly unable to conduct presidential business. More and more, his wife, Edith, had to select issues for his attention and delegate other matters to his cabinet heads. Advised to placate Lodge and other "Reservationist" senatorial critics so the Versailles treaty would have a chance of being approved by Congress, Wilson rejected "dishonorable compromise." From Senate Democrats he demanded utter loyalty—a vote against all reservations.

20-7d Senate Rejection of the Treaty and League

Twice in November the Senate rejected the Treaty of Versailles and thus U.S. membership in the League. In the first vote, Democrats joined sixteen "Irreconcilables," mostly Republicans who opposed any treaty whatsoever, to defeat the treaty with reservations (39 for and 55 against). In the second vote, Republicans and Irreconcilables turned down the treaty without reservations (38 for and 53 against). In March 1920, the Senate again voted; this time, a majority (49 for and 35 against) favored the treaty with reservations, but the tally fell short of the two-thirds needed. Had Wilson permitted Democrats to compromise—to accept reservations—he could have achieved his fervent goal of membership in the League, which, despite the U.S. absence, came into being.

At the core of the debate lay a basic issue in American foreign policy: whether the United States would endorse collective security or continue to travel the more solitary path articulated in George Washington's Farewell Address and in the Monroe Doctrine. In a world dominated by imperialist states unwilling to subordinate their strategic ambitions to an international organization, Americans preferred their traditional nonalignment and freedom of choice over binding commitments to collective action. That is why so many of Wilson's critics targeted Article 10. Wilson countered that this argument amounted to embracing the status quo—the European imperialist states are selfish, so the United States should be, too. Acceptance of Article 10 and membership in the League promised something better, he believed, for the United States and for the world; it promised collective security in place of the frail protection of alliances and the instability of a balance of power.

Library of Congress

▲ In October 1919, President Woodrow Wilson (1856–1924) receives assistance after his massive stroke, which made it difficult for him to maintain his train of thought and manage government affairs. Historians continue to debate the influence of Wilson's poor health on the president's losing battle for U.S. membership in the League of Nations.

20-7e An Unsafe World

In the end, World War I did not make the world safe for democracy. Wilson failed to create a new world order through reform. Still, the United States emerged from the First World

Freedom of Speech and the ACLU

Although freedom of speech is enshrined in the U.S. Constitution, for more than a century after the nation's founding the concept had little standing in American jurisprudence. Before World War I, those with radical views often met with harsh treatment for exercising what today would be termed their freedom of speech. During the war, however, the Wilson administration's suppression of dissidents led some Americans to reformulate the traditional definition of allowable speech. Two key figures in this movement were Roger Baldwin, a conscientious objector, and woman suffrage activist Crystal Eastman. Baldwin and Eastman were among the first to advance the idea that the content of political speech could be separated from the identity of the speaker and that patriotic Americans could—indeed should—defend the right of others to express political beliefs abhorrent to their own. After working during the war to defend the rights of conscientious objectors, Baldwin and Eastman—joined by activists such as Jane Addams, Helen Keller, and Norman Thomas—formed the American Civil Liberties Union (ACLU).

Since 1920, the ACLU—which today has some three hundred thousand members in three hundred chapters nationwide—has aimed to protect the basic civil liberties of all Americans and to extend them to those to whom they have traditionally been denied. The organization has been involved in almost every major civil liberties case contested in U.S. courts, among them the John Scopes "monkey trial" (1925), concerning the teaching of evolution at a Tennessee school, and the landmark *Brown v. Board of Education* case (1954), which ended federal tolerance of racial segregation. More recently, the ACLU was involved in a 1997 case in which the Supreme Court decided that the 1996 Communications Act banning "indecent speech" violated First Amendment rights.

Conservatives have long criticized the ACLU for its opposition to official prayers in public schools and its support of the legality of abortion, as well as for what they see as its selectivity in deciding whose freedom of speech to defend. Backers of the organization counter that it has also defended those on the right, such as Oliver North, a key figure in the Iran-Contra scandal of the 1980s.

Either way, the principle of free speech is today broadly accepted by Americans, so much so that even ACLU bashers take it for granted. Membership rose sharply after the terrorist attacks on September 11, 2001, due to concern among some people that government policies have eroded privacy and legal protections, not only for Americans but also for foreign detainees at the Guantánamo Bay detention facility. Ironically, the Wilson administration's crackdown on dissent produced an expanded commitment to freedom of speech for a people and a nation.

CRITICAL THINKING

- The ACLU has traditionally fought to protect American civil liberties, perhaps most notably our freedom of speech. Has social media allowed for an increase in "hate speech"?
- If so, should that type of speech still fall under the protection of the ACLU's efforts?

War an even greater world power. By 1920, the United States had become the world's leading economic power, producing 40 percent of its coal, 70 percent of its petroleum, and half of its pig iron. It also rose to first rank in world trade. American companies took advantage of the war to nudge the Germans and British out of foreign markets, especially in Latin America. Meanwhile, the United States shifted from a debtor to a creditor nation, becoming the world's leading banker.

After the disappointment of Versailles, appeals for arms control accelerated, and the peace movement revitalized. At the same time, the military became better armed and more professional. The Reserve Officers Training Corps (ROTC) became permanent; military "colleges" provided upper-echelon training; and the Army Industrial College, founded in 1924, pursued business-military cooperation in the area of logistics and planning. The National Research Council, created in 1916 with government money and Carnegie and Rockefeller funds, continued after the war as an alliance of scientists and businesspeople engaged in research relating to national defense. Tanks, quick-firing guns, armor-piercing explosives, and oxygen masks for high-altitude-flying pilots were just some of the technological advances that emerged from the First World War.

The international system born in these years was unstable and fragmented. Espousing decolonization and taking to heart the Wilsonian principle of self-determination, nationalist leaders active during the First World War, such as Ho Chi Minh of Indochina and Mohandas K. Gandhi of India, vowed to achieve independence for their peoples. Communism became a disruptive force in world politics, and the Soviets bore a grudge against those invaders who had tried to thwart their revolution. The new states in central and eastern Europe proved weak, dependent on outsiders for security. Germans bitterly resented the harsh peace settlement, and German war debts and reparations problems dogged international order for many years (Germany finally finished making reparations payments in 2010). As it entered the 1920s, the international system that Woodrow Wilson had vowed to reform was fraught with unresolved problems.

B eth and Robert Gordon did not seem to be compatible marriage partners. Beth was frumpy and demanding; Robert liked to party. One evening at a nightclub, he met Sally Clark, who liked to party, too. They danced close together, and when Robert came home, Beth smelled perfume on his suit. The spouses argued, and shortly they divorced. It was not long, however, before Robert found that Sally's appeal had worn off; he missed Beth's intellect and wisdom. Meanwhile, Beth concluded that she needed to change her dowdy image. She bought new clothes and makeup, turning herself into a glamorous beauty. By coincidence, Beth and Robert visited the same summer resort and rekindled their romance. When Robert was injured in an accident, Beth took him home and nursed him back to health, much to Sally's disappointment. In the end, Beth and Robert remarried, and Sally accepted her loss of Robert philosophically, concluding with the wry remark "The only good thing about marriage, anyway, is the alimony."

The experiences of Beth, Robert, and Sally make up the plot of the 1920 motion picture *Why Change Your Wife?*—one of dozens of films directed by Cecil B. DeMille. DeMille succeeded by giving audiences what they wanted to see and what they fantasized about doing. Beth, Robert, and Sally dressed stylishly, went out dancing, listened to phonograph records, rode in cars, and visited resorts. Although DeMille's films and others of the 1920s usually ended by reinforcing marriage, ruling out premarital sex, and supporting the work ethic, they also exuded a new morality. Female lead characters were not mothers tied to the home; both males and females shed old-style values for the pursuit of luxury, fun, and sexual freedom, just as the actors and actresses themselves, such as Gloria

◀ Dressed in stylish fashions and indulging in some flirtatious banter, Thomas Meighan and Gloria Swanson, stars of Cecil B. DeMille's romantic comedy *Why Change Your Wife?* represent ways that movies and movie personalities gave the public images, sometimes accurate but often exaggerated, of new social mores in the 1920s. Everett Collection

Chronology

1920
- Volstead Act implements prohibition (Eighteenth Amendment)
- Nineteenth Amendment ratified, legalizing vote for women in federal elections
- Harding elected president
- KDKA transmits first commercial radio broadcast

1920–21
- Postwar deflation and depression

1921
- Federal Highway Act funds national highway system
- Emergency Quota Act establishes immigration quotas
- Sacco and Vanzetti convicted
- Sheppard-Towner Act allots funds to states to set up maternity and pediatric clinics
- Washington Conference limits naval arms

1922
- Economic recovery raises standards of living
- *Coronado Coal Company v. United Mine Workers* rules that strikes may be illegal actions in restraint of trade
- *Bailey v. Drexel Furniture Company* voids restrictions on child labor
- Federal government ends strikes by railroad shop workers and miners
- Fordney-McCumber Tariff raises rates on imports

1923
- Harding dies; Coolidge assumes presidency
- *Adkins v. Children's Hospital* overturns a minimum wage law affecting women

1923–24
- Government scandals (Teapot Dome) exposed

1924
- Snyder Act grants citizenship to all Indians not previously citizens
- National Origins Act revises immigration quotas
- Coolidge elected president

1925
- Scopes trial highlights battle between religious fundamentalists and modernists

1927
- Lindbergh pilots solo transatlantic flight
- *The Jazz Singer*, first movie with sound, released

1928
- Stock market soars
- Kellogg-Briand Pact outlaws war
- Hoover elected president

1929
- Stock market crashes; Great Depression begins

Swanson and Thomas Meighan, the stars of *Why Change Your Wife?* did in their off-screen lives. Just like the characters they played, the actors were icons for America's new mass culture. In this way, *Why Change Your Wife?* was a harbinger, though an inexact one, of a new era.

Experience an interactive version of this story in MindTap®.

During the 1920s, consumerism flourished, represented by the products, entertainment, and leisure that film characters and the stars who played them enjoyed. Although poverty beset small farmers, workers in declining industries, and nonwhites everywhere, most other people enjoyed a high standard of living relative to that of previous generations. Spurred by advertising and installment buying, Americans eagerly acquired radios, automobiles, real estate, and stocks. Changes in work habits, family responsibilities, and health care fostered new uses of time and new attitudes about behavior, including encouragements to "think young." Winds of change also stirred up waves of resistance from those who held tight to traditional beliefs, and cultural divisions roiled politics.

As in the Gilded Age, the federal government nurtured a favorable climate for business. In contrast to the Progressive Era, crusades for change at the national level cooled. Yet state and local governments, extending the reach of public authority, undertook important reforms. Endeavors for reform also extended into international affairs, as both the federal government and private organizations searched for ways to secure world peace and prevent the horrors that had occurred in the First World War. Though many Americans now regarded themselves as isolationists, meaning they wanted no part of Europe's political squabbles, military alliances, or the League of Nations, the nation remained active in global affairs, as government and business leaders worked to facilitate American prosperity and security.

An unseen storm lurked on the horizon, however. The glitter of consumer culture that dominated DeMille's films and their audiences' everyday lives blinded Americans to rising debt and uneven prosperity. Just before the decade closed, a devastating depression brought the era to a brutal close.

- *How did developments in technology stimulate social change and influence foreign policy during the 1920s?*

■ *What were the benefits and costs of consumerism, and how did people deal with challenges to old-time values?*

■ *What caused the stock market crash and the ensuing deep depression that signaled the end of the era?*

21-1 Economic Expansion

▶ **What factors contributed to the recovery and expansion of the American economy after World War I?**

▶ **How did the development of the American economy become globally oriented after World War I?**

▶ **How did the federal government help businesses thrive in the 1920s?**

The 1920s began with a jolting economic decline. Shortly after the First World War ended, industrial output dropped as wartime orders dried up. As European agriculture recovered from war, American exports diminished and farm incomes plunged. In the West, railroads and the mining industry suffered. As demobilized soldiers flooded the workforce, unemployment, around 2 percent in 1919, passed 12 percent in 1921. Layoffs spread through New England as textile companies abandoned outdated factories for the convenient raw materials and cheap labor of the South. As a consequence of these patterns, consumer spending dwindled, causing more contraction and joblessness.

21-1a Business Triumphant

Aided by electric energy, a recovery began in 1922 and continued unevenly until 1929. Electric motors enabled manufacturers to replace steam engines and produce goods more cheaply and efficiently. Using new metal alloys, such as aluminum, and synthetic materials, such as rayon, producers could turn out an expanded array of consumer goods, including refrigerators, toasters, vacuum cleaners, and clothing. In addition, most urban households now had electric service, enabling them to utilize new appliances. The expanding economy gave Americans more spending money for these products, as well as for restaurants, beauty salons, and movie theaters. More important, installment, or time-payment, plans ("A dollar down and a dollar forever," one critic quipped) drove the new consumerism. Of 3.5 million automobiles sold in 1923, 80 percent were bought on credit. By the late 1920s, the United States produced nearly half of the world's industrial goods and ranked first among exporters.

Economic expansion brought a continuation of the corporate consolidation that had created trusts and holding companies in the late nineteenth century. Although Progressive Era trust-busting had achieved some regulation of big business, it had not eliminated oligopoly, the control of an entire industry by one or a few large firms. Now, sprawling companies such as U.S. Steel and General Electric dominated basic industries, and oligopolies dominated much of marketing, distribution, and finance as well.

21-1b Languishing Agriculture

The picture was different in farming. Pressed into competition with growers in other countries and trying to increase productivity by investing in machines, such as harvesters and tractors, American farmers found themselves steeped in hardship. Irrigation and mechanization had created "factories in the fields," making large-scale farming so efficient that fewer farmers could produce more crops than ever before. As a result, crop prices plunged, big agribusinesses took over, and small landholders and tenants could not make a living. Shortly after the end of the First World War, for example, the price that farmers could get for cotton dropped by two-thirds and that for livestock fell by half. Incomes of small farmers (but not agribusinesses) plummeted, and debts rose.

21-1c Economic Expansion Abroad

Flush with industrial expansion at home, business and government leaders attempted to use American prosperity to create economic stability at home and profits abroad. The First World War had left Europe in shambles. Between 1914 and 1924, Europe suffered tens of millions of casualties from world war, civil war, massacres, the influenza epidemic, and famine. Germany and France both lost 10 percent of their workers. Crops, livestock, factories, trains, bridges—little was spared. The American Relief Administration and private charities delivered food to needy people, including Russians wracked by famine in 1921 and 1922.

These efforts accompanied a move to strengthen America's prominence in the international economy. Because of World War I, the United States became a creditor nation and the financial capital of the world (see Figure 21.1). From 1914 to 1930, private investment abroad grew fivefold, to more than $17 billion. For example, General Electric invested heavily in Germany, and U.S. firms began to challenge British control of oil in the Middle East. Also, American know-how became an export product. Germans marveled at Henry Ford's economic success and industrial techniques ("Fordismus"), buying out translations of his autobiography, *My Life and Work* (1922). Further advertising the American capitalist model were the Phelps-Stokes Fund, exporting to black Africa Booker T. Washington's Tuskegee philosophy of education, and the Rockefeller Foundation, battling diseases in Latin America and Africa, supporting colleges to train doctors in Lebanon and China, and funding medical research and nurses' training in Europe.

21-1d Investments in Latin America

American companies focused especially on Latin America, where they began to exploit Venezuela's rich petroleum resources, where the United Fruit Company became a huge landowner, and where Pam American Airways first developed

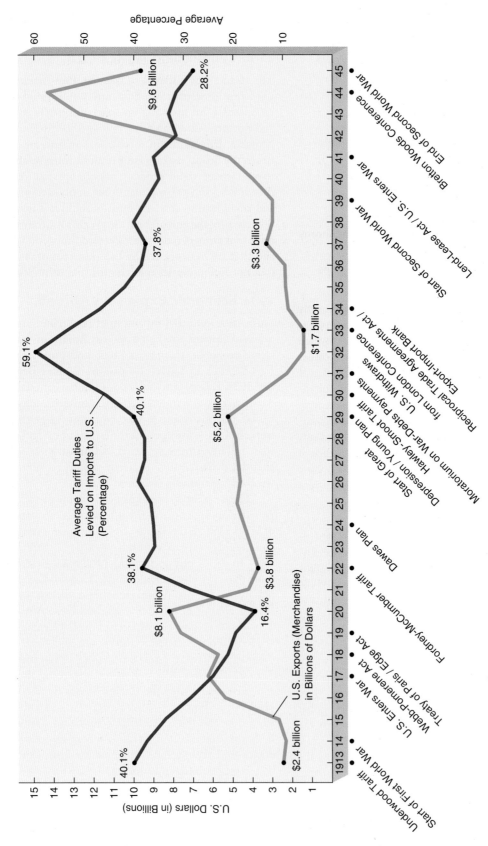

Figure 21.1 The United States in the World Economy

In the 1920s and 1930s, global depression and war scuttled the United States' hope for a stable economic order. This graph suggests, moreover, that high American tariffs meant lower exports, further impeding world trade. The Reciprocal Trade Agreements program initiated in the early 1930s was designed to ease tariff wars with other nations. *Source: U.S. Bureau of the Census, Historical Statistics of the United States, Colonial Times to 1970 (Washington, D.C., 1975).*

Margaret Mead and *Coming of Age in Samoa*

In 1925, Margaret Mead, age twenty-four, journeyed to the South Pacific where for nine months she lived among and studied natives who inhabited the island territory of American Samoa. Having just earned a masters degree from Columbia University, where she had studied with Franz Boas and Ruth Benedict, two of the country's most noted anthropologists, Meade set out to investigate whether a supposed "primitive" people might have their own highly developed culture that was not inferior to that of Americans and Europeans but only different. What she observed and later wrote about in her best-selling book, *Coming of Age in Samoa* (1928), shocked the nation, not only exposing Americans to manners and ethical standards much different from their own but also making Americans reconsider how they were raising their own children.

In Samoa, Mead focused her attention primarily on adolescent girls with the object of finding out how their experiences differed from those of American teenagers. She wanted to consider whether those experiences could teach anything to Americans and whether, as she wrote, "societies could be changed by changing the way children were brought up." Based on interviews of and psychological tests on 68 girls from three villages, Mead concluded that because of relaxed and more open attitudes toward sex in Samoan culture, adolescence there was a much less stressful stage of life than it was among American girls, who were pressured to conform to a particular kind of sexual behavior. Samoan children were allowed to observe, even experience, nudity, masturbation, intercourse, and homosexuality without adult-imposed judgments about whether such acts were shameful. As a result, Mead concluded, Samoans had less stormy adolescence because of Samoan culture—what anthropologists and psychologists would call "nurture"—rather than because they biologically were teenagers (what would be called "nature").

Mead's book had considerable impact, not just because it exposed Americans to much different customs, some of which were deemed scandalous, but also because it included a critique of American culture in which, according to Mead, children were "denied all firsthand knowledge of birth and love and death, harried by a society which will not let adolescents grow up at their own pace, imprisoned in the small, fragile, nuclear family from which there is no escape and in which there is little security." At the time, and later, critics accused Mead of being too gullible and admiring in her dealings with Samoans, and that "nature" had more importance than she would admit. Though the "nature vs. nurture" argument remains unresolved today, Mead's descriptions and the influence of her work on the field of anthropology have had lasting effect.

CRITICAL THINKING

- Although Margaret Mead's study of Samoan adolescence was widely criticized by those who argued that she had failed to view Samoan culture with an objective eye, how did deeply ingrained American ideas about gender likely influence many Americans' refusal to accept her findings as valid?

Manuscript Division, Library of Congress

▲ Posing in 1925 with two young Samoan women, Margaret Mead, who was just twenty-four years old at the time of this photograph, captured world attention three years later with publication of her study *Coming of Age in Samoa*. The book, based on Mead's observations of Samoan culture, caused controversy by concluding that adolescence was not a stressful time for Samoan girls because the native culture was more open about sexuality than American culture. Some critics complained that Mead romanticized Samoan life, but others found her findings revealing about American ways of raising children.

air service. By 1929, direct American investment in the region totaled $3.5 billion and U.S. exports dominated trade. Country after country experienced repercussions from American economic and political decisions. For example, the price that Americans set for Chilean copper determined the health of Chile's economy. North American oil executives bribed Venezuelan politicians for tax breaks.

Latin American nationalists protested that their resources were being drained away as profits for U.S. companies. A distinguished Argentine writer, Manuel Ugarte, asserted that the United States had become a new Rome, annexing wealth rather than territory, and that unapologetic Americans wrongly believed they were bringing only material improvements and blessings of liberty to Latin American neighbors. Criticism mounted as years passed. In 1928, at the Havana Inter-American conference, U.S. officials unsuccessfully tried to kill a resolution stating that "no state has a right to intervene in the internal affairs of another." Two years later, a Chilean newspaper warned that the American "Colossus" had "financial might" without "equal in history" and that its aim was "Americas for the Americans—of the North."

21-1e Associations and "New Lobbying"

Business and professional organizations that had arisen around 1900 also expanded in the 1920s. Retailers and manufacturers formed trade associations to swap information and coordinate planning. Farm bureaus promoted scientific agriculture and tried to stabilize markets for agricultural products. Lawyers, engineers, and doctors expanded their professional societies. In a complex society where government was playing an increasingly influential role, hundreds of organizations sought to convince federal and state legislators to support their interests through "new lobbying." One Washington, D.C., observer contended that "lobbyists were so thick they were constantly falling over one another."

Government policies helped business thrive, and legislators depended on lobbyists' expertise in making decisions. Prodded by lobbyists, Congress cut taxes on corporations and wealthy individuals in 1921 and passed the Fordney-McCumber Tariff (1922) to raise tariff rates. Presidents Warren G. Harding, Calvin Coolidge, and Herbert Hoover appointed cabinet officers who were favorable toward business. Regulatory agencies, such as the Federal Trade Commission and the Interstate Commerce Commission, monitored company activities but, under the influence of lobbyists, cooperated with corporations more than they regulated them.

The Supreme Court, led by Chief Justice William Howard Taft, the former president whom Harding nominated to the Court in 1921, protected business and private property as aggressively as in the Gilded Age and abandoned its Progressive Era antitrust stance. Key decisions sheltered business from government regulation and hindered organized labor's ability to achieve its ends through strikes and legislation. In *Coronado Coal Company v. United Mine Workers* (1922), Taft ruled that a striking union, like a trust, could be prosecuted for illegal restraint of trade, yet in *Maple Floor Association v. U.S.* (1929), the Court decided that trade associations that distributed anti-union information were not acting in restraint of trade. The Court also voided the federal law restricting child labor (*Bailey v. Drexel Furniture Company*, 1922) because it infringed on state power, and it overturned a minimum wage law affecting women because it infringed on liberty of contract (*Adkins v. Children's Hospital*, 1923).

21-1f Setbacks for Organized Labor

Organized labor suffered other setbacks during the 1920s. Fearful of communism allegedly being brought into the country by radical immigrants, public opinion turned against workers who disrupted everyday life with strikes. Perpetuating tactics used during the Red Scare of 1919, the Harding administration in 1922 obtained a court injunction to quash a strike by 400,000 railroad shop workers. The same year, the Justice Department helped end a nationwide strike by 650,000 miners. Courts at both the state and federal levels issued injunctions to prevent strikes and permitted businesses to sue unions for damages suffered because of labor actions.

Meanwhile, corporations fought unions directly. To prevent labor organization, employers imposed "yellow-dog contracts" that, as a condition of employment, compelled an employee to agree not to join a union. Companies also countered the appeal of unions by offering pensions, profit sharing, and company-sponsored picnics and sporting events—a policy known as "welfare capitalism." State legislators aided employers by prohibiting closed shops (workplaces where unions required that all employees be members of their labor organization) and permitting open shops (in which employers could hire nonunion employees). As a result of court action, welfare capitalism, and ineffective leadership, union membership fell from 5.1 million in 1920 to 3.6 million in 1929.

21-2 Government, Politics, and Reform

▶ How were women politically active in the postwar period?

▶ How did the national government demonstrate "goodwill" toward businesses during the presidencies of Warren G. Harding and Calvin Coolidge?

▶ How were efforts to achieve international peace advanced at the social and political levels in the 1920s?

During the 1920s, politics reflected a shift away from the activism of the Progressive Era, yet certain continuities remained, and women, enfranchised nationally by the Nineteenth Amendment, brought new influence to national and international affairs. A series of Republican presidents reinforced economic expansion by reinforcing

Theodore Roosevelt's notion of government-business cooperation, but they saw government as a compliant coordinator rather than the active manager Roosevelt had advocated. At the same time, the government extended reform programs at home and embarked on new efforts for peace and disarmament abroad.

21-2a Women and Politics

Though they had achieved suffrage through the Nineteenth Amendment, ratified in 1920, politically active women remained excluded from local and national power structures. But like business associations, women's voluntary organizations used tactics that advanced pressure-group politics. Whether the issue was birth control, world peace, education, American Indian affairs, or opposition to lynching, women in these associations lobbied for legislation to support their causes. For example, the League of Women Voters reorganized out of the National Woman Suffrage Association, encouraged women to run for office, and actively lobbied for laws to improve conditions for employed women, the mentally ill, and the poor.

In 1921, action by women's groups persuaded Congress to pass the **Sheppard-Towner Act**, which allotted funds to states to create maternity and pediatric clinics as means to reduce infant mortality. (The measure ended in 1929 when Congress, pressured by the American Medical Association, which believed the act was socialistic and threatened a doctor's professional prerogatives, canceled funding.) The Cable Act of 1923 reversed the law under which an American woman who married a foreigner lost her U.S. citizenship and had to assume her husband's citizenship. At the state level, women achieved rights such as the ability to serve as jurors.

Internal divisions, however, complicated women's tasks in achieving their goals. Members of the National Association of Colored Women, for example, fought for the rights of minority women and men without support from white women's groups. Some organizations, such as the National Woman's Party, pressed for a constitutional amendment to ensure women's equality with men under the law. But such activity alienated the National Consumers League, the Women's Trade Union League, the League of Women Voters, and other groups that supported special protective legislation to limit hours and improve conditions for employed women.

21-2b American Indian Affairs

Disturbed by the federal government's generally apathetic American Indian policy, reform organizations such as the Indian Rights Association, the Indian Defense Association, and the General Federation of Women's Clubs worked to obtain justice and social services, including better education and return of tribal lands. But because most Americans perceived American Indians as no longer a threat to whites' ambitions, they expected them to assimilate like other minorities. Such an assumption overlooked important problems. Severalty, the federal policy created by the Dawes Act of 1887 that allotted land to individuals rather than to tribes, had failed to make American Indians self-supporting. Native American farmers had to suffer poor soil, unavailable irrigation, and scarce medical care. Deeply attached to their land, they showed little inclination to move to cities. Whites still hoped to convert native peoples into "productive" citizens, but in a way that ignored indigenous cultures. Reformers were especially critical of Native American women, who refused to adopt middle-class homemaking habits and balked at sending their children to boarding schools.

Meanwhile, the federal government struggled to clarify American Indians' citizenship status. The Dawes Act had conferred citizenship on all Native Americans who accepted land allotments, but not on those who remained on reservations. Also, the government retained control over Native Americans that it did not exercise over others. For example, because of alleged drunkenness on reservations, federal law banned the sale of liquor to American Indians even before ratification of prohibition. After several court challenges, Congress finally passed an Indian Citizenship Act (Snyder Act) in 1924, granting full citizenship to all Native Americans who previously had not received it in hopes that American Indians would help each other to assimilate.

21-2c Presidency of Warren Harding

A symbol of the federal government's goodwill toward business was President **Warren G. Harding**, elected in 1920 over Democratic nominee and Ohio Governor James M. Cox, whose running mate was New York Governor Franklin D. Roosevelt (Teddy's cousin). Garnering 16 million popular votes to Cox's 9 million, Harding won the most lopsided victory in a presidential election to that date. (The total vote in the 1920 presidential election was 36 percent higher than in 1916, reflecting participation of women voters for the first time.) A small-town newspaperman and senator from Ohio who relished jokes and poker, Harding seemed suited to a nation recovering from world war and domestic hard times.

Harding also benefited from voter disillusionment with the League of Nations and the collective world security system envisioned by Woodrow Wilson and previously rejected by the Senate (see "Senate Rejection of the Treaty and League," Section 20-7d). The League proved feeble as a peacemaker, not just because the United States refused to join, but also because League members failed to utilize it to settle important disputes. In due course, however, American officials participated discreetly in League meetings on public health, prostitution, drug and arms trafficking, counterfeiting of currency, and other international issues. American jurists served on the Permanent Court of International Justice, and the Rockefeller Foundation donated $100,000 a year to support League work in public health.

Sheppard-Towner Act Sought to reduce infant mortality by providing matching funds to states to create prenatal and child health clinics. It was repealed in 1929.

Warren G. Harding The twenty-ninth president of the United States (1921–1923).

21-2d Scandals of the Harding Administration

Once in office, Harding gave primary attention to economic matters, and he appointed some capable assistants who helped promote business growth, notably Secretary of State Charles Evans Hughes, Secretary of Commerce Herbert Hoover, Secretary of the Treasury Andrew Mellon, and Secretary of Agriculture Henry C. Wallace. But Harding had personal weaknesses, and these soon took a toll on his presidency. As a senator, he had an extramarital liaison with the wife of an Ohio merchant. In 1917, he began a relationship with Nan Britton, who was thirty-one years his junior and who had been obsessed with Harding since her girlhood. A daughter was born from the affair in 1919, and Britton revealed the secret in a book, *The President's Daughter*, published in 1927. Unlike Grover Cleveland, Harding never acknowledged his illegitimate offspring.

Of more consequence than his sexual escapades, Harding appointed cronies who saw office holding as an invitation to personal gain. Charles Forbes, head of the Veterans Bureau, went to federal prison, convicted of fraud and bribery in connection with government contracts. Attorney General Harry Daugherty resigned after being implicated in a kickback scheme involving bootleggers of illegal liquor; he escaped prosecution by refusing to testify against himself. Most notoriously, a congressional inquiry in 1923–1924 revealed that Secretary of the Interior Albert Fall had accepted bribes to lease government property to private oil companies. For his role in the affair—called the **Teapot Dome scandal** after a Wyoming oil reserve that he handed to the Mammoth Oil Company—Fall was fined $100,000 and spent a year in jail, the first cabinet member ever to be so disgraced.

By mid-1923, Harding had become disillusioned. Amid rumors of mismanagement and crime, he told a journalist, "My God, this is a hell of a job. I have no trouble with my enemies. . . . But my friends, my God-damned friends . . . they're the ones that keep me walking the floor nights." On a speaking tour that summer, Harding became ill and died in San Francisco on August 2. Although his death preceded revelation of the Teapot Dome scandal, some people speculated that, to avoid impeachment, Harding committed suicide or was poisoned by his wife. Most evidence, however, points to death from natural causes, probably heart disease. Regardless, Harding was widely mourned.

Teapot Dome scandal Scandal that rocked the Harding administration after Harding's secretary of the interior was found guilty of secretly leasing government oil reserves to two oilmen in exchange for a bribe.

Calvin Coolidge The thirtieth president of the United States (1923–1929); took office after the death of President Warren Harding in 1923.

21-2e Coolidge Prosperity

Vice President **Calvin Coolidge**, who now became president, was far less outgoing than his predecessor. Journalists nicknamed him "Silent Cal," and one quipped that Coolidge could say nothing in five languages. As governor of Massachusetts, Coolidge attracted national attention in 1919 when he used the National Guard to end a strike by Boston policemen, an action that won him business support and the vice presidential nomination in 1920. Coolidge's presidency coincided with and assisted business prosperity. Respectful of private enterprise and aided by treasury secretary Andrew Mellon, Coolidge's administration reduced federal debt, lowered income tax rates (especially for the wealthy), and began construction of a national highway system. But Coolidge refused to apply government power to assist struggling farmers. Responding to farmers'

◄ President Calvin Coolidge felt comfortable among leaders of big business. He is shown here autographing a bucket for Henry Ford, with Harvey Firestone (from the Firestone Tire Company) on Ford's right, Thomas Edison on Coolidge's immediate left, Russell Firestone (Harvey's son) standing, and the president's father, Col. John Coolidge, seated next to Edison.

Library of Congress Prints and Photographs Division [LC-USZ62-14793] complaints of falling prices, Congress twice passed bills to establish government-backed price supports for staple crops (the McNary-Haugen bills of 1927 and 1928). Resembling the subtreasury scheme that Farmers' Alliances had advocated in the 1890s, these bills proposed to establish a system whereby the government would buy surplus farm products and either hold them until prices rose or sell them abroad. Farmers argued that they deserved as much government protection as manufacturers got. Coolidge, however, vetoed the measures both times as improper government interference in the market economy.

"Coolidge prosperity" was the decisive issue in the 1924 presidential election. Both major parties ran candidates who favored private initiative over government intervention. Republicans nominated Coolidge with little dissent. At their national convention, Democrats first debated whether to denounce the revived Ku Klux Klan, voting 546 to 543 against condemnation. They then endured 103 ballots, deadlocked between southern prohibitionists, who supported former treasury secretary William G. McAdoo, and antiprohibition easterners, who backed New York's governor, Alfred E. Smith. They finally compromised on John W. Davis, a New York corporate lawyer. Remnants of the Progressive movement formed a new Progressive Party and nominated Robert M. La Follette, the aging Wisconsin reformer. The new party stressed previous reform issues: public ownership of railroads and power plants, conservation of natural resources, aid to farmers, rights for organized labor, and regulation of business. The electorate, however, endorsed Coolidge prosperity. Coolidge beat Davis by 15.7 million to 8.4 million popular votes, and 382 to 136 electoral votes. La Follette finished third, receiving 4.8 million popular votes and 13 electoral votes.

In Congress and the presidency, the urgency for political and economic reform that had moved the generation of Progressive reformers faded in the 1920s. Much reform, however, occurred at state and local levels. Following initiatives begun before the First World War, thirty-four states instituted or expanded workers' compensation laws and public welfare programs in the 1920s. In cities, social workers strove for better housing and poverty relief. By 1926, every major city and many smaller ones had planning and zoning commissions to harness physical growth to the common good. As a result of their efforts, a new generation of reformers who later influenced national affairs acquired valuable experience in statehouses, city halls, and universities.

21-2f The Search for Lasting Peace

The Progressive quest for justice and humanity combined with a desire to prevent future world wars to energize a widespread peace movement in the United States. Societies such as the Fellowship of Reconciliation and the National Council for Prevention of War worked to keep alive Woodrow Wilson's dream for a world body to preserve peace. Women peace advocates, blocked by male leaders from influence in these groups, formed their own organization. Carrie Chapman

Catt's moderate National Conference on the Cure and Cause of War formed in 1924, and the more radical U.S. section of the Women's International League for Peace and Freedom (WILPF), organized in 1915 under leadership from Jane Addams and Emily Greene Balch, became the largest women's peace group. When Addams won the Nobel Peace Prize in 1921, she donated the money to the League of Nations.

Most peace groups worked to prevent war from becoming a means of solving international disputes, but they differed over strategies to ensure world order. Some urged cooperation with the League of Nations and World Court. Others championed such causes as the arbitration of disputes, disarmament, the outlawing of war, and neutrality by non-combatants during armed conflict. The WILPF called for an end to U.S. economic imperialism and military intervention

▲ The Women's Peace Union (WPU) distributed this flier in the 1920s to remind Americans of the human costs of the First World War. One of many peace societies active in the interwar years, the WPU lobbied for a constitutional amendment requiring a national referendum on a declaration of war. In the 1930s, Representative Louis Ludlow (Democrat from Indiana) worked to pass such a measure in Congress, but he failed.

in Latin America to protect business interests. The Women's Peace Union, organized in 1921, lobbied for a constitutional amendment to require a national referendum on a declaration of war. Quakers, YMCA officials, and Social Gospel clergy in 1917 created the American Friends Service Committee to promote alternatives to warmaking. In all, peace seekers believed that their reform activities could and must deliver a world without war.

21-2g Washington Naval Conference and Kellogg-Briand Pact

In this climate, peace advocates convinced President Harding to convene the **Washington Naval Conference** of November 1921–February 1922. Delegates from Great Britain, France, Japan, Italy, China, Portugal, Belgium, and the Netherlands joined a U.S. team led by Secretary of State Charles Evans Hughes to discuss limits on naval armaments. Britain, the United States, and Japan were facing a naval arms race whose huge military spending endangered economic recovery. American leaders also worried that an expansionist Japan, with the world's third-largest navy, would overtake the United States, ranked second behind Britain.

Hughes opened the conference with a stunning announcement: he proposed to achieve real disarmament by offering to scrap thirty major U.S. ships, totaling 846,000 tons. He then turned to the shocked British and Japanese delegations and urged them to do away with smaller amounts. The final limit, Hughes declared, should be 500,000 tons each for the Americans and British, 300,000 tons for the Japanese, and 175,000 tons each for the French and Italians—a ratio of 5:3:1.75. These totals were ratified in the Five-Power Treaty, which also set a ten-year moratorium on construction of battleships and aircraft carriers. The governments also pledged not to build new fortifications in their Pacific possessions (such as the Philippines).

Next, the conferees in Washington passed the Nine-Power Treaty, reaffirming the Open Door in China and recognizing Chinese sovereignty. Finally, in the Four-Power Treaty, the United States, Britain, France, and Japan agreed to respect one another's Pacific possessions. The three treaties did not limit submarines, destroyers, or carriers, nor did they provide enforcement powers. Still, the conference was a major accomplishment for Hughes. He achieved genuine arms limitations and at the same time improved America's strategic position vis-à-vis Japan in the Pacific.

Peace advocates also applauded the Locarno Pact of 1925, a set of agreements among European nations that sought to reduce tensions between Germany and France, and the Kellogg-Briand Pact of 1928. The latter document, named for U.S. secretary of state Frank B. Kellogg and French premier Aristide Briand, pledged sixty-two nations to "condemn recourse to war for the solution of international controversies, and renounce it as an instrument of national policy." The accord passed the U.S. Senate 85–1, but many lawmakers considered it little more than a statement of moral preference because it lacked enforcement provisions. Nevertheless, the agreement reflected popular aversion to war, and it stimulated further discussions of keeping the peace.

Washington Naval Conference Multinational conference led by U.S. Secretary of State Hughes to address the problem of the United States, Great Britain, and Japan edging toward a dangerous (and costly) naval arms race.

21-3 A Consumer Society

▶ How did the development of the automobile alter individual lives and American society?

▶ How did radio and advertising encourage consumption in American society?

The consumerism depicted in *Why Change Your Wife?* and that expanded American influence abroad reflected important economic changes affecting the people and the nation. Between 1919 and 1929, the gross national product—the total value of goods and services produced in the United States—swelled by 40 percent. Wages and salaries also grew (though not as drastically), while the cost of living remained relatively stable. People had more purchasing power, and they spent as Americans had never spent (see Table 21.1).

Table 21.1 **Consumerism in the 1920s**

1900	
2 bicycles	$ 70.00
Wringer and washboard	5.00
Brushes and brooms	5.00
Sewing machine (mechanical)	25.00
TOTAL	$ 105.00
1928	
Automobile	$ 700.00
Radio	75.00
Phonograph	50.00
Washing machine	150.00
Vacuum cleaner	50.00
Sewing machine (electric)	60.00
Other electrical equipment	25.00
Telephone (per year)	35.00
TOTAL	$ 1,145.00

Source: From an article in Survey Magazine *in 1928 reprinted in* Another Part of the Twenties, *by Paul Carter. Copyright 1977 by Columbia University Press. Reprinted with permission of the publisher.*

Technology's benefits reached more households than ever before. New products and services were available to more than just the rich, especially to people living in cities. By 1929, two-thirds of all Americans lived in dwellings that had electricity, compared with one-sixth in 1912. Indoor plumbing became more common in private residences, and canned foods and ready-made clothes were more affordable. In 1929, one-fourth of all families owned electric vacuum cleaners and one-fifth had toasters. Many could afford these goods plus radios, cosmetics, and movie tickets because more than one family member earned wages or because the breadwinner took a second job.

21-3a Effects of the Automobile

The automobile stood as vanguard of the era's material wonders. During the 1920s, automobile registrations soared from 8 million to 23 million, and by 1929 one in every five Americans had a car. Mass production and competition made autos affordable even to some working-class families. A Ford Model T cost less than $300, and a Chevrolet sold for $700 by 1926—when factory workers earned about $1,300 a year and clerical workers about $2,300. Used cars cost less. At those prices, people could consider the car a necessity rather than a luxury. "There is no such thing as a 'pleasure automobile,'" proclaimed one newspaper ad in 1925. "You might as well talk of 'pleasure fresh air,' or of 'pleasure beef steak.' . . . The automobile increases length of life, increases happiness, represents above all other achievements the progress and the civilization of our age."

Automobiles altered American life as railroads had seventy-five years earlier. Owners acquired a new "riding habit" and abandoned crowded, slow trolleys. Streets became cleaner as autos replaced horse-drawn carriages. Female drivers achieved newfound independence, taking touring trips with friends, conquering muddy roads, and making repairs when their vehicles broke down. Families created "homes on wheels," packing food and camping equipment to "get away from it all." By 1927, most autos were enclosed (they previously had open tops), offering young people new private space for courtship and sex. A vast choice of models (108 automobile manufacturers in 1923) and colors allowed owners to express personal tastes.

Americans' passion for driving necessitated extensive road construction and abundant fuel supplies. Since the late 1800s, farmers and bicyclists had been lobbying for improved roads. After the First World War, motorists joined the campaign, and in the 1920s government aid made "automobility" truly feasible. In 1921, Congress passed the Federal Highway Act, providing funds for state roads, and in 1923 the Bureau of Public Roads planned a national highway system. Roadbuilding in turn inspired such technological developments as mechanized graders and concrete mixers. The oil-refining industry, which produced gasoline, became vast and powerful. In 1920, the United States produced about 65 percent of the world's oil. Automobiles also forced public officials to pay attention to safety and traffic control. General Electric Company produced the first timed stop-and-go traffic light in 1924.

◀ Automobiles supposedly gave women new independence and skills as well as new mobility. Though it is unlikely that a woman dressed in furs and high heels, such as the woman posing in this photograph, would have changed a flat tire, the automobile nevertheless did give middle-class women exposure to and knowledge about a new technology with all its complexity and potential problems.

H. Armstrong Roberts/Getty Images

21-3b Advertising and Radio

Advertising, an essential component of consumerism, acquired new prominence. By 1929, more money was spent on advertising goods and services than on all types of formal education. Blending psychological theory with practical cynicism, advertising theorists confidently asserted that any person's tastes could be manipulated, and marketers developed new techniques to achieve their ends. For example, cosmetics manufacturers like Max Factor, Helena Rubenstein, and African American entrepreneur Madame C. J. Walker used movie stars and beauty advice in magazines to induce women to buy their products. Other advertisers hired baseball star Babe Ruth and football's Red Grange to endorse food and sporting goods.

Radio became a powerful advertising and entertainment agent. By 1929, 10 million families owned radios, and Americans spent $850 million a year on radio equipment. In the early 1920s, Congress decided that broadcasting should be a private enterprise, not a tax-supported public service as in Great Britain. As a result, American radio programming consisted mainly of entertainment rather than educational content because drama. music, and comedy attracted larger audiences and higher profits from advertisers. Station KDKA in Pittsburgh, owned by Westinghouse Electric Company, pioneered commercial radio in 1920, broadcasting results of the 1920 presidential election. Then, in 1922, an AT&T-run station in New York City broadcast recurring advertisements—"commercials"—for a real estate developer. Other stations began airing commercials; by the end of 1922, there were 508 such stations. In 1929, the National Broadcasting Company began assembling a network of stations and soon was charging advertisers $10,000 (equivalent to about $121,000 today) to sponsor an hour-long show.

21-3c Export of American Consumerism

While radio and advertising expanded consumerism at home, America's economic prominence stimulated interest in its products abroad. Though some foreigners warned against American economic domination, others eagerly accepted the products. Coca-Cola opened a bottling plant in Essen, Germany. Ford built an automobile assembly factory in Cologne, and General Motors built one for trucks near Berlin. German writer Hans Joachim claimed that cultural adoption might promote a peaceful, democratic world because "our interest in elevators, radio towers, and jazz was . . . an attitude that wanted to convert the flame thrower into a vacuum cleaner."

Products such as automobiles and radios helped create a new American people. As a result of its mass marketing and standardized programming, radio had the effect of blurring ethnic boundaries and creating—at least in one way—a homogeneous culture. And the automobile served as a social equalizer, prompting some observers to believe that it might calm social unrest among different ethnic groups. As one writer wrote in 1924, "It is hard to convince Steve Popovich, or Antonio Branca, or plain John Smith that he is being ground into the dust by Capital when at will he may drive the same highways, view the same country, and get as much enjoyment from his trip as the modern Midas."

◀ Even more than movies and books, radio reached corners of American society that previously had not been exposed to new popular culture. Note the elaborate equipment, such as headphones and large antenna, needed by this farmer in order to receive a radio signal in the 1920s.

Library of Congress Prints and Photographs Division[LC-US262-60682]

21-4 Cities, Migrants, and Suburbs

▶ What factors contributed to the expansion of urban areas in the 1920s?

▶ How did the racial and ethnic demographic makeup of urban areas change in the 1920s?

▶ Why did suburban growth occur in the 1920s?

Consumerism signified not merely an economically mature nation but also an urbanized one. The 1920 federal census revealed that, for the first time, a majority of Americans lived in urban areas (places with 2,500 or more people); the city had become the focus of national experience. In addition to growth in metropolises like Chicago and New York, manufacturing and services helped propel expansion in dozens of regional centers. Industries like steel, oil, and auto production energized Birmingham, Houston, and Detroit; services and retail trades boosted Seattle, Atlanta, and Minneapolis. Explosive growth also occurred in warm-climate cities—notably Miami and San Diego—where promises of comfort and profit attracted thousands of real estate speculators.

As cities grew, the agrarian way of life waned. During the 1920s, 6 million Americans left farms for the city. Young people who felt stifled when they compared their existence with the flashy openness of urban life moved to regional centers like Kansas City and Indianapolis or to the West. Between 1920 and 1930, California's population increased 67 percent, and California became a highly urbanized state while retaining its status as a leader in agricultural production. Meanwhile, streams of rural southerners moved to western industrial cities or rode railroads northward to Chicago and Cleveland.

21-4a African American Migration

African Americans, continuing their Great Migration that had begun in 1910, made up a sizable portion of people on the move. Pushed from cotton farming by a boll weevil plague and lured by industrial jobs, 1.5 million blacks migrated, doubling African American populations of New York, Chicago, Detroit, and Houston. Black communities also enlarged in Los Angeles, San Francisco, and San Diego. In these cities, they found work just as exploitive as that in the South—menial labor as janitors, longshoremen, and domestic servants. But the move northward included psychological release because a parcel of freedom was available in New York and Chicago that did not exist in Charleston or Atlanta. In the North, a black person did not always have to act subordinately to a white. As one migrant wrote back home, "I . . . am living well. . . . I can ride in the [streetcar] anywhere I can get a seat."

Forced by low wages and discrimination to seek the cheapest housing, African American newcomers squeezed into ghettos such as Chicago's South Side, New York's Harlem, and Los Angeles's Central Avenue. On the West Coast, however, black homeownership rates were higher than in other regions. Many took advantage of Los Angeles's "bungalow boom," in which they could purchase a small, one-story house for as little as $900. But unlike white migrants, who were free to move away from the inner city when they could afford to, blacks everywhere found better neighborhoods closed to them. They could either crowd further into already densely populated black neighborhoods or spill into nearby white neighborhoods, a process that sparked resistance and violence. Fears of such "invasion" prompted neighborhood associations to adopt restrictive covenants, whereby white homeowners pledged not to sell or rent property to blacks.

21-4b Marcus Garvey

In response to discrimination, threats, and violence, thousands of urban African Americans joined movements that glorified racial independence. The most influential of these black nationalist groups was the Universal Negro Improvement Association (UNIA), headquartered in New York City's Harlem area and led by **Marcus Garvey**, a Jamaican immigrant who believed blacks should separate from corrupt white society. Proclaiming, "I am the equal of any white man," and appealing for pride in African heritage, Garvey spread his message with mass meetings and parades. Unlike the NAACP, which had been formed by elite African American and white liberals, the UNIA was comprised exclusively of blacks, most of whom occupied lower rungs of the economic hierarchy.

Garvey promoted economic independence by encouraging black-owned businesses that would manufacture and sell products to black consumers, and his proposed Phillis Wheatley Hotel (named after a notable African American poet) would enable any black person to make a reservation. His newspaper, *Negro World*, preached black pride, and he founded the Black Star steamship line to transport manufactured goods and raw materials to black businesses in North America, the Caribbean, and Africa. In an era when whites were pouring money into stock market speculation, thousands of hopeful blacks invested their dollars in the Black Star Line.

The UNIA declined in the mid-1920s after mismanagement plagued Garvey's plans. In 1923, Garvey was imprisoned for mail fraud involving the bankrupt Black Star Line and then deported to Jamaica in 1927 for trying to sell stock by advertising a ship that his company did not own. His prosecution, however, was politically motivated. Middle-class black leaders, such as W.E.B. Du Bois, and several clergymen opposed the UNIA, fearing that its extremism would undermine their efforts and influence. Beginning in 1919, the U.S. Bureau of Investigation (BOI), forerunner to the FBI, had been monitoring Garvey's radical activities by infiltrating the UNIA, and the BOI's deputy head, J. Edgar Hoover, proclaimed Garvey to be one of the most dangerous blacks in America. Du Bois also became incensed when word leaked

Marcus Garvey Charismatic black leader who promoted racial pride and independence and believed blacks should separate from white society.

out in 1922 that Garvey had met secretly with leaders of the Ku Klux Klan, who supported Garvey's idea of enabling blacks to move to Africa. Nevertheless, for several years the UNIA attracted a large following (contemporaries estimated 500,000; Garvey claimed 6 million), and Garvey's speeches instilled in many African Americans a heightened sense of racial pride.

21-4c Newcomers from Mexico and Puerto Rico

The newest immigrants came from Mexico and Puerto Rico, where, as in rural North America, declining fortunes pushed people off the land. In parts of California and the Southwest, Mexicans had been among the original inhabitants and Anglo-Europeans were the immigrants. But by the twentieth century, Anglos had settled and taken control of many communities and businesses. During the 1910s, Anglo farmers' associations encouraged immigration from Mexico in order to obtain a source of cheap workers; by the 1920s, Mexican migrants constituted three-fourths of farm labor in the American West. Growers treated these laborers as slaves, paying them extremely low wages. Resembling other immigrant groups, Mexican newcomers lacked resources and skills, and men outnumbered women. Although some achieved middle-class status as shopkeepers and professionals, most crowded into low-rent districts in growing cities like Denver, San Antonio, Los Angeles, and Tucson, where they suffered poor sanitation, poor police protection, and poor schools. Both rural and urban Mexicans moved back and forth between their homeland and the United States, seeking jobs and creating a way of life that Mexicans called *sin fronteras*—without borders.

The 1920s also witnessed an influx of Puerto Ricans to the mainland. Puerto Rico had been a U.S. possession since 1898, and its natives were granted U.S. citizenship in 1916. When a shift in the island's economy from sugar to coffee production created a labor surplus, Puerto Ricans left for New York and other cities, attracted by employers seeking cheap labor. In the cities, they created *barrios* (communities) and found jobs in factories, restaurants, and domestic service. Puerto Ricans developed businesses—*bodegas* (grocery stores), cafes, boardinghouses—and social organizations to help them adapt to American society. As with Mexicans, educated Puerto Rican elites—doctors, lawyers, business owners—became community leaders.

21-4d Suburbanization

As urbanization peaked, suburban growth accelerated. Though towns had sprouted around major cities since the nation's earliest years, prosperity and automobile transportation in the 1920s made suburbs more accessible to those wishing to leave urban neighborhoods. Between 1920 and 1930, suburbs of Chicago (such as Oak Park and Evanston), Cleveland (Shaker Heights), and Los Angeles (Burbank and Inglewood) grew five to ten times faster than did nearby central cities. They sparked an outburst of home construction; Los Angeles builders alone erected 250,000 homes for auto-owning suburbanites. Although some suburbs, such as Highland Park (near Detroit) and East Chicago, were industrial satellites, most were middle- and upper-class bedroom communities.

Suburbanites wanted to escape big-city crime, grime, and taxes, and they fought to preserve control over their police, schools, and water and gas services. Consequently, suburbs increasingly resisted annexation to core cities. Particularly in the Northeast and Midwest, suburbs' fierce independence choked off expansion by the central cities and prevented them from access to the resources and tax bases of wealthier suburban residents. Suburban expansion had other costs, too, as automobiles and the dispersal of population spread the environmental problems of city life—trash, pollution, noise—across the entire metropolitan area.

◀ Over half a million Mexicans immigrated to the United States during the 1920s. Many of them traveled in families and worked together in the fields and orchards of California and other western states. This family is shown pitting apricots in Los Angeles County in 1924.

Library of Congress, Prints & Photographs Division, Reproduction number LC-DIG-nclc-00258 (color digital file from b&w original print)

Expansion of Suburbs in the 1920s

An outburst of housing and highway construction made possible the rapid growth of suburbs in the 1920s. The Chicago suburb of Niles Center, ultimately called the Village of Skokie, was incorporated in 1888. Aided by the service of commuter railroads, the village began to grow in the early 1900s, and in 1913 the first permanently paved road in Cook County was built there. After 1920, a real estate boom began, and by the mid-1920s the village had its own water, sewer, and street lighting services, along with many more paved roads. Wealthy Chicagoans such as utilities and railroad investor Samuel Insull built lavish homes in Niles Center, and soon commercial and office buildings sprang up along its major thoroughfares. Population grew so rapidly that the community boasted that it was "The World's Largest Village." The Great Depression halted the boom in 1929, but significant growth resumed after the Second World War.

CRITICAL THINKING

■ How do you think daily life changed as a result of the growth of suburbs?

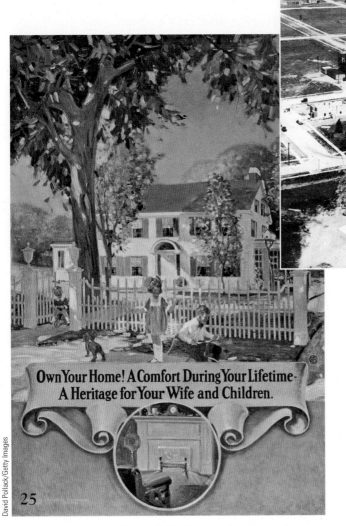

▲ During the 1920s, the ideal of a "home of one's own" became a motivating factor for buying a house in the suburbs. The ideal included not only a spacious cottage but also a grassy yard, white picket fence, shade trees, and an environment where children could play in safety.

▲ In some areas, real estate developers laid out streets and blocks in burgeoning suburbs, enticing offices, stores, and institutions before residences were even built. This photograph of Niles Center, Illinois, taken from an airplane around 1927, reveals how roads and automobiles had become essential to suburban expansion.

Own Your Home! A Comfort During Your Lifetime— A Heritage for Your Wife and Children.

David Pollack/Getty Images

Provided by the Skokie Historical Society

25

Together, cities and suburbs fostered the mass culture that gave the decade its character. Most consumers who jammed shops, movie houses, and sporting arenas and who embraced fads like crossword puzzles and miniature golf lived in or around cities. In these places, people defied older morals by patronizing speakeasies (illegal saloons during prohibition), wearing outlandish clothes, and dancing to jazz. Yet the ideal of small-town society survived. While millions thronged cityward, Americans reminisced about the simplicity of a world gone by, however mythical that world might have been. This was the dilemma the modern nation faced: how does one anchor oneself in a world of rampant materialism and rapid social change?

21-5 New Rhythms of Everyday Life

▶ How did Americans experience changes in the allocation of time to work, family, and leisure in the 1920s?

▶ What new social values and behaviors emerged in the 1920s?

▶ How did views of gender and sexuality shift in the 1920s?

Amid expanded consumerism, American people experienced new patterns of everyday life. One new pattern involved uses of time. People increasingly split their day into distinct time-based compartments: work, family, and leisure. For many, time on the job shrank as mechanization and resulting higher productivity enabled employers to shorten the workweek for many industrial laborers from six days to five and a half. White-collar employees often worked a forty-hour week, enjoyed the weekend off, and received paid vacations as a job benefit.

Family time is harder to measure, but certain trends emerged. Family size decreased between 1920 and 1930 as birth control became more widely practiced. Among American women who married in the 1870s and 1880s, over half who survived to age fifty had five or more children; of their counterparts who married in the 1920s, however, just 20 percent had five or more children. Lower birth rates and longer life expectancy meant that adults were devoting a smaller portion of their lives to raising children and having more time for nonfamily activities. Meanwhile, divorce rates rose. In 1920, there was 1 divorce for every 7.5 marriages; by 1929, the national ratio was 1 in 6, and in many cities it was 2 in 7.

21-5a Household Management

At home, housewives still toiled long hours cleaning, cooking, and raising children, but machines now lightened some tasks and enabled women to use time differently than their forebears had. Especially in middle-class households, electric irons and washing machines simplified some chores. Gas- and oil-powered central heating and hot water heaters eliminated the hauling of wood, coal, and water, the upkeep of a kitchen fire, and the removal of ashes.

Even as technology and economic change simplified some tasks, they also created new demands on a mother's time. The pool of those who could help housewives with cleaning, cooking, and childcare shrank because daughters stayed in school longer, and alternative forms of employment caused a shortage of domestic servants. In addition, the availability of washing machines, hot water, vacuum cleaners, and commercial soap put greater pressure on housewives to keep everything clean. Advertisers of these products tried to make women feel guilty for not devoting enough attention to cleaning the home. No longer a producer of food and clothing as her ancestors had been, a mother instead became the chief shopper, responsible for making sure her family spent money wisely. And the automobile made the wife chief chauffeur. One survey found that urban housewives spent on average seven and one-half hours per week driving to shop and transport children.

21-5b Health and Life Expectancy

Emphasis on nutrition added a scientific dimension to housewives' responsibilities. With the discovery of vitamins between 1915 and 1930, nutritionists began advocating consumption of certain foods to promote health. Producers of milk, canned fruits and vegetables, and other foods exploited the vitamin craze with claims about benefits that were hard to dispute because little was known about these invisible, tasteless ingredients. Welch's Grape Juice, for example, avoided mentioning the excess sugars in its product when it advertised that it was "Rich in Health Values" and "the laxative properties you cannot do without." Even chocolate candy manufacturers plugged their bars as vitamin packed.

Better diets and improved hygiene made Americans generally healthier. Life expectancy at birth increased from fifty-four to sixty years between 1920 and 1930, and infant mortality decreased by two-thirds. Public sanitation and research in bacteriology combined to reduce risks of life-threatening diseases such as tuberculosis and diphtheria. Medical progress did not benefit all groups equally; race and class mattered in health trends as they did in everything else. Infant mortality rates were 50 to 100 percent higher among nonwhites than among whites, and tuberculosis in *barrios* and inner-city slums remained alarmingly common. Moreover, fatalities from automobile accidents rose 150 percent, and deaths from heart disease and cancer—ailments of old age—increased 15 percent. Nevertheless, Americans in general were living longer: the total population over age sixty-five grew 35 percent between 1920 and 1930, while other age groups increased only 15 percent.

21-5c Older Americans and Retirement

As numbers of elderly increased, their worsening economic status stirred interest in pensions and other forms of old-age assistance. Industrialism put premiums on youth and agility, pushing older people into poverty from forced retirement and reduced income. Recognizing the needs of aging citizens, most European countries established state-supported pension systems in the early 1900s. Many Americans, however, believed that individuals should prepare for old age by saving in their youth; pensions, they felt, smacked of socialism. As late as 1923, the Pennsylvania Chamber of Commerce labeled old-age assistance "un-American and socialistic . . . an entering wedge of communistic propaganda."

Yet conditions were alarming. Most inmates in state poorhouses were older people, and almost one-third of Americans age sixty-five and older depended financially on someone else. Few employers, including the federal government, provided for retired employees. Noting that the government fed retired horses until they died, one postal worker complained, "For the purpose of drawing a pension, it would have been better had I been a horse than a human being." Resistance finally broke at the state level in the 1920s. Led by physician Isaac Max Rubinow and journalist Abraham Epstein, reformers persuaded voluntary associations, labor unions, and legislators to endorse old-age assistance through pensions, insurance, and retirement homes. By 1933, almost every state provided at least minimal support to needy elderly people, and a path had been opened for a national program of old-age insurance—social security.

21-5d Social Values

As Americans encountered new ways to use their time, altered behaviors and values were inevitable. Aided by new fabrics and chemical dyes, clothes became a means of self-expression as women and men wore more casual and gaily colored styles than their parents would have considered. The line between acceptable and inappropriate behavior blurred as smoking, drinking, and frankness about sex became fashionable. Birth control gained a large following in respectable circles. Newspapers, magazines, motion pictures (such as *Why Change Your Wife?*), and popular songs (such as "I Don't Care") made certain that Americans did not suffer from "sex starvation."

A typical movie ad promised "brilliant men, beautiful jazz babies, champagne baths, midnight revels, petting parties in the purple dawn, all ending in one terrific smashing climax that makes you gasp."

Other trends weakened inherited customs. Because restrictive child labor laws and compulsory attendance rules kept children in school longer than ever before, peer groups rather than parents played an influential role in socializing youngsters. In earlier eras, different age groups had often shared the same activities: children interacted with adults in fields and kitchens, and young apprentices toiled in workshops beside older journeymen and craftsmen. Now, graded school classes, sports, and clubs constantly brought together children of the same age, separating them from the company and influence of adults.

Furthermore, the ways that young people interacted with each other underwent fundamental changes. Between 1890 and the mid-1920s, ritualized middle- and upper-class courtship, consisting of men formally "calling" on women and of chaperoned social engagements, faded in favor of unsupervised "dating," in which a man "asked out" a woman and spent money on her. Unmarried young people, living in cities away from family restraints, eagerly went on dates to new commercial amusements, such as movies and nightclubs, and automobiles made dating even more extensive. A woman's job seldom provided sufficient income for her to afford these entertainments, but she could enjoy them if a man escorted and "treated" her. Companionship, romance, and, at times, sexual exploitation accompanied the practice, especially when a woman was expected to give sexual favors in return for being treated. A date thus ironically weakened a woman's prerogative at the same time that it expanded her opportunities. Under the courtship system, a woman had control over who could "call" on her. But once she entered a system in which a man's money enabled her to fulfill her desire for entertainment and independence, she might find herself faced with difficult moral choices.

◀ Department stores provided women with new responsibilities for handling money. When a customer paid the sales clerk for a purchase on the store's display floor and needed change and a receipt, the clerk would send the money by pneumatic (vacuum) tubes to another floor (here, the basement) where a cashier would make the change and send it back to the sales clerk who would then hand it to the customer. Previously, store owners would trust only men to make the change, but by the 1920s women were deemed responsible enough to make the transaction.

Underwood Archives/Getty Images

21-5e Women in the Workforce

The practice of dating burgeoned because, after the First World War, women streamed into the labor force. By 1930, 10.8 million women held paying jobs, an increase of 2 million since war's end (see Figure 21.2). The sex segregation that had long characterized workplaces persisted; most women took work that men seldom sought. Thus, more than 1 million women held jobs as teachers and nurses. In the clerical category, some 2.2 million women were typists, bookkeepers, and filing clerks, a tenfold increase since 1920. Another 736,000 were store clerks, and growing numbers could be found in the personal service category as waitresses and hairdressers. Wherever women were employed, their wages seldom exceeded half of those paid to men for similar work. Even though the vast majority of married women did not hold paying jobs (only 12 percent were employed in 1930), married women as a proportion of the workforce rose by 30 percent during the 1920s, and the number of employed married women swelled from 1.9 million to 3.1 million. These figures omit countless widowed, divorced, and abandoned women who held jobs and who, like married women, often had children to support.

The proportion of racial and ethnic minority women in paid labor was double that of white women. Often they entered the workforce because their husbands were unemployed or underemployed. The majority of employed African American women held domestic jobs doing cooking, cleaning, and laundry. The few who had manufacturing jobs, such as in cigarette factories and meatpacking plants, performed the least desirable, lowest-paying tasks. Some opportunities opened for educated black women in social work, teaching, and nursing, but these women also faced discrimination and low incomes. More than white mothers, employed black mothers called on a family network of grandmothers and aunts to help with child care. Economic necessity also drew other minority women into the labor force. Mexican women worked as domestic servants, operatives in garment factories, and agricultural laborers. Next to black women, Japanese American women were the most likely to hold paying jobs. They toiled as field hands and domestics, jobs in which they encountered racial bias and low pay.

21-5f Alternative Images of Femininity

Employed or not, women remade the image of femininity. In contrast to the heavy, floor-length dresses and long hair of previous generations, the short skirts and bobbed hair of the 1920s "flapper" symbolized independence and sexual freedom. Although few women lived the flapper life, the look became fashionable among office workers and store clerks as well as college students. As Cecil B. DeMille's movies showed, chaste models of female behavior were eclipsed by movie temptresses, such as Clara Bow, known as the "'It' Girl," and Gloria Swanson, notorious for torrid love affairs on and off the screen. Many women asserted social equality with men. One observer described "the new woman" as intriguingly independent.

> She takes a man's point of view as her mother never could. . . . She will never make you a hatband or knit you a necktie, but she'll drive you from the station . . . in her own little sports car. She'll don knickers and go skiing with you, . . . she'll dive as well as you, perhaps better, she'll dance as long as you care to, and she'll take everything you say the way you mean it.

21-5g Gay and Lesbian Culture

The era's openness regarding sexuality also enabled the underground homosexual culture to surface a little more than in previous eras. In nontraditional city neighborhoods, such as New York's Greenwich Village and Harlem, cheap rents

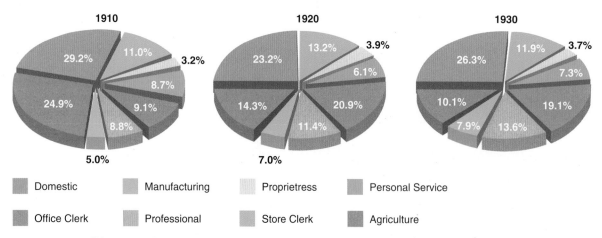

Figure 21.2 Changing Dimensions of Paid Female Labor, 1910–1930

These charts reveal the extraordinary growth in clerical and professional occupations among employed women and the accompanying decline in agricultural labor in the early twentieth century. Notice that manufacturing employment peaked in 1920 and that domestic service fluctuated as white immigrant women began to move out of these jobs and were replaced by women of color.

and a tolerance for alternate lifestyles attracted gay men and lesbians, who patronized dance halls, speakeasies, cafes, and other gathering places. Establishments that catered to a gay clientele remained targets for police raids, however, demonstrating that gays and lesbians could not expect acceptance from the rest of society.

These trends represented a break with the more restrained culture of the nineteenth century. But social change rarely proceeds smoothly. As the decade wore on, various groups mobilized to defend older values.

21-6 Lines of Defense

▶ How was the pluralism of American society challenged socially and politically in the 1920s?

▶ What were the key characteristics of the anti-immigrant sentiment in the 1920s?

▶ How did Protestant Christianity respond to the shift in social values and behavior in modern society?

Early in 1920, the leader of a newly formed organization, using a tactic adopted by modern businesses, hired two public relations experts to recruit members. Edward Clarke and Elizabeth Tyler canvassed communities in the South, Southwest, and Midwest, where they found countless people eager to pay a $10 membership fee and $6 for a white uniform. Clarke and Tyler pocketed $2.50 from each membership they sold. Their success helped build the organization to 5 million members and four thousand chapters by 1923.

21-6a Ku Klux Klan

No ordinary civic club, this was the Ku Klux Klan (KKK), a revived version of the hooded order that terrorized southern communities after the Civil War. Reconstituted in 1915 by William J. Simmons, an Atlanta, Georgia, evangelist and insurance salesman, the Klan adopted the hoods, intimidating tactics, and mystical terminology of its forerunner (its leader was the Imperial Wizard; its book of rituals, the Kloran). But the new Klan had broader objectives than the old. It fanned outward from the Deep South and for a time wielded political power in places as diverse as Oregon, where Portland's mayor was a Klan member, and Indiana, where Klansmen held the governorship and several seats in the legislature. Its membership included men from the urban middle class who were fearful of losing social and economic gains achieved from postwar prosperity and nervous about immigration and a new youth culture that seemed to be eluding family control. It also included a women's adjunct, Women of the Ku Klux Klan, boasting an estimated half-million members.

One phrase summed up Klan goals: "Native, white, Protestant supremacy." Native meant no immigration, no "mongrelization" of American culture. According to Imperial Wizard Hiram Wesley Evans, white supremacy was a matter of survival. "The world," he warned, "has been so made so that each race must fight for its life, must conquer, accept slavery, or die. The Klansman believes the whites will not become slaves, and he does not intend to die before his time." Evans praised Protestantism for promoting "unhampered individual development," and accused the Catholic Church of discouraging assimilation and enslaving people to priests and a foreign pope.

Using threatening assemblies, violence, and economic pressure, the new Klan menaced many communities. Klansmen meted out vigilante justice to suspected bootleggers, wife beaters, and adulterers; forced schools to stop teaching the theory of evolution; campaigned against Catholic and Jewish political candidates; urged members not to buy from merchants who did not share their views; and fueled racial tensions against Mexicans in Texas border cities, immigrants in northern cities, and African Americans everywhere. Although men firmly controlled Klan activities, women not only promoted native white Protestantism but also, with male approval, worked for moral reform and enforcement of prohibition. Because the KKK vowed to protect the "virtue" of women, housewives and other women sometimes appealed to the Klan for help in punishing abusive, unfaithful, or irresponsible husbands and fathers when legal authorities would not intervene. Rather than an arrest and trial, the Klan's method of justice was flogging.

By 1925, however, the Invisible Empire was weakening, as scandal undermined its moral base. Most notably, in 1925 Indiana grand dragon David Stephenson was convicted of second-degree murder after he kidnapped and raped a woman who later died either from taking poison or from infection caused by bites on her body. More generally, the Klan's negative, exclusive brand of patriotism and purity could not compete in a pluralistic society.

The KKK had no monopoly on bigotry; intolerance pervaded American society. Nativists had urged an end to open immigration since the 1880s. They charged that Catholic and Jewish immigrants clogged city slums and stubbornly embraced alien religious and political beliefs. Fear of immigrant radicals also fueled a dramatic trial in 1921, when two Italian anarchists, **Nicola Sacco and Bartolomeo Vanzetti**, were convicted of murdering a paymaster and guard in Braintree, Massachusetts. Evidence for their guilt was flimsy, but Judge Webster Thayer openly sided with the prosecution, privately calling the defendants "anarchistic bastards."

21-6b Immigration Quotas

Guided by such sentiments, the movement to restrict immigration gathered support. Labor leaders charged that alien workers depressed wages and caused unemployment of native-born men. Business executives, who formerly had opposed restrictions because they desired cheap immigrant laborers, changed their minds, having realized that they could keep wages low by

Nicola Sacco and Bartolomeo Vanzetti Italian immigrants found guilty of a Massachusetts murder and sentenced to death. Sacco and Vanzetti were also anarchists and much of their murder trial focused on their radicalism.

mechanizing. Even some humanitarian reformers supported restriction as a means of reducing poverty and easing assimilation. Drawing support from such groups, Congress reversed previous policy and, in the Emergency Quota Act of 1921, set yearly immigration allocations for each nationality. Reflecting preference for Anglo-Saxon Protestant immigrants and prejudice against Catholics and Jews from southern and eastern Europe, Congress stipulated that annual immigration of a given nationality could not exceed 3 percent of the number of immigrants from that nation residing in the United States in 1910. The act thereby discriminated against immigrants from southern and eastern Europe, whose numbers were small in 1910 relative to those from northern Europe.

In 1924, Congress replaced the Quota Act with the **National Origins Act**.

National Origins Act of 1924 Restricted annual immigration from any foreign country to 2 percent of that nationality residing in the United States in 1890 (but barred Asians); also limited total annual immigration to 150,000.

This law limited annual immigration to 150,000 people and set quotas at 2 percent of each nationality residing in the United States in 1890, except for Asians, who were banned completely (Chinese immigration had been banned since 1882 by the Chinese Exclusion Act). The National Origins Act further restricted southern and eastern Europeans because even fewer of those groups lived in the United States in 1890 than in 1910. The law did, however, allow foreign-born wives and children of U.S. citizens to enter as nonquota immigrants. In 1927, a revised National Origins Act apportioned new quotas to begin in 1929. It retained the annual limit of 150,000 but redefined quotas to be distributed among European countries in proportion to the "national-origins" (country of birth or descent) of American inhabitants in 1920. People coming from the Western Hemisphere did not fall under the quotas (except for those whom the Labor Department defined as potential paupers), and soon they became the largest immigrant groups (see Figure 21.3).

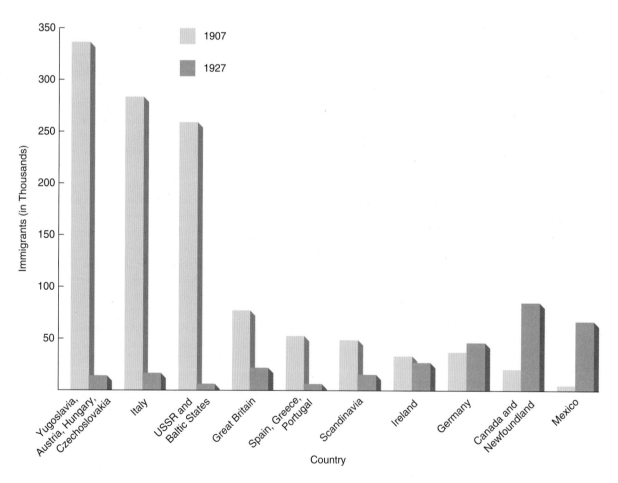

Figure 21.3 **Sources of Immigration, 1907 and 1927**

Immigration peaked in 1907 and 1908, when newcomers from southern and eastern Europe poured into the United States. After immigration restriction laws were passed in the 1920s, the greatest number of immigrants came from the Western Hemisphere (Canada and Mexico), which was exempted from the quotas, and the number coming from eastern and southern Europe shrank.

21-6c Fundamentalism and the Scopes Trial

Whereas nativists tried to establish ethnic and racial purity, the pursuit of spiritual purity stirred religious fundamentalists. Millions of Americans sought certainty and salvation by following Protestant evangelical denominations that interpreted the Bible literally. Resolutely believing that God's miracles created the world and its living creatures, they condemned the theory of evolution as heresy and argued that wherever fundamentalists constituted a majority of a community, as they did in many places, they should be able to determine what would be taught in schools. Their enemies were "modernists," who used reasoning from social sciences, such as psychology and anthropology, to interpret behavior. To modernists, God was important to the study of culture and history, but science was responsible for advancing knowledge.

In 1925, Christian **fundamentalism** clashed with modernism in a celebrated case in Dayton, Tennessee, that came to be known as the **Scopes Trial**. Early that year, the state legislature passed a law forbidding public school instructors to teach the theory that humans had evolved from lower forms of life rather than descended from Adam and Eve. Shortly thereafter, high-school teacher John Thomas Scopes volunteered to serve in a test case and was arrested for violating the law. Scopes's trial that summer became a headline event. William Jennings Bryan, former secretary of state and three-time presidential candidate, argued for the prosecution, and a team of civil liberties lawyers headed by noted defense attorney Clarence Darrow represented Scopes. News correspondents crowded into the small town, and radio stations broadcast the trial.

Although Scopes was convicted—clearly he had broken the law—modernists claimed victory. The testimony, they believed, showed fundamentalism to be illogical. The trial's climax occurred when Bryan took the witness stand as an expert on the Bible. Responding to Darrow's probing, Bryan asserted that Eve really had been created from Adam's rib, that the Tower of Babel was responsible for the diversity of languages, and that Jonah had been swallowed by a big fish. Spectators in Dayton cheered Bryan for his declarations, but the liberal press mocked him and his allies. Nevertheless, fundamentalism continued to expand. For example, the evangelical Southern Baptist Convention became the fastest-growing Protestant sect, and, along with other fundamentalist groups, pressured school boards to stop teaching about evolution. Advocates for what they believed to be basic values of family and conduct, these churches created an independent subculture, with their own schools, camps, radio ministries, and missionary societies.

21-6d Religious Revivalism

Religious fervor spread wherever people struggling with economic insecurity became nervous about modernism's attack on old-time religion. Countless urban and rural Pentecostal churches attracted blacks and whites swayed by their pageantry and depiction of a personal Savior. Using modern advertising techniques and elaborately staged broadcasts on radio, magnetic "revivalist" preachers—such as the flamboyant Aimee Semple McPherson, whose radio broadcasts drew hundreds of thousands of listeners and who built the nation's first "megachurch"; former baseball player Billy Sunday, who preached to large crowds as on his nationwide travels; and Father Divine, an African American who amassed an interracial following from his base on Long Island—stirred revivalist fervor.

Revivalism represented only one means of sustaining old-fashioned values and finding comfort in a fast-moving consumer society. Millions who did not belong to the KKK firmly believed that nonwhites and immigrants were inferior people who imperiled national welfare. Clergy and teachers of all faiths condemned dancing, new dress styles, and sex in movies and parked cars. Many urban dwellers supported prohibition, believing that eliminating the temptation of drink would help win the battle against poverty, vice, and corruption. Yet even while mourning a lost past, most Americans sincerely sought some kind of balance as they tried to adjust to the modern order in one way or another. Few refrained from listening to the radio and seeing movies like *Why Change Your Wife?*—activities that proved less corrupting than critics feared. More than ever, Americans sought fellowship in civic organizations such as Rotary, Elks, and women's clubs. Perhaps most important, more people were finding release in recreation and new uses of leisure time.

21-7 The Age of Play

▶ What form of entertainment and leisure did Americans engage in during the 1920s?

▶ What role did "heroes" play in American society in the 1920s?

▶ What cultural expressions were created and nurtured by African Americans in the 1920s?

Americans in the 1920s embraced commercial entertainment as never before. In 1919, they spent $2.5 billion on leisure activities; by 1929, such expenditures topped $4.3 billion, a figure not again equaled until after the Second World War. Spectator amusements—movies, music, and sports—accounted for 21 percent of the 1929 total; the rest involved participatory recreation such as games, hobbies, and travel. Entrepreneurs responded to an appetite for fads and spectacles. Early in the 1920s, mahjong, a Chinese tile game, was the craze. In the mid-1920s, devotees popularized crossword puzzles, printed in mass-circulation newspapers and magazines. Next, fun seekers adopted miniature golf. By 1930, the nation boasted thirty thousand miniature golf courses featuring tiny castles, windmills, and waterfalls. Dances like the

fundamentalism Twentieth-century movement within Protestantism that taught literal interpretation of the Bible.

Scopes Trial Trial that took place after high school teacher John Scopes challenged a Tennessee law that banned teaching the theory of evolution in public schools.

Charleston won fans throughout the country, aided by live and recorded music and the growing popularity of jazz.

21-7a Movies and Sports

In addition to indulging actively, Americans were avid spectators, particularly of movies and sports. In total capital investment, motion pictures became one of the nation's leading industries. Nearly every community had at least one theater, whether a hundred-seat, small-town establishment or a big-city "picture palace" with ornate lobbies and two thousand cushioned seats. In 1922, movies attracted 40 million viewers weekly; by 1929, the number neared 100 million—at a time when the nation's population was 120 million and total weekly church attendance was 60 million. New technology increased movies' appeal. Between 1922 and 1927, the Technicolor Corporation developed a means of producing movies in color. This process, along with the introduction of sound in *The Jazz Singer* in 1927, made movies even more exciting and realistic.

Responding to tastes of mass audiences, the movie industry produced escapist entertainment. Although DeMille's romantic comedies like *Why Change Your Wife?* explored worldly themes, his most popular films—*The Ten Commandments* (1923) and *The King of Kings* (1927)—were biblical. Lurid dramas like *Souls for Sale* (1923) and *A Woman Who Sinned* (1924) also drew big audiences, as did slapstick comedies starring Harold Lloyd and Charlie Chaplin. Movie content was tame by current standards. In 1927, producers, bowing to pressure from legislators and religious leaders, instituted self-censorship, forbidding nudity, rough language, and plots that did not end with justice and morality triumphant. Movies also reproduced social prejudices. Although white actresses and actors played roles as glamour queens and action heroes, what few black actors there were had to take roles as maids and butlers.

Spectator sports also boomed as each year millions packed stadiums and ballparks. In an age when technology and mass production had robbed experiences and objects of their uniqueness, sports provided the unpredictability and drama that people craved. Newspapers and radio magnified this tension, feeding sports news to eager readers and glorifying events with such dramatic narrative that sports promoters did not need to buy advertising space.

Baseball's drawn-out suspense, diverse plays, and potential for keeping statistics attracted a huge following. After the "Black Sox scandal" of 1919, when eight members of the Chicago White Sox were banned from the game for allegedly throwing the World Series to the Cincinnati Reds (even though a jury acquitted them), baseball regained respectability by transforming itself. Discovering that home

National Baseball Hall of Fame, Cooperstown, N.Y.

▲ Excluded from playing in white-dominated professional baseball, African Americans organized their own teams and leagues. The Indianapolis ABCs, named after the American Brewing Company, was one of the more successful teams in the Negro National League during the 1920s and featured some of the best black baseball players of the era, including Oscar Charleston, Elwood "Bingo" DeMoss, and "Cannonball" Dick Redding.

runs excited fans, the leagues redesigned the ball so that batters more easily could hit home runs. Game attendance skyrocketed. A record 300,000 people attended the six-game 1921 World Series between the New York Giants and New York Yankees. Millions gathered regularly to watch local teams, and even more listened to professional games on the radio. Although African American ballplayers were prohibited from playing in the major leagues, they formed their own teams, and in 1920 the first successful Negro League was founded, consisting of eight teams from places such as Chicago, Kansas City, and Indianapolis.

21-7b Sports Heroes

Sports, movies, and the news created a galaxy of heroes. As technology and mass society made the individual less significant, people clung to heroic personalities as a means of identifying with the unique. Athletes like Bill Tilden in tennis, Gertrude Ederle in swimming (in 1926, she became the first woman to swim across the English Channel), and Bobby Jones in golf had national and international reputations. The power and action of boxing, football, and baseball produced the most popular sports heroes. Heavyweight champion Jack Dempsey attracted the first of several million-dollar gates in his fight with Frenchman Georges Carpentier in 1921. Harold "Red" Grange, running back for the University of Illinois football team, thrilled fans and sportswriters (who called him "The Galloping Ghost") with his speed and agility.

Baseball's foremost hero was George Herman "Babe" Ruth, who began his career as a pitcher but found he could use his prodigious strength to better advantage hitting home runs. Ruth hit twenty-nine homers in 1919, fifty-four in 1920 (the year the Boston Red Sox sold him to the New York Yankees), fifty-nine in 1921, and sixty in 1927—each year a record. His talent and boyish grin endeared him to millions. Known for overindulgence in food, drink, and sex, he charmed fans into forgiving his excesses by appearing at public events and visiting hospitalized children.

21-7c Movie Stars and Public Heroes

Americans also fulfilled a yearning for romance and adventure through movie idols. The films and personal lives of Douglas Fairbanks, Gloria Swanson, and Charlie Chaplin were discussed in parlors and pool halls across the country. One of the decade's most adored movie personalities was Italian-born Rudolph Valentino, whose looks and suave manner made women swoon and men imitate his pomaded hairdo and slick sideburns. Valentino's image exploited the era's sexual liberalism and flirtation with wickedness. In his most famous film, Valentino played a passionate sheik who carried away beautiful women to his tent, combining the roles of abductor and seducer. When he died at thirty-one of complications from ulcers and appendicitis, the press turned his funeral into a public extravaganza. Mourners lined up for a mile to file past his coffin.

◀ Named the "Spirit of St. Louis" to honor the St. Louis businessmen who financed Lindbergh's flight, the plane was a custom-built single-engine, single-seat monoplane built in San Diego, California, for a total cost of $10,580—$2,000 of which was paid by Lindbergh himself from his earnings as an air mail pilot. The plane is shown here arriving in Boston and being thronged by spectators and soldiers, some of them mounted, during Lindbergh's triumphant tour of the United States after his historic flight.

Bettmann/Getty Images

The era's most celebrated hero, however, was **Charles A. Lindbergh**, an intrepid aviator who in May 1927 flew a plane solo from New York to Paris. The flight seized the attention of millions, as newspaper and telegraph reports followed Lindbergh's progress. After the pilot landed successfully, President Coolidge dispatched a warship to bring "Lucky Lindy" back home. Celebrants sent Lindbergh 55,000 telegrams and some 3 million to 4 million people celebrated him in a triumphant homecoming parade. Among countless prizes, Lindbergh received the Distinguished Flying Cross and the Congressional Medal of Honor. Promoters offered him millions of dollars to tour the world and $700,000 for a movie contract. Through it all, Lindbergh, nicknamed "The Lone Eagle," remained dignified, even aloof. Although his flight and its aftermath symbolized the new combination of technology and mass culture of the 1920s, Lindbergh himself epitomized individual achievement, self-reliance, and courage—old-fashioned values that attracted public respect amid the media frenzy.

21-7d Prohibition

In their quest for fun and self-expression, some Americans became lawbreakers by refusing to give up drinking. The Eighteenth Amendment (1919), which prohibited the manufacture, sale, and transportation of alcoholic beverages, and the federal law that implemented it (the Volstead Act of 1920) worked well at first. Per capita consumption of liquor dropped, as did arrests for drunkenness, and the price of illegal booze exceeded what average workers could afford. But federal and state authorities for the most part refrained from enforcing the new law. In 1922, Congress gave the Prohibition Bureau only three thousand employees and less than $7 million for nationwide enforcement, and by 1927 most state budgets omitted funds to enforce prohibition.

After 1925, the so-called noble experiment faltered as thousands of people made their own wine and gin illegally, and bootleg importers along the country's borders and shorelines easily evaded the few patrols that attempted to intercept them. Moreover, drinking, like gambling and prostitution, was a business with willing customers, and criminal organizations capitalized on public demand. The most notorious of such mobs belonged to Al Capone, a burly thug who seized control of illegal liquor, gambling, and prostitution in Chicago, maintaining power over politicians and the vice business through intimidation, bribery, and violence. Other mobsters, such as Charles "Lucky" Luciano (born Salvatore Lucania) and Arnold "the Brain" Rothstein, also netted huge incomes from the illegal production and sale of alcoholic beverages. Capone contended, in a statement revealing of the era, "Prohibition is a business. All I do is supply a public demand." Americans wanted their liquor and beer, and until 1931, when a federal court convicted and imprisoned him for income tax evasion (the only charge for which authorities could obtain hard evidence), Capone supplied them. Reflecting on contradictions inherent in prohibition,

Charles A. Lindbergh Popular aviator who flew solo across the Atlantic in his small single-engine plane, the *Spirit of St. Louis*, in May 1927.

columnist Walter Lippmann wrote in 1931, "The high level of lawlessness is maintained by the fact that Americans desire to do so many things which they also desire to prohibit."

At the same time that consumerism inspired Americans to do "so many things," the era's hardships and crassness spawned unease, and intellectuals like Lippmann were quick to point to persisting hypocrisies. Serious authors and artists felt at odds with society, and their rejection of materialism and conformity was both biting and bitter. In protest, several writers from the so-called Lost Generation, including novelist Ernest Hemingway and poets Ezra Pound and T. S. Eliot, abandoned the United States for Europe. Others, like novelists William Faulkner, Sinclair Lewis, and Edith Wharton remained in America but, like the expatriates, expressed disillusionment with the materialism that they witnessed.

21-7e Harlem Renaissance

Discontent quite different from that of white authors characterized a new generation of African American artists. Middle class, educated, and proud of their African heritage, black writers rejected white culture and exalted the militantly assertive "New Negro." Most of them lived in New York's Harlem; in this "Negro Mecca," intellectuals and artists, aided by a few white patrons, celebrated black culture during what became known as the Harlem Renaissance.

The 1921 musical comedy *Shuffle Along* is often credited with launching the Harlem Renaissance. The show featured talented black artists, such as lyricist Noble Sissle; composer Eubie Blake; and singers Florence Mills, Josephine Baker, and Mabel Mercer. The Harlem Renaissance also showcased several gifted writers, among them poets Langston Hughes, Countee Cullen, and Claude McKay; novelists Zora Neale Hurston, Jessie Fauset, and Jean Toomer; and essayist Alain Locke. The movement also included painter Aaron Douglas and sculptress Augusta Savage. Black writers from other parts of the country also flourished during the decade. They included novelist Sutton E. Griggs of Houston and Memphis and journalist and historian Drusilla Dunjee Houston from Oklahoma.

These artists and intellectuals grappled with notions of identity. Though cherishing their African heritage and the folk culture of the slave South, they realized that blacks had to come to terms with themselves as free American people. Thus, Alain Locke urged that the New Negro should become "a collaborator and participant in American civilization." But Langston Hughes wrote, "We younger Negro artists who create now intend to express our individual dark-skinned selves without fear or shame. If white people are pleased, we are glad. If they are not, it doesn't matter. We know we are beautiful."

21-7f Jazz

The Jazz Age, as the 1920s is sometimes called, owes its name to the music of black culture. Evolving from African and African American folk music, early jazz communicated exuberance, humor, and autonomy that black people seldom experienced in their public and political lives. With its emotional rhythms

Frank Driggs Collection/Getty Images

▲ African American blues and jazz music fueled much of the cultural outburst of the 1920s and gave opportunities to both male and female talent. This photograph, taken at the Sunset Café in Chicago in 1922, features singer and actor Clarence Muse on the floor with blues singers Mary Stafford and Frankie "Half-Pint" Jaxon behind him, performing with the Carroll Dickerson Band.

and improvisation, jazz blurred the distinction between composer and performer and created intimacy between performer and audience. Jazz arose in New Orleans (where it replaced African American ragtime music), and as African Americans moved northward and westward after slavery, their music traveled with them. Centers of jazz formed in Kansas City, Chicago, and San Diego. Urban dance halls and nightclubs, some of which included interracial audiences, featured gifted jazz performers like trumpeter Louis Armstrong, trombonist Kid Ory, and blues singer Bessie Smith. They and others enjoyed wide fame thanks to phonograph records and radio. Music recorded by black artists and aimed at black consumers (sometimes called "race records") gave African Americans a place in commercial culture. More important, jazz endowed the nation with its own distinctive art form.

In many ways, the 1920s were the most creative years the nation had yet experienced. Painters such as Georgia O'Keeffe and John Marin forged a uniquely American style of visual art. Composer Henry Cowell pioneered electronic music, and Aaron Copland built orchestral works around native folk motifs. George Gershwin blended jazz rhythms, classical forms, and folk melodies in serious works (*Rhapsody in Blue*, 1924, and *Piano Concerto in F*, 1925), musical dramas (*Funny Face*, 1927), and hit tunes such as "The Man I Love."

At the beginning of the decade, essayist Harold Stearns complained that "the most . . . pathetic fact in the social life of America today is emotional and aesthetic starvation." By 1929, that contention had been disproved.

21-8 The Election of 1928 and End of the New Era

▶ How did Herbert Hoover and Al Smith represent the changing nature of American society in the 1920s?

▶ What domestic and international factors contributed to the stock market crash and the economic depression that followed?

Intellectuals' uneasiness about materialism seldom altered the confident rhetoric of politics. Herbert Hoover voiced that confidence when he accepted the Republican nomination for president in 1928. "We in America today," Hoover boasted, "are nearer to the final triumph over poverty than ever before in the history of any land. . . . We have not yet reached the goal, but, given a chance to go forward with the policies of the last eight years, we shall soon, with the help of God, be in sight of the day when poverty will be banished from this nation."

21-8a Herbert Hoover

Hoover was an apt Republican candidate (Coolidge chose not to seek reelection) because he fused the traditional value of individual hard work with modern emphasis on corporate action. A Quaker from Iowa, orphaned at age ten, Hoover worked his way through Stanford University and became a wealthy mining engineer. During and after the First World War, he distinguished himself as U.S. food administrator and head of food relief for Europe.

As secretary of commerce under Presidents Harding and Coolidge, Hoover promoted "associationalism." Recognizing the extent to which nationwide associations dominated commerce and industry, Hoover wanted to stimulate a cooperative, associational relationship between business and government. He took every opportunity to make the Commerce Department a center for the promotion of business, encouraging the formation of trade associations, holding conferences, and issuing reports, all aimed at improving productivity and profits. His active leadership prompted one observer to quip that Hoover was "Secretary of Commerce and assistant secretary of everything else."

21-8b Al Smith

As their candidate, Democrats in 1928 chose New York's governor Alfred E. Smith, whose background contrasted with Hoover's. Hoover had rural, native-born, Protestant, and business roots and had never previously run for public office. Smith was an urbane, gregarious politician of Irish stock with a career embedded in New York City's Tammany Hall political machine. His relish for the give-and-take of city streets is apparent in his response to a heckler during the campaign. When the heckler shouted, "Tell them all you know, Al. It won't take long!" Smith unflinchingly retorted, "I'll tell them all we both know, and it won't take any longer!"

Smith was the first Roman Catholic to run for president on a major party ticket. His religion enhanced his appeal among urban ethnics (including women), who were voting in increasing numbers, but anti-Catholic sentiments lost him southern and rural votes. Smith had compiled a strong record on Progressive reform and civil rights during his governorship, but his campaign failed to build a coalition of farmers and city dwellers because he stressed issues unlikely to unite these groups, particularly his opposition to prohibition.

Hoover, who emphasized national prosperity under Republican administrations, won the popular vote by 21 million to 15 million and the electoral vote by 444 to 87. Smith's candidacy nevertheless had beneficial effects on the Democratic Party. By luring millions of foreign-stock voters to the polls, he carried the nation's twelve largest cities, which formerly had given majorities to Republican presidential candidates. For the next forty years, the Democratic Party solidified this urban base, which in conjunction with its traditional strength in the South made the party a formidable force in national elections.

21-8c Hoover's Administration

At his inaugural, Hoover proclaimed a New Day, "bright with hope." His cabinet, composed mostly of businessmen committed to the existing order, included six millionaires. To the lower ranks of government, Hoover appointed young professionals who agreed with him that a scientific approach could solve national problems. If Hoover was optimistic, so were the people who voted for him. There was widespread belief among them that success resulted from individual effort and that unemployment and poverty signaled personal weakness. Prevailing opinion also held that fluctuations of the business cycle were natural and therefore not to be tampered with by government.

21-8d Stock Market Crash

This trust dissolved on October 24, 1929, known as Black Thursday, when stock market prices suddenly plunged, wiping out $10 billion in value (worth over $100 billion today). Panic selling set in. Prices of many stocks hit record lows; some sellers could find no buyers. Stunned crowds gathered outside the frantic New York Stock Exchange. At noon, leading bankers met at the headquarters of J. P. Morgan and Company. To restore faith, they put up $20 million and ceremoniously began buying stocks. The mood brightened, and some stocks rallied. The bankers, it seemed, had saved the day.

But as news of Black Thursday spread, frightened investors decided to sell stocks rather than risk further losses. On Black Tuesday, October 29, with so many people trying to sell, prices plummeted again. Hoover, who had never approved of what he called "the fever of speculation," assured Americans that "the crisis will be over in sixty days." Three months later, he still believed that "the worst is over without a doubt." He shared the popular assumptions that the stock market's ills could be quarantined and that the economy was strong enough to endure until the market righted itself. Instead, the crash ultimately helped to unleash a devastating worldwide depression.

In hindsight, it is evident that the Depression began long before the stock market crash. Prosperity in the 1920s was not as widespread as optimists believed. Agriculture had been languishing for decades, and many areas, especially in the South, had been excluded from the bounty of consumer society. Racial minorities suffered from economic as well as social discrimination in both urban and rural settings. Industries such as mining and textiles failed to sustain profits throughout most of the decade, and even the high-flying automotive and household goods industries stagnated after 1926. The fever of speculation that concerned Hoover included rash investments in California and Florida real estate, as well as in the stock market, and masked much of what was unhealthy in the national economy.

21-8e Declining Demand

More generally, the economic weakness that underlay the Great Depression had several interrelated causes. One was declining demand. Since mid-1928, demand for new housing had faltered, leading to declining sales of building materials and unemployment among construction workers. Growth

▲ As the stock market tumbled on October 24, 1929, a crowd of concerned investors gathered outside the New York Stock Exchange on Wall Street, unprepared for an unprecedented economic decline that would send the country into a tailspin for the next decade.

industries, such as automobiles and electric appliances, had been able to expand as long as consumers bought their products. Expansion, however, could not continue unabated. When demand leveled off, factory owners had to cut production and pare workforces. Retailers had amassed large inventories that were going unsold and, in turn, they started ordering less from manufacturers. Farm prices continued to sag, leaving farmers with less income to purchase new machinery and goods. As wages and employment fell, families could not afford things they needed and wanted. Thus, by 1929, a sizable population of underconsumers was causing serious repercussions.

Underconsumption also resulted from widening divisions in income distribution. As the rich grew richer, middle- and lower-income Americans made modest gains at best. Although average per capita disposable income (income after taxes) rose about 9 percent between 1920 and 1929, income of the wealthiest 1 percent rose 75 percent, accounting for most of the general increase. Much of this money went for stock market speculation, not consumer goods.

21-8f Corporate Debt and Stock Market Speculation

Furthermore, in their eagerness to boost profits, many businesses overloaded themselves with debt. To obtain loans, they misrepresented their assets in ways that hid their inability to repay if forced to do so. Such practices, overlooked by lending agencies, put the nation's banking system on a precarious footing. When one part of the edifice collapsed, the entire structure crumbled.

Risky stock market speculation also precipitated the Depression. Individuals and corporations bought millions of stock shares on margin, meaning that they invested by placing a down payment of only a fraction of a stock's actual price and then used stocks they had bought, but not fully paid for, as collateral for more stock purchases. When stock prices stopped rising, investors tried to minimize losses by selling holdings they had bought on margin. But numerous investors selling at the same time caused prices to plunge. As stock values crumbled, brokers demanded full payment for stocks bought on margin. Investors attempted to comply by withdrawing savings from banks or selling stocks for whatever they could get. Cash-short bankers pressured businesses to pay back their loans, tightening the vise further. The more obligations went unmet, the more the system tottered. Inevitably, banks and investment companies collapsed.

21-8g Economic Troubles Abroad; Federal Failure at Home

International economic conditions also contributed to the Depression. During the First World War and postwar reconstruction, Americans loaned billions of dollars to war-torn European nations. By the late 1920s, however, American

Intercollegiate Athletics

College sports spread widely in the late nineteenth century, but by the 1920s violence and cheating seemed to be rampant. Reports of brutality, academic fraud, and illegal payments to recruits prompted the Carnegie Foundation for the Advancement of Higher Education in 1924 to undertake an investigation of college sports. Its 1929 report condemned coaches and alumni supporters for violating the amateur code and recommended the abolition of varsity football, where violence and corruption seemed most widespread. The report had minimal effect. As the career of Red Grange illustrated, college football was immensely popular during the 1920s, and scores of schools built massive stadiums and arenas to attract spectators, bolster alumni allegiance, enhance revenues, and promote school spirit.

From the 1920s to the present, big-time intercollegiate sports, with highly paid coaches and highly recruited athletes, have become one of the nation's major commercial entertainments. At the same time, American higher education has struggled to reconcile conflicts between the commercialism of athletic competition on one hand and the academic mission and ideal of amateurism on the other. No other country developed as extensive a link between high-caliber sport and education as the United States. Supposedly, cultivation of the mind is the objective of higher education. But the economic potential of competition and accompanying urge to win at all costs have spawned expanding athletic departments that include administrators, practice, training, and study facilities, and tutors, as well as multiple coaches and trainers, with the result that athletic programs compete with and sometimes overshadow an institution's academic mission.

Publicity about scandals, fraud, and felonious behavior has sparked controversy in college sports since the 1920s. In 1952, after revelations of point-shaving (fixing the outcome) of basketball games involving colleges in New York City and elsewhere, the American Council on Education (ACE) undertook a study similar to that of the Carnegie Foundation a generation earlier. The ACE's recommendations, including the elimination of football bowl games, went largely unheeded. In 1991, further abuses, especially in admission and academic eligibility, prompted the Knight Foundation Commission on Intercollegiate Athletics to conduct a study that urged college presidents to take the lead in reforming intercollegiate athletics. Few significant changes resulted, even after a follow-up study in 2001.

The most sweeping changes followed court rulings in the 1990s, mandating under Title IX of the Educational Amendments Act of 1972 that women's sports be treated equally with men's sports. Enforcement, however, provoked a backlash that aimed to prevent men's teams from being cut or reduced in roster size in order to satisfy Title IX's gender equity requirements. Also, by 2015, money from television and donations large and small enabled big-time schools and conferences to flex their muscles in a variety of ways. That year, for example, the five power college athletic conferences, the ones with big-time football and men's basketball programs—Big Ten, SEC, Pac 12, Big 12, and ACC—induced the NCAA to grant them autonomy to raise athletic scholarship amounts several thousand dollars to cover "full cost" of college education plus other prerogatives that most schools cannot afford. Recently the NCAA has made efforts to regulate academic standards and reward academic success by monitoring athletes' academic progress, but reform's effectiveness depends on cooperation from member institutions. As long as millions of dollars are involved and sports remain a vital component of college as well as national culture, the system established in the 1920s has shown ability to withstand most pressures for change.

CRITICAL THINKING

- College sports, particularly men's football and basketball, garner massive amounts of money for successful institutions. In many cases, these institutions of higher learning capitalize on the popularity of their athletes (well after they have stopped playing) through restrictions on the use of their images among other things. Some protests to this practice have arisen in recent years. Do institutions of higher education owe anything other than an education to the athletes that make millions of dollars in revenue for them?

---

investors were keeping their money at home, investing instead in the stock market. Europeans, unable to borrow funds and unable to sell goods in the American market because of high tariffs, began to buy less from the United States. Moreover, the Allied nations depended on German war reparations so they could pay their war debts to the United States, and the German government depended on American bank loans to pay those reparations. When the crash choked off American loans, Germany could not meet obligations to the Allies, and in turn the Allies were unable to pay war debts to the United States. The Western economy ground to a halt.

Some Europeans also branded the United States as stingy for its handling of World War I debts and reparations. Twenty-eight nations became entangled in a web of inter-Allied government debts, which totaled $26.5 billion ($9.6 billion of them owed to the U.S. government). Europeans owed private American creditors another $3 billion. Europeans urged Americans to erase these debts as a magnanimous contribution to the war effort. During the war, they angrily charged, Europe had bled while America profited. "There is only one way we could be worse with the Europeans," remarked the humorist Will Rogers, "and that is to have helped them out in two wars instead of one." American leaders, however, insisted on repayment, some pointing out that the victorious European nations had gained vast territory and resources as war spoils. Senator George Norris of Nebraska, emphasizing domestic priorities, declared that the United States could build highways in "every county seat" if only the Europeans would pay their debts.

21-8h Lack of Federal Regulation

Federal policies also underlay the crisis. The government refrained from regulating speculation and only occasionally scolded undisciplined bankers and businesspeople. In keeping with its support of business expansion, the Federal Reserve Board pursued easy credit policies, charging low discount rates (interest on its loans to member banks) even though such loans were financing the speculative mania.

Partly because of optimism and partly because of relatively unsophisticated economic analysis, neither experts nor people on the street realized what really had happened in 1929. Conventional wisdom, based on experiences from previous depressions, held that little could be done to correct economic downturns; they simply had to run their course. So in 1929, people waited for the tailspin to ease, never realizing that the "new era" had come to an end and that the economy, politics, and society would have to be rebuilt.

Summary

Two critical events, the end of the First World War and beginning of the Great Depression, marked the boundaries of the 1920s. In the war's aftermath, traditional customs and values weakened as the American people sought new forms of self-expression and gratification. A host of effects from science and technology—automobiles, electric appliances, and mass media, especially radio—touched the lives of rich and poor alike. Sports and movies made entertainment more accessible. Moreover, the decade's freewheeling consumerism enabled ordinary Americans to emulate wealthier people not only by purchasing more but also by trying to get rich through stock market speculation. The depression that followed the stock market crash stifled these habits, at least for a while. Overseas, meanwhile, U.S. administrations and humanitarian groups worked to preserve the peace even as they sought to expand America's global political and economic power.

Beneath the "new era" lurked two important phenomena rooted in previous eras. One was the continued prejudice and ethnic tensions that had long tainted the American dream. As Klansmen and immigration restrictionists made their voices heard, they encouraged discrimination against racial minorities and slurs against supposedly inferior ethnic groups. Meanwhile, the distinguishing forces of twentieth-century life—technological change, bureaucratization, mass culture, and growth of the middle class—accelerated, making the decade truly "new." Both phenomena would recur as major themes in the nation's history for the rest of the twentieth century.

Suggestions for Further Reading

Patrick Cohrs, *The Unfinished Peace After World War I: America, Britain and the Stabilization of Europe, 1919–1932* (2006)

Lynn Dumenil, *The Modern Temper: American Culture and Society in the 1920s* (1995)

Colin Grant, *Negro with a Hat: The Rise and Fall of Marcus Garvey* (2008)

Owen Gutfreund, *Twentieth-Century Sprawl: Highways and the Reshaping of the American Landscape* (2004)

Maury Klein, *Rainbow's End: The Crash of 1929* (2003)

Lisa McGirr, *The War on Alcohol: Prohibition and the Rise of the American State* (2016)

Nathan Miller, *New World Coming: The 1920s and the Making of Modern America* (2004)

Mae M. Ngai, *Impossible Subjects: Illegal Aliens and the Making of Modern America* (2004)

Martha L. Olney, *Buy Now, Pay Later: Advertising, Credit, and Consumer Durables in the 1920s* (1991)

Thomas R. Pegram, *One Hundred Percent American: The Rebirth and Decline of the Ku Klux Klan in the 1920s* (2011)

George Sanchez, *Becoming Mexican American: Ethnicity, Culture and Identity in Chicano Los Angeles, 1900–1945* (1993)

Susan Thistle, *From Marriage to the Market: The Transformation of Women's Lives and Work* (2006)

The Great Depression and the New Deal, 1929–1939

I n 1931, the rain stopped in the Great Plains. Montana and North Dakota became as arid as the Sonora Desert. Temperatures reached 115 degrees in Iowa. The soil baked. Farmers watched rich black dirt turn to gray dust.

Then the winds began to blow. Farmers had stripped the Plains of native grasses in the 1920s, using tractors to plow up fifty thousand acres of new land every day. Now, with nothing to hold the earth, it began to blow away. The dust storms began in 1934—and worsened in 1935. Dust obscured the noonday sun; some days it was pitch black at noon. Cattle, blinded by blowing grit, ran in circles until they died. A seven-year-old boy in Smith Center, Kansas, suffocated in a dust drift. Boiling clouds of dust filled the skies in parts of Kansas, Colorado, Oklahoma, Texas, and New Mexico—the Dust Bowl.

In late 1937, on a farm near Stigler, Oklahoma, Marvin Montgomery made a difficult decision. "The drought and such as that, it just got so hard," he told a congressional committee conducting hearings at a migratory labor camp in 1940. "I decided it would help me to change countries." So on December 29, 1937, Montgomery and his wife and four children loaded a secondhand Hudson automobile with their worldly goods—furniture, bedding, pots and pans—and headed for California.

The Montgomerys were not alone. At least a third of farms in the Dust Bowl were abandoned in the 1930s, and many families made the westward trek, lured by circulars and newspaper advertisements promising work in the fields of California. Some three hundred thousand people migrated to California in the 1930s. Most of these were not displaced and poverty-stricken farm

◀ This 1939 photograph, titled "Mother and Children on the Road," was taken in Tule Lake, California, by Farm Security Administration photographer Dorothea Lange. The FSA used photos like this one to build public support for New Deal programs to assist migrant workers and the rural poor. Library of Congress Prints and Photographs Division[LC-USF34-T01-020993-E]

Chronology

1929	■ Stock market crash (October); Great Depression begins
1930	■ Hawley-Smoot Tariff raises rates on imports ■ Motion Picture Production Code creates industry censorship of U.S. movies
1931	■ "Scottsboro Boys" arrested in Alabama
1932	■ Banks fail throughout nation ■ Bonus Army marches on Washington ■ Hoover's Reconstruction Finance Corporation tries to stabilize banks, insurance companies, railroads ■ Roosevelt elected president
1933	■ 13 million Americans unemployed ■ "First Hundred Days" of Roosevelt administration offer major legislation for economic recovery and poor relief ■ Adolf Hitler becomes chancellor of Germany
1934	■ Populist demagogues draw large following ■ Indian Reorganization (Wheeler-Howard) Act restores lands to tribal ownership
1935	■ The "Second New Deal" creates government programs to offer immediate relief, enhance economic security, and guarantee workers' right to organize ■ Congress passes first Neutrality Act
1936	■ 9 million Americans unemployed ■ United Auto Workers begin sit-down strike against General Motors
1937	■ Roosevelt's Court-packing plan fails ■ Memorial Day massacre of striking steelworkers ■ "Roosevelt recession" begins ■ Sino-Japanese War breaks out
1938	■ 10.4 million Americans unemployed ■ Munich Conference grants part of Czechoslovakia to Germany
1939	■ Marian Anderson performs at Lincoln Memorial ■ Germany invades Poland; Second World War begins

families like the Montgomerys; many were white-collar workers seeking better opportunities in California's cities. It was the plight of families like the Montgomerys, however, captured in federal government–sponsored Farm Security Administration (FSA) photographs and immortalized in John Steinbeck's best-selling 1938 novel *The Grapes of Wrath*, that came to represent the human suffering of the Great Depression.

The Montgomerys' trip was not easy. The family ran out of money somewhere in Arizona and worked in the cotton fields there for five weeks before they moved on. Once in California, "I hoed beets some; hoed some cotton, and I picked some spuds," Montgomery reported, but wages were low, and migrant families found little welcome. As they took over the agricultural labor formerly done by Mexicans and Mexican Americans, they learned that, by doing fieldwork, they had forfeited their "whiteness" in the eyes of many rural Californians. "Negroes and Okies upstairs," read a sign in a San Joaquin Valley movie theater.

Most migrants to rural California lived in squalid makeshift camps, but the Montgomerys were lucky. They got space in housing provided for farmworkers by the FSA. The FSA camp at Shafter in Kern County had 240 tents and 40 small houses. For nine months the Montgomery family of six lived in a fourteen-by-sixteen-foot tent, which rented for 10 cents a day plus four hours of volunteer labor a month. Then they proudly moved into an FSA house, "with water, lights, and everything, yes sir; and a little garden spot furnished." Montgomery, homesick for the farm, told the congressional committee that he hoped to return to Oklahoma, but his seventeen-year-old son, Harvey, saw a different future. "I like California," he said. "I would rather stay out here." And soon there were plentiful employment opportunities in California, not only for Harvey Montgomery but for many other newcomers, in aircraft factories and shipyards mobilizing for the Second World War.

Experience an interactive version of this story in MindTap®.

The Montgomerys' experience shows the human costs of the Great Depression, but statistics are necessary to give a sense of its magnitude. In the 1930s, as nations worldwide plunged into depression, the United States confronted a crisis of enormous proportions. Between 1929 and 1933, the gross national product was cut in half. Corporate profits fell from $10 billion to $1 billion; 100,000 businesses shut their doors altogether. Four million workers were unemployed in January 1930; by November, the number had jumped to 6 million. When President **Herbert Hoover** left office in 1933, 13 million Americans—about one-fourth of the labor force—were idle, and millions more worked only part time. There was no national safety net: no welfare system, no unemployment compensation, no Social Security. And as banks failed by the thousands, with no federally guaranteed deposit insurance, families' savings simply disappeared.

Herbert Hoover, who had been elected president in the prosperity and optimism of the late 1920s, looked first to private enterprise for solutions. By the end of his term, he had extended the federal government's role in managing an economic crisis further than any of his predecessors. Nonetheless, the depression deepened and Americans became increasingly desperate. In the United States the economic catastrophe exacerbated existing racial and class tensions, while in Germany it propelled **Adolf Hitler** to power. Although America's leaders did not really expect the United States to turn to fascism, they also knew that the German people had not anticipated Hitler's rise. By late 1932, the depression seemed more than just "hard times." Many feared it was a crisis of capitalism, even of democracy itself.

In 1932, voters replaced Hoover with a man who promised a New Deal and projected hope in a time of despair. **Franklin Delano Roosevelt** seemed willing to experiment, and although his scattershot approach did not end the economic depression (only the massive mobilization for World War II did that), New Deal programs did alleviate suffering. For the first time, the federal government assumed responsibility for the nation's economy and its citizens' welfare.

Although some Americans saw the depression crisis as an opportunity for major economic change—even revolution— New Deal programs did not fundamentally alter the existing capitalist system or the distribution of wealth. Roosevelt did not directly challenge legal segregation in the South, either— in part because he relied on the votes of southern white Democrats to pass New Deal legislation.

Despite its limits, the New Deal preserved America's democratic experiment through a time of uncertainty and crisis. By decade's end, the widening force of world war shifted America's focus from domestic to foreign policy. But the changes set in motion by the New Deal continued to transform the United States for decades to come.

- *How did economic hard times during the 1930s affect Americans, and what differences were there in the experiences of specific groups and regions?*

- *How and why did the power of the federal government expand during the Great Depression, and what were the successes and failures of the New Deal?*

- *How do the responses of the United States compare to those of other nations during the international crisis of the 1930s?*

22-1 Hard Times, 1929–1933

▶ **How did the Great Depression exacerbate discrimination against minority groups?**

▶ **How did the Great Depression impact lower- and middle-class workers?**

▶ **What methods did Herbert Hoover employ to address the economic crisis?**

▶ **How did Americans respond to the economic crisis of the Great Depression?**

By the early 1930s, as the depression continued to deepen, tens of millions of Americans were desperately poor. In the cities, hungry men and women lined up at soup kitchens. People survived on potatoes, crackers, or dandelion greens; some scratched through garbage cans for bits of food. In West Virginia and Kentucky, hunger was so widespread—and resources so limited— that the American Friends Service Committee distributed food only to those who were at least 10 percent below the normal weight for their height. In November 1932, *The Nation* told its readers that one-sixth of the American population risked starvation over the coming winter. Social workers in New York reported there was "no food at all" in the homes of many of the city's black children. In Albany, New York, a ten-year-old girl died of starvation in her elementary school classroom.

Families, unable to pay rent, were evicted. The new homeless poured into shantytowns, called

Herbert Hoover The thirty-first president of the United States, 1929–1933.

Adolf Hitler German chancellor and Nazi dictator whose efforts to restore his nation's prominence included a brutal program to purify it of Jews and others he deemed "inferior races."

Franklin Delano Roosevelt The thirty-second president of the United States (1933–1945).

"Hoovervilles" in ironic tribute to the formerly popular president. Over a million men took to the road or the rails in desperate search of any sort of work. Teenage boys and girls also left destitute families to strike out on their own. With uncertain futures, many young couples delayed marriage; the average age at marriage rose by more than two years during the 1930s. Married people put off having children, and in 1933 the birth rate sank below replacement rates. (Sales of condoms—at $1 per dozen—did not fall during the depression.) More than a quarter of women who were between the ages of twenty and thirty during the Great Depression never had children.

22-1a Farmers and Industrial Workers

Farmers were hit especially hard by the economic crisis. The agricultural sector, which employed almost one-quarter of American workers, had never shared in the good times of the 1920s. But as urbanites cut back on spending and foreign competitors dumped agricultural surpluses into the global market, farm prices hit rock bottom. Farmers tried to compensate for lower prices by producing more, thus adding to the surplus and depressing prices even further. By 1932, a bushel of wheat that cost North Dakota farmers 77 cents to produce brought only 33 cents. Throughout the nation, cash-strapped farmers could not pay their property taxes or mortgages. Banks, facing their own ruin, foreclosed. In Mississippi, it was reported in 1932, on a single day in April approximately one-fourth of all the farmland in the state was being auctioned off to meet debts. By the middle of the decade, the ecological crisis of the Dust Bowl would drive thousands of farmers from their land.

Unlike farmers, America's industrial workers had seen a slow but steady rise in their standard of living during the 1920s. In 1929, almost every urban American who wanted a job had one, and workers' spending on consumer goods had bolstered the nation's economic growth. But as Americans had less money to spend, sales of manufactured goods plummeted and factories closed—more than seventy thousand had gone out of business by 1933. As car sales dropped from 4.5 million in 1929 to 1 million in 1933, Ford laid off more than two-thirds of its Detroit workers. The remaining workers at U.S. Steel, America's first billion-dollar corporation, were put on "short hours"; the huge steel company had no full-time workers in 1933. Almost one-quarter of industrial workers were unemployed, and those who managed to hang onto a job saw the average wage fall by almost one-third.

22-1b Marginal Workers

For workers on the lowest rungs of the employment ladder, the depression was a crushing blow. In the South, where opportunities were already most limited for African Americans, jobs that many white men had considered below their dignity before the depression—street cleaner, bellhop, garbage collector—seemed suddenly desirable. In 1930, a short-lived fascist-style organization, the Black Shirts, recruited forty thousand members with the slogan "No Jobs for Niggers Until Every White Man Has a Job!" Northern blacks did not fare much better. As industry cut production, African Americans were the first fired. An Urban League survey of 106 cities found black unemployment rates averaged 30 to 60 percent higher than rates for whites. By 1932, African American unemployment reached almost 50 percent.

Mexican Americans and Mexican nationals trying to make a living in the American Southwest also felt the twin impacts of economic depression and racism. Their wages on California farms fell from a miserable 35 cents an hour in 1929 to a cruel 14 cents an hour by 1932. Throughout the Southwest, Anglo-Americans claimed that foreign workers were stealing their jobs. Campaigns against "foreigners" hurt not only Mexican immigrants but also American citizens of Hispanic descent whose families had lived in the Southwest for centuries, long before the land belonged to the United States. In 1931, the Labor Department announced plans to deport illegal immigrants to free jobs for American citizens. This policy fell hardest on people of Mexican origin. Even

◀ During the 1920s, farmers deep plowed land in the Great Plains, opening new farmland but destroying the deep-rooted grasses that had trapped moisture and held soil even when little rain fell. During the severe drought of the 1930s, soil turned to dust and, swept up by high winds, formed huge dark clouds—such as this dust storm in Baca County, Colorado.

Library of Congress Prints and Photographs Division[LC-USF34-001615-ZE]

those who had immigrated legally often lacked full documentation. Officials often ignored the fact that children born in the United States were U.S. citizens. The U.S. government officially deported 82,000 Mexicans between 1929 and 1935, but a much larger number—almost half a million people—repatriated to Mexico during the 1930s. Some left voluntarily, but many were coerced or tricked into believing they had no choice.

Even before the economic crisis, women of all classes and races were barred from many jobs and were paid significantly less than men. As the economy worsened, discrimination increased. Most Americans already believed that men should be breadwinners and women homemakers. With so many men unemployed, it was easy to believe that women who worked took jobs from men. In fact, men laid off from U.S. Steel would not likely have been hired as elementary schoolteachers, secretaries, "salesgirls," or maids. Nonetheless, when a 1936 Gallup poll asked whether wives should work if their husbands had jobs, 82 percent of the respondents (including 75 percent of the women) answered no. Such beliefs translated into policy. Of fifteen hundred urban school systems surveyed in 1930 and 1931, 77 percent refused to hire married women as teachers, and 63 percent fired female teachers who married while employed.

The depression had a mixed impact on women workers. At first, women lost jobs more quickly than men. Women in low-wage manufacturing jobs were laid off before male employees, who were presumed to be supporting families. Hard times hit domestic workers especially hard, as middle-class families economized by dispensing with household help. Almost one-quarter of women in domestic service—a high percentage of them African American—were unemployed by January 1931. And as jobs disappeared, women of color lost even these poorly paid positions to white women who were newly willing to do domestic labor. Despite discrimination and a poor economy, however, the number of women working outside the home rose during the 1930s. "Women's jobs," such as teaching, clerical work, and switchboard operating, were not hit as hard as "men's jobs" in heavy industry, and women—including married women who previously did not work for wages—increasingly sought employment to keep their families afloat during hard times. Still, by 1940, only 15.2 percent of married women worked outside the home.

22-1c Middle-Class Workers and Families

Although unemployment rates climbed to 25 percent, most Americans did not lose their homes or their jobs during the depression. Professional and white-collar workers did not fare as badly as industrial workers and farmers. Many middle-class families, however, while never hungry or homeless, "made do" with less. "Use it up, wear it out, make it do, or do without," the saying went, and middle-class women cut back on household expenses by canning food or making their own clothes. Newspapers offered imaginative suggestions for cooking cheap cuts of meat ("Liverburgers") or for

▲ As the economic depression deepened, manufacturers of consumer goods struggled to sell their products and stay in business. Americans had less money to spend, and even those who were economically secure sought to make dollars stretch further. Here, a woman browses through sale ads in her newspaper.

using "extenders," cheap ingredients to make food go further ("Cracker-Stuffed Cabbage"). Although most families' incomes fell, the impact was cushioned by the falling cost of consumer goods, especially food. In early 1933, for example, a cafe in Omaha offered a ten-course meal, complete with a rose for ladies and a cigar for gentlemen, for 60 cents.

As housewives scrambled to make do, men who could no longer provide well for their families often blamed themselves for their "failures." But even for the relatively affluent, the psychological impact of the depression was inescapable. The human toll of the depression was visible everywhere, and no one took economic security for granted anymore. Suffering was never equal, but all Americans had to contend with years of uncertainty and with fears about the future of their family and their nation.

22-1d Hoover's Limited Solutions

Although Herbert Hoover, "the Great Engineer," had a reputation as a problem solver, the economic crisis was not easily solved, and no one, including Hoover, really knew what to do. Experts and leaders disagreed about the causes of the depression, and they disagreed about the proper course of action as well. Many prominent business leaders believed that financial panics and depressions, no matter how painful, were part of a natural and ultimately beneficial "business cycle." Economic depressions, according to this theory, brought down inflated prices and cleared the way for real economic growth. Herbert Hoover disagreed. "The economic fatalist," he said, "believes that these crises are inevitable. . . . I would remind these pessimists that exactly the same thing was once said of typhoid, cholera, and smallpox." Hoover put his faith in a voluntary system of "associationalism," in which the federal government coordinated efforts of business and professional organizations to solve the nation's economic problems by crafting programs that state and local governments, along with private industry, could then choose—voluntarily—to implement.

While many Americans thought that Hoover was doing nothing to fight the economic downturn, in truth he stretched his core beliefs about the proper role of government to their limit. He tried voluntarism, exhortation, and limited government intervention. First, he sought voluntary pledges from hundreds of business groups to keep wages stable and renew economic investment. But when individual business-people looked at their own bottom lines, few could live up to those promises.

As unemployment climbed, Hoover continued to encourage voluntary responses to mounting need, creating the President's Organization on Unemployment Relief (POUR) to generate private contributions to aid the destitute. Although 1932 saw record charitable contributions, they were nowhere near adequate. By mid-1932, one-quarter of New York's private charities, funds exhausted, had closed their doors. Atlanta's Central Relief Committee could provide only $1.30 per family per week to those seeking help. State and city officials found their treasuries drying up, too. Hoover, however, held firm. "It is not the function of the government to relieve individuals of their responsibilities to their neighbors," he insisted.

Hoover feared that government "relief" would destroy the spirit of self-reliance among the poor. Thus, he authorized federal funds to feed the drought-stricken livestock of Arkansas farmers but rejected a smaller grant to provide food for impoverished farm families. Many Americans were becoming angry at Hoover's seeming insensitivity. When Hoover, trying to restore confidence to the increasingly anxious nation, said, "What this country needs is a good big laugh. . . . If someone could get off a good joke every ten days, I think our troubles would be over," the resulting jokes were not exactly what he had in mind. "Business is improving," one man tells another. "Is Hoover dead?" asks his companion. In the two short years since his election, Hoover had become the most hated man in America.

Hoover eventually endorsed limited federal action to combat the economic crisis, but it was much too little. Federal public works projects, such as the Grand Coulee Dam in Washington, created some jobs. Hoover also signed into law the Hawley-Smoot Tariff (1930), which was meant to support American farmers and manufacturers by raising import duties on foreign goods to a staggering 40 percent. Instead, it hampered international trade as other nations created their own protective tariffs. And as other nations sold fewer goods to the United States, they had less money to repay their U.S. debts or buy American products. Exports of American merchandise continued to slide, falling by more than half from their pre-Great Depression high of $5.2 billion. Fearing the collapse of the international monetary system, Hoover in 1931 announced a moratorium on the payment of First World War debts and reparations.

In January 1932, the administration took its most forceful action, creating the **Reconstruction Finance Corporation (RFC)** to provide federal loans to banks, insurance companies, and railroads, an action Hoover hoped would shore up those industries and halt the disinvestment in the American economy. Here, Hoover had compromised his ideological principles. This was direct government intervention, not "voluntarism." If he would support direct assistance to private industries, why not direct relief to the millions of unemployed?

22-1e Protest and Social Unrest

More and more Americans were asking that question. Although most people met the crisis with bewilderment or quiet despair, social unrest grew as the depression deepened. In scattered incidents, farmers and unemployed workers took direct action against what they saw as the causes of their plight. Others lashed out in anger, scapegoating those even weaker than themselves. Increasing violence raised the specter of popular revolt, and Chicago mayor Anton Cermak told Congress that if the federal government did not send his citizens aid, it would have to send troops instead.

Throughout the nation, tens of thousands of farmers took the law into their own hands. Angry crowds forced auctioneers to accept just a few dollars for foreclosed property, and then returned it to the original owners. In August 1932, a new group, the Farmers' Holiday Association, encouraged farmers to take a "holiday"—to hold back agricultural products to limit supply and drive prices up. In the Midwest, farmers barricaded roads with spiked logs and telegraph poles to stop other farmers' trucks, and then dumped the contents in roadside ditches.

In cities, the most militant actions came from Unemployed Councils, local groups similar to unions for unemployed workers that were created and led by Communist Party members. Communist leaders believed the depression demonstrated capitalism's failure and offered an opportunity for revolution. Few of the quarter-million Americans who joined the local Unemployed Councils sought revolution, but they did demand action. "Fight, Don't Starve," read banners in a Chicago demonstration. Demonstrations often turned ugly. When three thousand members of Detroit Unemployment Councils marched on Ford's River Rouge plant in 1932, Ford security guards opened fire on the crowd, killing four men and wounding fifty. Battles between protesters and police broke out in cities from the East Coast to the West Coast but rarely were covered as national news.

As social unrest spread, so, too, did racial violence. For example, vigilante committees offered bounties to force

Reconstruction Finance Corporation (RFC) Agency set up under the Hoover administration during the Great Depression to make loans to shore up banks and other industries.

African American workers off the Illinois Central Railroad's payroll: $25 for maiming and $100 for killing black workers. Ten men were murdered and at least seven more wounded. The Ku Klux Klan also gained strength. Thirty-eight black men were tortured, hanged, and mutilated by white mobs in the early years of the Great Depression, while local authorities prevented more than a hundred attempted lynchings. Racial violence was not restricted to the South; lynchings also took place in Pennsylvania, Minnesota, Colorado, and Ohio.

22-1f Bonus Army

The worst public confrontation shook the nation in the summer of 1932. More than fifteen thousand unemployed World War I veterans and their families converged on the nation's capital as Congress debated a bill authorizing immediate payment of cash "bonuses" that veterans had been scheduled to receive in 1945. Calling themselves the Bonus Expeditionary Force, or Bonus Army, they set up a sprawling "Hooverville" shantytown just across the river from the Capitol. Concerned about the impact on the federal budget, President Hoover opposed the bonus bill, and after much debate the Senate voted it down.

Most of the Bonus Marchers left Washington after this defeat, but several thousand stayed on. Some were simply destitute, with nowhere to go; others stayed to press their case. The president called them "insurrectionists" and set a deadline for their departure. On July 28, Hoover sent in the U.S. Army, led by General Douglas MacArthur. Four infantry companies, four troops of cavalry, a machine gun squadron, and six tanks converged on the veterans and their families. What followed shocked the nation. Men and women were chased down by horsemen; children were tear-gassed; shacks were set afire. The next day, newspapers carried photographs of U.S. troops attacking their own citizens. Hoover was unrepentant, insisting in a campaign speech, "Thank God we still have a government that knows how to deal with a mob."

While desperation-driven social unrest raised fears of revolution, some saw an even greater danger in the growing disillusionment with democracy itself. As the depression worsened, the appeal of a strong leader—someone who would take decisive action, unencumbered by constitutionally mandated checks and balances—grew. In early 1933, media magnate William Randolph Hearst released the film *Gabriel over the White House*, in which a political hack of a president is possessed by the archangel Gabriel and, divinely inspired, assumes dictatorial powers to end the misery of the Great Depression. More significantly, in February 1933, the U.S. Senate passed a resolution calling for newly elected president Franklin D. Roosevelt to assume "unlimited power." The rise to power of Hitler and his National Socialist Party in depression-ravaged Germany was an obvious parallel, adding to the sense of crisis that would come to a head in early 1933.

▲ In the summer of 1932, unemployed veterans of the First World War demanded Congress authorize early payment of promised soldiers' bonuses. This cartoon shows the "Bonus Expeditionary Forces"—doctors, laborers, farmers, merchants, "Americans All"—marching to seek "Justice" in Washington, D.C.

22-2 Franklin D. Roosevelt and the Launching of the New Deal

▸ What actions did Franklin D. Roosevelt take to address the banking crisis?

▸ How did New Deal programs seek to institute economic recovery in industry and agriculture?

▸ What attitudes and practices guided the federal government when providing relief for workers?

▸ How did the Great Depression impact U.S. foreign policy and international relations?

In the presidential campaign of 1932, voters were presented with a clear choice. In the face of the Great Depression, incumbent Herbert Hoover held to a platform of limited federal intervention. Democratic challenger Franklin Delano Roosevelt insisted that the federal government had to play a much greater role. He supported direct relief payments for the unemployed, declaring that such governmental aid was not charity but instead "a matter of social duty." He pledged "a new deal for the American people." During the campaign, he was never very explicit about the outlines of his New Deal. His most concrete proposals, in fact, were sometimes contradictory

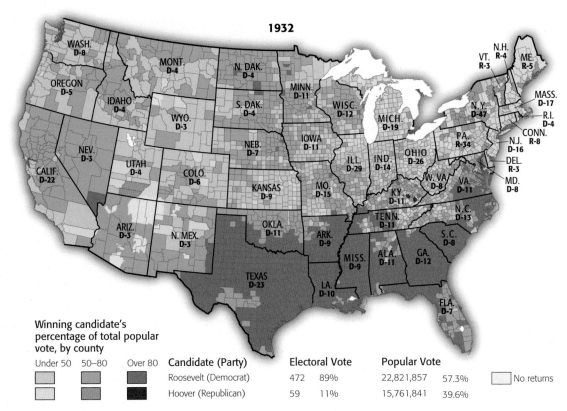

1932

Winning candidate's
percentage of total popular
vote, by county

Under 50	50–80	Over 80	Candidate (Party)	Electoral Vote		Popular Vote			No returns
			Roosevelt (Democrat)	472	89%	22,821,857	57.3%		
			Hoover (Republican)	59	11%	15,761,841	39.6%		

Map 22.1 Presidential Election, 1932

One factor above all decided the 1932 presidential election: the Great Depression. Roosevelt won 42 states and Hoover 6.

(in a nation without national news media, this was less a problem than it would be today). But all understood that he had committed to use the power of the federal government to combat the economic crisis that was paralyzing the nation. Voters chose Roosevelt over Hoover overwhelmingly: 22.8 million to 15.8 million in the popular vote (see Map 22.1).

Franklin Roosevelt, the twentieth-century president most beloved by America's "common people," had been born into a world of old money and upper-class privilege. The talented son of a politically prominent family, he seemed destined for political success. After graduating from Harvard College and Columbia Law School, he had married **Eleanor Roosevelt**, Theodore Roosevelt's niece and his own fifth cousin, once removed. He served in the New York State legislature; was appointed assistant secretary of the navy by Woodrow Wilson; and at the age of thirty-eight, ran for vice president in 1920 on the Democratic Party's losing ticket.

Then, in 1921, Roosevelt was stricken with polio. For two years he was bedridden, fighting one of the most feared diseases of the early twentieth century. He lost the use of his legs but gained, according to his wife Eleanor, a new strength of character that would serve him well as he reached out to depression-scarred America. As

Eleanor Roosevelt Widely popular and influential—and sometimes controversial—First Lady of the United States from 1933 to 1945.

Roosevelt explained it, "If you had spent two years in bed trying to wiggle your big toe, after that anything would seem easy." By 1928, Roosevelt was sufficiently recovered to run for—and win—the governorship of New York and then to accept the Democratic Party's presidential nomination in 1932.

Elected in November 1932, Roosevelt would not take office until March 4, 1933. (The Twentieth Amendment to the Constitution—the so-called Lame Duck Amendment, ratified in 1933—shifted all future inaugurations to January 20.) In this long interregnum, the American banking system reached the verge of collapse.

22-2a Banking Crisis

The origins of the banking crisis lay in the flush years of World War I and the 1920s, when American banks made countless risky loans. After real estate and stock market bubbles burst in 1929 and agricultural prices collapsed, many of these loans went bad, leaving many banks without sufficient funds to cover their customers' deposits. Depositors, afraid of losing their savings in a bank collapse, pulled money out of banks and put it into gold or under mattresses. "Bank runs," in which crowds of angry, frightened customers lined up to demand their money, became a common sight in economically ravaged towns throughout the nation. By Roosevelt's inauguration on March 4, every state in the Union had either suspended banking operations or restricted depositors' access to their money. The new president understood that this was more than a test of his administration. The total collapse of the U.S. banking system would threaten the nation's survival.

Roosevelt (who reportedly saw the film *Gabriel over the White House* several times before his inauguration) used his inaugural address to promise the American people decisive action. Standing in a cold rain on the Capitol steps, he vowed to face the crisis "frankly and boldly." The lines we best remember from his speech are words of comfort: "Let me assert my firm belief," the new president told the thousands gathered on the Capitol grounds and the millions gathered around their radios, "that the only thing we have to fear is fear itself—nameless, unreasoning, unjustified terror." But the only loud cheers that day came when Roosevelt proclaimed that, if need be, "I shall ask the Congress for the one remaining instrument to meet the crisis—broad Executive power to wage a war against the emergency, as great as the power that would be given to me if we were in fact invaded by a foreign foe."

The next day Roosevelt, using powers legally granted by the World War I Trading with the Enemy Act, closed the nation's banks for a four-day "holiday" and summoned Congress to an emergency session. He immediately introduced the Emergency Banking Relief Bill, which was passed sight unseen by unanimous House vote, approved 73 to 7 in the Senate, and signed into law the same day. This bill provided federal authority to reopen solvent banks and reorganize the rest, and authorized federal money to shore up private banks. In his inaugural address, Roosevelt had attacked "unscrupulous money changers," and many critics of the failed banking system had hoped he planned to remove the banks from private hands. Instead, as one North Dakota congressman complained, "the President drove the money changers out of the Capitol on March 4th and they were all back on the 9th." Roosevelt's banking policy was much like Hoover's—a fundamentally conservative approach that upheld the status quo.

The banking bill could save the U.S. banking system only if Americans were confident enough to deposit money in the reopened banks. So Roosevelt, in the first of his radio "Fireside Chats," asked the support of the American people. "We have provided the machinery to restore our financial system," he said. "It is up to you to support and make it work." The next morning, when the banks opened their doors, people lined up—but this time, most waited to deposit money. It was an enormous triumph for the new president. It also demonstrated that Roosevelt, though unafraid to take bold action, was not as radical as some wished or as others feared.

22-2b First Hundred Days

During the ninety-nine-day-long special session of Congress, dubbed by journalists "The First Hundred Days," the federal government took on dramatically new roles. Roosevelt, aided by a group of advisers—lawyers, university professors, and social workers, who were collectively nicknamed "the

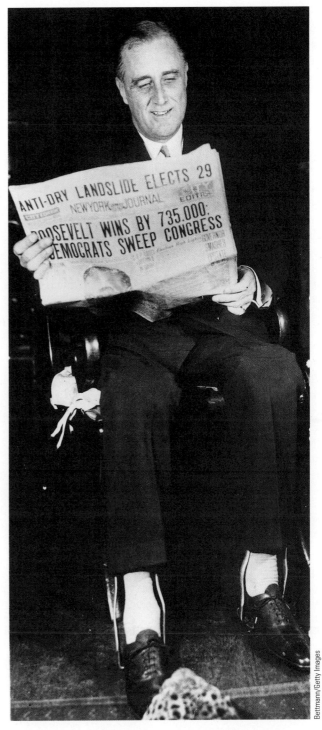

▲ In November 1930, Franklin D. Roosevelt (1882–1945) read the good news. Reelected governor of New York by 735,000 votes, he immediately became a leading contender for the Democratic presidential nomination. Notice Roosevelt's leg braces, rarely shown because of an unwritten agreement by photographers to shoot him from the waist up.

Bettmann/Getty Images

Brain Trust"—and by the enormously capable First Lady, set out to revive the American economy. These "New Dealers" had no single, coherent plan, and Roosevelt's economic policies fluctuated between attempts to balance the budget and massive deficit spending (spending more than is taken in in taxes and borrowing the difference). But with a strong mandate for action and the support of a Democrat-controlled Congress, the new administration produced a flood of legislation. The first priority was economic recovery. Two basic strategies emerged during the First Hundred Days. New Dealers experimented with national economic planning, and they created a range of "relief" programs to help those in need.

22-2c National Industrial Recovery Act

At the heart of the New Deal experiment in planning were the **National Industrial Recovery Act (NIRA)** and the Agricultural Adjustment Act (AAA). The NIRA was based on the belief that "destructive competition" had worsened industry's economic woes. Skirting antitrust regulation, the NIRA authorized competing businesses to cooperate in crafting industrywide codes. Thus, for example, automobile manufacturers would cooperate to limit production, establish industrywide prices, and set workers' wages. Competition among manufacturers would no longer drive down prices and wages. With wages and prices stabilized, the theory went, consumer spending would increase, thus allowing industries to rehire workers. Significantly, Section 7(a) guaranteed industrial workers the right to "organize and bargain collectively"—in other words, to unionize.

Individual businesses' participation in this program, administered by the **National Recovery Administration (NRA)**, was voluntary—with one catch. Businesses that adhered to the industrywide codes could display the Blue Eagle, the NRA symbol; the government urged consumers to boycott businesses that did not fly the Blue Eagle. This voluntary program, though larger in scale than any previous government–private sector cooperation, was not very different from Hoover-era "associationalism."

From the beginning, the NRA faced serious problems. As small-business owners had feared, big business easily dominated the NRA-mandated cartels. NRA staff lacked the training and experience to stand up to the representatives of corporate America. The twenty-six-year-old NRA staffer who oversaw the creation of the petroleum industry code was "helped" by twenty highly-paid oil industry lawyers. The majority of the 541 codes eventually approved by the NRA reflected the interests of major corporations, not small-business owners, labor, or consumers. Most fundamentally, the NRA did not deliver economic recovery. In 1935, the Supreme Court put an end to the fragile, floundering system. Using an old-fashioned (what Roosevelt called a "horse-and-buggy") definition of interstate commerce, the Supreme Court found that the NRA extended federal power past its constitutional bounds.

22-2d Agricultural Adjustment Act

The **Agricultural Adjustment Act (AAA)** had a more enduring effect on the United States. Establishing a national system of crop controls, the AAA offered subsidies to farmers who agreed to limit production of specific crops. (Overproduction drove crop prices down.) But to reduce production in 1933, the nation's farmers agreed to destroy 8.5 million piglets and to plow under crops in the fields. Although limiting production did raise agricultural prices, millions of hungry Americans found it difficult to understand the economic theory behind this waste of food.

Government crop subsidies had unintended consequences: they were a disaster for tenant farmers and sharecroppers, for as landlords cut production they turned tenant farmers off their land. In the South, the number of sharecropper farms dropped by almost one-third between 1930 and 1940 and dispossessed farmers—many of them African American—headed to cities and towns. But the subsidies did help many. In the depression-ravaged Dakotas, for example, government payments accounted for almost three-quarters of the total farm income for 1934.

In 1936, the Supreme Court found that the AAA, like the NRA, was unconstitutional. But the AAA (unlike the NRA) was too popular with its constituency—American farmers—to disappear. The legislation was rewritten to meet the Supreme Court's objections, and farm subsidies continue into the twenty-first century.

22-2e Relief Programs

With millions of Americans in desperate poverty, Roosevelt also moved quickly to implement poor relief: $3 billion in federal aid was allocated in 1935. New Dealers, however—like many other Americans—disapproved of direct relief payments. "Give a man a dole and you save his body and destroy his spirit; give him a job and pay him an assured wage and you save both the body and the spirit," wrote Harry Hopkins, Roosevelt's trusted adviser and head of the president's major relief agency, the Federal Emergency Relief Administration (FERA). Thus New Deal programs emphasized "work relief." By January 1934, the Civil Works Administration had hired 4 million people, most earning $15 a week. And the **Civilian Conservation Corps (CCC)** paid unmarried young men (young women were not eligible) $1 a day to do hard outdoor labor: building dams and reservoirs, creating trails in national parks. The program was segregated by race but brought together young men from very different backgrounds. By 1942, the CCC had employed 2.5 million men, including 80,000 American Indians who worked on western Indian reservations.

National Industrial Recovery Act (NIRA) Agency that brought together business leaders to draft codes of "fair competition" for their industries.

National Recovery Administration (NRA) Agency that established industrywide codes authorized by NIRA and which oversaw individual businesses' voluntary adherence to them. The program was struck down by the Supreme Court in 1935.

Agricultural Adjustment Act (AAA) New Deal program that sought to curb the surplus farm production that depressed crop prices by offering farmers payments for reducing production of seven farm products.

Civilian Conservation Corps (CCC) Government relief program that employed jobless young men in such projects as reforestation, park maintenance, and erosion control.

Table 22.1 New Deal Achievements

Year	Labor	Agriculture and Environment	Business and Industrial Recovery	Relief	Reform
1933	Section 7(a) of NIRA	Agricultural Adjustment Act Farm Credit Act	Emergency Banking Relief Act Economy Act Beer-Wine Revenue Act Banking Act of 1933 (guaranteed deposits) National Industrial Recovery Act	Civilian Conservation Corps Federal Emergency Relief Act Home Owners Refinancing Act Public Works Administration Civil Works Administration	TVA Federal Securities Act
1934	National Labor Relations Board	Taylor Grazing Act			Securities Exchange Act Reciprocal Trade Agreements Act Export-Import Bank
1935	National Labor Relations (Wagner) Act	Resettlement Administration Rural Electrification Administration		Works Progress Administration National Youth Administration	Social Security Act Public Utility Holding Company Act Revenue Act (wealth tax)
1937		Farm Security Administration		National Housing Act	
1938	Fair Labor Standards Act	Agricultural Adjustment Act of 1938			

Source: Adapted from Charles Sellers, Henry May, and Neil R. McMillen, *A Synopsis of American History,* 6th ed. Copyright © 1985 by Houghton Mifflin Company. Reprinted by permission.

Work relief programs rarely addressed the needs of poor women. Mothers of young children were usually classified as "unemployable" and were offered relief instead of jobs. But in North Carolina, for example, the "mother's-aid" grant was one-sixth of the wage paid in a federal works program. While federal relief programs rejected the poor-law tradition that distinguished between the "deserving" and the "undeserving" poor, local officials often did not. As journalist Lorena Hickok reported to Harry Hopkins, "a woman who isn't a good housekeeper is apt to have a pretty rough time of it. And heaven help the family in which there is any 'moral problem.'"

The **Public Works Administration (PWA)**, created by Title II of the National Industrial Recovery Act, used public funds to create jobs for men in the construction industry and building trades. In 1933, Congress appropriated $3.3 billion—or 165 percent of federal revenues for that year—to New Deal public works programs that would strengthen the nation's infrastructure. PWA workers built the Triborough Bridge in New York City, the Grand River Dam in Oklahoma, school buildings in almost half of the nation's counties, and most of the new sewer systems created during the depression years.

The special session of Congress, convened by FDR in March, adjourned on June 16, 1933, having passed fifteen major pieces of legislation (see Table 22.1). In just over three months, the United States had rebounded from near collapse, returning (in columnist Walter Lippmann's words) from a collection of "disorderly panic-stricken mobs and factions" to "an organized nation confident of our power to provide for our own security and to control our own destiny." And as New Deal programs continued to be passed and implemented, unemployment fell steadily from 13 million in 1933 to 9 million in 1936, farm prices rose, along with wages and salaries, and business failures abated (see Figure 22.1).

Public Works Administration (PWA) New Deal relief agency that appropriated $3.3 billion for large-scale public works projects to provide jobs and stimulate the economy.

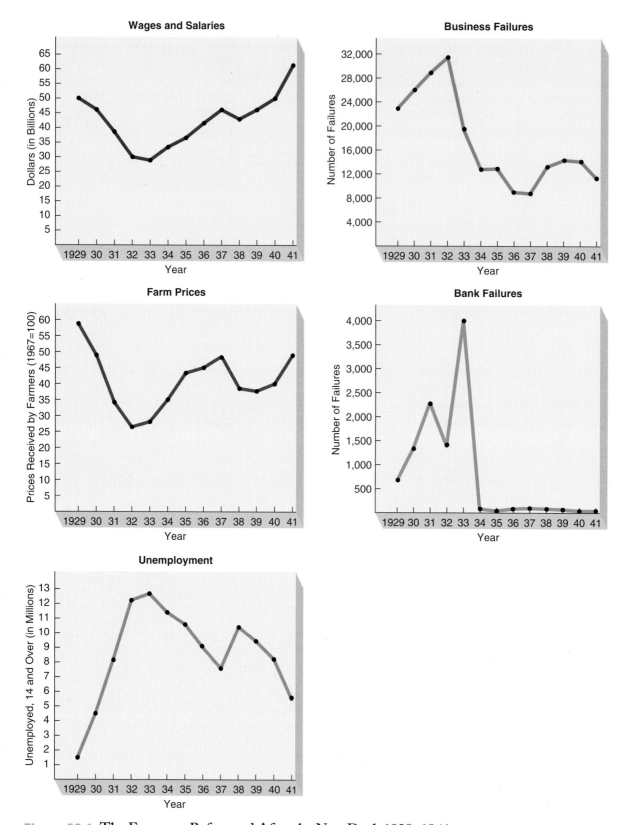

Figure 22.1 **The Economy Before and After the New Deal, 1929–1941**

The New Deal reduced bank closings, business failures, and unemployment, and it increased farm prices, wages, and salaries. Some of the nation's most persistent economic problems, however, did not disappear until the advent of the Second World War.

22-2f Lowering Tariffs

Internationally, meanwhile, the Roosevelt administration worked to expand trade. Increased trade, Secretary of State Cordell Hull insisted, would not only help the United States pull itself out of the economic doldrums but also boost the chances for global peace. Calling the protective tariff the "king of evils," he successfully pressed Congress to pass the Reciprocal Trade Agreements Act in 1934. This important legislation empowered the president to reduce U.S. tariffs by as much as 50 percent through special agreements with foreign countries. The central feature of the act was the most-favored-nation principle, whereby the United States was entitled to the lowest tariff rate set by any nation with which it had an agreement. If, for example, Belgium and the United States granted each other most-favored-nation status, and Belgium then negotiated an agreement with Germany that reduced the Belgian tariff on German typewriters, American typewriters would receive the same low rate.

In 1934, Hull also helped create the Export-Import Bank, a government agency that provided loans to foreigners for the purchase of American goods. The bank stimulated trade and became a diplomatic weapon, allowing the United States to exact concessions through the approval or denial of loans. But in the short term, Hull's ambitious programs—examples of America's independent internationalism—brought only mixed results.

22-2g U.S. Recognition of the Soviet Union

Economic imperatives also lay behind another major foreign policy decision in these years: the move by the Roosevelt administration to extend diplomatic recognition to the Soviet Union. Throughout the 1920s, the Republicans had refused to open diplomatic relations with the Soviet government, which had failed to pay $600 million for confiscated American-owned property and had repudiated preexisting Russian debts. To many Americans, the communists ranked as godless, radical malcontents bent on destroying the American way of life through world revolution. Nonetheless, in the late 1920s U.S. businesses such as General Electric and International Harvester entered the Soviet marketplace, and Henry Ford signed a contract to build an automobile plant there. By 1930 the Soviet Union had become the largest buyer of American farm and industrial equipment.

Upon entering the White House, Roosevelt concluded that nonrecognition had failed to alter the Soviet system, and he speculated that closer Soviet-American relations might help the economy and also deter Japanese expansion. In 1933, Roosevelt granted U.S. diplomatic recognition to the Soviet Union in return for Soviet agreement to discuss the debts question and to grant Americans in the Soviet Union religious freedom and legal rights.

22-2h Good Neighbor Policy

In Latin America, too, Roosevelt moved to reorient the direction of U.S. policy. He pledged that the United States would be a **"Good Neighbor,"** by which he meant in essence that Washington would be less blatant in its domination—less willing to defend exploitative business practices, less eager to launch military expeditions, and less reluctant to consult with Latin Americans. The policy was not without effect—in Mexico, for example, Roosevelt showed a level of restraint that his predecessors lacked. Overall, though, his administration continued to support and bolster dictators in the region, believing they would promote stability and preserve U.S. economic interests. ("He may be an S.O.B.," Roosevelt supposedly remarked of the Dominican Republic's ruthless leader Rafael Leonidas Trujillo, "but he is our S.O.B.") And when a revolution brought a radical government to power in Cuba in 1933, FDR proved unwilling to let the matter be. Although he refrained from sending U.S. ground troops to Cuba, he instructed the American ambassador in Havana to work with conservative Cubans to replace the new government with a regime more friendly to U.S. interests. With Washington's support, army sergeant Fulgencio Batista took power in 1934.

22-3 Political Pressure and the Second New Deal

▶ **Which groups of Americans opposed the New Deal, and why?**

▶ **Who proposed alternative ways to address the economic crisis, and what did those programs have in common?**

▶ **How did the programs of the Second New Deal seek to meet Americans' demands for relief and social justice?**

Roosevelt's New Deal had enjoyed unprecedented popular and congressional support, but that would not last. The seeming unity of the First Hundred Days masked deep divides within the nation, and once the immediate crisis was averted, the struggle over solutions began in earnest. As some tried to stop the expansion of government power, others pushed for increased governmental action to combat continuing poverty and inequality. Pressure came from all directions as the president considered the next phase of New Deal action.

22-3a Business Opposition

As the economy partially recovered, many wealthy business leaders started publicly criticizing the New Deal. They condemned budget-busting government spending for relief and jobs programs, as well as the regulations and rising taxes that affected them directly. In 1934, several corporate leaders joined with former presidential candidate Al Smith and disaffected conservative Democrats to establish the American Liberty League, an economically conservative organization that waged a highly visible campaign against New Deal "radicalism." Attempting to

"Good Neighbor" Implemented by President Roosevelt, this Latin American policy stated that no nation had the right to intervene in the affairs of another; it replaced direct U.S. intervention with diplomacy and support for various leaders, businesses, and programs.

CANADA

Ottawa ✪

ATLANTIC OCEAN

UNITED STATES

• San Francisco

40°N

Washington, D.C. ✪ — Roosevelt's Good Neighbor Policy, 1933

U.S. troops, 1917–1922
U.S. investors dominate sugar industry
Revolution of 1933
U.S. abrogates Platt Amendment, 1934
Batista era, 1934–1959

U.S. upholds right of intervention at Pan American Conference, 1928

U.S. troops, 1915–1934
Financial supervision, 1916–1941

MEXICO

Gulf of Mexico

Miami •

THE BAHAMAS
✪ Nassau

Constitution of 1917 challenges U.S. interests
Nationalization of foreign oil companies, 1938
U.S.-Mexico agreement settles oil dispute, 1942

✪ Havana

CUBA
Guantánamo •

U.S. financial supervision, 1905–1941
U.S. troops withdrawn, 1924
Trujillo era, 1930–1961

DOMINICAN REP.

San Juan

VIRGIN IS. (U.S./U.K.)

✪ Mexico City

Belmopan ✪ Kingston
BELIZE **JAMAICA** **HAITI** ✪

Santo Domingo

PUERTO RICO (U.S.)

U.S. colony since 1917

GUATEMALA ✪
Guatemala City ✪
San Salvador ✪
HONDURAS
✪ Tegucigalpa
Port-au-Prince

Caribbean Sea

U.S. colony
Jones Act grants U.S. citizenship, 1917

EL SALVADOR
NICARAGUA
✪ Managua

COSTA RICA
✪ San José

U.S. invasion, 1924
United Fruit Company active

PANAMA
✪ Panama

✪ Caracas

VENEZUELA

GUYANA
✪ Georgetown

SURINAME
• Cayenne
— **FRENCH GUIANA (Fr.)**

U.S. financial supervision, 1911–1924
U.S. military occupation, 1912–1925
U.S. war against Sandino, 1926–1933
Somoza era, 1936–1979

✪ Bogotá

COLOMBIA

Paramaribo

U.S. control of Canal Zone
Declaration of Panama, 1939

✪ Quito

ECUADOR

SURINAME

Equator – 0°

U.S. oil investments

Amazon R.

PACIFIC OCEAN

PERU

Lima ✪

BRAZIL

BOLIVIA
✪ La Paz

✪ Brasília

20°S

U.S. copper interests

Paraná R.

PARAGUAY
✪ Asunción

N

CHILE

URUGUAY

Santiago ✪

Buenos Aires ✪ ✪ Montevideo

ARGENTINA

U.S. votes for nonintervention pledge at Pan-American Conference, 1936

40°S

40°W

0   500   1000 Km.

0   500   1000 Mi.

80°W   60°W

Map 22.2 The United States and Latin America Between the Wars

The United States often intervened in other nations to maintain its hegemonic power in Latin America, where nationalists resented outside meddling in their sovereign affairs. The Good Neighbor policy decreased U.S. military interventions, but U.S. economic interests remained strong in the hemisphere.

splinter the Democratic Party by turning southern whites against the New Deal, the Liberty League also secretly channeled funds to a racist group in the South that circulated pictures of the First Lady with African Americans.

22-3b Demagogues and Populists

While many prominent business leaders fought the New Deal, other Americans (sometimes called "populists") thought the government favored business too much and paid too little attention to the needs of the common people. Unemployment had decreased—but 9 million people were still without work. In 1934, 1.5 million workers went on strike. In 1935, enormous dust storms enveloped the southern plains, killing livestock and driving families like the Montgomerys from their land. Millions of Americans still suffered. As their dissatisfaction mounted, so, too, did the appeal of various demagogues, who played to the prejudices and unreasoning passions of the people.

Father Charles Coughlin, a Roman Catholic priest whose weekly radio sermons reached up to 30 million listeners, spoke to those who felt they had lost control of their lives to distant elites and impersonal forces. Increasingly anti–New Deal, he was also increasingly anti-Semitic, telling his listeners that an international conspiracy of Jewish bankers caused their problems.

Another challenge came from Dr. Francis E. Townsend, a public health officer in Long Beach, California, who was thrown out of work at age sixty-seven with only $100 in savings. His situation was not unusual. With social welfare left to the states, only about 400,000 of the 6.6 million elderly Americans received any sort of state-supplied pension, and many lost both jobs and savings during the depression. Townsend proposed that Americans over the age of sixty should receive a government pension of $200 a month, financed by a new "transaction" (sales) tax. In fact, this plan was fiscally impossible (almost three-quarters of working Americans earned $200 a month or less) and profoundly regressive (because sales tax rates are the same for everyone, they take a larger share of income from those who earn the least). Nonetheless, 20 million Americans, or 1 in 5 adults—concerned about the plight of the elderly and not about details of funding—signed petitions supporting this plan.

Then there was Huey Long, perhaps the most successful populist demagogue in American history. Long was elected governor of Louisiana in 1928 with the slogan "Every Man a King, But No One Wears a Crown." As a U.S. senator, Long initially supported the New Deal but soon decided that Roosevelt had fallen captive to big business. Long countered in 1934 with the Share Our Wealth Society. Declaring that no family needed more than $5 million, he argued that the government should take any wealth over that amount, along with any income beyond $1 million a year, and use those funds to give each American family an annual income of $2,000 and a one-time homestead allowance of $5,000. (Long's plan was fiscally impossible but definitely not regressive.) By mid-1935, Long's movement claimed 7 million members, and few doubted that he aspired to the presidency. But Long was killed by a bodyguard's bullet during an assassination attempt in September 1935.

22-3c Left-Wing Critics

The political left also gained ground as hard times continued. Socialists and communists alike criticized the New Deal for trying to save capitalism instead of working to lessen the inequality of power and wealth in American society. In California, muckraker and socialist Upton Sinclair won the Democratic gubernatorial nomination in 1934 with the slogan "End Poverty in California," while in Wisconsin, the left-wing Progressive Party provided seven of the state's ten representatives to Congress. The U.S. Communist Party also gained support as it campaigned for social welfare and relief. Changing its strategy to disclaim any intention of overthrowing the U.S. government, the party proclaimed that "Communism Is Twentieth Century Americanism" and began to cooperate with left-wing labor unions, student groups, and writers' organizations in a **"Popular Front"** against fascism abroad and racism at home. It continued to fight racial discrimination through the League of Struggle for Negro Rights (founded in the late 1920s to fight lynching), and sent lawyers and funds to support the "Scottsboro Boys," who were falsely accused of raping two white women in Alabama (see "Race and the Limits of the New Deal," Section 22-6d). As one

"Popular Front" Coalition of communist and politically left groups against fascism and racism.

Bettmann/Getty Images

▲ Senator Huey Long was probably the most flamboyant member of the U.S. Congress, fond of white silk suits, pink ties, strong whiskey, and women who were not his wife. His appeals to populist anger and resentment led FDR to call him one of the most dangerous men in the nation.

◄ Mary McLeod Bethune, pictured with her friend and supporter Eleanor Roosevelt, became the first African American woman to head a federal agency as director of the Division of Negro Affairs for the National Youth Administration.

Bettmann/Getty Images

black worker who became a communist organizer in Alabama explained, the Communist Party "fought selflessly and tirelessly to undo the wrongs perpetrated upon my race. Here was no dilly-dallying, no pussyfooting on the question of full equality of the Negro people." In 1938, at its high point for the decade, the party had fifty-five thousand members.

22-3d Shaping the Second New Deal

It was not only external critics who pushed Roosevelt to focus on social justice. His administration—largely due to Eleanor Roosevelt's influence—included many progressive activists. **Frances Perkins**, America's first woman cabinet member, came from a social work background, as did Roosevelt's close adviser Harold Ickes. A group of women social reformers who coalesced around the First Lady became important figures in government and in the Democratic Party. And African Americans had an unprecedented voice in this White House. By 1936, at least fifty black Americans held relatively important positions in New Deal agencies and cabinet-level departments. Journalists called these officials—who met on Friday evenings at the home of Mary McLeod Bethune, a distinguished educator who served as director of the Division of Negro Affairs for the National Youth Administration—the "black cabinet." Finally, Eleanor Roosevelt herself worked tirelessly to put social justice issues at the center of the New Deal agenda.

As Roosevelt faced the election of 1936, he understood that he had to appeal to Americans who had seemingly contradictory desires. Those who had been hit hard by the depression looked to the New Deal for help and for social justice. If that help was not forthcoming, Roosevelt would lose their support. Other Americans—not the poorest, but those with a tenuous hold on the middle class—were afraid of the continued chaos and disorder. They wanted security and stability. Still others, with more to lose, were frightened by the populist promises of people like Long and Coughlin. They wanted the New Deal to preserve American capitalism. With these lessons in mind, Roosevelt took the initiative once more.

During the period historians call the Second New Deal, Roosevelt introduced a range of progressive programs aimed at providing, as he said in a 1935 address to Congress, "greater security for the average man than he has ever known before in the history of America." The first triumph of the Second New Deal was an innocuous-sounding but momentous law that Roosevelt called "the Big Bill." The Emergency Relief Appropriation Act provided $4 billion in new deficit spending, primarily to create massive public works programs for the jobless. It also established the Resettlement Administration, which resettled destitute families and organized rural homestead communities and suburban greenbelt towns for low-income workers; the Rural Electrification Administration, which brought electricity to isolated rural areas; and the National Youth Administration, which sponsored work-relief programs for young adults and part-time jobs for students.

22-3e Works Progress Administration

The largest and best-known program funded by the Emergency Relief Appropriation Act was the **Works Progress Administration (WPA)**, later renamed the Work Projects

Frances Perkins Served as Secretary of Labor from 1933 to 1945, former Progressive reformer, and first woman cabinet member.

Works Progress Administration (WPA) New Deal agency that hired millions of people to work on public works construction projects, including highways, roads, and public buildings; it also provided jobs for artists, actors, and writers in cultural programs.

Administration. The WPA employed more than 8.5 million people who built 650,000 miles of highways and roads and 125,000 public buildings, as well as bridges, reservoirs, irrigation systems, sewage treatment plants, parks, playgrounds, and swimming pools throughout the nation. Critics labeled these projects "boondoggles" or argued that they were simply to buy political favor, but WPA workers built schools and hospitals, operated nurseries for preschool children, and taught 1.5 million adults to read and write.

The WPA also employed artists, musicians, writers, and actors, commissioning artists to decorate post office walls with murals depicting ordinary life in America, sponsoring theater performances in cities and towns throughout the nation, and hiring fifteen thousand musicians to play in government-sponsored orchestras. Through the Federal Writers' Project (FWP), authors created guidebooks for every state and territory and wrote about the plain people of the United States, including a collection of "slave narratives" from more than two thousand elderly men and women who had been held in bondage before the Civil War. These cultural programs were also controversial, for many of the WPA artists, musicians, actors, and writers created works that showed sympathy for the political struggles of workers and farmers, attempting to recover a tradition of American radicalism by celebrating the lives and labor of America's plain folk.

Photographs in the Carol M. Highsmith Archive, Library of Congress, Prints and Photographs Division. [LC-DIG-highsm-13584]

▲ The Works Progress Administration commissioned twenty-six artists to create a mural depicting scenes of life in modern California for San Francisco's Coit Tower, which had been completed in 1933.

22-3f Social Security Act

Big Bill programs and agencies were part of a short-term "emergency" strategy to address the immediate needs of the nation. Roosevelt's long-term strategy centered around the second major piece of Second New Deal legislation, the **Social Security Act**. It created a federal pension system in which eligible workers paid mandatory Social Security taxes on their wages and their employers contributed an equivalent amount; these workers then received federal retirement benefits. The Social Security Act also created several welfare programs, including a cooperative federal-state system of unemployment compensation and Aid to Dependent Children (later renamed Aid to Families with Dependent Children, or AFDC) for needy children in families without fathers present. Over the course of the twentieth century, benefits provided through the Social Security system would save tens of millions of Americans, especially the elderly, from poverty and despair.

Compared with the social security systems already in place in most western European nations, the U.S. Social Security system was fairly conservative. First, the government did not pay for old-age benefits; workers and their employers did. Second, the tax was regressive in that the more workers earned, the less they were taxed proportionally. Finally, the law did not cover agricultural labor, domestic service, and "casual labor not in the course of the employer's trade or business" (for example, janitorial work at a hospital). That meant that people of color, who disproportionately worked as farm laborers, as domestic servants, and in service jobs in hospitals and restaurants, were often ineligible. The act also excluded public-sector employees, so that many teachers, nurses, librarians, and social workers, the majority of whom were women, went uncovered. (Although the original Social Security Act provided no retirement benefits for spouses or widows of covered workers, Congress added these benefits in 1939.) Despite these limits, the Social Security Act was highly significant because the federal government took some responsibility for the economic security of the aged, the temporarily unemployed, dependent children, and people with disabilities.

22-3g Roosevelt's Populist Strategies

As the election of 1936 approached, Roosevelt adopted the populist language of his critics. Denouncing big business's "entrenched greed" and the "unjust concentration of wealth and power," he supported a new tax on business profits and increased taxes on inheritances, large gifts, and profits from the sale of property (see Figure 22.2).

In November 1936, Roosevelt won the presidency by a landslide. The Democrats also won such huge majorities in the House and Senate that some worried the two-party system might collapse. In fact, Roosevelt and the Democrats had forged a powerful "New Deal coalition" that pulled together groups from very

Social Security Act New Deal relief measure that launched a federal retirement benefits system as well as unemployment compensation, aid to low-income children, and other welfare benefits.

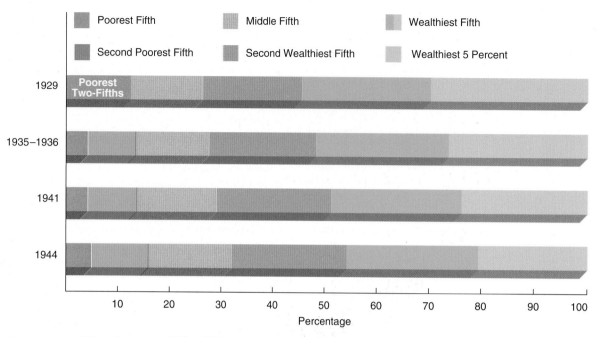

Figure 22.2 **Distribution of Total Family Income Among the American People, 1929–1944 (Percentage)**

Although the New Deal provided economic relief to the American people, it did not, as its critics so often charged, significantly redistribute income downward from the rich to the poor. *Source: Adapted from U.S. Bureau of the Census, Historical Statistics of the United States, Colonial Times to 1970. Bicentennial Edition, Washington, D.C.: U.S. Government Printing Office, 1975, page 301.*

different backgrounds and with different interests: the urban working class (especially immigrants from southern and eastern Europe and their sons and daughters), organized labor, the eleven states of the Confederacy (the "Solid South"), and northern blacks. By this time, the African American population in northern cities was large enough to constitute voting blocs, and New Deal benefits drew them away from the Republican Party, which they had long supported as the party of Lincoln. This New Deal coalition ensured that Democrats would occupy the White House for most of the next thirty years.

22-4 Labor

▶ **How did federal, state, and local governments intervene in labor relations during the Great Depression?**

▶ **What is the difference between craft and industrial unions, and how did the Great Depression exacerbate tensions between the two?**

▶ **What were the consequences of labor conflicts during the Great Depression?**

National Labor Relations (Wagner) Act Guaranteed workers the rights to organize and bargain collectively and outlawed unfair labor practices.

During the worst years of the depression, American workers continued to organize and to struggle for the rights of labor. Management,

however, fought back. Refusing to recognize unions, some even hired armed thugs to intimidate workers. One business publication declared that "a few hundred funerals will have a quieting influence." As employers refused to negotiate with union representatives, workers walked off the job. Local police or National Guard troops frequently intervened on the side of management, smashing workers' picket lines. Violence erupted in the steel, automobile, and textile industries; among lumber workers in the Pacific Northwest; and among teamsters in the Midwest. In 1934, police met a longshoremen's strike with violence on the docks of San Francisco; two union members were killed, and workers' anger spread to other industries. Eventually, 130,000 workers joined the general strike.

Workers pushed the Roosevelt administration for support, which came in the 1935 **National Labor Relations (Wagner) Act**. This act guaranteed workers the right to organize unions and to bargain collectively. It outlawed "unfair labor practices," such as firing workers who joined unions; prohibited management from sponsoring company unions; and required employers to bargain with labor's elected union representatives to set wages, hours, and working conditions. The Wagner Act also created a mechanism for enforcement: the National Labor Relations Board (NLRB). With federal protection, union membership grew. Organizers in the coalfields told miners that "President Roosevelt wants you to join the union," and join they did—along with workers in dozens of industries. In 1929 union membership stood at 3.6 million; in mid-1938 it surpassed 7 million.

The Wagner Act further alienated business leaders from the New Deal. "No Obedience," proclaimed an editorial in a leading business magazine. The business-sponsored Liberty League insisted—incorrectly—that the Supreme Court would soon find the Wagner Act unconstitutional.

22-4a Rivalry Between Craft and Industrial Unions

The growth and increasing militancy of the labor movement exacerbated an existing division between "craft" and "industrial" unions in the United States. Craft unions represented labor's elite: the skilled workers in a particular trade, such as carpentry. Industrial unions represented all the workers, skilled and unskilled, in a given industry such as automobile manufacture. In the 1930s, it was the industrial unions that had grown dramatically.

Craft unions dominated the American Federation of Labor, the powerful umbrella organization for individual unions. Most AFL leaders offered little support for industrial organizing. Many looked down on the industrial workers, disproportionately immigrants from southern and eastern Europe—"the rubbish at labor's door," in the words of the Teamsters' president. Skilled workers had economic interests different from those of the great mass of unskilled workers, and more conservative craft unionists were often alarmed at what they saw as the radicalism of industrial unions.

In 1935, the industrial unionists made their move. John L. Lewis, head of the United Mine Workers and the nation's most prominent labor leader, resigned as vice president of the AFL. He and other industrial unionists created the Committee for Industrial Organization (CIO); the AFL responded by suspending all CIO unions. By 1938, the slightly renamed **Congress of Industrial Organizations** had 3.7 million members, slightly more than the AFL's 3.4 million. Unlike the AFL, the CIO included women and people of color in its membership. Union membership gave these "marginal" workers greater employment security and the benefits of collective bargaining.

22-4b Sit-Down Strikes

The most decisive labor conflict of the decade came in late 1936, when the United Auto Workers (UAW), an industrial union, demanded recognition from General Motors (GM), Chrysler, and Ford. When GM refused, UAW organizers responded with a relatively new tactic: a "sit-down strike." On December 30, 1936, workers at the Fisher Body plant in Flint, Michigan, went on strike *inside* the Fisher One factory. They refused to leave the building, thus immobilizing a key part of the GM production system. GM tried to force the workers out by turning off the heat. When police attempted to take back the plant, strikers hurled steel bolts, coffee mugs, and bottles. The police tried tear gas. Strikers turned the plant's water hoses on the police.

As the sit-down strike spread to adjacent plants, auto production plummeted. General Motors obtained a court order to evacuate the plant, but the strikers stood firm, risking imprisonment and fines. In a critical decision, Michigan's governor refused to send in the National Guard to clear workers from the buildings. After forty-four days, the UAW triumphed. GM agreed to recognize the union, and Chrysler quickly followed. Ford held out until 1941.

22-4c Memorial Day Massacre

On the heels of this triumph, however, came a grim reminder of the costs of labor's struggle. On Memorial Day 1937, a group of picnicking workers and their families marched toward the Republic Steel plant in Chicago, intending to show support for strikers on a picket line in front of the plant. Police blocked their route and ordered them to disperse. One of the marchers threw something at the police, and the police attacked. Ten men were killed, seven of them shot in the back. Thirty marchers were wounded, including a woman and three children. Many Americans, fed up with labor strife and violence, showed little sympathy for the workers. The anti-labor *Chicago Tribune* blamed the marchers and praised police for repelling "a trained military unit of a revolutionary body."

At great cost, organized labor made great gains during the 1930s. Violence decreased as the NLRB effectively mediated disputes. And unionized workers—about 23 percent of the nonagricultural workforce—saw their standard of living rise. By 1941, the average steelworker could afford to buy a new coat for himself and his wife every six years and, every other year, a pair of shoes for each of his children.

22-5 Federal Power and the Nationalization of Culture

▶ How did the federal government expand its control of and influence over the West?

▶ What was the impact of the Indian Reorganization Act?

▶ How did the federal government respond to widespread poverty in the South?

▶ What role did popular culture play in providing relief during the Great Depression?

In the 1930s, national culture, politics, and policies played an increasingly important role in the lives of Americans from different regions, classes, and ethnic backgrounds as the reach of the national mass media grew and the power of the federal government expanded. During the decade-long economic crisis, political power moved from the state and local level to the White House and Congress, and individual Americans, in far more ways, found their lives bound up with the federal government. By the end of the 1930s, almost 35 percent of the population had received some sort of federal government benefit, whether crop subsidies through the

Congress of Industrial Organizations Association of 3.7 million members of industrial unions; included women and people of color.

The Women's Emergency Brigade and General Motors Sit-Down Strike

During the 1937 sit-down strike by automobile workers in Flint, Michigan, a women's "emergency brigade" of wives, daughters, sisters, and sweethearts demonstrated daily at the plant. When police tried to force the men out of Chevrolet Plant No. 9 by filling it with tear gas, the women used clubs to smash the plant's windows and let in fresh air. Sixteen people were injured that day in the riot between police and strikers. The following day the Women's Emergency Brigade marched again.

CRITICAL THINKING

Using this photograph as visual evidence:

- How did these women attempt to demonstrate the respectability and mainstream nature of their protest?
- How does that message fit with the clubs several still carry?

Bettmann/Getty Images

▲ Gerenda Johnson, wife of a striker, leads a march past the GM Chevrolet small parts plant on the day following a violent conflict between police and strikers.

federal AAA or a WPA job or relief payments through FERA. Americans in the 1930s began to look to the federal government to play a major and active role in the life of the nation.

22-5a New Deal in the West

The New Deal changed the American West more than any other region, as federally sponsored construction of dams and other public works projects reshaped the region's economy and environment. During the 1930s, the federal Bureau of Reclamation, an obscure agency created in 1902 to provide irrigation for small farms and ranches, dramatically expanded its mandate to build large multipurpose dams that controlled entire river systems. For example, the Boulder Dam (later renamed for Herbert Hoover) harnessed the Colorado River, providing water to southern California and using hydroelectric power to produce electricity for Los Angeles and southern Arizona. The water from these dams opened new areas to agriculture and allowed western cities to expand; the cheap electricity they produced attracted industry to the region. These federally managed projects also gave the federal government an unprecedented role in the West. Especially after the completion of Washington State's Grand Coulee Dam in 1941, the federal government controlled both a great deal of water and hydroelectric power in the region. And in the West, control of water meant control over the region's future.

The federal government also brought millions of acres of western land under its control in the 1930s as it attempted to combat the environmental disaster of the Dust Bowl and to keep crop and livestock prices from falling further. To reduce pressure on the land from overgrazing, the federal government bought 8 million cattle from farmers in a six-month period in 1934–1935 and transported the healthy cattle out of the region. In 1934, the Taylor Grazing Act imposed new restrictions on ranchers' use of public lands for grazing stock. Federal stock reduction programs probably saved the western cattle industry, but they destroyed the traditional economy of the Navajos by forcing them to reduce the size of sheep herds on their federally protected reservation lands. Despite new restrictions, federal subsidies and AAA crop supports greatly benefited the owners of large farms and ranches, but such programs also increased federal government control in the region. As historian Richard White argues, by the end of the 1930s, "federal bureaucracies were quite literally remaking the American West."

22-5b New Deal for American Indians

New federal activism extended to the West's people as well. Over the past several decades, federal policy toward American Indians, especially those on western reservations, had been disastrous. The Bureau of Indian Affairs (BIA) was riddled with corruption; in its attempts to "assimilate" Native peoples, it had separated children from their parents, suppressed Native languages, and outlawed tribal religious practices. Such BIA-enforced assimilation was not successful. Division of tribal lands had failed to promote individual landownership—almost half of those living on reservations in 1933 owned no land. In the early 1930s, American Indians were the poorest group in the nation, plagued by epidemics and malnutrition, with an infant mortality rate twice that of white Americans.

In 1933, Roosevelt named one of the BIA's most vocal critics to head the agency. John Collier, founder of the American Indian Defense Agency, meant to completely reverse the course of America's Indian policy, and his initiatives had many positive results. The **Indian Reorganization Act (IRA)** of 1934 went a long way toward ending the forced assimilation of Native peoples and restoring American Indian lands to tribal ownership. It also gave federal recognition to tribal governments. American Indian tribes had regained their status as semisovereign nations, guaranteed "internal sovereignty" in all matters not specifically limited by acts of Congress.

Not all Native peoples supported the IRA. Some saw it as a "back-to-the-blanket" measure based on romantic notions of "authentic" Native American culture. The tribal government structure specified by the IRA was culturally alien—and quite perplexing—to tribes such as the Papagos, whose language had no word for "representative." The Navajo nation also refused to ratify the IRA; in a terrible case of bad timing, the vote took place during the federally mandated destruction of Navajo sheep herds. Eventually, however, 181 tribes organized under the IRA. Collier had succeeded in reversing some of the destructive policies of the past, and the IRA laid the groundwork for future economic development and limited political autonomy among Native peoples.

22-5c New Deal in the South

New Dealers did not set out to transform the American West, but they did intend to transform the American South. Well before the Great Depression, the South was mired in widespread and debilitating poverty. In 1929, the South's per capita income of $365 per year was less than half of the West's $921. More than half of the region's farm families were tenants or sharecroppers with no land of their own. "Sickness, misery, and unnecessary death," in the words of a contemporary study, plagued the southern poor. Almost 15 percent of South Carolina's people could not read or write.

Roosevelt, who sought a cure for his polio in the pools of Warm Springs, Georgia, had seen southern poverty first-hand and understood its human costs. But in describing the South as "the Nation's No. 1 economic problem" in 1938, he was referring to the economic theory that underlay many New Deal programs. As long as its people were too poor to participate in the nation's mass consumer economy, the South would be a drag on national economic recovery.

Indian Reorganization Act (IRA) A 1934 measure that sought to restore Native peoples' lands to tribal ownership and provided federal recognition of tribes as semisovereign nations.

Map 22.3 The Tennessee Valley Authority

To control flooding and generate electricity, the Tennessee Valley Authority constructed dams along the Tennessee River and its tributaries from Paducah, Kentucky, to Knoxville, Tennessee.

The largest federal intervention in the South was the **Tennessee Valley Authority (TVA)**, authorized by Congress during Roosevelt's First Hundred Days. The TVA was created to develop a water and hydroelectric power project similar to the multipurpose dams of the West; dams would not only control flooding but also produce electric power for the region (see Map 22.3). However, confronted with the poverty and hopelessness of the Tennessee River Valley region (which included parts of Virginia, North Carolina, Tennessee, Georgia, Alabama, Mississippi, and Kentucky), the TVA quickly extended its focus. Through the TVA, the federal government promoted economic development, helped bring electricity to rural areas, restored fields worn out from overuse, and fought the curse of malaria.

Although it benefited many poor southerners, over time the TVA proved to be a monumental environmental disaster. TVA strip mining caused soil erosion. Its coal-burning generators released sulfur oxides, which combined with water vapor to produce acid rain. Above all, the TVA degraded the water by dumping untreated sewage, toxic chemicals, and metal pollutants from strip mining into streams and rivers.

During the 1930s, the Roosevelt administration faced a very difficult political situation in the South. The southern senators whose support Roosevelt so desperately needed

benefited from the flow of federal dollars to their states. But they were also suspicious of federal intervention and determined to preserve states' rights. Especially when federal action threatened the South's racial hierarchy, they resisted passionately. As the nation's poorest and least educated region, the South would not easily be integrated into the national culture and economy. But New Deal programs began that process and in so doing improved the lives of at least some of the region's people.

22-5d Mass Media and Popular Culture

It was not only federal government programs that broke down regional boundaries and fostered national connections during the 1930s. America's national mass media and popular culture helped millions survive hard times.

Photojournalism magazines *Life* and *Look* began publishing during the 1930s, and each quickly drew millions of readers. But it was the sound of the radio that filled the days and nights of the depression era. Manufacturers rushed to produce cheaper models, and by 1937 Americans were buying radios at the rate of twenty-eight a minute. By the end of the decade, 27.5 million households owned radios, and families listened on average five hours a day. Roosevelt understood the importance of the radio in American life, going directly to the American people with radio "Fireside Chats" throughout his presidency—and Americans ranked him eleventh among America's top "radio personalities" in 1938.

Tennessee Valley Authority (TVA) Ambitious plan of economic development that centered on creating an extensive hydroelectric power project in the poor Appalachian area.

The 1936 Olympic Games

The 1936 Olympic Games that were scheduled to take place in Berlin, under the Nazi regime, created a dilemma for the United States and other nations. Should they go to Berlin? Would participation in the Nazi-orchestrated spectacle lend credence to Hitler's regime? Or would victories won by other nations undermine Hitler's claims about the superiority of Germany's "Aryan race"?

Universal History Archive/Universal Images Group/Getty Images

Although the modern Olympic Games had been founded in 1896 with high hopes that they might help unite the nations of the world in peace and understanding, international politics were never far from the surface. Germany had been excluded from the 1920 and 1924 games following its aggression and defeat in World War I, and the International Olympic Committee's choice (in 1931) of Berlin for the XI Olympiad was intended to welcome Germany back into the world community. However, with Hitler's rise to power in 1933, Germany determined to use the games as propaganda for the Nazi state and to demonstrate the superiority of its pure "Aryan" athletes. Soon thereafter, campaigns to boycott the Berlin Olympics emerged in several nations, including Great Britain, Sweden, France, Czechoslovakia, and the United States.

The American people were divided over the question of a boycott. Some U.S. Jewish groups led campaigns against U.S. participation in Berlin, while others took no public position, concerned that their actions might lead to increased anti-Semitic violence within Germany. Jewish athletes made individual decisions

about whether or not to boycott the Olympics. The president of the United States Olympic Committee, Avery Brundage, attributed the boycott movement to a "conspiracy" of Jews and communists and instructed American athletes not to get involved in the "present Jew-Nazi altercation." African Americans, overwhelmingly, opposed boycotting the games. Well aware of Hitler's attitudes toward "mongrel" peoples, many looked forward to demonstrating on the tracks and fields of Berlin just how wrong Hitler's notions of Aryan superiority were. Some also pointed out the hypocrisy of American officials who criticized Germany while ignoring U.S. discrimination against black athletes.

In the end, the United States sent 312 athletes to Berlin; of these, 18 were African American. These African American athletes won fourteen medals, almost one-quarter of the U.S. total of fifty-six. Track and field star Jesse Owens came home with four gold medals. Jewish athletes won thirteen medals in the 1936 Olympics; one of those athletes was American. But German athletes won eighty-nine medals to U.S. athletes' fifty-six, and despite the initial controversy, the XI Olympiad was a

Bettmann/Getty Images

◀ The eleventh summer Olympic Games in Berlin were carefully crafted as propaganda for the Nazi state. And the spectacle of the 1936 games, as represented in the poster above, was impressive. But on the athletic fields, Nazi claims of Aryan superiority were challenged by athletes such as African American Jesse Owens, who is shown at left breaking the Olympic record in the 200-meter race.

(Continued)

public relations triumph for Germany. The *New York Times*, impressed by the spectacle of the games and the hospitality of the Germans, proclaimed that the XI Olympiad had put Germany "back in the fold of nations."

The idealistic vision of nations linked together through peaceful athletic competition hit a low point at the 1936 Olympics. The 1940 Olympic Games, scheduled for Tokyo, were cancelled because of the escalating world war.

CRITICAL THINKING

- Despite the idealistic intent of the Olympics to link the world's nations together through peaceful athletic competition, politics have gotten in the way on numerous occasions, including in 1936.
- What other instances can you think of where politics influenced an Olympic competition?
- Is it possible for international politics not to affect the Olympics and other sporting events that occur on a world stage?

The radio offered Americans many things. In a time of uncertainty, radio gave citizens immediate access—as never before—to the political news of the day and to the actual voices of their elected leaders. During hard times, radio offered escape: for children, the adventures of *Flash Gordon*; for housewives, new soap operas, such as *The Romance of Helen Trent*. Entire families gathered to listen to the comedy of ex-vaudevillians Jack Benny, George Burns, and Gracie Allen.

Radio also gave people a chance to participate—however vicariously—in events they could never have experienced before. Listeners were carried to New York City for performances of the Metropolitan Opera on Saturday afternoons, to the Moana Hotel on the beach at Waikiki through the live broadcast of *Hawaii Calls*, to major league baseball games (begun by the St. Louis Cardinals in 1935) in distant cities. Millions shared the horror of the kidnapping of aviator Charles Lindbergh's son in 1932; black Americans in the urban North and rural South experienced the triumphs of African American boxer Joe Louis ("the Brown Bomber"). Radio lessened the isolation of individuals and communities. It helped create a more homogeneous mass culture as people throughout the nation listened to the same programs; by offering a set of shared experiences, it also lessened the gulfs among Americans from different regions and class backgrounds.

Hollywood movies also offered shared experiences. During the first years of the depression almost one-third of all movie theaters closed, and ticket prices fell from 30 to 20 cents. By the mid-1930s, however, Americans were going to the movies again, and a nation of fewer than 130 million bought 80 million to 90 million movie tickets each week. Many Americans sought escape from grim realities at the movies. Comedies were especially popular, from the slapstick of the Marx Brothers to the sophisticated banter of *My Man Godfrey* or *It Happened One Night*. However, the appeal of upbeat movies was in the context of economic hard times. The song "Who's Afraid of the Big Bad Wolf?" from Disney's *Three Little Pigs* was a big hit in 1933—as the economy hit bottom.

When sales of undershirts plummeted in 1934 after Clark Gable took off his shirt to reveal a bare chest in *It Happened One Night*, it seemed clear that film influenced American attitudes and behavior. But some Americans had long worried about the power of film, criticizing their frequent use of sexual innuendo as well as the gangster movies that drew crowds in the early 1930s. No matter that the gangster hero always met death or destruction; critics argued that these films seemed to glamorize crime. Faced with a boycott

The Granger Collection, NYC

▲ *King Kong* broke all box-office records in 1933, as Americans flocked to see the giant ape fighting off airplanes from the top of New York's new Empire State Building—the tallest building in the world.

organized by the Roman Catholic Legion of Decency, in 1934 the film industry established a production code that would determine what American film audiences saw—and did not see—for decades. Pledged the Production Code Administration: "There is no room . . . for pictures which offend against common decency."

Finally, in an unintended consequence, federal policies intended to channel jobs to male heads of households strengthened the power of national popular culture. During Roosevelt's first two years in office, 1.5 million youths lost jobs; many young people who would have gone to work at the age of fourteen in better times decided to stay in school. By the end of the decade, three-quarters of American youth went to high school—up from one-half in 1920—and graduation rates doubled. School was free, classrooms were warm, and education seemed to promise a better future. The exuberant, fad-driven peer cultures that had developed in 1920s high schools and colleges were no more, but consumer-oriented youth culture had not died out. And as more young people went to high school, more participated in that national youth culture. Increasingly, young people listened to the same music. More than ever before, they adopted the same styles of clothing, of dance, of speech. Paradoxically, the hard times of the depression did not destroy youth culture; instead, they caused youth culture to spread more widely among America's young.

22-6 The Limits of the New Deal

▶ How did Franklin D. Roosevelt's actions weaken the effectiveness of the New Deal agenda?

▶ How did the New Deal fail minority groups, and why?

▶ Why did African Americans support Franklin D. Roosevelt?

▶ What role did First Lady Eleanor Roosevelt play in her husband's presidency?

Roosevelt began his second term with great optimism and a strong mandate for reform. Almost immediately, however, the president's own actions undermined his New Deal agenda. Labor strife and racial issues divided the American people. As fascism spread in Europe, the world inched toward war, and domestic initiatives lost ground to foreign affairs and defense. By the end of 1938, New Deal reform had ground to a halt, but it had already had a profound impact on the United States.

22-6a Court-Packing Plan

Following his landslide electoral victory in 1936, Roosevelt set out to safeguard his progressive agenda. The greatest danger he saw was from the U.S. Supreme Court. In ruling unconstitutional both the National Industrial Recovery Act (in 1935) and the Agricultural Adjustment Act (in 1936), the Court rejected not only specific provisions of hastily drafted New Deal legislation but also the expansion of presidential and federal power such legislation entailed. Only three of the nine justices were consistently sympathetic to New Deal "emergency" measures, and Roosevelt was convinced the Court would invalidate most of the Second New Deal legislation. Citing the advanced age and heavy workload of the nine justices, he asked Congress for authority to appoint up to six new justices to the Supreme Court. But in an era that had seen the rise to power of Hitler, Mussolini, and Stalin, many Americans saw Roosevelt's plan as an attack on constitutional government. Even those sympathetic to the New Deal worried about politicizing the Court. "Assuming, which is not at all impossible," wrote prominent journalist William Allen White, "a reactionary president, as charming, as eloquent and as irresistible as Roosevelt, with power to change the court, and we should be in the devil's own fix." Congress rebelled, and Roosevelt experienced his first major congressional defeat.

The episode had a final, ironic twist. During the long public debate over Court packing, the ideological center of the Supreme Court shifted. Key swing-vote justices began to vote in favor of liberal, pro–New Deal rulings. In short order, the Court upheld both the Wagner Act and the Social Security Act. Moreover, a new judicial pension program encouraged older judges to retire, allowing Roosevelt to appoint seven new associate justices in the next four years, including such notables as Hugo Black, Felix Frankfurter, and William O. Douglas. In the end, Roosevelt got what he wanted from the Supreme Court, but the Court-packing plan damaged his political credibility.

22-6b Roosevelt Recession

Another New Deal setback was the renewed economic recession of 1937–1939, sometimes called the Roosevelt recession. Despite his use of deficit spending, Roosevelt had never abandoned his commitment to a balanced budget. In 1937, confident that the depression had reversed, he began to cut government spending. At the same time, the Federal Reserve Board, concerned about a 3.6 percent inflation rate, tightened credit. The two actions sent the economy into a tailspin: unemployment climbed from 7.7 million in 1937 to 10.4 million in 1938. Soon Roosevelt resumed deficit financing.

The New Deal was in trouble in 1937 and 1938, and New Dealers struggled over the direction of liberal reform. Some urged vigorous trust-busting; others advocated the resurrection of national economic planning as it had existed under the National Recovery Administration. But in the end, Roosevelt rejected these alternatives and chose deficit financing as a means of stimulating consumer demand and creating jobs. And in 1939, with conflict over the world war that had begun in Europe commanding more and more of the nation's attention, the New Deal came to an end. Roosevelt sacrificed further domestic reforms in return for conservative support for his programs of military rearmament and preparedness.

22-6c Election of 1940

No president had ever served more than two terms, and many Americans speculated about whether Franklin Roosevelt would run for a third term in 1940. Roosevelt seemed undecided until that spring, when Adolf Hitler's military advances in Europe apparently convinced him to stay on (see "The Expanding Conflict," Section 23-1a). Roosevelt headed off the predictable attacks from his opponent, Republican Wendell Willkie, by expanding military and naval contracts and thus reducing unemployment. Roosevelt also promised Americans, "Your boys are not going to be sent into any foreign wars."

Roosevelt did not win this election in a landslide, as he had in 1936 (see Map 22.4). But the New Deal coalition held. Once again Roosevelt won in the cities, supported by blue-collar workers, ethnic Americans, and African Americans. He also carried every state in the South. Although New Deal reform was over at home, Roosevelt was still riding a wave of public approval.

22-6d Race and the Limits of the New Deal

While the New Deal directly touched the lives of a great many Americans, not all benefited equally. More than anything else, differences were based on race. The New Deal fell short of equality for people of color for two major reasons.

First was the relationship between local and national power. National programs were implemented at the local level, and where local custom conflicted with national intent, as in the South and West, local custom won. In the South, African Americans received lower relief payments than whites and were paid lower wages in WPA jobs. The situation was

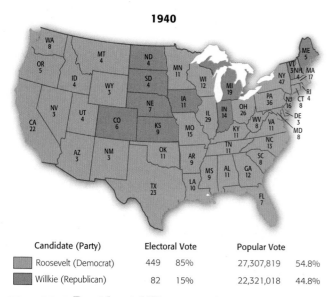

1940

Candidate (Party)	Electoral Vote		Popular Vote	
Roosevelt (Democrat)	449	85%	27,307,819	54.8%
Willkie (Republican)	82	15%	22,321,018	44.8%

Map 22.4 Presidential Election, 1940

Roosevelt won an unprecedented third term in the 1940 presidential election. He did not repeat his landslide 1936 victory, in which he won all but two states. But he did capture 38 states in 1940 to Republican Wendell Willkie's 10.

similar in the Southwest. In Tucson, Arizona, for example, Federal Emergency Relief Agency officials divided applicants into four groups—Anglos, Mexican Americans, Mexican immigrants, and Indians—and allocated relief payments in descending order.

Such discriminatory practices were rooted not only in racism but also in the economic interests of whites/Anglos. The majority of African American and Mexican American workers were paid so poorly that they *earned* less than impoverished whites got for "relief." Why would these workers take low-paying private jobs if government relief or government work programs provided more income? Local communities understood that federal programs threatened a political, social, and economic system based on racial hierarchies.

The case of the Scottsboro Boys illustrates the power of racism in the conflict between local and national power in 1930s America. One night in March 1931, a fight broke out between groups of young black and white "hobos" on a Southern Railroad freight train as it passed through Alabama. The black youths won the fight and tossed the whites off the train. Not long afterward, a posse stopped the train, arrested the black youths, and threw them in the Scottsboro, Alabama, jail. The posse also discovered two white women "riding the rails," who claimed that the young men had raped them. Word spread, and the youths were barely saved from a lynch mob. Medical evidence later showed that the women were lying. But within two weeks, eight of the so-called Scottsboro Boys were convicted of rape by all-white juries and sentenced to death. The ninth, a boy of thirteen, was saved from the death penalty by one vote. The case—so clearly a product of southern racism—became a cause célèbre, both in the nation and, through the efforts of the Communist Party, around the world.

The Supreme Court intervened, ruling that Alabama deprived black defendants of equal protection under the law by systematically excluding African Americans from juries and that the defendants had been denied counsel. Alabama, however, staged new trials. Five of the young men were convicted (four would be paroled by 1950, and one escaped from prison). Despite federal action through the Supreme Court, Alabama prevailed. Southern resistance to federal intervention—centered around issues of race—would not yield easily to federal power.

Second, the gains made by people of color under the New Deal were limited by the political realities of southern resistance. Roosevelt needed the support of southern Democrats to pass his legislative program, and they were willing to hold him hostage over race. In 1938, for example, southern Democrats blocked an antilynching bill with a six-week-long filibuster in the Senate. Roosevelt refused to use his political capital to break the filibuster and pass the bill. Politically, he had much to lose and little to gain. He knew that blacks would not desert the Democratic Party, but without southern senators, his legislative agenda was dead. Roosevelt wanted all Americans to enjoy the benefits of democracy, but he had no strong commitment to the cause of civil rights. As the NAACP's Roy Wilkins put it, "Mr. Roosevelt was no friend of the Negro. He wasn't an enemy, but he wasn't a friend."

22-6e African American Support

Why, then, did African Americans support Roosevelt and the New Deal? Because despite discriminatory policies, the New Deal helped African Americans. By the end of the 1930s, almost one-third of African American households survived on income from a WPA job. African Americans held some significant positions in the Roosevelt administration. Finally, there was the First Lady. When the acclaimed black contralto Marian Anderson was barred from performing in Washington's Constitution Hall by its owners, the Daughters of the American Revolution, Eleanor Roosevelt responded by resigning her membership in the DAR; she then helped arrange for Anderson to sing at the Lincoln Memorial on Easter Sunday, 1939. Such public commitment to racial equality was enormously important to African American citizens.

Despite widespread support for Roosevelt and the New Deal, many African Americans were well aware of the limits of New Deal reform. Some concluded that they could depend only on themselves and organized self-help and direct-action movements. In 1934, black tenant farmers and sharecroppers joined with poor whites to form the Southern Tenant Farmers' Union. In the North, the militant Harlem Tenants League fought rent increases and evictions, and African American consumers began to boycott white merchants who refused to hire blacks as clerks. Their slogan was "Don't Buy Where You Can't Work." And the Brotherhood of Sleeping Car Porters, under the astute leadership of A. Philip Randolph, fought for the rights of black workers.

22-6f An Assessment of the New Deal

Any analysis of the New Deal must begin with Franklin Delano Roosevelt himself. Assessments of Roosevelt varied widely during his presidency: he was passionately hated and just as passionately loved. Roosevelt personified the presidency for the American people. When he spoke directly to Americans in his Fireside Chats, hundreds of thousands wrote to him, sharing their problems, asking for his help, offering their advice.

Eleanor Roosevelt, the nation's First Lady, played a crucial and unprecedented role in the Roosevelt administration. As First Lady, she worked tirelessly for social justice and human rights, bringing reformers, trade unionists, and advocates for the rights of women and African Americans to the White House. Described by some as the conscience of the New Deal, she took public positions—especially on African American civil rights—far more progressive than those of her husband's administration. In some ways she served as a lightning rod, deflecting conservative criticism from her husband to herself. But her public stances also cemented the allegiance of other groups, African Americans in particular, to the New Deal.

Most historians and political scientists consider Franklin Roosevelt a truly great president, citing his courage and buoyant self-confidence, his willingness to experiment, and his capacity to inspire the nation during the most somber days of the depression. Some, who see the New Deal as a squandered opportunity for true political and economic change, charge that Roosevelt lacked vision and courage. They judge Roosevelt by goals that were not his own: Roosevelt was a pragmatist whose goal was to preserve the

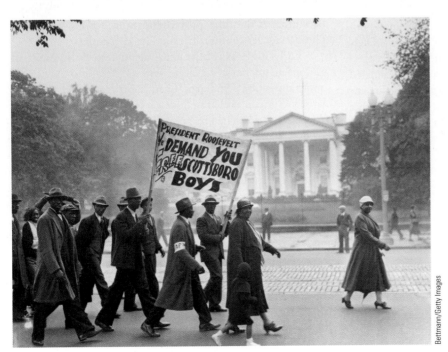

◀ Marchers in Washington, D.C., demand freedom for the Scottsboro Boys, young African American men who were falsely accused and convicted of raping two white women in Alabama in 1931. This 1933 march was organized by the International Labor Defense, the legal arm of the Communist Party of the United States of America, which waged a strong campaign on behalf of the nine young men.

Bettmann/Getty Images

system. Nonetheless, Franklin Delano Roosevelt transformed the American presidency, increasing its strength and independence and fostering a more direct connection with the American people.

During his more than twelve years in office, Roosevelt helped to expand the role of the federal government. For the first time, the federal government took primary responsibility for safeguarding the economic security of the American people. New Deal programs pumped money into the economy and saved millions of Americans from hunger and misery. However, as late as 1939, more than 10 million men and women were still jobless, and the nation's unemployment rate stood at 19 percent. In the end, it was not the New Deal, but massive government spending during the Second World War that brought full economic recovery. In 1941, as a result of mobilization for war, unemployment declined to 10 percent, and in 1944, at the height of the war, only 1 percent of the labor force was jobless. World War II, not the New Deal, would reinvigorate the American economy.

22-7 The Approach of War

▶ **What methods did the Nazis use to gain control inside and outside of Germany?**

▶ **How did American isolationist views influence the federal government's response to foreign affairs?**

▶ **How did Franklin D. Roosevelt's views on foreign affairs evolve during his presidency?**

▶ **What developments contributed to increased tension between Japan and the United States?**

The U.S. domestic struggles—economic, political, and social—took place within a larger international crisis and, by the late 1930s, a rapidly expanding war. On March 5, 1933, one day after Roosevelt's inauguration, Germany's parliament granted dictatorial powers to the new chancellor, Adolf Hitler, leader of the **Nazi Party**. The act marked the culmination of a stunning rise to power for Hitler, whose Nazis very likely would have remained a fringe party had the Great Depression not hit Germany with such force. Production plummeted 40 percent, and unemployment ballooned to 6 million, meaning that two workers out of five did not have jobs. Together with a disintegrating banking system, which robbed millions of their savings, as well as widespread resentment among Germans over the Versailles peace settlement, the plummeting employment figures brought mass discontent to the country. While the communists preached a workers' revolution, German business executives and property owners threw their support behind Hitler and the Nazis, many of them believing they could manipulate him once he had thwarted the communists. They were wrong.

Like Benito Mussolini, who had gained control of

Nazi Party National Socialist German Workers' Party; founded in Germany in 1919, it rose to prominence under the leadership of Adolf Hitler and stressed fascism and anti-Semitism.

appeasement The process of making concessions to pacify, quiet, or satisfy the other party.

Italy in 1922, Hitler was a fascist. Fascism (called Nazism, or National Socialism, in Germany) was a collection of ideas and prejudices that celebrated supremacy of the state over the individual; of dictatorship over democracy; of authoritarianism over freedom of speech; of a regulated, state-oriented economy over a free-market economy; and of militarism and war over peace. The Nazis vowed not only to revive German economic and military strength but also to cripple communism and "purify" the German "race" by destroying Jews and other people, such as homosexuals and Romani people, whom Hitler disparaged as inferiors. The Nuremberg Laws of 1935 stripped Jews of citizenship and outlawed intermarriage with Germans. Teachers, doctors, and other professionals could not practice their craft, and half of all German Jews were without work.

22-7a German Aggression Under Hitler

Determined to get Germany out from under the Versailles treaty system, Hitler withdrew Germany from the League of Nations, ended reparations payments, and began to rearm. While secretly laying plans for the conquest of neighboring states, he watched admiringly as Mussolini's troops invaded the African nation of Ethiopia in 1935. The next year, Hitler ordered his own troops into the Rhineland, an area that the Versailles treaty had demilitarized. When Germany's timid neighbor France did not resist this act, Hitler crowed, "The world belongs to the man with guts!"

Soon the aggressors joined hands. In 1936, Italy and Germany formed an alliance called the Rome-Berlin Axis. Shortly thereafter, Germany and Japan united against the Soviet Union in the Anti-Comintern Pact. To these events Britain and France responded with a policy of **appeasement**, hoping to curb Hitler's expansionist appetite by permitting him a few territorial nibbles. The policy of appeasing Hitler, though not altogether unreasonable in terms of what could be known at the time, proved disastrous, for the hate-filled German leader continually raised his demands.

Early in 1938, Hitler once again tested the limits of European tolerance when he sent soldiers into Austria to annex the nation of his birth. Then, in September, he seized the largely German-speaking Sudeten region of Czechoslovakia. Appeasement reached its apex that month when France and Britain, without consulting the Czechs, agreed at Munich to allow Hitler this territorial bite, in exchange for a pledge that he would not take more. British prime minister Neville Chamberlain returned home to proclaim "peace in our time," confident that Hitler was satiated. In March 1939, Hitler swallowed the rest of Czechoslovakia (see Map 22.5).

22-7b Isolationist Views in the United States

Americans had watched this buildup of tension in Europe with apprehension. Many sought to distance themselves from the tumult by embracing isolationism, whose key elements were abhorrence of war and fervent opposition to U.S. alliances with other nations. A 1937 Gallup poll found that nearly two-thirds of the respondents thought U.S.

Map 22.5 The German Advance

Hitler's drive to dominate Europe pushed German troops deep into France and the Soviet Union. Great Britain took a beating but held on with the help of American economic and military aid before the United States entered the Second World War in late 1941.

participation in World War I had been a mistake. The vast majority of isolationists opposed fascism and condemned aggression, but they did not think the United States should have to do what Europeans themselves refused to do: block Hitler. Isolationist sentiment was strongest in the Midwest and among anti-British ethnic groups, especially Americans of German or Irish descent, but it was a nationwide phenomenon that cut across socioeconomic, ethnic, party, and sectional lines, and it attracted a majority of the American people.

Some isolationists charged that corporate "merchants of death" had promoted war and were assisting the aggressors. In an era newly critical of business as unemployment rates hovered around 20 percent, a congressional committee headed by Senator Gerald P. Nye held hearings from 1934 to 1936 on the role of business and financiers in the U.S. decision to enter the First World War. The Nye committee did not prove that American munitions makers had dragged the nation into that war, but it did uncover evidence that corporations practicing "rotten commercialism" had bribed foreign politicians to bolster arms sales in the 1920s and 1930s and had lobbied against arms control.

Reflecting the popular desire for distance from Europe's disputes, Roosevelt signed a series of **neutrality acts,** in which Congress sought to protect the nation by outlawing the kinds

of contacts that had compromised U.S. neutrality during World War I. The Neutrality Act of 1935 prohibited arms shipments to either side in a war, once the president had declared the existence of belligerency. Roosevelt had wanted the authority to name the aggressor and apply an arms embargo against it alone, but Congress would not grant the president such discretionary power. The Neutrality Act of 1936 forbade loans to belligerents. After a joint resolution in 1937 declared the United States neutral in the Spanish Civil War, Roosevelt embargoed arms shipments to both sides. The Neutrality Act of 1937 introduced the cash-and-carry principle: warring nations wishing to trade with the United States would have to pay cash for their nonmilitary purchases and carry the goods from U.S. ports in their own ships. The act also forbade Americans from traveling on the ships of belligerent nations.

22-7c Roosevelt's Evolving Views

President Roosevelt shared the prevailing popular isolationism in the early 1930s. Although prior to World War I he was an expansionist and interventionist like his older cousin Theodore, during the interwar period FDR talked less about

neutrality acts Laws passed in the mid-1930s to keep the United States out of any European wars.

preparedness and more about disarmament and the horrors of war, less about policing the world and more about handling problems at home. In a passionate speech delivered in August 1936 at Chautauqua, New York, Roosevelt expressed prevailing isolationist opinion and made a pitch for the pacifist vote in the upcoming election: "I have seen war. . . . I have seen blood running from the wounded. I have seen men coughing out their gassed lungs. . . . I have seen the agony of mothers and wives. I hate war." The United States, he promised, would remain unentangled in the European conflict. During the crisis over Czechoslovakia in 1938, Roosevelt endorsed appeasement and greeted the Munich accord with a "universal sense of relief."

At the same time, Roosevelt grew increasingly troubled by the behavior of Germany. When, in November 1938, the Nazi leadership used the shooting of a German diplomat in Paris by a Jewish man (whose parents had just been deported to Poland by the Nazi government) as an excuse to launch *Kristallnacht* (or Crystal Night, after the shattered glass that littered German streets after the attacks on Jewish synagogues, businesses, and homes) and sent tens of thousands of Jews to concentration camps, FDR recalled the U.S. ambassador to Germany and allowed fifteen thousand refugees on visitor permits to remain longer in the United States. But he went no further, and Congress—motivated by economic concerns and spreading anti-Semitism—voted to uphold U.S. immigration restrictions as Jews attempted to flee Hitler's Germany.

Even the tragic voyage of the *St. Louis* did not change government policy. The vessel left Hamburg in mid-1939 carrying 930 desperate Jewish refugees, none of whom had proper immigration documents. Denied entry to Havana, the *St. Louis* headed for Miami, where Coast Guard cutters prevented it from docking. The ship was forced back to Europe, where some refugees took shelter in nations soon to be overrun by Hitler's legions.

Roosevelt, however, had quietly begun readying the country for war. In early 1938, he successfully pressured the House of Representatives to defeat a constitutional amendment proposed by Indiana Democrat Louis Ludlow to require a majority vote in a national referendum before a congressional declaration of war could go into effect (unless the United States were attacked). Later that year, in the wake of the Munich crisis, Roosevelt asked Congress for funds to build up the air force, which he believed essential to deter aggression. In January 1939, the president secretly decided to sell bombers to France, saying privately that "our frontier is on the Rhine." Although the more than five hundred combat planes delivered to France did not deter war, French orders spurred growth of the U.S. aircraft industry.

For Roosevelt and for other Western leaders, Hitler's swallowing of the whole of Czechoslovakia in March 1939 proved a turning point, forcing them to face a stark new reality. Until now, they had been able to explain away Hitler's actions by saying he was only trying to reunite German-speaking peoples. That argument no longer worked. Leaders in Paris and London realized that, if the German leader were to be stopped, it would have to be by force. When Hitler began eyeing his neighbor Poland, London and Paris announced they would stand by the Poles. The Soviets made a different choice. Soviet leader Joseph Stalin believed that the West's appeasement of Hitler had left him no choice but to cut a deal with Berlin, and he signed a non-aggression pact with Germany in 1939. But Stalin also coveted territory: a top-secret protocol attached to the pact carved eastern Europe into German and Soviet zones and permitted the Soviets to grab the eastern half of Poland and the three Baltic states of Lithuania, Estonia, and Latvia, formerly part of the Russian Empire.

22-7d Poland and the Outbreak of World War II

In the early morning hours of September 1, 1939, German tank columns rolled into Poland. German fighting planes covered the advance, thereby launching a new type of warfare, the *blitzkrieg* (lightning war)—highly mobile land forces and armor combined with tactical aircraft. Within forty-eight hours, Britain and France responded by declaring war on Germany. "It's come at last," Franklin Roosevelt murmured. "God help us all."

▲ German leader Adolf Hitler (1889–1945) is surrounded in this propagandistic painting by images that came to symbolize hate, genocide, and war: Nazi flags with emblems of the swastika, the iron cross on the dictator's pocket, Nazi troops in loyal salute. The anti-Semitic Hitler denounced the United States as a "Jewish rubbish heap" of "inferiority and decadence" that was "incapable of conducting war."

U.S. Army Center of Military History

When Europe descended into the abyss of war in September 1939, Roosevelt declared neutrality and pressed for repeal of the arms embargo. Isolationist senator Arthur Vandenberg of Michigan roared back that the United States could not be "an arsenal for one belligerent without becoming a target for the other." After much debate, however, Congress in November lifted the embargo on contraband and approved cash-and-carry exports of arms. Using "methods short of war," Roosevelt thus began to aid the Allies.

22-7e Asian Tensions

In Asia, meanwhile, Japan was on the march. The United States had interests at stake in the region: the Philippines and Pacific islands, religious missions, trade and investments, and the Open Door in China. In traditional missionary fashion, Americans also believed that they were China's special friend and protector. "With God's help," Senator Kenneth Wherry of Nebraska once proclaimed, "we will lift Shanghai up and up, ever up, until it is just like Kansas City." By contrast, the aggressive Japan loomed as a threat to American attitudes and interests. The Tokyo government seemed bent on subjugating China and unhinging the Open Door doctrine of equal trade and investment opportunity.

In the late 1920s, civil war broke out in China when Jiang Jieshi (Chiang Kai-shek) ousted Mao Zedong and his communist followers from the ruling Guomindang Party. Americans applauded this display of anti-Bolshevism and Jiang's conversion to Christianity in 1930. Jiang's new wife, Soong Meiling, also won their hearts. American educated, Madame Jiang spoke flawless English, dressed in Western fashion, and cultivated ties with prominent Americans. Warming to Jiang, U.S. officials abandoned one imperial vestige by signing a treaty in 1928 restoring control of tariffs to the Chinese.

Japan continued to pressure the Chinese (see Map 22.6). In mid-1937, owing to Japanese provocation, the Sino-Japanese War erupted. Japanese forces seized Beijing and cities along the coast. The gruesome bombing of Shanghai intensified anti-Japanese sentiment in the United States. Senator Norris, an isolationist who moved further away from isolationism with each Japanese thrust, condemned the Japanese as "disgraceful, ignoble, barbarous, and cruel, even beyond the power of language to describe." In an effort to help China by permitting it to buy American arms, Roosevelt refused to declare the existence of war, thus avoiding activation of the Neutrality Acts.

22-7f Roosevelt's Quarantine Speech

In a speech denouncing the aggressors on October 5, 1937, the president called for a "quarantine" to curb the "epidemic

Map 22.6 Japanese Expansion Before Pearl Harbor

The Japanese quest for predominance began at the turn of the century and intensified in the 1930s. China suffered the most at the hands of Tokyo's military. Vulnerable U.S. possessions in Asia and the Pacific proved no obstacle to Japan's ambitions for a Greater East Asia Co-Prosperity Sphere.

Social Security

The New Deal's Social Security system expanded over subsequent decades, and now covers almost 99 percent of American workers. It has dramatically reduced the poverty rate among the nation's elderly, giving millions a more secure and enjoyable old age, and it provides financial support for the disabled and for dependent children.

Despite its successes, today's Social Security system faces an uncertain future. Its troubles are due in part to decisions made during the 1930s. President Franklin Roosevelt did not want Social Security to be confused with poor relief. Therefore, he rejected the European model of government-funded pensions and instead created a system financed by payments from workers and their employers—a system based on individual accounts. This system, however, presented a short-term problem. If benefits came from their own contributions, workers who began receiving Social Security payments in 1940 would have received less than $1 a month. Therefore, Social Security payments from current workers paid the benefits of those already retired.

Over the years, this system of financing has become increasingly unstable, as an ever-larger pool of retirees has to be supported by those currently in the workforce. People are living longer. In 1935, when the system was created, average life expectancy was lower than sixty-five years, the age one could begin to collect benefits. Today, on average, American men live almost sixteen years past sixty-five, and women come close to twenty more years. In 1935, there were 16 current workers paying into the system for each person receiving retirement benefits. In 2010, there were 2.8 workers per retiree. The 77 million baby boomers born in the 1940s, 1950s, and 1960s are now retiring (though current retirees do not receive full Social Security benefits until age 66). Unless the system is reformed, many argue, the retirement of the baby-boom cohort could even bankrupt the system.

While the stock market was rising rapidly during the 1990s, some proposed that, because Social Security paid only a fraction of what individuals might have earned by investing their Social Security tax payments in the stock market, Americans be allowed to do just that. Some opponents declared this proposal too risky; others simply pointed to the structure of Social Security retirement. If current workers kept their money to invest, where would benefits for current retirees come from? The stock market's huge drop in 2001 and then the long-lasting economic downturn that began in 2008 (and the losses sustained by private pension funds) slowed the push for privatization. Nonetheless, as baby boomers retire in growing numbers, questions about the future of Social Security remain an important part of the system's legacy.

CRITICAL THINKING

- What should be done to shore up Social Security?
- Is privatization the answer to the looming shortfalls in the Social Security System?
- Should the age of full benefits be raised?
- What other possible solutions are there?

---

of world lawlessness." People who thought Washington had been too gentle with Japan cheered. Isolationists warned that the president was edging toward war. On December 12, Japanese aircraft sank the American gunboat *Panay*, an escort for Standard Oil Company tankers on the Yangtze River. Two American sailors died during the attack. Roosevelt was much relieved when Tokyo apologized and offered to pay for damages.

Japan's declaration of a "New Order" in Asia, in the words of one American official, "banged, barred, and bolted" the Open Door. Alarmed, the Roosevelt administration during the late 1930s gave loans and sold military equipment to Jiang's Chinese government. Secretary Hull declared a moral embargo on the shipment of airplanes to Japan. Meanwhile, the U.S. Navy continued to grow, aided by a billion-dollar congressional appropriation in 1938. In mid-1939, the United States abrogated its trade treaty with Tokyo, yet Americans continued to ship oil, cotton, and machinery to Japan. The administration hesitated to initiate economic sanctions because such pressure might spark a Japanese-American war at a time when Germany posed a more serious threat and the

United States was unprepared for war. When war broke out in Europe in the late summer of 1939, Japanese-American relations were stalemated.

Summary

In the 1930s, a major economic crisis and the approach of another world war threatened the future of the nation. By 1933, almost one-quarter of America's workers were unemployed. Millions of people did not have enough to eat or adequate places to live. Herbert Hoover, elected president in 1928, believed that government should play only a limited role in managing the nation's economy and rejected both public jobs programs and aid to the poor. In the 1932 presidential election, voters turned to the candidate who promised them a "New Deal." President Franklin Delano Roosevelt acted decisively to stabilize America's capitalist system and then worked to ameliorate its harshest impacts on the nation's people.

The New Deal was a liberal reform program that developed within the parameters of America's capitalist and democratic system. The New Deal expanded the role and power of the federal government. Because of New Deal reforms, banks, utilities, stock markets, farms, and most businesses operated under rules set by the federal government. Federal law guaranteed workers' right to join unions without fear of employer reprisals and required employers to negotiate with workers' unions. New Deal programs offered public jobs to the unemployed and guaranteed many Americans the basic protection of a national welfare system.

The New Deal faced challenges from many directions. As the depression wore on, populist demagogues blamed scapegoats or offered overly simple explanations for the plight of the American people. Business leaders attacked the New Deal for its new regulation of business and its support of organized labor. As the federal government expanded its role throughout the nation, tensions between national and local authority sometimes flared up. Both the West and the South were transformed by federal government action, but citizens of both regions were suspicious of federal intervention, and white southerners strongly resisted any attempt to challenge systems of racial discrimination. The political realities of a fragile New Deal coalition and strong opposition shaped—and limited—New Deal programs of the 1930s and the social welfare systems with which Americans still live today.

New Deal programs helped many of America's people live better, more secure lives. And the New Deal fundamentally changed the way that the U.S. government would deal with future economic downturns and with the needs of its citizens in good times and in bad.

Yet the New Deal by itself did not end the Great Depression; it took World War II and the economic boom it created to make that happen. As the crises in Europe and Asia deepened in the last years of the 1930s, the Roosevelt administration sought to keep the United States out of the fray; even after Nazi forces invaded Poland in September 1939, thus sparking a new European struggle, the president declared American neutrality. As he did so, however, he sent aid to the Allies and began preparing the country for war.

Suggestions for Further Reading

Anthony J. Badger, *The New Deal: The Depression Years, 1933–1940* (1989)

Alan Brinkley, *The End of Reform: New Deal Liberalism in Recession and War* (1995)

Alan Brinkley, *Voices of Protest: Huey Long, Father Coughlin, and the Great Depression* (1982)

Lizabeth Cohen, *Making a New Deal: Industrial Workers in Chicago* (1990)

Blanche Wiesen Cook, *Eleanor Roosevelt*, Vols. 1 and 2 (1992, 1999)

Kirsten Downey, *The Woman Behind the New Deal: The Life and Legacy of Frances Perkins—Social Security, Unemployment Insurance* (2009)

Timothy Egan, *The Worst Hard Time* (2005)

Sidney Fine, *Sitdown: The General Motors Strike of 1936–37* (1969)

James E. Goodman, *Stories of Scottsboro* (1994)

Ira Katznelson, *Fear Itself: The New Deal and the Origins of Our Time* (2014)

David M. Kennedy, *Freedom from Fear: The American People in Depression and War* (1999)

Eric Rauchway, *The Great Depression and the New Deal: A Very Short Introduction* (2008)

Jason Scott Smith, *Building New Deal Liberalism: The Political Economy of Public Works, 1933–1956* (2005)

Donald Worster, *Dust Bowl: The Southern Plains in the 1930s* (2004)

MINDTAP
From Cengage

MindTap® is a fully online personalized learning experience built upon Cengage Learning content. MindTap® combines student learning tools—readings, multimedia, activities, and assessments—into a singular Learning Path that guides students through the course and helps students develop the critical thinking, analysis, and communication skills that are essential to academic and professional success.

The Second World War at Home and Abroad, 1939–1945

The first wave of planes launched before dawn from Japanese aircraft carriers two hundred and thirty miles north of O'ahu; a second wave followed soon thereafter. At the island's north shore, one group circled leeward toward the battleships anchored at Pearl Harbor; a second swept down the center of the island between the Ko'olau and the Waianae mountain ranges. Most of the people outside that lovely Sunday morning paid them little mind; war games were so common in Hawai'i by that point that even seasoned military men were fooled. Watching planes diving on Pearl Harbor from the control tower at the adjacent army air base, Colonel William Farthing mused, "I wonder what the marines are doing to the navy so early on Sunday morning." Seconds later, as a Japanese bomber dived toward the air base, a rising sun emblazoned on its fuselage, one soldier pointed: "Look! There goes one of the red team." Then the plane dropped a bomb.

On the battleship *West Virginia*, Ship's Cook Third Class Doris Miller was collecting laundry when the general quarters alarm sounded. Miller, a 6´3˝, three-hundred-pound African American man whom the navy restricted to mess service because of his race, followed officers' orders to report to the bridge. Miller took over a .50-caliber Browning anti-aircraft gun—a weapon he'd never before fired—manning it until he ran out of ammunition and the order came to abandon the sinking ship. At Wheeler Field an army fighter pilot, Second Lieutenant Philip Rasmussen, commandeered an obsolete P-36 and took off to battle the Japanese, still wearing the purple pajamas in which he'd been sleeping. And in Honolulu, seventeen-year-old Daniel Inouye—the son of a Japanese immigrant who would win the Medal of Honor for heroism in the coming war and eventually serve as president pro tempore of the U.S. Senate—headed for the volunteer Red Cross station at Lunalilo School, where he worked for twenty-four hours without rest, treating the wounded and ferrying the dead to a makeshift morgue. Huddled in an air raid shelter, sixteen-year-old Mary Ann Ramsey saw the injured brought in "with filthy black oil covering shredded flesh." As casualties mounted, prostitutes turned

◄ The stricken USS *West Virginia* was one of eight battleships caught in the surprise Japanese attack at Pearl Harbor, Hawai'i, on December 7, 1941. In this photograph, sailors on a launch attempt to rescue a crew member from the water as oil burns around the sinking ship. National Archives

Chronology

1939	■ Germany invades Poland; World War II begins
1940	■ France and the Low Countries fall to the Germans
1941	■ Lend-Lease Act passed by Congress
	■ Atlantic Charter issued by Roosevelt and Churchill
	■ Japan attacks Pearl Harbor
	■ United States enters World War II
1942	■ War Production Board created to oversee conversion to military production
	■ Allies losing war in Pacific to Japan; U.S. victory at Battle of Midway in June is turning point
	■ Office of Price Administration creates rationing system for food and consumer goods
	■ United States pursues "Europe First" war policy; Allies reject Stalin's demands for a second front and invade North Africa
	■ West Coast Japanese Americans relocated to internment camps
	■ Manhattan Project set up to create atomic bomb
	■ Congress of Racial Equality established
1943	■ Soviet army defeats German troops at Stalingrad
	■ Congress passes War Labor Disputes (Smith-Connally) Act following coal miners' strike
	■ "Zoot suit riots" in Los Angeles; race riots break out in Detroit, Harlem, and other cities
	■ Allies invade Italy
	■ Roosevelt, Churchill, and Stalin meet at Tehran Conference
1944	■ Allied troops land at Normandy on D-Day, June 6
	■ Roosevelt elected to fourth term as president
	■ United States retakes Philippines
1945	■ Roosevelt, Stalin, and Churchill meet at Yalta Conference
	■ British and U.S. forces firebomb Dresden, Germany
	■ Battles of Iwo Jima and Okinawa result in heavy Japanese and American losses
	■ Roosevelt dies; Truman becomes president
	■ Germany surrenders; Allied forces liberate Nazi death camps
	■ Potsdam Conference calls for Japan's "unconditional surrender"
	■ United States uses atomic bombs on Hiroshima and Nagasaki
	■ Japan surrenders

the infamous brothels of Hotel Street into temporary hospital wards and nursed the badly wounded.

Japanese planes sank or severely damaged all eight of America's Pacific Fleet battleships. They destroyed or badly damaged 188 planes, most of them parked nose to tail on the island's airfields. More than 2,400 people died in the two-hour attack, 1,177 from the battleship *Arizona*, which sank within seconds after an armor-piercing bomb hit its forward ammunition compartment. That night the people of Hawai'i spent their first night under martial law, the islands completely dark against the threat of another attack. "Shortly before midnight," wrote one who sat in Honolulu's darkness that night, "the moon began to rise, and a vivid lunar rainbow, the old Hawaiian omen of victory, arched over the dark city."

By December 7, 1941, Europe and Asia were already in flames. Now the United States would join the world war.

Experience an interactive version of this story in MindTap®.

The Second World War marked a turning point in the lives of millions of Americans as well as in the history of the United States. Most deeply affected were those who fought the war, on the beaches and battlefields, in the skies and at sea. For forty-five months, Americans fought abroad to subdue the German, Italian, and Japanese aggressors. Although the war began badly for the United States, by mid-1942 the Allies had halted the Axis powers' advance. In June 1944, American troops, together with Canadian, British, and Free French units, launched a massive invasion across the English Channel, landing at Normandy and pushing into Germany by the following spring. Battered by merciless bombing raids, leaderless after Adolf Hitler's suicide, and pressed by a Soviet advance from the east, the Nazis capitulated in May 1945. In the Pacific, Americans drove Japanese forces back, island by island, toward Japan. America's devastating conventional bombing of Japanese cities, followed by the atomic bombs that demolished Hiroshima and Nagasaki in August 1945 and the Soviet Union's declaration of war on Japan, led to surrender. At the end of the war, prospects for international cooperation seemed bleak. The nations that made up the

"Grand Alliance"—Britain, the Soviet Union, and the United States—had very different visions of the postwar world.

The war was fought far from the United States, but it touched the lives of all Americans. This was a total war, in which the United States mobilized all sectors of American society and economy—industry, finance, agriculture, and labor; the civilian population and the military—to defeat the Axis powers. The federal government, which had the monumental task of managing the war on all fronts, expanded its reach and power.

Committed to becoming the "arsenal of democracy," the United States built a massive war industry that demanded workers for seven-days-a-week, twenty-four-hours-a-day production. These factories created new opportunities for formerly marginal workers: women, African Americans, Latinos. During the war, nearly one of every ten Americans moved permanently to another state, most headed for work in war production centers. After a decade of economic depression, Americans found new prosperity in the midst of global conflagration. The war strengthened unity and national purpose, but it also gave new shape to long-standing prejudices: the United States interned 112,000 Japanese nationals and Japanese Americans in remote "relocation camps" and fought the Axis with a racially segregated military. At war's end, although many Americans grieved for loved ones lost in battle and worried about the stability of the emerging postwar order, the United States had unprecedented power and unmatched prosperity among the world's nations.

■ *What factors brought the United States into the war?*

■ *What military, diplomatic, and social factors influenced decisions about how to fight the Second World War?*

■ *How did World War II transform the United States?*

23-1 America's Entry into the Conflict

▶ How did Franklin D. Roosevelt draw the United States closer to war?

▶ How did American attitudes about involvement in the war evolve after 1939?

▶ What was the nature of the relationship between Japan and the United States prior to the bombing of Pearl Harbor?

When a new European war broke out in 1939, many Americans hoped their country could stand apart. But would it be possible? Roosevelt remarked that the United States could not "draw a line of defense around this country and live completely and solely to ourselves," noting that when Thomas Jefferson had tried that with his 1807 embargo, "the damned thing didn't work," and "we got into the War of 1812." America, the president insisted, could not insulate itself from world war. But even as polls showed that Americans strongly favored the Allies and that most supported aid to Britain and France, the great majority also wanted the United States to remain at peace. Troubled by this conflicting advice—oppose Hitler, aid the Allies, but stay out of the war—the president gradually moved the nation from neutrality to undeclared war against Germany and then, after Japan attacked Pearl Harbor, to full-scale war itself.

From 1939 through 1941, Americans vigorously debated their nation's proper role in the growing war. Groups such as the American Legion, the League of Women Voters, labor unions, and local chapters of the Committee to Defend America by Aiding the Allies and the isolationist America First Committee (both organized in 1940) participated vigorously in the national debate. Most Americans understood the high stakes of U.S. foreign policy, but public interest also was fed by the chilling immediacy of radio news reports. Americans' ethnic affiliations with belligerents and victims of aggression also mattered. African American churches organized anti-Italian boycotts to protest Mussolini's pummeling of Ethiopia, and the German American Bund drew German Americans—in relatively small numbers—to rallies supporting the Nazi cause.

23-1a The Expanding Conflict

As Americans debated, the stakes grew higher. In March 1940, the Soviet Union—which had signed a non-aggression pact with Hitler shortly before Germany invaded Poland in 1939—invaded Finland. In April, Germany conquered Denmark and Norway (see Map 22.5). "The small countries are smashed up, one by one, like matchwood," sighed **Winston Churchill**, who became Britain's prime minister on May 10, 1940—the same day that Germany attacked Belgium, the Netherlands, and France. German divisions pushed French and British forces back to the English Channel, and between May 26 and June 6, more than 300,000 Allied soldiers escaped from Dunkirk to Britain on a flotilla of small boats. The Germans occupied Paris a week later. The French government plunged into disunion and chaos, from which emerged a new regime located in the town of Vichy, France, concluded an armistice with Germany on June 22 and collaborated with the conquering Nazis for the remainder of the war. With France out of the picture, the German Luftwaffe

Winston Churchill British wartime prime minister; close friend of FDR and staunch ally of the United States; served 1940–1945 and 1951–1955.

(air force) launched massive bombing raids against Great Britain in preparation for a full-scale invasion.

Alarmed by the swift defeat of one European nation after another, Americans increasingly questioned isolationist principles. Some liberals left the isolationist fold; it became more and more the province of conservatives. Emotions ran high. Roosevelt called the isolationists "ostriches" and charged that some were pro-Nazi subversives. More significantly, the president worked to prevent the fall of Britain. In May 1940, he ordered the sale of old surplus military equipment to Britain and France. In July, he cultivated bipartisan support by naming Republicans Henry L. Stimson and Frank Knox, ardent backers of aid to the Allies, secretaries of war and the navy, respectively. In September, by executive agreement, the president traded fifty over-age American destroyers for leases to eight British military bases, including Newfoundland, Bermuda, and Jamaica.

Recognizing America's move toward war, Germany, Italy, and Japan signed the Tripartite Pact in late September, 1940. The pact formalized existing alliances among the three nations, formally creating the Axis Powers. It officially recognized two separate spheres of influence, with Japan controlling Greater East Asia and—significantly—made clear that if the United States joined the war it would face enemies in both Europe and the Pacific.

23-1b Supporting the Allies

Also in September, Roosevelt signed into law the hotly debated and narrowly passed **Selective Training and Service Act of 1940**, the first peacetime military draft in American history. All men between the ages of twenty-one and thirty-five were required to register, and President Roosevelt himself read out the first number drawn in the national draft lottery. Meanwhile, Roosevelt won reelection in November 1940 with promises of peace: "Your boys are not going to be sent into any foreign wars." Republican candidate Wendell Willkie, who in the emerging spirit of bipartisanship had not made an issue of foreign policy, snapped, "That hypocritical son of a bitch! This is going to beat me!" And it did.

Roosevelt portrayed America's role as "the arsenal of democracy," and claimed that the United States could stay out of the war by enabling the British to win. To that end, he proposed a "Lend-Lease" bill. Because Britain was broke, the president explained, the United States should lend rather than sell weapons, much as a neighbor lends a garden hose to fight a fire. Most lawmakers needed little persuasion. In March 1941, with pro-British sentiment running high, Congress passed the **Lend-Lease Act** with overwhelming support. The initial appropriation was $7 billion, but by the end of the war the amount had reached $50 billion, more than $31 billion of it for Britain.

To make sure Lend-Lease supplies were delivered safely, Roosevelt ordered the U.S. Navy to patrol halfway across the Atlantic and stationed U.S. troops in Greenland and Iceland. He also sent Lend-Lease aid to the Soviet Union, which Hitler had attacked in June (thereby shattering the 1939 Nazi-Soviet nonaggression pact). If the Soviets could hold off two hundred German divisions in the east, Roosevelt calculated, Britain would gain some breathing room. Churchill, with dark humor, responded: "If Hitler invaded Hell, I would make at least a favorable reference to the Devil in the House of Commons."

23-1c Atlantic Charter

In August 1941, Churchill and Roosevelt met for four days on a British battleship off the coast of Newfoundland. They got along well, trading naval stories and making much of the fact that Churchill was half American (his mother was from New York). This meeting produced the **Atlantic Charter**, a set of war aims reminiscent of Wilsonianism: collective security, disarmament, self-determination, economic cooperation, and freedom of the seas. Churchill later recalled that Roosevelt told him in Newfoundland that he could not ask Congress for a declaration of war against Germany, but "he would wage war" and "become more and more provocative."

Within days of that meeting, German and American ships came into direct contact in the Atlantic. On September 4, a German submarine launched torpedoes at (but did not hit) the American destroyer *Greer*. In response, Roosevelt gave the U.S. Navy authority to fire first when under threat. He also publicly announced what he had promised Churchill in private: American warships would convoy British merchant ships across the ocean. The United States thus entered into an undeclared naval war with Germany. When a German submarine torpedoed the U.S. destroyer *Kearny* off the coast of Iceland a month later, Roosevelt declared that "the shooting has started. And history has recorded who fired the first shot." Later in October, when the destroyer *Reuben James* went down with the loss of more than one hundred American lives, Congress revised the Neutrality Acts (see "Isolationist Views in the United States," Section 22-b) to allow armed American merchant ships to carry weapons to Britain. The United States was edging very close to being a belligerent.

23-1d The Growing Crisis with Japan

It seems ironic, therefore, that the Second World War came to the United States by way of Asia. Roosevelt had wanted

Selective Training and Service Act of 1940 Controversial 1940 law that required all men between twenty-one and thirty-five (later expanded to eighteen through forty-five) to register with local draft boards; began the first peacetime military draft in U.S. history.

Lend-Lease Act Program proposed by Roosevelt and enacted by Congress in early 1941 to supply war material to cash-strapped Britain.

Atlantic Charter 1941 agreement between the United States and Great Britain that stated the two countries' war aims; it condemned international aggression, affirmed the right of national self-determination, and endorsed the principles of free trade, disarmament, and collective security.

to avoid war with Japan in order to concentrate American resources on the defeat of Germany. In September 1940, after Germany, Italy, and Japan had signed the Tripartite Pact to form the Axis powers, Roosevelt halted shipments of aviation fuel and scrap metal to Japan. Because the president believed the Japanese would consider a cutoff of oil a life-or-death matter, he did not embargo that vital commodity. But in July 1941 Japanese troops occupied French Indochina, seeking to cut off Western shipments of oil and other supplies to China, with whom Japan was at war, while also positioning Japanese troops to seize much of southeast Asia. In response, Washington froze Japanese assets in the United States, virtually ending trade (including oil) with Japan.

Tokyo proposed a summit meeting between President Roosevelt and Prime Minister Prince Konoye, but the United States rejected the idea. American officials insisted that the Japanese first agree to respect China's sovereignty and territorial integrity and to honor the Open Door policy—in short, to get out of China. For Roosevelt, Europe still claimed first priority, but he supported Secretary Hull's hard-line policy against Japan's pursuit of the Greater East Asia Co-Prosperity Sphere—the name Tokyo gave to the vast Asian region it intended to dominate. Fundamentally, the United States was unwilling to cede control of East Asia to Japan, and Japan understood that U.S. terms required it to abandon its growing empire and claims to power in the region, remaining subject to U.S. economic power.

◄ Men doing exercises as they become part of America's first peacetime military draft in 1940.

Ralph Morse/Getty Images

Roosevelt told his advisers to string out ongoing Japanese-American talks as a way to gain time—time to fortify the Philippines and to deal with the crisis in Europe. But because the United States had broken Japan's diplomatic code through Operation MAGIC, officials knew that Tokyo's patience with diplomacy was waning rapidly. In late November, the Japanese rejected American demands to withdraw from Indochina. On December 6, the United States intercepted a 14-part message to the Japanese embassy in Washington, D.C., along with instructions to destroy their cipher machines once it was received. American officials understood the significance of such instructions and, once the document was fully decrypted, sent warnings to American military installations in the Pacific. However, due to some questionable decisions about how to transmit the material, coupled with technical difficulties, the warnings arrived too late.

23-1e Japan's Surprise Attack

Japan had planned a daring raid on U.S. and British territory in the Pacific, one that required coordinating forces for near-simultaneous attacks on sites stretching over nearly seven thousand miles of the Pacific Ocean. In order to hit the most distant site—the U.S. Territory of Hawai'i—an armada of sixty Japanese ships, with a core of six carriers bearing 360 airplanes, had crossed three thousand miles of the Pacific Ocean in total radio silence. Early in the morning of December 7, some 230 miles north of Honolulu, the carriers unleashed their planes, each stamped with a red sun representing the Japanese flag. They swept down on the unsuspecting American naval base and nearby airfields, dropping torpedoes and bombs and strafing buildings.

In Pearl Harbor, the battleship USS *Arizona* fell victim to a Japanese bomb that ignited explosives below deck, killing more than a thousand sailors. The USS *Nevada* tried to escape the inferno by heading out to sea, but when a second wave of aerial attackers struck the ship the crew ran her aground to avoid blocking the harbor channel. Japanese forces sank or damaged eight battleships and many smaller vessels and destroyed more than 160 aircraft on the ground. By chance, all three of the Pacific Fleet's aircraft carriers were at sea and escaped the bombing.

The attack on Pearl Harbor would become a rallying cry for Americans at war, but on that same day (it was December 8 on the other side of the International Date Line), Japan also attacked the neutral nation of Thailand, as well as Malaya, Shanghai, Singapore, Guam, the Philippines, Hong Kong, Wake Island, and Midway—all of which were Pacific possessions of Western powers. Pearl Harbor was one piece of Japan's broader strategy.

Some critics at the time—and later—charged that Roosevelt had conspired to leave the fleet vulnerable to attack so that the United States could enter the Second World War through the "back door" of Asia. However, historians agree that no evidence supports that claim. American officials did believe, based on decrypted diplomatic cables,

that war was likely on the horizon. But they knew nothing more. The decrypted messages never discussed the coming attacks, and most military commanders in Hawai'i were confident—wrongly—that distance offered protection from Japanese attack.

23-1f Declaration of War

On December 8, referring to the previous day as "a date which will live in infamy," Roosevelt vowed that Americans would never forget "the character of the onslaught against us" and asked Congress to declare war against Japan. A unanimous vote in the Senate and a 388-to-1 vote in the House thrust America into war. Representative Jeannette Rankin of Montana voted no, repeating her vote against entry into the First World War. Britain declared war on Japan, but the Soviet Union did not. Three days later, Germany and Italy, honoring the Tripartite Pact they had signed with Japan in September 1940, declared war against the United States. "Hitler's fate was sealed," Churchill later wrote. "Mussolini's fate was sealed. As for the Japanese, they would be ground to powder. . . . I went to bed and slept the sleep of the saved and thankful."

23-2 The United States at War

▶ Why was the United States unprepared for the military conflict of World War II?

▶ How did the war develop in the Pacific after U.S. entry into World War II?

▶ How did the war in Europe develop after U.S. entry into World War II?

As Japanese bombs fell in the U.S. territory of Hawai'i, American antiwar sentiment evaporated. Some former critics of intervention, seeking a persuasive explanation, turned to the popular children's story *Ferdinand the Bull*. Ferdinand, though huge and powerful, just liked to "sit and smell the flowers"—until the day he was stung by a bee. It was a comforting tale about America's role, but it wasn't true. As the world went to war, the United States had not been, like Ferdinand, just "smell[ing] the flowers." America's embargo of shipments to Japan and refusal to accept Japan's expansionist policies had brought the two nations to the brink of war, and the United States was deeply involved in an undeclared naval war with Germany well before Japan's attack on Pearl Harbor. By December 1941, Roosevelt had long since instituted an unprecedented peacetime draft, created war mobilization agencies, and commissioned war plans for simultaneous struggle in Europe and the Pacific.

23-2a A Nation Unprepared

Nonetheless, the nation was not ready for war. Throughout the 1930s, military funding had been a low priority. In September 1939 (when Hitler invaded Poland and began what would become the Second World War), the U.S. Army ranked forty-fifth in size among the world's armies and could fully equip only one-third of its 227,000 men. The peacetime draft instituted in 1940 expanded the U.S. military to 2 million men, but Roosevelt's 1941 survey of war preparedness, the "Victory Plan," estimated that the United States could not be ready to fight before June 1943.

In December 1941, many analysts thought U.S. victory unlikely. In Europe, the Allies were losing the war (see Map 22.5). Hitler had claimed Austria, Czechoslovakia, Poland, the Netherlands, Denmark, and Norway. Romania was lost, then Greece and Bulgaria. France had fallen in June 1940. Britain fought on, but German planes rained bombs on London. More than 3 million soldiers under German command had penetrated deep into the Soviet Union and Africa. German U-boats controlled the Atlantic from the Arctic to the Caribbean. Within months of America's entry into the war, German submarines sank 216 vessels—some so close to American shores that people could see the glow of burning ships.

23-2b War in the Pacific

In the Pacific, the war was largely America's to fight. The Soviets had not declared war on Japan, and there were too

▲ "Let's Go Get 'Em!," proclaims this 1942 recruiting poster for the United States Marine Corps. Over the course of the war, 6 percent of servicemen overall were killed or wounded; the casualty ratio for Marines was 13 percent.

Library of Congress, Prints & Photographs Division, Reproduction number LC-USZC4-9891 (color film copy transparency)

few British troops protecting Great Britain's Asian colonies to make much difference. By late spring of 1942, Japan had captured most European colonial possessions in Southeast Asia: the Dutch East Indies (Indonesia); French Indochina (Vietnam, Laos, and Cambodia); and the British colonies of Malaya, Burma, Western New Guinea, Hong Kong, and Singapore. In the American Philippines, the struggle went on longer, but also in vain. The Japanese attacked the Philippines hours after Pearl Harbor and, finding the entire force of B-17 bombers sitting on the airfields, destroyed U.S. air capability in the region. American and Filipino troops retreated to the Bataan Peninsula, hoping to hold the main island, Luzon, but Japanese forces were superior. In March 1942, under orders from Roosevelt, General Douglas MacArthur, the commander of U.S. forces in the Far East, departed the Philippines for Australia, proclaiming, "I shall return."

Left behind were almost eighty thousand American and Filipino troops. Starving and weakened by disease, they held on for almost another month before surrendering. Those who survived long enough to surrender faced worse horror. Japanese troops, lacking supplies themselves, were not prepared to deal with a large number of prisoners, and most believed the prisoners had forfeited honorable treatment by surrendering. In what came to be known as the Bataan Death March, the Japanese force-marched their captives to prison camps more than 65 miles away, denying them food and water and bayoneting or beating to death those who fell behind. As many as ten thousand Filipinos and six hundred Americans died on the march. Tens of thousands of Filipino civilians also died under Japanese occupation.

As losses mounted, the United States began to strike back. On April 18, sixteen American B-25 bombers appeared in the skies over Japan. The Doolittle raid (named after the mission's leader) did little harm to Japan, but it had an enormous psychological impact, pushing Japanese commander Admiral Isoroku Yamamoto to bold action. Instead of consolidating control close to home, Yamamoto concluded, Japan must move quickly to lure the weakened United States into a "decisive battle." The target was Midway—two tiny islands about one thousand miles northwest of Honolulu, where the U.S. Navy had a base. If Japan could take Midway—not implausible, given Japan's string of victories—it would have a secure defensive perimeter far from the home islands (see Map 23.3). By using Guam, the Philippines, and perhaps even Australia as hostages, Japan believed, it could negotiate a favorable peace agreement with the United States.

Admiral Yamamoto did not know that America's MAGIC code-breaking machines could decipher Japanese messages. This time, surprise was on the side of the United States, and the Japanese fleet found the U.S. Navy and its carrier-based dive-bombers lying in wait. The Battle of Midway in June 1942 was a turning point in the Pacific war. Japanese strategists had hoped that the United States, discouraged by

Japan's early victories, would withdraw and leave Japan to control the Pacific. That outcome was no longer a possibility. Now Japan was on the defensive.

23-2c "Europe First" Strategy

Despite the importance of these early Pacific battles, America's war strategy was "Europe First." Germany, American war planners recognized, was a greater danger to the United States than Japan. If Germany conquered the Soviet Union, they believed, it might directly threaten the United States. Roosevelt also feared that the Soviet Union, suffering almost unimaginable losses as its military battled Hitler's invading army, might pursue a separate peace with Germany and so undo the Allied coalition. Therefore, the United States would work first with Britain and the USSR to defeat Germany, then deal with an isolated Japan.

British prime minister Winston Churchill and Soviet premier **Joseph Stalin** disagreed vehemently, however, over how to wage the war against Germany. By late 1941, before the fierce Russian winter stalled their onslaught, German troops had nearly reached Moscow and Leningrad (present-day St. Petersburg) and had slashed deeply into Ukraine, taking Kiev. Over a million Soviet soldiers had died defending their country. Stalin pressed for British and American troops to attack Germany from the west, through France, to draw German troops away from the Soviet front. Roosevelt believed "with heart and *mind*" that Stalin was right and promised to open a "second front" to Germany's west before the end of 1942. Churchill, however, blocked this plan. He had not forgotten Stalin's nonaggression pact with Hitler (see "Roosevelt's Evolving Views," Section 22-7c), and British military commanders, remembering the agonies of prolonged trench warfare in World War I, did not want to launch a large-scale invasion of Europe. Churchill promoted air attacks on Germany. He wanted to win control of the North Atlantic shipping lanes and to launch a smaller, safer attack on Axis positions in North Africa; halting the Germans there would protect British imperial possessions in the Mediterranean and the oil-rich Middle East.

Against his advisers' recommendation, Roosevelt accepted Churchill's plan. The U.S. military was not yet ready for a major campaign and Roosevelt needed to show the American public some success in the European war. Thus, instead of coming to the rescue of the USSR, the British and Americans made a joint landing in North Africa in November 1942. American troops, facing relatively light resistance, won quick victories in Algeria and Morocco. In Egypt, the British confronted General Erwin Rommel and his Afrika Korps in a struggle for control of the Suez Canal and the Middle East oil fields. Rommel's army, trapped between British and American troops, was forced to retreat into northern Tunisia and surrendered after six months. And in Russia, against all odds, the Soviet army hung on, fighting block by block for control of the city of Stalingrad in the deadly cold, to defeat the German Sixth Army in early 1943. Stalingrad, like Midway, was a major turning point in the war. By the spring of 1943, Germany, like Japan, was on the defensive. But relations among the Allies remained precarious. The Soviet Union had lost 1.1 million men in the Battle of Stalingrad. The United States and Britain, however, continued to resist Stalin's demand that they immediately open a second front. The death toll, already in the millions, continued to mount.

23-3 The Production Front and American Workers

▶ How did the American economy shift to production for the war?

▶ What role did the government play in wartime production and labor?

▶ What was the nature of wartime labor relations between workers and employers?

In late December 1940—almost a year before the United States entered the war—Franklin Roosevelt pledged that America would serve as the world's "great arsenal of democracy," making the machines that would win the war for the Allies. After Pearl Harbor, U.S. strategy remained much the same. The United States would prevail through a "crushing superiority of equipment," Roosevelt told Congress. Although the war would be fought on the battlefields of Europe and the Pacific, the nation's strategic advantage lay on the "production front" at home.

Goals for military production were staggering. In 1940, with war looming, American factories had built only 3,807 airplanes. Following Pearl Harbor, Roosevelt asked for 60,000 aircraft in 1942 and double that number in 1943. Plans called for building 16 million tons of shipping and 120,000 tanks. The military needed supplies to train and equip a force that would grow to almost 16 million men. Thus, for the duration of the war, military production took precedence. Turning from consumer desires to military needs, jukebox manufacturer Rock-Ola produced M1 carbines and Eureka Vacuum made gas masks, while automobile plants manufactured tanks and dress factories sewed military uniforms. The **War Production Board**, established in early 1942, had the enormous task of allocating resources and coordinating production among thousands of independent factories.

23-3a Businesses, Universities, and the War Effort

During the war, American businesses overwhelmingly cooperated with government war-production plans. Patriotism

Joseph Stalin Soviet premier and dictator of the Soviet Union who came to power after the death of Vladimir Lenin in 1924 and ruled until his death in 1953.

War Production Board U.S. government agency that allocated resources, coordinated production among thousands of independent factories, and awarded government contracts for wartime production during World War II.

was one reason, but generous incentives were another. Major American industries had at first resisted government pressure to shift to military production. In 1940, as the United States produced armaments for the Allies, the American economy had begun to recover from the Great Depression. Consumer spending increased, and industrialists gained confidence: automobile manufacturers, for example, expected to sell 25 percent more cars in 1941 than in 1939. Manufacturers understood that it would be enormously expensive to retool factories to produce planes or tanks instead of cars, and that such retooling would leave them totally dependent on a single client—the federal government. Many major industrialists, such as General Motors head Alfred Sloan, were suspicious of Roosevelt and what they saw as his antibusiness policies.

Government, however, met business more than halfway. The federal government paid for expensive retooling and factory expansions; it guaranteed profits by allowing corporations to charge the government for production costs plus a fixed profit; it created generous tax write-offs and exemptions from antitrust laws. War mobilization did not require America's businesses to sacrifice profits. Instead, corporations doubled their net profits between 1939 and 1943. As Secretary of War Henry Stimson explained, when a "capitalist country" goes to war, it must "let business make money out of the process or business won't work."

Most military contracts went to America's largest corporations, which had the facilities and experience to guarantee rapid, efficient production. From mid-1940 through September 1944, the government awarded contracts totaling $175 billion, with about two-thirds going to the top hundred corporations. General Motors alone received 8 percent of the total. This approach made sense for a nation that wanted enormous quantities of war goods manufactured in the shortest possible time; most small businesses simply did not have the necessary capacity. However, wartime government contracts further consolidated American manufacturing in the hands of a few giant corporations.

23-3b Manhattan Project

Wartime needs also created a new relationship between science and the U.S. military. Millions of dollars went to fund research programs at America's largest universities: $117 million to Massachusetts Institute of Technology alone. Such federally sponsored research programs developed new technologies of warfare, such as vastly improved radar systems and the proximity fuse. The most important government-sponsored scientific research program was the **Manhattan Project**, a $2 billion secret effort to build an atomic bomb. Roosevelt had been convinced by scientists fleeing the Nazis in 1939 that Germany was working to create an atomic weapon, and he resolved to beat them at their own efforts. But secrecy was paramount. The handful of key Congressional leaders who knew about the project hid its funding in the budget of the U.S. Army; almost all of Congress, and even FDR's vice president, remained in the dark.

The Manhattan Project achieved the world's first sustained nuclear chain reaction in 1942 at the University of Chicago, and in 1943 the federal government set up a secret community for atomic scientists and their families at Los Alamos, New Mexico. In this remote, sparsely populated, and beautiful setting, some of America's most talented scientists worked with Jewish refugees from Nazi Germany to develop the weapon that would change the world.

23-3c New Opportunities for Workers

America's new defense factories, running around the clock, required millions of workers. At first, workers were plentiful: 9 million Americans were still unemployed in 1940 when war mobilization began, and 3 million remained without work in December 1941. But during the war, the armed forces took almost 16 million men out of the potential civilian labor pool, forcing industry to look elsewhere for workers. Women, African Americans, Mexican Americans, poor whites from the isolated mountain hollows of Appalachia and the tenant farms of the Deep South—all streamed into jobs in defense plants.

In some cases, federal action eased their path. In 1941, as the federal government poured billions of dollars into war industries, many industries refused to hire African Americans. "The Negro will be considered only as janitors and other similar capacities," one executive notified black applicants. **A. Philip Randolph**, head of the Brotherhood of Sleeping Car Porters, proposed a march on Washington, D.C., to demand equal access to defense industry jobs. Roosevelt, fearing that the march might provoke race riots and that communists might infiltrate the movement, offered the March on Washington movement a deal. In exchange for canceling the march, the president issued Executive Order No. 8802, which prohibited discrimination in the defense industry and established the Fair Employment Practices Committee (FEPC) to deal with violations. Although enforcement was uneven, this official act led hundreds of thousands of black Americans to leave the South, seeking work and new lives in the industrial cities of the North and West.

Mexican workers also filled wartime jobs in the United States. Although the U.S. government had deported Mexicans as unemployment rose during the Great Depression, about 200,000 Mexican workers, or *braceros*, were offered short-term contracts to fill agricultural jobs left vacant as Americans sought well-paid war work. Mexican and Mexican American workers alike faced discrimination and segregation, but they seized the economic opportunities newly available to them. In 1941, the Los Angeles shipyards employed not a single Mexican American; by 1944, 17,000 worked there.

Manhattan Project Secret U.S. government-sponsored research program to develop an atomic bomb during World War II.

A. Philip Randolph Labor leader whose threatened march on Washington led President Roosevelt to issue Executive Order No. 8802, which prohibited racial discrimination in war industries and government jobs.

braceros Seasonal farm laborers from Mexico who were offered short-term contracts under a wartime "temporary worker" measure.

◀ War production plans called for defense factories to build 120,000 new aircraft in 1943. Here, women workers take on "men's jobs" at Vultee Aircraft Corporation, using riveting guns and bucking bars to build the center section of wings for training planes.

Bettmann/Getty Images

Early in the war production boom, employers insisted that women were not suited for industrial jobs. But as labor shortages began to threaten the war effort, employers did an about-face. The government's War Manpower Commission glorified the invented worker "**Rosie the Riveter**," who was featured on posters, in magazines, and in the recruiting jingle "Rosie's got a boyfriend, Charlie / Charlie, he's a marine / Rosie is protecting Charlie / Working overtime on the riveting machine."

Rosie the Riveter was an inspiring image, but she did not represent most women workers. Only 16 percent of female employees worked in defense plants, and women filled only 4.4 percent of "skilled" jobs (such as riveting). Nonetheless, the number of women in the workforce grew by 57 percent, as more than 6 million women took wartime jobs, while other women—including over 400,000 African American domestic workers—moved to higher-paying industrial jobs, often with union benefits.

Workers in defense plants were often expected to work ten days for every day off or to accept difficult night shifts. In an effort to keep employees on the job, both businesses and the federal government offered new forms of support. The West Coast Kaiser shipyards paid very well, but also provided child care, subsidized housing, and health care: the Kaiser Permanente Medical Care Program, a forerunner of today's health maintenance organization (HMO), cost workers a weekly payroll deduction of 50 cents. The federal government also funded child care centers and before- and after-school programs.

Rosie the Riveter Symbol of the woman war worker; the bulging muscles represented her strength as she aided the nation's war effort by taking jobs vacated by men who fought in the war.

23-3d Organized Labor During Wartime

Because America's war strategy relied on industrial production, the federal government tried to prevent the labor strikes that had been so common in the 1930s. Just days after Pearl Harbor, a White House labor-management conference agreed to a no-strike/no-lockout pledge, and in 1942, Roosevelt created the National War Labor Board (NWLB) to settle labor disputes. The NWLB forged a temporary compromise between labor union demands for a "closed shop," in which only union members could work, and management's desire for "open" shops: workers could not be required to join a union, but unions could enroll as many members as possible. Between 1940 and 1945, union membership ballooned from 8.5 million to 14.75 million.

However, the government did not hesitate to restrict union power if it threatened war production. When coal miners in the United Mine Workers union went on strike in 1943 after the NWLB attempted to limit wage increases to a cost-of-living adjustment, railroads and steel mills shut down for lack of coal. Few Americans supported this strike. One air force pilot claimed he'd "just as soon shoot down one of those strikers as shoot down Japs—they're doing as much to lose the war for us." As antilabor sentiment grew, Congress passed the War Labor Disputes (Smith-Connally) Act. This act gave the president authority to seize and operate any strike-bound plant deemed necessary to the national security. It also created criminal penalties for leading strikes and tried to constrain union power by prohibiting unions from contributing to political campaigns during time of war.

23-3e Success on the Production Front

For close to four years, American factories operated twenty-four hours a day, seven days a week, fighting the war on the production front. By war's end, the United States was producing 40 percent of the world's weaponry. Between 1940 and 1945, American factories turned out roughly 300,000 airplanes, 102,000 armored vehicles, 77,000 ships, 20 million small arms, 40 billion bullets, and 6 million tons of bombs. To reach such numbers, American factories had transformed skilled work in industries such as shipbuilding into an assembly-line process of mass production. Henry Ford, now seventy-eight years old, created a massive bomber plant on farmland along Willow Run Creek not far from Detroit. Willow Run's assembly lines, almost a mile long, turned out B-24 Liberator bombers at the rate of one an hour. On the West Coast, William Kaiser used mass-production techniques to cut construction time for Liberty ships—the huge, 440-foot-long cargo ships that transported the tanks and guns and bullets overseas—from 355 to 56 days. (As a publicity stunt, Kaiser's Richmond shipyard, near San Francisco, built one Liberty ship in 4 days, 15 hours, and 26 minutes.) The ships were not well made; their welded hulls sometimes split in rough seas, and one ship even foundered while still docked at the pier. However, as the United States struggled to produce cargo ships faster than German U-boats could sink them, speed of production counted for more than quality.

A visitor to the Willow Run plant described "the roar of the machinery, the special din of the riveting gun absolutely deafening nearby, the throbbing crash of the giant metal presses . . . the far-reaching line of half-born skyships growing wings under swarms of workers." His words reveal the might of American industry but also offer a glimpse of the experience of workers, who did dirty, repetitive, and physically exhausting work day after day "for the duration." Although American propaganda during the war badly overreached when comparing the contributions of well-paid war workers to those of men in combat, 102,000 men and women were killed doing war production work during the first two years of the war and more than 350,000 were seriously injured.

23-4 Life on the Home Front

▶ How did Americans feel the presence of the war in their lives on the home front?

▶ What racial and ethnic tensions emerged in the United States during the war?

▶ How did the war destabilize families?

The United States, protected by two oceans from its enemies, was spared the war that other nations experienced (Hawai'i was a U.S. territory and the Philippines a U.S. possession, but neither was part of the nation proper). Americans worried about loved ones fighting in distant places; they grieved the loss of sons and brothers and fathers and husbands and friends. Their lives were often profoundly disrupted. But bombs did not fall on American cities; invading armies did not burn and rape and kill. Instead, war mobilization brought prosperity in the midst of global conflagration.

23-4a Supporting the War Effort

The fighting was distant, but the war was a constant presence in the lives of Americans on "the home front." Although Americans were never so unified as the widespread images of "the greatest generation" suggest, civilians supported the war effort in many ways, and "shared sacrifice" was a powerful ideal and significant reality. During the war, families planted 20 million "victory gardens" to replace food that went to America's fighting men. Housewives saved fat from cooking and returned it to butchers, for cooking fat yielded glycerin to make the gunpowder used in shells or bullets. Children collected scrap metal, aware that the iron in one old shovel blade was enough for four hand grenades and that every tin can helped make a tank or Liberty ship.

Many consumer goods were rationed or unavailable. To save wool for military use, the War Production Board directed that men's suits would have narrow lapels, shorter jackets, and no vests or pant cuffs. Bathing suits, the WPB specified, must shrink by 10 percent. When silk and nylon were diverted from stockings to parachutes, women used makeup on their legs and drew in the "stocking" seam with eyebrow pencil. The Office of Price Administration (OPA), created by Congress in 1942, established a nationwide rationing system for sugar, coffee, gasoline, and other consumer goods. By early 1943, the OPA had instituted a point system for rationing food, and feeding a family required complex calculations. Each citizen—regardless of age—was allotted forty-eight blue points (canned fruits and vegetables) and sixty-four red points (meat, fish, and dairy) a month. In September 1944 a small bottle of ketchup "cost" twenty blue points and sirloin steak thirteen red points a pound (in addition to their cost in dollars and cents), while pork shoulder required only dollars. Sugar was tightly rationed, and people saved for months to make a birthday cake or holiday dessert. Rationed goods were available on the black market, but most Americans understood that sugar produced alcohol for weapons manufacture and meat went to feed "our boys" overseas.

23-4b Propaganda and Popular Culture

Although Americans strongly supported the war, government leaders worried that they would gradually become less willing to sacrifice. The Office of War Information (OWI), created in 1942, used Hollywood filmmakers and New York copywriters to sell the war at home. OWI posters exhorted Americans to save and sacrifice, and reminded them to watch what they said, for "loose lips sink ships."

Popular culture also reinforced wartime messages. Songs urged Americans to "Remember December 7th" or to "Accentuate the Positive." Others made fun of America's enemies ("You're a sap, Mr. Jap / You make a Yankee cranky / You're a sap, Mr. Jap / Uncle Sam is gonna spanky") or, like "Cleanin' My Rifle (and Dreamin' of You)," dealt with the hardship of wartime separation.

Movies drew 90 million viewers a week in 1944—out of a total population of 132 million. During the war "Draftee Duck" joined the army, chickens produced for the war effort at "Flockheed," and audiences sang along with an animated version of the song "Der Fuehrer's Face" ("When der fuehrer says we is de master race/We heil (pffft) heil (pffft) right in der fuehrer's face") in pre-film cartoons. For the most part, Hollywood tried to meet Eleanor Roosevelt's challenge to "Keep 'em laughing," though some films, such as *Bataan* or *Wake Island*, portrayed actual—if sanitized—events in the war. But even at the most frivolous comedies, the war was present. Theaters held "plasma premieres" with free admission to those who donated a half-pint of blood to the Red Cross. Before the film began, audiences sang "The Star-Spangled Banner" and watched newsreels with carefully censored footage of recent combat. On D-Day, June 6, 1944, as Allied troops landed at Normandy, theater managers across the nation led audiences in the Lord's Prayer or the Twenty-third Psalm ("The Lord is my shepherd . . ."). It was in movie theaters that Americans saw the horror of Nazi death camps in May 1945. The Universal newsreel narrator ordered audiences, "Don't turn away. Look."

23-4c Wartime Prosperity

The war disrupted the lives of all Americans and demanded profound sacrifice from some. But it also offered many Americans new prosperity. Per capita income rose from $691 in 1939 to $1,515 at war's end. OPA-administered price controls kept inflation down so that wage increases did not disappear to higher costs. And with little to buy, people saved money.

Fighting World War II cost the United States approximately $304 billion (more than $3 trillion in today's dollars). The national debt skyrocketed from $49 billion in 1941 to $259 billion in 1945 (and was not paid off until 1970). The government did not just defer those costs to later generations. It sold war bonds—thus borrowing money from those who bought them. And wartime legislation increased the number of Americans paying personal income tax from 4 million to 42.6 million—at rates ranging from 6 to 94 percent—and introduced a new system in which employers "withheld" taxes from employee paychecks. For the first time, individual Americans paid more in taxes than corporations.

23-4d A Nation in Motion

Despite hardships and fears, the war offered home-front Americans new opportunities, and millions of Americans took them. More than 15 million civilians moved during the war (see Map 23.1). More than half moved to another state, and half that number moved to another region. Seven hundred thousand black Americans left the South during the war years; in 1943, ten thousand black migrants poured into Los Angeles

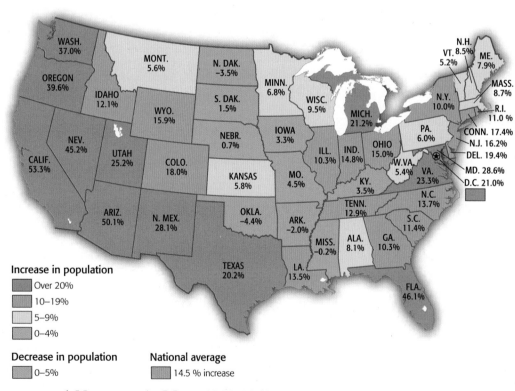

Map 23.1 A Nation on the Move, 1940–1950

American migration during the 1940s was the largest on record to that time. The farm population dropped dramatically as men, women, and children moved to war-production areas and to army and navy bases, particularly on the West Coast. Well over 30 million Americans (civilian and military) migrated during the war. Many returned to their rural homes after the war, but 12 million migrants stayed in their new locations. Notice the population increases on the West Coast as well as in the Southwest and Florida.

Portraying the Enemy

Racial stereotyping affected how both the Americans and the Japanese waged war. The Americans badly underestimated the Japanese, leaving themselves open for the surprise attack on Pearl Harbor and American forces in the Philippines. And the Japanese, believing Americans were barbarians who lacked a sense of honor, mistakenly expected that the United States would withdraw from East Asia once confronted with Japanese power and determination. This poster, aimed at workers for Texaco oil company, appeared in the first year of the war, not long after Japan's attack on Pearl Harbor.

CRITICAL THINKING

- How is the Japanese soldier portrayed here?
- Why does he urge American workers to take a day off?
- And how might the fact that Japan had launched an immensely successful surprise attack on the United States have shaped this image, or Americans' reactions to it?

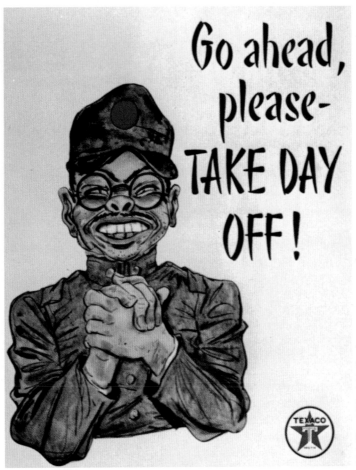

Galerie Bilderwelt/Hulton Archive/Getty Images

▲ American propaganda often portrayed the Japanese enemy as animalistic or subhuman.

every month. More than forty thousand Native Americans left reservations to work in the defense industry. People who had never traveled farther than the next county found themselves on the other side of the country—or of the world. People moved for defense jobs or to be close to loved ones at stateside military postings. Southerners moved north, northerners moved south, and 1.5 million people moved to California.

The rapid influx of war workers to major cities and small towns strained community resources. Migrants crowded into substandard housing—even woodsheds, tents, or cellars—and into trailer parks without adequate sanitary facilities. Disease spread: scabies and ringworm, polio, tuberculosis. Many long-term residents found the newcomers—especially the unmarried male war workers—a rough bunch. In the small town of Lawrence, Kansas, civic leaders bragged of the economic boost a new war plant gave the town but fretted over the appearance of bars, "dirty windowed dispensaries" that sold alcohol to the war workers.

In and around Detroit, where car factories now produced tanks and planes, established residents called war workers freshly arrived from southern Appalachia "hillbillies" and "white trash." A new joke circulated: "How many states are there in the Union? Forty-five. Tennessee and Kentucky moved to Michigan, and Michigan went to hell." Many of these migrants knew little about urban life. One young man from rural Tennessee, unfamiliar with traffic lights and street signs, navigated by counting the number of trees between his home and the war plant where he worked. Some Appalachian "trailer-ites" appalled their neighbors by building outdoor privies or burying garbage in their yards.

23-4e Racial Conflicts

As people from different backgrounds confronted one another under difficult conditions, tensions rose. Widespread racism made things worse. In 1943, almost 250 racial conflicts exploded in forty-seven cities. Outright racial warfare bloodied the streets of Detroit in June. White mobs, undeterred by police, roamed the city, attacking blacks. Blacks hurled rocks at police and dragged white passengers off streetcars. At the end of thirty hours of rioting, twenty-five blacks and nine whites lay dead. Surveying the damage, an elderly black woman said, "There ain't no North anymore. Everything now is South."

The heightened racial and ethnic tensions of wartime also led to riots in Los Angeles in 1943. Young Mexican American gang members, or *pachucos*, had adopted the zoot suit: a long jacket with wide padded shoulders, loose pants "pegged" below the knee, a wide-brimmed hat, and dangling watch chain. With cloth rationed, wearing pants requiring five yards of fabric was a political statement, and some young men wore the zoot suit as a purposeful rejection of wartime ideals of service and sacrifice. Although in fact a high percentage of Mexican Americans served in the armed forces, many white servicemen believed otherwise. Racial tensions were not far from the surface in overcrowded L.A., and rumors that *pachucos* had attacked white sailors quickly led to violence. For four days, mobs of white men—mainly soldiers and sailors—roamed the streets, attacking zoot-suiters and stripping them of their clothes. The city of Los Angeles outlawed zoot suits and arrested men who wore them. The "zoot suit riots" ended only when naval personnel were removed from the city.

23-4f Families in Wartime

The dislocations of war also had profound impacts on the nation's families. Despite policies that exempted married men and fathers from the draft during most of the war, almost 3 million families were broken up. Young children grew up not knowing their fathers. The divorce rate of 16 per 1,000 marriages in 1940 almost doubled to 27 per 1,000 in 1944.

Members of the Vega family pose for the camera in uniforms of the Marine Corps, National Guard, and U.S. Navy.

At the same time, hundreds of thousands of men and women were getting married. The number of marriages rose from 73 per 1,000 unmarried women in 1939 to 93 in 1942. Some couples scrambled to get married before the man was sent overseas; others sought military deferments. The birth rate climbed as well: 2.4 million babies were born in 1939 and 3.1 million in 1943. Many were "goodbye babies," conceived with the idea that the father might not survive the war.

On college campuses, some virtually stripped of male students, women complained, along with the song lyrics, "There is no available male." But other young women found an abundance of male company and their elders worried that the war was undermining sexual morality. *Youth in Crisis*, a 1943 newsreel, featured a girl with "experience far beyond her age" necking with a soldier on the street, while *Newsweek* warned of the "victory girls" or "cuddle bunnies" who were said to support the war effort by giving their all to men in uniform. Many young men and women, caught up in the emotional intensity of war, behaved as they never would in peacetime. Often that meant hasty marriages to virtual strangers, especially if a baby was on the way. Despite changes in behavior, taboos against unwed motherhood remained strong, and only 1 percent of births during the war were to unmarried women. Wartime mobility also increased opportunities for same-sex relationships, and gay communities grew in such cities as San Francisco.

In many ways, the war reinforced traditional gender roles that had been weakened during the depression, when many men lost the role of breadwinner. Now men defended their nation while women "kept the home fires burning." Some women took "men's jobs," but most understood that they were "for the duration"—the home-front equivalent to men's wartime military service. Even so, women who worked were frequently blamed for neglecting their children and creating an "epidemic" of juvenile delinquency—evidenced by the "victory girl." Nonetheless, millions of women took on new responsibilities in wartime, whether on the factory floor or within their family.

23-5 The Limits of American Ideals

▶ How did the American government attempt to balance democratic claims with wartime needs?

▶ What was the impact of internment on Japanese Americans during World War II?

▶ How did African Americans resist segregation of the military and discrimination during World War II?

During the war, the U.S. government worked hard to explain to its citizens the reasons for their sacrifices. In 1941, Roosevelt had pledged America to defend "four essential human freedoms"—freedom of speech, freedom of religion, freedom from want, and freedom from fear—and government-sponsored films contrasted democracy and totalitarianism, freedom and fascism, equality and oppression.

Despite such confident proclamations, as America fought the totalitarian regimes of the Axis powers, the nation confronted questions with no easy answers: What limits on civil liberties were justified in the interest of national security? How freely could information flow to the nation's citizens without revealing military secrets to the enemy and costing American lives? How could the United States protect itself against the threat of spies or saboteurs, especially from German, Italian, or Japanese citizens living in the United States? And what about America's ongoing domestic problems—particularly the problem of race? Could the nation address its own citizens' demands for reform as it fought the war against the Axis? The answers to these questions often revealed tensions between the nation's democratic claims and its wartime practices.

For the most part, America handled the issue of civil liberties well. American leaders embraced a "strategy of truth," declaring that citizens of a democratic nation required a truthful accounting of the war's progress. However, the government closely controlled information about military matters. Censorship was serious business, as even seemingly unimportant details might tip off enemies about troop movements or invasion plans: radio stations were forbidden to broadcast weather reports—or even to mention weather conditions—leaving residents without warning of impending

storms and sportscasters with no way to explain why play had been suspended or games had been called. During the war, government-created propaganda sometimes dehumanized the enemy, most especially the Japanese. Nonetheless, the American government resorted to hate-mongering much less frequently than during the First World War.

More complex was the question of how to handle dissent and how to guard against the possibility that enemy agents were operating within the nation's borders. The Alien Registration (Smith) Act, passed in 1940, made it unlawful to advocate the overthrow of the U.S. government by force or violence, or to join any organization that did so. After Pearl Harbor, the government used this authority to take thousands of Germans, Italians, and other Europeans into custody as suspected spies and potential traitors. During the war, the government interned 14,426 Europeans in Enemy Alien Camps. Fearing subversion, the government also prohibited ten thousand Italian Americans from living or working in restricted zones along the California coast, including San Francisco and Monterey Bay.

23-5a Internment of Japanese Americans

In March 1942, Roosevelt ordered that all 112,000 foreign-born Japanese and Japanese Americans living in California, Oregon, and the state of Washington (the vast majority of the mainland population) be removed from the West Coast to "relocation centers" for the duration of the war. Each of the Italian and German nationals interned by the U.S. government faced specific, individual charges. That was not the case for Japanese nationals and Japanese Americans. They were imprisoned as a group, under suspicion solely because they were of Japanese descent.

American anger at Japan's "sneak attack" on Pearl Harbor fueled the calls for internment, as did fears that West Coast cities might yet come under enemy attack. Long-standing racism was evident, as the chief of the Western Defense Command warned, "The Japanese race is an enemy race." Finally, people in economic competition with Japanese Americans strongly supported internment. Although Japanese nationals could not become U.S. citizens or own property, American-born Nissei (second generation) and Sansei (third generation), all U.S. citizens, were increasingly successful in business and agriculture. The eviction order forced Japanese Americans to sell property valued at $500 million for a fraction of its worth. West Coast Japanese Americans also lost their positions in the truck-garden, floral, and fishing industries.

The internees were sent to camps carved out of tax-delinquent land in Arkansas's Mississippi River floodplain, to the intermountain terrain of Wyoming and the desert of western Arizona, and to other arid and desolate spots in the West. The camps were bleak and demoralizing. Behind barbed wire stood tar-papered wooden barracks where entire families lived in a single room furnished only with cots, blankets, and a single bare light bulb. Most had no running water. Toilets and dining and bathing facilities were communal; privacy was almost nonexistent. In such difficult circumstances,

Radio News

In radio's early years, stations broadcast little news. Network executives believed their job was to entertain Americans and that current affairs should be left to newspapers. Yet radio could do something that no previous medium of communication could do: it could report not merely what had happened, but what was happening as it happened.

Franklin Roosevelt was among the first to grasp radio's potential in this regard. As governor of New York, he occasionally went on the air, and after becoming president, he commenced his Fireside Chats. With a voice perfectly suited to the medium, he reassured Americans suffering through the depression that, although current conditions were grim, the government was working hard to help them. So successful were these broadcasts that, in the words of one journalist, "The President has only to look toward a radio to bring Congress to terms."

Across the Atlantic, another leader also understood well the power of radio. Adolf Hitler determined early that he would use German radio to carry speeches directly to the people. His message: Germany had been wronged by enemies abroad and by Marxists and Jews at home. But the Nazis under Hitler's direction would lead the country back to its former greatness. As "Sieg Heil!" thundered over the airwaves, millions of Germans came to see Hitler as their salvation.

In 1938, as events in Europe reached a crisis, American radio networks increased their news coverage. When Hitler annexed Austria in March, NBC and CBS broke into scheduled programs to deliver news bulletins. Then, on the evening of Saturday, March 13, CBS went its rival one better by broadcasting the first international news roundup, a half-hour show featuring live reports on the annexation from the major capitals of Europe. A new era in American radio was born. In the words of author Joseph Persico, what made the broadcast revolutionary "was the listener's sensation of being on the scene" in far-off Europe.

When leaders from France and Britain met with Hitler in Munich later that year, millions of Americans listened with rapt attention to live radio updates. Correspondents soon became well known, none more so than Edward R. Murrow of CBS. During the Nazi air blitz of London in 1940–1941, Murrow's rich, understated, nicotine-scorched voice kept Americans spellbound. "This—is London," he would begin each broadcast, then proceed to give graphic accounts that tried, as he put it, to "report suffering to people [Americans] who have not suffered."

Murrow was resolutely pro-Allies, and there is little doubt his reports strengthened the interventionist voices in Washington by emphasizing Winston Churchill's greatness and England's bravery. More than that, though, radio reports from Europe made Americans feel more closely linked than before to people living thousands of miles and an ocean away. As American writer Archibald MacLeish said of Murrow's broadcasts, "Without rhetoric, without dramatics, without more emotion than needed be, you destroyed the superstition of distance and of time."

CRITICAL THINKING

- Radio broadcasts from Europe in the early days of World War II played an important role in convincing many Americans that intervention was necessary. Does the radio, or specifically today talk radio, continue to be a force in American life?

Library of Congress Prints and Photographs Division [LC-USZ62-119757]

▲ Edward R. Murrow at his typewriter in wartime London.

people nonetheless attempted to sustain community life, setting up consumer cooperatives and sports leagues (one Arkansas baseball team called itself the Chiggers), and for many, maintaining Buddhist worship in the face of pressure to adopt Christian beliefs.

Betrayed by their government, many internees were profoundly ambivalent about their loyalty to the United States. Some sought legal remedy, but the Supreme Court upheld the government's action in *Korematsu v. U.S.* (1944). Almost one-quarter of all adults in one Arkansas camp, when asked if they would "swear unqualified allegiance to the United States," answered "no" or expressed some reservation. And almost 6,000 of the 120,000 internees renounced U.S. citizenship and demanded to be sent to Japan. Far more sought to demonstrate their loyalty. The all–Japanese American 442nd Regimental Combat Team, drawn heavily from young men in internment camps, was the most decorated unit of its size. Suffering heavy casualties in Italy and France, members of the 442nd were awarded a Congressional Medal of Honor, 47 Distinguished Service Crosses, 350 Silver Stars, and more than 3,600 Purple Hearts. In 1988, Congress issued a public apology and largely symbolic payment of $20,000 to each of the 60,000 surviving Japanese American internees.

23-5b African Americans and "Double V"

As America mobilized for war, some African American leaders attempted to force the nation to confront the uncomfortable parallels between the racist doctrines of the Nazis and the persistence of Jim Crow segregation in the United States. Proclaiming a "Double V" campaign (victory at home and abroad), groups such as the National Association for the Advancement of Colored People (NAACP) hoped to "persuade, embarrass, compel and shame our government and our nation . . . into a more enlightened attitude toward a tenth of its people." Membership in civil rights organizations soared. The NAACP, 50,000 strong in 1940, had 450,000 members by 1946. And in 1942, civil rights activists, influenced by the philosophy of India's Mohandas Gandhi, founded the Congress of Racial Equality (CORE), which stressed "nonviolent direct action" and staged sit-ins to desegregate restaurants and movie theaters in Chicago and Washington, D.C.

Military service was a key issue for African Americans, who understood the traditional link between the duty to defend one's country and the rights of full citizenship. But the U.S. military remained segregated by race and strongly resisted efforts to use black units as combat troops. As late as 1943, less than 6 percent of the armed forces were African American, compared with more than 10 percent of the population. The marines at first refused to accept African Americans at all, and the navy approximated segregation by assigning black men to service positions in which they would rarely interact with nonblacks as equals or superiors.

23-5c A Segregated Military

Why did the United States fight a war for democracy with a segregated military? The U.S. military understood that its sole priority was to stop the Axis and win the war, and

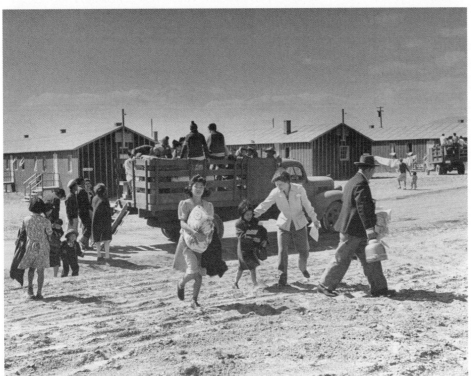

◄ Families arrive at the Heart Mountain Relocation Center in January 1942. One of the "internment camps" for Japanese Americans and Japanese resident aliens who were incarcerated under Executive Order 9066, Heart Mountain was in a remote area of northwestern Wyoming. Eventually 10,767 people were held in its barren confines, surrounded by barbed wire fence and monitored from nine guard towers.

Myron Davis/Getty Images

the federal government and War Department decided that the midst of world war was no time to try to integrate the armed forces. The majority of Americans (approximately 89 percent of Americans were white) opposed integration, many of them vehemently. As a sign of how deeply racist beliefs penetrated the United States, the Red Cross segregated blood plasma during the war. In most southern states, racial segregation was not simply custom; it was the law. Integration of military installations and training camps, the majority of which were in the South, would have provoked a crisis as federal power contradicted state law. Pointing to outbreaks of racial violence in southern training camps as evidence, government and military officials argued that wartime integration would almost certainly provoke even more racial violence, create disorder within the military, and hinder America's war effort. Such resistance might have been short term, but the War Department did not take that chance. Justifying its decision, the War Department argued that it could not "act outside the law, nor contrary to the will of the majority of the citizens of the Nation." General George C. Marshall, Army Chief of Staff, proclaimed that it was not the job of the army to "solve a social problem that has perplexed the American people throughout the history of this nation. . . . The army is not a sociological laboratory." Hopes for racial justice, so long deferred, were another casualty of the war.

Despite such discrimination, many African Americans stood up for their rights. Lieutenant Jackie Robinson refused to move to the back of the bus while training at the army's Camp Hood, Texas, in 1944—and faced court-martial, even though military regulations forbade racial discrimination on military vehicles, regardless of local law or custom. Black sailors disobeyed orders to return to work after surviving an explosion that destroyed two ships, killed 320 men, and shattered windows 35 miles away—an explosion caused by the navy practice of assigning men who were completely untrained in handling high explosives to load bombs from the munitions depot at Port Chicago, near San Francisco, onto Liberty ships. When they were court-martialed for mutiny, future Supreme Court justice and chief counsel for the NAACP Thurgood Marshall asked why only black sailors did this work. Marshall argued, "This is not fifty men on trial for mutiny. This is the Navy on trial for its whole vicious policy toward Negroes."

As the war wore on, African American servicemen did fight on the front lines, and fought well. The Marine Corps commandant in the Pacific proclaimed that "Negro Marines are no longer on trial. They are Marines, period." The "Tuskegee Airmen," pilots trained at the Tuskegee Institute in Alabama, saw heroic service in all-black units, such as the Ninety-ninth Pursuit Squadron, which won eighty Distinguished Flying Crosses. After the war, African Americans—as some white Americans had feared—called on their wartime service to claim the full rights of citizenship. African Americans' wartime experiences were mixed, but the war was a turning point in the movement for equal rights.

▲ During World War II, for the first time, the War Department sanctioned the training and use of African American pilots. These members of the Ninety-ninth Pursuit Squadron—known as "Tuskegee Airmen" because they trained at Alabama's all-black Tuskegee Institute—joined combat over North Africa in June 1943. Like most African American units in the racially segregated armed forces, the men of the Ninety-ninth Pursuit Squadron were under the command of white officers.

23-5d America and the Holocaust

America's inaction in the face of what we now call the Holocaust is a tragic failure, though the consequences are clearer in retrospect than they were at the time. As the United States turned away refugees on the MS *St. Louis* (see "Roosevelt's Evolving Views," Section 22-7c) in early 1939 and refused to relax its immigration quotas to admit European Jews and others fleeing Hitler's Germany, almost no one foresaw that the future would bring death camps like Auschwitz or Treblinka. Americans knew they were turning away people fleeing dire persecution, and while anti-Semitism played a significant role in that decision, it was not unusual to refuse those seeking refuge, especially in the midst of a major economic crisis that seemed to be worsening.

As early as 1942, American newspapers reported the "mass slaughter" of Jews and other "undesirables" (Gypsies, homosexuals, the physically and mentally handicapped) under Hitler. Many Americans, having been taken in by manufactured atrocity tales during World War I, wrongly discounted

National Archives and Records Administration, College Park

▲ Millions of civilians were starved, gassed, machine gunned, or worked to death by their Nazi jailers during the war. Here, U.S. Army troops force Nazi Party members to exhume the bodies of two hundred Russian officers and others who were shot by the SS near Wuelfel, while the residents of Hannover watch. Allied troops often compelled local townspeople to watch exhumations of mass graves, attempting to make them confront the atrocities that many insisted they never knew were happening.

these stories. But Roosevelt knew about the existence of Nazi death camps capable of killing up to two thousand people an hour using the gas Zyklon-B.

In 1943, British and American representatives met in Bermuda to discuss the situation but took no concrete action. Many Allied officials, though horrified, saw Hitler's "Final Solution" as just one part of a larger, worldwide holocaust in which tens of millions were dying. Appalled by the reluctance to act, Secretary of the Treasury Henry Morgenthau Jr. charged that the State Department's foot dragging made the United States an accessory to murder. "The matter of rescuing the Jews from extermination is a trust too great to remain in the hands of men who are indifferent, callous, and perhaps even hostile," he wrote bitterly in 1944. Later that year, stirred by Morgenthau's well-documented plea, Roosevelt created the War Refugee Board, which set up refugee camps in Europe and played a crucial role in saving 200,000 Jews from death. But, lamented one American official, "by that time it was too damned late to do too much." By war's end, the Nazis had systematically murdered almost 11 million people.

23-6 Life in the Military

▶ How was manpower allocated and organized during World War II?

▶ What was the nature of the wartime experience for men and women during World War II?

More than 15 million men and approximately 350,000 women served in the U.S. armed forces during World War II. Eighteen percent of American families had a father, son, or brother in the armed forces. Some of these men (and all of the women) volunteered, eager to defend their nation. But most who served—more than 10 million—were draftees. By presidential order, the military stopped accepting draft-age volunteers in December 1942 as, faced with the challenge of filling the military ranks while maintaining war production and the civilian economy, the Selective Service system and the new War Manpower Commission tried to centralize control over manpower allocation. The draft reached broadly and mostly equitably through the American population during World War II, and most Americans believed that it operated fairly.

23-6a Selective Service

The Selective Service Act did allow deferments, but they did not disproportionately benefit the well-to-do. Almost ten thousand Princeton students or alumni served—as did all four of Franklin and Eleanor Roosevelt's sons—while throughout the nation judges offered minor criminal offenders the choice of the military or jail. The small number of college deferments was more than balanced by deferments for a long list of "critical occupations," including not only war industry workers but also almost 2 million agricultural workers. Most exemptions from military service were for men deemed physically or mentally unqualified to serve. Army physicians discovered what a toll the depression had taken on the nation's youth as draftees arrived with rotted teeth and deteriorated eyesight—signs of malnutrition. Army dentists pulled 15 million teeth and fitted men with dentures; optometrists prescribed 2.5 million pairs of glasses. Hundreds of thousands of men with venereal diseases were cured by sulfa drugs, developed in 1942. Military examiners also found evidence of the impact of racism and poverty. Half of African American draftees had no schooling beyond the sixth grade, and up to one-third were functionally illiterate. Forty-six percent of African Americans and almost one-third of European Americans called for the draft were classified "4-F"—unfit for service.

Nonetheless, almost 12 percent of America's total population served in the military. Regiments were created rapidly, throwing together men from very different backgrounds. Regional differences were profound, and northerners and southerners often—literally—could not understand one another. Ethnic differences complicated things further. Although African Americans and Japanese Americans served in their own separate units, Hispanics, Native Americans, and Chinese Americans served in "white" units. Furthermore, the differences among "whites"—the "Italian" kid from Brooklyn and the one from rural Mississippi (or rural Montana)—were profound. The result was often tension, but many Americans became less prejudiced and less provincial as they served with men unlike themselves.

23-6b Fighting the War

Although military service was widespread, the burdens of combat were not equally shared. Women served their nation honorably and often courageously, but women's roles in the U.S. military were much more restricted than in the British or Soviet militaries, where women served as anti-aircraft gunners and in other combat-related positions. U.S. women served as nurses, in communications offices, and as typists or cooks. The recruiting slogan for the WACs (Women's Army Corps) was "Release a Man for Combat." However, most men in the armed forces never saw combat either; one-quarter never left the United States. The United States had the most extreme "teeth-to-tail" ratio of any of the combatants, with each combat soldier backed up by eight or more support personnel. Japan's ratio was almost one to one. One-third of U.S. military personnel served in clerical positions, filled mainly by well-educated men. African Americans, though assigned dirty and dangerous tasks, were largely kept from combat service. In World War II, lower-class, less-educated white men bore the brunt of the fighting.

For those who fought, combat in World War II was as horrible as anything humans have experienced. Home-front audiences for the war films Hollywood churned out saw men die bravely, shot cleanly through the heart and comforted by their buddies in their last moments. What men experienced was carnage. Less than 10 percent of casualties were caused by bullets. Most men were killed or wounded by mortars, bombs, or grenades. Seventy-five thousand American men remained missing in action at the end of the war, lost at sea or other inaccessible locations or blown into fragments of flesh too small to identify. Combat meant days and weeks of unrelenting rain in malarial jungles, sliding down a mud-slicked hill to land in a pile of putrid corpses. It meant drowning in the waters of the frigid North Atlantic amid burning wreckage of a torpedoed ship. It meant using flamethrowers that burned at 2,000 degrees Fahrenheit on other human beings. It meant being violently ill on a landing craft steering through floating body parts of those who had attempted the landing first, knowing that if you tripped you would likely drown under the sixty-eight-pound weight of your pack, and that if you made it ashore you would likely be blown apart by artillery shells. Service was "for the duration" of the war. Only death, serious injury, or victory offered release. In this hard world, men fought to victory.

In forty-five months of war, close to three hundred thousand American servicemen died in combat. Almost 1 million American troops were wounded, half of them seriously. Medical advances, such as the development of penicillin and the use of blood plasma to prevent shock, helped wounded men survive—but many never fully recovered from those wounds. Between 20 and 30 percent of combat casualties were psychoneurotic, as men were pushed past the limits of endurance. The federal government strictly censored images of American combat deaths for most of the war, consigning them to a secret file known as "the chamber of horrors." Americans at home rarely understood what combat had been like, and many men, upon return, never talked about their experiences in the war.

23-7 Winning the War

▶ What issues emerged among the Allied Powers during World War II?

▶ How did the Allied Powers achieve victory in Europe and the Pacific?

▶ Why did the United States choose to use the atom bomb?

Axis hopes for victory depended on a short war. Leaders in Germany and Japan knew that, if the United States had time to fully mobilize, flooding the theaters of war with armaments

Map 23.2 The Allies on the Offensive in Europe, 1942–1945

The United States pursued a "Europe First" policy: first defeat Germany, then focus on Japan. American military efforts began in North Africa in late 1942 and ended in Germany in 1945 on May 8 (V-E Day).

and reinforcing Allied troops with fresh, trained men, the war was lost. However, powerful factions in the Japanese military and German leadership believed that the United States would concede if it met with early, decisive defeats. Hitler, blinded by racial arrogance, had stated shortly after declaring war on the United States, "I don't see much future for the Americans. . . . It's a decayed country. . . . American society [is] half Judaized, and the other half Negrified. How can one expect a State like that to hold together." By mid-1942, the Axis powers understood that they had underestimated not only American resolve but also the willingness of other Allies to sacrifice unimaginable numbers of their citizens to stop the Axis advance (see Map 23.2). The chance of an Axis victory grew increasingly slim as the months passed, but though the outcome was virtually certain after spring 1943, two years of bloody fighting lay ahead.

23-7a Tensions Among the Allies

As the war continued, the Allies' suspicions of one another undermined cooperation. The Soviets continued to press Britain and the United States to open a second front to the

west of Germany and so draw German troops away from the USSR, but the United States and Britain continued to delay. Stalin was not mollified by the massive "thousand-bomber" raids on Germany that Britain's Royal Air Force began in 1942, nor by the Allied invasion of Italy in the summer of 1943. With the alliance badly strained, Roosevelt turned to personal diplomacy. The three Allied leaders met in Tehran, Iran, in December 1943. Churchill again proposed a peripheral attack, this time through the Balkans to Vienna. But Stalin had had enough, and this time Roosevelt joined him. The three finally agreed to launch **Operation Overlord**—the cross-channel invasion of France—in early 1944. And the Soviet Union promised to aid the Allies against Japan once Germany was defeated.

23-7b War in Europe

The second front opened in the dark morning hours

Operation Overlord Code name for the largest amphibious invasion in history, in which Allied troops stormed a sixty-mile stretch of the Normandy coast on June 6, 1944 (D-Day).

◀ Allied ships unloading cargo during the first days of the Normandy Invasion, June 1944. As this photograph shows, the scale of the operation was immense: Operation Overlord relied on 326,547 Allied troops, 11,590 aircraft and 6,939 naval vessels.

Regional Council of Basse-Normandie/U.S. National Archives

of June 6, 1944: D-Day. In the largest amphibious landing in history, more than 140,000 Allied troops under the command of American general Dwight D. Eisenhower scrambled ashore at Normandy, France. Thousands of ships ferried the men within one hundred yards of the sandy beaches. Landing craft and soldiers immediately encountered the enemy; they triggered mines and were pinned down by fire from cliffside pillboxes. Meanwhile, 15,500 Allied airborne troops, along with thousands of dummies meant to confuse the German defense, dropped from aircraft. Although heavy aerial and naval bombardment and the clandestine work of saboteurs had softened the German defenses, the fighting was ferocious.

By late July, 1.4 million Allied troops were fighting in France. They spread across the countryside, liberating France and Belgium by the end of August but leaving a path of devastation in their wake. Allied bombing, one British soldier wrote, left villages appearing "dead, mutilated and smothered, a gigantic sightless rubble heap so confounded by devastation as to suggest an Apocalypse." Almost 37,000 Allied troops died in that struggle, and up to 20,000 French civilians were killed. In September, the Allies pushed into Germany. German armored divisions counterattacked in Belgium's Ardennes Forest in December, hoping to push on to Antwerp to halt the flow of Allied supplies through that Belgian port. After weeks of heavy fighting in what

Battle of the Bulge The final German military offensive against the Western Allies in the Ardennes region of Belgium (December 16, 1944–January 25, 1945). Named for the shape of the "bulge" formed by the German forces where they penetrated the Allied lines.

has come to be called the **Battle of the Bulge**—because of the "bulge" created as German troops had pushed back the Allied line—the Allies gained control in late January 1945.

By that point, "strategic" bombing (though not nearly as precise as was publicly claimed) had destroyed Germany's war-production capacity and devastated its economy. In early 1945, the British and Americans began "morale" bombing, killing tens of thousands of civilians in aerial attacks on Berlin and then Dresden. Meanwhile, battle-hardened Soviet troops marched through Poland and cut a path to Berlin. American forces crossed the Rhine River in March 1945 and captured the heavily industrial Ruhr Valley. Several units peeled off to enter Austria and Czechoslovakia, where they met up with Soviet soldiers.

23-7c Yalta Conference

Even as Allied forces faced the last, desperate resistance from German troops in the Battle of the Bulge, Allied leaders began planning the peace. In early 1945, Franklin Roosevelt, by this time very ill, called for a summit meeting to discuss a host of political questions—including what to do with Germany. The three Allied leaders met at Yalta, in the Russian Crimea, in February 1945. Each had definite goals for the shape of the postwar world. Britain, its formerly powerful empire now vulnerable and shrinking, sought to protect its colonial possessions and to limit Soviet power. The Soviet Union, with 21 million dead, wanted Germany to pay reparations to fund its massive rebuilding effort. The Soviets hoped to expand their sphere of influence throughout eastern Europe and to guarantee their

national security; Germany, Stalin insisted, must be permanently weakened. Two German invasions in a quarter-century were more than enough.

The United States, like the other powers, hoped to expand its influence and to control the peace. To that end, Roosevelt lobbied for the United Nations Organization, approved in principle the previous year at Dumbarton Oaks in Washington, D.C., through which the United States hoped to exercise influence. The lessons of World War I also shaped American proposals; seeking long-term peace and stability, the United States hoped to avoid the debts-reparations fiasco that had plagued Europe after the First World War. U.S. goals included self-determination for liberated peoples; gradual and orderly decolonization; and management of world affairs by what Roosevelt had once called the Four Policemen: the Soviet Union, Great Britain, the United States, and China. (Roosevelt hoped China might help stabilize Asia after the war; the United States abolished the Chinese Exclusion Act in 1943 in an attempt to consolidate ties between the two nations.) The United States was also determined to limit Soviet influence in the postwar world. Obviously, there was much about which to disagree.

Military positions at the time of the Yalta conference helped shape the negotiations. Soviet troops occupied eastern European nations they had liberated, including Poland, where Moscow had installed a pro-Soviet regime despite a British-supported Polish government-in-exile in London. With Soviet troops in place, Britain and the United States had limited negotiating power over eastern Europe. As for Germany, the Big Three agreed that some eastern German territory would be transferred to Poland and the remainder divided into four zones—the fourth zone to be administered by France, which Britain had pressed to be included in plans for postwar control of Germany, so as to reduce the Soviet zone from one-third to one-quarter. Berlin, within the Soviet zone, would also be divided among the four victors. Yalta marked the high point of the Grand Alliance; in the tradition of diplomatic give-and-take, each of the Allies came away with something it wanted. In exchange for U.S. promises to support Soviet claims on territory lost to Japan in the Russo-Japanese War of 1904–1905, Stalin agreed to sign a treaty of friendship with Jiang Jieshi (Chiang Kai-shek), America's ally in China, rather than with the communist Mao Zedong (Mao Tse-tung), and to declare war on Japan two or three months after Hitler's defeat.

23-7d Harry Truman

Franklin D. Roosevelt, reelected to an unprecedented fourth term in November 1944, did not live to see the war's end. He died on April 12, and Vice President Harry S Truman became president and commander-in-chief. Truman, a senator from Missouri who had replaced former vice president Henry Wallace as Roosevelt's running mate in 1944, was inexperienced in foreign policy. He was not even informed about the top-secret atomic weapons project until after he became president. The day after Roosevelt's death, Truman sought out old friends, Democrats and Republicans, in Congress, to ask their help in this "terrible job." Shortly afterward, he told reporters, "Boys, if you ever pray, pray for me now. I don't know whether

◀ The three Allied leaders— Winston Churchill, Franklin D. Roosevelt, and Joseph Stalin— met at Yalta in February 1945. Having been president for twelve years, Roosevelt showed signs of age and fatigue. Two months later, he died of a massive cerebral hemorrhage.

Franklin D. Roosevelt Library

Map 23.3 The Pacific War

The strategy of the United States was to "island-hop"—from Hawai'i in 1942 to Iwo Jima and Okinawa in 1945. Naval battles were also decisive, notably the Battles of the Coral Sea and Midway in 1942. The war in the Pacific ended with Japan's surrender on August 15, 1945 (V-J Day).

you fellows ever had a load of hay fall on you, but when they told me yesterday what had happened, I felt like the moon, the stars, and all the planets had fallen on me." Eighteen days into Truman's presidency, Adolf Hitler killed himself in a bunker in bomb-ravaged Berlin. On May 8, Germany surrendered.

As the great powers jockeyed for influence after Germany's surrender, the Grand Alliance began to crumble. At the Potsdam Conference in mid-July, Truman—a novice at international diplomacy—was less patient with the Soviets than Roosevelt had been. And Truman learned during the conference that a test of the new atomic weapon had been successful. The United States, possessing such a weapon, no longer needed the Soviet Union's help in fighting the Pacific war. Roosevelt had secretly promised Stalin territory from Japan's wartime holdings in exchange for help in defeating Japan; the bomb made those concessions unnecessary. The Allies did agree that Japan must surrender unconditionally. But with the defeat of Hitler and the end of the European war, the wartime bonds among the Allies were strained to breaking.

23-7e The Pacific Campaign

In the Pacific, the war continued. Since halting the Japanese advance in the Battle of Midway in June 1942, American strategy had been to "island-hop" toward Japan, skipping the most strongly fortified islands whenever possible and taking the weaker ones, aiming to strand the Japanese armies on their island outposts. To cut off supplies being shipped from Japan's home islands, Americans also targeted the Japanese merchant marine. Allied and Japanese forces fought savagely for control of tiny specks of land scattered throughout the Pacific. By 1944, Allied troops—from the United States, Britain, Australia, and New Zealand—had secured the Solomon, Gilbert, Marshall, and Mariana Islands. General Douglas MacArthur landed at Leyte to retake the Philippines for the United States in October 1944 (see Map 23.3).

In February 1945, while the Big Three were meeting at Yalta, U.S. and Japanese troops battled for Iwo Jima, an island less than five miles long, located about seven hundred miles south of Tokyo. Twenty-one thousand Japanese defenders occupied the island's high ground.

◄ Navajo "code talkers" in the U.S. Marines were among the first assault forces to land on Pacific beaches. Dodging enemy fire, they set up radio equipment and transmitted vital information to headquarters using a code based on Diné, the Navajo language. In 1942 there was no written version of this complex language and fewer than thirty non-Navajos in the world— none of them Japanese—could understand it. While Navajo Marines made up the majority of the code talkers, members of twenty other tribes and nations served as code talkers in the U.S. military during World War II.

Hidden in a network of caves, trenches, and underground tunnels, they were protected from the aerial bombardment that U.S. forces used to clear the way for an amphibious landing. The stark volcanic island offered no cover, and marines were slaughtered as they came ashore. For twenty days, U.S. forces fought their way, yard by yard, up Mount Suribachi, the highest and most heavily fortified point on Iwo Jima. The struggle for Iwo Jima cost the lives of 6,821 Americans and more than 20,000 Japanese—some of whom committed suicide rather than surrender. Only 200 Japanese soldiers survived.

A month later, American troops landed on Okinawa, an island in the Ryukyus chain at the southern tip of Japan, from which Allied forces planned to invade the main Japanese islands. Fighting raged for two months; death was everywhere. The monsoon rains began in May, turning battlefields into seas of mud filled with decaying corpses. The supporting fleet endured waves of mass kamikaze (suicide) attacks, in which Japanese pilots intentionally crashed bomb-laden planes into American ships. Almost 5,000 seamen perished in these attacks. On Okinawa, 7,374 American soldiers and marines died in battle. Almost the entire Japanese garrison of 100,000 was killed. More than one-quarter of Okinawa's people, or approximately 80,000 civilians, perished as the two powers struggled over their island.

23-7f Bombing of Japan

Even with American forces entrenched just 350 miles from Japan's main islands, Japanese leaders still refused to admit defeat. A powerful military faction was determined to preserve the emperor's sovereignty and to avoid the humiliation of an unconditional surrender. They hung on even while American bombers leveled their cities. On the night of March 9, 1945, 333 American B-29 Superfortresses commanded by General Curtis LeMay dropped a mixture of explosives and incendiary devices on a four-by-three-mile area of Tokyo. Attempting to demonstrate the strategic value of airpower, they created a firestorm, a blaze so fierce that it sucked all the oxygen from the air, producing hurricane-force winds and growing so hot it could melt concrete and steel. Almost 100,000 people were incinerated, suffocated, or boiled to death in canals where they had taken refuge from the fire. Over the following five months, American bombers attacked sixty-six Japanese cities, leaving 8 million people homeless, killing almost 900,000.

Japan, at the same time, was attempting to bomb the U.S. mainland. Thousands of bomb-bearing high-altitude balloons, constructed out of rice paper and potato-flour paste by schoolgirls, were launched into the jet stream. Those that did reach the United States fell on unpopulated areas, occasionally starting forest fires. The only mainland U.S. casualties in the war were five children and an adult on a Sunday school picnic in Oregon who accidentally detonated a balloon bomb that they found in the underbrush. As Admiral Yamamoto had realized at the war's beginning, American resources would far outlast Japan's.

Early in the summer of 1945, Japan began to send out peace feelers through the Soviets. Japan was not, however, willing to accept the "unconditional surrender" terms on

◄ On Okinawa, a wounded GI prays while awaiting evacuation to a field hospital. Medical advances, such as the discovery of penicillin and the use of glucose saline solution to replace lost blood, greatly improved the survival rate for those wounded in combat. But where combat was especially horrific, as it was on Okinawa, psychiatric casualties might outnumber combat deaths three to one.

W. Eugene Smith/Getty Images

which the Allied leaders had agreed at Potsdam, and Truman and his advisers chose not to pursue a negotiated peace. By this time, U.S. troops were mobilizing for an invasion of the Japanese home islands. The experiences of Iwo Jima and Okinawa weighed heavily in the planning; Japanese troops had fought on, well past any hope of victory, and death tolls for Japanese and American troops alike had been enormous. News of the success of the Manhattan Project offered another option, and President Truman took it. Using atomic bombs on Japan, Truman believed, would end the war quickly and save American lives.

Historians still debate Truman's decision to use the atomic bomb. Why would he not negotiate surrender terms? Was Japan on the verge of an unconditional surrender, as some argue? Or was the antisurrender faction of Japanese military leaders strong enough to prevail? Truman knew the bomb could give the United States both real and psychological power in negotiating the peace; how much did his desire to demonstrate the bomb's power to the Soviet Union, or to prevent the Soviets from playing a major role in the last stages of the Pacific war, influence his decision? Did racism or a desire for retaliation play a role? How large were the projected casualty figures for invasion on which Truman based his decision, and were they accurate? No matter the answers to these ongoing debates, bombing (whether conventional or atomic) fit the established U.S. strategy of using machines rather than men whenever possible.

The decision to use the bomb did not seem as momentous to Truman as it does in retrospect. The moral line had already been crossed, as the move to wholesale bombing of civilian populations continued throughout the war: The Japanese had bombed the Chinese city of Shanghai in 1937. Germans had "terror-bombed" Warsaw, Rotterdam, and London. British and American bombers had purposely created firestorms in German cities; on a single night in February 1945, 25,000 people perished in the bombing of Dresden. The American bombing of Japanese cities—accomplished with conventional weapons—had already killed close to a million people and destroyed fifty-six square miles of Tokyo alone. What distinguished the atomic bombs from conventional bombs was their power and their efficiency—not that they killed huge numbers of innocent civilians in unspeakably awful ways.

On July 26, 1945, the Allies delivered an ultimatum to Japan: promising that the Japanese people would not be "enslaved," the **Potsdam Declaration** called for the Japanese to surrender unconditionally or face "prompt and utter destruction." Tokyo radio announced that the government would respond with *mokusatsu* (literally, "kill with silence," or ignore the ultimatum). On August 6, 1945, a B-29 bomber named after the pilot's mother, the *Enola Gay*, dropped an atomic bomb above the city of Hiroshima. A flash of dazzling light shot across the sky; then a huge, purplish mushroom cloud boiled forty thousand feet into the atmosphere. Much of the city was leveled by the blast. The bomb ignited a firestorm, and thousands who survived the initial blast burned to death. Approximately 130,000 people were killed. Tens of thousands more would suffer the effects of radiation poisoning.

Potsdam Declaration 1945 ultimatum of the Western Allies to Japan to surrender unconditionally or face "prompt and utter destruction."

National Archives

▲ The photo of Hiroshima shown above was taken eight months after the attack. The shock waves and fires caused by the atomic bomb leveled great expanses of the city. Radiation released by the bomb caused lingering deaths for thousands who survived the explosion.

American planes continued their devastating conventional bombing. On August 8, the Soviet Union declared war on Japan. On August 9, the United States dropped a second atomic bomb on Nagasaki, killing at least 60,000 people. Five days later, on August 14, Japan surrendered. Recent histories argue that the Soviet declaration of war played a more significant role in Japan's decision to surrender than America's use of atomic weapons. In the end, the Allies promised that the Japanese emperor could remain as the nation's titular head. Formal surrender ceremonies were held September 2 aboard the battleship *Missouri* in Tokyo Bay. The Second World War was over.

Summary

Hitler once prophesied, "We may be destroyed, but if we are, we shall drag a world with us—a world in flames." In that, Hitler was right. World War II devastated much of the globe. In Asia and in Europe, ghostlike people wandered through rubble, searching desperately for food. One out of nine people in the Soviet Union had perished: a total of at least 21 million civilian and military war dead. The Chinese calculated their war losses at 10 million; the Germans and Austrians at 6 million; the Japanese at 2.5 million. Up to 1 million died of famine in Japanese-controlled Indochina. Almost 11 million people had been systematically murdered in Nazi death camps. Across the globe, the Second World War killed at least 55 million people.

Waging war required the cooperation of Allied nations with very different goals and interests. Tensions among them remained high throughout the war, as the United States and Britain resisted Stalin's demands that they open a second front to draw German soldiers away from the Soviet Union. The United States, meanwhile, was fighting a brutal war in the Pacific, pushing Japanese forces back toward their home islands. By the time Japan surrendered in August 1945, the strains between the Soviet Union and its English-speaking Allies made postwar peace and stability unlikely.

American men and machines were a critical part of the Allied war effort. Although Americans did not join in the perfect unity and shared sacrifice suggested by recent descriptions of "the greatest generation," American servicemen covered the globe, from the Arctic to the tropics. And on the home front, Americans worked around the clock to make the weapons that would win the war. Although they

Nuclear Proliferation

Virtually from the moment of the Hiroshima and Nagasaki atomic bombings, American strategists grappled with the problem of erecting barriers to membership in the "nuclear club." The early focus was on the Soviet Union. How long, analysts wondered, before Stalin gets the bomb? On September 23, 1949, came the answer, as President Truman informed a shocked American public that the Soviets had successfully tested an atomic device.

In the years thereafter, membership in the nuclear club grew, through a combination of huge national investments, espionage, and a black market of willing Western suppliers of needed raw materials and technologies. There were successful detonations by Great Britain (1952), France (1960), China (1964), India (1974), and Pakistan (1998). Israel crossed the nuclear weapon threshold on the eve of the 1967 Six-Day War but to this day has always refused to confirm or deny that it has the bomb. More recently, creditable reports indicate that North Korea has a small nuclear arsenal and that Iran is working to get one.

If this is a sizable number of nuclear states, it is far fewer than experts predicted in the 1960s. "If three nations made nuclear weapons in the 1970s," one senior British analyst warned then, "ten might do so in the 1980s and thirty in the 1990s." It did not happen, and the main reason is that the five existing nuclear powers committed themselves in the mid-1960s—for a complex set of self-interested reasons—to promoting nonproliferation. Subsequently, the rate of proliferation steadily declined; all told, 22 of 31 states that started down the nuclear path changed course and renounced the bomb. By late 2006, the Treaty on the Non-Proliferation of Nuclear Weapons (NPT), enacted on July 1, 1968, had 187 signatories and was widely hailed as one of the great international agreements of the post-1945 era.

Skeptics took a different view. They noted that three states outside the NPT (Israel, India, and Pakistan) became nuclear powers, and they charged the "original five" with hypocrisy, for doing everything possible to prevent others from obtaining nuclear arms while keeping large stockpiles for themselves. With the world in 2013 awash in some 17,000 nuclear weapons (97 percent of which belong to the United States and Russia), critics feared a new kind of proliferation, in which a terrorist group or other nonstate actor got its hands on one or more bombs. In that nightmare scenario, they warned, the de facto post-Nagasaki international moratorium on the use of nuclear weapons would soon be—literally—blown away.

CRITICAL THINKING

- With the rise in non-state terrorism, what actions, if any, should the world's signees of the NPT, particularly the United States and Russia, take regarding existing nuclear stockpiles?

---

made sacrifices during the war—including almost three hundred thousand who gave their lives—many Americans found that the war had changed their lives for the better. Mobilization for war ended the Great Depression, reducing unemployment practically to zero. War jobs demanded workers, and Americans moved in huge numbers to war-production centers. The influx of workers strained the resources of existing communities and sometimes led to social friction and even violence. But many Americans—African Americans, Mexican Americans, women, poor whites from the South—found new opportunities for employment in well-paid war jobs.

The federal government, in order to manage the nation's war efforts, became a stronger presence in the lives of individual Americans—regulating business and employment; overseeing military conscription, training, and deployment; and even controlling what people could buy to eat or to wear. The Second World War was a powerful engine of social change.

Americans emerged from World War II fully confident that theirs was the greatest country in the world. It was certainly the most powerful. At war's end, only the United States had the capital and economic resources to spur international recovery; only the United States was more prosperous and more secure than when war began. In the coming struggle to fashion a new world out of the ashes of the old, soon to be called the Cold War, the United States held a commanding position. For better or worse—and clearly there were elements of each—the Second World War was a turning point in the nation's history.

Suggestions for Further Reading

Michael C. C. Adams, *The Best War Ever: America and World War II* (1993)

Tsuyoshi Hasegawa, *Racing the Enemy: Stalin, Truman, and the Surrender of Japan* (2005)

William I. Hitchcock, *The Bitter Road to Freedom: A New History of the Liberation of Europe* (2008)

John Howard, *Concentration Camps on the Homefront: Japanese Americans in the House of Jim Crow* (2008)

David M. Kennedy, *Freedom from Fear: The American People in Depression and War, 1929–1945* (1999)

Warren F. Kimball, *Forged in War: Roosevelt, Churchill, and the Second World War* (1997)

Nelson Lichtenstein, *Labor's War at Home: The CIO in World War II* (1983)

Gerald F. Linderman, *The World Within War: America's Combat Experience in World War II* (1997)

Leisa Meyers, *Creating G.I. Jane: Sexuality and Power in the Women's Army Corps During World War II* (1996)

Williamson Murray and Allan Reed Millett, *A War to Be Won: Fighting the Second World War* (2009)

George Roeder, Jr., *The Censored War: American Visual Experience During World War II* (1993)

James Sparrow, *Warfare State: World War II Americans and the Age of Big Government* (2011)

Ronald Takaki, *Double Victory: A Multicultural History of America in World War II* (2000)

Nancy Beck Young, *Why We Fight: Congress and the Politics of World War II* (2013)

MINDTAP
From Cengage

MindTap® is a fully online personalized learning experience built upon Cengage Learning content. MindTap® combines student learning tools—readings, multimedia, activities, and assessments—into a singular Learning Path that guides students through the course and helps students develop the critical thinking, analysis, and communication skills that are essential to academic and professional success.

The Cold War and American Globalism, 1945–1961

On July 16, 1945, the Deer Team leader parachuted into northern Vietnam, near Kimlung, a village in a valley of rice paddies. Colonel Allison Thomas could not know that the end of the Second World War was just weeks away, but he and the other five members of his Office of Strategic Services (OSS) unit knew their mission: to work with the Vietminh, a nationalist Vietnamese organization, to sabotage Japanese forces that in March had taken direct control of Vietnam from France. After disentangling himself from the banyan tree into which his parachute had slammed him, Thomas spoke a "few flowery sentences" to two hundred Vietminh soldiers assembled near a banner proclaiming, "Welcome to Our American Friends." Ho Chi Minh, head of the Vietminh, ill but speaking in good English, cordially greeted the OSS team and offered supper. The next day Ho denounced the French but remarked that "we welcome 10 million Americans." "Forget the Communist Bogy," Thomas radioed OSS headquarters in China.

A communist who had worked for decades to win his nation's independence from France, Ho joined the French Communist Party after World War I and sought to use it as a vehicle for Vietnamese independence. For the next two decades, living in China, the Soviet Union, and elsewhere, he patiently planned and fought to free his nation from French colonialism. During World War II, Ho's Vietminh warriors harassed both French and Japanese forces and rescued downed American pilots. In March 1945, Ho met with U.S. officials in China, where he read the *Encyclopaedia Americana* and *Time* magazine at an Office of War Information facility. Receiving no aid from his ideological allies in the Soviet Union, Ho hoped that the United States would favor his nation's long quest for liberation from colonialism.

Other OSS personnel soon parachuted into Kimlung, including a male nurse who diagnosed Ho's ailments as malaria and dysentery. Quinine and sulfa drugs restored his health, but Ho

◀ **Ho Chi Minh (in shorts) and his chief lieutenant, Gen. Vo Nguyen Giap (in white suit), with members of an Office of Strategic Services (OSS) team at Tan Trao in northern Vietnam, August 1945.** Vietnam: Ho Chi Minh (in shorts) and Vo Nguyen Giap (in white suit) with members of an American Office of Strategic Services (OSS) team at Tan Trao in northern Vietnam, August 1945/PICTURES FROM HISTORY/Bridgeman Images

Chronology

1945	■ Roosevelt dies; Truman becomes president ■ Atomic bombings of Japan
1946	■ Kennan's "long telegram" criticizes USSR ■ Vietnamese war against France erupts
1947	■ Truman Doctrine seeks aid for Greece and Turkey ■ Marshall offers Europe economic assistance ■ National Security Act reorganizes government
1948	■ Communists take power in Czechoslovakia ■ Truman recognizes Israel ■ United States organizes Berlin airlift
1949	■ NATO founded as anti-Soviet alliance ■ Soviet Union explodes atomic bomb ■ Mao's communists win power in China
1950	■ NSC-68 recommends major military buildup ■ Korean War starts in June; China enters in fall
1951	■ United States signs Mutual Security Treaty with Japan
1953	■ Eisenhower becomes president ■ Stalin dies ■ United States helps restore shah to power in Iran ■ Korean War ends
1954	■ Geneva Accords partition Vietnam ■ CIA-led coup overthrows Arbenz in Guatemala
1955	■ Soviets create Warsaw Pact
1956	■ Soviets crush uprising in Hungary ■ Suez crisis sparks war in Middle East
1957	■ Soviets fire first ICBM and launch *Sputnik*
1958	■ U.S. troops land in Lebanon ■ Berlin crisis
1959	■ Castro ousts Batista in Cuba
1960	■ Eighteen African colonies become independent ■ Vietcong organized in South Vietnam

remained frail. As a sign of friendship, the Americans in Vietnam named Ho "OSS Agent 19." Everywhere the Americans went, impoverished villagers thanked them with gifts of food and clothing, despite the devastating famine of 1944–1945 in which at least a million Vietnamese people died. The villagers interpreted the foreigners' presence as a sign of U.S. anticolonial and anti-Japanese sentiments. In early August, the Deer Team began to give Vietminh soldiers weapons training. During many conversations with the OSS members, Ho said he hoped young Vietnamese could study in the United States and that American technicians could help build an independent Vietnam. Citing history, Ho remarked that "your statesmen make eloquent speeches about . . . self-determination. We are self-determined. Why not help us? Am I any different from . . . your George Washington?"

A second OSS unit, the Mercy Team, headed by Captain Archimedes Patti, arrived in the city of Hanoi on August 22. When Patti met Ho—"this wisp of a man," as Patti put it—the Vietminh leader applauded America's assistance and called for future "collaboration." But unbeknownst to these OSS members, who believed that President Franklin D. Roosevelt's general sympathy for eventual Vietnamese independence remained U.S. policy, the new Truman administration in Washington had decided to let France decide the fate of Vietnam. That change in policy explains why Ho never received answers to the several letters and telegrams he sent to Washington—the first dated August 30, 1945.

On September 2, 1945, amid great fanfare in Hanoi, with OSS personnel present, an emotional Ho Chi Minh read his declaration of independence for the Democratic Republic of Vietnam: "All men are created equal; they are endowed by their Creator with certain unalienable Rights; among these are Life, Liberty, and the pursuit of

Happiness." Having borrowed from the internationally renowned American document of 1776, Ho then itemized Vietnamese grievances against France.

By early autumn, both OSS teams had departed Vietnam. In a last meeting with Captain Patti, Ho expressed his sadness that the United States had armed the French to reestablish their colonial rule in Vietnam. Sure, Ho said, U.S. officials in Washington judged him a "Moscow puppet" because he was a communist. But Ho claimed that he drew inspiration from the American struggle for independence and that he was foremost "a free agent," a nationalist. If necessary, Ho insisted, the Vietnamese would go it alone, with or without American or Soviet help. And they did—first against the French and eventually against more than half a million U.S. troops in what became America's longest war up to that time. How different world history might have been had President Harry S Truman responded favorably to Ho Chi Minh's last letter to Washington, dated February 16, 1946, which asked the United States "as guardians and champions of World Justice to take a decisive step in support of our independence."

Experience an interactive version of this story in MindTap®.

Because Ho Chi Minh and many of his nationalist followers had declared themselves communists, U.S. leaders rejected their appeal. Endorsing the containment doctrine to draw the line against communism everywhere, American presidents from Truman to George H. W. Bush believed that a ruthless Soviet Union was directing a worldwide communist conspiracy against peace, free-market capitalism, and political democracy. Soviet leaders from Joseph Stalin to Mikhail Gorbachev protested that a militarized, economically aggressive United States sought nothing less than world domination. This protracted contest between the United States and the Soviet Union acquired the name "the Cold War."

The primary feature of world affairs for more than four decades, the Cold War was fundamentally a bipolar contest between the United States and the Soviet Union over spheres of influence and world power. Decisions made in Washington and Moscow dominated world politics as the capitalist "West" squared off against the communist "East." The contest dominated international relations and eventually took the lives of millions, cost trillions of dollars, spawned doomsday fears, and destabilized one nation after another. On occasion, the two superpowers negotiated at summit conferences and signed agreements to temper their dangerous arms race; at other times they went to the brink of war and armed allies to fight vicious Third World conflicts. Sometimes these allies had their own ideas and ambitions, and they often proved adept at resisting pressure applied on them by one or both of the superpowers. Over time, American and Soviet leaders came to realize that, notwithstanding the immense military might at their disposal, their power to effect change was in key respects limited.

Vietnam was part of the "Third World," a general term for those nations that during the Cold War era wore neither the "West" (the "First World") nor the "East" (the "Second World") label. Sometimes called "developing countries," Third World nations were on the whole nonwhite, nonindustrialized, and located in the southern half of the globe—in Asia, Africa, the Middle East, and Latin America. Many had been colonies of European nations or Japan, and they were vulnerable to the Cold War rivalry that intruded on them. U.S. leaders often interpreted their anticolonialism, political instability, and restrictions on foreign-owned property as Soviet- or communist-inspired, or capable of being exploited by Moscow—in short, as Cold War matters rather than as expressions of profound indigenous nationalism. As an example, Vietnam became one among many sites where Cold War fears and Third World aspirations intersected, prompting American intervention. Such intervention bespoke a globalist foreign policy, meaning that U.S. officials now regarded the entire world as the appropriate sphere for America's influence.

Critics in the United States challenged the architects of the Cold War, questioning their exaggerations of threats from abroad, meddlesome interventions in the Third World, and expensive militarization of foreign policy. But when leaders like Truman described the Cold War in extremist terms as a life-and-death struggle against a monstrous enemy, legitimate criticism became suspect and dissenters were discredited. Critics' searching questions about America's global, interventionist foreign policy and its reliance on nuclear weapons were drowned out by charges that dissenters were "soft on communism," if not un-American. Decision makers in the United States successfully cultivated a Cold War consensus that stifled debate and shaped the mind-set of millions of Americans.

- ■ *Why did relations between the Soviet Union and the United States turn hostile soon after their victory in World War II?*

- ■ *When and why did the Cold War expand from a struggle over the future of Europe and central Asia to one encompassing virtually the entire globe?*

- ■ *By what means did the Truman and Eisenhower administrations seek to expand America's global influence in the late 1940s and the 1950s?*

24-1 From Allies to Adversaries

▶ **What were the respective postwar goals of the Soviet Union and the United States?**

▶ **What issues contributed to escalating tensions between the Soviet Union and the United States and the emergence of the Cold War?**

▶ **How did the personalities of Joseph Stalin and Harry S Truman shape the relationship between the Soviet Union and the United States?**

The Second World War had a deeply unsettling effect on the international system. At its end, Germany was in ruins. Great Britain was badly overstrained and exhausted; France, having endured five years of Nazi occupation, was rent by internal division. Italy also emerged drastically weakened and, in Asia, Japan was decimated and under occupation and China was headed toward a renewed civil war. Throughout Europe and Asia, factories, transportation, and communications links had been reduced to rubble. Agricultural production plummeted, and displaced persons wandered about in search of food and family. How would the devastated economic world be pieced back together? The United States and the Soviet Union, though allies in the war, offered very different answers and models. The collapse of Germany and Japan, moreover, had created power vacuums that drew the two major powers into collision as they sought influence in countries where the Axis aggressors had once held sway. And the political turmoil that many nations experienced after the war also spurred Soviet-American competition. For example, in Greece and China, where civil wars raged between leftists and conservative regimes, the two powers supported different sides.

24-1a Decolonization

The international system also experienced instability because empires were disintegrating, creating the new Third World. Financial constraints and nationalist rebellions forced the imperial states to set their colonies free. Britain exited India (and Pakistan) in 1947 and Burma and Sri Lanka (Ceylon) in 1948. The Philippines gained independence from the United States in 1946. After four years of battling nationalists in Indonesia, the Dutch left in 1949. In the Middle East, Lebanon (1943), Syria (1946), and Jordan (1946) gained independence, while in Palestine British officials faced growing pressure from Zionists intent on creating a Jewish homeland and from Arab leaders opposed to the prospect. In Iraq, too, nationalist agitation increased against the British-installed government. Washington and Moscow paid close attention to this anticolonial ferment, seeing these new or emerging Third World states as potential allies that might provide military bases, resources, and markets. Not all new nations were willing to play along; some chose nonalignment in the Cold War. "We do not intend to be the playthings of others," declared India's leader, Jawaharlal Nehru.

24-1b Stalin's Aims

Driven by different ideologies and different economic and strategic needs in this volatile international climate, the United States and the Soviet Union assessed their most pressing tasks in very different terms. The Soviets, though committed to seeking ultimate victory over the capitalist countries, were most concerned about preventing another invasion of their homeland. It was a territory much less secure than the United States, for reasons both geographic and historical. Its landmass was huge—three times as large as that of the United States—but it had only ten thousand miles of seacoast, much of which was under ice for a large part of the year. Russian leaders both before and after the revolution had made increased maritime access a chief foreign policy aim.

Worse, the geographical frontiers of the USSR were hard to defend. Siberia, vital for its mineral resources, lay six thousand miles east of Moscow and was vulnerable to encroachment by Japan and China. In the west, the border with Poland had generated violent clashes ever since World War I, and eastern Europe had been the launching pad for Hitler's invasion in 1941: the resulting war cost the lives of more than 20 million Soviet citizens and caused massive physical destruction. Henceforth, Soviet leaders determined, they could have no dangers along their western borders.

Overall, however, Soviet territorial objectives were limited. Although many Americans were quick to compare Stalin to Hitler, Stalin did not have the Nazi leader's grandiose plans for world hegemony. In general, his aims resembled those of the czars before him: he wanted to push the USSR's borders to include the Baltic states of Estonia, Latvia, and Lithuania, as well as the eastern part of prewar

Stalin: Ally to Adversary

These two *Look* magazine portrayals of Soviet leader Stalin indicate how quickly the Grand Alliance of World War II disintegrated into the superpower confrontation of the Cold War. In the first piece, from mid-1944, correspondent Ralph Parker writes that Stalin spends half his time writing poetry and the other half reading it to the schoolchildren who clamor to sit on his knee. "Stalin," Parker adds, "is undoubtedly among the best-dressed of all world leaders making Churchill in his siren suit look positively shabby." Four years later, Louis Fischer paints a very different picture. "This small man with drooping shoulders tyrannizes one-fifth of the world," Fischer writes of the Soviet leader, adding that neither Hitler nor any Russian czar was as powerful or as menacing as the "Great Red Father."

CRITICAL THINKING

- What do these two items suggest about American attitudes toward the outside world?
- What do they suggest about the role of the press in U.S. society?

▲ "A Guy Named Joe" cover story of *Look* magazine by Ralph Parker, June 27, 1944.

▲ "Life Story of Stalin" by Louis Fischer in *Look* magazine, June 8, 1948.

Poland. Fearful of a revived Germany, he sought to ensure pro-Soviet governments in eastern Europe. To the south, Stalin wanted to have a presence in northern Iran, and he pressed the Turks to grant him naval bases and free access out of the Black Sea. The Soviet government promoted economic independence more than trade with other countries; suspicious of their European neighbors, they did not promote rapid rebuilding of the war-ravaged economies of the region or, more generally, expanded world trade.

24-1c U.S. Economic and Strategic Needs

The United States, by contrast, came out of the war secure in its borders. Separated from the other world powers by two vast oceans, the American home base had been virtually immune from attack during the fighting—only an occasional shell from a submarine or a hostile balloon from Japan reached the shores of the continental United States. American casualties were fewer than those of any of the other major combatants—hugely so in comparison with the Soviet Union. With its fixed capital intact, its resources more plentiful than ever, and in lone possession of the atomic bomb, the United States was the strongest power in the world at war's end.

Yet this was no time for complacency, Washington officials reminded one another. Some other power—almost certainly the USSR—could take advantage of the political and economic instability in war-torn Europe and Asia, and eventually seize control of these areas, with dire implications for American security. To prevent this outcome, officials in Washington sought forward bases overseas, in order to keep an airborne enemy at bay. To further enhance U.S. security, American planners, in direct contrast to their Soviet counterparts, sought the quick reconstruction of nations—including the former enemies Germany and Japan—and a world economy based on free trade. Such a system, they reasoned, was essential to preserve America's economic well-being.

The Soviets, on the other hand, refused to join the new World Bank and International Monetary Fund (IMF), created at the July 1944 Bretton Woods Conference by forty-four nations to stabilize trade and finance. They held that the United States dominated both institutions and used them to promote private investment and open international commerce, which Moscow saw as capitalist tools of exploitation. With the United States as its largest donor, the World Bank opened its doors in 1945 and began to make loans to help members finance reconstruction projects; the IMF, also heavily backed by the United States, helped members meet their balance-of-payments problems through currency loans.

24-1d Stalin and Truman

The personalities of the two countries' leaders also mattered. Joseph Stalin, though hostile to the Western powers and capable of utter ruthlessness against his own people (his periodic purges since the 1930s had taken the lives of millions), did not want war. With the huge Russian losses in World War II, he was all too aware of his country's weakness vis-à-vis the United States. For a time at least, he appears to have believed he could achieve his aspirations peacefully, through continued cooperation with the Americans and the British. Over the long term, though, Stalin envisaged more conflict. He believed that Germany and Japan would rise again to threaten the USSR, probably by the 1960s, and his suspicion of the other capitalist powers was boundless. Many have concluded that Stalin was clinically paranoid: the first to do so, a leading Russian neuropathologist in 1927, died a few days later! As historian David Reynolds has noted, this paranoia, coupled with Stalin's xenophobia (fear of anything foreign) and his Marxist-Leninist ideology, created in the Soviet leader a mental map of "them" versus "us" that decisively influenced his approach to world affairs.

Harry Truman had none of Stalin's capacity for deception or ruthlessness, but to a lesser degree he, too, was prone to a "them" versus "us" worldview. Truman often glossed over nuances, ambiguities, and counterevidence; he preferred the simple answer stated in either/or terms. As Winston Churchill, who admired Truman's decisiveness, once observed, the president "takes no notice of delicate ground, he just plants his foot firmly on it." Truman constantly exaggerated, as when he declared in his undelivered farewell address that he had "knocked the socks off the communists" in Korea. Shortly after Roosevelt's death in early 1945, Truman met the Soviet commissar of foreign affairs, V. M. Molotov, at the White House. When the president sharply protested that the Soviets were not fulfilling the Yalta agreement on Poland, Molotov stormed out. Truman had self-consciously developed what he called his "tough method," and he bragged after the encounter that "I gave it to him straight one-two to the jaw." Truman's display of toughness became a trademark of American Cold War diplomacy.

24-1e The Beginning of the Cold War

At what point did the Cold War actually begin? No precise start date can be given. The origins must be thought of as a process, one that arguably began in 1917 with the Bolshevik Revolution and the Western powers' hostile response, but in a more meaningful sense began in mid-1945, as World War II drew to a close. By the spring of 1947, certainly, the struggle had begun.

One of the first Soviet-American clashes came in Poland in 1945, when the Soviets refused to allow the Polish government-in-exile in London to be a part of the communist government that Moscow sponsored. The Soviets also snuffed out civil liberties in the former Nazi satellite of Romania, justifying their actions by pointing to what they claimed was an equivalent U.S. manipulation of Italy. Moscow initially allowed free elections in Hungary and Czechoslovakia, but as the Cold War accelerated and U.S. influence in Europe expanded, the Soviets encouraged communist coups in Hungary (1947) and Czechoslovakia (1948). Yugoslavia stood as a unique case: its independent communist government, led by Josip Broz Tito, successfully broke with Stalin in 1948.

To defend their actions, Moscow officials noted that the United States was reviving their traditional enemy, Germany. Twice in the lifetime of Soviet leaders Germany had wrought enormous suffering on Russia, and Stalin and his associates were determined to prevent a third occurrence. The Soviets also protested that the United States was meddling in Eastern Europe. They cited clandestine American meetings with anti-Soviet groups, repeated calls for elections likely to produce anti-Soviet regimes, and the use of loans to gain political influence (financial diplomacy). Moscow charged that the United States was pursuing a double standard—intervening in the affairs of Eastern Europe but demanding that the Soviet Union stay out of Latin America and Asia. Americans called for free elections in the Soviet sphere, Moscow noted, but not in the U.S. sphere in Latin America, where several military dictatorships ruled.

24-1f Atomic Diplomacy

The atomic bomb also divided the two major powers. The Soviets believed that the United States was practicing "atomic diplomacy"—maintaining a nuclear monopoly to scare the Soviets into diplomatic concessions. Secretary of State James F. Byrnes thought that the atomic bomb gave the United States bargaining power and could serve as a deterrent to Soviet expansion, but Secretary of War Henry L. Stimson thought otherwise in 1945. If Americans continued to have "this weapon rather ostentatiously on our hip," he warned Truman, the Soviets' "suspicions and their distrust of our purposes and motives will increase."

In this atmosphere of suspicion and distrust, Truman refused to turn over the weapon to an international control authority. In 1946, he backed the Baruch Plan, named after its author, financier Bernard Baruch. Largely a propaganda ploy, this proposal provided for U.S. abandonment of its atomic monopoly only after the world's fissionable materials were brought under the authority of an international agency. The Soviets retorted that this plan would require them to shut down their atomic bomb development project while the United States continued its own. Washington and Moscow soon became locked in an expensive and frightening nuclear arms race.

By the middle of 1946, the wartime Grand Alliance was but a fading memory; that year, Soviets and Americans clashed on every front. When the United States turned down a Soviet request for a reconstruction loan but gave a loan to Britain, Moscow upbraided Washington for using its dollars to manipulate foreign governments. The two Cold War powers also backed different groups in Iran, where the United States helped bring the pro-West shah to the throne. Unable to agree on the unification of Germany, the former allies built up their zones independently.

24-1g Warnings from Kennan and Churchill

After Stalin gave a speech in February 1946 that depicted the world as threatened by capitalist acquisitiveness, the American chargé d'affaires in Moscow, **George F. Kennan**, sent a pessimistic "long telegram" to Washington. Kennan asserted that Soviet fanaticism made even a temporary understanding impossible. His widely circulated report fed a growing belief among American officials that only toughness would work with the Soviets. The following month, Winston Churchill delivered a stirring speech in Fulton, Missouri. The former British prime minister warned that a Soviet-erected "iron curtain" had cut off Eastern European countries from the West. With an approving Truman sitting on the stage, Churchill called for an Anglo-American partnership to resist the new menace.

The growing Soviet-American tensions had major implications for the functioning of the United Nations. The delegates who gathered in San Francisco in April 1945 to sign the UN charter had agreed on an organization that would include a General Assembly of all member states, as well as a smaller Security Council that would take the lead on issues of

▲ Smiles all around as President Truman waves his hat during his and Winston Churchill's 1946 visit to Fulton, Missouri.

peace and security. Five great powers were given permanent seats on the council—the United States, the Soviet Union, Great Britain, China, and France. These permanent members could not prohibit discussion of any issue, but they could exercise a veto against any proposed action. To be effective on the major issues of war and peace, therefore, the UN needed great-power cooperation of the type that had existed in wartime but was a distant memory by mid-1946. Of the fifty-one founding states, twenty-two came from the Americas and another fifteen from Europe, which in effect gave the United States a large majority in the assembly. In retaliation, Moscow began to exercise its veto in the Security Council.

Some high-level U.S. officials were dismayed by the administration's harsh anti-Soviet posture. Secretary of Commerce Henry A. Wallace, who had been Roosevelt's vice president before Truman, charged that Truman's get-tough policy was substituting atomic and economic coercion for diplomacy. Wallace told a Madison Square Garden audience in September 1946 that "getting tough never brought anything real and lasting—whether for schoolyard bullies or businessmen or world powers. The tougher we get, the tougher the Russians will get." Truman soon fired Wallace from the cabinet, blasting him privately as "a real Commie and a dangerous man" and boasting that he, Truman, had now "run the crackpots out of the Democratic Party."

24-1h Truman Doctrine

East-West tensions escalated further in early 1947, when the British requested American help in Greece to defend their conservative

George F. Kennan American diplomat in Moscow, architect of the Cold War policy of containment.

client-government (a government dependent on the economic or military support of a more powerful country) in a civil war against leftists. In his March 12, 1947, speech to Congress, Truman requested $400 million in aid to Greece and Turkey. He had a selling job to do. The Republican Eightieth Congress wanted less, not more, spending; many of its members had little respect for the Democratic president whose administration the voters had repudiated in the 1946 elections by giving the GOP ("Grand Old Party," the Republican Party) majorities in both houses of Congress. Republican senator Arthur Vandenberg of Michigan, a bipartisan leader who backed Truman's request, bluntly told the president that he would have to "scare hell out of the American people" to gain congressional approval.

With that advice in mind, the president delivered a speech laced with alarmist language intended to stake out the American role in the postwar world. Truman claimed that communism, feeding on economic dislocations, imperiled the world. "If Greece should fall under the control of an armed minority," he gravely concluded in an early version of the domino theory, "the effect upon its neighbor, Turkey, would be immediate and serious (see "Unrelenting Cold War," Section 24-5). Confusion and disorder might well spread throughout the entire Middle East." Truman articulated what became known as the **Truman Doctrine**: "I believe that it must be the policy of the United States to support free peoples who are resisting attempted subjugation by armed minorities or by outside pressures."

Critics correctly pointed out that the Soviet Union was little involved in the Greek civil war, that the communists in Greece were more pro-Tito than pro-Stalin, and that the resistance movement had noncommunist as well as communist members. Nor was the Soviet Union threatening Turkey at the time. Others suggested that such aid should be channeled through the United Nations. Truman countered that, should communists gain control of Greece, they might open the door to Soviet power in the Mediterranean. After much debate, the Senate approved Truman's request by 67 to 23 votes. Using U.S. dollars and military advisers, the Greek government defeated the insurgents in 1949, and Turkey became a staunch U.S. ally on the Soviets' border.

Truman Doctrine U.S. policy designed to contain the spread of communism; began with President Truman's 1947 request to Congress for economic and military aid to the struggling countries of Greece and Turkey to prevent them from succumbing to Soviet pressure.

containment U.S. policy uniting military, economic, and diplomatic strategies to prevent the spread of Soviet communism and to enhance America's security and influence abroad.

24-1i Inevitable Cold War?

In the months after Truman's speech, the term *Cold War* slipped into the lexicon as a description of the Soviet-American relationship. Less than two years had passed since the glorious victory over the Axis powers, and the two Grand Alliance members now found themselves locked in a tense struggle for world dominance. It would last almost half a century. Could the confrontation have been avoided? Not altogether, it seems clear. Even before World War II had ended, perceptive observers anticipated that the United States and the USSR would seek to fill the power vacuum that would exist after the armistice, and that friction would result. The two countries had a history of hostility and tension, and both were militarily powerful. Most of all, the two nations were divided by sharply differing political economies with widely divergent needs and by a deep ideological chasm. Some kind of confrontation was destined to occur.

It is far less clear that the conflict had to result in a Cold War. The "cold peace" that had prevailed from the revolution in 1917 through World War II could conceivably have been maintained into the postwar years as well. Neither side's leadership wanted war. Both hoped—at least in the initial months—that a spirit of cooperation could be maintained. The Cold War resulted from decisions by individual human beings who might well have chosen differently, who might have done more, for example, to maintain diplomatic dialogue, to seek negotiated solutions to complex international problems. For decades, many Americans would wonder if the high price they were paying for victory in the superpower confrontation was necessary.

24-2 Containment in Action

▶ How did the United States implement containment in western Europe?

▶ What domestic and international organizations were created to assist the United States in the area of national security?

▶ How did the Soviet Union respond to American containment efforts?

Having committed themselves to countering Soviet and communist expansion, the Truman team had to figure out just how to fight the Cold War. The policy they chose, **containment**, was in place before the term was coined. George Kennan, having moved from the U.S. embassy in Moscow to the State Department in Washington, published an influential statement of the containment doctrine. Writing as "Mr. X" in the July 1947 issue of the magazine *Foreign Affairs*, Kennan advocated a "policy of firm containment, designed to confront the Russians with unalterable counterforce at every point where they show signs of encroaching upon the interests of a peaceful and stable world." Such counterforce, Kennan argued, would check Soviet expansion and eventually foster a "mellowing" of Soviet behavior. Along with the Truman Doctrine, Kennan's "X" article became a key manifesto of Cold War policy.

24-2a Lippmann's Critique

The veteran journalist Walter Lippmann took issue with the containment doctrine in his slim but powerful book *The Cold War* (1947), calling it a "strategic monstrosity" that failed to distinguish between areas vital and peripheral to U.S. security. If American leaders defined every place on earth as strategically important, Lippmann reasoned, the nation's patience and resources soon would be drained. Nor did Lippmann share Truman's conviction that the Soviet Union was plotting to take over the world. The president, he asserted, put too little emphasis on diplomacy. Ironically, Kennan himself agreed with much of Lippmann's critique, and he soon began to distance himself from the doctrine he had helped to create.

Invoking the containment doctrine, the United States in 1947 and 1948 began to build an international economic and defensive network to protect American prosperity and security, and to advance U.S. hegemony. In Western Europe, the region of primary concern, American diplomats pursued a range of objectives, including economic reconstruction and the fostering of a political environment friendly to the United States. They sought the ouster of communists from governments, as occurred in 1947 in France and Italy, and blockage of "third force" or neutralist tendencies. To maintain political stability in key capitals, U.S. officials worked to keep the decolonization of European empires orderly. In Germany, they advocated the unification of the western zones. At the same time, American culture—consumer goods, music, consumption ethic, and production techniques—permeated European societies. Some Europeans resisted Americanization, but transatlantic ties strengthened.

24-2b Marshall Plan

The first instrument designed to achieve U.S. goals in Western Europe was the **Marshall Plan**. European nations, still reeling economically and unstable politically, lacked the dollars to buy vital American-made goods. Americans, who had already spent billions of dollars on European relief and recovery by 1947, remembered all too well the troubles of the 1930s: global depression, political extremism, and war born of economic discontent. Such cataclysms could not be allowed to happen again; communism must not replace fascism. Western Europe, said one State Department diplomat, was "the keystone in the arch which supports the kind of a world which we have to have in order to conduct our lives."

In June 1947, Secretary of State George C. Marshall announced that the United States would finance a massive European recovery program. Launched in 1948, the Marshall Plan sent $12.4 billion to Western Europe before the program ended in 1951 (see Map 24.1). To stimulate business at home, the legislation required that Europeans spend the foreign aid dollars in the United States on American-made products. The Marshall Plan proved a mixed success; some scholars today even argue that Europe could have revived without it. The program caused inflation, failed to solve a balance-of-payments problem, took only tentative steps toward economic integration, and further divided Europe between "East" and "West." But the program spurred impressive Western European industrial production and investment and started the region toward self-sustaining economic growth. From the American perspective, moreover, the plan succeeded because it helped contain communism.

24-2c National Security Act

To streamline the administration of U.S. defense, Truman worked with Congress on the **National Security Act of 1947**. The act created the Office of Secretary of Defense (which became the Department of Defense two years later) to oversee all branches of the armed services, the National Security Council (NSC) of high-level officials to advise the president, and the Central Intelligence Agency (CIA) to conduct spy operations and information gathering overseas. By the early 1950s, the CIA had become a significant element in national security policy and had expanded its functions to include covert (secret) operations aimed at overthrowing unfriendly foreign leaders and, as a high-ranking American official put it, a "Department of Dirty Tricks" to stir up economic trouble in "the camp of the enemy." Taken together, the components of the National Security Act gave the president increased powers with which to conduct foreign policy.

In response, Stalin forbade communist satellite governments in Eastern Europe to accept Marshall Plan aid and ordered communist parties in Western Europe to work to thwart the plan. He also created the Cominform, an organization designed to coordinate communist activities around the world. Whereas American planners saw the Marshall Plan as helping their European friends achieve security against a potential Soviet threat, in Stalin's mind it raised anew the specter of capitalist penetration. He tightened his grip on Eastern Europe—most notably, he engineered a coup in Czechoslovakia in February 1948 that ensured full Soviet control of the country—which in turn created more anxiety in the United States. In this way, the U.S.-Soviet relationship became a downward spiral that seemed to gain in velocity with each passing month.

24-2d Berlin Blockade and Airlift

The German problem remained especially intractable. In June 1948, the Americans, French, and British agreed to fuse their German zones, including their three sectors of Berlin. They sought to integrate West Germany (the Federal Republic of Germany) into the Western European economy, complete with a reformed German currency. Fearing a resurgent Germany tied to the American Cold War camp, the Soviets cut off western land access to the jointly occupied city of Berlin, located well inside the Soviet zone. In response to this bold move,

Marshall Plan The Truman administration's proposal for massive U.S. economic aid to speed the recovery of war-torn Europe.

National Security Act of 1947 Act that unified the armed forces under a single agency, later called the Department of Defense. It also established the National Security Council to advise the president on matters of national security and created the Central Intelligence Agency (CIA).

Map 24.1 Divided Europe

After the Second World War, Europe broke into two competing camps. When the United States launched the Marshall Plan in 1948, the Soviet Union countered with its own economic plan the following year. When the United States created NATO in 1949, the Soviet Union answered with the Warsaw Pact in 1955. On the whole, these two camps held firm until the late 1980s.

Legend (map):

Participants in the Marshall Plan

$ Member of NATO,* formed in 1949

Member of COMECON,** formed in 1949, and the Warsaw Pact, organized in 1955

● Member of the European Common Market, formed in 1958

Iron Curtain

* North Atlantic Treaty Organization
** Council for Mutual Economic Assistance

Map labels:

ATLANTIC OCEAN

ICELAND — Reykjavik — Joined Common Market, 1973

IRELAND — Dublin — Joined Common Market, 1973

UNITED KINGDOM — London — U.S. loan of $3.5 billion, 1946 / Exploded first atomic bomb, 1952 / Joined Common Market, 1973

NORWAY — Oslo

SWEDEN — Stockholm

FINLAND — Helsinki

DENMARK — Copenhagen — Joined Common Market, 1973

NETHERLANDS — Amsterdam

BELGIUM — Brussels

LUX. — Paris

FRANCE — Exploded first atomic bomb, 1960 / Withdrew from NATO, 1966

WEST GERMANY — Bonn — Joined NATO, 1955

SWITZ. — Bern

AUSTRIA — Vienna — Zones of occupation ended, 1955

EAST GERMANY — West Berlin / East Berlin / Berlin blockade, 1948–1949

POLAND — Warsaw

CZECHOSLOVAKIA — Prague — Communist coup, 1948 / U.S.S.R. invasion, 1968

HUNGARY — Budapest — Revolution, 1956

UNION OF SOVIET SOCIALIST REPUBLICS — Moscow — Exploded first atomic bomb, 1949

ITALY — Rome

YUGOSLAVIA — Belgrade — Tito-Stalin schism, 1948

ALBANIA — Tiranë — Left COMECON, 1961 / Withdrew from WP, 1968

ROMANIA — Bucharest

BULGARIA — Sofia

GREECE — Athens — Truman Doctrine, 1947 / Joined NATO, 1952 / Joined Common Market, 1981

TURKEY — Ankara — Truman Doctrine, 1947 / Joined NATO, 1952

CYPRUS — Nicosia

PORTUGAL — Lisbon — Joined Common Market, 1986

SPAIN — Madrid — Joined NATO, 1982 / Joined Common Market, 1986

North Sea, Baltic Sea, Black Sea, Caspian Sea, Mediterranean Sea

Volga R., Don R., Dnieper R., Danube R.

Corsica, Sardinia, Sicily, Balearic Is.

Arctic Circle, 20°W, 0°, 20°E

400 Mi. / 400 Km. / 200 / 0

▲ Under official postwar relief and recovery programs, including the Marshall Plan, the United States shipped billions of dollars' worth of food and equipment to Western European nations struggling to overcome the destruction of the Second World War. Private efforts, such as this one in 1950, also succeeded. The people of Jersey City, New Jersey, sent this snowplow to the mountainous village of Capracotta, Italy.

President Truman ordered a massive airlift of food, fuel, and other supplies to Berlin. Their spoiling effort blunted, the Soviets finally lifted the blockade in May 1949 and founded the German Democratic Republic, or East Germany.

The successful airlift may have saved Harry Truman's political career: he surprised pundits by narrowly defeating Republican Thomas E. Dewey in the presidential election that occurred in the middle of the crisis in November 1948. Safely elected, Truman took the major step of formalizing what was already in essence a military alliance among the United States, Canada, and the nations of Western Europe. In April 1949, twelve nations signed a mutual defense treaty, agreeing that an attack on any one of them would be considered an attack on all, and establishing the **North Atlantic Treaty Organization (NATO)** (see Map 24.1).

The treaty aroused considerable domestic debate, for not since 1778 had the United States entered a formal European military alliance, and some critics, such as Senator Robert A. Taft, Republican of Ohio, claimed that NATO would provoke rather than deter war. Other skeptics argued that the Soviet threat was political, not military. Administration officials themselves did not anticipate a Soviet military thrust against Western Europe, but they responded that, should the Soviets ever probe westward, NATO would function as a

"tripwire," bringing the full force of the United States to bear on the Soviet Union. Truman officials also hoped that NATO would keep Western Europeans from embracing communism or even neutralism in the Cold War. The Senate ratified the treaty by 82 votes to 13, and the United States soon began to spend billions of dollars under the Mutual Defense Assistance Act.

By the summer of 1949, Truman and his advisers were basking in the successes of their foreign policy. Containment was working splendidly, they and many outside observers had concluded. West Germany was on the road to recovery. The Berlin blockade had been defeated, and NATO had been formed. In Western Europe, the threat posed by communist parties seemed lessened. True, there was trouble in China, where the communists under **Mao Zedong** were winning that country's civil war. But that struggle would likely wax and wane for years or even decades to come, and besides, Truman could not

North Atlantic Treaty Organization (NATO) A mutual defense pact between the United States and eleven other nations promising to stand united in the face of military aggression, specifically by the Soviet Union.

Mao Zedong Chinese military and political leader who established the communist People's Republic of China.

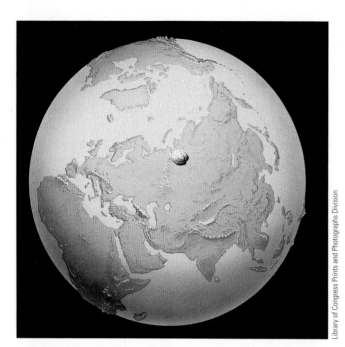

Library of Congress Prints and Photographs Division

▲ Richard Edes Harrison's illustration of the Soviet Union's detonation of an atomic bomb appeared in the October 1949 issue of *Life* magazine. A leading journalist-cartographer of the mid-twentieth century, Harrison was known for incorporating a global perspective in his work. Here, he uses a single cloud of smoke to suggest the potentially far-reaching effects of an isolated bomb explosion.

be held responsible for events there. Just possibly, some dared to think, Harry Truman was on his way to winning the Cold War.

24-2e Twin Shocks

Then, suddenly, in late September, came the "twin shocks," two momentous developments that made Americans feel in even greater danger than ever before—two decades later, they were still dealing with the reverberations. First, an American reconnaissance aircraft detected unusually high radioactivity in the atmosphere. The news stunned U.S. officials: the Soviets had exploded an atomic device. With the American nuclear monopoly erased, Western Europe seemed more vulnerable. At the same time, the communists in China completed their victory in that nation's civil war—the end came more quickly than many expected. Now the world's largest and most populous countries were ruled by communists, and one of them had the atomic bomb. The bipartisan foreign policy of 1945–1948 broke down, as Republicans, bitter over Truman's reelection, declared that traitors in America must have given Stalin the bomb and allowed China to be "lost."

Rejecting calls by Kennan and others for

NSC-68 Secret report by the National Security Council that would characterize U.S. Cold War strategy for decades; it saw the clash between the United States and the Soviet Union as a fight between good and evil and reversed the post–World War II military demobilization, focusing instead on a military buildup.

high-level negotiations, Truman in early 1950 gave the go-ahead to begin production of a hydrogen bomb, the "Super," and ordered his national security team to undertake a thorough review of policy. Kennan bemoaned the militarization of the Cold War and was replaced at the State Department by Paul Nitze. The National Security Council delivered to the president in April 1950 a significant top-secret document labeled **NSC-68**. Predicting continued tension with expansionistic communists all over the world and describing "a shrinking world of polarized power," the report, whose primary author was Nitze, appealed for a much-enlarged military budget and the mobilization of public opinion to support such an increase. The Cold War was about to become a vastly more expensive, more far-reaching affair.

24-3 The Cold War in Asia

▶ How did the implementation of containment differ in Japan and China?

▶ Why did the United States choose to support the French effort to restore colonial rule in Indochina?

Although Europe was the principal battleground in the early Cold War, Asia gradually became ensnared in the conflict as well. Indeed, it was in Asia that the consequences of an expansive containment doctrine would exact their heaviest price on the United States, in the form of large-scale and bloody wars in Korea and Vietnam. Though always less important to both superpowers than Europe, Asia would be the continent where the Cold War most often turned hot.

From the start, Japan was crucial to U.S. strategy. The United States monopolized Japan's reconstruction through a military occupation directed by General Douglas MacArthur, who envisioned turning the Pacific Ocean into "an Anglo-Saxon lake." Truman did not like "Mr. Prima Donna, Brass Hat" MacArthur, but the general initiated "a democratic revolution from above," as the Japanese called it, that reflected Washington's wishes. MacArthur wrote a democratic constitution, gave women voting rights, revitalized the economy, and destroyed the nation's weapons. U.S. authorities also helped Americanize Japan through censorship; films that hinted at criticism of the United States (for the destruction of Hiroshima, for example) or that depicted traditional Japanese customs, such as suicide, arranged marriages, and swordplay, were banned. In 1951, the United States and Japan signed a separate peace that restored Japan's sovereignty and ended the occupation. A Mutual Security Treaty that year provided for the stationing of U.S. forces on Japanese soil, including a base on Okinawa.

24-3a Chinese Civil War

The administration had less success in China. The United States had long backed the Nationalists of Jiang Jieshi (Chiang Kai-shek) against Mao Zedong's communists. But after the Second World War, Generalissimo Jiang became an unreliable partner who rejected U.S. advice. His government had become corrupt, inefficient, and out of touch with discontented peasants, whom the communists enlisted with promises of land reform. Jiang also subverted American efforts to negotiate a cease-fire and a coalition government. "We picked a bad horse," Truman admitted, privately denouncing the Nationalists as "grafters and crooks." Still, seeing Jiang as the only alternative to Mao, Truman backed him to the end.

American officials divided on the question of whether Mao was a puppet of the Soviet Union. Some considered him an Asian Tito—communist but independent—but most believed him to be part of an international communist movement that might give the Soviets a springboard into Asia. Thus, when the Chinese communists made secret overtures to the United States to begin diplomatic talks in 1945 and again in 1949, American officials rebuffed them. Mao decided to "lean" to the Soviet side in the Cold War. Because China always maintained a fierce independence that rankled the Soviets, before long a Sino-Soviet schism opened. Indeed, Mao deeply resented the Soviets' refusal to aid the communists during the civil war.

Then came Mao's victory in September 1949. Jiang fled to the island of Formosa (Taiwan), and in Beijing (formerly Peking) Mao proclaimed the People's Republic of China (PRC). Truman hesitated to extend diplomatic recognition to the new government, even after the British prime minister asked him, "Are we to cut ourselves off from all contact with one-sixth of the inhabitants of the world?" U.S. officials became alarmed by the 1950 Sino-Soviet treaty of friendship and by the harassment of Americans and their property in China. Truman also chose nonrecognition because a vocal group of Republican critics, the so-called China lobby, pinned Jiang's defeat on the administration. The president insisted that the self-defeating Jiang, despite billions of dollars in American aid, had proven a poor instrument of the containment doctrine. The administration nonetheless took the politically safe route and rejected recognition. (Not until 1979 did official Sino-American relations resume.)

24-3b Vietnam's Quest for Independence

Mao's victory in China drew urgent American attention to Indochina, the territory in Southeast Asia that had been held by France for the better part of a century. The Japanese had wrested control over Indochina during World War II, but even then Vietnamese nationalists dedicated to independence grew in strength. One leading nationalist, Ho Chi Minh, hoped to use Japan's defeat to assert Vietnamese independence, and he asked for U.S. support. American officials had few kind things to say about French colonial policy, and many were pessimistic that France could achieve a military solution to the conflict. Nevertheless, they rejected Ho's appeals in favor of a restoration of French rule, mostly to ensure France's cooperation in the emerging Soviet-American confrontation. In addition, the Truman administration was wary of Ho Chi Minh's communist politics. Ho, the State Department declared, was an "agent of international communism" who, it was assumed, would assist Soviet and, after 1949, Chinese expansionism. Overlooking the native roots of the nationalist rebellion against French colonialism, and the tenacious Vietnamese resistance to foreign intruders, Washington officials interpreted events in Indochina through a Cold War lens.

Even so, when war between the Vietminh and France broke out in 1946, the United States initially took a hands-off approach. But when Jiang's regime collapsed in China three years later, the Truman administration made two crucial decisions—both of them in early 1950, before the Korean War. First, in February, Washington recognized the French puppet government of Bao Dai, an intelligent but lazy former emperor who had collaborated with both the French and

◀ Mao Zedong was a military theoretician who also involved himself in day-to-day military decision making. He was responsible for, or at least approved, all of the major strategic moves the communists made on their way to power. This image shows him applauding soldiers and other supporters on Tiananmen Square in Beijing.

Apic/Getty Images

the Japanese. In the eyes of many Vietnamese, the United States thus became in essence a colonial power, an ally of the hated French. Second, in May, the administration agreed to send weapons and other assistance to sustain the French in Indochina. From 1945 to 1954, the United States gave $2 billion of the $5 billion that France spent to keep Vietnam within its empire—to no avail. How Vietnam ultimately became the site of a major American war, and how the world's most powerful nation failed to subdue a peasant people who suffered enormous losses, is one of the most remarkable and tragic stories of modern U.S. history.

24-4 The Korean War

▶ What factors contributed to American involvement in the war between North and South Korea?

▶ How did the Korean War change with the entrance of China into the conflict?

▶ What were the domestic and international consequences of the Korean War?

In the early morning of June 25, 1950, a large military force of the Democratic People's Republic of Korea (North Korea) moved across the thirty-eighth parallel into the Republic of Korea (South Korea). Colonized by Japan since 1910, Korea had been divided in two by the victorious powers after Japan's defeat in 1945.

Korean War War between North Korea and South Korea with heavy involvement by the superpowers and by the People's Republic of China, which lasted from 1950 to 1953 and which claimed the lives of millions.

Although the Soviets had armed the North and the Americans had armed the South (U.S. aid had reached $100 million a year), the **Korean War** began as a civil war. Virtually from the moment of the division, the two parts had been skirmishing along their supposedly temporary border while antigovernment (and anti-U.S.) guerrilla fighting flared in the South.

Both the North's communist leader, Kim Il Sung, and the South's president, Syngman Rhee, sought to reunify their nation. Kim's military in particular gained strength when tens of thousands of battle-tested Koreans returned home in 1949 after serving in Mao's army. Displaying the Cold War mentality of the time, however, President Truman claimed that the Soviets had masterminded the North Korean attack. "Communism was acting in Korea just as Hitler, Mussolini, and the Japanese had acted," he said, recalling Axis aggression.

Actually, Kim had to press a doubting Joseph Stalin, who only reluctantly approved the attack after Kim predicted an easy, early victory and after Mao backed Kim. Whatever Stalin's reasoning, his support for Kim's venture remained lukewarm. When the UN Security Council voted to defend South Korea against the invasion from the north, the Soviet representative was not even present to veto the resolution because the Soviets were boycotting the United Nations to protest its refusal to grant membership to the People's Republic of China. During the war, Moscow gave limited aid to North Korea and China, which grew angry at Stalin for reneging on promised Soviet airpower. Stalin, all too aware of his strategic inferiority vis-à-vis the United States, did not want to be dragged into a costly war.

◀ Men of the 3rd Battalion, 34th Infantry Regiment, 35th Infantry Division, take cover to avoid incoming mortar shells, near the Hantan River in central Korea, in April 1951.

24-4a U.S. Forces Intervene

The president first ordered General Douglas MacArthur to send arms and troops to South Korea. He did not seek congressional approval—he and his aides feared that lawmakers would initiate a lengthy debate—and thereby set the precedent of waging war on executive authority alone. Worried that Mao might use the occasion to take Formosa, Truman also directed the Seventh Fleet to patrol the waters between the Chinese mainland and Jiang's sanctuary on Formosa, thus inserting the United States again into Chinese politics. After the Security Council voted to assist South Korea, MacArthur became commander of UN forces in Korea. Sixteen nations contributed troops to the UN command, but 40 percent were South Korean and about 50 percent American. In the war's early weeks, North Korean tanks and superior firepower sent the South Korean army into chaotic retreat. The first American soldiers, taking heavy casualties, could not stop the North Korean advance. Within weeks, the South Koreans and Americans had been pushed into the tiny Pusan perimeter at the tip of South Korea (see Map 24.2).

General MacArthur planned a daring amphibious landing at heavily fortified Inchon, several hundred miles behind North Korean lines. After U.S. guns and bombs pounded Inchon, marines splashed ashore on September 15, 1950. The operation was a brilliant success, and the troops soon liberated the South Korean capital of Seoul and pushed the North Koreans back to the thirty-eighth parallel. Even before Inchon, Truman had redefined the U.S. war goal, changing it from the containment of North Korea to the reunification of Korea by force. Communism not only would be stopped; it would be rolled back.

24-4b Chinese Entry into the War

In September, Truman authorized UN forces to cross the thirty-eighth parallel. These troops drove deep into North Korea, and American aircraft began strikes against bridges on the Yalu River, the border between North Korea and China. The Chinese watched warily, fearing that the Americans would next stab at the People's Republic. Mao publicly warned that China could not permit the bombing of its transportation links with Korea and would not accept the annihilation of North Korea itself. MacArthur shrugged off the warnings, and Washington officials agreed with the strong-willed general, drawing further confidence from the fact that, as MacArthur had predicted, the Soviets were not preparing for war.

MacArthur was right about the Soviets, but wrong about the Chinese. Mao, concluding that the "Americans would run more rampant" unless stopped, on October 25 sent Chinese soldiers into the war near the Yalu. Perhaps to lure American forces into a trap or to signal willingness to begin negotiations, they pulled back after a brief and successful offensive against South Korean troops. Then, after MacArthur sent the U.S. Eighth Army northward, tens of thousands of Chinese troops counterattacked on November 26, surprising American forces and driving them pell-mell southward. One

Map 24.2 The Korean War, 1950–1953

Beginning as a civil war between North and South, this war became international when the United States—under the auspices of the United Nations—and the People's Republic of China intervened with their military forces.

U.S. officer termed it "a sight that hasn't been seen for hundreds of years: the men of a whole United States Army fleeing from a battlefield, abandoning their wounded, running for their lives."

24-4c Truman's Firing of MacArthur

By early 1951, the front had stabilized around the thirty-eighth parallel. A stalemate set in. Both Washington and Moscow welcomed negotiations, but MacArthur had other ideas. The theatrical general recklessly called for an attack on China and for Jiang's return to the mainland. Now was the time, he insisted, to smash communism by destroying its Asian flank. Denouncing the concept of limited war (war without nuclear weapons, confined to one place), MacArthur hinted that the president was practicing appeasement. In April, backed by the Joint Chiefs of Staff (the heads of the various armed services), Truman fired MacArthur. The general, who had not set foot in the United States for more than a decade, returned home a hero, with ticker-tape parades and cheers on the lecture circuit. Truman's popularity sagged, but he weathered scattered demands for his impeachment.

Armistice talks began in July 1951, but the fighting and dying went on for two more years. The most contentious point in the negotiations was the fate of prisoners of war (POWs). Defying the Geneva Prisoners of War Convention (1949), U.S. officials announced that only those North Korean and Chinese POWs who wished to go home would be returned. Responding to the American statement that there would be no forced repatriation, the North Koreans denounced forced retention. Both sides undertook "reeducation" or "brainwashing" programs to persuade POWs to resist repatriation.

24-4d Peace Agreement

As the POW issue stalled negotiations, U.S. officials made deliberately vague public statements about using atomic weapons in Korea. American bombers obliterated dams (whose rushing waters then destroyed rice fields), factories, airfields, and bridges in North Korea. Casualties on all sides mounted. Not until July 1953 was an armistice signed. Stalin's death in March and the advent of new leaders in both Moscow and Washington helped ease the way to a settlement that all sides welcomed. The combatants agreed to hand over the POW question to a special panel of neutral nations, which later gave prisoners their choice of staying or leaving. (In the end, 70,000 of about 100,000 North Korean and 5,600 of 20,700 Chinese POWs elected to return home; 21 American and 325 South Korean POWs of some 11,000 decided to stay in North Korea.) The North Korean–South Korean borderline was set near the thirty-eighth parallel, the prewar boundary, and a demilitarized zone was created between the two Koreas.

American casualties totaled 54,246 dead and 103,284 wounded. Close to 5 million Asians died in the war: 2 million North Korean civilians and 500,000 soldiers; 1 million South Korean civilians and 100,000 soldiers; and at least 1 million Chinese soldiers—ranking Korea as one of the costliest wars of the twentieth century.

John Foster Dulles Secretary of state under Dwight D. Eisenhower. He expressed skepticism about merely "containing" communism and spoke instead of rolling it back, but in practice moved cautiously.

24-4e Consequences of the War

The Korean War carried major domestic political consequences. The failure to achieve victory and the public's impatience with a stalemated war undoubtedly helped to elect Republican Dwight Eisenhower to the presidency in 1952, as the former general promised to "go to Korea" to end the war. The powers of the presidency grew as Congress repeatedly deferred to Truman. The president had never asked Congress for a declaration of war, believing that, as commander-in-chief, he had the authority to send troops wherever he wished. He saw no need to consult Congress—except when he wanted the $69.5 billion Korean War bill paid. In addition, the war, which occurred in the midst of the "who lost China?" debate, inflamed party politics in the United States. Republican lawmakers, including Wisconsin senator Joseph McCarthy, accused Truman and Secretary of State Dean Acheson of being "soft on communism" in failing first to prevent, and then to go all out to win, the war; their verbal attacks strengthened the administration's determination to take an uncompromising position in the negotiations.

The impact on foreign policy was even greater. The Sino-American hostility generated by the war ensured that there would be no U.S. reconciliation with the Beijing government and that South Korea and Formosa would become major recipients of American foreign aid. The alliance with Japan strengthened as the island's economy boomed after filling large procurement orders from the United States. Australia and New Zealand joined the United States in a mutual defense agreement, the ANZUS Treaty (1951). The U.S. Army sent four divisions to Europe, and the administration initiated plans to rearm West Germany. The Korean War also persuaded Truman to do what he had been unwilling to do before the outbreak of hostilities—approve NSC-68. Indeed, the military budget shot up from $14 billion in 1949 to $44 billion in 1953; it remained between $35 billion and $44 billion a year throughout the 1950s. The Soviet Union sought to match this military buildup, and the result was a major arms race between the two nations. In sum, Truman's legacy was a highly militarized U.S. foreign policy active on a global scale.

24-5 Unrelenting Cold War

▶ How did Cold War policy change during the presidency of Dwight D. Eisenhower?

▶ What role did the CIA play in American foreign policy during Eisenhower's presidency?

▶ How did Eisenhower respond to the crises in Suez and Hungary?

The new foreign policy team of President Eisenhower and Secretary of State **John Foster Dulles** largely sustained Truman's Cold War policies. Both brought abundant experience in foreign affairs to their posts. Eisenhower had lived and traveled in Europe, Asia, and Latin America and, as a general during the Second World War, had negotiated with world leaders. After the war, he had served as army chief of staff and NATO supreme commander. Dulles had been closely involved with U.S. diplomacy since the first decade

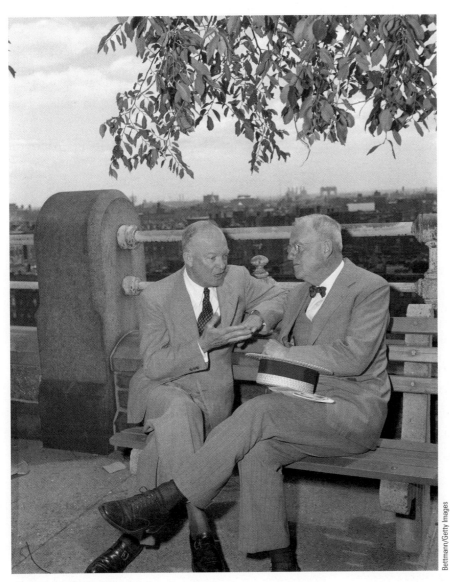

◄ President Eisenhower *(left)* confers with Secretary of State John Foster Dulles (1888–1959), known for his strong anti-communism and his often self-righteous lecturing style. Dulles once remarked that the United States "is almost the only country strong enough and powerful enough to be moral."

Bettmann/Getty Images

of the century. "Foster has been studying to be secretary of state since he was five years old," Eisenhower observed, exaggerating only slightly. He relied heavily on Dulles to be his emissary abroad. The secretary of state spent so much time traveling to world capitals that critics exclaimed, "Don't do something, Foster, just stand there!"

Eisenhower and Dulles accepted the Cold War consensus about the threat of communism and the need for global vigilance. Although Democrats promoted an image of Eisenhower as a bumbling, passive, aging hero, deferring most foreign policy matters to Dulles, the president in fact commanded the policymaking process and on occasion tamed the more hawkish proposals of Dulles and Vice President Richard Nixon. Even so, the secretary of state's influence was vast. Though polished and authoritative, he impressed people as arrogant, stubborn, and hectoring—and averse to compromise, an essential ingredient in successful diplomacy. Behind closed doors Dulles could show a different side, one considerably more flexible and pragmatic, but there is little evidence

that he saw much utility in negotiations, at least where communists were involved. His assertion that neutrality was an "immoral and short-sighted conception" did not sit well with Third World leaders, who resented being told they had to choose between East and West.

24-5a "Massive Retaliation"

Dulles said that he considered containment too defensive a stance toward communism. He called instead for "liberation," although he never explained precisely how the countries of Eastern Europe could be freed from Soviet control. "Massive retaliation" was the administration's plan for the nuclear obliteration of the Soviet state or its assumed client, the People's Republic of China, if either one took aggressive actions. Eisenhower said that it "simply means the ability to blow hell out of them in a hurry if they start anything." The ability of the United States to make such a threat was thought to provide "deterrence," the prevention of hostile Soviet behavior.

In their "New Look" for the American military, Eisenhower and Dulles emphasized airpower and nuclear weaponry. The president's preference for heavy weapons stemmed in part from his desire to trim the federal budget ("more bang for the buck," as the saying went). Galvanized by the successful test of the world's first hydrogen bomb in November 1952, Eisenhower oversaw a massive stockpiling of nuclear weapons—from 1,200 at the start of his presidency to 22,229 at the end. Backed by its huge military arsenal, the United States could practice "brinkmanship": not backing down in a crisis, even if it meant taking the nation to the brink of war. Eisenhower also popularized the "**domino theory**": that small, weak neighboring nations would fall to communism like a row of dominoes if they were not propped up by the United States.

24-5b CIA as Foreign Policy Instrument

Eisenhower increasingly utilized the Central Intelligence Agency as an instrument of foreign policy. Headed by Allen Dulles, brother of the secretary of state, the CIA put foreign leaders (such as King Hussein of Jordan) on its payroll; subsidized foreign labor unions, newspapers, and political parties (such as the conservative Liberal Democratic Party of Japan); planted false stories in newspapers through its "disinformation" projects; and trained foreign military officers in counterrevolutionary methods. It hired American journalists and professors, secretly funded the National Student Association to spur contacts with foreign student leaders, used business executives as "fronts," and conducted experiments on unsuspecting Americans to determine the effects of "mind control" drugs (the MK-ULTRA program). The CIA also launched covert operations (including assassination schemes) to subvert or destroy governments in the Third World. The CIA helped overthrow the governments of Iran (1953) and Guatemala (1954) but failed in attempts to topple regimes in Indonesia (1958) and Cuba (1961).

The CIA and other components of the American intelligence community followed the principle of plausible deniability: covert operations should be conducted in such a way, and the decisions that launched them concealed so well, that the president could deny any knowledge of them. Thus, President Eisenhower disavowed any U.S. role in Guatemala, even though he had ordered the operation. He and his successor, John F. Kennedy, also denied that they had instructed the CIA to assassinate Cuba's Fidel Castro, whose regime after 1959 became stridently anti-American.

24-5c Nuclear Buildup

Leaders in Moscow soon became aware of Eisenhower's expanded use of covert action as well as his stockpiling of nuclear weapons. They increased their own intelligence activity and tested their first H-bomb in 1953. Four years later, they shocked Americans by firing the world's first intercontinental ballistic missile (ICBM) and then propelling the satellite **Sputnik** into orbit in outer space. Americans felt more vulnerable to air attack and inferior in rocket technology, even though in 1957 the United States had 2,460 strategic weapons and a nuclear stockpile of 5,543, compared with the Soviet Union's 102 and 650. As President Eisenhower said, "If we were to release our nuclear stockpile on the Soviet Union, the main danger would arise not from retaliation but from fallout in the earth's atmosphere." The administration enlarged its fleet of long-range bombers (B-52s) and deployed intermediate-range missiles in Europe, targeted against the Soviet Union. At the end of 1960, the United States began adding Polaris missile-bearing submarines to its navy. To foster future technological advancement, the National Aeronautics and Space Administration (NASA) was created in 1958.

Overall, though, Eisenhower sought to avoid any kind of military confrontation with the Soviet Union and China; notwithstanding Dulles's tough talk of "liberation" and "massive retaliation," the administration was content to follow Truman's lead and emphasize the *containment* of communism. Eisenhower rejected opportunities to use nuclear weapons, and he proved more reluctant than many other Cold War presidents to send American soldiers into battle. He preferred to fight the Soviets at the level of propaganda. Convinced that the struggle against Moscow would in large measure be decided in the arena of international public opinion, he wanted to win the "hearts and minds" of people overseas. The "People-to-People" campaign, launched in 1956, sought to use ordinary Americans and nongovernmental organizations to enhance the international image of the United States and its people.

In the same way, American cultural exchanges and participation in trade fairs in the Eisenhower years were used to create a favorable atmosphere abroad for U.S. political, economic, and military policies. Sometimes, the propaganda war was waged on the Soviets' own turf. In 1959, Vice President Richard Nixon traveled to Moscow to open an American products fair. In the display of a modern American kitchen, part of a model six-room ranch-style house, Nixon extolled capitalist consumerism, while Soviet premier Nikita Khrushchev, Stalin's successor, touted the merits of communism. The encounter became famous as the "kitchen debate."

24-5d Rebellion in Hungary

Eisenhower showed his restraint in 1956 when turmoil rocked parts of Eastern Europe. In February, Khrushchev called for "peaceful coexistence" between capitalists and communists, denounced Stalin, and suggested that Moscow would tolerate different brands of communism. Revolts against Soviet power promptly erupted in Poland and Hungary, testing Khrushchev's new permissiveness. After a new Hungarian government in 1956 announced its withdrawal from the Warsaw Pact (the Soviet military alliance formed in 1955

domino theory Eisenhower's prediction that if Vietnam went communist, then the smaller, neighboring communities of Thailand, Burma, Indonesia, and ultimately all of Asia would fall like dominoes.

Sputnik Soviet satellite that was the world's first successful launch in space in 1957; it dashed the American myth of unquestioned technological superiority.

The People-to-People Campaign

Not long after the start of the Cold War, U.S. officials determined that the Soviet-American confrontation was as much psychological and ideological as military and economic. One result was the People-to-People campaign, a state-private venture initiated by the United States Information Agency (USIA) in 1956, which aimed to win the "hearts and minds" of people around the world. In this program, American propaganda experts sought to channel the energies of ordinary Americans, businesses, civic organizations, labor groups, and women's clubs to promote confidence abroad in the basic goodness of the American people and, by extension, their government. In addition, the campaign was designed to raise morale at home by giving Americans a sense of personal participation in the Cold War struggle. The People-to-People campaign, one USIA pamphlet said, made "every man an ambassador."

Campaign activities resembled the home-front mobilization efforts of World War II. If, during the war, Americans were exhorted by the Office of War Information to purchase war bonds, now they were told that $30 could send a ninety-nine-volume portable library of American books to schools and libraries overseas. Publishers donated magazines and books for free distribution to foreign countries—*Woman's Day*, for example, volunteered six thousand copies of the magazine per month. People-to-People committees organized sister-city affiliations and "pen-pal" letter exchanges, hosted exchange students, and organized traveling "People-to-People delegations" representing their various communities. The travelers were urged to behave like goodwill ambassadors when abroad and to "help overcome any feeling that America is a land that thinks money can buy everything." They were to "appreciate [foreigners'] manners and customs, not to insist on imitations of the American way of doing things."

To extol everyday life in the United States, Camp Fire Girls in more than three thousand communities took photographs on the theme "This is our home. This is how we live. These are my People." The photographs, assembled in albums, were sent to girls in Latin America, Africa, Asia, and the Middle East. The Hobbies Committee, meanwhile, connected people with interests in radio, photography, coins, stamps, and horticulture. One group represented dog owners, in the belief that "dogs make good ambassadors and are capable of hurdling the barriers of language and ideologies in the quest for peace."

Just what effect the People-to-People campaign had on foreign images of the United States is hard to say. The persistence to this day of the widespread impression that Americans are a provincial, materialistic people suggests that skepticism is in order. But alongside this negative image is a more positive one that sees Americans as admirably open, friendly, optimistic, and pragmatic; if the campaign did not erase the former impression, it may have helped foster the latter. Whatever role the People-to-People campaign played in the larger Cold War struggle, it certainly achieved one of its chief objectives: to link ordinary Americans more closely to people in other parts of the world.

CRITICAL THINKING

- The People-to-People campaign was meant to cultivate abroad the idea that Americans were good, hard-working people who respected others' cultures and customs. Why was it important to spread this view of Americans in the Cold War atmosphere?

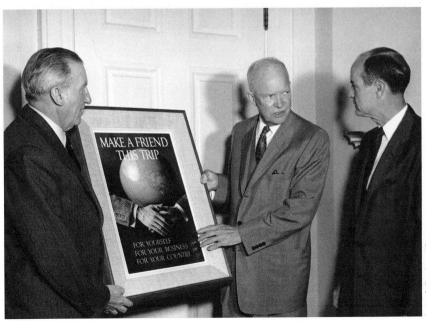

◀ "Make a friend this trip," urges this framed People-to-People poster, delivered to President Eisenhower in May 1957, "for yourself, for your business, for your country." With the president are two of the campaign's leaders, John W. Hanes Jr. and Edward Lipscomb.

with communist countries of Eastern Europe), Soviet troops and tanks battled students and workers in the streets of Budapest and crushed the rebellion.

Although the Eisenhower administration's propaganda had been encouraging liberation efforts, U.S. officials found themselves unable to aid the rebels without igniting a world war. Instead, they promised only to welcome Hungarian immigrants in greater numbers than American quota laws allowed. Even so, the West could have reaped some propaganda advantage from this display of Soviet brute force had not British, French, and Israeli troops—U.S. allies—invaded Egypt during the Suez crisis just before the Soviets smashed the Hungarian uprising (see "Suez Crisis," Section 24-6g).

The turmoil had hardly subsided when the divided city of Berlin once again became a Cold War flash point. The Soviets railed against the placement in West Germany of American bombers capable of carrying nuclear warheads, and they complained that West Berlin had become an escape route for disaffected East Germans. In 1958, Khrushchev announced that the Soviet Union would recognize East German control of all of Berlin unless the United States and its allies began talks on German reunification and rearmament. The United States refused to give up its hold on West Berlin or to break West German ties with NATO. Khrushchev backed away from his ultimatum but promised to press the issue again.

24-5e U-2 Incident

Khrushchev hoped to do just that at a summit meeting planned for Paris in mid-1960. But two weeks before the conference, on May 1, a U-2 spy plane carrying high-powered cameras crashed 1,200 miles inside the Soviet Union. Moscow claimed credit for shooting down the plane, which the Soviets put on display along with Francis Gary Powers, the captured CIA pilot, and the pictures he had been snapping of Soviet military sites. Khrushchev demanded an apology for the U.S. violation of Soviet airspace. When Washington refused, the Soviets walked out of the Paris summit—"a graveyard of lost opportunities," as a Soviet official put it.

While sparring over Europe, both sides kept a wary eye on the People's Republic of China, which denounced the Soviet call for peaceful coexistence. Despite evidence of a widening Sino-Soviet split, most American officials still treated communism as a monolithic world movement. The isolation separating Beijing and Washington stymied communication and made continued conflict between China and the United States likely. In 1954, in a dispute over some miniscule islands off the Chinese coast—Mazu (Matsu) and the chain known as Jinmen (Quemoy)—the United States and the People's Republic of China lurched toward the brink. Taiwan's Jiang Jieshi held these islands and hoped to use them as a launching point for the counterrevolution on the mainland. Communist China's guns bombarded the islands in 1954. Thinking that U.S. credibility was at stake, Eisenhower decided to defend the outposts; he even hinted that he might use nuclear weapons. Why massive retaliation over such an insignificant issue? "Let's keep the Reds guessing," advised John Foster Dulles. "But what if they guessed wrong?" critics replied.

24-5f Formosa Resolution

In early 1955, Congress passed the Formosa Resolution, authorizing the president to deploy American forces to defend Formosa and adjoining islands. In so doing, Congress formally surrendered to the president what it had informally given up at the time of the Korea decision in 1950: the constitutional power to declare war. Although the crisis passed in April 1955, war loomed again in 1958 over Jinmen and Mazu. This time, after Washington strongly cautioned him not to use force against the mainland, Jiang withdrew some troops from the islands, and China relaxed its bombardments. But Eisenhower's nuclear threats persuaded the Chinese that they, too, needed nuclear arms. In 1964, China exploded its first nuclear bomb.

24-6 The Struggle for the Third World

▶ How did the United States become involved and intervene in Third World countries?

▶ How did Third World countries resist U.S. influence and intervention?

▶ What economic and political factors influenced the development of U.S. foreign policy in the Middle East?

▶ How did American actions in Vietnam evolve during Eisenhower's presidency?

In much of the Third World, the process of decolonization that began during the First World War accelerated after the Second World War, when the economically wracked imperial countries proved incapable of resisting their colonies' demands for freedom. A cavalcade of new nations cast off their colonial bonds (see Map 24.3). In 1960 alone, eighteen new African nations did so. From 1943 to 1994, a total of 125 countries became independent (the figure includes the former Soviet republics that departed the USSR in 1991). The emergence of so many new states in the 1940s and after, and the instability associated with the transfer of authority, shook the foundations of the international system. Power was redistributed, creating "near chaos," said one U.S. government report. In the traditional U.S. sphere of influence, Latin America, nationalists once again challenged Washington's dominance.

24-6a Interests in the Third World

By the late 1940s, when Cold War lines were drawn fairly tightly in Europe, Soviet-American rivalry shifted increasingly to the Third World. Much was at stake. The new

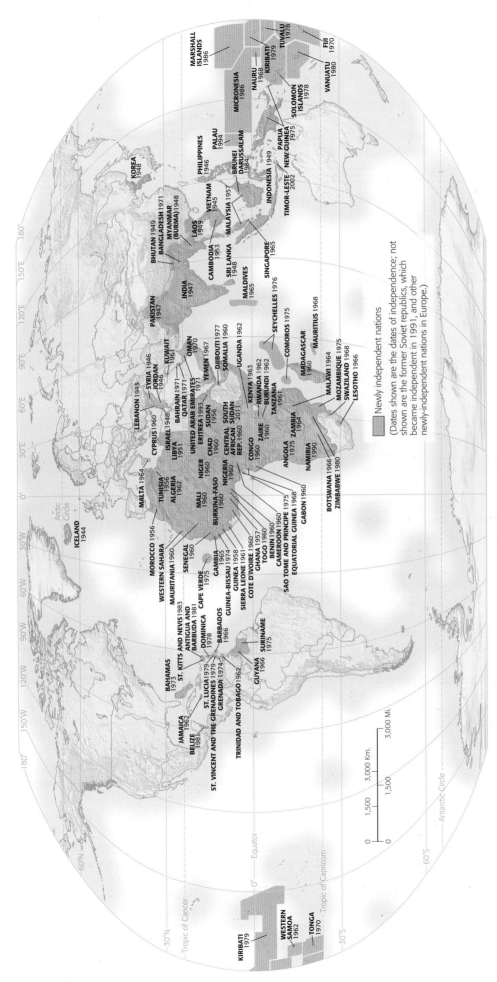

Map 24.3 The Rise of the Third World: Newly Independent Nations Since 1943

Accelerated by the Second World War, decolonization liberated many peoples from imperial rule. New nations emerged in the postwar international system dominated by the Cold War rivalry of the United States and the Soviet Union. Many newly independent states became targets of great-power intrigue but chose nonalignment in the Cold War.

Newly independent nations

(Dates shown are the dates of independence; not shown are the former Soviet republics, which became independent in 1991, and other newly-independent nations in Europe.)

KIRIBATI 1979

WESTERN SAMOA 1962

TONGA 1970

BAHAMAS 1973

BELIZE 1981

JAMAICA 1962

ST. LUCIA 1979
ST. VINCENT AND THE GRENADINES 1979
GRENADA 1974

ST. KITTS AND NEVIS 1983
ANTIGUA AND BARBUDA 1981
DOMINICA 1978

BARBADOS 1966

TRINIDAD AND TOBAGO 1962

GUYANA 1966

SURINAME 1975

ICELAND 1944

MOROCCO 1956

WESTERN SAHARA

MAURITANIA 1960

SENEGAL 1960

CAPE VERDE 1975

GAMBIA 1965

GUINEA-BISSAU 1974

GUINEA 1958

SIERRA LEONE 1961

COTE D'IVOIRE 1960

TUNISIA 1956

ALGERIA 1962

MALI 1960

BURKINA-FASO 1960

NIGER 1960

GHANA 1957

TOGO 1960

BENIN 1960

NIGERIA 1960

CAMEROON 1960

SAO TOME AND PRINCIPE 1975

EQUATORIAL GUINEA 1968

GABON 1960

MALTA 1964

LEBANON 1943

CYPRUS 1960

ISRAEL 1948

JORDAN 1946

SYRIA 1946

KUWAIT 1961

BAHRAIN 1971
QATAR 1971

UNITED ARAB EMIRATES 1971

OMAN 1970

YEMEN 1967

LIBYA 1951

CHAD 1960

SUDAN 1956

SOUTH SUDAN 2011

CENTRAL AFRICAN REP. 1960

ERITREA 1993

DJIBOUTI 1977

SOMALIA 1960

UGANDA 1962

CONGO 1960

ZAIRE 1960

KENYA 1963

RWANDA 1962

BURUNDI 1962

TANZANIA 1961

ANGOLA 1975

ZAMBIA 1964

MALAWI 1964

MOZAMBIQUE 1975

NAMIBIA 1990

BOTSWANA 1966

ZIMBABWE 1980

SWAZILAND 1968

LESOTHO 1966

SEYCHELLES 1976

COMOROS 1975

MADAGASCAR 1960

MAURITIUS 1968

PAKISTAN 1947

INDIA 1947

BHUTAN 1949

BANGLADESH 1971

MYANMAR (BURMA) 1948

LAOS 1949

CAMBODIA 1953

SRI LANKA 1948

MALDIVES 1965

SINGAPORE 1965

VIETNAM 1945

MALAYSIA 1957

KOREA 1948

PHILIPPINES 1946

PALAU 1994

BRUNEI DARUSSALAM 1984

INDONESIA 1949

TIMOR-LESTE 2002

PAPUA NEW GUINEA 1975

MICRONESIA 1986

MARSHALL ISLANDS 1986

NAURU 1968

KIRIBATI 1979

TUVALU 1978

FIJI 1970

SOLOMON ISLANDS 1978

VANUATU 1980

180° 150°W 120°W 90°W 60°W 30°W 0° 30°E 60°E 90°E 120°E 150°E 180°

Arctic Circle

Tropic of Cancer

Equator

Tropic of Capricorn

Antarctic Circle

60°N

30°N

0°

30°S

60°S

0   1,500   3,000 Km.
0   1,500   3,000 Mi.

nations could buy American goods and technology, supply strategic raw materials, and invite investments (more than one-third of America's private foreign investments were in Third World countries in 1959). And they could build cultural ties with the United States. Both great powers, moreover, looked to these new states for votes in the United Nations and sought sites within their borders for military and intelligence bases. But often poor and unstable—and rife with tribal, ethnic, and class rivalries—many new nations sought to end the economic, military, and cultural hegemony of the West. Many learned to play off the two superpowers against each other to garner more aid and arms. U.S. interventions—military and otherwise—in the Third World, American leaders believed, became necessary to impress Moscow with Washington's might and to resolve and counter the nationalism and radical anticapitalist social change that threatened American strategic and economic interests.

To thwart nationalist, radical, and communist challenges, the United States directed massive resources—foreign aid, propaganda, development projects—toward the Third World. By 1961, more than 90 percent of U.S. foreign aid was going to developing nations. Washington also allied with native elites and with undemocratic but anticommunist regimes, meddled in civil wars, and unleashed CIA covert operations. These American interventions often generated resentment among the local populace. When some of the larger Third World states—notably India, Ghana, Egypt, and Indonesia—refused to take sides in the Cold War, Secretary of State Dulles declared that neutralism was a step on the road to communism. Both he and Eisenhower insisted that every nation should take a side in the life-and-death Cold War struggle.

American leaders argued that technologically "backward" Third World countries needed Western-induced capitalist development and modernization in order to enjoy economic growth, social harmony, and political moderation. Often these U.S. officials also ascribed stereotyped race-, age-, and gender-based characteristics to Third World peoples, seeing them as dependent, emotional, and irrational, and therefore dependent on the fatherly tutelage of the United States. Cubans, CIA director Allen Dulles told the National Security Council in early 1959, "had to be treated more or less like children. They had to be led rather than rebuffed. If they were rebuffed, like children, they were capable of almost anything." At other times, American officials suggested that Third World countries were weak women—passive and servile, unable to resist the menacing appeals of communists and neutralists.

24-6b Racism and Segregation as U.S. Handicaps

Race attitudes and segregation practices in the United States especially influenced U.S. relations with Third World countries. In 1955, G. L. Mehta, the Indian ambassador to the United States, was refused service in the whites-only section of a restaurant at Houston International Airport. The insult stung deeply, as did many similar indignities experienced by other Third World diplomats. Fearing damaged relations with India, a large nation whose allegiance the United States sought in the Cold War, John Foster Dulles apologized to Mehta. The secretary thought racial segregation in the United States was a "major international hazard," spoiling American efforts to win friends in Third World countries and giving the Soviets a propaganda advantage. American practices and ideals did not align.

Thus, when the U.S. attorney general appealed to the Supreme Court to strike down segregation in public schools, he underlined that the humiliation of dark-skinned diplomats "furnished grist for the Communist propaganda mills." When the Court announced its *Brown* decision in 1954, the government quickly broadcast news of the desegregation order around the world in thirty-five languages on its Voice of America overseas radio network (see "Supreme Court Victories and School Desegregation," Section 25-4b). But the problem did not go away. For example, after the 1957 Little Rock crisis (see "Federal Authority and States' Rights," Section 25-4e), Dulles remarked that racial bigotry was "ruining our foreign policy. The effect of this in Asia and Africa will be worse for us than Hungary was for the Russians." Still, when an office of the Department of State decided to counter Soviet propaganda by creating for the 1958 World's Fair in Brussels an exhibit titled "The Unfinished Work"—on race relations in the United States and strides taken toward desegregation—southern conservatives kicked up such a furor that the Eisenhower administration closed the display.

American hostility toward revolution also obstructed the quest for influence in the Third World. In the twentieth century, the United States openly opposed revolutions in Mexico, China, Russia, Cuba, Vietnam, Nicaragua, and Iran, among other nations. Preferring, like most other great powers in history, to maintain the status quo, the United States usually supported its European allies or the conservative, propertied classes in the Third World. In 1960, for example, when forty-three African and Asian states sponsored a UN resolution endorsing decolonization, the United States abstained from the vote.

24-6c Development and Modernization

Yet idealism also inspired U.S. policy. Believing that Third World peoples craved modernization and that the American economic model of private enterprise and cooperation among business, labor, and government was best for them, American policymakers launched various "development" projects. Such projects held out the promise of sustained economic growth, prosperity, and stability, which the benefactors hoped would undermine radicalism. In the 1950s, the Carnegie, Ford, and Rockefeller Foundations worked with the U.S. Agency for International Development (AID) to sponsor a Green Revolution, a dramatic increase in agricultural production—for example, by the use of hybrid seeds. The Rockefeller Foundation supported foreign universities' efforts to train national leaders committed to non-radical development; from 1958 to 1969, the philanthropic agency spent $25 million in Nigeria. Before Dean Rusk became secretary of state in 1961, he served as president of the Rockefeller Foundation.

To persuade Third World peoples to abandon radical doctrines and neutralism, American leaders, often in cooperation with the business-sponsored Advertising Council, directed propaganda at developing nations. The United States Information Agency (USIA), founded in 1953, used films, radio broadcasts, the magazine *Free World*, exhibitions, exchange programs, and libraries (in 162 cities worldwide by 1961) to trumpet the theme of "People's Capitalism." Citing America's economic success—contrasted with "slave-labor" conditions in the Soviet Union—the message showcased well-paid American workers, political democracy, and religious freedom. To counter ugly pictures of segregation and white attacks on African Americans and civil rights activists in the South, the USIA applauded success stories of individual African Americans, such as boxers Floyd Patterson and Sugar Ray Robinson. In 1960 alone, some 13.8 million people visited U.S. pavilions abroad, including 1 million at the consumer products exhibit "Tradeways to Peace and Prosperity" in Damascus, Syria.

Undoubtedly, the American way of life appealed to some Third World peoples. They, too, wanted to enjoy American consumer goods, rock music, economic status, and educational opportunities. Hollywood movies offered enticing glimpses of middle-class materialism, and U.S. films dominated many overseas markets. Blue jeans, advertising billboards, and soft drinks flooded these societies. But if foreigners often envied Americans, they also resented them for having so much and wasting so much and for allowing their corporations to extract such high profits from overseas. Americans often received blame for the persistent poverty of the developing world, even though the leaders of those nations made decisions that hindered their own progress, such as pouring millions of dollars into their militaries while their people went hungry. Nonetheless, anti-American resentments could be measured in the late 1950s in attacks on USIA libraries in Calcutta, India; Beirut, Lebanon; and Bogotá, Colombia.

24-6d Intervention in Guatemala

When the more benign techniques of containment—aid, trade, cultural relations—proved insufficient to get Third World nations to line up on the American side in the Cold War, the Eisenhower administration often showed a willingness to press harder, by covert or overt means. Guatemala was an early test case. In 1951, leftist Jacobo

National Archives and Records Administration

▲ In the 1950s, the United States Information Agency—known overseas as the United States Information Service or USIS—sought to generate favorable international perceptions of American ideas and culture, including in what the State Department called "isolated areas." Here, people crowd around a USIS mobile library on a road near Rangoon, Burma, in June 1953.

Arbenz Guzmán was elected president of Guatemala, a poor country whose largest landowner was the American-owned United Fruit Company. United Fruit was an economic power throughout Latin America, where it owned 3 million acres of land and operated railroads, ports, ships, and telecommunications facilities. To fulfill his promise of land reform, Arbenz expropriated United Fruit's uncultivated land and offered compensation. The company dismissed the offer and charged that Arbenz posed a communist threat—a charge that CIA officials had already floated because Arbenz employed some communists in his government. The CIA began a secret plot to overthrow Arbenz. He turned to Moscow for military aid, thus reinforcing American suspicions. The CIA airlifted arms into Guatemala, dropping them at United Fruit facilities, and in mid-1954, CIA-supported Guatemalans struck from Honduras. U.S. planes bombed the capital city, and the invaders drove Arbenz from power. The new pro-American regime returned United Fruit's land, but an ensuing civil war staggered the Central American nation for decades.

24-6e The Cuban Revolution and Fidel Castro

Eisenhower also watched with apprehension as turmoil gripped Cuba in the late 1950s. In early 1959, Fidel Castro's rebels, or *barbudos* ("bearded ones"), driven by profound anti-American nationalism, ousted Fulgencio Batista, a longtime U.S. ally who had welcomed North American investors, U.S. military advisers, and tourists to the Caribbean island. Batista's corrupt, dictatorial regime had helped turn Havana into a haven for gambling and prostitution run by organized crime. Cubans had resented U.S. domination ever since the early twentieth century, when the Platt Amendment had compromised their independence. Curbing U.S. influence became a rallying cry of the Cuban revolution, all the more so after the CIA conspired secretly but futilely to block Castro's rise to power in 1958. From the start, Castro sought to roll back the influence of American business, which had invested some $1 billion on the island, and to break the U.S. grasp on Cuban trade.

Castro's increasing authoritarianism, anti-Yankee declarations, and growing popularity in the hemisphere alarmed Washington. In early 1960, after Cuba signed a trade treaty with the Soviet Union, Eisenhower ordered the CIA to organize an invasion force of Cuban exiles to overthrow the Castro government. The agency also began to plot an assassination of the Cuban leader. When Eisenhower drastically cut U.S. purchases of Cuban sugar, Castro seized all North American–owned companies that had not yet been nationalized. Threatened by U.S. decisions designed to bring him and his revolution down, Castro appealed to the Soviet Union, which offered loans and expanded trade. Just before leaving office in early 1961, Eisenhower broke diplomatic relations with Cuba and advised president-elect John F. Kennedy to advance plans for the invasion,

which came—and failed—in early 1961 (see "Bay of Pigs Invasion," Section 26-1e).

24-6f Arab-Israeli Conflict

In the Middle East, meanwhile, the Eisenhower administration confronted challenges posed by ongoing tensions between Arabs and Jews, and by nationalist leaders in Iran and Egypt (see Map 29.2, Section 29-3f). Prior to the end of World War II, only France and Britain among the great powers had been much concerned with this region of the world; they had effectively dominated the area during the prior three decades. But the dissolution of empires and the rise of Cold War tensions drew Washington into the region, as did the deepening tensions in British-held Palestine. From 1945 to 1947, Britain tried to enlist U.S. officials in the effort to find a solution to the vexing question of how to split Palestine between the Arabs and Jews who lived there. The Truman administration rejected London's solicitations, and the British, despairing at the violence between Arabs and Jews and at the rising number of British deaths, in 1947 turned the issue over to the United Nations, which voted to partition Palestine into separate Arab and Jewish states. Arab leaders opposed the decision, but in May 1948 Jewish leaders announced the creation of Israel.

The United States, which lobbied hard to secure the UN vote, extended recognition to the new state mere minutes after the act of foundation. A moral conviction that Jews deserved a homeland after the suffering of the Holocaust, and that Zionism was a worthy movement that would create a democratic Israel, influenced Truman's decision, as did the belief that Jewish votes might swing some states to the Democrats in the 1948 election. These beliefs trumped concerns that Arab oil producers might turn against the United States and that close Soviet-Israeli ties could turn Israel into a pro-Soviet bastion in the Middle East. The Soviet Union did promptly recognize the new nation, but Israeli leaders kept Moscow at arm's length, in part because they had more pressing concerns. Palestinian Arabs, displaced from land they considered theirs, joined with Israel's Arab neighbors to make immediate war on the new state. The Israelis stopped the offensive in bloody fighting over the next six months until a UN-backed truce was called.

Thereafter, U.S. Middle East policy centered on ensuring Israel's survival and cementing ties with Arab oil producers. American companies produced about half of the region's petroleum in the 1950s. Eisenhower consequently sought to avoid actions that might alienate Arab states, such as drawing too close to Israel, and he cultivated close relations with oil-rich Iran. Its ruling shah had granted American oil companies a 40 percent interest in a new petroleum consortium in return for CIA help in the successful overthrow, in 1953, of his rival, and prime minister, Mohammed Mossadegh, who had attempted to nationalize

▲ In the years 1948–1950, hundreds of thousands of Jewish refugees arrived in the state of Israel. Legendary war photographer Robert Capa snapped this picture of refugees arriving on a boat in Haifa in 1949. A few years later, while on assignment for *Life* magazine, Capa would be killed by a land mine in Indochina.

foreign oil interests. Nor was it only about petroleum: Iran's position on the Soviet border made the shah a particularly valuable friend.

American officials faced a more formidable foe in Egypt, in the form of Gamal Abdul Nasser, a towering figure in a pan-Arabic movement to reduce Western interests in the Middle East. Nasser vowed to expel the British from the Suez Canal and the Israelis from Palestine. The United States wished neither to anger the Arabs, for fear of losing valuable oil supplies, nor to alienate its ally Israel, which was supported at home by politically active American Jews. But when Nasser declared neutrality in the Cold War, Dulles lost patience.

24-6g Suez Crisis

In 1956, the United States abruptly reneged on its offer to Egypt to help finance the Aswan Dam, a project to provide inexpensive electricity and water for thirsty Nile valley farmland. Secretary Dulles's blunt economic pressure backfired, for Nasser responded by nationalizing the British-owned Suez Canal, intending to use its profits to build the dam. At a mass rally in Alexandria, Nasser expressed the profound nationalism typical of Third World peoples shedding an imperial past: "Tonight our Egyptian canal will be run by Egyptians. Egyptians!" Fully 75 percent of Western Europe's oil came from the Middle

East, most of it transported through the Suez Canal. Fearing an interruption in this vital trade, the British and French conspired with Israel to bring down Nasser. On October 29, 1956, the Israelis invaded Suez, joined two days later by British and French forces.

Eisenhower fumed. America's allies had not consulted him, and the attack had shifted attention from Soviet intervention in Hungary. The president also feared that the invasion would cause Nasser to seek help from the Soviets, inviting them into the Middle East. Eisenhower sternly demanded that London, Paris, and Tel Aviv pull their troops out, and they did. Egypt took possession of the canal, the Soviets built the Aswan Dam, and Nasser became a hero to Third World peoples. French and British influence in the region declined sharply. To counter Nasser, the United States determined to "build up" as an "Arab rival" the conservative King Ibn Saud of Saudi Arabia. Although the monarch renewed America's lease of an air base, few Arabs respected the notoriously corrupt Saud.

24-6h Eisenhower Doctrine

Washington officials worried that a "vacuum" existed in the Middle East—and that the Soviets might fill it. Nasserites insisted that there was no vacuum but rather a growing Arab nationalism that provided the best defense against communism. In an effort to improve the deteriorating

Western position in the Middle East and to protect American interests there, the president in 1957 proclaimed the **Eisenhower Doctrine**. The United States would intervene in the Middle East, he declared, if any government threatened by a communist takeover asked for help. In 1958, fourteen thousand American troops scrambled ashore in Lebanon to quell an internal political dispute that Washington feared might be exploited by pro-Nasser groups or communists. Concentrating the troops in the area of Beirut, Eisenhower said their mission was "not primarily to fight" but merely to show the flag. The restrained use of U.S. military power served to defuse the crisis, as Lebanese officials agreed to work for a peaceful transition to a new leadership. In Dulles's view, the intervention also served to "reassure many small nations that they could call on us in a time of crisis."

Cold War concerns also drove Eisenhower's policy toward Vietnam, where nationalists battled the French for independence. Despite a substantial U.S. aid program initiated under Truman, the French lost steadily to the Vietminh. Finally, in early 1954, Ho's forces surrounded the French fortress at Dien Bien Phu in northwest Vietnam (see Map 26.2, Section 26-4d). Although some of Eisenhower's advisers recommended a massive American air strike against Vietminh positions, perhaps even using tactical atomic weapons, the president moved cautiously. The United States had been advising and bankrolling the French, but it had not committed its own forces to the war. If American airpower did not save the French, would ground troops be required next, and in hostile terrain? As one high-level doubter remarked, "One cannot go over Niagara Falls in a barrel only slightly."

Worrying aloud about a communist victory, Eisenhower pressed the British to help form a coalition to address the Indochinese crisis, but they refused. At home, influential members of Congress—including Lyndon Baines Johnson of Texas, who as president would wage large-scale war in Vietnam—told Eisenhower they wanted "no more Koreas" and warned him against any unilateral U.S. military intervention. Some felt very uneasy about supporting colonialism. The issue became moot on May 7, when the weary French defenders at Dien Bien Phu surrendered.

24-6i Geneva Accords on Vietnam

Peace talks, already under way in Geneva, brought Cold War and nationalist contenders together—the United States, the Soviet Union, Britain, the People's Republic of China, Laos, Cambodia, and the competing Vietnamese regimes of Bao Dai and Ho Chi Minh. John Foster Dulles, a reluctant participant, feared the communists would get

Eisenhower Doctrine The 1957 proclamation that the United States would send military aid and, if necessary, troops to any Middle Eastern nation threatened by "Communist aggression."

the better of any agreement, yet in the end the Vietminh received less than their dominant military position suggested they should. The 1954 Geneva Accords, signed by France and Ho's Democratic Republic of Vietnam, temporarily divided Vietnam at the seventeenth parallel; Ho's government was confined to the North, Bao Dai's to the South. Only after pressure from the Chinese and the Soviets, who feared U.S. intervention in Vietnam without an agreement, did Ho's government agree to this compromise. The seventeenth parallel was meant to serve as a military truce line, not a national boundary, with elections for reunification slated to follow in 1956. Meanwhile, neither North nor South was to join a military alliance or permit foreign military bases on its soil.

Confident that the Geneva agreements ultimately would mean communist victory, the United States from an early point set about trying to undermine them. Soon after the conference, a CIA team entered Vietnam and undertook secret operations against the North, including commando raids across the seventeenth parallel. In the South, the United States helped Ngo Dinh Diem push Bao Dai aside and inaugurate the Republic of Vietnam. A Catholic in a Buddhist nation, Diem was a dedicated nationalist and anticommunist, but he had little mass support. He staged a fraudulent election in South Vietnam that gave him 99 percent of the vote (in Saigon, he received 200,000 more votes than there were registered voters). When Ho and some in the world community pressed for national elections in keeping with the Geneva agreements, Diem and Eisenhower refused, fearing that the popular Vietminh leader would win. From 1955 to 1961, the Diem government received more than $1 billion in American aid, most of it military. American advisers organized and trained Diem's army, and American agriculturalists worked to improve crops. Diem's Saigon regime became dependent on the United States for its very existence, and the culture of South Vietnam became increasingly Americanized.

24-6j National Liberation Front

Diem proved a difficult ally. He acted dictatorially, abolishing village elections and appointing to public office people beholden to him. He threw dissenters in jail and shut down newspapers that criticized his regime. When U.S. officials periodically urged him to implement meaningful land reform, he blithely ignored them. Noncommunists and communists alike began to strike back at Diem's repressive government. In Hanoi, Ho's government initially focused on solidifying its control on the North, but in the late 1950s it began to send aid to southern insurgents, who embarked on a program of terror, assassinating hundreds of Diem's village officials. In late 1960, southern communists, acting at the direction of Hanoi, organized the National Liberation Front (NLF), known as the Vietcong. The Vietcong in turn attracted other anti-Diem groups

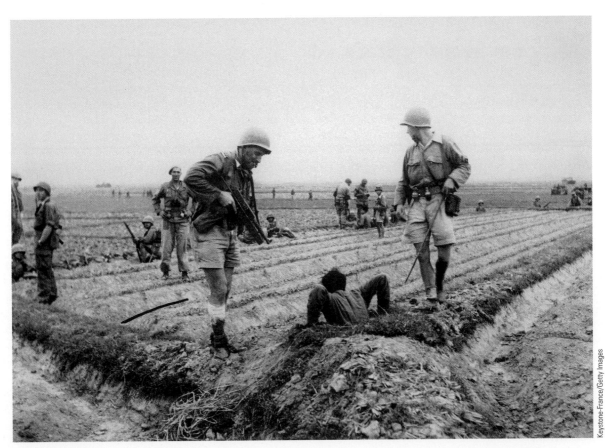

Keystone-France/Getty Images

▲ French troops capture a Vietminh soldier during an operation in the Red River Delta in Tonkin (northern Vietnam) in March 1952. The Vietminh were adept at camouflage, but this soldier could not escape detection while hidden in a dyke.

in the South. And the Eisenhower administration, all too aware of Diem's shortcomings and his unwillingness to follow American advice, continued to affirm its commitment to the preservation of an independent, noncommunist South Vietnam.

Summary

The United States emerged from the Second World War as the preeminent world power. Confident in the nation's immediate physical security, Washington officials nevertheless worried that the unstable international system, an unfriendly Soviet Union, and the decolonizing Third World could upset American plans for the postwar peace. Locked with the Soviet Union in a "Cold War," U.S. leaders marshaled their nation's superior resources to influence and cajole other countries. Foreign economic aid, atomic diplomacy, military alliances, client states, covert operations, interventions, propaganda, cultural infiltration—these and more became the instruments for waging the Cold War, a war that began as a conflict over the future of Europe but soon spread to encompass the globe.

America's claim to international leadership was welcomed by many in Western Europe and elsewhere who feared Stalin's intentions and those of his successors in the Soviet Union. The reconstruction of former enemies Japan and (West) Germany helped those nations recover swiftly and become staunch members of the Western alliance. But U.S. policy also sparked resistance. Communist countries condemned financial and atomic diplomacy, while Third World nations, many of them newly independent, sought to undermine America's European allies and sometimes identified the United States as an imperial coconspirator. On occasion, even America's allies bristled at a United States that boldly proclaimed itself economic master and global policeman, and haughtily touted its hegemonic status.

At home, liberal and radical critics protested that Presidents Truman and Eisenhower exaggerated the communist threat, wasting U.S. assets on immoral foreign ventures; crippled legitimate nationalist aspirations; and displayed racial bias. Still, these presidents and their successors held firm to the mission of creating a nonradical, capitalist, free-trade international order in the mold of domestic America. Determined to

The National Security State

To build a cathedral, someone has observed, you first need a religion, and a religion needs inspiring texts that command authority. For decades, America's Cold War religion has been national security; its texts, the Truman Doctrine, the "X" article, and NSC-68; and its cathedral, the national security state. The word *state* in this case means "civil government." During the Cold War, embracing preparedness for total war, the U.S. government essentially transformed itself into a huge military headquarters that interlocked with corporations and universities. Preaching the doctrine of national security, moreover, members of Congress strove to gain lucrative defense contracts for their districts.

Overseen by the president and his advisory body, the National Security Council, the national security state has had as its core what the National Security Act of 1947 called the National Military Establishment; in 1949, it became the Department of Defense. This department ranks as a leading employer; its payroll by 2007 included 1.4 million people on active duty and almost 600,000 civilian personnel, giving it more employees than Exxon Mobil, Ford, General Motors, and GE combined. Almost 700,000 of these troops and civilians served overseas, in 177 countries covering every time zone. Although spending for national defense declined in the years after the end of the Cold War, it never fell below $290 billion. In the aftermath of the 9/11 terrorist attacks and the invasion of Iraq, the military budget rose again, reaching $439 billion in 2007. By 2016, it topped $600 billion. That figure tops the entire economies of Poland and Belgium and equals the combined military spending of the twenty countries with the next-largest defense budgets. Nor does that sum include tens of billions of dollars in supplementary funds allocated by Congress to pay for operations in Afghanistan and Iraq.

Joining the Department of Defense as instruments of national security policy were the Joint Chiefs of Staff, the Central Intelligence Agency, and dozens more government bodies. The focus of all these entities was on finding the best means to combat real and potential threats from foreign governments. But what about threats from within? The terrorist attacks of September 2001 made starkly clear that enemies existed who, while perhaps beholden to a foreign entity—it need not be a government—launched their attacks from inside the nation's borders. Accordingly, in 2002 President George W. Bush proposed the creation of a Department of Homeland Security (DHS), which would have 170,000 employees and would include all or part of twenty-two agencies, including the Coast Guard, the Customs Service, the Federal Emergency Management Administration (FEMA), and the Internal Revenue Service. It would involve the biggest overhaul of the federal bureaucracy since the Department of Defense was created, and it signified a more expansive notion of national security. By 2017, the number of DHS employees had risen to 240,000.

In 1961, President Eisenhower warned against a "military-industrial complex," while others feared a "garrison state" or a "warfare state." Despite the warnings, by the start of the twenty-first century, the national security state remained vigorous, a lasting legacy of the early Cold War period for a people and a nation.

CRITICAL THINKING

- The Department of Homeland Security was established after the attacks of September 11, 2001 to combat homegrown terrorists. Despite this, domestic terrorism has continued to cause American civilians' deaths with the Boston Marathon bombing (2013), Charleston Church shooting (2015), San Bernardino shooting (2015), and Orlando nightclub shooting (2016) as prime examples. What steps should the nation take to avoid future massacres such as these?

---

contain Soviet expansion, fearful of domestic charges of being "soft on communism," they worked to enlarge the U.S. sphere of influence and shape the world. In their years of nurturing allies and applying the containment doctrine worldwide, Truman and Eisenhower held the line—against the Soviet Union and the People's Republic of China, and against nonalignment, communism, nationalism, and revolution everywhere. One consequence was a dramatic increase in presidential power in the realm of foreign affairs—what the historian Arthur M. Schlesinger Jr. called "the Imperial Presidency"—as Congress ceded constitutional power.

Putting itself at odds with many in the Third World, the United States usually stood with its European allies to slow decolonization and to preach evolution rather than revolution. The globalist perspective of the United States prompted Americans to interpret many troubles in the developing world as Cold War conflicts, inspired if not directed by Soviet-backed communists. The intensity of the Cold War obscured for Americans the indigenous roots of most Third World troubles, as the wars in Korea and Vietnam attested. Nor could the United States abide developing nations' drive for economic independence—for gaining control of their own raw materials and economies. Deeply intertwined in the global economy as importer, exporter, and investor, the United States read challenges from this "periphery" as threats to the American standard of living and a way of life characterized by private enterprise. The Third World, in short, challenged U.S. strategic power by forming a third force in the

Cold War, and it challenged American economic power by seeking a new economic order of shared interests. Overall, the rise of the Third World introduced new actors to the world stage, challenging the bipolarity of the international system and diffusing power.

All the while, the threat of nuclear war unsettled Americans and foreigners alike. In the film *Godzilla* (1956), a prehistoric monster, revived by atomic bomb tests, rampages through Tokyo. Stanley Kramer's popular but disturbing movie *On the Beach* (1959), based on Nevil Shute's best-selling 1957 novel, depicts a nuclear holocaust in which the last humans on earth choose to swallow government-issued poison tablets so that they can die before H-bomb radiation sickness kills them. Such doomsday or Armageddon attitudes contrasted sharply with official U.S. government assurances that Americans would survive a nuclear war. In *On the Beach*, a dying wife asks her husband, "Couldn't anyone have stopped it?" His answer: "Some kinds of silliness you just can't stop." Eisenhower did not halt it, even though he told Khrushchev in 1959 that "we really should come to some sort of agreement in order to stop this fruitless, really wasteful rivalry."

Suggestions for Further Reading

Campbell Craig and Fredrik Logevall, *America's Cold War: The Politics of Insecurity* (2009)

Nick Cullather, *The Hungry World: America's Cold War Battle Against Poverty in Asia* (2013)

Bruce Cumings, *The Korean War: A History* (2010)

Mary L. Dudziak, *Cold War Civil Rights: Race and the Image of American Democracy* (2000)

John Lewis Gaddis, *Strategies of Containment*, 2nd ed. (2005)

Stephen Kinzer, *The Brothers: John Foster Dulles, Allen Dulles, and Their Secret World War* (2013)

Fredrik Logevall, *Embers of War: The Fall of an Empire and the Making of America's Vietnam* (2012)

Geoffrey Roberts, *Stalin's Wars: From World War to Cold War, 1939–1953* (2007)

Marc Trachtenberg, *A Constructed Peace: The Making of the European Settlement, 1945–1963* (1999)

MINDTAP
From Cengage

MindTap® is a fully online personalized learning experience built upon Cengage Learning content. MindTap® combines student learning tools—readings, multimedia, activities, and assessments—into a singular Learning Path that guides students through the course and helps students develop the critical thinking, analysis, and communication skills that are essential to academic and professional success.

America at Midcentury, 1945–1960

saac and Oleta Nelson wrapped themselves in blankets against the predawn winter cold that morning in late January 1951 as they waited for the brilliant flash of light that would shatter the desert darkness. They, along with a hundred or so friends and neighbors from Cedar City, Utah, had driven out to watch the first atomic test on U.S. soil since the end of World War II. "Everybody was really excited," Isaac remembered. "We wanted to help out what little we could" and "show our patriotism." Soon the bomb's red-orange flare lit up the trees on the other side of the valley, more than ten miles away. And later that afternoon, residents of Kanarraville and Cedar City watched as pinkish-tan clouds drifted across the sky.

In the years immediately following World War II, the United States had tested atomic weapons on isolated islands in the South Pacific. U.S. officials were already aware of the dangers of radioactivity, but its unpredictability was driven home by the grisly deaths of crewmembers from a Japanese fishing boat, the *Daigo Fukuryū Maru* (Lucky Dragon 5), that had been unexpectedly caught in the path of fallout from the U.S. Bikini Atoll test in 1954. Despite that knowledge, as the USSR developed its own atomic weapon and the outbreak of hostilities in Korea signaled an escalation of the Cold War, members of the Atomic Energy Commission (AEC) argued that atomic testing outside U.S. borders presented a threat to national security. The danger to American public health and safety, they concluded (in a phrase from 1957 legal testimony), was offset by the threat of "total annihilation" by the Soviet enemy.

In late 1950, President Truman approved use of a large tract of land in Nevada for the nation's nuclear testing. It had meteorological advantages: the prevailing wind blew eastward, away from

◀ In the Nevada desert in May 1955, the U.S. government used its forty-fourth nuclear test explosion to evaluate the survivability of a nuclear blast. These department store mannequins inhabited a small village, built at the cost of a million dollars, its houses stocked with everything from living room furniture to canned soup. *Life* magazine reported: "The condition of the figures—one charred, another only scorched, another almost untouched—showed that the blast, equivalent to 35,000 tons of TNT . . . make[s] clear that even amid atomic holocaust careful planning could save lives." Loomis Dean/Getty Images

Chronology

population centers of Los Angeles and Las Vegas. Advisers portrayed the land downwind, which stretched across portions of Nevada, Arizona, and Utah, as "virtually uninhabitable." Yet almost 100,000 people occupied farms and small towns in its desert valleys; many were descendants of Mormon settlers who had arrived in the 1840s or members of the Western Shoshone Nation, on whose land the test site lay. And as radioactive clouds from subsequent tests drifted over those small towns and farms, children played in the fallout as if it were snow.

After fallout from "Harry," a thirty-two-kiloton blast, saturated the region in 1953, forty-five hundred of the fourteen thousand sheep on local ranches died. The AEC issued a press release blaming the deaths on "unprecedented cold weather." Lambs were born that spring without wool or skin, their organs covered only by a thin membrane. The commission suppressed veterinary reports that documented lethal levels of radiation. By 1955, the Atomic Energy Commission had mounted a campaign to reassure "downwinders" that the tests posed no danger. AEC medical staff visited small towns armed with blatant and calculated lies: radiation from nuclear tests, they told residents, amounted to only "about one-twentieth of that experienced in an X-ray." That same year, Oleta Nelson stood outside her home, watching a fallout cloud drift across the sky. Within hours, her exposed skin turned bright red. She vomited and had violent diarrhea. A month later, her hair—beautiful, raven black, shoulder length—fell out. It never grew back. Oleta was diagnosed with a brain tumor in 1962. She died in 1965. By that time, the cancer rate for "downwinders" was one and a half times that of the rest of the U.S. population.

Experience an interactive version of this story in MindTap®.

The Cold War did not affect most Americans so directly. Nonetheless, Cold War fears and policies shaped American life during the postwar era in ways both blatant and subtle, even as many people worked hard to leave the difficult years of depression and war behind and create good lives for themselves and their families.

Of all the major nations in the world, only the United States had emerged from World War II stronger and more prosperous. While Europe and Asia had been devastated, America's farms and cities and factories were intact. U.S. production capacity had increased during the war, and despite social tensions and inequalities, the fight against fascism gave Americans a unity of purpose. Victory seemed to confirm their struggles. But sixteen years of depression and war shadowed the U.S. victory, and memories of these experiences would continue to shape the choices Americans made in their private lives, their domestic policies, and their relations with the world.

In the postwar era, the actions of the federal government and the choices made by individual Americans reconfigured American society. Postwar social policies—many of them shaped by Cold War concerns—that sent millions of veterans to college on the GI Bill linked the nation with high-speed interstate highways, fostered the growth of suburbs and the Sunbelt, and disrupted regional isolation helped to create a national middle-class culture that encompassed an unprecedented majority of the nation's citizens. Countless individual decisions—to go to college, to marry young, to have a large family, to move to the suburbs, to start a business—were made possible by these federal initiatives. The cumulative weight of these individual decisions would change the meanings of class and ethnicity in American society. Americans in the postwar era defined a new American Dream—one that centered on the family, on a new level of material comfort and consumption, and on a shared sense of belonging to a common culture. Elite cultural critics roundly denounced this ideal of suburban comfort as "conformism," but many Americans found satisfaction in this new way of life.

Almost one-quarter of the American people did not share in the postwar prosperity—but they were ever less visible to the middle-class majority. Rural poverty continued, and inner cities became increasingly impoverished as more affluent Americans moved to the suburbs and new migrants—poor black and white southerners, new immigrants from Mexico, Puerto Ricans, and Native Americans resettled by the federal government from tribal lands—arrived.

As class and ethnicity became less important in suburbia, race continued to divide the American people. African Americans faced racism and discrimination throughout the nation, but the war had been a turning point in the struggle for equal rights. During this period, African Americans increasingly

took direct action, and in 1955 the yearlong Montgomery bus boycott launched the modern civil rights movement. Gradually the federal government began to protect the civil rights of black Americans, including the Supreme Court's school desegregation decision in *Brown v. Board of Education.*

Compared to the dramatic accomplishments of the New Deal, postwar domestic achievements were modest. Truman pledged to expand the New Deal but was stymied by a conservative Congress. **Dwight D. Eisenhower**, elected in 1952 as the first Republican president in twenty years, offered a solid Republican platform, seeking—though rarely attaining—a balanced budget, reduced taxes, and lower levels of government spending. Both presidents focused primarily on the foreign policy challenges of the Cold War.

The economic boom that began with the end of the war lasted twenty-five years, bringing new prosperity to the American people. Although fears—of nuclear war, of returning hard times—lingered, prosperity bred complacency by the late 1950s. At decade's end, people sought satisfaction in their families and in the consumer pleasures newly available to so many.

- *How did the Cold War affect American society and politics?*

- *How did federal government actions following World War II change the nation?*

- *During the 1950s, many people began to think of their country as a middle-class nation. Were they correct?*

25-1 Shaping Postwar America

▶ **What challenges did the United States face as veterans returned from war?**

▶ **What were the consequences of the GI Bill?**

▶ **What factors contributed to suburbanization in the postwar period?**

▶ **How did postwar federal programs contribute to long-term inequality in American society?**

As Americans celebrated the end of World War II and mourned those who would never return, many feared the challenges that lay ahead. The nation had to reintegrate war veterans into civilian society and find

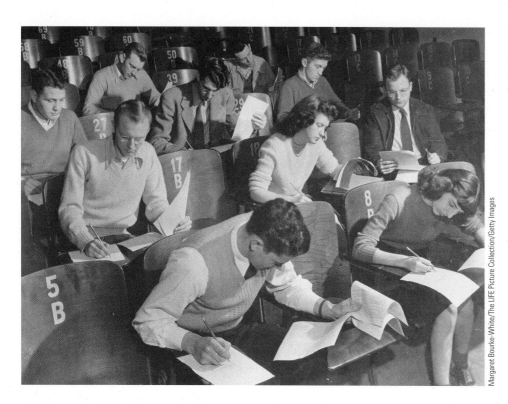

◀ Classroom at the University of Iowa, 1947, where 60 percent of students were war veterans. GI Bill education benefits transformed American universities.

Margaret Bourke-White/The LIFE Picture Collection/Getty Images

places for young families to live. It had to transform a wartime economy to peacetime functions. And it had to contend with the domestic implications of the Cold War and the new global balance of power. Though unemployment rose and a wave of strikes rocked the nation in the immediate aftermath of the war, the economy soon flourished. This strong economy, along with new federal programs, transformed the shape of American society.

25-1a The Veterans Return

In 1945, as Germany and then Japan surrendered, the nation had to demobilize almost 15 million servicemen. Seeking fairness, authorities decided not to demobilize unit by unit, but instead on an individual basis. Each man received a "service score" based on length of time in military service, time overseas, and time in combat—plus the number of his children. Men with the highest scores went home first; those with the lowest numbers were finally demobilized in June 1947.

Veterans' homecomings were often joyful, but in general, Americans were anxious about veterans' return. In one midwestern small town, elected officials estimated that 20 percent of returning veterans would be "debauched and wild," and that many were likely "deadbeats" who "expect too much." Such concerns were so widespread that *Time* magazine, in mid-1945, reassured readers that "the returned overseas soldier is no nerve-shattered civilian-hater who will explode into violent action if he does not get all he thinks he deserves."

GI Bill Popular name for the Servicemen's Readjustment Act (1944), which sought to aid returning veterans—and maintain economic stability—by providing college tuition, job training, unemployment benefits, and low-interest home and farm loans.

Most men found their way—but it was not always easy. Many veterans returned to wives whose lives had gone on without them, to children they barely knew, to a world grown unfamiliar. Some had serious physical injuries. Almost half a million veterans were diagnosed with neuropsychiatric disabilities, and the National Mental Health Act of 1946 passed, in large part, because of awareness of the psychological toll of war on those who fought. In 1946, Americans flocked to the movie *The Best Years of Our Lives*, which won seven Academy Awards for its depiction of three veterans struggling to adjust to the world to which they had returned.

Americans also worried about the economic impact of demobilization. As the end of the war approached and the American war machine slowed, factories had begun to lay off workers. Ten days after the Allied victory over Japan, 1.8 million people nationwide received pink slips, and 640,000 filed for unemployment compensation. How was the shrinking job base to absorb millions of returning veterans?

25-1b The GI Bill

Though the federal government had done little to prepare for U.S. entry into World War II, it had begun planning for demobilization even while some of the war's most difficult battles lay ahead. In the spring of 1944—a year before V-E Day—Congress unanimously passed the Servicemen's Readjustment Act, known as the GI Bill of Rights. The **GI Bill** showed the nation's gratitude to the men who fought, but it also attempted to keep the flood of demobilized veterans (almost all of them male) from swamping the U.S. economy. Roughly half of all veterans received unemployment benefits, meant to stagger veterans' entry into the civilian job market. The GI Bill also provided low-interest loans to buy a house or start a business, and—perhaps most significantly— stipends to cover the cost of college or technical school tuition and living expenses.

The GI Bill, as written, covered all veterans discharged "under conditions other than dishonorable," regardless of race or gender. It was not so inclusive in practice. Congress assigned the Veteran's Administration to administer the GI Bill, even though leaders knew that it didn't have the capacity to manage such a vast program. Thus, left with little oversight, state and local agencies had great control over implementation—and often discriminated against racial and ethnic minorities. And because men and women charged with homosexuality were given "blue" or administrative discharges, the ambiguous wording of the bill ("other than dishonorable") allowed them to be denied benefits, as well.

Nonetheless, the GI Bill offered new opportunities to many, and as individuals grasped these opportunities they changed their own lives and the shape of American society. Almost half of returning veterans used GI education benefits, which cost the nation more than the postwar Marshall Plan. Sub-college programs drew 5.6 million veterans, while 2.2 million attended college, graduate, or professional school. In 1947, about two-thirds of America's college students were veterans. Enrollment swelled at Syracuse University, tripling in a single year. Admissions quotas meant to limit the number of Jewish students largely disappeared, and while racial segregation persisted, Historically Black Colleges ("Negro Colleges") grew and strengthened. Facing the influx of nontraditional students, University of Chicago president Robert Maynard Hutchins protested that the GI Bill would turn universities into "educational hobo jungles," but the flood of students and federal dollars into the nation's colleges and universities created a golden age for higher education, and the resulting increase in well-educated or technically trained workers benefited the American economy.

Education obtained through the GI Bill created social mobility: children of barely literate menial laborers became white-collar professionals. And postwar universities, like the military, brought together people from vastly different backgrounds. The GI Bill helped to create a national middle-class culture, for as colleges exposed people to new ideas and to new experiences, their students tended to become less provincial, less rooted in ethnic or regional cultures.

25-1c Economic Growth

American concerns that economic depression would return with war's end proved unfounded. Adjustment to a peacetime economy was difficult at first, but the economy recovered quickly, fueled by consumer spending. Although Americans had brought home steady paychecks during the war, there was little on which to spend them: no new cars had been built since 1942, and new household appliances were scarce.

Americans had saved their money for four years, and they were ready to buy. Companies like General Motors, which flouted conventional wisdom about a coming depression and expanded its operations just after the war, found millions of eager customers. And because most other factories around the world were in ruins, U.S. corporations expanded their global dominance. Farming was also revolutionized, as increased use of fertilizers and pesticides, along with new machines such as mechanical cotton and tobacco pickers, tripled productivity. Potential profits attracted large investors, and the average size of farms increased from 195 to 306 acres.

25-1d Baby Boom

During the Great Depression, young people had delayed marriage and America's birth rate had plummeted. Marriage and birth rates began to rise as war brought economic recovery. But the end of the war brought a boom. In 1946, the U.S. marriage rate was higher than that of any record-keeping nation (except Hungary) in the history of the twentieth century. The birth rate soared, reversing the downward trend of the past 150 years. "Take the 3,548,000 babies born in 1950," wrote Sylvia F. Porter in her syndicated newspaper column. "Bundle them into a batch, bounce them all over the bountiful land that is America. What do you get?" Porter's answer: "Boom. The biggest, boomiest boom ever known in history. Just imagine how much these extra people, these new markets, will absorb—in food, clothing, in gadgets, in housing, in services. Our factories must expand just to keep pace." Although the **baby boom** peaked in 1957, more than 4 million babies were born every year until 1965 (see Figure 25.1).

25-1e Suburbanization

Where were all these baby boom families to live? Scarcely any new housing had been built since the 1920s. Almost 2 million families were doubled up with relatives in 1948; 50,000 people were living in Quonset huts, and in Chicago housing was so tight that 250 used trolley cars were sold as homes.

A combination of market forces, government actions, and individual decisions solved the housing crisis and, in so doing, changed the way large numbers of Americans lived. In the postwar years, white Americans moved to the suburbs. Their reasons varied. Some moved to escape the crowds and noise of the city. People from rural areas moved closer to city jobs. Some white families moved out of urban neighborhoods because African American families were moving in. Many new suburbanites wanted more political influence and more control over their children's education. More than anything else, however, those who moved wanted to own their own home—and it was the suburbs that offered affordable housing. Although suburban development predated World War II, the massive migration of

baby boom The soaring birth rate that occurred in the United States from 1946 through 1964.

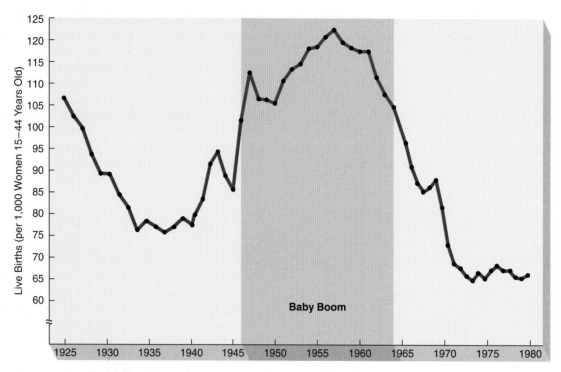

Figure 25.1 **Birth Rate, 1945–1964**

The birth rate began to rise in 1942 and 1943, but it skyrocketed during the postwar years beginning in 1946, reaching its peak in 1957. From 1954 to 1964, the United States recorded more than 4 million births every year. *Source: Adapted from U.S. Bureau of the Census,* Historical Statistics of the United States, Colonial Times to 1970, *Bicentennial Edition (Washington, D.C.: U.S. Government Printing Office, 1975), p. 49.*

18 million Americans to the suburbs from cities, small towns, and farms between 1950 and 1960 was on a wholly different scale (see Table 25.1).

In the years following World War II, suburban developers used mass production techniques to create acres of modest suburban houses in what had recently been pastures and fields. In 1947, builder William Levitt adapted Henry Ford's assembly-line methods to revolutionize homebuilding. By 1949, instead of 4 or 5 custom homes per year, Levitt's

Table 25.1 **Geographic Distribution of the U.S. Population, 1930–1970 (in Percentages)**

Year	Central Cities	Suburbs	Rural Areas and Small Towns
1930	31.8	18.0	50.2
1940	31.6	19.5	48.9
1950	32.3	23.8	43.9
1960	32.6	30.7	36.7
1970	31.4	37.6	31.0

Source: Adapted from U.S. Bureau of the Census, *Decennial Censuses, 1930–1970* (Washington, D.C.: U.S. Government Printing Office).

company built 180 houses a week. They were very basic—four and a half rooms on a 60-by-100-foot lot, all with identical floor plans—the Model Ts of houses. But the same floor plan could be disguised by four different exteriors, and by rotating seven paint colors Levitt guaranteed that only 1 in every 28 houses would be identical. In the Levittown on Long Island, a tree was planted every 28 feet (two and a half trees per house). The basic house, appliances included, sold for $7,990. Other homebuilders quickly adopted Levitt's techniques.

Suburban development could never have happened on such a large scale, however, without federal policies that encouraged it. Federal Housing Administration (FHA) mortgage insurance made low-interest GI mortgages and loans possible. New highways also promoted suburban development. Congress authorized construction of a 37,000-mile chain of highways in 1947 and in 1956 passed the Highway Act to create a 42,500-mile interstate highway system. These highways were built to facilitate commerce and to allow the military to mobilize quickly in case of a threat to national security, but they also allowed workers to live farther and farther from their jobs in central cities.

25-1f Inequality in Benefits

Postwar federal programs did not benefit all Americans equally. First, federal policies often assisted men at the expense of women. The federal Selective Service Act guaranteed that

Bettmann/Getty Images

▲ Housing was so tight in the years following World War II that many young couples had to move in with one set of their parents—or accept some unusual housing options. Former marine lieutenant Willard Pedrick and his family made their home in a Quonset hut on the campus of Northwestern University in Evanston, Illinois, where Pedrick was an associate professor in the economics department.

veterans (overwhelmingly men) had priority in postwar hiring. As industry laid off civilian workers to make room for veterans, women lost their jobs at a rate 75 percent higher than men. Many women stayed in the workforce but were pushed into less well-paying jobs. Universities made room for veterans on the GI Bill by excluding qualified women students; a much smaller percentage of college degrees went to women after the war than before.

Inequities were also based on race. Like European American veterans, African American, Native American, Mexican American, and Asian American veterans received educational benefits and hiring preference in civil service jobs following the war. But war workers from these groups were among the first laid off as factories made room for white, male veterans. Federal housing policies also exacerbated racial inequality. Federal loan officers and bankers often labeled African American or racially mixed neighborhoods "high risk" for lending, denying mortgages to members of racial minorities regardless of individual creditworthiness. This practice, called "redlining" because such neighborhoods were outlined in red on lenders' maps, kept African Americans and many Hispanics from buying into the great economic explosion of the postwar

era. White families who bought homes with federally guaranteed mortgages saw their small investments grow dramatically over the years. Discriminatory policies denied most African Americans and other people of color that opportunity.

25-2 Domestic Politics in the Cold War Era

▶ What challenges did Harry S Truman face in managing the transition from a wartime to peacetime economy?

▶ How did the Truman administration seek to continue a New Deal legislative agenda?

▶ Why was there a shift from New Deal liberalism to conservatism after World War II?

Although federal policies and programs shaped American society in the postwar era, domestic politics were not at the forefront of American life. Democratic president Harry Truman attempted to build on the New Deal's liberal agenda, while Republican President Dwight D. Eisenhower called for balanced budgets and business-friendly policies. But both administrations focused on the challenges of the expanding Cold War, and neither came close to the political and legislative activism of the 1930s New Deal.

25-2a Harry S Truman and Postwar Liberalism

Harry Truman, the plainspoken former haberdasher from Missouri, had never expected to be president. In 1944, when Franklin Roosevelt asked him to join the Democratic ticket as the vice-presidential candidate, he almost refused. Roosevelt, the master politician, played hardball. "If he wants to break up the Democratic Party in the middle of the war, that's his responsibility," the president said flatly. "Oh shit," said Truman, "if that's the situation, I'll have to say yes." But the president, with his hands full as America entered its fourth year of war, had little time for his new vice president and left Truman in the dark about everything from the Manhattan Project to plans for postwar domestic policy. When Roosevelt died, suddenly, in April 1945, Truman was unprepared to take his place.

Truman stepped forward, however, placing a sign on his desk that proclaimed, "The Buck Stops Here." Most of Truman's presidency focused on foreign relations, as he led the nation through the last months of World War II and into the new Cold War with the Soviet Union. Domestically, he oversaw the process of reconversion from war to peace and attempted to keep a liberal agenda—the legacy of Roosevelt's New Deal—alive.

In his 1944 State of the Union address, President Roosevelt had offered Americans a "Second Bill of Rights": the right to employment, health care, education, food, and housing. This declaration of government responsibility for the welfare of the nation and its citizens was the cornerstone of postwar liberalism. The Truman administration intended to preserve the federal government's active role in guaranteeing social welfare, promoting social justice, managing the economy, and regulating the power of business corporations. Truman proposed to increase the minimum wage; he supported the **Full Employment Act**, introduced by congressional Democrats in the winter of 1945, which guaranteed work to all who were able and willing, through public-sector employment if necessary.

To pay for his proposed social welfare programs, Truman gambled that full employment would generate sufficient tax revenue and that consumer spending would fuel economic growth. The gamble on economic growth paid off, but Truman quickly learned the limits of his political influence. The conservative coalition of Republicans and southern Democrats that had stalled Roosevelt's New Deal legislation in the late 1930s was even less inclined to support Truman. Congress refused to raise the minimum wage and gutted the Full Employment Act. By the time Truman signed it into law in early 1946, key provisions regarding guaranteed work had virtually disappeared. But the act did reaffirm the federal government's responsibility for managing the economy and created a Council of Economic Advisers to help the president prevent economic downturns.

25-2b Postwar Strikes and the Taft-Hartley Act

The difficulties of converting to a peacetime economy helped to undermine Truman's domestic influence. As the end of wartime price controls sent inflation skyrocketing and people struggled to feed their families, more than 5 million workers went on strike. Unions shut down the coal, automobile, steel, and electric industries, and halted railroad and maritime transportation. The strikes were so disruptive that Americans began hoarding food and gasoline.

By the spring of 1946, Americans were losing patience with the strikes and with the Democratic administration, which many saw as partly responsible. When unions threatened a national railway strike, President Truman made a dramatic appearance before a joint session of Congress. If strikers in an industry deemed vital to national security refused a presidential order to return to work, he announced, he would ask Congress to immediately draft into the armed forces "all workers who are on strike against their government." The Democratic Party, Truman made clear, would not offer unlimited support to organized labor.

Making the most of public anger at the strikes, a group of pro-business Republicans and their conservative Democratic allies worked to restrict the power of labor unions. The 1947 **Taft-Hartley Act** allowed states to adopt right-to-work legislation that outlawed "closed shops" (which required all to join the union if a majority of them favored a union shop). The law also mandated an eighty-day cooling-off period before unions could begin strikes that imperiled national security. Truman vetoed the Taft-Hartley Act; though he had threatened action to avert a national railroad strike, he did not support such limits on union power. But Congress passed the Taft-Hartley Act over Truman's veto. The resulting restrictions limited union growth, especially in the South and West, where states passed right-to-work laws.

As Truman presided over the rocky transition from a wartime to a peacetime economy, he had to deal with massive inflation (briefly hitting 35 percent), shortages of consumer goods, and the wave of postwar strikes that slowed production of eagerly awaited consumer goods and drove prices up further. With powerful congressional opposition, he had little chance of major legislative accomplishments. But his inexperience had contributed to the political impasse. "To err is Truman," people began to joke. Truman's approval rating plunged from 87 percent in late 1945 to 32 percent in 1946.

25-2c 1948 Election

By 1948, it seemed that Republicans would win the White House in November. A confident Republican Party nominated Thomas Dewey, the man Roosevelt had defeated in 1944, as its presidential candidate. The Republicans were counting on schisms in the Democratic Party to give them victory. Former New Dealer Henry A. Wallace was running on the **Progressive Party** ticket advocating friendly relations with the Soviet Union, racial desegregation, and nationalization of basic industries. And when the Democratic Party adopted a pro–civil rights plank in 1948, a group of white southerners had created the States' Rights Democratic Party (the Dixiecrats), which nominated the fiercely segregationist governor Strom Thurmond of South Carolina. If Wallace's candidacy did not destroy Truman's chances, experts said, the Dixiecrats certainly would.

Truman, however, refused to give up. He denounced Henry Wallace for accepting communist support. He also reached out to African American voters in northern cities, becoming the first presidential candidate to campaign in Harlem. In the end, Truman prevailed. African American voters made the difference, giving Truman the electoral votes of key northern states. Roosevelt's New Deal coalition—African Americans, union members, northern urban voters, and most southern whites—had endured.

Full Employment Act Postwar liberal initiative that created mechanisms to help the federal government manage the economy. Although the original bill sought to stimulate economic growth by raising the minimum wage and guaranteeing jobs to those willing and able to work, through public-sector employment if necessary, the act passed without either of these provisions, which were blocked in Congress.

Taft-Hartley Act A 1947 law, passed over Truman's veto, that undermined some of the pro-labor provisions of the 1935 Wagner Act and restricted the power of labor unions.

Progressive Party Party formed from a splintering within the Democratic Party in 1948 by those dissatisfied with Truman. It advocated friendly relations with the Soviet Union, racial desegregation, a ban on monopolies, and nationalization of basic industries.

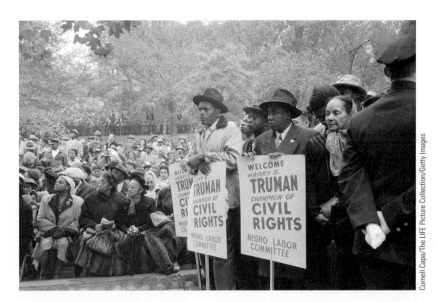

◀ African American voters were an increasingly important political force in the postwar era. President Truman had political reasons for appealing to black voters, but he also felt a moral obligation to support their struggle for civil rights. Here, a crowd waits to greet the president in 1952.

Cornell Capa/The LIFE Picture Collection/Getty Images

25-2d Truman's Fair Deal

Truman began his new term brimming with confidence. It was time, he believed, for government to fulfill its responsibility to provide economic security for the poor and the elderly. As he worked on his 1949 State of the Union message, he penciled in his intentions: "I expect to give every segment of our population a **fair deal**." Truman, unlike Roosevelt, pushed forward legislation to support the civil rights of African Americans, including the antilynching bill that Roosevelt had given only lukewarm support. He proposed a national health insurance program and federal aid for education. Once again, however, his proposals were defeated. A filibuster by southern conservatives in Congress destroyed his civil rights legislation, the American Medical Association denounced his health insurance plan as "socialized medicine," and the Roman Catholic Church opposed aid to education because it would not include parochial schools.

When the postwar peace proved short-lived and Truman ordered troops to Korea in June 1950, many reservists and National Guardsmen resented being called to active duty. Americans, remembering the shortages of the last war, tried to stockpile sugar, coffee, and canned goods—thus causing inflation. In 1951, the president's approval rating was only 23 percent.

25-2e Eisenhower's Dynamic Conservatism

In 1952 the Republicans insisted "It's Time for a Change," and voters agreed, especially with General Dwight D. Eisenhower as the Republican presidential nominee. Americans hoped that the immensely popular World War II hero could end the Korean War. And Eisenhower appealed to moderates in both parties; the Democrats also had tried to recruit him as their presidential candidate.

With a Republican in the White House for the first time in twenty years, conservatives hoped to roll back such New Deal liberal programs as the mandatory Social Security system. Eisenhower, however, had no such intention. As a moderate Republican, Eisenhower embraced an approach he called "dynamic conservatism": being "conservative when it comes to money and liberal when it comes to human beings." On the liberal side, in 1954 Eisenhower signed legislation that raised Social Security benefits and added 7.5 million workers, mostly self-employed farmers, to the Social Security rolls. The Eisenhower administration also increased funding for education—though increases were motivated by Cold War fears, not liberal principles, in the wake of the Soviet launch of *Sputnik* in 1957 (see "Links to the World: *Sputnik*," Section 26-6).

25-2f Growth of the Military-Industrial Complex

Overall, Eisenhower's administration was unabashedly fiscally conservative and pro-business. The president tried to reduce federal spending and to balance the budget. However, faced with three recessions (in 1953–1954, 1957–1958, and 1960–1961) and the tremendous cost of America's global activities, the Republican administration steadily turned to deficit spending. In 1959, federal spending climbed to $92 billion, about half of which went to defense spending: to support a standing military of 3.5 million men and to develop new weapons for the ongoing Cold War.

Eisenhower worried about this trajectory. In early 1961, as he bid farewell to the nation, the outgoing president condemned this new "conjunction of an immense military establishment and a large arms industry" and warned that its "total influence—economic, political, even

Dwight D. Eisenhower Thirty-fourth president of the United States (1953–1961) and U.S. Army five-star general during World War II; Republican known for his moderate politics, steering a middle course between Democratic liberalism and traditional Republican conservatism.

fair deal Agenda proposed by President Truman that included civil rights, national health care legislation, and federal aid to education.

spiritual"—threatened the nation's democratic process. Eisenhower, the former five-star general and war hero, urged Americans to "guard against . . . the **military-industrial complex**."

During Eisenhower's presidency, both liberal Democrats and moderate Republicans occupied what historian Arthur M. Schlesinger Jr. called "the vital center." And with the Cold War between the United States and the Soviet Union portrayed as a battle between good and evil and a struggle for the future of the world, criticism of American society seemed suspect—even unpatriotic. British journalist Godfrey Hodgson would later describe this time as an era of "consensus," when Americans were "confident to the verge of complacency about the perfectibility of American society, anxious to the point of paranoia about the threat of communism."

25-3 Cold War Fears and Anticommunism

▸ What developments contributed to the growth of anticommunist sentiment in the postwar period?

▸ How did the federal government attempt to locate communists in American society? What role did Senator Joseph McCarthy (R, WI) play in the postwar red scare?

▸ How and why did the search for communists and communist spies become excessive, and what impact did it have on American society?

International relations profoundly influenced America's domestic politics in the years following World War II. Americans were frightened by the Cold War tensions between the United States and the Soviet Union—and there were legitimate reasons for fear. Reasonable fears, however, spilled over into anticommunist demagoguery and witch hunts. Fear allowed the trampling of civil liberties, the suppression of dissent, and the persecution of thousands of innocent Americans.

military-industrial complex Term made famous by President Eisenhower's farewell speech in 1961; it refers to the U.S. military, arms industries, and related government and business interests, which together grew in power, size, and influence in the decades after World War II.

House Un-American Activities Committee Powerful Congressional committee popularly known as HUAC, originally created in 1938, which investigated communist influence in America and contributed to anticommunist hysteria in the postwar United States.

Anticommunism was not new in American society. A Red Scare had swept the nation following the Russian Revolution of 1917, and opponents of America's labor movement had used charges of communism to block unionization through the 1930s. Many saw the Soviet Union's virtual takeover of Eastern Europe in the late 1940s as an alarming parallel to Nazi Germany's takeover of neighboring states. People remembered the failure of "appeasement" at Munich and worried that the United States was "too soft" in its policy toward the Soviet Union.

25-3a Espionage and Nuclear Fears

In addition, top U.S. government officials knew that the Soviet Union was spying on the United States (as the United States was spying on the Soviet Union). A top-secret project, code-named "Venona," decrypted almost three thousand Soviet telegraphic cables that proved Soviet spies had infiltrated U.S. government agencies and nuclear programs. Intelligence officials resolved to prosecute Soviet spies, but they kept their evidence from the American public so that the Soviets would not realize their codes had been compromised. Thus even legitimate prosecution often appeared as government excess, persecution based on no real evidence.

Fear of nuclear war also contributed to American anticommunism. For four years, the United States alone possessed what seemed the ultimate weapon, but in 1949 the Soviet Union exploded its own atomic device. President Truman, initiating a national atomic civil defense program shortly thereafter, told Americans, "I cannot tell you when or where the attack will come or that it will come at all. I can only remind you that we must be ready when it does come." Children practiced "duck-and-cover" in their school classrooms, learning how to shield themselves "when the bomb falls." *Life* magazine featured backyard fallout shelters. As the stakes of the global struggle increased, Americans worried that the United States was newly vulnerable to attack on its own soil.

25-3b Politics of Anticommunism

At the height of the Cold War, American leaders, including Presidents Truman and Eisenhower, did not always draw a sufficient line between prudent attempts to prevent Soviet spies from infiltrating important government agencies and anticommunist scaremongering for political gain. Truman purposely invoked "the communist threat" to gain support for aid to Greece and Turkey in 1947. Republican politicians "red-baited" Democratic opponents, eventually targeting the Truman administration as a whole. In 1947, President Truman ordered investigations into the loyalty of more than 3 million U.S. government employees. As anticommunist hysteria grew, the government began discharging people deemed "security risks," among them alcoholics, homosexuals, and debtors thought susceptible to blackmail. It rarely had any evidence of disloyalty.

Leading the anticommunist crusade was the **House Un-American Activities Committee** (popularly known as HUAC). Created in 1938 to investigate "subversive and un-American propaganda," the viciously anti–New Deal committee had quickly lost credibility by charging that film stars—including eight-year-old Shirley Temple—were dupes of the Communist Party. In 1947, HUAC attacked Hollywood again. This time it relied on FBI files and on the testimony of Hollywood figures including Walt Disney and Screen Actors Guild president Ronald Reagan, who was also a secret

◀ The Cold War shaped American popular culture as well as foreign policy. Cartoonist Jay Ward's *Rocky and His Friends* premiered on television in 1959. In its first story sequence, "Jet Fuel Formula," Rocky the Flying Squirrel and Bullwinkle J. Moose—urged on by American military leaders—tried to re-create their secret formula for lunar propulsion while evading the tricks and explosive traps of Boris Badenov and Natasha Fatale, spies whose supposed "Pottsylvanian" origins did nothing to mask their heavy Russian accents.

informant for the FBI, complete with code name. Ten screenwriters and directors, known as the "Hollywood Ten," were sent to prison for contempt of Congress when they refused to "name names" of suspected communists for HUAC. Studios panicked and blacklisted hundreds of actors, screenwriters, directors, even makeup artists who were suspected of communist affiliations. With no evidence of wrongdoing, these men and women had their careers—and sometimes their lives—ruined.

25-3c McCarthyism and the Growing "Witch Hunt"

University professors became targets of the growing "witch hunt" in 1949, when HUAC demanded lists of the textbooks used in courses at eighty-one universities. When the board of regents at the University of California, Berkeley, instituted a loyalty oath for faculty, firing twenty-six who resisted on principle, protests from faculty members across the nation forced the regents to back down. But many professors, afraid of the reach of HUAC, began to downplay controversial material in their courses. In the labor movement, the CIO expelled eleven unions, with more than 900,000 members, for alleged communist domination.

The red panic reached its nadir in February 1950, when a relatively obscure U.S. senator came before an audience in Wheeling, West Virginia, to charge that the U.S. State Department was "thoroughly infested with Communists." Republican Senator **Joseph R. McCarthy** of Wisconsin was not an especially credible source. He made charges and then retracted them, claiming first that there were 205 communists in the State Department, then 57, then 81. He had a severe drinking problem; downing a water glass full of Scotch in a single gulp, he would follow it with a quarter-pound stick of butter, hoping to counteract the effects of the liquor. He had a record of dishonesty as a lawyer and judge in his

hometown of Appleton, Wisconsin. But McCarthy crystallized the anxieties many felt as they faced a new and difficult era in American life, and the anticommunist excesses of this era came to be known as McCarthyism.

With HUAC and McCarthy on the attack, Americans began pointing accusing fingers at one another. The anticommunist crusade was embraced by labor union officials, religious leaders, and the media, as well as by politicians. A bootblack at the Pentagon was questioned by the FBI seventy times because he was alleged to have given $10 during the 1930s to a defense fund for the Scottsboro Boys, who had been represented by an attorney from the Communist Party. Women in New York who lobbied for the continuation of wartime day care programs were denounced as communists by the *New York World Telegram*. "Reds, phonies, and parlor pinks," in Truman's words, seemed to lurk everywhere.

25-3d Anticommunism in Congress

In such a climate, most public figures found it too risky to stand up against McCarthyist tactics. And most Democrats did support the domestic Cold War and its anticommunist actions. In 1950, with bipartisan support, Congress passed the Internal Security (McCarran) Act, which required members of "Communist-front" organizations to register with the government and prohibited them from holding government jobs or traveling abroad. In 1954, the Senate unanimously passed the Communist Control Act (there were two dissenting votes in the House), which effectively made membership in the Communist Party illegal. Its chief sponsor, Democratic senator Hubert H. Humphrey of Minnesota,

Joseph R. McCarthy Wisconsin senator who used the media to stoke anti-communist hysteria, charging that Soviet spies and sympathizers had infiltrated the federal government. He was later discredited.

▲ Senator Joseph McCarthy (R, WI), whose name became shorthand for zealous anticommunism. McCarthy was at the forefront of anticommunist witch hunts in postwar America, but he was far from alone.

told his colleagues just before he cast his vote, "We have closed all of the doors. The rats will not get out of the trap."

The anticommunist fervor was fueled by spectacular and controversial trials of Americans accused of passing secrets to the Soviet Union. In 1948, Congressman Richard Nixon of California, a member of HUAC, was propelled onto the national stage when he accused former State Department official Alger Hiss of espionage. In 1950, Hiss was convicted of lying about his contacts with Soviet agents. That same year, **Ethel and Julius Rosenberg** were arrested for passing atomic secrets to the Soviets; they were found guilty of treason and executed in 1953. For decades, many historians believed that the Rosenbergs were primarily victims of a witch hunt. In fact, there was strong evidence of Julius Rosenberg's guilt in cables decrypted at

Ethel and Julius Rosenberg Couple found guilty of conspiracy to commit espionage and executed in 1953.

the time (as well as evidence that Ethel Rosenberg was less involved than had been charged), but this evidence was not presented at their trial for reasons of national security. The cables remained top secret until 1995, when a Clinton administration initiative opened the files to historians.

25-3e Waning of the Red Scare

Some of the worst excesses of Cold War anticommunism waned when Senator McCarthy was discredited on national television in 1954. McCarthy had used the press masterfully: knowing that newspapers usually buried corrections in their back pages, McCarthy made sensational, headline-worthy accusations just before reporters' deadlines, leaving them no time to verify his claims. But even after journalists knew McCarthy was unreliable they continued to report even his wildest charges. Sensational stories sell papers, and McCarthy had become a celebrity.

But McCarthy eventually miscalculated. When he pushed the Senate to investigate his charge that the U.S. Army was protecting communists within its ranks, both ABC and DuMont broadcast gavel-to-gavel coverage of the resulting Army-McCarthy hearings and Americans watched McCarthy in action. Apparently drunk, he ranted, slurred his words, and browbeat witnesses. Finally, after McCarthy maligned a young lawyer who was not even involved in the hearings, army counsel Joseph Welch intervened. "Have you no sense of decency, sir, at long last?" Welch asked, and the gallery erupted in applause. McCarthy's career as a witch-hunter was over. In December 1954, the Senate voted to "condemn" McCarthy for sullying the dignity of the Senate. He remained a senator, but exhaustion and alcohol took their toll and he died in 1957 at the age of forty-eight. With McCarthy discredited, the most virulent strand of anticommunism had run its course. However, the use of fear tactics for political gain, and the narrowing of American freedoms and liberties, were chilling domestic legacies of the Cold War.

25-4 The Struggle for Civil Rights

▶ What international and domestic developments contributed to increased support for African American civil rights?

▶ How did the federal government simultaneously support and undermine the advancement of African American civil rights?

▶ What methods did African Americans use to push for civil rights?

▶ In what ways did white Americans respond to the civil rights movement?

The Cold War—at home and abroad—also shaped African American struggles for social justice and the nation's responses to them. Some African American leaders saw their struggle for equal rights in the United States as part of a larger, international movement. And American diplomats understood that if the United States continued to allow segregation, discrimination, disenfranchisement, and racial violence against its own nonwhite citizens, it would struggle to pull the newly formed African and Asian nations into its sphere of influence. As the Soviet Union was quick to point out, the United States could hardly pose as the leader of the free world or condemn the Soviet Union's record on human rights while it practiced segregation at home. Cold War pressures supported domestic reform: to win the support of nonaligned nations, the United States would have to change its own practices. At the same time, many white Americans saw any criticism of their society as a Soviet-inspired attempt to weaken the United States in the ongoing Cold War. Opponents of the civil rights movement played the communist card, while the FBI and local law enforcement agencies used Cold War fears to claim legitimacy as they investigated civil rights activists. In this heated environment, African Americans struggled to seize the political initiative.

25-4a Black Political Power and Presidential Action

African Americans who had helped win World War II were determined that their lives in postwar America would be better because of their sacrifices. Moreover, politicians like Harry Truman were beginning to pay attention to black aspirations, especially as black voters in some urban-industrial states began to strongly influence the political balance of power.

President Truman had compelling political reasons for supporting African American civil rights. But he also felt a moral obligation. Truman genuinely believed it was only fair that every American, regardless of race, should enjoy the full rights of citizenship. He also was appalled by a resurgence of racial terrorism in the wake of the war, as a revived Ku Klux Klan tried to turn back the clock, threatening, beating, maiming, and murdering Americans who were not willing to accept their old place in the racial hierarchy. Reports that police in Aiken, South Carolina, had gouged out the eyes of a black sergeant just three hours after he had been discharged from the army made Isaac Woodard a national symbol of injustice, as filmmaker Orson Welles and folksinger Woody Guthrie took up his cause.

Popular opinion was beginning to shift, but not enough to prompt congressional action. Instead, Truman used the power of the presidency. In December 1946, he signed an executive order establishing the President's Committee on Civil Rights. The committee's report, *To Secure These Rights*, would become the civil rights movement's agenda for the next twenty years. It called for laws to end lynching and segregation and to guarantee voting rights and equal employment opportunity. For the first time since Reconstruction, a president had acknowledged the federal government's responsibility to protect all its citizens and to strive for racial equality.

In 1948 Truman issued two more executive orders, intended to end racial discrimination in the federal government. One proclaimed a policy of "fair employment" in federal jobs. The other, prompted in part by African American leaders who promised massive draft resistance if the military remained segregated, ordered the armed forces to end racial segregation "as rapidly as possible . . . without impairing efficiency or morale." The military did not readily comply, but by the beginning of the Korean War it had begun to phase out segregated units.

25-4b Supreme Court Victories and School Desegregation

African Americans successfully challenged racial discrimination both in the courts and in state and local legislatures. Northern state legislatures, in response to pressure by civil rights activists, passed measures prohibiting employment discrimination in the 1940s and 1950s. National successes came through the Supreme Court. During the 1940s the NAACP's Legal Defense and Educational Fund, led by Thurgood Marshall, carried forward a plan to destroy the separate but equal doctrine established in *Plessy v. Ferguson* (1896) by insisting on its literal interpretation. In higher education, the NAACP calculated, the cost of true equality in racially separate schools would be prohibitive. "You can't build a cyclotron for one student," the president of the University of Oklahoma acknowledged. NAACP lawsuits won African American students admission to professional and graduate schools at several formerly segregated state universities. The NAACP also won major victories through the Supreme Court in *Smith v. Allwright* (1944), which outlawed the whites-only primaries held by the Democratic Party in some southern states; *Morgan v. Virginia* (1946), which struck down segregation in interstate bus transportation; and *Shelley v. Kraemer* (1948), in which the Court held that racially restrictive covenants (private agreements among white homeowners not to sell to blacks) could not legally be enforced.

Even so, segregation was still standard practice in the 1950s, and blacks continued to suffer disfranchisement, job discrimination, and violence, including the 1951 bombing murder of the Florida state director of the NAACP and his wife. But in 1954, the NAACP won a historic victory that stunned the white South and energized African Americans to challenge segregation on several fronts. ***Brown v. Board of Education of Topeka***, which Thurgood Marshall argued before the high court, incorporated school desegregation cases from several states. The Court's unanimous decision was written by Chief Justice Earl Warren, who, as California's attorney general, had pushed for the internment of Japanese Americans during World War II and had come to regret that action. The

Brown v. Board of Education of Topeka Landmark Supreme Court case (1954) that overturned *Plessy v. Ferguson* (1896); it desegregated public schools by finding that racially separate schools are inherently unequal.

◀ Jackie Robinson cracked the color line in major league baseball when he joined the Brooklyn Dodgers for the 1947 season. Here, in a 1952 game at Ebbetts Field (Brooklyn), one of the greatest base runners of all time steals home plate.

Fred J. Sass/The New York Times Archive

Court concluded that "in the field of public education the doctrine of 'separate but equal' has no place. Separate educational facilities are inherently unequal." But the ruling that overturned *Plessy v. Ferguson* did not demand immediate compliance. A year later, the Court finally ordered school desegregation, but only "with all deliberate speed."

25-4c Montgomery Bus Boycott

By the mid-1950s, African Americans were engaged in a growing grassroots struggle for civil rights in both the North and the South, though southern struggles drew the most national attention. In 1955, Rosa Parks, a department store seamstress and longtime NAACP activist, was arrested when she refused to give up her seat to a white man on a public bus in Montgomery, Alabama. Her arrest gave local black women's organizations and civil rights groups a cause around which to organize a boycott of the city's bus system. They selected **Martin Luther King Jr.**, a recently ordained minister who had just arrived in Montgomery, as their leader. King launched the boycott with a moving speech, declaring, "If we are wrong, the Constitution is wrong. If we are wrong, God Almighty is wrong. If we are wrong, Jesus of Nazareth was merely a utopian dreamer. . . . If we are wrong, justice is a lie."

Martin Luther King Jr. was a twenty-six-year-old Baptist minister with a recent PhD from Boston University. Committed to the transforming potential of Christian love and schooled in the teachings of India's leader Mohandas K. Gandhi, King believed in nonviolent protest and civil disobedience. By refusing to obey unjust and racist laws, he hoped to focus the nation's attention on the immorality of Jim Crow. King persisted in this struggle even as opponents bombed his house and he was jailed for "conspiring" to boycott.

During the yearlong Montgomery bus boycott, blacks young and old rallied in their churches, sang hymns, and prayed that the nation would awaken to the evils of segregation and racial discrimination. They maintained their boycott through heavy rains and the steamy heat of summer, often walking miles a day. One elderly black woman, offered a ride to work by a white reporter, told him, "No, my feets is tired, but my soul is rested." With the bus company near bankruptcy and downtown merchants suffering from declining sales, city officials adopted harassment tactics to bring an end to the boycott. But the black people of Montgomery persevered. Thirteen months after the boycott began, the Supreme Court declared Alabama's bus segregation laws unconstitutional.

25-4d White Resistance

As the civil rights movement won significant victories, white reactions varied. Some communities in border states like Kansas and Maryland quietly implemented the school desegregation order, and many southern moderates advocated a gradual rollback of segregation. But others urged defiance. The Klan experienced another resurgence, and white violence against blacks increased. In August 1955, white men in Mississippi beat, mutilated, and murdered Emmett Till, a fourteen-year-old from Chicago, because they took offense at the way he spoke to a white woman; an all-white jury

Martin Luther King Jr. African American minister and leader of the Civil Rights Movement. His philosophy of civil disobedience fused the spirit of Christianity with the strategy of achieving racial justice through nonviolent resistance.

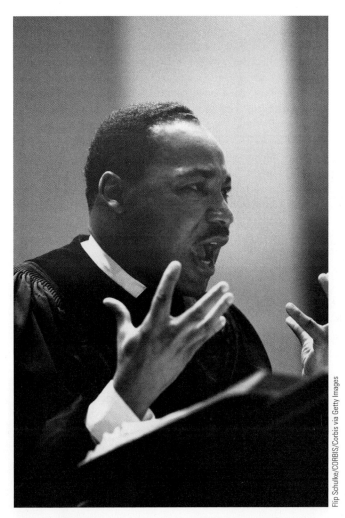

Flip Schulke/CORBIS/Corbis via Getty Images

▲ Reverend Martin Luther King Jr (1929–1968), leader of the African American Civil Rights Movement, delivers a sermon in Atlanta's Ebenezer Baptist Church. King was baptized there as a child and later served with his father, Martin Luther King Sr., as its co-pastor.

took only sixty-seven minutes to acquit those charged with the crime. Business and professional people created White Citizens' Councils for the express purpose of resisting the school desegregation order. Sometimes called "uptown Ku Klux Klans," the councils brought their economic power to bear against black civil rights activists. In keeping with the program of "massive resistance" proposed by Virginia's U.S. senator, Harry F. Byrd Sr., they pushed through state laws that paid private-school tuition for white children who left public schools to avoid integration and, in Virginia, refused state funding to integrated schools. When FBI director J. Edgar Hoover briefed President Eisenhower on southern racial tensions in 1956, he warned of communist influences among the civil rights activists and even suggested that, if the Citizens' Councils did not worsen the racial situation, their actions might "control the rising tension."

White resistance to civil rights also grew stronger in large northern cities. Chicago's African American population had increased from 275,000 in 1940 to 800,000 in 1960. These newcomers often found better jobs than they had left, and their numbers gave them political power. But they faced racism and segregation in the North as well. Many department stores and factories refused to hire blacks, who were also denied jobs in skilled trades. Whites welcomed a black family to a Columbus, Ohio, suburb by burning a cross on their front lawn. In 1951 in Cicero, a town adjoining Chicago, several thousand whites who were determined to keep blacks from moving into their neighborhood provoked a race riot. So racially divided was Chicago that the U.S. Commission on Civil Rights in 1959 described it as "the most residentially segregated city in the nation." Detroit and other northern cities were not far behind. And because children attended neighborhood schools, education in the North was in fact often segregated as well, though not by law, as it had been in the South.

25-4e Federal Authority and States' Rights

Unlike Truman, President Eisenhower wanted to avoid taking action on civil rights. Although he disapproved of racial segregation, Eisenhower objected to "compulsory federal law" as a solution, for he believed that race relations would improve "only if [desegregation] starts locally." He also feared that rapid desegregation under his administration would jeopardize Republican inroads in the South. Thus, Eisenhower did not state forthrightly that the federal government would enforce the *Brown* decision as the nation's law. In short, instead of leading, he spoke ambiguously and thereby tacitly encouraged white resistance. In 1956, 101 congressmen and senators from eleven southern states, all Democrats, issued "The Southern Manifesto." This document condemned the *Brown* decision as an "unwarranted exercise of power by the Court," which violated the principle of states' rights, and commended those states that sought to "resist forced integration by any lawful means."

Events in Little Rock, Arkansas, forced the president to act. In September 1957, Arkansas governor Orval E. Faubus defied a court-supported desegregation plan for Little Rock's Central High School. Faubus went on television the night before school began and told Arkansans that "blood would run in the streets" if black students tried to enter the high school the next day. On the second day of school, eight black teenagers tried to enter Central High, but they were turned away by Arkansas National Guard troops the governor had deployed to block their entrance. The ninth student, separated from the others, was surrounded by jeering whites and narrowly escaped the mob with the help of a sympathetic white woman.

It was more than two weeks after school began that the "Little Rock Nine" first entered Central High—and then only because a federal judge intervened. As an angry crowd surrounded the school and television broadcast the scene to the nation and the world, Eisenhower decided to nationalize the Arkansas National Guard (placing it under federal, not state, control) and dispatch one thousand army paratroopers to Little Rock. Troops guarded the students for the rest of the year. Eisenhower's use of federal power in Little Rock was a critical step in America's struggle over racial equality, for he had directly confronted the conflict between federal authority and states' rights. However, state power triumphed the following year, when Faubus closed all public high schools in Little Rock rather than desegregate them. Nonetheless, federal action continued. In 1957, Congress passed the first Civil Rights Act since Reconstruction, creating the United States Commission on Civil Rights to investigate systemic discrimination, such as in voting. Although this measure, like a voting rights act passed three years later, was not fully effective, it was another federal recognition of the centrality of civil rights.

Most important, however, was the growing strength of a new, grassroots civil rights activism. In 1957, Martin Luther King Jr. became the first president of the Southern Christian Leadership Conference (SCLC), organized to coordinate civil rights activities. With the success in Montgomery and the gains won through the Supreme Court and the Truman administration, African Americans were poised to launch a major national movement for civil rights in the years to come.

25-5 Creating a Middle-Class Nation

▶ What factors contributed to the creation of a shared "suburban culture"?

▶ Why was postwar economic growth and prosperity relatively widespread, and what were its limits?

▶ What were the main characteristics of the postwar middle-class culture?

Even as African Americans encountered massive resistance in their struggles for civil rights during the 1950s, in other ways the United States was becoming a more inclusive society. More Americans than ever before participated in a broad middle-class and suburban culture, and divisions among Americans based on class, ethnicity, religion, and regional identity became less important. Old European ethnic identities were fading, as an ever-smaller percentage of America's people were first- or second-generation immigrants. Ever greater numbers of Americans found material comfort and economic security in this time of broadly shared prosperity, with the least economic inequality between the wealthy and the middle class in the past one hundred years.

In the new suburbs, people from different backgrounds worked together to create communities and build schools, churches, and other institutions. Middle-class Americans increasingly looked to powerful national media rather than to regional or ethnic traditions for advice on matters ranging from how to celebrate Thanksgiving to what car to buy to how to raise children. New opportunities for consumption—whether the fads of a powerful teenage culture or the suburban ranch-style house—also tied together Americans from different backgrounds. In the postwar years, a new middle-class way of life was transforming the United States.

25-5a Prosperity for More Americans

During the 1950s, a growing economy gave more Americans than ever before middle-class comforts and economic security (see Figure 25.2). The nation's economic boom was driven by consumer spending, as Americans eagerly bought the cars and kitchen appliances and silk stockings and foodstuffs that had not been available during the war, and industries expanded production to meet consumer demand. Government spending was also important. As the Cold War deepened, the government poured money into defense industries, creating jobs and stimulating the economy. Such spending was made possible, in part, by steep tax rates on the richest Americans—with federal taxes topping out at 91 percent.

Cold War military and aerospace spending changed American society and culture in unintended ways. Weapons development and space programs required highly educated scientists, engineers, and other white-collar workers, so the professional middle class expanded. And as universities received billions of dollars to fund such research, they grew and claimed greater roles in American life. This government-funded research had other unanticipated results: the transistor, invented during the 1950s, made possible both the computer revolution and the transistor radio, without which 1950s youth culture would have looked very different.

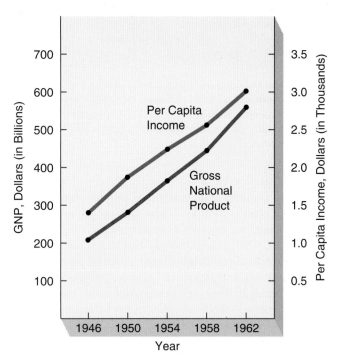

Figure 25.2 **Gross National Product and Per Capita Income, 1946–1962**

Both gross national product and per capita income soared during the economic boom from 1946 to 1962. *Source: Adapted from U.S. Bureau of the Census,* Historical Statistics of the United States, Colonial Times to 1970, *Bicentennial Edition (Washington, D.C.: U.S. Government Printing Office, 1975), p. 224.*

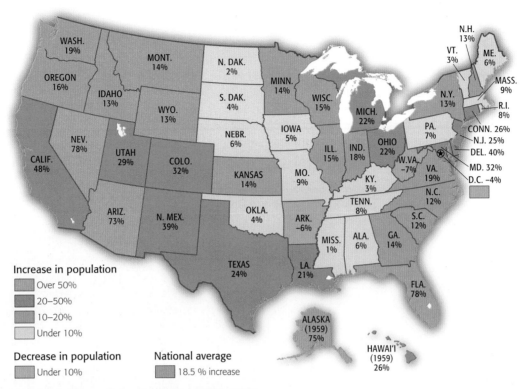

Map 25.1 Rise of the Sunbelt, 1950–1960

The years after the Second World War saw a continuation of the migration of Americans to the Sunbelt states of the Southwest and the West Coast.

A new era of labor relations also helped bring economic prosperity to more Americans. By 1950, labor and management created a new, more stable relationship. In peaceful negotiations, the United Auto Workers (UAW) and General Motors led the way in providing workers with health insurance, pension plans, and guaranteed cost-of-living adjustments, or COLAs, to protect wages from inflation. The 1950 agreement that *Fortune* magazine called "The Treaty of Detroit" gave GM's workers a five-year contract, with regular wage increases tied to corporate productivity. This was a turning point for the labor movement. In exchange for wages and benefits, organized labor gave up its demands for greater control in corporate affairs. And with wage increases tied to corporate productivity, labor cast its lot with management: workplace stability and efficiency, not strikes, would bring higher wages. During the 1950s, union wages and benefits often rivaled those of college-educated professionals and propelled union families into the ranks of the economic middle class.

25-5b Sunbelt and Economic Growth

Just as labor agreements helped create prosperity for union members and their families, government policies helped bring the nation's poorest region into the American economic mainstream. In the 1930s, Roosevelt had called the South "the nation's No. 1 economic problem." During World War II, new defense industry plants and military training camps channeled federal money to the region, stimulating economic growth. In the postwar era, huge levels of defense spending, especially for the nation's aerospace industry, continued to shift economic development from the Northeast and Midwest to the South and Southwest—the **Sunbelt** (see Map 25.1). Government actions—including generous tax breaks for oil companies, siting of military bases, and awarding of defense and aerospace contracts—were crucial to the region's new prosperity.

The Sunbelt's spectacular growth was also due to agribusiness, the oil industry, real estate development, and recreation. Sunbelt states aggressively—and successfully—sought foreign investment. Industry was drawn to the South by right-to-work laws, which outlawed closed shops, and by low taxes and low heating bills. Air conditioning, which was first used in office buildings during the 1930s, made the hottest summer days bearable (though few residences had even window units before the 1960s). Houston, Phoenix, Los Angeles, San Diego, Dallas, and Miami all boomed; the population of Houston, a center of the aerospace industry and also of oil and petrochemical production, more than tripled between 1940 and 1960. California absorbed no less than one-fifth of

Sunbelt Southern and southwestern states whose rapid economic development brought many new residents during the postwar years.

Moving to Levittown

Builder William Levitt's assembly-line methods created affordable homes for young families—although initially only "Caucasians" were allowed to buy homes in Levittown. Here, truck supervisor Bernard Levey and his family stand in front of their new Levitt-built home in 1950. The Leveys would have received a copy of the Levittown *Homeowners* *Guide*, which contained a list of "do's" and "don'ts": for example, residents were not to hang laundry on Sundays, when their neighbors were "most likely to be relaxing on the rear lawn."

CRITICAL THINKING

■ What does this photograph reveal about the new Levittown development?

■ Compare the structures you see here (the new home behind the Levey family and one under construction in 1948) with the average new suburban home today. What does their size and layout suggest about the extent of "consumer culture" in the early 1950s?

Bernard Hoffman/Time & Life Pictures/Getty Images

▲ Truck supervisor Bernard Levey standing with his family in front of his new Levitt-built home.

Tony Linck/The LIFE Picture Collection/Getty Images

▲ Aerial view of a concrete foundation and prefabricated components of a home under construction in the planned community of Levittown, New York, June 1948.

the nation's entire population increase in the 1950s. By 1963, it was the most populous state in the Union.

25-5c A New Middle-Class Culture

By the 1950s, it seemed that America was becoming a middle-class nation. Unionized blue-collar workers gained middle-class incomes, and veterans with GI Bill college educations swelled the growing managerial and professional class. In 1956, for the first time, the United States had more white-collar than blue-collar workers, and in 1957 there were 61 percent more salaried middle-class workers than just a decade earlier. Also for the first time, a majority of families—60 percent—had incomes in the middle-class range (approximately $3,000 to $9,000 a year in the mid-1950s), and the gap between the rich and the middle class shrank dramatically.

However, middle-class identity was not simply a matter of economics. Half of teenagers whose fathers did unskilled menial labor or whose mothers had only a sixth-grade education, a major 1952 survey discovered, believed their family was "middle class" (not working class or lower class). Paradoxically, the strength of unions in the postwar era contributed to a decline in working-class identity: as large numbers of blue-collar workers participated fully in the suburban middle-class culture, the lines separating working class and middle class seemed less important. Increasingly, a family's standard of living mattered more than what sort of work made the standard of living possible. People of color did not share equally in America's postwar prosperity and were usually invisible in American representations of "the good life." However, many middle-income African Americans, Latinos, and Asian Americans did participate in the broad middle-class culture.

25-5d Whiteness and National Culture

The emergence of a national middle-class culture was possible in part because America's population was more homogeneous in the 1950s than before or since. In the nineteenth and early twentieth centuries, the United States had restricted or prohibited immigration from Asia, Africa, and Latin America while accepting millions of Europeans to America's shores. This large-scale European immigration had been shut off in the 1920s, so that by 1960 only 5.7 percent of Americans were foreign born (compared with approximately 15 percent in 1910 and 13.7 percent in 2015). In 1950, 88 percent of Americans were non-Hispanic whites (compared with less than 64 percent in 2010), 10 percent of the population was African American, roughly 2 percent was Hispanic, and Native Americans and Asian Americans each accounted for about one-fifth of 1 percent. But almost all European Americans were at least a generation removed from immigration. Instead of "Italians" or "Russians" or "Jews," they were increasingly likely to describe themselves as "white." In 1959, the addition of two new states, Alaska and Hawai'i, brought more people of Native, Asian, or Pacific origin to the U.S. population.

Although the new suburbs were peopled mostly by white families, these suburbs were usually more diverse than the communities from which their residents had come. America's small towns and urban ethnic enclaves were quite homogeneous and usually intolerant of difference and of challenges to traditional ways. In the suburbs, people from different backgrounds came together: migrants from the city and the country; from different regions of the nation, different ethnic cultures, and different religious backgrounds. It was in the suburbs, paradoxically, that many people encountered different customs and beliefs. But as they joined with neighbors to forge new communities, the new suburbanites frequently adopted the norms of the developing national middle class. They traded the provincial homogeneity of specific ethnic or regional cultures for a new sort of homogeneity: a national white middle-class culture.

25-5e Television

Because many white Americans were new to the middle class, they were uncertain about what behaviors were proper and expected of them. They found instruction, in part, in the national mass media. Women's magazines helped housewives replace the ethnic and regional dishes with which they had grown up with "American" recipes created from national brand name products—such as casseroles made with Campbell's Cream of Mushroom soup. Television also fostered America's shared national culture and taught Americans how to be middle class. Although television sets cost about $300—the equivalent of $2,500 today—almost half of American homes had TVs by 1953. Television ownership rose to 90 percent by 1960, when more American households had a television set than a washing machine or an electric iron.

On television, suburban families like the Andersons (*Father Knows Best*) and the Cleavers (*Leave It to Beaver*) ate dinner at a properly set dining room table. The mothers were always well groomed; June Cleaver did housework in a carefully ironed dress. When children faced moral dilemmas, parents gently but firmly guided them toward correct decisions. Every crisis was resolved through paternal wisdom—and a little humor. In these families, no one ever yelled or hit. These popular family situation comedies portrayed and reinforced the suburban middle-class ideal that so many American families sought.

The "middle-classness" of television programming was due in part to the economics of the television industry. Advertising paid for television programming, and the corporations that bought advertising did not want to offend potential consumers. Thus, although African American musician Nat King Cole drew millions of viewers to his NBC television show, it never found a sponsor. National corporations were afraid that being linked to a black performer like Cole would hurt their sales among whites—especially in the South. Because African Americans made up only about 10 percent of the population and many had limited disposable income, they had little power in this economics-driven system. The *Nat King Cole Show* was canceled within a year; it was a decade before the networks again tried to anchor a show around a black performer.

Television's reach extended beyond the suburbs. People from the inner cities and from isolated rural areas also watched family sitcoms or laughed at the antics of Milton Berle and Lucille Ball. With only network television available—ABC, CBS, and NBC (and, until 1956, DuMont)—70 percent or more of all viewers might be watching the same popular program at the same time. (In the early twenty-first century, the most popular shows might attract 12 percent of the live viewing audience—a group that is steadily shrinking as other viewing platforms develop.) Television gave Americans a shared set of experiences; it also helped create a more homogeneous, white-focused, middle-class culture.

25-5f Consumer Culture

Linked by a shared national culture, Americans also found common ground in a new abundance of consumer goods. After decades of scarcity, Americans had what seemed a dazzling array of consumer goods from which to choose, and they embraced them with unmatched exuberance. Even the most utilitarian objects got two-tone paint jobs or rocket ship details; there was an optimism and vulgar joy in the popularity of turquoise refrigerators, furniture shaped like boomerangs, and cars designed to resemble fighter jets. In this consumer society, people used consumer choices to express their personal identity and to claim status within the broad boundaries of the middle class.

Cars more than anything else embodied the consumer fantasies and exuberance of newly prosperous Americans. Expensive Cadillacs were the first to develop tail fins, and fins soon soared from midrange Chevys, Fords, and Plymouths as well. Americans spent $65 billion on automobiles in 1955—a figure equivalent to almost 20 percent of the gross national product. To pay for all those cars—and for suburban houses with modern appliances—America's consumer debt rose from $5.7 billion in 1945 to $58 billion in 1961.

25-5g Religion

In the same years, Americans turned in unprecedented numbers to organized religion. Membership (primarily in mainline Christian churches) doubled between the end of World War II and the beginning of the 1960s. The uncertainties of the nuclear age likely contributed to the resurgence of religion, and some Americans may have sought spiritual consolation in the wake of the immensely destructive world war. The increasingly important national mass media played a role, as preachers like Billy Graham created national congregations from television audiences, preaching a message that combined the promise of salvation with Cold War patriotism. But along with religious teachings, local churches and synagogues offered new suburbanites a sense of community. They welcomed

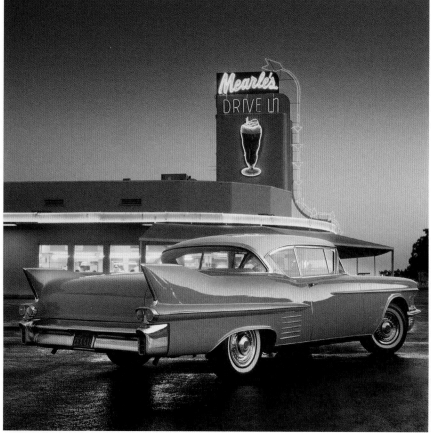

◀ Consumer goods reflected a new exuberance during the 1950s, and none more than that decade's automobiles. This candy-pink 1958 Cadillac coupe, complete with swooping tail fins, stands in front of another 1950s institution: a California drive-in.

Car Culture/Getty Images

newcomers, celebrated life's rituals, and supported the sick and the bereaved, who were often far from their extended families and old communities. It is difficult to measure the depth of religious belief in postwar America, but church fellowship halls were near the center of the new postwar middle-class culture.

25-6 Men, Women, and Youth at Midcentury

▶ What were the dominant postwar attitudes and ideas about gender roles, marriage, and sexuality?

▶ How did the postwar economy and culture shape assumptions about men's and women's work?

▶ What made the postwar "youth culture" distinctive?

Most of all, Americans pursued "the good life" and sought refuge from the tensions of the Cold War world through their homes and families. Having survived the Great Depression and a world war, many sought fulfillment in private life rather than public engagement; they saw their commitment to home and family as an expression of faith in the future. However, despite the real satisfactions that many Americans found in family life, both men and women found their life choices limited by powerful social pressures to conform to narrowly defined gender roles.

25-6a Marriage and Families

During the 1950s, few Americans remained single, and most people married very young. By 1959, half of American brides were twenty or younger; their husbands were not much older. This trend toward early marriage was endorsed by experts and approved by most parents, in part as a way to prevent premarital sex. As Americans accepted psychotherapeutic insights in the years following the war, they worried not only that premarital sex might leave the young woman pregnant or ruin her "reputation," but also that the experience could so damage her psychologically that she could never adjust to "normal" marital relations. One popular women's magazine argued, "When two people are ready for sexual intercourse at the fully human level they are ready for marriage. . . . Not to do so is moral cowardice. And society has no right to stand in their way."

Many young couples—still teenagers—found autonomy and freedom from parental authority by marrying and setting up their own household. Most newlyweds quickly had babies—an average of three—completing their family while still in their twenties. Birth control (condoms and diaphragms) was widely available and widely used, for most couples planned the size of their family. But almost all married couples, regardless of race or class, wanted a large family. Two children were the American ideal in 1940; by 1960, most couples wanted four. And though many families looked nothing like television's June, Ward, Wally, and Beaver Cleaver, 87 percent

of children under eighteen lived with two married parents (in 2015, the figure was 61 percent). Fewer children were born outside marriage then; only 3.9 percent of births were to unmarried women in 1950 (compared with about 40 percent of births today). Divorce rates were also lower, escalating from a new high of 9 divorces per 1,000 married couples in 1960 to a peak of 22 in the early 1980s, and down to approximately 16 divorces per 1,000 married couples today.

25-6b Gender Roles in 1950s Families

In these 1950s families, men and women usually took distinct and different roles, with male breadwinners and female homemakers. This division of labor, contemporary commentators insisted, was based on the timeless and essential differences between the sexes. In fact, the economic and social structure and the cultural values of postwar American society largely determined what choices were available to American men and women.

During the 1950s, it was possible for many white families to live in modest middle-class comfort on one (male) salary. (Racial discrimination made this much more difficult for black families.) There were strong incentives for women to stay at home, especially while children were young. Good child care was rarely available, and fewer families lived close to the grandparents or other relatives who had traditionally helped with the children. A new cohort of child care experts, including **Dr. Benjamin Spock**, whose 1946 *Baby and Child Care* sold millions of copies, insisted that a mother's full-time attention was necessary for her children's well-being. Because of hiring discrimination, women who could afford to stay home often did not find the jobs available to them attractive enough to justify a double shift, with paid employment simply added to their responsibilities for cooking and housework. Many women thus chose to devote their considerable energies to family life. America's schools and religious institutions also benefited immensely from their volunteer labor.

25-6c Women and Work

A great number of women, however, found that their lives did not completely match the ideal of 1950s family life. Suburban domesticity left many women feeling isolated, cut off from the larger world of experiences their husbands still inhabited. The popular belief that one should find complete emotional satisfaction in private life put unrealistic pressures on marriages and family relationships. And finally, despite near-universal celebration of women's domestic roles, many women found themselves managing both job and family responsibilities (see Figure 25.3). Twice as many women were employed in 1960 as in 1940, including 39 percent of women with children between the ages of six and seventeen. A majority of these women worked part time

Dr. Benjamin Spock Physician and author of *Baby and Child Care,* the best-selling child-rearing manual for parents of the baby boom generation.

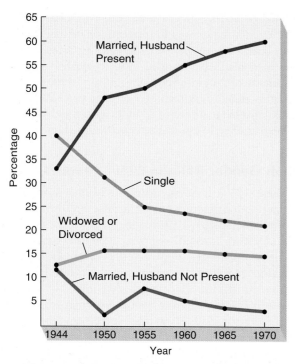

Figure 25.3 **Marital Distribution of the Female Labor Force, 1944–1970**

The composition of the female labor force changed dramatically from 1944 to 1970. In 1944, 41 percent of women in the labor force were single; in 1970, only 22 percent were single. During the same years, the percentage of the female labor force who had a husband in the home jumped from 34 to 59. The percentage who were widowed or divorced remained about the same from 1944 to 1970. *Source: Adapted from U.S. Bureau of the Census, Historical Statistics of the United States, Colonial Times to 1970, Bicentennial Edition (Washington, D.C.: U.S. Government Printing Office, 1975), p. 133.*

for some specific family goal: a new car, college tuition for the children. They did not see these jobs as violating their primary role as housewife; these jobs were in service to the family, not a means to independence from it.

Whether she worked to supplement a middle-class income, to feed her children, or to support herself, however, a woman faced discrimination in the world of work. Want ads were divided into "Help Wanted—Male" and "Help Wanted—Female" categories. Female full-time workers earned, on average, just 60 percent of what male full-time workers were paid and were restricted to less well-paid "female" fields, as maids, secretaries, teachers, and nurses. Women with exceptional talent or ambition often found their aspirations blocked. A popular book, *Modern Woman: The Lost Sex*, explained that ambitious women and "feminists" suffered from "penis envy." Textbooks for college psychology and sociology courses warned women not to "compete" with men; magazine articles described "career women" as a "third sex." Medical schools commonly limited the admission of women to 5 percent of each class. In 1960, less than 4 percent of lawyers and judges were female. When future Supreme

Court Justice Ruth Bader Ginsburg graduated at the top of her Columbia Law School class in 1959, she could not find a job.

25-6d "Crisis of Masculinity"

While academics and mass media critics alike stressed the importance of "proper" female roles, they devoted equal attention to the plight of the American male. American men faced a "crisis of masculinity," proclaimed the nation's mass-circulation magazines, quoting an array of psychological experts. In a best-selling book, sociologist William H. Whyte explained that postwar corporate employees had become "organization men," succeeding through cooperation and conformity, not through individual initiative and risk. Women, too, were blamed for men's crisis: women's "natural" desire for security and comfort, experts insisted, was stifling men's natural instinct for adventure. Some even linked concerns about masculinity to the Cold War, arguing that, unless America's men recovered masculinity diminished by white-collar work or a suburban, family-centered existence, the nation's future was at risk. At the same time, however, men who did not conform to current standards of male responsibility—husband, father, breadwinner—were forcefully condemned, sometimes in the same magazines that preached the crisis of masculinity. One influential book advocated mandatory psychotherapy for men who reached thirty without having married; such single men were open to charges of "emotional immaturity" or "latent homosexuality."

25-6e Sexuality

Sexuality was complicated terrain in postwar America. Only heterosexual intercourse within marriage was deemed socially acceptable, and consequences for sexual misconduct could be severe. Women who became pregnant outside marriage were often ostracized by friends and family and expelled from schools or colleges. Homosexuality was grounds for dismissal from a job, expulsion from college, even jail. At the same time, a great many Americans were breaking the sexual rules of the era. In his major works on human sexuality, *Sexual Behavior in the Human Male* (1948) and *Sexual Behavior in the Human Female* (1953), Dr. Alfred Kinsey, director of the Institute for Sex Research at Indiana University, informed Americans that, despite the fact that more than 80 percent of his female sample disapproved of premarital sex on "moral grounds," half of these women had had premarital sex. He also reported that at least 37 percent of American men had had "some homosexual experience." Americans made best sellers of Kinsey's dry, quantitative studies—as many rushed to condemn him. One congressman charged Kinsey with "hurling the insult of the century against our mothers, wives, daughters and sisters"; the *Chicago Tribune* called him a "menace to society." Although Kinsey's population samples did not provide a completely accurate picture of American sexual behavior, his findings made many Americans aware that they were not alone in breaking certain rules.

Another challenge to the sexual rules of 1950s America came from Hugh Hefner, who launched *Playboy* magazine in 1953. Within three years, the magazine had a circulation of 1 million. Hefner saw *Playboy* as an attack on America's "ferocious anti-sexuality [and] dark antieroticism" and his nude "playmates" as a means for men to combat what he considered the increasingly "blurred distinctions between the sexes" in a family-centered suburban culture.

25-6f Youth Culture

As children grew up in relative stability and prosperity, a distinctive "youth culture" developed. Youth culture was really a set of subcultures; the culture of white, middle-class, suburban youth was not the same as that of black, urban teens or even of the white working class. Youth culture was, however, distinct from the culture of adults. Its customs and rituals were created within peer groups and shaped by national media—teen magazines, movies, radio, advertising, music—targeted toward this huge potential audience.

The sheer numbers of "baby boom" youth made them a force in American society. People sometimes described the baby boom generation as "a pig in a python," and as this group moved from childhood to youth, communities successively built elementary schools, junior high schools, and high schools. America's corporations quickly learned the power of youth, as children's fads launched multimillion-dollar industries. Slinky, selling for a dollar, began loping down people's stairs in 1947; Mr. Potato Head—probably the first toy advertised on television—had $4 million in sales in 1952. Barbie, introduced by Mattel in 1959, would sell its billionth copy in 1997. In the mid-1950s, when Walt Disney's television show *Disneyland* featured Davy Crockett, "King of the Wild Frontier," every child in America (and more than a few adults) just *had* to have a coonskin cap. When the price of raccoon fur skyrocketed from 25 cents to $8 a pound, many children had to make do with a Davy Crockett lunchbox or toothbrush instead. As these baby boom children grew up, their buying power shaped American popular culture.

By 1960, America's 18 million teenagers were spending $10 billion a year. Seventy-two percent of movie tickets in the 1950s were sold to teenagers, and Hollywood catered to this audience with films that ranged from forgettable B movies like *The Cool and the Crazy* and *Senior Prom* to controversial and influential movies, such as James Dean's *Rebel Without a Cause*. Adults worried that teens would be drawn to romantic images of delinquency in *Rebel Without a Cause*, and teenage boys did copy Dean's rebellious look. The film, however, blamed parents for teenage confusion, drawing heavily on popular psychological theories about sexuality and the "crisis of masculinity." "What can you do when you have to be a man?," James Dean's character implored his father.

Movies helped shape teen fads and fashions, but nothing defined youth culture as much as its music. Young Americans were electrified by the driving energy and beat of Bill Haley and the Comets, Chuck Berry, Little Richard, and Buddy Holly. **Elvis Presley**'s 1956 appearance on TV's *Ed Sullivan Show* touched off a frenzy of teen adulation—and

▲ Elvis Presley's first RCA recording, *Heartbreak Hotel*, went to number one on the charts in 1956, and teenage girls went wild for him. Drafted in December 1957, Elvis served in the U.S. Army from 1958 to 1960.

Bettmann/Getty Images

a flood of letters from parents scandalized by his "gyrations." As one reviewer noted, "When Presley executes his bumps and grinds, it must be remembered that even the 12-year-old's curiosity may be overstimulated." Although few white musicians acknowledged the debt, the roots of rock 'n' roll lay in African American rhythm and blues. The raw energy and sometimes sexually suggestive lyrics of early rock music faded as the music industry sought white performers, like Pat Boone, to do blander, more acceptable "cover" versions of music by black artists.

The distinct youth culture that developed in the 1950s made many adults uneasy. Parents worried that the common practice of "going steady" made it more likely that teens would "go too far" sexually. Juvenile delinquency was a major concern. Crime rates for young people had risen dramatically in the years following World War II, but much was "status" crime—curfew violations, sexual experimentation, underage drinking—activities that were criminal because of the person's age, not because of the action itself. Congress held extensive hearings on juvenile delinquency, with experts testifying to the corrupting power of youth-oriented popular culture, comic books in

Elvis Presley Popular rock 'n' roll musician who melded country, gospel, and rhythm and blues influences; his sexually charged style drew young fans and alarmed many adults.

Sputnik

On October 4, 1957, the Soviet Union launched the first human-made satellite into space. *Sputnik*—roughly the size of a basketball, weighing 184 pounds—fell into orbit 500 miles above the earth's surface, emitting a steady beeping sound (A-flat, for 3/10 of a second) that could be picked up not only by sophisticated scientific instruments but by ham radio operators around the world. In the United States, an NBC radio announcer broadcast the beep, telling his listeners: "Listen now for the sound that forevermore separates the old from the new." The Soviets had begun a new era in human history.

Underlining the scientific and psychological triumph that *Sputnik* represented in the ongoing Cold War, Soviets framed it—in Cold War terms—as a triumph of communism. And *Sputnik's* propaganda value was undeniable. In the fall of 1957, Soviet technological and scientific achievement made headlines around the world; the United States, in contrast, offered scenes of racial violence. Radio Moscow, ever eager to make that point, announced the precise moment that *Sputnik* passed over Little Rock, Arkansas, where white mobs had attacked black students attempting to integrate its high school.

Some Americans worried about *Sputnik's* symbolic value. More, however, worried that America had become more vulnerable to Soviet attack. The little beeping sphere mattered little, but the missile that propelled it into outer space was another story. Such a missile could carry a nuclear warhead from

Soviet territory to the United States: the Soviets had created an intercontinental ballistic missile (ICBM). Said Soviet First Secretary Nikita Khrushchev: "[W]e now have all the rockets we need: long range rockets, intermediate-range rockets. And short-range rockets . . . [which] now make it possible to hit a target in any area of the globe."

Khrushchev's claim was more bluster than fact, as U.S. president Eisenhower well knew. American aerial reconnaissance showed that the Soviet missile program was not nearly so advanced or production so prolific. Eisenhower tried to calm the fears of his countrymen, going so far as to play five rounds of golf in the subsequent week. But he was not going to reveal America's top secret program of aerial surveillance.

Within hours of Sputnik's launch, however, Senator Lyndon Johnson (D-TX) had launched a Senate investigation: How had the Republican administration allowed the Soviets to beat the United States into space? Eisenhower, in response to increasing pressure (and surprising the not terribly well funded team in charge of the U.S. satellite program) announced that the United States would have its own satellite in orbit before the end of the year. On December 6, the United States launched a rocket, topped with a grapefruit-sized satellite, from Cape Canaveral, Florida. It rose about four feet into the air and exploded.

U.S. scientists would do better on the next try, successfully launching a satellite into orbit less than two months

later. But the combination of Soviet triumph and U.S. failure left Americans seeking an explanation. One answer seemed to lie in the U.S. educational system. *Life* magazine made the case: "Where there are young minds of great promise, there are rarely the means to advance them." In the heated atmosphere of the Cold War, Congress passed the National Defense Education Act of 1958. "An educational emergency exists," it claimed, which "requires action by the federal government. . . . to help develop as rapidly as possible those skills necessary for national defense."

In the wake of *Sputnik's* launch, federal money began to flow into higher education, funding scientific research and the study of foreign languages and societies. Federal money went to graduate fellowships and, in an attempt to draw more talented students to college, to fund high school college counselors and establish the first college student loan program. In this rise of federal support for American universities, we see a clear link to the world.

CRITICAL THINKING

- In the wake of the Soviet launch of Sputnik, the United States began investing more heavily in higher education through the National Defense Education Act of 1958. With the recent uptick in the use of cyberattacks by foreign governments and non-state entities, should the federal government again take a leading role in the promotion of certain kinds of education?

---

particular. In 1955, *Life* magazine reported, "Some American parents, without quite knowing what it is their kids are up to, are worried that it's something they shouldn't be." Most youthful behavior, however—from going steady to fads in music and dress—fit squarely into the consumer culture that youth shared

with their parents. "Rebellious youth" rarely questioned the logic of postwar American culture.

25-6g Challenges to Middle-Class Culture

Despite the growing reach and power of this middle-class culture, there were pockets of cultural dissent. **Beat** (a word that suggested both "down and out" and "beatific") writers rejected both middle-class social decorum and contemporary literary conventions. Jack Kerouac, author of *On the*

Beat Term used to describe a generation of nonconformist writers, such as Allen Ginsberg, who expressed scorn for the middle-class ideals of conformity, religion, family values, and materialism.

◀ Soviet postcard celebrating the launch of Sputnik I (October 4, 1957) and Sputnik II (November 3, 1957).

Mark Rykoff/Getty Images

Road, traced his inspiration to "weariness with all forms of the modern industrial state." The Beat Generation embraced spontaneity in their art, in their lives sought freedom from the demands of everyday life, and enjoyed a more open sexuality and drug use. Perhaps the most significant beat work was Allen Ginsberg's angry, incantational poem "Howl" (1956), the subject of an obscenity trial whose verdict opened American publishing to a much broader range of works. The mainstream press made fun of the beats, dubbing them and their followers "beatniks" (after *Sputnik,* suggesting their un-Americanness). Although their numbers were small in the 1950s, their rebellion helped shape America's counterculture in the 1960s and 1970s.

25-7 The Limits of the Middle-Class Nation

▶ What did critics find problematic about the postwar middle-class culture?

▶ How did the postwar economy affect the environment?

▶ What groups of Americans were left behind in the nation's economic expansion, and why?

During the 1950s, America's popular culture and mass media celebrated the opportunities available to the nation's people. At the same time, a host of influential critics rushed to condemn the new middle-class culture as a wasteland of conformity, homogeneity, and ugly consumerism.

25-7a Critics of Conformity

These critics were not lone figures crying out in the wilderness. Americans, obsessed with self-criticism even as most participated wholeheartedly in the celebratory "consensus" culture of their age, rushed to buy books like John Keats's *The*

Crack in the Picture Window (1957), which portrayed three families—the "Drones," the "Amiables," and the "Fecunds"—who lived in identical suburban tract houses "vomited" up by developers and sacrificed their remaining individuality in the quest for consumer goods. Some of the most popular fiction of the postwar era, such as J. D. Salinger's *The Catcher in the Rye* and Norman Mailer's *The Naked and the Dead,* was profoundly critical of American society. Americans even made best sellers of difficult academic works, such as David Riesman's *The Lonely Crowd* (1950) and William H. Whyte's *The Organization Man* (1955), both of which criticized the rise of conformity in American life. Versions of these critiques also appeared in mass-circulation magazines like *Ladies' Home Journal* and *Reader's Digest.* Steeped in such cultural criticism, many Americans even understood *Invasion of the Body Snatchers*—a 1956 film in which zombielike aliens grown in huge pods gradually replace a town's human inhabitants—as criticism of suburban conformity and the bland homogeneity of postwar culture.

Most of these critics were attempting to understand large-scale and significant changes in American society. Americans had lost some autonomy as large corporations replaced smaller businesses; they experienced the homogenizing force of mass production and a national consumer culture; they saw distinctions among ethnic groups and even among socioeconomic classes decline in importance. Many wanted to understand these social dislocations better. Critics of the new culture, however, were often elitist and antidemocratic. Many saw only bland conformity and sterility in the emerging middle-class suburban culture and so missed something important. Identical houses did not produce identical souls; instead, inexpensive suburban housing gave healthier, and perhaps happier, lives to millions who had grown up in dank, dark tenements or ramshackle farmhouses without indoor plumbing. In retrospect, however, other criticisms are obvious.

25-7b Environmental Degradation

First, the new consumer culture encouraged wasteful habits and harmed the environment. *BusinessWeek* noted during the 1950s that corporations need not rely on "planned obsolescence," purposely designing a product to wear out so that consumers would have to replace it. Americans replaced products because they were "out of date," not because they did not work, and automakers, encouraging the trend, revamped designs every year. New and inexpensive plastic products and detergents made consumers' lives easier—but were not biodegradable. And America's new consumer society used an ever-larger share of the world's resources. By the 1960s, the United States, with only 5 percent of the world's population, consumed more than one-third of its goods and services.

The rapid economic growth that made the middle-class consumer culture possible exacted environmental costs. Steel mills, coal-powered generators, and internal-combustion car engines burning lead-based gasoline polluted the atmosphere and imperiled people's health. As suburbanites commuted greater distances to their jobs, and neighborhoods were built without public transportation or shopping within walking distance of people's homes, Americans relied on private automobiles, consuming the nonrenewable resources of oil and gasoline and filling cities and suburbs with smog. Vast quantities of water were diverted from lakes and rivers to meet the needs of America's burgeoning Sunbelt cities, including the swimming pools and golf courses that dotted parched Arizona and southern California.

Defense contractors and farmers were among the country's worst polluters. Refuse from nuclear weapons facilities at Hanford, Washington, and at Colorado's Rocky Flats arsenal poisoned soil and water resources for years. Agriculture began employing massive amounts of pesticides and other chemicals. DDT, a chemical used on Pacific islands during the war to kill mosquitoes and lice, was used widely in the United States from 1945 until after 1962, when wildlife biologist Rachel Carson specifically indicted DDT for the deaths of mammals, birds, and fish in her best-selling book *Silent Spring.*

In the midst of prosperity, few understood the consequences of the economic transformation taking place. The nation was moving toward a postindustrial economy in which providing goods and services to consumers was more important than producing goods. Therefore, though union members prospered during the 1950s, union membership grew slowly—because most new jobs were being created not in heavy industries that hired blue-collar workers but in the union-resistant white-collar service trades. Technological advances increased productivity, as automated electronic processes replaced slower mechanical ones—but they pushed people out of relatively well-paid blue-collar jobs into the growing and less well-paid service sector.

25-7c Continuing Racism

Largely oblivious to the environmental degradation and work sector shifts that accompanied economic growth and consumerism, the new middle-class culture also largely ignored those who did not belong to its ranks. Race remained a major dividing line in American society, even as fewer Americans were excluded because of ethnic identity. Racial discrimination stood unchallenged in most of 1950s America. Suburbs, both North and South, were almost always racially segregated. Many white Americans had little or no contact in their daily lives with people of different races—not only because of residential segregation but also because the relatively small populations of nonwhite Americans were not dispersed equally throughout the nation. In 1960, there were 68 people of Chinese descent and 519 African Americans living in Vermont; 181 Native Americans lived in West Virginia; and Mississippi had just 178 Japanese American residents. Most white Americans in the 1950s—especially those outside the South, where there was a large African American population—gave little thought to race. They did not think of the emerging middle-class culture as "white," but as "American," marginalizing people of color in image as in reality (see Map 25.2).

◀ During the Second World War, DDT was used to protect American troops from bug-borne diseases and was hailed as a miracle insecticide. The use of DDT spread in postwar America, but little attention was paid to its often-fatal consequences for birds, mammals, and fish. In 1945, even as children ran alongside, this truck sprayed DDT as part of a mosquito control program at New York's Jones Beach State Park.

Bettmann/Getty Images

1950

2000

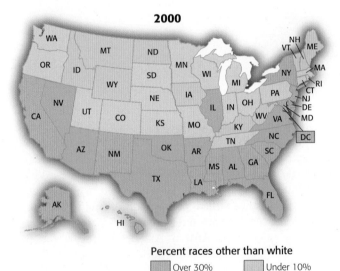

Percent races other than white

▨	Over 30%	▨	Under 10%
▨	20–29%	▨	Not applicable
▨	10–19%		

Map 25.2 **Racial Composition of the United States, 1950 and 2000**

Compared with present-day America, most states were fairly racially homogeneous in 1950. The exception was the Deep South, where most African Americans still lived. *Source: Adapted from "Demographic Trends in the Twentieth Century," U.S. Census Bureau; www.census.gov/population/www/censusdata/hiscendata.html.*

The new middle-class culture was also indifferent to the plight of the poor. In an age of abundance, more than one in five Americans lived in poverty. One-fifth of the poor were people of color, including almost half of the nation's African American population and more than half of all Native Americans. Two-thirds of the poor lived in households headed by a person with an eighth-grade education or less, one-fourth in households headed by a single woman. More than one-third of the poor were under age eighteen; one-fourth were over age sixty-five. Social Security payments helped the elderly, but many retirees were not yet covered, and

medical costs drove many older Americans into poverty. Few of these people had much reason for hope.

25-7d Poverty in an Age of Abundance

As millions of Americans (most of them white) were settling in the suburbs, the poor were ever more concentrated in the inner cities. African American migrants from the South were joined by poor whites from the southern Appalachians, many of whom moved to Chicago, Cincinnati, Baltimore, and Detroit. Meanwhile, Latin Americans were arriving in growing numbers from Mexico, the Dominican Republic, Colombia, Ecuador, and Cuba. According to the 1960 census, over a half-million Mexican Americans had migrated to the barrios of the Los Angeles–Long Beach area since 1940. And New York City's Puerto Rican population exploded from 70,000 in 1940 to 613,000 in 1960.

All of these newcomers to the cities came seeking better lives and greater opportunities. Because of the strong economy and low unemployment rate, many did gain a higher standard of living. But discrimination limited their advances, and they endured crowded and decrepit housing and poor schools. In addition, the federal programs that helped middle-class Americans sometimes made the lives of the poor worse. For example, the National Housing Act of 1949, passed to make available "a decent home . . . for every American family," provided for "urban redevelopment." Redevelopment meant slum clearance. Many poor people lost what housing they had as entire neighborhoods were leveled and replaced with luxury high-rise buildings, parking lots, and even highways.

Rural poverty was a long-standing problem in America, but the growth of large agribusinesses pushed more tenant farmers and owners of small farms off the land. From 1945 to 1961, the nation's farm population declined from 24.4 million to 14.8 million. When the harvesting of cotton in the South was mechanized in the 1940s and 1950s, more than 4 million people were displaced. Southern tobacco growers dismissed their tenant farmers, bought tractors to plow the land, and hired migratory workers to harvest the crops. Many of these displaced farmers traded southern rural poverty for northern urban poverty. And in the West and Southwest, Mexican citizens continued to serve as cheap migrant labor under the *bracero* program. Almost 1 million Mexican workers came legally to the United States in 1959; many more were undocumented workers. Entire families labored, enduring conditions little better than in the Great Depression.

Native Americans were America's poorest people, with an average annual income barely half that of the poverty level. Conditions for Native peoples were made worse by a federal policy implemented during the Eisenhower administration: termination. Termination reversed the Indian Reorganization Act of 1934, allowing Native peoples to terminate their tribal status and so remove reservation lands from federal protection that prohibited their sale. Sixty-one tribes were terminated between 1954 and 1960. Termination could take place only with a tribe's agreement, but pressure was sometimes intense—especially when reservation land

◀ After the war, American Indians lost sacred land to both big corporations and the federal government. In 1948, George Gillette (*left*), chairman of the Fort Berthold, North Dakota, Indian Tribal Council, covers his face and weeps as Secretary of the Interior J. A. Krug signs a contract buying 155,000 acres of tribal land for a reservoir.

AP Photo/William Chaplis

was rich in natural resources. The Klamaths of Oregon, for example, lived on a reservation rich in ponderosa pine, which lumber interests coveted. Enticed by cash payments, almost four-fifths of the Klamaths accepted termination and voted to sell their shares of the forestland. With termination, their way of life collapsed. Many Native Americans left reservation land for the city, joining the influx of other poor Americans seeking jobs and new lives. By the time termination was halted in the 1960s, observers compared the situation of Native Americans to the devastation their forebears had endured in the nineteenth century. Like most of the poor, these Americans were invisible to the growing middle class in the suburbs.

Overall, Americans who had lived through the devastation of the Great Depression and World War II enjoyed the relative prosperity and economic security of the postwar era. But those who had made it to the comfortable middle class often ignored the plight of those left behind. It would be their children—the generation of the baby boom, many reared in suburban comfort—who would see racism, poverty, and the self-satisfaction of postwar suburban culture as a failure of American ideals.

Summary

As the experiences of economic depression and world war receded, Americans worked to create good lives for themselves and their families. People married and had children in record numbers. Millions of veterans used the GI Bill to attend college, buy homes, and start businesses. Although American leaders feared that the nation would lapse back into economic depression after wartime government spending ended, consumer spending brought economic growth. The sustained economic growth of the postwar era, supported by strong labor unions and government policies, lifted a majority of Americans into an expanding middle class and lessened economic inequality.

The Cold War presidencies of Truman and Eisenhower focused on international relations and a global struggle against communism, rather than on domestic politics. Within the United States, Cold War fears provoked an extreme anticommunism that stifled political dissent and diminished Americans' civil liberties and freedoms.

The continuing African American struggle for civil rights drew national attention during the Montgomery bus boycott. African Americans won important victories in the Supreme Court, including the landmark decision in *Brown v. Board of Education*, and both Truman and Eisenhower used federal power to guarantee the rights of black Americans. With these victories, a national civil rights movement began to coalesce, and racial tensions within the nation increased.

Despite continued racial divisions, the United States became in many ways a more inclusive nation in the 1950s, as a majority of Americans participated in a national, consumer-oriented, middle-class culture. This culture largely ignored the poverty that remained in the nation's cities and rural areas, and contributed to rapidly increasing economic degradation. But for the growing number of middle-class Americans who, for the first time, lived in modest material comfort, the American dream seemed a reality.

Suggestions for Further Reading

Glenn C. Altschuler and Stuart M. Blumin, *The GI Bill: A New Deal for Veterans* (2009)

Taylor Branch, *Parting the Waters: America in the King Years, 1954–1963* (1988)

The Pledge of Allegiance

The Pledge of Allegiance that Americans recite in school classrooms and sports stadiums throughout the nation today was shaped by America's Cold War struggle against the Soviet Union. Congress added the phrase "under God" to the existing pledge in 1954, as part of an attempt to emphasize the difference between the God-fearing United States and the "godless communists" of the Soviet Union.

The Pledge of Allegiance was not always an important part of American public life. The original version was written in 1892 by Francis Bellamy, editor of *The Youth's Companion*, to commemorate the four hundredth anniversary of Columbus's arrival in North America. On October 11, 1892, more than 11 million schoolchildren recited the words "I pledge allegiance to my flag and the Republic for which it stands; one nation indivisible, with liberty and justice for all." In 1942, Congress officially adopted a revised version of this pledge as an act of wartime patriotism. The Supreme Court ruled in 1943, however, that

schoolchildren could not be forced to say the "Pledge to the Flag."

During the Cold War years, the pledge became more and more important as a way to demonstrate loyalty to the United States. Cold War fears lent force to a campaign by the Knights of Columbus, a Catholic men's service organization, to include "under God" in the pledge. Supporting the bill, President Eisenhower proclaimed that

in this way we are reaffirming the transcendence of religious faith in America's heritage and future; in this way we shall constantly strengthen those spiritual weapons which forever will be our country's most powerful resource in peace and war. From this day forward, the millions of our schoolchildren will daily proclaim in every city and town, every village and every rural schoolhouse, the dedication of our nation and our people to the Almighty.

Some Americans, citing the doctrine of separation of church and state, have protested the inclusion of "under God" in the nation's pledge. In June 2002, the Ninth District Court (covering California and eight other western states) touched off a major controversy by ruling that the 1954 version of the pledge was unconstitutional because it conveyed a "state endorsement" of a religious belief. Questions about the proper role of religion in American life are sure to remain controversial, a legacy for a people and a nation as America's people become even more diverse in the twenty-first century.

CRITICAL THINKING

■ The tensions of the Cold War helped to produce the first efforts to identify the United States as a Christian nation encapsulated by the addition of "under God" to the Pledge of Allegiance. In 2002, a federal district court ruled the 1954 version of the pledge to be in violation of the constitutional separation of church and state. The battle over the relationship of the nation to religion continues today. What evidence of this struggle can you identify in the United States today?

Lizabeth Cohen, *A Consumer's Republic: The Politics of Mass Consumption in Postwar America* (2003)

Stephanie Coontz, *The Way We Never Were: American Families and the Nostalgia Trap* (1992)

Thomas Patrick Doherty, *Cold War, Cool Medium: Television, McCarthyism, and American Culture* (2003)

Mary Dudziak, *Cold War Civil Rights: Race and the Image of American Democracy* (2000)

James Gregory, *The Southern Diaspora: How the Great Migrations of Black and White Southerners Transformed the Nation* (2007)

Thomas Hine, *Populuxe* (1986)

Grace Palladino, *Teenagers* (1996)

Michael Sherry, *In the Shadow of War* (1995)

Thomas J. Sugrue, *Sweet Land of Liberty: The Forgotten Struggle for Civil Rights in the North* (2008)

The Tumultuous Sixties, 1960–1968

t was late at night, and Ezell Blair had a big exam the next day. But there he was with his friends in the dormitory, talking—as they so often did—about injustice, and discrimination, and about living in a nation that proclaimed equality for all but denied full citizenship to some of its people because of the color of their skin. They were complaining about all the do-nothing adults, condemning pretty much the entire black community of Greensboro—and not for the first time—when Franklin McCain said, as if he meant it, "It's time to fish or cut bait." And Joe McNeil said, "Yes, we're a bunch of hypocrites. Come on, let's do it. Let's do it tomorrow." McCain's roommate, David Richmond, agreed. Blair hesitated. "I was thinking about my grades," he said later, just "trying to deal with that architecture and engineering course I was taking."

But Blair was outvoted. The next day, February 1, 1960, after their classes at North Carolina Agricultural and Technical College were over, the four freshmen walked into town. At the F. W. Woolworth's on South Elm Street, one of the most profitable stores in the national chain, each bought a few small things, mostly school supplies. Then, nervously, they sat down on the vinyl-covered stools at the lunch counter and tried to order coffee. These young men—seventeen and eighteen years old—were prepared to be arrested, even physically attacked. But nothing happened. The counter help ignored them as long as possible; they never got their coffee. When one worker finally reminded them, "We don't serve colored here," the four made their point: they had already been served just a few feet away when they made their purchases. Why not at the lunch counter? An elderly white woman came up to the boys and told them how proud she was of them. "We got so much courage and so much pride" from that "little old lady," McCain said later. But still nothing happened. The store closed; the manager turned out the lights. After sitting in near darkness for about forty-five minutes, the

◀ When four freshmen from North Carolina Agricultural and Technical College sat down and tried to order coffee at the whites-only Woolworth's lunch counter in Greensboro, North Carolina, they did not know if they would be arrested or even physically attacked. This photograph is from the second day of the sit-in, when the four were joined by classmates. Bettmann/Getty Images

Chronology

1960
- Sit-ins begin in Greensboro
- Birth control pill approved
- John F. Kennedy elected president
- Young Americans for Freedom write Sharon Statement

1961
- Freedom Riders protest segregation in transportation

1962
- Students for a Democratic Society issues Port Huron Statement
- Cuban missile crisis courts nuclear war

1963
- Civil rights March on Washington for Jobs and Freedom draws more than 250,000
- South Vietnamese leader Diem assassinated following U.S.-sanctioned coup d'état
- John F. Kennedy assassinated; Lyndon B. Johnson becomes president

1964
- Civil Rights Act passed by Congress
- Race riots break out in first of the "long, hot summers"
- Gulf of Tonkin Resolution passed by Congress
- Free Speech Movement begins at University of California, Berkeley
- Lyndon B. Johnson elected president

1965
- Lyndon Johnson launches Great Society programs
- United States commits ground troops to Vietnam and initiates bombing campaign
- Voting Rights Act outlaws practices preventing most African Americans from voting in southern states
- Immigration and Nationality Act lowers barriers to immigration from Asia and Latin America
- Malcolm X assassinated

1966
- National Organization for Women founded

1967
- "Summer of love" in San Francisco's Haight-Ashbury district
- Race riots erupt in Newark, Detroit, and other cities

1968
- Tet Offensive deepens fear of losing war in Vietnam
- Martin Luther King Jr. assassinated
- Robert Kennedy assassinated
- Violence erupts at Democratic National Convention
- Richard Nixon elected president

four men who had begun the sit-in movement got up and walked from the store.

The next day they returned, but they were not alone. Twenty fellow students joined the sit-in. By February 3, sixty-three of the sixty-five seats were taken. On February 4, students from other colleges arrived, and the sit-in spread to the S. H. Kress store across the street. By February 7, there were sit-ins in Winston-Salem; by February 8, in Charlotte; on February 9, sit-ins began in Raleigh. By the third week in February, students were picketing Woolworth's stores in the North, and at lunch counters throughout the South, well-dressed young men and women sat, politely asking to be served. On July 26, 1960, they won. F. W. Woolworth's ended segregation, not only in Greensboro but in all of its stores.

Experience an interactive version of this story in MindTap®.

When these four college freshmen sat down at the Woolworth's lunch counter in Greensboro, they signaled the beginning of a decade of public activism rarely matched in American history. During the 1960s, millions of Americans—many of them young people—took to the streets. Some marched for civil rights or against the war in Vietnam; others lashed out in anger over the circumstances of their lives. Passion over the events of the day revitalized democracy—and threatened to tear the nation apart.

John F. Kennedy, the nation's youngest elected president, told Americans as he took office in 1961, "The torch has been passed to a new generation." Despite his inspirational language, Kennedy had only modest success implementing his domestic agenda. As he began his third year as president, pushed by the bravery of civil rights activists and the intransigence of their white opponents, Kennedy began to offer more active support for civil rights and to propose more ambitious domestic policies. But Kennedy was assassinated in November 1963. His death seemed, to many, the end of an era of hope.

Lyndon Johnson, Kennedy's successor, called on the memory of the martyred president to launch an ambitious program of civil rights and other liberal legislation. Johnson meant to use the power of the federal government to eliminate poverty and to guarantee equal rights to all America's people. He called his vision **the Great Society**.

Despite liberal triumphs in Washington, D.C., and real gains by the African American civil rights movement, social tensions escalated during the mid-1960s. A revitalized conservative movement emerged, and Franklin Roosevelt's old New Deal coalition fractured as white southerners abandoned the Democratic Party. Many African Americans, especially in the North, were angry that poverty and racial discrimination persisted despite the passage of landmark civil rights laws, and their discontent exploded during the "long, hot summers" of the mid-1960s. White youth culture, which seemed intent on rejecting everything an older generation had worked for, created a division that Americans came to call "the generation gap."

Developments overseas also contributed to a growing national instability. After the Cuban missile crisis of 1962 brought the Soviet Union and the United States close to nuclear disaster, President John F. Kennedy and Soviet leader Nikita Khrushchev moved to reduce bilateral tensions in 1963, with the result that Cold War pressures in Europe lessened appreciably. In the rest of the world, however, the superpowers continued their intense competition. Throughout the 1960s, the United States used a variety of approaches—including foreign aid, CIA covert actions, military assaults, cultural penetration, economic sanctions, and diplomacy—in its attempts to win the Cold War, draw unaligned nations into its orbit, and defuse revolutionary nationalism. In Vietnam, Kennedy chose to expand U.S. involvement significantly. Johnson "Americanized" the war, increasing the troop-count to more than half a million in 1968.

By 1968, the war in Vietnam had divided the American people and undermined Johnson's Great Society. With the assassinations of Martin Luther King Jr. and Robert F. Kennedy—two of America's brightest leaders—that spring, with cities in flames, and with tanks in the streets of Chicago in August, the fate of the nation seemed to hang in the balance.

- *What were the successes and failures of American liberalism in the 1960s?*
- *Why did the United States expand its participation in the war in Vietnam and continue in the war so long?*
- *By 1968, many believed the fate of the nation hung in the balance. What did they think was at stake? What divided Americans, and how did they express their differences?*

26-1 Kennedy and the Cold War

▶ Why did John F. Kennedy capture the attention of the country?

▶ What position did John F. Kennedy take on the Cold War and foreign policy?

▶ How did Cuba become part of the Cold War tensions between the United States and the Soviet Union?

President **John F. Kennedy**, was, as writer Norman Mailer observed, "our leading man." Young, handsome, and vigorous, the new chief executive was the first president born in the twentieth century. Kennedy had a genuinely inquiring mind, and as a patron of the arts he brought wit and sophistication to the White House. He was born to wealth and politics: his Irish American grandfather had been mayor of Boston, and his millionaire father, Joseph P. Kennedy, had served as ambassador to Great Britain. In 1946, the young Kennedy, having returned from the Second World War a naval hero (the boat he commanded had been rammed and sunk by a Japanese destroyer in 1943, and Kennedy had saved his crew), continued the family tradition by campaigning to represent Boston in the U.S. House of Representatives. He won easily, served three terms in the House, and in 1952 was elected to the Senate.

26-1a John Fitzgerald Kennedy

As a Democrat, Kennedy inherited the New Deal commitment to America's social welfare system. He generally cast liberal votes in line with the pro-labor sentiments of his low-income, blue-collar constituents. But he avoided controversial issues, such as civil rights and the censure of Joseph McCarthy. Kennedy won a Pulitzer Prize for his *Profiles in Courage* (1956), a study of politicians who had acted on principle, but he shaded the truth when he claimed sole authorship of the book, which had been drafted substantially by aide Theodore Sorensen (though based on more than one hundred pages of notes dictated by Kennedy). In foreign policy, Senator Kennedy endorsed the Cold War policy of containment, and his interest in world affairs deepened as the 1950s progressed. His record as a legislator was not impressive, but he enjoyed an enthusiastic following, especially after his landslide reelection to the Senate in 1958.

Kennedy and his handlers worked hard to cultivate an image of him as a happy and healthy family man. To some extent, it was a ruse. He was a chronic womanizer, and his liaisons continued even after he married Jacqueline Bouvier in 1953. Nor was he the picture of physical vitality

The Great Society President Johnson's vision for America; LBJ believed the federal government must act to alleviate poverty, end racial injustice, and improve the lives of all Americans.

John F. Kennedy Thirty-fifth president of the United States (1961–1963). Assassinated in Dallas, Texas on November 22, 1963.

that his war hero status and youthful handsomeness seemed to project. As a child, he had almost died of scarlet fever, and he spent large portions of his early years in bed, suffering from one ailment after another. He developed severe back problems, made worse by his fighting experience in World War II. After the war, Kennedy was diagnosed with Addison's disease, an adrenaline deficiency that required daily injections of cortisone in order to be contained. At the time, the disease was thought to be terminal; though Kennedy survived, he was often in acute pain. As president, he would require plenty of bed rest and frequent therapeutic swims in the White House pool.

26-1b Election of 1960

Kennedy's rhetoric and style captured the imagination of many Americans. Yet his election victory over Republican

▲ Many Americans were enchanted with the youthful and photogenic Kennedys. Here, the president and his family pose outside the Palm Beach, Florida, home of the president's father after a private Easter service, April 14, 1963.

Richard Nixon in 1960 was extraordinarily narrow—118,000 votes out of nearly 69 million cast. Kennedy achieved only mixed success in the South, but he ran well in the Northeast and Midwest. His Roman Catholic faith hurt him in some states, where voters feared he would take direction from the pope, but helped in states with large Catholic populations. As the sitting vice president, Nixon was saddled with the handicaps of incumbency; he had to answer for sagging economic figures and the Soviet downing of a U-2 spy plane. Nixon also looked disagreeable on TV; in televised debates against the telegenic Kennedy, he looked alternately nervous and surly, and the camera made him appear unshaven. Perhaps worse, Eisenhower gave Nixon only a tepid endorsement. Asked to list Nixon's significant decisions as vice president, Eisenhower replied, "If you give me a week, I might think of one."

In a departure from the Eisenhower administration's staid, conservative image, the new president surrounded himself with mostly young advisers of intellectual verve, who proclaimed that they had fresh ideas for invigorating the nation; writer David Halberstam called them "the best and the brightest." Secretary of Defense Robert McNamara (age forty-four) had been an assistant professor at Harvard at twenty-four and later the whiz-kid president of the Ford Motor Company. Kennedy's special assistant for national security affairs, McGeorge Bundy (age forty-one) had become a Harvard dean at thirty-four with only a bachelor's degree. Secretary of State Dean Rusk, the old man in the group at fifty-two, had been a Rhodes Scholar in his youth. Kennedy himself was only forty-three, and his brother Robert, the attorney general, was thirty-five.

It was no accident that most of these "best and brightest" operated in the realm of foreign policy. From the start, Kennedy gave top priority to waging the Cold War. In the campaign, he had criticized Eisenhower's foreign policy as unimaginative, accusing him of missing chances to reduce the threat of nuclear war with the Soviet Union and of weakening America's standing in the Third World. Kennedy and his advisers exuded confidence that they would change things. As national security adviser McGeorge Bundy put it, "The United States is the engine of mankind, and the rest of the world is the caboose." Kennedy's inaugural address suggested no halfway measures: "Let every nation know that we shall pay any price, bear any burden, meet any hardship, support any friend, oppose any foe to assure the survival and the success of liberty."

26-1c Nation Building in the Third World

In reality, Kennedy in office would not be prepared to pay any price or bear any burden in the struggle against communism. He came to understand, sooner than many of his advisers, that there were limits to American power abroad; overall, he showed himself to be cautious and pragmatic in foreign policy. More than his predecessor, he proved willing to initiate dialogue with the Soviets, sometimes using his brother Robert as a secret back channel to Moscow. Yet

Kennedy also sought victory in the Cold War. After Soviet leader Nikita Khrushchev endorsed "wars of national liberation," such as the one in Vietnam, Kennedy called for "peaceful revolution" based on the concept of nation building. The administration set out to help developing nations through the early stages of nationhood with aid programs aimed at improving agriculture, transportation, and communications. Kennedy thus oversaw the creation of the multibillion-dollar Alliance for Progress in 1961 to spur economic development in Latin America. In the same year, he also created the Peace Corps, dispatching thousands of American teachers, agricultural specialists, and health workers, many of them right out of college, to assist authorities in developing nations.

Cynics then and later dismissed the Alliance and the Peace Corps as Cold War tools by which Kennedy sought to counter anti-Americanism and defeat communism in the developing world. The programs did have those aims, but both were also born of genuine humanitarianism. The Peace Corps in particular embodied both the idealistic, can-do spirit of the 1960s and Americans' long pursuit of moral leadership in the world. "More than any other entity," historian Elizabeth Cobbs Hoffman has written, "the Peace Corps broached an age-old dilemma of U.S. foreign policy: how to reconcile the imperatives and temptations of power politics with the ideals of freedom and self-determination for all nations."

It was one thing to broach the dilemma, and quite another to resolve it. Kennedy and his aides considered themselves supportive of social revolution in the Third World, but they could not imagine the legitimacy of communist involvement in any such uprising, or that developing countries might wish to be neutral in the East-West struggle. In addition to largely benevolent programs like the Peace Corps, therefore, the administration also relied on the more insidious concept of counterinsurgency to defeat revolutionaries who challenged pro-American Third World governments. American military and technical advisers trained native troops and police forces to quell unrest.

Nation building and counterinsurgency encountered numerous problems. The Alliance for Progress was only partly successful; infant mortality rates improved, but Latin American economies registered unimpressive growth rates, and class divisions continued to widen, exacerbating political unrest. Americans assumed that the U.S. model of capitalism and representative government could be transferred successfully to foreign cultures. Although many foreign peoples welcomed U.S. economic assistance and craved American material culture, they resented interference by outsiders. And because aid was usually transmitted through a self-interested elite, it often failed to reach the very poor.

26-1d Soviet-American Tensions

Nor did the new president have success in relations with the Soviet Union. A summit meeting with Soviet leader Nikita Khrushchev in Vienna in June 1961 went poorly, with the two leaders disagreeing over the preconditions for peace and stability in the world. Consequently, the administration's first year witnessed little movement on controlling the nuclear arms race or even on getting a superpower ban on testing nuclear weapons in the atmosphere or underground. The latter objective mattered a great deal to Kennedy, who saw a test ban as a prerequisite to preventing additional nations from getting the terrifying weapon. Instead, both superpowers continued testing and accelerated their arms production. In 1961, the U.S. military budget shot up 15 percent; by mid-1964, U.S. nuclear weapons had increased by 150 percent. Government advice to citizens to build fallout shelters in their backyards intensified public fear of devastating war.

If war occurred, many believed it would be over the persistent problem of Berlin. In mid-1961, Khrushchev ratcheted up the tension by demanding an end to Western occupation of West Berlin and a reunification of East and West Germany. Kennedy replied that the United States would stand by its commitment to West Berlin and West Germany. In August, the Soviets—at the urging of the East German regime—erected a concrete and barbed-wire barricade across the divided city to halt the exodus of East Germans into the more prosperous and politically free West Berlin. The Berlin Wall inspired protests throughout the noncommunist world, but Kennedy privately mused that "a wall is a hell of a lot better than a war." The ugly barrier shut off the flow of refugees, and the crisis passed.

26-1e Bay of Pigs Invasion

Yet Kennedy knew that Khrushchev would continue to press for advantage in various parts of the globe. The president was particularly rankled by the growing Soviet assistance to the Cuban government of Fidel Castro. Kennedy once acknowledged that most American allies thought the United States had a "fixation" with Cuba; whether true of the country as a whole, he and his inner circle certainly did. The Eisenhower administration had contested the Cuban revolution and bequeathed to the Kennedy administration a partially developed CIA plan to overthrow Fidel Castro: CIA-trained Cuban exiles would land and secure a beachhead; the Cuban people would rise up against Castro and welcome a new government brought in from the United States.

Kennedy approved the plan, and the attack took place on April 17, 1961, as twelve hundred exiles landed at the swampy Bay of Pigs in Cuba. But no discontented Cubans were there to greet them, only troops loyal to the Castro government. The invaders were quickly surrounded and captured. Kennedy had tried to keep the U.S. participation in the operation hidden—for this reason, he refused to provide air cover for the attackers—but the CIA's role swiftly became public. Anti-American sentiment shot up throughout Latin America. Castro, concluding that the United States would not take defeat well and might launch another invasion, looked even more toward the Soviet Union for a military and economic lifeline.

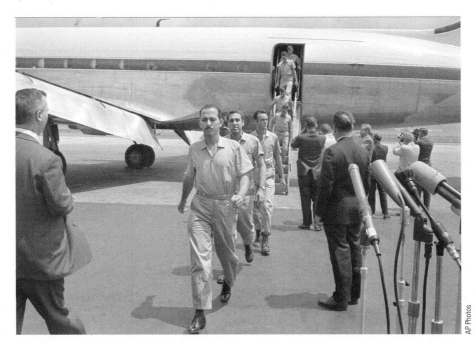

▲ Cuban commandos march from their plane at National Airport in Washington, on May 22, 1961. The commandos were released by Fidel Castro as part of a plan to swap five hundred U.S. tractors or bulldozers for 1214 men captured in the failed Bay of Pigs operation.

Embarrassed by the Bay of Pigs fiasco, Kennedy ratcheted up the pressure on Castro. The CIA soon hatched a project called Operation Mongoose to disrupt the island's trade, support raids on Cuba from Miami, and plot to kill Castro. The agency's assassination schemes included providing Castro with cigars laced with explosives and deadly poison, and an attempt to harpoon him while he was snorkeling at a Caribbean resort. The United States also tightened its economic blockade and undertook military maneuvers in the Caribbean. The Joint Chiefs of Staff sketched plans to spark a rebellion in Cuba that would be followed by an invasion of U.S. troops. "If I had been in Moscow or Havana at that time," defense secretary Robert McNamara later remarked, "I would have believed the Americans were preparing for an invasion."

26-1f Cuban Missile Crisis

McNamara knew whereof he spoke, for both Castro and Khrushchev believed an invasion was coming. This was one reason for the Soviet leader's risky decision in 1962 to secretly deploy nuclear missiles in Cuba: he hoped the presence of such weapons on the island would deter any attack. But Khrushchev also had other motives. Installing atomic weaponry in Cuba would instantly improve the Soviet position in the nuclear balance of power, he believed, and might also force Kennedy to resolve the German problem once and for all. Khrushchev still wanted to oust the West from Berlin, and he also worried that Washington might provide West Germany with nuclear weapons. What better way to prevent such a move than to put Soviet missiles just ninety miles off the coast of Florida? With Castro's support, Khrushchev moved to install the weapons. The world soon faced brinkmanship at its most frightening.

In mid-October 1962, a U-2 plane flying over Cuba photographed the missile sites. The president immediately organized a special Executive Committee (ExComm) of advisers to find a way to force the missiles and their nuclear warheads out of Cuba. Options that the ExComm considered ranged from full-scale invasion to limited bombing to quiet diplomacy. Most participants favored military action, but Kennedy demurred; patiently, he steered the group toward a less confrontational position. McNamara then proposed the formula the president ultimately accepted: a naval quarantine of Cuba.

Kennedy addressed the nation on television on October 22 and demanded that the Soviets retreat. U.S. warships began crisscrossing the Caribbean, while B-52s with nuclear bombs took to the skies. Khrushchev replied that the missiles would be withdrawn if the United States pledged never to attack Cuba. And he added that American Jupiter missiles aimed at the Soviet Union must be removed from Turkey. Edgy advisers predicted war, and for several days the world teetered on the brink of disaster. Then, on October 28, came a compromise. The United States promised not to invade Cuba, secretly pledging to withdraw the Jupiters from Turkey in exchange for the withdrawal of Soviet offensive forces from Cuba. Fearing accidents or some provocative action by Castro that might start a "real fire," Khrushchev decided to settle without consulting the Cubans. The missiles were removed from the island.

Many observers then and later called it Kennedy's finest hour. Tapes of the ExComm meetings recorded during the crisis reveal a deeply engaged, calmly authoritative commander-in-chief, committed to removing the missiles peacefully if possible. Critics claim that Kennedy helped cause the crisis in the first place with his anti-Cuban projects; some contend that quiet diplomacy could have achieved the same result, without the extraordinary tension. Other skeptics assert that Kennedy rejected a diplomatic solution because he feared the Republicans would ride the missiles to victory in the upcoming midterm elections. Still, it cannot be denied that the president handled the crisis skillfully, exercising both restraint and flexibility. At this most tense moment of the Cold War, Kennedy had proven equal to the task.

The **Cuban missile crisis** was a watershed in the Soviet-American relationship. Both Kennedy and Khrushchev acted with greater prudence in its aftermath, taking determined steps toward improved bilateral relations. Much of the hostility drained out of the relationship. In August, the adversaries signed a treaty banning nuclear tests in the atmosphere, the oceans, and outer space. They also installed a coded wire-telegraph "hot line" staffed around the clock by translators and technicians, to allow near-instant communication between the capitals. Both sides refrained from further confrontation in Berlin.

Together, these steps reversed the trend of the previous years and began to build much-needed mutual trust. By the autumn of 1963, Cold War tensions in Europe were subsiding as both sides accepted the status quo of a divided continent and a fortified border. Still, the arms race continued and in some respects accelerated, and the superpower competition in the Third World showed little sign of cooling down.

26-2 Marching for Freedom

▶ What methods did Americans who fought for civil rights adopt to challenge segregation and disfranchisement in the 1960s?

▶ What was the relationship between the federal government and the civil rights movement in the 1960s?

▶ How did national coverage of attacks on those struggling for equal rights affect the civil rights movement?

From the beginning of his presidency, John Kennedy believed that the Cold War was the most important issue facing the American people. But in the early 1960s, young civil rights activists—building on a decades-long struggle—seized the national stage and demanded that the force of the federal government be mobilized behind them. They won victories in their struggle for racial justice, but their gains were paid for in blood.

26-2a Students and the Movement

The Woolworth's lunch counter sit-in begun by the four freshmen from North Carolina A&T marked a turning point in the African American struggle for civil rights. In 1960, six years after the *Brown* decision had declared "separate but equal" unconstitutional, only 10 percent of southern public schools had begun desegregation. Fewer than one in four adult black Americans in the South had access to the voting booth, and water fountains in public places were still labeled "White Only" and "Colored Only." But one year after the young men had sat down at the all-white lunch counter in Greensboro, more than seventy thousand Americans—most of them college students—had participated in the sit-in movement, challenging segregation at lunch counters in the South and protesting at the northern branches of national chains that practiced segregation in their southern stores.

The young people who created the **Student Nonviolent Coordinating Committee (SNCC)** in the spring of 1960 to help coordinate the sit-in movement were, like Martin Luther King Jr., committed to nonviolence. In the years to come, such young people would risk their lives in the struggle for social justice.

26-2b Freedom Rides and Voter Registration

On May 4, 1961, thirteen members of the Congress of Racial Equality (CORE), a nonviolent civil rights organization formed during World War II, purchased bus tickets in Washington, D.C., for a 1,500-mile trip through the South to New Orleans. This racially integrated group, calling themselves Freedom Riders, meant to show that, despite Supreme Court rulings ordering the desegregation of interstate buses and bus stations, Jim Crow still ruled in the South. These men and women knew they were risking their lives, and some suffered injuries from which they never recovered. One bus was firebombed outside Anniston, Alabama. Riders were badly beaten in Birmingham. In Montgomery, after reinforcements replaced the injured, a mob of more than a thousand whites attacked riders on another bus with baseball bats and steel bars. Police were nowhere to be seen; Montgomery's police commissioner declared, "We have no intention of standing guard for a bunch of troublemakers coming into our city."

News of the violent attacks made headlines around the world. In the Soviet Union, commentators pointed out the "savage nature of American freedom and democracy." One southern business leader, in Tokyo to promote Birmingham as a site for international business development, saw Japanese interest evaporate when photographs of the Birmingham attacks appeared in Tokyo newspapers.

In America, the violence—reported by the national news media—forced Americans to confront the reality of racial discrimination and hatred in their nation. In the south, significant numbers of middle-class whites who rejected Klan violence had nonetheless participated in the "massive resistance" to integration following the *Brown* decision, and even racial moderates remained highly suspicious of interference by the "Yankee" federal government almost a century after the Civil War. The Freedom Rides

Cuban missile crisis Confrontation between the Soviet Union and the United States in 1962 regarding the Soviet deployment of nuclear missiles in Cuba. It put the world on the brink of nuclear disaster until the two nations reached a compromise.

Student Nonviolent Coordinating Committee (SNCC) Civil rights organization founded by young people that played a key role in grassroots organizing in the South in the early 1960s.

made some think differently. The *Atlanta Journal* editorialized: "[I]t is time for the decent people . . . to muzzle the jackals." The national and international outcry pushed a reluctant President Kennedy to act. In a direct challenge to southern doctrines of states' rights, Kennedy sent federal marshals to Alabama to safeguard the Freedom Riders and their supporters. At the same time, bowing to white southern pressure, he allowed the Freedom Riders to be arrested in Mississippi.

While some activists pursued these "direct action" tactics, others worked to build black political power in the South. Beginning in 1961, thousands of SNCC volunteers, many of them high school and college students, risked their lives walking the dusty back roads of Mississippi and Georgia, encouraging African Americans to register to vote. Some SNCC volunteers were white, and some were from the North, but many were black southerners, and many were from low-income families. These volunteers understood from experience how racism, powerlessness, and poverty intersected in the lives of African Americans.

26-2c Kennedy and Civil Rights

President Kennedy was generally sympathetic—though not terribly committed—to the civil rights movement, and he realized that racial oppression hurt the United States in the Cold War struggle for international opinion. However, like Franklin D. Roosevelt, he also understood that if he alienated conservative southern Democrats in Congress, his legislative programs would founder. Thus, he appointed five die-hard segregationists to the federal bench in the Deep South and delayed issuing an executive order forbidding segregation in federally subsidized housing (a pledge made in the 1960 campaign) until late 1962. Furthermore, he allowed FBI director J. Edgar Hoover to harass Martin Luther King and other civil rights leaders, using wiretaps and surveillance to gather personal information and circulating rumors of communist connections and of personal improprieties in efforts to discredit their leadership.

But grassroots civil rights activism—and the violence of white mobs—relentlessly forced Kennedy's hand. In September 1962, the president ordered 500 U.S. marshals to protect James Meredith, the first African American student to attempt to enroll at the University of Mississippi. In response, thousands of whites attacked the marshals with guns, gasoline bombs, bricks, and pipes. The mob killed two men and seriously wounded 160 federal marshals. The marshals did not back down, nor did James Meredith. He broke the color line at "Ole Miss."

26-2d Birmingham and the Children's Crusade

In 1961, the Freedom Riders had captured the attention of the nation and the larger Cold War world, and had forced the hand of the president. Martin Luther King Jr., having risen through the Montgomery bus boycott to leadership in the movement, drew a lesson from the Freedom Rides. He and his allies, while still committed to principles of nonviolence, concluded that the only way to advance the struggle for civil rights was to provoke a crisis that would create pressure for further change. King and his Southern Christian Leadership Conference (SCLC) began to plan a 1963 campaign in one of the most violently racist cities in America: Birmingham, Alabama. Fully aware that their nonviolent protests would draw a violent response, they called their plan "Project C"—for "confrontation." King wanted all Americans to see the racist hate and violence that marred their nation.

Through most of April 1963, nonviolent protests in Birmingham led to hundreds of arrests. Then, on May 2, in a highly controversial action, King and the parents of Birmingham raised the stakes. They put children, some as young as six, on the front lines of protest. As about a thousand black children marched for civil rights, police commissioner Eugene "Bull" Connor ordered his police to train monitor water guns—powerful enough to strip bark from a tree at 100 feet—on them. The water guns mowed the children down. Then police loosed attack dogs. As footage played on the evening news, the nation watched with horror. President Kennedy, once again, was pushed into action. He demanded that Birmingham's white business and political elite negotiate a settlement. Under pressure, they agreed. The Birmingham movement had won a concrete victory. Even more, activists had pushed civil rights to the fore of President Kennedy's political agenda.

26-2e "Segregation Forever!"

The Kennedy administration also confronted the defiant governor of Alabama, George C. Wallace. On June 11, Wallace fulfilled a promise to "bar the schoolhouse door" himself to prevent the desegregation of the University of Alabama. Hearing echoes of Wallace's January 1963 inaugural pledge "Segregation now, segregation tomorrow, segregation forever!" and facing a nation rocked by hundreds of civil rights protests, many of them met with white mob violence, Kennedy committed the power of the federal government to guarantee racial justice—even over the opposition of individual states. The next evening, June 12, in a televised address, Kennedy told the American people, "Now the time has come for this nation to fulfill its promise." A few hours later, thirty-seven-year-old civil rights leader Medgar Evers was murdered—in front of his children—in his driveway in Jackson, Mississippi. The next week, the president asked Congress to pass a comprehensive civil rights bill that would end legal discrimination on the basis of race in the United States.

26-2f March on Washington

On August 28, 1963, a quarter-million Americans gathered in the steamy heat on the Washington Mall. They came from all over America to show Congress their support for Kennedy's civil rights bill; many also wanted federal action to guarantee work opportunities. Behind the scenes, organizers from major civil rights groups—SCLC, CORE, SNCC, the NAACP, the Urban League, and A. Philip Randolph's Brotherhood of Sleeping Car Porters—grappled with growing tensions within the movement. SNCC activists saw Kennedy's

"Project C" and National Opinion

This photograph of a police dog attacking a seventeen-year-old demonstrator during a civil rights march in Birmingham, Alabama, appeared on the front page of the *New York Times* on May 4, 1963, just above a second photograph of a fireman spraying a group that included three teenage girls with a high-pressure fire hose.

The following day, President Kennedy discussed this photo in a meeting in the White House.

CRITICAL THINKING

- Some historians argue that photographs not only document history, they make it. Is that statement true in this case?

- How does this photograph fit into Martin Luther King's plans for "Project C" (see "Birmingham and the Children's Crusade," Section 26-2d)?

- What difference might it make that the *New York Times* editors chose to run this photograph rather than one of the many others taken that day?

▲ Mass media coverage helped galvanize public opinion in support of civil rights protesters.

proposed legislation as too little, too late; they wanted radical action. King and other older leaders counseled the virtues of moderation. The movement was beginning to splinter.

Those divisions were not completely hidden. SNCC's John Lewis proclaimed his "misgiving," asking, "Where is the political party that will make it unnecessary to march on Washington?" What most Americans saw, however, was a celebration of unity. Black and white celebrities joined hands; folksingers sang songs of freedom. Television networks cut away from afternoon soap operas as Martin Luther King Jr., in southern preacher cadences, prophesied a day when "all God's children, black men and white men, Jews and Gentiles, Protestants and Catholics, will be able to join hands and sing in the words of the old Negro spiritual, Free at last!

Free at last! Thank God Almighty, we are free at last!" The 1963 March on Washington for Jobs and Freedom was a moment of triumph, powerfully demonstrating to the nation the determination of its African American citizens to secure equality and justice. But the struggle was far from over. Just days later, white supremacists bombed the Sixteenth Street Baptist Church in Birmingham, killing four black girls.

26-2g Freedom Summer

In the face of violence, the struggle for racial justice continued. During the summer of 1964, more than one thousand white students joined the voter mobilization project in Mississippi. These workers formed Freedom Schools, teaching literacy and constitutional rights, and helped organize the Mississippi

Freedom Democratic Party as an alternative to Mississippi's white-only Democratic Party. Key SNCC organizers also believed that large numbers of white volunteers would focus national attention on Mississippi repression and violence. Not all went smoothly: local black activists were sometimes frustrated when well-educated white volunteers stepped into decision-making roles. Far worse, project workers were arrested, shot at, bombed, and beaten. On June 21, local black activist James Cheney and two white volunteers, Michael Schwerner and Andrew Goodman, were murdered by a Klan mob. Four days later, before their bodies had been found, Walter Cronkite told the nightly news audience that all of America was watching Mississippi. CBS played footage of black and white workers holding hands, singing "We Shall Overcome." That summer, black and white activists risked their lives together, challenging the racial caste system of the Deep South.

26-3 Liberalism and the Great Society

▶ How did Lyndon B. Johnson seek to use the federal government to improve the quality of Americans' lives?

▶ How did different groups of Americans, including political parties, respond to the federal government's active social agenda in the 1960s?

▶ What were the features of the federal government's "War on Poverty"?

By 1963, with civil rights at the top of his domestic agenda, Kennedy seemed to be taking a new path. Campaigning in 1960, he had promised to lead Americans into a "New Frontier," a society in which the federal government would work to eradicate poverty, restore the nation's cities, guarantee health care to the elderly, and provide decent schools for all America's children. But few of Kennedy's domestic initiatives were passed into law, in part because Kennedy did not use his political capital to support them. Lacking a popular mandate in the 1960 election, fearful of alienating southern Democrats in Congress, and without a strong vision of domestic reform, Kennedy let his administration's social policy agenda languish.

Instead, Kennedy focused on less controversial attempts to fine-tune the American economy, believing that continued economic growth and prosperity would solve America's social problems. Kennedy's vision was perhaps best realized in America's space program. As the Soviets drew ahead in the Cold War space race, Kennedy vowed in 1961 to put a man on the moon before decade's end. With billions in new funding, the National Aeronautics and Space Administration (NASA) began the Apollo program. And in February 1962, astronaut John Glenn orbited the earth in the space capsule *Friendship* 7.

Lyndon B. Johnson Thirty-sixth president of the United States (1963–1969); champion of civil rights legislation and the war on poverty, who presided over America's entry into large-scale war in Vietnam.

26-3a Kennedy Assassination

The nation would not learn what sort of president John Kennedy might have become. On November 22, 1963, Kennedy visited Texas, the home state of his vice president, **Lyndon B. Johnson**. In Dallas, riding with his wife, Jackie, in an open-top limousine, Kennedy was cheered by thousands of people lining the motorcade's route. Suddenly, shots rang out. The president crumpled, shot in the head. Tears ran down the cheeks of CBS anchorman Walter Cronkite as he told the nation their president was dead. The word spread quickly, in whispered messages to classroom teachers, by somber announcements in factories and offices, through the stunned faces of people on the street.

That same day, police captured a suspect: Lee Harvey Oswald, a former U.S. Marine (dishonorably discharged) who had once attempted to gain Soviet citizenship. Just two days later, in full view of millions of TV viewers, Oswald himself was shot dead by a shady nightclub owner named Jack Ruby. Americans, already in shock, didn't know what to think. What was Ruby's motive? Was he silencing Oswald to prevent him from implicating others? (The seven-member Warren Commission, appointed by Lyndon Johnson and headed by U.S. Supreme Court Chief Justice Earl Warren, concluded the following year that Oswald had acted alone.) For four days, the tragedy played uninterrupted on American television. Millions of Americans watched their president's funeral: the brave young widow behind a black veil; a riderless horse; three-year-old "John-John" saluting his father's casket. In one awful moment in Dallas, the reality of the Kennedy presidency had been transformed into myth, the man into martyr. People would remember Kennedy less for any specific accomplishment than for his youthful enthusiasm, his inspirational rhetoric, and the romance he brought to American political life. In a peculiar way, he accomplished more in death than in life. In the post-assassination atmosphere of grief and remorse, Lyndon Johnson, sworn in as president aboard *Air Force One*, invoked Kennedy's memory to push through the most ambitious program of legislation since the New Deal.

26-3b Johnson and the Great Society

The new president was a big and passionate man, different from his predecessor in almost every respect. While Kennedy had been raised to wealth and privilege, Johnson had grown up in modest circumstances in the Texas hill country. He was as earthy as Kennedy was elegant, prone to colorful curses and willing to use his physical size to his advantage. Advisers and aides reported that he expected them to follow him into the bathroom and conduct business while he showered or used the toilet. But Johnson had been in national politics most of his adult life. He filled an empty congressional seat from Texas in 1937, and as Senate majority leader from 1954 through 1960, he had learned how to manipulate people and wield power to achieve his ends. Now, as president, he used these political skills in an attempt to unite and reassure the nation. "Let us here highly resolve," he told a joint session of

▲ Poverty in America was not only an urban problem, and President Johnson visited poverty-stricken areas throughout the nation during the summer of 1964. Here he talks with the Marlow family of Rocky Mount, North Carolina, on the steps of their farmhouse.

Congress five days after the assassination, "that John Fitzgerald Kennedy did not live—or die—in vain."

Johnson, a liberal in the style of Franklin D. Roosevelt, believed that the federal government must work actively to improve the lives of Americans. In a 1964 commencement address at the University of Michigan, he described his vision of a nation built on "abundance and liberty for all . . . demand[ing] an end to poverty and racial injustice . . . where every child can find knowledge to enrich his mind and to enlarge his talents . . . where every man can renew contact with nature . . . where men are more concerned with the quality of their goals than the quantity of their goods." Johnson called this vision "the Great Society."

26-3c Civil Rights Act

Johnson made civil rights his top legislative priority, and in July he signed into law the **Civil Rights Act of 1964**. This legislation grew from the civil rights protests of the early 1960s: In the wake of violent attacks on civil rights protesters in Birmingham, the Kennedy administration had crafted a bill outlawing *legal* discrimination on the basis of race, color, religion, or national origin in employment, federal programs, voting, and public accommodation. This legislation was hard won, passing only after Kennedy's assassination. In the Senate a "southern bloc" filibustered for 57 days, preventing not only a vote on the bill but any other congressional business. In

the end, growing public support for civil rights, pressure from the Johnson administration, savvy legislative maneuvering, compromise, and a few acts of political heroism brought the bill to a vote.

The Civil Rights Act of 1964 gave the civil rights movement a major legislative victory, in part because it provided means to enforce its provisions: federal authority to withhold funds from public agencies or federal contractors that discriminated, and an Equal Employment Opportunity Commission (EEOC) to investigate claims of job discrimination.

The Civil Rights Act did not only prohibit racial discrimination; it also made it illegal to discriminate on the basis of sex. The original bill had not included sex discrimination. That provision was introduced by a southern congressman who—though he had long supported the pro-women's rights National Woman's Party—meant to undermine the bill. His proposal was met with laughter and jeers by members of the House of Representatives who found the notion of women's legal equality ridiculous. Representative Martha Griffiths, however, saw an opening. In the end, a strange coalition of eleven female representatives (of twelve total), Republicans,

Civil Rights Act of 1964 The most significant civil rights law in modern U.S. history; outlawed legal discrimination based on race color, religion, national origin, and sex, and created means to enforce its provisions.

and anti–civil rights Democrats (who later voted against the bill as a whole) backed the amendment that listed sex as a protected category. (Most liberal Democrats, focused on race, opposed the addition.) In the first years after the bill was passed the EEOC did not take sex discrimination seriously, despite a flood of complaints from women. As one EEOC staffer argued in 1965, complaints about sex discrimination "undermine the efforts on behalf of minority groups" because they divert "attention and resources from the more serious allegations by members of racial, religious, and ethnic communities." Frustrated by such responses, a group of about three hundred prominent women and men came together in 1966 to form the **National Organization for Women (NOW)**, an organization created to pressure the EEOC to enforce the law and to work for women's equality in American society. NOW would play a key role in the developing women's movement, which expanded dramatically during the late 1960s and the 1970s (see "The Women's Movement," Section 27-1d).

Many Americans did not believe it was the federal government's job to fight poverty or to end racial discrimination. Racism bolstered opposition to federal action, as it remained powerful, and not only in the South. Throughout the nation, millions of conservative Americans believed that the federal government had been overstepping its constitutional boundaries since the New Deal. They wanted to reinforce local control and states' rights in the face of growing federal power. In the 1964 election, this conservative vision was championed by the Republican candidate, Arizona senator Barry Goldwater.

26-3d Election of 1964

Goldwater had not only voted against the 1964 Civil Rights Act; he also opposed the national Social Security system. Like many conservatives, he believed that individual *liberty*, not equality, was the most important American value. Goldwater's calls for "law and order" drew cheers from voters. He argued that the United States needed a more powerful national military to fight communism; in campaign speeches, he suggested that the United States might use tactical nuclear weapons against its enemies. "Extremism in the defense of liberty is no vice," he told delegates at the 1964 Republican National Convention.

Goldwater's campaign slogan, "In your heart you know he's right," was turned against him by Johnson's supporters: "In your heart you know he's right . . . far right," one punned. Another version warned of Goldwater's willingness to use nuclear weapons: "In your heart you know he might." Johnson campaigned on his record, with an unemployment rate under 4 percent and economic growth at better than 6 percent. But he knew that his support of civil rights had broken apart the New Deal coalition. Shortly after signing the Civil Rights Act of 1964, he told an aide, "I think we just delivered the south to the Republican Party for my lifetime and yours."

The tension between Johnson's support of civil rights and his need for southern Democratic support came to a head at the 1964 Democratic National Convention. Two delegations had arrived from Mississippi, a state in which discriminatory literacy tests and violence disfranchised its black citizens: an official, all-white delegation and a multiracial delegation from the Mississippi Freedom Democratic Party (MFDP). In response, white representatives from southern states threatened to walk out if the MFDP delegates were seated. MFDP delegate Fannie Lou Hamer offered powerful testimony to the convention's credentials committee, concluding, "[If] the Freedom Party is not seated now, I question America." Johnson tried to engineer a compromise, but the MFDP had no interest in political deals. "We didn't come all this way for no two seats," Hamer said, and the delegation walked out.

Johnson lost the MFDP, and he also lost the Deep South—the first Democrat since the Civil War to do so. Yet he won the election by a landslide, and American voters also gave him the most liberal Congress in American history. With the mandate provided by a record 61.1 percent of the popular vote, Johnson launched his Great Society. Congress responded to Johnson's election with the most sweeping reform legislation since 1935.

Civil rights remained a critical issue. In late 1964, Martin Luther King Jr. and other leaders turned to Selma, Alabama—a town with a history of vicious response to civil rights protest—seeking another public confrontation that would mobilize national support and federal action to support voting rights. That confrontation came on March 6, 1965, when state troopers turned electric cattle prods, chains, and tear gas against peaceful marchers as they crossed the Edmund Pettus Bridge on the way to Montgomery. On March 15, the president addressed Congress and the nation, offering full support for a second monumental civil rights bill, the **Voting Rights Act of 1965**. This act outlawed practices that had prevented most black citizens in the Deep South from voting and provided for federal oversight of elections in districts where there was evidence of past discrimination (see Map 26.1). Within two years, African American voter registration in Mississippi jumped from 7 percent to almost 60 percent. Black elected officials became increasingly common in southern states over the following decade.

26-3e Improving American Life

Seeking to improve the quality of American life, the Johnson administration established new student loan and grant programs to help low- and moderate-income Americans

National Organization for Women (NOW) Founded in 1966, a civil rights group for women that lobbied for equal opportunity, filed lawsuits against gender discrimination, and mobilized public opinion against sexism.

Voting Rights Act of 1965 Law that outlawed practices that prevented African Americans in the South from voting, and provided for federal oversight of elections in districts where African Americans had been disfranchised.

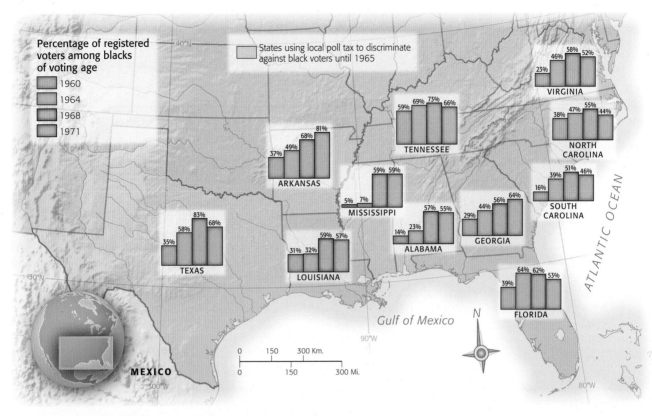

Map 26.1 African American Voting Rights, 1960–1971

After passage of the 1965 Voting Rights Act, African American registration skyrocketed in Mississippi and Alabama, and rose substantially in other southern states. *Source: From* Voter Mobilization and the Politics of Race: The South and Universal Suffrage, 1952–1984 *by Harold W. Stanley. Copyright © 1987 by Praeger Publishers. Reproduced with permission of ABC-CLIO, LLC.*

attend college, and created the National Endowment for the Arts and the National Endowment for the Humanities. The **Immigration Act of 1965** ended the racially-based quotas that had shaped American immigration policy for decades. And Johnson supported important consumer protection legislation, including the 1966 National Traffic and Motor Vehicle Safety Act, which was inspired by Ralph Nader's exposé of the automobile industry, *Unsafe at Any Speed* (1965).

Environmentalists found an ally in the Johnson administration. First Lady Claudia Alta Taylor Johnson (known to all as "Lady Bird") successfully campaigned for laws restricting the billboards and junkyards that had sprung up along the nation's new interstate highway system. Johnson signed "preservation" legislation to protect wilderness areas and supported laws to control environmental pollution.

26-3f War on Poverty

At the heart of Johnson's Great Society was the **War on Poverty**. Johnson and other liberals believed that, in a time of great economic affluence, the nation should devote its resources to programs that could end "poverty, ignorance and hunger as intractable, permanent features of American society." Beginning in 1964, the Johnson administration passed more than a score of major laws meant to do so (see Table 26.1).

Johnson's goal, in his words, was "to offer the forgotten fifth of our people opportunity, not doles." Thus, many new laws focused on increasing opportunity. Billions of federal dollars went to local governments and school districts to pay for programs meant to improve opportunities for the poor, from preschoolers (Head Start) to high schoolers (Upward Bound) to young adults (Job Corps). The Model Cities program targeted "blighted" urban neighborhoods with federal funds for employment, housing, education, and health. Community Action Programs, working from the assumption that community residents best understood their own needs, channeled federal funds for antipoverty programs directly to neighborhood groups.

Immigration Act of 1965 Law that abolished the national origins quotas of the 1920s, transforming U.S. immigration policy.

War on Poverty Campaign launched by Johnson administration in 1964, based on a set of major laws meant to offer greater opportunity to Americans living in poverty.

Table 26.1 Great Society Achievements, 1964–1966

	1964	1965	1966
Civil Rights	Civil Rights Act Equal Employment Opportunity Commission Twenty-fourth Amendment	Voting Rights Act	
War on Poverty	Economic Opportunity Act Office of Economic Opportunity Job Corps Legal Services for the Poor VISTA		Model Cities
Education		Elementary and Secondary Education Act Head Start Upward Bound	
Environment		Water Quality Act Air Quality Act	Clean Water Restoration Act
New Government Agencies		Department of Housing and Urban Development National Endowments for the Arts and Humanities	Department of Transportation
Other		Medicare and Medicaid Immigration and Nationality Act	

Note: The Great Society of the mid-1960s saw the biggest burst of reform legislation since the New Deal of the 1930s.

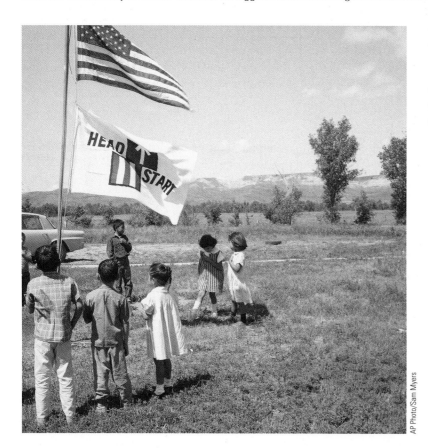

◀ Sioux children pledge allegiance to the U.S. flag in a reservation-based Head Start program, Red Shirt, South Dakota, 1965. One of several programs established by the 1964 Economic Opportunity Act, Head Start prepared pre-schoolers from low-income families for grade school.

AP Photo/Sam Myers

The Johnson administration also tried to ensure basic economic safeguards, expanding the existing Food Stamp program and earmarking billions of dollars to construct public housing and subsidize rents. Aid to Families with Dependent Children (AFDC), the basic welfare program created during the New Deal, expanded both benefits and eligibility. And comprehensive health care—a goal of liberals since the 1940s—made progress as, for the first time, federal programs guaranteed health care for those aged sixty-five and older (**Medicare**) and the poor (**Medicaid**).

The War on Poverty was controversial from its beginnings. Leftists believed the government was doing too little to change fundamental structural inequality. Conservatives argued that Great Society programs created dependency among America's poor. Policy analysts noted that some programs were ill conceived and badly implemented. Even supporters acknowledged that programs were vastly underfunded and marred by political compromises. Responding to criticisms, Joseph Califano, one of the "generals" in the War on Poverty, claimed, "Whatever historians of the Great Society say twenty years later, they must admit we tried, and I believe they will conclude that America is a better place because we did."

Decades later, most historians judge the War on Poverty a mixed success. War on Poverty programs offered better housing, health care, and nutrition to the nation's poor. By 1975, for instance, the number of eligible Americans receiving food stamps had increased from 600,000 (in 1965) to 17 million. Poverty among the elderly fell from about 40 percent in 1960 to 16 percent in 1974, due largely to increased Social Security benefits and to Medicare. As federal spending for Social Security, health care, welfare, and education more than doubled between 1965 and 1970, the War on Poverty undoubtedly improved the quality of life for many low-income Americans (see Figure 26.1).

But War on Poverty programs less successfully addressed the root causes of poverty. Neither the Job Corps nor Community Action Programs showed significant results. Economic growth, not Johnson administration policies, was primarily responsible for the dramatic decrease in overall poverty rates—from 22.4 percent of Americans in 1959 to 11 percent in 1973. And one measure of poverty remained unchanged: 11 million Americans in female-headed households remained poor at the end of the decade—the same number as in 1963.

Political compromises that shaped Great Society programs also created long-term problems. For example, Congress accommodated the interests of doctors and hospitals in its Medicare legislation by allowing federal reimbursements of hospitals' "reasonable costs" and doctors' "reasonable charges" in treating elderly patients. With no incentives for doctors or hospitals to hold prices down, the cost of health care rose dramatically. National health care expenditures as a percentage of the gross national product rose by almost 44 percent from 1960 to 1971.

Johnson's Great Society was not an unqualified success, but it was a moment in which many Americans believed they could solve the problems of poverty and disease and discrimination—and that it was necessary to try.

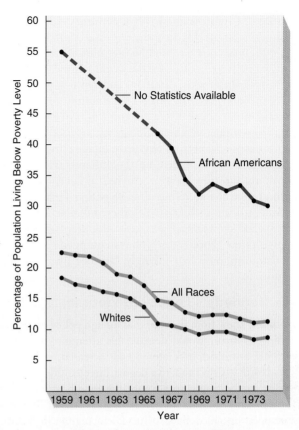

Figure 26.1 Poverty in America for Whites, African Americans, and All Races, 1959–1974

Because of rising levels of economic prosperity, combined with the impact of Great Society programs, the percentage of Americans living in poverty in 1974 was half as high as in 1959. African Americans still were far more likely than white Americans to be poor. In 1959, more than half of all blacks (55.1 percent) were poor; in 1974, the figure remained high (30.3 percent). The government did not record data on African American poverty for the years 1960 through 1965.

26-4 Johnson and Vietnam

▶ Why did the Johnson administration escalate American involvement in Vietnam?

▶ How did the North Vietnamese counter increased U.S. military involvement?

▶ What was the nature of American military involvement and the soldier's experience in the war?

▶ What divisions emerged within the government over America's presence in Vietnam?

Johnson's domestic ambitions were threatened from an early point by turmoil overseas. In foreign policy,

Medicare Program providing government health insurance for Americans aged sixty-five and older; created by Congress under President Johnson's leadership in 1965.

Medicaid Program providing health care for the poor; created by Congress under President Johnson's leadership in 1965.

he held firmly to ideas about U.S. superiority and the menace of communism. He saw the world in simple, bipolar terms—them against us—and he saw a lot of "them." But, mostly, he preferred not to see the world beyond America's shores at all. International affairs had never much interested him, and he had little appreciation for foreign cultures. Once, on a visit to Thailand while vice president, he flew into a rage when an aide gently advised him that the Thai people recoil from physical contact with strangers. Dammit, Johnson exploded, he shook hands with people everywhere, and they loved it. At the Taj Mahal in India, Johnson tested the monument's echo with a Texas cowboy yell. And on a trip to Senegal, he ordered that an American bed, a special showerhead, and cases of Cutty Sark be sent along with him. "Foreigners," Johnson quipped early in his administration, only half-jokingly, "are not like the folks I am used to."

26-4a Kennedy's Legacy in Vietnam

Yet Johnson knew from the start that foreign policy, especially regarding Vietnam, would demand his attention. Since the late 1950s, hostilities in Vietnam had increased, as Ho Chi Minh's North assisted and, to a degree, directed the Vietcong guerrillas in the South to advance the reunification of the country under a communist government. President Kennedy had stepped up aid dollars to the Diem regime in Saigon, increased the airdropping of raiding teams into North Vietnam, and launched crop destruction by herbicides to starve the Vietcong and expose their hiding places. Kennedy also strengthened the U.S. military presence in South Vietnam, to the point that by 1963 more than sixteen thousand military advisers were in the country, some authorized to take part in combat alongside the U.S.-equipped Army of the Republic of Vietnam (ARVN).

Meanwhile, opposition to Diem's repressive regime increased, and not just by communists. Peasants objected to programs that removed them from their villages for their own safety, and Buddhist monks, protesting the Roman Catholic Diem's religious persecution, poured gasoline over their robes and ignited themselves in the streets of Saigon. Although Diem was personally honest, he countenanced corruption in his government and concentrated power in the hands of family and friends. He jailed critics to silence them. Eventually, U.S. officials, with Kennedy's approval, encouraged ambitious South Vietnamese generals to remove Diem. On November 1, 1963, the generals struck, murdering Diem. Just a few weeks later, Kennedy himself was assassinated.

The timing of Kennedy's murder ensured that Vietnam would be the most controversial aspect of his legacy. Just what would have happened in Southeast Asia had Kennedy returned from Texas alive can never be known, of course, and the speculation is made more difficult by his contradictory record on the conflict. He expanded U.S. involvement and approved a coup against Diem, but despite the urgings of top advisers he refused to commit American ground forces to the struggle. Over time, he became increasingly skeptical about South Vietnam's prospects and hinted that he would end the American commitment after winning reelection in 1964. Some authors have gone further and argued that he was ending U.S. involvement even at the time of his death, but the evidence for this claim is thin. More likely, Kennedy arrived in Dallas that fateful day still uncertain about how to solve the Vietnam problem, postponing the truly difficult choices until later.

26-4b Tonkin Gulf Incident and Resolution

Lyndon Johnson, too, was unsure on Vietnam, wanting to do nothing there that could complicate his aim of winning the 1964 election. Yet Johnson also sought victory in the struggle. As a result, throughout 1964 the administration secretly laid plans to expand the war to North Vietnam and never seriously considered negotiating a settlement.

In early August 1964, an incident in the Gulf of Tonkin, off the coast of North Vietnam, drew Johnson's involvement (see Map 26.2). Twice in three days, U.S. destroyers reported coming under attack from North Vietnamese patrol boats. Despite a lack of evidence that the second attack occurred, Johnson ordered retaliatory air strikes against selected North Vietnamese patrol boat bases and an oil depot. He also directed aides to rework a long-existing congressional resolution on the use of force. By a vote of 416 to 0 in the House and 88 to 2 in the Senate, Congress quickly passed the Gulf of Tonkin Resolution, which gave the president the authority to "take all necessary measures to repel any armed attack against the forces of the United States and to prevent further aggression." In so doing, Congress essentially surrendered its warmaking powers to the executive branch. The resolution, Secretary of Defense McNamara later noted, served "to open the floodgates."

26-4c Decision for Escalation

President Johnson, delighted with the broad authority the resolution gave him, used a different metaphor. "Like grandma's nightshirt," he quipped, "it covered everything." He also appreciated what the Gulf of Tonkin affair did for his political standing—his public approval ratings went up dramatically, and his show of force effectively removed Vietnam as a campaign issue for GOP presidential nominee Barry Goldwater. On the ground in South Vietnam, however, the outlook remained grim in the final weeks of 1964, as the Vietcong continued to make gains. U.S. officials responded by laying secret plans for an escalation of American involvement.

In February 1965, in response to Vietcong attacks on American installations in South Vietnam that killed thirty-two Americans, Johnson ordered Operation Rolling Thunder, a bombing program planned the previous fall, which continued, more or less uninterrupted, until October 1968. Then, on March 8, the first U.S. combat battalions came ashore near Danang. The North Vietnamese, however,

Legend

- Ho Chi Minh Trail
- → Enemy supply routes
- ★ Major battle of the Tet offensive, January 1968
- ■ Major U.S. base during the war
- Boat-people refugees after 1975

Map labels

CHINA

MYANMAR (BURMA)

Red R.

Black R.

• Dienbienphu

Hanoi •

Haiphong •

Harbor mined, 1972

NORTH VIETNAM

Gulf of Tonkin

U.S. bombing begins, 1964 Communist-Pathet Lao victory, 1975

PLAIN OF JARS

Co. R.

Mekong R.

• Vinh

Maddox incident, 1964

LAOS

• Vientiane

Keo Nua Pass

Mu Gia Pass

U.S. Seventh Fleet operations during the war

Udon Thani •

Nakhon Phanom •

Demilitarized Zone

Demarcation Line, 1954

17°N

THAILAND

Khon Kaen •

Sépone •
Khe Sanh
Lang Vei

Quang Tri
Hue

A Shau Valley

Da Nang

South China Sea

• Ta Khli

Ubon Ratchathani •

Chu Lai
My Lai
Quang Ngai

15°N

Ratchasima •

Kham Duc

Dak To
Kontum
Pleiku
An Khe

Duc Co

Qui Nhon

• Don Muang

• Bangkok

CAMBODIA (KAMPUCHEA)

U.S. bombing begins, 1969

CENTRAL HIGHLANDS

Tuy Hoa

Ban Me Thuot

Sattahip •

Nha Trang

U.S. invasion, 1970

Bu Dop

Dalat

Cam Ranh Bay

110°E

Communist-Khmer Rouge victory, 1975

Phnom Penh •

Vietnamese invasion, 1978

SOUTH VIETNAM

N

Gulf of Thailand

Chau Duc

Saigon
Tan Son Nhut
Cholon
My Tho
Vinh Long
Can Tho
Ben Tre

Bien Hoa
Long Binh
Vung Tau

10°N

Mayaguez incident, 1975

CA MAU PENINSULA

Mekong Delta

• Ca Mau

Vietcong-North Vietnamese victory and U.S. withdrawal, 1975

100°E

105°E

20°N

Map 26.2 Southeast Asia and the Vietnam War

To prevent communists from coming to power in Vietnam, Cambodia, and Laos in the 1960s, the United States intervened massively in Southeast Asia. The interventions failed, and the remaining American troops made a hasty exit from Vietnam in 1975, when the victorious Vietcong and North Vietnamese took Saigon and renamed it Ho Chi Minh City.

would not give up. They hid in shelters and rebuilt roads and bridges with a perseverance that frustrated and awed American decision makers. They also increased infiltration into the South. In Saigon, meanwhile, coups and countercoups by self-serving military leaders undermined U.S. efforts to turn the war effort around. "I don't think we ought to take this government seriously," Ambassador Henry Cabot Lodge told a White House meeting. "There is simply no one who can do anything."

In July 1965, Johnson convened a series of high-level discussions about U.S. policy in the war. Although these deliberations had about them the character of a charade—Johnson wanted history to record that he agonized over a choice he had in fact already made—they did confirm that the American commitment would be more or less open-ended. On July 28, the president publicly announced a significant troop increase, disclosing that others would follow. By the end of 1965, more than 180,000 U.S. ground troops were in South Vietnam. In 1966, the figure climbed to 385,000. In 1967 alone, U.S. warplanes flew 108,000 sorties and dropped 226,000 tons of bombs on North Vietnam. In 1968, U.S. troop strength reached 536,100 (see Figure 26.2). Each American escalation

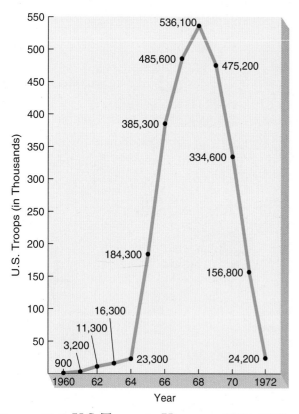

Figure 26.2 **U.S. Troops in Vietnam, 1960–1972**

These numbers show the Americanization of the Vietnam War under President Johnson, who ordered vast increases in troop levels. President Nixon gradually reversed the escalation, so that by the time of the cease-fire in early 1973, fewer than 25,000 American troops remained in Vietnam. Data are for December 31 of each year. *Source: U.S. Department of Defense*

brought not victory, but a new North Vietnamese escalation. The Soviet Union and China responded to the stepped-up U.S. involvement by increasing their material assistance to the Hanoi government.

26-4d Opposition to Americanization

The initiation of Rolling Thunder and the U.S. troop commitment "Americanized" the war. What could have been seen as a civil war between North and South, or a war of national reunification, was now clearly an American war against the communist Hanoi government. This "Americanization" of the war in Vietnam came despite deep misgivings on the part of influential and informed voices at home and abroad. In the key months of decision, Democratic leaders in the Senate, major newspapers such as the *New York Times* and the *Wall Street Journal*, and prominent columnists like Walter Lippmann warned against deepening involvement. So did some within the administration, including Vice President Hubert H. Humphrey and Undersecretary of State George W. Ball. Abroad, virtually all of America's allies—including France, Britain, Canada, and Japan—cautioned against escalation and urged a political settlement, on the grounds that no military solution favorable to the United States was possible. Still more remarkable, top U.S. officials themselves shared this pessimism. Most of them knew that the odds of success were not great. They certainly hoped that the new measures would cause Hanoi to end the insurgency in the South, but it cannot be said they were confident.

Why, then, did America's leaders choose war? At stake was "credibility." They feared that, if the United States failed to prevail in Vietnam, friends and foes around the world would find American power less credible. The Soviets and Chinese would be emboldened to challenge U.S. interests elsewhere in the world, and allied governments might conclude that they could not depend on Washington. For at least some key players, too, including the president himself, domestic political credibility and personal credibility were also on the line. Johnson worried that failure in Vietnam would harm his domestic agenda; even more, he feared the personal humiliation that he imagined would inevitably accompany a defeat—and for him, a negotiated withdrawal constituted defeat. As for the stated objective of helping a South Vietnamese ally repulse external aggression, that, too, figured into the equation, but not as much as it would have had the Saigon government—racked with infighting among senior leaders and possessing little popular support—done more to assist in its own defense.

26-4e American Soldiers in Vietnam

Even as Johnson Americanized the Vietnam War, he sought to keep the publicity surrounding the action as low as possible. Thus, he rejected the Joint Chiefs' view that U.S. reserve forces should be mobilized and a national emergency declared. This decision not to call up reserve units had a momentous impact on the makeup of the American fighting force sent to Vietnam. It forced the military establishment to rely more heavily on the draft, which in turn meant that Vietnam became a young man's war—the average age of soldiers was twenty-two, as compared with twenty-six in World War II. It also became a war of the poor and the working class. Through the years of heavy escalation (1965–1968), college students could get deferments, as could teachers and engineers. (In 1969, the draft was changed so that some students were called up through a lottery system.) The poorest and least-educated young men were less likely to be able to avoid the draft and more likely to volunteer. The armed services recruited hard in poor communities, many of them heavily African American and Latino, advertising the military as an avenue of training and advancement; very often, the pitch worked. Once in uniform, those with fewer skills were far more likely to see combat, and hence to die.

Infantrymen on maneuvers in South Vietnam carried heavy rucksacks into thick jungle growth, where every step was precarious. Booby traps and land mines were a constant threat. Insects swarmed, and leeches sucked at weary bodies. Boots and human skin rotted from the rains, which alternated with withering suns. "It was as if the sun and the land itself were in league with the Vietcong," recalled marine officer Philip Caputo in *A Rumor of War* (1977), "wearing us down, driving us mad, killing us." The enemy, meanwhile, was hard to find, often burrowed into elaborate underground tunnels or melded into the population, where any Vietnamese might be a Vietcong.

The American forces fought well, and their entry into the conflict in 1965 helped stave off a South Vietnamese defeat. In that sense, Americanization achieved its most immediate and basic objective. But if the stepped-up fighting that year demonstrated to Hanoi leaders that the war would not swiftly be won, it also showed the same thing to their counterparts in Washington. As the North Vietnamese matched each American escalation with one of their own, the war became a stalemate. The U.S. commander, General William Westmoreland, proved mistaken in his belief that a strategy of attrition represented the key to victory—the enemy had a seemingly endless supply of recruits to throw into battle. Under Westmoreland's strategy, the measure of success became the "body count"—that is, the number of North Vietnamese and Vietcong corpses found after battle. From the start, the counts were subject to manipulation by officers eager to convince superiors of the success of an operation. Worse, the American reliance on massive military and other technology—including carpet bombing, napalm (jellied gasoline), and crop defoliants that destroyed entire forests—alienated many South Vietnamese and brought new recruits to the Vietcong.

▲ Wounded American soldiers after a battle in Vietnam.

Larry Burrows/Getty Images

26-4f Divisions at Home

Increasingly, Americans divided into those who supported the war and those who did not. As television coverage brought the war—its body counts and body bags, its burned villages and weeping refugees—into homes every night, the number of opponents grew. On college campuses, professors and students organized debates and lectures on American policy. Sometimes going around the clock, these intense public discussions became a form of protest, called "teach-ins" after the sit-ins of the civil rights movement. The big campus and street demonstrations were still to come, but pacifist groups organized early protests.

In early 1966, Senator William Fulbright held televised public hearings on whether the national interest was being served by pursuing the war. What exactly was the threat? senators asked. To the surprise of some, George F. Kennan testified that his containment doctrine was meant for Europe, not the volatile environment of Southeast Asia. America's "preoccupation" with Vietnam, Kennan asserted, was undermining its global obligations. Whether many minds were changed by the Fulbright hearings is hard to say, but they constituted the first in-depth national discussion of the U.S. commitment in Vietnam. They provoked Americans to think about the conflict and the nation's role in it. No longer could anyone doubt that there were deep divisions on Vietnam among public officials, or that two of them, Lyndon Johnson and William Fulbright, formerly close political associates, had broken completely over the war.

Defense secretary Robert McNamara, who despite private misgivings championed the Americanization of the war in 1965, became increasingly troubled by the killing and destructiveness of the bombing. Already in November 1965 he expressed skepticism that victory could ever be achieved, and in the months thereafter he agonized over how the United States looked in the eyes of the world. American credibility, far from being protected by the staunch commitment to the war, was suffering grievous damage, McNamara feared. "The picture of the world's greatest superpower killing or seriously injuring 1,000 noncombatants a week, while trying to pound a tiny backward nation into submission on an issue whose merits are hotly disputed, is not a pretty one," he told Johnson in mid-1967.

But Johnson was in no mood to listen or reconsider. Determined to prevail in Vietnam, he dug in, snapping at "those little shits on the campuses." Although on occasion he halted the bombing to encourage North Vietnam to negotiate (on America's terms), and to disarm critics, such pauses often were accompanied by increases in American troop strength. And the United States sometimes resumed or accelerated the bombing just when a diplomatic breakthrough seemed possible. Hanoi demanded a complete suspension of bombing raids before sitting down at the conference table. And North Vietnamese leaders could not accept American terms, which amounted to abandonment of their determination to achieve an independent, unified Vietnam.

26-5 A Nation Divided

▶ **What factors contributed to urban unrest in the 1960s?**

▶ **What new forms of leadership emerged from the civil rights movement in the 1960s?**

▶ **What causes did the Mexican American civil rights movement embrace during the 1960s?**

▶ **How did young people seek to change their lives and the society in which they lived?**

As Johnson struggled to overcome an implacable foe in Vietnam, his liberal vision of a Great Society faced challenges at home. The divisions among Americans over policy in Vietnam were only one fissure in a society that was fracturing along many different lines: black and white, young and old, radical, liberal, and conservative.

Even as the civil rights movement was winning important victories in the mid-1960s, many African Americans had given up on the promise of liberal reform. In 1964, shortly after President Johnson signed the landmark Civil Rights Act, racial violence erupted in northern cities. Angry residents of Harlem took to the streets after a white police officer shot a black teenager. The following summer, in the predominantly black Watts section of Los Angeles, crowds burned, looted, and battled police for five days and nights. The uprising, which began when a white police officer attempted to arrest a black resident on suspicion of drunken driving, left thirty-four dead and more than one thousand injured. In July 1967, twenty-six people were killed in street battles between African Americans and police and army troops in Newark, New Jersey. A week later, in Detroit, forty-three died as three square miles of the city went up in flames. In 1967 alone, there were 167 violent outbreaks in 128 cities (see Map 26.3).

The "long, hot summers" of urban unrest in the 1960s differed from almost all previous race riots. Past riots were typically started by whites. Here, black residents exploded in anger and frustration over the conditions of their lives. They looted and burned stores, most of them white-owned. But in the process they devastated their own neighborhoods.

In 1968, the National Advisory Commission on Civil Disorders, chaired by Governor Otto Kerner of Illinois, warned that America was "moving towards two societies, one white, one black—separate and unequal," and blamed white racism for the violence. "What white Americans have never fully understood—but what the Negro can never forget—is that white society is deeply implicated in the ghetto. White institutions created it, white institutions maintain it, and white society condones it," concluded the

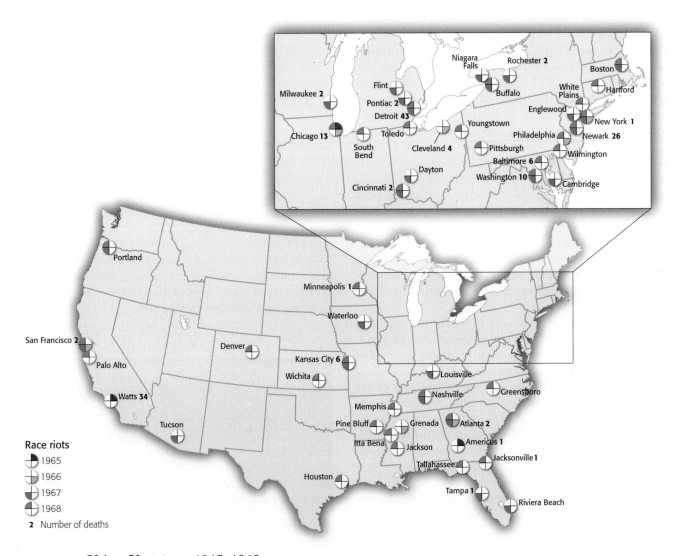

Map 26.3 Urban Uprisings, 1965–1968

The first major violent black uprising of the 1960s exploded in the Los Angeles neighborhood of Watts in 1965. The bloodiest uprisings of 1967 were in Newark, New Jersey, and Detroit, Michigan. Scores of uprisings erupted in the aftermath of Martin Luther King Jr.'s assassination in 1968.

Kerner Commission. Some white Americans rejected this interpretation. Others, shocked at what appeared to be senseless violence, wondered why African Americans were venting their frustration so destructively just when they were making real progress in the civil rights struggle.

The answer stemmed in part from regional differences. Although the *legal* disfranchisement and discrimination in the South was a clear focal point for civil rights activism, African Americans outside the South also suffered racial discrimination. Increasingly concentrated in the deteriorating ghettos of inner cities, the majority lived in societies as segregated as any in the Deep South. They faced discrimination in housing, in the availability of credit and mortgages, and in employment. The median income of northern blacks was little more than half that of northern

whites, and their unemployment rate was twice as high. Many northern blacks had given up on the civil rights movement, and few believed that Great Society liberalism would solve their plight.

26-5a Black Power

In this climate, a new voice urged blacks to seize their freedom "by any means necessary." Malcolm X, a onetime pimp and street hustler who had converted while in prison to the Nation of Islam faith, offered African Americans a new direction of leadership. Members of the Nation of Islam, commonly known as Black Muslims, espoused black pride and separatism from white society. Their faith, combining elements of traditional Islam with a belief that whites were subhuman "devils" whose race would soon be destroyed, also emphasized the importance of sobriety, thrift, and social responsibility. By the early 1960s, Malcolm X had become the Black Muslims' chief spokesperson, and his advice was straightforward: "If someone puts a hand on you, send him to the cemetery." But Malcolm X was murdered in early 1965 by members of the Nation of Islam who believed he had betrayed their cause by breaking with the Black Muslims to start his own, more racially tolerant organization. In death, Malcolm X became a powerful symbol of black defiance and self-respect.

A year after Malcolm X's death, Stokely Carmichael, SNCC chairman, denounced "the betrayal of black dreams by white America." To be truly free from white oppression, Carmichael proclaimed, blacks had to "stand up and take over"—to elect black candidates, to organize their own schools, to control their own institutions, to embrace "**Black Power**." That year, SNCC expelled its white members and repudiated both nonviolence and integration. CORE followed suit in 1967.

The best-known black radicals of the era were the Black Panthers, an organization formed in Oakland, California, in 1966. Blending black separatism and revolutionary communism, the Panthers dedicated themselves to destroying both capitalism and "the military arm of our oppressors," the police in the ghettos. In direct contrast to earlier, nonviolent civil rights protesters, who had worn suits and ties or dresses to demonstrate their respectability, male Panthers wore black leather coats, carried weapons, and talked about killing "pigs"—and did kill eleven officers by 1970. Police targeted the Panthers; most infamously, Chicago police murdered local Panther leader Fred Hampton in his bed. However, the Panthers also worked to improve life in their neighborhoods by creating free breakfast and health care programs for children, offering courses in African American history, and demanding jobs and decent housing for the poor.

26-5b Mexican American Activism

In 1965, Mexican Americans made up about 4 percent of the U.S. population, concentrated in the Southwest and California. Although the federal census counted all Hispanics as "white," they were often discriminated against in the job market, pay, housing, schools, and the courts. Organizations such as the League of United Latin American Citizens (LULAC), a middle-class–oriented group founded in 1929, had long sought full assimilation of Hispanic citizens—most of whom were of Mexican origin. But a national Mexican American movement for social justice began outside this growing middle class, first focused on the plight of Mexican and Mexican American migrant farm workers.

Black Power Advocated in 1966 by SNCC president Stokely Carmichael, it promoted black nationalism, self-determination, and greater militance as a means of self-defense.

Grape growers in California relied heavily on migrant farm workers, paying them as little as 10 cents an hour in 1965 (the minimum wage was $1.25), and too frequently the housing they provided lacked running water and indoor toilets. Mexican American and Filipino grape workers launched a strike (*huelga*) against large growers in California's San Joaquin Valley in 1965, and labor organizers César Chávez and Delores Huerta offered leadership. A national consumer boycott of table grapes, led by Chávez and the AFL-CIO-affiliated United Farm Workers (UFW), brought the growers to the bargaining table, winning better wages and working conditions in 1970. The UFW's roots in the Mexican and Mexican American communities were critical to its success, as the union resembled nineteenth-century Mexican *mutualistas*, or cooperative associations, as much as it did a traditional American labor union. Its members founded cooperative groceries, a Spanish-language newspaper, and a theater group; they called on the Virgin de Guadalupe for assistance in their struggle.

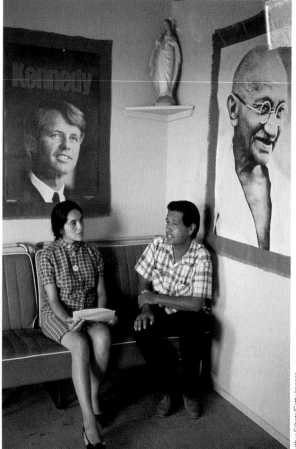

Arthur Schatz/Getty Images

▲ United Farm Workers leaders César Chávez and Dolores Huerta talk during the 1968 grape pickers' strike. The statue of the Virgin Mary, poster for presidential candidate Robert Kennedy, and photograph of Mahatma Gandhi suggest the guiding religious, political, and philosophical underpinnings of the movement.

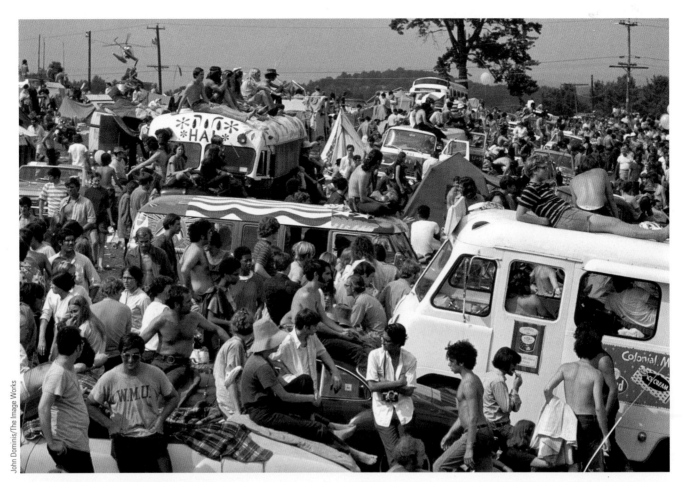

John Dominis/The Image Works

▲ Hundreds of thousands of young people came together for the Woodstock Music and Art Fair in August 1969. In its coverage, *Time* magazine warned adults that "the children of the welfare state and the atom bomb do indeed march to the beat of a different drummer, as well as to the tune of an electric guitarist," but the local sheriff called them "the nicest bunch of kids I've ever dealt with."

Although the New Left criticized the counterculture as apolitical, many freaks did envision revolutionary change. As John Sinclair, manager of the rock band MC5, explained, mind-blowing experiences with sex, drugs, or music were far more likely to change young peoples' minds than earnest speeches: "Rather than go up there and make some speech about our moral commitment in Vietnam, you just make 'em so freaky they'd never want to go into the army in the first place."

The nascent counterculture had first burst on the national consciousness during the summer of 1967, when tens of thousands of young people poured into the Haight-Ashbury district of San Francisco, the heart of America's psychedelic culture, for the "Summer of Love." As an older generation of "straight" (or Establishment) Americans watched with horror, white youth came to look—and act—more and more like the counterculture. Coats and ties disappeared, as did stockings—and bras. Young men grew long hair, and parents throughout the nation complained, "You can't tell the boys from the girls." Millions used marijuana or hallucinogenic drugs, read underground newspapers, and thought of themselves as alienated from "straight" culture even though they were attending high school or college and not completely "dropping out" of the Establishment.

Some of the most lasting cultural changes involved attitudes about sex. The mass media were fascinated with "free love," and some people did embrace a truly promiscuous sexuality. More important, however, premarital sex no longer destroyed a woman's "reputation." The birth control pill, distributed since 1960 and widely available to single women by the late 1960s, greatly lessened the risk of unplanned pregnancy, and venereal diseases were easily cured by a basic course of antibiotics. The number of couples living together—"without benefit of matrimony," as the phrase went at the time—increased 900 percent from 1960 to 1970; many young people no longer tried to hide the fact that they were sexually active. Still, 68 percent of American adults disapproved of premarital sex in 1969.

Adults were baffled and often angered by the behavior of youth. A generation that had grown up in the hard decades of depression and war, many of whom saw middle-class respectability as crucial to success and stability, just did not understand. How could young people put such promising futures at risk by having sex without marriage, taking drugs, or opposing the American government over the war in Vietnam?

The British Invasion

The British invasion began in earnest on February 7, 1964. London and Paris had already fallen, reported *Life* magazine, and New York was soon to follow. Three thousand screaming American teenagers were waiting when Pan Am's *Yankee Clipper* touched down at Kennedy Airport with four British "moptops" aboard. "I Want to Hold Your Hand" was already at the top of the U.S. charts, and the Beatles' conquest of America was quick. Seventy-three million people—at that time the largest television audience in history—watched them on the *Ed Sullivan Show* the following Sunday night.

Although the Beatles led the invasion, they did not conquer America alone. The Rolling Stones' first U.S. hit single also came in 1964. The Dave Clark Five appeared on *Ed Sullivan* eighteen times. And there was a whole list of others, some now forgotten, some not: Freddie and the Dreamers, Herman's Hermits, the Animals, the Yardbirds, the Hollies, the Kinks, Gerry and the Pacemakers, Chad and Jeremy, Petula Clark.

The British invasion was, at least in part, the triumphal return of American music, part of a transatlantic exchange that reinvigorated both nations. American rock 'n' roll had lost much of its early energy by the early 1960s, and in England, the London-centered popular music industry was pumping out a highly produced, saccharine version of American pop. But other forms of American music had made their way across the Atlantic, often carried by travelers through port cities like Liverpool, where the Beatles were born. By the late 1950s, young musicians in England's provincial cities were listening to the music of African American bluesmen Muddy Waters and Howlin' Wolf; they were playing cover versions of the early rock 'n' roll of Buddy Holly and Chuck Berry; and they were experimenting with skiffle, a sort of jazz- and blues-influenced folk music played mostly with improvised instruments. None of this music had a large popular audience in the United States, where *Billboard* magazine's number one hit for 1960 was Percy Faith's "Theme from *A Summer Place*" (a movie starring Sandra Dee and Troy Donahue), and the Singing Nun was at the top of the charts just before the Beatles arrived.

Young British musicians, including John Lennon, Eric Clapton, and Mick Jagger, re-created American musical forms and reinvented rock 'n' roll. By the mid-1960s, the Beatles and the other bands of the British invasion were at the heart of a youth culture that transcended the boundaries of nations. This music not only connected Britain and America but also reached across the Atlantic and the Pacific to link America's youth with young people throughout the world.

CRITICAL THINKING

- Music, specifically rock and roll music, was at the heart of the youth culture and the counterculture of the 1960s. It was also a mainstay in many of the protest movements of the era both in the United States and abroad. Why is music so well-suited to the culture of protest?

◄ The Beatles perform on the *Ed Sullivan Show* in February 1964. Although Britain's Queen Mother thought the Beatles "young, fresh, and vital," American parents were appalled when the "long" Beatles haircut swept the nation.

AP Photo

26-6 1968

▶ Why did it seem that the "nation was coming apart" in 1968?

▶ What were the consequences of the Tet Offensive?

▶ How was social unrest a global issue in 1968?

By the beginning of 1968, it seemed that the nation was coming apart. Divided over the war in Vietnam, frustrated by the slow pace of social change, or angry over the racial violence that wracked America's cities, Americans looked for solutions as the nation faced the most serious domestic crisis of the postwar era.

26-6a The Tet Offensive

The year opened with a major attack in Vietnam. On January 31, 1968, the first day of the Vietnamese New Year (Tet), Vietcong and North Vietnamese forces struck all across South Vietnam, capturing provincial capitals (see Map 26.2 in "Opposition to Americanization," Section 26-4d). During the carefully planned offensive, the Saigon airport, the presidential palace, and the ARVN headquarters came under attack. Even the U.S. embassy compound was penetrated by Vietcong soldiers, who occupied its courtyard for six hours. American and South Vietnamese units eventually regained much of the ground they had lost, inflicting heavy casualties and devastating numerous villages.

Although the Tet Offensive did not achieve the resounding battlefield victory that Hanoi strategists had hoped for, the heavy fighting called into question American military leaders' confident predictions in earlier months that the war would soon be won. Had not the Vietcong and North Vietnamese demonstrated that they could strike when and where they wished? If America's airpower, dollars, and half a million troops could not now defeat the Vietcong, could they ever do so? Had the American public been deceived? In February, the highly respected CBS television anchorman Walter Cronkite went to Vietnam to find out. The military brass in Saigon assured him that "we had the enemy just where we wanted him." The newsman recalled, "Tell that to the Marines, I thought—the Marines in the body bags on that helicopter."

26-6b Johnson's Exit

Top presidential advisers sounded notes of despair. Clark Clifford, who had succeeded Robert McNamara as secretary of defense, told Johnson that the war—"a sinkhole"—could not be won, even with the 206,000 additional soldiers requested by Westmoreland. Aware that the nation was suffering a financial crisis prompted by rampant deficit spending to sustain the war and other global commitments, they knew that taking the initiative in Vietnam would cost billions more, further derail the budget, panic foreign owners

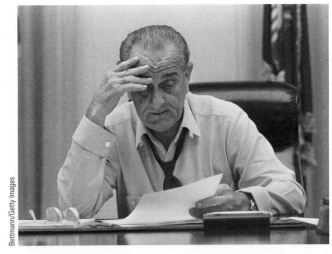

▲ In early October 1968, as his presidency draws to a close, a weary-looking Lyndon Johnson prepares to address the nation on the war in Vietnam.

of dollars, and wreck the economy. Clifford heard from his associates in the business community; "These men now feel we are in a hopeless bog," he told the president. To "maintain public support for the war without the support of these men" was impossible.

Controversy over the war split the Democratic Party, just as a presidential election loomed in November. Senator Eugene McCarthy of Minnesota and Robert F. Kennedy (now a senator from New York), both strong opponents of Johnson's war policies, forcefully challenged the president in early primaries. Strained by exhausting sessions with skeptical advisers, troubled by the economic implications of escalation, and sensing that more resources would not bring victory, Johnson changed course. During a March 31 television address, he announced a halt to most of the bombing, asked Hanoi to begin negotiations, and stunned his listeners by withdrawing from the presidential race. He had become a casualty of the war, his presidency doomed—as he had always feared it might be—by a seemingly interminable struggle ten thousand miles from Washington. Peace talks began in May in Paris, but the war ground on.

26-6c Assassinations

Less than a week after Johnson's shocking announcement, Martin Luther King Jr. was murdered in Memphis, where he had traveled to support striking sanitation workers. It is still not clear why James Earl Ray, a white forty-year-old drifter and petty criminal, shot King—or whether he acted alone or as part of a conspiracy. By 1968, King, the senior statesman of the civil rights movement, had become an outspoken critic of the Vietnam War and of American capitalism. Despite the continuing power of racism in American society, King was widely respected and honored, and most Americans mourned his death. In the days following his assassination, black rage and grief exploded in 130 cities. Once again, ghetto neighborhoods burned; thirty-four blacks and five whites died. The violence provoked a backlash from whites—primarily urban, working-class people who were tired of violence and who had little sympathy for the demands of black radicals. In Chicago, Mayor Richard Daley ordered police to shoot rioters.

An already shaken nation watched in disbelief as another leader fell to violence only two months later. Antiwar Democratic presidential candidate Robert Kennedy was shot and killed as he celebrated his victory in the California primary. His assassin, Sirhan Sirhan, an Arab nationalist, targeted Kennedy because of his support for Israel.

26-6d Chicago Democratic National Convention

Violence erupted again in August at the Democratic National Convention in Chicago. Thousands of protesters converged on the city: students who'd gone "Clean for Gene," cutting long hair and donning "respectable" clothes to campaign for antiwar candidate Eugene McCarthy; members of America's counterculture drawn by a promise from the anarchist group,

the Yippies, of a "Festival of Life" to counter the "Convention of Death"; members of antiwar groups that ranged from radical to mainstream. Mayor Daley, resolving that no one would disrupt "his" convention, assigned twelve thousand police to twelve-hour shifts and had twelve thousand army troops with bazookas, rifles, and flamethrowers on call as backup. Police attacked peaceful antiwar protesters and journalists. "The whole world is watching," chanted the protesters, as club-swinging police indiscriminately beat people to the ground, and Americans gathered around their television sets, despairing over the future of their nation.

26-6e Global Protest

Although American eyes were focused on the clashes in Chicago, upheavals burst forth around the world that spring and summer. In France, university students protested both rigid academic policies and the Vietnam War. They received support from French workers, who occupied their factories and paralyzed public transport; the turmoil contributed to the collapse of Charles de Gaulle's government the following year. In Italy, Germany, England, Ireland, Sweden, Canada, Mexico, Chile, Japan, and

Hulton Archive/Getty Images

▲ A military truck with civilians waving Czech flags drives past a Soviet truck in Prague on August 21, 1968, shortly after Warsaw Pact troops invaded Czechoslovakia. More than one hundred people were killed in the clashes, and several Prague Spring leaders, including Alexander Dubček, were arrested and taken to Moscow. Dubček's attempts to create "socialism with a human face" are often seen as historical and ideological forerunners to Mikhail Gorbachev's reform policies in the 1980s in the Soviet Union.

South Korea, students also protested—sometimes violently—against universities, governments, and the Vietnam War. In Czechoslovakia, hundreds of thousands of demonstrators flooded the streets of Prague, demanding democracy and an end to repression by the Soviet-controlled government. This so-called Prague Spring developed into a full-scale national rebellion before being crushed by Soviet tanks.

Why so many uprisings occurred in so many places simultaneously is not altogether clear. Sheer numbers had an impact. The postwar baby boom experienced by many nations produced by the late 1960s a huge mass of teenagers and young adults, many of whom had grown up in relative prosperity, with high expectations for the future. The expanded reach of global media also mattered. Technological advances allowed the nearly instantaneous transmittal of televised images around the world, so protests in one country could readily inspire similar actions in others. Although the worldwide demonstrations might have occurred even without the Vietnam War, television news footage showing the wealthiest and most industrialized nation carpet-bombing a poor and developing one—whose longtime leader was the charismatic revolutionary Ho Chi Minh—surely helped fuel the agitation.

26-6f Nixon's Election

The presidential election of 1968, coming at the end of such a difficult year, did little to heal the nation. Democratic nominee Hubert Humphrey, Johnson's vice president, seemed a continuation of the old politics. Republican candidate Richard Nixon, like Goldwater in 1964, called for "law and order"—a phrase some understood as racist code words—to appeal to those who were angry about racial violence and tired of social unrest. Promising to "bring us together," he reached out to those he called "the great, quite forgotten majority—the nonshouters and the nondemonstrators, the millions who ask principally to go their own way in decency and dignity." On Vietnam, Nixon vowed he would "end the war and win the peace." Governor George Wallace of Alabama, who only five years before had vowed, "Segregation forever!" and who proposed using nuclear weapons on Vietnam, ran as a third-party candidate. Wallace carried five southern states, drawing almost 14 percent of the popular vote, and Nixon was elected president with the slimmest of margins (see Map 26.4). Divisions among Americans deepened.

Yet on Christmas Eve 1968—in a step toward fulfilling the pledge John Kennedy had made at the opening of a tumultuous decade—*Apollo* 8 entered lunar orbit. Looking down on a troubled world, the astronauts broadcast photographs of the earth seen from space, a fragile blue orb floating in darkness. As people around the world listened, the astronauts read aloud the opening passages of Genesis, "In the beginning, God created the heaven and the earth . . . and God saw that it was good," and many listeners found themselves in tears.

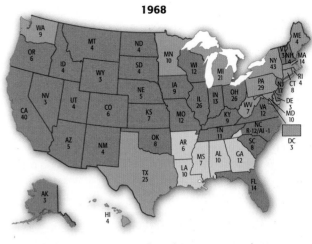

1968

Candidate (Party)	Electoral Vote		Popular Vote	
Nixon (Republican)	301	56.1%	31,710,470	43.4%
Humphrey (Democrat)	191	35.5%	30,898,055	42.3%
Wallace (American Independent)	46	8.4%	9,446,167	12.9%

Map 26.4 Presidential Election, 1968

The popular vote was almost evenly split between Richard M. Nixon and Hubert Humphrey, but Nixon won 31 states to Humphrey's 14 and triumphed easily in electoral votes. George Wallace, the American Independent Party candidate, won 5 states in the Deep South.

Summary

The 1960s began with high hopes for a more democratic America. Civil rights volunteers, often risking their lives, carried the quest for racial equality to all parts of the nation. Gradually, the nation's leaders put their support behind the movement, and the 1964 Civil Rights Act and the 1965 Voting Rights Act were major landmarks in the quest for a more just society. America was shaken by the assassination of President John Kennedy in 1963, but under President Johnson's Great Society, the liberal vision of using government power to improve the lives of the nation's citizens reached new heights.

But throughout this period, the nation was troubled by threats to its stability. The Cold War between the United States and the USSR grew in size and scope during the early 1960s. The world came close to nuclear war in the 1962 Cuban missile crisis, and meanwhile the United States became steadily more involved in the ongoing war in Vietnam. Determined not to let South Vietnam "fall" to communists, Lyndon Johnson in 1965 sent military forces to prevent the victory of communist Vietnamese nationalists led by Ho Chi Minh in that nation's civil war. By 1968, there were more than half a million American ground troops in Vietnam. America's war in Southeast Asia divided the country, undermined

The Immigration Act of 1965

When President Johnson signed the 1965 Immigration Act in a ceremony at the foot of the Statue of Liberty, he stated, "This bill that we sign today is not a revolutionary bill. It does not affect the lives of millions. It will not reshape the structure of our daily lives, or really add importantly to our wealth and power." Johnson believed the act was important in an era of struggle over the role of race in American society because it "repair[ed] a very deep and painful flaw in the fabric of American justice" by ending national origins quotas that all but excluded "Polynesians, orientals, and Negroes" (as Hawai'i's senator Hiram Fong pointed out in 1963). Nevertheless, the president and his advisers saw it as primarily symbolic. They were wrong. This relatively obscure act may have had greater long-term impact on Americans' lives than any other piece of Great Society legislation.

The 1965 Immigration Act ended national quotas (see "Improving American Life," Section 26-3e) and established a policy of family reunification that allowed immediate relatives of U.S. citizens to immigrate to the United States regardless of numerical ceilings on immigration. Those who created the Immigration Act did not expect the numbers of immigrants to rise or the sources of immigration to change. But world events decreed otherwise. As population increased rapidly in many of the world's poorer countries, the continuing prosperity of the United States drew those seeking opportunity. Other immigrants fled political instability, including wars in Southeast Asia and civil conflict in Latin America and Africa. U.S. immigration rates skyrocketed.

Following the National Origins Act of 1924, the percentage of U.S. foreign-born residents had dropped steadily, reaching a low of 5 percent in 1970. In 2014, more than 13 percent of American residents were foreign born—a figure last reached in 1920. (And it's important to note that not all immigration is controlled by legislation, as both figures include unauthorized immigrants—approximately 4 percent of the U.S. population in 2014, according to Pew Research Center estimates.) Moreover, no longer were most immigrants from western Europe. As of 2014 the majorities came from (in order) Mexico, India, China, and the Philippines, followed by El Salvador, Vietnam, Cuba, and Korea.

More than two-thirds of the post-1965 immigrants settled in six states—New York, California, Florida, New Jersey, Illinois, and Texas—but many found their way to parts of America that had previously been much more homogeneous. By the late twentieth century, Spanish-language signs appeared in South Carolina, and Hmong farmers from the mountains of Southeast Asia offered their produce at the farmers' market in Missoula, Montana. The legacy of the 1965 Immigration Act was unintended but profound: the people and the nation are today much more diverse than they otherwise would have been.

CRITICAL THINKING

- In keeping with other legislation intended to end legal racism in the United States, the Immigration Act of 1965 addressed "a flaw in the fabric of American Justice"—laws that prevented individuals from immigrating to the United States because of their country of origin (a category usually tied to race or ethnicity). Today, some Americans propose returning to the practice of excluding potential immigrants because of their national origin, religion, or race/ethnicity. What type of immigration policies should the United States have, and why?

Great Society domestic programs, and ultimately destroyed Johnson's presidency.

Despite real gains in civil rights and in attempts to promote justice and to end poverty, divisions among Americans grew in the second half of the decade. Many African Americans turned away from the civil rights movement, seeking more immediate change in their lives. Poor African American neighborhoods burned as violent unrest spread through the nation. Vocal young people—and some of their elders—questioned whether democracy truly existed in the United States. Large numbers of the nation's white youth embraced another form of rebellion, claiming membership in a "counterculture" that rejected white middle-class respectability. With great passion, Americans struggled over the future of their nation.

Suggestions for Further Reading

Beth Bailey, *Sex in the Heartland* (1999)
David Farber, *The Age of Great Dreams* (1994)
Lawrence Freedman, *Kennedy's Wars: Berlin, Cuba, Laos, and Vietnam* (2000)

George C. Herring, *LBJ and Vietnam: A Different Kind of War* (1994)

Peniel Joseph, *Waiting 'Til the Midnight Hour: A Narrative History of Black Power in America* (2006)

Michael Kazin and Maurice Isserman, *America Divided: The Civil War of the 1960s* (1999)

Fredrik Logevall, *Choosing War: The Lost Chance for Peace and the Escalation of War in Vietnam* (1999)

Lisa McGirr, *Suburban Warriors: The Origins of the New American Right* (2001)

Charles Payne, *I've Got the Light of Freedom: The Organizing Tradition and the Mississippi Freedom Struggle* (1995)

Fred Turner, *From Counterculture to Cyberculture: Stewart Brand, The Whole Earth Network, and the Rise of Digital Utopianism* (2006)

Julian Zelizer, *The Fierce Urgency of Now: Lyndon Johnson, Congress, and the Battle for the Great Society* (2015)

A Pivotal Era, 1969–1980

On the morning of November 4, 1979, a Sunday, a mob of several thousand young Iranians gathered outside the U.S. embassy in Tehran. They were supporters of Iran's new leader, Ayatollah Ruhollah Khomeini, a shia cleric who had been living in exile in Paris. Most were men, but there were women too, dressed in black and shrouded in chadors. At 10:30, a small group cut the chain that secured the main gate to the embassy compound and made their way inside the grounds. Hundreds followed them. Hearing the commotion and sensing trouble, Bill Daugherty, a CIA officer newly arrived in the country, set about destroying sensitive embassy documents as fast as he could, hand-feeding the papers into a small incinerator in a back room. Soon he could hear the Iranians in the building. Cooly and methodically, he kept going, until the machine seized up and would take no more documents.

By early afternoon, Daugherty and the few dozen other American personnel still present in the embassy had been captured and handcuffed. Though a few (mostly women and African Americans) were released, fifty-two of them languished under Iranian guard. Thus began the Iran hostage crisis, which would last 444 days and go down as one of the defining events in the modern history of U.S.-Iran relations.

Dramatic though were the events of that fall day in the Iranian capital, they were not wholly shocking to outside observers. Early in the year, the U.S.-supported leader of Iran, Shah Mohammad Reza Pahlavi, had been deposed by revolutionary forces loyal to Khomeini, following years of unrest fueled by resentment of the shah's autocratic style and the growing gap

◀ **A blindfolded American hostage is paraded by his Iranian captors at the U.S. embassy in Tehran, on November 1, 1979.** Alain Mingam/Gamma-Rapho/Getty Images

Chronology

1969
- Stonewall Inn uprising begins gay liberation movement
- *Apollo 11* astronaut Neil Armstrong becomes first person to walk on the moon's surface
- National Chicano Liberation Youth Conference held in Denver
- Indians of All Tribes occupies Alcatraz Island
- Nixon administration begins affirmative action plan

1970
- United States invades Cambodia
- Students at Kent State and Jackson State universities shot by National Guard troops
- First Earth Day celebrated
- Environmental Protection Agency created

1971
- Pentagon Papers published

1972
- Nixon visits China and Soviet Union
- CREEP stages Watergate break-in
- Congress approves ERA and passes Title IX, which creates growth in women's athletics

1973
- Peace agreement in Paris ends U.S. involvement in Vietnam
- OPEC increases oil prices, creating U.S. energy crisis
- *Roe v. Wade* legalizes abortion
- Agnew resigns; Ford named vice president

1974
- Nixon resigns under threat of impeachment; Ford becomes president

1975
- In deepening economic recession, unemployment hits 8.5 percent
- New York City saved from bankruptcy by federal loan guarantees
- Congress passes Indian Self-Determination and Education Assistance Act in response to Native American activists

1976
- Carter elected president

1977
- *Regents of the University of California v. Bakke* outlaws quotas but upholds affirmative action
- California voters approve Proposition 13

1979
- Three Mile Island nuclear accident raises fears
- Camp David accords signed by Israel and Egypt
- American hostages seized in Iran
- Soviet Union invades Afghanistan
- Consumer debt doubles from 1975 to hit $315 billion

between Iran's rich and poor. A succession of U.S. administrations had backed his government, and these close ties had produced deep hostility among the shah's critics on both right and left. For many months before the hostage-taking, the U.S. embassy had been the scene of demonstrations against the American presence in the country, as well as the decision by the Carter administration to allow the ailing shah to travel to the United States for medical treatment; in February 1979, the embassy was attacked and briefly occupied. In response, the Carter administration cut the embassy staff from a pre-revolutionary high of 1400 to about seventy. Most of them now found themselves blindfolded and paraded before the television cameras of the world.

As the days and weeks passed, President Carter became consumed by the crisis. About to begin his campaign for reelection and already facing right-wing accusations of weakness, he groped for some way to free the hostages. It was a political nightmare, made worse be the intense daily attention American media organizations paid to the standoff. Determining that military action was too risky, the White House tried to squeeze Iran through economic sanctions and froze its assets in the United States. It pursued every diplomatic angle, official as well as secret. Nothing worked. The public, initially inclined to rally around the president, grew frustrated.

Finally, on April 11, 1980 Carter approved a high-risk rescue operation, called "Operation Eagle Claw." It failed spectacularly after equipment malfunction in the sandy Iranian desert at a staging area called "Desert One," and during the hasty withdrawal two aircraft collided, killing eight American servicemen. Daugherty and his fellow hostages were not freed until January 1981, after Carter left office and the United States unfroze some Iranian assets and promised not to intervene again in Iran's internal affairs.

How much the crisis contributed to Carter's election defeat is hard to say, but certainly it harmed his prospects. And if he deserves sympathy for his predicament, he can also be criticized for his response to it, a point historian

Gaddis Smith has made well: "President Carter inherited an impossible situation—and he and his advisers made the worst of it." Divided among themselves, they groped for a response to something Americans had scarcely encountered before, at least in sustained fashion: Islamic fundamentalism. It was a harbinger of things to come.

Experience an interactive version of this story in MindTap®.

Most Americans experienced the 1970s as a series of jolts and crises, an era of continuing divisions, betrayed expectations, and new limits. Exposure of Richard Nixon's illegal acts in the political scandal known as "Watergate" shook the faith of Americans not already disillusioned by discovery that the Nixon administration had lied to the public about its conduct of the war in Vietnam. The movements for racial equality and social justice that had flowered in the 1960s became more radical by the early 1970s, as some activists called for social revolution or embraced a form of "cultural nationalism" that emphasized the differences among America's peoples. The United States faced an economic crisis that sent the "misery index" (a combination of the unemployment rate and inflation) skyrocketing and shocked Americans who had grown to expect continued economic growth and widening prosperity. Americans worried about social crisis as the divorce rate soared, as did the rate of violent crime. Environmental crises also challenged the nation: in 1969, Ohio's sludge-filled Cuyahoga River caught fire; in 1979, a partial meltdown at Pennsylvania's Three Mile Island nuclear power plant became America's worst nuclear accident.

Overseas, too, Americans faced challenges. Nixon and his national security adviser, Henry Kissinger, understood that the United States and the Soviet Union, weakened by the costs of their competition and challenged by other nations, faced a world where power was more diffused. Accordingly, even as they pressed for victory in Vietnam, Nixon and Kissinger sought improved relations with the People's Republic of China and the Soviet Union. They failed in Vietnam, but the great-power negotiations bore fruit, and the diplomatic efforts continued under Nixon's successors, Gerald Ford and Jimmy Carter. But Carter's presidency was undermined by international events beyond his control. In the Middle East—a region of growing importance in U.S. foreign policy—Carter helped broker a peace deal between Egypt and Israel but proved powerless to end the hostage crisis in Iran. An economic downturn caused by changes in the global economy and international trade worsened Carter's woes, and on his watch Cold War tensions revived following a Soviet invasion of Afghanistan in 1979.

Despite—and sometimes because of—these crises, the 1970s was a pivotal era in American history. It was a time of triumph for many who sought a more egalitarian American society, as women and people of color fought and won battles against discrimination. It was also a time of major economic transformation. As international economic competition increased, the United States continued to lose well-paid industrial jobs. America's developing postindustrial economy increased economic disparities. Well-educated Americans would soon benefit from new opportunities in technology, finance, and creative fields, while less-educated Americans suffered as low-paid slots in the service sector replaced often-unionized manufacturing jobs. The 1970s economic crisis compounded Americans' loss of confidence in their political leaders; as federal government attempts to manage the economy failed, many Americans rejected the notion of an active federal government. In the 1970s, the growth of a New Deal, Great Society model in which the federal government attempted to protect Americans from the insecurity of the market was challenged by a broad—though contested—turn toward the competitive marketplace as the means to address the political, social, and economic problems of the nation. Thus, as women and racial and ethnic minorities won battles against discrimination, they found increased opportunity to compete in a tough new economy rather than widespread economic and social equality.

- *How did American foreign policy change as a result of involvement in Vietnam?*

- *Why did Americans see this era as an age of limits?*

- *Some historians describe the period between 1968 and 1980 as a time when many Americans lost faith—in their government, in the possibility of joining together in a society that offered equality to all, in the possibility of consensus instead of conflict. Do you agree, or were the struggles and divisions of this era similar to those of previous decades?*

27-1 Rights, Liberation, and Nationalism

▶ How did minority groups embrace cultural nationalism as a means to assert their identity?

▶ What methods did minority groups use to fight for their social and economic rights?

▶ How did the women's movement evolve in the 1960s and 1970s?

▶ What opposition emerged to the efforts of minority groups to obtain equal rights?

The social change movements of the 1960s evolved into new and powerful forms during the 1970s. By the end of the 1960s, as divisions continued to deepen among the American people, movements for social justice and racial equality had become stronger, louder, and often more radical. The civil rights movement splintered as many young African Americans turned away from the tactics of nonviolence, rejected integration in favor of separatism, and embraced a distinct African American culture. By the early 1970s Mexican Americans and Native Americans, inspired by African American claims, had created powerful "Brown Power" and "Red Power" movements that demanded recognition of their own distinct cultures, and the voices of Puerto Rican nationalists had emerged from New York City and Chicago. As women claimed new rights, some feminists—along with gay men and lesbians—called for "liberation." All these claims were controversial, and Americans disagreed both on possible remedies and on the very definition of the problem.

27-1a African American Cultural Nationalism

By the late 1960s many black Americans, disillusioned by the racism that outlasted the end of legal segregation, believed that integration would leave them subordinated in a white-dominated society that did not respect their history or cultural traditions. Mainstream groups such as the NAACP continued to use the nation's courts and ballot boxes to fight for social and political equality, but other activists (like the white youth of the counterculture) looked to culture rather than to narrow political action for social change. Rejecting current European American standards of beauty, young people let their hair grow into "naturals" and "Afros"; they claimed the power of black "soul." Black students and young faculty members sought strength in their own histories and cultural heritages, as colleges and universities met their demands for black studies programs. African traditions were reclaimed—or sometimes created. The new holiday Kwanzaa, invented in 1966 by Maulana Karenga, professor of black studies at California State University, Long Beach, celebrated African heritage. Many African Americans found pride in their history and culture;

the most radical activists gave up on the notion of a larger "American" culture altogether.

27-1b Chicano and Puerto Rican Activism

Mexican Americans, likewise, struggled over the best path to social justice and good lives in the United States. Although growing numbers of the nation's 9 million Mexican Americans (4.3 percent of the U.S. population) were middle class, almost one-quarter of Mexican American families fell below the official poverty line. Almost half of Mexican Americans were functionally illiterate, and dropout rates were phenomenal: in 1974, only 21 percent of Mexican American young men graduated high school.

Confronting widespread discrimination and social inequality, some groups, including the League of United Latin American Citizens (LULAC, founded in 1929) and the new Mexican American Legal Defense and Education Fund (MALDEF, founded in 1968), pursued traditional paths: courts, ballot boxes, and schools. Other groups embraced radical approaches. In northern New Mexico, Reies Tijerina created the Alianza Federal de Mercedes (Federal Alliance of Grants) to fight for the return of land that the organization claimed belonged to local *hispano* villagers (whose ancestors had occupied the territory before it was claimed by the United States) under the 1848 Treaty of Guadalupe Hidalgo. In Denver, former boxer Rudolfo "Corky" Gonzáles drew Mexican American youth to his "Crusade for Justice"; those who gathered there for the National Chicano Liberation Youth Conference in 1969 adopted a manifesto, *El Plan Espiritual de Aztlan*, which condemned the "brutal 'Gringo' invasion of our territories" and declared "the Independence of our . . . Nation."

These young activists did not seek equal rights through integration; instead, they wanted to liberate "La Raza" (from *La Raza de Bronze*, "the brown people") from the oppressive force of American society and culture. They also rejected a hyphenated "Mexican-American" identity. The "Mexican American," they explained in *El Plan Espiritual de Aztlan*, "lacks respect for his culture and ethnic heritage . . . [and] seeks assimilation as a way out of his 'degraded' social status." These young people called themselves "Chicanos" or "Chicanas"—a term drawn from barrio slang and associated with *pachucos*, the hip, rebellious, and definitely not respectable young men.

Many middle-class Mexican Americans and members of the older generations never embraced the term *Chicano* or the separatist, cultural nationalist agenda of *el movimiento*. Throughout the 1970s, however, younger activists continued to seek "Brown Power" based on a separate and distinct Chicano/Chicana culture. They succeeded in introducing Chicano studies into local high school and college curricula and in creating a strong and unifying sense of cultural identity for Mexican American youth.

Most Latinos in the United States were of Mexican ancestry. The number of Puerto Ricans, however, had expanded steadily since World War II, and by 1970 more than a million Puerto Ricans made their homes in northeastern and midwestern cities, especially New York City and Chicago. Although Puerto Rico was a U.S. commonwealth and Puerto Ricans held U.S. citizenship, migrants often encountered discrimination; by the mid-1970s Puerto Rican households had among the lowest per capita income in the nation. Like black and Chicano youth, young Puerto Ricans embraced cultural nationalism and worked to improve the conditions in their communities. In this case, though, nationalism meant something more: many activists also sought Puerto Rican independence from the United States.

Neither Puerto Rican activism nor the Chicano movement ever had as much national influence as the African American civil rights movement or the Black Power movement. However, both challenged discrimination on the local level and created a basis for political action as the Latino population of the United States grew dramatically over the following decades.

27-1c American Indian Activism

Between 1968 and 1975, American Indian activists forced American society to hear their demands and to reform U.S. government policies toward Native peoples. Many young activists, seeking a return to the "old ways," joined with "traditionalists" among their elders to challenge tribal leaders who advocated assimilation and cooperation with federal agencies.

In November 1969, a small group that called itself "Indians of All Tribes" occupied Alcatraz Island in San Francisco Bay, demanding that the land be returned to Native peoples. The protest, which over time drew more than four hundred people from fifty different tribes or nations, lasted nineteen months and consolidated a new "pan-Indian" approach to activism. Before Alcatraz, protests tended to be concerned with specific local issues on individual reservations. Many of the Alcatraz activists, however, were urban Indians whose lives had been shaped by government policies that led Native peoples to leave reservations and seek jobs in the nation's cities. They were interested in claiming a shared "Indian" identity that transcended tribal differences. These protesters did not succeed in reclaiming Alcatraz Island, but they drew national attention to their struggle and inspired the growing "Red Power" movement. In 1972, members of the radical American Indian Movement occupied a Bureau of Indian Affairs office in Washington, D.C., and then in 1973 a trading post at Wounded Knee, South Dakota, where U.S. Army troops had massacred three hundred Sioux men, women, and children in 1890.

At the same time, more moderate activists, working through such pan-tribal organizations as the National Congress of American Indians and the Native American Rights Fund, lobbied Congress for greater rights and resources to govern themselves and to strengthen their tribal cultures. In response to those demands, Congress and the federal courts returned millions of acres of land to tribal ownership,

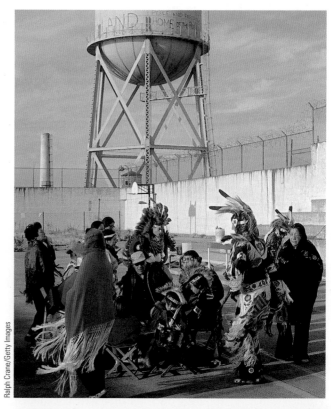

Ralph Crane/Getty Images

▲ Calling their movement "Red Power," these American Indian activists dance in 1969 while "reclaiming" Alcatraz Island in San Francisco Bay. Arguing that an 1868 Sioux treaty entitled them to possession of unused federal lands, the group occupied the island until mid-1971.

and in 1975 Congress passed the **Indian Self-Determination and Education Assistance Act**. Despite these successes, conditions for most Native Americans remained grim during the 1970s and 1980s: They had higher rates of tuberculosis, alcoholism, and suicide than any other group; nine of ten lived in substandard housing; and the unemployment rate for American Indians hovered around 40 percent.

27-1d The Women's Movement

During the 1950s, even as more and more women joined the paid workforce and participated in the political life of the nation, Americans emphasized women's private roles as wives and mothers; it seemed as if the women's movement that won American women the vote in the 1920s had all but disappeared. But during the 1960s, a "second wave" of the American women's movement emerged, and by the 1970s activists waged a multifront battle for "women's liberation." Feminists did not always agree on methods or goals, but their struggles and successes made the 1970s a pivotal decade for American women.

Indian Self-Determination and Education Assistance Act The 1975 act granted Native American tribes control of federal aid programs on the reservations and oversight of their own schools.

In 1963, the surprise popularity of Betty Friedan's *The Feminine Mystique* signaled there was ample fuel for a revived women's movement. Writing as a housewife and mother (though she had a long history of political activism as well), Friedan described "the problem with no name," the dissatisfaction of educated, middle-class wives and mothers like herself, who—looking at their nice homes and families—wondered guiltily if that was all there was to life. This "problem" was not new; the vague sense of dissatisfaction plaguing housewives had been a staple topic for women's magazines in the 1950s. But Friedan, instead of blaming individual women for failing to adapt to women's proper role, blamed the role itself and the society that created it.

The organized, liberal wing of the women's movement emerged in 1966, with the founding of the **National Organization for Women (NOW)**. NOW was initially a small group of educated, professional women. It served as a traditional lobbying group; its goal was to pressure the EEOC to enforce the 1964 Civil Rights Act (see Section 26-3c "Civil Rights Act"). Racial discrimination was the EEOC's focus, and discrimination on the basis of sex was such a low priority that the topic could be treated as a joke. When a reporter asked EEOC chair Franklin Roosevelt Jr., "What about sex?" Roosevelt laughed, "Don't get me started. I'm all for it." Women who faced workplace discrimination were not amused by such comments, and by 1970, NOW had one hundred chapters with more than three thousand members nationwide.

Another strand of the women's movement developed from the nation's increasingly radical movements for social change and justice. Many women, as they worked for civil rights or against the war in Vietnam, found themselves subordinate to men—making coffee, not policy. As they analyzed inequality in America's social and political structure, these young women began to discuss their own oppression, and the oppression of all women, in American society. In 1968, a group of women gathered outside the Miss America Pageant in Atlantic City to protest the "degrading mindless-boob girlie symbol" represented by the beauty pageant. Although nothing was burned, the pejorative 1970s term for feminists, "bra-burners," came from this event, in which women threw items of "enslavement" (girdles, high heels, curlers, and bras) into a "Freedom Trash Can."

27-1e Feminist Goals and Accomplishments

The feminism embraced by these young activists and others who challenged women's oppression was never a single, coherent set of beliefs. Some argued that the world should be governed by peaceful, noncompetitive values, which they believed were intrinsically female; others claimed that society imposed gender roles and that there were no innate differences between men and women. Most radical feminists, however, practiced what they called

National Organization for Women (NOW) Women's rights organization founded in 1966 that lobbied for equal opportunity, filed lawsuits against gender discrimination, and mobilized public opinion against sexism.

"personal politics." They believed, as feminist author Charlotte Bunch explained, that "there is no private domain of a person's life that is not political, and there is no political issue that is not ultimately personal." Some of these young women began to meet in "consciousness-raising" groups to discuss how, in their personal, everyday lives, women were subordinated by men and by a patriarchal society. By the early 1970s, consciousness-raising groups were meeting in suburban kitchens, college dorm rooms, and churches or synagogues, as women talked about power and patriarchy, romance and marriage, sexuality, abortion, health care, work, and family.

Such conversations left many women convinced that it was crucial to gain the right to control their own bodies. The Boston Women's Health Collective published *Our Bodies, Ourselves* in 1971 (the original edition sold more than 3 million copies), offering women new understanding of their own sexual and reproductive health. And women who sought the right to safe and legal abortions won a major victory in 1973 when the Supreme Court, in a 7-to-2 decision in *Roe v. Wade*, ruled that privacy rights protected a woman's choice to end a pregnancy.

Women's opportunities expanded enormously in the 1970s. When the decade began, help-wanted ads specified "male" or "female." Unmarried women could be denied birth

▲ Gloria Steinem, one of the co-founders of *Ms.* magazine, later said of its founding: "I realized as a journalist that there really was nothing for women to read that was controlled by women." *Ms.* premiered in January 1972 and the first issue, with comic book hero Wonder Woman on its cover, sold out within eight days.

control; women were systematically excluded from juries; women (married, divorced, or widowed) frequently could not obtain credit in their own names. U.S. rape law mirrored the claim of a psychiatrist at the University of Kansas student health center: "A woman sometimes plays a big part in provoking her attacker by . . . her overall attitude and appearance"; courts allowed attorneys to use women's sexual histories to discredit them and did not recognize spousal rape. Only 4 percent of American attorneys were female; women made up only 1.3 percent of the military, and there was not a single female general. National Airlines advertisements featured pretty young stewardesses with suggestive captions: "Hi, I'm Linda, and I'm going to FLY you like you've never been flown before." Less than 2 percent of college and university athletic budgets went to women's sports—and women received no athletic scholarships. No woman had ever been named a Rhodes Scholar, served as president of the *Harvard Law Review*, or been ordained as a pastor, rabbi, or (Episcopal) priest. All that would change by the end of the decade.

27-1f Opposition to the Women's Movement

Initially, the nation's elected representatives supported women's claims to equal rights. On March 22, 1972, Senate Republicans and Democrats joined to approve the **Equal Rights Amendment**—the same amendment first proposed by the National Women's Party in the 1920s. By a vote of 82 to 8, senators confirmed that "equality of rights under the law shall not be denied or abridged by the United States or by any State on account of sex." States rapidly fell in line to endorse the amendment; by the end of the year, twenty-two states (of the thirty-eight necessary to amend the Constitution) had ratified the ERA.

While the women's movement encompassed a broad range of women and found many male supporters, it was also met by powerful opposition—much of it from women. Many women believed that middle-class feminists did not understand the realities of their world. They had no desire to be "equal" if that meant giving up traditional gender roles in marriage or going out to work at low-wage, physically exhausting jobs. African American women and Latinas, many of whom had been active in movements for the liberation of their peoples and some of whom had helped create second-wave feminism, often came to regard feminism as a "white" movement that ignored their cultural traditions and needs; some believed the women's movement diverted time and energy away from the fight for racial equality.

Organized opposition to feminism came primarily from conservative, often religiously motivated men and women. As one conservative Christian writer claimed, "The Bible clearly states that the wife is to submit to her husband's leadership . . . just as she would to Christ her Lord." Such beliefs, along with fears about changing gender roles and expectations, fueled the STOP-ERA movement led by Phyllis Schlafly, a lawyer and prominent conservative political activist. Schlafly argued that ERA supporters were "a

bunch of bitter women seeking a constitutional cure for their personal problems." She attacked the women's movement as "a total assault on the role of the American woman as wife and mother, and on the family as the basic unit of society." Schlafly and her supporters argued that the ERA would foster federal intervention in personal life, decriminalize rape, force Americans to use unisex toilets, and make women subject to the military draft.

Many women saw feminism as an attack on the choices they had made and felt that by opposing the ERA they were defending their traditional roles. In fighting the ERA, tens of thousands of women became politically experienced; they fed a growing grassroots conservative movement that would come into its own in the 1980s. By the mid-1970s, the STOP-ERA movement had stalled the Equal Rights Amendment. Despite Congress's extension of the ratification deadline, the amendment would fall three states short of ratification and expire in 1982.

27-1g Gay Liberation

In the early 1970s, consensual sexual intercourse between people of the same sex was illegal in almost every state, and until 1973 homosexuality was labeled a mental disorder by the American Psychiatric Association. Homosexual couples did not receive partnership benefits, such as health insurance; they could not adopt children. The issue of gay and lesbian rights divided even progressive organizations: in 1970, the New York City chapter of NOW expelled its lesbian officers. Gay men and lesbians faced discrimination in both private and public life, but unlike most members of racial minorities, they could conceal the identity that made them vulnerable. Remaining "in the closet" offered protection from discrimination and harassment, but also foreclosed the possibility of an openly gay identity or sexual/romantic relationships. Reliance on "the closet" also made it very difficult to organize a political movement. There were small "homophile" organizations, such as the Mattachine Society (named for the Société Mattachine—a medieval musical organization whose members performed in masks, which allowed them to criticize the nobility without fear of reprisal—to evoke the "masked" lives of gay Americans) and the Daughters of Bilitis (after a work of love poems between women), which had worked for gay rights since the 1950s. But the symbolic beginning of the gay liberation movement came on June 28, 1969, when New York City police raided the Stonewall Inn, a gay bar in Greenwich Village, for violating the New York City law that made it illegal for more than three homosexual patrons to occupy a bar at the same time. That night, for the first time, patrons stood up to the police. As word spread through New York's gay community, hundreds more joined the confrontation. The next morning, New

Equal Rights Amendment Proposed constitutional amendment guaranteeing equal rights for women; passed with strong support of both Democrats and Republicans in congress, but fell short of ratification by the states by the congressionally-extended deadline of 1982.

Yorkers found a new slogan spray-painted on neighborhood walls: "Gay Power."

Inspired by the Stonewall riot, some men and women worked openly and militantly for gay rights. They focused on a dual agenda: legal equality and the promotion of Gay Pride. In a version of the identity politics adopted by racial and ethnic communities, some rejected the notion of fitting into straight (heterosexual) culture and helped create distinctive gay communities. By 1973, there were about eight hundred gay organizations in the United States. Centered in big cities and on college campuses, most organizations tried to create supportive environments for gay men and lesbians to come "out of the closet." Once "out," they could use their numbers ("We are everywhere" was a popular slogan) to push for political reform, such as nondiscrimination statutes similar to those that protected women and racial minority groups. By the end of the decade, gay men and lesbians were a political force in cities including New York, Miami, and San Francisco, and they played an increasingly visible role in the social and political life of the nation.

27-1h Affirmative Action

As activists made Americans increasingly aware of discrimination and inequality, policymakers struggled to frame remedies. As early as 1965, President Johnson had acknowledged the limits of civil rights legislation. "You do not take a person who, for years, has been hobbled by chains and liberate him, bring him up to the starting line of a race and then say, 'you are free to compete with all the others,'" Johnson told an audience at Howard University, "and still justly believe that you have been completely fair." In this speech, Johnson called for "not just legal equality . . . but equality as a fact and equality as a result." Here Johnson joined his belief that the federal government must help *individuals* attain the skills necessary to compete in American society to a new concept: equality could be measured by *group* outcomes or results.

Practical issues helped shift emphasis to group outcomes, as well. The 1964 Civil Rights Act had outlawed discrimination, but seemed to stipulate that action could be taken only when an employer "intentionally" discriminated against an individual. This individual, case-by-case approach to equal rights created a nightmare for the Equal Employment Opportunity Commission (EEOC). The tens of thousands of cases filed suggested that racial and sexual discrimination were widespread, but each alleged incident required proof that the employer intended to discriminate against an individual. Some argued that it was possible, instead, to prove discrimination by "results"—by the relative number of African Americans or women, for example, an employer had hired or promoted.

In 1969, the Nixon administration implemented the first major government affirmative action program to promote "equality of results." The Philadelphia Plan (so called because it targeted government contracts in that city) required businesses contracting with the federal government to show (in the words of President Nixon) "affirmative action to meet the goals of increasing minority employment" and set specific numerical "goals," or quotas, for employers. Major government contracts soon required affirmative action for women and members of racial and ethnic minorities, and many large corporations and universities began their own programs.

Supporters saw affirmative action as a remedy for the lasting effects of past discrimination. Critics (some of whom supported racial and sexual equality) argued that attempts to create proportional representation for women and minorities meant discrimination against other individuals who had not created past discrimination, and that group-based remedies violated the principle that individuals should be judged on their own merits. As affirmative action programs began to have an impact in hiring and college admissions, a deepening recession made jobs scarce. Thus, because the job market was not expanding, hiring more minorities and women often meant hiring fewer white men. White working-class men were most adversely affected by the policy, and many resented it. And while women and people of color had new protections, they gained them just as individual competition for jobs became fierce.

27-2 The End in Vietnam

▶ How did Richard Nixon simultaneously deescalate and expand the war in Vietnam?

▶ What were the domestic and international consequences of American involvement in Vietnam?

▶ Why does American involvement in Vietnam remain a controversial issue?

Of all the divisions in American politics and society at the end of the 1960s, none was as pervasive as that over the war in Vietnam. "I'm not going to end up like LBJ," Richard Nixon vowed after winning the 1968 presidential election, recalling that the war had destroyed Johnson's political career. "I'm going to stop that war. Fast." But he did not. He understood that the conflict was generating deep divisions at home and hurting the nation's image abroad, yet—like officials in the Johnson administration—he feared that a precipitous withdrawal would harm American credibility on the world stage as well as his own domestic standing. Anxious to get American troops out of Vietnam, Nixon was at the same time no less committed than his predecessors to preserving an independent, noncommunist South Vietnam. To accomplish these aims, he set upon a policy that at once contracted and expanded the war.

27-2a Invasion of Cambodia

A centerpiece of Nixon's policy was "Vietnamization"—the building up of South Vietnamese forces to replace U.S. forces. Nixon hoped that such a policy would quiet domestic opposition and advance the peace talks under way in Paris since May 1968. Accordingly, the president began to withdraw American troops from Vietnam, decreasing their number from 543,000 in the spring of 1969 to 156,800 by the end

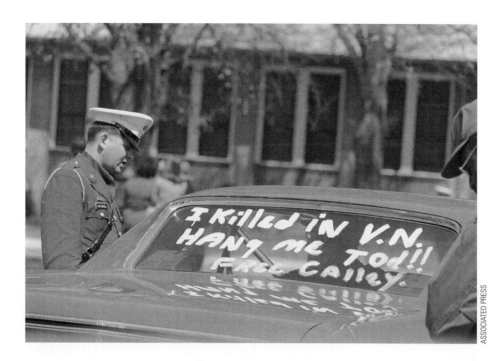

The court-martial of Lieutenant William Calley for his role in the My Lai massacre of more than 300 unarmed Vietnamese civilians, like the war in Vietnam, divided Americans.

ASSOCIATED PRESS

of 1971, and to 60,000 by the fall of 1972. Vietnamization did help limit domestic dissent, but it did nothing to end the stalemate in the Paris negotiations. Even as he embarked on this troop withdrawal, Nixon intensified the bombing of North Vietnam and enemy supply depots in neighboring Cambodia, hoping to pound Hanoi into concessions (see Map 26.2 in "Johnson and Vietnam," Section 26-4).

The bombing of neutral Cambodia commenced in March 1969. Over the next fourteen months, B-52 pilots flew 3,600 missions and dropped over 100,000 tons of bombs on that country. At first, the administration went to great lengths to keep the bombing campaign secret. When the North Vietnamese refused to buckle, Nixon turned up the heat: in April 1970, South Vietnamese and U.S. forces invaded Cambodia in search of arms depots and North Vietnamese army sanctuaries. The president announced publicly that he would not allow "the world's most powerful nation" to act "like a pitiful, helpless giant."

27-2b Protests and Counter-demonstrations

Instantly, the antiwar movement rose up, as students on about 450 college campuses went out on strike and hundreds of thousands of demonstrators gathered in various cities to protest the administration's policies. The crisis atmosphere intensified further on May 4, when National Guardsmen in Ohio fired into a crowd of students at Kent State University, killing four young people and wounding eleven. Ten days later, police and state highway patrolmen armed with automatic weapons blasted a women's dormitory at Jackson State, a historically black university in Mississippi, killing two students and wounding nine others. The police claimed they had been shot at, but no evidence of sniping could be found. In Congress, where opposition to the war had been

building over the previous months, Nixon's widening of the war sparked outrage, and in June the Senate terminated the Gulf of Tonkin Resolution of 1964. After two months, U.S. troops withdrew from Cambodia, having accomplished little.

Americans still remained divided on the war. Although a majority told pollsters they thought the original U.S. troop commitment to Vietnam had been a mistake, 50 percent said they believed Nixon's claim that the Cambodia invasion would shorten the war. Angered by the sight of demonstrating college students, many backed the president and the war effort. In Washington, an "Honor America Day" program attracted more than 200,000 people who heard Billy Graham and Bob Hope laud administration policy. Nevertheless, though Nixon welcomed these expressions of support, the tumult over the invasion served to reduce his options on the war. Henceforth, solid majorities could be expected to oppose any new missions for U.S. ground troops in Southeast Asia.

Nixon's troubles at home mounted in June 1971, when the *New York Times* and other newspapers began to publish the **Pentagon Papers**, a top-secret official study of U.S. decisions in the Vietnam War commissioned by former Secretary of Defense Robert McNamara. In 1969 Daniel Ellsberg, a thirty-eight-year-old former Pentagon aide who had contributed to a portion of the study and now felt increasingly disillusioned with the war, gained access to a copy being stored at the Rand Corporation in California. He spent months poring over the forty-seven volumes and determined he

Pentagon Papers A forty-seven-volume U.S. government study from the end of World War II to the Vietnam War, tracing U.S. involvement in Southeast Asia. Released to the press by former Pentagon employee Daniel Ellsberg, the papers revealed military mistakes and a long history of White House lies to Congress, foreign leaders, and the American people.

must disclose their contents to the public. The study showed incontrovertibly, Ellsberg believed, that presidents had repeatedly escalated the American commitment in Vietnam despite pessimistic estimates from their advisers. Perhaps disclosure of this information could force a change in policy. With the help of a Rand colleague, Ellsberg surreptitiously photocopied the entire study, then spent months pleading with antiwar senators and representatives to release it. When they refused, he went to the press.

Nixon secured an injunction to prevent publication, but the Supreme Court overturned the order. Americans learned from this study that political and military leaders frequently had lied to the public about their aims and strategies in Southeast Asia.

Equally troubling was the growing evidence of decay within the armed forces. Morale and discipline among troops had been on the decline even before Nixon took office, and there were growing reports of drug addiction, desertion, racial discord, even the murder of unpopular officers by enlisted men (a practice called "fragging"). Stories of atrocities committed by U.S. troops also began to make their way home. The court-martial and conviction in 1971 of Lieutenant William Calley, who was charged with overseeing the killing of more than three hundred unarmed South Vietnamese civilians in the hamlet of **My Lai** in 1968, got particular attention. An army photographer captured the horror in graphic pictures. For many, the massacre signified the dehumanizing impact of the war on those who fought it.

27-2c Paris Peace Accords

The Nixon administration, meanwhile, stepped up its efforts to pressure Hanoi into a settlement. Johnson had lacked the will to "go to the brink," Nixon told Kissinger, but "I have the will in spades." When the North Vietnamese launched a major offensive across the border into South Vietnam in March 1972, Nixon responded with a massive aerial onslaught against North Vietnam. In December 1972, after an apparent peace agreement collapsed when the South Vietnamese refused to moderate their position, the United States launched a massive air strike on the North—the so-called "Christmas bombing."

But a diplomatic agreement was close. Months earlier, Kissinger and his North Vietnamese counterpart in the negotiations, Le Duc Tho, had resolved many of the outstanding issues. Most notably, Kissinger agreed that North Vietnamese troops could remain in the South after the settlement, while Tho abandoned Hanoi's insistence that the Saigon government of Nguyen Van Thieu be removed. Nixon had instructed Kissinger to make concessions because the president was eager to improve relations with the Soviet Union and China, to win back the allegiance of America's allies, and to restore stability at home. On January 27, 1973, Kissinger and Le Duc Tho signed a cease-fire agreement in Paris, and Nixon compelled a reluctant Thieu to accept it by threatening to cut off U.S. aid while at the same time promising to defend the South if the North violated the agreement. In the accord, the United States promised to withdraw all of its troops within sixty days. North Vietnamese troops would be allowed to stay in South Vietnam, and a coalition government that included the Vietcong eventually would be formed in the South.

The United States pulled its troops out of Vietnam, leaving behind some military advisers. Soon, both North and South violated the cease-fire, and full-scale war erupted once more. The feeble South Vietnamese government, despite holding a clear superiority in the number of tanks and combat-ready troops, could not hold out. Just before its surrender, hundreds of Americans and Vietnamese who had worked for them were hastily evacuated from Saigon. On April 29, 1975, the South Vietnamese government collapsed, and Vietnam was reunified under a communist government based in Hanoi. Shortly thereafter, Saigon was renamed Ho Chi Minh City for the persevering patriot, who had died in 1969.

27-2d Costs of the Vietnam War

The overall costs of the war were immense. More than 58,000 Americans and somewhere between 1.5 to 3 million Vietnamese had died. Civilian deaths in Cambodia and Laos numbered in the hundreds of thousands. The war cost the United States at least $170 billion, and billions more would be paid out in veterans' benefits. The vast sums spent on the war became unavailable for investment in domestic programs. Instead, the nation suffered inflation and retreat from reform, as well as political schism and abuses of executive power. The war also delayed accommodation with the Soviet Union and the People's Republic of China, fueled friction with allies, and alienated Third World nations.

In 1975, communists assumed control and formed repressive governments in Vietnam, Cambodia, and Laos, but beyond Indochina the domino effect once predicted by U.S. officials never occurred. Acute hunger afflicted the people of those devastated lands. Soon refugees—"boat people"—crowded aboard unsafe vessels in an attempt to escape their battered homelands. Many emigrated to the United States, where they were received with mixed feelings by Americans reluctant to be reminded of defeat in Asia. But many Americans faced the fact that the United States, which had relentlessly bombed, burned, and defoliated once-rich agricultural lands, bore considerable responsibility for the plight of the Southeast Asian peoples.

27-2e Debate Over the Lessons of Vietnam

Americans seemed both angry and confused about the nation's war experience. Hawkish observers claimed that America's failure in Vietnam undermined the nation's credibility and tempted enemies to exploit opportunities at the expense of

My Lai South Vietnamese village and site of an intended search-and-destroy mission by U.S. soldiers that evolved into a brutal massacre of more than 300 unarmed civilians, including women and children; some were lined up in ditches and shot, with their village then burned to the ground.

The Image of War

The Vietnam War has been called the first "television war." More than ever before (or arguably since), news clips and photos brought Americans and others around the world face to face with the fighting and its victims. On June 8, 1972, as children and their families fled the village of Trang Bang, their bodies seared by napalm, Huynh Cong "Nick" Ut took this iconic photograph that became an antiwar rallying point and symbol of hope. The girl in the center, Phan Thi Kim Phuc, survived the attack but had to endure fourteen months of painful rehabilitation to treat the third-degree burns that covered more than half of her body. Kim later became a Canadian citizen and a Goodwill Ambassador for the United Nations Educational, Scientific and Cultural Organization (UNESCO).

CRITICAL THINKING

■ Some analysts have argued that a single image can become the voice of popular protest; others say that even indelible images such as this one cannot have that power. What do you think?

Nick Ut/AP Images

U.S. interests. They pointed to a "Vietnam syndrome"—a resulting American suspicion of foreign entanglements—which they feared would inhibit the future exercise of U.S. power. America lost in Vietnam, they asserted, because Americans had lost their guts at home.

Dovish analysts drew different conclusions, denying that the military had suffered undue restrictions. Some blamed the war on an imperial presidency that had permitted strong-willed men to act without restraint and on a weak Congress that had conceded too much power to the executive branch. Make the president adhere to the checks-and-balances system—make him go to Congress for a declaration of war—these critics counseled, and America would become less interventionist. This view found expression in the War Powers Act of 1973, which sought to limit the president's war-making freedom. Henceforth, Congress would have to approve any commitment of U.S. forces to combat action lasting more than sixty days. In the same year, the draft (which

◀ On Memorial Day 2010, a Vietnam veteran prays over the name of a friend, one of the few American women killed in the war. The national Vietnam Veterans Memorial in Washington, D.C., was designed in 1980 by Maya Lin, then an undergraduate at Yale University. Critics called the memorial a "scar" and a "black gash of shame," but it has become the most visited site on the National Mall.

AP Photo/Jose Luis Magana

had been shifted to a lottery system in 1969) came to an end; the U.S. military would henceforth be a volunteer army.

27-2f Vietnam Veterans

Public discussion of the lessons of the Vietnam War was also stimulated by veterans' calls for help in dealing with posttraumatic stress disorder, which afflicted thousands of the 2.8 million Vietnam veterans. Once home, they suffered nightmares and extreme nervousness. Doctors reported that the disorder stemmed primarily from the soldiers' having seen so many children, women, and elderly people killed. Some GIs inadvertently killed these people; some killed them vengefully and later felt guilt. Other veterans heightened public awareness of the war by publicizing their deteriorating health from the effects of exposure to the defoliant Agent Orange and other herbicides they had handled or were accidentally sprayed with in Vietnam. The Vietnam Veterans Memorial, erected in Washington, D.C., in 1982, has kept the issue alive, as have many oral history projects of veterans conducted by school and college students in classes to this day.

27-3 Nixon, Kissinger, and the World

▶ How did Richard Nixon and Henry Kissinger seek to adapt the United States to a more multipolar world?

▶ How did Nixon seek to improve relations with the Soviet Union and China?

▶ How did Nixon and Kissinger seek to assert U.S. influence in the Middle East and Third World countries?

Even as Nixon and Kissinger tried to achieve victory in Vietnam, they understood that the United States had overreached in the 1960s with a military commitment that had caused massive bloodshed, deep domestic divisions, and economic dislocation. The difficulties of the war signified to them that American power was limited and, in relative terms, in decline. This reality necessitated a new approach to the Cold War, and both moved quickly to reorient American policy. In particular, they believed the United States had to adapt to a new, multipolar international system; no longer could that system be defined simply by the Soviet-American rivalry. Western Europe was becoming a major player in its own right, as was Japan. The Middle East loomed increasingly large, due in large part to America's growing dependence on oil from the region. Above all, Americans had to come to grips with the reality of China by rethinking the policy of hostile isolation followed by the United States since the communist takeover in 1949.

They were an unlikely duo—the reclusive, ambitious Californian, born of Quaker parents, and the sociable, dynamic Jewish intellectual who had fled Nazi Germany as a child. Nixon, ten years older, was more or less a career politician, while Kissinger had made his name as a Harvard professor and foreign policy consultant. Whereas Nixon was a staunch Republican, Kissinger had no strong partisan commitments and indeed said disparaging things about Republicans to his Democratic friends. What the two men had in common was a tendency toward paranoia about rivals and a capacity to think in broad conceptual terms about America's place in the world.

In July 1969, Nixon and Kissinger acknowledged the limits of American power and resources when they announced the Nixon Doctrine. The United States, they said, would continue to provide economic aid to allies in Asia

◀ "This was the week that changed the world," Richard Nixon said of his visit to China in February 1972. Many historians agree and consider the China opening Nixon's greatest achievement as president. When he and wife Pat visited the Great Wall, the president reportedly remarked: "This is a great wall."

AP Images

and elsewhere, but these allies should no longer count on American troops. It was an admission that Washington could no longer afford to sustain its many overseas commitments and therefore would have to rely more on regional allies—including, it turned out, many authoritarian regimes—to maintain an anticommunist world order. Although Nixon did not say so, his doctrine amounted to a partial retreat from the 1947 Truman Doctrine, with its promise to support noncommunist governments facing internal or external threats to their existence.

27-3a Détente

If the Nixon Doctrine was one pillar of the new foreign policy, the other was **détente**: measured cooperation with the Soviets through negotiations within a general environment of rivalry, drawn from the French word for "relaxation." Détente's primary purpose, like that of the containment doctrine it resembled, was to check Soviet expansion and limit the Soviet arms buildup, though now that goal would be accomplished through diplomacy and mutual concessions. The second part of the strategy sought to curb revolution and radicalism in the Third World so as to quash threats to American interests. More specifically, the Cold War and limited wars like that in Vietnam were costing too much; expanded trade with friendlier Soviets and Chinese might reduce the huge U.S. balance-of-payments deficit. And improving relations with both communist giants, at a time when Sino-Soviet tensions were increasing, might exacerbate feuding between the two, weakening communism.

The Soviet Union's leadership had its own reasons for wanting détente. The Cold War was a drain on its resources, too, and by the late 1960s defense needs and consumer demands were increasingly at odds. Improved ties with Washington would also allow the USSR to focus more on its increasingly fractious relations with China and might generate serious progress on outstanding European issues, including the status of Germany and Berlin. Some ideologues in the Moscow leadership remained deeply suspicious of cozying up to the American capitalists, but they did not prevail over advocates of change. Thus, in May 1972, the United States and the USSR agreed in the ABM Treaty (officially the Treaty on the Limitation of Anti-Ballistic Missile Systems) to slow the costly arms race by limiting the construction and deployment of intercontinental ballistic missiles and antiballistic missile defenses.

27-3b Opening to China

While cultivating détente with the Soviet Union, the United States took dramatic steps to end more than two decades of Sino-American hostility. The Chinese welcomed the change because they wanted to spur trade and hoped that friendlier Sino-American relations would make their onetime ally and now enemy, the Soviet Union, more cautious. Nixon reasoned the same way: "We're using the Chinese thaw to get the Russians shook." In early 1972, Nixon made a historic trip to "Red China," where he and the venerable Chinese leaders Mao Zedong and Zhou Enlai agreed to disagree on a number of issues, except one: the Soviet Union should not be permitted to make gains in Asia. Sino-American relations improved slightly, and official diplomatic recognition and the exchange of ambassadors came in 1979.

The opening to communist China and the policy of détente with the Soviet Union reflected Nixon's and Kissinger's belief in the importance of maintaining stability among the great

détente Nixon's foreign policy initiative with the Soviet Union; it focused on mutual cooperation and sought to check expansion and reduce arms buildup through diplomacy and negotiation.

OPEC and the 1973 Oil Embargo

If one date can be said to have marked the relative decline of American power in the Cold War era and the arrival of the Arab nations of the Middle East as important players on the world stage, it would be October 20, 1973. That day, the Arab members of the Organization of Petroleum Exporting Countries (OPEC)—Saudi Arabia, Iraq, Kuwait, Libya, and Algeria—imposed a total embargo on oil shipments to the United States and to other allies of Israel. The move was in retaliation against U.S. support of Israel in the two-week-old Yom Kippur War. The embargo followed a decision by the members three days earlier to unilaterally raise oil prices, from $3.01 to $5.12 per barrel. In December, the five Arab countries, joined by Iran, raised prices again, to $11.65 per barrel, close to a fourfold increase from early October. "This decision," said National Security Adviser Henry Kissinger of the price hike, "was one of the pivotal events in the history of this century."

Kissinger exaggerated, but not by much. Gasoline prices surged across America, and some dealers ran low on supplies. Frustrated Americans endured endless lines at the pumps and shivered in underheated homes. Letters to newspaper editors expressed anger not merely at the Arab governments but also at the major oil companies, whose profits soared. When the embargo was lifted after five months, in March 1974, oil prices stayed high, and the aftereffects of the embargo would linger through the decade. Like no other event could, it confirmed the extent to which Americans no longer exercised full control over their own economic destiny.

Just twenty years before, in the early 1950s, Americans had produced at home all the oil they needed. Detroit automakers had no difficulty selling ever larger gas-guzzlers with ever more outrageous tail fins. By the early 1960s, the picture had begun to change, as American factories and automobiles then were dependent on foreign sources for one out of every six barrels of oil they used. By 1972, the figure had gone up to about two out of six,

or more than 30 percent. Although in absolute terms the amount was massive—U.S. motorists consumed one of every seven barrels used in the world each day—few Americans worried; hence the shock of the embargo. As author Daniel Yergin has put it, "The shortfall struck at fundamental beliefs in the endless abundance of resources, convictions so deeply rooted in the American character and experience that a large part of the public did not even know, up until October 1973, that the United States imported any oil at all."

Although Americans resumed their wasteful ways after the embargo ended, an important change had occurred, whether people understood it or not. The United States had become a dependent nation, its economic future linked to decisions by Arab leaders half a world away.

CRITICAL THINKING

- What lessons did the United States learn from the oil embargo?
- How did it affect foreign policy and national economic policies?

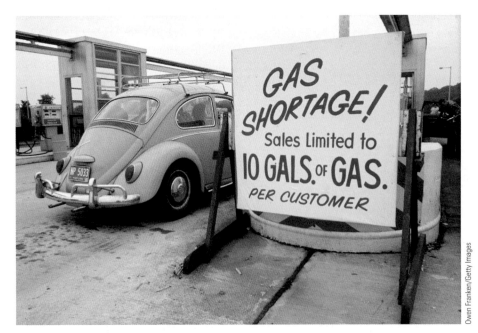

▲ A common sight during the oil crisis of 1973–74 was long lines and ominous signs at service stations in the United States. In this image, taken in early 1974, a station in Connecticut makes its point clearly.

powers. In the Third World, too, they sought stability, though there they hoped to get it not by change but by maintaining the status quo. As it happened, events in the Third World would provide the Nixon-Kissinger approach with its greatest test, and not merely because of Vietnam.

In the Middle East, the situation had grown more volatile in the aftermath of the Arab-Israeli Six-Day War in 1967. In that conflict, Israel had scored victories against Egypt and Syria, seizing the Sinai Peninsula and the Gaza Strip from Egypt, the West Bank and East Jerusalem from Jordan, and the Golan Heights from Syria (see Map 29.2). Instantly, Israel's regional position was transformed, as it gained 28,000 square miles and could henceforth defend itself more easily against invading military forces. But the victory came at a price. Gaza and the West Bank were the ancestral home of hundreds of thousands of Palestinians and the more recent home of additional hundreds of thousands of Palestinian refugees from the 1948 Arab-Israeli conflict (see Section 24-6f "Arab-Israeli Conflict,"). Suddenly, Israel found itself governing large numbers of people who wanted nothing more than to see Israel destroyed. When the Israelis began to establish Jewish settlements in their newly won areas, Arab resentment grew even stronger. Terrorists associated with the Palestinian Liberation Organization (PLO) made hit-and-run raids on Jewish settlements, hijacked jetliners, and murdered eleven Israeli Olympic team members at the 1972 Olympic Games in Munich, West Germany. The Israelis retaliated by assassinating PLO leaders.

In October 1973, on the Jewish High Holy Day of Yom Kippur, Egypt and Syria attacked Israel. Their motives were complex, but primarily they sought revenge for the 1967 defeat. Caught by surprise, Israel reeled before launching an effective counteroffensive against Soviet-armed Egyptian forces in the Sinai. In an attempt to punish Americans for their pro-Israel stance, the Organization of Petroleum Exporting Countries (OPEC), a group of mostly Arab nations that had joined together to raise the price of oil, embargoed shipments of oil to the United States and other supporters of Israel. An energy crisis and dramatically higher oil prices rocked the nation. Soon Kissinger arranged a cease-fire in the war, but OPEC did not lift the oil embargo until March 1974. The next year, Kissinger persuaded Egypt and Israel to accept a UN peacekeeping force in the Sinai. But peace did not come to the region, for Palestinians and other Arabs still vowed to destroy Israel, and Israelis insisted on building more Jewish settlements in occupied lands.

27-3c Antiradicalism in Latin America and Africa

In Latin America, meanwhile, the Nixon administration sought to preserve stability and to thwart radical leftist challenges to authoritarian rule. In Chile, after voters in 1970 elected a Marxist president, Salvador Allende, the CIA began secret operations to disrupt Chile and encouraged military officers to stage a coup. In 1973, a military junta ousted Allende and installed an authoritarian regime under

General Augusto Pinochet. (Allende was subsequently murdered.) Washington publicly denied any role in the affair that implanted iron-fisted tyranny in Chile for two decades.

In Africa as well, Washington preferred the status quo. Nixon backed the white-minority regime in Rhodesia (now Zimbabwe), while in South Africa he tolerated the white rulers who imposed the segregationist policy of apartheid on blacks and mixed-race "coloureds" (85 percent of the population), keeping them poor, disfranchised, and ghettoized in prisonlike townships. Elsewhere on the continent, Washington built economic ties and sent arms to friendly black nations, such as Kenya and the Republic of the Congo (Léopoldville) (now the Democratic Republic of the Congo). The administration also began to distance the United States from the white governments of Rhodesia and South Africa. America had to "prevent the radicalization of Africa," said Kissinger.

27-4 Presidential Politics and the Crisis of Leadership

▶ How did Nixon's personality and political beliefs shape his domestic policy record and lead to his downfall?

▶ In what ways was Nixon's domestic political agenda both liberal and conservative?

▶ What effect did the "Watergate" crisis have on American society and government?

Richard Nixon's foreign policy accomplishments were overshadowed by his failures at home. He betrayed the public trust and broke laws, large and small. His misconduct, combined with Americans' growing belief that their leaders had lied to them repeatedly about the war in Vietnam, shook Americans' faith in government. This new mistrust joined with conservatives' traditional suspicion of big, activist government to create a crisis of leadership and undermine liberal policies that had governed the nation since the New Deal, even in the Eisenhower era. The profound suspicion of presidential leadership and government action that enveloped the nation by the end of the Watergate hearings would limit what Gerald Ford and Jimmy Carter, Nixon's successors to the presidency, could accomplish.

27-4a Nixon's Domestic Agenda

Richard Nixon was brilliant, driven, politically cunning, able to address changing global realities with creativity. He was also crude, prejudiced against Jews and African Americans, happy to use dirty tricks and presidential power against those he considered his enemies, and driven by a sense of resentment that bordered on paranoia. Despite his tenacity and intelligence, Nixon—the son of a grocer from an agricultural region of southern California—was never accepted by the sophisticated northeastern liberal elite. (After Nixon's election, *Washingtonian* magazine joked that "cottage cheese with ketchup" had replaced elegant desserts at White House dinners.) Nixon loathed the liberal establishment, which loathed him back, and his presidency was driven by that hatred as much as by any strong philosophical commitment to conservative principles.

Nixon's domestic policy initiatives have long confused historians. Much of his agenda was liberal, expanding federal programs to improve society. The Nixon administration pioneered affirmative action. It doubled the budgets of the new National Endowment for the Humanities (NEH) and National Endowment for the Arts (NEA). Nixon supported the ERA, signed major environmental legislation, created the Occupational Safety and Health Administration (OSHA), actively attempted to manage the economy using deficit spending, and even proposed a guaranteed minimum income for all Americans.

At the same time, Nixon pursued a conservative agenda. One of his major legislative goals was "devolution," or shifting federal government authority to states and localities. He promoted revenue-sharing programs that distributed federal funds back to the states to use as they saw fit, thus appealing to those who were angry about, as they saw it, paying high taxes to support liberal "giveaway" programs for poor and minority Americans. As president, Nixon worked to equate the Republican Party with law and order and the Democrats with permissiveness, crime, drugs, radicalism, and the "hippie lifestyle." To capitalize on the backlash against the 1960s movements for social change and consolidate the support of those he called "the silent majority," Nixon fostered division, using his outspoken vice president, Spiro Agnew, to attack war protesters and critics as "naughty children," "effete . . . snobs," and "ideological eunuchs." He appointed four conservative justices to the Supreme Court: Warren Burger, Harry Blackmun, Lewis Powell Jr., and William Rehnquist.

With such a confusing record, was Nixon liberal, conservative, or simply pragmatic? The answer is complicated. For example, when the Nixon administration proposed a guaranteed minimum income for all Americans, including the working poor, his larger goal was to dismantle the federal welfare system and destroy its liberal bureaucracy of social workers (no longer necessary under Nixon's model). And though Nixon doubled funding for the NEA, he redirected awards from the northeastern art establishment—the "elite" that he thought of as an enemy—toward local and regional art groups that sponsored popular art forms, such as representational painting or folk music. Nixon did not reject a powerful role for the federal government, but he was suspicious of federal bureaucrats, social change activists, and intellectual elites.

In addition, recognizing the possibility of attracting white southerners to the Republican Party, Nixon pursued a highly pragmatic "southern strategy." He nominated two southerners for positions on the Supreme Court—one of whom had a segregationist record—and when Congress declined to confirm either nominee, Nixon protested angrily, saying, "I understand the bitter feelings of millions of Americans who live in the South." After the Supreme Court upheld a school desegregation plan that required a North Carolina school system—still highly segregated fifteen years after the *Brown* decision—to achieve racial integration by removing both black and white children from their neighborhood schools and busing them to schools elsewhere in the county (*Swann v. Charlotte-Mecklenburg*, 1971), Nixon denounced busing as a reckless and extreme remedy. (Neither resistance to busing nor continuing segregation was a purely southern phenomenon, as Boston showed in 1974 when residents protested—sometimes violently—court-ordered busing to combat school segregation.)

27-4b Enemies and Dirty Tricks

Nixon was almost sure of reelection in 1972. His Democratic opponent was **George McGovern**, a progressive senator from South Dakota and strong opponent of the Vietnam War. McGovern appealed to the left and essentially wrote off the middle, declaring, "I am not a centrist candidate." Alabama governor George Wallace, running on a third-party ticket, withdrew from the race after he was paralyzed in an assassination attempt. The Nixon campaign, however, was taking no chances. On June 17, four months before the election, five men tied to the Committee to Re-elect the President (CREEP) were caught breaking into the Democratic National Committee's offices at the Watergate complex in Washington, D.C. The break-in got little attention at the time, and Nixon was swept into office with 60 percent of the popular vote in November. McGovern carried only Massachusetts and the District of Columbia. But even as Nixon triumphed, his downfall had begun.

From the beginning of his presidency, Nixon was obsessed with the idea that, in a time of national turmoil, he was surrounded by enemies. He made "enemies lists," hundreds of names long, that included all black members of Congress and the presidents of most Ivy League universities. The Nixon administration worked, in the words of one of its members, to "use the available federal machinery to screw our political enemies." On Nixon's order, his aide Charles Colson (best known for his maxim "When you've got them by the balls, their hearts and minds will follow") formed a secret group called the Plumbers. Their first assignment was to break into the office of the psychiatrist treating Daniel Ellsberg, the former Pentagon employee who had gone public with the Pentagon Papers, looking for material to discredit him. The Plumbers expanded their "dirty tricks" operations during the 1972 presidential campaign, bugging phones, infiltrating campaign staffs, even writing and distributing anonymous letters falsely accusing Democratic candidates of sexual misconduct. They had already bugged the Democratic National Committee offices and were going back to plant more surveillance equipment when they were caught by the D.C. police at the Watergate complex.

George McGovern Liberal senator from South Dakota and Democratic candidate for president in 1972.

27-4c Watergate Cover-up and Investigation

Nixon was not directly involved in the Watergate break-in. But instead of distancing himself and firing those responsible, he tried to cover it up, ordering the CIA to stop the FBI's investigation, claiming it imperiled national security. At this point, Nixon had obstructed justice—a felony and, under the Constitution, an impeachable crime—but he had also, it seemed, halted the investigation. However, two young, relatively unknown reporters for the *Washington Post*, Carl Bernstein and Bob Woodward, stayed on the story. Aided by an anonymous, highly placed government official whom they code-named Deep Throat (the title of a notorious 1972 X-rated film), they followed a money trail that led straight to the White House. (W. Mark Felt, who was second in command at the FBI in the early 1970s, publicly identified himself as Watergate's Deep Throat in 2005.)

From May to August 1973, the Senate held televised public hearings on the Watergate affair. White House Counsel John Dean, fearful that he was being made the fall guy for the entire Watergate fiasco, gave damning testimony. Then, on July 13, a White House aide told the Senate Committee that Nixon regularly recorded his conversations in the Oval Office. These tape recordings were the "smoking gun" that could prove Nixon's direct involvement in the cover-up—but Nixon refused to turn the tapes over to Congress.

27-4d Impeachment and Resignation

As Nixon and Congress fought over the tapes, Nixon faced scandals on other fronts. In October 1973, Vice President Spiro Agnew resigned, following charges that he had accepted bribes while governor of Maryland. Following constitutional procedures, Nixon appointed and Congress approved Michigan's **Gerald Ford**, the House minority leader, as Agnew's replacement. Meanwhile, Nixon's staff grew increasingly concerned about his excessive drinking and seeming mental instability. Then, on October 24, 1973, the House of Representatives began impeachment proceedings against the president.

Under court order, Nixon began releasing edited portions of the Oval Office tapes to Congress. Although the first tapes revealed no criminal activity, the public was shocked by Nixon's constant obscenities and racist slurs. Finally, in July 1974, the Supreme Court ruled that Nixon must release all the tapes. Despite "mysterious" erasures on two key tapes, the House Judiciary Committee found evidence of three impeachable offenses: obstruction of justice, abuse of power, and contempt of Congress. On August 9, 1974, facing certain impeachment and conviction, Richard Nixon became the first president of the United States to resign his office.

The Watergate scandal shook the confidence of American citizens in their government. It also prompted Congress to reevaluate the balance of power between the executive and legislative branches. New laws intended to restrict presidential power included the War Powers Act and the 1974 Budget and Impoundment Control Act, which made it impossible for the president to disregard congressional spending mandates.

27-4e Ford's Presidency

Gerald Ford, the nation's first unelected president, faced a nation awash in cynicism. The presidency was discredited. The economy was in decline. The nation's people were divided. When, in one of his first official acts as president, Ford issued a full pardon to Richard Nixon, forestalling any attempts to bring criminal charges, his approval ratings plummeted from 71 to 41 percent. Some suggested, with no evidence, that he had struck some sort of sordid deal with Nixon. Ford insisted, for decades, that he had simply acted in the interest of the nation, but shortly before his death in late 2006 he told a reporter that, though few knew it, he and Nixon had been good friends and that he "didn't want to see my real friend have the stigma" of criminal charges.

While Ford was, overall, a decent and honorable man who did his best to end what he called "the long national nightmare," he accomplished little domestically during his two and a half years in office. The Democrats gained a large margin in the 1974 congressional elections and, after Watergate, Congress was willing to exercise its power. Ford almost routinely vetoed its bills—thirty-nine in one year—but Congress often overrode his veto. And Ford had become the object of constant mockery, portrayed as a buffoon and a klutz in political cartoons, comedy monologues, and especially on the new hit television show *Saturday Night Live*. When Ford slipped on the steps exiting *Air Force One*, all major newscasts showed the footage. The irony of portraying Ford—who had turned down a chance to play in the National Football League in order to attend Yale Law School—as physically inept was extraordinary. But as Ford understood, these portrayals began to give the impression that he was a "stumbler," in danger of making blunders of all kinds. Ford caught the fallout of disrespect that Nixon's actions had unleashed. No longer would respect for the office of the presidency prevent the mass media from reporting presidential slips, stumbles, frailties, or misconduct. Ford was the first president to discover how much the rules had changed.

27-4f Carter as "Outsider" President

Jimmy Carter, who was elected in 1976 by a slim margin, initially benefited from Americans' suspicion of politicians. Carter was a one-term governor of Georgia, one of the new southern leaders who were committed to racial equality and integration. He had grown up in the rural Georgia town of Plains, where his family owned a peanut farm, graduated from the U.S. Naval Academy, then served as an engineer in the navy's nuclear submarine program. Carter, a deeply religious born-again Christian, made a virtue of his lack of political experience. Promising the American people, "I will

Gerald Ford Michigan congressman who took the place of Vice President Spiro Agnew when Agnew resigned following charges of corruption. Ford became the thirty-eighth president of the United States when Nixon resigned in 1974.

Jimmy Carter Thirty-ninth president of the United States (1977–1981).

▲ Resigning in disgrace as impeachment for his role in the Watergate cover-up became a certainty, Richard Nixon flashes the "V for victory" sign as he leaves the White House for the last time.

never lie to you," he emphasized his distance from Washington and the political corruption of recent times.

From his inauguration, when he broke with the convention of a motorcade and walked down Pennsylvania Avenue holding hands with his wife and close adviser, Rosalynn, and their young daughter, Amy, Carter rejected the trappings of the imperial presidency and emphasized his populist, outsider appeal. But the outsider status that gained him the presidency would make Carter a less effective president. Though he was an astute policymaker, he scorned the sort of deal making necessary to get legislation through Congress.

Carter faced problems that would have challenged any leader: the economy continued to decline, energy shortages had not abated, the American people distrusted their government. More than any other American leader of the post–World War II era, Carter was willing to tell the American people things they did not want to hear. As shortages of natural gas forced schools and businesses to close during the bitterly cold winter of 1977, Carter went on television—wearing a cardigan sweater—to call for "sacrifice" in a new era of limits. Carter tried to model that sacrifice: he had White House thermostats lowered to a daytime temperature of 65 degrees and asked all Americans to do the same. He also tried to shape policy, submitting a detailed, conservation-based energy plan to Congress. And he moved beyond concrete solutions. In the defining speech of his

presidency Carter told Americans that the nation suffered from a crisis of the spirit. He talked about the false lures of "self-indulgence and consumption," about "paralysis and stagnation and drift." And he called for a "new commitment to the path of common purpose." But his words failed to inspire Americans to break free of what was then described as a national malaise.

Carter did score some noteworthy domestic accomplishments. He worked to ease burdensome government regulations without destroying consumer and worker safeguards, and created the Department of Energy and the Department of Education. He also established a $1.6 billion "superfund" to clean up abandoned chemical waste sites and placed more than 100 million acres of Alaskan land under the federal government's protection as national parks, national forests, and wildlife refuges.

27-5 Economic Crisis

▶ What were the causes of the economic crisis in the 1970s?

▶ How did the federal government attempt to manage the economic crisis in the 1970s?

▶ How did Americans respond to the economic crisis of the 1970s?

Americans' loss of confidence in their political leaders was intensified by a growing economic crisis. Since World War II, except for a few brief downturns, prosperity had been a fundamental condition of American life. A steadily rising gross national product, based largely on growing rates of productivity, had propelled large numbers of Americans into the economically comfortable middle class. Prosperity had made possible the great liberal initiatives of the 1960s and improved the lives of America's poor and elderly citizens. But in the early 1970s, that long period of economic expansion and prosperity came to an end. Almost every economic indicator drove home bad news. In 1974 alone, the gross national product dropped 2 full percentage points. Industrial production fell 9 percent. Inflation—the increase in costs of goods and services—skyrocketed, and unemployment grew.

27-5a Stagflation and Its Causes

Throughout most of the 1970s, the U.S. economy floundered in a condition that economists dubbed "stagflation": a stagnant economy characterized by high unemployment combined with out-of-control inflation (see Figure 27.1). Stagflation was almost impossible to manage with traditional economic remedies. When the federal government increased spending to stimulate the economy and so reduce unemployment, inflation grew. When the federal government tried to rein in inflation by cutting government spending or tightening the money supply, the recession deepened and unemployment rates skyrocketed.

The causes of the economic crisis were complex. Federal management of the economy was in part to blame: President Johnson had reversed conventional economic wisdom and created inflationary pressure by insisting that the United States could have both "guns and butter" as he waged a very expensive war in Vietnam while greatly expanding domestic spending in his Great Society programs. But America's changing role in the global economy also created problems. After World War II, with most leading industrial nations in ruins, the United States had stood alone at the pinnacle of the global economy. But in the decades that followed, the war-ravaged nations—often with major economic assistance from the United States—had built new, technologically advanced industrial plants. By the early 1970s, both of America's major wartime adversaries, Japan and Germany, had become major economic powers—and major competitors in global trade. U.S. trade laws allowed easy access to American consumers even as those nations restricted American imports. In 1971, for the first time since the end of the nineteenth century, the United States imported more goods than it exported, beginning an era of American trade deficits.

American corporations were also to blame. During the years of global dominance, few American companies saw the need to improve production techniques or educate workers, and thus American productivity—that is, the average

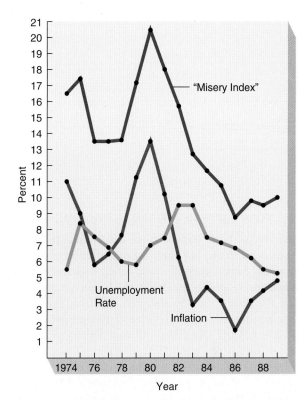

Figure 27.1 **"Misery Index" (Unemployment Plus Inflation), 1974–1989**

Americans' economic discomfort directly determined their political behavior. When the "misery index" was high in 1976 and 1980, Americans voted for a change in presidents. When economic discomfort declined in 1984 and 1988, Ronald Reagan and George Bush were the political beneficiaries. *Source: Adapted from* Economic Report of the President, 1992 *(Washington, D.C.: 1992), pp. 340, 365.*

output of goods per hour of labor—had begun to decline. As workers' productivity declined, however, their wages rarely did. High labor costs combined with falling productivity made American goods more and more expensive—both for Americans and for consumers in other nations. Even worse, without significant competition from foreign manufacturers, American companies had allowed the quality of their goods to decline. From 1966 to 1973, for example, American car and truck manufacturers had to recall almost 30 million vehicles because of serious defects.

America's global economic vulnerability was driven home by the energy crisis that began in 1973. Americans had grown up with cheap and abundant energy, and their lifestyles showed it. American passenger cars got an average of 13.4 miles per gallon in 1973, when a gallon of gas cost 38 cents (about $2.07 in 2016 dollars); neither home-heating nor household appliances were designed to be energy efficient. The country, however, depended on imported oil for almost one-third of its energy supply. When OPEC cut off oil shipments to the United States, U.S. oil prices rose 350 percent. The increases reverberated through the economy: heating costs, shipping costs, and manufacturing costs increased, and so did the cost of goods and services. Inflation jumped from 3 percent in early 1973 to 11 percent in 1974. Sales of gas-guzzling American cars plummeted as people rushed to buy energy-efficient subcompacts from Japan and Europe. American car manufacturers, stuck with machinery for producing large cars, were hit hard. GM laid off 6 percent of its domestic workforce and put an even larger number on rolling unpaid leaves. As the ailing automobile industry quit buying steel, glass, and rubber, manufacturers of these goods laid off workers, too.

27-5b Attempts to Fix the Economy

American political leaders tried desperately to manage the economic crisis, but their actions often exacerbated it instead. As America's rising trade deficit undermined international confidence in the dollar, the Nixon administration ended the dollar's link to the gold standard; free-floating exchange rates increased the price of foreign goods in the United States and stimulated inflation. President Ford created a voluntary program, Whip Inflation Now (complete with red and white "WIN" buttons), in 1974 to encourage grassroots anti-inflation efforts. Following the tenets of monetary theory, which held that, with less money available to "chase" the supply of goods, price increases would gradually slow down, ending the inflationary spiral, Ford curbed federal spending and encouraged the Federal Reserve Board

to tighten credit—and prompted the worst recession in forty years. In 1975, unemployment climbed to 8.5 percent.

Carter first attempted to bring unemployment rates down by stimulating the economy, but inflation careened out of control; he then tried to slow the economy down—and prompted a major recession during the election year of 1980. One approach pointed in a new direction: both Ford and Carter pinned their hopes less on government regulation than on market competition, and the Carter administration led a bipartisan effort to deregulate airline, trucking, banking, and communications industries. But at the end of the decade, the economy was still in crisis and Americans were losing faith in the American economy and in the ability of their political leaders to manage it.

27-5c Impacts of the Economic Crisis

The economic crisis of the 1970s accelerated the nation's transition from an industrial to a service economy. During the 1970s, the American economy "deindustrialized." Automobile companies laid off workers. Massive steel plants shut down, leaving entire communities devastated. Other manufacturing concerns moved overseas, seeking lower labor costs and fewer government regulations. New jobs were created—27 million of them—but they were overwhelmingly in the lower end of what economists call the "service sector": retail sales, restaurants, warehouse and transportation work. As heavy industries collapsed, formerly highly paid, unionized workers took

▲ Long lines of people seeking unemployment benefits formed in this St. Louis suburb after nearby Chrysler auto and truck assembly plants shut down.

Bettmann/Getty Images

jobs in the growing—but not unionized—service sector, most of which paid lower wages and lacked health care benefits. Formerly successful blue-collar workers saw their middle-class standard of living slipping away.

In addition, more people were chasing fewer jobs. Married homemakers looked for work because inflation steadily ate away at their husbands' wages. Baby boomers added pressure; even in the best of times the economy would have been hard pressed to produce jobs for the millions of young people who entered the labor market in the 1970s. Young people graduating from high school or college in the 1970s had been raised with high expectations. Instead, they found new limits.

The economic crisis also helped to shift the economic and population centers of the nation. As the old industrial regions of the North and Midwest went into decline, people fled the "snow belt" or the "rust belt," speeding up the Sunbelt boom already in progress (see Map 27.1). The Sunbelt was where the jobs were. The federal government had invested heavily in the South and West during the postwar era, especially in military and defense industries, and in the infrastructures necessary for them. Never a major center for heavy manufactures, the Sunbelt was primed for the rapid growth of modern industries and services—aerospace, defense, electronics, transportation, research, banking and finance, and leisure. City and state governments competed to lure businesses and investment dollars, in part by preventing the growth of

unions. Atlanta, Houston, and other southern cities marketed themselves as cosmopolitan, sophisticated, and racially tolerant; they bought sports teams and built museums.

This population shift south and west, combined with the flight of middle-class taxpayers to the suburbs, created disaster in northern and midwestern cities. New York City, close to financial collapse by late 1975, was saved only when the House and Senate Banking Committees approved federal loan guarantees. Cleveland defaulted on its debts in 1978, the first major city to do so since Detroit declared bankruptcy in 1933.

27-5d Tax Revolts

Even as stagflation and Sunbelt growth transformed American politics, a "tax revolt" movement emerged in the rapidly growing American West. In California, inflation had driven property taxes up rapidly, hitting middle-class taxpayers hard. In this era of economic decline and post-Watergate suspicion, angry taxpayers saw government as the problem. Instead of calling for wealthy citizens and major corporations to pay a larger share of taxes, voters rebelled against taxation itself. California's Proposition 13, passed by a landslide in 1978, rolled back property taxes and restricted future increases. Within months of Proposition 13's passage, thirty-seven states cut property taxes, and twenty-eight lowered their state income tax rates.

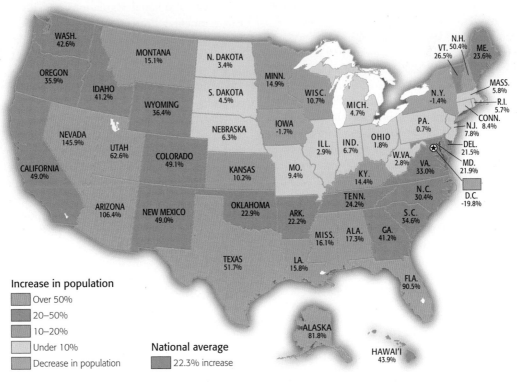

Map 27.1 The Continued Shift to the Sunbelt in the 1970s and 1980s

Throughout the 1970s and 1980s, Americans continued to leave economically declining areas of the North and East in pursuit of opportunity in the Sunbelt. States in the Sunbelt and in the West had the largest population increases. *Source: "Shift to the Sunbelt," Newsweek, September 10, 1990.*

The impact of Proposition 13 and similar initiatives was initially cushioned by state budget surpluses, but as those surpluses turned to deficits, states cut services—closing fire stations and public libraries, ending or limiting mental health services and programs for the disabled. Public schools were hit especially hard. The tax revolt movement signaled the growth of a new conservatism; voters who wanted lower taxes and smaller government would help bring Ronald Reagan to the White House in the election of 1980.

27-5e Credit and Investment

The runaway inflation of the 1970s also changed how Americans managed their money. Before this era, home mortgages and auto loans were the only kind of major debt most Americans would venture. National credit cards had become common only in the late 1960s, and few Americans—especially those who remembered the Great Depression—were willing to spend money they did not have. In the 1970s, however, thriftiness stopped making sense. Double-digit inflation rates meant double-digit declines in the purchasing power of a dollar. It was economically smarter to buy goods before their prices went up—even if it meant borrowing the money. Because debt was paid off later with devalued dollars, the consumer came out ahead. In 1975, consumer debt hit a high of $167 billion; by 1979 that figure had almost doubled, to $315 billion.

The 1970s were also the decade in which average Americans became investors rather than savers. Throughout the 1970s, because of regulations created during the Great Depression, the interest rates that banks could pay on individual savings accounts were capped. An average savings account bearing 5 percent interest actually *lost* more than 20 percent of its value from 1970 through 1980 because of inflation. That same money, invested at market rates, would have grown dramatically. Fidelity Investments, a mutual fund company, saw a business opportunity: its money market accounts combined many smaller investments to purchase large-denomination Treasury bills and certificates of deposit, thus allowing small investors to get the high interest rates normally available only to major investors. Money flooded out of passbook accounts and into money funds, and money market investments grew from $1.7 billion in 1974 to $200 billion in 1982. At the same time, deregulation of the New York Stock Exchange spawned discount brokerage houses, whose low commission rates made it affordable for middle-class investors to trade stocks.

27-6 An Era of Cultural Transformation

▶ Why were Americans uneasy about the state of the environment and technological change?

▶ How did sexual behavior and expectations about the family change during this decade?

▶ How does the emphasis on "diversity" emerge, and how does it differ from affirmative action?

During the 1970s, as Americans struggled with economic recession, government betrayal, and social division, they also transformed critical parts of American culture. The current environmental movement, the growth of technology, the rise of born-again Christianity and a "therapeutic culture," contemporary forms of sexuality and the family, new roles for youth, and America's emphasis on diversity all have roots in this pivotal decade.

27-6a Environmentalism

Just as Americans were forced to confront the end of postwar prosperity, a series of ecological crises drove home the limits on natural resources and the fragility of the environment. In 1969, a major oil spill took place off the coast of Santa Barbara, California; that same year, the polluted Cuyahoga River, flowing through Cleveland, caught fire. Although the energy crisis of the 1970s was due to an oil embargo, not a scarcity of oil, it drove home the real limits of the world's supplies of oil and natural gas. In 1979, human error contributed to a nuclear accident at the Three Mile Island nuclear power plant near Harrisburg, Pennsylvania; in 1980, President Carter declared a federal emergency in the Niagara Falls, New York neighborhood of Love Canal—which had previously served as a dump site for a local chemical manufacturer—after it was discovered that over 30 percent of local residents had suffered chromosomal damage from exposure to toxic chemicals that had leaked from the dump. Public activism during the 1970s produced major environmental regulations and initiatives, from the Environmental Protection Agency (EPA), created (under strong public pressure) in 1970 by the Nixon administration, to eighteen major environmental laws enacted by Congress during the decade.

When 20 million Americans—half of them schoolchildren—gathered in local communities to celebrate the first Earth Day on April 22, 1970, they signaled the triumph of a relatively new understanding of environmentalism. Traditional concerns about preserving "unspoiled" wilderness had joined with a new focus on "ecology," which stressed the connections between the earth and all living organisms, including humans. Central to this movement was a recognition that the earth's resources were finite and must be both conserved and protected from the consequences of human action, such as pollution. In 1971, biologist Barry Commoner insisted, "The present course of environmental degradation . . . is so serious, that, if continued, it will destroy the capability of the environment to support a reasonably civilized human society." Many of those concerned about the strain on earth's resources also identified rapid global population growth as a problem, and state public health offices frequently dispensed contraceptives as a way to stem this new "epidemic."

27-6b Technology

During these years, Americans became increasingly uneasy about the science and technology that had been one source

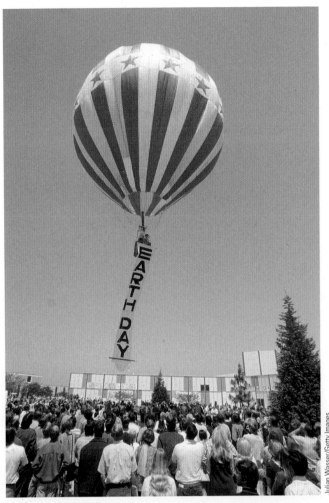

▲ Students at Cerritos College celebrate the first Earth Day, April 22, 1970. More than 20 million Americans participated in local teach-ins, celebrations, and protests to draw attention to environmental issues. By 1990, Earth Day was observed throughout the world, drawing 200 million participants from 141 nations.

of America's might. In a triumph of technology, American astronaut **Neil Armstrong** stepped onto the lunar surface on July 20, 1969, as people worldwide watched the grainy television transmission and heard, indistinctly, his first words—"That's one small step for [a] man, one giant leap for mankind." But the advances that could take a man to the moon seemed unable to cope with earthbound problems of poverty, crime, pollution, and urban decay; and the failure of technological warfare to deliver victory in Vietnam came at the same time antiwar protesters were questioning the morality of using such technology. Some Americans joined a movement for "appropriate technology" and human-scale development, but the nation was profoundly dependent on complex technological systems. And it was during the 1970s that the foundation was laid for America's computer revolution. The integrated circuit was created in 1970, and by 1975 the MITS Altair

8800—operated by toggle switches that entered individual binary numbers, boasting 256 bytes of memory, and requiring about thirty hours to assemble—could be mail-ordered from Albuquerque, New Mexico.

27-6c Religion and the Therapeutic Culture

As Americans confronted material limits, they increasingly sought spiritual fulfillment and well-being. Some turned to religion, though not to traditional mainstream Protestantism. Methodist, Presbyterian, and Episcopalian churches all lost members during this era, while membership in evangelical and fundamentalist Christian churches grew dramatically. Protestant evangelicals, professing a personal relationship with their savior, described themselves as "born again" and emphasized the immediate, daily presence of God in their lives. Even some Catholics, such as the Mexican Americans who embraced the *cursillo* movement (a "little course" in faith), sought a more personal relationship with God. Other Americans looked to the variety of beliefs and practices described as "New Age." The New Age movement drew from, and often combined, versions of nonwestern spiritual and religious practices, including Zen Buddhism, yoga, and shamanism, along with insights from Western psychology and a form of spiritually oriented environmentalism. Some desires for spiritual comfort went badly wrong, as when 907 members of the People's Temple, a religious cult led by James Jones, committed "revolutionary suicide" by drinking cyanide-laced Kool-Aid at "Jonestown," the group's compound in Guyana, in 1978.

Also in the 1970s, America saw the full emergence of a "therapeutic" culture. Although some Americans were disgusted with the self-centeredness of the "Me Decade," bestselling books by therapists and self-help gurus insisted that individual feelings offered the ultimate measure of truth; emotional honesty and self-awareness were social goods surpassing the bonds of community, friendship, or family. Self-help books with titles like *I Ain't Much Baby—But I'm All I've Got*, or *I'm OK—You're OK* (first published in 1967, it became a best seller in the mid-1970s) made up 15 percent of all best-selling books during the decade.

27-6d Sexuality and the Family

One such self-help book was *The Joy of Sex* (1972), which sold 3.8 million copies in two years. Sex became much more visible in America's public culture during the 1970s, as network television loosened its regulation of sexual content. At the beginning of the 1960s, married couples in television shows were required to occupy twin beds; in the 1970s, hit television shows included *Three's Company*, a situation comedy based on the then-scandalous premise that a single man shared an apartment with two beautiful female roommates—and got away with it only by pretending to their suspicious landlord

Neil Armstrong First person to set foot on the moon.

that he was gay. *Charlie's Angels*, another major television hit, capitalized on what people called the "jiggle factor" and displayed (for the time) lots of bare female flesh. A major youth fad of the era was "streaking," running naked through public places. Donna Summers's 1975 disco hit "Love to Love You Baby" contained sixteen minutes of sexual moaning. Discos were sites of sexual display, both for gay men and for macho working-class cultures; the hustle (a dance) originated in a Latino section of the Bronx, and the 1977 hit film *Saturday Night Fever* portrayed an Italian American young man who escaped the confines of his family and the limits of his dead-end job in sexually charged dance at a Brooklyn disco. And though very few Americans participated in heterosexual orgies at New York City's Plato's Retreat, many knew about them through a *Time* magazine feature story.

Sexual behaviors had also changed. The 1970s were the era of singles bars and gay bathhouses, and some Americans led sexual lives virtually unrestrained by the old rules. For most Americans, however, the major changes brought about by the "sexual revolution" were a broader public acceptance of premarital sex and a limited acceptance of homosexuality, especially among more educated Americans. More and more heterosexual young people lived together without marriage during the 1970s; the census bureau even coined the term *POSSLQ* ("persons of opposite sex sharing living quarters") to describe the relationship. When First Lady Betty Ford said on 60 *Minutes* that she would not be surprised if her then-seventeen-year-old daughter Susan began a sexual relationship, it was clear that much had changed in the course of a decade.

Changes in sexual mores and in the roles possible for women helped to alter the shape of the American family as well. Both men and women married later than in recent decades, and American women had fewer children. By the end of the 1970s, the birth rate had dropped almost 40 percent from its 1957 peak. Almost one-quarter of young single women in 1980 said that they did not plan to have children. And a steadily rising percentage of babies was born to unmarried women, as the number of families headed by never-married women rose 400 percent during the 1970s. The divorce rate also rose, in part because states implemented "no fault" divorce. Although families seemed less stable in the 1970s than in the previous postwar decades, Americans also developed a greater acceptance of various family forms (the blended family of television's *Brady Bunch*, for example), and many young couples sought greater equality between the sexes in romantic relationships or marriages.

27-6e Youth

Young people gained new freedoms and responsibilities in American society during the 1970s, but they also confronted economic crisis and social upheaval. In 1971, partly in recognition that the eighteen-year-old men who were eligible for the draft were not eligible to vote, Congress passed—and the states quickly ratified—the Twenty-sixth Amendment, which guaranteed the right of eighteen-year-olds to vote. In a similar impulse, twenty-nine states lowered their minimum drinking age. Marijuana use skyrocketed, and several states moved toward decriminalization. As young people graduated from high school or college, they were more likely to live with others their own age than with their parents. In the early part of the decade, some young people established communes—both urban and rural—and attempted to create countercultural worlds outside "the system." Later in the decade, a very different group of young people, partly in reaction to a postindustrial landscape of limited opportunity and the seeming impossibility of political change, created the punk movement, which offered new physical and cultural spaces for youth both through music and its do-it-yourself ethic.

27-6f Diversity

The racial justice and identity movements of the late 1960s and the 1970s made all Americans more aware of differences among the nation's peoples—an awareness made stronger by the great influx of new immigrants, not from Europe but from Latin America and Asia. It was a challenge, however, to figure out how to acknowledge the new importance of "difference" in public policy. The solution developed in the 1970s was the idea of "diversity." Difference was not a problem but a strength; the nation should not seek policies to diminish differences among its peoples but should instead seek to foster the "diversity" of its schools, workplaces, and public culture.

One major move in this direction came in the 1978 Supreme Court decision *Regents of the University of California v. Bakke*. Allan Bakke, a thirty-three-year-old white man with a strong academic record, had been denied admission to the medical school of the University of California at Davis. Bakke sued, charging that he had been denied "equal protection" of the law because the medical school's affirmative action program reserved 16 percent of its slots for racial minority candidates, who were held to lower standards than other applicants. The case set off furious debates nationwide over the legitimacy of affirmative action. In 1978, the Supreme Court, in a split decision, decided in favor of Bakke. Four justices argued that any race-based decision violated the Civil Rights Act of 1964; four saw affirmative action programs as constitutionally acceptable remedies for past discrimination. The deciding vote, though for Bakke, contained an important qualification. A "diverse student body," Justice Lewis Powell wrote, is "a constitutionally permissible goal for an institution of higher education." To achieve the positive quality of "diversity," educational institutions could take race into account when making decisions about admissions.

27-7 Renewed Cold War and Middle East Crisis

▶ What challenges did Jimmy Carter face in implementing his foreign policy?

▶ How did the relationship between the United States and the Middle East develop during Jimmy Carter's presidency?

▶ What factors contributed to tense relations between the Soviet Union and the United States?

When Jimmy Carter took office in 1977, he asked Americans to put their "inordinate fear of Communism" behind them. With reformist zeal, Carter vowed to reduce the U.S. military presence overseas, to cut back arms sales (which had reached the unprecedented height of $10 billion per year under Nixon), and to slow the nuclear arms race. At the time, more than 400,000 American military personnel were stationed abroad, the United States had military links with ninety-two nations, and the CIA was active on every continent. Carter promised to avoid new Vietnams through an activist preventive diplomacy in the Third World and to give more attention to environmental issues as well as relations between rich and poor nations. He especially determined to improve human rights abroad—the freedom to vote, worship, travel, speak out, and get a fair trial. Like his predecessors, however, Carter identified revolutionary nationalism as a threat to America's prominent global position.

27-7a Carter's Divided Administration

Carter spoke and acted inconsistently, in part because in the post-Vietnam years, no consensus existed in foreign policy and in part because his advisers squabbled among themselves. One source of the problem was the stern-faced Zbigniew Brzezinski, a Polish-born political scientist who became Carter's national security adviser. An old-fashioned Cold Warrior, Brzezinski blamed foreign crises on Soviet expansionism. Carter gradually listened more to Brzezinski than to Secretary of State Cyrus Vance, an experienced public servant who advocated quiet diplomacy. Vocal neoconservative intellectuals, such as Norman Podhoretz, editor of *Commentary* magazine, and the Committee on the Present Danger, founded in 1976 by such Cold War hawks as Paul Nitze, who had composed NSC-68 in 1950, criticized Carter for any relaxation of the Cold War and demanded that he jettison détente.

Nitze got his wish. Under Carter, détente deteriorated, and the Cold War deepened. But it did not happen right away. Initially, Carter maintained fairly good relations with Moscow and was able to score some foreign policy successes around the world. In Panama, where citizens longed for control over the Canal Zone, which they believed had been wrongfully taken from them in 1903, Carter reenergized negotiations that had begun after anti-American riots in Panama in 1964. The United States signed two treaties with Panama in 1977. One provided for the return of the Canal Zone to Panama in 2000, and the other guaranteed the United States the right to defend the canal after that time. With conservatives denouncing the deal as a sellout, the Senate narrowly endorsed both agreements in 1978. The majority agreed with Carter's argument that relinquishing the canal was the best way to improve U.S. relations with Latin America.

27-7b Camp David Accords

Important though it was, the Panama agreement paled next to what must be considered the crowning accomplishment of Carter's presidency: the **Camp David Accords**, the first mediated peace treaty between Israel and an Arab nation. Through tenacious personal diplomacy at a Camp David, Maryland, meeting in September 1978 with Egyptian and Israeli leaders, the president persuaded Israel and Egypt to agree to a peace treaty, gained Israel's promise to withdraw from the Sinai Peninsula, and forged a provisional agreement that provided for continued negotiations on the future status of the Palestinian people living in the occupied territories of Jordan's West Bank and Egypt's Gaza Strip (see Map 29.2). Other Arab states denounced the agreement for not requiring Israel to relinquish all occupied territories and for not guaranteeing a Palestinian homeland. But the accord at least ended warfare along one frontier in that troubled area of the world. On March 26, 1979, Israeli prime minister Menachem Begin and Egyptian president Anwar al-Sadat signed the formal treaty on the White House lawn, with a beaming Carter looking on.

27-7c Soviet Invasion of Afghanistan

Carter's moment of diplomatic triumph did not last long, for soon other foreign policy problems pressed in. Relations with Moscow had deteriorated, with U.S. and Soviet officials sparring over the Kremlin's reluctance to lift restrictions on Jewish emigration from the USSR, and over the Soviet decision to deploy new intermediate-range ballistic missiles aimed at Western Europe. Then, in December 1979, the Soviets invaded Afghanistan. A remote, mountainous country, Afghanistan had long been a source of great-power conflict because of its strategic position. In the nineteenth century, it was the fulcrum of the Great Game, the contest between Britain and Russia for control of Central Asia and India. Following World War II, Afghanistan settled into a pattern of ethnic and factional squabbling; few in the West paid attention until the country spiraled into anarchy in the

Camp David Accords Agreements that were signed by Egypt's President Sadat and Israel's Prime Minister Begin following twelve days of secret negotiations—arranged by President Carter—at Camp David.

▲ Egyptian President Anwar al-Sadat, U.S. President Jimmy Carter, and Israeli Prime Minister Menachem Begin sit together outside the White House on March 26, 1979, ready to sign the peace treaty based on the Camp David Accords of September 1978. The treaty ended the long-standing state of war between Egypt and Israel.

1970s. In late 1979, the Red Army bludgeoned its way into Afghanistan to shore up a faltering communist government under siege by Muslim rebels. Moscow officials calculated that they could be in and out of the country before anyone really noticed, including the Americans.

To their dismay, Carter not only noticed but reacted forcefully—no doubt in part because of the test he faced simultaneously with the hostage crisis in neighboring Iran. He suspended shipments of grain and high-technology equipment to the Soviet Union, withdrew a major new arms control treaty from Senate consideration, and initiated an international boycott of the 1980 Summer Olympics in Moscow. He also secretly authorized the CIA to distribute aid, including arms and military support, to the Mujahidin (Islamic guerillas) fighting the communist government and sanctioned military aid to their backer, Pakistan. Announcing the Carter Doctrine, the president asserted that the United States would intervene, unilaterally and militarily if necessary, should Soviet aggression threaten the petroleum-rich Persian Gulf. This string of measures represented a victory of the hawkish Brzezinski over the pro-détente Vance. Indeed, Carter seemed more ardent than Brzezinski in his denunciations of the Kremlin. He warned aides that the Soviets, unless checked, would likely attack elsewhere in the Middle East, but declassified documents confirm

what critics at the time said: that the Soviet invasion was limited in scope and did not presage a push southwest to the Persian Gulf.

The Iranian revolution, together with the rise of the Mujahidin in Afghanistan, signified the emergence of Islamic fundamentalism as a force in world affairs. Socialism and capitalism, the great answers that the two superpowers offered to the problems of modernization, had failed to solve the problems in Central Asia and the Middle East, let alone satisfy the passions and expectations they had aroused. Nor had they assuaged deeply held feelings of humiliation generated by centuries of Western domination. As a result, Islamic orthodoxy found growing support for its message: that secular leaders such as Nasser in Egypt and the shah in Iran had taken their peoples down the wrong path, necessitating a return to conservative Islamic values and Islamic law. The Iranian revolution in particular expressed a deep and complex mixture of discontent within many Islamic societies.

27-7d Rise of Saddam Hussein

U.S. officials took some consolation from the fact that Iran faced growing friction from the avowedly secular government in neighboring Iraq. Ruled by the Ba'athist Party (a secular and quasi-socialist party with branches in several Arab countries), Iraq had already won favor in Washington

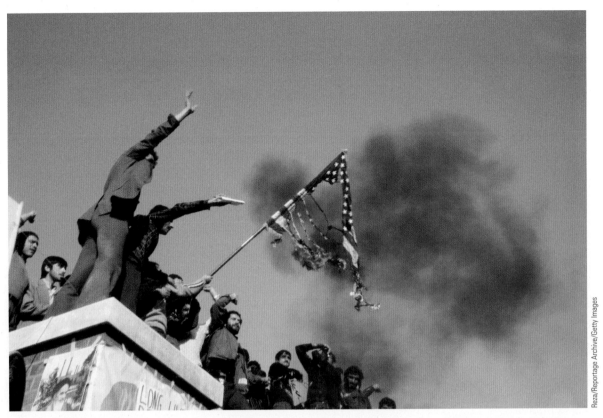

▲ In June 1980, midway through the Iran Hostage Crisis, a group of anti-American protesters set fire to a U.S. flag on the roof of the occupied U.S. embassy in Tehran.

Reza/Reportage Archive/Getty Images

for its ruthless pursuit and execution of Iraqi communists. When a Ba'athist leader named Saddam Hussein took over as president of Iraq in 1979 and began threatening the Tehran government, U.S. officials were not displeased; to them, Saddam seemed likely to offset the Iranian danger in the Persian Gulf region. As border clashes between Iraqi and Iranian forces escalated in 1980, culminating in the outbreak of large-scale war in September, Washington policymakers took an officially neutral position but soon tilted toward Iraq.

Jimmy Carter's record in foreign affairs sparked considerable criticism from both left and right. He had earned some diplomatic successes in the Middle East, Africa, and Latin America, but the revived Cold War and the prolonged Iranian hostage crisis had hurt the administration politically. Contrary to Carter's goals, more American military personnel were stationed overseas in 1980 than in 1976; the defense budget climbed and sales of arms abroad grew to $15.3 billion in 1980. On human rights, the president proved inconsistent. He practiced a double standard by applying the human rights test to some nations (the Soviet Union, Argentina, and Chile) but not to U.S. allies (South Korea, the shah's Iran, and the Philippines). Still, if inconsistent, Carter's human rights policy was not unimportant: he gained the release and saved the lives of some political prisoners, and he popularized and institutionalized concern

for human rights around the world. But Carter did not satisfy Americans who wanted a post-Vietnam restoration of the economic dominance and military edge the United States once enjoyed. He lost the 1980 election to the hawkish Ronald Reagan, former Hollywood actor and governor of California.

Summary

The 1970s were a difficult decade for Americans. From the crisis year of 1968 on, it seemed that Americans were ever more polarized—over the war in Vietnam, over the best path to racial equality and equal rights for all Americans, over the meaning of equality, and over the meaning of America itself. As many activists for social justice turned to "cultural nationalism," notions of American unity seemed a relic of the past. And though a new women's movement won great victories against sex discrimination, a powerful opposition movement arose in response.

During this era, Americans became increasingly disillusioned with politics and presidential leadership. Richard Nixon's abuses of power in the Watergate scandal and cover-up, combined with growing awareness that several administrations had lied to the citizenry repeatedly about America's role in Vietnam, produced a profound suspicion of government. A major economic crisis ended the post–World War II

The All-Volunteer Force

On June 30, 1973, the United States ended its military draft. From that date on, the nation relied on an all-volunteer force (AVF). The draft had been in effect, with only a brief interruption in the late 1940s, since the United States had begun to mobilize in 1940 for World War II. Never before had the United States had a peacetime draft. But as the country took on new roles of global leadership after the war, and as the dark shadow of the Cold War grew, the draft became an accepted part of American life. More than 50 million American men had been inducted into the nation's military between the end of World War II and the end of conscription in 1973.

Richard Nixon had promised to end the draft during his presidential campaign in 1968. It was an astute political move, for the draft had become a focus for widespread protest during the failing—and increasingly unpopular—war in Vietnam. Ending the draft was not feasible during the war, but Nixon kept his promise and began planning for an all-volunteer force as soon as he took office. Many Americans supported the shift because they believed it would be more difficult for a president to send an all-volunteer military to war. According to this logic, if people did not support the war, there would be no draft to compel them to fight.

The military, however, was not enthusiastic about Nixon's plan. The war in Vietnam had shattered morale and left much of the nation's military—particularly the army—in disarray. Public opinion of the military was at an all-time low. How were the military services to fill their ranks?

The army, as the largest of the four services, had to draw the largest number of volunteers. It faced a difficult task. Reform was the first step: getting rid of "chickenshit" (unrelated to military skills) tasks such as cutting grass, "Kitchen Police" (KP) and the like, and enhancing military professionalism. The army also turned to state-of-the-art market research and advertising. Discovering that many young men were afraid they would lose their individuality in the army, the army's advertising agency launched a new campaign. Instead of the traditional poster of Uncle Sam proclaiming, "I Want You," the new volunteer army claimed, "Today's Army Wants to Join You."

The AVF had a rough beginning. The army had to recruit about 225,000 new soldiers each year (compared to about 62,500 per year in 2016) and had difficulty attracting enough capable young men and women. Within a decade, however, America's military boasted a higher rate of high school graduates and higher mental "quality" (as measured by standardized tests) than the comparable age population

in the United States. During an era of relative peace, many young men and women found opportunities for education and training through military service. Military service was particularly attractive to capable but economically disadvantaged young people, a high percentage of whom were African American.

The move to a volunteer force had major legacies for the American people. The military understood that, without a draft, it would have to turn to women in order to fill the ranks. The proportion of women in the active military increased from 1.9 percent in 1972 to about 15 percent currently, and the roles they were allowed to fill widened dramatically. At the same time, the nation's understanding of military service changed. With a volunteer force, military service was no longer an obligation of (male) citizenship. Instead, the military had to compete in the national labor market, often portraying military service to potential recruits as "a good job." The implications seemed less urgent in peacetime. But in time of war, the legacy of the move to an AVF is highly charged.

CRITICAL THINKING

- What does it mean when only a small number of volunteers bears the burden of warfare and most Americans never have to consider the possibility of going to war?

expansion that had fueled the growth of the middle class and social reform programs alike, and Americans struggled with the psychological impact of a new age of limits and with the effects of stagflation: rising unemployment rates coupled with high rates of inflation.

Overseas, a string of setbacks—defeat in Vietnam, the oil embargo, and the Iranian hostage crisis—signified the waning of American power during the 1970s. The nation seemed increasingly unable to have its own way on the world stage. Détente with the Soviet Union had flourished for a time, as both superpowers sought to adjust to the new

geopolitical realities; however, by 1980 Cold War tensions were again on the rise. But if the nation's most important bilateral relationship remained that with the USSR, an important change, not always perceptible at the time, was under way: more and more, the focus of U.S. foreign policy was on the Middle East.

Plagued by political, economic, and foreign policy crises, America ended the 1970s bruised, battered, and frustrated. The age of liberalism was long over; the turn toward marketplace solutions had begun, and the elements for a conservative resurgence were in place.

Suggestions for Further Reading

Thomas Borstelman, *The 1970s: A New Global History from Civil Rights to Economic Inequality* (2012)

Jefferson R. Cowie, *Stayin' Alive: The 1970s and the Last Days of the Working Class* (2010)

Donald T. Critchlow, *Phyllis Schlafly and Grassroots Conservatism: A Woman's Crusade* (2005)

Daniel Ellsberg, *Secrets: A Memoir of Vietnam and the Pentagon Papers* (2002)

David Farber, *Taken Hostage: The Iran Hostage Crisis and America's First Encounter with Radical Islam* (2004)

Ken Hughes, *Fatal Politics: The Nixon Tapes, the Vietnam War, and the Casualties of Reelection* (2015)

Nancy MacLean, *Freedom Is Not Enough: The Opening of the American Workplace* (2006)

Rick Perlstein, *Nixonland: The Rise of a President and the Fracturing of America* (2008)

Ruth Rosen, *The World Split Open: How the Modern Women's Movement Changed America* (2000)

Hal Rothman, *The Greening of a Nation: Environmentalism in the U.S. Since 1945* (1997)

Odd Arne Westad, *The Global Cold War: Third World Interventions and the Making of Our Times* (2005)

Natasha Zaretsky, *No Direction Home: The American Family and the Fear of National Decline, 1968—1980* (2007)

MINDTAP
From Cengage

Conservatism Revived, 1980–1992

The train to DC was late, and Sheila and Joe Kerley waited with their still-sleepy children for it to arrive at the Charlottesville, Virginia, station, surrounded by people in "Washington for Jesus" T-shirts, singing hymns to pass the time. Joe and Sheila had taken off work for this trip to the nation's capital, Joe from his father-in-law's small plumbing company, Sheila from her position as teacher's aide at the Christian school their children, 6-year-old Joey and 4-year-old Nikki, attended.

On the morning of April 29, 1980, the Kerleys were headed to a Christian rally on the mall in Washington, DC. Joe and Sheila believed strongly in the power of prayer. He'd been a rebellious teenager who'd dropped out of high school in Tennessee; they'd married young, and both of them were certain Joe's conversion had saved their marriage. Once saved, Sheila said, he became "a different person."

The Kerleys were going to the rally because they believed the Equal Rights Amendment would "tear down family life" (though they had difficulty explaining how), and because they didn't want their children taught about evolution, and because they were worried about the threat of communism. More than anything else, though, they believed that the United States was suffering because it had lost God's favor.

That morning, 200,000 people—most of them charismatic, Pentecostal, and evangelical Christians—massed on the national mall. They carried Bibles and American flags, hoisted signs and banners: "The Bible—It's True"; "America Must Repent or Perish." The day began with steady rain, but with the words of an opening prayer, the skies cleared. The air echoed with cries of "Praise the Lord." Groups joined hands to pray. Some men and women spoke in tongues.

◀ In 1988, on the eighth anniversary of the original "Washington for Jesus" rally, President Reagan addressed the crowd gathered for the second such rally by videotape. Cynthia Johnson/Getty Images

Chronology

1980
- Reagan elected president

1981
- AIDS first observed in United States
- Economic problems continue; prime interest rate reaches 21.5 percent
- "Reaganomics" plan of budget and tax cuts approved by Congress

1982
- Unemployment reaches 10.8 percent, highest rate since Great Depression
- ERA defeated after STOP ERA campaign prevents ratification in key states

1983
- Reagan introduces SDI
- Terrorists kill U.S. Marines in Lebanon
- U.S. invasion of Grenada

1984
- Reagan aids Contras despite congressional ban
- Economic recovery; unemployment rate drops and economy grows without inflation
- Reagan reelected
- Gorbachev promotes reforms in USSR

1986
- Iran-Contra scandal erupts

1987
- Palestinian *intifada* begins

1988
- George H. W. Bush elected president

1989
- Tiananmen Square massacre in China
- Berlin Wall torn down
- U.S. troops invade Panama
- Gulf between rich and poor at highest point since 1920s

1990
- Americans with Disabilities Act passed
- Communist regimes in Eastern Europe collapse
- Iraq invades Kuwait
- South Africa begins to dismantle apartheid

1991
- Persian Gulf War
- USSR dissolves into independent states
- United States enters recession

1992
- Annual federal budget deficit reaches high of $300 billion at end of Bush presidency

In the keynote speech Bill Bright, the head of Campus Crusade for Christ, chronicled America's descent into "a world aflame." He recounted a "series of plagues"—the war in Vietnam, racial conflict, Watergate, the rise in divorce, unwed pregnancy, abortion, drug use—and warned: "Unless we repent and turn from our sin, we can expect to be destroyed."

The organizers of the rally had begun with a clearly political purpose, crafting a "Christian Declaration" with a list of legislative goals, including ending legal abortion and cutting spending on social programs. Public opposition from other Christian leaders led them to pull that document. Nonetheless, delegates were sent to lobby their congressional representatives. When James Farmer, the founder of the Congress of Racial Equality, said, "We must fight to defeat their use of religious rhetoric to conceal their rightwing objectives," Reverend Pat Robertson told reporters that the rally was for prayer, not politics. But, he insisted, "Every leader in this city holds his tenure only so long as God wills it, and they have no authority except as God gives it to them. So the Congress and the President are secondary to us. And God was here today to hear us."

Experience an interactive version of this story in MindTap®.

In the wake of the economic crisis and social divisions of the 1970s, the United States entered a new era of conservatism in the 1980s—one in which the growing religious right would play a critical role. A new conservative coalition comprised of widely different groups joined to elect Ronald Reagan president; his support came from wealthy people who liked his pro-business economic policies; the religious New Right who sought the creation of "God's America"; and white middle- and working-class Americans attracted by Reagan's charisma and his embrace of "old-fashioned" values. The election of Ronald Reagan in 1980 began a twelve-year period of Republican rule, as Reagan was succeeded by his vice president, George Bush, in 1988.

Members of this new coalition had different goals, but all expected the presidential administration to embrace their causes. Reagan did support New Right social issues: he was anti-abortion, he embraced prayer in schools, he ended Republican Party support for the Equal Rights Amendment, and he appointed judges to both the Supreme Court and the federal bench whose rulings strengthened social-conservative agendas. Nonetheless, the Reagan administration focused primarily on the agendas of political and economic conservatives: reducing the size and power of the federal government and creating favorable conditions for business and industry. The U.S. economy recovered from the stagflation that had plagued the nation, and through much of the 1980s, it boomed. But corruption flourished in financial institutions freed from government oversight, and taxpayers paid the bill for bailouts. By the end of the Reagan-Bush era, a combination of tax cuts and massive increases in defense spending left a budget deficit five times larger than when Reagan took office.

The 1980s saw increasing divisions between rich and poor in America. A host of social problems—drugs, violence, homelessness, the growing AIDS epidemic—made life even more difficult for the urban poor, especially as government aid was cut. But for those on the other side of the economic divide, the 1980s were an era of luxury and ostentation. One of the most poignant images from the time was of a homeless man huddled just outside the Reagan White House—the two Americans, divided by a widening gulf.

The most dramatic events of the Reagan-Bush years were not domestic, however, but international. In the span of a decade, the Cold War intensified drastically and then ended. The key figure in the intensification was Reagan, who entered office promising to reassert America's military might and stand up to the Soviet Union, and he delivered on both counts. The key figure in ending the Cold War was Soviet leader Mikhail Gorbachev, who came to power in 1985 determined to address the USSR's long-term economic decline and needed a more amicable superpower relationship to do so. Gorbachev, though no revolutionary—he hoped to reform the Soviet system, not eradicate it—lost control of events as a wave of revolutions in Eastern Europe toppled one communist regime after another. In 1991, the Soviet Union itself disappeared, and the United States found itself the world's lone superpower. The Persian Gulf War of that same year demonstrated America's unrivaled world power and the unprecedented importance of the Middle East in U.S. foreign policy.

■ *Ronald Reagan, campaigning for president in 1984, told voters, "It's morning again in America." How might Americans from different backgrounds judge the accuracy of his claim?*

■ *What issues, beliefs, backgrounds, and economic realities divided Americans in the 1980s, and how do those divisions continue to shape the culture and politics of contemporary America?*

■ *Why did the Cold War intensify and then wane during the decade of the 1980s?*

28-1 A New Conservative Coalition

▶ **Why did the New Deal coalition come to an end?**
▶ **What groups in American society comprised the conservative coalition?**

The 1970s had been a hard decade for Americans: defeat in Vietnam, the resignation of a president in disgrace, the energy crisis, economic "stagflation," and the Iranian hostage crisis. Increasingly, Americans had lost faith in their government and in government-based solutions to the nation's problems. Many turned away from the liberal policies that had dominated American politics since the New Deal. Conservatives, ranging from wealthy business interests to an emerging religious right, saw an opportunity in this national disillusion. In the election year of 1980, when President Carter's public approval rating stood at 21 percent, a diverse set of conservative groups forged a new coalition, coalescing around Republican candidate **Ronald Reagan**. The election of 1980 marked a sea change in American politics. Its victor, Ronald Reagan—as much as any president since Franklin Roosevelt—defined the era over which he presided.

28-1a The End of the New Deal Coalition

The New Deal coalition—the combination of organized labor, urban ethnic and working-class whites, African Americans, and white southerners who, since the days of Franklin Roosevelt, had dependably voted Democratic—had begun to splinter by the late 1960s, as large numbers of white southerners abandoned the Democratic Party. By 1980, the votes of urban working-class white Americans outside the South were also in play. These voters offered a compelling target for conservative organizers such as Richard Viguerie, founder of *Conservative Digest* magazine, who meant to make the white working class the foundation of a new conservative movement.

Changes in the American economy had helped shift working-class politics. Labor unions had traditionally supported and been supported by the Democratic Party; as factories relocated to "right-to-work" states or shut down altogether during the 1970s,

Ronald Reagan Former actor and California governor (1967–1975) who served as the fortieth president of the United States (1981–1989).

union membership fell. Labor offered the Democratic Party smaller numbers, and loyalty to the Democratic Party had less pull on nonunionized workers.

As working-class whites faced new economic limits, government action often seemed incomprehensible or even harmful. New government-mandated affirmative action programs further reduced opportunities for working-class white men in a time of shrinking employment. White working-class parents often saw busing (sending children from racially segregated neighborhoods to other school districts to integrate schools) as government interference that threatened the quality of their children's education and even their safety. Watching the growth of liberal social programs for the poor, some working-class whites felt outraged that they worked hard to support their families while others lived on taxpayer-funded welfare. Racial prejudice played a role here; while the majority of welfare recipients were white, opponents of such government programs frequently portrayed welfare as a transfer of money from hardworking white families to indolent black ones.

Finally, many white working-class Americans were socially conservative. Catholics, who filled many urban ethnic working-class neighborhoods, worried not only about changes in sexual behaviors and women's roles but about government support for social change, including the Supreme Court's recognition of abortion rights in *Roe v. Wade*. As working-class whites felt economically beleaguered and often frustrated by government actions, conservative questions about the proper limits of the liberal state gained a new hearing.

28-1b Growth of the Religious Right

By 1980, a newly powerful movement of social conservatives, based in fundamentalist Christian churches, was poised to influence American politics. Their new prominence surprised many Americans; at the beginning of the decade, historians commonly argued that the 1925 Scopes trial over the teaching of evolution had been the last gasp of fundamentalist Christianity in the United States. They were wrong. Since the 1960s, America's mainline liberal Protestant churches—Episcopalian, Presbyterian, Methodist—had been losing members, while Southern Baptists and other denominations that offered the spiritual experience of being "born again" through belief in Jesus Christ and that accepted the literal truth of the Bible (fundamentalism) had grown rapidly. Fundamentalist and evangelical preachers reached out to vast audiences through television: by the late 1970s, televangelist Oral Roberts was drawing an audience of 3.9 million. Close to 20 percent of Americans identified themselves as fundamentalist Christians in 1980.

Most fundamentalist Christian churches stayed out of the social and political conflicts of the 1960s and early 1970s, arguing that preaching the "pure saving gospel of Jesus Christ" was more important. But in the late 1970s—motivated by what they saw as the betrayal of God's will in an increasingly permissive American society—some influential preachers began to mobilize their flocks for political struggle.

The Moral Majority, founded in 1979 by Jerry Falwell, sought to create a "Christian America," which Falwell believed required fighting against the ERA and women's rights (he called NOW the "National Order of Witches"), gay rights, abortion, pornography, and the teaching of evolution and sex education in public schools.

28-1c Economic Conservatives

America's business community had also developed a strong political presence by the beginning of the 1980s. The Business Roundtable, founded in 1972, brought together chief executive officers from America's largest corporations—the Fortune 500. These corporations controlled billions of dollars and millions of jobs; their leaders meant to leverage this financial power to shape American politics and public policy. CEOs of corporations such as Sears, General Foods, and Westinghouse personally lobbied politicians, as the Roundtable pushed for deregulation and corporate tax breaks and investment credits.

The U.S. Chamber of Commerce, which traced its origins to 1912, had also become more politically active. Unlike the Business Roundtable, which emphasized the quiet influence of powerful CEOs, the U.S. Chamber of Commerce

▲ At the Republican National Convention, a delegate from Texas supports Ronald Reagan. Reagan's favorite campaign slogan was "Let's make America great again."

built a broadly based grassroots movement that celebrated entrepreneurship and welcomed businesses of any size. Attempting to build a mass movement for capitalism, the chamber relied on individual members to persuade their local public schools to adopt its education module, "Economics for Young Americans." By 1981, the chamber had 2,700 local Congressional Action Committees to lobby congressional representatives; they pushed to weaken government regulations, lower taxes, and restrict the power of labor unions. And unlike the Business Roundtable, the chamber joined the religious right in its socially conservative agenda.

28-1d The Election of 1980

As the American presidential election season began in 1980, inflation was in double digits. Mortgage rates approached 14 percent. Oil prices were three times what they'd been at the start of the decade. Unemployment lingered at the then-high rate of 7 percent. And fifty-two American hostages remained in captivity in Iran. None of that offered any advantage to Democratic incumbent Jimmy Carter. Conservative leaders understood their opportunity.

Several strong Republican candidates entered the race, but support quickly coalesced around Ronald Reagan, a former movie star and two-term governor of California. Reagan offered (in marked contrast to Carter) an optimistic vision of America's future. With his Hollywood charm and strong conservative credentials, he succeeded in forging very different sorts of American conservatives into a new political coalition.

Turnout was low on Election Day, but Reagan crushed Carter at the polls. And for the first time since 1952, the Senate majority went to the Republicans.

28-2 Reagan's Conservative Agenda

▶ What vision of America's future did the Reagan administration offer?

▶ What federal programs and policies did the Reagan administration seek to reform, and why?

▶ Why did Ronald Reagan appeal to the New Right?

Reagan's conservative credentials were strong. In the 1940s, as president of Hollywood's Screen Actors Guild, Reagan had been a New Deal Democrat. But in the 1950s, as a corporate spokesman for General Electric, he became increasingly conservative. In 1964, Reagan's televised speech supporting Republican presidential candidate Barry Goldwater catapulted him to the forefront of conservative politics. America, Reagan said, had come to "a time for choosing" between free enterprise and big government, between individual liberty and "the ant heap of totalitarianism."

Elected governor of California just two years later, Reagan became known for his right-wing rhetoric: America should "level Vietnam, pave it, paint stripes on it, and make

a parking lot out of it," Reagan claimed. And in 1969, when student protesters occupied "People's Park" near the University of California in Berkeley, he threatened a "bloodbath" and dispatched National Guard troops in full riot gear. Reagan was often pragmatic, however, about policy decisions. He denounced welfare but presided over reform of the state's social welfare bureaucracy. And he signed one of the nation's most liberal abortion laws.

Ronald Reagan, at age sixty-nine the oldest American to that point elected to the presidency, restored the pomp and circumstance Jimmy Carter had resolutely stripped from the office. For example, Reagan spent $19.4 million for his inaugural balls; Carter's cost $3.5 million. (Private donors pay for these events.) And Reagan, as president, was not especially focused on the details of governing or the specifics of policies and programs. When outgoing president Jimmy Carter briefed him on urgent issues of foreign and domestic policy, Reagan listened politely but took not a single note and asked no questions. Critics argued that his lack of knowledge could prove dangerous—as when he insisted that intercontinental ballistic missiles carrying nuclear warheads could be called back once launched, or when he said that "approximately 80 percent of our air pollution stems from hydrocarbons released by vegetation."

But supporters insisted that Reagan was a great president in large part because he focused on the big picture. When he spoke to the American people, he offered what seemed to be simple truths—and he did it with the straightforwardness of a true believer and the warmth and humor of an experienced actor. Although many—even among Reagan supporters—winced at his willingness to reduce complex policy issues to simple (and often misleading) stories, Reagan was to most Americans the "Great Communicator." He won admiration for his courage after he was seriously wounded in an assassination attempt just sixty-nine days into his presidency. Reagan quipped to doctors preparing to remove the bullet lodged near his heart, "I hope you're all Republicans."

Most important, Reagan had a clear vision for America's future. He and his advisers wanted to roll back fifty years of liberal policies that had made government increasingly responsible for the health of the nation's economy and for the social welfare of its citizens. In the words of David Stockman, a Reagan appointee who headed the Office of Management and Budget, the administration meant to "create a minimalist government" and sever "the umbilical cords of dependency that run from Washington to every nook and cranny of the nation."

28-2a Attacks on Social Welfare Programs

Traditional conservatives believed that the federal government could not solve America's social problems. But a broader and less coherent backlash against Great Society programs strengthened conservatives' hands. Many Americans who struggled to make ends meet during the economic crises of the 1970s and early 1980s resented paying taxes that, they believed, funded government "handouts" to people who did not work. Reagan himself used existing racial tensions to undermine support for welfare, repeatedly describing a "welfare queen" from Chicago's South Side (a primarily African American area) who had collected welfare checks under eighty different last names and defrauded the government of $150,000 (the actual case involved two aliases and $8,000). In 1981, the administration cut welfare programs for the poor by $25 billion. But programs such as Aid to Families with Dependent Children and food stamps were a small part of the budget compared with Social Security and Medicare—social welfare programs that benefited Americans of all income levels, not just the poor. Major budget cuts for these popular, broadly based programs proved impossible. The Reagan administration did shrink the *proportion* of the federal budget devoted to social welfare programs (including Social Security and Medicare) from 28 to 22 percent by the late 1980s—but only because it increased defense spending by $1.2 trillion.

28-2b Pro-Business Policies and the Environment

The Reagan administration also attacked federal environmental, health, and safety regulations that conservatives believed reduced business profits and discouraged economic growth. Administration officials claimed that removing the stifling hand of government regulation would restore the energy and creativity of America's free-market system. However, they did not so much end government's role as deploy government power to aid corporate America.

President Reagan appointed opponents of federal regulations to head the agencies charged with enforcing them—letting foxes guard the chicken coop, critics charged. Environmentalists were appalled when Reagan appointed James Watt, a well-known anti-environmentalist, as secretary of the interior. Watt was a leader in the "Sagebrush Rebellion," which sought to shift publicly owned lands in the West, such as national forests, from federal to state control. Land control issues were complicated: the federal government controlled more than half of western lands—including 83 percent of the land in Nevada, 66 percent in Utah, and 50 percent in Wyoming—and many westerners believed that eastern policymakers did not understand the realities of western life. But states' ability to control land within their borders was not the sole issue; Watt and his group wanted to open western public lands to private businesses for logging, mining, and ranching.

Telling senators in his 1981 confirmation hearing, "I don't know how many generations we can count on until the Lord returns," Watt saw no need to protect national resources and public wilderness for future generations. As interior secretary, he allowed private corporations to acquire oil, mineral, and timber rights to federal lands for minuscule payments. Watt was forced to resign in 1983 after he dismissively referred to a federal advisory panel as "a black . . . a woman, two Jews, and a cripple." But his appointment had already backfired, for his actions reenergized the nation's environmental movement

and even provoked opposition from business leaders who understood that uncontrolled strip-mining and clear-cut logging of western lands could destroy lucrative tourism and recreation industries in western states.

28-2c Attacks on Organized Labor

As part of its pro-business agenda, the Reagan administration undercut organized labor's ability to negotiate wages and working conditions. Union power was already waning; labor union membership declined in the 1970s as jobs in heavy industry disappeared, and efforts to unionize the high-growth electronics and service sectors of the economy had failed. Setting the tone for his administration, in August 1981 Reagan intervened in a strike by the Professional Air Traffic Controllers Organization (PATCO). The air traffic controllers—federal employees, for whom striking was illegal—were protesting working conditions they believed compromised the safety of American air travel. Only forty-eight hours into the strike, Reagan fired the 11,350 strikers, stipulating that they could never be rehired by the Federal Aviation Administration.

With the support of Reagan appointees to the National Labor Relations Board and an anti-union secretary of labor, businesses took an increasingly hard line with labor during the 1980s and unions failed to mount an effective opposition. By 1990, only 12 percent of private sector workers were unionized. Yet roughly 44 percent of union families had voted for Reagan in 1980, drawn to his geniality, espousal of old-fashioned values, and vigorous anticommunist rhetoric.

28-2d The New Right

Although Reagan's domestic agenda focused on traditional conservative political and economic goals, New Right issues played an increasingly important role in Reagan-era social policy. It is surprising that the strongly religious New Right was drawn to Reagan, a divorced man without strong ties to religion or, seemingly, his own children. But the non-churchgoing Reagan lent his support to the New Right, endorsing the anti-abortion cause and supporting prayer in public schools.

Reagan's judicial nominations also pleased the religious New Right. Though the Senate, in a bipartisan vote, refused to confirm Supreme Court nominee Robert Bork after eighty-seven hours of antagonistic hearings, Congress eventually confirmed Anthony M. Kennedy instead. Reagan also appointed Antonin Scalia, who would become a key conservative force on the Court, and Sandra Day O'Connor (the first female appointee) and elevated Nixon appointee William Rehnquist to chief justice. In 1986, the increasingly conservative Supreme Court upheld a Georgia law that punished consensual sex between men with up to twenty years in jail (*Bowers v. Hardwick*); in 1989, the justices ruled that a Missouri law restricting the right to an abortion was constitutional (*Webster v. Reproductive Health Services*), thus encouraging further challenges to *Roe v. Wade*. In federal courts, U.S. Justice Department lawyers argued New Right positions on such social issues, and Reagan's 378 appointees to the federal bench usually ruled accordingly. Overall, however, the Reagan administration did not push a conservative social agenda as strongly as some members of the new Republican coalition had hoped.

28-3 Economic Conservatism

▶ What economic theories and ideas shaped the Reagan administration's economic agenda?

▶ How did implementation of "Reaganomics" affect the American economy and the American people?

▶ What impact did deregulation have on the banking and finance industries?

▶ Who benefited from the economic and financial policies implemented during the Reagan administration?

The U.S. economy was in bad shape at the beginning of the 1980s. In 1981, the economy plunged deeper into recession and unemployment rates jumped. Everyone agreed that something had to be done.

Business elites, conservative economists, and the president himself argued that New Deal remedies, emphasizing government intervention in the economy through spending, had failed. Reagan offered the American people a simple diagnosis of the nation's economic woes. Instead of focusing on the complexities of global competition, deindustrialization, and OPEC's control of oil, Reagan argued that U.S. economic problems were caused by government intrusion in the "free-market" economic system. At fault were intrusive government regulation of business and industry, expensive government social programs that offered "handouts" to nonproductive citizens, high taxes, and deficit spending—in short, government itself. The Reagan administration's economic agenda—often called "Reaganomics"—was closely tied to its larger conservative ideology of limited government: it sought to "unshackle" the free-enterprise system from government regulation and control, to slash spending on social programs, to limit government's use of taxes to redistribute income among the American people, and to balance the budget by reducing the role of the federal government.

28-3a Harsh Medicine for Inflation

Before this new approach could have any real impact, the administration had to solve the continuing problem of inflation. Here the Federal Reserve Bank, an autonomous federal agency, stepped in. In 1981, the Federal Reserve Bank raised interest rates for bank loans to an unprecedented 21.5 percent, battling inflation by tightening the money supply and slowing the economy down. The nation plunged into recession. During the last three months of the year, the gross national product (GNP) fell 5 percent, and sales of cars and houses dropped sharply. With declining economic activity, unemployment soared to 8 percent, the highest level in almost six years.

By late 1982, unemployment had reached 10.8 percent, the highest rate since 1940. For African Americans, it was 20 percent. Many of the unemployed were blue-collar workers in ailing "smokestack industries," such as steel and automobiles. Reagan and his advisers promised that consumers would lift the economy out of the recession by spending their tax cuts. But as late as April 1983, unemployment still stood at 10 percent, and people were angry. Jobless steelworkers paraded through McKeesport, Pennsylvania, carrying a coffin that bore the epitaph "American Dream." Agriculture, too, was faltering and near collapse. Farmers suffered not only from falling crop prices due to overproduction but also from floods, droughts, and burdensome debts with high interest rates. Many lost their property to mortgage foreclosure; others filed for bankruptcy. As the recession deepened, poverty rose to its highest level since 1965.

It was harsh medicine, but the Federal Reserve Bank's plan to end stagflation worked. High interest rates helped drop inflation from 12 percent in 1980 to less than 7 percent in 1982. The economy also benefited from OPEC's 1981 decision to stop engineering an artificial scarcity and increase oil production, thus lowering prices—and inflation.

28-3b Supply-Side Economics

With inflation tamed, proponents of conservative economic policy could develop their pro-business agenda. The Reagan administration's economic policy was based largely on supply-side economics, the theory that tax cuts (rather than government spending) will create economic growth. According to a theory proposed by economist Arthur Laffer—his soon-to-be-famous Laffer curve—at some point rising tax rates discourage people from engaging in taxable activities (such as investing their money): if profits from investments simply disappear to taxes, what is the incentive to invest? As people invest less, the economy slows. Even though tax rates remain high, the government collects less in tax revenue because the economy stalls. Cutting taxes, according to this theory, reverses the cycle and increases tax revenues.

Although economists accepted the Laffer curve's broader principle, almost none believed that U.S. tax rates were anywhere close to the point of disincentive. Even conservative economists were suspicious of supply-side principles. Reagan and his staff, however—on the basis of the unproven assumption that both corporate and personal tax rates in the United States were so high that they discouraged investment—sought a massive tax cut. They argued that American corporations and individuals would invest funds freed up by lower tax rates, producing new plants, new jobs, and new products. This economic growth would more than make up for the tax revenues lost. And as prosperity returned, the profits at the top would "trickle down" to the middle classes and even to the poor.

Reagan proposed to balance the federal budget through economic growth (created by tax cuts) and deep spending cuts, primarily in social programs. Congress cooperated with a three-year, $750 billion tax cut, at that point the largest ever in American history. Cutting the federal budget, however, proved more difficult; while Reagan's plan assumed $100 billion in cuts from programs including Social Security and Medicare, Congress was not about to cut those benefits. Reagan, meanwhile, canceled out domestic spending cuts by dramatically increasing defense spending.

Major tax cuts, big increases in defense spending, small cuts in social programs: the numbers did not add up. The annual federal budget deficit exploded—from $59 billion in 1980 to more than $100 billion in 1982 to almost $300 billion by the end of George H. W. Bush's presidency in 1993. The Republican administrations borrowed money to make up the difference, transforming the United States from the world's largest creditor nation to its largest debtor (see Figure 28.1). The national debt grew to almost $3 trillion. Because an ever-greater share of the federal budget went to pay the interest on this ballooning debt, less was available for federal programs, foreign or domestic.

28-3c Deregulation

Supply-side economics was not the only policy that transformed America's economy in the 1980s. Deregulation, begun under Jimmy Carter and expanded vastly under Reagan (the Federal Register, which contains all federal regulations, shrank from 87,012 pages in 1980 to 47,418 pages in 1986), created new opportunities for American business and industry. The 1978 deregulation of the airline industry lowered ticket prices both short term and long term; airline tickets cost almost 45 percent less in the early twenty-first century (in constant dollars) than in 1978. Deregulation of telecommunications industries created serious competition for the giant AT&T, and long-distance calling became inexpensive.

The Reagan administration loosened regulation of the American banking and finance industries and purposely

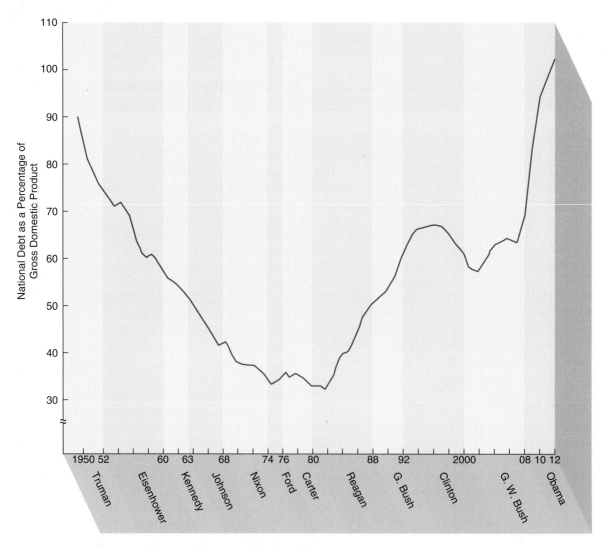

Figure 28.1 **America's Rising National Debt, 1974–2012**

America's national debt, which rose sporadically throughout the 1970s, soared to record heights during the 1980s. Under President Reagan, large defense expenditures and tax cuts caused the national debt to grow by $1.5 trillion.

Source: Adapted from U.S. Bureau of the Census, Statistical Abstract of the United States *(Washington, D.C.: 1992), p. 315.*

▲ President Ronald Reagan, who created a major budget deficit by pairing large tax cuts with large increases in defense spending, brandishes his "Tax Ax" at a Chamber of Commerce lunch in 1986.

cut the ability of the Securities and Exchange Commission (SEC), which oversees Wall Street, to enforce those regulations. In 1984, the GNP rose 7 percent, the sharpest increase since 1951, and midyear unemployment fell to a four-year low of 7 percent. The economy was booming, but without sparking inflation.

28-3d "Morning in America"

By the presidential election of 1984, the recession was only a memory. Reagan got credit for the recovery. The Democratic candidate, former Vice President Walter Mondale, talked about fairness and compassion; not all Americans, Mondale told the American public, were prospering in Reagan's America. Reagan, in contrast, proclaimed, "It's morning again in America." Television ads showed heartwarming images of American life, as an off-screen narrator told viewers, "Life is better. America is back. And people have a sense of pride they never felt they'd feel again." Reagan won in a landslide, with 59 percent of the vote. Mondale, with running mate Geraldine Ferraro—U.S. congresswoman from New York

and the first woman vice presidential candidate—carried only his home state of Minnesota.

28-3e Junk Bonds and Merger Mania

Reagan's reelection in 1984 guaranteed the continuation of deregulation and pro-business economic policies, which facilitated economic risk taking and new financial practices. On Wall Street, for example, a reclusive bond trader for the firm Drexel Firestone named Michael Milken pioneered the "junk bond" industry and created wildly lucrative investment possibilities. Milken offered financing to debt-ridden or otherwise weak corporations that could not get traditional, low-interest bank loans to fund expansion, using bond issues that paid investors high interest rates because they were high-risk (thus "junk") bonds. Many of these corporations, Milken realized, were attractive targets for takeover by other corporations or investors—who, in turn, could finance takeovers with junk bonds. Such "predators" could use the first corporation's existing debt as a tax write-off, sell off unprofitable units, and lay off employees to create a more efficient—and thus more profitable—corporation. Investors in the original junk bonds could make huge profits by selling their shares to the corporate raiders.

By the mid-1980s, it was no longer only weak corporations that were targeted for these "hostile takeovers"; hundreds of major corporations—including giants Walt Disney and Conoco—fell prey to merger mania. Profits for investors were staggering, and by 1987 Milken, the guru of junk bonds, was earning $550 million a year—about $1,046 a minute—in salary; counting investment returns, Milken's income was about $1 billion a year.

In the 1980s, new conservative economic policies led to large-scale economic reorganization and increased economic growth. Heightened competition and corporate downsizing often created more efficient businesses and industries. Deregulation helped smaller and often innovative corporations challenge the virtual monopolies of giant corporations in fields like telecommunications. And through much of the 1980s, following the "Reagan recession," the American economy boomed.

28-3f The Costs of Economic Conservatism

The conservative policies of the 1980s and the high-risk boom they unleashed also had significant costs. Corporate downsizing meant layoffs for white-collar employees, many of whom (especially those past middle age) had difficulty finding comparable positions. The wave of mergers and takeovers left American corporations as a whole more burdened by debt. It also helped to consolidate sectors of the economy—such as the media—under the control of an ever-smaller number of players.

The high-risk, deregulated boom of the 1980s, furthermore, was rotten with corruption. By the late 1980s, insider trading scandals—in which people used "inside" information about corporations that wasn't available to the general public to make huge profits trading stocks—rocked financial markets and sent some of the most prominent figures on Wall Street to jail (albeit comfortable, "country club" jails). Congress's deregulation of the nation's savings and loan institutions (S&Ls) also fostered corruption and left regular Americans at risk. By ending government oversight of investment practices, while guaranteeing to cover losses from bad S&L investments, Congress left no penalties for failure. S&Ls increasingly put depositors' money into high-risk investments and engaged in shady—even criminal—deals. S&Ls lost billions of dollars in bad investments, sometimes turning to fraud to cover them up. Scandal reached all the way to the White House: Vice President Bush's son Neil was involved in shady S&L deals. The Reagan-Bush administration's bailout of the S&L industry had a total price tag of more than half a trillion dollars.

Finally, during the 1980s, the rich got richer, and the poor got poorer (see Figure 28.2). Ten times as many Americans reported an annual income of $500,000 in 1989 as in 1980. By 1989, CEOs received, on average, 71 times an average worker's pay, up from a 20-to-1 ratio in 1965 (the ratio was 303 to 1 in 2015, down from a 2000 high of 383 to 1). In 1987, the United States had forty-nine billionaires—up from one in 1978. While the number of very wealthy Americans grew, middle-class incomes were stagnant.

Most of the new inequality was due to conservative economic policies, which benefited the wealthy at the expense of middle- and lower-income Americans. Reagan's tax policies decreased the "total effective tax rates"—income taxes plus Social Security taxes—for the top 1 percent of American families by 14.4 percent. But they increased tax rates for the poorest 20 percent of families by 16 percent. By 1990, the richest 1 percent of Americans controlled 40 percent of the nation's wealth; fully 80 percent of wealth was controlled by the top 20 percent. Not since the 1920s had America seen such economic inequality.

28-4 Challenges and Opportunities Abroad

▶ Why did Ronald Reagan's approach to the Soviet Union shift from his first to his second term in office?

▶ How was the Reagan Doctrine implemented in the Caribbean and Latin America?

▶ What new challenges did the United States face in developing foreign policy toward the Middle East?

A key element in Reagan's winning strategy in the 1980 election was his forthright call for the United States to assert itself on the world stage. Though lacking a firm grasp of international issues, history, and geography—friends and associates often marveled at his ability to get even elementary facts wrong—Reagan adhered to a few core principles. One was a deep and abiding anticommunism, which had dictated his worldview for decades and which formed the foundation of his presidential campaign. A second was an underlying optimism about the ability of American power and values to bring positive change in the world. Reagan liked to quote Thomas Paine of the American Revolution: "We have it in our power to begin the world over again." Yet Reagan was also a political pragmatist, particularly as time went on and his administration became mired in scandal. Together, these elements help explain both his aggressive anticommunist foreign policy and his willingness to respond positively in his

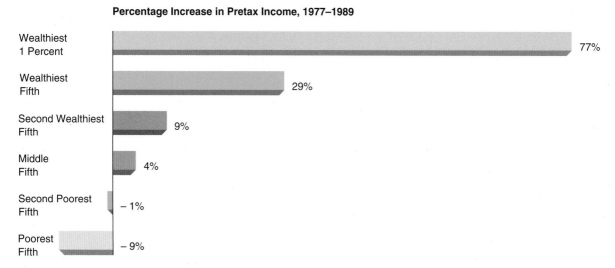

Percentage Increase in Pretax Income, 1977–1989

Wealthiest 1 Percent — 77%
Wealthiest Fifth — 29%
Second Wealthiest Fifth — 9%
Middle Fifth — 4%
Second Poorest Fifth — −1%
Poorest Fifth — −9%

Figure 28.2 While the Rich Got Richer in the 1980s, the Poor Got Poorer

Between 1977 and 1989, the richest 1 percent of American families reaped most of the gains from economic growth. In fact, the average pretax income of families in the top percentage rose 77 percent. At the same time, the typical family saw its income edge up only 4 percent. And the bottom 40 percent of families had actual declines in income. *Source: Data from the* New York Times, *March 5, 1992.*

second term to Soviet leader Mikhail Gorbachev's call for "new thinking" in world affairs.

28-4a Soviet-American Tension

Initially, toughness vis-à-vis Moscow was the watchword. Embracing the strident anticommunism that characterized U.S. foreign policy in the early Cold War, Reagan and his advisers rejected both the détente of the Nixon years and the Carter administration's focus on extending human rights abroad. Where Nixon and Carter perceived an increasingly multipolar international system, the Reagan team reverted to a bipolar perspective defined by the Soviet-American relationship. Much of the intellectual ballast and moral fervor for this shift toward confrontation with Moscow was provided by **neoconservatives**, a small but influential group composed primarily of academics and intellectuals, many of them former Democrats who believed the party had lost its way after Vietnam and who rejected the old conservatism as backward looking. Key figures in this group included Richard Perle and Paul Wolfowitz, who held mid-level positions in the administration.

In his first presidential press conference, Reagan described a malevolent Soviet Union, whose leaders thought they had "the right to commit any crime, to lie, to cheat." When Poland's pro-Soviet leaders in 1981 cracked down on Solidarity, an independent labor organization, Washington responded by restricting Soviet-American trade and hurling angry words at Moscow. In March 1983, Reagan told an audience of evangelical Christians in Florida that the Soviets were "the focus of evil in the modern world . . . an evil empire." That same year, Reagan restricted commercial flights to the Soviet Union after a Soviet fighter pilot mistakenly shot down a South Korean commercial jet that had strayed some three hundred miles off course into Soviet airspace, killing 269 passengers.

Reagan believed that a substantial military buildup would thwart the Soviet threat and intimidate Moscow. Accordingly, the administration launched the largest peacetime arms buildup in American history, driving up the federal debt. In 1985, when the military budget hit $294.7 billion (a doubling since 1980), the Pentagon spent an average of $28 million an hour. Assigning low priority to arms control talks, Reagan announced in 1983 his desire for a space-based defense shield against incoming ballistic missiles: the **Strategic Defense Initiative (SDI)**. His critics tagged it "Star Wars" and said perfecting such a system was scientifically impossible—some enemy missiles would always get through the shield. Moreover, the critics warned, SDI would have the effect of elevating the arms race to dangerous new levels. But Reagan was undaunted, and in the years that followed, SDI research and development consumed tens of billions of dollars.

28-4b Reagan Doctrine

Because he attributed Third World disorders to Soviet intrigue, the president declared the Reagan Doctrine: the United States would openly support anticommunist movements—"freedom fighters"—wherever they were battling the Soviets or Soviet-backed governments. In Afghanistan, the president continued Jimmy Carter's policy of providing covert assistance, through Pakistan, to the Mujahidin rebels in their war against the Soviet occupation. CIA director William J. Casey made numerous trips to Pakistan to coordinate the flow of arms and other assistance. When the Soviets stepped up the war in 1985, the Reagan administration sent more high-tech weapons. Particularly important were the Stinger anti-aircraft missiles. Easily transportable and fired by a single soldier, the Stingers turned the tide of the Afghan war by making Soviet jets and helicopters vulnerable below twelve thousand feet. Soviet commanders had no effective response.

The administration also applied the Reagan Doctrine aggressively in the Caribbean and Central America. Senior officials believed that the Soviets and Castro's Cuba were fomenting disorder in the region (see Map 28.1). Accordingly, in October 1983 the president sent U.S. troops into the tiny Caribbean island of Grenada to oust a pro-Marxist government that appeared to be forging ties with Moscow and Havana. In El Salvador, he provided military and economic assistance to a military-dominated government struggling against left-wing revolutionaries. The regime used (or could not control) right-wing death squads, which by the end of the decade had killed forty thousand dissidents and other citizens, as well as several American missionaries who had been working with landless peasants. By then, the United States had spent more than $6 billion there in a counterinsurgency war. In January 1992, the Salvadoran combatants finally negotiated a UN-sponsored peace.

28-4c Contra War in Nicaragua

In nearby Nicaragua, too, the administration made its presence felt. In 1979, leftist insurgents in Nicaragua had overthrown Anastasio Somoza, a longtime ally of the United States and member of the dictatorial family that had ruled the Central American nation since the mid-1930s. The revolutionaries called themselves Sandinistas in honor of Augusto César Sandino—who had headed the nationalistic, anti-imperialist Nicaraguan opposition against U.S. occupation in the 1930s and been assassinated by Somoza henchmen—and they denounced the tradition of U.S. imperialism in their country. When the Sandinistas aided rebels in El Salvador, bought Soviet weapons, and invited Cubans to work in Nicaragua's hospitals and schools and help reorganize the Nicaraguan army, Reagan officials charged that Nicaragua was becoming a Soviet client. In 1981, the CIA began to train, arm, and direct more than ten thousand counterrevolutionaries, known as *contras*, to overthrow the Nicaraguan government.

neoconservatives A small but influential group of intellectuals—typically former Democrats disillusioned with the party after Vietnam—who became part of Republican Ronald Reagan's conservative coalition.

Strategic Defense Initiative (SDI) Reagan's proposed program for developing a high-tech, space-based defense shield that would protect the United States against incoming ballistic missiles; nicknamed "Star Wars" by critics.

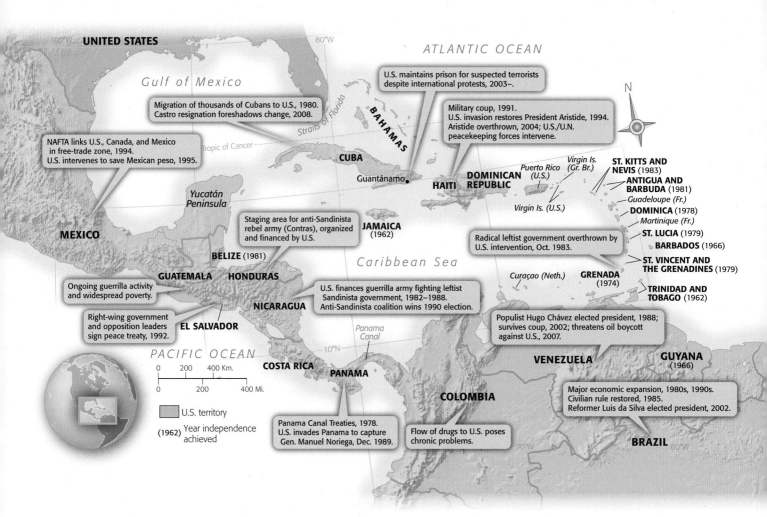

Map 28.1 **The United States in the Caribbean and Central America**

The United States has often intervened in the Caribbean and Central America. Geographical proximity, economic stakes, political disputes, security links, trade in illicit drugs, and Cuban leader Fidel Castro's longtime defiance of Washington have kept U.S. eyes fixed on events in the region.

Not everyone accepted the administration's interpretation of the stakes. Many Americans, including Democratic leaders in Congress, were skeptical about the communist threat to the region and warned that Nicaragua could become another Vietnam. Consequently, Congress in 1984 voted to stop U.S. military aid to the contras. Secretly, the Reagan administration lined up other countries, including Saudi Arabia, Panama, and South Korea, to funnel money and weapons to the contras, and in 1985 Reagan imposed an economic embargo against Nicaragua. The president might have opted for a diplomatic solution, but he rejected a plan proposed by Costa Rica's president Oscar Arias Sanchez in 1987 to obtain a cease-fire in Central America through negotiations and cutbacks in military aid to all rebel forces. (Arias won the 1987 Nobel Peace Prize.) Three years later, after Reagan had left

Oliver North U.S. Marine colonel who became a central figure in the Iran-contra, arms-for-hostages scandal.

office, all of the Central American presidents at last brokered a settlement; in the national election that followed, the Sandinistas lost to a U.S.-funded party. After nearly a decade of civil war, thirty thousand Nicaraguans had died, and the ravaged economy had dwindled to one of the poorest in the hemisphere.

28-4d Iran-Contra Scandal

Reagan's obsession with defeating the Sandinistas almost caused his political undoing. In November 1986, it became known that the president's national security adviser, John M. Poindexter, and an aide, marine lieutenant colonel **Oliver North**, in collusion with CIA director Casey, had covertly sold weapons to Iran as part of a largely unsuccessful attempt to win the release of several Americans being held hostage by Islamic fundamentalist groups in the Middle East. During the same period, Washington had been condemning Iran as a terrorist nation and demanding that America's allies not trade with the Islamic state. Still more damaging was the revelation that money from the Iran arms deal had been illegally diverted to a fund to aid the contras—this after Congress had unambiguously rejected providing such aid. North later admitted he had illegally destroyed government documents and lied to Congress to keep the operation clandestine.

Although Reagan survived the **Iran-Contra scandal**—it remained unclear just what he did and did not know about the operation—his presidency suffered a major blow. His personal popularity declined, and an emboldened Congress began to reassert its authority over foreign affairs. In late 1992, outgoing President George Bush pardoned several former government officials convicted of lying to Congress. Critics smelled a cover-up, for Bush himself, as vice president, had participated in high-level meetings on Iran-contra deals. As for North, his conviction was overturned on a technicality. In view of its deliberate thwarting of congressional authority, the Iran-contra secret network, the scholar William LeoGrande has argued, "posed a greater threat to democracy in the United States than Nicaragua ever did."

28-4e U.S. Interests in the Middle East

The Iran-contra scandal also pointed to the increased importance in U.S. foreign policy of the Middle East and terrorism (see Map 29.2). As before, the United States had as its main goals in the Middle East preserving access to oil and supporting its ally Israel, while at the same time checking Soviet influence in the region. But in the 1980s American leaders faced new pressures, in the form of a deepened Israeli-Palestinian conflict and an anti-American and anti-Israeli Islamic fundamentalist movement that began to spread after the ouster of the shah of Iran in 1979.

The 1979 Camp David Accords between Israel and Egypt had raised hopes of a lasting settlement involving self-government for the Palestinian Arabs living in the Israeli-occupied Gaza Strip and West Bank. It did not happen, as Israel and the Palestinian Liberation Organization (PLO) remained at odds. In 1982, in retaliation for Palestinian shelling of Israel from Lebanon, Israeli troops invaded Lebanon, reaching the capital, Beirut, and inflicting massive damage. The beleaguered PLO and various Lebanese factions called on Syria to contain the Israelis. Thousands of civilians died in the multifaceted conflict, and a million people became refugees. Reagan made no effort to halt the Israeli offensive, but he agreed to send U.S. Marines to Lebanon to join a peacekeeping force. Soon the American troops became embroiled in a war between Christian and Muslim factions, as the latter accused the marines of helping the Christian-dominated government rather than acting as neutral peacekeepers. In October 1983, terrorist bombs demolished a barracks, killing 241 American servicemen. Sensing the futility of the mission, Reagan pulled the remaining marines out four months later.

28-4f Terrorism

The attack on the marine barracks showed the growing danger of terrorism to the United States and other Western countries. In the 1980s, numerous otherwise powerless groups, many of them associated with the Palestinian cause or with Islamic fundamentalism, relied on terrorist acts to further their political aims. Often they targeted American citizens and property, on account of Washington's support of Israel and U.S. involvement in the Lebanese civil war. Of the 690 hijackings, kidnappings, bombings, and shootings around the world in 1985, for example, 217 were against Americans. Most of these actions originated in Iran, Libya, Lebanon, and the Gaza Strip. In June 1985, for example, Shi'ite

Iran-Contra scandal Scandal in which the Reagan administration illegally sold weapons to Iran to finance contras in Nicaragua.

◄ A U.S. Marine lieutenant stands guard as rescue workers comb the ruins of the American embassy in Beirut after a suicide bombing on April 18, 1983. The attack killed 63, including 17 Americans. The U.S. Marines were there as part of a multinational peacekeeping intervention in Lebanon's Civil War.

Francoise De Mulder/Getty Images

Muslim terrorists from Lebanon hijacked an American jetliner, killed one passenger, and held thirty-nine Americans hostage for seventeen days. Three years later, a Pan American passenger plane was destroyed over Scotland by a bomb that, investigators later determined, had been concealed in a cassette player. Several organizations claimed responsibility for the bombing, but questions remain about who did it.

Washington, firmly allied with Israel, continued to propose peace plans designed to persuade the Israelis to give back occupied territories and the Arabs to give up attempts to push the Jews out of the Middle East (the "land-for-peace" formula). As the peace process stalled in 1987, Palestinians living in the West Bank began an *intifada* (Arabic for "uprising") against Israeli forces. Israel refused to negotiate, but the United States decided to talk with PLO chief Yasir Arafat after he renounced terrorism and accepted Israel's right to live in peace and security. For the PLO to recognize Israel and, in effect, for the United States to recognize the PLO were major developments in the Arab-Israeli conflict, even as a lasting settlement remained elusive.

In South Africa, too, American diplomacy became more aggressive as the decade progressed. At first, the Reagan administration followed a policy of "constructive engagement"—asking the increasingly isolated government to reform its apartheid system, designed to preserve white supremacy. But many Americans demanded economic sanctions: cutting off imports from South Africa and pressuring some 350 American companies—top among them Texaco, General Motors, Ford, and Goodyear—to cease operations there. Some American cities and states passed divestment laws, withdrawing dollars (such as pension funds used to buy stock) from American companies active in South Africa. Public protest and congressional legislation forced the Reagan administration in 1986 to impose economic restrictions against South Africa. Within two years, about half of the U.S. companies in South Africa had pulled out.

28-4g Enter Gorbachev

Many on the right disliked the South Africa sanctions policy—they believed the main black opposition group, the African National Congress (ANC), was dominated by communists, and they doubted the efficacy of sanctions—and the more extreme among them soon found another reason to be disenchanted with Reagan. A new Soviet leader, Mikhail S. Gorbachev, had come to power, and Reagan, his own popularity sagging, showed a newfound willingness to enter negotiations with the "evil empire." Gorbachev called for a friendlier superpower relationship and a new, more cooperative world system. At a 1985 Geneva summit meeting between the two men, Reagan agreed in principle with Gorbachev's contention that strategic weapons should be substantially reduced, and at a 1986 meeting in Reykjavik, Iceland, they came very close to a major reduction agreement. SDI, however, stood in the way: Gorbachev insisted that the initiative be shelved, and Reagan refused to part with it, despite continuing scientific objections that the plan would cost billions of dollars and never work.

But Reagan and Gorbachev got along well, despite the language barrier and their differing personalities. Reagan's penchant for telling stories rather than discussing the intricacies of policy did not trouble the detail-oriented Gorbachev. As General Colin Powell commented, though the Soviet leader was far superior to Reagan in mastery of specifics, he never exhibited even a trace of condescension. He understood that Reagan was, as Powell put it, "the embodiment of his people's down-to-earth character, practicality, and optimism." And Reagan toned down his strident anti-Soviet rhetoric, particularly as his more hawkish advisers left the administration in the late 1980s.

28-4h *Perestroika* and *Glasnost*

The turnaround in Soviet-American relations stemmed more from changes abroad than from Reagan's decisions. As Reagan said near the end of his presidency, he had been "dropped into

▲ In one of several summit meetings, top Soviet leader Mikhail Gorbachev (b. 1931) and President Ronald Reagan (1911–2004) met in Moscow in May 1988 in hopes of signing a Strategic Arms Reduction Talks (START) agreement. The chemistry of warm friendship that Reagan later claimed characterized his personal relationship with Gorbachev fell short of producing cuts in dangerous strategic weapons. But their cordial interaction encouraged the diplomatic dialogue that helped end the Cold War.

AFP/Getty Images

a grand historical moment." Under the dynamic Gorbachev, a younger generation of Soviet leaders came to power in 1985. They began to modernize the highly bureaucratized, decaying economy through a reform program known as *perestroika* ("restructuring") and to liberalize the authoritarian political system through *glasnost* ("openness"). For these reforms to work, however, Soviet military expenditures had to be reduced and foreign aid decreased.

In 1987, Gorbachev and Reagan signed the **Intermediate-Range Nuclear Forces (INF) Treaty**, which banned all land-based intermediate-range nuclear missiles in Europe. Soon began the destruction of 2,800 missiles, including Soviet missiles targeted at Western Europe and NATO missiles aimed at the Soviet Union. Gorbachev also unilaterally reduced his nation's armed forces, helped settle regional conflicts, and began the withdrawal of Soviet troops from Afghanistan. After more than forty chilling years, the Cold War was coming to an end.

28-5 American Society in the 1980s

▶ What were the origins of the "culture wars" of the 1980s?

▶ What social crises did the United States face in the 1980s?

▶ How did immigration change American society in the 1970s and 1980s?

As the Cold War waned, so, too, did Americans' belief that the nation was united by a set of shared, middle-class values. By the 1980s, after years of social struggle and division, few Americans believed in the reality of that vision; many rejected it as undesirable. And though the 1980s were never as contentious and violent as the era of social protest in the 1960s and early 1970s, deep social and cultural divides existed among Americans. A newly powerful group of Christian conservatives challenged the secular culture of the American majority. A growing class of affluent, well-educated Americans seemed a society apart from the urban poor, and new technologies reshaped both work and leisure. At the same time, immigration was dramatically changing the composition of the American population.

28-5a "Culture Wars"

Throughout the 1980s, a coalition of conservative Christians known as the New Right waged campaigns against America's secular culture. Rejecting the "multiculturalist" belief that different cultures and lifestyle choices were equally valid, the New Right worked to make "God's law" the basis for American society. Concerned Women for America, founded by Beverly LaHayes in 1979, attempted to have elementary school readers containing "unacceptable" religious beliefs (including excerpts from *The Diary of Anne Frank* and *The Wizard of Oz*) removed from school classrooms, and

fundamentalist Christian groups once again began to challenge the teaching of evolutionary theory in public schools. The Reagan administration frequently turned to James Dobson, founder of the conservative Focus on the Family organization, for policy advice.

Although the New Right often found an ally in the Reagan White House, many other Americans vigorously opposed a movement they saw as preaching a doctrine of intolerance and threatening basic freedoms—including freedom of religion for those whose beliefs did not accord with the conservative Christianity of the New Right. In 1982, prominent figures from the fields of business, religion, politics, and entertainment founded People for the American Way to support American civil liberties and freedoms, the separation of church and state, and the values of tolerance and diversity. The struggle between the religious right and their opponents for the future of the nation came to be known as the "culture wars."

It was not only organized groups, however, that opposed the agenda of the religious right. Many New Right beliefs ran counter to the way most Americans lived—especially when it came to women's roles. By the 1980s, a generation of girls had grown up expecting freedoms and opportunities that their mothers never had. Legislation such as the Civil Rights Act of 1964 and Title IX had opened both academic and athletic programs to girls and women. In 1960, there were 38 male lawyers for every female lawyer in the United States; by 1983, the ratio was 5.5 to 1. By 1985, more than half of married women with children under three worked outside the home—many from economic necessity. The religious right's insistence that women's place was in the home, subordinated to her husband, contradicted not only the gains made toward sexual equality in American society but also the reality of many women's lives.

28-5b The New Inequality

As Americans fought the "culture wars" of the 1980s, another major social divide threatened the nation. A 1988 national report on race relations looked back to the 1968 Kerner Commission report to claim, "America is again becoming two separate societies," white and black. It argued that African Americans endured poverty, segregation, and crime in inner-city ghettos while most whites lived comfortably in suburban enclaves. In fact, America's separate societies of comfort and hardship were not wholly determined by race. The majority of America's poor were white, and the black middle class was strong and expanding. But people of color made up a disproportionate share of America's poor. In 1980, 33 percent of blacks and 26 percent of Latinos lived in poverty, compared with 10 percent of whites (see Figure 28.3).

Reasons for poverty varied. For people of color,

Intermediate-Range Nuclear Forces (INF) Treaty Treaty signed by U.S. president Reagan and Soviet leader Mikhail Gorbachev banning all land-based intermediate-range nuclear missiles in Europe, and resulting in the destruction of 2,800 missiles.

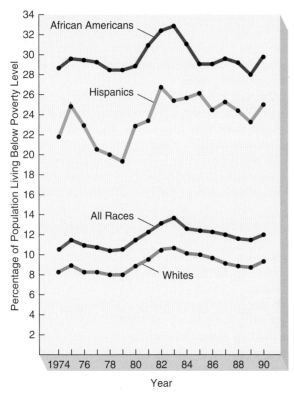

Figure 28.3 **Poverty in America by Race, 1974–1990**

Poverty in America rose in the early 1980s but subsided afterward. Many people of color, however, experienced little relief during the decade. Notice that the percentage of African Americans living below the poverty level was three times higher than that for whites. It was also much higher for Hispanics.

the legacies of racism played a role. The changing job structure was partly responsible, as the overall number of well-paid jobs for both skilled and unskilled workers decreased, replaced by lower-paid service jobs. New York alone had 234,000 fewer blue-collar workers in 1980 than at the beginning of the 1970s. In addition, families headed by a single mother were more likely to be poor—five times more likely than families of the same race with two parents present. By 1990, a high rate of unwed pregnancy and a rising divorce rate meant that about one-quarter of all children lived in a single-parent household. Racial differences were significant: in 1992, 59 percent of African American children and 17 percent of white children lived in households headed by a single woman, and almost half of black children lived in poverty.

28-5c Social Crises in American Cities

As inequality increased, so, too, did social pathology. In impoverished and often hopeless inner-city neighborhoods, violent crime—particularly homicides and gang warfare—grew alarmingly, as did school dropout rates, crime rates, and child abuse. Some people tried to find escape in hard drugs, especially crack, a derivative of cocaine, which first struck New York City's poorest neighborhoods in 1985. Crack's legacy included destroyed families, abused children, and heavily armed teenage drug dealers. Gang shootouts over drugs were deadly: the toll in Los Angeles in 1987 was 387 deaths, more than half of them innocent bystanders. Shocked by the violence, many states instituted mandatory prison sentences for possessing small amounts of crack. The federal government made penalties for a gram of crack equivalent to those for 100 grams of cocaine, the drug of choice for more affluent,

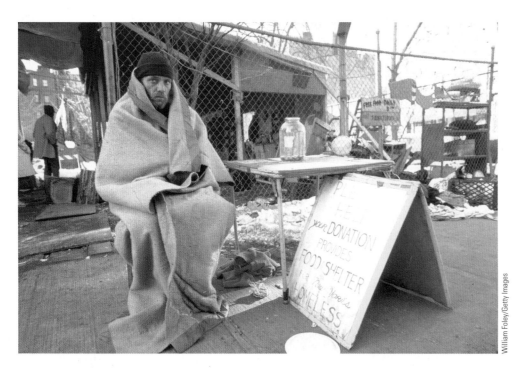

◀ A homeless man collects donations for the Temple of Rainbow food kitchen in a vacant lot, 1988. Americans increasingly recognized homelessness as a major national problem during the 1980s.

Combating the Spread of AIDS

During the 1960s and 1970s, with penicillin offering a quick and painless cure for venereal diseases, and with dependable contraceptives, such as the birth control pill, widely available, nonmonogamous sex had fewer physical risks than at any time in history. But new sexually transmitted diseases appeared during the 1980s. By far the most serious was HIV/AIDS (Human Immunodeficiency Virus/Acquired Immune Deficiency Syndrome). Because AIDS initially was diagnosed in communities of gay men, many heterosexual Americans were slow to understand that they, too, might be at risk. Public health agencies and activist groups worked to raise awareness and promote safe sex.

CRITICAL THINKING

How is the couple in this ad portrayed?

- How does this image complicate widespread assumptions about who is at risk?
- How does this public service advertisement make the case for "safe sex"?

Courtesy New York City Department of Health with permission of Saatchi & Saatchi North America, Inc.

▲ Campaigns for "safe sex," such as this New York City subway ad, urged people to use condoms.

white Americans during the 1980s. This war on drugs, along with a crackdown on rapidly rising violent crime and a far more punitive criminal justice system, increased America's prison population almost fourfold. By 2000, young black men were more likely to have been arrested than to have graduated from a four-year college.

Rates of homelessness also grew during the 1980s, in part because of major cuts to low-income housing subsidies. Some of the homeless were impoverished families; many of the people living on the streets had problems with drugs or alcohol. About one-third of the homeless were former psychiatric patients discharged from psychiatric wards in a burst of enthusiasm for "deinstitutionalization." By 1985, 80 percent of the total number of beds in state mental hospitals had been eliminated on the premise that small neighborhood programs would be more responsive to people's needs than large state hospitals. Such local programs failed to materialize. Without adequate medical supervision and medication, many of America's mentally ill citizens wandered the streets.

28-5d The AIDS Epidemic

Another social crisis confronting Americans in the 1980s was the global spread of acquired immune deficiency syndrome, or **AIDS**. Caused by the human immunodeficiency virus (HIV), which attacks cells in the immune system, AIDS leaves its victims susceptible to deadly infections and cancers. The human immunodeficiency virus itself is spread through the exchange of blood or body fluids, often through sexual intercourse or needle sharing by intravenous drug users.

AIDS was first diagnosed in the United States in 1981. During the 1980s it seemed an almost certain death sentence. Politicians were slow to devote resources to combating AIDS, in part because it was initially perceived as a "gay man's disease" and as such drew little concern from many of the nation's leaders. "A man reaps what he sows," declared the Reverend Jerry Falwell of the Moral Majority. A new group, ACT UP (the AIDS Coalition to Unleash Power), staged guerilla, agitprop demonstrations to confront "the system" that was so slow to address the threat of AIDS; ACT UP wrapped the home of conservative senator Jesse Helms in a huge, custom-made condom, and when Northwest Airlines refused to carry passengers with AIDS, the group bought millions of dollars' worth of Northwest tickets—and refused to pay for them. AIDS, along with other sexually transmitted diseases, such as genital herpes and chlamydia, ended an era defined by penicillin and "the Pill," in which sex was freed from the threat of serious disease or unwanted pregnancy.

AIDS Acquired Immune Deficiency Syndrome, first diagnosed in the United States in 1981; it had a very high mortality rate in the 1980s.

28-5e New Immigrants from Asia

Social divisions were further complicated by the arrival of new groups of immigrants. Between 1970 and 1990, the United States absorbed more than 13 million new arrivals, most from Latin America and Asia.

Before the immigration act reforms of 1965, less than 1 percent of Americans were of Asian ancestry; that percentage more than tripled by 1990. The new immigrants came from different nations. Before 1965, more than half of Asian Americans were of Japanese ancestry; Chinese or Filipino Americans made up most of the rest. There were only 603 Vietnamese residents of the United States in 1964. By 1990, the United States had absorbed almost 800,000 refugees from Indochina, casualties of the war in Vietnam and surrounding nations. Immigrants flooded in from South Korea, Thailand, India, Pakistan, Bangladesh, Indonesia, Singapore, Laos, Cambodia, and Vietnam. Japanese Americans became a much smaller portion of the Asian American population, at 15 percent surpassed by Chinese and Filipino Americans and rivaled by the Vietnamese.

Immigrants from Asia tended to be either highly skilled or unskilled. Unsettled conditions in the Philippines in the 1970s and 1980s created an exodus of well-educated Filipinos to the United States. India's economy was not able to support its abundance of well-trained physicians and health care workers, who increasingly found employment in the United States and elsewhere. Korea, Taiwan, and China also lost skilled and educated workers to the United States. Other immigrants from China, however, had few job skills and spoke little or no English. Large numbers of new immigrants crowded into neighborhoods like New York City's Chinatown, where women worked long hours under terrible conditions in the city's nonunion garment industry.

◄ Applicants for visas wait in line at the U.S. embassy in New Delhi, India. In 1985, 140,000 people were on the waiting list for one of 20,000 annual immigrant visas. Many poorer nations, such as India, experienced a "brain drain" of highly educated people to the United States and Western Europe.

Sandro Tucci/Getty Images

Immigrants from Southeast Asia were the most likely to be unskilled and to live in poverty in the United States, though some found opportunities for success.

But even highly educated immigrants often found their options limited. A 1983 study found that Korean immigrants or Korean Americans owned three-quarters of the approximately twelve hundred greengroceries (small stores that sell fresh vegetables and fruit) in New York City. Though often cited as a great immigrant success story, Korean greengrocers usually had descended the professional ladder: 78 percent of them had college or professional degrees.

28-5f The Growing Latino Population

Although immigration from Asia was high, unprecedented rates of immigration coupled with a high birth rate made Latinos the fastest-growing group of Americans. New immigrants from Mexico joined Mexican Americans and other Spanish-surnamed Americans, many of whose families had lived in this land even before it became the United States. In 1970, Latinos comprised 4.5 percent of the nation's population; that percentage jumped to 9 percent by 1990, when one out of three Los Angelenos and Miamians were Hispanic, as were 48 percent of the population of San Antonio and 70 percent of El Paso. Mexican Americans, concentrated in California and the Southwest, made up the majority of this population, but Puerto Ricans, Cubans, Dominicans, and other immigrants from the Caribbean also lived in the United States, clustered principally in East Coast cities.

During the 1980s, people from Guatemala and El Salvador fled civil war and government violence. Many found their way to the United States even though the U.S. government commonly refused to grant them political asylum (about 113,000 Cubans received political refugee status during the 1980s, compared with fewer than 1,400 El Salvadorans) until 1989. Economic troubles in Mexico and throughout Central and South America also produced a flood of a different sort of refugee: undocumented workers who crossed the two-thousand-mile border between the United States and Mexico, seeking economic opportunities. Some were sojourners who moved back and forth between nations. A majority meant to stay. These new Americans created a hybrid culture that became an important part of the American mosaic. "We want to be here," explained Daniel Villanueva, a TV executive in Los Angeles, "but without losing our language and our culture. They are a richness, a treasure that we don't care to lose."

The incorporation of so many newcomers into American society was not always easy, as many Americans believed new arrivals threatened their jobs and economic security, and nativist violence and simple bigotry increased. In 1982, twenty-seven-year-old Vincent Chin was beaten to death in Detroit by an unemployed autoworker and his uncle. American auto plants were losing the competition with Japanese imports, and the two men seemingly mistook the Chinese American Chin for Japanese, reportedly shouting at him, "It's because of you little [expletive deleted] that we're out of work." In New York, Philadelphia, and Los Angeles,

inner-city African Americans boycotted Korean groceries. Riots broke out in Los Angeles schools between black students and newly arrived Mexicans. In Dade County, Florida, voters passed an antibilingual measure that led to the removal of Spanish-language signs on public transportation, while at the state and national level people debated initiatives declaring English the "official" language of the United States. Public school classrooms, however, struggled with practical issues: in 1992, more than one thousand school districts in the United States enrolled students from at least eight different language groups.

Concerned about the flow of illegal aliens into the United States, Congress passed the **Immigration Reform and Control (Simpson-Rodino) Act** in 1986. The act's purpose was to discourage illegal immigration by imposing sanctions on employers who hired undocumented workers, but it also provided amnesty to millions who had immigrated illegally before 1982. As immigration continued at a high rate into the 1990s, however, it would further transform the face of America, offering both the richness of diverse cultures and the potential for continued social conflict.

28-5g New Ways of Life

Many Americans found their ways of life transformed during the 1980s, in large part due to new technologies and new models of distribution and consumption. American businesses made huge capital investments in technology during the 1980s as computers became increasingly central to the workplace. Such new communications technology made it possible to locate large office parks on the outskirts of cities, where building costs were low; these new workplaces fostered the development of "edge cities" or "technoburbs" filled with residents who lived, worked, and shopped outside the old city centers. New single-family homes grew larger and more expensive; the average cost of a new home rose from two and a half times the median household salary in 1980 to more than four times the median salary in 1988, and 42 percent of new homes had three or more bathrooms.

While the very rich embraced ostentation (Donald Trump's $29 million yacht had gold-plated bathroom fixtures) during this decade, people of more modest means also consumed more. Between 1980 and 1988, Wal-mart's sales jumped from $1.6 billion to $20.6 billion. The number of American shopping malls increased by two-thirds during the decade, and supermarkets stocked twice as many different items as they had ten years before. Eating out became common; by the end of the decade McDonald's was serving 17 million people a day, while "nouvelle cuisine" (artfully presented small portions, emphasizing fresh ingredients) appeared in upscale restaurants. The percentage of Americans who were overweight or

Immigration Reform and Control (Simpson-Rodino) Act A 1986 law that sought to discourage illegal immigration by fining employers who hired undocumented workers, but that also provided amnesty and a path to citizenship for millions who had immigrated illegally before 1982.

obese increased dramatically during the 1980s, even as more and more people began to run marathons (or compete in the much more demanding triathlons), tens of millions took aerobics classes or bought actress Jane Fonda's aerobics exercise videos, and the rapidly growing Nike brand launched its new slogan: "Just Do It."

New technology was not restricted to the workplace. Apple, founded by Steve Jobs and Steve Wozniak in 1976, introduced the Apple II computer in 1977; 2.1 million had been sold by 1985. IBM introduced its PC (personal computer) in 1981: for $1,565 (equivalent to $4,080 2015 dollars), purchasers got only 16 kilobytes of RAM. But the industry grew quickly, as did computer capacity, and almost half of American families owned some form of home computer by 1990.

Cable television expanded the choices offered by broadcast TV; about half of all families subscribed by the middle of the decade. When MTV (Music Television) was launched in 1981, only a few thousand cable subscribers in New Jersey had access, but it quickly grew to a national phenomenon. The first generation of MTV stars included Michael Jackson, whose fourteen-minute "Thriller" video premiered there in 1983, and Madonna, whose creative manipulation of her own image, from "Boy Toy" sexuality to celebration of female empowerment in "Express Yourself," infuriated both sides in the decade's culture wars. Newly affordable VCRs also gave consumers more choice. Movie attendance dropped as Americans rented movies to view at home, and children no longer had to wait for the annual and much-anticipated airing of *Cinderella* or *The Wizard of Oz* on television, but could instead watch *The Muppets Take Manhattan* or a host of other child-focused videos on demand—or as often as parents would allow.

28-6 The End of the Cold War and Global Disorder

▶ How did George H. W. Bush respond to events and developments on the international stage?

▶ What movements for democratization emerged in the 1980s?

▶ Why did the United States intervene militarily in the Middle East?

George H. W. Bush The forty-first president of the United States (1989–1993).

Americans with Disabilities Act Law that barred discrimination against disabled persons in employment, transportation, public accommodation, communications, and governmental activities.

Clarence Thomas African American judge nominated for the Supreme Court by George H.W. Bush in 1991. As a justice, he has interpreted the Constitution narrowly, championing conservative social issues.

The departure of Ronald Reagan from the presidency coincided with a set of changes in world affairs that would lead in short order to the end of the Cold War and the dawn of a new international system. Reagan's vice president, **George H. W. Bush**, would become president and oversee the transition. The scion of a Wall Street banker who had been a U.S. senator from Connecticut, Bush had attended an exclusive boarding school and then gone on to Yale. An upper-class, eastern Establishment figure of the type that was becoming increasingly rare in the Republican Party, he had the advantage over his rivals for the presidential nomination in that he had been a loyal vice president. And he possessed a formidable résumé—he had been ambassador to the United Nations, chairman of the Republican Party, special envoy to China, and director of the CIA. He had also been a war hero, flying fifty-eight combat missions in the Pacific in World War II and receiving the Distinguished Flying Cross.

28-6a George Herbert Walker Bush

In 1988, the Democratic Party nominated Massachusetts governor Michael Dukakis for president; Vice President Bush, with Reagan's support, gained the Republican nomination. Bush built on Reagan's popularity, the nation's economic prosperity, and international stability. His camp also waged one of the most racially negative campaigns in recent American history, airing a television commercial featuring a black convicted murderer, Willie Horton, who had terrorized a Maryland couple, raping the woman, while on weekend furlough—a temporary release program begun under Dukakis's Republican predecessor but used in the ad to suggest that Dukakis was "soft on crime." Bush defeated Dukakis by 8 percentage points in the popular vote, but the Democrats retained control of both houses of Congress.

From the start, Bush focused most of his attention on foreign policy, but domestic issues demanded his attention. Though the most-quoted line from his presidential campaign was "Read my lips: no new taxes," when confronted with a rapidly growing federal deficit, Bush chose to do what he thought necessary for the good of the nation: he compromised with Congress and raised taxes. Bush believed that government could not solve the nation's social problems, and he praised private charitable organizations as "a thousand points of light" and called for more "hands-on" activism from the American people. Yet he believed government played an important role in the "kinder, gentler nation" he envisioned. In 1990, Bush signed the **Americans with Disabilities Act (ADA)** (see "Legacy for a People and a Nation"). Much to the disappointment of conservatives who opposed increased government regulation, Bush signed the Clean Air Act, which sought to reduce acid rain by limiting emissions from factories and automobiles. And in 1991, after months of contentious debate, Bush and Congress agreed on a civil rights bill that expanded the remedies victims of job discrimination could seek. However, Bush also nominated the highly conservative **Clarence Thomas** to the Supreme Court.

In world affairs, Bush was by nature cautious and reactive, even in the face of huge changes in the international system and much to the chagrin of neoconservatives. Mikhail Gorbachev's reforms in the Soviet Union were now taking

▲ President George H. W. Bush signs the Americans with Disabilities Act (ADA) on the White House lawn, July 26, 1990. As he lifted his pen, the president said: "Let the shameful wall of exclusion finally come tumbling down."

on a life of their own, stimulating reforms in Eastern Europe that ultimately led to revolution. In 1989, many thousands of people in East Germany, Poland, Hungary, Czechoslovakia, and Romania, longing for personal freedom, startled the world by repudiating their communist governments and staging mass protests against a despised ideology. In November 1989, Germans scaled the Berlin Wall and then tore it down; the following October, the two Germanys reunited after forty-five years of separation. By then, the other communist governments in Eastern Europe had either fallen or were about to do so.

28-6b Pro-Democracy Movements

Challenges to communist rule in China met with less success. In June 1989, hundreds—perhaps thousands—of unarmed students and other citizens who for weeks had been holding peaceful pro-democracy rallies in Beijing's Tiananmen Square were slaughtered by Chinese armed forces. The Bush administration, anxious to preserve influence in Beijing, did no more than denounce the action, allowing the Chinese government, whose successful economic reforms had won much admiration in the 1980s, to emphatically reject political liberalization.

Elsewhere, however, the forces of democratization proved too powerful to resist. In South Africa, a new government under F. W. de Klerk, responding to increased domestic and international pressure (including from college campuses in the United States, where students erected shantytowns and called for universities to divest their investments in financial institutions with holdings in South Africa), began a cautious retreat from the apartheid system. In February 1990, de Klerk legalized all political parties in South Africa, including the ANC, and ordered the release of Nelson Mandela, a hero to black South Africans, after a twenty-seven-year imprisonment. Then, in a staged process lasting several years, the government repealed its apartheid laws and opened up the vote to all citizens, regardless of color. Mandela, who became South Africa's first black president in 1994, called the transformation of his country "a small miracle."

28-6c Collapse of Soviet Power

In 1990, the Soviet Union itself began to disintegrate. First the Baltic states of Lithuania, Latvia, and Estonia declared independence from Moscow's rule. The following year, the Soviet Union itself ceased to exist, disintegrating into fifteen

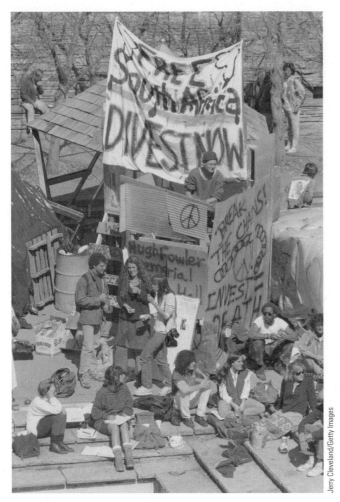

Jerry Cleveland/Getty Images

▲ The 1980s witnessed the rise of organized "divestment campaigns" on American college campuses in opposition to South Africa's apartheid system. Here protestors gather outside their shantytown at the University of Colorado in Boulder in early 1988. Some 80 students lived in shacks and tents built to protest the South African government and the university's investments in that country.

independent successor states—Russia, Ukraine, Belarus, Armenia, Tajikistan, and many others (see Map 28.2). Muscled aside by Russian reformers who thought he was moving too slowly toward democracy and free-market economics, Gorbachev himself lost power. The breakup of the Soviet empire, the dismantling of the Warsaw Pact (the Soviet military alliance formed in 1955 with communist countries of eastern Europe), the repudiation of communism by its own leaders, German reunification, and a significantly reduced risk of nuclear war signaled the end of the Cold War. The Soviet-American rivalry that for half a century had dominated international politics—and circumscribed domestic prospects in both countries—was over.

The United States and its allies had won. The containment policy followed by nine presidents—from Truman through Bush—had many critics over the years, on both the left and the right, but it had succeeded on a most basic level: it had

contained communism for four-plus decades without blowing up the world and without obliterating freedom at home. Two systems competed in this East-West confrontation, and that of the West had clearly triumphed—as anyone who experienced life in both a NATO country and a Warsaw Pact nation quickly realized. Next to the glitz and bustle and well-stocked store shelves of the former were the drab housing projects, polluted skies, and scarce consumer goods of the latter. Over time, the Soviet socialist economy proved less and less able to compete with the American free-market one, less and less able to cope with the demands of the Soviet and Eastern European citizenry.

Yet the Soviet empire might have hobbled along for years more had it not been for Gorbachev, one of the most influential figures of the twentieth century. His ascension to the top of the Soviet leadership was the single most important event in the final phase of the Cold War, and it is hard to imagine the far-reaching changes of the 1985–1990 period without his influence. Through a series of unexpected overtures and decisions, Gorbachev fundamentally transformed the nature of the superpower relationship in a way that could scarcely have been anticipated a few years before. Ronald Reagan's role was less central but still vitally important, not so much because of his hard-line policies in his first term as because of his later willingness to enter into serious negotiations and to treat Gorbachev more as a partner than as an adversary. George H. W. Bush, too, followed this general approach. In this way, just as personalities mattered in starting the Cold War, so they mattered in ending it.

28-6d Costs of Victory

The victory in the Cold War elicited little celebration among Americans. The struggle had exacted a heavy price in money and lives. The confrontation may never have become a hot war on a global level, but the period after 1945 nevertheless witnessed numerous bloody Cold War–related conflicts claiming millions of lives. In the Vietnam War alone, between 1.5 million and 2 million people died, more than 58,000 of them Americans. Military budgets, meanwhile, had eaten up billions upon billions of dollars that could have been allocated to domestic programs. Some Americans wondered whether the steep price had been necessary, whether the communist threat had ever been as grave as officials, from the late 1940s on, had claimed.

Bush proclaimed a "new world order," but for him and his advisers the question was: what happens next? As the Cold War closed, they struggled to describe the dimensions of an international system that they said would be based on democracy, free trade, and the rule of law. The administration signed important arms reduction treaties with the Soviet Union in 1991 and with the post-breakup Russia in 1993, leading to major reductions in nuclear weapons on both sides, but the United States sustained a large defense budget and continued to station large numbers of military forces overseas. As a result, Americans were denied the "peace dividend" that

Map 28.2 **The End of the Cold War in Europe**

When Mikhail Gorbachev came to power in the Soviet Union in 1985, he initiated reforms that ultimately undermined the communist regimes in Eastern Europe and East Germany and led to the breakup of the Soviet Union itself, ensuring an end to the Cold War.

they hoped would reduce taxes and free up funds to address domestic problems.

28-6e Saddam Hussein's Gamble

The strongest test of Bush's foreign policy came in the Middle East. The Iran-Iraq War had ended inconclusively in August 1988, after eight years of fighting and almost four hundred thousand dead. The Reagan administration had assisted the Iraqi war effort with weapons and intelligence, as had many other NATO countries. In mid-1990, Iraqi president Saddam Hussein, facing massive war debts and growing domestic discontent, invaded neighboring Kuwait, hoping thereby to enhance his regional power and his oil revenues and shore up domestic support. He counted on Washington to look the other way. Instead, George Bush condemned the invasion and vowed to defend Kuwait. He was outraged by Hussein's act of aggression and also feared that Iraq might

threaten U.S. oil supplies, not merely in Kuwait but also in petroleum-rich Saudi Arabia next door.

Within weeks, Bush had convinced virtually every important government, including most of the Arab and Islamic states, to sign on to an economic boycott of Iraq. Then, in Operation Desert Shield, Bush dispatched more than 500,000 U.S. forces to the region, where they were joined by more than 200,000 from the allies. Likening Saddam to Hitler and declaring the moment the first post–Cold War "test of our mettle," Bush rallied a deeply divided Congress to authorize "all necessary means" to oust Iraq from Kuwait (by a vote of 250 to 183 in the House and 52 to 47 in the Senate). Although Bush did not invoke the 1973 War Powers Act, numerous observers saw his seeking a congressional resolution of approval as reinforcing the intent of the act. Many Americans believed that economic sanctions imposed on Iraq should be given more time

CNN

When Ted Turner launched CNN, his Cable News Network, on June 1, 1980, few people took it seriously. CNN, with a staff of three hundred—mostly young, mostly inexperienced— operated out of the basement of a converted country club in Atlanta. Dismissed by critics as the Chicken Noodle Network, CNN was at first best known for its on-air errors, as when a cleaning woman walked onto the set and emptied anchor Bernard Shaw's trash during his live newscast. But by 1992, against all expectations, CNN was seen in more than 150 nations worldwide, and *Time* magazine named Ted Turner its "Man of the Year" for realizing media theorist Marshall McLuhan's vision of the world as a "global village" united by mass media.

Throughout the 1980s, CNN steadily built relations with local news outlets in nations throughout the world. As critical—and sometimes unanticipated—events reshaped the world, CNN reported live from Tiananmen Square and from the Berlin Wall in 1989. Millions watched as CNN reporters broadcast live from Baghdad in the early hours of the Gulf War in 1991. CNN changed not only viewers' experience of these events but diplomacy itself. When the Soviet Union wanted to denounce the 1989 U.S. invasion of Panama, officials called CNN's Moscow bureau instead of the U.S. embassy. During the Gulf War, Saddam Hussein reportedly kept televisions in his bunker tuned to CNN, and U.S. generals relied on its broadcasts to judge the effectiveness of missile attacks. In 1992, President George H. W. Bush noted, "I learn more from CNN than I do from the CIA."

Although Turner's twenty-four-hour news network had a global mission, its American origins were often apparent. During the U.S. invasion of Panama, CNN cautioned correspondents not to refer to the American military forces as "our" troops. Turner himself once sent his staff a memo insisting that anyone who used the word *foreign* instead of *international* would be fined $100. What CNN offered was not so much international news but a global experience: people throughout the world joined in watching the major moments in contemporary history as they unfolded. America's CNN created new links among the world's people. But as *Time* magazine noted (while praising Turner as the "Prince of the Global Village"), such connections "did not produce instantaneous brotherhood, just a slowly dawning awareness of the implications of a world transfixed by a single TV image."

CRITICAL THINKING

- If people throughout the world receive news from the same source, why do they all not understand the events and their meaning the same way?

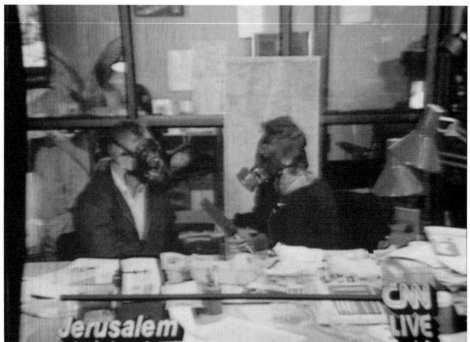

▲ A CNN correspondent interviews Israeli deputy foreign minister Benjamin Netanyahu on January 19, 1991. Following an alarm indicating an Iraqi missile attack on Israeli targets, those in the Jerusalem CNN studios had donned gas masks. CNN changed media history in the way its live coverage reported events as they unfolded.

AP Images/Mario Suriani

◀ In the Persian Gulf War of early 1991, Operation Desert Storm forced Iraqi troops out of Kuwait. Much of that nation's oil industry was destroyed by bombs and by the retreating Iraqis, who torched oil facilities as they left. Oil wells burned for months, darkening the sky over these American forces and causing environmental damage.

Bruno Barbey/Magnum Photos

to work, but Bush would not wait. "This will not be another Vietnam," the president said, by which he meant it would not be a lengthy and frustrating affair. Victory would come swiftly and cleanly.

28-6f Operation Desert Storm

Operation Desert Storm began on January 16, 1991, with the greatest air armada in history pummeling Iraqi targets. American cruise missiles reinforced round-the-clock bombing raids on Baghdad, Iraq's capital. It was a television war, in which CNN reporters broadcast live from a Baghdad hotel while bombs were falling in the city, and millions of Americans sat transfixed in their living rooms, eyes glued to the TV. In late February, coalition forces under General Norman Schwarzkopf launched a ground war that quickly routed the Iraqis from Kuwait. When the war ended on March 1, at least 40,000 Iraqis had been killed, while the death toll for allied troops stood at 240 (148 of them Americans). Almost one-quarter of the American dead were killed by "friendly fire"—by weapons fired by U.S. or allied troops.

Bush rejected a call from some of his advisers to take Baghdad and topple Saddam Hussein's regime. Coalition members would not have agreed to such a plan—it would go beyond the original objective of forcing Iraq out of Kuwait—and it was also not clear who in Iraq would replace the dictator. Some also warned that the drive to Baghdad could bog down, subjecting U.S. forces to a costly and drawn-out campaign. So Saddam survived in power, though with his authority curtailed. The UN maintained an arms and economic embargo, and the Security Council issued Resolution 687, demanding that Iraq provide full disclosure of all aspects of its program to develop weapons of mass destruction and ballistic missiles with a range greater than 150 kilometers. In Resolution 688, the Security Council condemned a brutal crackdown by the Iraqi regime against Kurds in northern Iraq and Shi'ite Muslims in the south and demanded access for humanitarian groups. The United States, Britain, and France seized on Resolution 688 to create a northern "no-fly zone" prohibiting Iraqi aircraft flights. A similar no-fly zone was set up in southern Iraq in 1992 and expanded in 1996.

Although in time some would question President Bush's decision to stop short of Baghdad, initially there were few objections. In the wake of Desert Storm, the president's popularity in the polls soared to 91 percent, beating the previous high of 89 percent set by Harry Truman in June 1945 after the surrender of Germany. Cocky White House advisers thought Bush could ride his popularity right through the 1992 election and beyond. In the afterglow of military victory it seemed a good bet, but in the months following the Gulf War the nation entered a full-fledged recession. Unemployment climbed to 8 percent. By late 1991, fewer than 40 percent of Americans felt comfortable with the way the country was going. By the time George H. W. Bush and the Republicans entered the election year of 1992, the glow of military victory in the Gulf War had faded completely.

Summary

When Ronald Reagan left the White House in 1988, succeeded by his vice president, George Bush, the *New York Times* summed up his presidency: "Ronald Reagan leaves no Vietnam War, no Watergate, no hostage crisis. But he

The Americans with Disabilities Act

The Americans with Disabilities Act (ADA), passed by large bipartisan majorities in Congress and signed into law by President George H. W. Bush on July 26, 1990, built on the legacy of America's civil rights movement; President Bush called it "the world's first comprehensive declaration of equality for people with disabilities." But the ADA did more than prohibit discrimination against people with physical and mental disabilities. It mandated that public and private entities—including schools, stores, restaurants and hotels, libraries and other government buildings, and public transportation authorities—provide "reasonable accommodations" to allow people with disabilities to participate fully in the life of their communities and their nation.

In less than two decades, the equal-access provisions of the ADA have changed the landscape of America. Steep curbs and stairs once blocked access to wheelchair users; now ramps and lifts are common. Buses "kneel" for passengers with limited mobility; crosswalks and elevators use audible signals for the sight impaired. At colleges and universities, qualified students (including those with learning disabilities) receive a wide range of assistance or accommodation. The National Park Service's "accessibility" program has enabled people with a whole spectrum of disabilities to travel into the Grand Canyon and on trails in many parks. Lee Page, a wheelchair user and sports fan from Virginia, described the impact of ADA standards for sports stadiums: "We were able to see over the standing spectators as the anthem was sung. I could see the flag and everything that was happening down on the field. . . . I finally felt like a part of the crowd."

At the same time that the ADA has offered greater opportunity to many Americans, regulations covering employment have generated some difficult legal questions. Which conditions are covered by the ADA? (The Supreme Court has ruled that asymptomatic HIV infection is a covered disability and carpal tunnel syndrome is not.) Employers may not discriminate against qualified people who can, with "reasonable" accommodation, perform the "essential" tasks of a job—but what is "reasonable" and what is "essential"? The specific provisions of the ADA will likely continue to be contested and redefined in the courts. But as Attorney General Janet Reno noted, as she celebrated the tenth anniversary of the ADA with a ceremony at Warm Springs, Georgia, where President Franklin Roosevelt had sought therapy for the effects of polio, the true legacy of the ADA is the determination "to find the best in everyone and to give everyone equal opportunity."

CRITICAL THINKING

- Terms such as "reasonable" and "essential" do not give specific guidance. What should employers consider in their efforts to offer equal opportunity?

---

leaves huge question marks—and much to do." George H. W. Bush met the foreign policy promises of the 1980s, as the Soviet Union collapsed and America achieved victory in the decades-long Cold War. He also led the United States into war with Iraq—a war that ended in swift and decisive victory but left Saddam Hussein in power.

During the 1980s, the United States moved from deep recession to economic prosperity. However, deep tax cuts and massive increases in defense spending created huge budget deficits, increasing the national debt from $994 billion to more than $2.9 trillion. This enormous debt would limit the options of subsequent presidential administrations. Pro-business policies, such as deregulation, created opportunities for the development of new technologies and prompted economic growth but also opened the door to corruption and fraud. Policies that benefited the wealthy at the expense of middle-class or poor Americans widened the gulf between the rich and everyone else. And drug addiction, crime, and violence grew during this era, especially in the nation's most impoverished areas.

The 1980s also saw the coalescence of the "culture wars" between fundamentalist Christians who sought to "restore" America to God and opponents who championed separation of church and state and embraced liberal values. The nation shifted politically to the right, though the coalitions of economic and social conservatives that supported Reagan were fragile and did not guarantee continued Republican dominance.

Finally, during the 1980s, the face of America changed. A society that many had thought of as comprised of white and black Americans became ever more diverse. The nation's Latino population grew in size and visibility. New immigrants from Asia arrived in large numbers; though still a small part of the population, they would play an increasingly important role in American society. During the Reagan-Bush years, America had become both more divided and more diverse. In the years to come, Americans and their leaders would struggle with the legacies of the Reagan era.

Suggestions for Further Reading

Elijah Anderson, *Streetwise: Race, Class, and Change in an Urban Community* (1992)

Lou Cannon, *President Reagan: The Role of a Lifetime* (2000)

Robert M. Collins, *Transforming America: Politics and Culture During the Reagan Years* (2006)

Campbell Craig and Fredrik Logevall, *America's Cold War* (2009)

Andrew Hartman, *A War for the Soul of America: A History of the Culture Wars* (2015)

Bradford Martin, *The Other Eighties: A Secret History of America in the Age of Reagan* (2011)

James Patterson, *The Restless Giant: The United States from Watergate to Bush vs. Gore* (2005)

Kim Phillips-Fein, *Invisible Hands: The Making of the Conservative Movement from the New Deal to Reagan* (2009)

Daniel T. Rogers, *Age of Fracture* (2012)

James Graham Wilson, *The Triumph of Improvisation: Gorbachev's Adaptability, Reagan's Engagement, and the End of the Cold War* (2014)

MINDTAP
From Cengage

MindTap® is a fully online personalized learning experience built upon Cengage Learning content. MindTap® combines student learning tools—readings, multimedia, activities, and assessments—into a singular Learning Path that guides students through the course and helps students develop the critical thinking, analysis, and communication skills that are essential to academic and professional success.

Into the Global Millennium: America Since 1992

At 8:46 AM on that fateful Tuesday morning, Jan Demczur, a window washer, stepped into an elevator in the North Tower of the World Trade Center in New York City. The elevator started to climb, but before it reached its next landing, one of the six occupants recalled, "We felt a muted thud. The whole building shook. And the elevator swung from side to side like a pendulum." None of the occupants knew it, but American Airlines Flight 175 had just crashed into the building, at a speed of 440 miles per hour.

The elevator started plunging. Someone pushed the emergency stop button, and the descent stopped. For several minutes, nothing happened. Then a voice came over the intercom to deliver a blunt message: there had been an explosion. The line went dead, as smoke began to seep through the elevator's doors. Using the wooden handle of Demczur's squeegee, several of the men forced open the doors but discovered they were on the fiftieth floor, five hundred feet above the ground, where this elevator did not stop. In front of them was a wall.

Demczur, a Polish immigrant who once worked as a builder, saw that the wall was made of Sheetrock, a plasterboard he knew could be cut. Using the squeegee, he started to scrape the metal edge against the wall, back and forth, over and over again. When the blade broke and fell down the shaft, he used a short metal handle that he had in his bucket. It took more than an hour, but the six men took turns scraping and poking, and finally burst through to a men's bathroom. Startled firefighters guided them to a stairwell. After an agonizingly slow descent through the heavy smoke, they finally burst onto the street at 10:23 a.m. Five minutes later, the tower collapsed.

It was September 11, 2001.

Only later that day did Demczur learn what had happened: terrorists had hijacked four airliners and turned them into missiles. Two had been flown into the World Trade Center; one had

◄ "The Tribute of Light," dedicated to the memory of the victims of the World Trade Center terrorist attacks, lights up the sky above Lower Manhattan on March 11, 2002, the six-month anniversary of the attacks. The Brooklyn Bridge is seen in the foreground. AP Photo/Daniel P. Derella

Chronology

1992	■ Violence erupts in Los Angeles over Rodney King verdict
	■ Major economic recession
	■ Clinton elected president
1993	■ Congress approves North American Free Trade Agreement (NAFTA)
1994	■ Republican "Contract with America"
	■ Genocide in Rwanda
	■ U.S. intervention in Haiti
1995	■ Domestic terrorist bombs Oklahoma City federal building
	■ U.S. diplomats broker peace for Bosnia
1996	■ Welfare reform bill places time limits on welfare payments
	■ Clinton reelected president
1999	■ NATO bombs Serbia over Kosovo crisis
	■ Antiglobalization demonstrators disrupt World Trade Organization (WTO) meeting in Seattle
2000	■ Nation records longest economic expansion in its history
	■ Supreme Court settles contested presidential election in favor of George W. Bush
2001	■ Economy dips into recession
	■ Al Qaeda terrorists attack World Trade Center and Pentagon
	■ United States attacks Al Qaeda positions in Afghanistan, topples ruling Taliban regime
2003	■ United States invades Iraq, ousts Saddam Hussein regime
2004	■ Bush reelected
2005	■ Hurricane Katrina strikes Gulf Coast
2006	■ By end of year, U.S. war deaths in Iraq reach three thousand
2007	■ Major economic recession begins in December
2008	■ Barack Obama elected president
2009	■ Obama announces increased U.S. military commitment to Afghanistan; U.S. continues troop drawdown in Iraq
2010	■ Congress passes Patient Protection and Affordable Care Act
2011	■ U.S. Navy SEALs kill Osama bin Laden
2012	■ Obama reelected president
2015	■ Iran nuclear deal
	■ Reestablishment of U.S.-Cuba relations
2016	■ Donald Trump elected president

slammed into the Pentagon in Washington, D.C.; and one had crashed in a field in rural Pennsylvania after passengers tried to wrest control of the plane from the hijackers. Both World Trade Center towers had collapsed, killing close to three thousand people, including Demczur's close friend Roko Camaj, a window washer from Albania.

It was the deadliest attack the United States had ever suffered on its soil, and it would lead to far-ranging changes in American life. But the events of the day sent shock waves well beyond the country's shores, indeed around the globe, and made starkly clear just how interconnected the world had become at the dawn of the twenty-first century. At the World Trade Center alone, nearly five hundred foreigners from more than eighty countries lost their lives. Sixty-seven Britons died, twenty-one Jamaicans, and twenty-seven Japanese. Mexico lost seventeen of its citizens; India lost thirty-four. Sixteen Canadians perished, as did fifteen Australians and seven Haitians. The tiny Caribbean nation of Trinidad and Tobago counted fifteen deaths.

The list of victims revealed the extraordinary diversity of people who inhabited New York, showing the city once again to be a mélange of world cultures. According to a chaplain at "Ground Zero," the victims' families communicated their grief in well over a hundred languages. Many of the victims were, like Demczur and Camaj, immigrants who had come to New York to seek a better life for themselves and their families; others were there on temporary work visas. But all helped to make the World Trade Center a kind of global city within a city, where some 50,000 people worked and another 140,000 visited on any given day.

A symbol of U.S. financial power, the World Trade Center towers were also—as their very name suggested—a symbol of the globalization of world trade that had been a central phenomenon of the 1980s and 1990s. The towers housed the offices and Wall Street infrastructure of more than four hundred businesses, including some of the world's leading financial institutions—Bank of America, Switzerland's Credit Suisse Group, Germany's Deutsche Bank, and Japan's Dai-Ichi Kangyo Bank.

Experience an interactive version of this story in MindTap®.

One of the buzzwords produced by the 1990s is *globalization*; by most definitions, globalization went beyond trade and investment to include the web of connections—in commerce, communications, and culture—that increasingly bound the world together. The terrorists, who were tied to a radical Islamic group called Al Qaeda, sought to strike a blow at that globalization, yet their attack was also an expression of it. In other words, Al Qaeda depended on the same international technological, economic, and travel infrastructure that had fueled global integration. Cell phones, computers, intercontinental air travel—the plotters made full use of these instruments of globalization in preparing to carry out their attack, then turned four modern jetliners into lethal weapons.

Americans struggled to comprehend the meaning of the attacks. For a broad majority of them, the last decade of the century offered good times. The stock market soared, unemployment dropped, and more Americans than ever before owned their own homes. But the 1990s were also marked by violence and cultural conflict—the first multiethnic uprising in Los Angeles, domestic terrorism in Oklahoma City, shootings by students at their schools, hate crimes that shocked the nation.

These were also years of political volatility and divisions. From the first days of Clinton's presidency, conservative Republicans blocked the Democrats' legislative programs. With a conservative agenda of limited government and "family values," the GOP routed Democrats in the 1994 midterm elections. But Republicans overestimated their power, alienating many voters by forcing the federal government to shut down during the winter of 1995–1996 in a standoff over the federal budget, and Clinton was reelected in 1996. However, Clinton's impeachment over sexual impropriety compromised his ability to lead the nation.

Clinton's successor, George W. Bush, responded to the 9/11 attacks by declaring a "war on terrorism." In so doing, he committed his administration and the nation to a complex and dangerous campaign of undefined scope and duration. Twice within eighteen months, Bush ordered U.S. forces into large-scale military action, first in Afghanistan, where Al Qaeda had its headquarters with the blessing of the ruling Taliban regime, then in Iraq to oust the government of Saddam Hussein. Both operations initially went well militarily, as the Taliban and the Iraqi government were quickly beaten. Al Qaeda, however, did not cease to be a threat, and in Afghanistan fighting eventually resumed. In Iraq, U.S. occupying forces battled a large-scale insurgency. Bush saw his high approval ratings begin to drop, and though he won reelection in 2004, his second term was undermined by continued bloodshed in Iraq and scandal at home. In 2008, Democratic candidate Barack Obama won the presidency on a platform of hope and change. The election of the nation's first African American president was a moment of great symbolic importance, but Obama, who inherited two wars and a major recession, found it difficult to create the domestic transformations he had promised. The depth of the economic crisis drastically limited the scope for substantive policy initiatives, and Obama also operated in a deeply polarized climate. Nevertheless, in his two terms in office, he brought the recession to an end, concluded American combat involvement in Iraq, and got Congress to pass the Patient Protection and Affordable Care Act, the most significant regulatory overhaul of the U.S. healthcare system since 1965. In 2016, a divided nation split the popular and electoral college vote, sending Donald J. Trump to the White House.

globalization The removal of barriers to the flow of capital, goods, and ideas across national borders.

■ *What was "the new economy" of the 1990s, and how did it contribute to the globalization of business?*

■ *Did the attacks of September 11, 2001, change America in fundamental ways? Explain.*

■ *Why did the United States wage wars in Iraq and Afghanistan in the decade after 9/11, and why did it struggle to prevail in both despite its massive technological superiority?*

29-1 Social Strains and New Directions

▶ **What did the Los Angeles riots reveal about the complexity of race relations in the United States?**

▶ **How did the Democrats and Republicans simultaneously compromise with one another and challenge one another on public policy?**

▶ **How did Bill Clinton respond to international events and address foreign policy issues?**

Although the 1990s would be remembered as an era of relative peace and prosperity, the decade did not start that way. Scourges of drugs, homelessness, and crime plagued America's cities. Racial tensions had worsened; the gulf between rich and poor had grown more pronounced. The economy, slowing since 1989, had tipped into recession. Public disillusionment with political leaders ran strong. As the 1992 presidential election year began, Americans were frustrated and looking for a change.

29-1a Turmoil in L.A.

The racial tensions that troubled the nation erupted in the South Central neighborhood of Los Angeles in 1992. The violence in Los Angeles (which the Korean community called Sa-I-Gu, or 4/29, for the date it began) was a multiethnic uprising that left at least fifty-three people dead. Like most such outbreaks, there was an immediate cause. A jury with no African American members had acquitted four white police officers charged with beating a black man, Rodney King, who had fled a pursuing police car at speeds exceeding 110 miles per hour.

Bill Clinton Forty-second president of the United States (1993–2001). Clinton served as the governor of Arkansas for twelve years prior to his election to the U.S. presidency.

Hillary Rodham Clinton Wife of President Bill Clinton, she was directly involved in policymaking during her husband's presidency. She later served as a New York senator (2001–2009), ran for president (2008 and 2016), and served as secretary of state (2009–2013) in the first Obama administration.

The roots of the violence went deeper. After well-paid jobs disappeared during the deindustrialization of the 1970s and 1980s, almost one-third of South Central residents lived in poverty. Tensions increased as new immigrants—Latinos from Mexico and Central America who competed with African American residents for jobs, as well as Koreans who established small businesses—sought a foothold in the area. Outside the legitimate economy, the 40 Crips (an African American gang) and the 18th Street gang (Latino) struggled over territory as the crack epidemic further decimated the neighborhood and the homicide rate soared. Police tactics had alienated most neighborhood residents, and relations were especially strained between African Americans and the new Korean population, as many African American and Latino residents saw high prices in Korean-owned shops as exploitation, while Korean shopkeepers complained of shoplifting, robberies, and violence.

Other sources of the conflict extended well beyond Los Angeles. During the Bush (senior) administration, the nation's economy had grown slowly or not at all. Factory employment was at its lowest level since the recession of 1982, and corporate downsizing meant that well-educated white-collar workers were also losing jobs. In 1992, poverty was at its highest level since 1964.

29-1b Clinton and the "New Democrats"

As the American economy suffered, so did President George H. W. Bush's approval rating. Despite the credit Bush gained for foreign policy—the end of the Cold War and the quick victory in the Gulf War—economic woes and a lack of what he once called the "vision thing" left him vulnerable in the 1992 presidential election. On Election Day, Democratic nominee **Bill Clinton** and his running mate, Tennessee senator Al Gore, swept New England, the West Coast, and much of the industrial Midwest, even making inroads into what had become an almost solidly Republican South and drawing "Reagan Democrats" back into the fold.

Bill Clinton was a larger-than-life figure, a born politician from a small town called Hope who had wanted to be president most of his life. In college during the 1960s he had protested the Vietnam War and (like many of his generation) had maneuvered to keep himself from being sent to Vietnam. Clinton had won a Rhodes Scholarship to Oxford, earned his law degree from Yale, and returned to his home state of Arkansas, where he was elected governor in 1978 at the age of thirty-two. Bill Clinton's wife, **Hillary Rodham Clinton**, was the first First Lady to have a significant career of her own during her married life; they had met when they were both law students at Yale, where Hillary Rodham had made Law Review (an honor not shared by her husband).

Politically, Bill Clinton was a "new Democrat." He, along with other members of the new Democratic Leadership Council, advocated a more centrist—though still socially progressive—position for the Democratic Party. Clinton and his colleagues asked whether large

AP Images/Reed Saxon

◀ Presidential candidate and tenor saxophonist Bill Clinton plays Elvis Presley's *Heartbreak Hotel* on the Arsenio Hall show, June 3, 1992. Many Washington commentators deemed it undignified, but Clinton's turn to late-night TV—a first in presidential campaigning—appealed to young and non-white Americans and transformed his campaign.

government bureaucracies were still appropriate tools for addressing social problems in modern America. They emphasized private-sector economic development rather than public jobs programs, focusing on job training and other policies that they believed would promote opportunity, not dependency. They championed a global outlook in both foreign policy and economic development. Finally, they emphasized an ethic of "mutual responsibility" and "inclusiveness."

Clinton plunged into an ambitious program of reform and revitalization. His major goal was to make health care affordable and accessible for all Americans, including the millions who had no insurance coverage. But special interests mobilized in opposition: the insurance industry worried about lost profits; the business community feared higher taxes to support the uninsured; the medical community was concerned about more regulation, lower government reimbursement rates, and reduced healthcare quality. The administration's healthcare task force, co-chaired by Hillary Rodham Clinton, could not create a political coalition strong enough to defeat these forces. Within a year, the centerpiece of Clinton's fledgling presidency had failed.

29-1c "Republican Revolution" and Political Compromise

With Clinton beleaguered, Republicans mounted a challenge. In September 1994, conservative Republicans championed a new "Contract with America." Developed under the leadership of Georgia congressman **Newt Gingrich**, the "Contract" called for a balanced-budget amendment to the Constitution, reduction of the capital gains tax, a two-year limit on welfare payments (while making unmarried mothers under eighteen ineligible), and increased defense spending.

In the midterm elections, the Republican Party mobilized socially conservative voters, gaining control of both houses of Congress for the first time since 1954 and increasing their share in state legislatures and governorships. Many Republicans believed their ongoing attempts to weaken federal power and to dismantle the welfare state would now succeed.

The Republicans of the 104th Congress, however, had miscalculated. Although many Americans liked the idea of cutting government spending, they opposed cuts to specific programs: Medicare and Medicaid, education and college loans, highway construction, farm subsidies, veterans' benefits, and Social Security. Republicans made a bigger mistake when they issued President Clinton an ultimatum on the federal budget. Clinton refused to accept their terms, and Republicans shut down the federal government in response. An angry public blamed the Republicans.

Such actions showed Clinton's resolve. But Clinton also compromised with those to his political right. He signed the 1996 Personal Responsibility and Work Opportunity Act, a welfare reform measure that required heads of families on welfare to find work within two years (though states could exempt up to 20 percent of recipients), limited welfare benefits to five years over an individual's lifetime, and made many legal immigrants ineligible. He also signed the Telecommunications Act of 1996, which reduced diversity in America's media by permitting companies to own more television and radio stations.

Clinton and Gore were reelected in 1996 (defeating Republican Bob Dole and Reform Party candidate Ross Perot), in part

Newt Gingrich Republican congressman from Georgia (1979–1999) who co-authored the 1994 "Contract with America." Gingrich served as Speaker of the House from 1995–1999, and led the Congressional shutdown of the U.S. federal government that lasted for 27 days in 1995–1996.

◀ Congressman Newt Gingrich (R., GA) led the opposition to President Bill Clinton and the Democratic Party's agenda. Here, at a rally on Capitol Hill in September 1994, Gingrich secures the support of Republican congressional candidates for his "Contract with America."

John Duricka/AP Images

because Clinton stole some of the conservatives' thunder. He declared that "the era of big government is over" and invoked family values, a centerpiece of the Republican campaign. Some of Clinton's actions were true compromises with conservative interests; other times he attempted to reclaim issues from the conservatives, as when he redefined family values as "fighting for the family-leave law or the assault-weapons ban or . . . trying to keep tobacco out of the hands of kids."

29-1d Political Partisanship and Domestic Terrorism

Despite widespread economic security and Clinton's moves toward the political center, politics were divisive, often ugly, and sometimes violent during the Clinton era. The political right attacked Clinton with a vehemence not seen since Franklin Roosevelt's New Deal. Hillary Clinton was a frequent target; when she told a hostile interviewer during her husband's first presidential campaign, "I suppose I could have stayed home and baked cookies and had teas. But what I decided to do was pursue my profession, which I entered before my husband was in public life," the *New York Post* called her "a buffoon, an insult to most women."

A political extremism that existed well beyond the bounds of Washington politics exploded into view on April 19, 1995, when 168 children, women, and men were killed in a blast that destroyed the nine-story Alfred P. Murrah Federal Building in downtown Oklahoma City. Many thought the bomb had been set by Middle Eastern terrorists. But evidence from a charred piece of truck axle found two blocks from the explosion led investigators to Timothy McVeigh, a native-born white American and a decorated veteran of the Persian Gulf War. McVeigh was seeking revenge for the deaths of members of the Branch Davidian religious sect,

whom he believed the FBI had deliberately slaughtered in a standoff over firearms charges on that date two years before in Waco, Texas.

In the months that followed, reporters and government investigators discovered networks of militias, tax resisters, and various white-supremacist groups throughout the nation. These groups were united by distrust of the federal government. Many saw federal gun control laws, such as the Brady Bill, signed into law in 1993, as a dangerous usurpation of citizens' right to bear arms. Members of these groups believed that the federal government was controlled by "sinister forces," including Jews, cultural elitists, Queen Elizabeth, and the United Nations.

Inside Washington, partisan politics grew more divisive. Republicans demanded an open-ended investigation of alleged wrongdoings by Bill and Hillary Clinton. The special counsel's investigation, which cost taxpayers $72 million, found no wrongdoing in the Clintons' financial or political affairs, but did offer evidence that Bill Clinton had committed perjury when he testified to a grand jury that he had not engaged in sexual relations with twenty-two-year-old White House intern Monica Lewinsky. In the wake of these charges, in 1998 Clinton became the second president—and the first in 130 years—to be impeached by the House of Representatives. However, the Republican-controlled Senate, responding at least in part to popular opinion, acquitted Clinton. Ironically, both Republican Speaker of the House Newt Gingrich and his successor, Robert Livingston, subsequently resigned when faced with evidence of their own extramarital affairs.

29-1e Clinton's Diplomacy

Internationally, the Clinton team faced less tumult; the United States still occupied a uniquely powerful position on the world stage. The demise of the Soviet Union had created a one-superpower world, in which the United States stood far above other powers in political, military, and economic might. Yet in his first term Clinton was more wary in traditional aspects of foreign policy—great-power diplomacy, arms control, regional disputes—than in facilitating American cultural and trade expansion. He was deeply suspicious of foreign military involvements. The Vietnam debacle had taught him that the American public had limited patience for wars lacking a clear-cut national interest, a lesson he found confirmed by George Bush's failure to gain lasting political strength from the Gulf War victory.

This mistrust of foreign interventions was cemented for Clinton by the difficulties he inherited from Bush in Somalia. In 1992, Bush had sent U.S. Marines to the East African nation as part of a UN effort to ensure that humanitarian supplies reached starving Somalis. But in summer 1993, when Americans came under deadly attack from forces loyal to a local warlord, Clinton withdrew U.S. troops. And to his later regret he did not intervene in Rwanda, where in 1994 the majority Hutus butchered 800,000 of the minority Tutsis in a brutal civil war.

29-1f Balkan Crisis

That Somalia and Rwanda were on the policy agenda at all testified to the growing importance of humanitarian concerns in post–Cold War U.S. policy. Many administration officials argued for using America's power to contain ethnic hatreds, support human rights, and promote democracy worldwide. The notion faced a severe test in the Balkans, which erupted in a series of ethnic wars. Bosnian Muslims, Serbs, and Croats were soon killing one another by the tens of thousands. Clinton talked tough against Serbian aggression and atrocities in Bosnia-Herzegovina, especially the Serbs' "ethnic cleansing" of Muslims through massacres and rape camps.

He occasionally ordered air strikes, but he primarily emphasized diplomacy. In late 1995, American diplomats brokered a fragile peace.

But Yugoslav president Slobodan Milosevic continued the anti-Muslim and anti-Croat fervor. When Serb forces moved to violently rid Serbia's southern province of Kosovo of its majority ethnic Albanians, Clinton was pressed to intervene. Initially he resisted. But reports of Serbian atrocities and a major refugee crisis stirred world opinion and convinced Clinton to respond. In 1999, U.S.-led NATO forces launched a massive aerial bombardment of Serbia. Milosevic withdrew from Kosovo, where U.S. troops joined a UN peacekeeping force. That same year, the International War Crimes Tribunal indicted Milosevic and his top aides for atrocities.

29-1g Agreements in the Middle East

In the Middle East, Clinton took an active role in trying to bring the Palestine Liberation Organization (PLO) and Israel together to settle their differences. In September 1993, the PLO's Yasir Arafat and Israeli prime minister Yitzhak Rabin signed an agreement at the White House for Palestinian self-rule in the Gaza Strip and the West Bank's Jericho. The following year Israel signed a peace accord with Jordan, further reducing the chances of another full-scale Arab-Israeli war. But radical anti-Arafat Palestinians continued terrorist attacks on Israelis, while extremist Israelis killed Palestinians and, in November 1995, Rabin himself. Only after American-conducted negotiations and renewed violence in the West Bank did Israel agree in early 1997 to withdraw its forces from the Palestinian city of Hebron. Thereafter, the peace process alternately sagged and spurted.

The same could be said of international efforts to protect the environment, which gained momentum in the 1990s. The George H. W. Bush administration had opposed many

◀ Villagers flee towards the town of Glogovac, in the Pristina district of central Kosovo, at the height of the Kosovo crisis in 1999.

David Brauchli/Getty Images

provisions of the 1992 Rio de Janeiro Treaty protecting the diversity of plant and animal species, and resisted stricter rules to reduce **global warming**. Clinton, urged on by Vice President Al Gore, signed the 1997 Kyoto Protocol, which aimed to combat emissions of carbon dioxide and other gases that most scientists believe trap heat in the atmosphere. The treaty required the United States to reduce its emissions by 2012 to 7 percent below its 1990 levels. (It failed to meet that target.) But facing strong congressional opposition, Clinton never submitted the protocol for ratification to the Republican-controlled Senate.

29-1h Bin Laden and Al Qaeda

Meanwhile, the administration was increasingly concerned about the threat to U.S. interests by Islamic fundamentalism. In particular, senior officials worried about the rise of **Al Qaeda** (Arabic for "the base"), an international terrorist network led by **Osama bin Laden**, which was dedicated to purging Muslim countries of what it saw as the profane influence of the West and installing fundamentalist Islamic regimes.

The son of a Yemen-born construction tycoon in Saudi Arabia, bin Laden had supported the Afghan Mujahidin in their struggle against Soviet occupation. He then founded Al Qaeda and financed terrorist projects with his substantial inheritance. U.S. officials grew more concerned, particularly as bin Laden focused on American targets. In 1995, a car bomb in Riyadh killed seven people, five of them Americans. In 1998, simultaneous bombings at the American embassies in Kenya and Tanzania killed 224 people, including twelve Americans.

In Yemen in 2000, a boat laden with explosives hit the destroyer USS *Cole*, killing seventeen American sailors. Although bin Laden masterminded and financed these attacks, he eluded U.S. attempts to apprehend him. In 1998, Clinton approved a plan to assassinate bin Laden at an Al Qaeda camp in Afghanistan, but the attempt failed.

Clinton's accomplishments during his two terms in office were modest. Domestic achievements included programs that made life easier for American families. The Family and Medical Leave Act gave employees the right to take time off work to care for ailing relatives or newborn children; health insurance reforms guaranteed that Americans would not lose health insurance when they changed jobs because of preexisting medical conditions. Clinton also created national parks and monuments that protected 3.2 million acres of American land and made unprecedented progress cleaning up toxic waste dumps throughout the nation. In foreign policy, meanwhile, he brokered a durable if incomplete peace in the Balkans and facilitated negotiations between Palestinian and Israeli officials, but he failed to act quickly or decisively to stop the mass killings in Rwanda.

29-2 Globalization and Prosperity

▶ **What factors contributed to a period of economic prosperity in the 1990s?**

▶ **How did globalization evolve in the 1990s?**

▶ **Why was globalization a controversial development?**

Despite conflicts abroad and partisan struggles in Washington, the majority of Americans experienced the late 1990s as a time of unprecedented peace and prosperity, fueled by the dizzying rise of the stock market. Between 1991 and 1999, the Dow Jones Industrial Average climbed from 3,169 to a high of 11,497 (see Figure 29.1). The booming market benefited the middle class and the wealthy, as mutual funds, 401(k) plans, and other new investment vehicles drew a majority of Americans into the stock market. In 1952, only 4 percent of American households were invested in stocks; by 2000, almost 60 percent were.

At the end of the 1990s, the unemployment rate stood at 4.3 percent—the lowest peacetime rate since 1957. That made it easier to implement welfare reform, and welfare rolls declined 50 percent. Both the richest 5 percent and the least-well-off 20 percent of American households saw their incomes rise almost 25 percent. But that translated to an average gain of $50,000 for the top 5 percent and only $2,880 for the bottom 20 percent, further widening the gap between rich and poor. Still, by decade's end, more than two-thirds of Americans were homeowners—the highest percentage in history.

Just how much credit Clinton deserved for the improved economy is debatable. Presidents typically get too much blame when the economy struggles and too much credit when times are good. The roots of the 1990s boom were in the 1970s, when American corporations began investing in automation, retooling plants to become more energy efficient, and cutting labor costs by moving to the union-weak South and West and to countries such as China and Mexico, where labor was cheap and pollution controls were lax.

29-2a Digital Revolution

Economic growth during the 1980s and 1990s was also driven by new digital technology: the rapid development of computers, fax machines, cell phones, and the Internet. New

global warming, or climate change, is the worldwide increase in average temperatures of the Earth's surface caused by greenhouse gas emissions.

Al Qaeda A radical Islamic group founded in the late 1980s and headed by Osama bin Laden until his death; it relies on an international network of cells to carry out terrorist attacks against the West, particularly the United States and its allies, in the name of Islamic fundamentalism.

Osama bin Laden A wealthy Islamic fundamentalist militant expelled from his native Saudi Arabia in 1991; he took refuge in Sudan, where he financed large-scale construction and agricultural projects and amassed followers of his Al Qaeda terrorist organization. He masterminded several attacks, among them the September 11, 2001, attack on the United States.

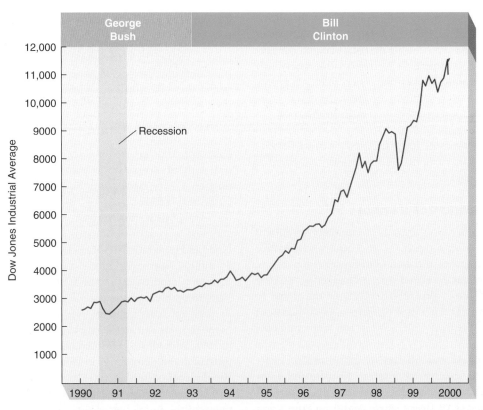

Figure 29.1 **The American Stock Market**

This graph of the Dow Jones Industrial Average, climbing steadily in the bull market of the 1990s, illustrates the great economic expansion of the decade.

companies and industries sprang up, many headquartered in the "Silicon Valley" near San Francisco. By the second half of the 1990s, the Forbes list of the four hundred richest Americans featured high-tech leaders such as Microsoft's Bill Gates, who became the wealthiest person in the world with worth approaching $100 billion at that point, as his company produced the operating software for most personal computers. The high-tech industry had considerable spillover effects, generating improved productivity, new jobs, and sustained economic growth.

◀ Students and their teacher gather around a laptop at an elementary school in Hebei Province, China. This then-innovative tool for learning connected these students to resources that were not easily accessible before.

The heart of this technological revolution was the microprocessor. Introduced in 1970 by Intel, the microprocessor miniaturized the central processing unit of a computer, meaning small machines could now perform calculations previously requiring large machines. Computing chores that took a week in the early 1970s took one minute by 2000; the cost of storing one megabyte of information, or enough for 320 pages of text, fell from more than $5,000 in 1975 to 17 cents in 1999 to 0.07 (7/100ths) of a cent in 2009; and while it cost $100,000 to store a gigabyte in 1975, by 2015 the figure was three or four cents. The implications for business were enormous.

29-2b Globalization of Business

Clinton perceived early on that the technology revolution would shrink the world and make it more interconnected. He was convinced that, with the demise of Soviet communism, capitalism—or at least the introduction of market forces, freer trade, and deregulation—was spreading around the globe.

Globalization was not a new phenomenon—it had been under way for a century—but now it had unprecedented momentum. Journalist Thomas L. Friedman asserted that the post–Cold War world was "the age of globalization," characterized by the integration of markets, finance, and technologies. U.S. officials lowered trade and investment barriers, completing George H.W. Bush's **North American Free Trade Agreement (NAFTA)** with Canada and Mexico in 1993, and in 1994 concluding the Uruguay Round of the General Agreement on Tariffs and Trade (GATT), which lowered tariffs for the seventy member nations that accounted for about 80 percent of world trade. The administration also endorsed the 1995 creation of the **World Trade Organization (WTO)** to administer and enforce agreements made at the Uruguay Round. Finally, the president formed a National Economic Council to promote trade missions around the world.

Multinational corporations were the hallmark of this global economy. By 2007, there were 79,000 parent companies worldwide and 790,000 foreign affiliates. Some, such as Nike and Gap, Inc., subcontracted production of certain merchandise to whichever developing countries had the lowest labor costs. Such arrangements created a "new international division of labor" and generated a boom in world exports, which, at $5.4 trillion in 1998, had doubled in two decades. U.S. exports reached $680 billion in 1998, but imports rose even higher, to $907 billion (for a trade deficit of $227 billion). Sometimes the multinationals directly affected foreign policy, as when Clinton in 1995 extended full diplomatic recognition to Vietnam partly in response to pressure from such corporations as Coca-Cola, Citigroup, General Motors, and United Airlines, which wanted to enter that emerging market.

North American Free Trade Agreement (NAFTA) Pact that admitted Mexico to the free-trade zone that the United States and Canada had created earlier.

World Trade Organization (WTO) International organization that regulates the global trading system and provides dispute resolution between member nations.

29-2c The Debate over Globalization

While the administration promoted open markets, labor unions argued that free-trade agreements exacerbated the trade deficit and exported American jobs. Other critics maintained that globalization widened the gap between rich and poor countries, creating a mass of "slave laborers" in poor countries working under conditions that would never be tolerated in the West. Environmentalists charged that globalization also exported pollution to countries unprepared to deal with. Still other critics warned about the power of multinational corporations and the global financial markets over traditional cultures.

Antiglobalization activists staged mass demonstrations and also targeted corporations such as the Gap, Starbucks, Nike, and especially McDonald's, which by 1995 was serving 30 million customers daily in twenty thousand franchises in over one hundred countries. Critics assailed the company's slaughterhouse techniques, alleged exploitation of workers, its high-fat menu, and its role in creating an increasingly homogeneous and sterile world culture. For six years starting in 1996, McDonald's endured hundreds of often-violent protests, including bombings in Rome, Prague, London, Macao, Rio de Janeiro, and Jakarta.

Others decried the violence and the underlying arguments of the antiglobalization campaigners. True, some economists acknowledged, statistics showed that global inequality had grown in recent years. But if one included quality-of-life measurements, such as literacy and health, global inequality

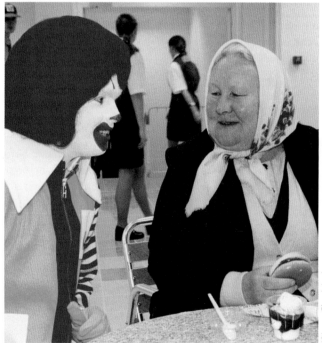

▲ McDonald's restaurants circled the globe by the early twenty-first century, exemplifying the globalization of American culture. This Ukrainian woman in Kiev seems to enjoy both her hamburger and a conversation with the human symbol of the fast-food chain, Ronald McDonald.

AP Images/Efrem Lukatsky

had actually declined. And globalization is responsible for only a small percentage of wage and job losses for U.S. workers; the major cause is automation. Other researchers saw no evidence that governments' sovereignty had been seriously compromised or that there was a "race to the bottom" in environmental standards from globalization.

As for creating a homogeneous global culture, McDonald's, others said, tailored its menu and operating practices to local tastes. And although American movies, TV programs, music, computer software, and other "intellectual property" often dominated world markets, foreign competition also made itself felt in America. Millions of American children were gripped by the Japanese Pokémon fad, and satellite television established a worldwide following for European soccer teams. An influx of foreign players added to the international appeal of both the National Basketball Association and Major League Baseball, while in the National Hockey League some 20 percent of players hailed from Europe by the late 1990s.

29-3 9/11 and the War in Iraq

▶ What domestic and international counterterrorism policies did George W. Bush's administration institute after 9/11?

▶ How did George W. Bush's foreign policy actions affect U.S. relations with other nations?

▶ Why was the U.S. decision to go to war with Iraq controversial?

George W. Bush was the unlikely winner of the 2000 presidential election. The strong U.S. economy seemed to favor his opponent, Vice President **Al Gore**, and Gore did win the popular vote (see Map 29.1). But the election came down to the twenty-five electoral votes of Florida, where Bush's brother Jeb was governor. According to the initial tally, Bush won the state—but by so close a margin that a recount was legally required. Thirty-six days later, in the midst of highly contested recount, the Supreme Court voted 5 to 4 along narrowly partisan lines to end the process. Florida's electoral votes—and the presidency—went to **George W. Bush**. Struggles over the election outcome further polarized the nation, and as Bush waited for the January inaugural, critics and comics began referring to him as the "president select."

In view of the close election, many believed that Bush would govern from the center. Some also thought that he was philosophically centrist, as his father had been, and that he had moved to the right only to ensure turnout among evangelical Christians, who made up an increasing portion of the Republican base. From the administration's first days, however, Bush governed from the right, arguably further to the right than any previous administration of modern times.

In international affairs, the administration charted a unilateralist course. Given America's preponderant power, senior Bush officials reasoned, it did not need other countries' help.

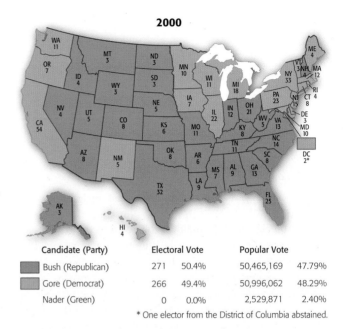

2000

Candidate (Party)	Electoral Vote		Popular Vote	
Bush (Republican)	271	50.4%	50,465,169	47.79%
Gore (Democrat)	266	49.4%	50,996,062	48.29%
Nader (Green)	0	0.0%	2,529,871	2.40%

*One elector from the District of Columbia abstained.

Map 29.1 Presidential Election, 2000

Democratic candidate Al Gore won the popular vote, but George W. Bush succeeded in gaining electoral victory by four votes. Among white males, Bush ran extremely well, while Gore won a majority of minority and women voters. Ralph Nader's Green Party won less than 3 percent of the national vote, but his votes in Florida may have detracted from the Gore tally, helping Bush win the critical electoral votes.

Accordingly, Bush withdrew the United States from the 1972 Anti-Ballistic Missile Treaty with Russia to develop a National Missile Defense system (forbidden under the treaty) broadly similar to Reagan's "Star Wars." The White House also renounced the 1997 **Kyoto Protocol** on controlling global warming and opposed a carefully negotiated protocol to strengthen the 1972 Biological and Toxin Weapons Convention. These decisions and the administration's hands-off policy toward the Israeli-Palestinian peace process caused consternation in Europe.

29-3a 9/11

Then came September 11. On that sunny Tuesday morning, nineteen hijackers seized control of four commercial jets departing from East Coast airports. At 8:46 AM, one plane crashed

Al Gore Longtime Democratic representative (1977–1985) and senator (1985–1993) from Tennessee; vice president under Bill Clinton (1993–2001); unsuccessfully ran for president in the highly contested 2000 race; won a 2007 Nobel Peace Prize for his advocacy and expertise on environmental issues, particularly global warming.

George W. Bush Forty-third president of the United States (2001–2009); governor of Texas from 1995 to 2000, when he resigned upon election to the presidency; son of forty-first President George H. W. Bush.

Kyoto Protocol A protocol setting strict emission targets for industrialized nations. President George W. Bush refused to sign the agreement, making the United States one of only four nations that declined participation.

into the 110-story North Tower of the World Trade Center in New York City. At 9:03 AM, a second plane flew into the South Tower. In less than two hours, both buildings collapsed, killing thousands of office workers, firefighters, and police officers. At 9:43, the third plane crashed into the Pentagon, leaving a huge hole in its west side. The fourth plane was also headed toward Washington, but several passengers—learning of the World Trade Center attacks through cell phone conversations—stormed the cockpit; in the ensuing scuffle, the plane crashed in Somerset County, Pennsylvania, killing all aboard.

More than three thousand people died, making this the deadliest act of terrorism in history. Not since the Japanese assault on Pearl Harbor in 1941 had the United States experienced such a devastating attack on its soil. The hijackers—fifteen Saudi Arabians, two Emiratis, one Lebanese, and, leading them, an Egyptian—had ties to Al Qaeda, Osama bin Laden's radical Islamic organization. Some officials in the Clinton and Bush administrations had warned that an Al Qaeda attack was inevitable, but neither administration made counterterrorism a foreign policy priority.

29-3b Afghanistan War

In an instant, counterterrorism was priority number one. President Bush responded quickly with large-scale military force. Al Qaeda operated out of Afghanistan with the blessing of the ruling Taliban, a repressive Islamic fundamentalist group that had gained power in 1996. In early October, the United States launched a sustained bombing campaign against Taliban and Al Qaeda positions and sent special operations forces to help a resistance organization in northern Afghanistan. Within two months, the Taliban was driven from power, although bin Laden and top Taliban leaders eluded capture.

As administration officials acknowledged, the swift military victory did not end the terrorist threat. Bush spoke of a long struggle against evil forces, in which the nations of the world were either with the United States or against it. Some questioned whether a "war on terrorism" could ever be won in a meaningful sense, given that the foe was a nonstate actor weak in the traditional measures of power—territory and governmental power—and with little to lose. Most Americans, however, were ready to believe. Stunned by September 11, they experienced a renewed sense of national unity and pride. Flag sales soared, and Bush's approval ratings skyrocketed. Citizenship applications from immigrants rose dramatically.

Colin Powell Four-star general, United States Army, who served as national security adviser (1987–1989), chairman of the Joint of Chiefs of Staff (1989–1993), and secretary of state (2001–2005) in the first George W. Bush administration. He was the first African-American to hold each of these positions.

Economic concerns, evident before 9/11, deepened thereafter with a four-day closing of Wall Street and a subsequent sharp drop in stock prices. The week after the markets reopened, the Dow Jones Industrial Average plunged 14.26 percent—the fourth largest weekly drop in percentage terms since 1900. The markets eventually rebounded, but questions remained about the economy's overall health. Such was Bush's political strength after 9/11, however, that neither this economic uncertainty nor the failure to capture Osama bin Laden and top Taliban leaders dented his popularity. In the 2002 midterm elections, Republicans retook the Senate and increased their majority in the House.

29-3c International Responses

Overseas, the president's standing was not nearly so high. Immediately after September 11, there was an outpouring of support from people everywhere. "We are all Americans now," said the French newspaper *Le Monde* after the attacks. Moments of silence in honor of the victims were held in many countries, and governments worldwide announced they would work with Washington against terrorism. But within a year, attitudes changed dramatically. Bush's bellicose stance and good-versus-evil terminology had put off many foreign observers from the start, but they initially swallowed their objections. When the president hinted that America might unilaterally strike Saddam Hussein's Iraq or deal forcefully with North Korea or Iran—the three countries of Bush's "axis of evil"—many allied governments strongly objected.

At issue was not merely the prospect of an American attack on one of these countries but the underlying rationale that would accompany it. Bush and other top officials argued that in an age of terrorism, the United States would not wait for a potential security threat to become real; henceforth, it would strike first. Critics, among them many world leaders, called it recklessly aggressive and contrary to international law, and they wondered what would happen if dictators around the world claimed the same right of preemption.

But Bush was determined, particularly on Iraq. Several of his top advisers, including Secretary of Defense Donald Rumsfeld and Vice President Dick Cheney, had wanted to oust Saddam Hussein for years, indeed since the end of the Gulf War in 1991. After the Twin Towers fell, they folded Iraq into the larger war on terrorism—even though counterterrorism experts saw no link between Saddam and Al Qaeda. For a time, Secretary of State **Colin Powell**, the first African American in that post, kept the focus on Afghanistan, but gradually the thinking in the White House shifted. In November 2001, Bush ordered the Pentagon to initiate war planning for Iraq; by spring 2002, a secret consensus was reached: Saddam Hussein would be removed by force.

29-3d Why Iraq?

In September 2002, Bush challenged the United Nations to enforce its resolutions against Iraq or the United States would act on its own. In subsequent weeks, he and his aides offered shifting reasons for getting tough with Iraq. They said Saddam was a major threat to the United States and its allies, a leader who possessed and would use banned biological and chemical "weapons of mass destruction" (WMDs) and who sought to acquire nuclear weapons. They claimed, contrary to their own intelligence estimates, that he had ties to Al Qaeda and could be linked to the 9/11 attacks. They said that he brutalized his own people and generated regional instability with his tyrannous rule.

Beneath the surface lurked other motivations. Neoconservatives saw in Iraq a chance to use U.S. power to reshape the region in America's image, to oppose tyranny and spread democracy. Ousting Saddam, they said, would enhance the security of Israel, America's key Middle East ally, and likely start a chain reaction that would extend democracy throughout the region. White House political strategists, meanwhile, believed a swift removal of a hated dictator would cement Republican domination in Washington and virtually ensure Bush's reelection. Finally, Bush wanted to prevent an Iraq potentially armed with WMDs from destabilizing an oil-rich region.

29-3e Congressional Approval

Like his father in 1991, Bush claimed he did not need congressional authorization for military action against Iraq; also like his father, he nevertheless sought it. In early October 2002, the House of Representatives voted 296 to 133 and the Senate 77 to 23 to authorize force against Iraq. Many who voted in favor were unwilling to defy a president so close to a midterm election, even though they opposed military action without UN sanction. Critics complained that the president had not presented evidence that Saddam Hussein constituted an imminent threat or was connected to the 9/11 attacks. Bush switched to a less hawkish stance, and in early November, the UN Security Council unanimously approved Resolution 1441, imposing rigorous new arms inspections on Iraq.

Behind the scenes, though, the Security Council was divided over the next move. As the debate continued, and as massive antiwar demonstrations took place around the world, Bush sent about 250,000 soldiers to the region. Britain sent about 45,000 troops.

29-3f Fall of Baghdad

In late February, the United States floated a draft resolution to the UN that proposed issuing an ultimatum to Iraq, but only three of the fifteen Security Council members affirmed support. Bush abandoned the resolution and all further diplomatic efforts on March 17, when he ordered Saddam Hussein to leave Iraq within forty-eight hours or face an attack. Saddam ignored the ultimatum, and on March 19 the United States and Britain launched an aerial bombardment of Baghdad and other areas. A ground invasion followed (see Map 29.2). The Iraqis initially offered stiff resistance, but on April 9, Baghdad fell.

When violence and lawlessness soon erupted, American planners seemed powerless to respond. The plight of ordinary Iraqis deteriorated as the occupation authority proved unable to maintain order. In Baghdad, electricity worked only a few hours each day, and telephone service was nonexistent. Decisions by the Coalition Provisional Authority (CPA), headed by Ambassador Paul Bremer, made matters worse—notably Bremer's move in May to disband the Iraqi army, which left tens of thousands of men, angry and armed, out of work. A multisided insurgency of Saddam loyalists, Iraqi nationalists of various stripes, and foreign Islamic revolutionaries took shape; soon, U.S. occupying forces faced frequent ambushes and hit-and-run attacks. By October 2003, more troops had died from these attacks than had perished in the initial invasion.

The mounting chaos in Iraq and the failure to find weapons of mass destruction had critics questioning the war's validity. The much-derided sanctions and UN inspections, it was now clear, had in fact been successful in rendering Saddam a largely toothless tyrant, with a hollow military and no chemical or biological weapons. Prewar claims of a "rush to war" resounded again. Even defenders of the invasion castigated the administration for its failure to anticipate the occupation problems. In spring 2004, graphic photos showing Iraqi detainees being abused by American guards at Abu Ghraib prison were broadcast worldwide, generating international condemnation.

29-3g Election of 2004

President Bush, facing reelection that fall, expressed disgust at the Abu Ghraib images and fended off charges that he and his top aides knew of and condoned the abuse. Many were skeptical, but voters that fall were prepared to give Bush the benefit of the doubt. His Democratic opponent, Senator **John Kerry** of Massachusetts, a Vietnam veteran who had reluctantly voted for the Iraq resolution in October 2001, had difficulty finding his campaign footing and never articulated a clear alternative strategy on the war. With the electorate deeply split, Bush won reelection with 51 percent of the popular vote to Kerry's 48 percent. The GOP also increased its majorities in the House and Senate.

29-3h America Isolated

Internationally, too, Bush faced criticism, not only on account of Iraq and Abu Ghraib, but also because of his administration's lack of engagement in the Israeli-Palestinian dispute and seeming disdain for diplomacy generally. The White House, critics said, rightly sought to prevent North Korea and Iran from joining the nuclear club but seemed incapable of working imaginatively and multilaterally to make it happen.

Iraq, though, remained the chief problem. The Bush administration denied that the struggle had become a Vietnam-like quagmire, but it seemed uncertain about how to end the fighting. In Congress and the press, calls for withdrawal from Iraq multiplied, but skeptics cautioned it could make things worse, triggering sectarian bloodshed and a collapse of the Baghdad government. The power and regional influence of neighboring Iran would increase, and American credibility would be undermined throughout

John Kerry Senator from Massachusetts (1985–2013) and Vietnam War veteran; Democratic nominee for president in 2004; served as secretary of state (2013–2017) in the second Obama administration.

BULGARIA

Black Sea

RUSSIA

KAZAKHSTAN

UZBEKISTAN

GEORGIA

Ankara

TURKEY

ARMENIA   AZERBAIJAN

Caspian Sea

TURKMENISTAN

CHINA

Soviet occupation, 1979–1989
U.S. aid to rebels, 1980s
International and Northern Alliance
forces defeat Taliban, 2001

Mazar e
Sharif

Kabul

AFGHANISTAN

Islamabad

Mediterranean Sea

20°E

Crete

CYPRUS

U.S. troops, 1958, 1983–1984

SYRIA

Tigris R.

Euphrates R.

Tikrit   Kirkuk

Tehran

Herat

Kandahar

PAKISTAN

Quetta

LEBANON

Damascus

ISRAEL

Tel Aviv

Amman

JORDAN

Fallujah   Baghdad

IRAQ

IRAN

U.S. arms sales, 1955–1978:
$20.8 billion
Shah overthrown, 1979
American hostages taken,
1979–1981

30°N

30°N

INDIA

Cairo

Basra

LIBYA

EGYPT

Nile R.

Tropic of Cancer

Aswan
Dam

Red Sea

Kuwait

KUWAIT

U.S. arms sales, 1980s,
during Iran-Iraq War
Iraq invades Kuwait, 1990
Second U.S.-Iraq War, 2003

Persian Gulf

U.S. and allies launch
First U.S.-Iraq War, 1991

Manama

BAHRAIN   QATAR

Doha

Riyadh

SAUDI ARABIA

Dubayy

Abu Dhabi

UNITED ARAB
EMIRATES

Strait of Hormuz

Muscat

Karachi

Partner in U.S. efforts to
eradicate al-Qaeda, 2001–

70°E

Oil embargo, 1973
Source of 17% of U.S. oil imports
in 1975
Largest buyer of U.S. arms, 1978

OMAN

Arabian Sea

SUDAN

30°E

20°N

40°E

Mecca

Jewish state after UN partition
of Palestine, 1947

Israel after War of 1948–1949

Area controlled by Israel after
Six-Day War, 1967

Israeli-occupied area after
Yom Kippur War, 1973

By Egyptian-Israeli agreements of 1975 and
1979, Israel withdrew from the Sinai in 1982.
In 1981 Israel annexed the Golan Heights.
Through negotiations between Israel and
the PLO, Jericho and the Gaza Strip were
placed under Palestinian self-rule, and Israeli
troops were withdrawn in 1994. In 1994
Israel and Jordan signed an agreement
opening their borders and normalizing their
relations.

ERITREA

LEBANON

Beirut

Damascus

SYRIA

Haifa

GOLAN
HEIGHTS

Sea
of Galilee

Mediterranean
Sea

Tel Aviv

WEST
BANK

ISRAEL

Jerusalem

Jordan R.

Amman

Gaza

Dead
Sea

32°E

Port Said

Suez
Canal

EGYPT

Cairo

Suez

Gulf of Suez

SINAI
PENINSULA

Elath

Gulf of Aqaba

JORDAN

SAUDI
ARABIA

ARAB-ISRAELI
CONFLICT

Sharm
el-Sheikh

Red Sea

28°E

32°E

YEMEN

Sana

Mukalla

50°E

Aden

Gulf of Aden

Socotra
(Yemen)

60°E

INDIAN
OCEAN

DJIBOUTI

Djibouti

10°N

ETHIOPIA

SOMALIA

U.S. troops assist in relief
of famine, 1992–1993; U.S.
troops withdrawn, 1994

Mogadishu

Members of the Organization of
Petroleum Exporting Countries
(OPEC)

Oil field

0   250   500 Km.

0   250   500 Mi.

0° Equator

N

Map 29.2 The Middle East

The nations of the Middle East maintained precarious relations with the United States. To protect its interests, the United States extended large amounts of economic and military aid and sold huge quantities of weapons to the area. At times, Washington ordered U.S. troops to the region. The Arab-Israeli dispute particularly upended order, although the peace process moved forward intermittently.

the Middle East. Some commentators instead called for an increase of U.S. forces in Iraq, and Bush heeded their advice. The "surge" of 2007 contributed to a drastic reduction in violence, as commanders shifted the focus to a counterinsurgency strategy emphasizing protection of the population. But the surge did not achieve meaningful results in its second goal: promoting political reconciliation among the competing factions in Iraq. That objective remained elusive when Bush left office in early 2009.

29-4 Domestic Politics and Foreign Policy in Post–9/11 America

▶ How did George W. Bush implement a conservative domestic agenda and respond to social crises?

▶ What was the significance of the presidential election of 2008?

▶ How did Barack Obama respond to the international issues he inherited?

While the Bush administration focused on what Bush had labeled "the global war on terrorism" (or GWOT), it also pursued domestic goals. The centerpiece of the Bush domestic agenda, achieved before the attacks of 9/11, was a $1.3 trillion tax cut—the largest in U.S. history. As Bush intended, this tax cut wiped out the $200 billion budget surplus he had inherited from the Clinton administration.

29-4a The Presidency of George W. Bush

Throughout his years as president, George W. Bush embraced conservative ideals, though sometimes in ways that seemed paradoxical. Much of his agenda fit smoothly with conservative principles. Religious conservatives were pleased by the newly prominent role of religion in the political process. The president spoke frequently of his faith; Bush's attorney general, John Ashcroft, a Pentecostal Christian who had stated, prior to his confirmation, that America had "no king but Jesus," held prayer meetings at 8 a.m. every morning in the Justice Department. And Bush appointed the medical director of a Christian pregnancy-counseling center whose website claimed that the "distribution of birth control is demeaning to women, degrading of human sexuality and adverse to human health and happiness" to head the nation's federal family planning program.

Bush was also a strong advocate of economic deregulation. His administration dismantled environmental restrictions on the oil, timber, and mining industries, and as Wall Street developed an incredible array of new and risky financial instruments, he maintained a full hands-off approach to regulation. While he failed to privatize the Social Security system, he did reshape the Supreme Court. Fifty-year-old conservative U.S. Circuit Court judge John Roberts was

confirmed as chief justice following the death of Chief Justice William Rehnquist at age eighty, and another strong conservative, fifty-five-year-old Samuel Alito, became junior associate justice following the resignation of Sandra Day O'Connor, who had often voted with the more liberal faction of the court.

At the same time, Bush turned to big government solutions. While Ronald Reagan had tried to abolish the federal Department of Education, Bush dramatically increased the federal government's role in public education in an attempt to fix a "broken system of education that dismisses certain children and classes of children as unteachable." Under his **"No Child Left Behind"** initiative, schools could only receive federal funding if their state set "high standards" for all students, mandated standardized tests to evaluate their progress, and held failing schools accountable. And while conservatives traditionally argued that the federal government was not responsible for individuals' medical care costs, the Bush administration created an enormously expensive new entitlement program that covered prescription drugs for American seniors, regardless of income, under Medicare.

Although Bush won the presidential election in 2004, growing perceptions of administrative incompetence began to undermine the American people's confidence in the president and his administration. In late August 2005, a major hurricane hit the U.S. Gulf Coast and New Orleans. **Hurricane Katrina** destroyed the levees that kept low-lying parts of New Orleans from being swamped by water from Lake Pontchartrain and surrounding canals. Floodwater covered 80 percent of New Orleans. More than 1,800 people died in the storm and the floods that followed.

Tens of thousands of people who lacked the resources to flee New Orleans sought shelter at the Superdome. Supplies of food and water quickly ran low and toilets backed up; people wrapped the dead in blankets and waited for rescue. Those outside the Gulf region, watching the suffering crowd of mainly poor, black New Orleanians, began a soul-searching conversation about what Democratic Party leader Howard Dean called the "ugly truth": that poverty remains linked to race in this nation.

29-4b Economic Recession

Economic troubles were also brewing: American home prices—a huge "housing bubble"—were on the verge of collapse. Following the beginnings of deregulation in the financial markets during the 1980s, financial institutions had sought new ways to expand their market and their

"No Child Left Behind" Bush administration initiative intended to improve public schools for all children. This legislation expanded the federal government's role in education; many criticized its reliance on standardized testing for leading teachers to "teach to the test."

Hurricane Katrina Worst natural disaster in U.S. history; resulting flooding destroyed much of New Orleans and the Gulf Coast in August 2005; poor handling of the crisis fueled cries of racism and tarnished the Bush administration.

profits. They began experimenting with "subprime" mortgages for people who, in previous years, would not have qualified for credit. For example, "NINA" loans went to homebuyers with "No Income, No Assets." By 2006, one-fifth of all home loans were subprime. As more Americans bought homes, increased demand and rabid speculation kept housing prices rising. In 2000, a median-priced house "cost" 3 full years of a (median-earning) family's income. At the height of the bubble in 2006, it cost 4.6 years of work. This was good news for lenders: because housing prices kept going up, they saw little risk. If a family defaulted on their mortgage and lost their house, the property could be sold for more—sometimes much more—than the mortgage was worth. Wall Street firms saw an opportunity for rapid short-term profit. They began buying up mortgages, bundling them together, good and bad, into multibillion-dollar packages to sell to investors. These mortgage-backed securities were complex and difficult to value—but because conservatives had cut government oversight (deregulation), large financial institutions got away with risky—and unethical—practices. Some bankers and mortgage rating agencies purposely deceived investors.

This unstable structure began to fail in 2007, as more and more borrowers began to default on their mortgages. People tried to escape unaffordable mortgages by selling their houses, but housing prices dropped rapidly. Increasingly, mortgages were larger than the declining value of houses. And the huge financial institutions that had gambled on mortgage-backed securities did not have enough capital to sustain such losses. America's major financial institutions—indeed, key banks around the world—were on the verge of collapse.

Barack Obama Forty-fourth president of the United States (2009–2017) and the nation's first African American president, who took office in the midst of the worst economic crisis since the Great Depression.

The U.S. economy depends on the availability of credit—for business loans, car loans, home loans, credit cards. This housing crisis paralyzed the credit markets. Businesses couldn't get the loans they needed to buy raw materials or inventory; consumers couldn't get the credit they needed to buy large items, such as cars. And many Americans were already deeply in debt. They had taken out home equity loans against the rising value of their houses; they owed money on several credit cards. In 1981, families saved more than 10 percent of their post-tax income; in 2005, the average family spent more than it earned—and for those under thirty-five, the savings rate was minus 16 percent. As credit tightened, people bought less. Businesses began laying off workers, and the unemployment rate began to climb. Those who were unemployed or worried about their jobs spent less money, and the cycle continued. The Bush administration attempted to prevent the collapse of the financial system by bailing out some of America's largest banks and credit providers—those that were deemed "too big to fail." The Troubled Asset Relief Program (TARP) eventually provided $700 billion in loans to failing institutions, but as "Main Street" recovered more slowly than Wall Street, many Americans were angry that tax dollars had gone to rescue wealthy bankers, none of whom would face prosecution for their misdeeds.

29-4c Barack Obama's Presidency

The presidential election of 2008 was shaped by the growing worldwide economic crisis. As Americans worried about the economy and Bush's approval rating fell to 27 percent, the Democratic candidate, Illinois Senator **Barack Obama**, prevailed over John McCain, the senior senator from Arizona (Map 29.3). Barack Hussein Obama, who would become the nation's first African American president, made

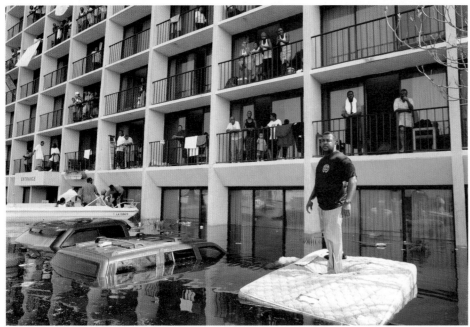

◀ New Orleans police officers and volunteers rescue residents from a flooded neighborhood during the devastation following Hurricane Katrina in August 2005. Katrina destroyed not only New Orleans, but much of the Gulf Coast from Louisiana into Alabama.

AP Photo/Eric Gay

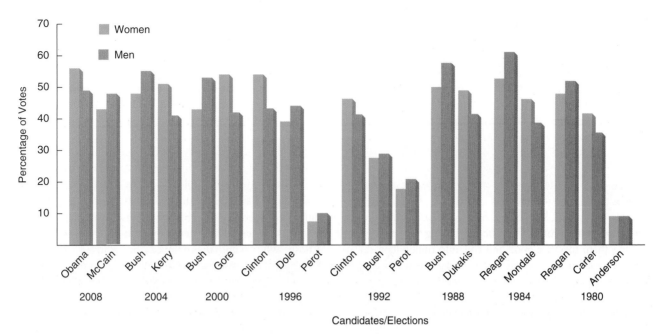

Figure 29.2 **The Gender Gap in American Presidential Elections**

The gender gap, or the difference in voting patterns between men and women, was first identified in 1980 by National Organization for Women president Eleanor Smeal and has been recognized as an important force in American politics ever since. In virtually every presidential election portrayed here, greater percentages of women (no matter their race or ethnicity, income, level of education, or marital status) than men voted for the Democratic candidate. *Source: Based on data from the Center for American Women and Politics.*

headlines in 2002 by opposing the coming war in Iraq; he caught the nation's attention when he delivered a powerful keynote speech at the 2004 Democratic national convention; three years later, as a first-term senator, he was running for the presidency.

Obama was born in Hawai'i in 1961. His mother was a young white woman from Kansas, his father a Kenyan graduate student at the University of Hawai'i. (The couple divorced when their child was two years old and each married again, giving Barack both African and Indonesian half-siblings.) Obama spent part of his childhood in Indonesia with his mother, attended high school in Hawai'i, and moved to the U.S. mainland for college. After graduating from Harvard Law School, where he served as president of the *Harvard Law Review*, Obama moved to Chicago. There he met and married fellow Harvard Law graduate Michelle Robinson and joined the law school faculty at the University of Chicago.

Obama was an inspirational speaker who offered messages of "hope" and "change." Supporters were passionate about him, expecting in some cases that he would almost miraculously solve the nation's problems and bring bipartisan harmony to a deeply divided Congress (see Figure 29.2). Obama began his presidency with big ideas and ambitious goals, but he also had to confront his inheritance: two unresolved wars, a massive federal deficit, and a major recession that threatened to spin into a global meltdown.

In February 2009, Obama signed legislation creating a $787 billion economic stimulus package in an attempt to

jump-start the economy, and supported expanding TARP and bailing out auto giants GM and Chrysler, both on the verge of failing. The economy began a slow recovery in 2009, but unemployment rates remained high. In 2010, one in eight Americans was receiving food stamps from the government, and Wal-mart pointed to evidence of hard times: a big jump in the purchase of kitchen storage containers for leftovers.

As the recession continued, Republicans won a landslide victory in the 2010 elections, gaining control of the House of Representatives. Spearheading this Republican victory was a new grassroots movement: the Tea Party. The Tea Party mobilized Republican middle-class voters who were angry about big government and expensive federal programs aimed at lower-income Americans, but wealthy conservatives provided essential financial and organizational support.

Obama's victory in 2012 (over Republican Mitt Romney) was narrower than his first, but his coalition held and he drew critical support from the growing Latinx electorate. Treating his election as a mandate, Obama took firmer positions. Despite Obama's renewed political will, however, the nation continued to face fierce struggles over annual debt, budget deficits, taxes, and government expenditures.

Throughout the Obama years, Congress was mired in partisan gridlock, and Republicans frequently stymied administrative actions. Refusing to compromise on the budget in 2013, Republicans shut down the federal government for sixteen days. And after conservative Supreme Court Justice Anton Scalia died in early 2016, Republic Senate leaders

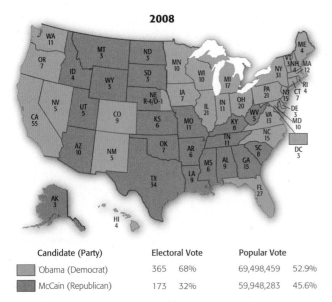

2008

Candidate (Party)	Electoral Vote		Popular Vote	
Obama (Democrat)	365	68%	69,498,459	52.9%
McCain (Republican)	173	32%	59,948,283	45.6%

Map 29.3 **Presidential Election, 2008**

The economy was the deciding factor in the 2008 election. McCain's claim, in the midst of Wall Street's meltdown in September 2008, that "the fundamentals of our economy are strong" backfired. Americans found Obama's calm and deliberate presence a better bet for dealing with the economic crisis, and gave him victory in November.

refused to consider Merrick Garland, Obama's nominee to the court.

Obama's greatest domestic achievement may have been shepherding the national economy back to health; by the end of his second term, unemployment had dropped from nearly 10 percent to 4.7 percent (see Figure 29.3). During the Obama years, 15.8 million new jobs were created, and in 2014—2015,

real median household income (the inflation-adjusted earning of households in the middle of income distribution) grew 5.2 percent. That said, well-paid manufacturing jobs continued to disappear, replaced by jobs in the service economy, and some who left the job market during the depths of the recession never found a way back into employment.

Obama's most significant achievement was the Affordable Care Act (often called Obamacare). Signed into law in 2010, the ACA is a market-based plan that relies on for-profit insurance companies to provide coverage. The ACA had significant problems in its initial roll out, but by 2016 an additional 20 million Americans had gained insurance as the plan removed lifetime insurance caps, added coverage for preventative care, and prohibited insurance companies from excluding or charging higher premiums to individuals with preexisting medical conditions. In order to pay for this expansion in size and coverage, the plan mandated that all individuals have insurance coverage and taxed the wealthy to subsidize premiums for lower-income Americans. The program drew strong opposition from Republicans, who attempted to repeal it, in full or in part, more than sixty times during Obama's presidency.

Obama committed his presidency to environmental protection. Under his leadership, in 2016 the United States signed the first comprehensive global plan to reduce global warming. He created new national monuments, protecting more than 553 million acres of land and water—more than the past eighteen presidents combined. These monuments conserved the land, but they also celebrated a more inclusive vision of American history, commemorating events central to women, American Indian, African American, and LGBT Americans.

Throughout his presidency, Obama was a measured champion of equal rights and social justice. Some Americans

◀ More than seventy-five thousand people gathered in Chicago's Grant Park to celebrate Barack Obama's election on November 4, 2008.

REUTERS/Gary Hershorn

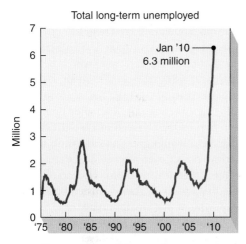

Total long-term unemployed

Jan '10 —
6.3 million

Figure 29.3 **Long-Term Unemployment**

Unemployment rates skyrocketed during the recession. But perhaps most striking is the dramatic increase in long-term unemployment. In January 2010, 6.3 million job seekers had been unemployed for twenty-seven weeks or longer. *Source: "Long Term Unemployment" graphs, New York Times, February 21, 2010, from http://www.nytimes.com/2010/02/21/business/economy/21unemployed.html?hp. Reprinted by permission of The New York Times.*

believed that his election signaled the beginning of a "post-racial America." But rising racial tensions, in large part tied to police shootings of black men and the resulting protests, showed how wrong that claim was. Obama, here as in most arenas, emphasized the need for mutual understanding—leaving both advocates for the police and protestors against racialized policing unsatisfied. Under Obama's watch, the Supreme Court guaranteed marriage equality for same-sex couples nationwide; the "Don't Ask, Don't Tell" policy that barred gay men and lesbians from serving openly in the U.S. military was repealed, and women were allowed to join military combat units for the first time. Finally, the Obama years were notable for the grace and dignity with which the president and his family filled their roles.

29-4d Obama and the World

In foreign affairs, Obama focused initially on fulfilling a campaign promise to reduce the nation's involvement in Iraq. U.S. casualty figures continued to decline in 2009, and Obama stuck to a timeline for withdrawal that would have all combat forces out of the country by August 2010. In August 2010, he declared that "the American combat mission in Iraq has ended. Operation Iraqi Freedom is over, and the Iraqi people now have lead responsibility for the security of their country." Though some U.S. troops remained in Iraq as "advise and assist brigades" assigned to noncombat operations, in late 2011 these too were removed. On December 15, 2011, U.S. Defense Secretary Leon Panetta officially pronounced the Iraq War over at a flag-lowering ceremony in Baghdad. The last U.S. troops left Iraqi territory on December 18, 2011, but political stability in the country remained elusive.

Even as he drew down in Iraq, Obama ramped up U.S. involvement in Afghanistan. During the 2008 campaign he had stressed the importance of the ongoing struggle there, and when he took office in early 2009, the situation was deteriorating. The Taliban were regaining a foothold and appeared ready to threaten the existence of the government in Kabul, headed by Hamid Karzai. Obama judged trends to be sufficiently alarming that he ordered 17,000 more American combat troops to Afghanistan even before completion of the first review he'd ordered.

In December, following another policy review, Obama announced a "surge" that would commit 33,000 additional U.S. troops to the struggle (for a total of 100,000), as well as 7,000 troops from NATO members and other allies. He rejected the advice of skeptics such as Vice President Joseph Biden, who questioned whether the surge would work and whether Karzai's government could be counted on to take responsibility for its own security. To placate concerns that he was committing America to an open-ended war, Obama promised that "our troops will begin to come home" by the summer of 2011.

The president didn't make the deadline, but by the summer of 2012 the surge troops had been withdrawn, leaving some 68,000 U.S. forces still in place. Although a constant barrage of drone strikes and special operations raids took a harsh toll on Al Qaeda, it was difficult for the administration to make the case that Afghanistan had achieved stability or that Karzai's government could stand on its own without U.S. assistance.

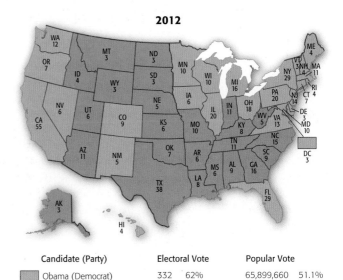

2012

Candidate (Party)	Electoral Vote		Popular Vote	
Obama (Democrat)	332	62%	65,899,660	51.1%
Romney (Republican)	206	38%	60,932,152	47.2%

Map 29.4 **Presidential Election, 2012**

In the 2012 election, Barack Obama held on to most of his 2008 winning coalition. A fractured Republican party nominated Mitt Romney, who was the first member of the Church of Jesus Christ of Latter-day Saints to run for president as a major political party's candidate.

Notwithstanding the continuing problems in Afghanistan, most voters in the 2012 presidential campaign gave Obama high marks on foreign policy. His trump card was an altogether more dramatic event: the violent death of the mastermind behind the 9/11 attacks, the man who had become the symbolic leader of global *jihad* against the West. In the very early hours of May 2, 2011, American Navy SEALs, in a daring operation later immortalized in the Hollywood film *Zero Dark Thirty*, shot and killed Osama bin Laden in Abbottabad, a garrison town north of Islamabad, Pakistan.

The operation took forty minutes, but the groundwork had been laid years before. Thanks to information acquired by interrogating detainees, CIA analysts identified one of the few Al Qaeda couriers trusted by bin Laden. Eventually, they pinpointed the area of Pakistan in which the courier operated, and in August 2010 they tracked him to a high-walled compound in Abbottabad they speculated was bin Laden's location. On April 29, 2011, Obama gave the go-ahead for the operation, even though there was no certainty bin Laden was there. Three days later, the U.S. commandos swooped down on the compound in stealth helicopters in the dead of a moonless night, moved through the buildings, and shot dead a total of five people, including bin Laden.

In his second term, Obama faced greater pressures abroad, especially with the challenge from ISIL (Islamic State in Iraq and the Levant, also known as ISIS, or Daesh, from the initial letters in the group's earlier Arabic name), a jihadist organization that catapulted onto the global scene in 2013 and 2014 when it conquered significant swaths of territory in Iraq and Syria. Tracing its lineage to the aftermath of the U.S. invasion of Iraq in 2003, ISIS expanded its capabilities after Abu Bakr al-Baghdadi became leader in 2010.

It soon became notorious for its wanton brutality, including mass executions, abductions, and beheadings.

The terror group's rise took U.S. officials by surprise, particularly as the Syrian civil war (which began in 2011 as a broad-based uprising against President Bashar al-Assad) created a power vacuum in parts of the country that ISIS filled. As the fighting raged and a major humanitarian crisis unfolded in Syria, Obama faced intense criticism from some quarters for his unwillingness to intervene more forcefully with American power, even after evidence emerged of Assad's use of banned chemical weapons. Instead, Obama targeted the Islamic State with an American-led bombing campaign and the deployment of a small number of U.S. special forces. The effort gradually achieved results, and by the time Obama left office the amount of ISIS-held territory in Iraq and Syria had been cut in half.

The misery in Syria continued, however, and seemed likely to tarnish Obama's legacy. His supporters hoped his record would be buoyed by other developments, including a landmark nuclear deal with Iran and a diplomatic opening to Cuba, and by the prevention of a 9/11-type attack on American soil on his watch.

29-4e Election of 2016

In 2016, a divided America went to the polls. Although former secretary of state Hillary Clinton won the popular vote by almost 3 million, the electoral college went to businessman and reality TV star Donald Trump, who became the forty-fifth president of the United States. Following a peaceful transfer of power on January 20, 2017, opponents of Trump's agenda gathered in cities throughout the nation. More than half a million people flooded the streets of the nation's capital

◀ On May 1, 2011, photographer Pete Souza captured President Obama and his senior advisers watching in real time the secret raid by American forces against Osama bin Laden's Pakistan compound. Obama had made the decision to launch the attack, but here he can only be spectator like everyone else in the room.

The White House/Getty Images

◀ President-elect Donald Trump delivers his acceptance speech in New York City, November 9, 2016.

for the Women's March on Washington, while up to 4 million more marched in other cities and towns, waving signs and banners, chanting "This is what democracy looks like."

29-5 Americans in the New Millennium

▶ In what ways are Americans divided in recent years? What are the sources of those divisions?

▶ How do American families of the new millennium compare to those of fifty and seventy-five years ago?

▶ What were the consequences of increased connectivity of persons across the globe via technology?

In the twenty-first century, the United States is a nation of extraordinary diversity. For much of the twentieth century, however, it had seemed that the United States was moving in the opposite direction. Very few immigrants had been allowed into the United States from the 1920s through 1965. New technologies, such as radio and television, had a homogenizing effect at first, for these mass media were dependent on reaching the broadest possible audience—a mass market. Although local and ethnic traditions persisted, more and more Americans participated in a shared mass culture. During the last third of the twentieth century, however, those homogenizing trends were reversed. Immigration reform in the mid-1960s opened American borders to large numbers of people from a wider variety of nations than ever before. New technologies—the Internet, and cable and satellite television, with their proliferation of channels—replaced mass markets with niche markets. Everything from cosmetics to cars to politics could be targeted toward specific groups defined by age, ethnicity, class, gender, sexuality, or lifestyle choices.

These changes had mixed results. They may have helped to make Americans' understandings of identity more fluid and more complex. They also created echo chambers, fragmenting the American public into groups whose lifestyle choices, values, and politics were constantly reinforced.

29-5a A Nation Divided

America has become, in fundamental ways, a nation divided. Some of that division is based on concrete differences in circumstances, while some is tied to the political weight Americans give various choices or beliefs.

For example, more than half of American adults see a fundamental conflict between religious belief and science, though two-thirds see no conflict between science and their own beliefs. In the United States, only 32 percent of adults believe that evolution took place solely through natural processes, while 33 percent believe that humans and other living things have existed in their present-day form since the beginning of time. Conflicts have arisen as fundamentalist Christians have struggled to prevent the teaching of evolution in the nation's science classes or to introduce parallel instruction of biblical "creationism" or theories of "intelligent design," which hold that an intelligent creator lies behind the development of life on earth.

Gun ownership has become a key symbolic divide in the American public. According to recent surveys (and such findings are always controversial), approximately 36 percent of American adults either own a firearm or live with someone who does, down from a height of 53 percent in 1994. But who owns such weapons—and why—has changed. Of the somewhere between 265 and 310 million guns in the United States, research suggests that more than half are owned by 3 percent of the population. Many fewer Americans today own guns intended for hunting, while purchases of AR-15 style rifles and of handguns, which

63 percent say they purchased for "protection against people," have risen. Conflicts over Second Amendment rights to gun ownership and potential limits to or regulations of such rights further divide Americans, and the National Rifle Association plays a major role in American politics.

More concrete divisions are tied to the distribution of wealth (see Figure 29.4). Globally, the divide is shocking: in 2015 it took the combined wealth of 3.5 billion people at the bottom of the economic scale to match the wealth owned by 62 individuals at the top (in 2010, it required the combined wealth of 388 billionaires to match that 3.5 billion). And by global standards, even America's poorest five percent are wealthier (in cost-corrected measures) than 68 percent of the globe—although the United States does not measure nearly so well when compared to other developed nations. But within the United States, the economic divide has continued to grow. In 2013, families in the top 1 percent claimed an average income 25 times that of the average family in the bottom 99 percent, the widest gulf in more than three decades. And the divide between the wealthy 1 percent and the super-rich 0.001 percent is growing even faster.

In September 2011, new protests against this growing divide first gained significant attention. New York City's Occupy Wall Street effort was modeled on a variety of international protests, and Occupy was an international movement, but it captured a widespread sense of outrage and frustration within the United States, particularly among well-educated whites, and more than six hundred U.S. communities began local occupations. The movement was often criticized for its lack of clear goals or demands, and it often struggled with its consensus-based governance. But while the U.S. movement faded in 2012—*The New York Times* headlined "The Frenzy that Fizzled"—Occupy drew attention to economic inequality and offered a framework for discussing that divide: "We are the 99%."

Race continues to divide the nation, and despite the diversity of the American public, that divide is most often framed in black and white. Economics play a role: almost a quarter of African Americans live below the poverty line, compared to less than 10 percent of whites. Despite a large black middle class, overall black infant mortality is more than twice the rate for whites; black children are more likely to attend failing schools; and the homicide rate—19.4 per 100,000—falls just below violence-torn Nigeria (and compares to 2.5 per 100,000 for white Americans). According to one 2015 study, young unarmed black men were twice as likely as young unarmed white men to be shot and killed by police officers; of unarmed suspects shot by police in 2015, 41 percent were black.

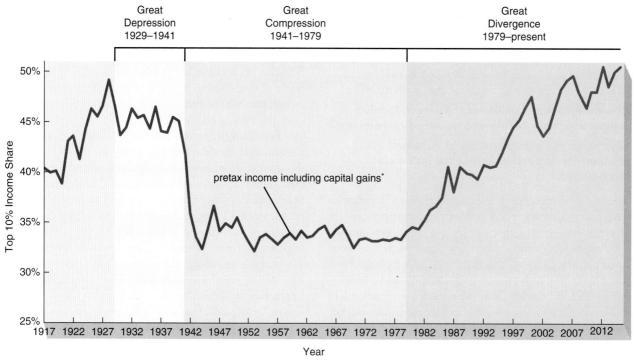

*Income does not include government transfer payments (e.g. Social Security or unemployment).

Figure 29.4 The Great Divergence

This chart shows the share of income received by the top ten percent of American households from 1917 forward. During what economic historians Claudia Golden and Robert Mango labeled "the great compression," Americans' household income was more equal, or compressed. Beginning in the late 1970s, growing income inequality appears as "the great divergence" (economist Paul Krugman's term). In 2015, the top ten percent received slightly more than 50 percent of US household income. Twenty-two percent went to the top one percent of households. *Source:* Emmanuel Saez, "Striking it Richer: The Evolution of Top Incomes in the United States" (Updated with 2015 preliminary estimates), UC Berkeley, June 30, 2016, available at https://eml.berkeley.edu/~saez/saez-UStopincomes-2015.pdf.

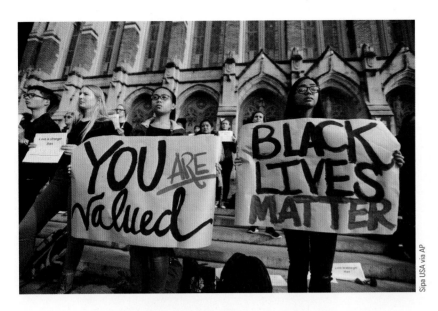

◀ Black Lives Matter was created by black community organizers Patrisse Cullors, Alicia Garza, and Opal Tometi in 2013. It became a national and then international movement. Here, students at the University of Washington carry BLM signs in a 2017 protest.

Sipa USA via AP

Such losses gave rise to the Black Lives Matter movement. BLM emerged first as a hashtag (#BlackLivesMatter) in 2013, after neighborhood watch coordinator George Zimmerman was acquitted for the shooting death of Trayvon Martin, an unarmed 17-year-old who was visiting the gated community where the shooting occurred in Sanford, Florida. BLM moved from online protests to demonstrations in the streets following the police shooting of Michael Brown in 2014 and, focusing on the broader issue of systemic racism, showed significant political force during the 2016 election and in the protests that followed.

In the first decade and a half of the twenty-first century, few people in positions of power paid much attention to the plight of white working-class Americans, whose incomes were stagnating or dropping and whose communities suffered in kind. While no organized protest movement captured their frustrations, increasing suicide rates, along with heroin, opioid, and other prescription drug addictions pointed toward a growing crisis. Fueled by economic concerns, anger over what many perceived as declining status in a more diverse America, and rejection of fundamental social change, these Americans would prove a significant political force in the election of 2016.

29-5b Immigration and the Changing Face of America

On October 17, 2006, the United States population officially passed the 300 million mark, and its people were more diverse than at any time in the nation's history (see Map 29.5). (For comparison, U.S. population was approximately 321 million in 2015; 100 million in 1915; and 200 million in 1967.) During the 1990s, the population of people of color grew twelve times as fast as the white population, fueled by both immigration and birth rates. In 2003, Latinxs moved past African Americans to become the second largest ethnic or racial group in the nation, following non-Hispanic whites (see Figure 29.5). Immigration from Asia also remained high, and according to the 2010 census 5.6 percent of the U.S.

population was Asian or Asian American. Most immigration to the United States is legal, but the number of people in the United States without official documentation peaked in 2007 at 12 million (up from 3 million in 1980), before falling to

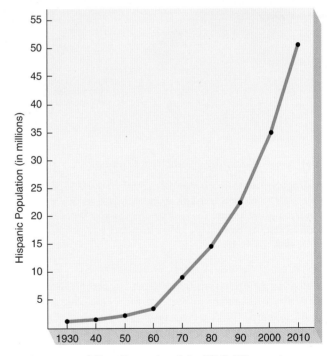

Figure 29.5 **The Growth of the U.S. Hispanic Population**

"Hispanic" combines people from a wide variety of national origins or ancestries—including all the nations of Central and South America, Mexico, Cuba, Puerto Rico, the Dominican Republic, Spain—as well as those who identify as Californio, Tejano, Nuevo Mexicano, and Mestizo. *Source: Adapted from the U.S. Department of Commerce, Economics and Statistics Information, Bureau of the Census, 1993 report "We, the American. . . Hispanics"; also recent Census Bureau figures for the Hispanic population.*

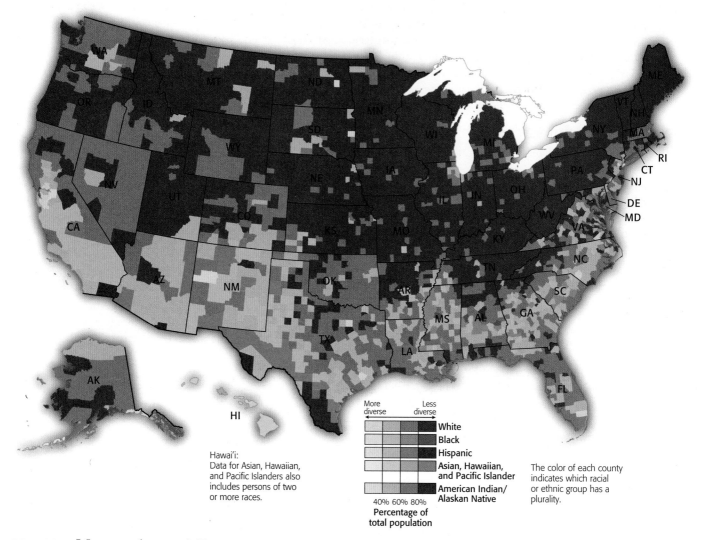

Hawai'i:
Data for Asian, Hawaiian, and Pacific Islanders also includes persons of two or more races.

More diverse ← → Less diverse

White
Black
Hispanic
Asian, Hawaiian, and Pacific Islander
American Indian/ Alaskan Native

40% 60% 80%
Percentage of total population

The color of each county indicates which racial or ethnic group has a plurality.

Map 29.5 Mapping America's Diversity

Aggregate figures (more than 12 percent of the U.S. population was black and about 4 percent Asian in 2000, for example) convey America's ethnic and racial diversity. However, as this map shows, members of racial and ethnic groups are not distributed evenly throughout the nation. *Source: From* The New York Times, *© April 1, 2001 The New York Times. All rights reserved. Used by permission and protected by the Copyright Laws of the United States. The printing, copying redistribution, or retransmission of the material without express written permission is prohibited.*

about 11 million during the economic recession that began that year, a level that did not rise with economic recovery. Undocumented workers made up almost 8 percent of the U.S. labor force in 2014, including almost 17 percent of agricultural laborers.

These rapid demographic changes have altered the face of America. At a Dairy Queen in the far southern suburbs of Atlanta, six miles from the Gone with the Wind Historical District, teenage children of immigrants from India and Pakistan serve Blizzards and Brownie Earthquakes. In western Kansas, where immigrants from Somalia, Myanmar, Mexico, Sudan, Ethiopia, and Burma now work in Garden City's meatpacking plants, pho is a lunchtime staple on Garden City's main street, a Buddhist prayer space fills the old Kwik Shop, and the Tyson plant offers male and female

prayer rooms to its Muslim employees. Overwhelmingly, Garden City residents have welcomed the new immigrants and their diverse cultures: "This town is so nice," says Ahmed Ali, a young Somali man who works in the meat packing plant. Town leaders credit immigrant workers for the town's vibrant economy and low unemployment rate. But with almost three dozen native languages brought into the town's classrooms, and as children who spent much of their previous lives in the difficult circumstances of refugee camps face difficult adjustments, the town also encounters practical challenges that demand both funding and policy solutions.

Many of America's schools and neighborhoods remain racially segregated and public debates about illegal immigration are heated. At the same time, American popular culture has embraced the influences of this new multiethnic population.

Economics were important: in 2015 the buying power of the growing Latino population exceeded $1.3 trillion, up 167 percent since 2000, while average income for Asian American households tops that for all other groups. But American audiences also crossed racial and ethnic lines as, for example, African American rap and hip-hop attracted large followings of young white men.

29-5c The Changing American Family

The American family takes many different shapes in the twenty-first century (see Figure 29.6). Fewer and fewer American adults are married—barely half in 2015, compared with almost three-quarters in 1960. The median age at marriage continues to rise, reaching 29.2 for men and 27.4 for women in 2015. People are increasingly likely to marry someone of a different race or ethnicity: fewer than 1 percent of couples did so in 1970, compared to more than 15 percent in 2010. About 7 percent of couples live together without marriage, and roughly 14 percent of American adults live alone.

In the early twenty-first century, a vocal antigay movement coexisted with rising support for the legal equality of gay, lesbian, transgendered, and bisexual Americans. Although the federal Defense of Marriage Act (DOMA), passed by Congress in 1996, defined marriage as "only" a union between one man and one woman, many states and private corporations extend domestic partner benefits to gay couples, and in 2002 the American Academy of Pediatrics endorsed adoption by gay couples. Between 2003 and 2013, same-sex marriage was legalized in twelve states, though DOMA prevented the

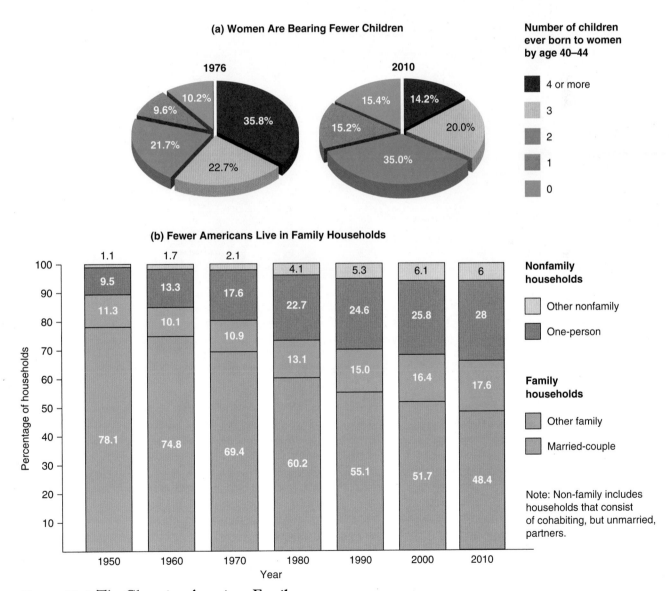

Figure 29.6 **The Changing American Family**

American households have become smaller, as more people live alone and women have, on average, fewer children. *Source: Adapted from U.S. Bureau of the Census, http://www.census.gov/prod/2002pubs/censr-4.pdf and http://www.census.gov/population/pop-profile/2000 /chap04.pdf.*

American War Dead

In 1991, as the United States prepared to go to war in the Persian Gulf, Defense Secretary Dick Cheney banned the media from photographing American war dead being returned to U.S. soil. The ban imposed by the George H. W. Bush administration may stem from a moment in the 1989 U.S. invasion of Panama, when ABC, CBS, and CNN chose to run coverage of caskets arriving at Dover Air Force Base and President Bush's White House news conference simultaneously on a split screen, making it appear that the president was not paying appropriate respect to those killed in battle. During the twenty-first-century wars in Iraq and Afghanistan, the George W. Bush administration enforced a blanket ban on media photographs.

Critics argued that the Bush administration was hiding the tragic cost of America's wars, while supporters insisted that the policy protected the privacy of American military families. The ban was lifted by Robert M. Gates, President Obama's secretary of defense, in 2009, with the support of the U.S. Army. However, media access was granted only when the fallen soldier's family gave permission.

CRITICAL THINKING

- In cases such as this, is it possible that what Americans do not see is as important as what they do see?

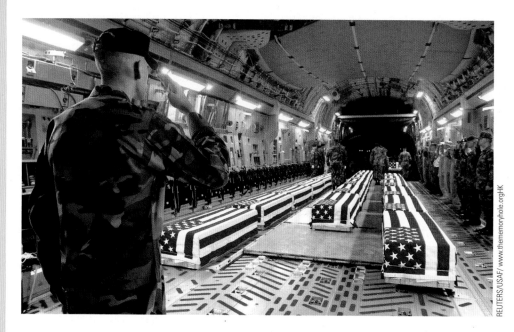

◄ *Coffins of U.S. military personnel arriving at Dover Air Force Base in Dover, Delaware. This undated photograph was released in response to a Freedom of Information Act request.*

REUTERS/USAF/ www.thememoryhole.orgHK

federal government from recognizing any same-sex couples as married. In June 2013 the Supreme Court, in a 5-to-4 decision (*United States v. Windsor*), ruled DOMA unconstitutional, arguing that the legislation "humiliates" children raised by same-sex couples and undermines state power to define marriage. Marriage equality had practical implications: for example, it made legally married same-sex couples eligible for military, health, and other federal benefits.

In the early twenty-first century, babies were almost as likely to be born to unmarried women as to married ones. (In the United States, about 40 percent of babies were born to unmarried women, compared to 54 percent in Sweden and 2 percent in Japan.) Although almost one-third of families with children had only one parent present—most frequently the mother—children also lived in blended families created by second marriages or moved back and forth between households of parents who had joint custody. Based on current statistical analysis, for couples who married in the mid-1990s the woman's level of education was the clearest predictor of divorce: if the woman graduated from a four-year college, the couple had a 25 percent likelihood of divorce; if she had not, the rate jumped to 50 percent.

In 2016, the leading edge of the baby boom generation turned 70; the median age of the American population was 37.8 in 2015, up from 29.5 in 1967. Although baby boomers are not aging in the same manner as their parents and grandparents—"Sixty is the new forty," the saying goes—the large and growing proportion of older people will have a major impact on American society. As life expectancy increases, the growing number of elderly Americans will put enormous pressure on the nation's healthcare system and family structure—who will care for people when they can no longer live independently?—and strain the Social Security and Medicare systems.

29-5d Violence, Crime, and Incarceration

In past decades, the nation has been haunted by increasingly frequent and inexplicable mass shootings. Americans were shocked in 1999 when two academically successful students at Columbine High School in Colorado murdered thirteen people (and injured twenty-three more) before committing suicide, but students also massacred classmates and teachers in Paducah, Kentucky; Springfield, Oregon; Jonesboro, Arkansas, and on the campuses of Virginia Tech and Okiah College in California. Armed men, most of them young, white, and mentally ill, committed mass murders at coffee shops and nursing homes, at workplaces, hotels, and places of worship, at a mall and a movie theater and an army post and an air force base. Among the most horrific events were a gunman's shooting of ten young girls in a one-room Amish schoolhouse in 2006, the murder of twenty small children and six adults at Sandy Hook Elementary School in Newtown, Connecticut, in 2012, and the slaughter of nine African American worshipers by a 22-year-old white supremacist during a prayer service in Charleston, South Carolina.

Such mass shootings, however, account for less than one-half of 1 percent of gun-related homicides. Shooting deaths, along with other homicides, occur far more frequently in poor, inner-city neighborhoods. In Chicago, for example, close to four hundred school-aged children were shot and killed between 2009 and 2017, and in early 2012 Chicago's death toll exceeded the number of U.S. servicemen and servicewomen killed in Afghanistan. At the same time, the majority of Americans saw rapidly declining rates of violent crime after 1993; according to the FBI, U.S. homicide rates hit a fifty-year low in 2014, and violent crime dropped 16.5 percent between 2006 and 2015.

The U.S. prison population increased dramatically from the mid-1970s through the first decade of the twenty-first century; rates have begun to drop, but still exceed those of almost every nation in the world. In 2008, the U.S. imprisonment rate of 751 per 100,000 compared to Russia's 577, Canada's 117, and Japan's 59. While the United States does have a higher rate of violent (often gun-related) crime than most other developed nations, high incarceration rates are due in part to the length of sentences mandated for nonviolent criminals (including those convicted of drug crimes). Thus it is not so much the number of people sentenced to prison as the length of their sentences that accounts for America's outlier rates. For example, in 2005 the average convicted burglar in Scotland served three and a half months, while his U.S. counterpart stayed in jail fifteen months longer.

While African Americans are still incarcerated at much higher rates than white or Latinx Americans, the racial disparity has begun to shrink. According to the U.S. Bureau of Justice Statistics, the imprisonment rate for black men has dropped 22 percent since 2000, while it has risen slightly for white men; the rate for black women has dropped by almost half, as the rate for white women has grown by 56 percent. In general, although more than nine out of ten inmates are male, women make up the fastest-growing prison population in the United States.

America's prison system, according to the White House Council of Economic Advisors in 2016, costs taxpayers over $80 billion a year; eleven states spent more on their corrections systems than on higher education. Carceral system costs top out at $168,000 per inmate per year in New York City; Kentucky, in contrast, spends less than $15,000. Social costs are extraordinary, as men and women emerging from prison, due in part to their criminal records, are too often unable to become productive members of society or to rejoin stable families and communities.

29-5e Health and Medicine

The leading causes of death in the United States today are heart disease and cancer; almost 1.7 million new cases of cancer were diagnosed in 2016. At the same time, middle-aged whites are dying in increasing numbers not because of these major killers, but due to suicide, alcohol-linked liver disease, and overdoses of prescription opioids and heroin. On the positive side, the CDC reports that new HIV infections are dropping significantly.

Other health issues have become increasingly important. In a rapid change over the course of a decade, more than two-thirds of American adults are now overweight or obese—conditions linked to hypertension, cardiovascular disease, and diabetes. In 1995, no state had an adult obesity rate that hit 20 percent. By 2012, not a single state fell below that 20 percent mark. Twelve states topped 30 percent obesity rates in 2012; three years later, twenty-five states did.

Cigarette smoking continues a slow but steady decline. Slightly less than one-fifth of American adults smoked in 2010, down from about one-third of adults in 1980 and from 42 percent in 1965. According to the Centers for Disease Control, smoking causes one of every five U.S. deaths, and smoking-related medical costs and lost productivity total about $300 billion a year. With clearer understanding of the danger of secondhand smoke, local governments have overwhelmingly banned smoking in public spaces, including restaurants and bars.

In efforts to combat disease and improve quality of life, scientists and medical researchers are making important breakthroughs in a variety of fields, from improved HIV medication to targeted cancer therapies to the development of bionic limbs for amputees. Research on stem cells, the unspecialized cells that can be induced to become cells with specialized functions, is promising. Stem cells may become insulin-producing cells of the pancreas, and thus make possible a cure for diabetes, or they might become dopamine-producing neurons, offering therapy for Parkinson's disease, a progressive disorder of the nervous system that affects over 1 million Americans. Finally, research on the human genome helps to identify the genetic origins of disease and thus paths to more effective treatment.

29-5f Century of Change

The twentieth century had seen more momentous change than any previous century—change that brought enormous benefits to human beings, change that threatened the very existence of the human species. Research in the physical and biological sciences had provided insight into the structure of matter and of the universe. Technology—the application of science—had made startling advances that benefited Americans in nearly every aspect of life: better health, more wealth, more mobility, less drudgery, greater access to information.

Through these advances, Americans at the start of the new century were more connected to the rest of humankind than ever before. This interconnection was perhaps the most powerful product of globalization. A commodities trader in Chicago in February 2010 could send a text message to her fiancé in Tokyo while she spoke on the phone to a trader in Frankfurt, and e-mailed another one in Bombay, all while keeping one eye on NBC's live coverage of the Winter Olympics in Vancouver; within a minute or two, she could receive a reply from her fiancé saying that he missed her, too. If she felt sufficiently lovesick, she could board an airplane and be in Japan the following day.

The world had shrunk to the size of an airplane ticket. In 1955, 51 million people a year traveled by plane. By the turn of the century, 1.6 billion were airborne every year, and 530 million—or about 1.5 million each day—crossed international borders. This permeability of national boundaries brought many benefits, as did the integration of markets and the global spread of information that occurred alongside it.

29-5g Globalization and World Health

But there was a flip side to this growing connectivity, which even advocates of globalization perceived. The rapid increase in international air travel was a particularly potent force for the dissemination of global disease, as flying made it possible for people to reach the other side of the world in far less time than the incubation period for many ailments. Environmental degradation also created major global health threats. In 2003, the World Health Organization (WHO) estimated that nearly one-quarter of the global burden of disease and injury was related to environmental disruption and decline. For example, some 90 percent of diarrheal diseases (such as cholera), which were killing 3 million people a year, resulted from contaminated water. WHO also pointed to globalization and environmental disruption as contributing to the fact that, in the final two decades of the twentieth century, more than thirty infectious diseases were identified in humans for the first time—including AIDS, Ebola virus, hantavirus, and hepatitis C and E. Environmentalists, meanwhile, insisted that the growing interaction of national economies was having a deleterious impact on the ecosystem through climate change, ozone depletion, hazardous waste, and damage to fisheries.

29-5h Confronting Terrorism

In military and diplomatic terms, the years after 9/11 witnessed important changes. The attacks that day brought home what Americans had only dimly perceived before then: that globalization had shrunk the natural buffers that distance and two oceans provided the United States. Al Qaeda, it was clear, had used the increasingly open, integrated, globalized world to give itself new power and reach. It had shown that small cells of terrorists could become true transnational threats—thriving around the world without any single state sponsor or home base. According to American intelligence, Al Qaeda operated in more than ninety countries—including the United States.

How would one go about vanquishing such a foe? Was a decisive victory even possible? These remained open questions in the years after the World Trade Center collapsed.

◀ In this August 25, 2013, photo, inmate firefighters walk along Highway 120 after battling the Rim Fire near Yosemite National Park, California. Caused by a hunter's illegal campfire that got out of control, the blaze was one of the largest in California's history, and the largest ever in the Sierra Nevada mountain range, burning 257,000 acres over a period of nine weeks.

AP Images/Jae C. Hong, File

The "Swine Flu" Pandemic

When United Flight 803 from Washington, D.C., landed at Tokyo's Narita airport on May 20, 2009, Japanese health officials boarded the plane. Garbed in respirator masks, goggles, and disposable scrubs, they used thermal scanners to check passengers for elevated temperatures. Passengers waited anxiously as officials interviewed each person on board, aware that, if any symptoms or suspicious travel patterns were discovered, the entire plane might be quarantined. Japan had already closed its borders to all travelers from Mexico, where the H1N1 "swine flu" virus had emerged about three weeks earlier. Mexico took extraordinary actions, closing schools and businesses and drawing on public health expertise from around the world. Nevertheless, the H1N1 virus had, by mid-May, already spread to more than twenty-two countries. It was much too late to stem the spread of swine flu by isolating travelers from its country of origin.

Soon after a series of deaths in Mexico in late April, the World Health Organization had raised its alert level to stage 5, signaling that officials expected the virus to create the first major flu pandemic in more than forty years. Articles in the world media reminded readers of the flu pandemic of 1918 while emphasizing how much had changed. International air travel had brought the world into much closer contact, with more than 2 billion passengers traveling by airline each year. Health analysts made clear that the "right" pathogen, if it emerged in the "right" place, might spread throughout the world in the space of a day, well before anyone was conscious of the threat it posed.

On the other hand, global connections also offered new tools to combat pandemics: global surveillance of disease, though not equally well developed or dependable in all countries, might head off developing health threats. Individual nations and global organizations pool expertise as they develop vaccines and techniques to cope with pandemics, should one emerge. Because of lessons learned during the 2003 SARS outbreak, Hong Kong provided a model to the rest of the world with its plans for the prevention and management of major outbreaks of infectious disease. Finally, some believe that a global culture where borders present little barrier may facilitate the growth of global immunities to infectious diseases.

People around the world were relieved when the swine flu, after the initial deaths in Mexico, turned out to be no more deadly than a usual flu strain. In previous years, SARS (severe, acute respiratory syndrome) and the H5N1 "bird flu" had also failed to develop into major worldwide heath threats, as did later threats from Ebola. But the World Health Organization and the U.S. Centers for Disease Control cautioned that the emergence of a major pandemic was simply a matter of time, especially as drug-resistant strains of infectious disease emerge. "We live in one world, with one health," observed a UN official. In the era of globalization, diseases do not stop at borders or respect wealth and power, and the links between Americans and the rest of the world's peoples cannot be denied.

CRITICAL THINKING

■ In this era of globalization, diseases cannot be contained within the borders of one country. What responsibility does the United States have to cooperate with and offer support to other nations when outbreaks of disease occur?

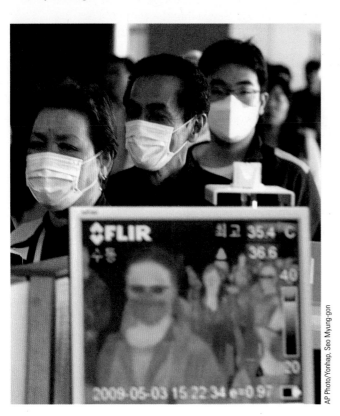

AP Photo/Yonhap, Seo Myung-gon

◀ As the H1N1 virus—"swine flu"—spread rapidly in the spring of 2009, nations around the world attempted to prevent the spread of infection. Here, thermal cameras check the body temperatures of passengers arriving at Incheon International Airport in South Korea.

Unchallenged militarily and seeing no rival great power, the United States felt few constraints about intervening in Afghanistan and then Iraq, but the problems in both countries showed that it could take scant comfort from this superiority. It continued to spend colossal sums on its military, more indeed than the next fourteen highest-spending countries combined (the Pentagon in 2016 spent $600 billion, not including supplemental appropriations for Iraq and Afghanistan). America had taken on military commitments all over the globe, from the Balkans and Iraq to Afghanistan and Korea (see Table 29.1). Its armed forces looked colossal, but its obligations looked even larger.

And more than ever, Americans debated whether the nation should maintain commitments all over the globe. Was it the case, as proponents of a global posture maintained, that the United States had benefited in countless ways from its post–World War II dominance of the international system, whatever the costs associated with that policy, whatever misadventures that occasionally had resulted? Or could it be, as the critics of "global hegemony" maintained, that the nation

Table 29.1 U.S. Military Personnel on Active Duty in Foreign Countries, 2012[1]

Region/Country[2]	Personnel	Region/Country[2]	Personnel
United States and Territories		Singapore	180
Continental U.S.	1,123,219	Thailand	114
Alaska	21,280	Bahrain	2,902
Hawai'i	49,242	Diego Garcia	516
Guam	5,646	Egypt	292
Puerto Rico	162	Israel	41
Europe		Oman	37
Belgium*	1,165	Pakistan	42
France*	70	Qatar	800
Germany*	45,596	Saudi Arabia	278
Greece*	361	United Arab Emirates	193
Greenland*	138	**Sub-Saharan Africa**	
Hungary	62	Djibouti	139
Italy*	10,916	Kenya	40
Netherlands*	374	South Africa	35
Norway*	90	**Western Hemisphere**	
Portugal*	713	Bahamas, The	50
Russia	67	Brazil	48
Spain*	1,600	Canada	146
Turkey*	1,491	Chile	38
United Kingdom*	9,310	Colombia	64
East Asia and Pacific		Cuba (Guantanamo)	988
Australia	183	Honduras	388
China, People's Republic of	49	Peru	51
Japan	52,692	**Total Worldwide**[2]	1,372,522
Philippines	131	Undistributed[3]	39,157

*NATO countries

[1]Only countries with 30 or more U.S. military personnel are listed.

[2]Includes all regions/countries, not simply those listed.

[3]Undistributed includes Afghanistan, Iraq, Kuwait, Republic of Korea, and any unknown/classified locations.

Source: U.S. Department of Defense, Defense Manpower Data Center (http://siadapp.dmdc.osd.mil/personnel/MILITARY/miltop.htm Accessed July 1, 2013)

Twitter Revolution

When Barack Obama won reelection as president of the United States on November 7, 2012, he celebrated by tweeting a photograph of himself hugging his wife, Michelle. The Tweet read, "Four more years. pic.twitter.com/bAJE6Vom." Almost immediately, it became the most popular Tweet of all time, with more than half a million Retweets.

Twitter, a social networking and microblogging service founded in 2006 by Jack Dorsey and Biz Stone, has become one of the ten most visited websites on the planet, with more than 200 million monthly active users communicating via short bursts of information called Tweets.

Along with Facebook, Flickr, and other social media sites, Twitter has spawned an important structural change in how information spreads. No longer is there a need to rely on the smoke signals and carrier pigeons used by early Americans, or even the phone calls, faxes, and television shows so prized by the Baby Boom generation. In addition to announcing personal opinions and achievements, the new sites have been used to organize protests—indeed, they have been credited with reinventing social activism. Thus the Arab Spring uprisings of 2010–11 and the Iranian election protests of 2009–10 were called "Twitter Revolutions" for the ways they upended the traditional relationship between political authority and popular will and enabled activists to collaborate and coordinate.

That social media and mass political protests are closely connected is a beguiling notion, but also a problematic one. Social networks did not cause these upheavals, and indeed had little connection to the underlying factors behind the protests. In Egypt, for example, the sociopolitical tension between the tiny ruling elite and the mass of the populace had long been acute, prompting many analysts to expect a major upheaval in due course. Egyptian activists, for their part, insisted that old-fashioned grassroots organizing on the ground, not social media, drove their revolution. They further noted that, at the time of the protests, very few Twitter accounts existed in the country.

Yet if Twitter and other social media are not particularly effective at boosting popular *motivation* for a given cause, they can have an outsized impact on increasing *participation*, at least in the short term. The Occupy Wall Street movement of 2011–12, for example, began as a Twitter experiment in July 2011, when the Canadian anti-consumerism magazine *Adbusters* posted the idea of a march in Lower Manhattan. The proposal took hold, and in subsequent months, protesters used Twitter, YouTube, and Facebook to coordinate efforts in cities and towns all over the country as well as abroad.

Twitter has shown other uses as well, including as a de facto emergency communication system for breaking news. The Boston Police, for example, tweeted news of the arrest of a suspect in the 2013 Boston Marathon terrorist attack in order to calm residents' nerves. Researchers are also studying using Twitter to track epidemics and how they spread, while college professors are seeing promising results when they use Twitter to promote student interaction, especially in large lecture classes. For these and other dedicated tweeters, there could be no more fitting legacy of the twentieth century than the Internet and the social media it spawned.

CRITICAL THINKING

- During the 2016 election cycle, George Will, a Washington Post political pundit famously said of Republican nominee and the eventual winner of the election, Donald Trump, "He has an advantage on me. He can say everything he knows about any subject in 140 characters, and I can't." What role have Twitter and other social media outlets played in American politics in the last decade?
- Has social media been beneficial or detrimental to the political process of democracy?

could and should draw down its overseas commitments significantly, passing the burdens of regional security in various locales to allied governments, thereby allowing more time, money, and attention to be devoted to improving the lives of Americans at home?

Summary

The 1990s were, for most Americans, good times. A digitized revolution in communications and information—as fundamental as the revolution brought about by electricity and the combustion engine a century earlier, or the steam engine a century before that—was generating prosperity and transforming life in America and around the globe. The longest economic expansion in American history—from 1991 to 2001—meant that most Americans who wanted jobs had them, that the stock market boomed, that the nation had a budget surplus instead of a deficit, and that more Americans than ever before owned their own homes. In addition, America was not only prosperous; it was powerful. With the Soviet Union gone and no other formidable rival on the horizon, the United States stood as the world's lone superpower, its economic and military power daunting to friend and foe alike.

Although America seemed at the apex of power and prosperity, unsettling events troubled the nation, abroad and at home. Just minutes before midnight on December 31, 1999, President Clinton called on the American people not to fear the future, but to "welcome it, create it, and embrace it." The challenges of the future would be greater than Americans imagined as they welcomed the new millennium that night. In 2000, the contested presidential election was decided by the Supreme Court in a partisan 5-to-4 vote; in 2001, the ten-year economic expansion came to an end.

Then, on September 11 of that year, radical Islamic terrorists attacked the World Trade Center and the Pentagon, killing thousands and altering many aspects of American life. The new president, George W. Bush, declared a "war on terrorism," one with both foreign and domestic components. Bush won reelection in 2004, but his fortunes soon waned. The combination of two costly wars abroad and a severe economic crisis at home paved the way for Barack Obama's historic election in 2008, but also shaped the limits and possibilities of Obama's two-term presidency. As he departed the White House for the last time on the morning of January 20, 2017, to attend the inauguration of his successor, it remained to be seen where the wondrous American story would go next.

The world that Americans found in the first years of the twenty-first century was much different from the one they had looked forward to with confidence and high hopes as they celebrated the coming of the new millennium on New Year's Eve 1999. The horror of the terror attacks of September 11, 2001, shook America to its core. Then came two lengthy and inconclusive wars, to be followed in turn by the most severe economic downturn since the Great Depression. By the start of the new decade, Americans were deeply divided over how to respond to the nation's problems. To some, the obstacles seemed impossibly daunting. Yet the American people had faced difficult times before in their history; each time, they had proved their resilience and weathered the storm. As Donald Trump's term began, Americans faced the need to struggle over foreign and domestic policy priorities, over the direction of their nation, with the controlled passion and the commitment to reason that a healthy democracy demands.

Suggestions for Further Reading

Andrew Bacevich, *America's War for the Greater Middle East: A Military History* (2016)

Derek Chollet and James Goldgeier, *America Between the Wars: From 11/9 to 9/11* (2008)

Barbara Ehrenreich, *Nickel and Dimed: On (Not) Getting by in America* (2002)

John F. Harris, *The Survivor: Bill Clinton in the White House* (2005)

Jennifer L. Hochschild, *Facing Up to the American Dream: Race, Class, and the Soul of the Nation* (1995)

Alejandro Portes and Reuben G. Rumbaut, *Immigrant America: A Portrait*, 3rd ed. (2006)

Samantha Power, *"A Problem from Hell": America and the Age of Genocide* (2002)

Emma Sky, *The Unraveling: High Hopes and Missed Opportunities in Iraq* (2015)

Joseph E. Stiglitz, *Globalization and Its Discontents* (2002)

Joby Warrick, *Black Flags: The Rise of ISIS* (2015)

Declaration of Independence in Congress, July 4, 1776

When, in the course of human events, it becomes necessary for one people to dissolve the political bonds which have connected them with another, and to assume, among the powers of the earth, the separate and equal station to which the laws of nature and of nature's God entitle them, a decent respect to the opinions of mankind requires that they should declare the causes which impel them to the separation.

We hold these truths to be self-evident: That all men are created equal; that they are endowed by their Creator with certain unalienable rights; that among these are life, liberty, and the pursuit of happiness; that, to secure these rights, governments are instituted among men, deriving their just powers from the consent of the governed; that whenever any form of government becomes destructive of these ends, it is the right of the people to alter or to abolish it, and to institute new government, laying its foundation on such principles, and organizing its powers in such form, as to them shall seem most likely to effect their safety and happiness. Prudence, indeed, will dictate that governments long established should not be changed for light and transient causes; and accordingly all experience hath shown that mankind are more disposed to suffer, while evils are sufferable, than to right themselves by abolishing the forms to which they are accustomed. But when a long train of abuses and usurpations, pursuing invariably the same object, evinces a design to reduce them under absolute despotism, it is their right, it is their duty, to throw off such government, and to provide new guards for their future security. Such has been the patient sufferance of these colonies; and such is now the necessity which constrains them to alter their former systems of government. The history of the present King of Great Britain is a history of repeated injuries and usurpations, all having in direct object the establishment of an absolute tyranny over these states. To prove this, let facts be submitted to a candid world.

He has refused his assent to laws, the most wholesome and necessary for the public good.

He has forbidden his governors to pass laws of immediate and pressing importance, unless suspended in their operation till his assent should be obtained; and, when so suspended, he has utterly neglected to attend to them.

He has refused to pass other laws for the accommodation of large districts of people, unless those people would relinquish the right of representation in the legislature, a right inestimable to them, and formidable to tyrants only.

He has called together legislative bodies at places unusual, uncomfortable, and distant from the depository of their public records, for the sole purpose of fatiguing them into compliance with his measures.

He has dissolved representative houses repeatedly, for opposing, with manly firmness, his invasions on the rights of the people.

He has refused for a long time, after such dissolutions, to cause others to be elected; whereby the legislative powers, incapable of annihilation, have returned to the people at large for their exercise; the state remaining, in the mean time, exposed to all the dangers of invasions from without and convulsions within.

He has endeavored to prevent the population of these states; for that purpose obstructing the laws for naturalization of foreigners; refusing to pass others to encourage their migration hither, and raising the conditions of new appropriations of lands.

He has obstructed the administration of justice, by refusing his assent to laws for establishing judiciary powers.

He has made judges dependent on his will alone, for the tenure of their offices, and the amount and payment of their salaries.

He has erected a multitude of new offices, and sent hither swarms of officers to harass our people and eat out their substance.

He has kept among us, in times of peace, standing armies, without the consent of our legislatures.

He has affected to render the military independent of, and superior to, the civil power.

He has combined with others to subject us to a jurisdiction foreign to our constitution, and unacknowledged by our laws, giving his assent to their acts of pretended legislation:

For quartering large bodies of armed troops among us;

For protecting them, by a mock trial, from punishment for any murders which they should commit on the inhabitants of these states;

For cutting off our trade with all parts of the world;

For imposing taxes on us without our consent;

For depriving us, in many cases, of the benefits of trial by jury;

For transporting us beyond seas, to be tried for pretended offenses;

For abolishing the free system of English laws in a neighboring province, establishing therein an arbitrary government, and enlarging its boundaries, so as to render it at once an example and fit instrument for introducing the same absolute rule into these colonies;

For taking away our charters, abolishing our most valuable laws, and altering fundamentally the forms of our governments;

For suspending our own legislatures, and declaring themselves invested with power to legislate for us in all cases whatsoever.

He has abdicated government here, by declaring us out of his protection and waging war against us.

He has plundered our seas, ravaged our coasts, burned our towns, and destroyed the lives of our people.

He is at this time transporting large armies of foreign mercenaries to complete the works of death, desolation, and tyranny already begun with circumstances of cruelty and perfidy scarcely paralleled in the most barbarous ages, and totally unworthy the head of a civilized nation.

He has constrained our fellow-citizens, taken captive on the high seas, to bear arms against their country, to become the executioners of their friends and brethren, or to fall themselves by their hands.

He has excited domestic insurrection among us, and has endeavored to bring on the inhabitants of our frontiers the merciless Indian savages, whose known rule of warfare is an undistinguished destruction of all ages, sexes, and conditions.

In every stage of these oppressions we have petitioned for redress in the most humble terms; our repeated petitions have been answered only by repeated injury. A prince, whose character is thus marked by every act which may define a tyrant, is unfit to be the ruler of a free people.

Nor have we been wanting in our attentions to our British brethren. We have warned them, from time to time, of attempts by their legislature to extend an unwarrantable jurisdiction over us. We have reminded them of the circumstances of our emigration and settlement here. We have appealed to their native justice and magnanimity; and we have conjured them, by the ties of our common kindred, to disavow these usurpations, which would inevitably interrupt our connections and correspondence. They, too, have been deaf to the voice of justice and of consanguinity. We must, therefore, acquiesce in the necessity which denounces our separation, and hold them, as we hold the rest of mankind, enemies in war, in peace friends.

We, therefore, the representatives of the United States of America, in General Congress assembled, appealing to the Supreme Judge of the world for the rectitude of our intentions, do, in the name and by the authority of the good people of these colonies, solemnly publish and declare, that these United Colonies are, and of right ought to be, FREE AND INDEPENDENT STATES; that they are absolved from all allegiance to the British crown, and that all political connection between them and the state of Great Britain is, and ought to be, totally dissolved; and that, as free and independent states, they have full power to levy war, conclude peace, contract alliances, establish commerce, and do all other acts and things which independent states may of right do. And for the support of this declaration, with a firm reliance on the protection of Divine Providence, we mutually pledge to each other our lives, our fortunes, and our sacred honor.

Articles of Confederation

Whereas the Delegates of the United States of America in Congress assembled did on the fifteenth day of November in the Year of our Lord One Thousand Seven Hundred and Seventy seven, and in the Second Year of the Independence of America agree to certain articles of Confederation and perpetual Union between the States of Newhampshire, Massachusetts Bay, Rhode Island and Providence Plantations, Connecticut, New York, New Jersey, Pennsylvania, Delaware, Maryland, Virginia, North Carolina, South Carolina and Georgia in the Words following, viz. "Articles of Confederation and perpetual Union between the states of Newhampshire, Massachusetts Bay, Rhode Island and Providence Plantations, Connecticut, New York, New Jersey, Pennsylvania, Delaware, Maryland, Virginia, North Carolina, South Carolina and Georgia.

Article I The Stile of this confederacy shall be "The United States of America."

Article II Each state retains its sovereignty, freedom and independence, and every Power, Jurisdiction and right, which is not by this confederation expressly delegated to the United States, in Congress assembled.

Article III The said states hereby severally enter into a firm league of friendship with each other, for their common defence, the security of their Liberties, and their mutual and general welfare, binding themselves to assist each other, against all force offered to, or attacks made upon them, or any of them, on account of religion, sovereignty, trade, or any other pretence whatever.

Article IV The better to secure and perpetuate mutual friendship and intercourse among the people of the different states in this union, the free inhabitants of each of these states, paupers, vagabonds and fugitives from Justice excepted, shall be entitled to all privileges and immunities of free citizens in the several states; and the people of each state shall have free ingress and regress to and from any other state, and shall enjoy therein all the privileges of trade and commerce, subject to the same duties, impositions and restrictions as the inhabitants thereof respectively, provided that such restriction shall not extend so far as to prevent the removal of property imported into any state, to any other state of which the Owner is an inhabitant; provided also that no imposition, duties or restriction shall be laid by any state, on the property of the united states, or either of them.

If any Person guilty of, or charged with treason, felony, or other high misdemeanor in any state, shall flee from Justice, and be found in any of the united states, he shall upon demand of the Governor or executive power, of the state from which he fled, be delivered up and removed to the state having jurisdiction of his offence.

Full faith and credit shall be given in each of these states to the records, acts and judicial proceedings of the courts and magistrates of every other state.

Article V For the more convenient management of the general interests of the united states, delegates shall be annually appointed in such manner as the legislature of each state shall direct, to meet in Congress on the first Monday in November, in every year, with a power reserved to each state, to recall its delegates, or any of them, at any time within the year, and to send others in their stead, for the remainder of the Year.

No state shall be represented in Congress by less than two, nor by more than seven Members; and no person shall be capable of being a delegate for more than three years in any term of six years; nor shall any person, being a delegate, be capable of holding any office under the united states, for which he, or another for his benefit receives any salary, fees or emolument of any kind.

Each state shall maintain its own delegates in a meeting of the states, and while they act as members of the committee of the states.

In determining questions in the united states, in Congress assembled, each state shall have one vote.

Freedom of speech and debate in Congress shall not be impeached or questioned in any Court, or place out of Congress, and the members of congress shall be protected in their persons from arrests and imprisonments, during the time of their going to and from, and attendance on congress, except for treason, felony, or breach of the peace.

Article VI No state without the Consent of the united states in congress assembled, shall send any embassy to, or receive any embassy from, or enter into any conference, agreement, or alliance or treaty with any King, prince or state; nor shall any person holding any office of profit or trust under the united states, or any of them, accept of any present, emolument, office or title of any kind whatever from any king, prince or foreign state; nor shall the united states in congress assembled, or any of them, grant any title of nobility.

No two or more states shall enter into any treaty, confederation or alliance whatever between them, without the consent of the united states in congress assembled, specifying accurately the purposes for which the same is to be entered into, and how long it shall continue.

No state shall lay any imposts or duties, which may interfere with any stipulations in treaties, entered into by the united states in congress assembled, with any king, prince or state, in pursuance of any treaties already proposed by congress, to the courts of France and Spain.

No vessels of war shall be kept up in time of peace by any state, except such number only, as shall be deemed necessary by the united states in congress assembled, for the defence of such state, or its trade; nor shall any body of forces be kept up by any state, in time of peace, except such number only, as in the judgment of the united states, in congress assembled, shall be deemed requisite to garrison the forts necessary for the defence of such state; but every state shall always keep up a well regulated and disciplined militia, sufficiently armed and accoutred, and shall provide and constantly have ready for use, in public stores, a due number of field pieces and tents, and a proper quantity of arms, ammunition and camp equipage.

No state shall engage in any war without the consent of the united states in congress assembled, unless such state be actually invaded by enemies, or shall have received certain advice of a resolution being formed by some nation of Indians to invade such state, and the danger is so imminent as not to admit of a delay, till the united states in congress assembled can be consulted: nor shall any state grant commissions to any ships or vessels of war, nor letters of marque or reprisal, except it be after a declaration of war by the united states in congress assembled, and then only against the kingdom or state and the subjects thereof, against which war has been so declared, and under such regulations as shall be established by the united states in congress assembled, unless such state be infested by pirates, in which case vessels of war may be fitted out for that occasion, and kept so long as the danger shall continue, or until the united states in congress assembled shall determine otherwise.

Article VII When land-forces are raised by any state for the common defence, all officers of or under the rank of colonel, shall be appointed by the legislature of each state respectively by whom such forces shall be raised, or in such manner as such state shall direct, and all vacancies shall be filled up by the state which first made the appointment.

Article VIII All charges of war, and all other expences that shall be incurred for the common defence or general welfare, and allowed by the united states in congress assembled, shall be defrayed out of a common treasury, which shall be supplied by the several states, in proportion to the value of all land within each state, granted to or surveyed for any Person, as such land and the buildings and improvements thereon shall be estimated according to such mode as the united states in congress assembled, shall from time to time direct and appoint. The taxes for paying that proportion shall be laid and levied by the authority and direction of the legislatures of the several states within the time agreed upon by the united states in congress assembled.

Article IX The united states in congress assembled, shall have the sole and exclusive right and power of determining on peace and war, except in the cases mentioned in the sixth article—of sending and receiving ambassadors—entering into treaties and alliances, provided that no treaty of commerce shall be made whereby the legislative power of the respective states shall be restrained from imposing such imposts and duties on foreigners, as their own people are subjected to, or from prohibiting the exportation or importation of any species of goods or commodities whatsoever—of establishing rules for deciding in all cases, what captures on land or water shall be legal, and in what manner prizes taken by land or naval forces in the service of the united states shall be divided or appropriated—of granting letters of marque and reprisal in times of peace—appointing courts for the trial of piracies and felonies committed on the high seas and establishing courts for receiving and determining final appeals in all cases of captures, provided that no member of congress shall be appointed a judge of any of the said courts.

The united states in congress assembled shall also be the last resort on appeal in all disputes and differences now subsisting or that hereafter may arise between two or more states concerning boundary, jurisdiction or any other cause whatever; which authority shall always be exercised in the manner following. Whenever the legislative or executive authority or lawful agent of any state in controversy with another shall present a petition to congress, stating the matter in question and praying for a hearing, notice thereof shall be given by order of congress to the legislative or executive authority of the other state in controversy, and a day assigned for the appearance of the parties by their lawful agents, who shall then be directed to appoint by joint consent, commissioners or judges to constitute a court for hearing and determining the matter in question: but if they cannot agree, congress shall name three persons out of each of the united states, and from the list of such persons each party shall alternately strike out one, the petitioners beginning, until the number shall be reduced to thirteen; and from that number not less than seven, nor more than nine names as congress shall direct, shall in the presence of congress be drawn out by lot, and the persons whose names shall be so drawn or any five of them, shall be commissioners or judges, to hear and finally determine the controversy, so always as a major part of the judges who shall hear the cause shall agree in the determination: and if either party shall neglect to attend at the day appointed, without showing reasons, which congress shall judge sufficient, or being present shall refuse to strike, the congress shall proceed to nominate three persons out of each state, and the secretary of congress shall strike in behalf of such party absent or refusing; and the judgment and sentence of the court to be appointed, in the manner before prescribed, shall be final and conclusive; and if any of the parties shall refuse to submit to the authority of such court, or to appear to defend their claim or cause, the court shall nevertheless proceed to pronounce sentence, or judgment, which shall in like manner be final and decisive, the judgment or sentence and other proceedings being in either case transmitted to congress, and lodged among the acts of congress for the security of the parties concerned: provided that every commissioner, before he sits in judgment, shall take an oath to be administered by one of the judges of the supreme or superior court of the state, where the cause shall be tried, "well and truly to hear and determine the matter in question, according to the best of his judgment, without favour, affection or hope of reward:" provided also that no state shall be deprived of territory for the benefit of the united states.

All controversies concerning the private right of soil claimed under different grants of two or more states, whose jurisdictions as they may respect such lands, and the states which passed such grants are adjusted, the said grants or either of them being at the same time claimed to have originated antecedent to such settlement of jurisdiction, shall on the petition of either party to the congress of the united states, be finally determined as near as may be in the same manner as is before prescribed for deciding disputes respecting territorial jurisdiction between different states.

The united states in congress assembled shall also have the sole and exclusive right and power of regulating the alloy and value of coin struck by their own authority, or by that of the respective states—fixing the standard of weights and measures throughout the united states—regulating the trade and managing all affairs with the Indians, not members of any of the states, provided that the legislative right of any state within its own limits be not infringed or violated—establishing and regulating post-offices from one state to another, throughout all the united states, and exacting such postage on the papers passing thro' the same as may be requisite to defray the expences of the said office—appointing all officers of the land forces, in the service of the united states, excepting regimental officers—appointing all the officers of the naval forces, and commissioning all officers whatever in the service of the united states—making rules for the government and regulation of the said land and naval forces, and directing their operations.

The united states in congress assembled shall have authority to appoint a committee, to sit in the recess of congress, to be denominated "A Committee of the States," and to consist of one delegate from each state; and to appoint such other committees and civil officers as may be necessary for managing the general affairs of the united states under their direction—to appoint one of their number to preside, provided that no person be allowed to serve in the office of president more than one year in any term of three years; to ascertain the necessary sums of Money to be raised for the service of the united states, and to appropriate and apply the same for defraying the public expences—to borrow money, or emit bills on the credit of the united states, transmitting every half year to the respective states an account of the sums of money so borrowed or emitted—to build and equip a navy—to agree upon the number of land forces, and to make requisitions from each state for its quota, in proportion to the number of white inhabitants in such state; which requisition shall be binding, and thereupon the legislature of each state shall appoint the regimental officers, raise the men and cloath, arm and equip them in a soldier like manner, at the expence of the united states, and the officers and men so cloathed, armed and equipped shall march to the place appointed, and within the time agreed on by the united states in congress assembled: But if the united states in congress assembled shall, on consideration of circumstances judge proper that any state should not raise men, or should raise a smaller number than its quota, and that any other state should raise a greater number of men than the quota thereof, such extra number shall be raised, officered, cloathed, armed and equipped in the same manner as the quota of such state, unless the legislature of such state shall judge that such extra number cannot be safely spared out of the same, in which case they shall raise, officer, cloath, arm and equip as many of such extra number as they judge can be safely spared. And the officers and men so cloathed, armed and equipped, shall march to the place appointed, and within the time agreed on by the united states in congress assembled.

The united states in congress assembled shall never engage in a war, nor grant letters of marque and reprisal in time of peace, nor enter into any treaties or alliances, nor coin money, nor regulate the value thereof, nor ascertain the sums and expences necessary for the defence and welfare of the united states, or any of them, nor emit bills, nor borrow money on the credit of the united states, nor appropriate money, nor agree upon the number of vessels of war, to be built or purchased, or the number of land or sea forces to be raised, nor appoint a commander in chief of the army or navy, unless nine states assent to the same: nor shall a question on any other point, except for adjourning from day to day be determined, unless by the votes of a majority of the united states in congress assembled.

The congress of the united states shall have power to adjourn to any time within the year, and to any place within the united states, so that no period of adjournment be for a longer duration than the space of six Months, and shall publish the Journal of their proceedings monthly, except such parts thereof relating to treaties, alliances or military operations as in their judgment require secresy; and the yeas and nays of the delegates of each state on any question shall be entered on the Journal, when it is desired by any delegate; and the delegates of a state, or any of them, at his or their request shall be furnished with a transcript of the said Journal, except such parts as are above excepted, to lay before the legislatures of the several states.

Article X The committee of the states, or any nine of them, shall be authorised to execute, in the recess of congress, such of the powers of congress as the united states in congress assembled, by the consent of nine states, shall from time to time think expedient to vest them with; provided that no power be delegated to the said committee, for the exercise of which, by the articles of confederation, the voice of nine states in the congress of the united states assembled is requisite.

Article XI Canada acceding to this confederation, and joining in the measures of the united states, shall be admitted into, and entitled to all the advantages of this union: but no other colony shall be admitted into the same, unless such admission be agreed to by nine states.

Article XII All bills of credit emitted, monies borrowed and debts contracted by, or under the authority of congress, before the assembling of the united states, in pursuance of the present confederation, shall be deemed and considered as a charge against the united states, for payment and satisfaction whereof the said united states, and the public faith are hereby solemnly pledged.

Article XIII Every state shall abide by the determinations of the united states in congress assembled, on all questions which by this confederation are submitted to them. And the Articles of this confederation shall be inviolably observed by every state, and the union shall be perpetual; nor shall any alteration at any time hereafter be made in any of them; unless such alteration be agreed to in a congress of the united states, and be afterwards confirmed by the legislatures of every state.

AND WHEREAS it hath pleased the Great Governor of the World to incline the hearts of the legislatures we respectively represent in congress, to approve of, and to authorize us to ratify the said articles of confederation and perpetual union. Know Ye that we the under-signed delegates, by virtue of the power and authority to us given for that purpose, do by these presents, in the name and in behalf of our respective constituents, fully and entirely ratify and confirm each and every of the said articles of confederation and perpetual union, and all and singular the matters and things therein contained: And we do further solemnly plight and engage the faith of our respective constituents, that they shall abide by the determinations of the united states in congress assembled, on all questions, which by the said confederation are submitted to them. And that the articles thereof shall be inviolably observed by the states we respectively represent, and that the union shall be perpetual. In Witness whereof we have hereunto set our hands in Congress. Done at Philadelphia in the state of Pennsylvania the ninth Day of July in the Year of our Lord one Thousand seven Hundred and Seventy-eight, and in the third year of the independence of America.

Constitution of the United States of America and Amendments*

Preamble

We the people of the United States, in order to form a more perfect union, establish justice, insure domestic tranquillity, provide for the common defense, promote the general welfare, and secure the blessings of liberty to ourselves and our posterity, do ordain and establish this Constitution for the United States of America.

Article I

Section 1 All legislative powers herein granted shall be vested in a Congress of the United States, which shall consist of a Senate and a House of Representatives.

Section 2 The House of Representatives shall be composed of members chosen every second year by the people of the several States, and the electors in each State shall have the qualifications requisite for electors of the most numerous branch of the State Legislature.

No person shall be a Representative who shall not have attained to the age of twenty-five years, and been seven years a citizen of the United States, and who shall not, when elected, be an inhabitant of that State in which he shall be chosen.

Representatives and direct taxes shall be apportioned among the several States which may be included within this Union, according to their respective numbers, *which shall be determined by adding to the whole number of free persons, including those bound to service for a term of years and excluding Indians not taxed, three-fifths of all other persons.* The actual enumeration shall be made within three years after the first meeting of the Congress of the United States, and within every subsequent term of ten years, in such manner as they shall by law direct. The number of Representatives shall not exceed one for every thirty thousand, but each State shall have at least one Representative; *and until such enumeration shall be made, the State of New Hampshire shall be entitled to choose three, Massachusetts eight, Rhode Island and Providence Plantations one, Connecticut five, New York six, New Jersey four, Pennsylvania eight, Delaware one, Maryland six, Virginia ten, North Carolina five, South Carolina five, and Georgia three.*

When vacancies happen in the representation from any State, the Executive authority thereof shall issue writs of election to fill such vacancies.

The House of Representatives shall choose their Speaker and other officers; and shall have the sole power of impeachment.

Section 3 The Senate of the United States shall be composed of two Senators from each State, *chosen by the legislature thereof,* for six years; and each Senator shall have one vote.

Immediately after they shall be assembled in consequence of the first election, they shall be divided as equally as may be into three classes. The seats of the Senators of the first class shall be vacated at the expiration of the second year, of the second class at the expiration of the fourth year, and of the third class at the expiration of the sixth year, so that one-third may be chosen every second year; and if vacancies happen by resignation or otherwise, during the recess of the legislature of any State, the Executive thereof may make temporary appointments until the next meeting of the legislature, which shall then fill such vacancies.

No person shall be a Senator who shall not have attained to the age of thirty years, and been nine years a citizen of the United States, and who shall not, when elected, be an inhabitant of that State for which he shall be chosen.

The Vice-President of the United States shall be President of the Senate, but shall have no vote, unless they be equally divided.

The Senate shall choose their other officers, and also a President *pro tempore,* in the absence of the Vice-President, or when he shall exercise the office of President of the United States.

The Senate shall have the sole power to try all impeachments. When sitting for that purpose, they shall be on oath or affirmation. When the President of the United States is tried, the Chief Justice shall preside: and no person shall be convicted without the concurrence of two-thirds of the members present.

Judgment in cases of impeachment shall not extend further than to removal from the office, and disqualification to hold and enjoy any office of honor, trust or profit under the United States: but the party convicted shall nevertheless be liable and subject to indictment, trial, judgment and punishment, according to law.

Section 4 The times, places and manner of holding elections for Senators and Representatives shall be prescribed in each State by the legislature thereof; but the Congress may at any time by law make or alter such regulations, except as to the places of choosing Senators.

The Congress shall assemble at least once in every year, and such meeting *shall be on the first Monday in December, unless they shall by law appoint a different day.*

Section 5 Each house shall be the judge of the elections, returns and qualifications of its own members, and a majority of each shall constitute a quorum to do business; but a smaller number may adjourn from day to day, and may be authorized to compel the attendance of absent members, in such manner, and under such penalties, as each house may provide.

---

* Passages no longer in effect are printed in italic type.

Each house may determine the rules of its proceedings, punish its members for disorderly behavior, and with the concurrence of two-thirds, expel a member.

Each house shall keep a journal of its proceedings, and from time to time publish the same, excepting such parts as may in their judgment require secrecy; and the yeas and nays of the members of either house on any question shall, at the desire of one-fifth of those present, be entered on the journal.

Neither house, during the session of Congress, shall, without the consent of the other, adjourn for more than three days, nor to any other place than that in which the two houses shall be sitting.

Section 6 The Senators and Representatives shall receive a compensation for their services, to be ascertained by law and paid out of the treasury of the United States. They shall in all cases except treason, felony and breach of the peace, be privileged from arrest during their attendance at the session of their respective houses, and in going to and returning from the same; and for any speech or debate in either house, they shall not be questioned in any other place.

No Senator or Representative shall, during the time for which he was elected, be appointed to any civil office under the authority of the United States, which shall have been created, or the emoluments whereof shall have been increased, during such time; and no person holding any office under the United States shall be a member of either house during his continuance in office.

Section 7 All bills for raising revenue shall originate in the House of Representatives; but the Senate may propose or concur with amendments as on other bills.

Every bill which shall have passed the House of Representatives and the Senate, shall, before it become a law, be presented to the President of the United States; if he approve he shall sign it, but if not he shall return it with objections to that house in which it originated, who shall enter the objections at large on their journal, and proceed to reconsider it. If after such reconsideration two-thirds of that house shall agree to pass the bill, it shall be sent, together with the objections, to the other house, by which it shall likewise be reconsidered, and, if approved by two-thirds of that house, it shall become a law. But in all such cases the votes of both houses shall be determined by yeas and nays, and the names of the persons voting for and against the bill shall be entered on the journal of each house respectively. If any bill shall not be returned by the President within ten days (Sundays excepted) after it shall have been presented to him, the same shall be a law, in like manner as if he had signed it, unless the Congress by their adjournment prevent its return, in which case it shall not be a law.

Every order, resolution, or vote to which the concurrence of the Senate and House of Representatives may be necessary (except on a question of adjournment) shall be presented to the President of the United States; and before the same shall take effect, shall be approved by him, or being disapproved by him, shall be repassed by two-thirds of the Senate and House of Representatives, according to the rules and limitations prescribed in the case of a bill.

Section 8 The Congress shall have power

To lay and collect taxes, duties, imposts, and excises, to pay the debts and provide for the common defense and general welfare of the United States; but all duties, imposts and excises shall be uniform throughout the United States;

To borrow money on the credit of the United States;

To regulate commerce with foreign nations, and among the several States, and with the Indian tribes;

To establish an uniform rule of naturalization, and uniform laws on the subject of bankruptcies throughout the United States;

To coin money, regulate the value thereof, and of foreign coin, and fix the standard of weights and measures;

To provide for the punishment of counterfeiting the securities and current coin of the United States;

To establish post offices and post roads;

To promote the progress of science and useful arts by securing for limited times to authors and inventors the exclusive right to their respective writings and discoveries;

To constitute tribunals inferior to the Supreme Court;

To define and punish piracies and felonies committed on the high seas and offenses against the law of nations;

To declare war, grant letters of marque and reprisal, and make rules concerning captures on land and water;

To raise and support armies, but no appropriation of money to that use shall be for a longer term than two years;

To provide and maintain a navy;

To make rules for the government and regulation of the land and naval forces;

To provide for calling forth the militia to execute the laws of the Union, suppress insurrections, and repel invasions;

To provide for organizing, arming, and disciplining the militia, and for governing such part of them as may be employed in the service of the United States, reserving to the States respectively the appointment of the officers, and the authority of training the militia according to the discipline prescribed by Congress;

To exercise exclusive legislation in all cases whatsoever, over such district (not exceeding ten miles square) as may, by cession of particular States, and the acceptance of Congress, become the seat of government of the United States, and to exercise like authority over all places purchased by the consent of the legislature of the State, in which the same shall be, for erection of forts, magazines, arsenals, dockyards, and other needful buildings; —and

To make all laws which shall be necessary and proper for carrying into execution the foregoing powers, and all other powers vested by this Constitution in the government of the United States, or in any department or officer thereof.

Section 9 *The migration or importation of such persons as any of the States now existing shall think proper to admit shall not be prohibited by the Congress prior to the year 1808; but a tax or duty may be imposed on such importation, not exceeding $10 for each person.*

The privilege of the writ of habeas corpus shall not be suspended, unless when in cases of rebellion or invasion the public safety may require it.

No bill of attainder or ex post facto law shall be passed.

No capitation, or other direct, tax shall be laid, unless in proportion to the census or enumeration herein before directed to be taken.

No tax or duty shall be laid on articles exported from any State.

No preference shall be given by any regulation of commerce or revenue to the ports of one State over those of another; nor shall vessels bound to, or from, one State, be obliged to enter, clear, or pay duties in another.

No money shall be drawn from the treasury, but in consequence of appropriations made by law; and a regular statement and account of the receipts and expenditures of all public money shall be published from time to time.

No title of nobility shall be granted by the United States: and no person holding any office of profit or trust under them, shall, without the consent of the Congress, accept of any present, emolument, office, or title, of any kind whatever, from any king, prince, or foreign state.

Section 10 No State shall enter into any treaty, alliance, or confederation; grant letters of marque and reprisal; coin money; emit bills of credit; make anything but gold and silver coin a tender in payment of debts; pass any bill of attainder, ex post facto law, or law impairing the obligation of contracts, or grant any title of nobility.

No State shall, without the consent of Congress, lay any imposts or duties on imports or exports, except what may be absolutely necessary for executing its inspection laws: and the net produce of all duties and imposts, laid by any State on imports or exports, shall be for the use of the treasury of the United States; and all such laws shall be subject to the revision and control of the Congress.

No State shall, without the consent of Congress, lay any duty of tonnage, keep troops or ships of war in time of peace, enter into any agreement or compact with another State, or with a foreign power, or engage in war, unless actually invaded, or in such imminent danger as will not admit of delay.

Article II

Section 1 The executive power shall be vested in a President of the United States of America. He shall hold his office during the term of four years, and, together with the Vice-President, chosen for the same term, be elected as follows:

Each State shall appoint, in such manner as the legislature thereof may direct, a number of electors, equal to the whole number of Senators and Representatives to which the State may be entitled in the Congress; but no Senator or Representative, or person holding an office of trust or profit under the United States, shall be appointed an elector.

The electors shall meet in their respective States, and vote by ballot for two persons, of whom one at least shall not be an inhabitant of the same State with themselves. And they shall make a list of all the persons voted for, and of the number of votes for each; which list they shall sign and certify, and transmit sealed to the seat of government of the United States, directed to the President of the Senate. The President of the Senate shall, in the presence of the Senate and House of Representatives, open all the certificates, and the votes shall then be counted. The person having the greatest number of votes shall be the President, if such number be a majority of the whole number of electors appointed; and if there be more than one who have such majority, and have an equal number of votes, then the House of Representatives shall immediately choose by ballot one of them for President; and if no person have a majority, then from the five highest on the list said house shall in like manner choose the President. But in choosing the President the votes shall be taken by States, the representation from each State having one vote; a quorum for this purpose shall consist of a member or members from two-thirds of the States, and a majority of all the States shall be necessary to a choice. In every case, after the choice of the President, the person having the greatest number of votes of the electors shall be the Vice-President. But if there should remain two or more who have equal votes, the Senate shall choose from them by ballot the Vice-President.

The Congress may determine the time of choosing the electors and the day on which they shall give their votes; which day shall be the same throughout the United States.

No person except a natural-born citizen, *or a citizen of the United States at the time of the adoption of this Constitution,* shall be eligible to the office of President; neither shall any person be eligible to that office who shall not have attained to the age of thirty-five years, and been fourteen years a resident within the United States.

In cases of the removal of the President from office or of his death, resignation, or inability to discharge the powers and duties of the said office, the same shall devolve on the Vice-President, and the Congress may by law provide for the case of removal, death, resignation, or inability, both of the President and Vice-President, declaring what officer shall then act as President, and such officer shall act accordingly, until the disability be removed, or a President shall be elected.

The President shall, at stated times, receive for his services a compensation, which shall neither be increased nor diminished during the period for which he shall have been elected, and he shall not receive within that period any other emolument from the United States, or any of them.

Before he enter on the execution of his office, he shall take the following oath or affirmation:—"I do solemnly swear (or affirm) that I will faithfully execute the office of the President of the United States, and will to the best of my ability preserve, protect and defend the Constitution of the United States."

Section 2 The President shall be commander in chief of the army and navy of the United States, and of the militia of the several States, when called into the actual service of the United States; he may require the opinion, in writing, of the principal officer in each of the executive departments, upon any subject relating to the duties of their respective offices, and he shall have power to grant reprieves and pardons for offenses against the United States, except in cases of impeachment.

He shall have power, by and with the advice and consent of the Senate, to make treaties, provided two-thirds of the Senators present concur; and he shall nominate, and by and with the advice and consent of the Senate, shall appoint ambassadors, other public ministers and consuls, judges of the Supreme Court, and all other officers of the United States, whose appointments are not herein otherwise provided for, and which shall be established by law: but Congress may by law vest the appointment of such inferior officers, as they think proper, in the President alone, in the courts of law, or in the heads of departments.

The President shall have power to fill up all vacancies that may happen during the recess of the Senate, by granting commissions which shall expire at the end of their next session.

Section 3 He shall from time to time give to the Congress information of the state of the Union, and recommend to their consideration such measures as he shall judge necessary and expedient; he may, on extraordinary occasions, convene both houses, or either of them, and in case of disagreement between them, with respect to the time of adjournment, he may adjourn them to such time as he shall think proper; he shall receive ambassadors and other public ministers; he shall take care that the laws be faithfully executed, and shall commission all the officers of the United States.

Section 4 The President, Vice-President and all civil officers of the United States shall be removed from office on impeachment for, and on conviction of, treason, bribery, or other high crimes and misdemeanors.

Article III

Section 1 The judicial power of the United States shall be vested in one Supreme Court, and in such inferior courts as the Congress may from time to time ordain and establish. The judges, both of the Supreme and inferior courts, shall hold their offices during good behavior, and shall, at stated times, receive for their services a compensation which shall not be diminished during their continuance in office.

Section 2 The judicial power shall extend to all cases, in law and equity, arising under this Constitution, the laws of the United States, and treaties made, or which shall be made, under their authority;—to all cases affecting ambassadors, other public ministers and consuls;—to all cases of admiralty and maritime jurisdiction;—to controversies to which the United States shall be a party;—to controversies between two or more States;— *between a State and citizens of another*

State;—between citizens of different States;—between citizens of the same State claiming lands under grants of different States, and between a State, or the citizens thereof, and foreign states, citizens or subjects.

In all cases affecting ambassadors, other public ministers and consuls, and those in which a State shall be party, the Supreme Court shall have original jurisdiction. In all the other cases before mentioned, the Supreme Court shall have appellate jurisdiction, both as to law and fact, with such exceptions, and under such regulations, as the Congress shall make.

The trial of all crimes, except in cases of impeachment, shall be by jury; and such trial shall be held in the State where said crimes shall have been committed; but when not committed within any State, the trial shall be at such place or places as the Congress may by law have directed.

Section 3 Treason against the United States shall consist only in levying war against them, or in adhering to their enemies, giving them aid and comfort. No person shall be convicted of treason unless on the testimony of two witnesses to the same overt act, or on confession in open court.

The Congress shall have power to declare the punishment of treason, but no attainder of treason shall work corruption of blood, or forfeiture except during the life of the person attainted.

Article IV

Section 1 Full faith and credit shall be given in each State to the public acts, records, and judicial proceedings of every other State. And the Congress may by general laws prescribe the manner in which such acts, records, and proceedings shall be proved, and the effect thereof.

Section 2 The citizens of each State shall be entitled to all privileges and immunities of citizens in the several States.

A person charged in any State with treason, felony, or other crime, who shall flee from justice, and be found in another State, shall on demand of the executive authority of the State from which he fled, be delivered up, to be removed to the State having jurisdiction of the crime.

No person held to service or labor in one State, under the laws thereof, escaping into another, shall, in consequence of any law or regulation therein, be discharged from such service or labor, but shall be delivered up on claim of the party to whom such service or labor may be due.

Section 3 New States may be admitted by the Congress into this Union; but no new State shall be formed or erected within the jurisdiction of any other State; nor any State be formed by the junction of two or more States, or parts of States, without the consent of the legislatures of the States concerned as well as of the Congress.

The Congress shall have power to dispose of and make all needful rules and regulations respecting the territory or other property belonging to the United States; and nothing in this Constitution shall be so construed as to prejudice any claims of the United States, or of any particular State.

Section 4 The United States shall guarantee to every State in this Union a republican form of government, and shall protect each of them against invasion; and on application of the legislature, or of the executive (when the legislature cannot be convened), against domestic violence.

Article V

The Congress, whenever two-thirds of both houses shall deem it necessary, shall propose amendments to this Constitution, or, on the application of the legislatures of two-thirds of the several States, shall call a convention for proposing amendments, which, in either case, shall be valid to all intents and purposes, as part of this Constitution, when ratified by the legislatures of three-fourths of the several States, or by conventions in three-fourths thereof, as the one or the other mode of ratification may be proposed by the Congress; provided *that no amendments which may be made prior to the year one thousand eight hundred and eight shall in any manner affect the first and fourth clauses in the ninth section of the first article;* and that no State, without its consent, shall be deprived of its equal suffrage in the Senate.

Article VI

All debts contracted and engagements entered into, before the adoption of this Constitution, shall be as valid against the United States under this Constitution, as under the Confederation.

This Constitution, and the laws of the United States which shall be made in pursuance thereof; and all treaties made, or which shall be made, under the authority of the United States, shall be the supreme law of the land; and the judges in every State shall be bound thereby, anything in the Constitution or laws of any State to the contrary notwithstanding.

The Senators and Representatives before mentioned, and the members of the several State legislatures, and all executive and judicial officers, both of the United States and of the several States, shall be bound by oath or affirmation to support this Constitution; but no religious test shall ever be required as a qualification to any office or public trust under the United States.

Article VII

The ratification of the conventions of nine States shall be sufficient for the establishment of this Constitution between the States so ratifying the same.

Done in Convention by the unanimous consent of the States present, the seventeenth day of September in the year of our Lord one thousand seven hundred and eighty-seven and of the Independence of the United States of America the twelfth. In witness whereof we have hereunto subscribed our names.

Amendments to the Constitution*

Amendment I

Congress shall make no law respecting an establishment of religion, or prohibiting the free exercise thereof; or abridging the freedom of speech, or of the press; or the right of the people peaceably to assemble, and to petition the government for a redress of grievances.

Amendment II

A well-regulated militia being necessary to the security of a free State, the right of the people to keep and bear arms shall not be infringed.

Amendment III

No soldier shall, in time of peace, be quartered in any house without the consent of the owner, nor in time of war, but in a manner to be prescribed by law.

Amendment IV

The right of the people to be secure in their persons, houses, papers, and effects, against unreasonable searches and seizures, shall not be violated, and no warrants shall issue but upon probable cause, supported by oath or affirmation, and particularly describing the place to be searched, and the persons or things to be seized.

Amendment V

No person shall be held to answer for a capital, or otherwise infamous crime, unless on a presentment or indictment of a grand jury, except in cases arising in the land or naval forces, or in the militia, when in actual service in time of war or public danger; nor shall any person be subject for the same offense to be twice put in jeopardy of life or limb; nor shall be compelled in any criminal case to be a witness against himself, nor be deprived of life, liberty, or property, without due process of law; nor shall private property be taken for public use without just compensation.

Amendment VI

In all criminal prosecutions, the accused shall enjoy the right to a speedy and public trial, by an impartial jury of the State and district wherein the crime shall have been committed,

---

* The first ten Amendments (the Bill of Rights) were adopted in 1791.

which district shall have been previously ascertained by law, and to be informed of the nature and cause of the accusation; to be confronted with the witnesses against him; to have compulsory process for obtaining witnesses in his favor, and to have the assistance of counsel for his defense.

Amendment VII

In suits at common law, where the value in controversy shall exceed twenty dollars, the right of trial by jury shall be preserved, and no fact tried by a jury shall be otherwise reexamined in any court of the United States, than according to the rules of the common law.

Amendment VIII

Excessive bail shall not be required, nor excessive fines imposed, nor cruel and unusual punishments inflicted.

Amendment IX

The enumeration in the Constitution, of certain rights, shall not be construed to deny or disparage others retained by the people.

Amendment X

The powers not delegated to the United States by the Constitution, nor prohibited by it to the States, are reserved to the States respectively, or to the people.

Amendment XI

[Adopted 1798]

The judicial power of the United States shall not be construed to extend to any suit in law or equity, commenced or prosecuted against one of the United States by citizens of another State, or by citizens or subjects of any foreign state.

Amendment XII

[Adopted 1804]

The electors shall meet in their respective States, and vote by ballot for President and Vice-President, one of whom, at least, shall not be an inhabitant of the same State with themselves; they shall name in their ballots the person voted for as President, and in distinct ballots the person voted for as Vice-President, and they shall make distinct lists of all persons voted for as President, and of all persons voted for as Vice-President, and of the number of votes for each, which lists they shall sign and certify, and transmit sealed to the seat of government of the United States, directed to the President of the Senate;—the President of the Senate shall, in the presence of the Senate and House of Representatives, open all the certificates and the votes shall then be counted;—the person having the greatest number of votes for President shall be the President, if such number be a majority of the whole number of electors appointed; and if no person have such majority, then from the persons having the highest numbers not exceeding three on the list of those voted for as President, the House of Representatives shall choose immediately, by ballot, the President. But in choosing the President, the votes shall be taken by States, the representation from each State having one vote; a quorum for this purpose shall consist of a member or members from two-thirds of the States, and a majority of all the States shall be necessary to a choice. And if the House of Representatives shall not choose a President whenever the right of choice shall devolve upon them, before *the fourth day of March* next following, then the Vice-President shall act as President, as in the case of the death or other constitutional disability of the President.

The person having the greatest number of votes as Vice-President shall be the Vice-President, if such number be a majority of the whole number of electors appointed; and if no person have a majority, then from the two highest numbers on the list the Senate shall choose the Vice-President; a quorum for the purpose shall consist of two-thirds of the whole number of Senators, and a majority of the whole number shall be necessary to a choice. But no person constitutionally ineligible to the office of President shall be eligible to that of Vice-President of the United States.

Amendment XIII

[Adopted 1865]

Section 1 Neither slavery nor involuntary servitude, except as a punishment for crime whereof the party shall have been duly convicted, shall exist within the United States, or any place subject to their jurisdiction.

Section 2 Congress shall have power to enforce this article by appropriate legislation.

Amendment XIV

[Adopted 1868]

Section 1 All persons born or naturalized in the United States, and subject to the jurisdiction thereof, are citizens of the United States and of the State wherein they reside. No State shall make or enforce any law which shall abridge the privileges or immunities of citizens of the United States; nor shall any State deprive any person of life, liberty, or property, without due process of law; nor deny to any person within its jurisdiction the equal protection of the laws.

Section 2 Representatives shall be apportioned among the several States according to their respective numbers, counting the whole number of persons in each State, excluding Indians not taxed. But when the right to vote at any election for the choice of Electors for President and Vice-President of the United States, Representatives in Congress, the executive and judicial officers of a State, or the members of the legislature thereof, is denied to any of the male inhabitants of such State, being twenty-one years of age and citizens of the United States, or in any way abridged, except for participation in rebellion, or other crime, the basis of representation therein shall be reduced in the proportion which the number of such male citizens shall bear to the whole number of male citizens twenty-one years of age in such State.

Section 3 No person shall be a Senator or Representative in Congress, or Elector of President and Vice-President, or hold any office, civil or military, under the United States, or under any State, who, having previously taken an oath, as a member of Congress, or as an officer of the United States, or as a member of any State legislature, or as an executive or judicial officer of any State, to support the Constitution of the United States, shall have engaged in insurrection or rebellion against the same, or given aid or comfort to the enemies thereof. Congress may, by a vote of two-thirds of each house, remove such disability.

Section 4 The validity of the public debt of the United States, authorized by law, including debts incurred for payment of pensions and bounties for services in suppressing insurrection or rebellion, shall not be questioned. But neither the United States nor any State shall assume or pay any debt or obligation incurred in aid of insurrection or rebellion against the United States, or any claim for the loss of emancipation of any slave; but all such debts, obligations, and claims shall be held illegal and void.

Section 5 The Congress shall have power to enforce, by appropriate legislation, the provisions of this article.

Amendment XV
[Adopted 1870]

Section 1 The right of citizens of the United States to vote shall not be denied or abridged by the United States or by any State on account of race, color, or previous condition of servitude.

Section 2 The Congress shall have power to enforce this article by appropriate legislation.

Amendment XVI
[Adopted 1913]

The Congress shall have power to lay and collect taxes on incomes, from whatever source derived, without apportionment among the several States, and without regard to any census or enumeration.

Amendment XVII
[Adopted 1913]

Section 1 The Senate of the United States shall be composed of two Senators from each State, elected by the people thereof, for six years; and each Senator shall have one vote. The electors in each State shall have the qualifications requisite for electors of [voters for] the most numerous branch of the State legislatures.

Section 2 When vacancies happen in the representation of any State in the Senate, the executive authority of such State shall issue writs of election to fill such vacancies: Provided, that the Legislature of any State may empower the executive

thereof to make temporary appointments until the people fill the vacancies by election as the Legislature may direct.

Section 3 This amendment shall not be so construed as to affect the election or term of any Senator chosen before it becomes valid as part of the Constitution.

Amendment XVIII
[Adopted 1919; Repealed 1933]

Section 1 After one year from the ratification of this article the manufacture, sale, or transportation of intoxicating liquors within, the importation thereof into, or the exportation thereof from the United States and all territory subject to the jurisdiction thereof, for beverage purposes, is hereby prohibited.

Section 2 The Congress and the several States shall have concurrent power to enforce this article by appropriate legislation.

Section 3 This article shall be inoperative unless it shall have been ratified as an amendment to the Constitution by the legislatures of the several States, as provided by the Constitution, within seven years from the date of the submission thereof to the States by the Congress.

Amendment XIX
[Adopted 1920]

Section 1 The right of citizens of the United States to vote shall not be denied or abridged by the United States or by any State on account of sex.

Section 2 The Congress shall have power to enforce this article by appropriate legislation.

Amendment XX
[Adopted 1933]

Section 1 The terms of the President and Vice-President shall end at noon on the 20th day of January, and the terms of Senators and Representatives at noon on the 3rd day of January, of the years in which such terms would have ended if this article had not been ratified; and the terms of their successors shall then begin.

Section 2 The Congress shall assemble at least once in every year, and such meeting shall begin at noon on the 3rd day of January, unless they shall by law appoint a different day.

Section 3 If, at the time fixed for the beginning of the term of the President, the President-elect shall have died, the Vice-President-elect shall become President. If a President shall not have been chosen before the time fixed for the beginning of his term, or if the President-elect shall have failed to qualify, then the Vice-President-elect shall act as President until a President shall have qualified; and the Congress may by law provide for the case wherein neither a President-elect nor a Vice-President-elect shall have qualified, declaring who shall then act as President, or the manner in which one who is to act shall be selected, and such persons shall act accordingly until a President or Vice-President shall have qualified.

Section 4 The Congress may by law provide for the case of the death of any of the persons from whom the House of Representatives may choose a President whenever the right of choice shall have devolved upon them, and for the case of the death of any of the persons from whom the Senate may choose a Vice-President whenever the right of choice shall have devolved upon them.

Section 5 Sections 1 and 2 shall take effect on the 15th day of October following the ratification of this article.

Section 6 This article shall be inoperative unless it shall have been ratified as an amendment to the Constitution by the Legislatures of three-fourths of the several States within seven years from the date of its submission.

Amendment XXI

[Adopted 1933]
Section 1 The eighteenth article of amendment to the Constitution of the United States is hereby repealed.

Section 2 The transportation or importation into any State, Territory, or Possession of the United States for delivery or use therein of intoxicating liquors, in violation of the laws thereof, is hereby prohibited.

Section 3 This article shall be inoperative unless it shall have been ratified as an amendment to the Constitution by conventions in the several States, as provided in the Constitution, within seven years from the date of submission thereof to the States by the Congress.

Amendment XXII

[Adopted 1951]
Section 1 No person shall be elected to the office of President more than twice, and no person who has held the office of President, or acted as President, for more than two years of a term to which some other person was elected President shall be elected to the office of President more than once. But this article shall not apply to any person holding the office of President when this article was proposed by the Congress, and shall not prevent any person who may be holding the office of President, or acting as President, during the term within which this article becomes operative from holding the office of President or acting as President during the remainder of such term.

Section 2 This article shall be inoperative unless it shall have been ratified as an amendment to the Constitution by the legislatures of three-fourths of the several States within seven years from the date of its submission to the States by the Congress.

Amendment XXIII

[Adopted 1961]
Section 1 The District constituting the seat of Government of the United States shall appoint in such manner as the Congress may direct:

A number of electors of President and Vice-President equal to the whole number of Senators and Representatives in Congress to which the District would be entitled if it were a State, but in no event more than the least populous State; they shall be in addition to those appointed by the States, but they shall be considered for the purposes of the election of President and Vice-President, to be electors appointed by a State; and they shall meet in the District and perform such duties as provided by the twelfth article of amendment.

Section 2 The Congress shall have the power to enforce this article by appropriate legislation.

Amendment XXIV

[Adopted 1964]
Section 1 The right of citizens of the United States to vote in any primary or other election for President or Vice-President, for electors for President or Vice-President, or for Senator or Representative in Congress, shall not be denied or abridged by the United States or any State by reason of failure to pay any poll tax or other tax.

Section 2 The Congress shall have the power to enforce this article by appropriate legislation.

Amendment XXV

[Adopted 1967]
Section 1 In case of the removal of the President from office or of his death or resignation, the Vice-President shall become President.

Section 2 Whenever there is a vacancy in the office of the Vice-President, the President shall nominate a Vice-President who shall take office upon confirmation by a majority vote of both Houses of Congress.

Section 3 Whenever the President transmits to the President pro tempore of the Senate and the Speaker of the House of Representatives his written declaration that he is unable to discharge the powers and duties of his office, and until he transmits to them a written declaration to the contrary, such powers and duties shall be discharged by the Vice-President as Acting President.

Section 4 Whenever the Vice-President and a majority of either the principal officers of the executive departments or of such other body as Congress may by law provide, transmit to the President pro tempore of the Senate and the Speaker of the House of Representatives their written declaration that the President is unable to discharge the powers and duties of his office, the Vice-President shall immediately assume the powers and duties of the office as Acting President.

Thereafter, when the President transmits to the President pro tempore of the Senate and the Speaker of the House of Representatives his written declaration that no inability exists, he shall resume the powers and duties of his office unless the Vice-President and a majority of either the principal officers of the executive department[s] or of such other body as Congress may by law provide, transmit within four days to the President pro tempore of the Senate and the Speaker of the House of Representatives their written declaration that the President is unable to discharge the powers and duties of his office. Thereupon Congress shall decide the issue, assembling within forty-eight hours for that purpose if not in session. If the Congress, within twenty-one days after receipt of the latter written declaration, or, if Congress is not in session, within twenty-one days after Congress is required to assemble, determines by two-thirds vote of both Houses that the President is unable to discharge the powers and duties of his office, the Vice-President shall continue to discharge the same as Acting President; otherwise, the President shall resume the powers and duties of his office.

Amendment XXVI
[Adopted 1971]

Section 1 The right of citizens of the United States, who are eighteen years of age or older, to vote shall not be denied or abridged by the United States or by any State on account of age.

Section 2 The Congress shall have power to enforce this article by appropriate legislation.

Amendment XXVII
[Adopted 1992]

No law, varying the compensation for the services of the Senators and Representatives, shall take effect, until an election of Representatives shall have intervened.

Presidential Elections

Year	Number of States	Candidates	Parties	Popular Vote	% of Popular Vote	Electoral Vote	% Voter Participation[a]
1789	10	**George Washington**	No party			69	
		John Adams	designations			34	
		Other candidates				35	
1792	15	**George Washington**	No party			132	
		John Adams	designations			77	
		George Clinton				50	
		Other candidates				5	
1796	16	**John Adams**	Federalist			71	
		Thomas Jefferson	Democratic-Republican			68	
		Thomas Pinckney	Federalist			59	
		Aaron Burr	Democratic-Republican			30	
		Other candidates				48	
1800	16	**Thomas Jefferson**	Democratic-Republican			73	
		Aaron Burr	Democratic-Republican			73	
		John Adams	Federalist			65	
		Charles C. Pinckney	Federalist			64	
		John Jay	Federalist			1	
1804	17	**Thomas Jefferson**	Democratic-Republican			162	
		Charles C. Pinckney	Federalist			14	
1808	17	**James Madison**	Democratic-Republican			122	
		Charles C. Pinckney	Federalist			47	
		George Clinton	Democratic-Republican			6	
1812	18	**James Madison**	Democratic-Republican			128	
		DeWitt Clinton	Federalist			89	
1816	19	**James Monroe**	Democratic-Republican			183	
		Rufus King	Federalist			34	
1820	24	**James Monroe**	Democratic-Republican			231	
		John Quincy Adams	Independent Republican			1	

Presidential Elections (continued)

Year	Number of States	Candidates	Parties	Popular Vote	% of Popular Vote	Electoral Vote	% Voter Participation[a]
1824	24	**John Quincy Adams**	Democratic-Republican	108,740	30.5	84	26.9
		Andrew Jackson	Democratic-Republican	153,544	43.1	99	
		Henry Clay	Democratic-Republican	47,136	13.2	37	
		William H. Crawford	Democratic-Republican	46,618	13.1	41	
1828	24	**Andrew Jackson**	Democratic	647,286	56.0	178	57.6
		John Quincy Adams	National Republican	508,064	44.0	83	
1832	24	**Andrew Jackson**	Democratic	701,780	54.2	219	55.4
		Henry Clay	National Republican	484,205	37.4	49	
		Other candidates		107,988	8.0	18	
1836	26	**Martin Van Buren**	Democratic	764,176	50.8	170	57.8
		William H. Harrison	Whig	550,816	36.6	73	
		Hugh L. White	Whig	146,107	9.7	26	
1840	26	**William H. Harrison**	Whig	1,274,624	53.1	234	80.2
		Martin Van Buren	Democratic	1,127,781	46.9	60	
1844	26	**James K. Polk**	Democratic	1,338,464	49.6	170	78.9
		Henry Clay	Whig	1,300,097	48.1	105	
		James G. Birney	Liberty	62,300	2.3		
1848	30	**Zachary Taylor**	Whig	1,360,967	47.4	163	72.7
		Lewis Cass	Democratic	1,222,342	42.5	127	
		Martin Van Buren	Free Soil	291,263	10.1		
1852	31	**Franklin Pierce**	Democratic	1,601,117	50.9	254	69.6
		Winfield Scott	Whig	1,385,453	44.1	42	
		John P. Hale	Free Soil	155,825	5.0		
1856	31	**James Buchanan**	Democratic	1,832,955	45.3	174	78.9
		John C. Frémont	Republican	1,339,932	33.1	114	
		Millard Fillmore	American	871,731	21.6		
1860	33	**Abraham Lincoln**	Republican	1,865,593	39.8	180	81.2
		Stephen A. Douglas	Democratic	1,382,713	29.5	12	
		John C. Breckinridge	Democratic	848,356	18.1	72	
		John Bell	Constitutional Union	592,906	12.6	39	

Year	Number of States	Candidates	Parties	Popular Vote	% of Popular Vote	Electoral Vote	% Voter Participation[a]
1864	36	**Abraham Lincoln**	Republican	2,206,938	55.0	212	73.8
		George B. McClellan	Democratic	1,803,787	45.0	21	
1868	37	**Ulysses S. Grant**	Republican	3,013,421	52.7	214	78.1
		Horatio Seymour	Democratic	2,706,829	47.3	80	
1872	37	**Ulysses S. Grant**	Republican	3,596,745	55.6	286	71.3
		Horace Greeley[b]	Democratic	2,843,446	43.9		
1876	38	**Rutherford B. Hayes**	Republican	4,036,572	48.0	185	81.8
		Samuel J. Tilden	Democratic	4,284,020	51.0	184	
1880	38	**James A. Garfield**	Republican	4,453,295	48.5	214	79.4
		Winfield S. Hancock	Democratic	4,414,082	48.1	155	
		James B. Weaver	Greenback-Labor	308,578	3.4		
1884	38	**Grover Cleveland**	Democratic	4,879,507	48.5	219	77.5
		James G. Blaine	Republican	4,850,293	48.2	182	
		Benjamin F. Butler	Greenback-Labor	175,370	1.8		
		John P. St. John	Prohibition	150,369	1.5		
1888	38	**Benjamin Harrison**	Republican	5,447,129	47.9	233	79.3
		Grover Cleveland	Democratic	5,537,857	48.6	168	
		Clinton B. Fisk	Prohibition	249,506	2.2		
		Anson J. Streeter	Union Labor	146,935	1.3		
1892	44	**Grover Cleveland**	Democratic	5,555,426	46.1	277	74.7
		Benjamin Harrison	Republican	5,182,690	43.0	145	
		James B. Weaver	People's	1,029,846	8.5	22	
		John Bidwell	Prohibition	264,133	2.2		
1896	45	**William McKinley**	Republican	7,102,246	51.1	271	79.3
		William J. Bryan	Democratic	6,492,559	47.7	176	
1900	45	**William McKinley**	Republican	7,218,491	51.7	292	73.2
		William J. Bryan	Democratic; Populist	6,356,734	45.5	155	
		John C. Wooley	Prohibition	208,914	1.5		
1904	45	**Theodore Roosevelt**	Republican	7,628,461	57.4	336	65.2
		Alton B. Parker	Democratic	5,084,223	37.6	140	
		Eugene V. Debs	Socialist	402,283	3.0		
		Silas C. Swallow	Prohibition	258,536	1.9		
1908	46	**William H. Taft**	Republican	7,675,320	51.6	321	65.4
		William J. Bryan	Democratic	6,412,294	43.1	162	
		Eugene V. Debs	Socialist	420,793	2.8		
		Eugene W. Chafin	Prohibition	253,840	1.7		

Presidential Elections (continued)

Year	Number of States	Candidates	Parties	Popular Vote	% of Popular Vote	Electoral Vote	% Voter Participation[a]
1912	48	**Woodrow Wilson**	Democratic	6,296,547	41.9	435	58.8
		Theodore Roosevelt	Progressive	4,118,571	27.4	88	
		William H. Taft	Republican	3,486,720	23.2	8	
		Eugene V. Debs	Socialist	900,672	6.0		
		Eugene W. Chafin	Prohibition	206,275	1.4		
1916	48	**Woodrow Wilson**	Democratic	9,127,695	49.4	277	61.6
		Charles E. Hughes	Republican	8,533,507	46.2	254	
		A. L. Benson	Socialist	585,113	3.2		
		J. Frank Hanly	Prohibition	220,506	1.2		
1920	48	**Warren G. Harding**	Republican	16,143,407	60.4	404	49.2
		James M. Cox	Democratic	9,130,328	34.2	127	
		Eugene V. Debs	Socialist	919,799	3.4		
		P. P. Christensen	Farmer-Labor	265,411	1.0		
1924	48	**Calvin Coolidge**	Republican	15,718,211	54.0	382	48.9
		John W. Davis	Democratic	8,385,283	28.8	136	
		Robert M. La Follette	Progressive	4,831,289	16.6	13	
1928	48	**Herbert C. Hoover**	Republican	21,391,993	58.2	444	56.9
		Alfred E. Smith	Democratic	15,016,169	40.9	87	
1932	48	**Franklin D. Roosevelt**	Democratic	22,821,857	57.4	472	56.9
		Herbert C. Hoover	Republican	15,761,841	39.7	59	
		Norman Thomas	Socialist	884,781	2.2		
1936	48	**Franklin D. Roosevelt**	Democratic	27,752,869	60.8	523	61.0
		Alfred M. Landon	Republican	16,674,665	36.5	8	
		William Lemke	Union	882,479	1.9		
1940	48	**Franklin D. Roosevelt**	Democratic	27,307,819	54.8	449	62.5
		Wendell L. Willkie	Republican	22,321,018	44.8	82	
1944	48	**Franklin D. Roosevelt**	Democratic	25,606,585	53.5	432	55.9
		Thomas E. Dewey	Republican	22,014,745	46.0	99	
1948	48	**Harry S Truman**	Democratic	24,179,345	49.6	303	53.0
		Thomas E. Dewey	Republican	21,991,291	45.1	189	
		J. Strom Thurmond	States' Rights	1,176,125	2.4	39	
		Henry A. Wallace	Progressive	1,157,326	2.4		

Year	Number of States	Candidates	Parties	Popular Vote	% of Popular Vote	Electoral Vote	% Voter Participation[a]
1952	48	**Dwight D. Eisenhower**	Republican	33,936,234	55.1	442	63.3
		Adlai E. Stevenson	Democratic	27,314,992	44.4	89	
1956	48	**Dwight D. Eisenhower**	Republican	35,590,472	57.6	457	60.6
		Adlai E. Stevenson	Democratic	26,022,752	42.1	73	
1960	50	**John F. Kennedy**	Democratic	34,226,731	49.7	303	62.8
		Richard M. Nixon	Republican	34,108,157	49.5	219	
1964	50	**Lyndon B. Johnson**	Democratic	43,129,566	61.1	486	61.7
		Barry M. Goldwater	Republican	27,178,188	38.5	52	
1968	50	**Richard M. Nixon**	Republican	33,045,480	43.4	301	60.6
		Hubert H. Humphrey	Democratic	31,850,140	42.7	191	
		George C. Wallace	American Independent	171,422	13.5	46	
1972	50	**Richard M. Nixon**	Republican	47,169,911	60.7	520	55.2
		George S. McGovern	Democratic	29,170,383	37.5	17	
		John G. Schmitz	American	1,099,482	1.4		
1976	50	**James E. Carter**	Democratic	40,830,763	50.1	297	53.5
		Gerald R. Ford	Republican	39,147,793	48.0	240	
1980	50	**Ronald W. Reagan**	Republican	43,904,153	50.7	489	52.6
		James E. Carter	Democratic	35,483,883	41.0	49	
		John B. Anderson	Independent	5,720,060	6.6		
		Ed Clark	Libertarian	921,299	1.1		
1984	50	**Ronald W. Reagan**	Republican	54,455,075	58.8	525	53.3
		Walter F. Mondale	Democratic	37,577,185	40.6	13	
1988	50	**George H. W. Bush**	Republican	48,886,097	53.4	426	50.1
		Michael S. Dukakis	Democratic	41,809,074	45.6	111[c]	
1992	50	**William J. Clinton**	Democratic	44,909,326	43.0	370	55.2
		George H. W. Bush	Republican	39,103,882	37.4	168	
		H. Ross Perot	Independent	19,741,048	18.9		
1996	50	**William J. Clinton**	Democratic	47,402,357	49.2	379	49.1
		Robert J. Dole	Republican	39,196,755	40.7	159	
		H. Ross Perot	Reform	8,085,402	8.4		
		Ralph Nader	Green	684,902	0.7		
2000	50	**George W. Bush**	Republican	50,456,169	47.9	271	51.2
		Albert Gore	Democratic	50,996,116	48.4	266	
		Ralph Nader	Green	2,783,728	2.7		

Presidential Elections (continued)

Year	Number of States	Candidates	Parties	Popular Vote	% of Popular Vote	Electoral Vote	% Voter Participation[a]
2004	50	George W. Bush	Republican	62,039,073	50.7	286	55.3
		John F. Kerry	Democratic	59,027,478	48.2	251	
		Ralph Nader	Independent	240,896	0.2		
2008	50	Barack Obama	Democratic	69,498,459	53.0	365	61.7
		John McCain	Republican	59,948,283	46.0	173	
		Ralph Nader	Independent	739,165	0.55		
2012	50	Barack Obama	Democratic	65,907,213	51.07	332	
		Mitt Romney	Republican	60,931,767	47.21	206	
		Gary Johnson	Independent	1,275,804	0.99		
2016	50	Donald J. Trump	Republican	62,984,825	46.1	304	59.7
		Hillary Clinton	Democratic	65,853,516	48.2	227	

Candidates receiving less than 1 percent of the popular vote have been omitted. Thus the percentage of popular vote given for any election year may not total 100 percent.

Before the passage of the Twelfth Amendment in 1804, the electoral college voted for two presidential candidates; the runner-up became vice president.

Before 1824, most presidential electors were chosen by state legislatures, not by popular vote.

[a]Percent of voting-age population casting ballots.

[b]Greeley died shortly after the election; the electors supporting him then divided their votes among minor candidates.

[c]One elector from West Virginia cast her electoral college presidential ballot for Lloyd Bentsen, the Democratic Party's vice-presidential candidate.

Presidents and Vice Presidents

		Office	Term of Service
1st	**George Washington**	President	1789–1797
	John Adams	Vice President	1789–1797
2nd	**John Adams**	President	1797–1801
	Thomas Jefferson	Vice President	1797–1801
3rd	**Thomas Jefferson**	President	1801–1809
	Aaron Burr	Vice President	1801–1805
	George Clinton	Vice President	1805–1809
4th	**James Madison**	President	1809–1817
	George Clinton	Vice President	1809–1813
	Elbridge Gerry	Vice President	1813–1817
5th	**James Monroe**	President	1817–1825
	Daniel Tompkins	Vice President	1817–1825
6th	**John Quincy Adams**	President	1825–1829
	John C. Calhoun	Vice President	1825–1829
7th	**Andrew Jackson**	President	1829–1837
	John C. Calhoun	Vice President	1829–1833
	Martin Van Buren	Vice President	1833–1837
8th	**Martin Van Buren**	President	1837–1841
	Richard M. Johnson	Vice President	1837–1841
9th	**William H. Harrison**	President	1841
	John Tyler	Vice President	1841
10th	**John Tyler**	President	1841–1845
	None	Vice President	
11th	**James K. Polk**	President	1845–1849
	George M. Dallas	Vice President	1845–1849
12th	**Zachary Taylor**	President	1849–1850
	Millard Fillmore	Vice President	1849–1850
13th	**Millard Fillmore**	President	1850–1853
	None	Vice President	
14th	**Franklin Pierce**	President	1853–1857
	William R. King	Vice President	1853–1857
15th	**James Buchanan**	President	1857–1861
	John C. Breckinridge	Vice President	1857–1861
16th	**Abraham Lincoln**	President	1861–1865
	Hannibal Hamlin	Vice President	1861–1865
	Andrew Johnson	Vice President	1865

Presidents and Vice Presidents (continued)

		Office	Term of Service
17th	**Andrew Johnson**	President	1865–1869
	None	Vice President	
18th	**Ulysses S. Grant**	President	1869–1877
	Schuyler Colfax	Vice President	1869–1873
	Henry Wilson	Vice President	1873–1877
19th	**Rutherford B. Hayes**	President	1877–1881
	William A. Wheeler	Vice President	1877–1881
20th	**James A. Garfield**	President	1881
	Chester A. Arthur	Vice President	1881
21st	**Chester A. Arthur**	President	1881–1885
	None	Vice President	
22nd	**Grover Cleveland**	President	1885–1889
	Thomas A. Hendricks	Vice President	1885–1889
23rd	**Benjamin Harrison**	President	1889–1893
	Levi P. Morton	Vice President	1889–1893
24th	**Grover Cleveland**	President	1893–1897
	Adlai E. Stevenson	Vice President	1893–1897
25th	**William McKinley**	President	1897–1901
	Garret A. Hobart	Vice President	1897–1901
	Theodore Roosevelt	Vice President	1901
26th	**Theodore Roosevelt**	President	1901–1909
	Charles Fairbanks	Vice President	1905–1909
27th	**William H. Taft**	President	1909–1913
	James S. Sherman	Vice President	1909–1913
28th	**Woodrow Wilson**	President	1913–1921
	Thomas R. Marshall	Vice President	1913–1921
29th	**Warren G. Harding**	President	1921–1923
	Calvin Coolidge	Vice President	1921–1923
30th	**Calvin Coolidge**	President	1923–1929
	Charles G. Dawes	Vice President	1925–1929
31st	**Herbert C. Hoover**	President	1929–1933
	Charles Curtis	Vice President	1929–1933
32nd	**Franklin D. Roosevelt**	President	1933–1945
	John N. Garner	Vice President	1933–1941
	Henry A. Wallace	Vice President	1941–1945
	Harry S Truman	Vice President	1945

		Office	Term of Service
33rd	**Harry S Truman**	President	1945–1953
	Alben W. Barkley	Vice President	1949–1953
34th	**Dwight D. Eisenhower**	President	1953–1961
	Richard M. Nixon	Vice President	1953–1961
35th	**John F. Kennedy**	President	1961–1963
	Lyndon B. Johnson	Vice President	1961–1963
36th	**Lyndon B. Johnson**	President	1963–1969
	Hubert H. Humphrey	Vice President	1965–1969
37th	**Richard M. Nixon**	President	1969–1974
	Spiro T. Agnew	Vice President	1969–1973
	Gerald R. Ford	Vice President	1973–1974
38th	**Gerald R. Ford**	President	1974–1977
	Nelson A. Rockefeller	Vice President	1974–1977
39th	**James E. Carter**	President	1977–1981
	Walter F. Mondale	Vice President	1977–1981
40th	**Ronald W. Reagan**	President	1981–1989
	George H. W. Bush	Vice President	1981–1989
41st	**George H. W. Bush**	President	1989–1993
	J. Danforth Quayle	Vice President	1989–1993
42nd	**William J. Clinton**	President	1993–2001
	Albert A. Gore	Vice President	1993–2001
43rd	**George W. Bush**	President	2001–2009
	Richard B. Cheney	Vice President	2001–2009
44th	**Barack H. Obama**	President	2009–2017
	Joseph R. Biden	Vice President	2009–2017
45th	**Donald J. Trump**	President	2017–
	Michael R. Pence	Vice President	2017–

Justices of the Supreme Court

	Term of Service	Years of Service	Life Span
John Jay	1789–1795	5	1745–1829
John Rutledge	1789–1791	1	1739–1800
William Cushing	1789–1810	20	1732–1810
James Wilson	1789–1798	8	1742–1798
John Blair	1789–1796	6	1732–1800
Robert H. Harrison	1789–1790	—	1745–1790
James Iredell	1790–1799	9	1751–1799
Thomas Johnson	1791–1793	1	1732–1819
William Paterson	1793–1806	13	1745–1806
*John Rutledge**	1795	—	1739–1800
Samuel Chase	1796–1811	15	1741–1811
Oliver Ellsworth	1796–1800	4	1745–1807
Bushrod Washington	1798–1829	31	1762–1829
Alfred Moore	1799–1804	4	1755–1810
John Marshall	1801–1835	34	1755–1835
William Johnson	1804–1834	30	1771–1834
H. Brockholst Livingston	1806–1823	16	1757–1823
Thomas Todd	1807–1826	18	1765–1826
Joseph Story	1811–1845	33	1779–1845
Gabriel Duval	1811–1835	24	1752–1844
Smith Thompson	1823–1843	20	1768–1843
Robert Trimble	1826–1828	2	1777–1828
John McLean	1829–1861	32	1785–1861
Henry Baldwin	1830–1844	14	1780–1844
James M. Wayne	1835–1867	32	1790–1867
Roger B. Taney	1836–1864	28	1777–1864
Philip P. Barbour	1836–1841	4	1783–1841
John Catron	1837–1865	28	1786–1865
John McKinley	1837–1852	15	1780–1852
Peter V. Daniel	1841–1860	19	1784–1860
Samuel Nelson	1845–1872	27	1792–1873
Levi Woodbury	1845–1851	5	1789–1851
Robert C. Grier	1846–1870	23	1794–1870
Benjamin R. Curtis	1851–1857	6	1809–1874
John A. Campbell	1853–1861	8	1811–1889
Nathan Clifford	1858–1881	23	1803–1881
Noah H. Swayne	1862–1881	18	1804–1884
Samuel F. Miller	1862–1890	28	1816–1890
David Davis	1862–1877	14	1815–1886

	Term of Service	Years of Service	Life Span
Stephen J. Field	1863–1897	34	1816–1899
Salmon P. Chase	1864–1873	8	1808–1873
William Strong	1870–1880	10	1808–1895
Joseph P. Bradley	1870–1892	22	1813–1892
Ward Hunt	1873–1882	9	1810–1886
Morrison R. Waite	1874–1888	14	1816–1888
John M. Harlan	1877–1911	34	1833–1911
William B. Woods	1880–1887	7	1824–1887
Stanley Mathews	1881–1889	7	1824–1889
Horace Gray	1882–1902	20	1828–1902
Samuel Blatchford	1882–1893	11	1820–1893
Lucius Q. C. Lamar	1888–1893	5	1825–1893
Melville W. Fuller	1888–1910	21	1833–1910
David J. Brewer	1890–1910	20	1837–1910
Henry B. Brown	1890–1906	16	1836–1913
George Shiras Jr.	1892–1903	10	1832–1924
Howell E. Jackson	1893–1895	2	1832–1895
Edward D. White	1894–1910	16	1845–1921
Rufus W. Peckham	1895–1909	14	1838–1909
Joseph McKenna	1898–1925	26	1843–1926
Oliver W. Holmes	1902–1932	30	1841–1935
William D. Day	1903–1922	19	1849–1923
William H. Moody	1906–1910	3	1853–1917
Horace H. Lurton	1910–1914	4	1844–1914
Charles E. Hughes	1910–1916	5	1862–1948
Willis Van Devanter	1911–1937	26	1859–1941
Joseph R. Lamar	1911–1916	5	1857–1916
Edward D. White	1910–1921	11	1845–1921
Mahlon Pitney	1912–1922	10	1858–1924
James C. McReynolds	1914–1941	26	1862–1946
Louis D. Brandeis	1916–1939	22	1856–1941
John H. Clarke	1916–1922	6	1857–1945
William H. Taft	1921–1930	8	1857–1930
George Sutherland	1922–1938	15	1862–1942
Pierce Butler	1922–1939	16	1866–1939
Edward T. Sanford	1923–1930	7	1865–1930
Harlan F. Stone	1925–1941	16	1872–1946
Charles E. Hughes	1930–1941	11	1862–1948
Owen J. Roberts	1930–1945	15	1875–1955
Benjamin N. Cardozo	1932–1938	6	1870–1938
Hugo L. Black	1937–1971	34	1886–1971

Justices of the Supreme Court (continued)

	Term of Service	Years of Service	Life Span
Stanley F. Reed	1938–1957	19	1884–1980
Felix Frankfurter	1939–1962	23	1882–1965
William O. Douglas	1939–1975	36	1898–1980
Frank Murphy	1940–1949	9	1890–1949
Harlan F. Stone	1941–1946	5	1872–1946
James F. Byrnes	1941–1942	1	1879–1972
Robert H. Jackson	1941–1954	13	1892–1954
Wiley B. Rutledge	1943–1949	6	1894–1949
Harold H. Burton	1945–1958	13	1888–1964
Fred M. Vinson	1946–1953	7	1890–1953
Tom C. Clark	1949–1967	18	1899–1977
Sherman Minton	1949–1956	7	1890–1965
Earl Warren	1953–1969	16	1891–1974
John Marshall Harlan	1955–1971	16	1899–1971
William J. Brennan Jr.	1956–1990	34	1906–1997
Charles E. Whittaker	1957–1962	5	1901–1973
Potter Stewart	1958–1981	23	1915–1985
Byron R. White	1962–1993	31	1917–
Arthur J. Goldberg	1962–1965	3	1908–1990
Abe Fortas	1965–1969	4	1910–1982
Thurgood Marshall	1967–1991	24	1908–1993
Warren C. Burger	1969–1986	17	1907–1995
Harry A. Blackmun	1970–1994	24	1908–1998
Lewis F. Powell Jr.	1972–1987	15	1907–1998
William H. Rehnquist	1972–2005	33	1924–2005
John P. Stevens III	1975–2010	35	1920–
Sandra Day O'Connor	1981–2006	25	1930–
Antonin Scalia	1986–2016	30	1936–2016
Anthony M. Kennedy	1988–	—	1936–
David H. Souter	1990–2009	19	1939–
Clarence Thomas	1991–	—	1948–
Ruth Bader Ginsburg	1993–	—	1933–
Stephen Breyer	1994–	—	1938–
John G. Roberts	2005–	—	1955–
Samuel A. Alito, Jr.	2006–	—	1950–
Sonia Sotomayor	2009–	—	1954–
Elena Kagan	2010–	—	1960–
Neil Gorsuch	2017–	—	1967–

Note: Chief justices are in italics.

*Appointed and served one term, but not confirmed by the Senate.

INDEX